ENVIRONMENTAL POLICY MAKING IN ECONOMIES WITH PRIOR TAX DISTORTIONS

NEW HORIZONS IN ENVIRONMENTAL ECONOMICS

Series Editors: Wallace E. Oates, *Professor of Economics, University of Maryland, USA* and Henk Folmer, *Professor of General Economics, Wageningen University and Professor of Environmental Economics, Tilburg University, The Netherlands*

This important series is designed to make a significant contribution to the development of the principles and practices of environmental economics. It includes both theoretical and empirical work. International in scope, it addresses issues of current and future concern in both East and West and in developed and developing countries.

The main purpose of the series is to create a forum for the publication of high quality work and to show how economic analysis can make a contribution to understanding and resolving the environmental problems confronting the world in the twenty-first century.

Recent titles in the series include:

Instruments for Climate Policy
Limited versus Unlimited Flexibility
Edited by Johan Albrecht

Environmental Co-operation and Institutional Change
Theories and Policies for European Agriculture
Edited by Konrad Hagedorn

Valuing Environmental and Natural Resources
The Econometrics of Non-Market Valuation
Timothy C. Haab and Kenneth E. McConnell

The Economics of Household Garbage and Recycling Behavior
Edited by Don Fullerton and Thomas C. Kinnaman

Controlling Global Warming
Perspectives from Economics, Game Theory and Public Choice
Edited by Christoph Böhringer, Michael Finus and Carsten Vogt

Environmental Regulation in a Federal System
Framing Environmental Policy in the European Union
Tim Jeppesen

The International Yearbook of Environmental and Resource Economics 2002/2003
A Survey of Current Issues
Edited by Tom Tietenberg and Henk Folmer

International Climate Policy to Combat Global Warming
An Analysis of the Ancillary Benefits of Reducing Carbon Emissions
Dirk T.G. Rübbelke

Pollution, Property and Prices
An Essay in Policy-making & Economics
J.H. Dales

The Contingent Valuation of Natural Parks
Assessing the Warmglow Propensity Factor
Paulo A.L.D. Nunes

Environmental Policy Making in Economies
with Prior Tax Distortions
Edited by Lawrence H. Goulder

Environmental Policy Making in Economies with Prior Tax Distortions

Edited by

Lawrence H. Goulder

Shuzo Nishihara Professor of Environmental and Resource Economics, Department of Economics and Institute for International Studies, Stanford University, USA

NEW HORIZONS IN ENVIRONMENTAL ECONOMICS

Edward Elgar

Cheltenham, UK • Northampton, MA, USA

Published by
Edward Elgar Publishing Limited
Glensanda House
Montpellier Parade
Cheltenham
Glos GL50 1UA
UK

Edward Elgar Publishing, Inc.
136 West Street
Suite 202
Northampton
Massachusetts 01060
USA

A catalogue record for this book
is available from the British Library

Library of Congress Cataloguing in Publication Data
Environmental policy making in economies with prior tax distortions / edited by Lawrence H. Goulder.
p. cm. — (New Horizons in environmental economics series)
Includes bibliographical references (p.) and index.
1. Environmental impact charges. 2. Environmental policy—Economic aspects. I. Goulder, Lawrence H. (Lawrence Herbert) II. New horizons in environmental economics

HJ5316 .E5793 2002
333.7—dc21 2002024376

ISBN 1 84064 727 2

Printed and bound in Great Britain by MPG Books Ltd, Bodmin, Cornwall

Contents

PART IV ENVIRONMENTAL INSTRUMENT CHOICE IN A SECOND-BEST SETTING

PART V EFFICIENCY–DISTRIBUTION TRADE-OFFS IN ENVIRONMENTAL POLICY

Acknowledgements

The editor wishes to thank Wallace Oates for suggesting a collection of papers on the topic of this volume, and for helping make this volume possible.

The editor and publishers wish to thank the following who have kindly given permission for the use of copyright material.

Academic Press Inc. for Roberton C. Williams III, 'Environmental Tax Interactions When Pollution Affects Health or Productivity', *Journal of Environmental Economics and Management*, April 2002; Ian W.H. Parry, 'Pollution Taxes and Revenue Recycling', *Journal of Environmental Economics and Management*, **29** (3), November 1995, S-64–S-77; Lawrence H. Goulder, 'Effects of Carbon Taxes in an Economy with Prior Tax Distortions: An Intertemporal General Equilibrium Analysis', *Journal of Environmental Economics and Management*, **29** (3), November 1995, 271–97; Ian W.H. Parry and Antonio M. Bento, 'Tax Deductions, Environmental Policy, and the "Double Dividend" Hypothesis', *Journal of Environmental Economics and Management*, **39** (1), January 2000, 67–96; Ian W.H. Parry, Roberton C. Williams III and Lawrence H. Goulder, 'When Can Carbon Abatement Policies Increase Welfare? The Fundamental Role of Distorted Factor Markets', *Journal of Environmental Economics and Management*, **37** (1), January 1999, 52–84.

American Economic Association for A. Lans Bovenberg and Ruud A. de Mooij, 'Environmental Levies and Distortionary Taxation', *American Economic Review*, **84** (4), September 1994, 1085–9; A. Lans Bovenberg and Lawrence H. Goulder, 'Optimal Environmental Taxation in the Presence of Other Taxes: General-Equilibrium Analyses', *American Economic Review*, **86** (4), September 1996, 985–1000; Don Fullerton, 'Environmental Levies and Distortionary Taxation: Comment', *American Economic Review*, **87** (1), March 1997, 245–51; A. Lans Bovenberg and Ruud A. de Mooij, 'Environmental Levies and Distortionary Taxation: Reply', *American Economic Review*, **87** (1), 1997, 252–3.

Blackwell Publishers for Agnar Sandmo, 'Optimal Taxation in the Presence of Externalities', *The Swedish Journal of Economics*, **77** (1), 1975, 86–98; A. Lans Bovenberg and Frederick van der Ploeg, 'Tax Reform, Structural Unemployment and the Environment', *Scandinavian Journal of Economics*, **100** (3), 1998, 593– 610.

Elsevier Science b.v. for A. Lans Bovenberg and Frederick van der Ploeg, 'Environmental Policy, Public Finance and the Labour Market in a Second-Best World', *Journal of Public Economics*, **55**, 1994, 349–90; Helmuth Cremer, Firouz Gahvari and Norbert Ladoux, 'Externalities and Optimal Taxation', *Journal of Public Economics*, **70** (3), 1998, 343–64; Don Fullerton and Gilbert E. Metcalf, 'Environmental Controls, Scarcity Rents, and Pre-Existing Distortions', *Journal of Public Economics*, **80** (2), May 2001, 249–67; Lawrence H. Goulder, Ian W.H. Parry, Roberton C. Williams III and Dallas Burtraw, 'The Cost-Effectiveness of Alternative Instruments for Environmental Protection in a Second-Best Setting', *Journal of Public Economics*, **72** (3), 1999, 329–60; Roberton C. Williams III, 'Tax Normalizations, the Marginal Cost of Funds, and Optimal Environmental Taxes', *Economics Letters*, **71**, 2001, 137–42; Erkki Koskela and Ronnie Schöb, 'Alleviating Unemployment: The Case for Green Tax Reforms', *European Economic Review*, **43** (9), October 1999, 1723–46; Ian W.H. Parry, 'Environmental Taxes and Quotas in the Presence of Distorting Taxes in Factor Markets', *Resource and Energy Economics*, **19**, 1997, 203–20.

John Wiley and Sons for Ian W.H. Parry and Wallace E. Oates, 'Policy Analysis in the Presence of Distorting Taxes', *Journal of Policy Analysis and Management*, **19** (4), Fall 2000, 603–13.

Journal of Applied Economics for Lawrence H. Goulder, 'Environmental Policy Making in a Second-Best Setting', **1** (2), 1998, 279–328.

Kluwer Academic Publishers for Lawrence H. Goulder, 'Environmental Taxation and the Double Dividend: A Reader's Guide', *International Tax and Public Finance*, **2**, 1995, 157–83; A. Lans Bovenberg, 'Green Tax Reforms and the Double Dividend: An Updated Reader's Guide', *International Tax and Public Finance*, **6** (3), August 1999, 421–43; Ronnie Schöb, 'Environmental Taxes and Pre-Existing Distortions: The Normalization Trap', *International Tax and Public Finance*, **4** (2), 1997, 167–76; Ruud A. de Mooij and A. Lans Bovenberg, 'Environmental Taxes, International Capital Mobility and Inefficient Tax Systems: Tax Burden vs. Tax Shifting', *International Tax and Public Finance*, **5** (1), 1998, 7–39; Ian W.H. Parry, 'A Second-Best Analysis of Environmental Subsidies', *International Tax and Public Finance*, **5** (2), 1998, 153–70; S. Proost and D. van Regemorter, 'The Double Dividend and the Role of Inequality Aversion and Macroeconomic Regimes', *International Tax and Public Finance*, **2** (2), 1995, 207–19.

National Tax Association for A. Lans Bovenberg and Lawrence H. Goulder, 'Costs of Environmentally Motivated Taxes in the Presence of Other Taxes: General Equilibrium Analyses', *National Tax Journal*, **L** (1), 1997, 59–87; Louis Kaplow, 'The Optimal Supply of Public Goods and the Distortionary Cost of Taxation', *National Tax Journal*, **XLIX** (4), 1996, 513–33.

RAND Journal of Economics for Lawrence H. Goulder, Ian W.H. Parry and Dallas Burtraw, 'Revenue-Raising versus Other Approaches to Environmental Protection: The Critical Significance of Preexisting Tax Distortions', **28** (4), Winter 1997, 708–31.

University of Chicago Press for A. Lans Bovenberg and Lawrence H. Goulder, 'Neutralizing the Adverse Industry Impacts of CO_2 Abatement Policies: What Does It Cost?', in *Behavioral and Distributional Effects of Environmental Policy*, C. Carraro and G. Metcalf (eds), 2001, 45–85.

Every effort has been made to trace all the copyright holders but if any have been inadvertently overlooked the publishers will be pleased to make the necessary arrangements at the first opportunity.

Introduction

Lawrence H. Goulder

A Span of the volume

The last three decades have brought significant growth in the use of economic analysis to guide the design and evaluation of environmental policies. This increase has taken place not only in the USA but in many other countries as well. There is wider use of benefit–cost analysis, and increased sophistication in the measurement of both benefits and costs. In addition, policy analysts have become considerably more adept at determining the relative cost-effectiveness of alternative methods for achieving given targets for environmental quality.

In performing evaluations of the costs of environmental policies, researchers have tended to focus on the industry, sector or market that is targeted by the regulation, and to disregard policy impacts in other parts of the economy. This focus has some appeal. At first blush, one would expect that the cost-impacts on the rest of the economy are second order – that most of the impacts occur in the targeted industry or market. This approach thus economizes on detail and adds to transparency, apparently without losing critical information.

Recent research indicates, however, that in realistic settings the impacts outside of the targeted industry, sector or market actually are of first-order importance. In particular, in economies where governments rely on distortionary taxes (such as income and sales taxes) for revenue, a substantial part – and sometimes the lion's share – of the overall cost or efficiency impact occurs in other markets. This research indicates that environmental regulations, by altering supplies or demands in other markets, affect the efficiency of these markets, sometimes profoundly. The greater the pre-existing distortions in such markets, the larger those other-market effects will be.

These findings signal the importance of using a general equilibrium framework to evaluate many types of environmental policy, a framework that can capture interactions across industries, sectors or markets. Indeed, general equilibrium analysis frequently yields results dramatically different from those one would obtain from narrower, partial equilibrium analyses. The differences can be striking. In some plausible cases, policies that appear to be efficiency improving under partial equilibrium analyses emerge as efficiency *reducing* when pre-existing taxes and associated general equilibrium interactions are taken into account. Moreover, general equilibrium interactions sometimes alter the relative costs of different environmental policy instruments, overturning conventional wisdom regarding the rankings of different regulatory approaches in terms of cost-effectiveness. These analyses uphold the notion that well-designed environmental policies improve efficiency by internalizing environmental externalities. But some policies that emerge near the top in a partial equilibrium framework fall significantly in the ranks after a general equilibrium analysis, and (under typical conditions) even the policies that remain top-ranked lose some of their luster.

For this volume I have assembled a set of important papers on the impacts of environmental regulations in the presence of prior distortionary taxes. With the exception of a seminal paper written by Agnar Sandmo in 1975, the papers collected here were published no earlier than 1994. Sandmo's paper was widely regarded as an important contribution at the time of its publication, yet there was fairly little additional work on interactions between environmental policy initiatives and the rest of the tax system until the early 1990s, when growing interest in 'green tax reform' revived interest in these interconnections.

Many of the insights in the recent environmental economics papers have antecedents in earlier work in public economics, such as Anthony Atkinson and Nicholas Stern's (1974) article on optimal taxation to finance a public good in the presence of tax distortions, and Peter Diamond and James Mirrlees's (1971) article on optimal taxation and production efficiency. But in many ways the recent work has broken new ground, identifying previously unrecognized relationships and producing new and policy-relevant insights. Some of the methods and findings from this research are now diffusing back from environmental economics to public economics and other fields, such as the economics of regulation. Interest in this aspect of environmental policy analysis continues to grow and spawn additional theoretical and empirical work. No doubt several additional important papers in this area will emerge over the next few years.

Since this research considers economies with distortionary taxes, it falls within the general domain of second-best policy analysis. One often is reminded of the notion that 'anything can happen in a second-best setting'. From this perspective, nothing in the results from the recent research is altogether surprising. However, the current research goes well beyond demonstrating the possible. An important contribution is to show which outcomes, within the universe of all conceivably possible outcomes, will in fact occur under empirically plausible economic assumptions or conditions. By adding reasonable structure – for example, plausible assumptions about household preferences, production technologies and market structure – this research offers specific predictions that are useful for real-world policy analysis.

B An overview

Part I of this volume offers some surveys of this research. The year 2000 article by Ian Parry and Wallace Oates and my 1998 article offer an overview of results on impacts of environmental policies in the presence of distortionary taxes. The policies examined include both environmental taxes and non-tax policies such as tradeable emissions permits and mandated technologies. The other two papers in this section – my 1995 piece and the 1999 article by Lans Bovenberg – are somewhat narrower in focus. Both are 'reader's guides' for the 'double dividend' issue – the question as to whether the revenue-neutral substitution of an environmental tax for existing distortionary tax (such as the income tax) might produce two benefits by both (1) improving the environment and (2) reducing the cost of the tax system, apart from environmental considerations. If the second 'dividend' obtains, then the gross costs of the revenue-neutral reform (that is, the costs before netting out environmental benefits) are negative. The possibility of a negative-cost environmental policy has considerable attraction for advocates of green tax reform, and has stimulated a great deal of interest among policy makers and analysts.

Part II focuses on the optimal rates of environmental taxes in the second-best setting of concern. It begins with Sandmo's fundamental contribution, which appeared in the *Swedish* (now *Scandinavian*) *Journal of Economics* in 1975. Sandmo examined the optimal setting of commodity taxes in a setting where one of the commodities involved an externality. He showed that if the government needs to raise more revenue than generated by environmental taxes set at 'Pigovian' levels (that is, at rates equal to marginal external costs), then the optimal commodity tax system is a blend of ordinary 'Ramsey' commodity taxation and Pigovian taxation. The optimal system includes taxes on all commodities – both ordinary commodities and the environmentally harmful commodity. The optimal tax rate on the environmentally harmful commodity, in particular, involves both a non-environmental 'Ramsey' component as well as an environmental component that reflects the magnitude of the externality.

More recent analyses reinforce and expand on the Sandmovian insights. In a paper published in 1994 in the *Journal of Public Economics*, Bovenberg and Fredrick van der Ploeg analyze the (realistic) situation where the government employs both income (labor) taxes and taxes on at least some commodities. This contrasts with Sandmo's paper, which examined the case where the government employs only commodity taxes. Bovenberg and van der Ploeg find, as in Sandmo, that the optimal tax rate on an environmentally offensive commodity is the sum of a Ramsey component and an environmental component. The environmental component generally differs from the Pigovian rate (the marginal damage). In particular, if the marginal cost of public funds (MCPF) exceeds unity, the environmental component is less than the Pigovian rate. This result was only implicit in Sandmo's earlier contribution. In the absence of prior taxes, the marginal social cost of an environmental tax is the tax rate. Hence one achieves the optimum – a balancing of marginal social cost and marginal benefit (avoided marginal environmental damage) – by setting the environmental tax rate equal to the marginal environmental damage. This is the Pigovian rate. The intuition for the Bovenberg–van der Ploeg result is that, in a second-best setting with prior distortionary taxes, the marginal social cost of an environmental tax exceeds the tax rate (for reasons discussed below). Hence to equate marginal social cost and marginal social damage (thus achieving the optimum), one needs to set the environmental tax rate below the marginal environmental damage.

Bovenberg and Ruud de Mooij's paper in the 1994 *American Economic Review* was another important contribution. This paper also shows that the environmental component of the optimal environmental tax rate is equal to the marginal environmental damage divided by the MCPF. In addition to providing insights in the area of optimal environmental taxation, this paper made a seminal contribution to the double dividend issue; for this reason I discuss this paper in some detail below in connection with Part III.

Bovenberg and Goulder's 1996 paper in the *American Economic Review* generalized the Bovenberg–van der Ploeg analysis to include attention to taxes on intermediate inputs. (Many fuel taxes fall into this category.) The paper also applies the theory in a detailed, computable general equilibrium (CGE) model of the US economy. In the CGE model, the MCPF is approximately 1.2, and thus the optimal environmental tax rate is about 5/6 of the marginal damages. Bovenberg and Goulder also consider constrained optimal policies and find that the constrained optimal environmental tax rate may be well below the optimal rate. Thus, if the government is unable to set 'non-environmental' taxes optimally (or, equivalently, is unable to use revenues from an environmental tax to finance cuts in distortionary factor taxes), the optimal environmental tax rate may approach zero or even be negative.

In interpreting optimal tax formulas, a potential source of confusion arises from the fact that different tax systems involve different 'tax normalizations'. If the government has access to *n* different tax instruments, it is often the case that functionally equivalent tax systems – that is, systems that produce identical real outcomes – can be generated by setting *n – 1* of the taxes to non-zero levels and setting the *n*th tax equal to zero. Although the tax systems are functionally the same, they may appear to imply different optimal tax rules. Some readers misinterpreted the Bovenberg–de Mooij paper as indicating that the *overall* environmental tax rate is always below the marginal environmental damage. Two subsequent papers – a comment by Don Fullerton published in 1997 in the *American Economic Review* and an article by Ronnie Schöb published the same year in *International Tax and Public Finance* – indicated that the relationship between the overall environmental tax rate and the marginal damage depends on the tax normalization. These papers emphasize that functionally equivalent tax systems can be introduced by employing either (1) a labor tax and commodity taxes (with one commodity tax set to zero), or (2) only commodity taxes (with the labor tax set to zero). The papers indicate that in the former case the overall environmental tax is below the marginal damage (or 'Pigovian' rate), while in the latter it is above such damage.

What remains true irrespective of the tax normalization is that the *environmental component* of the optimal environmental tax rate is equal to the marginal environmental damage divided by the MCPF. Most studies indicate that the MCPF is above unity; hence the environmental component is less than the marginal damage. Bovenberg and de Mooij make this point in their reply to Fullerton, and the issue is generalized very effectively in Roberton Williams's 2001 paper in *Economics Letters*. The tax normalization affects the *overall* environmental tax rate for the following reason. Under the first normalization, the labor tax effectively picks up all the non-environmental aspects of taxation, so that the Ramsey component of the environmental tax is zero. In contrast, under the second normalization the non-environmental aspects of taxation are captured through non-zero Ramsey taxes on all commodities, including a non-zero Ramsey component on the environmentally offensive (or 'dirty') consumption good. As a result, under the second normalization the overall tax on the environmentally offensive good – the sum of the Ramsey and environmental components – is above the marginal environmental damage. Williams's paper also shows that the MCPF is affected by the tax normalization. Hence the environmental component (marginal damages divided by the MCPF) depends on the tax normalization.

Bovenberg and de Mooij's paper also argued that a higher MCPF weakens the case for environmental taxes. Fullerton's comment clarifies the sense in which this is so while helping to dispel a potential misinterpretation. The claim is correct in the sense that a higher MCPF reduces the environmental component of the optimal environmental tax. Fullerton shows, however, that under the second tax normalization, an increase in the MCPF (reflecting an increase in the government's need for revenue) will imply a higher overall environmental tax rate. This happens because the Ramsey component increases. A higher MCPF implies a lower environmental component, but the need for additional revenue raises the Ramsey component by more than enough to compensate. The overall tax rate rises.

As previously mentioned papers point out, the environmental component of the optimal environmental tax is lower in the world with distortionary taxes (if the MCPF exceeds unity). This does not mean, however, that the level of pollution must be higher in a world with distortionary taxes, compared with the level in a world in which lump-sum taxes could be employed to generate any needed revenue beyond that obtained from environmental taxes set at Pigovian rates. Indeed, a working paper by Thomas Gaube[1] showed that, in a world with distortionary taxes, the level of emissions could well be *lower* than in the world where the government has access to lump-sum taxes, despite the lower environmental tax rate in the former, second-best case. Thus the level of environmental quality may in fact be higher in the second-best setting. As shown in Gaube's paper, this reflects the negative impact of distortionary taxes on incomes and economic activity. In a world where distortionary taxes are needed for government revenue, the reduced economic activity can imply a lower level of pollution, despite the lower environmental tax rate.

Roberton Williams's 2002 paper in the *Journal of Environmental Economics and Management* examines the costs of environmental taxes in a model that explicitly considers impacts on health and labor productivity. In most of the models already discussed, environmental quality affects individuals directly in that it is an argument of the utility function. In such models, the 'marginal environmental damage' is the monetary equivalent of the loss of utility from a reduction in environmental quality. Williams's paper extends earlier analyses by allowing changes in environmental quality to affect health, which in turn affects time sick (away from work or leisure) or expenditure on medical care. In this model, for reasonable parameter values the costs of environmental regulations are even higher than in the simpler models, and the optimal environmental tax rate is lower than the marginal damage divided by the MCPF. Williams also considers the case where environmental quality affects the economy solely through impacts on labor productivity. In this case, the Pigovian rule again applies: the optimal rate equals the marginal damage. The result mirrors that obtained by Bovenberg and van der Ploeg (1994), although Williams's paper generalizes the Bovenberg–van der Ploeg analysis in several ways.

Helmuth Cremer, Firouz Gahvari and Norbert Ladoux consider a different dimension of optimal taxation. In contrast to the previously mentioned studies, they consider the heterogeneity among households and a tax system that differentially treats those households through a nonlinear income tax. If the government does not have access to specific taxes on environmentally offensive commodities, it can address externalities indirectly through the income tax. In a paper published in the *Journal of Public Economics* in 1998, Cremer, Gahvari and Ladoux examine how the structure of the optimal nonlinear income tax is changed when externalities are present. Under the optimal tax structure, households with relatively higher demands for environmentally damaging goods face relatively higher rates than they would in the absence of externalities.

Part III includes papers that focus on environmental tax *reforms*. Such reforms involve the introduction of a new environmentally motivated tax, perhaps accompanied by adjustments to some existing tax or set of taxes. But there is no claim to optimality of the overall tax system, either before or after the reform.

Proposals for environmental (or 'green') tax reform tend to involve the revenue-neutral substitution of environmentally motivated taxes for ordinary taxes such as income or sales taxes. Environmentally motivated taxes might include taxes on pollution, on energy fuels or on other commodities or activities associated with pollution. A potential attraction of green tax reform is the possibility of using environmental tax revenues to finance reductions in the rates of existing distortionary taxes, thus avoiding some of the efficiency costs that these prior taxes impose. As mentioned above, the issue that has sparked the greatest interest and debate amid discussions of green tax reform is that of the double dividend: the possibility that a revenue-neutral environmental tax could both improve environmental quality and reduce the overall gross costs of the tax system (where 'gross costs' denote the costs before netting out any environmental benefits stemming from the tax reform).

Bovenberg and de Mooij's 1994 *American Economic Review* paper (included in Part II) was a seminal contribution to this issue. The authors consider a revenue-neutral policy in which an environmental tax is imposed on a 'dirty' consumption good and the revenues are used to finance a reduction in the rate of the pre-existing distortionary tax on labor. They find that, under plausible assumptions, the revenue-neutral reform does not lower the gross costs of the tax system. Their model demonstrates that environmental taxes – for example, taxes on a 'dirty' consumption good – are implicit taxes on labor. By raising the costs of a given consumption good and of consumption in general, the environmental tax lowers the real wage, thus implicitly taxing labor. For an infinitesimal environmental tax, the gross distortionary[2] impact of the implicit tax on labor (that is, the environmental tax) is exactly offset by the gross efficiency gain from using the revenues to reduce the labor tax. But for any 'large' environmental tax, the cost from the implicit tax exceeds the gain from the reduction in the explicit tax: the overall cost of the tax system increases. Hence the double dividend does not materialize. The intuition is that a broad tax on commodities is equivalent to a labor tax. Hence substituting a broad commodity tax for a labor tax would involve no change in the cost of the tax system. But substituting a narrow commodity tax (that is, an environmental tax) for a labor tax introduces inter-commodity distortions without lowering the effective tax on labor. Hence the overall (gross) distortionary cost of the tax system increases.

It is important to recognize that the absence of the second dividend does not imply that green tax reform will reduce efficiency. To the contrary, in the Bovenberg–de Mooij paper and in other studies, an appropriately scaled environmental tax confers gross benefits (welfare gains stemming from environmental improvement) that exceed the gross costs of the reform. Hence green tax reform remains attractive as an efficiency-improving venture. On the other hand, the absence of the second dividend surely makes it more difficult to garner political support for such reform.

Parry's 1995 article in the *Journal of Environmental Economics and Management* obtained results similar to those in the Bovenberg–de Mooij paper. A very important contribution of Parry's paper is its decomposition of the overall gross costs of revenue-neutral environmental taxes. The gross costs can be divided into a *primary cost*, a *revenue-recycling effect* and a *tax-interaction effect*.[3] The primary cost is approximately the 'partial equilibrium' cost accounted for in studies that focus on the taxed industry, sector or market. The revenue-recycling effect is the efficiency benefit from lowering the explicit labor tax. The tax-interaction effect is the efficiency cost from the implicit taxation of labor through the environmental tax. The overall cost is the primary cost plus the tax-interaction effect minus the revenue-recycling effect.

Parry's article shows that if the 'dirty' commodity on which the environmental tax is imposed is an average substitute for leisure, then the (beneficial) revenue-recycling effect will only partly undo the (costly) tax-interaction effect. Not only does revenue recycling fail to bring overall gross costs below zero (a requirement for the double dividend), it fails to bring them down to the level of primary costs. Thus in a second-best setting, the costs of a given environmental tax tend to exceed primary costs – the only costs that apply in a world without prior taxes. Because the environmental tax is a narrow tax, it is a less efficient (on non-environmental grounds) source of revenue than the income tax it replaces. The environmental tax 'distorts' the choice among intermediate inputs and among consumption goods, and also (under neutral assumptions) creates the same labor-market distortion as the labor tax. In contrast, the income tax only distorts the labor market. This helps explain why the tax-interaction effect exceeds the revenue-recycling effect. Parry's decomposition has proven to be enormously helpful in understanding the cost impacts of other environmental policies, as discussed below in connection with the papers in Part IV.

The papers by Goulder, published in 1995 in the *Journal of Environmental Economics and Management*, and by Dale Jorgenson and Peter Wilcoxen, published in a Stanford Energy Modeling Forum compendium in 1996, apply detailed CGE models to assess the impacts of green tax reforms – of revenue-neutral carbon tax policies, in particular. The additional complexity of these models rules out the possibility of obtaining analytical solutions; these models must be solved numerically. Information obtained from these models complements the findings from simpler analytical models, indicating whether the predictions of simpler models hold up in more complex settings. Both papers indicate significant reductions in costs when carbon tax revenues are recycled through cuts in marginal income tax rates. In the Goulder paper, such recycling lowers the costs by about 50 percent, relative to the costs that would occur if the revenues were returned to the economy in a lump-sum fashion. However, recycling does not make the costs negative, as required for a double dividend. The Jorgenson–Wilcoxen paper, in contrast, obtains the double dividend when revenues are recycled through cuts in marginal rates of taxes on capital. A potential explanation is provided below in the discussion of inefficient factor taxation.

Subsequent to the initial analytical work by Bovenberg, de Mooij, van der Ploeg, Parry and others, a second wave of research investigated the impacts of green tax reform in more complex, yet analytically tractable models that incorporated other channels that could influence the cost impacts and the possibilities for a double dividend. By considering these new channels, such models offer insights about the generality of the analytical results obtained in earlier studies. These models clarify in particular the significance of assumptions about the nature of household preferences, market structure and the pre-existing tax system.

One additional important channel materializes in models that incorporate more than one primary factor of production. The Bovenberg–Goulder paper from the 1997 *National Tax Journal* and the de Mooij–Bovenberg paper from the 1998 volume of *International Tax and Public Finance* employ models incorporating both capital and labor as primary factors of production. These papers show that a double dividend can occur if the revenue-neutral environmental tax reform shifts the burden of factor taxation from the factor that was overtaxed to the factor that was undertaxed under the pre-existing tax structure. Thus if capital is initially overtaxed relative to labor (in the sense that the marginal excess burden per dollar of revenue raised is higher for capital than for labor), and if the green tax reform shifts the burden from capital to labor, the double dividend can occur. In this case, the reform introduces a 'tax shifting' effect that promotes improved efficiency of the tax system.

While this effect works in favor of a double dividend, it does not guarantee it. The effect must be strong enough to overcome both the primary cost and the inherent handicap of the environmental tax relative to other taxes as a source of revenue – a handicap stemming from its relatively narrow base, as discussed above. The Bovenberg–Goulder paper includes simulations with a CGE model of the US economy, experiments focusing on the impacts of revenue-neutral energy (Btu and gasoline) taxes. In those simulations, the tax-shifting effect is not large enough to generate the double dividend under central parameter values. However, if the supply for capital is made sufficiently elastic and the inefficiency in the pre-existing tax system is thereby made sufficiently great, the double dividend arises. The tax-shifting effect may explain the presence of the double dividend in the Jorgenson–Wilcoxen model. That model assumes more elastic capital supply (from higher savings elasticities) than the model employed in the Bovenberg–Goulder study. As a result, shifting the burden of taxation from capital to labor – for example, through a carbon tax policy in which revenues are devoted exclusively to cuts in capital taxes – yields an especially strong (beneficial) tax-shifting effect in the Jorgenson–Wilcoxen model.

A second additional channel can be provided by imperfectly competitive labor markets. In their paper in the 1999 *European Economic Review*, Erkki Koskela and Ronnie Schöb show that a double dividend can indeed arise in a setting involving involuntary unemployment. In addition, they point out the possibilities for achieving an 'employment dividend' from green tax reform. Bovenberg and van der Ploeg's paper in the 1998 *Scandinavian Journal of Economics* arrives at similar conclusions. These papers indicate that the indexation of employment benefits importantly influences the real-wage impact of green tax reforms and the prospects for a double dividend.

A third channel arises when the prior tax system offers tax deductions for certain forms of consumer spending. In their paper in the year 2000 *Journal of Environmental Economics and Management*, Parry and Antonio Bento point out that the tax deductibility of certain forms of consumer spending – including home mortgage payments and medical expenditures – creates distortions in the allocation of consumer spending. The magnitude of these distortions is a function of the income (labor) tax rate. To the extent that an environmental tax leads to reduced labor taxes, these distortions are reduced. Thus when the prior tax system favors certain forms of spending, the revenue-recycling effect associated with a revenue-neutral environmental tax reform gains added strength. Parry and Bento find that, under reasonable parameter values, the efficiency benefit from revenue recycling will (contrary to the simplest models) outweigh the costly tax-interaction effect. Indeed, under some parameter specifications the benefit from revenue recycling will be strong enough to overcome both the tax-interaction effect and primary cost, thus yielding the double dividend.[4]

A fourth channel is provided by inelastically supplied exhaustible resources. To the extent that the burden of environmental taxes falls on the owners of inelastically supplied stocks of exhaustible resources, the environmental tax functions as a rent tax and involves no efficiency cost. A recent working paper by Bento[5] shows that this phenomenon is a mixed blessing. To the extent that the environmental tax is a rent tax, its gross cost is lowered and the prospects for the second dividend improve. However, this also implies that the environmental tax will be borne by producers, with little impact on output prices and demand. Hence the impact on emissions will be small. The prospects for the first (environmental) dividend worsen.

Although these studies consider a variety of complications that influence the prospects for a double dividend, the results from the studies all fall under a common general principle. The general principle is that to obtain the double dividend, three conditions must obtain: (1) the initial tax system must be inefficient along some non-environmental dimension; (2) the revenue-neutral environmental tax swap must reduce this inefficiency; and (3) the efficiency improvement along this dimension must more than compensate for both the primary and the environmental tax's inherent efficiency disadvantage relative to an income tax (attributable to its narrow base). This principle explains whether the double dividend occurs in the presence of inefficient factor taxation, imperfectly competitive labor markets, tax deductions for certain types of spending, (inelastically supplied) exhaustible resources and other economic circumstances.[6]

The principle makes clear that the presence or absence of the double dividend depends on the nature of the prior tax system and how revenues are recycled. This does not mean, however, that the double dividend is as likely to occur as not. The narrow base of green taxes constitutes an inherent efficiency handicap. The green tax reform's impact on pre-existing inefficiencies in the tax system could offset this handicap, but could also add to it. Moreover, even if prior inefficiencies were such as to allow a green tax reform to overcome the efficiency handicap, the reform would also have to overcome primary cost to generate the double dividend. This is a very significant hurdle.

Part IV offers a collection of articles on the choice of environmental policy instrument in economies with prior tax distortions. As indicated above, general equilibrium tax interactions importantly affect the absolute and relative costs of alternative instruments.

The 1997 articles by Parry from *Resource and Energy Economics* and by Goulder, Parry and Dallas Burtraw from the *RAND Journal of Economics*, as well as the 1999 article by Parry, Williams and Goulder from the *Journal of Environmental Economics and Management*, compare the costs of environmental taxes and quotas (or tradeable permits) in economies with and without prior distortionary taxes. Like environmental taxes, emissions quotas or tradeable permits systems lead to higher production costs, higher commodity prices and reductions in real factor returns. As a result, regulating pollution through quotas or tradeable permits generates a tax-interaction effect similar to that produced by environmental taxes. If the quota rights or permits are auctioned, and the revenues are used to finance cuts in prior distortionary taxes, the tax-interaction effect will be partly offset by the revenue-recycling effect. On the other hand, if the quotas rights are assigned rather than auctioned, or if the permits are given out free, there can be no such offset.

These studies indicate that when policies exploit the revenue-recycling effect, such recycling does not fully offset the tax-interaction effect. Hence the costs of given amounts of abatement exceed primary costs. This suggests that the costs of given amounts of abatement are higher in a second-best setting than in a world with no prior distortionary taxes.[7] The costs of given amounts of abatement tend to rise with the magnitude of prior taxes.

In these studies the presence or absence of the revenue-recycling effect has dramatic implications for economic costs. The Goulder–Parry–Burtraw paper indicates that the costs of reducing sulfur dioxide emissions under Title IV of the 1990 Clean Air Act could have been reduced by about 25 percent if the tradeable permits employed under the Act had been auctioned (and revenues recycled) rather than given out free. For policies involving very small amounts of abatement, the failure to exploit the revenue-recycling effect can raise costs by several hundred percent. In some plausible cases, whether the overall efficiency impact is positive or negative depends on the decision whether freely to allocate or to auction tradeable permits. In this connection, the Parry–Williams–Goulder paper shows that while reducing carbon dioxide (CO_2) emissions through auctioned permits is efficiency improving (provided that the revenues are recycled), a system of freely provided CO_2 permits is likely to be an efficiency-reducing proposition: under plausible values for the environmental benefits per ton of CO_2 abatement, *any* level of emissions reduction yields environmental benefits that fall short of society's costs of abatement!

The paper by Fullerton and Gilbert Metcalf from the 2001 *Journal of Public Economics* offers an additional perspective on the relative costs of quotas (or tradeable permits) and taxes. The paper indicates that the higher efficiency cost of policies such as systems of freely offered tradeable permits, compared with the costs of systems of auctioned tradeable permits, can be explained by the fact that the former policies leave policy-generated rents in private hands, while the latter policies collect these rents as government revenue. The paper also examines the cost of another potential environmental policy instrument: a government-mandated restriction on private technology. For incremental amounts of abatement, this 'command and control' policy involves lower costs than a system of freely offered tradeable permits. This is explained in terms of the fact that the technology restriction does not leave rents in private hands, while the system of freely offered permits does.

In their paper in the 1999 *Journal of Public Economics*, Goulder, Parry, Williams and Burtraw investigate a wide range of policy instruments, including both 'conventional' policies such as performance standards and technology mandates, as well as emissions taxes, quotas and permits. In contrast to the Fullerton–Metcalf study, they consider 'large' as well as incremental amounts of abatement, explaining the cost differences in terms of primary cost and the tax-interaction and revenue-recycling effects.[8] They find that pre-existing taxes imply significantly higher abatement costs for every policy instrument. The cost impact of such taxes differs sharply across instruments at low levels of abatement, but this impact converges across policies as abatement approaches 100 percent. The tax-interaction effect is especially large for emissions taxes or permits. As a result, the costs of such 'incentive based' policies exceed those of other, command-and-control policies if the revenues from the former policies are not directed towards cuts in prior taxes.

Economists had long argued that tradeable emissions permits and emissions taxes are more cost-effective than performance standards, technology mandates and other traditional forms of regulation. Both the Fullerton–Metcalf and the Goulder–Parry–Williams–Burtraw papers indicate that this is not necessarily the case. Systems of freely offered tradeable permits, as well as environmental taxes whose revenues are returned lump sum, can involve higher costs than command-and-control policies that achieve the same amount of abatement. This finding deserves qualification, however. None of the studies included in this section considers the heterogeneity in the abatement cost schedules of firms within given industries, or the associated information problems faced by regulators. Incentive-based regulations have important advantages over command-and-control policies in the presence of such heterogeneity, because they can bring about equality in marginal abatement costs even when regulators have relatively little information about the differing abatement cost schedules of the various firms. Such advantages deserve consideration in any overall comparison of the cost-effectiveness of incentive-based and traditional regulations.

Parry's 1998 article in *International Tax and Public Finance* examines the impacts of environmental subsidies in economies with prior tax distortions. Parry shows that environmental subsidies involve a revenue-financing effect: the cost associated with needing to raise the rates of ordinary taxes to finance the subsidy. This is the mirror image of the revenue-recycling effect from environmental taxes. In addition, subsidies involve a *beneficial* tax-interaction effect because they lower the prices of the subsidized good and of goods in general, thereby raising the real wage. Parry's analysis shows that, under typical conditions, the (costly) revenue-financing effect is larger than the (beneficial) tax-interaction effect. Thus the second-best considerations imply that subsidies are more costly in a second-best setting than in a first-best world, where neither the revenue-financing nor the tax-interaction effect would apply. At the same time, some prior studies had recognized the costs of financing subsidies, and thus had concluded that the optimal subsidy is significantly lower than would apply in a setting with no prior taxes. Parry's study indicates that such studies overstate the subsidy cost and understate the size of the optimal subsidy, because they ignore the tax-interaction effect.

The final Part pulls together papers that address connections between efficiency and distribution in economies with tax distortions. Louis Kaplow's article from the 1996 *National Tax Journal* shows that if the government can fully offset distributional effects, the MCPF may be unity after all. This would imply that (the environmental component of) the optimal environmental tax is equal to the marginal damage – the Pigovian rule. Kaplow's result requires some particular conditions relating to individuals' utility functions, the separability between leisure and other elements of household utility functions, and the government's capacity to neutralize distributional effects through adjustments to the tax system. In one particular case, the improvement in environmental quality from an environmental tax has a positive labor supply effect that exactly offsets the negative labor supply effect from adjustments to the income tax schedule. Hence there is no labor supply impact and no gross efficiency cost, and thus the MCPF is unity. Even if the assumed conditions in Kaplow's analysis do not hold, the paper carries very important messages for policy analysis. It reveals the importance of considering factor supply effects stemming from the changes in environmental quality. (Williams's 'Environmental Tax Interactions' paper in Part II addresses some of these issues.) In addition, it indicates that, where possible, it is useful to assess efficiency impacts subject to the constraint of 'distributional neutrality' – the requirement that the distribution of individual well-being remain unchanged.

In many cases, however, the policies 'on the table' are not distributionally neutral, so that efficiency rankings do not reliably indicate social welfare rankings. Yet these policies demand evaluation. In such cases it is helpful to examine efficiency and distributional impacts in an integrated fashion, so that trade-offs between efficiency and distribution can be exposed. In a paper published in 1995 in *International Tax and Public Finance*, Stef Proost and Denise van Regemorter explore connections between distributional concerns, efficiency costs and social welfare as they arise from a carbon tax in the European Community. The analysis is distinct from many other studies in distinguishing several household income groups and in examining together the efficiency and income distributional impacts of environmental policies. A common suggestion in much of the second-best literature is that it is advisable to exploit the revenue-recycling effect: that it is better to devote environmental tax revenues to cuts in marginal tax rates than to return them in a lump-sum fashion (for example, by raising personal tax exemptions). The efficiency advantage of the former recycling method over the latter is sometimes termed the 'weak' second dividend. Proost and Regemorter's analysis shows that the former recycling method may worsen the income distribution and that, under reasonable specifications for a social welfare function, the latter recycling method may in fact achieve higher social welfare. This analysis demonstrates the usefulness of considering efficiency and distributional issues in an integrated fashion.

The final paper in the volume is an article that Bovenberg and Goulder contributed to *Behavioral and Distributional Effects of Environmental Policy*. In that paper, Bovenberg and Goulder evaluate efficiency–distribution trade-offs in US climate-change policy. The most cost-effective policies for reducing domestic CO_2 emissions – a carbon tax or a system of auctioned carbon permits – meet stiff political opposition in part because of their distributional impacts. A large share of the overall economic cost of these policies is borne by a few, highly mobilized, energy industries. Bovenberg and Goulder examine the efficiency cost of avoiding adverse impacts on the profits of these industries (and thereby enhancing political feasibility). They find that these distributional objectives can be met with a small sacrifice of efficiency. The key recognition behind this finding is that CO_2 abatement policies generate very large potential rents. These potential rents either materialize as government revenue (when permits are auctioned) or as rents to the fossil fuel-supplying industries (when permits are freely offered). The potential rents are quite large relative to the potential losses in profit to the major energy industries. By designing policies that enable firms to retain just a small fraction of the potential rents, profits can be maintained. Government revenue has an efficiency value because it can be used to finance cuts in pre-existing distortionary taxes; that is, to exploit the revenue-recycling effect. Because these policies forego little of this potential revenue, they involve only a small efficiency sacrifice.

C Where from here?

These papers reveal the first-order significance of general equilibrium interactions to the evaluation of efficiency impacts of environmental policies. Partial equilibrium analyses may reach incorrect conclusions as to the magnitudes, and even the sign, of the efficiency impacts. At present, most evaluations of the costs of environmental regulations continue to be partial equilibrium in nature. In many cases, economy-wide costs are assumed to be simply the sum of the abatement costs in targeted industries. One implication of the research reported in this volume is the significant potential benefit from the wider use of general equilibrium techniques in policy evaluations.

Although these papers focus on environmental policies, their findings have important implications for policy evaluation in other domains. The tax-interaction effect applies broadly: to the extent that agricultural policies or international trade policies raise the costs of output and thereby reduce real factor returns, they exacerbate the factor-market distortions from pre-existing taxes and imply higher social costs than would be indicated by partial equilibrium analyses. The call for wider use of general equilibrium assessments has validity in many policy areas.

These papers pave the way for further productive research. Additional empirical work could be especially valuable. A central point from the existing theoretical work is that the efficiency impacts of environmental policies depend on the nature and extent of prior inefficiencies in the tax system. These inefficiencies depend not only on the structure of the prior tax system but also on preference parameters, technical parameters and market stucture. These determine the magnitudes of inefficiencies stemming from a given tax structure. As often happens, theory has outpaced empirical work. There remain considerable uncertainties about key parameters. Improved estimates of these parameters will help reduce uncertainties about cost impacts and environmental benefits.

Further work that integrates efficiency and distributional impacts could also be quite useful. In the real world, efficiency gains rarely translate into actual Pareto improvements, since compensation of the losers by the winners typically is not possible. The distributional impacts of policies can be dramatic, and thus the efficiency rankings of policies may be a poor indicator of social welfare rankings. Hence further attention to efficiency–distribution trade-offs can produce very useful results. Such work might not only examine existing environmental policy instruments – taxes, quotas, permits, standards, and so on – but also devise new instruments that lower the efficiency cost of meeting distributional concerns. Such work could help policy makers confront more effectively a major political challenge: namely, the achievement of efficiency goals without producing unacceptable distributional outcomes.

Notes

1. See Gaube (1998). Because this paper had not been published at the time this collection went to print, we were unable to reproduce it here.
2. The word 'gross' is inserted here to indicate that this distortionary cost does not take account of the benefits from environmental improvement.
3. Parry originally referred to the latter two effects as the *revenue effect* and the *interdependency effect*.
4. Parry and Bento distinguish an 'intermediate' version of the double dividend from the 'strong' version under discussion in this Introduction. (We discuss a 'weak' version below.) The intermediate version occurs if the revenue-recycling effect outweighs the tax-interaction effect. In this case, the overall costs of the revenue-neutral reform are less than primary costs, although still positive.
5. Bento (2001).
6. See the Goulder (1995) and Bovenberg (1999) review articles for a discussion of other settings.
7. These analytical studies show that second-best overall costs exceed *second-best* primary costs. If second-best primary costs were identical to primary costs in a setting with no prior taxes, one could conclude that second-best costs also exceed the overall costs in the no-prior-tax setting, since in that setting primary cost is the only component of cost. However, primary costs in that setting need not be identical to second-best primary costs. Still, numerical studies indicate that second-best overall costs also exceed first-best costs, because there is very little difference between primary costs between economies with or without prior distortionary taxes. (See Goulder, Parry and Burtraw (1997) and Goulder, Parry, Williams and Burtraw (1999).)
8. The two explanations of costs – one in terms of privately retained rents and the other in terms of tax-interaction and revenue-recycling effects – yield the same answers when applied to policies involving *incremental* amounts of pollution abatement. Under both explanations, the initial costs of tradeable permits are zero if the permits are auctioned and revenues recycled, but are positive if the permits are given out free. (The latter policy leaves rents in private hands. It also fails to offset the tax-interaction effect with a revenue-recycling effect.) Similarly, both explanations indicate that the cost of incremental abatement under a technology mandate is zero. (This policy creates no rents, and thus leaves none in private hands. It also generates no tax-interaction effect, and thus has zero cost even without revenue recycling.) However, when 'large' amounts of abatement are involved, one cannot explain differences in policy costs simply by examining whether rents are generated and left in private hands. In these cases it helps to focus on differences across policies in the magnitudes of tax-interaction and revenue-recycling effects. The Goulder–Parry–Williams–Burtraw paper in this volume discusses these issues.

References (papers not contained in this volume)

Atkinson, Anthony and Nicholas Stern, 1974, 'Pigou, Taxation, and Public Goods', *Review of Economic Studies*, **41**, 119–28.

Bento, Antonio, 2001.

Diamond, Peter and J. Mirrlees, 1971, 'Optimal Taxation and Public Production I: Production Efficiency and II: Tax Rules', *American Economic Review*, **61**.

Gaube, Thomas, 1998, 'Distortionary Taxes Preserve the Environment', Discussion Paper No. A-579, Department of Economics, University of Bonn, August.

PART I

SURVEYS OF ENVIRONMENTAL POLICY MAKING IN THE PRESENCE OF DISTORTIONARY TAXES

[1]

Policy Analysis in the Presence of Distorting Taxes

Ian W.H. Parry
Wallace E. Oates

Abstract

This article first describes the new literature in environmental economics on the so-called "double-dividend" and then explores its implications for a broad range of economic issues. This literature reveals that in a second-best, general-equilibrium setting, environmental measures raise costs and prices and thereby reduce the real wage. This rise in the cost of living reduces slightly the quantity of labor supplied in an already highly distorted labor market, giving rise to losses in social welfare that can be large relative to the basic gains from a cleaner environment. These losses can be offset to some extent by using revenues (if any) from the environmental programs to reduce existing taxes on labor. This same line of analysis applies to many programs and institutions in the economy that raise the cost of living: tariffs and quotas on imports, agricultural price-support programs, monopoly pricing, programs of occupational licensure that limit entry, and many others. Thus, traditional, partial-equilibrium benefit–cost analysis appears, in many instances, to have unwittingly omitted from the calculations a potentially quite significant class of social costs. © 2000 by the Association for Public Policy and Management.

INTRODUCTION

There has appeared in the last few years a challenging new literature on the design of policy instruments in a setting with preexisting distortions in the economy (distortions that result, for example, from income, payroll, or sales taxes). In the jargon of economics, such a setting gives rise to the search for "second-best policies" since such preexisting distortions sometimes undermine the case for the standard (or "first-best") measures that economists typically recommend when they ignore these distortions. Such second-best considerations are obviously not a new issue in economics, but this recent round of research has produced some striking and, in certain respects, troubling findings. In particular, this research has found that the costs associated with corrective taxes (and other regulatory measures) can be much higher in a second-best setting, so much so that in some cases the economic improvements from the traditional prescriptions can be offset by the exacerbation of the preexisting distortions. To take one example, it has been shown that for plausible values of the key parameters, a "perfectly" designed system of tradeable emissions rights—one that precisely internalizes the environmental externality by placing the costs of the environmental damages on the polluting source—may actually result in an overall loss in social welfare (Parry, Williams, and Goulder, 1999)! How can this be?

Manuscript received October 1998; revise and resubmit recommended March 1999; revision received May 1999; paper accepted August 1999.

Journal of Policy Analysis and Management, Vol. 19, No. 4, 603–613 (2000)

Published by John Wiley & Sons, Inc.

The primary source of these findings has been a body of work in environmental economics that has been reexamining the traditional case for environmental taxes and various quantity instruments (like systems of tradeable emission permits) for mitigating the distortions caused by environmental externalities.[1] The analysis focuses on preexisting tax distortions in the economic system—particularly those in the labor market—and finds that emissions taxes or marketable discharge permits can increase the social costs (or "deadweight losses" as economists call them) stemming from these distortions.[2] Moreover, this increase in costs can be large relative to the welfare gains from the environmental improvement. As noted in the earlier example, gains from the reduction in pollution can be more than offset by welfare losses from the accentuation of preexisting distortions in the economy. More generally, the findings show that the levels of environmental taxes (or other measures) should be significantly lower when these "interactions" are integrated into the analysis than when they are ignored.

The purpose of this article is to explain to economists and policy analysts just what is going on here—and to explore its broader implications. Upon further reflection, it appears that the literature in environmental economics is really just the tip of the iceberg. The basic problem is one that infects any policy measure or institutional structure with an impact on the price of consumer goods, including tariffs and quotas in international trade, agricultural price-support and quota programs, airline safety regulations, occupational licensure measures, minimum-wage laws, monopoly pricing, and a host of other major features of the economic landscape. This body of findings presents some fundamental challenges to the design of a broad range of policy measures. In particular, it suggests that the scope of benefit–cost analysis must be expanded in some very basic ways. The full range of these implications is just beginning to become clear: It is something that policy analysts must think hard about.

To introduce the issue, it is useful to review briefly the way in which it has surfaced in the literature in environmental economics.

THE DOUBLE-DIVIDEND DEBATE

The traditional treatment of environmentally damaging activities (a case of what economists call "detrimental externalities") leads directly to the prescription for a corrective tax (or, alternatively, for a system of tradeable permits) to correct the allocative distortion. The familiar unit tax equal to marginal social damages serves to internalize the externality and redeploy economic activity in an efficient manner, or so the standard argument goes. In this literature, the issue of the revenues that such a tax generates was largely ignored. It was typically assumed that the revenues would be returned lump-sum to the economic actors (e.g., Baumol and Oates, 1998, ch. 4).

But it then occurred to several observers that we should be able to do better than this (e.g., Oates, 1993; Pearce, 1991; Repetto et al., 1992). Since the existing tax system is itself the source of some serious distortions in the economy, why not use the revenues from the environmental taxes (or auctioned permits) to reduce the rates on other distorting taxes (particularly taxes on labor and capital)? This seemed to offer a way

[1] See, for example, Bovenberg and de Mooij (1994); Bovenberg and van der Ploeg (1994); Bovenberg and Goulder (1996, 1997); Parry (1995, 1997); Goulder, Parry, and Burtraw (1997); Goulder et al. (1999); Parry, Williams, and Goulder (1999); and Fullerton and Metcalf (1997). For surveys of this literature, see Bovenberg and Goulder (in press) and Oates (1995).

[2] Economists frequently use the term "deadweight loss" to refer to the magnitude of the welfare loss from a distortion in the economic system. An income tax, for example, distorts the choice between work and leisure. This results in a deadweight loss that can, in principle, be measured.

to kill two birds with one stone: We could, at the same time, both protect the environment and reduce some of the deadweight losses from the tax system. Some referred to this as a potential "double dividend" from green taxes.

But more careful analysis has revealed that this treatment is too simplistic. Once the preexisting distortions associated with the tax system are acknowledged, the basic linkages between the proposed environmental measures and existing taxes must be fully taken into account. The insight provided in the new literature is that this interaction of environmental policies with the existing system of taxes is typically the source of enlarged deadweight losses, largely from the market for labor. The labor market is a significantly distorted market in the sense that there typically exists a large wedge between the gross wage paid by firms and the net wage received by workers (with the difference going to income and social insurance taxes). This implies that the value of the extra output produced by the last unit of labor is substantially higher than its social cost (i.e., the value of time foregone in nonmarket activities, such as child rearing or leisure pursuits).

A new environmental tax increases the cost of production. To the extent that this is passed on in higher prices of goods, it will reduce the real wage received by households. In consequence, the return to work effort as compared with nonmarket activities falls, and *ceteris paribus*, a slight reduction in labor supply typically occurs. To the extent that higher production costs reduce the net income received by producers, they will tend to reduce output and their demand for labor. Thus, the environmental tax, by inducing a fall in the overall level of employment, generates a welfare loss in the labor market. Preexisting taxes, in short, have created a distorted labor market with too little work effort. And the additional costs of the environmental measures induce yet further reductions in labor supply.

But surely a green tax on a polluting activity, operating only indirectly through a minor—indeed a tiny—effect on the real wage, cannot affect labor-market decisions sufficiently to offset much of the basic and direct welfare gains from internalizing the environmental externality. After all, macroeconomic simulations of the effects of environmental regulation on prices typically find only a very small inflationary impact.

But this turns out to be wrong! Although the effect on labor supply may be quite small, it does not take much of a response in such an enormously important market—and one that is significantly distorted at the margin—to generate significant welfare effects. Existing estimates suggest that the combined impact of income, payroll, and sales taxes effectively reduces the net wage at the margin to some 40 percent or so below the gross wage (Browning, 1987). Moreover, labor income accounts for some three-quarters of national income. So even a tiny movement from A to B along the horizontal axis in Figure 1 in the labor market generates a welfare-loss rectangle whose area can be sizable. The results both from simple theoretical models and larger, more complex models of the economy (solved by numerical simulation) make it clear that this effect operating through labor market decisions cannot be dismissed as "second order" in magnitude.[3]

A CLOSER LOOK

It is helpful next to provide in this section a more systematic treatment of the analytical approach used in this literature and a more detailed characterization of the findings.

[3] Much of this analysis has focused on the distortions operating through the labor market. But it is important to realize that other factor markets (like that for capital) are often seriously distorted. Interactions of environmental measures with other factor markets are important too. In this sense, the labor market in this literature may be viewed as a kind of proxy for all distorted factor markets.

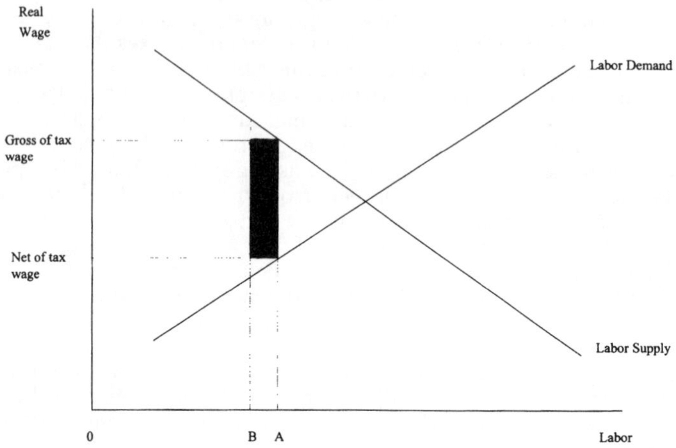

Figure 1. Distortions in the labor market.

The approach used in the analytical models is fairly straightforward (see, for example, Bovenberg and de Mooij, 1994, or Parry, 1995). Households have utility functions that contain, as arguments, consumption goods, leisure, and environmental quality, and they supply labor. Firms produce goods and, in the process, generate pollution that reduces environmental quality. In the simple models, the government employs two taxes: a tax on labor and a tax on pollution. The models are then used to study cases of "revenue-neutral" environmental taxes, where the revenues raised from unit taxes on pollution are used to reduce the tax on labor.

It is instructive to characterize the findings from this kind of analysis in terms of three distinct effects on economic welfare: the "primary welfare gain," a "revenue-recycling effect," and a "tax-interaction effect." The first is simply the familiar welfare gain whose source is the benefits net of the (partial–equilibrium) costs from the environmental improvement. In terms of Figure 2, this gain is the well-known triangle (OAB) that results from internalizing the external effect (or social cost) from waste emissions, in this case with a unit tax on emissions of Ot. In a first-best analysis, with environmental tax revenues returned lump-sum, this is all there is to the matter.

In the presence of preexisting tax distortions, however, there is more to worry about. Now the revenues raised by the environmental tax (EBCF in Figure 2) can be used to reduce the rates on existing distorting taxes. In the simple analytical models, this means that they replace revenues from the tax on labor. Hence, there is a second source of welfare gain: The revenue-recyling effect. This gain comes from the small reduction in the wedge between the gross and net wage with a resulting increase in the level of employment.

But, as mentioned earlier, a third effect involves the way in which the environmental tax interacts with the existing tax on labor. In the analytical models (which typically assume the demand for labor to be perfectly elastic) the environmental tax discourages work effort by reducing the real household wage. This is the tax-interaction effect—and it reduces welfare.

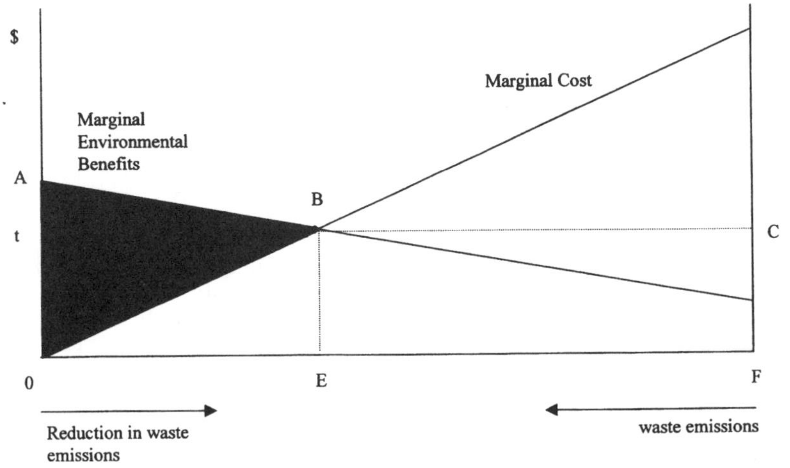

Figure 2. Primary welfare gain.

The effect of the environmental tax on economic welfare thus depends on the net impact of these three effects. The findings from the theoretical models (and many of the numerical simulations as well) indicate that, in general, the cost of the tax-interaction effect dominates the benefits from the revenue-recycling effect. That is, the welfare loss from the reduction in work effort from a reduced real wage is larger than the welfare gain from a reduced tax rate on labor. The implication is that the overall welfare (or efficiency) gain from taxing waste emissions is something less than the primary welfare gain associated with a first-best analysis.[4] Of course, environmental taxes can produce important benefits in terms of improved environmental quality and incentives for the development of cleaner production methods. However, these benefits generally do not include a reduction in the overall economic costs of the tax system—in other words, the double-dividend hypothesis is typically invalid.

This result should not be so surprising from the perspective of the earlier literature in public finance on optimal (or Ramsey) taxation (see Sandmo (1976) for a survey). This literature has established the principle that, on efficiency grounds, broad-based

[4] In the case where the environmental tax is "small," the tax-interaction and revenue-recycling effects exactly offset one another. Other qualifications are important to this result. For example, it can be reversed if output from the polluting industry is a sufficiently weaker substitute for leisure than other goods (as may be the case, for example, with pollutants in the agricultural sector). In addition, the models in this literature typically assume that environmental effects are separable in the utility function from leisure. In consequence, they effectively abstract from any feedback effects from improved environmental quality on labor/leisure decisions (e.g., health effects). A further noteworthy point is that the existing models may significantly understate the welfare gains from revenue recycling and hence the potential for a double dividend. Lowering tax rates on income, in addition to reducing the labor market distortion, decreases the effective subsidy for tax-favored expenditures, such as health insurance and mortgage interest. Some preliminary estimates by Martin Feldstein (1999) suggest that the welfare gains from reducing tax-favored expenditures may be as important as the welfare gains from increasing labor supply.

taxes generally are to be preferred to more narrow ones. Excess burden results from individuals and firms shifting away from taxed activities. There is typically much greater scope for such substitution when the tax base is narrow (for example, a polluting input in a specific industry) than when it encompasses a broad range of activity (such as a tax on all labor income or on general consumption). Replacing revenues from labor taxes with revenues from more narrowly focused taxes opens up a wider range of substitution possibilities for consumers and firms, and this typically raises the excess burden of the tax system.

The recent literature suggests that in a second-best setting, the optimal tax on waste emissions is somewhat less than the marginal social damages to the environment. Just how much less depends on the level of environmental damages, the way in which the revenues are recycled, and various parameters (notably the elasticity of labor supply). Table 1 shows some findings from a study by Lans Bovenberg and Lawrence Goulder (two of the major contributors to this literature). They make use, first, of a relatively simple model that can be solved by hand and, second, of a more complex model (solved by numerical simulation) that incorporates a more detailed treatment of the tax system. For both models, they have estimated the Pigouvian tax and optimal second-best taxes on carbon emissions for a variety of cases.[5] Column 2 gives the Pigouvian tax, which (reassuringly) is simply equal to the marginal environmental (social) damages in column 1. Column 3 shows that the optimal tax (as calculated from the analytical model) is somewhat less than the Pigouvian levy (on the order of 10 to 20 percent less); this assumes that the revenues are recycled in the form of a reduction in the personal income tax (PIT). The results from the numerical model suggest a somewhat larger divergence of the optimal, from the Pigouvian, tax; here the extent of the difference depends on whether the recycling takes an "optimized" or more realistic form of replacement of personal income taxes.[6] In the latter case, column 5 indicates that the optimal tax may fall far below the Pigouvian rate—in one instance by over 50 percent. But most striking is column 4, where the revenues are recycled in the form of the lump-sum rebate that appears in the academic literature. For this case, the optimal tax is zero for marginal environmental damages of $50 per ton or less. A positive tax for this range of cases would actually reduce welfare; this occurs because there is effectively no revenue-recycling effect (i.e., reduction in the tax on labor) to offset any of the tax-interaction effect.

This last result is of much more than purely academic interest for it immediately calls to mind the use of systems of tradeable emission permits where, to set the system in motion, the permits are simply given away. Under the Clean Air Act Amendment of 1990, for example, the United States is cutting aggregate national sulfur emissions by 50 percent under a program where the initial emissions allowances were simply distributed free of charge to sources. A similar emissions permit program is being

[5] The Pigouvian tax (named after the British economist A.C. Pigou) is a tax per unit of an activity equal to the marginal social damages. In the environmental context, this will typically take the form of a tax per unit of waste emissions equal to the monetary value of the damages to the environment resulting from the marginal unit of emissions. It is straightforward to show that, in the absence of other distortions, such a tax can completely remove any distortions in resource allocation stemming from environmentally damaging activities (such as the production of certain goods and services). See, for example, Baumol and Oates (1998). For this reason, it is sometimes referred to as a "first-best" tax (i.e., a tax that eliminates the sole distortion in the economic system). Ignoring preexisting distortions, environmental economists have typically made the case, in principle, for the Pigouvian tax as a measure to induce the socially efficient level of polluting activities.

[6] The "realistic" case uses a benchmark approximating the actual U.S. tax system that includes a variety of distorting taxes on intermediate and final goods; in contrast, the "optimized" case assumes a counterfactual benchmark where these taxes are eliminated and replaced by revenues from the personal income tax.

Table 1. Differences between Pigouvian and second-best taxes (all rates in dollars per ton).

			Optimal tax from numerical model		
Assumed marginal environmental damages	"Optimal" Pigouvian tax	Optimal tax implied by analytical model (PIT replacement)	Realistic benchmark, lump-sum replacement	Realistic benchmark, PIT replacement	Optimized benchmark, PIT replacement
25	25	22	0	7	17
50	50	45	0	27	41
75	75	67	13	48	64
100	100	89	31	68	85

Source: Bovenberg and Goulder (1996).

proposed as a means to meeting the U.S. pledge to limit future carbon emissions. The problem with these programs is that there is no revenue-recycling effect.[7] As recently shown by Parry, Williams, and Goulder (1999) and Parry (1997)+, even for "ideal" systems that set the quantity of permits by a Pigouvian rule, it is possible that for reasonable values of the key parameters, the adverse tax-interaction effect will be larger than the primary welfare gain from reducing pollution. Thus, the loss in welfare from reduced work effort can more than offset the gains from a cleaner environment. Such a system of tradeable allowances—a system strongly supported by environmental economists as a major step forward in the use of market incentives for environmental protection—could possibly reduce social welfare.

One lesson that emerges from the new literature is the potential importance of revenue recycling. From the second-best perspective, a system of tradeable allowances set in motion by an auction of the permits to sources should be much preferred to one in which the permits are distributed to the sources without charge. The former generates revenues that can be used to reduce other distorting taxes, while the latter does not. This admittedly raises some tricky matters of political economy. One of the attractions of marketable permits in the policy arena has been the receptivity to them of polluting firms, who would much prefer to receive a free allotment of valuable tradeable permits than to be subject to a tax on their emissions or, alternatively, to be forced to compete in an auction for the permits. But, in a second-best setting, such provisions for the free distribution of permits may compromise the welfare-improving potential of the system. Moreover, even if the program generates revenues through an auction of permits or some schedule of charges, there is no guarantee that the newly generated revenues will be employed to reduce rates on other distorting taxes.[8]

[7] This is not quite accurate. Emissions permits create rents for firms. These are reflected in higher profits (subject to corporate income taxation) and in additional taxes when distributed to households in the form of dividends or capital gains. As a result, about a third of these rents may accrue to the government in the form of tax revenues. Grandfathered emissions permits can produce a complete revenue-recycling effect equivalent to that under an emissions tax only in the limiting case where rents are 100 percent taxed.

[8] In fact, environmental programs that generate revenues often contain provisions that direct the revenues into some kind of trust fund that must be used for environmental enhancement. Of course such spending may produce a significant efficiency gain—but only if the social benefits per dollar of additional spending are well in excess of a dollar.

A further important point from the recent literature is that the relative importance of the tax-interaction effect is sensitive to the level of environmental regulation. When marginal environmental benefits in Figure 2 are more modest relative to marginal control costs (as is thought to be the case for carbon emissions), then the Pigouvian level of emissions reductions will tend to be relatively small, and it becomes more likely that the welfare loss rectangle in Figure 1 outweighs the Pigouvian welfare gain triangle in Figure 2 (Parry, Williams, and Goulder, 1999). In contrast, where marginal environmental benefits are relatively large (as estimates suggest for the case of sulfur emissions), the tax-interaction effect is unlikely to reverse the sign of the overall welfare impact from positive to negative (see Goulder, Parry, and Burtraw, 1997).

SOME BROADER IMPLICATIONS

Although most of the new literature focuses on programs for environmental management, upon reflection it becomes clear that this is a very general issue. Any program or institution that influences the costs of production, or in any other way affects the labor market, is going to generate some social gains or losses from the operation of the tax-interaction effect. In fact, an independent discovery of the importance of this phenomenon arose in a very different kind of study. Edgar Browning (1997), reexamining the welfare losses associated with monopoly pricing, found (somewhat to his astonishment) that the welfare costs of monopoly distortions in a second-best framework were many times larger than those implied by the familiar Harberger triangles.

Some further thought suggests that programs like tariffs and quotas on imports of manufactured goods, or agricultural price-supports and quotas, which drive up prices and effectively reduce the real wage, are likely to have substantial welfare costs stemming from labor-market distortions in addition to the more traditional forms of welfare losses that economists have measured. Indeed, as this second-best analytical framework is applied to a wide range of programs, the welfare losses associated with many of these programs may turn out significantly larger than previously thought. To take one such case, Williams (1999) and Parry (in press) have recently shown that the presence of preexisting taxes can raise the economic costs of tariffs and import quotas by a potentially substantial amount.[9]

It is easy to extend the list of potential applications. It would appear, for example, that the costs of airline safety regulations, programs of occupational licensure that limit entry and increase prices, and minimum-wage laws can be much magnified in their impact when preexisting taxes are taken into account.

It is not the case, however, that this second-best framework implies that public programs are inevitably more costly than a partial–equilibrium treatment would indicate. There may well be some important cases where there are significant complementarities to work effort. One that comes to mind is traffic congestion. A (revenue-neutral) toll on a congested roadway for commuters that reduces travel time may, under certain circumstances, effectively raise the real wage and induce an increase in employment.[10]

[9] In fact, interactions with the tax system can eliminate the well-known textbook case for an optimal tariff when a country has market power in trade, unless the tariff revenues are used to finance reductions in other distorting taxes.

[10] The analysis also has some important implications for subsidy programs, such as those for industrial R&D, public transport, and child care. Here the tax-interaction effect results in a welfare gain where such subsidies reduce the price of goods and services. This implies that the tax-interaction effect may offset much of the cost of financing a subsidy by distortionary taxes.

CONCLUDING REMARKS

This new literature thus raises a large red flag to those engaged in benefit–cost analysis: Beware of partial–equilibrium studies. In an economy with distorted factor markets, it is important to take into account the indirect welfare effects of public programs on the labor market and perhaps other factor markets as well.[11] In certain cases, these indirect effects (although seemingly small) can outweigh the primary welfare effects of the program.

This is a troubling and sobering finding because it complicates the task of policy analysis and can undermine the case for certain programs that have long been dear to economists working in a first-best setting. At the same time, the results from the recent literature are preliminary in a number of respects. We have much to learn about the properties and applicability of this analysis to the evaluation of public policy.

One issue, in particular, stands out: the structure and workings of the labor market. It is the indirect effect of these programs on levels of employment that is the source of most of the "secondary," but large, welfare effects in a general–equilibrium setting. The labor market is a very complex institution with many facets. The analyses described here treat it as a single, integrated, and competitive market. But, in truth, it is difficult to estimate the overall employment effects caused by policies that affect the real wage because these effects depend on a diverse set of decisions involving labor–market participation and hours worked for a variety of different groups in varying settings. In the labor literature a substantial range of estimates exist of the relevant labor supply elasticities so that any projections of the effects of changes in the real wage on employment are subject to a fair amount of uncertainty. The point here is simply that given the importance of the labor-market responses to the bottom line in benefit–cost studies of public programs, it is crucial to have a sound understanding and reliable estimates of labor-market behavior.

This is likely to be even more complicated and important outside the United States. It may be reasonable to characterize the U.S. labor market as a competitive market, but this seems less true in, say, Europe, where there are many more regulations (including more generous unemployment benefits, provisions for retirement, higher minimum wages, and higher taxes on labor) and much stronger labor unions that impinge on (and distort) the workings of the market. The high levels of unemployment that are plaguing many of the European nations appear, at least in part, to stem from these provisions. Perhaps the revenue-recycling effects that result in lower taxes on labor and the tax-interaction effects from a reduced real wage operate a bit differently in the context of some of these institutional features of European labor markets.

Finally these new findings are certainly not grounds for abandoning the economist's case for pricing incentives for environmental protection. The argument here has been limited to an essentially static framework. And, as economists have long argued, one of the most important properties (in fact, perhaps the most important) of incentive-based instruments for environmental management is the inducement that such

[11] Some of the numerical models are dynamic with capital accumulation and allow for tax distortions in the capital market (e.g., Bovenberg and Goulder (1997), and Jorgenson and Wilcoxen (1993). Tax interactions are more complex in this setting. To the extent that environmental regulations discourage investment by raising the cost of producing output in future periods, they tend to compound the welfare costs of taxes on capital. Bovenberg and Goulder (1997) show that incorporating capital can either strengthen or weaken the results from static one-factor models, depending on whether the revenue-neutral environmental tax reform expands or reduces inefficiencies associated with the uneven taxation of labor and capital. However, given that the capital market is only around one-third the size of the labor market, we would expect the results from the static models to be reasonably robust to incorporating capital.

instruments provide for the development and adoption of new techniques for pollution control. The welfare gains from such technical advances may well dominate the static gains from the more efficient deployment of resources within a given technological context. Moreover, even in a purely static analysis, it is still the case that pricing incentives typically yield a net benefit. In short, the absence of a double dividend does not eliminate the case for environmental taxes.

The central, and more general, point is that a potentially major element of social costs has been systematically overlooked in the analysis of a wide class of public programs and economic institutions. It is tempting simply to dismiss such findings on the grounds that, "We know that anything can happen in a second-best setting." But this really misses the point. The contribution of this new literature is to show specifically what can happen under certain, well-defined, and realistic circumstances; it reduces the ambiguity. And the results seem quite robust: There is now a large body of work, encompassing both analytical and numerical studies, that has firmly established the potential importance of these indirect effects operating through factor markets. Moreover, this work generates some valuable insights into the design of policy measures (most notably the importance of revenue recycling). The new second-best literature presents a serious challenge to much of traditional policy analysis.

The authors are most grateful for helpful comments from Lawrence Goulder and Paul Portney. Parry also thanks the Environmental Protection Agency for its support of this work under EPA Grant R825313-01.

IAN W.H. PARRY is a Research Fellow at Resources for the Future.

WALLACE E. OATES is Professor of Economics at the University of Maryland (College Park) and University Fellow at Resources for the Future.

REFERENCES

Baumol, W., & Oates, W. (1998). The theory of environmental policy (2nd ed.). Cambridge: Cambridge University Press.

Bovenberg, A., & de Mooij, R. (1994). Environmental levies and distortionary taxation. American Economic Review, 84, 1085–1089.

Bovenberg, A., & Goulder, L. (in press). Environmental taxation. In A. Auerbach & M. Feldstein (Eds.), Handbook of public economics (2nd ed.). New York: North-Holland.

Bovenberg, A., & Goulder, L. (1996). Optimal environmental Taxation in the presence of other taxes: General equilibrium analyses. American Economic Review, 86, 985–1000.

Bovenberg, A., & Goulder, L. (1997). Costs of environmentally motivated taxes in the presence of other taxes: General equilibrium analyses. National Tax Journal, 50, 59–88.

Bovenberg, A., & van der Ploeg, F. (1994). Environmental policy, public finance and the labor market in a second-best world. Journal of Public Economics, 55, 349–390.

Browning, E. (1987). On the marginal welfare cost of taxation. American Economic Review, 77, 11–23.

Browning, E. (1997). A neglected welfare cost of monopoly—And most other product market distortions. Journal of Public Economics, 66, 127–144.

Feldstein, M. (1999). Tax avoidance and the deadweight loss of the income tax. Review of Economics and Statistics, 81, 674–680.

Fullerton, D. & Metcalf, G. (1997). Environmental controls, scarcity rents, and preexisting distortions. National Bureau of Economic Research Working Paper No. 6091. Cambridge, MA.

Goulder, L., Parry I., & Burtraw, D. (1997). Revenue-raising vs. other approaches to environmental protection: The critical significance of preexisting tax distortions. RAND Journal of Economics, 28, 708–731.

Goulder, L., Parry, I., Williams, R., & Burtraw, D. (1999). The cost-effectiveness of alternative instruments for environmental protection in a second-best setting. Journal of Public Economics, 72, 329–360.

Jorgenson, D., & Wilcoxen, P. (1993). Reducing U.S. carbon emissions: An econometric general equilibrium assessment. Resource and Energy Economics, 15, 7–26.

Oates, W. (1995). Green taxes: Can we protect the environment and improve the tax system at the same time? Southern Economic Journal, 61, 915–922.

Oates, W. (1993). Pollution charges as a source of public revenues. In H. Giersch (Ed.), Economic progress and environmental concerns (pp. 135–152), Berlin: Springer-Verlag.

Parry, I. (1995). Pollution taxes and revenue recycling. Journal of Environmental Economics and Management, 29, S64–S77.

Parry, I. (1997). Environmental taxes and quotas in the presence of distorting taxes in factor markets. Resource and Energy Economics, 19, 203–220.

Parry, I. (in press). The costs of restrictive trade policies in the presence of factor tax distortions. International Tax and Public Finance.

Parry, I., Williams, R., & Goulder, L. (1999). When can carbon abatement policies increase welfare? The fundamental role of distorted factor markets. Journal of Environmental Economics and Management, 37, 52–84.

Pearce, D. (1991). The role of carbon taxes in adjusting to global warming. Economic Journal, 101, 938–948.

Repetto, R., Dower, R., Jenkins, R., & Geoghegan, J. (1992). Green fees: How a tax shift can work for the environment and the economy. Washington, DC: World Resources Institute.

Sandmo, A. (1976). Optimal taxation: An introduction to the literature. Journal of Public Economics, 6, 37–54.

Williams, R. (1999). Revisiting the cost of protectionism: The role of tax distortions in the labor market. Journal of International Economics, 47, 459–477.

[2]

Environmental Policy Making in a Second-Best Setting

Lawrence H. Goulder

Lawrence H. Goulder is Associate Professor of Economics at Stanford University, University Fellow at Resources for the Future, and Research Associate at the National Bureau of Economic Research.

I. Introduction

Economists have long been interested in ways that taxes and other policy instruments can address environmental problems associated with externalities. This interest dates back at least to Pigou (1938), who showed that taxes could usefully internalize externalities and thereby "get the prices right"—that is, bring prices into alignment with marginal social cost. In the last two decades, there has been increased attention to other, non-tax market instruments—including tradeable emission permits and deposit-refund systems—as tools for dealing with environmental problems in an effective way.

Since the publication of Pigou's classic article, the tradition in environmental economics has been to analyze environmental policies with an almost exclusive attention to the externality of immediate concern and little attention to other distortions or market failures. However, in recent years economists have come to recognize the importance of interactions between environmental policies and other (nonenvironmental) distortions in the economy. In particular, there has been increased attention to the interconnections between environmental taxes and the distortions imposed by preexisting income or commodity taxes.

These interactions were first examined in a seminal contribution by Sandmo (1975), although the insights from this article were largely ignored until recently. Sandmo analyzed the optimal setting of commodity taxes when the production or consumption of one of the commodities generates an externality. He showed that when the government's need for revenue exceeds the level that can be generated by taxes set according to the "Pigov-

"Environmental Policy Making in a Second-Best Setting," by Lawrence H. Goulder was prepared for the University of CEMA Twentieth Anniversary Conference on Applied Economics, Buenos Aires, Argentina, November 12–14, 1998. The original version of this paper appeared in the *Journal of Applied Economics*, 1(2) (November 1998). Section II of the present paper replaces the previous, more technical version of Section II. The author is grateful to Roberton C. Williams III for very helpful comments, and to the National Science Foundation (Grant SBR9613458) and U.S. Environmental Protection Agency (Grant R825313-01) for financial support.

ian principle" (that is, set equal to the marginal environmental damages), then the optimal tax system includes taxes not only on externality-generating goods and services but on other goods and services as well. In Sandmo's analysis, the optimal tax rates on environmentally damaging activities and on ordinary activities are intimately connected.

The interconnections between ordinary and environmental taxes, so central to Sandmo's optimal tax result, also figure importantly in the analysis of the impacts of marginal (that is, less than globally optimizing) environmental reforms. A line of research conducted during this decade shows that one cannot effectively evaluate the impacts of many environmental reforms without paying attention to the magnitudes and types of existing, distortionary taxes such as income, payroll, or sales taxes. There are two important interconnections here. First, as Terkla (1984), Lee and Misiolek (1986), Oates and Schwab (1988), Oates (1993), Repetto et al. (1992), and others have emphasized, the presence of distortionary taxes introduces opportunities to use revenues from new environmental taxes to finance cuts in the marginal rates of the ordinary distortionary taxes. To the extent that revenues from the environmental tax finance marginal rate cuts of this kind, some of the distortions that the ordinary taxes would have generated are avoided. This *revenue-recycling effect* suggests that the overall *gross*[1] costs of environmental taxes will be lower in a second-best world than in a first-best setting.

However, a second interconnection works in the opposite direction. Recent work by Bovenberg and de Mooij (1994a), Bovenberg and van der Ploeg (1994), Bovenberg and Goulder (1996, 1997), Parry (1995, 1997), and others[2] points out that environmental taxes are implicit taxes on factors of production such as labor and capital. By raising the costs of production and the costs of goods in general, environmental taxes (and many other environmental regulations) reduce real after-tax factor returns much like explicit factor taxes do. Thus, environmental taxes function as increments to existing factor taxes, tending to magnify the factor market distortions already generated by preexisting factor taxes. The additional efficiency costs of environmental taxes associated with the reduction in factor returns brought about by higher costs and output prices has been called the *tax-interaction effect*.[3] The larger the rates of preexisting factor taxes, the larger the tax-interaction effect, and thus the higher the gross costs from environmental taxes and other regulations that reduce after-tax returns to factors. The tax-interaction effect implies that, for any given method of recycling the revenues, the gross costs of environmental taxes are higher in a second-best setting with preexisting factor taxes than they would be if there

[1]The modifier "gross" indicates that the costs do not net out the policy-generated benefits associated with an improved environment.

[2]For earlier reviews of this recent literature, see Oates (1995) and Goulder (1995a).

[3]Parry (1995) was the first to isolate the tax-interaction and revenue-recycling effects in evaluating the second-best welfare impacts of environmental taxes. He termed these the "interdependency" and "revenue" effects.

were no prior taxes on factors. As will be discussed in more detail later in this paper, the tax-interaction effect tends to be of greater magnitude than the revenue-recycling effect; that is, it is only partly offset by the revenue-recycling effect.

The revenue-recycling and tax-interaction effects are highly relevant to the evaluation of "green tax reforms." A green tax policy of particular interest is a revenue-neutral carbon tax, which would address the prospect of global climate change by discouraging combustion of fossil fuels and the associated emissions of carbon dioxide, a principal contributor to the greenhouse effect. In discussions of carbon taxes, there has been great interest in the possibility that judicious recycling of the revenues from these taxes could cause the overall gross costs of this policy to be become zero or negative. Proponents of carbon taxes certainly would welcome this result, since it implies that policy makers must only establish that there are nonnegative environment-related *benefits* from the carbon tax policy to justify the policy on efficiency grounds. Given the vast uncertainties about the environment-related benefits from carbon abatement, it would significantly reduce the information burden faced by policy makers if they simply needed to determine the sign, rather than magnitude, of the environmental benefits. If one ignores the tax-interaction effect and concentrates only on revenue-recycling (and the revenue-recycling effect), the prospects for a zero-cost carbon tax will seem quite good. But the tax-interaction effect also has a key role here and, as will be discussed below, this latter effect significantly reduces the scope for the zero-cost result.

The absence of a zero-cost result does not imply that carbon taxes are a bad idea; it only means that justifying these taxes requires attention to the magnitudes (not just the sign) of the environmental benefits. Even if revenue-neutral carbon taxes or other green tax reforms do not make environmental improvement a free lunch, they may reduce its cost enough to make it very much worth buying. Indeed, in most analyses (see below) appropriately scaled revenue-neutral green tax reforms yield environmental benefits that exceed their gross costs.

A second area where the revenue-recycling and tax-interaction effects are important is in the choice among alternative policy instruments. Consider, for example, the choice between pollution tax policies (or pollution permits policies involving the auctioning of permits by the government) and freely allocated (or "grandfathered"[4]) emissions permits. The former policies raise revenue and thus are capable of taking advantage of the revenue-recycling effect. The latter policies, in contrast, do not raise revenue and therefore cannot exploit this effect. As discussed below, the tax-

[4]In keeping with common practice, we use the terms "grandfathered" and "freely allocated" interchangeably. Strictly speaking, however, grandfathering is not synonymous with free allocation. Grandfathering is a legal provision whereby "old" entities (e.g., firms subject to previous environmental rules) are waived of new regulatory requirements and instead remain bound only to the earlier (and perhaps more lax) regulatory provisions.

interaction effect arises under both policies, but only under the revenue-raising policies is the (costly) tax-interaction effect offset by the revenue-recycling effect. Recent work by Parry (1997), Goulder, Parry, and Burtraw (1997), Parry, Williams, and Goulder (1999), Fullerton and Metcalf (1997), and Goulder et al. (1999) reveals that the presence or absence of the revenue-recycling effect can fundamentally affect the overall efficiency impacts of these policies.[5] In fact, when marginal benefits from pollution abatement fail to exceed a certain threshold value, pollution permit policies that fail to enjoy the revenue-recycling effect may be unable to produce any efficiency improvements, no matter what the level of pollution abatement![6] This analysis shows that the decision to give out pollution permits free rather than to auction them (or, equivalent, to employ a pollution tax) comes at a high price in terms of efficiency, and indeed may affect the sign of the overall efficiency impact. Other considerations—such as distributional consequences—may tend to support the use of grandfathered permits rather than auctioned permits or pollution taxes, but this recent literature indicates that the efficiency disadvantage of grandfathered permits is more significant than was previously recognized.

This paper examines the efficiency impacts of pollution taxes and some other pollution-control policies in a second-best setting with prior distortionary taxes in factor markets. It aims to articulate and pull together some key ideas from recent papers on this subject. The next section heuristically describes some of the main results from recent work on the efficiency effects of environmental taxes and quotas (or tradeable permits) in a second-best setting.[7] Section III then elaborates on these results, first by offering additional interpretation related to environmental taxes and the double dividend issue, and then by considering the significance of second-best issues for the choice between taxes and other, non-tax instruments for environmental protection. Section IV briefly depicts some results from investigations that apply this second-best framework to assess the efficiency impacts of environmental taxes and regulations. It first considers the impacts of revenue-neutral environmental taxes; it then examines potential impacts of pollution permits, with a focus on the efficiency implications of the decision whether to auction or freely offer the permits. The final section offers conclusions.

---

[5]Fullerton and Metcalf explain differences in efficiency outcomes in terms of whether policies generate privately-retained scarcity rents, rather than in terms of whether they exploit the revenue-recycling effect. As discussed in Section III, the two issues are intimately connected.

[6]This result, for pollution permits, was foreshadowed by Bovenberg and Goulder's (1996) finding that a carbon tax with lump-sum replacement of the revenues will be efficiency-reducing if marginal environmental benefits from carbon abatement are below a certain threshold (about $50 per ton). Parry (1997) recognized that the same formal analysis applies to the case of pollution quotas and grandfathered pollution permits; thus the same "threshold" issue arises.

[7]This section offers a nontechnical presentation of the results generated in Goulder (1998). Other sections of this paper involve only incidental changes from the corresponding sections in Goulder (1998).

II. Impacts of Environmental Taxes and Quotas in a Second-Best Setting

A. The Conventional, Partial Equilibrium Analysis of Policy Impacts

To understand how environmental policies interact with preexisting factor-market distortions, it helps to consider first the impacts of environmental policies in a setting with no prior distortionary taxes. We can then observe how the situation changes in the presence of distortionary taxes and associated factor-market distortions.

Figure 1 offers the typical partial equilibrium framework for analyzing the welfare effects of an environmental tax or quota.[8] *MC* denotes the private marginal costs of producing the given commodity, which in this example is coal. MC_{soc} represents the social marginal-cost curve, incorporating the marginal external damage (marginal external cost) *MED*. *MB* represents the marginal benefit (demand) curve. If a tax is imposed on coal equal to the marginal external damage, the welfare gain is area *B*.[9] This is the value of the environmental improvement $(A + B)$ minus the gross costs of the tax (A).[10]

The same figure indicates the impacts of a quota on coal use. Suppose that the government restricts total coal use to the quantity Q_1. The government could do this, for example, by issuing licenses to coal-supplying firms, where the licenses authorize the sale of coal and where the total number of licenses limits aggregate sales to Q_1. (Assume that the licenses are given out free, rather than auctioned, so that the government does not earn revenue in issuing licenses. We will consider shortly the significance of auctioning the licenses.) The diagram indicates that the restriction in coal supply will cause the price of coal to rise by the same amount as in the case of the coal tax. Under this policy, the restriction on coal supply imposes gross costs of *A*; these gross costs are the lost potential surplus to users of coal such as steel manufacturers or electric utilities. The value of the environmental improvement is again $(A + B)$, and thus the welfare gain is again *B*.[11]

---

[8]Here the tax is a strict Pigovian tax in that it applies to a commodity with which pollution is associated rather than directly to pollution emissions. Similarly, the quota applies to the commodity (coal) rather than to pollution emissions from coal. The lessons from this section apply equally to taxes and quotas on emissions. For a general examination of issues surrounding the choice between regulating emissions and regulating a commodity closely associated with emissions, see Bovenberg and Goulder (1999).

[9]In the case with nonconstant private marginal costs or nonconstant marginal external costs, the presentation is slightly more complicated but the results are essentially the same.

[10]The environmental economics literature often refers to *abatement costs*. These are usually defined in a way that corresponds, in Figure 1, to the entire area below the *MB* curve (including the area below the *MC* curve) over the interval from Q_0 to Q_1.

[11]The efficiency impacts of the tax and quota are the same in this example. However, this example ignores uncertainty by the regulator with regard to firms' costs of coal (or pollution) abatement. In the presence of such uncertainty, taxes and quotas generally have different impacts. See Weitzman (1974) and Stavins (1995).

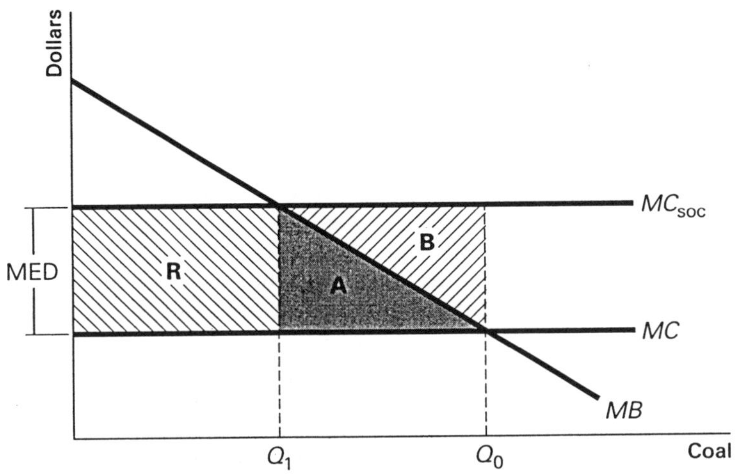

Figure 1 Typical Partial Equilibrium Framework for Analyzing Efficiency Impacts of Environmental Taxes and Quotas

B. Two Complications

Prior distortionary taxes complicate the analysis in two ways. The simple analysis usually assumes that there are no efficiency consequences associated with the transfer of the tax revenue *R* from those who pay the coal tax to the government and then back to the private sector.[12] However, in an economy with prior taxes, the revenues from an environmental tax can be used to finance reductions in the marginal rates of prior distortionary taxes such as income, payroll, or sales taxes. When revenues are "recycled" in this way, some of the distortions or excess burdens from prior taxes can be avoided. This beneficial efficiency impact is the revenue-recycling effect.

A second complicating effect works in the opposite direction. This second effect, the tax-interaction effect, occurs because the environmental tax or quote tends to reduce the real returns to factors such as labor and capital, discourage the supply of these factors, and thereby exacerbate preexisting distortions in factor markets. The tax-interaction effect is discussed in general terms in a number of recent studies.[13] For concreteness, in the present discussion we will illustrate the tax-interaction effect using our example with coal. In addition, we will describe the tax-interaction effect through its impact on the labor market. A recent paper by Williams (1999) shows that the tax-interaction effect applies to capital in much the same way it applies to labor.

The tax-interaction effect reflects the links from (1) the tax or quota to (2) the cost of living to (3) the real wage and finally to (4) the distortion in

[12]In the simplest case, the revenues are returned to the private sector in a lump-sum fashion.
[13]See Parry (1995, 1997), Goulder, Parry, and Burtraw (1997), and Goulder et al. (1999).

the labor market. As suggested by Figure 1, the tax or the quota causes the market price of coal to rise. The higher price of coal raises costs to users of coal, which implies increased prices of goods or services from coal-using industries. One might expect the price-increases to be most pronounced in the industries for which coal is a significant, direct input (e.g., electricity and steel). However, higher coal prices affect the costs and output prices of other industries too, since other industries use coal indirectly: for example, they use the steel that was made from coal. Through direct and indirect cost-impacts, the higher coal price leads to higher prices in many industries and contributes to a rise in the cost of living. This increase in the cost of living means that a given nominal wage, *w*, now represents a lower real wage.

By raising the costs of goods and services, environmental policies reduce the real return to labor. These policies are implicit taxes on labor (and other factors of production). These implicit taxes discourage labor (and other factor) supply, as indicated by Figure 2. In this figure, S_L and D_L represent the supply and demand curves for labor, respectively. Let τ_L denote the prior tax on labor implied by preexisting payroll or income taxes. In this setting, with a prior labor tax, the initial equilibrium labor supply is $L_I < L_0$. The prior distortion in the labor market is given by the triangular region defined by points *a*, *b*, and *c*. Now consider the labor-market impact of the environmental tax or quota. By raising the cost of living and lowering the real wage, the environmental policy induces a shift in the la-

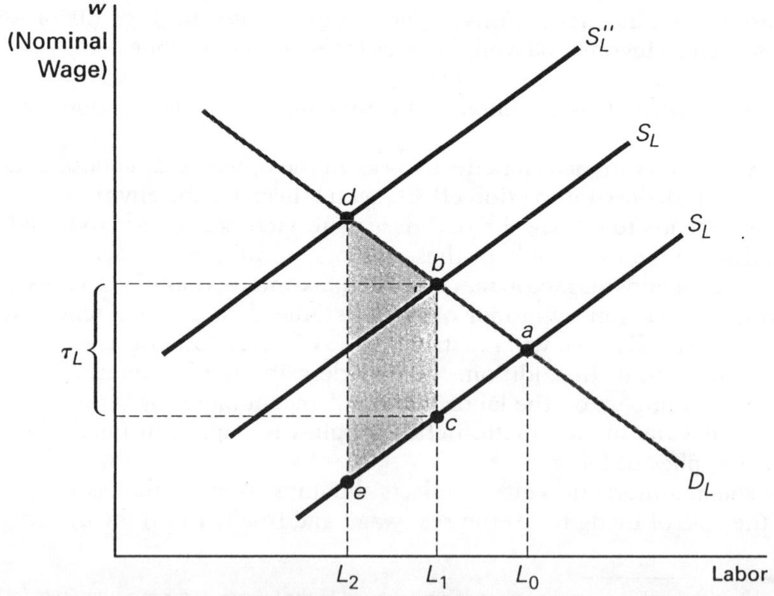

Figure 2 The Tax Interaction Effect

bor supply curve from S_L' to S_L''. This implies a further reduction (to L_2) in the equilibrium labor supply, and a further distortion in the labor market, represented by the trapezoidal area defined by points *b*, *d*, *e*, and *c*. This area is the tax-interaction effect. As suggested by Figure 2, the tax-interaction effect is an increasing function of the size of the prior tax on labor.[14] In the limiting case where the prior tax τ_L is zero, the tax-interaction effect disappears.

Thus, in a second-best setting, two effects complicate the efficiency analysis of environmental taxes and quotas. The revenue-recycling effect tends to imply lower costs of these policies than in a "first-best" setting with no prior taxes. But the tax-interaction effect tends to imply higher costs. Which effect is stronger? In the simple models developed in recent studies, the tax-interaction effect dominates. If the good to which the environmental tax applies in an average substitute for leisure, the tax-interaction effect is stronger than the revenue-recycling effect.[15] This implies that the costs of environmental taxes and quotas are higher in the presence of prior factor taxes than in their absence—even when the revenues are recycled through cuts in marginal income tax rates.

Why is the tax-interaction effect more powerful? Note that the environmental (coal) tax affects the relative prices of goods and services. It thus "distorts" not only the labor market (by lowering the real wage) but also "distorts" consumers' choices among these goods and services.[16] Recycling the revenues helps return the real wage to its original value and thereby helps reduce the labor-market distortion, but such recycling does not undo the change in relative consumer good prices and the associated "distortion" in consumption choices. For this reason the revenue-recycling effect only partly offsets the tax-interaction effect. The revenue-neutral environmental tax policy effectively substitutes (at the margin) a narrow environmental tax for a broader income tax. This makes the tax system less efficient along the nonenvironmental dimensions captured under the notion of gross cost. (At the same time, the tax system may well be more efficient overall, once one accounts for the environment-related benefits from the tax or quota.)

Figure 3 illustrates these findings. The figure shows the marginal efficiency costs of pollution abatement, at different levels of abatement, where the efficiency costs represented here are gross (that is, exclusive) of the benefits from environmental improvement. The lowermost line depicts the marginal costs of abatement in the "first-best" setting, by which we mean an economy with no distortionary taxes. In a first-best situation, the marginal costs of abatement are the same regardless of whether an environmental tax or quota is imposed.

---

[14]See Parry (1997) for a rigorous demonstration.

[15]We discuss below the significance of the "average substitute" assumption.

[16]The word "distort" is in quotes to acknowledge that we are ignoring environment-related benefits here. While the changes in relative prices of commodities occasioned by the environmental tax may contribute to higher gross costs, these same relative price changes may bring about an overall efficiency improvement, since overall efficiency incorporates the environment-related benefits (reduced pollution) associated with the relative price changes.

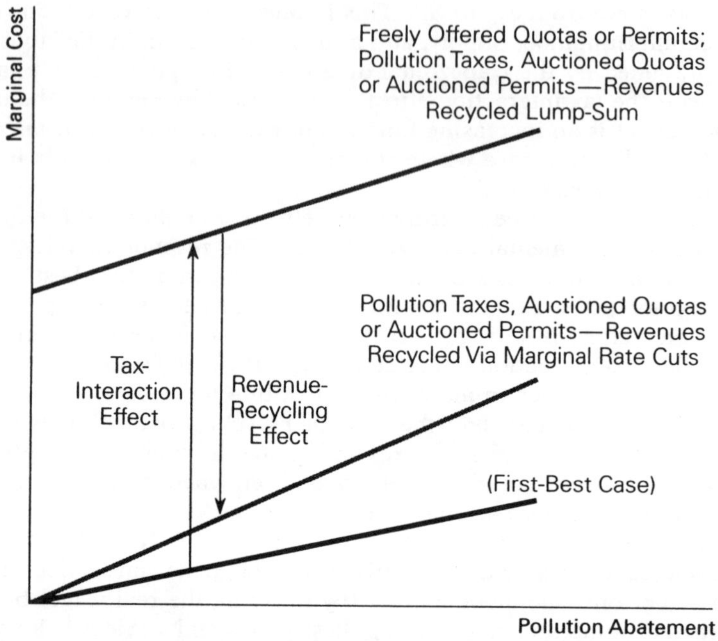

Figure 3 Marginal Costs of Pollution Abatement in First- and Second-Best Settings

The other lines represent the marginal costs in an economy with prior distortionary taxes. The top line depicts the marginal costs of abatement for policies that produce the tax-interaction effect but do not enjoy the revenue-recycling effect. Several policies fall into this category. One is the coal quota just discussed. Another is a system of tradeable coal permits, where the permits are given out free ("grandfathered"). A third is a coal tax policy in which the revenues are returned to the economy lump-sum rather than through cuts in marginal tax rates. In all of these cases, the revenue-recycling effect is absent. For these policies, at all levels of abatement, the marginal costs of abatement are higher than in the first-best case. This is the case even at incremental abatement: the second-best marginal cost curve has a positive intercept, whereas the marginal cost of incremental abatement for these policies is zero (dashed line) in the first-best case.[17] At any level of abatement, the tax-interaction effect is represented by the vertical distance between the top and bottom (dashed) marginal cost curve.

The intercept of the top marginal cost curve represents the critical value for marginal environmental *benefits* from pollution abatement through these policies. If the marginal benefits are (always) below this value, then pollution reductions through one of these policies will always involve costs

[17]So long as the prior tax rate on labor is positive, the introduction of these environmental policies augments a preexisting distortion and involves a first-order (i.e., nonincremental) efficiency cost.

that exceed the benefits. Under these circumstances, these policies will be efficiency-reducing regardless of the level of abatement!

The middle line in Figure 3 represents the marginal costs of abatement for policies that exploit the revenue-recycling effect by raising revenues and using these revenues to finance cuts in the marginal rates of prior distortionary taxes. Such policies include environmental taxes, *auctioned* coal quotas or *auctioned* tradeable permits, where revenues are recycled through marginal rate cuts. The revenue-recycling effect is represented by the vertical distance between the top and middle marginal cost curves. Revenue-recycling through marginal rate reductions can significantly reduce the general-equilibrium costs of environmental regulations. At incremental abatement, the revenue-recycling effect fully offsets the tax-interaction effect; hence, the marginal cost of abatement is zero at incremental abatement (as in the first-best case). However, for larger amounts of abatement, the revenue-recycling effect only partly offsets the tax-interaction effect (for the reasons given above), and thus the costs of abatement exceed the costs of comparable abatement in a first-best setting.

Figure 3 illustrates the idea that an environmental policy's potential to yield an overall efficiency gain can depend on whether it exploits the revenue-recycling effect. By definition, a policy yields an efficiency improvement if and only if its (environment-related) benefits exceed its overall gross costs (including the net contribution of the tax-interaction and revenue-recycling effects). The revenue-recycling effect may be necessary to make net benefits positive.

The figure also indicates that second-best considerations tend to imply higher costs from environmental policies. Even so, the news for environmental policy reform is not entirely bad. Note that for policies that exploit the revenue-recycling effect, the general equilibrium marginal costs are initially zero. Note also that, in general, one would expect the (gross) marginal *benefits* from pollution-abatement to be strictly positive at initial amounts of abatement. Together, these ideas imply that these policies generally will be justified on efficiency grounds—so long as the amount of abatement is not too great. In a second-best world, there remains potential for efficiency gains through pollution taxes and other policies that deal with pollution-related externalities.

It should be noted that Figure 3 illustrates the "central case" results from analytical models—that is, the results that stem from the assumption that the good on which the environmental tax is imposed is an average substitute for leisure. Suppose instead, that this good were a weaker than average substitute for leisure, that is, a relative complement to leisure. Analytical studies indicate that in this case, for a sufficiently small environmental tax (or sufficiently small amount of abatement in Figure 3), the revenue-recycling effect will outweigh the tax-interaction effect. Under these circumstances, the costs of abatement are *lower* in a second-best world than in a first-best world—at least up to a certain level of abatement. When a good is a relative complement to leisure, the environmental tax causes a reduction in both the demand for that good and the demand for leisure. The reduced demand for leisure, or increased supply of labor, helps alleviate preexisting labor market distortion. If, on the other hand, the taxed good were a stronger than average substitute for leisure, the tax-interaction effect would overtake the revenue-recycling effect by even more than in the average-substitute case, and the costs of given amounts of abatement would be greater than in the average-substitute case. There is a lack of solid empirical information regarding the extent to which various pollution-related goods are substitutes or complements with leisure. In the absence of such information, the assumption of "average substitutability" seems reasonable. Further empirical work that clarifies these substitutability or complementarity relationships could be of great value to researchers aiming to assess the costs of environmental regulations.

III. Interpretations, Qualifications, and Extensions

A. Can Pollution Taxes Deliver a "Double Dividend"?

In recent years there has been considerable debate about the possibilities for "green tax reform," that is, the substitution of taxes on pollution for ordinary, distortionary taxes. A general argument for such reform is that it makes sense to concentrate taxes on "bads" like pollution rather than "goods" like labor effort or capital formation (saving and investment). To buttress the case for green tax reform, some analysts have argued that the revenue-neutral swap of pollution taxes for ordinary taxes will produce a "double dividend:" not only (1) improve the quality of the environment but also (2) reduce certain costs of the tax system. This argument has occupied a prominent place in the debate about carbon taxes, as mentioned in the introduction. Few analysts deny the first dividend; it is the second dividend that generates controversy.

Can environmental taxes generate the second dividend? Different policy analysts have meant different things by this dividend, and this has led to confusion. Goulder (1995a) distinguishes a "strong" and "weak" version of the double dividend claim, as follows. Let $C(\tau_E\ \Delta\tau_L)$ refer to the gross cost of a revenue-neutral policy involving a new environmental tax τ_E that finances the change (reduction) $\Delta\tau_L$ in preexisting distortionary taxes.[18] Let $C(\tau_E, \Delta T)$ denote the gross cost of a revenue-neutral policy in which a new environmental tax τ_E finances the lump-sum reduction in taxes, ΔT. The weak double dividend claim is:

$$C(\tau_E, \Delta\tau_L) < C(\tau_E, \Delta T)$$

[18]In keeping with Section II's focus on labor-market distortions, we use the subscript "L" to refer to the distortionary factor tax. The points raised here apply to economies in which there are several distortionary taxes, including taxes on capital as well as labor.

The above expression asserts that a reform in which the environmental tax's revenues are recycled through cuts in the rates of distortionary tax involves lower gross costs than a policy in which the environmental tax's revenues are returned lump-sum. This weak double-dividend claim is easy to justify: environmental taxes, with revenues devoted to cuts in distortionary taxes, do indeed lower the costs of the tax system *relative to what the costs would be if the revenues were returned lump-sum.* As shown in Goulder (1995a), the weak double-dividend claim is upheld so long as the tax τ_L is appropriately labeled as distortionary. That is, the weak claim is upheld if and only if the tax τ_L has a positive marginal excess burden.

In terms of Figure 3, the weak double-dividend claim is verified by the fact that the marginal cost curve for the environmental tax with lump-sum revenue-replacement lies above the curve for the environmental tax accompanied by cuts in the marginal rates of a distortionary tax. In essence, the weak double-dividend claim amounts to the assertion that, in terms of efficiency, it pays to take advantage of the revenue-recycling effect. Thus it is closely related to the notion that pollution taxes that finance cuts in distortionary taxes are preferable on efficiency grounds to pollution quotas or grandfathered tradeable permits.

The stronger double-dividend claim is

$$C(\tau_E, \Delta\tau_L) \leq 0$$

that is, the revenue-neutral swap of an environmental tax for existing distortionary taxes involves zero or negative gross costs. This is equivalent to asserting that the gross distortionary cost directly attributable to the environmental tax is smaller than the avoided gross distortionary cost stemming from the environmental-tax-financed cut in the distortionary tax. If this strong double-dividend claim held for a carbon tax, then, as noted in the introduction, the tax would be justified on efficiency grounds so long as the environment-related gross *benefits* from the policy were nonnegative.

Is the stronger claim justified? Figure 3 sheds light on the answer. For the strong claim to be valid, the marginal cost curve for the pollution tax accompanied by cuts in distortionary taxes would have to lie on or below the horizontal axis. Clearly the curve does not fulfill this requirement—except at zero abatement. To support the stronger double-dividend claim, the revenue-recycling effect not only would have to fully offset the tax-interaction effect, but also would have to overcome the usual, first-best abatement costs represented by the dashed line. The analytical studies referred to in Section II, which form the basis for the positions of the marginal cost curves in Figure 3, do not support such an outcome. In these studies, for anything but an infinitesimal amount of abatement (infinitesimal environmental tax) the gross costs of a revenue-neutral environmental tax reform are positive.

Some qualifications are in order. As mentioned in the previous section, in most of the aforementioned analytical models the pollution-generating (or "dirty") good is assumed to be an average substitute for leisure. If instead the pollution-generating good were a weaker than average substitute for (stronger than average complement with) leisure, then the double dividend will arise after all—for a sufficiently small environmental tax. Further empirical work to gauge the extent of substitutability or complementarity could shed much light.

Second, more complex theoretical models can provide more scope for the strong double-dividend claim than is offered here.[19] To achieve greater tractability, many of the models examining this issue consider only one factor of production—labor. In models with both capital and labor, an environmental tax reform can produce the second dividend under certain circumstances. Specifically, if the tax system initially is highly inefficient in the sense that one factor is overtaxed relative to the other,[20] and if the environmental tax reform (the combination of the tax itself and the recycling of the revenues) serves to shift the tax burden from the overtaxed to the undertaxed factor, then the reform will produce a *tax-shifting effect* that works toward a more efficient tax system. If this beneficial tax-shifting effect is large enough, it (combined with the revenue-recycling effect) can entirely compensate for usual "first-best" abatement costs and the tax-interaction effect.[21] Thus, under these circumstances, the strong double-dividend materializes after all.

Most empirical studies indicate that in the United States, capital is overtaxed (in efficiency terms) relative to labor.[22] With these initial conditions, an environmental tax reform will produce a favorable tax-shifting effect if it shifts the burden away from capital and toward labor. Bovenberg and Goulder (1997) examine two environmentally motivated, revenue-neutral tax reforms—a Btu tax applied to fossil fuels and an increase in the Federal gasoline tax—and find that the latter policy produces a tax-shifting effect that significantly reduces the gross costs. However, the tax-shifting effect is generally not strong enough to make the gross costs zero or negative, except under extreme values for behavioral parameters. Although the results are somewhat mixed, other simulation studies have tended to support the idea that it is difficult to generate the strong double dividend under plausible parameter values and realistic policy specifications.[23]

The possibility of a (strong) double dividend through a powerful tax-shifting effect is illustrative of a general theme that emerges from recent theoretical work. In virtually all of the theoretical studies, a double

---

[19]Bovenberg (1996), Goulder (1995a), and Bovenberg and Goulder (1999) analyze a range of complicating issues.

[20]In efficiency terms, one factor of production is overtaxed relative to another if the tax on this factor has a larger marginal excess burden per dollar of revenue than the tax on the other factor.

[21]For a theoretical treatment of the tax-shifting issue, see Bovenberg and de Mooij (1994b), and Bovenberg and Goulder (1997).

[22]See, for example, Ballard, Shoven, and Whalley (1985), Fullerton and Mackie (1987), Jorgenson and Yun (1990), Lucas (1990), and Goulder and Thalmann (1993).

[23]Goulder (1995a) surveys these studies.

dividend becomes possible only when two general conditions are met: (1) prior to the introduction of the environmental tax reform, there is a significant inefficiency in the tax system along a nonenvironmental dimension, and (2) the environmental tax reform serves to reduce this "nonenvironmental" inefficiency. If this "non-green" benefit from green tax reform is large enough, it can compensate for the factors that work against the double dividend. The possibility of a double dividend through environmental tax policies that reduce prior inefficiencies in the relative taxation of labor and capital is an illustration of this general theme.[24]

It is important to recognize that the absence of the (strong) double dividend does not vitiate the case for green tax reform. It only means that the positive *sign* of the environmental benefits is not a sufficient condition for justifying such reform. If there is no double dividend, policy makers are obliged to consider the magnitudes of the environmental benefits and compare them with the (positive) gross costs. Also, the absence of a double dividend does not repudiate our intuition that it makes sense to orient the tax system, to a degree, on "bads" (polluting activities) rather than "goods" (labor and capital). *Even if the strong double-dividend claim fails, it is still the case that "Pigovian considerations" should be part of the design of an efficient tax system*: other things equal, the tax on a given good or activity should be higher, the larger the environmental externalities associated with that good or activity. Higher environmental benefits justify higher taxes on polluting activities. It is the larger environmental benefits—not the presumption of zero gross costs—that justify the greening of the tax system.

B. Significance of the Scale of Abatement for the Choice between Taxes and Quotas

The theoretical model indicated that the pollution taxes and auctioned permits have an efficiency advantage over pollution quotas and grandfathered pollution permits to the extent that the former policies exploit the revenue-recycling effect. However, the size of the efficiency advantage generally declines with the amount of abatement. In fact, this advantages approaches zero as the extent of abatement approaches 100 percent. This is illustrated by Figure 4, which is borrowed from Goulder, Parry, and Burtraw (1997), which we will refer to as GPB. Marginal costs rise faster for the pollution tax (or auctioned pollution permit) policy. Eventually—when the extent of abatement is substantial—marginal costs under this policy exceed those for the pollution quota (or grandfathered permit) policy.

[24]This theme also is illustrated in the case where the double dividend can arise because the pollution-generating good is a stronger than average complement with leisure. Ignoring environmental considerations, optimal "Ramsey" commodity taxation would tend to justify taxing this relative complement to leisure. In this setting, introducing an environmental tax both serves an environmental purpose and helps eliminate a preexisting inefficiency of the tax system along nonenvironmental dimensions. Thus the situation is conducive to a double dividend.

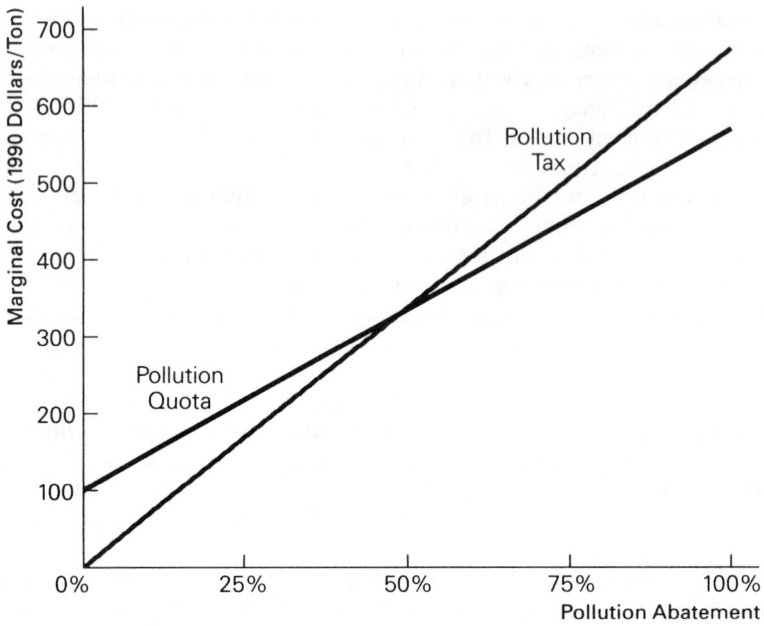

Figure 4 Marginal Costs Over the Entire Range of Possible Emissions Reductions

Why is this so? Consider the pollution tax. Because of this policy's negative impact on labor supply and on emissions, marginal tax revenue declines as the emissions tax rate rises. This means that, with greater abatement, the ability to exploit the revenue-recycling effect diminishes. Eventually, the point is reached where, at the margin, additional abatement (via an incrementally higher pollution tax) raises no more revenue than is raised under the quota policy.[25]

That is the point where the pollution tax and pollution quota marginal cost curves cross. To the right of that point, *at the margin* the tax policy is more costly than the quota policy, because at the margin it has a *negative* revenue-recycling effect (as compared with the negligible revenue-recycling effect of the quota policy). Indeed, if one pursues emissions reductions to the point of 100 percent abatement, the total costs of the two types of policies are identical. This makes sense: at 100 percent abatement neither policy earns any revenue, and thus there is no effective difference between a tax and a quota at that point. Thus the areas under the marginal cost curves from 0 to 100 percent abatement are the same for both policies.

These results demonstrate that the relative superiority (in terms of lower cost) of policies that exploit the revenue-recycling effect diminishes

[25]The quota policy does not necessarily raise zero revenue. This policy will tend to raise revenue insofar as quota rents are taxed, and will tend to lose revenue insofar as the policy causes a loss of overall real income and a reduction in the labor tax base.

with the extent of abatement. At low levels of abatement (as would be appropriate if marginal environmental *benefits* are low), these policies have a considerable cost advantage. But at high levels of abatement (as would be justified when marginal environmental benefits are high) the advantage of these policies is much smaller. In the limiting case of 100 percent abatement, these policies have no cost advantage.

C. Impacts of Other Environmental Policies in a Second-Best Setting

Thus far, all of the discussion in this paper has centered on pollution taxes, quotas, and permits. Recent papers by Fullerton and Metcalf (1997) and Goulder, Parry, Williams, and Burtraw (1999) examine the impacts of other policy instruments (in addition to pollution taxes and quotas) in a second-best setting.[26] Among the additional instruments considered in these recent papers are some "command-and-control" policies: namely, mandated technologies and performance standards.

Goulder et al. (1999) show that preexisting taxes also raise the costs of the command-and-control policies relative to their costs in a first-best world. Like emissions taxes and quotas, the command-and-control policies raise production costs and lead to higher output prices. If there are prior distortionary taxes in factor markets, the higher output prices produce the tax-interaction effect, which implies higher costs relative to the costs in a first-best setting.

Although second-best considerations raise the costs of all instruments, they do not increase costs in the same proportion. Indeed, when the amount of pollution-abatement is incremental or "small," preexisting taxes especially raise the costs of non-auctioned quotas or permits, and can put non-auctioned quotas or permits at a cost-disadvantage relative to command-and-control policies. Economists have long favored market-based policies as being more cost-effective than the command-and-control alternatives. Yet in a second-best setting, certain market-based policies can be at a disadvantage. The recent studies by Fullerton and Metcalf and Goulder et al. indicate that the marginal abatement costs of performance standards and technology mandates resemble those of the emissions tax in that marginal costs are zero at the first increment of abatement.[27] This contrasts with the strictly positive costs of initial abatement under a non-auctioned quota. Thus, for "low" amounts of abatement, a command-and-control policy can be less costly than grandfathered permits. However, it should be kept in mind that the command-and-control policies eventually involve higher costs as the amount of abatement becomes very extensive. As discussed in Goul-

---

[26]See also Ng (1980), who analyzed environmental subsidies in the presence of prior tax distortions.

[27]This point was first demonstrated by Fullerton and Metcalf. This was shown for a "technology restriction" policy, which was a constraint on the ratio of labor input to emissions. In their model, this is functionally equivalent to a policy involving a constraint on the ratio of emissions to output.

der et al. (1999), this reflects the inability of these alternative instruments to provide the appropriate prices of inputs and outputs.

It is worth considering further why the marginal cost curves of these alternative instruments emerge from the origin (as in the case of the pollution tax or auctioned quota—with revenues devoted to marginal rate reductions), while the marginal cost curves of grandfathered quotas (or emissions taxes with revenues returned lump sum) do not. Since the mandated technology and performance standard do not raise revenue, it is clear that raising revenue *per se* is not necessary for the zero-marginal-cost-at-initial-abatement property to obtain. One can explain these differences in terms of whether the tax-interaction and revenue-recycling effects cancel at initial abatement. At the first incremental amount of abatement, emissions taxes (with revenues returned through marginal rate cuts) produce a strictly positive tax-interaction effect that is exactly offset by the strictly negative revenue-recycling effect. Hence the marginal abatement costs are zero at initial abatement. The mandated technology and performance standard produce neither a tax-interaction effect nor a revenue-recycling effect. Hence the marginal costs of abatement are again zero at initial abatement.[28] In contrast, under grandfathered quotas there is a strictly positive tax-interaction effect and no offsetting revenue-recycling effect. Hence marginal costs are strictly positive. Thus, the tax-interaction and revenue-recycling effects can explain why marginal costs start out strictly positive under non-auctioned permits or quotas, and start out at zero under the other policies.

These differences at initial abatement can also be linked to the presence or absence of a lump-sum transfer. The government effectuates a lump-sum transfer to individuals when it introduces a pollution tax and returns the revenues lump-sum, when it implements a pollution quota (thus generating quota rents that are not entirely taxed away), or when it introduces a pollution tax and recycles the revenues through cuts in the marginal tax rate on a perfectly inelastically supplied factor of production.[29] In a second-best world, such transfers involve an efficiency cost because they must ultimately be financed through distortionary taxes. In contrast, under the pollution tax or fuels tax (with revenues financing cuts in prior taxes), or under the mandated technology or performance standard, there is no such transfer. Thus the presence or absence of a positive intercept of the marginal cost function corresponds to the presence or absence of this lump-sum transfer.[30]

[28]Alternatively, one can view the technology mandate as producing two tax-interaction effects and two revenue-recycling effects. As indicated by Fullerton and Metcalf, the mandated technology is equivalent to the combination of a subsidy to the use of the clean input and a tax on emissions. The subsidy and tax components respectively account for negative (in efficiency terms) and positive revenue-recycling effects, which cancel out, and positive and negative tax-interaction effects, which also cancel out (at the first unit of abatement).

[29]This last case is examined by Bovenberg and de Mooij (1996) and Williams (1998).

[30]Fullerton and Metcalf (1997) point out that pollution regulation through grandfathered permits creates scarcity rents that remain in private (that is, the regulated firm's) hands, and indicate that this accounts for the fact that the marginal costs of incremental abatement are strictly positive. The creation of scarcity rents is an example of the government's bringing about a lump-sum transfer to the private sector.

IV. Some Numerical Results

Thus far we have only considered results from analytical models. Analytical tractability comes at a price in that it necessitates the use of fairly simple models. In this section we briefly display results from some numerical models.[31]

First we present some results that pertain to the double-dividend issue. Here we display and briefly interpret results from the disaggregated computable general equilibrium model employed in Bovenberg and Goulder (1997). We will only sketch the results here; the reader is referred to the Bovenberg-Goulder article for details. In this discussion we also present a sampling of results from other numerical models.

Next we display numerical results indicating how preexisting taxes affect the choice between auctioned and grandfathered emissions permits, in the context of sulfur dioxide (SO_2) and carbon dioxide (CO_2) emissions reductions in the United States.

A. Numerical Explorations of the Double-Dividend Issue

1. Results from Bovenberg-Goulder (1997). Here we examine simulations in which a fossil fuel Btu tax or a consumer gasoline tax increase is implemented in revenue-neutral fashion, with the revenues devoted to reductions in the income tax. An important item to keep in mind when interpreting the results is the relative taxation of capital and labor. In the baseline, or reference equilibrium (and under central values for parameters), the marginal excess burden (MEB) of capital taxes is .43, while the MEB of labor taxes is .31. This means that the tax-shifting effect (see III.A above) works in favor of the second dividend when policies shift the burden of taxation from (overtaxed) capital to (undertaxed) labor. In this regard, note that while the Btu tax tends to fall more or less evenly on capital and labor, the gasoline tax tends to fall mainly on labor (by virtue of its being akin to a consumption tax). Hence the gasoline tax has more potential for tax-shifting that support the second dividend.

Figure 5 shows results when these taxes are introduced with *lump-sum* replacement of the revenues. Figure 5a shows that in the short term, the environmental (Btu and gas) taxes entail a greater GDP sacrifice than the personal income tax. Figure 5b shows that the gasoline tax has a much smaller investment cost than does the Btu tax or income tax. This reflects the fact that the gasoline tax tends to ease the tax burden on capital.

Table 1 shows the effects of these policies on factor prices and quantities. It indicates that the combination of gasoline tax increase and reduction in personal income tax reduces capital's tax burden and raises la-

[31]Real-world environmental taxes and other regulations involve "large," as opposed to incremental, changes in the level of pollution. Numerical simulation is usually necessary to evaluate the efficiency implications of these changes.

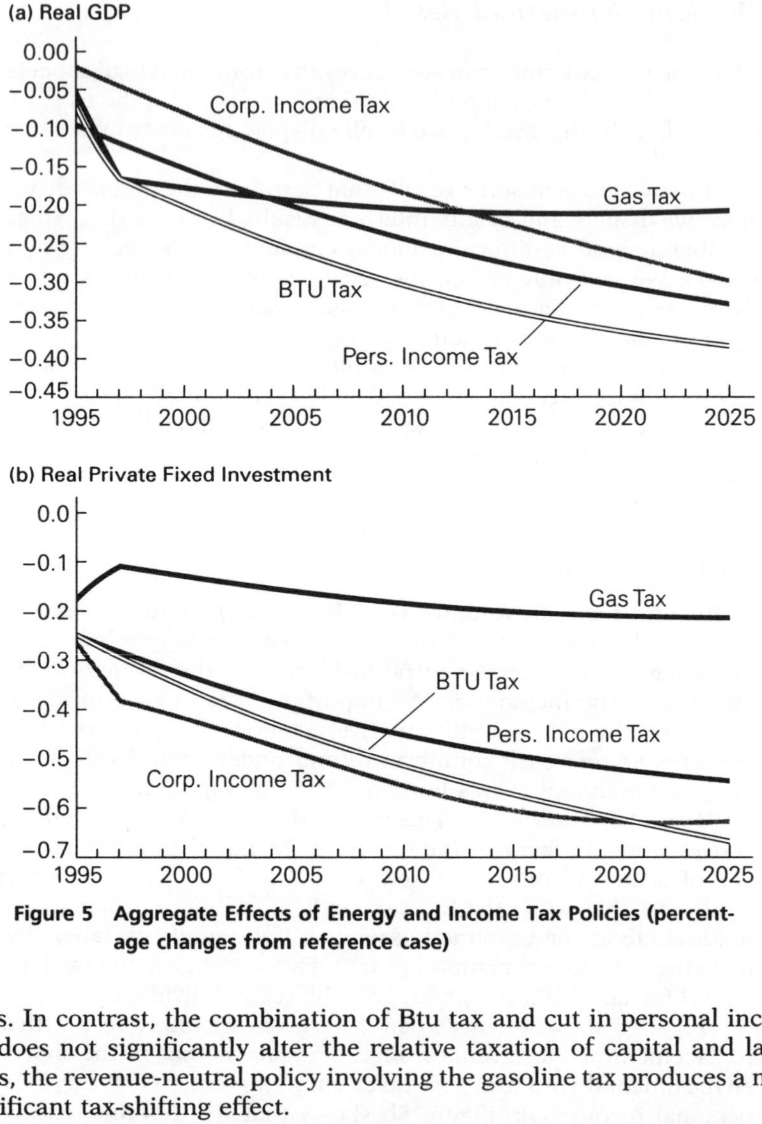

Figure 5 Aggregate Effects of Energy and Income Tax Policies (percentage changes from reference case)

bor's. In contrast, the combination of Btu tax and cut in personal income tax does not significantly alter the relative taxation of capital and labor. Thus, the revenue-neutral policy involving the gasoline tax produces a more significant tax-shifting effect.

Table 2 shows welfare effects. These are the monetary equivalent (using the equivalent variation) of the change in utility associated with the policy change. These welfare measures disregard welfare impacts associated with the changes in environmental quality; they refer only to the cost side of the benefit-cost ledger.

Comparing the left and right columns indicates the importance of the revenue-recycling effect; that is, of returning revenues through cuts in marginal tax rates instead of through lump-sum tax cuts. The welfare costs of the revenue-neutral reforms are significantly higher when revenues are returned in lump-sum fashion.

Table 1 Impacts of Taxes on Factor Prices and Supplies (percentage changes from baseline)

	Years after Policy Introduction			
	1	*2*	*5*	*30*
"Single Tax" Policies:				
Btu Tax, Lump-Sum Repl.				
w	−0.250	−0.390	−0.446	−0.655
r	−0.083	−0.239	−0.179	−0.084
L	−0.124	−0.140	−0.121	−0.049
K	−0.017	−0.035	−0.092	−0.364
Gasoline Tax Increase, Lump-Sum Repl.				
w	−0.722	−1.069	−1.058	−0.983
r	0.095	−0.007	−0.027	−0.005
L	−0.266	−0.335	−0.331	−0.298
K	−0.011	−0.019	−0.031	−0.069
Personal Tax Increase, Lump-Sum Repl.				
w	−0.333	−0.347	−0.404	−0.655
r	−0.104	−0.108	−0.105	−0.053
L	−0.277	−0.274	−0.265	−0.212
K	−0.015	−0.030	−0.072	−0.313
Substitution of Environmental Tax For Personal Tax:				
Btu Tax, Personal Tax Repl.				
w	0.083	−0.042	−0.042	0.014
r	0.031	−0.125	−0.074	−0.053
L	0.157	0.139	0.149	0.163
K	−0.001	−0.005	−0.019	−0.037
Gasoline Tax Increase, Personal Tax Repl.				
w	−0.375	−0.694	−0.571	−0.307
r	0.216	0.111	0.076	0.057
L	0.013	−0.057	−0.061	−0.084
K	0.004	0.012	0.041	0.252

Note: w, r, L, and K respectively refer to the after-tax real wage, after-tax real rate of return, aggregate real labor supply, and aggregate real capital stock.

Table 2 Welfare Impacts

	Welfare Cost Per Dollar of Revenue	
	Lump-Sum Tax Replacement	*Personal Income Tax Replacement*
BTU Tax	.656	.318
Consumer-Level Gasoline Tax Increase	.594	.253
Personal Income Tax Increase	.379	–
Corporate Income Tax Increase	.438	.093

Concentrate now on the right column, which displays results from revenue-neutral policies in which the environmental tax revenues finance reductions in the personal tax. There are two main results from this column. First, the second dividend does not arise: the gross welfare costs (i.e., the costs before netting out the environmental benefits) are positive. Second, the welfare cost is lower for the gasoline tax reform, despite the narrower base of the gasoline tax. This reflects the tax-shifting effect: as Table 1 indicated, under the gasoline tax reform the tax burden is shifted from capital to labor, which tends to reduce the gross costs. However, the tax-shifting effect is not strong enough to undo the cost associated with the tax-interaction effect.

Is it possible to make the tax-shifting effect large enough to give the second dividend? Yes. The tax-shifting effect will be stronger to the extent that (1) the initial inefficiencies in the relative taxation of capital and labor are large, and (2) the policy shifts the burden from the overtaxed to the undertaxed factor. To enhance the first condition, we have performed simulations with very elastic capital supply assumptions. Specifically, we assume that the elasticity of substitution in consumption (which affects the household's interest elasticity of saving) is "high" relative to most estimates. To enhance the second condition, we consider a policy in which a gasoline tax is introduced and all the revenues from this tax are recycled through cuts in capital taxes only. This combination produces a large enough tax-shifting effect to yield the second dividend if the intertemporal elasticity of substitution is 1.8 or more. Although this shows that the second dividend can arise, producing this dividend seems to require implausibly high values for the intertemporal elasticity of substitution (most estimates are between 0 and unity[32]).

2. Results from a Sampling of Other Models. Table 3 summarizes results from numerical studies of a revenue-neutral carbon tax policy. The table presents results from seven numerical models. These are the Goulder and Jorgenson-Wilcoxen intertemporal general equilibrium models of the United States, the Proost-Regemorter general equilibrium model of Belgium, the DRI and LINK econometric macroeconomic models of the United States, and the Shah-Larsen partial equilibrium model, which has been applied to five countries, including the United States.[33] The results in Table 3 are for the revenue-neutral combination of an environmental tax (usually a carbon tax) and reduction in the personal income tax, except in cases where this combination was not available.

---

[32]Using time-series data, Hall (1988) estimates that this elasticity is below 0.2. A cross-section analysis by Lawrance (1991) generates a central estimate of 1.1. Estimates from time-series tend to be lower than those from cross-section analyses.

[33]For a more detailed description of these models, see Goulder (1995b), Jorgenson and Wilcoxen (1990, 1996), Shackleton et al. (1996), Proost and Regemorter (1995), and Shah and Larsen (1992). The Shah-Larsen model is the simplest of the models, in part because it takes pretax factor prices as given. Despite its simplicity, the model addresses interactions between commodity and factor markets and thus incorporates some of the major efficiency connections discussed earlier.

Table 3 Numerical Assessments of Welfare Impacts of Revenue-Neutral Environmental Tax Reforms

Model	*Reference*	*Country*	*Type of Environmental Tax*	*Method of Revenue Replacement*	*Welfare Effect*
DRI	Shackleton et al. (1996)	U.S.	Phased-in Carbon Tax[a]	Personal Tax Cut	−0.39[b]
Goulder	Goulder (1995b)	U.S.	$25/ton Carbon Tax	Personal Tax Cut	−0.33[c]
"	Goulder (1994)	U.S.	Fossil Fuel Btu Tax	Personal Tax Cut	−0.28[c]
Jorgenson-Wilcoxen	Shackleton et al. (1996)	U.S.	Phased-in Carbon Tax[a]	Capital Tax Cut	0.19[d]
LINK	Shackleton et al. (1996)	U.S.	Phased-in Carbon Tax[a]	Personal Tax Cut	−0.51[b]
Proost-van Regemorter	Proost and van Regemorter (1995)	Belgium	Hybrid of Carbon and Energy Tax	Payroll (Social Security) Tax Cut	−3.45[d]
Shah-Larsen	Shah and Larsen (1992)	U.S.	$10/ton	Personal Tax Cut	−1049.[e]
"	"	India	"	"	−129.
"	"	Indonesia	"	"	−4.
"	"	Japan	"	"	−269.
"	"	Pakistan	"	"	−23.

Notes: [a]Beginning at $15/ton in 1990 (period 1), growing at five percent annually to $39.80 per ton in 2010 (period 21), and remaining at that level thereafter. [b]Percentage change in the present value of consumption; the model does not allow for utility-based welfare measures. [c]Welfare cost per dollar of tax revenue, as measured by the equivalent variation. [d]Equivalent variation as a percentage of benchmark private wealth. [e]Compensating variation in levels (millions of U.S. dollars).

All welfare changes abstract from changes in welfare associated with improvements in environmental quality (reductions in greenhouse gas emissions). Thus they correspond to the gross cost concept discussed above. In the Goulder, Jorgenson-Wilcoxen, and Proost-Regemorter models, welfare changes are reported in terms of the equivalent variation; in the Shah-Larsen model, the changes are based on the compensating variation.[34] In the DRI and LINK macroeconomic models, the percentage change in aggregate real consumption substitutes for a utility-based welfare measure.[35]

[34]The equivalent variation is the lump-sum change in wealth which, under the "business-as-usual" or base case, would leave the household as well off as in the policy-change case. Thus a positive equivalent variation indicates that the policy is welfare-improving. The compensating variation is the lump-sum change in wealth that, in the policy-change scenario, would cause the household to be as well off as in the base case. In reporting the Shah-Larsen results we adopt the convention of multiplying the compensating variation by −1, so that a positive number in the table signifies a welfare improvement here as well.

[35]The demand functions in these models are not derived from an explicit utility function. Hence they do not yield utility-based measures.

In most cases, the revenue-neutral green tax swap implies a reduction in welfare, that is, entails positive gross costs. This militates against the double dividend claim. Results from the Jorgenson-Wilcoxen model, however, support the double dividend notion. Relatively high interest elasticities of savings (a high capital supply elasticity) and the assumption of perfect capital mobility across sectors may partially explain this result, at least in the case where revenues from the carbon tax are devoted to cuts in marginal taxes on capital. These assumptions imply large marginal excess burdens from taxes on capital, considerably larger than the MEBs from labor taxes. As indicated above, if the MEB on capital significantly exceeds that on labor, and the environmental reform shifts the tax burden on to labor, the double dividend can arise. Thus, the large MEBs from capital taxes help explain why, in the Jorgenson-Wilcoxen model, a revenue-neutral combination of carbon tax and reduction in capital taxes involves negative gross costs, that is, produces a double dividend. Identifying the sources of differences in results across models is difficult, in large part because of the lack of relevant information on simulation outcomes and parameters. Relatively few studies have performed the type of analysis that exposes the channels underlying the overall impacts. There is a need for more systematic sensitivity analysis, as well as closer investigations of how structural aspects of tax policies (type of tax base, narrowness of tax base, uniformity of tax rates, etc.) influence the outcomes. In addition, key behavioral parameters need to be reported. Serious attention to these issues will help explain differences in results and, one hopes, lead to a greater consensus on likely policy impacts.

B. Preexisting Taxes and the Choice between Auctioned and Non-Auctioned Pollution Permits

Here we display numerical results that bear on the importance of preexisting taxes for the choice between auctioned and non-auctioned (or grandfathered) pollution permits. As the discussion in Section II indicates, these results display the significance of the revenue-recycling effect. Thus the principles here are somewhat broader than the choice between auctioned or grandfathered permits. The results for auctioned permits also would apply to emissions taxes that exploit the revenue-recycling effect by using the revenues to finance cuts in marginal rates of preexisting factor taxes. Likewise, the results for non-auctioned permits apply to emissions taxes that fail to exploit the revenue-recycling effect by returning the revenues in a lump-sum fashion.

1. Sulfur Dioxide Abatement. The GPB study includes an assessment of the costs of reducing emissions of sulfur dioxide (SO_2) from U.S. coal-fired electric power plants. Provisions of the 1990 Clean Air Act Amendments call for such reductions and introduce a system of grandfathered SO_2 emissions permits to achieve them.

Two questions arise. First, how much higher are the costs of reducing SO_2 emissions as a result of preexisting taxes? And how much of the increase in abatement costs could be avoided if the reductions were achieved through a policy that auctioned the permits (or imposed an SO_2 tax) and exploited the revenue-recycling effect, rather than through a policy that grandfathered the permits? Figure 6 gives GPB's best estimates of the answers to these questions. The two solid lines in the figure are the ratios of total costs in a second-best setting (with a positive preexisting tax rate on labor equal to 0.4) to total costs in a first-best setting (with no preexisting tax on labor). In the case of auctioned permits (or pollution taxes), the line is almost perfectly horizontal: this ratio is approximately constant throughout the entire range of possible emissions reductions (0 to 20 million tons). Second-best considerations raise the costs of auctioned permits by about 30 percent, regardless of the extent of emissions abatement. For the actual policy of grandfathered emissions permits, the ratio of total cost is very sensitive to the extent of abatement. Under this policy the ratio begins at infinity, in keeping with the fact that the intercept of the *marginal* cost function is positive for this policy in a second-best world and zero in a first-best world. As the level of abatement approaches 100 percent, the ratio of total costs approaches the ratio for auctioned permits. This is in keeping with the point made in Section III that the efficiency disadvantage of policies that forgo the revenue-recycling effect disappears at 100 percent abatement.

The 1990 Clean Air Act Amendments call for a 10-million-ton (or approximately 50 percent) reduction in SO_2 emissions. There may be significant distributional or political objectives that are served by grandfather-

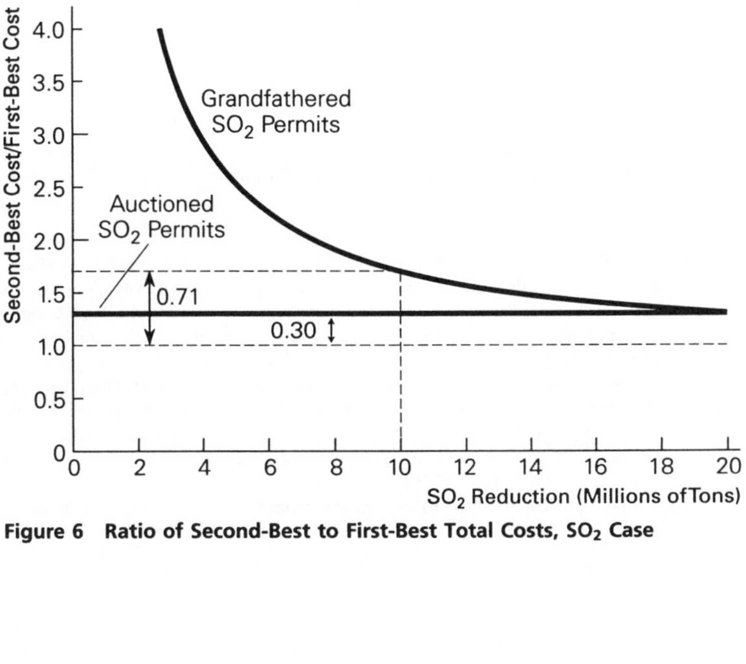

Figure 6 Ratio of Second-Best to First-Best Total Costs, SO_2 Case

ing, but Figure 6's results indicate that they come at a high price in terms of the social cost of abatement. At 10 million tons of abatement, annual total costs under the actual policy are estimated to be 71 percent (or $907 million) higher than they would be in a first-best world. As indicated in this figure, over half of this extra cost could be avoided by auctioning the permits or employing an SO_2 tax. The difference in cost between the two types of policy is $533 million.[36] These results indicate that preexisting taxes and the presence or absence of revenue-recycling have a very substantial impact on the costs of environmental policies.

Figure 7 brings in the benefit side in considering the overall efficiency gains from SO_2 abatement. The overall gains obviously depend on the marginal benefits from SO_2 reductions, and these are highly uncertain. Most estimates are in the range of $100–600 per ton, but some recent estimates are as high as $1000 per ton. The figure displays the net efficiency gains as a function of different values for the marginal benefits, ranging from zero to about $750 per ton.[37] It shows the efficiency gains that result under optimal levels of abatement, that is, abatement levels that equate marginal benefits with marginal costs. For low and intermediate values of the marginal benefits, the efficiency gains are considerably larger when SO_2 permits are auctioned than when they are grandfathered, in keeping with the lower marginal costs of abatement in the former case. Indeed, net gains under grandfathered permits are zero if marginal benefits are below $104 per ton, because in this circumstance the optimal policy is not to regulate SO_2; that is, the optimal reduction in SO_2 is zero. For very high values of the marginal benefits, there is less difference in the net efficiency gains. In fact the net efficiency gains are identical for marginal benefits greater than or equal to about $680 per ton. When marginal benefits go beyond this level, the optimal policy is to eliminate SO_2 emissions entirely. At this point it makes no difference whether permits are grandfathered or auctioned, since no permits are actually provided and thus no revenue can be raised in either case.

2. Carbon Dioxide Abatement. Recent work by Parry, Williams, and Goulder (1999) examines these issues in the context of carbon dioxide (CO_2) emissions abatement in the United States. Figures 8 and 9, based on re-

---

[36]The costs of a 10-million-ton reduction are $2182 and $1649 million under the grandfathering and auctioning of emissions allowances, respectively. Although this paper points out the efficiency drawbacks of the grandfathering element of SO_2 emissions regulation under the 1990 Clean Air Act Amendments, it is not intended to be a wholesale critique of this legislation. We would note that the 1990 legislation achieved major reforms in environmental regulation by introducing a flexible, incentive-based approach to regulation in the form of emissions allowance trading. This approach has a number of theoretical advantages over the traditional, less flexible methods (see, for example, Tietenberg [1985]), and empirical studies already indicate that this approach will yield a dramatic reduction in overall compliance costs, compared to conventional approaches (see, for example, Burtraw [1996], and Ellerman and Montero [1996]).

[37]The marginal benefits are assumed to be constant, that is, independent of the level of abatement.

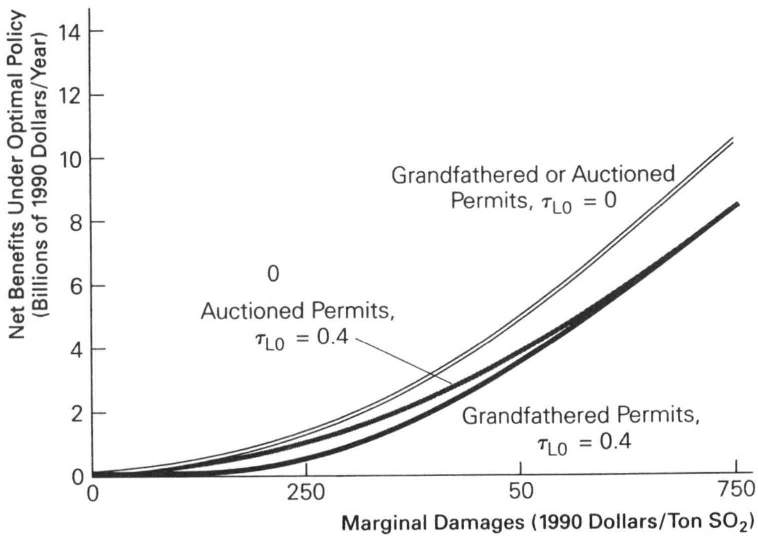

Figure 7 Net Welfare Gain from the Optimal Level of SO_2 Regulation

sults from this study, provide for CO_2 abatement policies the same sort of information as was displayed for SO_2 policies in Figures 6 and 7.

Figure 8 presents the ratio of second-best (τ_L = .4) and first-best (τ_L = 0) total costs, under a carbon (CO_2) tax and a carbon (CO_2) quota.[38] The carbon tax policy exploits the revenue-recycling effect: revenues from the tax are devoted to cuts in the preexisting distortionary (labor) tax. The results are qualitatively similar to the results that were shown in Figure 6. For the carbon tax, the ratio of total costs is virtually unaffected by the extent of carbon emissions abatement. For the carbon quota, in contrast, the ratio of total costs is highly sensitive to the amount of abatement, for the same reasons as were discussed earlier.

Figure 9 shows Parry, Williams, and Goulder's best estimates for net efficiency gains from carbon abatement policies, for a range of values for the marginal benefits from CO_2 abatement. Efficiency gains are considerably larger under the carbon tax than under the carbon quota. In fact, efficiency gains are zero (the optimal amount of abatement is zero) if marginal benefits are below \$18 per ton. This reflects the fact that the (gross) marginal costs of CO_2 abatement begin at \$18 per ton under the quota policy. Thus, any emissions abatement by way of this type of policy will be ef-

[38]The tax and quota policies actually would be oriented toward the use of carbon-based fuels (oil, coal, and natural gas) rather than emissions of CO_2 itself. Emissions from the combustion of these fuels are strictly proportional to carbon content, so that taxing or regulating the use of these fuels is virtually equivalent to taxing or regulating CO_2 emissions. A complication is posed by non-combustion or feedstock uses of these fuels. In the U.S. such uses represent a very small share (less than four percent) of total use.

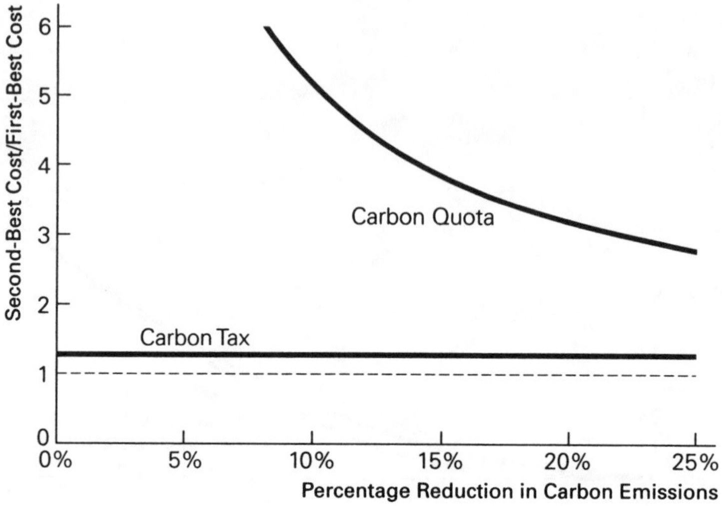

Figure 8 Ratio of Second-Best to First-Best Total Costs, CO_2 Case

ficiency-reducing if the marginal benefits are below this value. Most estimates of the marginal environmental benefits from carbon abatement obtain values below \$18 per ton.[39] Thus, these results suggest that any car-

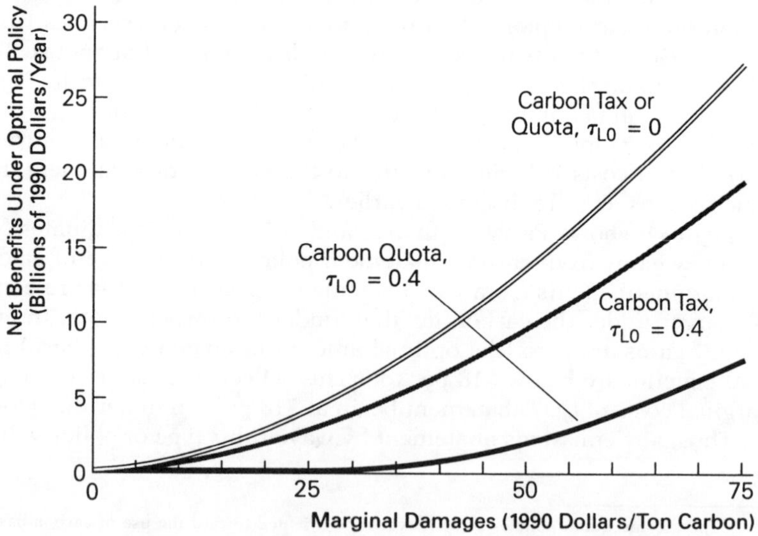

Figure 9 Net Welfare Gain from the Optimal Level of CO_2 Regulation

[39]See, for example, Nordhaus (1991), Peck and Teisberg (1993), and Fankhauser (1994).

bon abatement by way of a quota (or freely offered set of carbon permits) will be efficiency reducing![40]

Thus, in the context of regulating SO_2 and CO_2 emissions, second-best interactions have a very substantial effect on the gross costs and net efficiency gains. Preexisting taxes significantly raise the costs of achieving emissions reductions relative to the costs in a first-best setting. And they put policies involving emissions quotas or grandfathered permits policies at a very significant cost disadvantage relative to policies that raise revenue and finance cuts in preexisting taxes. Second-best interactions have first-order consequences.

V. Conclusions

This paper examines the significance of preexisting factor taxes for various environmental policies. It indicates that, under plausible assumptions, prior factor-market distortions raise the costs of revenue-neutral environmental policies, despite the potential to use the revenues from environmental taxes to finance cuts in the marginal rates of preexisting factor taxes. It also shows that prior factor taxes amplify the costs of other environmental policies, including pollution quotas and tradeable pollution permits, relative to what the costs would be in a first-best world.

Two effects underlie these results. The *tax-interaction effect* is the adverse impact in factor markets arising from reductions in after-tax returns to factors (labor) brought about by environmental regulation. In a world with prior taxes on factors, this effect leads to significantly higher costs of regulation relative to what would apply in a first-best world with no preexisting taxes. By generating revenues and using them to reduce preexisting tax rates, pollution taxes and auctioned pollution permits exploit a *revenue-recycling effect* that offsets some of the tax-interaction effect. In contrast, pollution quotas and grandfathered permits enjoy no such offset. Thus the costs of achieving given reductions in pollution are higher under these latter policies.

Even when they take advantage of the revenue-recycling effect, pollution abatement policies through pollution taxes or auctioned permits generally entail positive gross costs. If the good responsible for pollution emissions is an average substitute for leisure, the revenue-recycling effect only partly offsets the gross costs attributable to the tax-interaction effect. This implies that pollution-abatement through these policies is more costly in a second-best setting than it would be in a first-best world, and that the double dividend claim (in its strong form) is not upheld.

[40]Several studies suggest that the marginal climate-related damages increase with CO_2 concentrations. If this is the case, and if CO_2 concentrations increase through time, then marginal damages from CO_2 emissions (or marginal benefits from CO_2 emissions abatement) will increase over time. Under such circumstances the prospects for efficiency gains under a quota policy improve with time.

The interactions with factor markets affect the choice among alternative policy instruments. In particular, they put pollution quotas and grandfathered pollution permits at a serious efficiency disadvantage relative to revenue-raising policies whose revenues finance reductions in the marginal rates of existing taxes. Indeed, if the marginal environmental benefits from pollution reductions are below a certain threshold value, then *any* level of pollution abatement through quotas or grandfathered permits is efficiency-reducing. These results emerge from simple analytical models and are confirmed by numerical investigations in specific regulatory contexts.

In recognizing the efficiency advantages of these pollution-tax and auctioned-permit policies over policies involving pollution quotas or grandfathered permits, one should not lose sight of related equity issues. The decision whether to exploit the revenue-recycling effect fundamentally affects the distribution of wealth between taxpayers, on the one hand, and owners and employees of polluting firms, on the other. Clearly, there are important equity issues associated with the differences in distribution. The second-best considerations raised in this paper do not reduce the importance of the equity issues, but at the same time they indicate that the efficiency costs of forgoing the redistribution toward taxpayers are greater than what would be suggested by a first-best analysis.

The tax-interaction effect is relevant to government regulation outside the environmental area. To the extent that government regulations of international trade or agricultural production raise the costs of output and thereby reduce real factor returns, these regulations exacerbate the labor market distortions from preexisting taxes and thus involve higher social costs than would be indicated by partial equilibrium analyses.[41]

REFERENCES

Ballard, Charles, L., John B. Shoven, and John Whalley, 1985. "General Equilibrium Computations of the Marginal Welfare Costs of Taxes in the U.S." *American Economic Review* 75(1):128–38.

Bovenberg, A. Lans, 1996. "Environmental Policy, Distortionary Labor Taxation, and Employment: Pollution Taxes and the Double Dividend." In Carlo Carraro, Yiannis Katsoulacos, and Anastasios Xepapadeas, eds., *Environmental Policy and Market Structure.* Dordrecht: Kluwer Academic Publishers.

Bovenberg, A. Lans, and Ruud A. de Mooij, 1994a. "Environmental Levies and Distortionary Taxation." *American Economic Review* 84(4):1085–9.

Bovenberg, A. Lans, and Ruud A. de Mooij, 1994b. "Environmental Taxation and Labor Market Distortions." *European Journal of Political Economy* 10(4):655–83.

Bovenberg, A. Lans, and Ruud A. de Mooij, 1996. "Environmental Taxation and the Double-Dividend: The Role of Factor Substitution and Capital Mobility." In C.

[41]Similarly, Browning (1997) finds that monopoly pricing exacerbates preexisting distortions in factor markets. Hence the efficiency costs of monopoly pricing increase with the magnitude of preexisting factor tax rates. Browning estimates that monopoly pricing in the U.S. is ten times more costly than it would be in the absence of prior factor taxes.

Carraro and D. Siniscalco, eds., *Environmental Fiscal Reform and Unemployment.* Dordrecht: Kluwer.

Bovenberg, A. Lans, and Lawrence H. Goulder, 1996. "Optimal Environmental Taxation in the Presence of Other Taxes: General Equilibrium Analyses." *American Economic Review*, September.

Bovenberg, A. Lans, and Lawrence H. Goulder, 1997. "Costs of Environmentally Motivated Taxes in the Presence of Other Taxes: General Equilibrium Analyses." *National Tax Journal*, forthcoming March 1997.

Bovenberg, A. Lans, and Lawrence H. Goulder, 1999. "Environmental Taxation." In A. Auerbach and M. Feldstein, eds., *Handbook of Public Economics.* New York: North Holland, forthcoming.

Bovenberg, A. Lans, and F. van der Ploeg, 1994. "Environmental Policy, Public Finance, and the Labour Market in a Second-Best World." *Journal of Public Economics* 55:349–70.

Browning, E. K., 1997. "The Welfare Cost of Monopoly and Other Output Distortions." *Journal of Public Economics*, 66:127–44.

Browning, E. K., 1987. "On the Marginal Welfare Cost of Taxation." *American Economic Review* 77:11–23.

Burtraw, Dallas, 1996. "The SO_2 Emissions Trading Program: Cost Savings Without Allowance Trades," *Contemporary Economic Policy*, vol. XIV, no. 2 (April), 79–94.

Ellerman, A. Denny, and Juan Pablo Montero, 1996. "Why Are Allowance Prices So Low? An Analysis of the SO_2 Emissions Trading Program," CEEPR 96-001, Massachusetts Institute of Technology (February).

Fankhauser, Samuel, 1994. "The Social Costs of Greenhouse Gas Emissions: An Expected Value Approach." *The Energy Journal* 15:157–84.

Fullerton, Don, and J. Mackie, 1987. "Investment Allocation and Growth under the Tax Reform Act of 1986." *In Compendium of Tax Research 1987*, Office of Tax Analysis of the U.S. Department of the Treasury, Washington, D.C., pp. 131–171.

Fullerton, Don and Gilbert Metcalf, 1997. "Environmental Controls, Scarcity Rents, and Pre-Existing Distortions." NBER Working paper 6091, July.

Goulder, Lawrence H., 1995a. "Environmental Taxation and the 'Double Dividend': A Reader's Guide." *International Tax and Public Finance* 2(2):157–183.

Goulder, Lawrence H., 1995b. "Effects of Carbon Taxes in an Economy with Prior Tax Distortions: An Intertemporal General Equilibrium Analysis," *Journal of Environmental Economics and Management*, October.

Goulder, Lawrence H., 1998. "Environmental Policy Making in a Second-Best Setting," *Journal of Applied Economics*, 1(2).

Goulder, Lawrence H., Ian W. H. Parry, and Dallas Burtraw, 1997. "Revenue-Raising vs. Other Approaches to Environmental Protection: The Critical Significance of Pre-Existing Tax Distortions." *RAND Journal of Economics*, Winter.

Goulder, Lawrence H., Ian W. H. Parry, Roberton C. Williams III, and Dallas Burtraw, 1999. "The Cost-Effectiveness of Alternative Instruments for Environmental Protection in a Second-best Setting." *Journal of Public Economics* 72(3):329–60.

Goulder, Lawrence H., and Philippe Thalmann, 1993. "Approaches to Efficient Capital Taxation: Leveling the Playing Field vs. Living by the Golden Rule." *Journal of Public Economics* 50:169–96.

Hall, Robert, 1988. "Intertemporal Substitution in Consumption," *Journal of Political Economy* 96(2):339–57.

Jorgenson, Dale W. and Peter J. Wilcoxen, 1990. "Environmental Regulation and U.S. Economic Growth," *RAND Journal of Economics* 21(2), 314–340.

Jorgenson, Dale W. and Peter J. Wilcoxen, 1996. "Reducing U.S. Carbon Emissions: An Econometric General Equilibrium Assessment." In Darius Gaskins and John Weyant, eds., *Reducing Global Carbon Dioxide Emissions: Costs and Policy Options*. Energy Modeling Forum, Stanford University, Stanford, Calif.

Jorgenson, Dale, and Kun-Young Yun, 1990. "Tax Policy and the Cost of Capital." Oxford: Oxford University Press.

Lawrence, Emily, 1991, "Poverty and the Rate of Time Preference: Evidence from Panel Data," *Journal of Political Economy* 99(1):54–77.

Lee, Dwight R., and Walter S. Misiolek, 1986. "Substituting Pollution Taxation for General Taxation: Some Implications for Efficiency in Pollution Taxation." *Journal of Environmental Economics and Management* 13:338–347.

Lucas, Robert E., 1990. "Supply-Side Economics: An Analytical Review." *Oxford Economic Papers* 42:293–316.

Ng, Y. K., 1980. "Optimal Corrective Taxes or Subsidies when Revenue-Raising Imposes an Excess Burden." *American Economic Review* 70:744–51.

Nordhaus, William D., 1991. "To Slow or Not to Slow: The Economics of the Greenhouse Effect." *The Economic Journal* 101:920–37.

Oates, Wallace E., 1993. "Pollution Charges as a Source of Public Revenues." In Herbert Giersch, ed., *Economic Progress and Environmental Concerns*. Berlin: Springer-Verlag, pp. 135–52.

Oates, Wallace E., 1995. "Green Taxes: Can We Protect the Environment and Improve the Tax System at the Same Time?" *Southern Economic Journal* 61(4):914–922.

Oates, Wallace E., and Robert M. Schwab, 1988. "Economic Competition among Jurisdictions: Efficiency Enhancing or Distortion Inducing?" *Journal of Public Economics* 35:333–354, April.

Oates, Wallace E., and Diana L. Strassmann, 1984. "Effluent Fees and Market Structure." *Journal of Public Economics* 24:29–46.

Parry, Ian W. H., 1995. "Pollution Taxes and Revenue Recycling." *Journal of Environmental Economics and Management* 29:S64–S77.

Parry, Ian W. H., 1997. "Environmental Taxes and Quotas in the Presence of Distorting Taxes in Factor Markets." *Resource and Energy Economics* 19:203–220.

Parry, Ian W. H., Roberton Williams, and Lawrence H. Goulder, 1999. "When Can Carbon Abatement Policies Increase Welfare? The Fundamental Role of Distorted Factor Markets." *Journal of Environmental Economics and Management* 37:52–84.

Peck, Stephen C. and Thomas J. Teisberg, 1993. "Global Warming Uncertainties and the Value of Information: An Analysis Using CETA." *Resource and Energy Economics* 15:71–98.

Pigou, A. C., 1938. *The Economics of Welfare* (4th edition). London: Weidenfeld and Nicolson.

Proost, S., and D. van Regemorter, 1995. "The Double Dividend and the Role of Inequality Aversion and Macroeconomic Regimes." *International Tax and Public Finance* 2(2), August.

Repetto, Robert, Roger C. Dower, Robin Jenkins, and Jacqueline Geoghegan, 1992. *Green Fees: How a Tax Shift Can Work for the Environment and the Economy.* World Resources Institute, November.

Sandmo, Agnar, 1975. "Optimal Taxation in the Presence of Externalities." *Swedish Journal of Economics* 77.

Shackleton, Robert, Michael Shelby, Alex Cristofaro, Roger Brinner, Joyce Yanchar, Lawrence Goulder, Dale Jorgenson, Peter Wilcoxen, and Peter Pauly, 1996. "The Efficiency Value of Carbon Tax Revenues." In Darius Gaskins and John Weyant, eds., *Reducing Global Carbon Dioxide Emissions: Costs and Policy Options*. Stanford, Calif.: Energy Modeling Forum.

Shah, Anwar, and Bjorn Larsen, 1992. "Carbon Taxes, the Greenhouse Effect and Developing Countries," World Bank Policy Research Working Paper Series No. 957, The World Bank, Washington, D.C.

Stavins, Robert N., 1995. "Transactions Costs and Tradeable Permits." *Journal of Environmental Economics and Management* 29, 133–147.

Terkla, David, 1984. "The Efficiency Value of Effluent Tax Revenues." *Journal of Environmental Economics and Management* 11:107–23.

Tietenberg, T. H., 1985. *Emissions Trading: An Exercise In Reforming Pollution Policy*. Washington D.C.: Resources for the Future.

Weitzman, Martin L., 1974. "Prices vs. Quantities." *Review of Economic Studies* 41, 477–491.

Williams, Roberton C. III, 1998. "Revisiting the Cost of Protectionism: The Role of Tax Distortions in the Labor Market." *Journal of International Economics*, forthcoming.

Williams, Roberton C. III, 1999. "Tax-Interactions in a Dynamic Model with Capital Accumulation." Working paper, Stanford University.

[3]

International Tax and Public Finance, 2: 157–183 (1995)

Environmental Taxation and the Double Dividend: A Reader's Guide

LAWRENCE H. GOULDER
Department of Economics, Landau Economics Building, Stanford University, Stanford, CA 94305-6072, U.S.A., e-mail goulder@leland.stanford.edu; Resources for the Future; and National Bureau of Economic Research

Abstract

There has been considerable debate as to whether the revenue-neutral substitution of environmental taxes for ordinary income taxes might offer a double dividend: not only (1) improve the environment but also (2) reduce certain costs of the tax system. This paper articulates different notions of double dividend and examines the theoretical and empirical evidence for each. It also connects the double-dividend issue with principles of optimal environmental taxation in a second-best setting.

A weak double-dividend claim—that returning tax revenues through cuts in distortionary taxes leads to cost savings relative to the case where revenues are returned lump sum—is easily defended on theoretical grounds and (thankfully) receives wide support from numerical simulations. The stronger versions contend that revenue-neutral swaps of environmental taxes for ordinary distortionary taxes involve zero or negative gross costs. Theoretical analyses and numerical results tend to cast doubt on the strong double-dividend claim, although the theoretical case is not air-tight and the numerical evidence is mixed.

Key words: environmental taxation, environmental tax reform, second-best environmental taxation, double-dividend, general equilibrium tax analysis

Economists have long favored the use of taxes as instruments of environmental protection. To many economic analysts, in situations involving serious externalities taxes are the most effective mechanism for "getting the prices right"—that is, for helping prices closely approximate marginal social costs. The notion that taxes can improve welfare outcomes by internalizing externalities traces back at least as far as Pigou (1938) and is a central tenet of environmental economics.

Real-world economies obtain public revenues not only through environmental (corrective) taxes but also through distortionary taxes such as income, payroll, and sales taxes. What constitutes getting the prices right (or merely closer to right) is more complicated in a second-best setting where both types of taxes are present than in a world with environmental taxes alone. This is the case for at least two reasons. First, taxes interact. In particular, the *gross costs*[1] of newly imposed environmental taxes depend on the marginal rates of preexisting distortionary taxes.[2] Second, the presence of other taxes introduces the possibility of swapping an environmental tax for an existing tax. Consider a tax reform in which an environmental tax is introduced and its revenues are used to finance reductions in the income tax. The overall gross cost of this revenue-neutral package depends not only on the costs attributable to the environmental tax itself but also on certain efficiency benefits (avoided costs) associated with the reduction in income tax rates.[3]

These issues have come to life in recent analyses and policy debates surrounding the carbon tax option. Initial work on carbon taxes tended to ignore other distortionary taxes; most initial studies assumed that the revenues from this tax would be returned to the economy in a lump-sum fashion.[4] Subsequent analysis pointed out, however, that the revenues could be used to finance reductions in ordinary, distortionary taxes.[5] Several analysts have indicated that this could significantly reduce the costs of the carbon tax. Indeed, some have suggested that these costs could be zero or negative when opportunities to recycle the revenues through cuts in distortionary taxes are taken into account. However, some recent theoretical and empirical work points out an effect that works in the opposite direction, revealing ways that existing distortionary taxes may interact with the carbon tax and thereby enlarge the carbon tax's costs. While recognizing that recycling the revenues can reduce the costs of a carbon tax, this work shows that for any given method of recycling, pre-existing taxes augment the costs. Much of this work indicates that this *tax interaction effect* is larger than the *revenue-recycling effect*, so that, overall, a revenue-neutral carbon tax is likely to involve positive costs in a second-best setting.

The term *double dividend* relates directly to these discussions. Pearce (1991) noted that swaps of environmental taxes for distortionary taxes may produce a double dividend by not only (1) discouraging environmentally damaging activities but also (2) reducing the distortionary cost of the tax system. The double-dividend concept is relevant to many important ideas in second-best environmental taxation. Unfortunately, the term is used in different ways: the dividend given by (2) above, in particular, can have very different interpretations. This has led to some confusion. This paper distinguishes the different notions of double dividend and analyzes the theoretical and empirical support for each. The main motivation here is not to develop a taxonomy but rather to clarify key issues relevant to the formulation of environmental policy in second-best economies. The discussion is intended to help delineate the circumstances under which the substitution of green or environmentally motivated taxes for typical existing taxes is likely to be an efficiency-improving venture.

Before launching into the specifics of the double-dividend issue, it may be useful to view the issue in a broader context. There is widespread agreement as to the ability of environmental taxes to confer the first dividend above (environmental improvement), although the magnitude of this dividend usually is highly uncertain. On the other hand, there is much debate as to what kind of additional (second) dividend, if any, might be offered by environmental taxes. The preoccupation with the possibility of a second dividend, in my view, reflects the uncertainties about the magnitudes of the first. Much of the controversy about the second dividend is in terms of whether environmental taxes can be introduced in a way that is costless. Policymakers who are interested in green tax swaps are often frustrated by the uncertainties as to the values of the environmental benefits that would result from such swaps. Under these conditions, the no-cost idea is especially appealing. If revenue-neutral environmental tax policies are costless, then the burden of proof facing the policy-maker is much reduced: to justify the environmental tax on benefit-cost grounds, it suffices to know the *sign* of the environmental benefits—to know that they are positive. If costs are zero (or negative), this guarantees positive net benefits. On the other hand, if one cannot be assured that the costs are zero, then before one can recommend an environmental tax swap on efficiency grounds one has to be involved in the messy business of comparing (uncertain) environmental benefits with the economic costs.

Thus the debate about the double dividend reflects the desire to be able to make safe judgments about environmental reforms in the presence of uncertainty. In my view, it makes a difference how this debate is resolved because this could influence what policymakers view as the minimal information requirements for fruitful environmental tax reform.

The rest of this paper is organized as follows. Section 1 distinguishes three interpretations of the double-dividend concept and comments on the implications of each. The stronger interpretations are most relevant to policy evaluation, and subsequent sections of the paper deal primarily with them. Section 2 examines the theoretical evidence for or against the stronger double dividend notions. Section 3 presents numerical results. Section 4 discusses the relationship between this issue and optimal environmental taxation. The final section offers conclusions.

1. Three double-dividend propositions

One can distinguish several double-dividend claims that might be made about a given environmental tax initiative such as a carbon tax. Here are three: [6]

- *Weak form* By using revenues from the environmental tax to finance reductions in marginal rates of an existing distortionary tax, one achieves cost savings relative to the case where the tax revenues are returned to taxpayers in lump-sum fashion.
- *Intermediate form* It is possible to find a distortionary tax such that the revenue-neutral substitution of the environmental tax for this tax involves a zero or negative gross cost.
- *Strong form* The revenue-neutral substitution of the environmental tax for *typical* or *representative* distortionary taxes involves a zero or negative gross cost.

1.1. The weak form

These hypotheses differ in terms of what they propose about the costs of revenue-neutral environmental tax policies. Let *gross cost* refer to the reduction in individual welfare (in wealth equivalents) of a given tax initiative, abstracting from the welfare effect from changes in environmental quality.[7] Let $C(t_E, \Delta T_L)$ denote the gross cost of the new environmental tax t_E in combination with lump-sum tax reductions ΔT_L sufficient to make the policy revenue neutral. Similarly, let $C(t_E, \Delta t_X)$ denote the gross cost of the new tax t_E accompanied by cuts in the distortionary tax Δt_X sufficient to achieve revenue neutrality. The first proposition asserts that

$$C(t_E, \Delta t_X) < C(t_E, \Delta T_L). \tag{1}$$

The gross cost is lower when revenues are replaced through cuts in the distortionary tax than when revenues are replaced lump-sum. Under this proposition, the second dividend is the lower distortionary cost in the former case (left side) relative to the cost in the latter case (right side).

The weak double-dividend notion is relatively uncontroversial. This is fortunate because the key assumption on which it depends is relatively innocuous. The weak double-dividend claim can be shown to be equivalent to the claim that replacing, at the margin, a lump-sum tax by a distortionary tax entails a positive welfare cost (apart from environmental considerations).[8] This latter claim is not difficult to uphold, since the idea that swapping a distortionary tax for a lump-sum tax has a positive welfare cost is part of the usual definition of *distortionary*. So long as the tax t_X deserves its title as a distortionary tax, it will have a positive efficiency cost, and the weak double-dividend claim will hold.[9]

The weak form can be related to the elements of Figure 1. The figure offers the typical partial equilibrium and first-best framework for analyzing welfare effects of an environmental tax.[10] *MC* denotes the private marginal costs of producing the given commodity, which in this example is coal. MC_{soc} represents the social marginal-cost curve, incorporating the marginal external damage (marginal external cost), *MED*. *MB* represents the marginal benefit (demand) curve. If a tax is imposed on coal equal to the marginal external damage, social and private marginal costs become aligned. The usual textbook analysis regards the welfare gain as area *B*.[11] This is the value of the environmental improvement (*A* + *B*) minus the gross costs of the tax (*A*).[12]

This simple analysis suggests that the tax revenue *R* is transferred costlessly from those who pay the coal tax to the government and back to the private sector,[13] with no efficiency consequences. The weak notion of the double dividend recognizes the fact that this recycling of the revenues (R) may indeed have efficiency consequences. The assertion is that when revenues are used to cut existing distortionary taxes, in particular, they help reduce the overall (gross) costs of the tax system. *If* the gross costs under *lump-sum* replacement are given by area *A*, then under *distortionary-tax* replacement they are less than *A*.[14]

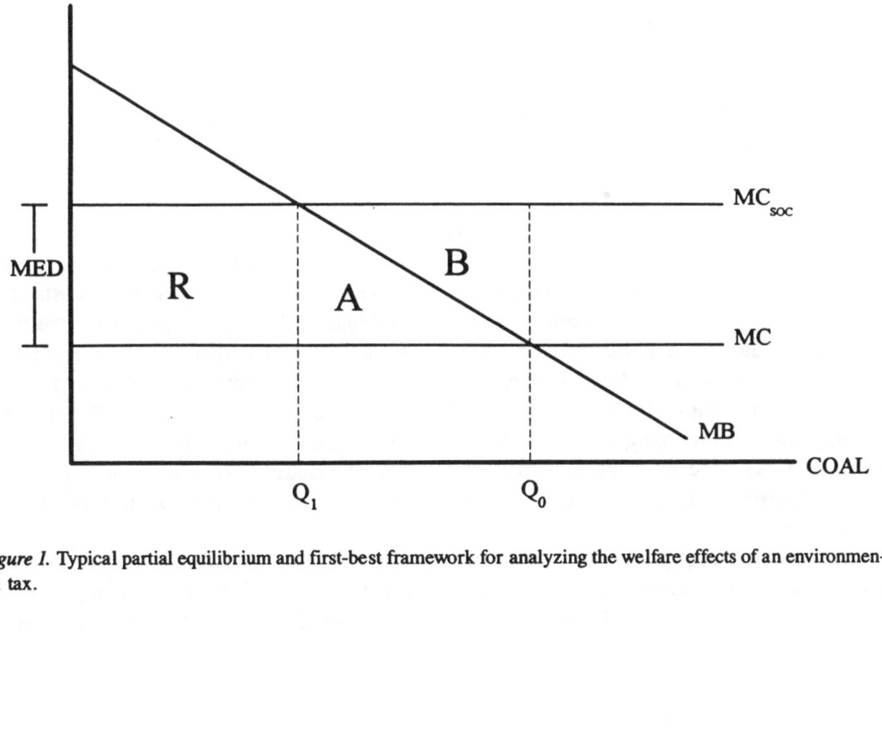

Figure 1. Typical partial equilibrium and first-best framework for analyzing the welfare effects of an environmental tax.

It is important to recognize, however, that other important cost considerations may be obscured by the first-best, partial-equilibrium framework embodied in Figure 1. In particular, when other taxes (such as income taxes) are present, the area A in Figure 1 is not a good indicator of the gross costs of the tax on coal. The weak double-dividend notion correctly claims that rebating revenues through cuts in distortionary taxes reduces gross costs relative to their level under lump-sum replacement, but the reference level from which the reduction occurs is generally quite different from that suggested by area A in the diagram. We return to this issue below.

1.2. The stronger forms

The intermediate and strong double-dividend notions involve assertions about the *sign* of the gross cost of a revenue-neutral policy in which an environmental tax replaces (some of) an existing distortionary tax. The assertion is

$$C(t_E, \Delta t_X) < 0. \tag{2}$$

The assertion here is that swapping an environmental tax for a distortionary tax involves a negative overall gross cost.

The intermediate and strong double-dividend notions differ in the strength of the claim regarding the extensiveness of the class of distortionary taxes for which (2) holds. The intermediate notion affirms that there exists at least one distortionary tax t_X for which (2) applies; the strong notion claims that (2) holds for typical or representative existing taxes. For any given distortionary tax (t_X) involved in the tax swap, condition (2) is stronger than (1) assuming $C(t_E, \Delta T_L) > 0$.

One can decompose the overall gross cost $C(t_E, \Delta t_X)$ into cost that is directly attributable to the environmental tax and cost that is directly attributable to the reduction in the distortionary tax.[15] The intermediate and strong double-dividend notions can be interpreted as claims that the first cost—the cost resulting from the environmental tax—is smaller in absolute magnitude than the second cost—the cost associated with the cut in the distortionary tax. In other words, when the taxes are scaled to imply the same revenue impact, the environmental tax introduces a smaller cost than an equal-revenue change in the distortionary tax.

It is important to keep in mind what is meant by *costs*. As mentioned earlier, costs (C) are a measure of the policy-induced changes in individual welfare (abstracting from welfare effects associated with policy-related changes in environmental quality). In the related theoretical work, welfare depends directly on individual consumption of goods and services and enjoyment of leisure. Measured this way, the economic cost can differ in sign and magnitude from changes in important macroeconomic variables such as GNP or the growth of GNP. The question whether a given revenue-neutral tax swap entails positive costs is different from the question whether the swap entails a reduction in GNP or its growth rate.[16]

Relative to the strong version, the intermediate double-dividend version makes a more modest claim about the circumstances in which gross costs will be zero or negative. It asserts the existence of at least one particularly burdensome distortionary tax whose replacement by an environmental tax would involve negative costs. It should be noted that the case for removing or reducing an unusually costly existing tax can be made without introducing environmental considerations. Even without bringing in the environmental dimension, there would be strong reasons for replacing this tax with other taxes on narrow (nonenvironmental) efficiency grounds.[17] Correspondingly, although the presence of this highly inefficient tax may supply a target for general tax reform, by itself it does not offer support for introducing the new environmental tax.

As mentioned in the introduction, the validity of the strong form of the double dividend would significantly reduce information hurdles associated with the evalution of environmental taxes. If the strong double dividend obtained, it would be necessary only to establish the positive sign of environmental benefits to justify a given revenue-neutral environmental tax on benefit-cost grounds. In light of the substantial uncertainties surrounding the magnitudes of environmental benefits from green taxes, the appeal of the strong form is quite understandable. Much of the debate about the potential for environmental tax reform revolves around whether the strong form holds. The remainder of this paper concentrates on this double-dividend notion.

2. Does the strong form hold? Theoretical considerations

2.1. A key result

This section examines the theoretical evidence related to the strong interpretation of the double-dividend idea. An important theoretical investigation of this issue was provided by Bovenberg and de Mooij (1992, 1994a). These authors develop a simple general equilibrium model with one primary factor of production—labor—and three produced commodities—a "clean" consumption good, a "dirty" consumption good, and a public good (nonrival in consumption). Production exhibits constant returns to scale, and the rates of transformation between the three produced commodities are constant and equal to unity. Environmental quality is negatively related to aggregate production of the dirty consumption good. A representative household derives utility from leisure, from consumption of the three produced goods, and from environmental quality. The two private goods and leisure are weakly separable from the public good and environmental quality in the utility function.

Bovenberg and de Mooij begin with the situation where the only tax is a labor income tax with a constant marginal tax rate. They then consider the effects of a revenue-neutral policy change in which a tax is imposed on the dirty consumption commodity and the revenues are devoted to a reduction in the labor tax rate. The commodity tax is noninfinitesimal.[18] The strong double-dividend claim is that this policy would yield an increase in nonenvironment-related welfare—that is, in the utility from the composite of consumption and leisure enjoyed by the representative household.[19] These authors find that this claim is substantiated if and only if the uncompensated wage elasticity of labor supply is negative—that is, if and only if the labor supply function is backward bending. Most empirical studies of labor supply yield positive values for the uncompensated elasticity (see, for example, Hausman, 1985). Thus, the Bovenberg-de Mooij results tend to reject the double-dividend proposition in its strong form.[20]

What lies behind the Bovenberg-de Mooij result? There are two key components. First, the tax on the environmentally harmful consumption good lowers the after-tax wage and generates distortions in the *labor* market, and these labor-market distortions are at least as great in magnitude as the labor market distortions from a labor-tax increment of equal revenue yield. Hence, the revenue-neutral swap in which the environmental tax replaces (some of) the labor tax leads to no reduction (and usually an increase) in labor-market distortions. Second, the tax on the environmentally damaging commodity induces changes in the commodity market—"distorting" the choice among alternative commodities.[21] These two distortionary effects—in labor and commodity markets—imply that, apart from environmental considerations, the revenue-neutral combination of an environmental tax and reduction in labor tax involves a reduction in the nonenvironmental component of welfare. In fact, the distortions in the commodity and labor markets are connected. To the extent that the environmentally motivated commodity tax leads households to substitute other commodities for the taxed commodity, there is a reduction in the gross revenue yield of the tax. This *tax base erosion effect* limits the extent to which the environmental tax can finance a reduction in the labor tax and augments the overall gross cost of the tax initiative.

The intuition for this result is as follows.[22] Consider a static model in which there is one labor market (no labor heterogeneity). Let case 1 refer to the situation where there is just one produced commodity. Suppose that initially there is a tax on labor but no commodity tax. Under these circumstances the commodity tax (even an infinitesimal one) produces a noninfinitesimal excess burden. This occurs because, under the circumstances just described, the introduction of a commodity tax is formally identical to an increase in the labor tax. It reduces the real wage in precisely the same way an increase in a labor tax would.[23] Now suppose, in contrast to this first case, that there are many distinct produced commodities. As before, suppose that the initial situation involves only a tax on labor. Now consider (case 2) the effect of introducing a uniform but small tax on *all* commodities and (case 3) the effect of introducing a small tax on just *one* of the commodities. Case 2 is formally similar to case 1; it will generate noninfinitesimal excess burdens because this tax is equivalent to an increase in the wage tax.[24] Case 3 is relevant to the imposition of an environmental tax on one commodity. Bovenberg and de Mooij show analytically that, for a given revenue yield, the excess burden in case 3 is noninfinitesimal and in fact is larger than in case 1 or 2. The reason is that case 3 generates the same or larger labor market distortion as in the other cases and a larger distortion in the commodity markets.[25]

These results indicate that there are *two* important omissions in Figure 1. They work in opposite directions. First (as emphasized by the weak double-dividend claim), the revenues *R* can be used to reduce gross distortionary costs. This suggests that the partial equilibrium analysis would overstate the cost of the environmental tax initiative. At the same time, the presence of other (labor) taxes implies that, for any given use of the tax revenues, the gross distortion from the environmental tax will be larger than implied by Figure 1. This implies the opposite bias from the partial equilibrium analysis. Bovenberg and de Mooij show that the latter effect is larger in magnitude than the former: overall, the presence of prior taxes implies higher gross costs from the environmental tax—even when revenues are recycled through cuts in the distortionary tax. These two effects are schematized in Figure 2. Adopting terminology similar to that introduced by Parry (1994) in a recent paper, I call the former effect the *revenue-recycling effect* and the latter the *tax-interaction effect*.[26] (The tax base erosion effect, mentioned three paragraphs above, contributes to the more general

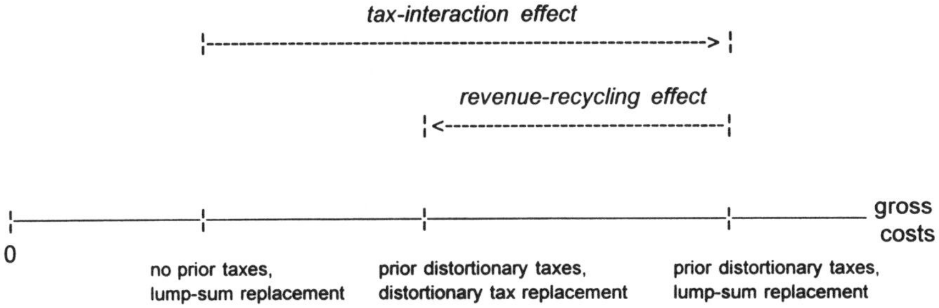

Figure 2. Gross costs of environmental tax under alternative initial conditions and recycling methods.

tax interaction effect.) Using a different analytical approach, Parry obtains results that conform to those of Bovenberg and de Mooij, showing that the tax interaction effect is of greater magnitude than the revenue-recycling effect under plausible values for parameters.[27]

Earlier analyses of revenue-neutral environmental taxes emphasized the revenue-recycling effect and did not recognize the tax-interaction effect. These analyses suggested that the strong double dividend was inevitable. An important contribution of Bovenberg-de Mooij, Parry, and others is to call attention to the tax-interaction effect and its implications for the costs of revenue-neutral environmental tax reforms. A related and important lesson from this work is that partial equilibrium analyses of the gross costs of environmental taxes can be highly misleading. This research shows that environmental taxes importantly affect resource use in markets other than the market in which the tax is applied—with significant implications for gross costs. These general equilibrium impacts are especially important if there are prior taxes in other markets such as the labor market.[28]

2.2. *How general are these results?*

The analytical results from Bovenberg-de Mooij and Parry stem from simplified models. What are the key simplifying assumptions of these models, and to what extent are these simplifications critical to the results?

2.2.1. Intermediate inputs. One simplification of the models is that they disregard intermediate inputs. However, in Bovenberg and Goulder (1994a), the Bovenberg-de Mooij model is extended to incorporate intermediate inputs, and the results above prevail in the extended model. Bovenberg and Goulder analyze the effects of environmentally motivated taxes on "dirty" intermediate goods and on "dirty" consumption goods. In each case, the strong double-dividend claim fails to materialize when the uncompensated wage elasticity of labor supply is positive. The economic basis for the result in the case of the intermediate good tax is the same as that provided above for the commodity (consumer good) tax. Similar results are obtained in Bovenberg and de Mooij (1994b).

2.2.2. Capital. Another simplification in the above models is their static nature. How would consideration of capital affect the results? Including capital introduces the possibility that a revenue-neutral environmental tax could shift the burden of taxation from one factor to another. This has efficiency implications to the extent that, in the initial tax system, the marginal efficiency costs of capital taxation and of labor taxation are different.[29] To assess the importance of including capital in the analysis, two considerations are important. First, one needs to consider the extent to which the marginal efficiency costs of capital taxation differ from those of labor taxation under the *status quo ante*. On what do these marginal efficiency costs depend? While labor taxes distort the labor-leisure margin—the margin of choice between enjoying leisure and enjoying consumption (by earning labor income)—capital taxes distort the intertemporal margin—the margin of choice between consuming today and consuming in the future (by saving). For a given labor tax, the distortion in the labor-leisure margin is greater the larger is the (compensated) wage elasticity of labor supply. For a given capital income tax, the distortion along the intertemporal dimension is greater the larger is the intertemporal elasticity of substitution in consumption. Thus, the relative marginal efficiency costs of labor and capital income taxes depend on these elasticities and on the magnitudes of labor and capital income tax rates.

The second consideration is whether the burden or incidence of the environmental tax falls largely on labor or on capital. As is well known (see Auerbach and Kotlikoff, 1987), taxes on consumption commodities (such as a consumer gasoline tax) are implicitly taxes on labor.[30] On the other hand, the burden of taxes on intermediate inputs (such as a tax on fossil fuels) could potentially fall primarily on capital. This can occur because such taxes can raise the cost of producing capital goods and thereby lower the rate of return. If this effect is large enouogh, the burden of the tax will fall primarily on capital.[31]

These considerations indicate that the gross costs of a revenue-neutral environmental tax will be lower to the extent that

1. In the initial tax system, the difference in marginal efficiency costs (marginal excess burdens) is large,
2. The burden of the environmental tax falls primarily on the factor with relatively low marginal efficiency cost,
3. The base of the environmental tax is relatively broad, so that the gross distortions it generates in intermediate good and consumer good markets are small, and
4. Revenues from the tax are devoted to reducing tax rates on the factor with relatively high marginal-efficiency cost.

These considerations raise the possibility of a zero or negative cost tax swap. For example, if the marginal excess burden of capital taxes is higher than that for labor, and if the burden of a new environmental tax falls primarily on labor, then introducing this new tax in combination with a revenue-preserving cut in capital taxes can involve zero or negative gross costs.

Would this result, if it occurred, resurrect the double dividend in its strong form? Or would it only confirm the intermediate double dividend claim? The issue is semantic: the answer depends on whether one classifies a (pure) tax on capital as a typical or representative tax. A more clear-cut confirmation of the strong double dividend notion would occur if the gross costs were negative in a case where revenues are returned through a general income tax cut (that is, through cuts in the marginal rates applicable to capital and labor).

Returning the revenues through a general income tax cut dilutes the gain associated with revenue replacement because it involves a reduction in the relatively efficient factor tax as well as the more inefficient one. This method of revenue replacement does not exploit the potential contribution of item (4) above, but foregoing (4) enables the policy to test unequivocally the strong double-dividend claim. The above considerations indicate that if the capital tax is extremely costly relative to the labor tax, the gross costs can be negative even if the potential contribution of (4) is not exploited.

Thus, once capital is considered, the theory gives more scope for the possibility of the strong double dividend. Is it likely empirically? Most empirical studies for the United States indicate that capital taxes have higher marginal excess burdens than do labor taxes (see Ballard, Shoven, and Whalley, 1985; Jorgenson and Yun, 1990). Under these circumstances, the prospects for a strong double dividend become more favorable to the extent that

1′. In the initial tax system, there is large difference in the marginal excess burden (MEB) per dollar of revenue for capital taxation, as compared with the MEB per dollar for labor taxation,
2′. The burden of the environmental tax falls primarily on labor, and
3′. The base of the environmental tax is broad.

Are these conditions met in the real world? Condition 2′ indicates that the strong double-dividend claim could potentially be upheld for an environmentally motivated commodity tax because such taxes tend to be borne largely by labor. An example of an environmentally motivated commodity tax is a tax on consumer purchases of gasoline. In a world where capital taxes have much higher excess burdens than labor taxes, the gasoline tax (with revenues returned through cuts in income taxes, or, even better, through cuts in capital taxes) is appealing because it helps shift the burden of taxation from capital to labor. Intuitively, this consumer-level tax functions like a consumption tax and shares the appeal of a consumption tax in reducing intertemporal distortions or distortions in capital markets. On the other hand, a tax on consumers' gasoline purchases is obviously much narrower than a general consumption tax. As indicated by condition 3′, the narrowness of the base is a liability. To the extent that substitution from gasoline is easy, a given gasoline tax will generate less revenue and introduce larger gross distortions in commodity markets, worsening the prospects for zero or negative gross costs.[32]

The prospects for the strong claim are worse in the case of a tax on intermediate inputs. Certain intermediate input taxes—for example, a tax on fossil fuel inputs—may have a strong justification when environmental benefits are taken into account. But the double-dividend issue relates only to the cost side, and intermediate input taxes do not have much promise on this side of the ledger. The reason is that these taxes are often borne to a significant degree by capital. To the extent that fossil fuels are employed more intensively in the production of capital goods than in the economy in general, an environmentally motivated tax on fossil fuels will raise the relative price of these goods and be borne more by capital. In the data set employed in my general equilibrium energy-economy-environment model of the United States (see Goulder, 1994a), capital-goods production is highly energy intensive. Consequently, in policy simulations the burden of fossil fuel (intermediate input) taxes falls primarily on capital, virtually ruling out the possibility of the double dividend in the strong form.[33]

The new dimension that arises when capital is considered is that of shifting the burden of taxes between factors and thereby exploiting differences in the marginal excess burdens of factor taxes. This dimension has force only insofar as the existing tax system is inefficient in the sense that the marginal excess burdens of different taxes are not equal. Arguably, the case for reducing these inefficiencies is independent of the case for a new environmental tax. The possibility of a double dividend in the strong form is more difficult if one considers only situations where the "rest of the tax system" is optimal in some sense. We return to this issue in Section 4.

2.2.3. Preexisting subsidies. The issue just raised also is relevant to evaluating the strong double-dividend claim in the presence of prior subsidies: there may be independent reasons for revoking the subsidies. Still, it is worthwhile noting that prior subsidies clearly offer scope for the strong double dividend. For example, a carbon tax can serve to undo prior subsidies on fossil fuels and thereby reduce or eliminate the gross distortionary costs in fuels markets. Shah and Larsen (1992) emphasize this point in considering the potential for carbon taxes in developing countries.

2.2.4. Emissions taxes. The analytical models discussed above consider taxes on commodities (consumer goods or intermediate inputs) whose production or use generates pollution. Other things equal (abstracting from monitoring costs, and so on), it is most efficient to tax the source of the externality—that is, emissions. Relative to commodity taxes, emissions taxes can yield higher *overall* efficiency gains. But the results concerning the double dividend are not changed. One can think of emissions as another intermediate input. As with taxes imposed on an ordinary intermediate input, emissions taxes alter the mix of all intermediate inputs and distort factor markets. The same mechanisms as discussed earlier indicate that emissions taxes will involve larger gross costs per dollar of revenue than the income (labor) taxes they replace. Whether they are more or less attractive in terms of gross costs than intermediate input taxes depends on the production technology. It may seem counterintuitive that emissions taxes do not automatically fare better than ordinary input taxes in terms of the double dividend. It helps to keep in mind that the issue here is gross costs per dollar of revenue, not overall gross costs. The same feature that makes emissions taxes attractive in terms of overall efficiency—their ability to induce larger emissions reductions per dollar of revenue than ordinary intermediate input taxes—curtails their attractiveness in terms of gross costs.

2.2.5. Exhaustible resources and decreasing returns. To this point we have only considered taxes on produced goods. In assessing the gross costs, we needed to consider the distortions produced in the markets for the factors that produced these goods. In particular, in examining the costs of a tax on fossil fuels, we regarded fossil fuels as produced intermediate goods and attended to the related distortions in the markets for labor and capital.

Of course, fossil fuels in their original form are primary resources, not produced goods. They are exhaustible resources whose reserves are given by nature.[34] The essential scarcity of natural resource stocks gives rise to scarcity rents. A basic result from the literature on the taxation of natural resources is that a constant tax on these rents does not alter the intertemporal allocation of these resources and has no efficiency cost (see, for example,

Sweeney, 1977, 1993; Dasgupta and Heal, 1979).[35] This suggests that an environmentally motivated tax on, say, fossil fuels, might not have a significant (gross) efficiency cost after all, given the exhaustible nature of these fuels. If this were the case, then swapping a tax on these fuels for ordinary income taxes might be a negative cost option, upholding the double-dividend claim in its strong form.

Should the previous results be discarded because they derive from models that ignored exhaustible resources? Not necessarily. It should be recognized that in most cases, the environmentally motivated taxes under actual consideration are not taxes on scarcity rents. The base of a carbon tax, for example, is not the scarcity rent but rather the quantity of fuel purchased (since carbon combustion and the amount of CO_2 emitted are functions of the quantity of fuel consumed). In contrast with a tax on pure rent, the tax on fuel output affects intertemporal choice and introduces a gross efficiency cost.[36] Despite the exhaustible nature of fossil fuels, a carbon tax does not attain the nondistortionary ideal.

Of course, this does not entirely disprove the significance of exhaustibility to the double-dividend issue. Even if the environmental taxes in question are related to fuel output rather than rent, it is possible that the gross efficiency costs of these taxes might be considerably lower when these "outputs" are extracted exhaustible resources. To continue with the fossil fuels example, *extracted* fossil fuels are the product of several primary factor inputs: natural resource stocks (fuels in the ground), capital and labor. The gross efficiency cost from taxes on these fuels will be a weighted average of the gross efficiency cost generated by the tax in the exhaustible-resource market, the capital market, and the labor market.[37] To discern this efficiency cost, one would need to know the extent to which the tax is borne by each of these factors and the marginal efficiency cost associated with reductions in scarcity rents, the return to capital, and the wage. This information is not easy to obtain, to say the least. Ascertaining the marginal efficiency cost in the resource market alone is exceedingly difficult. Despite these difficulties, further empirical work aimed at gauging these magnitudes might be of considerable value.

2.2.6. Involuntary unemployment. The above models assume all markets clear. However, introducing involuntary unemployment in the models by way of a fixed real wage above the market-clearing value would not change the basic results, assuming no other structural changes. In the original models, introducing the (revenue-neutral) environmental tax reduces labor productivity and shifts leftward the labor demand function. The same phenomenon occurs in a model in which the real wage is fixed above the original market-clearing level; the result is higher involuntary unemployment. The gross costs of this revenue-neutral policy are positive for the same reasons as in the market-clearing models.[38] However, the results differ when a further structural change is introduced. Bovenberg and van der Ploeg (1993) develop a model with involuntary unemployment (resulting from a fixed real wage) and three factors of production: labor, resources, and a fixed factor. In this model, under some circumstances the revenue-neutral combination of an environmental tax and a labor tax cut boosts employment and raises the nonenvironmental component of welfare (that is, the gross welfare cost is negative). This occurs when the production share of the fixed factor is large and substitution between labor and resources is easy. Under these circumstances a large share of the tax burden from the environmental tax is borne by the fixed factor, with relatively little efficiency cost. Hence the revenue-preserving cut in the labor tax yields a gross efficiency gain that more than offsets the gross efficiency cost attributable to the environmental tax.[39]

2.2.7. The environment as a capital good. In the analytical models discussed so far, environmental quality, if it is represented at all, enters as an argument of the utility function. It is a nonrival consumption good. The models that incorporate environmental quality usually assume that utility from consumption of ordinary goods and services is separable from utility from environmental quality. This permits a clean separation of gross costs and environmental benefits in the welfare analysis.

Environmental quality may also function as a capital good. That is, a cleaner environment may contribute positively to output, holding other inputs constant. Accounting for the productive contribution of environmental quality is a key element in developing truly integrated economy-environment models. Such integration permits models to capture an important potential benefit from environmental taxes—namely, the avoidance of the adverse impact of environmental deterioration on production.[40]

Once the capital goods aspect of environmental quality is included in an economic model, it becomes more difficult to separate cleanly the gross costs and (environmental) benefits of tax policies. *Gross costs* signifies the effect of the environmental tax on welfare, abstracting from welfare changes linked to changes in environmental quality. In a model with environment as a capital good, it is difficult (though not impossible) to perform this abstraction. In a very recent paper, Bovenberg and de Mooij (1994b) develop a model in which environmental quality functions both as a capital good and consumption good. They show that, under certain circumstances, an environmental tax produces the two dividends of a cleaner environment and faster economic growth. In my view, their result, strictly speaking, does not provide support for the strong double-dividend notion because it involves *benefit*-side issues; this is not a case of negative gross costs. Rather, their result supports the notion that *when production-related environmental benefits are taken into account*, environmental taxes sometimes can lead to faster growth as well as a cleaner environment.[41]

2.2.8. Terms of trade effects. All of the analyses discussed above adopt a closed-economy framework. In open economies, another economic dimension—changes in the terms of trade—can affect welfare. In certain cases an open economy can employ environmental taxes as a means of improving its terms of trade. Specifically, if the economy in question is a net importer of the good on which the environmental tax is imposed, and if this economy is large enough to exert monopsony power (that is, large enough to influence world prices of this good), then imposing the environmental tax can improve this economy's terms of trade. By taxing this imported good, this economy reduces national (and thus global) demands for the good and induces a reduction in the good's before-tax price in world markets. This shifts some of the burden of the domestic environmental tax onto foreigners, assuming that the revenues from the tax are devoted to cuts in taxes paid by domestic consumers or domestically owned firms. If the terms of trade gains are large enough, they could offset the other gross costs associated with the domestically imposed environmental tax and produce the strong double dividend from the point of view of the domestic economy.[42]

For the United States, an environmentally motivated tax on imported oil could fall in this category.[43] On the other hand, it is difficult to make the case that the United States would enjoy terms of trade gains from a (unilateral) carbon tax because this tax applies largely to coal, of which the United States is a net exporter.

2.3. A common theme

A unifying theme emerges from these considerations. Although the above analysis reveals circumstances in which the strong double dividend can occur, with one exception (the terms-of-trade case) these circumstances involve an essential inefficiency in the existing tax system on nonenvironmental dimensions. That is, the strong double dividend can arise only if the initial tax system involves inefficiencies in the form of differences in the marginal excess burdens of various taxes. If the environmental tax shifts the tax burden from factors associated with high MEBs to factors with relatively low MEBs, it can thereby reduce the nonenvironmental inefficiencies of the tax system and (if this effect is large enough) yield the strong double dividend. Thus, the strong double dividend presumes a need, based on nonenvironmental considerations, for factor tax reform. It is reasonable to ask why these inefficiencies cannot be addressed directly (through changes in factor tax rates) rather than through an environmental tax. It seems more natural to address these inefficiencies directly as part of general tax reform than indirectly as part of environmental policy.

One qualification to this last remark might be offered: there may be political opposition to reforms that directly alter the relative taxation of factors. Under these circumstances one could regard a revenue-neutral environmental tax policy as a more feasible alternative to direct reforms that are politically less palatable. The empirical support for this political argument is far from clear. Even if there were an empirical basis for the argument, one might feel uncomfortable rallying behind it since it essentially exploits the inability of voters to recognize the true incidence of environmental taxes.

3. Numerical findings

This section presents some numerical results applicable to the double dividend issue. Here I consider only the results that bear on the strong double-dividend notion defined above: the issue under investigation is the gross costs (nonenvironment-related welfare costs) of revenue-neutral tax swaps. As mentioned earlier (see note 6) some other studies define reductions in unemployment or increased profits as additional dividends from green taxes. I do not report results from these studies here because I do not have the information necessary to combine the reported changes in unemployment, profits, and other economic variables into the more general welfare notion expressed by *gross costs*.[44]

Table 1 presents results from five numerical models. These are the Goulder and Jorgenson-Wilcoxen intertemporal general equilibrium models of the United States, the DRI and LINK econometric macroeconomic models of the United States, and the Shah-Larsen partial equilibrium model, which has been applied to five countries, including the United States.[45] The results in Table 1 are for the revenue-neutral combination of an environmental tax (usually a carbon tax) and reduction in the personal income tax, except in cases where this combination was not available. I have focused on the case where revenues are returned through cuts in the personal income tax because this tax seems typical and representative; hence this case is relevant to the strong double-dividend claim.

All welfare changes abstract from changes in welfare associated with improvements in environmental quality (reductions in greenhouse gas emissions). Thus they correspond to

Table 1. Comparative numerical results.

Model	Reference	Country	Type of Environmental Tax	Form of Revenue Replacement	Results: Welfare Change	Percent Change in Real GNP: Period 1	Percent Change in Real GNP: Period 21
DRI	Shackleton et al. (1992)	U.S.	Phased-in carbon tax[a]	Personal tax cut	-0.39[b]	-0.00	-0.76
Goulder	Goulder (1994a)	U.S.	$25/ton carbon tax	Personal tax cut	-0.33[c]	-0.15	-0.22
Goulder	Goulder (1994b)	U.S.	Fossil fuel Btu tax	Personal tax cut	-0.28[c]	-0.09	-0.18
Jorgenson-Wilcoxen	Shackleton et al. (1992)	U.S.	Phased-in carbon tax[a]	Labor tax cut	1.01[d]	0.03	-0.41
Jorgenson-Wilcoxen	Shackleton et al. (1992)	U.S.	Phased-in carbon tax[a]	Capital tax cut	0.19[d]	0.20	0.95
LINK	Shackleton et al. (1992)	U.S.	Phased-in carbon tax[a]	Personal tax cut	-0.51[b]	0.00	-0.35
Shah-Larsen	Shah and Larsen (1992)	U.S.	$10/ton	Personal tax cut	-1049.[a]	-0.020[f]	
Shah-Larsen	Shah and Larsen (1992)	India	$10/ton	Personal tax cut	-129.	-0.060	
Shah-Larsen	Shah and Larsen (1992)	Indonesia	$10/ton	Personal tax cut	-4.	-0.005	
Shah-Larsen	Shah and Larsen (1992)	Japan	$10/ton	Personal tax cut	-269.	-0.008	
Shah-Larsen	Shah and Larsen (1992)	Pakistan	$10/ton	Personal tax cut	-23.	-0.070	

a. Beginning at $15/ton in 1990 (period 1), growing at 5 percent annually to $39.80 per ton in 2010 (period 21) and remaining at that level thereafter.
b. Percentage change in the present value of consumption; the model does not allow for utility-based welfare measures.
c. Welfare cost per dollar of tax revenue, as measured by the equivalent variation.
d. Equivalent variation as a percentage of benchmark private wealth.
e. Compensating variation in levels (millions of U.S. dollars).
f. Percentage change in GDP (not GNP). This is a one-period model.

the gross-cost concept discussed above. In the Goulder and Jorgenson-Wilcoxen models, welfare changes are reported in terms of the equivalent variation; in the Shah-Larsen model, the changes are based on the compensating variation.[46] In the DRI and LINK macroeconomic models, the percentage change in aggregate real consumption substitutes for a utility-based welfare measure.[47]

In most cases, the revenue-neutral green tax swap involves a reduction in welfare—that is, entails positive gross costs. This militates against the strong double-dividend claim. Results from the Jorgenson-Wilcoxen model, however, support the strong double-dividend notion.[48] To what might the differences in results be attributed?

A thorough examination of the differences in structure of these models and an extensive test of how these differences account for differences in model outcomes are beyond the scope of this paper. However, one potential explanation lies in the differences between the Jorgenson-Wilcoxen and Goulder models in the marginal excess burden of capital taxation.[49] The interest elasticity of saving is higher in the Jorgensen-Wilcoxen model than in the Goulder model. In addition, the Jorgenson-Wilcoxen model assumes that capital is fully mobile across sectors, while the Goulder model includes adjustment costs, which limit the speed at which capital can be reallocated and lower the elasticity of capital demand. Thus, elasticities of capital supply and capital demand are higher in the Jorgenson-Wilcoxen model; correspondingly, the marginal excess burden of capital taxation is considerably higher in the Jorgenson-Wilcoxen model than in the Goulder model, and the difference in the marginal excess burdens of capital and of labor is larger. In the Goulder model, the difference in MEBs per dollar is \$0.10;[50] the difference in the Jorgenson-Wilcoxen model appears to be considerably higher.[51] As indicated in the previous section, a large deviation in the MEBs on capital and labor taxes works in favor of the strong double dividend (particularly if the burden of the environmental tax falls on labor). This helps explain why, in the Jorgenson-Wilcoxen model, a revenue-neutral combination of carbon tax and reduction in *capital* tax involves negative gross costs (that is, a positive change in gross welfare). It is more difficult to account for the fact that substituting a carbon tax for a *labor* tax involves negative gross costs in the model.

Table 1 also includes GNP impacts. These are included simply because they may be of interest. As mentioned above, conceptually they bear no systematic relationship to welfare impacts. Indeed, in some of the numerical simulations the GNP and welfare changes are of opposite sign.

Like the theoretical results, the numerical outcomes in Table 1 tend to weigh against the strong double-dividend claim. But there is less than perfect agreement among the numerical results. Discerning the sources of differences in results across models is difficult and frustrating, in large part because of the lack of relevant information on simulation outcomes and parameters. Relatively few studies have performed the type of analysis that exposes the channels underlying the overall impacts. There is a need for more systematic sensitivity analysis, as well as closer investigations of how structural aspects of tax policies (type of tax base, narrowness of tax base, uniformity of tax rates, and so on) influence the outcomes. In addition, key behavioral parameters need to be reported. Serious attention to these issues will help explain differences in results and, one hopes, lead to a greater consensus on likely policy impacts.

4. Relationship to optimal environmental taxation

4.1. The optimal tax rate and the strong double-dividend claim

The previous discussions concerned the effects of incremental tax reforms. How do these issues relate to the optimal levels of environmental taxes?

The basic partial equilibrium analysis of the optimal environmental tax invokes the Pigovian principle: the optimal environmental tax is at a rate equal to the marginal external costs or marginal environmental damages (MED). This principle implicitly assumes that the gross marginal cost (or marginal abatement cost) associated with an environmental tax is equal to the tax rate. Hence if the tax is set equal to MED, gross costs and environmental benefits will be equated at the margin, ensuring optimality.[52]

The foregoing discussion indicates, however, that in a second-best setting a given environmental tax may give rise to marginal gross costs that differ from the tax rate. As indicated above, the revenue-replacement effect tends to reduce the gross costs; other things equal, it tends to imply a higher optimal tax rate—that is, a rate above MED. On the other hand, the tax interaction effect tends to raise gross costs; other things equal, it implies an optimal rate below MED. A central question underlying the strong notion of double dividend is whether the revenue replacement effect is strong enough to outweigh the tax interaction effect. The answer to this question also determines the relationship between the optimal tax rate and MED in a second-best setting. The previous discussion indicated that, under plausible conditions, the tax interaction effect is of greater magnitude than the revenue recycling effect. This implies that, under these conditions, the optimal environmental tax rate is below the rate implied by the Pigovian rule.

This result is supported by analytical work by Bovenberg and van der Ploeg (1994a) and by Parry (1994).[53] From Bovenberg and van der Ploeg's analysis, in a second-best setting the optimal environmental tax rate, t^*, is given by

$$t^* = MED/\mu \tag{3}$$

where μ is the marginal cost of public funds.[54] In their model, μ exceeds unity if and only if the uncompensated wage elasticity of labor supply is positive. This is precisely the condition that denies the double dividend in its strong form.

Bovenberg and van der Ploeg offer the following intuition for their optimal tax formula. Environmental quality can be viewed as a good which the public sector provides by obtaining public revenues through the environment tax. The higher the value of μ, the more costly it is to provide environmental quality. Thus, the higher is μ, the lower the optimal amount of environmental quality and the lower the value of t^*, other things equal.[55]

These issues are highly relevant to considerations of the optimal carbon tax. Nordhaus (1993) calculates the optimal carbon tax in the case where revenues are returned lump sum and compares that with the optimal tax when revenues are returned through cuts in distortionary taxes. In the former case, the optimal tax begins at about \$5 per ton, while in the latter case it begins at \$59 per ton! This seems to contradict the notion, indicated by the optimal tax formula above, that second-best considerations should *reduce* the optimal tax rate. It turns out, however, that although Nordhaus' experiments attend to the revenue-replacement effect, they do not capture the tax interaction effect because the model did not include preexisting taxes. Including preexisting taxes in the benchmark data would likely reverse the Nordhaus results. In this connection, simulations by Bovenberg and Goulder (1994b) indicate that the optimal carbon tax declines with the level of preexisting taxes.

4.2. Caveats

These models indicate that in the presence of other taxes, the optimal environmental tax rate is lower than MED. Although these results seem intuitive, they are no more compelling than the case against the strong double-dividend idea. To the extent that more complex models might expand the possibilities for a strong double dividend, they also offer scope for an optimal environmental tax above MED.

It is also important to recognize that the optimal tax formulas by Bovenberg-van der Ploeg and Parry assume that the optimal environmental tax is part of an optimal tax system. These formulas do not address the *constrained* second-best problem: how best to establish environmental taxes when the rest of the tax system is suboptimal. Much depends on how the rest of the system departs from optimality. Simulation experiments by Bovenberg and Goulder (1994b) for the U.S. economy indicate that the "suboptimality"[56] of the U.S. tax system implies a constrained second-best optimal carbon tax that is lower than that suggested by the Bovenberg-van der Ploeg formula. The intuition is that a given environmental tax generates a larger gross cost in a suboptimal setting than in a setting where other taxes are set optimally.

4.3. "Is a small tax efficiency-improving?" and related theoretical issues

The cost-side-oriented discussion of the double dividend is driven by the broader question as to whether the substitution of environmentally motivated or green taxes for ordinary taxes might be a welfare-improving venture. It is important to recognize that the difficulty of substantiating the strong double-dividend claim is not an indication that green tax swaps are ill-advised. Even if gross costs are positive, the environmental benefits could outweigh these costs, possibly by a substantial margin.

But in light of the uncertainties, are positive net benefits likely? There is a line of reasoning that suggests that policymakers can be assured that benefits will exceed costs provided that the environmental tax is sufficiently small. The argument is that the gross costs of an incremental environmental tax (with revenues devoted to reducing ordinary taxes) is infinitesimal; in contrast, the gross benefits from an incremental environmental tax are nonincremental. This argument prompts two questions: (1) Does a "small" environmental tax indeed have a "small" gross cost, and (2) if so, is this of practical value to policymakers?

A result from Bovenberg and de Mooij (1992, 1994a) is relevant to the first question. In their framework, an *incremental* environmental tax, with revenues returned as a reduced labor tax, indeed has a zero gross cost. When the environmental tax is small, it yields the same labor-market distortion as the labor tax it replaces, and the gross distortion in the commodity market is infinitesimal. Hence the overall gross cost is zero. So long as the tax yields a nonincremental environmental benefit, it offers an overall welfare improvement.[57]

However, the claim that a small tax yields an overall efficiency improvement may not apply in more general circumstances such as the case where the initial tax system is highly inefficient. The issue is an example of the general second-best tax problem investigated by Lipsey and Lancaster (1956), Bertrand and Vanek (1971), Dixit (1975), and others: in a suboptimal tax system, under what circumstances does introduction of a tax in one market that helps bring prices closer to marginal cost in that market yield an overall efficiency improvement? Although a number of authors have shown particular conditions under which this will occur (see, for example, Dixit, 1975), this cannot be guaranteed for tax systems that simultaneously involve labor, capital, and commodity taxation. These notions are reinforced by results from simulations of a carbon tax by Bovenberg and Goulder (1994b) and by Parry (1994). In these simulations, an incremental carbon tax has incremental gross costs when the initial tax situation is efficient in the sense that marginal excess burdens of taxes are equated. However, the incremental tax involves large gross costs when the initial situation reflects inefficiencies of the U.S. tax system.

This suggests that, in many cases, one cannot be assured that a small environmental tax will produce small gross costs. Moreover, even if this were the case, the knowledge that gross costs will be small seems to be of limited practical value. In my view, it cannot substitute for information about the magnitudes of environmental benefits. In the extreme case where analysts have virtually no information about the magnitudes of these benefits—except perhaps that they are nonnegative—one cannot tell how small is small enough. No matter how small the tax, it's possible that the (small) gross costs exceed the (even smaller) gross benefits. Although it is useful to know that incremental taxes produce negligible costs, to be of practical value this knowledge needs to be coupled with information about benefits.

This discussion was not meant to lead to pessimism. Rather, it was intended to serve the constructive purpose of drawing attention to significant issues in policy evaluation. The key implication of this discussion is that in evaluating possible green tax swaps, information about environmental benefits is indispensable.[58] Much of the interest in the possibility of a double dividend was fueled by a hope that benefits considerations could be pushed aside. This seems to have been a false hope. The benefits side is critical, and further research to reduce the uncertainties about environmental benefits is likely to be of great value to policy analysts.

5. Summary and conclusions

This paper has articulated different senses of the potential double dividend from environmental taxes and examined the theoretical and empirical support for each.

The weakest double-dividend claim is that returning tax revenues through cuts in distortionary taxes leads to cost savings relative to the case where revenues are returned lump sum. This claim is easily defended on theoretical grounds and (thankfully) receives wide support from numerical simulations.

The stronger versions contend that the costs of revenue-neutral swaps of environmental taxes for ordinary distortionary taxes involve zero or negative gross costs. The strongest version affirms that this is typically the case. An intermediate version asserts that this is the case in at least one instance. The existing theoretical analyses of this issue cast doubt on the strong double-dividend claim. At the same time, the theoretical case against the strong form is not air-tight. In simple models the strong version would obtain if the uncompensated wage elasticity of labor supply were negative. In more elaborate models, it could arise if the initial tax system were highly inefficient in factor markets (leading to significant differences across factors in marginal value products per dollar) and the environmental tax served to shift the burden of taxes to more efficient factors. These inefficiencies may offer more of a justification for direct attention to these inefficiencies than for indirect approaches through a revenue-neutral environmental tax.

Although the evidence is mixed, numerical results tend to militate against the strong double-dividend claim. There is a need for more systematic numerical investigations of revenue-neutral environmentally motivated tax policies. More extensive policy analyses and broader sensitivity analyses would help identify the channels driving the results and reveal the sources of differences in model outcomes. The extent to which the burden of environmentally motivated taxes is imposed on exhaustible resources (and on resource rents) remains a very interesting empirical issue, and greater attention to this issue in numerical models could generate important insights.

The difficulty of establishing the strong double dividend does not contradict the common numerical finding that an environmental tax can promote higher levels of national income when revenues are earmarked for capital formation. National income is distinct from welfare, and the double-dividend notions (at least as defined here) concern welfare costs.

The presence or absence of a strong double dividend is directly relevant to the issue of the optimal environmental tax. In simpler models, the conditions under which the strong double-dividend claim is absent (present) are closely related to the conditions under which the second-best optimal environmental tax is lower than (greater than) the marginal environmental damages. Existing analytical models, in casting doubt on the strongest double-dividend claim, also indicate that the optimal environmental tax is lower than the rate suggested by the simple Pigovian rule.

The keen interest in the double dividend—particularly in its strong form—reflects the uncertainties faced by policymakers concerning environmental benefits. The strong double-dividend notion, if true, would reduce significantly the amount of information that policymakers need to make a benefit-cost case for green tax swaps. The difficulty of establishing the strong claim implies, unfortunately, that assessing magnitudes of environmental benefits remains a crucial task in policy evaluation. This conclusion cannot be dodged by appeals to the net benefits from "small" environmental taxes. One never knows a priori how small is small enough, and, moreover, even small environmental taxes may have large gross costs when the existing tax system is suboptimal (in some sense).

The critical importance of attending to the environmental benefits may be the most fundamental message from this examination. Research that helps establish the environmental benefits associated with various environmental tax options will have considerable value to policy analysts. While research can reduce the uncertainties, they will remain a basic fact of life in environmental policymaking. Policymakers cannot afford to wait until circumstances permit riskless policy choices; they would wait forever. A better approach is to recognize the uncertainties and endorse environmental tax reforms when the prospects for gain make the risks worth taking.

Acknowledgments

The author is grateful to Lans Bovenberg, Sijbren Cnossen, Bill Hogan, Robert Kohn, Jenny Ligthart, Robert McMillan, Ian Parry, Jim Poterba, Robert Repetto, Ronnie Schöb, Jon Strand, Jim Sweeney, and two anonymous referees for helpful comments and to Jesse David and Steven Weinberg for excellent research assistance. Financial support from the National Science Foundation (Grant No. SBR 9310362), Resources for the Future, and the IBM Corporation is gratefully acknowledged.

Notes

1. *Gross costs* denotes the welfare sacrifices associated with environmental tax policies, abstracting from the welfare benefits associated with the change in environmental quality. The modifier *gross* is used to make clear that the (usually beneficial) environment-related welfare impacts are being disregarded. Under this method of accounting, the overall efficiency change from a policy initiative is the welfare benefit stemming from the change in environmental quality (the gross benefits) minus the gross costs. A more precise definition of *costs* will be offered in Section 1. In this paper, *costs* always means gross costs unless explicitly stated otherwise.
2. Partial equilibrium analysis suggests that the incremental efficiency cost of a new tax in a given market is higher, the larger are preexisting taxes in that market. This follows from the basic notion in public economics that the costs of a given tax tend to rise with the square of the overall tax rate. However, as emphasized later in this paper, tax interactions extend across markets: preexisting taxes in other markets significantly affect the costs of a new tax in a given market.
3. This idea was advanced several decades ago by Tullock (1967) and Kneese and Bower (1968) and somewhat more recently by Nichols (1984). Terkla (1984) appears to have been the first to perform a numerical assessment of the efficiency benefits associated with devoting environmental tax revenues to cuts in existing taxes.
4. For example, in its Model Comparison Project undertaken in 1990–1992, the OECD commissioned six models to investigate the costs of reducing CO_2 emissions through carbon taxes. In this investigation, costs were evaluated assuming lump-sum replacement of revenues. Only two of the six models were capable of assuming alternative forms of revenue-replacement. On this see OECD (1992).
5. For general discussions, see, for example, Pearce (1991), Poterba (1991), Pezzey (1992), and Repetto et al. (1992). For numerical assessments, see Shackleton et al. (1992) and Gaskins and Weyant (1995) for results from several models; see also Section 3's references to the models discussed in that section.
6. Other notions have appeared. In European discussions, reduced unemployment and increased profits are often referred to as the potential extra dividends (in addition to improved environmental quality) from environmental taxes. See, for example, Bovenberg and van der Ploeg (1993), Carraro, Galeotti, and Gallo (1994), and Sörenson, Pedersen, and Nielsen (1994). In this paper, the extra dividend is more fundamental: it relates to gross welfare costs rather than specific economic variables (such as employment or profits) that contribute to welfare.
7. I emphasize efficiency issues here, and thus I define *gross costs* in welfare terms. These costs are most easily defined with respect to a representative individual whose overall utility U can be defined by $U(u_1(E), u_2(G))$, where u_1 is utility from environmental quality (E) and u_2 is utility from ordinary goods and services (G). Policy initiatives generally lead to changes in both u_1 and u_2. Gross benefits are the wealth equivalent (as measured), for example, by the equivalent variation) of the change in u_1; gross costs are the negative of the wealth equivalent of the change in u_2.
8. This can be shown as follows. Consider the two postreform situations associated with (1). One (associated with the left-hand side) involves a reduction in a distortionary tax; the other (associated with the right-hand side) involves a lump-sum tax reduction. The two postreform situations are alike in other important respects: they involve the same tax revenue and all other tax rates (including t_E) are the same. One can write the levels of welfare associated with the two postreform situations as $W(t_E, t_X', T_L)$ and $W(t_E, t_X, T_L')$, where $t_X' = t_X + \Delta t_X$ and $T_L' = T_L + \Delta T_L$. (Note that $\Delta t_X < 0$, $\Delta T_L < 0$). The weak double-dividend assertion is equivalent to the assertion that $W(t_E, t_X', T_L) > W(t_E, t_X, T_L')$. This, however, is equivalent to the assertion that the gross efficiency cost of raising the distortionary tax from t_X' to t_X, where the change is financed through a reduction in lump-sum taxes from T_L to T_L', is positive. Thus, the weak double-dividend claim is upheld so long as the distortionary tax considered has a positive gross efficiency cost or excess burden.
9. Two clarifications are in order here. First, it should be kept in mind that this discussion only considers *efficiency* costs and benefits from environmental tax initiatives: distributional concerns are ignored. When distributional impacts are taken into account, it is no longer guaranteed that the social costs of a revenue-neutral environmental tax initiative are lower when revenues are recycled through cuts in distortionary taxes than when they are recycled in lump-sum fashion. For an exploration of these issues, see Proost and van Regemorter (1994).

Second, it is interesting to consider whether the weak double-dividend notion is upheld in the case where t_X is negative in the *status quo ante*. Starting from a negative value (or subsidy), a further reduction in this tax (financed through lump-sum taxes) may be efficiency worsening. Under these circumstances, if a new environmental tax is employed to finance reductions in a distortionary tax whose value is already negative, the weak double dividend will not obtain. This does not contradict the claims in the text. In the situation described here, the key requirement of the weak double-dividend notion—that the tax t_X have a positive marginal excess burden—is missing.

10. In this example, the tax is a strict Pigovian tax in that it applies to a commodity with which pollution is associated rather than directly to pollution emissions. The basic lessons apply to emissions taxes as well.
11. In the case with nonconstant private marginal costs or nonconstant marginal external costs, the presentation is slightly more complicated, but the results are essentially the same.
12. The environmental economics literature often refers to *abatement costs*. These are usually defined in a way that corresponds, in Figure 1, to the entire area below the *MB* curve (including the area below the *MC* curve) over interval from Q_0 to Q_1. Gross costs are smaller than abatement costs because they net out the avoided expenditure on polluting inputs. In Figure 1, this avoided expenditure is the area under the *MC* curve from Q_0 to Q_1.
13. In the simplest case, the revenues are returned to the private sector in a lump-sum fashion.
14. Of course, the government could waste the revenues—for example, by applying them to government projects with benefit-cost ratios below one. In this case the gross costs will be greater than A. In this paper I do not consider which use of revenues is most likely; I leave that to political scientists.
15. Since taxes interact, the attribution of the cost of the revenue-neutral policy change into direct effects of t_E and direct effects of Δt_X is not automatic. A reasonable decomposition is to split $C(t_E, \delta t_X)$ into $C(\Delta t_X, \Delta T_{L2})$, where ΔT_{L1} and ΔT_{L2} are the lump-sum tax changes necessary to make the component changes t_E and Δt_X revenue neutral.
16. GNP is an imperfect indicator of gross welfare for several reasons. One is that it only reflects the marginal welfare contributions of goods and services (to the extent that these are reflected in market prices); inframarginal surpluses are not incorporated. A second reason is that it disregards welfare contributions from nonmarketed goods and services such as leisure.
17. If efficiency were the only consideration, optimal tax reform would achieve equality in the marginal efficiency costs of all taxes with nonzero rates. Of course, efficiency is not the sole policy objective. A highly inefficient tax may be worth keeping if it has important virtues along other dimensions such as distribution.
18. Alternatively, the tax is incremental but superimposed on an existing noninfinitesimal tax on the dirty consumption commodity. The significance of the noninfinitesimal assumption is discussed in Section 4.
19. The separability assumption enables the authors to evaluate utility from the consumption-leisure composite apart from the utility from public goods or environmental quality.
20. At the same time, Bovenberg and de Mooij's analysis supports the weak notion of double dividend. Their paper concludes with "Hence, there exists a 'double dividend' in the sense that a cost reduction can be achieved by using revenues from pollution taxes to cut distortionary taxes rather than returning these revenues in a lump-sum fashion."
21. It should be kept in mind that we are concerned with distortions in the *gross* sense—abstracting from environmental considerations. Clearly environmental taxes can improve overall resource allocation—reduce overall distortions—when the environmental dimension is considered. We return to this issue below.
22. See Poterba (1993) for a complementary discussion.
23. The after-tax real wage is (1) the after-tax nominal wage divided by (2) the gross of tax price of consumption. Income taxes directly affect the after-tax real wage by reducing (1), whereas energy taxes directly influence this wage by raising (2).
24. A uniform commodity tax does not avoid distorting the commodity market in all circumstances. A sufficient set of conditions for its optimality is that commodity consumption be separable from leisure in utility and that the utility function be homothetic. See Bovenberg and de Mooij (1994a).
25. The gross cost is greater in case 3 than in case 2 under the stated assumption that the environmental tax is noninfinitesimal. With an infinitesimal environmental tax, the commodity market gross distortion is negligible, and the net distortionary impact in the labor market is zero (the effect of the new environmental tax just compensates for the effect of the reduction in the labor tax). With the "large" environmental tax, in contrast, the commodity market distortion is nonincremental. So long as there is some substitutability across commodities,

the tax on the environmental commodity leads to substitution away from this commodity in consumption. This implies a loss of tax base (relative to the case of no substitution) and, importantly, a reduction in the absolute magnitude of the cut in labor taxes that can be financed by the environmental tax. Because of this tax-base-erosion effect, the environmental tax is unable to finance a reduction in labor taxes large enough to compensate for the implicit increase in labor taxes represented by the environmental tax itself. Thus, when environmental taxes are "large," the revenue-neutral combination of environmental tax and labor tax cut involves a gross distortionary cost for two reasons: (1) labor market distortions are enlarged, and (2) a nonnegligible distortion is generated in the commodity market.

26. Parry terms these the *revenue effect* and *interdependency effect*.
27. In Parry's analysis, the revenue-recycling effect is greater than the tax-interaction effect only when two conditions simultaneously hold: (1) output from the polluting industry (which produces the good subject to the environmental tax) is a weaker than average substitute for leisure, and (2) the tax elasticity of emissions is well below unity.

    Figure 2 shows that to uphold the strong double-dividend claim, the magnitude of the revenue-recycling effect must in fact be *larger* than that of the tax-interaction effect—by enough to bring the gross costs to zero. In Bovenberg-de Mooij and Parry's analyses, since the tax-interaction effect is larger than the revenue-recycling effect, environmental taxes not only involve positive gross costs, but larger gross costs than would result from the same tax in a first-best setting where there are no preexisting taxes and where revenues are returned lump-sum.
28. On the other hand, the partial equilibrium welfare analysis is apt for a first-best world with no prior taxes.
29. The discussion here is not formal. To my knowledge, no one has yet examined the double-dividend issue analytically in a dynamic, closed model with capital and labor. Bovenberg and van der Ploeg (1994b) develop an analytical model for a small open economy that employs labor and capital. The efficiency issues I shall discuss here apply to an economy that is large in the sense that it influences the return to capital; these issues are largely absent in the Bovenberg-van der Ploeg model of a small, open economy, where the return to capital is given by the world market and the burden of domestically imposed green taxes is fully borne by labor. Ligthart and van der Ploeg (1994) develop a static model with labor and a fixed factor, capital. The issues I shall discuss here are of interest only when capital is not fixed in supply.
30. Indeed, this phenomenon underlies the Bovenberg-de Mooij result. The environmental (commodity) tax is an implicit labor tax that produces both labor and commodity market distortions.
31. Specifically, capital income will fall by a larger percentage than labor income. Labor income falls because the tax raises costs of production, leading to an increase in the prices of consumer goods and a reduction in the real wage.
32. Paradoxically, the very feature—a narrow base—that contributes to larger gross costs is the feature that often makes environmental taxes attractive in terms of overall efficiency. The narrower these taxes are, the closer they often are to the source of the externality (for example, certain types of emissions). Hence, even though the narrower base tends to amplify gross costs, it also tends to expand gross benefits and overall efficiency (gross benefits minus gross costs). To the extent that the objective is overall efficiency, large gross costs should not stand in the way of environmental taxes.

    This implicitly assumes that a uniform commodity tax is optimal (see note 24). Optimal commodity tax principles indicate that, other things equal, there is an efficiency rationale for relatively higher taxes on commodities that are highly complementary to leisure. See, for example, Atkinson and Stiglitz (1980, ch. 12).
33. Many of these issues are examined in detail in Goulder (1994b), in which the costs of a fossil fuels tax (Btu tax) and gasoline tax are compared.
34. *Known* reserves, of course, are endogenous, a function of exploration activity. This does not alter the main points discussed here.
35. It may be noted that under these circumstances the environmental tax does not yield any environmental benefits.
36. This is the case because, in general, the present value of the tax payment per unit of fuel is not constant through time. On this see, for example, Sweeney (1977).
37. Whether the strong double dividend arises depends on whether the government has already taxed fixed-factor rents. In a model with three factors of production—labor, resources, and a fixed factor—Bovenberg and van der Ploeg (1993) show analytically that a tax on a dirty consumption commodity fails to yield a double dividend (in the strong sense) if all the rents from the fixed factor are already taxed. On the other hand, if fixed-factor rents are not taxed, the same type of tax offers the double dividend. In the latter case the commodity tax proxies for the tax on fixed factor rents and enjoys much of its efficiency potential.

38. Labor taxes introduce a wedge between the marginal product of labor and the marginal disutility of labor. With a binding minimum wage, this wedge is even larger. Thus a leftward shift in labor demand is likely to be more costly with involuntary unemployment than under a market-clearing wage.
39. The same qualitative result would obtain if there were no involuntary unemployment in this model. In this model, the environmental tax serves as an implicit way to tax the rents from the fixed factor in the absence of a more direct instrument to do so.
40. This is an important dimension of the environmental benefits from a carbon tax. To the extent that a carbon tax slows the accumulation of greenhouse gases and reduces global warming, it avoids productivity losses in agriculture and other climate-sensitive sectors.
41. Consideration of the capital good aspect of environmental quality seems to be very important in the *overall* benefit-cost evaluation of environmental tax options and may help justify the replacement of ordinary taxes by environmental taxes in several instances. But the strength of the case for the strong double-dividend claim, as defined here, seems largely independent of whether the capital good function of environmental quality is accounted for.
42. Terms of trade effects do not support the strong double-dividend claim in global terms.
43. The analysis is made more complicated by the existence of the OPEC cartel and the imperfectly competitive nature of the world oil market.
44. Nor do I consider the evidence for the weak double-dividend notion. As mentioned earlier, there is virtually unanimous numerical support for this notion, so a weighing of this evidence seems unnecessary.
45. For a more detailed description of these models, see Goulder (1994a), Jorgenson and Wilcoxen (1990, 1995), Shackleton et al. (1992), and Shah and Larsen (1992). The Shah-Larsen model is by far the simplest of the five models, in part because it takes pretax-factor prices as given. Despite its simplicity, the model addresses interactions between commodity and factor markets and thus incorporates some of the major efficiency connections discussed earlier.
46. The equivalent variation is the lump-sum change in wealth which, under the business-as-usual or base case, would leave the household as well off as in the policy-change case. Thus a positive equivalent variation indicates that the policy is welfare improving. The compensating variation is the lump-sum change in wealth that, in the policy-change scenario, would cause the household to be as well off as in the base case. In reporting the Shah-Larsen results I adopt the convention of multiplying the compensating variation by -1, so that a positive number in the table signifies a welfare improvement here as well.
47. The demand functions in these models are not derived from an explicit utility function. Hence they do not yield utility-based measures. A difficulty with using consumption as a proxy for welfare is that it disregards welfare changes linked to changes in leisure.
48. It might also be noted that the Shah-Larsen model yields negative gross costs for four of five countries in simulations that combine a carbon tax and reduction in the corporate income tax. (Such results do not appear in Table 1.) Only in the case of the United States is such a tax swap a gross-welfare-reducing venture.
49. Of the five models in Table 1, these two are the most similar and allow for the most straightforward comparisons.
50. The MEBs per dollar are \$0.22 and \$0.12 for the tax on individual capital and individual labor income, respectively.
51. This assumption is based on reported values in Jorgenson and Yun (1990). The Jorgenson-Yun and Jorgenson-Wilcoxen models have some similarities in structure and parameters, but there are important differences as well. Marginal excess burden numbers from the Jorgenson-Wilcoxen model were not yet available.
52. Assuming the appropriate second-order conditions apply.
53. The seminal contribution to the theory of integrating environmental and distortionary taxes was by Sandmo (1975), who analyzed the optimal configuration of commodity taxes when one of the commodities generates an externality.

    Parry derives analytically the conditions under which the tax interaction effect will be greater than the revenue replacement effect. Conducting broad sensitivity analysis, he finds that under plausible parameter values the tax interaction effect is of greater magnitude. Parry suggests that in the United States the optimal environmental tax rate is typically between 60 and 90 percent of the MED.
54. The marginal cost of public funds (MCPF) is the welfare cost of an incremental increase in government spending financed by taxes. For an explication of this concept and its relationship to the notion of marginal excess burden, see Ballard and Fullerton (1992). For an analysis of how aggregare activity influences the MCPF, see Ligthart and van der Ploeg (1994). Brendemoen and Vennemo (1993) develop and assess numerically a broader notion of the MCPF that includes the environmental benefits from public projects.

55. The Bovenberg and van der Ploeg formula may appear to contradict an optimality requirement articulated by Lee and Misiolek (1986). In fact, the results are consistent. (For a close examination of this issue, see Schöb, 1994). The Lee-Misiolek requirement for an optimal environmental tax is that the difference between marginal abatement costs and marginal environmental benefits per marginal dollar of revenues must equal the marginal excess burden of existing distortionary taxes. This can be written as

$$\frac{\partial C/\partial t_E}{\partial R/\partial t_E} - \frac{\partial B/\partial t_E}{\partial R/\partial t_E} = \lambda(t_X),$$

where $C(t_E, t_X)$ is gross cost, B is total environmental benefit, R is revenue, λ is the marginal excess burden of other taxes, and t_E and t_X are the rates of the environmental and existing distortionary tax. Note that C is a function of both t_E and t_X. If t_X is zero, λ is zero and the equation above reduces to

$$\partial C/\partial t_E = \partial B/\partial t_E,$$

the Pigovian rule. Let t_E^* represent the tax rate that satisfies the above equation. Now consider the case where there are preexisting taxes ($t_X > 0$). How does t_E^{**}, the optimum when other taxes are present, differ from t_E^*? Oates (1991) points out that the tax elasticity at the Pigovian optimum is relevant here. If the derivative $\partial C/\partial t_E$ were independent of t_X, one could determine from this elasticity whether t_E^{**} is greater or less than t_E^*. However, as discussed above, higher preexisting taxes raise the value of $\partial C/\partial t_E$ evaluated at a given level of t_E. This means that in the presence of other taxes, a *lower* value of t_E may be required to satisfy the Lee-Misiolek requirement.
56. The tax system is suboptimal in the sense that marginal gross efficiency costs of different taxes are not equal. To the extent that the tax system is meeting other objectives, this need not be suboptimal in a broader sense.
57. A similar result appears in Bovenberg and van der Ploeg (1994a).
58. Ballard and Medema (1993) offer one of the first studies to incorporate environmental benefits in a computable general equilibrium assessment of environmental tax reforms.

References

Atkinson, Anthony B., and Joseph E. Stiglitz. (1980). *Lectures on Public Economics*. New York: McGraw-Hill.

Auerbach, Alan J., and Laurence J. Kotlikoff. (1987). *Dynamic Fiscal Policy*. Cambridge: Cambridge University Press.

Ballard, Charles L., and Don Fullerton. (1992). "Distortionary Taxes and the Provision of Public Goods." *Journal of Economic Perspectives* 6(3), 117-131.

Ballard, Charles L., and Steven G. Medema. (1993). "The Marginal Efficiency Effects of Taxes and Subsidies in the Presence of Externalities." *Journal of Public Economics* 52, 199-216.

Ballard, Charles L., John B. Shoven, and John Whalley. (1985). "General Equilibrium Computations of the Marginal Welfare Costs of Taxes in the U.S." *American Economic Review* 75(1), 128-138.

Bertrand, T.J., and J. Vanek. (1971). "The Theory of Tariffs, Taxes, and Subsidies: Some Aspects of the Second Best." *American Economic Review* 61, 925-931.

Bovenberg, A. Lans, and Ruud A. de Mooij. (1992). "Environmental Taxation and Labor Market Distortions," Working Paper, Ministry of Economic Affairs, The Hague, March. Forthcoming in *European Journal of Political Economy*.

Bovenberg, A. Lans, and Ruud A. de Mooij. (1994a). "Environmental Levies and Distortionary Taxation." *American Economic Review*, September, Vol. 84, No. 4, pp. 1085-1089.

Bovenberg, A. Lans, and Ruud A. de Mooij. (1994b). "Environmental Tax Reform and Endogenous Growth." Working Paper, Tilburg University.

Bovenberg, A. Lans, and Lawrence H. Goulder. (1994a). "Inegrating Environmental and Distortionary Taxes: General Equilibrium Analyses." Working Paper, Stanford University, March.

Bovenberg, A. Lans, and Lawrence H. Goulder. (1994b). "Optimal Environmental Taxataion in the Presence of Other Taxes: An Applied General Equilibrium Analysis." Working Paper, Stanford University, May.

Bovenberg, A. Lans, and F. van der Ploeg. (1993). "Consequences of Environmental Tax Reform for Involuntary Unemployment and Welfare." Working Paper, Tilburg University, September.

Bovenberg, A. Lans, and F. van der Ploeg. (1994a). "Environmental Policy, Public Finance and the Labor Market in a Second-Best World." *Journal of Public Economics* 55, 349–390.

Bovenberg, A. Lans, and F. van der Ploeg. (1994b). "Green Policies in a Small Open Economy." *Scandinavian Journal of Economics* 96(3), 343-363.

Brendemoen, Anne, and Haakon Vennemo. (1993). "The Marginal Cost of Funds in the Presence of External Effects." Discussion Paper No. 99, Research Department, Central Bureau of Statistics, Norway, August.

Carraro, Carlo, Marzio Geleotti, and Massimo Gallo. (1994). "Environmental Taxation and Unemployment: Some Evidence on the Double Dividend Hypothesis in Europe." Working Paper, GRETA Econometrics, May.

Dasgupta, Partha S., and Geoffrey M. Heal. (1979). *Economic Theory and Exhaustible Resources*. Cambridge: Cambridge University Press.

Deaton, Angus. (1987). "Econometric Issues for Tax Design in Developing Countries." In David Newbery and Nicholas Stern, (eds.), *The Theory of Taxation for Developing Countries*. New York: Oxford University Press.

Diamond, Peter, and J. Mirrlees. (1971). "Optimal Taxation and Public Production I: Production Efficiency and II: Tax Rules." *American Economic Review* 61.

Dixit, Avinash. (1975). "Welfare Effects of Tax and Price Changes." *Journal of Public Economics* 4(1), 103–123.

Gaskins, Darius, and John Weyant. (1995). *Reducing Global Carbon Dioxide Emissions: Costs and Policy Options*. Stanford, CA: Stanford University Press.

Goulder, Lawrence H. (1994a). "Effects of Carbon Taxes in an Economy with Prior Tax Distortions: An Intertemporal General Equilibrium Analysis." Working Paper, Stanford University, July. Forthcoming in *Journal of Environmental Economics and Management*.

Goulder, Lawrence H. (1994b). "Energy Taxes: Traditional Efficiency Effects and Environmental Implications." In James M. Poterba, (ed.), *Tax Policy and the Economy 8*. Cambridge, MA: MIT Press.

Hausman, Jerry A. (1985). "Taxes and Labor Supply." In A.J. Auerbach and Martin S. Feldstein (eds.), *Handbook of Public Economics* (Vol. 1). Amsterdam: North-Holland.

Jorgenson, Dale W., and Peter J. Wilcoxen. (1990). "Environmental Regulation and U.S. Economic Growth." *Rand Journal of Economics* 21(2), 314–340.

Jorgenson, Dale W., and Peter J. Wilcoxen. (1995). "Reducing U.S. Carbon Emissions: An Econometric General Equilibrium Assessment." In Darius Gaskins and John Weyant (eds.), *Reducing Global Carbon Dioxide Emissions: Costs and Policy Options*. Stanford, CA: Stanford University Press.

Jorgenson, Dale W., and Kun-Young Yun. (1990). *Tax Policy and the Cost of Capital*. Oxford: Oxford University Press.

Kneese, Allen V., and Blair T. Bower. (1968). *Managing Water Quality: Economics, Technology, Institutions*. Baltimore: Johns Hopkins Press.

Lee, Dwight, R., and Walter S. Misiolek. (1986). "Substituting Pollution Taxation for General Taxation: Some Implications for Efficiency in Pollution Taxation." *Journal of Environmental Economics and Management* 13, 338–347.

Ligthart, Jenny E., and Frederick van der Ploeg. (1994). "Pollution, the Cost of Public Funds and Endogenous Growth." Working Paper, University of Amsterdam, October. Forthcoming in *Economic Letters*.

Lipsey, R.G., and K. Lancaster. (1956). "The General Theory of the Second Best." *Review of Economic Studies* 24, 11–32.

Nichols, Albert L. (1984). *Targeting Economic Incentives for Environmental Protection*. Cambridge, MA: MIT Press.

Nordhaus, William D. (1993). "Optimal Greenhouse-Gas Reductions and Tax Policy in the 'DICE' Model." *American Economic Review* 83(2) (Papers and Proceedings), 313–317.

Oates, Wallace E. (1991). "Pollution Charges as a Source of Public Revenues." Resources for the Future Discussion Paper QE92-05. Resources for the Future, Washington, DC, November.

OECD. (1992). *The Economic Costs of Reducing CO_2 Emissions*. OECD Economic Studies 19. Paris: OECD.

Parry, Ian W.H. (1994). "Pollution Taxes and Revenue Recycling." Working Paper, Economic Research Service, U.S. Department of Agriculture, April.

Pearce, David W. (1991). "The Role of Carbon Taxes in Adjuting to Global Warming." *Economic Journal* 101, 938–948.

Pezzey, John. (1992). "Some Interactions between Environmental Policy and Public Finance." Working Paper, University of Bristol, June.

Pigou, A.C. (1938). *The Economics of Welfare* (4th ed.). London: Weidenfeld and Nicolson.

Poterba, James M. (1991). "Tax Policy to Combat Global Warming: On Designing a Carbon Tax." In Rudiger Dornbusch and James M. Poterba, (eds.), *Global Warming Economic Policy Responses*. Cambridge, MA: MIT Press.

Poterba, James M. (1993). "Global Warming: A Public Finance Perspective." *Journal of Economic Perspectives* 7(4), 47–63.

Proost, Stef, and Denise van Regemorter. (1994). "Testing the Double Dividend Hypothesis for a Carbon Tax in a Small Open Economy." Working Paper, Center for Economic Studies, Catholic University of Leuven, Leuven, Belgium.

Repetto, Robert, Roger C. Dower, Robin Jenkins, and Jacqueline Geoghegan. (1992). *Green Fees: How a Tax Shift Can Work for the Environment and the Economy.* World Resources Institute, November, Washington, D.C.

Sandmo, Agnar. (1975). "Optimal Taxation in the Presence of Externalities." *Swedish Journal of Economics* 77, pp. 86–98.

Schöb, Ronnie. (1994). "Environmental Levies and Distortionary Taxation: Environmental View vs. Public Finance View." Working Paper, Department of Economics, University of Munich, June.

Shackleton, Robert, Michael Shelby, Alex Cristofaro, Roger Brinner, Joyce Yanchar, Lawrence Goulder, Dale Jorgenson, Peter Wilcoxen, and Peter Pauly. (1992). "The Efficiency Value of Carbon Tax Revenues." U.S. Environmental Protection Agency, November, draft manuscript.

Shah, Anar, and Bjorn Larsen. (1992). "Carbon Taxes, the Greenhouse Effect and Developing Countries." World Bank Policy Research Working Paper Series No. 957. World Bank, Washington, DC.

Sörenson, Peter B., Lars H. Pedersen, and Soren B. Nielsen. (1994). "Taxation, Pollution, Unemployment and Growth: Could There Be a Triple Dividend from a Green Tax Reform?" Working Paper, Economic Policy Research Unit, Copenhagen Business School.

Sweeney, James L. (1977). "Economics of Depletable Resources: Market Forces and Intertemporal Bias." *Review of Economic Studies* 44, 125–142.

Sweeney, James L. (1993). "Economic Theory of Depletable Resources: An Introduction." In Allen V. Kneese and James L. Sweeney, (eds.), *Handbook of Natural Resource and Energy Economics* (Vol. 3). New York: North Holland.

Terkla, David. (1984). "The Efficiency Value of Effluent Tax Revenues." *Journal of Environmental Economics and Management* 11, 107–123.

Tullock, Gordon. (1967). "Excess Benefit." *Water Resources Research* 3, 643–644.

[4]

International Tax and Public Finance, 6, 421–443 (1999)

Green Tax Reforms and the Double Dividend: an Updated Reader's Guide

A. LANS BOVENBERG a.l.bovenberg@kub.nl
Tilburg University, P.O. Box 90153, 5000 LE Tilburg

Abstract

This paper draws on the literature on the double dividend to explore whether an environmental tax reform yields not only a cleaner environment but also non-environmental benefits. In doing so, it investigates how environmental tax reforms impact welfare, the distribution of income, and employment. Also the political economy of environmental taxation is discussed.

Keywords: environmental taxes, double dividend, employment, distribution

JEL Codes: D61, D62, H21

1. Introduction

Environmental tax reforms have become increasingly popular in recent years. One reason is increasing concern about the quality of the natural environment; environmental taxes are generally an efficient instrument for protecting the environment. A second reason involves the revenues from environmental taxes. These revenues can be used to cut other, distortionary taxes. In this way, the government may reap a 'double dividend'—not only a cleaner environment but also a less distortionary tax system. If the double dividend hypothesis holds, an environmental tax reform is a so-called 'no-regret' option; even if the environmental benefits are in doubt, an environmental tax reform may be desirable. In the first IIPF conference issue of International Tax and Public Finance, Goulder (1995) surveyed the theoretical and empirical evidence on the double dividend hypothesis. In doing so, he distinguished between the strong and the weak form of the double dividend.

The weak form of the double dividend hypothesis states that the efficiency costs of a revenue-neutral environmental tax reform are lower if the additional revenues from the environmental taxes are recycled in the form of lower distortionary taxes compared to the case that these revenues are recycled in a lump-sum fashion. A corollary of this hypothesis is that environmental taxes are more efficient instruments for environmental protection than environmental policy instruments that do not yield any revenues. The reason is that the additional revenues from the environmental taxes can be employed to cut distortionary taxes. In the case of non-revenue-raising instruments such as grandfathered pollution permits or regulation, in contrast, the rents associated with the cut in emissions accrue as a lump-sum benefit to the polluters rather than the government.

The strong form of the double dividend asserts that an environmental tax reform enhances not only environmental quality but also non-environmental welfare. In other words, the gross efficiency costs (i.e. the efficiency effects abstracting from environmental benefits) of substituting an environmental tax for a distortionary tax are negative. Whereas the weak double dividend thus compares two policy changes (with different recycling), the strong version of the double dividend hypothesis compares the equilibrium after a single policy change with the status quo.

This paper updates Goulder's reader's guide. On the one hand, it has a more limited scope than Goulder's contribution because it focusses mainly on the theoretical literature on the strong double dividend hypothesis. On the other hand, whereas Goulder concentrates on efficiency effects, the present paper explores also the equity effects of green tax reforms and related political-economy issues. As another extension of Goulder (1995), this paper explores the so-called employment dividend of green tax reforms by investigating the conditions under which an environmental tax reform boosts employment and reduces involuntary unemployment.

The paper is organized as follows. Section 2 constructs a small general equilibrium model to explore the main intuition behind the failure of the strong double-dividend hypothesis. As a related result, it is shown that the optimal environmental tax typically lies below the Pigovian tax. Intuitively, cutting pollution taxes below their Pigovian levels raises efficiency by alleviating non-environmental distortions. Section 3 investigates several cases in which the strong double dividend does hold. In all these cases, the initial tax system is inefficient from a non-environmental point of view. By bringing the tax system closer to its non-environmental optimum, green tax reforms yield both environmental and non-environmental benefits.

Section 4 turns to the distributional effects of environmental tax reforms. Distributional concerns may be one of the main reasons why the initial tax system is inefficient, thereby in principle offering room for a strong double dividend. To assess the scope for an improvement in social welfare (which accounts for both efficiency and equity considerations), however, one should analyse equity and efficiency together. Indeed, distributional issues are at the heart of the double dividend debate issue because in the absence of distributional concerns governments could freely use uniform lump-sum taxation to meet their revenue needs so that taxes would not need to be distortionary. Section 4 also discusses the political economy of green tax reform in a society populated by heterogeneous households with diverse interests.

In Europe, the interest in environmental tax reform originates primarily in the desire to raise employment and reduce involuntary unemployment. Defining the non-environmental dividend as an expansion of employment, section 5 extends the model introduced in section 2 by allowing for consumption out of non-labour income. It shows that the impact on employment depends on two effects: the *tax-level* effect and the *tax-shifting* effect. In particular, for an environmental tax reform to benefit employment by reducing the tax burden on labour, two conditions must be met. First, the overall tax level should be contained. Second, the distribution of the tax burden should be moved away from workers to others, *i.e.* capital owners, the owners of resources, and the recipients of income transfers. Section 5 also discusses the crucial role of the process of wage determination in affecting the impact of a green tax reform on involuntary unemployment. The analysis reveals that, in order to determine the employment effects of pollution taxes, an analysis of the ultimate incidence of pollution taxes is called for. Section 5 provides such an analysis. Finally, section 6 concludes.

2. The Strong Double-Dividend Hypothesis

This section develops the main intuition for how general equilibrium effects can cause the strong version of the double dividend to fail. In particular, it reveals how a change in a given tax affects not only the market being taxed but also other distorted markets. Subsection 2.1 constructs a small general equilibrium model based on Bovenberg and de Mooij (1994a). In this model, the only distorted market is the labour market. The main insights, however, continue to hold in larger models with several distorted markets (see de Mooij and Bovenberg (1998)). Defining the non-environmental dividend as an increase in non-environmental welfare, subsection 2.2 shows that in the simple model of subsection 2.1 a non-environmental dividend requires an expansion of employment. Subsection 2.3 reveals, however, that an environmental reform reduces employment if the initial pollution tax is positive. This result is used in subsection 2.4 to show that the strong double dividend fails in this model. Intuitively, in the absence of environmental concerns, the optimal pollution tax would be zero. By further increasing the pollution tax, the government takes the tax system further from its non-environmental optimum. Indeed, if the government has set taxes optimally ignoring, or being unaware of, environmental concerns, it cannot reap a double dividend by boosting non-environmental welfare. The reason is that non-environmental welfare has already been optimized in the initial equilibrium and thus cannot be increased (see Christiansen (1996)). Subsection 2.5 turns to the closely related issue of the optimal level of environmental taxes. It demonstrates that the optimal pollution tax lies below the Pigovian level because a marginal cut in the pollution tax below its Pigovian level alleviates the non-environmental distortions in the labour market.

2.1. The Model

Output is produced with a single production factor labour. It can be used for public consumption, G, and for private consumption of a 'clean' and a 'dirty' commodity (per capita consumption of these two commodities is denoted by, respectively, C and D). Accordingly, equilibrium on the commodity market is given by:

$$NL = G + NC + ND \qquad (1)$$

where L stands for per-capita employment and N represents the number of households. Units are normalized so that the constant rates of transformation between labour and the three produced commodities are unity.

The representative household faces the following budget constraint:

$$C + (1 + t_D)D = (1 - t_L)L \qquad (2)$$

where t_D and t_L represent taxes on dirty consumption and labour, respectively. We assume that the clean consumption commodity is untaxed. The government finances public consumption through the environmental tax on dirty consumption and the distortionary tax on labour:

$$G = t_D ND + t_L NL \qquad (3)$$

Environmental quality, E, deteriorates with dirty consumption, $E = e(ND)$, $e_{ND} < 0$, where a subscript denotes a partial derivative with respect to a particular variable.

Household utility is given by $u = u(M(Q(C, D), 1 - L), G, E)$.[1] Private goods are thus (weakly) separable from public goods G and E. Hence, environmental quality and public consumption do not directly affect private demands. The subutility function Q, aggregating clean and dirty consumption into a composite consumption good, is homothetic. Accordingly, in the absence of environmental externalities, a uniform tax on clean and dirty consumption is optimal. Households ignore environmental externalities. Optimization of household utility with respect to the budget constraint yields the following first-order conditions:

$$u_C = \lambda \tag{4}$$

$$u_D = \lambda(1 + t_D) \tag{5}$$

$$u_{1-L} = \lambda(1 - t_L) \tag{6}$$

where λ denotes the marginal utility of income.

2.2. *Marginal Welfare Effects and the Strong Double Dividend*

This subsection turns to the welfare effects of a marginal tax reform in order to more precisely define the strong double dividend from an environmental tax reform. The total differential of utility $U(C, D, 1-L, G, e(ND))$ produces the following expression for the welfare effects of a revenue-neutral change in the tax mix (i.e. a change in taxes such that government consumption is constant):

$$du = u_C dC + u_D dD - u_{1-L} dL + N u_E e_{ND} dD \tag{7}$$

Substituting the expressions for household behaviour (4), (5), and (6) into (7), we arrive at:

$$\frac{du}{u_C} = dC + (1 + t_D)dD - (1 - t_L)dL + \frac{N u_E e_{ND}}{u_C} dD \tag{8}$$

Taking the total differential of the goods-market equilibrium (1) and using the result to eliminate dC from (8), we find:

$$\frac{du}{u_C} = t_L dL + \left[t_D - \frac{N u_E(-e_{ND})}{u_C} \right] dD \tag{9}$$

Equation (9) reveals the welfare impacts due to changes in employment and dirty consumption. The first term on the right-hand side of (9) represents the distortionary effect in the labour market, which is regulated by the distortionary tax on labour income t_L. The second term corresponds to the welfare effects on the environmental margin. The welfare impact of a marginal increase in the demand for the dirty consumption good amounts to the difference between, on the one hand, a tax term (which measures the social benefits of additional tax revenue due to a broader revenue base) and, on the other hand, the marginal social damage from pollution.

In the 'first-best' case, in which there is no need to finance public spending through distortionary taxation (i.e., if $t_L = 0$), the optimal pollution tax amounts to the Pigovian tax. This tax fully internalizes the adverse external effects of pollution:

$$t_D = \frac{Nu_E(-e_{ND})}{u_C} \tag{10}$$

Substituting (10) into (9), we find that in this first-best case, the beneficial environmental effects associated with less dirty consumption (i.e., $Nu_E(-e_{ND}/u_C)dD]$) exactly offset the adverse welfare effects due to an erosion of the tax base (i.e., $t_D dD$). In this case, incremental changes in employment do not yield any first-order effects on welfare because the social opportunity costs of additional employment exactly offset the social benefits at the margin.

For the more general case in which distortionary taxes are present, we can diagnose the effects of tax changes by rearranging expression (9):

$$\frac{du}{u_C} = -\frac{u_E}{u_C}[N(-e_{ND}dD] + [t_L dL + t_D dD] \tag{11}$$

The first term on the right-hand side of equation (11) corresponds to the welfare effects of changes in environmental quality. The last term in square brackets on the right-hand side of (11) stands for the impact on the tax base. This tax-base effect represents the consequences of a different tax mix for the efficiency of the tax system as an instrument to raise revenue. In particular, an erosion of the tax base indicates that the tax system becomes less efficient as a revenue-raising device, as higher marginal tax rates are required to collect the same amount of revenue.

The tax-base effect can also be written as the change in real private (after-tax) income enjoyed by households, dY^D, by taking the total differential of the government budget constraint (3) (with $dG = 0$):

$$t_L dL + t_D dD = -L dt_L - D dt_D = dY^D \tag{12}$$

Expression (11) can be used to examine the double-dividend argument, as the two terms in square brackets on the right-hand side of equation (11) represent the two dividends. The tax-base effect corresponds to the non-environmental dividend of environmental taxes, i.e. the negative of the 'gross' distortionary costs (i.e., the costs before netting out the environmental benefits) of the tax-induced changes in the allocation of resources. If the double-dividend hypothesis were to hold, (small) environmental taxes not only would raise environmental quality, but also, by expanding the base of the distortionary labour income tax, would reduce the tax burden on private incomes. In this way, pre-existing distortions in the labour market would make pollution taxes more attractive.

2.3. *An Environmental Tax Reform and Employment*

This subsection explores how an environmental tax reform affects employment and thereby the non-environmental dividend as defined in the previous subsection. In implementing an environmental tax reform, the government raises the pollution taxes on dirty consumption and keeps the public budget balanced by adjusting the tax rate on labour. To find the general equilibrium effects of the pollution tax on dirty consumption, t_D, on employment, one first derives $(u_D/u_C) = (1 + t_D)$ from (4) and (5). Taking the total differential, we arrive at:

$$\tilde{C} - \tilde{D} = \sigma_H \tilde{t}_D \tag{13}$$

where $\tilde{t}_D \equiv dt_D/(1+t_D)$. For other variables, a $\tilde{}$ stands for a relative change. σ_H represents the substitution elasticity between clean and dirty consumption in the subutility function $Q(C, D)$. In deriving (13), we have used the assumption that leisure is weakly separable from the produced commodities C and D in private utility. Under these separability assumptions and a linear homogenous subutility function $Q(C, D)$, the first-order conditions for optimal household behaviour can be written as $u_Q/u_{1-L} = p_Q/w$, where p_Q is the ideal consumer price index of the consumption basket Q and $w \equiv (1 - t_L)$ stands for the after-tax wage. Taking the total differential of this first-order condition and using (13) and the total differential of the household budget constraint (2), we find:

$$\tilde{L} = V(\sigma_v - 1)\tilde{w}_R \tag{14}$$

$$\tilde{C} = \tilde{L} + \tilde{w}_R + (1 - \alpha_C)\sigma_H \tilde{t}_D \tag{15}$$

$$\tilde{D} = \tilde{L} + \tilde{w}_R - \alpha_C \sigma_H \tilde{t}_D \tag{16}$$

where σ_v stands for the substitution elasticity between leisure and composite consumption, $\alpha_C \equiv C/(1 - t_L)L$ is the share of non-polluting consumption in overall household consumption and $\tilde{w}_R \equiv \tilde{w} - \tilde{p}_Q$ represents the relative change in the real after-tax wage.

We can write the goods market equilibrium (1) as:

$$\tilde{L} = (1 - t_L)[\alpha_C \tilde{C} + ((1 - \alpha_C)/(1 + t_D))\tilde{D}] \tag{17}$$

Substituting (14), (15), and (16) into (17), we arrive at:

$$\tilde{L} = \frac{-\beta_L}{\Delta}\left[\theta_D \alpha_C (1 - \alpha_C)(1 - t_L)\sigma_H \tilde{t}_D\right] \tag{18}$$

where $\Delta \equiv S - \beta_L T > 0$; $S \equiv (1 - t_L)(1 - \theta_D(1 - \alpha_C))$; $T \equiv t_L + \theta_D(1 - \alpha_C)(1 - t_L)$; $\theta_D \equiv t_D/(1 + t_D)$ and $\beta_L \equiv V\sigma_v - V$ stands for the uncompensated wage elasticity of labour supply. The latter elasticity is positive because we assume that the substitution effect dominates the income effect, i.e., that the substitution elasticity between leisure and composite consumption, σ_v, exceeds unity.

We first consider the effects of introducing small environmental taxes in an equilibrium without any environmental taxes (i.e., $t_D = 0$). This reform does not affect employment (see equation (18)), although the revenues from the pollution taxes allow for lower taxes on labour. The reason is that the incidence not only of the labour tax but also of the pollution tax falls on labour. Substituting a pollution levy for a labour tax thus amounts to substituting an implicit tax on labour for an explicit tax on labour. In particular, the wage rate that affects the incentives to supply labour is the real after-tax wage (i.e., the wage not only after labour taxes but also after consumption taxes). Hence, the wedge between before-tax and real after-tax wages is widened not only by the distortionary tax on labour but also by the pollution tax on consumption. Given the constraint of revenue neutrality, the higher pollution tax exactly offsets the effect of a lower labour tax on the overall wedge between before- and after-tax wages.

We now discuss the case in which environmental taxes are raised from an initial equilibrium in which environmental taxes are positive (i.e., $t_D > 0$). In this case, an increase in the pollution tax reduces employment (see expression (18) with $\beta_L > 0$). The negative effect on employment is due to a decline in the real after-tax wage, which reduces the incentive to supply labour. The negative effect on the real after-tax wage comes about because the lower tax rate on labour income does not fully compensate workers for the adverse effect of the pollution levy on their real after-tax wage. This incomplete offset originates in the erosion of the base of the environmental taxes. In particular, the increase in environmental taxes causes private agents to reduce their demands for polluting goods. If the initial pollution tax is positive, these behavioural effects erode the base of the environmental tax. The associated adverse implications for public revenues imply that the government is not able to reduce the tax rate on labour sufficiently in order to offset the adverse effect of a higher pollution levy on the real after-tax wage. The resulting lower income from an additional unit of work reduces labour supply and thus employment.

2.4. Environmental Tax Reform and Welfare

Armed with the general equilibrium effects on employment, this subsection uses expression (9) to discuss the welfare effects of marginal increases in positive pollution taxes. By harming employment, higher pollution taxes narrow, rather than widen, the tax base. Accordingly, the gross distortionary costs of substituting pollution levies for labour taxes are positive and the double dividend hypothesis thus fails. Moreover, by eroding the base of the labour tax, environmental taxes exacerbate pre-existing tax distortions. Hence, the larger the magnitude of pre-existing tax distortions, the higher become the gross distortionary costs of revenue-neutral pollution taxes. In particular, in the presence of a distortionary tax on labour, welfare would rise if the government would marginally reduce the environmental tax below its Pigovian level (and, at the same time, would raise the tax on labour, t_L, to offset the revenue losses).

As an instrument to finance public spending with the least costs to after-tax wages, the environmental tax thus appears to be less efficient than a broad-based labour tax. In contrast to a labour tax, the pollution tax on dirty consumption 'distorts' the composition of the consumption basket.[2] These 'distortions' enhance environmental quality but at the same time reduce the real after-tax income from work. Whereas the environmental benefits are public and thus independent of private behaviour, the costs depend on the amount of labour supplied. Indeed, by enhancing environmental quality, the pollution tax expands the supply of public goods, thereby raising the overall tax burden (as measured by the burden of the provision of public goods on private incomes). This additional tax burden corresponds to the abatement costs. Indeed, a cleaner environment is not a free lunch: just as other public priorities that require public spending, environmental policy imposes costs on the private sector. Hence, the environmental tax reform amounts to replacing explicit labour taxes by higher implicit labour taxes. Indeed, as stressed by Christiansen (1996), a strong double dividend can not be reaped if the government has already set taxes optimally from a non-environmental point of view.

The term between square brackets in (18) represents the additional tax burden associated with a cleaner environment. This so-called *tax-level* effect, which corresponds to the costs of cleaner environment, depends on two elements: First, the initial pollution levies and, second, the substitution elasticities between clean and dirty commodities.

The initial pollution taxes measure the marginal abatement costs. Without prior pollution taxes, reducing a marginal unit of pollution comes free. However, the higher the initial pollution taxes are, the larger the marginal costs of increasing environmental quality become. Hence, while small environmental taxes impose only small abatement costs, large pollution taxes tend to impose a substantial burden on private incomes. Indeed, the erosion of the base of pollution taxes due to lower pollution yields more serious adverse consequences for tax revenues if initial pollution taxes are higher.

Whereas the initial tax rates determine the costs associated with each unit of reduced pollution, the substitution elasticities between clean and dirty commodities affect the magnitude of the reduction in pollution. The larger these elasticities are, the larger the improvement in environmental quality, and thus the larger the overall costs associated with the additional supply of this public good. Thus, a fundamental trade-off emerges between, on the one hand, beneficial environmental effects and, on the other hand, favourable employment effects. The more successful environmental policy is in improving the quality of the environment, the higher the overall tax burden and thus the less likely an expansion of employment becomes. Indeed, if a pollution levy is successful in changing behaviour, it does not generate much revenue, thereby reducing the scope for cutting distortionary taxes on labour.

2.5. The Optimal Environmental Tax

The failure of the strong double dividend in the previous subsection has direct consequences for the optimal environmental tax. In particular, if the environmental tax is reduced slightly below its Pigovian level, the first-order welfare effect on the environmental distortion (i.e. the second term on the right-hand side of (9)) is zero.[3] By raising employment, however, this marginal tax reform yields a positive first-order welfare effect by alleviating the labour-market distortions that are due to the pre-existing tax on labour (i.e. the first term on the right-hand side of (9)). Accordingly, reducing the pollution tax below its Pigovian level boosts overall welfare. This is a typical second-best result. The theory of the second best teaches that, in a world with remaining distortions, introducing an additional distortion (i.e., reducing the environmental tax below its Pigovian value) may not necessarily reduce overall efficiency. Intuitively, the introduction of the distortion on the environmental margin alleviates distortions in the labour market on account of the labour tax.

The rest of this subsection derives an explicit expression for the optimal pollution tax in the simple model presented in subsection 2.1. The government adopts the two tax instruments

(t_L, t_D) to maximize household utility subject to the government budget constraint and decentralized optimization by firms and households:

$$NV((1+t_D), (1-t_L), G, e(ND)) + \mu[t_L NL + t_D ND - G] \tag{19}$$

where V represents indirect utility, and μ denotes the marginal disutility of raising one unit of public revenue.

Maximizing with respect to t_L, we find the following first-order condition:

$$(\lambda - \mu)L + \mu\left[t_D \frac{\partial D}{\partial w} + t_L \frac{\partial L}{\partial w}\right] + N u_E e_{ND} \frac{\partial D}{\partial w} = 0 \tag{20}$$

where we have used Roy's identity $\partial V/\partial(1-t_L) = \lambda L$. Define:

$$t_D^E = \frac{N u_E(-e_{ND})}{\mu} \tag{21}$$

Substitution of (21) into (20) yields:

$$(\lambda - \mu)L + \mu\left[(t_D - t_D^E)\frac{\partial D}{\partial w} + t_L \frac{\partial L}{\partial w}\right] = 0 \tag{22}$$

In an analogous way, the first-order condition for t_D yields:

$$(\lambda - \mu)D - \mu\left[(t_D - t_D^E)\frac{\partial D}{\partial t_D} + t_L \frac{\partial L}{\partial t_D}\right] = 0 \tag{23}$$

where we have used Roy's identity $\partial V/\partial(1+t_D) = -\lambda D$.

The optimal tax on dirty consumption consists of two parts (see also Sandmo (1975) and Bovenberg and van der Ploeg (1994b)). The first part is the distortionary (or revenue-raising) component of the tax on polluting consumption. Together with the optimal labour tax, the optimal level of this distortionary component is determined on the basis of the familiar Ramsey formulas for raising revenues with the lowest costs to private incomes (see (22) and (23)). Since clean and dirty consumption are weakly separable from leisure and utility is homothetic, uniform taxation of clean and dirty goods is optimal from the point of view of raising revenues with the smallest burden on private incomes. Here, the optimum involves equal distortionary components of the two taxes on consumption. In this model, uniform distortionary taxes on consumption are equivalent to taxes on labour; the optimum is thus characterized by zero distortionary taxation of dirty consumption (i.e. $t_D = t_D^E$). In this particular case, the so-called marginal cost of public funds (MCPF) $\eta \equiv \mu/\lambda$ can be written with the aid of (22) as:

$$\eta = [1 - t_L \beta_L]^{-1} \tag{24}$$

The MCPF thus exceeds unity if, first, the uncompensated wage elasticity of labour supply, β_L, is positive and, second, Pigovian taxes do not suffice to finance public consumption so that the distortionary tax on labour, t_L, is positive.

The second part of the optimal tax on dirty consumption, t_D^E, corrects for the environmental externality (use (21) with $\lambda = u_C$):

$$t_D^E = \left[\frac{N u_E(-e_D)}{u_C}\right] \frac{1}{\eta} \tag{25}$$

The term between square brackets on the right-hand side of (25) corresponds to the Pigovian tax (see (10)). The Pigovian tax is optimal only if the marginal cost of public funds, $\eta \equiv \mu/\lambda$, equals unity. A unitary MCPF indicates that public funds are not scarcer than private funds (as is the case if distortionary taxes are absent or labour supply is completely inelastic). However, in a second-best world without lump-sum taxation, the MCPF typically differs from one. Indeed, the MCPF term in (25) reveals how second-best considerations affect optimal environmental taxation. In particular, the higher the MCPF is, *ceteris paribus*, the smaller becomes the optimal environmental tax.

The reason for the inverse relationship between the MCPF and the optimal environmental tax is as follows. The government employs the tax system to simultaneously accomplish two objectives: raising revenues and internalizing environmental externalities. If public revenues become scarcer, as indicated by a higher marginal cost of public funds, the optimal tax system focuses more on generating revenues and less on internalizing pollution externalities. The conflict between raising revenues and protecting the environment exists because an environmental levy reduces pollution by encouraging taxpayers to avoid taxes. Tax avoidance not only reduces pollution but also makes it necessary to levy higher distortionary taxes to finance public spending. Accordingly, the larger the government's revenue needs are (as indicated by a higher MCPF), the less the government can afford tax differentiation aimed at environmental protection. Indeed, the optimal pollution tax balances the social costs of pollution against the social benefits from additional tax revenues. Therefore, the higher the social value attached to tax revenue, the higher the marginal social costs of pollution have to be to justify a given environmental tax.

3. The Strong Double Dividend and Inefficient Tax Systems

As noted in the previous section, a strong double dividend is not feasible if the government has set taxes at their non-environmental optimum in the initial equilibrium. If the initial tax structure is not optimal from a non-environmental point of view, however, an environmental tax reform may be able to reduce the overall burden of taxation. The key requirement is that the tax reform moves the tax system closer to its non-environmental optimum. In that case, the welfare gains associated with moving towards a more efficient tax system from a non-environmental point of view may finance the improvement in environmental quality. This section illustrates this general point with a number of examples.

Clean Consumption as a Better Substitute for Leisure

The utility structure assumed in section 2 implies that leisure is an equally good substitute for dirty and clean consumption. Accordingly, a uniform tax on clean and dirty consumption (i.e. a labour tax) is optimal from a non-environmental point of view. If, compared to dirty consumption, clean consumption is a better substitute for leisure, however, the optimal (non-environmental) tax on dirty consumption exceeds that on clean consumption. In that case, therefore, an environmental tax reform that starts from a uniform tax on clean and dirty consumption moves the tax system closer to the non-environmental optimum (see e.g. Ng (1980), Parry (1995) and Fuest und Huber (1999)). Intuitively, by shifting the tax burden from clean consumption, which is a relatively good substitute for leisure, to dirty consumption, which is a relatively poor substitute for leisure, the government implicitly taxes leisure. The resulting higher level of labour supply alleviates the initial tax distortions.

The Environment as a Substitute for Leisure

Another reason why the optimal non-environmental tax on dirty consumption may exceed that on clean consumption is that environmental quality enters household utility in a non-separable fashion. In particular, if environmental quality is a close substitute for leisure, a higher level of environmental quality boosts labour supply, thereby alleviating the labour-market distortions on account of the distortionary labour tax (see e.g. Schwartz and Repetto (1999) and Mayeres and Proost (1997)). Hence, introducing an environmental tax yields a double dividend.

Environmental Taxes as Rent Taxes

Environmental taxes may be an implicit way to tax the scarcity rents associated with natural resources. Taxes on the demands for fossil fuels, for example, may be borne largely by the owners of the fossil fuels, especially if various countries simultaneously raise environmental taxes. The shifting of these taxes to the suppliers contains the non-environmental costs because taxing rents involves no efficiency cost (see also Fullerton and Metcalf (1997)). At the same time, this shifting to the supply side limits the environmental improvements, since it reduces the increase in (gross-of-tax) prices to those who demand the fuels.

Inefficient Factor Taxation

If the initial tax system involves differences in the marginal excess burdens of various taxes, an environmental tax reform can boost private incomes by shifting the tax burden away from factors with high marginal excess burdens to factors with low marginal excess burdens (see Goulder (1995) and de Mooij and Bovenberg (1998)). These considerations may be relevant for the mix between capital and labour taxation. To illustrate, most applied dynamic general equilibrium models of the economy suggest that, compared to taxes on labour income, taxes on capital income tend to produce larger marginal efficiency losses. The most direct way to improve the efficiency of the tax system as a revenue-raising device would be to finance a cut in capital taxes with higher taxes on labour. However, if the government does not want to adopt explicit labour taxes, it can use environmental taxes that are primarily borne by labour (i.e. implicit labour taxes).

The welfare effects associated with a sub-optimal initial tax system do not necessarily make environmental tax reforms more attractive, however, because the burden of the environmental tax could well fall on the factor that is already overtaxed from an efficiency point of view. Indeed, the numerical general equilibrium analysis in Bovenberg and Goulder (1997) suggests that inefficiencies in the initial tax system may make carbon taxes less rather than more attractive.

Environmental Taxes as Optimal Tariffs

In an open economy, governments can employ pollution taxes to improve the terms of trade. For example, a large oil-importing country may improve its terms of trade if it reduces the demand for oil by raising the tax burden on fossil fuels. Similarly, a large oil-exporting country can boost the prices of its exports by imposing pollution taxes that reduce the supply of its export commodities. If the terms-of-trade gains are sufficiently large, domestic non-environmental welfare may rise. In that case, foreigners, in effect, pay for the cleaner environment.

Pre-Existing Subsidies on Polluting Activities

The overall burden on polluting activities may be too low initially—even from the point of view of maximizing private income—because these activities are subsidized initially. The tax reform analysis in section 2 illustrates this. If the dirty consumption good is subsidized in the initial equilibrium (i.e. $t_D < 0$), employment (and hence private income) expands if this subsidy is reduced.

The Environment as a Public Input into Production

The basic model in section 2 assumes that the natural environment is a public consumption good. However, a cleaner environment could act not only as a public consumption good but also as a public input into production (see e.g. Ballard and Medema (1993)). For example, in agriculture, production benefits from a better quality of the soil and the air. Furthermore, less air pollution is likely to improve health and morale, thereby boosting labour productivity.

If the environment enters the economy in this way, environmental benefits accrue as part of the non-environmental dividend. Introducing a pollution tax yields a strong double dividend if the environment acts both as a public consumption good and a public input into production (see Bovenberg and de Mooij (1997)). In particular, more public consumption of environmental quality produces an environmental dividend. At the same time, the expansion of employment on account of the increased environmental inputs into production boosts utility from non-environmental commodities, thereby yielding a non-environmental dividend.

If the environment enters production as an input, environmental quality may well raise labour productivity. As a direct consequence, both the costs and the benefits of a cleaner environment rise with the amount of labour supplied, so that households with the highest supply of labour benefit most from the cleaner environment. Internalizing environmental externalities is thus less costly in terms of exacerbating labour-market distortions. Indeed, if the environment enters production as a public production factor (and does not enter utility), Bovenberg and van der Ploeg (1994a) demonstrate that the optimal environment tax equals the Pigovian tax, even in a second-best world with distortionary labour taxes. Intuitively, marginally reducing the environmental tax below the Pigovian tax does not alleviate the labour-market distortion by raising employment because both the benefits and costs of doing so are directly borne by labour.

4. The Double Dividend and the Income Distribution

The previous section showed that an environmental tax reform may raise non-environmental welfare by reducing non-environmental distortions. This raises the question why governments have not reformed their tax systems to address these inefficiencies. Indeed, in these circumstances, the efficiency case for tax reform is independent of environmental concerns. However, distributional considerations may have prevented the government from enhancing the efficiency of the tax system. Indeed, distributional issues are at the heart of the double-dividend issue: without distributional concerns, taxes would not need to be distortionary —as governments could freely use uniform lump-sum taxation to meet their revenue needs. In designing environmental tax reforms, governments typically face a trade-off between equity and efficiency. In particular, the revenues from pollution taxes can be used only once: either to compensate the poor or to reduce distortionary taxes.

This section first explores optimal taxation in the presence of heterogeneous households in subsection 4.1. Subsequently, sub-section 4.2 uses this analysis to investigate the political economy of green tax reform.

4.1. Optimal Taxation in the Presence of Heterogeneous Households

The literature on the optimal provision of public goods in the presence of heterogeneous households suggests that there may be cases in which distributional concerns should result in 'over providing' environmental quality (as measured by the relationship between the optimal environmental tax, on the one hand, and the Pigovian tax (defined as the sum of the marginal rates of substitution between the environmental public good and private goods) on the other). In particular, for environmental quality to be over provided, environmental quality should be less complementary with leisure than with private goods. In this case, the marginal willingness to pay for the environment (i.e. the marginal rate of substitution between environmental quality and private goods) declines with the amount of leisure. This relaxes the self-selection constraint that restricts the amount of redistribution (see

Boadway and Keen (1993)). In particular, if high-ability households mimic the low-ability households, the high-ability households enjoy more leisure. Their marginal willingness to pay for the environment is lower than that of the low-ability households because this willingness to pay declines with leisure. Accordingly, raising the ratio of environmental quality to private commodities increases the utility of the low-ability households compared to that of the high-ability households that are mimicking them. By relaxing the self-selection constraint, a higher environmental tax allows for a less progressive tax system—i.e. a lower (distortionary) marginal labour tax for the low-ability households. In this way, distributional concerns cause the environment to be 'over provided' (see also Pirttilä and Tuomala (1997) and Cremer, Gahvari and Ladoux (1998)).

In this case, environmental tax reforms enhance non-environmental efficiency not just by moving along the frontier that depicts the efficiency-equity trade-off, but by shifting out the frontier itself. Hence, a green tax reform enhances both equity, non-environmental efficiency, and environmental quality. Intuitively, environmental quality is used as an instrument to distribute resources to the low-ability households, which feature a higher marginal willingness to pay for the environment than the mimicking high-ability households. In this way, the provision of environmental quality is employed as a redistributive instrument. A similar argument holds if preferences are correlated with unobservable ability. In particular, the environment should be 'over provided' if low-ability households feature high preferences for the environment.

Distributional concerns, however, can sometimes tighten rather than relax second-best constraints. The literature on the optimal provision of public goods suggests that this is the case if, compared to private goods, leisure is more complementary with environmental quality—so that the marginal willingness to pay for the environment rises with the consumption of leisure. In that case, under providing the natural environment is an implicit way to tax leisure, thereby relaxing the second-best constraint. Indeed, environmental quality and leisure may well be complementary because a cleaner environment is likely to make leisure more enjoyable.

4.2. The Political Economy of Green Tax Reform

If the government aims for two objectives, it should in principle employ two instruments. Conceptually, therefore, one can view a green tax reform aimed at reaping a double dividend as consisting of two separate policies. One policy is aimed at improving the quality of the environment (i.e. the pollution tax). The other policy is targeted at the non-environmental objective. This section explores the political-economy case for linking these two policies, in part based on the analysis in the previous subsection (see also Pezzey and Park (1998)).

There may be a political case for linking two issues because such a linkage increases the number of instruments that can be used to compensate losers from separate reforms. In this way, the scope is increased for arriving at Pareto-improving reforms in political bargaining. To illustrate, an efficiency-enhancing tax reform that stimulates employment may not be politically acceptable because inactive households that rely on non-labour income lose from such a reform. If these latter households attach a high value to environmental quality, however, they may favour an environmental tax reform that shifts the tax burden away from labour. Indeed, for inactive households, the environmental benefits offset the non-environmental costs of such a reform. Hence, the government may be able to introduce a policy that reduces the real value of non-labour incomes while still satisfying the distributional constraint that the overall welfare of households relying on non-labour incomes must be maintained. Indeed, the taxes borne by the inactive households act as benefit taxes for benefits associated with the better quality of the environment: the households that benefit from the cleaner environment also pay for it.

This points to a key feature of environmental taxes that distinguishes these taxes from other taxes. In particular, environmental taxes not only finance ordinary public goods but also increase the supply of the environmental public good. The distribution of these environmental benefits can be such as to create more opportunities for political bargaining concerning an efficiency-enhancing reform. In this way, environmental taxes can 'grease the wheels' of tax reform.

Political considerations may make an employment-generating environmental tax reform difficult to attain if those who bear the incidence of the pollution taxes (i.e. the victims of the tax-shifting effect) do not attach much value to the cleaner environment. In that case, these victims pay twice: not only for the cleaner environment (through the tax-burden effect), but also for ordinary public goods (through the tax-shifting effect, which implies that they pay a larger share of ordinary public spending). Simultaneously raising employment and environmental quality thus implies that costs and benefits accrue to rather different groups in society. This complicates the processes of building political consensus on environmental policy.

5. Employment and Tax Incidence

The interest in environmental tax reform in Europe originates primarily in the desire to raise employment. This section shows that the impact on employment depends in general on two effects: the *tax-level* effect (discussed in section 2) and the so-called *tax-shifting* effect. To that end, subsection 5.1 extends the model introduced in subsection 2.1 by allowing for consumption out of non-labour income. Subsection 5.2 extends the analysis by allowing for involuntary unemployment. Subsections 5.1 and 5.2 reveal that pollution taxes do not need to be implicit taxes on labour income (as was the case in subsection 2.4). Accordingly, in order to determine the employment effects of pollution taxes, an analysis of the ultimate incidence of pollution taxes is called for. The key question is who bears the ultimate incidence of the pollution taxes. The incidence of pollution taxes on production and consumption is explored in, respectively, subsection 5.3 and subsection 5.4.

5.1. A Model with Two Household Types

There are two types of households. The first type, the 'active' household, relies entirely on labour income. The second type, the 'inactive' household is retired and finances its consumption exclusively out of transfer incomes provided by the government. Higher taxes on consumption reduce the purchasing power of the inactive households because transfers are fixed in terms of the producer prices of the consumption goods. Transfers are not subject to the tax on labour income. The relative changes in the demands for the two commodities (15) and (16) become:

$$\tilde{C} = (1-\varphi)(\tilde{w}_R + \tilde{L}) - \varphi(1-\alpha_C)\tilde{t}_D + (1-\alpha_C)\sigma_H\tilde{t}_D \quad (26)$$

$$\tilde{D} = (1-\varphi)(\tilde{w}_R + \tilde{L} - \varphi(1-\alpha_C)\tilde{t}_D - \alpha_C\sigma_H\tilde{t}_D \quad (27)$$

where φ denotes the share of non-labour income in aggregate household income (after labour taxes). Substitution of (14), (26) and (27) into (17) yields the following expression for employment:

$$\tilde{L} = \frac{\beta_L}{\Delta_T}[-\theta_D\alpha_C(1-\alpha_C)(1-t_L)\sigma_H + \varphi S(1-\alpha_C)]\tilde{t}_D \quad (28)$$

where $\Delta \equiv (1-\varphi)S - \beta_L T_T$ and $T_t \equiv t_L + \varphi(1-t_L+\theta_D(1-\alpha_C)(1-t_L)(1-\varphi)$. In the absence of transfer income, expression (18) reveals that an environmental tax reform does not affect employment if the initial pollution tax is zero. If transfers are positive, in contrast, such a reform boosts employment (see (28) with $\theta_D = 0$). The reason is that, unlike the case without non-labour income, the government is able to more than compensate workers for the real income loss due to a higher environmental tax. Intuitively, contrary to the labour tax, the environmental tax is borne not only by labour but also by non-labour incomes. Hence, the tax reform redistributes income from those receiving non-labour income (who pay the higher tax on dirty consumption but are not compensated by either lower labour income taxes or higher nominal transfers) towards those collecting labour income. As a direct consequence, real wages—and thus labour supply—rise. Accordingly, better environmental quality is accompanied by a higher level of employment.

With positive initial pollution taxes (i.e., $\theta_D > 0$), the overall impact on employment occurs through two channels. The first channel, represented by the first term in square brackets in (28), is the tax-level effect discussed in subsection 2.4. This effect reduces employment. It operates if the initial pollution tax is positive: only in that case does a cleaner environment require real resources at the margin.

The second channel through which an ecological tax reform impacts employment is what we call the *tax-shifting* effect. This channel, represented by the second term in square brackets in expression (28), involves redistribution of income between labour and non-labour incomes. Through this channel, an environmental tax reform can raise employment if it redistributes income away from non-labour incomes to labour income.

In terms of the model, the government can raise employment only if it cuts the real value of transfers. If the government would raise transfers to maintain the real purchasing power of these transfers after the introduction of a pollution tax, the employment impact of the higher labour taxes required to finance the additional transfers would exactly offset the positive employment effect of the tax-shifting effect (see Bovenberg and de Mooij (1994b)).[4]

The overall effect on employment depends on the balance between, on the one hand, the tax-level effect, and, on the other hand, the tax-shifting effect. Employment increases only if the tax-shifting effect dominates the tax-level effect. In that case, the cleaner environment is entirely paid for by the inactive household.

5.2. Involuntary Unemployment

The European interest in the double-dividend issue springs mainly from the existence of widespread involuntary unemployment. In the presence of unemployment, the tax burden can be shifted to those collecting unemployment benefits. As in subsection 5.1, lower unemployment benefits boost labour demand by reducing the need to raise labour taxes to finance these benefits. However, lower unemployment benefits raise employment also through another channel, namely the process of wage determination. In particular, less generous unemployment compensation induces workers to moderate wages, as a less attractive outside option weakens the bargaining position of workers. This transmission channel is important in Nielsen, Pedersen and Sørenson (1995), who develop an endogenous growth model with involuntary unemployment stemming from union monopoly power, and in Koskela and Schöb (1999), who construct a model with wage bargaining between unions and employers. These papers find that a green tax reform alleviates involuntary unemployment if such a reform shifts the tax burden away from workers to the unemployed.

Koskela and Schöb (1990), for example, show that the taxation of unemployment benefits is a crucial determinant of the unemployment effects of environmental tax reform. In particular, a green tax reform reduces unemployment if unemployment benefits are neither subject to the labour income tax nor indexed to the consumer price index. Since benefits are not indexed, higher pollution taxes on consumption depress the real value of unemployment benefits. Furthermore, the unemployed do not get compensated by the cut in the labour tax because they do not pay that tax. Hence, the environmental tax reform shifts the tax burden towards the unemployed and away from workers.

Whereas Koskela and Schöb (1990) focus on pollution taxes on consumption, Bovenberg and van der Ploeg (1998b) argue that also pollution taxes on intermediate inputs can redistribute income away from transfer recipients to workers if those not employed in the formal sector collect not only unemployment benefits but also incomes from activities in the informal sector. Bovenberg and van der Ploeg (1998b) analyse the consequences of an environmental tax reform in a model with involuntary unemployment due to hiring and search costs. These latter costs imply a rent on job matches. Wages are the outcome of a bargaining process between workers and employers about the distribution of these rents. Informal activities are not subject to the labour tax, so that the unemployed escape the burden of the labour tax. However, they may bear some of the burden of the pollution tax. In particular, a pollution tax on intermediate goods, by reducing labour productivity in the formal sector, also hurts incomes in the informal sector. An environmental reform thus substitutes a tax that is in part borne by the unemployed (i.e., the pollution tax) for a tax that does not affect the unemployed (i.e., the labour tax). The resulting shift in the tax burden away from the employed in the formal sector towards those who are not employed in the formal sector corresponds to yet another form of the tax-shifting effect. This tax-shifting effect, which makes the outside option of workers in the formal sector less attractive, induces these workers to moderate wages, thereby benefiting employment in the formal sector.

This tax-shifting effect is consistent with wage equations in which labour productivity is fully shifted towards employees in terms of higher after-tax wages, while labour taxes are only in part absorbed by workers, so that these labour taxes are in part borne by employers in terms of higher wage costs (see Graafland and Huizinga (1996)). In the presence of such a wage equation, a green tax reform moderates wages, thereby boosting labour demand. On the one hand, the pollution taxes do not affect labour costs per unit of output because the fall in labour productivity is offset by lower after-tax wages. On the other hand, the lower labour taxes reduce labour costs because the cuts in labour taxes are shared between employees (in terms of higher after-tax wages) and employers (in terms of lower (before-tax) wage costs).

The tax-level effect, representing the abatement costs associated with a cleaner environment, typically hurts employment. The overall effect on employment depends on the net impact of the tax-burden effect and the tax-shifting effect. Even if the increase in the tax burden is large, employment may rise if workers accept a large drop in their disposable income. An environmental tax reform succeeds in moderating wages if it makes work in the formal sector more attractive compared to being unemployed. With endogenous wage determination, therefore, a higher tax burden associated with a cleaner environment does not necessarily result in a higher level of unemployment. Intuitively, workers and the unemployed absorb the costs of the cleaner environment in terms of lower after-tax wages and lower incomes in unemployment rather than an increased risk of becoming (or staying) unemployed.

Another channel through which an environmental tax reform may reduce unemployment is a shift in the tax burden away from low-skilled towards high-skilled labour. Lower tax rates on low-skilled labour can facilitate the transition from unemployment to work in the official labour market (alleviating the so-called ‘unemployment trap’). The replacement rates for unemployment benefits tend to be the highest for low-income earners because the earnings of these workers are closest to the social minimum. Furthermore, the effective tax rates on work that are faced by low-income workers are particularly high due to the interaction of the tax system, social security contributions, means-tested social security benefits, and income-related prices.

In view of these concerns, the case is quite strong for a cut in the average tax burden on low-income workers. However, a substantial reduction in average tax rates facing low incomes is rather costly in terms of lost tax revenue. To mitigate the budgetary costs, governments may restrict the tax cuts to the lowest incomes only. This implies that marginal tax rates rise. The resulting more progressive tax system may actually reduce unemployment through its effect on wage-setting behaviour in non-competitive labour markets. In particular, a more progressive tax reduces the incentive for unions to bargain for higher wages. Moreover, firms find it less attractive to pay efficiency wages. Intuitively, marginal taxes moderate wages because they act like a tax on wage increases (see e.g. Pissarides (1998)).

Whereas lower taxes on low-skilled labour and higher marginal tax rates can reduce unemployment, they are likely to harm the incentives to supply labour and to acquire more skills. Moreover, price signals in the form of wage differentials are distorted by high marginal tax rates. This harms the flexibility of the labour market in responding to shocks, and reduces the efficiency with which labour is allocated across sectors and regions. Accordingly, governments face a trade-off between cutting unemployment and raising the quality and quantity of labour supply.

5.3. *Incidence of Pollution Taxes on Consumption*

The previous subsections demonstrated the important role of the ultimate tax incidence of green taxes in determining the employment effects of an environmental tax reform. This and the next subsection elaborate on the tax incidence of pollution taxes on, respectively, consumption and production.

Destination-based taxes are borne by consumers if they are imposed by a small open economy on tradable commodities. Producers can continue to sell their commodities abroad at fixed world-market prices. Hence, they escape the tax burden. The tax is paid not only by those who consume out of labour income, but also by those who consume out of transfer and capital incomes.

In some cases, consumers may share the burden of indirect taxes with other economic agents. In particular, a tax on non-tradable consumption commodities may in part be borne by the production factors that produce the taxed commodity. Depending on relative demand and supply elasticities, the burden is shared between consumers and the suppliers of production factors. Hence, workers are likely to suffer if the tax is imposed on a non-tradable labour intensive commodity

The burden of an indirect tax would also fall on producers if a large country or a group of countries with a dominant position in the world market were to increase a destination-based tax on a tradable commodity. In that case, the world-market price for the taxed commodity would decline, thereby imposing a burden on producers.

5.4. *The Incidence of Pollution Taxes on Production*

Pollution taxes can be levied on production in various ways. To illustrate, emissions of pollutants by industry can be subject to charges. Alternatively, the government may tax certain polluting inputs into production (*e.g.*, various forms of energy or fertilizers). These taxes are typically not refunded when the outputs of the production process are exported. Furthermore, imports of similar commodities do not face an equivalent tax. Consequently, if a small country imposes a tax on the production process of a tradable commodity, domestic consumers escape the tax burden and the factors engaged in production suffer the incidence of the tax.

Which of the factors actually bears the brunt of the tax incidence depends on both the production structure and the supply elasticities of the various production factors. A major determinant of the supply elasticities is the degree to which the various factors are mobile internationally. If all non-labour inputs (*e.g.*, capital and energy) are fully mobile internationally, these inputs can escape the tax burden by moving abroad. Accordingly, non-mobile labour bears the full incidence of the tax (see Bovenberg and van der Ploeg (1994a)).

Other non-labour inputs share some of the incidence of pollution taxes in a small open economy if these inputs cannot move costlessly abroad. Indeed, in the short run, physical capital is likely to be rather immobile internationally. As a result, not only human capital but also the owners of physical capital suffer capital losses as a result of unanticipated pollution taxes. In that case, the production structure becomes relevant. With a tax on the input of energy into production, capital bears a relatively large part of the burden of unanticipated environmental taxes if, compared to labour, capital is a poorer substitute for energy (see Bovenberg and van der Ploeg (1998a)).

In the long run, however, capital is likely to be mobile internationally. Accordingly, it is able to escape the burden of environmental taxes—at least in open economies. Capital can be taxed on a sustainable basis by reducing the after-tax return only if countries coordinate their tax policies. Even then, elastic saving behaviour can shift the burden to labour—as lower saving reduces capital formation, thereby hurting labour productivity.

Also the producers of the taxed input can bear part of the burden of environmental policy. To illustrate, if OECD countries would raise taxes on fossil fuels, the oil price could fall substantially. Accordingly, the terms of trade of the oil-importing countries would improve. The OPEC countries, in contrast, would suffer terms-of-trade losses. In this way, oil-producing countries, rather than consumers in OECD countries, would bear the brunt of the tax.

The terms of trade of a country pursuing ambitious environmental policies could improve also if that country exerts market power in its export markets. In particular, by reducing the supply of its export commodities, environmental policy may raise the world-market price of these goods. In this way, part of the incidence of pollution taxes can be shifted to foreign consumers.

6. Conclusions

The overall message of this paper is rather disappointing for those who expect substantial non-environmental benefits from green tax reform. The analysis shows that stringent conditions need to be met in order for an environmental tax reform to yield a double dividend. Moreover such a double dividend often yields negative political or distributional dividends.

More fundamentally, requiring environmental policy to serve not only environmental objectives but also other, non-environmental, goals may complicate the implementation of environmental policy by intensifying the distributional struggle about the property rights of the natural environment. In deciding on environmental policy instruments, the government implicitly determines the distribution of property rights of the environment. To illustrate, if the government imposes environmental taxes, the government, as the representative of the victims of the pollution, in effect owns the property rights. Hence, in order to be able to pollute, polluters have to compensate the victims by paying the government. If the polluters own the property rights, in contrast, the victims have to bribe the polluters to cut pollution, for example by providing subsidies for cleaner technologies. In view of the rather different distributional outcomes of the various policy instruments, it is not surprising that political discussions about environmental policy are often dominated by distributional issues rather than efficiency considerations.

If polluters have historically (i.e. before environmental concerns became important) enjoyed the right to freely pollute, the government's action in imposing environmental taxes amounts to nationalizing the pollution rights. Polluters often perceive these changes in the rules of the game as inequitable. In their view, by imposing unanticipated pollution taxes, the government breaks implicit promises about stable property rights. In this way, the government taxes away quasi-rents that originate in specific investments made in anticipation of free pollution rights. This government behaviour may thus raise uncertainty about the stability of property rights, thereby negatively affecting long-term investment decisions.

To avoid these adverse equity and efficiency effects, the government may use the revenues from environmental taxes to compensate polluters for the nationalization of property rights. Using revenues to compensate polluters, however, typically conflicts with the desire to boost employment and reduce non-environmental distortions in tax systems. Whereas reaping a double dividend requires tax shifting, political considerations (i.e. respecting property rights and creating political consensus) argue in favour of minimizing tax shifting so as to contain the distributional effects of environmental policy. Indeed, taxing away the quasi-rents from existing pollution rights creates the potential for a double dividend, but violates the desire to respect historical property rights.[5] It confirms the fear of polluters that the government uses environmental taxes primarily to redistribute rents rather than to protect the environment. In their view, a redistributive operation is conducted under the banner of environmental protection. The government talking about a double dividend convinces pollutors that their rents will indeed be taken away from them in order to be used for non-environmental objectives. Linking environmental policy to redistribution intensifies the distributional struggle associated with environmental policy and may result in rent-seeking behaviour. In this way, linking environmental policy to other objectives (such as employment creation) raises the political transaction costs of implementing environmental policy.

This paper should not be misread as suggesting that environmental taxes should not be employed. It does suggest, however, that the case for environmental taxes should be made primarily on environmental grounds. The attention for the double-dividend argument stems in part from the desire to justify environmental taxes despite the uncertainties about the size of the environmental dividend. In the presence of a non-environmental dividend, green tax reforms are worthwhile as long as the environmental benefits are non-negative. The discussion in this paper indicates that the attempt to argue in favour of environmental taxes on non-environmental grounds is likely to fail. Hence, empirical research on the magnitude of environmental benefits is essential. Indeed, the analysis suggests that environmental benefits not only determine the environmental dividend but may also impact the non-environmental dividend. In particular, the feedback of environmental benefits on the economy is an important determinant of the non-environmental dividend (see section 3). Moreover, the distribution of the environmental benefits importantly affects the impact of green tax reform on political and second-best constraints (see section 4). Accordingly, a high priority should be given to identifying and measuring environmental benefits.

Acknowledgments

I wish to thank Richard Blundell, Larry Goulder, Gilbert van Hagen, Ruud de Mooij and two anonymous referees for helpful comments on an earlier draft of this paper.

Notes

1. The number of hours available for work has been normalized at unity.
2. The word 'distort' is in quotes to acknowledge that the change in resource allocation may be efficient if environmental benefits are taken into account.
3. The effect on the environmental *distortion* differs from that on the environmental *dividend*. The environmental *dividend* is defined as the increase in welfare due to a higher level of environmental quality (i.e. the first term on the right-hand side of (12)). The impact on the environmental *distortion*, in contrast, represents the net effect of the environmental dividend and the adverse welfare effects of the erosion of the pollution tax (i.e. the second term on the right-hand side of (9)).
4. The tax-shifting effect would also be absent if transfers were indexed to consumer prices rather than producer prices.
5. Another reason why green taxes may be unattractive from a political point of view is that the nationalization of pollution rights may expand public spending. In particular, it may be feared that revenues from green taxes are not recycled to the private sector but rather are spent by the political process on wasteful public spending. This would further increase the tax-burden effect discussed in subsection 2.4.

References

Ballard, C. L., and S. G. Medema. (1993). "The Marginal Efficiency Effects of Taxes and Subsidies in the Presence of Externalities: A Computational General Equilibrium Approach." *Journal of Public Economics* 52(2), 199–216.

Boadway, R., and M. Keen. (1993). "Public Goods, Self-Selection and Optimal Income Taxation." *International Economic Review* 34(3), 463–478.

Bovenberg, A. L., and R. A. de Mooij. (1994a). "Environmental Levies and Distortionary Taxation." *American Economic Review* 84(4), 1085–1089.

Bovenberg, A. L., and R. A. de Mooij. (1994b). "Environmental Policy in a Small Open Economy with Distortionary Labor Taxes: A General Equilibrium Analysis." In E. C. van Ierland (ed.), *International Environmental Economics*. Amsterdam: Elsevier.

Bovenberg, A. L., and R. A. de Mooij. (1997). "Environmental Tax Reform and Endogenous Growth." *Journal of Public Economics* 63(2), 207–237.

Bovenberg, A. L., and F. van der Ploeg. (1994a). "Green Policies and Public Finance in a Small Open Economy." *Scandinavian Journal of Economics* 96(3), 343–363.

Bovenberg, A. L., and F. van der Ploeg. (1994b). "Environmental Policy, Public Finance and the Labour Market in a Second-Best World." *Journal of Public Economics* 55(3), 349–390.

Bovenberg, A. L., and F. van der Ploeg. (1998a). "Consequences of Environmental Tax Reform for Unemployment and Welfare." *Environmental and Resource Economics* 12(2), 137–150.

Bovenberg, A. L., and F. van der Ploeg. (1998b). "Tax Reform, Structural Unemployment, and the Environment." *Scandinavian Journal of Economics* 100(3), 593–610.

Bovenberg, A. L., and L. H. Goulder. (1997). "Costs of Environmentally Motivated Taxes in the Presence of Other Taxes: General Equilibrium Analyses." *National Tax Journal* 50(1), 59–87.

Christiansen, V. (1996). "Green Taxes: A Note on the Double Dividend and the Optimum Tax Rate." CES Working Paper No. 107, University of Munich.

Cremer, H., F. Gahvari, and N. Ladoux. (1998). "Externalities and Optimal Taxation." *Journal of Public Economics* 70(3), 343–364.

Fuest, C., and B. Huber. (1999). "Second-Best Pollution Taxes: An Analytical Framework and Some New Results." *Bulletin of Economic Research* 51, 31–38.

Fullerton, D., and G. E. Metcalf. (1997). "Environmental Taxes and the Double-Dividend Hypothesis: Did You Really Expect Something for Nothing?" NBER Working Paper No. W 6199.

Goulder, L. H. (1995). "Environmental Taxation and the "Double Dividend": A Reader's Guide." *International Tax and Public Finance* 2(2), 157–183.

Graafland, J. J., and F. H. Huizinga. (1996). "Taxes and Benefits in a Non-Linear Wage Equation." Research Memorandum no. 125, CPB Netherlands Bureau for Economic Policy Analysis, The Hague, Netherlands.

Koskela, E., and R. Schöb. (1999). "Alleviating Unemployment: The Case for Green Tax Reforms." *European Economic Review* 42, 1998.

Mayeres, I., and S. Proost. (1997). "Optimal Tax and Public Investment Rules for Congestion Type of Externalities." *Scandinavian Journal of Economics* 99(2), 261–279.

Mooij, R. A. de, and A. L. Bovenberg. (1998). "Environmental Taxes, International Capital Mobility, and Inefficient Tax Systems: Tax Burden vs. Tax Shifting." *International Tax and Public Finance* 5(1), 7–39.

Ng., Y.-K. (1980). "Optimal Corrective Taxes or Subsidies when Revenue Raising Imposes an Excess Burden." *American Economic Review* 70(4), 744–751.

Nielsen, S. B., L. H. Pedersen, and P. B. Sørensen. (1995). "Environmental Policy, Pollution, Unemployment, and Endogenous Growth." *International Tax and Public Finance* 2(2), 185–205.

Parry, I. W. H. (1995). "Pollution Taxes and Revenue Recycling." *Journal of Environmental Economics and Management* 29, 564–577.

Pezzey, J. C. V., and A. Park. (1998). "Reflections on the Double-Dividend Debate, The Importance of Interest Groups and Information Costs." *Environmental and Resource Economics* 11(3–4), 539–555.

Pirtillä, J., and M. Tuomala. (1997). "Income Tax, Commodity Tax, and Environmental Policy." *International Tax and Public Finance* 4(3), 379–393.

Pissarides, C. A. (1998). "The Impact of Employment Tax Cuts on Unemployment and Wages; the Role of Unemployment Benefits and Tax Structure." *European Economic Review* 42(1), 155–183.

Sandmo, A. (1975). "Optimal Taxation in the Presence of Externalities." *Swedish Journal of Economics* 77(1), 86–98.

Schwartz, J., and R. Repetto. (1999). "Nonseparable Utility and the Double Dividend Debate: Reconsidering the Tax-Interaction Effect." *Environmental and Resource Economics*, forthcoming.

PART II

OPTIMAL ENVIRONMENTAL TAXATION IN THE PRESENCE OF DISTORTIONARY TAXES

[5]

OPTIMAL TAXATION IN THE PRESENCE OF EXTERNALITIES

*Agnar Sandmo**

Norwegian School of Economics and Business Administration, Bergen, Norway

Summary

This paper attempts to integrate the theory of optimal taxation with the analysis of the use of indirect taxation to counteract negative external effects (Pigovian taxes). A first-best solution to the problem of the optimal tax on an externality-generating good is contrasted with the case where the government also needs other, distortionary taxes in order to satisfy its revenue requirements. The main result is that the Pigovian principle holds in a modified form in the latter case as well. The problem of the distributional impact of taxation is also studied for the special case of individuals with identical preferences and a utilitarian social welfare function.

1. Introduction

Since the idea was first introduced by Pigou (1920) economists have generally accepted that when externalities are present, indirect taxation can be used as a tool for correcting inefficiencies in the competitive allocation of resources. In particular, this is true if the externality in question is of the public good (or "bad") variety, so that negotiations between the parties concerned can be effectively ruled out. The effect of the tax in this case is to confront the generator of the externality with a price reflecting the damage (or benefit, as the case may be) which his production or consumption of the commodity in question inflicts on others.[1]

There is already considerable literature on the applicability of the Pigovian tax solution. This question has recently come to the foreground in connection with the choice of policies aimed at protecting the natural environment. However, practical difficulties of implementation are not the direct concern of this paper. Instead, we consider the theoretical problem of determining optimal taxes when externalities of the public good type are present.

The existing literature on this topic suffers from several shortcomings.

* I am indebted to Victor D. Norman, who has read the manuscript and given helpful comments. The advice of a referee is also appreciated.

[1] For a critical evaluation of Pigou's own analysis and of its applicability to the case where the parties can negotiate, see Coase (1960) and the discussion of Coase's arguments by Baumol (1972).

First, most of it is partial equilibrium in nature and does not contain satisfactory treatment of the benefits resulting from control of externalities. Second, the analyses do not take into account the second-best problems which arise as soon as it is realized that Pigovian taxes only constitute part of a more comprehensive system of commodity taxes. Thus, the form in which optimality conditions are stated must frequently be taken to imply that the proceeds from Pigovian taxes are distributed to consumers in a lump-sum manner and that the net tax requirement of the public sector is zero. These assumptions are surely unattractive. Third, distributional aspects of optimal taxes are ignored.

The first of these objections, although probably insufficiently emphasized, requires only fairly straightforward analysis. The second, however, raises more interesting problems. Taxes on commodities that do not involve external effects introduce distortions of their own and raise the familiar problem of second-best theory, i.e. since the remaining conditions for Pareto optimality are not satisfied, the imposition of a tax on the externality-generating commodity reflecting the marginal social damage may no longer be optimal. This point was made in a slightly different context by Buchanan (1969), who argued that the Pigovian tax may in fact reduce efficiency if the externality-generating commodity is produced by a monopolist. Buchanan seems to draw the conclusion that the Pigovian tax solution is only applicable under ideal competitive conditions. Finally, distributional aspects of optimal taxation are of particular interest in the context of environmental externalities, where there has been a good deal of concern about the distributional impact of economic policies.

These three points will be taken up in turn in this paper. The "first-best" model is introduced in Section 2, while Section 3 analyzes the second-best problem of the choice of an optimal set of commodity taxes under a budgetary constraint for the public sector. In this section the distributional problem is assumed away; it is taken up in Section 4. Section 5 contains some concluding remarks.

2. The Structure of the Model and the First-Best Solution

The basic model to be used in this paper is a very simple one; given the complexity of the problem, it is probably the simplest model imaginable. Thus, we assume that consumers have identical preferences. This assumption is useful when one wishes to ignore the problem of distribution as well as when one wants to come to grips with it. We also treat the production side of the economy in an aggregate fashion, assuming a simple linear production structure.

There are n consumers in the economy and $m+1$ consumer goods. Let x_i be the amount consumed of good i by the individual consumer and X_i the total amount consumed and produced in the economy. We assume now that x_0 denotes hours worked and that leisure can be written as $1-x_0$. It is also assumed that the consumption of good m creates a negative externality which is a function of the total consumption of that good X_m. We can then write the utility function of the representative consumer as

$$u^j = u(1-x_0, x_1 \ldots, x_m, X_m). \tag{1}$$

This function is assumed to be strictly concave[1] and to satisfy the usual differentiability requirements with the following sign assumptions for the first-order partial derivatives:

$$u_i > 0 \quad (i=0, 1, \ldots, m), \quad u_{m+1} < 0 \tag{2}$$

This treatment of the externality is of course highly stylized, although it does seem to capture some essential aspects of the concern over environmental externalities. Traffic congestion, air and water pollution resulting from the production of certain commodities, etc. can all be interpreted as examples of this general description.

The production side of the economy is summarized in a fixed-coefficients transformation function

$$-X_0 + \sum_{i=1}^{m} a_i X_i = 0 \quad (a_i > 0, \forall i). \tag{3}$$

The fixed-coefficients assumption is obviously a strong one, but at least in the present context it is less restrictive than it may seem (see footnote 6 below). It should be observed that only the total amount of labor enters in (3); all individuals are perfect substitutes for each other in production.

The welfare function is taken to be the utilitarian unweighted sum of utilities. Since each individual has the same preferences and the same productivity, the optimum will obviously be characterized by full equality, and we can write $X_i = nx_i$ for all i. To characterize the properties of an optimal allocation the Lagrangian can now be written

$$L = nu(1-x_0, x_1, \ldots, x_m, nx_m) - \alpha\left(-X_0 + \sum_{i=1}^{m} a_i X_i\right). \tag{4}$$

Setting the partial derivatives of L equal to zero, we can write the optimality conditions as

$$\frac{u_i}{u_0} = a_i. \quad (i=1, \ldots, m-1). \tag{5}$$

---

[1] While guaranteeing the sufficiency of the first-order maximum conditions, the assumption of strict concavity is stronger than necessary for the main results in Sections 2 and 3, which require only quasi-concavity. However, when we come to distributional problems we utilize arguments based on decreasing marginal utility of income, which imply strict concavity. For simplicity, the stronger assumption is made from the start.

$$\frac{u_m}{u_0}\left(1+n\frac{u_{m+1}}{u_m}\right)=a_m. \tag{6}$$

Eq. (5) says that for the first $m-1$ consumer goods the marginal rate of substitution between any one good and leisure should be equal to their marginal rate of transformation. Eq. (6) says that, for the mth good, its marginal rate of substitution for leisure should not be equated directly to the marginal rate of transformation; the former should be multiplied by a factor involving the sum of the marginal rates of substitution between the mth good as a private and as a public good.

To interpret these conditions in terms of a competitive equilibrium we define a consumer price vector $P=(P_0, P_1, ..., P_m)$ and a producer price vector $p=(p_0, p_1, ..., p_m)$. Prices may be normalized by choosing labor as our *numéraire*, setting $P_0=p_0=1$. In a competitive equilibrium consumers maximize utility subject to a budget constraint involving the prices P, while firms maximize profit, taking the price vector p as given. Thus, the consumer's optimum is found as the maximum of (1) subject to the budget constraint

$$-x_0+\sum_{i=1}^{m}P_i x_i - S=0, \tag{7}$$

where S is the amount of lump-sum transfers received from the public sector. When maximizing utility subject to this constraint the individual consumer, being very small compared to the market, will ignore the effect of a small change in his own consumption on the total quantity of good m consumed, effectively assuming that the derivative $\partial X_m/\partial x_m=0$.[1] This is simply the usual competitive assumption.

We can now reformulate the first-order conditions for the consumer as

$$\frac{u_i}{u_0}=P_i. \quad (i=1, \ldots, m). \tag{8}$$

Firms maximize profit subject to the production constraint (3) and the price vector p. Obviously, the only structure of producer prices which is compatible with competitive assumptions is

$$p_i=a_i \quad (i=1, ..., m). \tag{9}$$

This says that producer prices should be equal to marginal costs measured in labor units.

We now ask, what is the nature of the competitive price system that will lead to an efficient allocation of resources? Comparing (8) and (9) with (5) and (6) we see that efficiency requires

[1] However, the externality problem would remain, although in a slightly different form, if the individual were to assume (rightly) that $\partial X_m/\partial x_m=1$. The reason for this, of course, is that the individual only takes into account the externality effect on himself, while continuing to ignore the effects of his own consumption on others.

$$P_i = p_i \quad (i = 1, \ldots, m-1) \tag{10}$$

$$P_m\left(1 + n\frac{u_{m+1}}{u_m}\right) = p_m. \tag{11}$$

Thus, efficiency results when there is a price structure with equality between consumer and producer prices for the first $m-1$ goods and an inequality for the mth externality-creating good. The optimal rate of the Pigovian tax may now be defined as

$$\theta_m = -n\frac{u_{m+1}}{u_m}, \tag{12}$$

since $(1-\theta_m)$ is the optimal ratio between the producer and the consumer price for good m. For this solution to make sense we must obviously assume that $\theta_m < 1$ or

$$-\frac{u_{m+1}}{u_m} < \frac{1}{n}, \tag{13}$$

so that our local optimality conditions also describe a global optimum.

Conditions (10) and (11) provide a general equilibrium solution to the problem of the optimal Pigovian tax; from (12) we see that the optimal tax rate reflects the marginal "social damage" as the sum of the marginal rates of substitution between good m as a private and as a public good. But the underlying assumptions about the public sector are still unsatisfactory. Its only task is to correct for externalities by imposing Pigovian taxes and distribute the tax revenue through lump-sum payments. We now turn to a model which sets more realistic constraints for the public sector.

3. The Second-Best Problem

As in most of the recent contributions to the theory of optimal commodity taxation[1] we approach the optimization problem by way of the dual. Thus, let us define the consumer's indirect utility function as

$$v(P) \equiv u(x(P)), \tag{14}$$

where x is the consumption vector. The derivative of v with respect to the kth price is then

$$\frac{\partial v}{\partial P_k} = -u_0\frac{\partial x_0}{\partial P_k} + \sum_{i=1}^{m} u_i\frac{\partial x_i}{\partial P_k} + nu_{m+1}\frac{\partial x_m}{\partial P_k}.$$

Substituting from the first-order conditions we obtain

[1] See e.g. Diamond & Mirrlees (1971), Stiglitz & Dasgupta (1971), Dixit (1974) and Sandmo (1974).

$$\frac{\partial v}{\partial P_k} = -\lambda \frac{\partial x_0}{\partial P_k} + \lambda \sum_{i=1}^{m} P_i \frac{\partial x_i}{\partial P_k} + n u_{m+1} \frac{\partial x_m}{\partial P_k}.$$

But from the budget constraint (7) we have that

$$-\frac{\partial x_0}{\partial P_k} + \sum_{i=1}^{m} P_i \frac{\partial x_i}{\partial P_k} + x_k = 0,$$

so that we get

$$\frac{\partial v}{\partial P_k} = -\lambda x_k + n u_{m+1} \frac{\partial x_m}{\partial P_k}. \quad (k = 1, \ldots, m) \tag{15}$$

We can now formulate the second-best optimization model. We omit an explicit and detailed treatment of the expenditure side of the public sector's budget and simply assume that the public sector requires a given amount of tax revenue, T. As the required tax revenue is in labor units[1] we might interpret it as, e.g. the amount of labor required to keep up a pre-determined level of national defense. Unit taxes are defined as $t_i = P_i - p_i$. The government's budget constraint can then be written as

$$\sum_{i=1}^{m} t_i X_i = n \sum_{i=1}^{m} (P_i - p_i) x_i = T. \tag{16}$$

The optimization problem can be formulated as maximization of the sum of the indirect utility functions with respect to consumer prices subject to the budget constraint (16). The Lagrangian becomes

$$L = nv(P) - \beta \left[n \sum_{i=1}^{m} (P_i - p_i) x_i - T \right], \tag{17}$$

and the first-order conditions are

$$-\lambda x_k + n u_{m+1} \frac{\partial x_m}{\partial P_k} - \beta \left[\sum_{i=1}^{m} t_i \frac{\partial x_i}{\partial P_k} + x_k \right] = 0. \quad (k = 1, \ldots, m). \tag{18}$$

These are the fundamental optimality conditions. In general it is not possible to solve for the optimal taxes explicitly, since the quantities demanded depend on the taxes. However, it is illuminating to solve for the t_i from (18), although the resulting expressions still only give us implicit solutions.

The coefficient matrix of the t_i is the transpose of the Jacobian matrix of the demand functions for the taxed goods:

[1] The choice of labor as the untaxed *numéraire* good is of course arbitrary, and the reader is free to reinterpret the model so as to include labor among the taxed goods. However, the income tax considered is then only a proportional one; more complicated income tax schedules would require substantial extensions of the analysis.

$$J^* = \begin{pmatrix} \frac{\partial x_1}{\partial P_1} \cdots \frac{\partial x_m}{\partial P_1} \\ \vdots \\ \frac{\partial x_1}{\partial P_m} \cdots \frac{\partial x_m}{\partial P_m} \end{pmatrix} \tag{19}$$

Let J be the determinant of J^* and J_{ik} the cofactor of the element in the ith row, kth column of J. Assuming J^* to be non-singular we can then use Cramer's rule to solve for t_k from (18):

$$t_k = \frac{\sum_{i=1}^{m} \left[-\frac{\lambda+\beta}{\beta} x_i + \frac{1}{\beta} n u_{m+1} \frac{\partial x_m}{\partial P_i} \right] J_{ik}}{J}.$$

This expression can be rewritten as

$$t_k = -\frac{\lambda+\beta}{\beta} \frac{\sum_{i=1}^{m} x_i J_{ik}}{J} + \frac{1}{\beta} n u_{m+1} \frac{\sum_{i=1}^{m} \frac{\partial x_m}{\partial P_i} J_{ik}}{J}. \tag{20}$$

According to some well-known theorems about the expansion of determinants we have that

$$\sum_{i=1}^{m} \frac{\partial x_m}{\partial P_i} J_{ik} = \begin{cases} 0 & \text{for } k \neq m \\ J & \text{for } k = m. \end{cases} \tag{21}$$

Rewriting (20) in terms of the tax rates $\theta_k(=t_k/P_k)$, and defining $\mu = -\lambda/\beta$, we can then conclude that the optimal tax structure has the following form:

$$\theta_k = (1-\mu) \left[-\frac{1}{P_k} \frac{\sum_{i=1}^{m} x_i J_{ik}}{J} \right] \quad \text{for } k \neq m \tag{22}$$

$$\theta_m = (1-\mu) \left[-\frac{1}{P_m} \frac{\sum_{i=1}^{m} x_i J_{im}}{J} \right] + \mu \left[-n \frac{u_{m+1}}{u_m} \right]. \tag{23}$$

Two main conclusions follow from this analysis.

The first is that the optimal tax structure is characterized by what might be called an additivity property; the marginal social damage of commodity m enters the tax formula for that commodity additively, and does not enter the tax formulas for the other commodities, regardless of the pattern of complementarity and substitutability. Thus, the fact that a commodity involves a negative externality is not in itself an argument for taxing other commodities which are complementary with it, nor for subsidizing substitutes. This result has obvious relevance for economic policy and is not evident from the viewpoint of the theory of second best.

This conclusion should be interpreted with some caution, however It does not imply that the marginal social damage is the same under a system of commodity taxation as in the first-best situation described in Section 2. In general, both relative prices and incomes of consumers will differ between the two situations and so, therefore, will the marginal social damage. Thus, our conclusion is no more than a statement about the terms contained in the optimal tax formulas.

The second implication is that the optimal tax rate on the externality-creating commodity is a weighted average of two terms, of which the second is the marginal social damage of commodity m. The first term, similar to the corresponding terms in the formulas for the remaining commodities, is composed of the efficiency terms familiar from the theory of optimal taxation. To see that this is indeed so, consider the case of independent demands, so that $\partial x_j/\partial P_k=0$ for $j \neq k$. The determinant of the transposed Jacobian is then simply equal to the product of the diagonal terms, and formulas (22) and (23) reduce to

$$\theta_k = (1-\mu)\left(-\frac{1}{\varepsilon_k}\right) \quad \text{for } k \neq m \tag{24}$$

$$\theta_m = (1-\mu)\left(-\frac{1}{\varepsilon_m}\right) + \mu\left(-n\frac{u_{m+1}}{u_m}\right). \tag{25}$$

(24) is the inverse elasticity formula familiar from the literature and says that the highest tax rates should be levied on commodities with inelastic demand.[1] Eq. (25) shows that the optimal tax rate for the externality-creating commodity is a weighted average of the inverse elasticity and the marginal social damage. (We assume that $\varepsilon_k<0$ for all k.)

There remains the task of interpreting the weight factor μ. Recall that λ is the marginal utility of income (or leisure) and therefore positive. From the formulation of the Lagrangian (17) we see that β is the effect of an increase in the tax requirement T on social utility; β is therefore negative. Clearly, the public sector should employ its tax revenue in such a way that the marginal social utility of income in the public sector equals the value of the marginal amount withdrawn from the private sector, which is $-\beta$. Therefore, since $\mu=-\lambda/\beta$, we might interpret μ as the marginal rate of substitution between private and public income; the higher μ is, the higher the marginal value of private income compared with public income, and the lower the tax requirement, given that this is itself derived from an underlying optimization criterion. We also see that with increasing μ, the proportionallity factor of the effi-

[1] Supply elasticities do not enter these formulas because of our linearity assumption about the structure of production. The crucial assumption, however, is not that of fixed coefficients but of constant returns to scale; see Diamond & Mirrlees (1971). If some commodity is in completely inelastic demand, it is the ideal tax object from the efficiency viewpoint, but this extreme case is disregarded here.

ciency terms in our formulas decrease, and the marginal social damage comes to dominate the tax on good m. It is conceivable that $\mu > 1$, in which case the efficiency terms become formulas for optimal subsidies, since the marginal social damage alone implies a tax on good m which creates revenue in excess of the tax requirement.

What of the case $\mu = 1$? This obviously implies that we are back to the first-best solution with a tax on good m only, and at a rate reflecting the marginal social damage. This is the fortunate case where the Pigovian tax alone happens to satisfy the tax requirement exactly, so that no additional taxes or subsidies of a distortionary kind are called for.

4. Distributional Considerations

From the viewpoint of practical economic policy, a good case can be made for ignoring distributional considerations when using taxes to correct for external effects. Taxes on income and wealth as well as educational and social policy may all be more efficient means of achieving a socially desirable redistribution of welfare. However, if such policies are not in fact effective, a government committed to certain redistributional goals cannot ignore the distributional impact of taxes that are primarily designed for the purpose of "internalizing externalities".

There could be no distributional problem in the model in the preceding sections since everybody was alike. We continue to assume that all individuals have the same preferences, but we now let them have unequal productivities. The transformation function will be written as

$$-\sum_{j=1}^{n} a_{0j} x_{0j} + \sum_{i=1}^{m} a_i X_i = 0, \tag{26}$$

where

$$X_i = \sum_{j=1}^{n} x_{ij}. \quad (i = 1, \ldots, m). \tag{27}$$

Here a_{0j}/a_i is obviously individual j's marginal productivity in the production of good i.

In competitive equilibrium producer prices must necessarily be such that

$$p_i = a_i, \; p_{0j} = a_{0j}. \tag{28}$$

The indirect utility function is now[1]

$$v_j(P_j) \equiv u(x_j(P_j)) \tag{29}$$

[1] The price vector encountered by consumer j is $P_j = (p_{0j}, P_1, \ldots, P_m)$ and differs between consumers because they face different prices for the labor they supply. Note that since labor is still not taxed, $P_{0j} = p_{0j}$.

and its derivative with respect to the kth price is

$$\frac{\partial v_j}{\partial P_k} = -u_{0j}\frac{\partial x_{0j}}{\partial P_k} + \sum_{i=1}^{m} u_{ij}\frac{\partial x_{ij}}{\partial P_k} + u_{m+1,j}\sum_{j=1}^{n}\frac{\partial x_{mj}}{\partial P_k}.$$

Letting λ_j be the marginal utility of income for individual j, we proceed as in the preceding section to obtain

$$\frac{\partial v_j}{\partial P_k} = -\lambda_j x_{kj} + u_{m+1,j}\frac{\partial X_m}{\partial P_k}. \tag{30}$$

To find the optimal price structure we form the Lagrangian

$$L = \sum_{j=1}^{n} v_j(P_j) - \beta\left[\sum_{i=1}^{m}(P_i - p_i)X_i - T\right] \tag{31}$$

and set its partial derivatives equal to zero:

$$-\sum_{j=1}^{n}\lambda_j x_{kj} + \left(\sum_{j=1}^{n} u_{m+1,j}\right)\frac{\partial X_m}{\partial P_k} - \beta\left[\sum_{i=1}^{m} t_i\frac{\partial X_i}{\partial P_k} + X_k\right] = 0 \quad (k = 1, \ldots, m).$$

Solving for t_k we obtain

$$t_k = \frac{\sum_{i=1}^{m}\left[-\sum_{j=1}^{n}\frac{\lambda_j + \beta}{\beta}x_{kj} + \frac{1}{\beta}\left(\sum_{j=1}^{n} u_{m+1,j}\right)\frac{\partial X_m}{\partial P_i}\right]J_{ik}}{J} \quad (k = 1, \ldots, m).$$

Utilizing (21), the solution can be rewritten as

$$\theta_k = \sum_{j=1}^{n}(1-\mu_j)\left[-\frac{1}{P_k}\frac{\sum_{i=1}^{m} x_{ij}J_{ik}}{J}\right] \quad (k = 1, \ldots, m-1) \tag{32}$$

$$\theta_m = \sum_{j=1}^{n}(1-\mu_j)\left[-\frac{1}{P_k}\frac{\sum_{i=1}^{m} x_{ij}J_{im}}{J}\right] + \sum_{j=1}^{n}\mu_j\left(-\frac{u_{m+1,j}}{u_{mj}}\right). \tag{33}$$

Here $\mu_j = -\lambda_j/\beta$.

Perhaps the most striking feature of the solution is that the additive property carries over to this more general case. It is still true that the marginal social damage is only an argument in the tax formula for good m. For further insights into the properties of the solution we concentrate on the case of demand independence, in which (32) and (33) become

$$\theta_k = \frac{\sum_{j=1}^{n}(1-\mu_j)x_{kj}}{\sum_{j=1}^{n} x_{kj}}\left(-\frac{1}{\varepsilon_k}\right) \quad (k = 1, \ldots, m-1). \tag{34}$$

$$\theta_m = \frac{\sum_{j=1}^{n} (1-\mu_j) x_{mj}}{\sum_{j=1}^{n} x_{mj}} \left(-\frac{1}{\varepsilon_m}\right) + \sum_{j=1}^{n} \mu_j \left(-\frac{u_{m+1,j}}{u_{mj}}\right). \tag{35}$$

The efficiency terms of the optimal tax formulas are proportional to the aggregate demand elasticities as before. However, the proportionality factor has become somewhat more complicated. It is a weighted average across individuals of the factor $(1-\mu_j)$, the weights being in each case the amount of the commodity in question consumed by individual j. Now, $(1-\mu_j)$ varies positively with the level of income, being low (possibly negative) for low-income individuals and high (approaching one) for high-income individuals. Thus, the proportionality factor[1] takes a low (possibly negative) value if the consumption of commodity k is concentrated among low-income individuals and a high value if it is mainly consumed by high-income people. This distributional modification of the inverse elasticity rule is a natural implication of our utilitarian social welfare function.

These remarks also apply to the efficiency term of the externality-generating commodity m. But distributional factors also enter into the social damage term, since each individual's marginal rate of substitution is weighted by the factor μ_j, which varies negatively with income. Thus, the social damage term will be high if those who suffer the most from the externality tend to have low incomes and low if they are concentrated among the high-income groups.

In much of the literature on externalities there is a distinction between "polluters" and "pollutees". This distinction, although it may well be useful for some purposes, might be somewhat artificial—after all, the main victim of traffic congestion is the individual driver, who is also its source. In the present model there is no such sharp distinction, but when individuals differ with respect to income, it is still possible to make statements about various income classes as being "main polluters" and "main pollutees". From this point of view one might consider the total tax rate on good m. The conditions most favorable to a high tax rate exist when we have high-income polluters and low-income pollutees, while the opposite constellation would favor a low tax rate. The intermediate cases are when polluters and pollutees are both located either in low-income or high-income groups; this calls for a low efficiency term and a high social damage term or the opposite, as the case may be.

5. Concluding Remarks

As should be clear from the previous sections, this paper is not designed as a practical guide to the use of Pigovian taxes by economic planners. The models are extremely stylized, and the problems of estimating social damages and of

[1] In accordance with Pestieau (1973), we might refer to the proportionality factor for good k as the *distributional characteristic* of that good.

choosing the correct tax base, although of great practical importance, have been assumed away or ignored. Still, an exercise such as this may have some derived practical value. We have shown that the Pigovian taxation principle can be validated as part of a more comprehensive system of indirect taxation, and we have demonstrated that it holds in a modified form even when distributional considerations enter as correctives to the efficiency principles of taxation. Thus, even in a world of distortionary taxation where the allocative functions of the price system cannot be separated from its effects on distribution, there is scope for taxing externality-generating commodities according to the Pigovian principle. It should perhaps be stressed that our conclusions must be evaluated in relation to the framework of analysis, which is that of an *optimal* second-best set of commodity taxes. Thus, the conclusions cannot be expected to hold if some taxes are unalterable and have not been set according to the optimality criterion. To take an example, suppose that it is not possible to tax the externality-generating commodity. We would then naturally expect that the allocation of resources could be improved by taxing complementary goods or subsidizing substitutes, so that the tax rates for these goods should reflect the marginal social damage. There is no inconsistency between this and the preceding analysis.

Some of the assumptions used are admittedly rather special, but the essential features of the results carry over to more general models with suitable reinterpretations. Thus, the analysis of the first-best model in Section 2 and the resulting optimal tax formula (12) can be interpreted as an analysis of the Pareto optimal tax rate in more general models. The right-hand side of (12) would then be a proper sum of marginal rates of substitution, and this formula would describe a tax rate that is optimal in the welfare sense subject to the qualification that the distribution of income is optimal according to the welfare function used. Similarly, the problem dealt with in Section 3 could be regarded as an analysis of efficient taxation when the distributional problem can somehow be solved separately, presumably by lump-sum transfers. The difficulties and paradoxes inherent in this interpretation are obvious and well known. Finally, the model incorporating distributional effects could have been made more general by the adoption of a more general social welfare function. The individual weights in the optimal tax formulas could then be interpreted as *social* marginal utilities of income, and there would be no need to associate marginal social "deservingness" with income level alone.

These extensions and reinterpretations are not free from serious complications. This applies in particular when we wish to take distributional effects into account. In the more applied lines of welfare economics it sometimes has to be assumed that the foundations of the theory are more solid than they really are. This may not be as bad as it seems, however, since such a procedure may indicate more clearly the lines along which work on the foundations might most fruitfully be pursued.

References

Baumol, W. J.: On taxation and the control of externalities. *American Economic Review 62*, 307–322, 1972.

Buchanan, J. M.: External diseconomies, corrective taxes, and market structure. *American Economic Review 59*, 174–177, 1969.

Coase, R. H.: The problem of social cost. *Journal of Law and Economics 3*, 1–44, 1960.

Diamond, P. A. & Mirrlees, J. A.: Optimal taxation and public production I–II. *American Economic Review 61*, 8–27, 261–278, 1971.

Dixit, A. K.: Welfare effects of tax and price changes. Unpublished paper, 1974.

Pestieau, P.: Equity and efficiency rules for the provision of public goods. Unpublished paper, 1973.

Pigou, A. C.: *The economics of welfare*. London, 1920. (4th edition 1932.)

Sandmo, A.: A note on the structure of optimal taxation. *American Economic Review 64*, 701–706, 1974.

Stiglitz, J. E. & Dasgupta, P.: Differential taxation, public goods and economic efficiency. *Review of Economic Studies 38*, 151–174, 1971.

[6]

ELSEVIER

Journal of Public Economics 55 (1994) 349–390

JOURNAL OF PUBLIC ECONOMICS

Environmental policy, public finance and the labour market in a second-best world

A. L. Bovenberg,[a,b,c], F. van der Ploeg[d,e,*]

[a]*Center for Economic Research, Tilburg University, P.O. Box 90153, 5000 LE Tilburg, The Netherlands*
[b]*OCFEB, Erasmus University, P.O. Box 1738, 3000 DR Rotterdam, The Netherlands*
[c]*CEPR*
[d]*FEE, University of Amsterdam, Roetersstraat 11, 1018 WB Amsterdam, Netherlands*
[e]*Member of Parliament, Binnerhof, The Hague, The Netherlands*

Received November 1992, final version received July 1993

Abstract

Environmental and tax policies and the optimal provision of clean and dirty public goods are analysed within the context of a second-best framework of optimal taxation. Households consume both clean and dirty commodities. Degradation of the natural environment occurs due to the consumption of dirty private and public goods, but can be offset when the government engages in abatement activities. Increased environmental concern implies a higher dirt tax, a lower tax on labour, less employment, more public abatement, and a cleaner environment. If the elasticity of substitution between private consumption commodities and leisure is large and that between clean and dirty goods is small, public consumption may expand while private consumption contracts. Otherwise, public consumption falls.

Key words: Environmental externalities; Clean and dirty goods; Dirt tax; Labour tax; Excess burden; Public goods; Optimal taxation; 'Double dividend'; Second best.

JEL classification: E60; H21; H41; Q28

1. Introduction

One of the most pressing problems facing the world today is the

* Corresponding author.

SSDI 0047-2727(93)01398-T

degradation of the natural environment. Since the environmental issue can be viewed as a problem of missing markets, it requires public intervention. In particular, governments may introduce markets for pollution permits or, alternatively, resort to Pigovian taxes on pollution. However, another major task of governments is to provide public goods (other than the natural environment) and to undertake public abatement activities to clean up the environment. Financing public spending is straightforward if lump-sum taxes are available. In practice, however, governments have to resort to distortionary taxation. This raises the question of how governments should optimally set the level and structure of taxes and spending if the tax system faces the dual task of internalising environmental externalities and raising revenues to finance public spending. A related issue is the optimal design of environmental policy in a second-best world in which a sizeable public sector gives rise to serious tax distortions.

This paper explores the interaction between environmental policy and the public finances in a second-best world in which the government does not have access to lump-sum instruments. It builds on the work of Diamond (1973), Sandmo (1975) and Ng (1980), who combined the Ramsey (1927) and Pigovian (1947) objectives of taxation by analysing the optimal tax structure in the presence of environmental externalities and an exogenous revenue requirement. We extend their analysis in a number of ways. First, we consider the impact of environmental externalities not only on the optimal tax structure but also on the optimal level and composition of public spending. In analysing the optimal size of the public sector, we use the concept of the marginal cost of public funds, which has been developed in the literature on the optimal provision of public goods in the presence of distortionary taxation (see, for example, Atkinson and Stern, 1974, and, for a recent survey of this literature, Ballard and Fullerton, 1992). In doing so, we integrate environmental externalities and the optimal provision of the public good of the natural environment into this literature.

Most of the literature on optimal taxation and the optimal provision of public goods merely derives and interprets the first-order conditions for optimal policy. We go beyond the characterisation of first-order conditions by exploring the comparative statics of various preference shocks. In particular, for the case in which environmental quality, public consumption, and private welfare are perfect substitutes in social welfare, we investigate how a greater environmental concern ('greener' preferences) and a higher priority for public consumption ('redder' preferences), affect the optimal level and structure of taxes and spending.

Apart from examining the impact of changing social priorities on the public finances, we also investigate their aggregate implications for the labour market. In this connection, special attention is paid to how greener preferences impact the level of employment. One might argue that the best response to greener preferences would be to raise pollution taxes and to use the revenues to cut distortionary labour taxes. In this way, the government may reap two dividends: first, a better quality of the environment, and second, a higher level of employment and an expansion of the base of the distortionary labour tax. We call the hypothesis that an increase in environmental concern not only boosts environmental quality but also employment the double dividend hypothesis.[1]

We find that the government indeed finds it optimal to cut the labour tax in response to an increased concern for environmental quality. Nevertheless, if private goods, public consumption goods, and environmental quality enter social utility in a separable fashion, employment declines and the double dividend hypothesis fails. Intuitively, employment indirectly harms the environment because part of labour income is spent on dirty goods. The consumption of leisure, in contrast, is clean.[2] Hence, a decline in employment is optimal in response to more environmental concern.

The paper examines not only aggregate implications for employment and private consumption but also welfare outcomes. In particular, we investigate the trade-off between the three arguments of social welfare: the quality of the environment, public consumption, and private welfare. The colours green, red, and blue are associated with these three utility components. We explore under which conditions red and green priorities are 'compatible', by which we mean that a cleaner environment (higher public consumption) associated with greener (redder) preferences is associated with a rise in public consumption (environmental quality).

We find that red and green priorities may be compatible if the elasticity of substitution between produced goods and leisure in private utility is large while, at the same time, dirty and clean commodities are poor substitutes and the productivity of public abatement rapidly declines with the level of abatement. In that case, the improvement in environmental quality associated with greener preferences is achieved primarily through a lower level of employment and output rather than a cleaner composition of output (i.e.

[1] In our model without involuntary employment, the level of employment is not a goal in itself. Nevertheless, the level of employment is a major macroeconomic variable and is therefore of interest. Ulph (1992), Pezzey (1994), and Bovenberg and de Mooij (1994) employ alternative definitions of the double dividend. For a survey of the double dividend issue, see Smith (1992). Whereas Ulph (1992) and Pezzey (1992) examine the interaction between environmental and other taxes under the assumption of Cobb–Douglas preferences, our paper considers the more general class of homothetic preferences. Furthermore, we go beyond the analysis in Ulph (1992), Pezzey (1992), and Bovenberg and de Mooij (1994) by endogenising the level and structure of public spending, exploring the comparative statics of preference shocks, and investigating aggregate effects on employment and private consumption.

[2] Of course, one may consume polluting commodities while at the same time enjoying leisure (e.g. holiday travel). However, these polluting consumption goods can be acquired only after having earned sufficient income out of employment.

more public abatement and a cleaner composition of private consumption). The intuition behind the expansion of public consumption is that the disincentive effects on labour supply associated with a large public sector and a high overall tax level become less damaging if the only way to improve the environment in response to greener preferences is a lower level of economic activity. However, if substitution between dirty and clean goods is easy or the productivity of abatement does not decline rapidly, the environment can be enhanced through a 'greener' composition of economic activity. In that case, it is optimal to reduce the level of public consumption.

Section 2 investigates environmental and tax policy in a first-best world where lump-sum taxes and subsidies are available. In this setting it also analyses the optimal provision of clean and dirty public consumption goods and the optimal level of public abatement activities. Assuming that only distortionary taxes are feasible, Section 3 discusses the Ramsey tax rules and the optimal provision of public goods if environmental externalities are absent. Section 4 integrates the results of Sections 2 and 3. Within the framework of optimal distortionary taxation, it simultaneously considers the correction for environmental externalities, the provision of clean and dirty public consumption goods, and the level of public abatement activities. Section 5 restricts preferences in such a way that the demand for clean and dirty private commodities is weakly separable from leisure and that the demand for social goods is weakly separable from the demand for marketable goods. Sections 6 and 7 log-linearise the model of private behaviour and the conditions characterising optimal public policy, respectively, in order to perform comparative statics of optimal tax equilibria. Section 8 explores how an increase in environmental concern affects the public finances, employment, as well as private and public welfare. Section 9 explores the impact of more priority for public consumption. Section 10 concludes with a summary of results and suggestions for further research.

2. Environmental policy in a first-best world

2.1. The command economy

The representative consumer derives utility (U) from the consumption of marketable goods, namely clean private goods (C), dirty private goods (D), and leisure (V). Furthermore, social goods, i.e. clean public goods (X), dirty public goods (Y), and the quality of the environment (E), raise utility. The utility function for the representative consumer is thus denoted by $U = u(C,D,V,X,Y,E)$. See Table 1 for a complete list of notations. The quality of the environment deteriorates when private agents or the public sector consume more dirty goods. However, environmental quality improves

Table 1
Notation

N	number of households
U	social welfare
E	quality of the environment
A	level of abatement activities
M	utility of marketable goods
G	utility of the basket of clean and dirty public goods (i.e. public consumption)
X, Y	consumption of clean and dirty public goods
Q	utility of the basket of clean and dirty private goods
C, D	consumption of clean and dirty private goods
V, L	leisure and labour supply
T	(lump-sum) income transfer from government to private agents
P_C, P_D	consumption prices of clean and dirty products in private consumption
t_D	tax (rate) on private consumption of dirty products
t_{DP}	Pigovian component of the dirt tax
P_L, β	consumption wage ($\beta(1-t_L)$) and producer wage
t_L	tax rate on labour income
δ_D, δ	emission ratios of private and public dirty consumption
θ_D	t_D/P_D
θ_Y	$(\delta_Y/\delta_D)t_D/[1+(\delta_Y/\delta_D)t_D]$
θ_L	$t_L/(1-t_L)$
$\tilde{t}_i$	deviation of t_i from initial equilibrium, normalised by P_i, $i = D, L$
P_Q	ideal price index for the basket of private consumption goods
P_G	ideal price index of public consumption
λ	marginal private utility of private income
λ'	marginal social utility of private income
μ, η	marginal disutility and marginal cost (μ/λ) of public funds
η'	μ/λ'
α_D	budget share of dirty products in private consumption ($P_D D/P_L L$)
α_V	budget share of leisure in marketable goods ($M_V V/M = V$)
α_Y	budget share of dirty goods in public consumption ($G_Y Y/G$)
α_E	ratio of value of environment to national income ($(t_D/\delta_D)E/(N\beta L)$)
ω_i	national income share of good $i(I/\beta NL$, $i = X, Y, A$, $I/\beta L$, $i = C, D)$
ω_G	national income share of public spending ($(X+Y+A)/\beta NL = \omega_X + \omega_Y + \omega_A = t_L + (1-t_L)\theta_D\alpha_D$)
σ_M	elasticity of substitution between Q and V
σ_G, σ_Q	elasticities of substitution between X and Y and between C and D
σ_A	elasticity of productivity of public abatement ($-e^{A''}A/e^{A'}$)
$\overset{U}{\epsilon}_{ij}$	uncompensated elasticity of demand for good i with respect to price j
ϵ_{ij}	compensated elasticity of demand for good i with respect to price j
Γ_i	weight of I in social welfare $U = \Gamma_G G + \Gamma_E E + \Gamma_M M$
κ	$1 - t_L[1-(1-\alpha_V)(\sigma_M - 1)]$
Δ	$1 - \omega_G(1+\overset{U}{\epsilon}_{LL}) = 1 - \omega_G[1-\alpha_V(1-\sigma_M)]$
ρ_G	$(\omega_X + \omega_Y)\theta_Y\alpha_Y(1-\theta_Y\alpha_Y)^{-1}(1-\alpha_Y)$
ρ_Q	$(\omega_C + \omega_D)\theta_D\alpha_D(1-\theta_D\alpha_D)^{-1}(1-\alpha_D)$
ρ	$\rho_Q\sigma_Q + \rho_G\sigma_G + \omega_A(\theta_D\sigma_A)^{-1}$

when the government engages in abatement activities (A), i.e. $E = e(ND,Y,A)$ with $e_{ND}, e_Y < 0$ and $e_A > 0$, where N stands for the number of private agents in the economy. Private agents ignore environmental externalities when they decide on the consumption of dirty products.

Producers face a linear constant-returns-to-scale technology in which output is proportional to employment (L) and can be used for consumption of (clean and dirty) private and public goods and for public spending on abatement activities.[3] The material balance condition for the economy is thus given by

$$\beta NL = \beta N(1 - V) = \beta_C NC + \beta_D ND + \beta_X X + \beta_Y Y + \beta_A A, \beta_i > 0. \quad (1)$$

Each worker–consumer has one unit of time available which can be used for either work (L) or leisure (V). We assume, without loss of generality, that $\beta_i = 1$, $i = C,D,X,Y,A$. The production price associated with these goods therefore acts as the numeraire. The production price of labour, the product wage, is denoted by β.

It is of some interest to consider as a benchmark the first-best outcome, which is attainable in a command economy. In such an economy, the social planner maximises utility of the representative household subject to the material balance condition (1). This yields the following optimality conditions:

$$u_C = \beta^{-1} u_V = N u_X = u_D + N u_E e_{ND} = N(u_Y + u_E e_Y) = N u_E e_A. \quad (2)$$

The marginal rate of substitution between leisure and clean products must equal the relevant marginal rate of transformation, i.e. the product wage. The marginal utility of clean private products must be set to the sum of the marginal utilities of clean public goods for each of the private agents (cf. Samuelson, 1954). The marginal utility of clean products must equal that of dirty products minus a term correcting for the environmental externality (note $e_{ND}, e_Y < 0$). This condition must hold for both private and public goods. Finally, the sum of marginal utilities of a cleaner natural environment resulting from public abatement activities must equal the marginal utility of clean private products.

[3] Relaxing the assumption of fixed producer prices and linear technology does not affect the results as long as producer prices result from competitive behaviour and producers face constant returns to scale (or pure profits are taxed away under decreasing returns to scale) (cf. Auerbach, 1985).

2.2 Pollution taxes in a market economy: A Pigovian view

The first-best outcome discussed in Subsection 2.1 is sustainable in a decentralised market economy if lump-sum taxes and subsidies are available. To see this, interpret the material balance condition (1) as the equilibrium condition for the goods market and $V + L = 1$ as the condition for equilibrium in the labour market. If firms maximise profits under perfect competition, the producer prices of clean and dirty private products, clean and dirty public goods, and public abatement are unity and the producer wage is β. The budget constraint for a typical consumer is

$$P_C C + P_D D = (1 - t_L)\beta L + T, \tag{3}$$

where P_C and P_D denote the consumption prices of, respectively, clean and dirty products, t_L stands for the labour tax rate, and T represents lump-sum transfers provided by the government to each household. The consumption wage is denoted by $P_L \equiv (1 - t_L)\beta$ and corresponds to the opportunity cost of leisure. The government can levy also specific taxes on clean and dirty products, so that $P_i = 1 + t_i$, $i = C,D$, where t_C denotes the clean tax and t_D denotes the dirt tax. The optimality conditions for the representative consumer in a competitive market economy are

$$(u_C/P_C) = (u_D/P_D) = (u_V/[(1 - t_L)\beta]) = \lambda, \tag{4}$$

where λ stands for marginal private utility of income. The government can thus achieve the first-best outcome characterised by (2) if it levies no taxes on consumption of clean goods and on labour income, i.e. $t_C = t_L = 0$, sets the dirt tax equal to

$$t_D = -Nu_E e_{ND}(u_D + Nu_E e_{ND})^{-1} = -Nu_E e_{ND} u_C^{-1} > 0 \tag{5}$$

and determines the quantities of the two public goods and of abatement activities from (2). This Pigovian dirt tax can also be interpreted as the price of auctioned pollution permits. The government budget constraint then determines the amount of lump-sum taxes (transfers) that must be levied on (handed back to) the public if revenues from the dirt tax fall short of (exceed) public spending, i.e. $NT = t_D ND - X - Y - A$. Equivalent to the dirt tax (5) is a subsidy on clean goods combined with a labour tax of equal magnitude, i.e. $t_L = -t_C = -N(u_E e_{ND}/u_D) > 0$.

3. Distortions and public goods: Ramsey tax schemes

In practice, the government must resort to distortionary taxes as lump-sum taxes and subsidies are not available (i.e. $T = 0$). This section derives the Ramsey tax rules, which yield the least distortionary way of financing a given level of public spending if environmental externalities are absent (i.e. $u_E = 0$). It also examines the conditions for the optimal level of public spending. The remaining sections then turn to the general policy problem in which taxes face the dual task of generating revenues to finance public spending and internalising environmental externalities.

3.1. Tax structure

Since a labour tax is equivalent to a uniform tax on clean and dirty private products and a dirt tax is the natural candidate for inducing private agents to pollute less, we assume (without loss of generality) that C is the untaxed good. There is thus no explicit tax on clean private commodities (i.e. $P_C = 1$). This assumption accords most closely with the political debate about the interactions between optimal environmental and tax policies and, in particular, about the double dividend hypothesis. When a given amount of public spending, $X + Y + A$, has to be financed by distortionary taxation, the optimal tax structure must satisfy (cf. Atkinson and Stiglitz, 1980, Ch. 12, or Auerbach, 1985)

$$\lambda D - \mu\left[D + t_D\left(\frac{\partial D}{\partial P_D}\right) + t_L\beta\left(\frac{\partial L}{\partial P_D}\right)\right] = 0, \tag{6}$$

$$\lambda L - \mu\left[L - t_D\left(\frac{\partial D}{\partial P_L}\right) - t_L\beta\left(\frac{\partial L}{\partial P_L}\right)\right] = 0, \tag{7}$$

where μ denotes the marginal disutility of raising a unit of government revenues and thus measures the scarcity of public funds. Using the Slutsky decompositions $(\partial I/\partial P_D) = S_{iD} - (\partial I/\partial T)D$ and $(\partial I/\partial P_L) = S_{iL} + (\partial I/\partial T)L$, $I,i = D,L$, where S represents the (symmetric and negative definite) Slutsky matrix, one obtains

$$\begin{pmatrix} t_D \\ \beta t_L \end{pmatrix} = -\left(\frac{\mu - \lambda'}{\mu}\right)\begin{pmatrix} S_{DD} & S_{LD} \\ S_{DL} & S_{LL} \end{pmatrix}^{-1}\begin{pmatrix} D \\ -L \end{pmatrix},$$

$$\lambda' \equiv \lambda + \mu\left(t_D\frac{\partial D}{\partial T} + \beta t_L\frac{\partial L}{\partial T}\right). \tag{8}$$

The marginal *social* utility of private income (λ') may exceed the marginal *private* utility of income (λ) as it takes acount of the increased tax revenues resulting from additional private expenditures. Negative definiteness of the

Slutsky matrix in (8) implies that μ exceeds λ' for positive government revenues (cf. Auerbach, 1985, p.112). Defining $\varepsilon_{ik} \equiv P_k S_{ik}/I$ as the compensated elasticity of demand for commodity i (I) with respect to the price of commodity k and using Slutsky symmetry ($\varepsilon_{LD} = -\alpha_D \varepsilon_{DL}$, where α_D denotes the private budget share of dirty goods), one can rewrite Eq. (8) in terms of elasticities:

$$\begin{pmatrix} \theta_D \\ \theta_L \end{pmatrix} \equiv \begin{pmatrix} \dfrac{t_D}{1+t_D} \\ \dfrac{t_L}{1-t_L} \end{pmatrix} = \left(\frac{\mu - \lambda'}{\mu}\right) \begin{pmatrix} \varepsilon_{DD} & -\varepsilon_{DL} \\ -\varepsilon_{LD} & \varepsilon_{LL} \end{pmatrix}^{-1} \begin{pmatrix} -1 \\ 1 \end{pmatrix}. \tag{8'}$$

Eq.(8′) can be solved to give

$$\theta_D \equiv \left(\frac{t_D}{1+t_D}\right) = \left(\frac{\varepsilon_{LL} - \varepsilon_{DL}}{\varepsilon_{LD} - \varepsilon_{DD}}\right)\theta_L \tag{9}$$

and

$$\theta_L \equiv \left(\frac{t_L}{1-t_L}\right) = \left(\frac{\varepsilon_{LD} - \varepsilon_{DD}}{-\varepsilon_{DD}\varepsilon_{LL} + \varepsilon_{LD}\varepsilon_{DL}}\right)\left(\frac{\mu - \lambda'}{\mu}\right). \tag{10}$$

The marginal disutility of financing public spending (μ) exceeds the marginal social utility of private income (λ') if public revenues are positive. Moreover, negative definiteness of the Slutsky matrix implies that the denominator in the first term in brackets in the expression for θ_L in (10) is positive. Hence, the tax on labour is positive if and only if ε_{LD} exceeds ε_{DD}.[4]

Since compensated demand functions depend only on relative prices, $\varepsilon_{iL} = -(\varepsilon_{iC} + \varepsilon_{iD})$, $i = D,L$ must hold. Hence, using Slutsky symmetry (i.e. $\varepsilon_{LD} = -\alpha_D \varepsilon_{DL}$ and $\varepsilon_{LC} = -(1-\alpha_D)\varepsilon_{CL}$), we can write (9) as

$$\theta_D \equiv \left(\frac{t_D}{1+t_D}\right) = \left(\frac{\varepsilon_{CL} - \varepsilon_{DL}}{\varepsilon_{CD} - \varepsilon_{DD}}\right)\theta_L. \tag{9'}$$

Optimal government policy thus involves a tax on labour, which is a uniform tax on both clean and dirty products. On top of that the government should levy a dirt tax, the sign of which depends on the cross-

[4] If $\varepsilon_{LD} = \varepsilon_{DL} = 0$ and $\varepsilon_{LL} = -\varepsilon_{DD}$, Eq. (9) shows that it is optimal to have a uniform tax on dirty products and labour supply. It is optimal to have a higher (lower) dirt tax than labour tax if the own price elasticity of the compensated supply of labour (ε_{LL}) exceeds (falls short of) that for dirty private goods ($-\varepsilon_{DD}$). Similarly, it can be shown that, if $\varepsilon_{CD} = \varepsilon_{DC} = 0$ and $\varepsilon_{CC} = \varepsilon_{DD}$, it is optimal to levy a uniform tax on clean and dirty products (equivalent to a tax on labour). If the own price elasticity of the demand for clean products ($-\varepsilon_{CC}$) is lower (higher) than that of dirty products ($-\varepsilon_{DD}$), it is optimal to give (levy) an additional subsidy (tax) on dirty products. These special cases illustrate the Ramsey rule which states that it is optimal to tax goods with a low price elasticity more heavily than goods with a high price elasticity.

elasticities with leisure. In particular, the dirt tax is positive if clean goods are better substitutes for leisure than dirty goods are ($\varepsilon_{CL} > \varepsilon_{DL}$). In that case, dirty goods are the relative complement to leisure. Accordingly, it is optimal for the government to levy a uniform tax on clean and dirty products, i.e. tax labour, and to levy an additional tax on the product that is most complementary to leisure.[5]

3.2. Choice between public and private goods

In the absence of lump-sum taxes and subsidies, the marginal rate of transformation between private and public goods no longer corresponds to the sum of the marginal rates of substitution between private and public goods as in Samuelson (1954). This may be seen from the following condition for the optimal provision of public goods (cf. Atkinson and Stern, 1974):

$$N\left(\frac{u_X}{u_C}\right) = \eta\left[1 - t_D N\left(\frac{\partial D}{\partial X}\right) - t_L \beta N\left(\frac{\partial L}{\partial X}\right)\right] \quad \eta \equiv \left(\frac{\mu}{\lambda}\right), \tag{11}$$

where η denotes the marginal cost of public funds (in terms of the numeraire). There are two reasons why the marginal rate of transformation between private and public goods differs from the corresponding sum of the marginal rates of substitution.

The first reason is that, if public goods are complementary to taxed commodities ($t_D \partial D/\partial X > 0$ or $t_L \partial L/\partial X > 0$), raising public spending alleviates the excess burden of distortionary taxation by boosting the consumption of taxed commodities. For example, the construction of public highways between suburbs and cities may induce some agents to work more and, therefore, pay more tax on their labour income. Moreover, they may buy more heavily taxed commodities, such as petrol and cars. Public libraries, in contrast, may encourage private agents to enjoy more leisure, thereby eroding the base of the labour tax. The social cost of funds devoted to libraries is thus higher than that of funds allocated to highways.

The second reason for the divergence between the marginal rates of transformation and substitution is that the marginal cost of public funds (η) may differ from unity. If an increase in public revenues erodes the base of pre-existing distortionary taxes, it imposes costs over and above the revenue

[5] An alternative is to have a clean tax and a dirt tax with labour as the untaxed good. The implicit price of clean products then amounts to $(1 - t_L)^{-1}$ and the associated tax rate $t_L(1 - t_L)^{-1}$. The implicit price of dirty products equals $(1 + t_D)(1 - t_L)^{-1}$ and the implicit dirt tax rate is $(t_D + t_L)(1 - t_L)^{-1}$. See also Corlett and Hague (1953) and Diamond and Mirrlees (1971, p.263) for an analogous expression to (9′) and a related discussion.

collected by the government. Accordingly, the marginal cost of public funds exceeds unity. However, if taxed commodities are inferior, the marginal cost of funds may actually fall short of unity. The reason is that the negative income effect associated with a higher tax level may raise the consumption of taxed commodities. The indirect benefit of additional tax revenue from a broader revenue base causes the marginal cost of public funds to fall below unity.[6]

4. Pollution and labour taxation in a second-best world

This section again considers a second-best world in which lump-sum transfers are excluded (i.e. $T > 0$). In contrast to the previous section, however, environmental externalities are present in consumption (i.e. $u_E > 0$). Accordingly, labour and dirt taxes are employed not only to finance public spending but also to internalise environmental externalities. These externalities affect the Ramsey tax rules and the optimal provision of public goods.

4.1. Tax structure

In the presence of environmental externalities, Eq. (6) becomes

$$\lambda D - \mu\left[D + t_D \frac{\partial D}{\partial P_D} + \beta t_L \frac{\partial L}{\partial P_D}\right] - Nu'_E e_{ND} \frac{\partial D}{\partial P_D} = 0, \tag{12}$$

where u'_E denotes the marginal social utility of the environment:

$$u'_E \equiv \left(\frac{u_E + \mu\left[t_D \frac{\partial D}{\partial E} + \beta t_L \frac{\partial L}{\partial E}\right]}{1 - Ne_{ND} \frac{\partial D}{\partial E}} \right). \tag{13}$$

u'_E accounts not only for the direct impact of the environment on utility ($u_E > 0$), but also for the indirect effects of an improved environment on the tax base. Furthermore, if a better environmental quality raises the demand for dirty goods (i.e. $\partial D/\partial E > 0$), the net social utility of the environment is reduced (as $e_{ND} < 0$).

[6] The marginal cost of public funds is smaller than unity if, in the terminology of Atkinson and Stern (1974), the 'revenue effect' of a tax increase boosts the demand for tax commodities and is large enough to more than offset the 'distortionary effect' of tax increases. See also Ballard and Fullerton (1992).

Defining the non-distortionary (or externality-correcting) component of the optimal dirt tax, t_{DP}, as (using $\lambda = u_C$ and $\eta = \mu/\lambda$)

$$t_{DP} \equiv \left(\frac{-Ne_{ND}u'_E}{u_C}\right)\left(\frac{1}{\eta}\right) = \left(\frac{-Ne_{ND}}{1 - Ne_{ND}\dfrac{\partial D}{\partial E}}\right)\left(\frac{u_E}{\mu} + t_D\frac{\partial D}{\partial E} + \beta t_L\frac{\partial L}{\partial E}\right), \tag{14}$$

we can rewrite (12) as

$$\lambda D - \mu\left[D + (t_D - t_{DP})\frac{\partial D}{\partial P_D} + \beta t_L\frac{\partial L}{\partial P_D}\right] = 0. \tag{12'}$$

In the presence of externalities, Eq. (7) for the first-order condition for the optimal labour tax becomes

$$\lambda L - \mu\left[L - (t_D - t_{DP})\left(\frac{\partial D}{\partial P_L}\right) - \beta t_L\left(\frac{\partial L}{\partial P_L}\right)\right] = 0. \tag{15}$$

Comparing the conditions for the optimal tax structure without environmental externalities [i.e (6) and (7)] with those with externalities in consumption [i.e. (12) and (15)], one notices that the terms with the dirt tax t_D in (6) and (7) are replaced by terms with the dirt tax net of the non-distortionary tax term $(t_D - t_{DP})$ in (12) and (15). This latter term, which we call the Ramsey (or distortionary) component of the dirt tax, measures the social contribution (in terms of government revenues) of additional demand for dirty goods as the difference between a positive and a negative contribution. On the one hand, consumption of dirty private goods boosts the tax base and thus facilitates the financing of ordinary public goods. On the other hand, it damages the environment, thereby reducing the supply of the 'collective good' of the environment. It follows (from the same steps as in subsection 3.1) that the optimal dirt tax is the sum of the Ramsey and externality-correcting terms:[7]

[7] See Sandmo (1975). Ng (1980) explores the sign of the optimal dirt tax. He finds that, in the presence of environmental externalities (i.e. $u_E > 0$), the dirt tax is typically positive. However, if the revenue requirement is small and falls short of the revenues from the Pigovian tax, the optimal dirt tax may actually be negative. In this counterintuitive case, a lower consumption wage must be very effective in reducing dirty consumption, compared with a higher consumption price for dirty consumption. Hence, the combination of a wage tax and a subsidy on dirty consumption reduces pollution. Ng (1980) focuses on the sign of the optimal dirt tax but does not analyse its optimal magnitude. He assumes that public spending is exogenous and mostly deals with the case of a small revenue requirement.

$$\theta_D = \left(\frac{\varepsilon_{CL} - \varepsilon_{DL}}{\varepsilon_{CD} - \varepsilon_{DD}}\right)\theta_L + \theta_{DP}, \qquad \theta_{DP} \equiv \left(\frac{t_{DP}}{1 + t_D}\right), \tag{16}$$

which replaces (9′). Hence, even if the compensated elasticities of the demands for clean and dirty goods with respect to the price of leisure are identical (i.e. $\varepsilon_{CL} = \varepsilon_{DL}$), a zero dirt tax is not optimal. Although the Ramsey term (i.e. the first term on the right-hand side of (16)) is zero, a separate non-distortionary term corrects for the environmental externality, namely t_{DP}.

If the government has access to lump-sum instruments, expression (5) reveals that the optimal Pigovian tax measures the direct social damage of pollution in terms of the numeraire. In particular, the Pigovian tax [scaled by the environmental damage per unit of dirty private consumption, $(-e_{ND})$] amounts to the sum of the marginal rates of substitution between the public good of environmental quality and the clean commodity (i.e. the numeraire):

$$\left(\frac{t_{DP}}{-e_{ND}}\right) = \left(\frac{Nu_E}{u_C}\right). \tag{5′}$$

Comparing (5′) for the optimal Pigovian tax with expression (14) for the optimal non-distortionary component of the dirt tax in the presence of distortionary taxation, we notice that the two expressions coincide if two conditions are met. First, the marginal cost of public funds should be unity. Second, the direct impact of the environment on utility, u_E, should be the same as the overall impact, u'_E. This second condition is met if environmental quality is weakly separable from the other arguments in social utility.

If the marginal cost of funds exceeds unity ($\eta > 1$), the optimal non-distortionary component falls below the Pigovian tax (i.e. the marginal social damage of pollution as measured by the sum of the marginal rates of substitution between environmental quality and clean private consumption). The reason is that the optimal non-distortionary tax measures the social costs of pollution in terms of *public* rather than *private* income. In particular, the optimal environmental tax equates the social costs of pollution to the social benefit of the public goods that can be financed by the additional tax revenue generated by the pollution tax. This implies that each unit of pollution does not have to yield as much public revenue to offset the environmental damage if this revenue becomes more valuable as measured by a higher marginal cost of public funds. Intuitively, the government employs the tax system to simultaneously accomplish two objectives: first, to raise public revenues to finance public goods (other than the environment), and, second, to internalise pollution externalities, thereby protecting the public good of the natural environment. If public revenues become scarcer, as indicated by a higher marginal cost of public funds, the optimal tax system focuses more on generating revenues and less on internalising pollution externalities. In particular, the government can afford less tax differentiation aimed at environmental protection. Through this channel, ordinary public consumption competes with environmental quality as a high level of the cost of public funds reduces the demand not only for ordinary public consumption but also for the public good of the environment.[8]

In contrast to previous authors (e.g. Sandmo, 1975; Ng, 1980; and Auerbach, 1985), our definition of the non-distortionary dirt tax (14) incorporates a second factor that may cause the Pigovian tax to deviate from the sum of the marginal rates of substitution. In particular, the environmental quality may directly impact the consumption of taxed commodities. For example, if labour supply is taxed and an improved environment induces people to enjoy more leisure and work less (i.e. $\partial L/\partial E < 0$), the social value of environmental protection is reduced and the optimal environmental tax falls. In principle it is possible, albeit unlikely, that the Pigovian component of the dirt tax is negative, namely if tax rates are high and if a better environmental quality substantially reduces the demands for taxed goods.

The formula for the optimal labour tax in (10) is not affected by environmental externalities. This corresponds to the principle of targeting (e.g. Dixit, 1985), which states that a distortion is best addressed by the instrument that acts directly on the relevant margin. Hence, dirt taxes rather than labour taxes should deal with environmental externalities.

It is instructive to write the condition for the optimal dirt tax as the weighted sum of an externality-correction term and a revenue-raising term [using (10), (14) and (16)]:

$$\theta_D = (1 - \eta'^{-1})\left(\frac{(\varepsilon_{CL} - \varepsilon_{DL})(1 - \alpha_D)}{-\varepsilon_{DD}\varepsilon_{LL} + \varepsilon_{DL}\varepsilon_{LD}}\right) + \eta^{-1}\left(\frac{-Ne_{ND}u'_E}{(1 + t_D)u_C}\right). \tag{17}$$

The weight of the revenue-raising term [i.e. $(1 - \eta'^{-1})$] is positive if government revenue from non-dirt taxes is positive (as the Slutsky matrix is negative definite and $\eta' \equiv \mu/\lambda' > 1$). It rises with the scarcity of public funds (reflected in a high value for η'). The weight of the externality-correction term (i.e. η^{-1}), in contrast, falls with the marginal cost of public funds.[9] Hence, if public funds become scarcer, the revenue-raising term becomes more important relative to the externality-correction term. Intuitively, the

[8] Sections 7 and 8 provide a full general equilibrium analysis of the trade-offs between environmental quality and other public priorities.

[9] Typically, the weight given to the Pigovian term is less than one, but it may be greater than one if taxed goods are inferior.

tax structure focuses more on the revenue-raising rather than the environmental objective if government revenue becomes more 'expensive'.

In a command economy the marginal cost of public funds is unity ($\eta = 1$). In a market economy, in contrast, the marginal cost of public funds incorporates the costs of distortionary taxation. This may be seen upon solving Eq. (15) for the marginal cost of public funds:

$$\eta = \left(\frac{1}{1 - (\theta_D - \theta_{DP})\alpha_D \varepsilon^{U}_{DL} - \theta_L \varepsilon^{U}_{LL}} \right), \tag{18}$$

where we have defined $\varepsilon^{U}_{ik} \equiv (P_K/I)(\partial I/\partial P_K)$ as the uncompensated elasticity of demand for commodity i (I) with respect to the price of commodity k (K). The marginal cost of public funds exceeds unity if the financing of additional public spending erodes the base of existing Ramsey (or distortionary) taxes. This occurs if a positive labour tax coincides with an upward-sloping Marshallian labour supply curve ($\varepsilon^{U}_{LL} > 0$) or if the dirt tax exceeds the non-distortionary component ($\theta_D > \theta_{DP}$) and, at the same time, private demand for dirty goods falls as the tax on labour increases (i.e. $\varepsilon^{U}_{DL} > 0$).

4.2. Public consumption: Level and composition

The condition for the optimal provision of clean public goods (11) becomes

$$N\left(\frac{u_X}{u_C}\right) = \eta\left[1 - (t_D - t_{DP})N\left(\frac{\partial D}{\partial X}\right) - t_L N\beta\left(\frac{\partial L}{\partial X}\right)\right]. \tag{19}$$

Comparing (11) and (19), one notices that the dirt tax in (11) is again replaced by the Ramsey component of the dirt tax in (19). The reason is that only additional revenues from the distortionary (i.e. Ramsey) component of the dirt tax provide a net positive contribution to social welfare. The revenues from the non-distortionary (i.e. externality-correction) component of the dirt tax merely offset the environmental damage due to additional dirty consumption. To illustrate, if public highways are complementary to the consumption of taxed gasoline, the construction of highways boosts gasoline consumption. Whereas the additional consumption of gasoline boosts tax collections, it also pollutes the environment. The social cost of the environmental damage is measured by the additional revenue collected from the non-distortionary (i.e. externality-correction) component of the gasoline tax. Hence, only to the extent that the revenues from the Ramsey (distortionary) component of the gasoline tax rise, does the widening of the tax base yield a net social benefit, thereby reducing the social cost of financing highways.

The optimality condition for dirty public goods is

$$N\left(\frac{u_Y + u_E' e_Y}{u_C}\right) = \eta\left[1 - (t_D - t_{DP})N\left(\frac{\partial D}{\partial Y}\right) - t_L N\beta\left(\frac{\partial L}{\partial Y}\right)\right]. \tag{20}$$

Clearly, if public consumption pollutes the environment (i.e $e_Y < 0$), the direct marginal utility of public goods must be higher to compensate for the environmental damage caused by these public goods.

Note that, if public goods and the quality of the natural environment are weakly separable from the other arguments in $u(\cdot)$, the marginal rate of substitution between the environment and public consumption of clean commodities can, with the aid of (15) and (20), be written as

$$\frac{u_E}{u_X} = \left(\frac{u_Y - u_X}{u_X}\right)\left(\frac{1}{-e_Y}\right) = \left(\frac{t_{DP}}{-e_{ND}}\right). \tag{21}$$

The relative price of the environment in terms of clean public goods equals the dirt tax scaled by the damage done by dirty private goods to environmental quality. Clearly, the marginal utility of dirty public goods must exceed that of clean public goods (i.e. $u_Y > u_X$).

4.3. *Public abatement*

The government engages in abatement until the sum of the marginal rates of substitution between these activities and private consumption of clean goods equals the social cost of abatement activities:

$$N\left(\frac{u_E e_A}{u_C}\right) = \eta\left[1 - N\left((t_D - t_{DP})\frac{\partial D}{\partial E} + \beta t_L \frac{\partial L}{\partial E}\right)e_A\right]. \tag{22}$$

Using (14), we can rewrite (22) as

$$e_A = -(t_{DP}/e_{ND})^{-1}. \tag{22'}$$

The optimum level of abatement increases with the implicit price of the environment $-(t_D/e_{ND})$ and thus with the level of the dirt tax. This illustrates the principle that one should employ a mix of environmental policy instruments.

Substituting (22′) into (21) we find

$$u_X/u_E = e_A. \tag{21'}$$

The marginal rate of substitution between clean public consumption and environmental quality equals the marginal rate of transformation between public abatement and environmental quality (e_A). Unlike Eq. (19), (21′) features neither the marginal cost of public funds (η) nor the number of households (N). The reason is that both public consumption and public abatement are financed through distortionary taxation. Hence, the marginal cost of public funds affects the optimal demands for these public goods in similar ways.

5. Restrictions on preferences

5.1. The utility tree

To obtain more specific results, we put restrictions on preferences. In particular, we assume that the utility function of the representative consumer can be written in weakly separable form:

$$U = u(C,D,V,X,Y,E) = U(M(Q(C,D),V),G(X,Y),E). \tag{23}$$

We also assume that the utility function $U(\cdot)$ and the sub-utility functions $M(\cdot)$, $G(\cdot)$ and $Q(\cdot)$ are homothetic. Together with leisure, the basket of clean and dirty private goods (Q) determines the utility of marketable goods (M). Total utility of the representative consumer (U) is a function of the 'private' utility index M, the basket of clean and dirty public goods (G) and environmental quality (E).

The chosen structure of preferences implies strong restrictions on demand. In particular, the compensated elasticities ε_{CL} and ε_{DL} are identical. Accordingly, the Ramsey tax term in (16) is zero and the dirt tax reduces to the externality-correction term ($t_D = t_{DP}$). Moreover, neither private demand for dirty goods nor labour supply depends directly on public consumption or the quality of the environment. Hence, the social cost of public goods [i.e. the right-hand side of expressions (11), (19), (20) and (22)] reduces to the marginal cost of public funds (η). Furthermore, marginal social utility of the environment (u'_E) given in expression (13) boils down to the direct effect of environmental quality on utility (u_E).

We assume that the function describing the quality of the environment takes the following form:

$$E = e(ND,Y,A) \equiv E_0 - \delta_D ND - \delta_Y Y + e^{\mathrm{A}}(A),$$
$$\delta_D,\delta_Y,e'^{\mathrm{A}} \geq 0, e''^{\mathrm{A}} < 0, \tag{24}$$

where E_0 denotes the quality of the environment when it is neither spoilt by pollution nor improved through abatement, and δ_D (δ_Y) stands for the emission ratio for dirty private (public) consumption. There are decreasing returns to abatement activities.

5.2. The optimality conditions revisited

For the chosen structure of preferences, (13), (14) and (16) imply the following tax structure:

$$t_D = t_{DP} = \left(\frac{NU_E\delta_D}{u_C}\right)\left(\frac{1}{\eta}\right). \tag{25}$$

The optimal structure of public consumption follows from (19), (20) and (25):

$$\frac{G_X}{G_Y} = \frac{1}{1 + t_D(\delta_Y/\delta_D)}. \tag{26}$$

The marginal rate of substitution between clean and dirty public goods equals the ratio of the price of clean public goods (normalised to unity) to the social cost of dirty public goods. This latter cost consists of the production price (unity) plus a term that represents environmental costs.

From Eqs. (19), (20), (26) and $u_C = \lambda = U_M M_Q / P_Q$, where P_Q denotes the 'ideal' price index for the private consumption basket Q (i.e. $P_Q = [C + (1 + t_D)D]/Q$), one obtains the following expression for the trade-off between the optimal levels of public and private consumption:

$$\frac{NU_G}{U_M M_Q} = \eta\left(\frac{P_G}{P_Q}\right), \tag{27}$$

where P_G is the 'ideal' price index for the basket of public goods (i.e. $P_G = [X + (1 + t_D\delta_Y/\delta_D)Y]/G = 1/G_X$). Clearly, the sum of the marginal rates of substitution between public and private goods must equal the marginal cost of public funds (η) times the relative price of public goods in terms of private goods (P_G/P_Q).

Two elements cause the sum of the marginal rates of substitution to differ from the marginal rate of transformation in production. First, the relative price of public and private commodities (P_G/P_Q) depends not only on the relative costs in production but also on the relative social costs in terms of environmental damage. Second, the marginal cost of public funds (η) drives a wedge between the sum of the rates of substitution and the rate of transformation. It incorporates the costs of distortionary taxation and, in general, differs from unity. For the chosen structure of preferences, $\theta_D = \theta_{DP}$ so that the dirt tax does not affect the marginal cost of funds directly and (18) reduces to

$$\eta = \left(\frac{1}{1 - \theta_L \varepsilon_{LL}^{U}}\right). \tag{28}$$

In a decentralised market economy, distortionary taxes raise the marginal cost of public funds above unity if the financing of additional government spending erodes the base of existing distortionary taxes. This is the case if both the labour tax (t_L) and the uncompensated wage elasticity of labour supply (ε^{U}_{LL}) are positive. Note that Cobb–Douglas preferences imply inelastic labour supply so that the marginal cost of public funds is unity.

Combining (25) and (27), one obtains an expression for the trade-off between public consumption and environmental quality:

$$\frac{U_G}{U_E} = \left(\frac{P_G}{t_D/\delta_D}\right). \tag{29}$$

The marginal rate of substitution between public consumption and environmental quality must equal the ratio of the price of public goods to the price for dirty private environmental quality (i.e. the dirt tax scaled by the dirt-emission rate for consumption). As both public consumption and the environment are public goods, the marginal cost of public funds (η) does not enter (29).

6. Log-linearisation

In this section we start to log-linearise the model around its initial equilibrium in order to examine the comparative statics of optimal tax equilibria. This section derives the trade-offs the government faces between the three components of social utility, namely private welfare (M), public consumption (G), and environmental quality (E). These trade-offs follow from private behavior (Subsection 6.1), the government budget constraint (or the resource constraint) (Subsection 6.2), and ecological relationships (Subsection 6.3). Section 7 uses these trade-offs to characterise optimal government policy. Sections 8 and 9 examine how government policy should respond to a higher social priority for, respectively, environmental quality and public consumption. Logarithmic deviations from the initial equilibrium values are denoted by a tilde. The changes from initial equilibrium values for the tax rates t_i are normalised by P_i, and also denoted by a tilde, i.e. $\tilde{t}_i$, $i = D,L$.

6.1. Private behaviour

Table 2, part (a) contains the compensated elasticities associated with the Hicksian demand functions. Note that clean and dirty goods are Hicksian substitutes for a given sub-utility level Q. However, for a given utility level M (or U), clean and dirty goods may be Hicksian complements (if σ_M is large relative to σ_Q) as an increase in the price of dirty products induces

Table 2

(a) Compensated demand elasticities (ϵ_{ij})

	$\tilde{P}_C$	$\tilde{P}_D = \tilde{t}_D$	$\tilde{P}_L = -\hat{t}_L$	$\tilde{M}$
$\tilde{Q}$	$-\sigma_M\alpha_V(1-\alpha_D)$	$-\sigma_M\alpha_V\alpha_D$	$\sigma_M\alpha_V$	1
$\tilde{V}$	$\sigma_M(1-\alpha_V)(1-\alpha_D)$	$\sigma_M(1-\alpha_V)\alpha_D$	$-\sigma_M(1-\alpha_V)$	1
$\tilde{L}$	$-\sigma_M\alpha_V(1-\alpha_D)$	$-\sigma_M\alpha_V\alpha_D$	$\sigma_M\alpha_V$	$-\alpha_V/(1-\alpha_V)$
$\tilde{C}$	$-\alpha_D(\sigma_Q-\sigma_M\alpha_V)-\sigma_M\alpha_V$	$\alpha_D(\sigma_Q-\sigma_M\alpha_V)$	$\alpha_M\alpha_V$	1
$\tilde{D}$	$(1-\alpha_D)(\sigma_Q-\sigma_M\alpha_V)$	$\alpha_D(\sigma_Q-\sigma_M\alpha_V)-\sigma_Q$	$\sigma_M\alpha_V$	1

(b) Uncompensated demand elasticities (ϵ_{ij}^{U})

	$\tilde{P}_C$	$\tilde{P}_D = \tilde{t}_D$	$\tilde{P}_L = -\tilde{t}_L$	$\tilde{T}$
$\tilde{M}$	$-(1-\alpha_D)(1-\alpha_V)$	$-\alpha_D(1-\alpha_V)$	$1-\alpha_V$	$1-\alpha_V$
$\tilde{Q}$	$-(1-\alpha_D)[(\sigma_M-1)\alpha_V+1]$	$-\alpha_D[(\sigma_M-1)\alpha_V+1]$	$(\sigma_M-1)\alpha_V+1$	$1-\alpha_V$
$\tilde{V}$	$(1-\alpha_D)(\sigma_M-1)(1-\alpha_V)$	$\alpha_D(\sigma_M-1)(1-\alpha_V)$	$(1-\sigma_M)(1-\alpha_V)$	$1-\alpha_V$
$\tilde{L}$	$(1-\alpha_D)(1-\sigma_M)\alpha_V$	$\alpha_D(1-\sigma_M)\alpha_V$	$(\sigma_M-1)\alpha_V$	$-\alpha_V$
$\tilde{C}$	$-\alpha_D\sigma_Q-(1-\alpha_D)[(\sigma_M-1)\alpha_V+1]$	$\alpha_D[\sigma_Q-(\sigma_M-1)\alpha_V-1]$	$(\sigma_M-1)\alpha_V+1$	$1-\alpha_V$
$\tilde{D}$	$(1-\alpha_D)[\sigma_Q-(\sigma_M-1)\alpha_V-1]$	$-(1-\alpha_D)\sigma_Q-\alpha_D[(\sigma_M-1)\alpha_V+1]$	$(\sigma_M-1)\alpha_V+1$	$1-\alpha_V$

Note: The entries in Tables 2 parts (a) and (b) give the elasticities of the row variables with respect to the column variables. The final column of Table 2, part (b) gives semi-elasticities with respect to changes in $T/P_L L$. See Table 1 for an explanation of the symbols.

substitution away from clean (and dirty) products towards leisure. Both clean and dirty products are Hicksian substitutes for leisure. The ideal price indices are given by

$$\tilde{P}_Q = (1 - \alpha_D)\tilde{P}_C + \alpha_D \tilde{P}_D, \tag{30}$$

$$\begin{aligned}\tilde{P}_M &= (1 - \alpha_V)\tilde{P}_Q + \alpha_V \tilde{P}_L \\ &= (1 - \alpha_V)[(1 - \alpha_D)\tilde{P}_C + \alpha_D \tilde{P}_D] + \alpha_V \tilde{P}_L.\end{aligned} \tag{31}$$

Where $\alpha_V \equiv M_V/M$ denotes the budget share of leisure in marketable goods. Table 2, part (b) reveals that utility of marketable goods ($\tilde{M}$) rises if lump-sum transfers or the real consumption wage increase. Substitution of $\tilde{M}$ from Table 2, part (a) yields the Marshallian demand functions and the uncompensated demand elasticities reported in Table 2, part (b). For example, the uncompensated elasticity of the Marshallian demand for leisure with respect to the consumption wage (P_L) is given by $\varepsilon^{U}_{VL} \equiv (1 - \alpha_V)(1 - \sigma_M)$ and exceeds the compensated elasticity $\varepsilon_{VL} < 0$. An increase in the consumption wage has two effects on labour supply: first, substitution away from leisure towards clean and dirty commodities, thereby raising labour supply (measured by $\varepsilon_{LL} = \sigma_M \alpha_V > 0$); second, a boost in real income, which raises consumption of leisure, thereby reducing labour supply (measured by the term $-\alpha_V$). The substitution effect dominates the income effect if the elasticity of substitution between leisure and Q, i.e. σ_M, exceeds unity. Similarly, the uncompensated elasticity of the demand for clean products with respect to the price of dirty products (ε^{U}_{CD}) depends crucially on the relative magnitudes of the substitution elasticities σ_Q and σ_M. Clean and dirty private goods are likely to be gross substitutes (complements) when the elasticity of substitution between clean and dirty products is large (small) and the substitution elasticity between private goods and leisure is small (large).

6.2. Equilibrium and the government budget constraint

The log-linearised version of the material balance condition for the economy is given by [cf. Eq. (1)]

$$\omega_C \tilde{C} + \omega_D \tilde{D} + \omega_X \tilde{X} + \omega_Y \tilde{Y} + \omega_A \tilde{A} = \tilde{L}, \tag{32}$$

where $\omega_i \equiv I/\beta L$, $i = C,D$, and $\omega_j \equiv J/\beta NL$, $j = X,Y,A$. Substituting the uncompensated demand functions from Table 2, part (b), one finds (see the appendix):

$$\omega_X \tilde{X} + \omega_Y \tilde{Y} + \omega_A \tilde{A} = \Delta(\tilde{t}_L + \alpha_D \tilde{t}_D) - (1 - t_L)\theta_D \alpha_D (1 - \alpha_D)\sigma_Q \tilde{t}_D, \tag{33}$$

where $\omega_G \equiv \omega_X + \omega_Y + \omega_A = 1 - \omega_C - \omega_D = t_L + (1 - t_L)\theta_D\alpha_D$ denotes the national income share of public spending and $\Delta \equiv 1 - \omega_G(1 + \varepsilon^{U}_{LL})$. In view of Walras' law, (33) can also be viewed as the reduced-form government budget constraint. Public spending must be financed from labour and dirt tax revenues. Eq. (33) allows for the erosion of tax bases as tax rates rise. To illustrate, an increase in the labour tax rate increases revenues less than proportionally if the uncompensated wage elasticity of labour supply (ε^{U}_{LL}) exceeds zero. In that case, an increase in the labour tax induces people to work less, thereby eroding the base of the labour and dirt taxes. An increase in the dirt tax rate has an additional adverse effect on the tax base. It encourages consumers to shift from dirty to clean products, thereby eroding the base of the dirt tax.

Table 2, part (b) shows that private utility, $\tilde{M} = \alpha_V\tilde{V} + (1 - \alpha_V)\tilde{Q}$, may be written as a decreasing function of both the tax on labour and the dirt tax:

$$\tilde{M} = -(1 - \alpha_V)(\tilde{t}_L + \alpha_D\tilde{t}_D). \tag{34}$$

Using (33) and $\tilde{G} = \alpha_Y\tilde{Y} + (1 - \alpha_Y)\tilde{X}$ (where $\alpha_Y \equiv G_Y Y/G$ denotes the (shadow) budget share of dirty goods in public consumption), we can decompose the effect on private utility as follows (see the appendix):

$$\tilde{M} = -(1 - \alpha_V)\Delta^{-1}[(\omega_X + \omega_Y)\tilde{G} + \omega_A\tilde{A} + \rho_G(\tilde{X} - \tilde{Y}) + \rho_Q\sigma_Q\tilde{t}_D], \tag{35}$$

where

$$\rho_G \equiv (\omega_X + \omega_Y)\left(\frac{\theta_Y\alpha_Y}{1 - \theta_Y\alpha_Y}\right)(1 - \alpha_Y), \tag{36}$$

$$\rho_Q \equiv (\omega_C + \omega_D)\left(\frac{\theta_D\alpha_D}{1 - \theta_D\alpha_D}\right)(1 - \alpha_D), \tag{37}$$

where $\theta_Y \equiv (\delta_Y/\delta_D)t_D/[1 + (\delta_Y/\delta_D)t_D]$. Expression (35) reveals how the resource constraint implies trade-offs between private ('blue') welfare, utility from public consumption ('red' welfare), and the three instruments of environmental policy, namely the dirt tax, public abatement, and the composition of public consumption. In particular, a higher level of blue welfare requires either a lower level of red welfare [the first term in square brackets on the right-hand side of (35)] or a less ambitious environmental policy.

As far as environmental policy is concerned, the costs of public abatement are represented by the second term in square brackets. The third term in square brackets [i.e. $\rho_G(\tilde{X} - \tilde{Y})$] stands for the costs of a cleaner composition of public consumption. A cleaner composition of public consumption requires higher tax rates to achieve the same level of red welfare because, per unit of revenue raised, dirty public consumption yields more red welfare than does clean public consumption. Accordingly, cleaner public consumption, for a given level of red welfare, requires a higher tax level and thus lower private welfare.

The last term in square brackets (i.e. $\rho_Q \sigma_Q \tilde{t}_D$) corresponds to the costs that are associated with the shift toward a cleaner composition of private consumption on account of a higher dirt tax. Intuitively, compared with the broad-based labour tax, the dirt tax is a less effective instrument for raising public revenue because it affects the composition of consumption. Indeed, abstracting from environmental benefits, the dirt tax imposes a higher excess burden. Hence, a higher dirt tax depresses the level of private utility for a given level of public revenues and red welfare.

6.3. Environmental quality

Environmental quality depends on a number of effects (see the appendix):

$$\tilde{E} = \left(\frac{1}{\alpha_E(1-\theta_D\alpha_D)}\right)\left[-\theta_D\alpha_D\tilde{L} + \omega_A\tilde{A} + \rho_G(\tilde{X}-\tilde{Y}) + \rho_Q\sigma_Q\tilde{t}_D + \left(\frac{(\theta_D\alpha_D-\theta_Y\alpha_Y)(\omega_X+\omega_Y)}{1-\theta_Y\alpha_Y}\right)\tilde{G}\right], \qquad (38)$$

where from Table 2, part (b)

$$\tilde{L} = \alpha_V(1-\alpha_V)^{-1}(\sigma_M - 1)\tilde{M} \qquad (39)$$

and $\alpha_E \equiv (t_D/\delta_D)E/(N\beta L)$ represents the ratio of the value of the environment to national income. The first term in the square brackets in (38) shows that a shift to (clean) leisure improves environmental quality. This shift corresponds to a lower *level* of economic activity. The other three terms stand for changes in the *composition* of economic activity. In particular, the second term denotes an increase in public abatement. The third and fourth terms reflect a shift from dirty to clean commodities in public and private consumption. The last term stands for a different distribution of activity over the public and private sectors. If public consumption is cleaner than private consumption (i.e. $\theta_Y\alpha_Y < \theta_D\alpha_D$), a higher level of public consumption benefits the environment.

7. Optimal government policy revisited

To obtain explicit results about the way in which public policy should respond to a change in political preferences, marketable goods, public consumption, and the environment are assumed to be perfect substitutes in social utility. Hence, social utility can be written as $U = \Gamma_G G + \Gamma_E E + \Gamma_M M$.[10] Imperfect substitution would mitigate the allocational effects of a change in political preferences on M, E, and G. Furthermore, we assume that in the initial equilibrium public and private consumption are equally dirty (i.e. $\theta_Y \alpha_Y = \theta_D \alpha_D$). Hence, the fifth term in the square brackets of (38) drops out.

7.1. Environmental policy

The optimal trade-off between public consumption and environmental quality is given by expression (29). Substituting $\tilde{P}_G = (\theta_Y/\theta_D)\alpha_Y \tilde{t}_D$ into the log-linearised version of (29) yields

$$\tilde{t}_D/\theta_D = (\tilde{\Gamma}_E - \tilde{\Gamma}_G)/(1 - \theta_Y \alpha_Y). \tag{40}$$

If consumption pollutes the environment (i.e. $\theta_Y \alpha_Y > 0$), the relative increase in the dirt tax ($\tilde{t}_D/\theta_D$) exceeds the relative increase in environmental concern ($\tilde{\Gamma}_E - \tilde{\Gamma}_G$). Intuitively, more environmental concern requires an increase in the price of the environment (i.e. the dirt tax) relative to the price of public consumption. If public consumption damages the environment, a higher dirt tax raises not only the price of the environment but also the shadow price of public goods, thereby offsetting some of the effect of the higher dirt tax on the relative price of the environment to public consumption. Hence, the dirt tax has to rise more to accomplish the required increase in the relative price of the environment.

7.2. Composition of private and public spending

The solution for the dirt tax determines the optimal mix of dirty and clean public goods [i.e. log-linearise (26)]:

$$\tilde{X} - \tilde{Y} = \sigma_G(\theta_Y/\theta_D)\tilde{t}_D. \tag{41}$$

[10] This function may also be interpreted as a complex interest function in which the weights Γ_i, $i = G,E,M$, represent the bargaining strength of various social pressure groups. The solution to optimising this interest function also corresponds to an outcome of an electoral competition model (e.g. Drissen and van Winden, 1992).

It also determines the composition of public and private consumption from Table 2 and optimal abatement from (22′):

$$\tilde{C} - \tilde{D} = \sigma_Q \tilde{t}_D, \tag{42}$$

$$\tilde{A} = \left(\frac{\tilde{t}_D}{\sigma_A \theta_D}\right), \qquad \sigma_A \equiv \left(\frac{-e^{A\prime\prime}A}{e^{A\prime}}\right) > 0, \tag{43}$$

where σ_A denotes the elasticity of productivity of public abatement. The increase in environmental concern $(\tilde{\Gamma}_E - \tilde{\Gamma}_G)$ pushes up the shadow price of the environment (t_D), which changes the composition of public and private consumption toward clean commodities and raises public abatement. The possibilities for substitution, as reflected by the elasticities σ_G and σ_Q, determine the magnitude of the change in the composition of the consumption baskets. The rise in public abatement is inversely related to the concavity of the abatement function $e^A(\cdot)$.

7.3. Cost of public funds: Tax level and tax composition effects

Expression (27) determines the trade-off between public and private consumption. It can be written as

$$\left(\frac{N\Gamma_G}{\Gamma_M}\right)\left(\frac{P_Q}{P_G}\right) = M_Q \eta. \tag{44}$$

The dirt tax does not affect the price ratio P_Q/P_G if private and public consumption are equally dirty $(\theta_D \alpha_D = \theta_Y \alpha_Y)$. Accordingly, the left-hand side of (44) is fixed as public and private consumption (G and M) are perfect substitutes. The right-hand side corresponds to the marginal cost of public funds in terms of private utility (M). The log-linearised version of (44) is (see the appendix)

$$\begin{aligned}\tilde{\Gamma}_G &= \tilde{M}_Q + \tilde{\eta} \\ &= -\left(\frac{\alpha_V}{1 - t_L(1 - \alpha_V + \sigma_M \alpha_V)}\right)\left[(\sigma_M - 1)\alpha_D \tilde{t}_D + \left(\frac{\sigma_M \kappa}{1 - \alpha_V}\right)\tilde{M}\right] = 0.\end{aligned} \tag{45}$$

where

$$\kappa \equiv 1 - t_L[1 - (1 - \alpha_V)(\sigma_M - 1)]. \tag{46}$$

The first term in the square brackets on the right-hand side of (45) stands for the effect on the cost of public funds of substituting a non-distortionary (dirt) tax for a distortionary (labour) tax, while keeping private welfare constant. This change in the tax structure towards non-distortionary taxation cuts the cost of public funds if the elasticity of substitution between private consumption commodities and leisure exceeds unity ($\sigma_M > 1$) and the uncompensated wage elasticity of labour supply is thus positive ($\varepsilon_{LL}^{U} = \alpha_V(\sigma_M - 1) > 0$). Indeed, expression (28) reveals that lower distortionary labour taxation reduces the cost of public funds if and only if the uncompensated wage elasticity of labour supply is positive. Intuitively, public goods become easier to finance and the marginal cost of public funds declines if dirt taxes aimed at internalising externalities rather than distortionary taxes are employed. The impact of moving from distortionary to non-distortionary taxes is called the 'tax *composition*' effect because it involves a change in the composition of taxation without affecting the level of private utility and thus the overall tax level [i.e. $\tilde{M} = \tilde{t}_L + \alpha_D \tilde{t}_D = 0$, see (34)].

The second term in the square brackets on the right-hand side of (45) is the 'tax *level*' effect. It involves a fall in private welfare on account of an increase in the overall burden of taxation (i.e. $\tilde{M} < 0$, $\tilde{t}_L + \alpha_D \tilde{t}_D > 0$). The overall burden of taxation measures the costs (in terms of private welfare) of the 'social' sector, which includes not only ordinary public consumption (corresponding to 'red' welfare) but also the public good of environmental quality (corresponding to 'green' welfare). In particular, given the utility of public consumption (i.e. 'red' welfare), environmental policy aimed at 'greening' the composition of economic activity[11] raises the burden of taxation for three reasons [see expression (35)]: first, to finance public abatement activities; second, to pay for a cleaner (but also more expensive) composition of public consumption; and third, to offset the erosion of the tax base due to the change towards a cleaner private consumption basket induced by the dirt tax. These three factors that raise the overall tax burden are thus associated with the three instruments of environmental policy: public abatement, the composition of public consumption, and the dirt tax. Given the level of red welfare (i.e. $\tilde{G} = 0$), two of these environmental policy instruments raise the level of public spending, namely public abatement and the composition of public consumption. In the case of the dirt tax, the private sector rather than the public sector undertakes the activities aimed at improving environmental quality. Hence, the costs associated with a cleaner environment do not appear on the government budget in the form of public spending but are 'hidden' in a higher 'excess burden' per additional unit of public revenue raised. This additional excess burden corresponds to the costs the private sector incurs in changing the composition of its consumption basket for the benefit of the public good of the environment.

[11] Indeed, the tax *level* effect involves a different *composition* of economic activity (i.e. greener and redder). The tax *composition* effect, in contrast, involves the *level* of economic activity. See below.

Indeed, the public good of the environment is provided through activities in the private rather than the public sector.

Expression (45) reveals that a decline in private welfare, which is associated with a higher tax burden reflecting the costs associated with a larger social sector, raises the costs of public funds (in terms of private utility) as long as substitution between leisure and private goods is possible (i.e. $\sigma_M > 0$). Intuitively, the higher overall tax level reduces the marginal benefits from working, thereby exacerbating the distortionary effects of labour taxes.

The sign of the 'tax composition effect' is ambiguous and depends on the relative magnitude of income versus substitution effects. In particular, moving toward non-distortionary dirt taxation reduces the cost of public funds only if the substitution effect of a higher after-tax wage is sufficiently large relative to the income effect (i.e. $\sigma_M > 1$). The sign of the 'tax level' effect, in contrast, is unambiguous; given that κ is assumed to be positive[12], a rise in the tax level always raises the cost of public funds because only substitution effects determine the 'tax level' effect. Intuitively, a 'tax level' effect imposes a first-order loss in private utility, thereby raising marginal private utility from private consumption goods (M_Q). Hence, the income effects of a higher tax level on the costs of public funds in terms of private utility ηM_Q [i.e. the right-hand side of (44)] cancel out. On the one hand, adverse income effects associated with a higher tax level reduce the cost of public funds in terms of private consumption (η) by reducing the demand for leisure and thus raising taxed labour supply. On the other hand, these income effects increase the cost of public funds in terms of private utility by reducing private utility (M) thus raising the marginal private utility from private goods (M_Q).

8. Shift towards greener preferences

This section explores the consequences of a larger weight of environmental quality in social utility (higher Γ_E). This shift towards more environmental concern may be interpreted as a bigger influence (or bargaining strength) of green political parties in the political process. For example, if households feature identical sub-utility functions for private utility and public consumption but differ in their valuation of environmental quality, we may interpret this shock as a shift towards greener preferences for the median voter. Alternatively, this shock can be interpreted as the discovery that environmental problems cause more serious damage than previously thought. Table 3 contains the detailed impact of the shift towards greener preferences

[12] This will be the case if $t_L < 1/2$ or $\alpha_V = 1$ or $\sigma_M > 1$.

Table 3
Shift towards greener preferences

	Higher priority for environmental quality ($\tilde{\Gamma}_E > 0$)
$\tilde{t}_D$	$(1-\theta_D\alpha_D)^{-1}\theta_D > 0$
$\tilde{t}_L$	$-(1-\theta_D\alpha_D)^{-1}\theta_D\alpha_D\sigma_M^{-1}\kappa^{-1}\{1-\sigma_M t_L[1-(1-\alpha_V)(\sigma_M-1)]\} < 0$
$\tilde{A}$	$(1-\theta_D\alpha_D)^{-1}\sigma_A^{-1} > 0$
$\tilde{G}$	$(1-\theta_D\alpha_D)^{-1}\theta_D[\alpha_D\,\Delta\kappa^{-1}\sigma_M^{-1}(\sigma_M-1)-\rho](\omega_X+\omega_Y)^{-1}$
$\tilde{X}-\tilde{Y}$	$(1-\theta_D\alpha_D)^{-1}\theta_D\sigma_G > 0$
$\tilde{M}$	$(1-\theta_D\alpha_D)^{-1}\theta_D\alpha_D\kappa^{-1}\sigma_M^{-1}(1-\sigma_M)(1-\alpha_V) < 0$, if $\sigma_M > 1$
$\tilde{C}-\tilde{D}$	$(1-\theta_D\alpha_D)^{-1}\theta_D\sigma_Q > 0$
$\tilde{E}$	$(1-\theta_D\alpha_D)^{-1}\theta_D[\theta_D\alpha_D^2\kappa^{-1}\sigma_M^{-1}(\sigma_M-1)^2\alpha_V+\rho][\alpha_E(1-\theta_D\alpha_D)]^{-1} > 0$
$\tilde{L}$	$-(1-\theta_D\alpha_D)^{-1}\theta_D\alpha_D\kappa^{-1}\sigma_M^{-1}(\sigma_M-1)^2\alpha_V \leq 0$

for public finances, environmental policy, the three components of social welfare, and employment.

8.1. Labour tax and employment: The double dividend hypothesis

Upon elimination of $\tilde{M}$ in (45) by using (34), we obtain an inverse relationship between the tax on labour and the dirt tax (see the appendix). Hence, a rise in environmental concern, which is accompanied by a higher dirt tax, reduces the tax on labour. Conventional wisdom about environmental concern causing a shift away from labour taxation is thus correct.

Although the (explicit) tax on labour falls, employment does not rise (see Table 3). In fact, labour supply typically falls. If the (uncompensated) wage elasticity of labour supply is positive, the change in the tax structure away from distortionary to pollution taxation reduces the marginal cost of public funds, thereby expanding the size of the social sector at the expense of private welfare and thus the consumption wage. With upward-sloping labour supply, the lower wage depresses the supply of labour and hence employment. If the wage elasticity is negative, the change in the tax structure away from distortionary taxation *raises* rather than *reduces* the cost of public funds. Hence, the social sector contracts while private welfare expands. As the labour supply curve bends backwards, the associated higher consumption wage reduces labour supply. Accordingly, employment declines not only with an upward-sloping but also with a backward-bending labour supply curve. Only if labour supply is completely inelastic (i.e. $\sigma_M = 1$), does employment remain constant. Hence, the popular version of the 'double dividend' argument—increased environmental concern raises employment—fails. Intuitively, a reallocation from labour to leisure benefits the environment; the consumption of leisure does not pollute while employment indirectly harms the environment because part of labour income is spent on dirty goods.

Proposition 1. A higher political preference for a cleaner environment raises the dirt tax and reduces the labour tax. The higher dirt tax yields a cleaner composition of private and public consumption baskets and a higher level of public abatement. Despite a lower labour tax, employment falls unless labour supply is completely inelastic.

8.2. Public consumption: Are red and green policies compatible?

Public consumption is affected through two main channels. The first term in square brackets in the expression for public consumption in Table 3 stands for the 'tax composition' effect. This effect may make green and red preferences 'compatible', by which we mean that public consumption and environmental quality move together if there is a shift towards greener preferences (higher Γ_E). In particular, substituting dirt for labour taxes reduces the marginal cost of public funds if existing distortionary taxes imply a marginal cost of public funds (η) greater than unity, i.e. if the substitution effect of lower labour taxation dominates the income effect ($\sigma_M > 1$) [see expression (28)]. Intuitively, the shift away from distortionary taxation reduces the cost of financing public consumption.

The second term in square brackets in the expression for public consumption in Table 3 represents the 'tax level' effect. It implies a negative link between public consumption and environmental concern and reflects the expansion of the social sector due to a more ambitious environmental policy. The costs associated with a cleaner ('greener') composition of economic activity exacerbate the deadweight losses associated with distortionary taxation, thereby raising the cost of public funds and reducing public consumption. Hence, a higher priority for one public good, environmental quality, crowds out other public priorities, such as public consumption.

The overall effect of greener preferences on public consumption depends on the balance between the 'tax composition' and the 'tax level' effects. In particular, environmental quality and public consumption move together, and red and green preferences are thus compatible, only if the 'tax level' effect is small compared with the 'tax composition' effect. The 'tax level' effect is small if dirt taxes constitute a small part of the price of dirty goods (i.e. θ_D small) and, at the same time, the substitution elasticity between dirty and clean goods (σ_Q) is small [see expressions (45), (35) and (37)]. In that case, changes in the composition of the private consumption basket are not only small (because σ_Q is small) but also cheap (because of the small tax rate). The 'tax composition' effect gains in importance if substitution between leisure and private consumption goods is strong (i.e. if σ_M is large) and hence labour taxes are especially distortionary [see expression (45)]. Accordingly, the 'tax composition' effect is large relative to the 'tax level' effect if substitution between leisure and private commodities is easy compared with substitution between clean and dirty private commodities. Green and red preferences are thus compatible if dirty and clean private goods are complements. In that case, the tax on labour and the dirt tax yield similar effects. In particular, a labour tax is a good instrument to improve the environment as it reduces private consumption of dirty commodities by raising the consumption of clean leisure. Furthermore, by reducing the real after-tax wage, a dirt tax acts like a labour tax because it leaves the composition of private consumption largely unaffected if the substitution elasticity between clean and dirty goods is small. Hence, a dirt tax is a rather efficient instrument to fund public consumption.

Red and green political preferences can be compatible only if the substitution elasticity between leisure and private commodities (σ_M) is large. Table 3 reveals that in that case labour supply declines substantially. The intuition is that a fall in employment (i.e. more 'inactivity') is socially undesirable only if it is due to a distortionary tax on labour. Social welfare is enhanced, however, if employment declines on account of a dirt tax reflecting the social cost of environmental degradation. Indeed, increased environmental concern should make work less attractive, because part of labour income is spent on dirty goods. This may in fact be consistent with green parties advocating a reduction in the length of the working week.

Accordingly, red and green can be compatible only if most of the improvement in environmental quality is accomplished through a lower level of economic activity and employment. Hence, a tension emerges between the desire to increase the participation (of women) in the labour force while at the same time maintaining public consumption and improving environmental quality. The objectives of enhancing environmental quality and raising labour participation do not conflict only if the substitution elasticity between leisure and private commodities is close to unity ($\sigma_M \approx 1$) while substitution elasticities between clean and dirty goods in private and public consumption (σ_Q and σ_G) are large and the effectiveness of abatement actitivities in cleaning up the environment does not decline rapidly. In that case, the tax *level* effect dominates the tax *composition* effect and the improvement in environmental quality is accomplished primarily through a cleaner *composition* of economic activity rather than a lower *level* of that activity. This implies that activity and employment are not discouraged. Hence, the disincentive effects of high tax levels are undesirable and public consumption therefore becomes *more* rather than *less* expensive.

Proposition 2. Public consumption rises with a higher political preference for a cleaner environment (a 'social' double dividend) if and only if the uncompensated wage elasticity of labour supply is large and positive (i.e. σ_M is much greater than one) and, at the same time, clean and dirty commodities *are poor substitutes (i.e. σ_G and σ_Q small) and the effectiveness of public abatement declines rapidly (i.e. σ_A large). Most of the improvement in environmental quality is then achieved through a lower level of activity rather than a cleaner composition of that activity.*

8.3. Economic costs of an explicit green target

This subsection explores what the best policy instruments are to achieve a particular absolute green target for the quality of the environment, say $E = E^*$. It also examines the welfare costs of such a target. A green target implies an improvement in environmental quality and, if the economy was at an optimum before the green target was set, must reduce either utility from public consumption or private welfare or both.

8.3.1. Cleaner economic activity: Choice of instruments

If the income and substitution effects of wages on labour supply offset each other (i.e. $\sigma_M = 1$), the environment is improved by changing the composition rather than the level of economic activity. The higher implicit tax level associated with cleaner economic activity raises the marginal cost of public funds, thereby crowding out conventional public consumption. Private utility, labour supply and the level of economic activity are not affected in this special case.

Three environmental policy instruments can be employed to render economic activity more friendly to the environment, namely public abatement, cleaner public consumption, and a dirt tax aimed at cleaner private consumption. Abatement makes a major contribution to a cleaner environment if the productivity of abatement is not very sensitive to the level of abatement (i.e. σ_A is small). Cleaner public consumption is important if substitution between clean and dirty goods in public consumption is easy (i.e. σ_G is large). The dirt tax plays a large role if economic activity is dirty [i.e. $\theta_Y \alpha_Y = \theta_D \alpha_D$ large; see (40)], substitution between the two public goods is difficult, and the productivity of abatement diminishes rapidly with the level of abatement (σ_A large). In that case, most of the improvement in environmental quality must be accomplished by changing the composition of private consumption. This change may be brought about by a dirt tax or, perhaps more naturally, by auctioning off tradable polluton permits. In the latter case, the price that the government will fetch for a permit equals the dirt tax.

8.3.2. Change in the level of economic activity

Economic activity cannot become cleaner if substitution in private and public consumption is not possible ($\sigma_G = \sigma_Q = 0$) and the optimal level of abatement is constant (i.e. $\sigma_A \rightarrow \infty$). In this special case, environmental quality is enhanced only through a reduction in the level of economic activity and employment. If income effects dominate substitution effects ($\sigma_M < 1$), the public sector pays for the cleaner environment. The associated lower tax level increases private utility, thereby raising the demand for (clean) leisure. Accordingly, large private incomes due to a small public sector benefit the environment. In this case, there is a 'double dividend' in that both environmental quality and private utility increase while public consumption falls. Since private welfare and environmental quality move together (if $\sigma_M < 1$), we can say that green and blue preferences are compatible.

However, if substitution between leisure and private commodities is easy and the uncompensated wage elasticity of labour supply is thus positive (σ_M exceeds unity), the environment crowds out private utility and crowds in public consumption. In that case, a higher tax level encourages substitution towards clean leisure. Hence, a large public sector accompanied by a high tax level benefits the environment. In this case, green and red political preferences are compatible. This scenario amounts to a more social type of 'double dividend'.

Proposition 3. If labour supply bends backwards ($\sigma_M < 1$), a cleaner environment boosts private welfare and crowds out public consumption. Hence, a double dividend of a cleaner environment and higher private welfare emerges (i.e. blue and green political preferences are compatible). However, if labour supply slopes upwards ($\sigma_M > 1$), a cleaner environment crowds out private welfare. If labour supply is inelastic ($\sigma_M = 1$), environmental quality is enhanced entirely through a cleaner composition rather than a lower level of activity. Public consumption bears all costs associated with the cleaner composition of activity while private welfare is unaffected.

9. A shift towards redder preferences

This section investigates the implications of a higher social priority for public consumption, i.e. a shift towards redder political preferences ($\tilde{\Gamma}_G >$ 0). The effects are summarised in Table 4.

9.1. Tax structure and employment

Eq. (40) shows that the dirt tax falls. This seems counter-intuitive because a rise in public consumption requires higher tax rates. However, labour rather than dirt taxes rise to finance higher public spending. A higher priority for public consumption implies that society is willing to pay a higher

Table 4
Shift towards redder preferences

	Higher priority for public consumption ($\tilde{\Gamma}_G > 0$)
$\tilde{t}_D$	$-(1-\theta_D\alpha_D)^{-1}\theta_D < 0$
$\tilde{t}_L$	$(1-\theta_D\alpha_D)^{-1}[\Delta\kappa^{-1}\sigma_M^{-1}\alpha_V^{-1} + \theta_D\alpha_D] > 0$
$\tilde{t}_D + \tilde{t}_L$	$(1-\theta_D\alpha_D)^{-1}[\Delta\kappa^{-1}\sigma_M^{-1}\alpha_V^{-1} - (1-\alpha_D)\theta_D]$
$\tilde{A}$	$-(1-\theta_D\alpha_D)^{-1}\sigma_A^{-1} < 0$
$\tilde{G}$	$(1-\theta_D\alpha_D)^{-1}[\Delta^2\kappa^{-1}\sigma_M^{-1}\alpha_V^{-1} + \rho\theta_D](\omega_X + \omega_Y)^{-1} > 0$
$\tilde{X} - \tilde{Y}$	$-(1-\theta_D\alpha_D)^{-1}\theta_D\sigma_G < 0$
$\tilde{M}$	$-(1-\theta_D\alpha_D)^{-1}\Delta\sigma_M^{-1}k^{-1}(1-\alpha_V)\alpha_V^{-1} < 0$
$\tilde{C} - \tilde{D}$	$-(1-\theta_D\alpha_D)^{-1}\theta_D\sigma_Q < 0$
$\tilde{E}$	$(1-\theta_D\alpha_D)^{-1}\theta_D[\alpha_D\Delta\kappa^{-1}\sigma_M^{-1}(\sigma_M - 1) - \rho][\alpha_E(1-\theta_D\alpha_D)]^{-1}$
$\tilde{L}$	$(1-\theta_D\alpha_D)^{-1}(1-\sigma_M)\Delta\sigma_M^{-1}\kappa^{-1} < 0$, if $\sigma_M > 1$

Note: The entries in Table 3 and 4 give the elasticities of variables relating to government policy and private behaviour (the row variables) with respect to changes in the weight given to environmental quality and public consumption, respectively. See Table 1 for an explanation of the symbols.

price for additional public consumption in the form of a higher marginal cost of public funds. As public revenue gets more valuable, revenue-raising rather than environmental protection becomes a more important objective of the tax system. The government is thus less able to afford environmental taxes, which are less efficient from a revenue-raising point of view.

The effect on the dirt tax ($\tilde{t}_D$) is a good measure for how shocks affect the degree of tax differentiation aimed at environmental protection. However, the sum of the impacts on the two taxes ($\tilde{t}_L + \tilde{t}_D$) can be used to assess the effect on the overall tax burden on dirty consumption.[13] The information contained in Table 4 reveals that the sign of this latter effect depends on the magnitude of the substitution elasticity between leisure and private commodities. If σ_M is large, the overall tax burden on dirty consumption declines. With a small elasticity, however, the tax burden on dirty consumption may rise because of a substantial increase in public consumption and hence aggregate tax collections (see below).

This elasticity (σ_M) determines also the employment effect of redder preferences. In particular, employment declines if and only if this elasticity exceeds unity. In that case, the substitution effect of higher taxation reducing after-tax wages (i.e. the disincentive effect) exceeds the income effect of lower private utility.

[13] Indeed, as the tax on labour acts as a uniform tax on clean and dirty commodities, one could (if we normalise so that there is no labour tax) interpret $\tilde{t}_L$ as the effect on the clean tax and $\tilde{t}_L + \tilde{t}_D$ as the effect on the dirt tax.

Proposition 4. A higher social preference for public consumption raises the labour tax and reduces the dirt tax. Employment declines if and only if σ_M exceeds one. The lower dirt tax yields a dirtier composition of public and private consumption and less public abatement.

9.2. Public consumption, private welfare and environmental quality

Private utility always suffers. Hence, red and blue political preferences are not 'compatible' by which we mean that private utility falls if society gives more priority to public consumption (higher Γ_G). The magnitude of the fall in private welfare depends on the substitution elasticity between leisure and private commodities (σ_M). If this elasticity is large, private welfare suffers less. In that case, the cost of public funds increases rapidly as public consumption expands. Hence, public consumption does not rise much and the overall tax burden on dirty consumption declines (see above).

Comparison of Tables 3 and 4 reveals the following symmetry: the sign and nature of the effect of a shift towards redder preferences on the quality of the environment is the same as the effect of a shift towards greener preferences on public consumption. In particular, environmental quality and public consumption move together and red and green preferences are thus compatible, if dirty and clean goods are poor substitutes (i.e. σ_Q small), the wage elasticity of labour supply is large and positive (i.e. σ_M large), and if the composition of public spending is insensitive to the (shadow) price for pollution (i.e. σ_G small and σ_A large). If σ_Q and σ_G are small, the lower dirt tax does not induce a large shift toward dirty commodities in private and public consumption. Furthermore, public abatement does not fall much if the productivity of abatement rises rapidly as abatement falls (i.e. σ_A large). Moreover, the higher labour tax acts as an implicit dirt tax and, if σ_M is large, improves the environment by reducing economic activity. Indeed, one reaps a social double dividend of a cleaner environment and more public consumption only if employment falls. In that case, the change in the level and structure of taxes shifts private demand to (clean) leisure rather than dirty commodities.

The environment suffers if the substitution elasticity between leisure and other private goods (σ_M) is small, substitution in private and public consumption baskets is strong (σ_Q,σ_G large), and the productivity of abatement does not rise rapidly as abatement falls (σ_A small). In this case, both the level of economic activity (labour supply) rises and the composition of this activity becomes dirtier. In particular, the adverse private income effect associated with a higher tax level boosts labour supply. Not only does the income effect exceed the substitution effect, but the small substitution effect causes the marginal cost of public funds to rise only slowly as the public sector expands. Accordingly, the tax level, and therefore employment, rise substantially. Higher output raises the sum of private and public consumption. As regards the composition of economic activity, the lower dirt tax induces a lot of substitution towards dirty consumption goods if σ_Q and σ_G are large. Moreover, public abatement falls substantially if σ_A is small.

Public consumption rises most if labour taxes are not very distortionary (i.e σ_M is small) and the lower dirt tax makes a lot of room for public consumption (through less abatement and 'cheaper' (i.e. dirtier) public and private consumption). In other words, the lower dirt tax reduces the cost of public funds significantly while the higher labour tax does not raise this cost much. The environment pays for the lower dirt tax as it raises pollution. Private utility suffers on account of the higher labour tax.

Proposition 5. A higher social preference for public consumption crowds out private welfare (i.e. red and blue preferences are not compatible). Environmental quality is improved if and only if σ_M is large and, at the same time, σ_Q and σ_G are small and σ_A is large. In this case, economic activity declines but does not become much dirtier.

10. Concluding remarks

This paper has explored the interactions between environmental policy and the public finances in a second-best world with distortionary taxes. Our analysis illustrated the difficult trade-offs governments face in implementing a more ambitious environmental policy in response to increased environmental concern. We found that such an environmental policy reduces employment, even though part of the revenues generated by the higher dirt tax are used to reduce the labour tax. Moreover, in order to make the structure of economic activity more friendly towards the environment, other collective priorities may be crowded out. In particular, if households feature a high substitution elasticity between clean and dirty consumption commodities, the shift in the composition of the tax structure away from broad-based labour taxation toward pollution taxation is fairly successful in making the structure of private consumption more environmentally friendly. At the same time, however, a successful environmental policy implies avoidance of the dirt tax. The structural shift in the consumption pattern thus erodes the tax base, thereby making the tax system a less effective device for raising public revenue. Indeed, higher marginal tax rates, which are borne by labour, are required to raise the same amount of revenue. Hence, each unit of public revenue imposes a higher cost in terms of private utility and net wages. This encourages households to increase their consumption of leisure, thereby worsening pre-existing tax distortions by eroding the base of the distortionary labour tax. In order to prevent the marginal cost of public funds from rising, the government finds it optimal to cut public consumption. Hence, public ('red') rather than private ('blue') welfare is crowded out by the increased environmental care in the private sector. Intuitively, the public sector makes room for the costs the private sector incurs to increase the supply of the public good of the environment. Through this channel, although the public good is provided through private-sector activities, the public priority of a cleaner environment competes with other public priorities. This illustrates that countries with a large public sector often find it costly to implement a tough environmental policy because such a policy erodes the tax base and thus requires even higher marginal tax rates.

If public abatement expands substantially or if the composition of public consumption becomes cleaner, tax collections do not necessarily fall as a result of the different composition of the *tax* system. In this case, however, a shift in the composition of *public spending* toward public abatement causes utility from public consumption to fall. Hence, public (i.e. 'red') welfare is crowded out by public rather than private activities aimed at improving environmental quality.

Whether the size of the public sector as measured by revenue collections expands in response to more environmental concern depends on two factors. These two factors involve the two channels through which the environment can be improved: first, a lower level of economic activity, and, second, a cleaner composition of that activity.

An increase in environmental concern raises the consumption of clean leisure, thereby reducing economic activity and employment. An expansion of the public sector at the expense of the private sector depresses the net wage. This benefits the environment by reducing the consumption of leisure if the labour-supply curve slopes upward. If the labour-supply curve slopes downward, in contrast, a richer private sector, which is associated with a higher net wage, benefits the environment by reducing labour supply. In that case, therefore, it is optimal to boost private welfare in response to an increase in environmental concern.

The second factor determining the optimal size of the public sector is whether it is cheaper to make the composition of public or of private spending greener. If the productivity of public abatement does not decline rapidly and the government finds it easy to substitute away from dirty public consumption, it is more efficient to enhance environmental quality through activities in the public sector. In that case, environmental policy instruments that raise public spending play a major role thereby boosting public spending.

If private consumers find it easy to substitute away from dirty to clean consumption, however, the government prefers to improve the environment by encouraging the private sector to make its activities greener rather than greening its own spending. Under these circumstances, environmental policy relies more on tax rather than spending instruments. These tax instruments make the tax system a less effective device for raising revenues. Intuitively, a large share of the marginal tax level is aimed at improving environmental quality rather than raising revenues for public consumption. Accordingly, the size of the public sector as measured by collected revenues should be reduced. This makes room for private activities benefiting the collective priority of a cleaner environment.

Overall, then, the level of public spending expands if the labour-supply curve slopes upwards and, at the same time, environmental quality can be enhanced more cheaply by changing the composition of public rather than private spending. Red and green preferences are likely to be compatible, i.e. public consumption rises in response to increased environmental concern, if the wage elasticity of labour supply is large and positive, clean and dirty consumption goods are poor substitutes, and the effectiveness of public abatement in enhancing environmental quality declines rapidly. In that case the environment is mainly improved through a lower level of economic activity. Dirt taxes are then levied not so much because they correct pollutive behaviour through changing relative prices, but because they are an excellent source of public revenues. However, if substitution between clean and dirty goods is easy and labour supply is not very elastic, dirt taxes are a splendid device for encouraging clean consumption and not so good for generating revenues. In that case, public consumption falls while the level of economic activity does not fall very much.

An important direction of future research is to abandon the world of representative agents and extend the analysis of this paper to address equity issues. Since an equitable income distribution may be viewed as a public good (cf. Thurow, 1971; Smith, 1992), it is of interest to investigate the trade-off between the various public goods (public consumption of clean and dirty products, the quality of the natural environment, and an equitable income distribution). This line of analysis should benefit from abandoning the assumption of homothetic preferences. For example, if one allows for subsistence levels of consumption and thus for necessities, one can shed more light on the issue of basic needs and equity in relation to environmental policy.

Acknowledgements

The authors are grateful for the helpful comments of an editor and two referees. They have also benefited from the comments of participants in seminars at the University of Amsterdam, Athens University, Universidad Aotónama de Barcelona, Université Libres de Bruxelles, CERGE, Charles

University, the Copenhagen Business School, Groningen University, CentER, Tilburg University, and in the Conference 'The International Dimension of Environmental Policy' organised by FEEM, Milan.

Appendix

A.1. Derivation of (33)

Substituting expressions for $\tilde{L}$, $\tilde{C}$, $\tilde{D}$ and from Table 2, part (b) into (32) yields:

$$\omega_X \tilde{X} + \omega_Y \tilde{Y} + \omega_A \tilde{A} = (\sigma_M - 1)\alpha_V(\omega_C + \omega_D - 1)(\tilde{t}_L + \alpha_D \tilde{t}_D) + (\tilde{t}_L + \alpha_D \tilde{t}_D)(\omega_C + \omega_D) - \sigma_Q \tilde{t}_D[\omega_C \alpha_D - \omega_D(1 - \alpha_D)]\,. \quad (A.1)$$

Use of $\omega_C + \omega_D = 1 - \omega_G$, $\omega_C = (1 - t_L)(1 - \alpha_D)$ and $\omega_D = (1 - \theta_D)(1 - t_L)\alpha_D$ in (A.1) yields (33).

A.2. Derivation of (35)–(37)

With the aid of (33), we obtain

$$\hat{t}_L + \alpha_D \tilde{t}_D = \left(\frac{\omega_X \tilde{X} + \omega_Y \tilde{Y} + \omega_A \tilde{A}}{\Delta}\right) + \left(\frac{(1 - t_L)\theta_D \alpha_D (1 - \alpha_D)\sigma_Q \tilde{t}_D}{\Delta}\right) \quad (A.2)$$

which upon substitution into (34) yields

$$\tilde{M} = -(1 - \alpha_V)\,\Delta^{-1}[\omega_X \tilde{X} + \omega_Y \tilde{Y} + \omega_A \tilde{A} + (1 - t_L)\theta_D \alpha_D (1 - \alpha_D)\sigma_Q \tilde{t}_D]\,. \quad (A.3)$$

Using $\tilde{G} = \alpha_{\tilde{Y}} + (1 - \alpha_Y)\tilde{X}$ and (41) gives

$$\omega_X \tilde{X} + \omega_Y \tilde{Y} = (\omega_X + \omega_Y)\tilde{G} + \sigma_G \left(\frac{\theta_Y}{\theta_D}\right)\tilde{t}_D[\alpha_Y \omega_X - (1 - \alpha_Y)\omega_Y]\,. \quad (A.4)$$

Given that

$$\omega_X = (\omega_X + \omega_Y)\left(\frac{1 - \alpha_Y}{1 - \theta_Y \alpha_Y}\right) \quad \text{and}$$

$$\omega_Y = (\omega_X + \omega_Y)\left(\frac{\alpha_Y(1 - \theta_Y)}{1 - \theta_Y \alpha_Y}\right), \quad (A.5)$$

we can rewrite (A.4) as

$$\omega_X\tilde{X} + \omega_Y\tilde{Y} = (\omega_X + \omega_Y)\tilde{G} + (\omega_x + \omega_Y) \times \left(\frac{1}{1-\theta_Y\alpha_Y}\right)[(1-\alpha_Y)\alpha_Y\theta_Y]\sigma_G\left(\frac{\theta_Y}{\theta_D}\right)\tilde{t}_D\,. \tag{A.6}$$

Substitution of (A.6) into (A.3) and using $1 - t_L = (\omega_C + \omega_D)/(1-\theta_D\alpha_D)$ yields (35)–(37).

A.3. Derivation of (38)

When we log-linearise (24) and multiply by $\alpha_E \equiv t_D E/\delta_D N\beta L$, we obtain [after substituting (22′)]

$$\begin{aligned}\alpha_E\tilde{E} &= -\left(\frac{t_D D}{\beta L}\right)\tilde{D} - \left(\frac{\delta_Y t_D Y}{\delta_D N\beta L}\right)\tilde{Y} + \left(\frac{e^{A'}}{\delta_D}\right)\left(\frac{t_D A}{N\beta L}\right)\tilde{A}\\ &= -(\theta_D\alpha_D(1-t_L))\tilde{D} - (\omega_X+\omega_Y)\left(\frac{\theta_Y\alpha_Y}{1-\theta_Y\alpha_Y}\right)\tilde{Y} + \omega_A\tilde{A}\\ &= -((1-t_L)\theta_D\alpha_D)\left[\tilde{D} + \left(\frac{\omega_X\tilde{X}+\omega_Y\tilde{Y}+\omega_A\tilde{A}}{1-\omega_G}\right)\right]\\ &\quad + \left[\left(\frac{(1-t_L)\theta_D\alpha_D}{1-\omega_G}\right)(\omega_X\tilde{X}+\omega_Y\tilde{Y}+\omega_A\tilde{A})\right.\\ &\quad \left. - (\omega_X+\omega_Y)\left(\frac{\theta_Y\alpha_Y}{1-\theta_Y\alpha_Y}\right)\tilde{Y} + \omega_A\tilde{A}\right].\end{aligned} \tag{A.7}$$

Using (33) [after eliminating $\tilde{t}_L + \alpha_D\tilde{t}_D$ from (34)] and $\tilde{D}$ from Table 2, part (b), we can rewrite the term in the first set of square brackets on the (last) right-hand side of (A.7) as

$$\begin{aligned}\tilde{D} + \left(\frac{\omega_X\tilde{X}+\omega_Y\tilde{Y}+\omega_A\tilde{A}}{1-\omega_G}\right) &= \left[1-\alpha_V+\sigma_M\alpha_V - \frac{\Delta}{1-\omega_G}\right]\left(\frac{\tilde{M}}{1-\alpha_V}\right)\\ &\quad - (1-\alpha_D)\sigma_Q\tilde{t}_D\left[1+\frac{(1-t_L)\theta_D\alpha_D}{1-\omega_G}\right]\\ &= \left[\frac{\alpha_V(\sigma_M-1)}{1-\omega_G}\right]\left(\frac{\tilde{M}}{1-\alpha_V}\right)\\ &\quad - \left[\frac{(1-\alpha_D)\sigma_Q\tilde{t}_D}{1-\theta_D\alpha_D}\right].\end{aligned} \tag{A.8}$$

Using (A.6) and $(1-t_L)(1-\omega_G)^{-1} = (1-\theta_D\alpha_D)^{-1}$, the term in the second set of square brackets on the (last) right-hand side of (A.7) may be written as

$$\left[\frac{\theta_D\alpha_D - \theta_Y\alpha_Y}{(1-\theta_D\alpha_D)(1-\theta_Y\alpha_Y)}\right](\omega_X + \omega_Y)\tilde{G}$$
$$+\left(\frac{1}{1-\theta_D\alpha_D}\right)\left(\omega_A\tilde{A}\left(\frac{\omega_X+\omega_Y}{1-\theta_Y\alpha_Y}\right)\left(\frac{\theta_Y^2}{\theta_D}\right)\alpha_Y(1-\alpha_Y)\sigma_G\tilde{t}_D\right). \quad \text{(A.9)}$$

Finally, substituting (A.8) and (A.9) into (A.7), using $(1-t_L) = (\omega_C + \omega_D)(1-\theta_D\alpha_D)^{-1}$ and making use of definitions (36) and (37) yields (38).

A.4. Derivation of (45)

Using the demand functions of Table 2 and (34), we obtain

$$\tilde{V} - \tilde{Q} = \sigma_M(\tilde{t}_L + \alpha_D\tilde{t}_D) = -\left(\frac{\sigma_M}{1-\alpha_V}\right)\tilde{M} \quad \text{(A.10)}$$

which yields

$$\tilde{M}_Q = \left(\frac{\alpha_V}{\sigma_M}\right)(\tilde{V} - \tilde{Q}) = -\left(\frac{\alpha_V}{1-\alpha_V}\right)\tilde{M}\,. \quad \text{(A.11)}$$

We use ε_{LL}^{U} from Table 2, part (b) and $\alpha_V = V$ to rewrite (28) as

$$\eta^{-1} = \left[1 - \left(\frac{t_L}{1-t_L}\right)V(\sigma_M - 1)\right] \quad \text{(A.12)}$$

which upon log-linearisation yields

$$-\tilde{\eta} = -\left[\frac{t_L\alpha_V(\sigma_M-1)\tilde{V} + \alpha_V(\sigma_M-1)\tilde{t}_L}{1 - t_L(1+\alpha_V(\sigma_M-1))}\right]. \quad \text{(A.13)}$$

We substitute $\tilde{t}_L$ from (34) and $\tilde{V} = -(\sigma_M - 1)\tilde{M}$ [see Table 2, part (b)] and obtain

$$-\tilde{\eta} = \left[\frac{\alpha_V(\sigma_M-1)[t_L(\sigma_M-1) + (1-\alpha_V)^{-1}]\tilde{M} + \alpha_V(\sigma_M-1)\alpha_D\tilde{t}_D}{1 - t_L(1+\alpha_V(\sigma_M-1))}\right]. \quad \text{(A.14)}$$

Combining (A.11) and (A.14) we obtain

$$\tilde{\eta} + \tilde{M}_Q = -\left(\frac{\alpha_V}{1-\alpha_V}\right)\left[1 + (\sigma_M - 1)\left(\frac{1 + t_L(\sigma_M-1)(1-\alpha_V)}{1 - t_L(1+\alpha_V(\sigma_M-1)}\right)\right]\tilde{M}$$
$$-\left(\frac{\alpha_V(\sigma_M-1)}{1-t_L(1+\alpha_V(\sigma_M-1))}\right)\alpha_D\tilde{t}_D\,. \quad \text{(A.15)}$$

Upon substituting $\sigma_M\kappa[1 - t_L(1+\alpha_V(\sigma_M-1))]^{-1}$ for the term in square brackets in (A.15), we obtain (45).

A.5. Derivation of Tables 3 and 4

All entries can be written as functions of $\tilde{M}^* \equiv \tilde{M}/(1-\alpha_V) = -(\tilde{t}_L + \alpha_D \tilde{t}_D)$ [using (34)] and $\tilde{t}_D$. $\tilde{t}_L$ follows immediately from the definition of $\tilde{M}^*$. Eqs. (41), (42), and (43) give, respectively, $\tilde{X}-\tilde{Y}$, $\tilde{C}-\tilde{D}$, and $\tilde{A}$. Eliminating $\tilde{M}$ from the definition of $\tilde{M}^*$ and $\tilde{A}$ from (35) and using the definition of ρ (see Table 1), we obtain

$$(\omega_X + \omega_Y)\tilde{G} = -\Delta \tilde{M}^* - \left[\rho_Q \sigma_Q + \rho_G \sigma_G + \left(\frac{\omega_A}{\theta_D \sigma_A}\right)\right]\tilde{t}_D$$
$$= -\Delta \tilde{M}^* - \rho \tilde{t}_D \,. \tag{A.16}$$

Eqs. (38) and (39) with $\theta_D \alpha_D = \theta_Y \alpha_Y$ [and substituting (43) to eliminate $\tilde{A}$ and using the definition of ρ] give

$$\tilde{E} = \left[\frac{-\theta_D \alpha_D (\sigma_M - 1)\alpha_V \tilde{M}^* + \rho \tilde{t}_D}{\alpha_E (1-\theta_D \alpha_D)}\right]. \tag{A.17}$$

Eq. (39) gives $\tilde{L} = (\sigma_M - 1)\alpha_V \tilde{M}^*$.

To complete Tables 3 and 4, we need expressions for $\tilde{t}_D$ and $\tilde{M}^*$. Eq. (40) amounts to a reduced-form expression for $\tilde{t}_D$. Upon substitution of this expression for $\tilde{t}_D$ into (45), we obtain (using $\theta_D \alpha_D = \theta_Y \alpha_Y$)

$$\tilde{M}^* = -\left(\frac{\sigma_M - 1}{\sigma_M \kappa}\right)\left(\frac{\alpha_D \theta_D}{1-\theta_D \alpha_D}\right)\tilde{\Gamma}_E - \left[\frac{\Delta}{\alpha_V \sigma_M \kappa (1-\theta_D \alpha_D)}\right]\tilde{\Gamma}_G \,. \tag{A.18}$$

A.6. Proof that t_L falls if $\tilde{\Gamma}_E > 0$

Looking at the entry for $\tilde{t}_L$ in Table 3, we need to establish that

$$F(\sigma_M) \equiv \sigma_M t_L [1-(1-\alpha_V)(\sigma_M - 1)] \le 1 \,. \tag{A.19}$$

Since $\omega_G = t_L + (1-t_L)\theta_D \alpha_D$ and stability requires $\Delta > 0$, t_L cannot exceed $(1-\alpha_V + \sigma_M \alpha_V)^{-1}$. For $\sigma_M > 1$, it is then possible to show that

$$F(\sigma_M) < \sigma_M \left[\frac{1+(1-\alpha_V)-(1-\alpha_V)\sigma_M}{(1-\alpha_V)+\sigma_M \alpha_V}\right] < 1 \,. \tag{A.20}$$

For $\sigma_M < 1$, $t_L < 1$ and one can also establish that $F'(\sigma_M) > 0$, $F(1) = 1$ and thus $F(\sigma_M) < 1$. The only case that $\tilde{t}_L = 0$ is $\sigma_M = t_L = 1$.

References

Atkinson, A.B. and N.H. Stern, 1974, Pigou, taxation and public goods, Review of Economic Studies XLI, no. 1, 119–128.

Atkinson, A.B. and J.E. Stiglitz, 1980, Lectures on public economics (McGraw-Hill, London).

Auerbach, A.J., 1985, The theory of excess burden and optimal taxation, in: A.J. Auerbach and M. Feldstein, eds., Handbook of public economics, vol. I (North-Holland, Amsterdam) 61–127.

Ballard, C.L. and D. Fullerton, 1992, Distortionary taxes and the provision of public goods, Journal of Economic Perspectives 6, no. 3, 117–131.

Bovenberg, A.L. and R.A. de Mooij, 1994, Environmental levels and distorting taxation American Economic Review (forthcoming).

Corlett, W.J. and D.C. Hague, 1953, Complementarity and the excess burden of taxation, Review of Economic Studies 21, 21–30.

Diamond, P.A., 1973, Consumption externalities and imperfect corrective pricing, Bell Journal of Economics 4, 526–538.

Diamond, P.A. and J.A. Mirrlees, 1971, Optimal taxation and public production: II. Tax rules, American Economic Review 61, 261–278.

Dixit, A., 1985, Tax policy in open economies, in: A.J. Auerbach and M. Feldstein, eds., Handbook of public economics, vol. I (North-Holland, Amsterdam) 313–374.

Drissen, E. and F. van Winden, 1992, Social security in a general equilibrium model with endogeneous government behaviour, in: D. Bös and S. Cnossen, eds., Fiscal implications of an ageing population (Springer-Verlag, Berlin) 1–22.

Ng, Y.-K., 1980, Optimal corrective taxes or subsidies when revenue raising imposes an excess burden, American Economic Review 70, no. 4, 744–751.

Pezzey, J., 1992, Some interactions between environmental policy and public finance, presented to the Third Annual Conference of the EAERE.

Pigou, A.C., 1947, A study in public finance, 3rd edn. (Macmillan, London).

Ramsey, F.P., 1927, A contribution to the theory of taxation, Economic Journal 37, 47–61.

Samuelson, P.A., 1954, The pure theory of public expenditure, Review of Economics and Statistics 36, 387–389.

Sandmo, A., 1975, Optimal taxation in the presence of externalities, Swedish Journal of Economics 77, 86–98.

Smith, S., 1992, Taxation and the environment: A survey, Fiscal Studies 13, 21–57.

Ulph, D., 1992, A note on the 'double benefit' of pollution taxes, mimeo, University College London.

Thurow, L.G., 1971, The income distribution as a pure public good, Quarterly Journal of Economics 85, 321–336.

[7]

Environmental Levies and Distortionary Taxation

By A. Lans Bovenberg and Ruud A. de Mooij*

In the face of growing concerns about serious environmental problems, environmental taxes have attracted increasing attention. Many economists have argued that pollution levies are an efficient instrument for achieving environmental objectives (see e.g., William J. Baumol and Wallace E. Oates, 1988). Some have gone even further to suggest that environmental taxes may yield benefits over and above a cleaner environment. In particular, governments can use the revenues from pollution taxes to decrease other, distortionary taxes. In this way, environmental taxes may yield a "double dividend"—not only a cleaner environment, but also a less distortionary tax system. This argument suggests that one may wish to push the role of environmental taxes beyond that of solely an instrument for environmental protection and employ these instruments also as a revenue-raising device (see e.g., Oates, 1991). Furthermore, if pollution taxes are available, ambitious environmental policies may seem more attractive if public revenues become scarcer. Indeed, high estimates for the deadweight losses of current tax systems have been used to suggest that environmental taxes may yield important "side benefits" (see e.g., Oates, 1991; David W. Pearce, 1991).

The main contribution of this note is to show that environmental taxes typically exacerbate, rather than alleviate, preexisting tax distortions—even if revenues are employed to cut preexisting distortionary taxes. We demonstrate that, in the presence of preexisting distortionary taxes, the optimal pollution tax typically lies below the Pigovian tax, which fully internalizes the marginal social damage from pollution. Intuitively, the collective good of environmental quality directly competes with other collective goods. Hence, the marginal costs of environmental policy rise with the marginal cost of public funds.

I. The Model

A linear technology describes production:

$$(1) \qquad hNL = NC + ND + G.$$

Labor, L, is the only input into production. Labor productivity, h, is constant, while output can be used for public consumption, G, as well as for the consumption of clean and dirty private consumption commodities denoted by, respectively, C and D. We normalize units so that the constant rates of transformation between the three produced commodities are unity. All private commodities are expressed in per capita terms. N stands for the number of households.

Two public goods enter household utility $U = u(C, D, V, G, E)$, namely, public consumption and environmental quality, E. The household takes the supply of both of these goods as given. Hence, in optimizing its utility, the household adopts as instruments the demands for private goods (i.e., leisure $[V]$ and clean and dirty consumption). By including the quality of the natural environment in the utility function, we are able to perform explicit welfare analysis, and in particular, we can examine the interaction between environmental and labor-market distortions in a second-best framework. The

*Bovenberg: CentER for Economic Research, Tilburg University, P.O. Box 90153, 5000 LE Tilburg, Netherlands, Research Centre for Economic Policy (OCFEB), Erasmus University Rotterdam, and Centre for Economic Policy Research, London; de Mooij: Ministry of Economic Affairs, Netherlands, and Research Centre for Economic Policy (OCFEB), Rotterdam, Netherlands. The views expressed in this note are strictly personal. They do not necessarily represent the official positions of the Ministry of Economic Affairs in the Netherlands. We thank three anonymous referees for constructive comments on earlier drafts.

environmental distortion comes about because households do not take into account the adverse effect of their dirty consumption on environmental quality $E = e(ND)$; $de/d(ND) < 0$. The labor-market distortion originates in a tax on labor income. This tax is distortionary, as the model allows for endogenous labor supply by including leisure, V, in utility. The household-budget constraint amounts to

$$(2) \quad C + (1 + t_D)D = h(1 - t_L)(1 - V)$$

where t_L denotes the ad valorem tax rate on labor income and t_D stands for the pollution tax on dirty consumption. The labor endowment is normalized at 1 (hence, $V + L = 1$).

The law of Walras yields the government budget constraint by combining market equilibrium (1) and the household-budget constraint (2):

$$(3) \qquad G = t_D ND + t_L hNL.$$

The welfare effects of a revenue-neutral change in the tax mix (i.e., $dG = 0$) are found from

$$(4) \quad dU = -\frac{\partial u}{\partial V}dL + \frac{\partial u}{\partial C}dC + \frac{\partial u}{\partial D}dD + \frac{\partial u}{\partial E}\left[\frac{de}{d(ND)}\right]N dD.$$

Substituting the first-order conditions characterizing optimal household behavior and using (1), we arrive at the following:

$$(5) \quad \frac{dU}{\lambda} = ht_L\, dL + \left[t_D - N\frac{\partial u}{\partial E}\left(-\frac{de}{d(ND)}\right)\Big/\lambda\right] dD$$

where λ denotes marginal utility of income. The first term on the right-hand side of (5) stands for the effect on the labor-market distortion, which is due to the tax on labor income. The second term corresponds to the effect on the environmental distortion. The welfare impact of a marginal increase in dirty consumption amounts to the difference between a tax term, which measures the social benefits of additional tax revenue due to a wider revenue base, and a term representing the marginal social damage from pollution. In the absence of a pollution levy (i.e., $t_D = 0$), cutting the demand for the dirty commodity enhances overall welfare because the social costs of pollution exceed the social benefits.

In the "first-best" case, in which there is no need to finance public spending through distortionary taxation (i.e., $t_L = 0$), the optimal value of t_D would simply be the Pigovian tax. This tax fully internalizes the adverse external effects of pollution:

$$(6) \qquad t_D = N\frac{\partial u}{\partial E}\left(-\frac{de}{d(ND)}\right)\Big/\lambda.$$

At the Pigovian tax, the beneficial environmental effects associated with less dirty consumption would exactly offset the adverse welfare effects due to an erosion of the tax base. Changes in employment would not affect welfare; in the absence of distortionary labor taxation, the social opportunity costs of additional employment exactly offset the social benefits. In the presence of a distortionary tax on labor ($t_L > 0$), however, the optimal environmental tax depends on the response of employment to a change in the tax mix.

II. Employment

In order to explore the general-equilibrium impact of a higher pollution tax on employment, the model is log-linearized.[1] A tilde (~) denotes a relative change, unless indicated otherwise. Since we explore a change in the tax mix, we assume that the government does not change public consumption (i.e., $\tilde{G} = 0$). Log-linearizing the

[1]This approach amounts to an exercise in comparative statics. For a similar approach, see Wouter J. Keller (1980) and Bovenberg (1989).

government budget constraint (3) and dividing through by $(1-t_L)hNL$, we find

$$\tilde{b}' = -\tilde{t}_L - \Phi_D\tilde{t}_D. \tag{7}$$

Φ_D denotes the share of dirty goods in overall household consumption: $\Phi_D = (1+t_D)D/[C+(1+t_D)D]$; $\tilde{t}_L$ and $\tilde{t}_D$ are defined as $\tilde{t}_L = dt_L/(1-t_L)$ and $\tilde{t}_D = dt_D/(1+t_D)$. The "tax-base" effect is defined by

$$\tilde{b}' \equiv \frac{\left[t_L\tilde{L} + t_D a_D\tilde{D}\right]}{1-t_L} \tag{8}$$

where $a_D = (D/hL) = (1-t_L)\Phi_D/(1+t_D)$ is the output share of dirty goods. The two terms in square brackets in (8) stand for the effects on the bases of the labor tax and the pollution levy, respectively. Given a fixed before-tax wage, h, the right-hand side of (7) stands for the relative change in the after-tax real wage, $w = h(1-t_L)/p$, where p is the consumption price index:

$$\tilde{w} = -\tilde{t}_L - \Phi_D\tilde{t}_D. \tag{9}$$

Hence, expression (7) reveals that the real after-tax wage falls if the tax base erodes (i.e., $\tilde{b}' < 0$).

In order to find expressions for household labor supply, $\tilde{L}$, and demand for dirty goods, $\tilde{D}$, we make some separability assumptions regarding household utility:

$$U = u(G, E, H(V; Q(C, D))). \tag{10}$$

Private goods are (weakly) separable from public goods G and E. Environmental quality and public consumption thus do not directly affect private demand. The subutility function Q aggregates clean and dirty consumption into a composite consumption good, Q. This function is homothetic. Hence, in the absence of environmental externalities, a uniform tax on clean and dirty consumption would be optimal. Optimizing utility (10) subject to the household budget constraint (2), we find labor supply:

$$\tilde{L} = \theta_\ell\tilde{w} \tag{11}$$

where $\theta_\ell = V\sigma_V - V$ stands for the uncompensated wage elasticity of labor supply. The substitution effect dominates the income effect if the substitution elasticity between leisure and composite consumption, σ_V, exceeds unity. Labor supply depends only on the after-tax real wage. Neither the price of dirty goods nor environmental quality enters expression (11) because of the separability assumptions implicit in (10).

The following expression describes household demand for dirty consumption:

$$\tilde{D} = \tilde{L} + \tilde{w} - (1-\Phi_D)\sigma\tilde{t}_D \tag{12}$$

where σ represents the substitution elasticity between clean and dirty consumption in the subutility function $Q(C, D)$. The solution for employment is derived by substituting (8), (9), (11), and (12) into (7):

$$\Delta\tilde{L} = -\theta_\ell t_D a_D(1-\Phi_D)\sigma\tilde{t}_D \tag{13}$$

where $\Delta \equiv 1-(t_L + a_D t_D)(1+\theta_\ell) > 0$.[2] An increase in the pollution tax from a positive initial level (i.e, $t_D > 0$) reduces employment if the uncompensated wage elasticity of labor supply, θ_ℓ, is positive. We assume that the labor-supply curve is indeed upward-sloping, as most empirical studies yield positive estimates for this elasticity (see e.g., Jerry Hausman, 1985). The negative effect on employment is due to a decline in the real after-tax wage eroding the incentives to supply labor. The drop in the real after-tax wage comes about because the lower tax rate on labor income does not fully compensate workers for the adverse effect of the pollution levy on their real after-tax wage. This incomplete offset is due to the erosion of the base of the environmental tax. In particular, the higher environmental tax induces households to switch from dirty to clean consumption commodi-

[2] If $\Delta < 0$, the Laffer curve is downward-sloping, and the model is not stable.

ties. If the initial tax rate on the dirty commodities is positive, this behavioral effect erodes the base of the environmental tax and, therefore, produces a negative tax-base effect (i.e., $\tilde{b}' < 0$). Expressions (7) and (9) indicate that this reduces the real after-tax wage. Thus, if it needs to maintain overall tax revenues, the government is unable to reduce the labor tax sufficiently to offset the adverse effect of the higher pollution levy on the real after-tax wage. The resulting lower income from an additional unit of work erodes the incentives to supply labor.

Intuitively, as an instrument to finance public spending with the least costs to after-tax wages, the environmental tax, which amounts to a narrow-based tax, is less efficient than a broad-based labor tax because, in contrast to a labor tax, it "distorts" the composition of the consumption basket. These "distortions" enhance environmental quality but reduce the real after-tax income from work. Whereas the environmental benefits are public and independent of the amount of labor supplied, the costs depend on the amount of labor supplied. Indeed, by enhancing environmental quality, pollution taxes expand the overall supply of collective goods. This reduces the incentives to supply labor because the costs of all collective goods, including a cleaner environment, are borne by labor.

III. Optimal Pollution Tax

Armed with the general-equilibrium effects on employment, we can now return to expression (5) for the welfare effects of marginal tax changes. Without a preexisting distortionary tax (i.e., $t_L = 0$), welfare would not be affected if the government were to marginally reduce the environmental tax below its Pigovian level. If the initial tax on labor is positive ($t_L > 0$), in contrast, welfare would increase. Whereas the second term on the right-hand side of (5) would be zero, the rise in employment associated with a lower pollution tax would produce a positive first term. In this "second-best" case with distortionary taxation, therefore, the optimal environmental tax lies below the social damage from pollution.

In this way, high costs of public funds crowd out not only ordinary public consumption, but also the collective good of the environment. Following Anthony B. Atkinson and Nicholas H. Stern (1974) and David E. Wildasin (1984), Charles L. Ballard and Don Fullerton (1990) explore the conditions under which distortionary taxation crowds out public spending by raising the marginal cost of public funds above unity (i.e., the marginal costs of public funds in a first-best economy with lump-sum taxes). For public spending that is separable from consumers' choices on leisure and consumption, they derive that distortionary labor taxes raise the marginal costs of public spending above unity if the uncompensated wage elasticity of labor supply is positive. We find that the same condition on the uncompensated wage elasticity determines whether distortionary labor taxes raise the marginal cost of (the collective good of) environmental protection above its social benefit. This result depends on the separability assumptions regarding utility. If environmental quality were a closer substitute for private consumption than for leisure, a heavier reliance on environmental taxes would imply smaller income effects on labor supply. In the extreme case in which households would perceive an improvement in environmental quality as cash, compensated rather than uncompensated elasticities would govern the effect on the marginal cost of environmental protection (see Wildasin, 1984).

The government can use the revenues from pollution taxes to raise lump-sum transfers rather than to cut labor taxes. The associated higher levels of distortionary taxation and transfers imply that employment would decline more than in the case in which labor taxes are cut.[3] The lower level

[3]Note that the compensated wage elasticity of labor supply determines the employment impact of using labor taxes to raise income transfers. The reason is that the additional transfers offset the income effects of higher labor taxes. Hence, only the substitution effect of higher labor taxes remains.

of employment erodes the base of the labor tax, thereby further worsening preexisting tax distortions. In the presence of distortionary taxes, therefore, pollution taxes become more attractive if the revenues are not recycled in a lump-sum fashion, but rather are used to cut distortionary taxes.[4] Hence, there exists a "doubled dividend" in the sense that a cost reduction can be achieved by using revenues from pollution taxes to cut distortionary taxes rather than returning these revenues in a lump-sum fashion.

REFERENCES

Atkinson, Anthony B. and Stern, Nicholas H. "Pigou, Taxation and Public Goods." *Review of Economic Studies*, January 1974, *41*(1), pp. 119–28.

Ballard, Charles L. and Fullerton, Don. "Wage Tax Distortions and Public Good Provision." National Bureau of Economic Research (Cambridge MA) Working Paper No. 3506, 1990.

Baumol, William J. and Oates, Wallace E. *The theory of environmental policy*. Cambridge: Cambridge University Press, 1988.

Bovenberg, A. Lans. "The Effects of Capital Income Taxation on International Competitiveness and Trade Flows." *American Economic Review*, December 1989, *79*(5), pp. 1045–64.

Bovenberg, A. Lans and de Mooij, Ruud A. "Environmental Policy in a Small Open Economy with Distortionary Labor Taxes: A General Equilibrium Analysis." Mimeo, Research Centre for Economic Policy (OCFEB), Erasmus University, Rotterdam, 1993.

Hausman, Jerry A. "Taxes and Labor Supply," in Alan J. Auerbach and Martin S. Feldstein, eds., *Handbook of public economics*, Vol. 1. Amsterdam: North-Holland, 1985, pp. 213–63.

Keller, Wouter J. *Tax incidence: A general equilibrium approach*. Amsterdam: North-Holland, 1980.

Oates, Wallace E. "Pollution Charges as a Source of Public Revenues." Discussion Paper No. QE92-05, Resources for the Future, Washington, DC, 1991.

Pearce, David W. "The Role of Carbon Taxes in Adjusting to Global Warming." *Economic Journal*, July 1991, *101*(407), pp. 938–48.

Wildasin, David E. "On Public Good Provision with Distortionary Taxation." *Economic Inquiry*, April 1984, *22*(2), pp. 227–43.

[4] If the government uses environmental policy instruments that do not yield public revenues, it in effect distributes free pollution rights to the private sector. These free pollution rights amount to a lump-sum transfer. For a formal analysis, see Bovenberg and de Mooij (1993).

[8]

Optimal Environmental Taxation in the Presence of Other Taxes: General-Equilibrium Analyses

By A. LANS BOVENBERG AND LAWRENCE H. GOULDER *

Most economies feature levels of public spending that require more tax revenues than would be generated solely from the pollution taxes set according to the Pigovian principle, that is, set equal to marginal environmental damages. As a consequence, tax systems generally rely on both environmental (corrective) and other taxes. However, economists typically have analyzed environmental taxes without taking into account the presence of other, distortionary taxes. The omission is significant because the consequences of environmental taxes depend fundamentally on the levels of other taxes, including income and commodity taxes.

This paper examines how optimal environmental tax rates deviate from rates implied by the Pigovian principle in a second-best setting where other, distortionary taxes are present. Previous investigations of this issue include the partial equilibrium analyses of Dwight R. Lee and Walter S. Misiolek (1986) and Wallace E. Oates (1991), who derive formulas linking the optimal rate for a newly imposed environmental tax to the marginal excess burden from existing taxes. In a general-equilibrium setting, Agnar Sandmo (1975) and Bovenberg and Frederick van der Ploeg (1994) have demonstrated how the well-known ''Ramsey'' formula for optimal commodity taxes is altered when one of the consumption commodities generates an externality.[1]

The present paper contributes to the analytical and empirical literature in three ways. First, it extends earlier analytical work on optimal environmental taxation in a general-equilibrium setting by considering pollution taxes imposed on intermediate inputs. This is a useful extension because many actual environmental regulations and taxes affect the costs of intermediate inputs.[2] Second, the paper investigates second-best optimal environmental taxes numerically. Here we expand on the analytical work by employing a numerical general-equilibrium model of the United States. The use of a numerical model enables us to employ a realistic specification of taxes and adopt a fairly detailed representation of production and demand. Our paper thus combines the strengths of analytical and numerical approaches: a stylized analytical model uncovers the major mechanisms at play, while a numerical model explores the empirical significance of these mechanisms in a more realistic setting. Despite considerable differences in the complexity of the analytical and numerical models, we find a strong coherence between the two models' results.

The third contribution of the paper is its numerical investigation of optimal environmental tax policies in the presence of realistic policy constraints. The constraints involve either the inability to alter all tax rates (so that much of the initial, suboptimal tax system re-

* Bovenberg: CPB Netherlands Bureau for Economic Policy Analysis, P.O. Box 80510, 2508 GM The Hague, The Netherlands, and CentER for Economic Research, Tilburg University; Goulder: Department of Economics, Landau Economics Building 335, Stanford University, Stanford, CA 94305-6072. The authors are grateful to Jesse David and Steven Weinberg for excellent research assistance, to three anonymous referees for helpful comments, and to the National Science Foundation (Grant SBR-9310362) and IBM Corporation for financial support.

[1] A closely related issue is the extent to which the costs of environmental taxes are lowered when revenues from such taxes are devoted to reductions in existing distortionary taxes. A key question is whether ''recycling'' the revenues in this way can make the overall cost of the revenue-neutral policy zero or negative. For general discussions of this issue see, for example, David W. Pearce (1991), James M. Poterba (1993), Oates (1995) and Goulder (1995a). For analytical treatments see, for example, Bovenberg and Ruud A. de Mooij (1994) and Ian W. H. Parry (1995). For numerical investigations see, for example, Robert Shackleton et al. (1996) and Goulder (1995b).

[2] For example, taxes on fossil fuels raise the costs of fuel inputs; similarly, specific excises such as taxes on gasoline raise the costs to producers of the transportation services they might employ.

mains) or the inability to use revenues from environmental taxes in optimal ways. We find that these constraints substantially affect the optimal environmental tax rates.

The paper is organized as follows. Section I develops a stylized general-equilibrium model to uncover the main determinants of optimal environmental taxes in the presence of distortionary taxes. Section II describes the numerical model, and Section III applies this model to evaluate the departures from Pigovian tax rules implied by second-best considerations. The final section offers conclusions.

I. Theoretical Issues and Analytical Results

This section explores analytically how the presence of distortionary taxes affects the optimal setting of environmental taxes on both intermediate inputs and consumption goods. To this end, we extend the model in Bovenberg and Ruud de Mooij (1994) by incorporating intermediate inputs. Output derives from a constant-returns-to-scale production function $F(L, x_C, x_D)$ with inputs not only of labor (L) but also of "clean" and "dirty" intermediate goods (x_C and x_D, respectively). Output can be devoted to public consumption (G), to clean or dirty intermediate inputs, or to household consumption of a "clean" or "dirty" consumption good (denoted by C_C and C_D, respectively). Hence, the commodity market equilibrium is given by $F(L, x_C, x_D) = G + x_C + x_D + C_C + C_D$. We normalize units so that the constant rates of transformation between the five produced commodities are unity.

The representative household maximizes utility $U(C_C, C_D, l, G, Q) = u(N(H(C_C, C_D), l), G, Q)$. Private utility $N(\cdot)$ is homothetic, while commodity consumption $H(\cdot)$ is separable from leisure, l. In addition, private utility is weakly separable from the two public goods, environmental quality (Q) and (nonenvironmental) public consumption (G). These assumptions on utility match the specifications of household behavior in the numerical model (see Section II).

The household faces the budget constraint $C_C + (1 + \tau_D^C)C_D = (1 - \tau_L)wL$, where τ_D^C and τ_L denote, respectively, the tax rates on dirty consumption and labor. Without loss of generality, the tax on clean consumption is assumed to be zero.[3] The labor tax rate and the producer (before-tax) wage w yield the consumption (after-tax) wage, $w_N = (1 - \tau_L)w$.

The government budget constraint is $G = \tau_C^x x_C + \tau_D^x x_D + \tau_D^C C_D + \tau_L wL$, where τ_C^x and τ_D^x stand for the taxes on clean and dirty intermediate inputs, respectively. Environmental quality, Q, deteriorates with pollution, which is directly related to the quantity used of dirty intermediate and dirty consumption goods; thus, $Q = q(x_D, C_D)$, with $\partial q/\partial x_D, \partial q/\partial C_D < 0$. Private decision makers ignore environmental externalities.

To derive the optimal tax rates, we solve the government's problem of maximizing household utility subject to the government budget constraint and the decentralized optimizing behavior of firms and households. Accordingly, the government chooses values of its four tax instruments τ_L, τ_D^C, τ_C^x, and τ_D^x to maximize:

$$(1) \qquad u[V(w_N, \tau_D^C), G, q(x_D, C_D)] + \mu(\tau_C^x x_C + \tau_D^x x_D + \tau_D^C C_D + \tau_L wL - G)$$

where V represents indirect private utility and μ denotes the marginal utility associated with the public goods consumption made possible by one additional unit of public revenue.

Appendix A derives the optimal tax rates. The analysis reveals that the clean intermediate input should not be taxed (that is, $\tau_C^x = 0$). This is an application of the well-known result of Peter A. Diamond and James A. Mirrlees (1971a, b) demonstrating that, if production exhibits constant returns to scale,[4] an optimal tax system should not distort production.

[3] A positive tax on consumption is redundant in that the equivalent to any tax system with a positive tax on consumption can be obtained through suitable combinations of the labor tax and the tax on dirty consumption. This follows from the fact that the labor tax is equivalent to a uniform tax on the two consumption commodities.

[4] Under decreasing returns to scale, production efficiency continues to be optimal so long as a 100-percent tax on pure profits is available.

The optimal tax on the dirty intermediate input is (see Appendix A):

$$(2) \qquad \tau_D^x = \left[\frac{\dfrac{\partial U}{\partial Q}\left(-\dfrac{\partial q}{\partial x_D}\right)}{\dfrac{\partial U}{\partial C_C}} \right] \frac{1}{\eta}.$$

The term between the large square brackets on the right-hand side of (2) is the marginal environmental damage (MED) from this input. η ($\equiv \mu/(\partial U/\partial C_C)$) is defined as the ratio of the marginal (utility) value of public revenue to the marginal utility of private income; it is often referred to as the marginal cost of public funds (MCPF). Analogously, the optimal tax on the dirty consumption good is the marginal environmental damage from the use of this good divided by the MCPF (see Appendix A):[5]

$$(3) \qquad \tau_D^C = \left[\frac{\dfrac{\partial U}{\partial Q}\left(-\dfrac{\partial q}{\partial C_D}\right)}{\dfrac{\partial U}{\partial C_C}} \right] \frac{1}{\eta}.$$

Equations (2) and (3) indicate how the presence of distortionary taxation affects the optimal environmental tax rate. In general, an optimal pollution tax induces the level of emissions at which the marginal welfare benefit from emissions reductions (MWB_E) equals the marginal welfare cost of achieving such reductions (MWC_E).[6] In the special case of a first-best world without distortionary taxes, a one-unit reduction in emissions involves a welfare cost corresponding to the loss of tax revenue due to the erosion of the base of the pollution tax—thus the pollution tax rate represents the marginal welfare cost of emissions reductions (MWC_E). Hence, in a first-best setting, optimality requires that the pollution tax be set equal to the marginal (environmental) benefit from pollution reduction (or marginal damage from pollution), which is given by the term in the large square brackets in equation (2) or (3). This is the Pigovian tax rate.

The MCPF term in equations (2) and (3) reveals how the presence of distortionary taxes requires a modification of the Pigovian principle. In particular, it shows that the Pigovian rate is optimal if and only if the MCPF is unity. A unitary MCPF means that public funds are no more costly than private funds. The higher the MCPF, the greater the cost of public consumption goods, including the public good of environmental quality. When these goods are more costly, the government finds it optimal to cut down on public consumption of the environment by reducing the pollution tax.

In a second-best world with distortionary taxes, the MCPF is given by (see Appendix A)[7]:

$$(4) \qquad \eta = \left[l - \frac{\tau_L}{l - \tau_L} \theta_L \right]^{-1}.$$

The MCPF exceeds unity if 1) the uncompensated wage elasticity of labor supply, θ_L, is positive, and 2) the distortionary tax on labor, τ_L, is positive (which is required if Pigovian taxes are not sufficient to finance public consumption). Combining equation (4) with equation (2) (or (3)), we find that the presence of distortionary labor taxation reduces the optimal pollution tax below its Pigovian level if and only if θ_L is positive.[8] In a second-best

[5] With a different normalization of the tax system, the tax rate on clean consumption can be positive. In that case, the *difference* between the optimal rates on dirty and clean consumption equals the Pigovian tax divided by the MCPF. No matter what normalization is used and the level of tax on clean consumption, all of the difference between the optimal rates on dirty and clean consumption stems from environmental considerations. This reflects our assumption that commodity consumption is separable from leisure: in the absence of environmental externalities, uniform consumption taxation is optimal.

[6] The marginal welfare benefit is the welfare change associated with the increase in environmental quality Q that results from the reduction in pollution. The marginal welfare cost is the negative of the welfare impact from changes in arguments of the private-good subutility function $N(\cdot)$ that result from the pollution-reduction policy. The subscript "E" is employed to distinguish the marginal welfare cost *per unit of emissions reductions* (MWC_E) from the marginal welfare cost *per dollar of revenue* (MWC), which is equal to MCPF-1.

[7] This equation can be interpreted as an implicit expression for the optimal labor tax.

[8] This is consistent with the literature on the MCPF surveyed in Charles L. Ballard and Don Fullerton (1992). For

TABLE 1—INDUSTRY AND CONSUMER-GOOD CATEGORIES

Industries	Consumer goods
1. Coal mining	1. Food
2. Crude petroleum and natural gas extraction	2. Alcohol
3. Synthetic fuels	3. Tobacco
4. Petroleum refining	4. Utilities
5. Electric utilities	5. Housing services
6. Gas utilities	6. Furnishings
7. Agriculture and noncoal mining	7. Appliances
8. Construction	8. Clothing and jewelry
9. Metals and machinery	9. Transportation
10. Motor vehicles	10. Motor vehicles
11. Miscellaneous manufacturing	11. Services (except financial)
12. Services (except housing)	12. Financial services
13. Housing services	13. Recreation, reading, and miscellaneous
	14. Nondurable, nonfood household expenditure
	15. Gasoline and other fuels
	16. Education
	17. Health

setting, environmental taxes are more costly because they exacerbate the distortions imposed by the labor tax. In particular, by reducing the real after-tax wage, they decrease labor supply if the uncompensated wage elasticity of labor supply is positive. In the presence of a distortionary labor tax, the decline in labor supply produces a first-order loss in welfare by eroding the base of the labor tax. This additional welfare loss raises the overall welfare cost associated with a marginal reduction in emissions. As a result, and in contrast with the first-best case, here the marginal welfare cost of a unit of emissions reduction (MWC_E) exceeds the pollution tax rate. Thus, to equate marginal welfare costs and marginal social (environmental) benefits from emissions reduction, the optimal environmental tax must be set below the marginal social benefit, that is, below the Pigovian rate.

II. Basic Features of the Numerical Model

We employ a numerical model of the U.S. economy to examine further the issues of second-best optimal environmental taxation.[9] This model enables us to relax restrictions of the analytical model and thereby assess these issues in a more realistic setting. The additional realism includes greater industry disaggregation, a more detailed treatment of the tax system, and attention to capital (in addition to labor) as a primary factor, which permits attention to dynamic effects. The numerical simulations also allow us to evaluate constrained-optimal environmental tax policies, where the constraints involve either the inability to optimize over all tax rates (so that some prior "imperfections" in the tax system remain) or the inability to optimally recycle revenues from environmental taxes.

A. *Components and Behavioral Specifications*

The model distinguishes the 13 industries (of which 6 are energy-producing industries) and the 17 consumer products identified in Table 1. In each industry, a nested-CES production structure accounts for substitution between different forms of energy as well as between energy and other inputs. Managers of

public consumption that is separable from consumer's choice on leisure and consumption, this literature finds that distortionary labor taxes raise the marginal benefits of public consumption above its direct resource cost if the uncompensated wage elasticity of labor supply is positive.

[9] Some details on the model's structure and parameters are offered in Appendix B. A more complete description is in Goulder (1992). Miguel Cruz and Goulder (1992) provide data documentation.

firms choose input quantities and investment levels to maximize the value of the firm. Investment decisions take account of adjustment costs that are a convex function of the rate of gross investment.[10]

Consumption, labor supply, and saving result from the decisions of a representative household maximizing its intertemporal utility, defined on leisure and overall consumption in each period.[11] As in the analytical model of the previous section, the utility function is homothetic and leisure and consumption are weakly separable. Overall consumption in each period is an aggregate of the 17 types of consumer goods, where each consumer good is in turn a composite of a domestic and foreign consumer good of a given type.

Except for oil and gas imports, imported intermediate and consumer goods are imperfect substitutes for their domestic counterparts. Import prices are exogenous in foreign currency, but the domestic-currency price changes with variations in the exchange rate. Export demands are modeled as functions of the foreign price of U.S. exports and the level of foreign income. The exchange rate adjusts to balance trade in each period.

The government's tax instruments include energy taxes, output taxes, the corporate income tax, property taxes, sales taxes, and taxes on individual labor and capital income. In policy experiments, we require that real government spending and real government debt follow the same paths as in the reference case.[12]

B. *Equilibrium and Growth*

The model generates paths of equilibrium prices, outputs, and incomes for the United States and the "rest of the world" under specified policy scenarios. All domestic prices in the model are endogenous, except for the domestic price of oil and gas, which is determined by the exogenously specified world oil price.[13] The general-equilibrium solution requires that demand equal supply in all markets at all points in time.[14] Equilibria are calculated at yearly intervals beginning in the 1990 benchmark year and usually extending to the year 2070.

Economic growth reflects the growth of capital stocks and of potential labor resources. The growth of capital stocks stems from endogenous saving and investment behavior. Potential labor resources are specified as increasing at an exogenous rate.

III. Optimal Environmental Taxes in a Second-Best Setting: Numerical Results

We focus on the policy of a carbon tax. This is a tax on fossil fuels—coal, crude oil, and natural gas—in proportion to their carbon content. Since carbon dioxide (CO_2) emissions generally are proportional to the carbon content of these fuels, a tax based on carbon content is effectively a tax on CO_2 emissions.

A. *Marginal Costs of Emissions Reductions*

Our use of the general equilibrium model is summarized in Figure 1. We explain this figure in several steps, starting with the vertical axis of Figure 1B, which shows the carbon tax rate in dollars per ton. As a first step, this tax rate is set exogenously and the model is used to calculate the general equilibrium associated with each value of the tax rate. Each exogenous setting of the carbon tax rate results in a particular

[10] The oil and gas industry differs from the 12 other industries in incorporating a nonproduced input, oil and gas reserves. Unit production costs rise as these reserves are depleted. The "synfuels" industry produces a backstop substitute for oil and gas, which permits the model to achieve a steady state despite the waning production of oil and gas. Details on these specifications are in Goulder (1992).

[11] The central case value for θ_L, the uncompensated wage elasticity of labor supply, is 0.15, which is an average of estimates for primary and secondary earners. The sensitivity analysis (Section III.C) considers alternative values.

[12] In the reference case (or status quo) simulation, the debt-GNP ratio is constant over time and the government deficit is 2 percent of GNP.

[13] The world oil price path follows the assumptions of the Stanford Energy Modeling Forum. See Darius W. Gaskins and John P. Weyant (forthcoming).

[14] Households and producers are assumed to have perfect foresight. Hence the equilibrium in each period depends not only on current prices and taxes but on future levels as well.

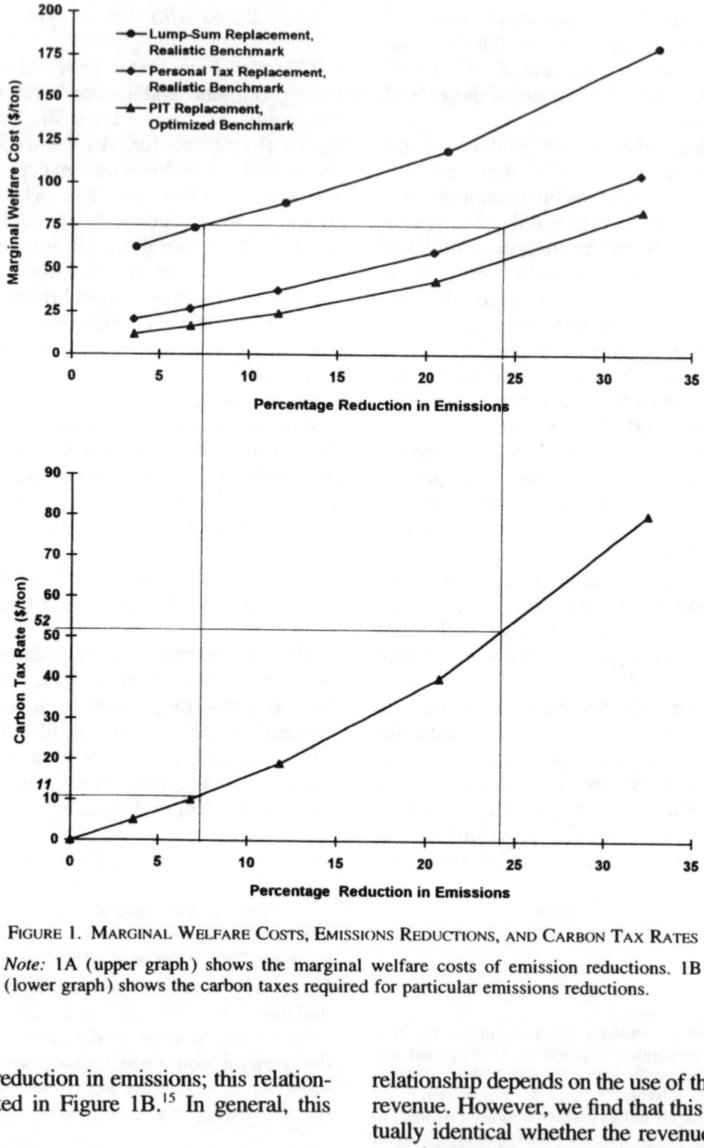

FIGURE 1. MARGINAL WELFARE COSTS, EMISSIONS REDUCTIONS, AND CARBON TAX RATES

Note: 1A (upper graph) shows the marginal welfare costs of emission reductions. 1B (lower graph) shows the carbon taxes required for particular emissions reductions.

percentage reduction in emissions; this relationship is plotted in Figure 1B.[15] In general, this relationship depends on the use of the carbon tax revenue. However, we find that this curve is virtually identical whether the revenue is returned as a lump sum to households or employed to reduce personal tax rates.[16] Although the use of

[15] Obviously, a given tax generates different percentage reductions at different times; we ''average'' these reductions by calculating the present value of the reductions (over an infinite time horizon). The percentage changes in emissions reductions shown in Figure 1 are the percentage changes in these present values. Present values are calculated using the household's real after-tax rate of return as the discount rate.

[16] The difference between returning revenues in lump-sum fashion or through reductions in personal tax rates is virtually undetectable on a graph. For this reason we present only one curve in Figure 1B. The relationships differ

the revenue does not much affect the percentage reduction in emissions, it does affect welfare. As a second step, therefore, we show marginal welfare effects for each use of revenue with separate curves in Figure 1A.[17] The top line in Figure 1A shows the welfare costs when revenues are returned to households in lump-sum fashion, while the middle line in this figure indicates welfare costs when revenues are used to finance cuts in personal income tax rates. Together, Figures 1A and 1B indicate the welfare costs of a given carbon tax under different uses of the revenues. A carbon tax of $11 per ton, for example, implies a reduction in emissions of about 8 percent (Figure 1B). The marginal welfare cost of this emissions reduction is $75 per ton when revenues are returned lump sum (top line of Figure 1A), and just over $25 dollars per ton when revenues are returned through cuts in personal tax rates (middle line of Figure 1A). Figure 1 shows that, for any given carbon tax rate, the marginal welfare costs are lower when revenues are devoted to reductions in marginal tax rates than when revenues are returned in lump-sum fashion. Using revenues to cut personal income tax rates decreases the distortionary costs of the income tax, thereby lowering the cost of this revenue-neutral environmental policy relative to the alternative policy with lump-sum revenue replacement.

B. *Optimal Taxes: Departures from Pigovian Rates*

1. *Lump-Sum Revenue Replacement.*—Once the relationships in Figure 1 are calculated and plotted, we can make use of them in the reverse order to calculate the optimal tax rates associated with given assumptions about the marginal environmental benefits from carbon emissions reductions. These optimal tax rates can be compared with the rates endorsed by the Pigovian principle. Consider first the optimal tax rates when revenues are returned lump sum (top line in Figure 1A). Suppose, for example, that the marginal benefits from reductions (or marginal damages from increases) in CO_2 were equal to $75. As discussed in connection with equations (2) and (3) above, the Pigovian principle would call for a carbon tax of the same value. However, the light horizontal and vertical lines in Figure 1A show that marginal benefits are equal to marginal costs when emissions are reduced by about 8 percent; according to Figure 1B, this requires a carbon tax of only $11 per ton. Thus, the optimal carbon tax rate in this case is only a fraction of the marginal environmental benefits.

The information in Figure 1 can be used similarly to derive the optimal rates associated with other values for marginal environmental benefits. Results for a range of marginal benefits are listed in column (3) of Table 2. When revenues are returned lump sum, the optimal carbon tax is always substantially lower than the marginal environmental benefit. Indeed, if marginal environmental benefits are $50 per ton or lower, the optimal carbon tax is negative![18]

2. *Revenue Replacement Through Cuts in Marginal Income Tax Rates.*—What accounts for these substantial departures from the Pigovian rule? One possible explanation invokes the way revenues are used. Lump-sum replacement of revenues constitutes a suboptimal use of revenues, since a given carbon tax would impose lower welfare costs if revenues were devoted instead to cuts in marginal income tax rates. Would optimal rates closely approximate the marginal environmental benefits if revenues were recycled through cuts in marginal income tax rates? The light horizontal

(slightly) because the method of revenue replacement influences emissions. Specifically, a given carbon tax rate implies somewhat larger emissions reductions in the lump-sum case relative to the case where revenues finance cuts in personal tax rates. This reflects the lower income and aggregate output in the lump-sum case.

[17] Figure 1A shows the marginal welfare cost of emissions reductions (MWC_E) evaluated at different levels of emissions reductions. As indicated in Section I, the MWC_E is the change in welfare (in dollar equivalents) from a marginal (one-ton) reduction in emissions. We evaluate the MWC_E by incrementing the carbon tax and observing, at different levels of emissions reductions, the changes in (nonenvironmental) welfare corresponding to the marginal changes in emissions.

[18] The optimal tax is negative because the carbon subsidy is an implicit subsidy to labor and capital which helps offset the distortions to labor and capital markets generated by explicit factor taxes. In this case the subsidy is financed by a nondistorting, lump-sum tax. For analytical treatments of how environmental taxes act as implicit factor taxes, see Bovenberg and de Mooij (1994) and Parry (1995).

TABLE 2—DIFFERENCES BETWEEN PIGOVIAN AND SECOND-BEST TAXES

		Realistic Tax System				Optimized Tax System		
Assumed marginal environmental damages (1)	"Optimal" Pigovian tax (2)	Optimal tax, lump-sum replacement (3)	Optimal tax, personal tax replacement (4)	$MCPF_P$ (5)	$MED/MCPF_P$ (6)	Optimal tax (7)	MCPF (8)	MED/MCPF (9)
25	25	−19	8	1.29	19	22	1.16	22
50	50	−10	30	1.28	39	46	1.11	45
75	75	11	52	1.25	60	70	1.10	68
100	100	28	73	1.24	81	93	1.10	91

Notes: All tax rates in 1990 dollars per ton. $MCPF_P$ denotes the marginal cost of public funds obtained through the personal income tax.

and vertical lines in Figure 1A show that if marginal environmental benefits are $75 per ton, under this form of revenue-replacement marginal costs are equated to marginal benefits when emissions are reduced by about 24 percent; this reduction requires a carbon tax of $52 per ton (Figure 1B). Optimal rates corresponding to different marginal environmental benefits (or damages) are displayed in column (4) of Table 2. When revenues are devoted to reductions in marginal income tax rates, the optimal tax lies midway between the optimal tax under lump-sum replacement and the "optimal" tax prescribed by the Pigovian rule. Thus, while suboptimal (lump-sum) use of revenues explains some of the deviation from Pigovian rates, departures from Pigovian rates remain even when revenues are returned through cuts in marginal income tax rates.

It is useful to compare these results with the ratio, MED/MCPF, which is the optimal rate implied by the analytical model (equation (2) of Section I). The MCPF depends, in general, on the configuration of all taxes, including whatever carbon taxes are present. We therefore evaluate the MCPF at the new equilibrium after the imposition of the carbon tax.[19] A comparison of columns (4) and (6) reveals that the optimal rates from the numerical model are somewhat lower than the rates prescribed by the analytical model.

3. *Fully Optimal Tax Policies.*—To what might the differences from the "analytical optimum" be attributed? A potential source of this discrepancy is the nature of the numerical model's benchmark. The analytical model presumes a fully optimized tax system—one in which *all* tax rates are set optimally. In contrast, the results from column (4) of Table 2 are based on a realistic, suboptimal benchmark reflecting the configuration of taxes in the U.S. economy.[20] Thus, the rates in column (4) are constrained optimal tax rates, since the policy involves only *incremental* changes in other, distortionary taxes to the extent that carbon tax revenues can finance such changes. These simulations do not involve a fully optimized tax system.

To enhance further the comparisons of results across models, we derive the optimal carbon tax in a new, counterfactual scenario in which *all* taxes are set optimally. Here we develop a configuration of other (noncarbon) taxes that is optimal according to the principles inherent in the analytical model. The optimized configuration of other taxes involves two changes relative to the original benchmark: 1) taxes on intermediate inputs, industry

[19] We are grateful to an anonymous referee for having pointed out the importance of measuring the MCPF at the post-tax equilibrium. The MCPF in column (5) of Table 2 ($MCPF_P$) applies to funds raised from the personal income tax.

[20] An indicator of this suboptimality is the fact that the MCPF differs depending on which tax is employed to raise funds. It is worth noting that we have defined "optimality" strictly in terms of efficiency. Under a broader notion of optimality, differences in MCPF's need not represent deficiencies in the tax system. For example, to the extent that distributional objectives are realized through uneven factor taxation and associated differences in MCPF's, these "suboptimal" features may be constructive elements of the tax system.

outputs, and consumer goods are eliminated, and 2) marginal rates of remaining (capital and labor income) taxes are adjusted so that the MCPF is the same for each tax. Since marginal rates of capital and labor taxes depend on the magnitude of the carbon tax (because the carbon tax finances cuts in factor taxes), the MCPF as well is a function of the magnitude of the carbon tax. Thus, the optimal carbon tax and the optimal configuration of other taxes must be determined simultaneously: for each value of marginal environmental benefits from CO_2 reductions, there is an optimal carbon tax and an optimal configuration of labor and capital taxes (that is, a set of factor tax rates that manages to equate the MCPF's from labor and capital taxes).[21]

Figure 1 and Table 2 include results based on this fully optimized system. Figure 1A shows that in this counterfactual scenario, the marginal welfare costs of given emissions reductions are significantly lower than under the realistic tax system.[22] Correspondingly, in Table 2 the optimal carbon tax associated with given marginal environmental damages is higher than the optimal tax arising in the realistic case. A comparison of columns (7) and (9) of Table 2 shows that the numerical model's results in this fully optimized case closely approximate the tax rates prescribed by the analytical model.[23,24]

C. *Sensitivity Analysis*

Table 3 indicates the sensitivity of optimal tax rates to key parameters. These simulations involve changes relative to the realistic (as opposed to optimized) tax system. The table reports results based on a posited value of $75 per ton for the marginal environmental benefits from the carbon tax. All results in the table are for simulations in which carbon tax revenues are recycled through cuts in personal income tax rates.

The general result from Table 3 is that, under the range of parameter values considered, the analytical and numerical models call for optimal tax rates below the Pigovian optimum. The analytical optimum is always below the Pigovian optimum because the MCPF consistently exceeds unity. The numerical model's optimum is always below the prescribed optimum from the analytical model; as discussed above, this reflects the suboptimal nature of the benchmark tax system.

To consider the significance of preexisting taxes, we reduce or increase the marginal rates of all preexisting taxes by 50 percent. The MCPF moves toward unity as the preexisting tax rates are reduced; accordingly, the optimal tax rates from the analytical and simulation models move toward the Pigovian rate of $75/ton.

Higher values for the intertemporal elasticity of substitution in consumption, the uncompensated elasticity of labor supply, or energy

[21] Thus, in Figure 1A, the lower-most marginal-welfare-cost schedule should be interpreted as the marginal welfare cost of achieving emissions reductions through a fully optimal tax system; the configuration of factor taxes changes with the extent of emissions reductions (although the path of real government spending is the same in all cases). However, we find that the optimal rates for capital and labor taxes change only slightly with changes in the assumed marginal benefits from CO_2 reductions.

[22] This reflects two aspects of the realistic benchmark. First, in this benchmark, the MCPF from capital taxes is larger than that from labor taxes. Second, the combination of the carbon tax and a cut in personal income taxes tends to raise the tax burden on capital relative to labor (because the carbon tax component falls primarily on capital). As a consequence, the revenue-neutral policy effectively emphasizes the high MCPF of capital. In the counterfactual, fully optimized tax setting, the MCPF from capital taxes is lower than in the realistic benchmark; thus the welfare costs of carbon taxes are lower as well.

[23] The slight differences between results in the two columns are due to approximation error. While numerical and analytical results virtually match under the optimized benchmark, they differ significantly under the realistic benchmark case (compare results of columns (4) and (6)). The differences under the realistic benchmark stem from the fact that the carbon tax imposes a higher cost in the realistic benchmark than under optimal benchmark conditions (for reasons given in the previous footnote). This implies a lower optimal tax than would be endorsed by the analytical formula, which presumes a fully optimized setting.

[24] Column (8) of Table 2 suggests the interconnections between marginal environmental damages and the MCPF in an optimized tax system. With marginal environmental damages of $25 per ton, the MCPF is $1.16. But with higher marginal environmental damages (and a higher optimal value for the carbon tax), the MCPF is somewhat lower, as revenues from the (higher) carbon tax permit lower marginal rates on labor and capital. The MCPF is $1.21 if zero marginal environmental damages are assumed (so that the optimal carbon tax is zero).

TABLE 3—SENSITIVITY ANALYSIS[a]

	MCPF	Optimal tax implied by analytical model	Optimal tax from numerical model
1. Central case	1.252	60	52
2. Marginal rates for preexisting taxes:			
Lowered 50 percent	1.113	67	61
Raised 50 percent	1.410	53	46
3. Intertemporal elasticity of substitution in consumption:[b]			
Low (0.33)	1.198	63	55
High (0.66)	1.406	53	43
4. Uncompensated elasticity of labor supply:[c]			
Low (0.00)	1.121	67	61
High (0.26)	1.398	54	48
5. Energy substitution elasticities:[d]			
Lowered by 50 percent	1.233	61	54
Raised by 50 percent	1.366	55	48

[a] Marginal environmental benefits are assumed to be $75 per ton. Results for the numerical model are from simulations of a carbon tax with revenue-preserving reductions in marginal rates of the personal income tax.

[b] Central case value is 0.5.

[c] These simulations involve changes in ν, the goods-leisure elasticity of substitution. The central case value of ν is 0.77, implying an uncompensated labor supply elasticity of 0.15. ν is 0.62 and 0.90 in the low and high elasticity cases. The compensated elasticities in the low, central and high cases are 0.47, 0.94, and 5.90, respectively.

[d] In the low (high) elasticity simulation, σ_{K2}, the elasticity of substitution between composite energy (E) and composite materials (M), is lowered (raised) in all industries by 50 percent from its central case value of 0.7.

substitution elasticities raise the potential for distortions in capital, labor, or energy markets from a given configuration of taxes. The numerical model generates a higher MCPF with increases in these elasticities; hence the optimal rates prescribed by the analytical model are lower. Changes in these parameters also induce changes in the optimal rates derived directly from the numerical model. These changes are in the same direction as the changes in optimal rates prescribed by the analytical model.

Under central case values for parameters, the optimal rate from the numerical model is 69 percent of the Pigovian rate. By comparison, the optimal rate is 57 (73) percent of the Pigovian rate under high (low) values for the intertemporal elasticity of substitution in consumption. It is 64 (81) percent of the Pigovian rate under high (low) values for the labor supply elasticity.

IV. Conclusions

This paper has employed analytical and numerical models to examine the general-equilibrium interactions between environmentally motivated taxes and distortionary taxes. The analytical model extends earlier work by examining environmental taxes that, like carbon taxes, apply to intermediate inputs. This model indicates that in the presence of distortionary taxes, optimal environmental tax rates are generally below the rates suggested by the Pigovian principle—even when revenues from environmental taxes are used to cut distortionary taxes.

The numerical simulations support this analytical result. Under central values for parameters, optimal carbon tax rates from the numerical model (when the tax system is fully optimized) are between six and twelve percent below the marginal environmental damages.

In addition, the numerical model shows that in the presence of realistic policy constraints, optimal carbon tax rates are far below the marginal environmental damages—and may even be negative. Simulations based on the U.S. tax system indicate that if policy makers can only incrementally alter existing distortionary taxes (rather than globally optimize the tax system), the optimal carbon tax may be substantially below the marginal environmental damages. Moreover, if the revenue changes from carbon taxes are absorbed through changes in lump-sum transfers (rather than through changes in marginal rates of existing distortionary taxes), the optimal rate for this tax becomes negative when marginal environmental damages from carbon emissions are below about $50 per ton.

These considerations suggest that estimates of optimal carbon taxes in integrated climate-economy models (for example, William D. Nordhaus, 1993,[25] and Stephen C. Peck and Thomas J. Teisberg, 1992) are biased upward. For example, Nordhaus has considered how recycling carbon-tax revenues through cuts in distortionary taxes affects the optimal carbon tax. When revenues from the carbon tax are returned in lump-sum fashion, the optimal tax rate for the first decade is about $5 per ton; the optimal rate rises to $59 per ton when revenues are devoted to reducing distortionary taxes. Importantly, that study does not consider how preexisting taxes increase the gross costs of the carbon tax itself (before the revenues are recycled). While the Nordhaus study accounts for the efficiency gains connected with the *reduction* (through recycling) of initial distortionary taxes, it does not consider the efficiency costs stemming from the interactions between *remaining* distortionary taxes and the newly imposed carbon tax. The analytical and simulation models in this paper indicate that these interactions augment the costs of the carbon tax and imply an optimal rate below the first-best or Pigovian rate—even in the case where revenues are recycled through cuts in marginal rates of distortionary taxes.

APPENDIX A: ANALYTICAL RESULTS

Firms maximize profits under perfect competition and thus equalize the marginal product of each factor to its user cost:

$$\text{(A1)} \qquad \frac{\partial F}{\partial L}(1, x_C/L, x_D/L) = w$$

$$\text{(A2)} \qquad \frac{\partial F}{\partial x_C}(1, x_C/L, x_D/L) = 1 + \tau_C^x$$

$$\text{(A3)} \qquad \frac{\partial F}{\partial x_D}(1, x_C/L, x_D/L) = 1 + \tau_D^x.$$

[25] Nordhaus has pioneered the integration of (environmental) benefits and (nonenvironmental) costs in simulation modeling of carbon taxes.

(A2) and (A3) yield the demands for the two intermediate inputs as functions (f_C and f_D) of τ_C^x and τ_D^x and the level of employment:

$$\text{(A4)} \qquad x_C = Lf_C(1 + \tau_C^x; 1 + \tau_D^x)$$

$$\text{(A5)} \qquad x_D = Lf_D(1 + \tau_C^x; 1 + \tau_D^x).$$

Substituting (A4) and (A5) into (A1), we can express the producer wage as a function ω of τ_C^x and τ_D^x:

$$\text{(A6)} \qquad w = \omega(1 + \tau_C^x; 1 + \tau_D^x)$$

where

$$\text{(A7)} \qquad \frac{\partial \omega}{\partial \tau_C^x} = \frac{-x_C}{L}; \qquad \frac{\partial \omega}{\partial \tau_D^x} = \frac{-x_D}{L}.$$

To find the optimal tax rates, we substitute (A4) and (A5) into equation (1) of Section I to eliminate x_C and x_D. Maximizing with respect to τ_L, we obtain the following first-order condition:

$$\text{(A8)} \qquad (\lambda - \mu)L + \mu\left[\tau_D^C \frac{\partial C_D}{\partial w_N} + (\tau_L wL + \tau_C^x x_C + \tau_D^x x_D)\frac{1}{L}\frac{\partial L}{\partial w_N}\right] + \frac{\partial U}{\partial Q}\left[\frac{\partial q}{\partial C_D}\frac{\partial C_D}{\partial w_N} + \frac{\partial q}{\partial x_D}\frac{x_D}{L}\frac{\partial L}{\partial w_N}\right] = 0$$

where we have used $\partial U/\partial w_N = \lambda L$ (Roy's identity) and $\lambda \equiv \partial U/\partial C_C$ is the marginal utility of income. Define

$$\text{(A9)} \qquad \bar{\tau}_D^x \equiv \frac{\frac{\partial U}{\partial Q}\left(-\frac{\partial q}{\partial x_D}\right)}{\mu}$$

$$\text{(A10)} \qquad \bar{\tau}_D^C \equiv \frac{\frac{\partial U}{\partial Q}\left(-\frac{\partial q}{\partial C_D}\right)}{\mu}.$$

Substitution of (A9) and (A10) into (A8) yields

$$\text{(A11)} \qquad (\lambda - \mu)L + \mu\left[(\tau_D^C - \bar{\tau}_D^C)\frac{\partial C_D}{\partial w_N} + \tau_L w \frac{\partial L}{\partial w_N}\right] + \mu[\tau_C^x x_C + (\tau_D^x - \bar{\tau}_D^x)x_D] \times \frac{1}{L}\frac{\partial L}{\partial w_N} = 0.$$

The first-order condition for maximizing (1) with respect to τ_C^x is

$$\text{(A12)} \quad \mu\left[x_C + \tau_C^x L \frac{\partial f_C}{\partial \tau_C^x} + (\tau_D^x - \bar{\tau}_D^x) L \frac{\partial f_D}{\partial \tau_C^x}\right] + (1 - \tau_L)\frac{\partial \omega}{\partial \tau_C^x} \times \left[\lambda L + \mu\left[(\tau_D^C - \bar{\tau}_D^C)\frac{\partial C_D}{\partial w_N} + \tau_L w \frac{\partial L}{\partial w_N}\right] + \mu[\tau_C^x x_C + (\tau_D^x - \bar{\tau}_D^x) x_D]\frac{1}{L}\frac{\partial L}{\partial w_N}\right] + \frac{\partial \omega}{\partial \tau_C^x}\mu \tau_L L = 0$$

where we have used (A9) and (A10). Substitution of (A7) and (A11) into (A12) yields:

$$\text{(A13)} \quad \tau_C^x \frac{\partial f_C}{\partial \tau_C^x} + (\tau_D^x - \bar{\tau}_D^x)\frac{\partial f_D}{\partial \tau_C^x} = 0.$$

In an analogous way, we derive the first-order condition for τ_D^x as

$$\text{(A14)} \quad \tau_C^x \frac{\partial f_C}{\partial \tau_D^x} + (\tau_D^x - \bar{\tau}_D^x)\frac{\partial f_D}{\partial \tau_D^x} = 0.$$

(A13) and (A14) together imply $\tau_C^x = 0$ and $\tau_D^x = \bar{\tau}_D^x$. With (A9), this implies equation (2) of Section I, where $\eta \equiv \mu/(\partial U/\partial C_C)$.

Applying $\tau_C^x = 0$ and $\tau_D^x = \bar{\tau}_D^x$ to (A11) yields

$$\text{(A15)} \quad (\lambda - \mu)L = -\mu\left[(\tau_D^C - \bar{\tau}_D^C)\frac{\partial C_D}{\partial w_N} + \tau_L w \frac{\partial L}{\partial w_N}\right].$$

By applying $\tau_C^x = 0$ and $\tau_D^x = \bar{\tau}_D^x$ to the first-order condition that results from maximizing (1) with respect to τ_D^C, we obtain

$$\text{(A16)} \quad (\lambda - \mu)C_D = \mu\left[(\tau_D^C - \bar{\tau}_D^C)\frac{\partial C_D}{\partial \tau_D^C} + \tau_L w \frac{\partial L}{\partial \tau_D^C}\right].$$

Define $\tau_D^{nC} \equiv \tau_D^C - \bar{\tau}_D^C$. (A15) and (A16) are modified versions of the familiar Ramsey equations, where the tax on dirty consumption has been replaced by τ_D^{nC}, the distortionary (or nonenvironmental) component of the tax on dirty consumption. If utility is homothetic and leisure is weakly separable from commodity consumption, (A15) and (A16) can be solved to yield $\tau_D^{nC} = 0$, implying $\tau_D^C = \bar{\tau}_D^C$. Substituting τ_D^C for $\bar{\tau}_D^C$ in (A10), we arrive at equation (3) of Section I. Applying $\tau_D^C - \bar{\tau}_D^C = 0$ to (A15) yields equation (4) of Section I.

APPENDIX B: STRUCTURE AND PARAMETER VALUES OF THE NUMERICAL MODEL[26]

A. *Production Technology*

In each industry i, gross output X_i is produced using inputs of labor (L_i), capital (K_i), and produced intermediate inputs x_{ji} ($j = 1, \ldots, 13$). We employ the following nested form

$$\text{(B1)} \quad X_i = F_i(L_i; K_i; x_{1i}, \ldots, x_{13i}; I_i) = f_i[g_{1i}(L_i, K_i), g_{2i}(E_i, M_i)] - \phi_i(I_i / K_i)I_i$$

where E_i and M_i represent composites of intermediate inputs of energy and materials, respectively. f_i, g_{1i}, and g_{2i} are constant-elasticity-of-substitution functions. Hence the function f, for example, can be written as

$$\text{(B2)} \quad f(g_1, g_2) = \gamma_f[\alpha_f g_1^{\rho_f} + (1 - \alpha_f)g_2^{\rho_f}]^{1/\rho_f}$$

where the industry subscript has been suppressed and where γ_f, α_f, and ρ_f are parameters. The parameter ρ_f is related to σ_f, the elasticity of substitution between g_1 and g_2: $\rho_f = (\sigma_f - 1)/\sigma_f$. Analogous expressions apply for the functions g_1 and g_2.

The second term in equation (B1) represents the loss of output associated with installing new capital (or dismantling existing capital). Per-unit adjustment costs, ϕ, are given by

$$\text{(B3)} \quad \phi(I/K) = \frac{(\beta/2)(I/K - \delta)^2}{I/K}$$

where I represents gross investment (purchases of new capital goods) and β and δ are parameters. The parameter δ denotes the rate of economic depreciation of the capital stock.

The energy composite E in equation (B1) is a CES function of the specific energy products of the different energy industries:

$$\text{(B4a)} \quad E = E(x_1, x_2 + x_3, x_4, x_5, x_6)$$

$$\text{(B4b)} \quad = \gamma_E\left[\sum_{j=1}^{5} \alpha_{Ej}\hat{x}_j^{\rho_E}\right]^{1/\rho_E}$$

where

$$\hat{x}_j = \begin{cases} x_1, & j = 1 \\ x_2 + x_3, & j = 2 \\ x_{j+1}, & j = 3, \ldots, 5 \end{cases}$$

and where $\Sigma_{j=1}^{5} \alpha_{Ej} = 1$. The subscripts to the x_j's in equations (B4a) and (B4b) correspond to energy industries as follows.

[26] A more comprehensive description of the structure of the model is in Goulder (1992). Detailed documentation of the data and parameters for the model is provided in Cruz and Goulder (1992).

Subscript	Energy industries
1	Coal mining
2	Oil and gas extraction
3	Synthetic fuels
4	Petroleum refining
5	Electric utilities
6	Processed natural gas

Oil and gas extraction and synthetic fuels combine as one input in the energy composite, reflecting the fact that these fuels are treated as perfect substitutes in production.

Similarly, the materials composite (M_i) in equation (B1) is a CES function of the specific materials products of the 7 nonenergy industries:

$$\text{(B5a)} \qquad M = M(x_7, x_8, \ldots, x_{13})$$

$$\text{(B5b)} \qquad = \gamma_M \left[\sum_{j=7}^{13} \alpha_{Mj} x_j^{\rho_M} \right]^{1/\rho_M}$$

where $\Sigma_{j=7}^{13} \alpha_{Mj} = 1$. The subscripts to the x_j's in equations (B5a) and (B5b) correspond to materials (nonenergy) industries as follows.

Subscript	Materials industries
7	Agriculture and mining (except coal mining)
8	Construction
9	Metals and machinery
10	Motor vehicles
11	Miscellaneous manufacturing
12	Services (except housing services)
13	Housing services

The elements x_j ($j = 1, \ldots, 13$) in the E and M functions are themselves CES composites of domestically produced and foreign made inputs:

$$\text{(B6)} \qquad x_j = \gamma_{xj}[\alpha_{xj} xD_j^{\rho_{xj}} + (1 - \alpha_{xj}) xF_j^{\rho_{xj}}]^{1/\rho_{xj}}, \quad j = 1, \ldots, 13$$

where xD_j and xF_j denote domestic and foreign intermediate inputs of type j. The overall nesting of the production system is summarized in Table A1.

γ_f in the oil and gas production function is endogenous. In industries other than oil and gas, the element γ_f in the production function is parametric. In the oil and gas industry, γ_f is a decreasing function of cumulative oil and gas extraction:

$$\text{(B7)} \qquad \gamma_{f,t} = \varepsilon_1[1 - (Z_t / \bar{Z})^{\varepsilon_2}]$$

where ε_1 and ε_2 are parameters, Z_t represents cumulative extraction as of the beginning of period t, and $\bar{Z}$ is the original estimated total stock of recoverable reserves of oil and gas (as estimated from the benchmark year). The following equation of motion specifies the evolution of Z_t:

$$\text{(B8)} \qquad Z_{t+1} = Z_t + X_t.$$

Equation (B7) implies that the production function for oil and gas shifts downward as cumulative oil and gas extraction increases. This addresses the fact that as reserves are depleted, remaining reserves become more difficult to extract and require more inputs per unit of extraction.

TABLE A1—NESTED PRODUCTION STRUCTURE

Function
$X = f(g_1, g_2) - \phi(I/K)I$
$g_1 = g_1(L, K)$
$g_2 = g_2(E, M)$
$E = E(x_1, \ldots, x_6)$
$M = M(x_7, \ldots, x_{13})$
$x_i = x_i(xD_i, xF_i) \qquad i = 1, \ldots, 13$

Note: All functions are CES in form except for $\phi(I/K)$, which is quadratic in I/K.

B. *Behavior of Firms*

In each industry, managers of firms serve stockholders in aiming to maximize the value of the firm. The objective of firm-value maximization determines firms' choices of input quantities and investment levels in each period of time.

While optimal demands for variable inputs (labor and intermediate inputs) depend only on current prices, optimal investment depends on both present and future prices. In specifying firms' investment decisions, we adopt the asset price approach of Lawrence H. Summers (1981). The investment decision is fundamentally intertemporal because the firm's current investment decisions affect future capital stocks and thereby influence future adjustment costs through the function $\phi(I/K)$ contained in equation (B1). As detailed in Goulder (1992), we assume that managers finance investments through retained earnings, new debt issues, and new share issues, where new share issues represent the marginal source of funds. Optimal investment is a function of tax-adjusted q (see Goulder, 1992).

C. *Household Behavior*

Consumption, labor supply, and saving result from the decisions of an infinitely-lived representative household maximizing its intertemporal utility with perfect foresight. The nested structure of the household's utility function is indicated in Table A2. In year t the household chooses a path of "full-consumption" C to maximize

$$\text{(B9)} \qquad U_t = \sum_{s=t}^{\infty} (1 + \xi)^{t-s} \frac{\sigma}{\sigma - 1} C_s^{(\sigma-1)/\sigma}$$

where ξ is the subjective rate of time preference and σ is the intertemporal elasticity of substitution in full consumption. C is a CES composite of consumption of goods and services $\tilde{C}$ and leisure l:

$$\text{(B10)} \qquad C_s = [\tilde{C}_s^{(\nu-1)/\nu} + \alpha_l^{1/\nu} l_s^{(\nu-1)/\nu}]^{\nu/(\nu-1)}.$$

ν is the elasticity of substitution between goods and leisure; α_l is an intensity parameter for leisure.

TABLE A2—NESTED UTILITY STRUCTURE

Function	Functional form
$U_t(C_t, C_{t+1}, \ldots, C_s, \ldots)$	Constant intertemporal elasticity of substitution
$C_s(\tilde{C}_s, l_s)$	CES
$\tilde{C}_s(\bar{C}_{1,s}, \ldots, \bar{C}_{i,s}, \ldots, \bar{C}_{17,s})$	Cobb-Douglas
$\bar{C}_{i,s}(CD_{i,s}, CF_{i,s})$	CES
Variable	**Definition**
U_t	Intertemporal utility evaluated from period t
C_s	Full consumption in period s
$\tilde{C}_s$	Overall goods consumption in period s
l_s	Leisure in period s
$\bar{C}_{i,s}$	Consumption of composite consumer good i in period s
$\mathrm{CD}_{i,s}$	Consumption of domestically produced consumer good i in period s
$\mathrm{CF}_{i,s}$	Consumption of foreign produced consumer good i in period s

The variable $\tilde{C}_s$ in (B10) is a Cobb-Douglas aggregate of 17 composite consumer goods:

$$\tilde{C}_s = \prod_{i=1}^{17} \bar{C}_{i,s}^{\alpha_{\tilde{C},i}} \tag{B11}$$

where the $\alpha_{\tilde{C},i}$ ($i = 1, \ldots, 17$) are parameters. The 17 types of consumer goods identified in the model are shown in Table 1 of the main text.

Consumer goods are produced domestically and abroad. Each composite consumer good $\bar{C}_i$, $i = 1, \ldots, 17$, is a CES aggregate of a domestic and foreign consumer good of a given type:

$$\bar{C} = \gamma_{\bar{C}}[\alpha_{\bar{C}}\mathrm{CD}^{\rho_{\bar{C}}} + (1 - \alpha_{\bar{C}})\mathrm{CF}^{\rho_{\bar{C}}}]^{1/\rho_{\bar{C}}}. \tag{B12}$$

In the above equation, CD and CF denote the household's consumption of domestically produced and foreign made consumer good of a given type at a given point in time. For simplicity, we have omitted subscripts designating the type of consumer good and the time period.

The household maximizes utility subject to the intertemporal budget constraint given by the following condition governing the change in financial wealth, WK:

$$\mathrm{WK}_{t+1} - \mathrm{WK}_t = \bar{r}_t\mathrm{WK}_t + \mathrm{YL}_t + \mathrm{GT}_t - \tilde{p}_t\tilde{C}_t. \tag{B13}$$

In the above equation, $\bar{r}$ is the average after-tax return on the household's portfolio of financial capital, YL is after-tax labor income, GT is transfer income, and $\tilde{p}$ is the price index representing the cost to the household of a unit of the consumption composite, $\tilde{C}$.

D. *Government Behavior*

A single government sector approximates government activities at all levels—federal, state, and local. The main activities of the government sector are purchasing goods and services (both nondurable and durable), transferring incomes, and raising revenue through taxes or bond issue.

1. *Components of Government Expenditure.*—Government expenditure, G, divides into nominal purchases of nondurable goods and services (GP), nominal government investment (GI), and nominal transfers (GT):

$$G_t = \mathrm{GP}_t + \mathrm{GI}_t + \mathrm{GT}_t \tag{B14}$$

In the reference case, the paths of real government purchases, investment, and transfers all are specified as growing at the steady-state real growth rate, g. In simulating policy changes we fix the paths of GP, GI, and GT so that the paths of real government purchases, investment and transfers are the same as in corresponding years of the reference case. Thus, the expenditure side of the government ledger is largely kept unchanged across simulations. This procedure is expressed by

$$\mathrm{GP}_t^P / p_{\mathrm{GP},t}^P = \mathrm{GP}_t^R / p_{\mathrm{GP},t}^R \tag{B15a}$$

$$\mathrm{GI}_t^P / p_{\mathrm{GI},t}^P = \mathrm{GI}_t^R / p_{\mathrm{GI},t}^R \tag{B15b}$$

$$\mathrm{GT}_t^P / p_{\mathrm{GT},t}^P = \mathrm{GT}_t^R / p_{\mathrm{GT},t}^R. \tag{B15c}$$

The superscripts P and R denote policy change and reference case magnitudes, while p_{GP}, p_{GI}, and p_{GT} are price indices for GP, GI, and GT. The price index for government investment, p_{GI}, is the purchase price of the representative capital good. The price index for transfers, p_{GT}, is the consumer price index. The index for government purchases, p_{GP}, is defined below.

2. *Allocation of Government Purchases.*—GP divides into purchases of particular outputs of the 13 domestic industries according to fixed expenditure shares:

$$\alpha_{G,i}\mathrm{GP} = \mathrm{GP}X_i p_i \qquad i = 1, \ldots, 13. \tag{B16}$$

$\mathrm{GP}X_i$ and p_i are the quantity demanded and price of output from industry i, and $\alpha_{G,i}$ is the corresponding expenditure share. The ideal price index for government purchases, p_{GP}, is given by

$$p_{\mathrm{GP}} = \prod_{i=1}^{13} p_i^{\alpha_{G,i}}. \tag{B17}$$

TABLE A3—PARAMETER VALUES

Panel A: Elasticities of substitution in production

	Parameter for substitution margin					
	σ_f g_1-g_2	σ_{g_1} $L-K$	σ_{g_2} $E-M$	σ_E E components	σ_M M components	σ_x Domestic-foreign inputs
Producing industry:						
1. Coal mining	0.7	0.80	0.7	1.08	0.6	1.14
2. Oil and gas extraction	0.7	0.82	0.7	1.04	0.6	(infinite)
3. Synthetic fuels	0.7	0.82	0.7	1.04	0.6	(not traded)
4. Petroleum refining	0.7	0.74	0.7	1.04	0.6	2.21
5. Electric utilities	0.7	0.81	0.7	0.97	0.6	1.0
6. Gas utilities	0.7	0.96	0.7	1.04	0.6	1.0
7. Agriculture and noncoal mining	0.7	0.68	0.7	1.45	0.6	2.31
8. Construction	0.7	0.95	0.7	1.04	0.6	1.0
9. Metals and machinery	0.7	0.91	0.7	1.21	0.6	2.74
10. Motor vehicles	0.7	0.80	0.7	1.04	0.6	1.14
11. Miscellaneous manufacturing	0.7	0.94	0.7	1.08	0.6	2.74
12. Services (except housing)	0.7	0.98	0.7	1.07	0.6	1.0
13. Housing services	0.7	0.80	0.7	1.81	0.6	(not traded)

Panel B: Parameters of stock effect function in oil and gas industry[a]

	Parameter			
	Z_0	$\bar{Z}$	ε_1	ε_2
Value	0	450	1.27	2.0

Panel C: Utility function parameters

	Parameter			
	ξ	σ	ν	α_1
Value	0.007	0.5	0.77	0.84

[a] This function is parametrized so that γ_f approaches 0 as Z approaches $\bar{Z}$ (see equation (B7)). The value of $\bar{Z}$ is 450 billion barrels (about 100 times the 1990 production of oil and gas, where gas is measured in barrel equivalents). $\bar{Z}$ is based on estimates from Charles D. Masters et al. (1987). Investment in new oil and gas capital ceases to be profitable before reserves are depleted: the values of ε_1 and ε_2 imply that, in the baseline scenario, oil and gas investment becomes zero in the year 2031.

REFERENCES

Ballard, Charles L. and Fullerton, Don. "Distortionary Taxes and the Provision of Public Goods." *Journal of Economic Perspectives*, Summer 1992, *6*(3), pp. 117–31.

Bovenberg, Lans and de Mooij, Ruud A. "Environmental Levies and Distortionary Taxation." *American Economic Review*, September 1994, *84*(4), pp. 1085–89.

Bovenberg, Lans and van der Ploeg, Frederick. "Environmental Policy, Public Finance and the Labor Market in a Second-Best World." *Journal of Public Economics*, November 1994, *55*(3), pp. 349–90.

Cruz, Miguel and Goulder, Lawrence H. "An Intertemporal General Equilibrium Model for Analyzing U.S. Energy and Environmental Policies: Data Documentation." Manuscript, Stanford University, 1992.

Diamond, Peter A. and Mirrlees, James A. "Optimal Taxation and Public Production: I—Production Efficiency." *American Economic Review*, March 1971a, *61*(1), pp. 8–27.

______. "Optimal Taxation and Public Production: II—Tax Rules." *American Economic Review*, June 1971b, *61*(3), pp. 261–78.

Gaskins, Darius W. and Weyant, John P. *Reducing global carbon dioxide emissions: Costs and policy options.* Stanford, CA: Stanford University Press, forthcoming 1996.

Goulder, Lawrence H. "An Intertemporal General Equilibrium Model for Analyzing U.S. Energy and Environmental Policies: Model Structure." Manuscript, Stanford University, November 1992.

______. "Effects of Carbon Taxes in an Economy with Prior Tax Distortions: An Intertemporal General Equilibrium Analysis." *Journal of Environmental Economics and Management*, November 1995b, *29*(3), pp. 271–97.

______. "Environmental Taxation and the 'Double Dividend': A Reader's Guide." *International Tax and Public Finance*, August 1995a, *2*(2), pp. 157–83.

Lee, Dwight R. and Misiolek, Walter S. "Substituting Pollution Taxation for General Taxation: Some Implications for Efficiency in Pollution Taxation." *Journal of Environmental Economics and Management*, December 1986, *13*(4), pp. 338–47.

Masters, Charles D.; Attanasi, Emil; Dietzman, William; Meyer, Richard; Michell, Robert and Root, David. "World Resources of Crude Oil, Natural Gas, Natural Bitumen, and Shale Oil." *Proceedings of the 12th World Petroleum Congress*, 1987, *5*, pp. 3–27.

Nordhaus, William D. "Optimal Greenhouse-Gas Reductions and Tax Policy in the 'DICE' Model." *American Economic Review*, May 1993 (*Papers and Proceedings*), *83*(2), pp. 313–17.

Oates, Wallace E. "Pollution Charges as a Source of Public Revenues," in Herbert Giersch, ed., *Economic progress and environmental concerns, 1991*. Berlin: Springer-Verlag, 1993, pp. 135–52.

______. "Green Taxes: Can We Protect the Environment and Improve the Tax System at the Same Time?" *Southern Economic Journal*, April 1995, *61*(4), pp. 915–22.

Parry, Ian W. H. "Pollution Taxes and Revenue Recycling." *Journal of Environmental Economics and Management*, November 1995, *29*(3), pp. 564–77.

Pearce, David W. "The Role of Carbon Taxes in Adjusting to Global Warming." *Economic Journal*, July 1991, *101*, pp. 938–48.

Peck, Stephen C. and Teisberg, Thomas J. "CETA: A Model for Carbon Emissions Trajectory Assessment." *Energy Journal*, 1992, *13*(1), pp. 55–77.

Poterba, James M. "Global Warming: A Public Finance Perspective." *Journal of Economic Perspectives*, Fall 1993, *7*(4), pp. 47–63.

Sandmo, Agnar. "Optimal Taxation in the Presence of Externalities." *Swedish Journal of Economics*, 1975, *77*(1), pp. 86–98.

Shackleton, Robert; Shelby, Michael; Cristofaro, Alex; Brinner, Roger; Yanchar, Joyce; Goulder, Lawrence; Jorgenson, Dale; Wilcoxen, Peter and Pauly, Peter. "The Efficiency Value of Carbon Tax Revenues," in Darius Gaskins and John Weyant, eds., *Reducing global carbon dioxide emissions: Costs and policy options*. Stanford, CA: Stanford University Press, forthcoming 1996.

Summers, Lawrence H. "Taxation and Corporate Investment: A *q*-Theory Approach." *Brookings Papers on Economic Activity*, January 1981, *1*, pp. 67–127.

[9]

Environmental Levies and Distortionary Taxation: Comment

By DON FULLERTON*

With no revenue requirement, or where government can use lump-sum taxes, Arthur C. Pigou (1947) shows that the first-best tax on pollution is equal to the marginal environmental damage. Consumers then pay the social marginal cost of each item, the direct cost of resources, plus the indirect cost of pollution.

Suppose government needs more revenue, however, and cannot use lump-sum taxes. In this second-best world, our intuition might tell us to raise all tax rates: the tax on any "clean" commodity should be raised above its first-best level of zero, and the tax on a "dirty" good should be raised above its first-best Pigovian level (the marginal environmental damage). Despite this intuition, a recent paper by A. Lans Bovenberg and Ruud A. de Mooij (1994 p. 1085) claims to "... demonstrate that, in the presence of preexisting distortionary taxes, the optimal pollution tax typically lies below the Pigovian tax... ."

This note argues that nothing is necessarily wrong with the intuition that all taxes should be raised. Nothing is wrong with the Bovenberg and de Mooij model either, but the above quote could be misinterpreted. I generalize their model to reconcile these opposing views.

Earlier writers have expressed several versions of the "double-dividend hypothesis."[1] These views are discussed more below, but a strong version of this hypothesis might claim that a revenue-neutral switch toward a tax on the dirty good and away from taxation of clean goods can improve environmental quality *and* reduce the overall cost of tax distortions. By implication, this view might suggest that any additional revenue requirements should be met by raising the tax on the dirty good by more than taxes on clean goods. The important and correct result of Bovenberg and de Mooij is that this strong view is flawed.[2] Even if the pollution tax helps solve an environmental problem, it likely worsens other tax distortions. Thus, the tax on the dirty good should rise by less than the tax on the clean good. Bovenberg and de Mooij focus on the *differential* between the tax rates on the clean and dirty goods, but they never quite say so. They assume the tax on the clean good is always zero, so their dirt tax *is* the differential. With this choice of normalization, starting with the dirt tax at the Pigovian rate, additional revenue would be raised by the labor tax while the dirt tax (differential) would fall.

However, other normalizations are equally valid and sometimes preferable. In their model, the extra labor tax is equivalent to a uniform tax on both goods. Thus, from the same starting point with the dirt tax at the Pigovian level, an equivalent policy would raise both the commodity tax rates. The total tax on the dirty good would then exceed the Pigovian level.

Bovenberg and de Mooij clearly understand this point, but their readers might not. Therefore, the first purpose of this note is just to clarify the interpretation of their results. The

* Department of Economics, University of Texas, Austin, TX 78712 (e-mail: dfullert@eco.utexas.edu). I am grateful for financial assistance from National Science Foundation grant SBR-9413334 and Environmental Protection Agency grant R824740-01, and for helpful suggestions from Lans Bovenberg, Larry Goulder, Gib Metcalf, Ian Parry, Ronnie Schöb, Pete Wilcoxen, Jay Wilson, Ann Wolverton, and two anonymous referees. This paper is part of the National Bureau of Economic Research's research program in Public Economics. Any opinions expressed are those of the author and not those of the National Science Foundation, the Environmental Protection Agency, or the National Bureau of Economic Research.

[1] Examples include David Terkla (1984), Dwight R. Lee and Walter S. Misiolek (1986), and Wallace E. Oates (1991).

[2] Other recent literature that refutes the strong view includes Bovenberg and F. van der Ploeg (1994), Ian W. H. Parry (1995), and Bovenberg and Lawrence H. Goulder (1996). Further discussion is provided by Oates (1995) and by Goulder (1995), who distinguishes weak and strong forms of the double-dividend hypothesis.

second purpose is to explore the role of "normalization" in a model with tax rates on both goods and on labor. Any one tax rate can be set to zero, as a conceptual matter, but implementation of some taxes might be easier than others as a practical matter.

In fact, I later reinterpret the model of Bovenberg and de Mooij to describe a case where production requires both a clean input and "emissions." This dirty input is difficult to monitor, because it is not purchased on the market. Enforcement is difficult, if midnight dumping is easy. Yet any one of these tax rates can be set to zero. Thus, the emissions tax can be entirely replaced by the equivalent combination of a subsidy to all clean inputs plus an additional tax on output. This "two-part instrument" provides the same changes in all relative prices, and thus the same outcome, as the emissions tax. And both parts apply to market transactions, with invoices to substantiate the tax due or the subsidy requested.

I. The Model

Bovenberg and de Mooij use a linear production technology where a unit of time can be retained as leisure V, or it can be supplied as labor L to produce the dirty good D, the clean good C, or government consumption G. The number of individuals is N, and labor productivity is h. They define units such that all unit production costs are one. Thus:

$$(1) \qquad hNL = NC + ND + G.$$

Their second-best optimum may involve a tax on the dirty good at rate t_D and on labor at rate t_L. Here, I add the possibility of a tax on the clean good at rate t_C. The procedure is to look at a revenue-neutral change that leaves G unaffected. Differentiate (1), use $dG = 0$, and divide by N:

$$(2) \qquad hdL = dC + dD.$$

Household utility depends on choices of private goods, given the public good G and the level of environmental quality E. Thus, households maximize:

$$(3) \qquad U = u(C, D, V, G, E)$$

subject to their budget constraint:

$$(4) \qquad hL(1 - t_L) = C(1 + t_C) + D(1 + t_D).$$

Environmental quality is a function of the output of the dirty industry, $E = e(ND)$, where $e' < 0$. Define τ as the dollar cost of environmental damage per unit of the dirty output:

$$(5) \qquad \tau = -\frac{\partial u}{\partial E} e' N/\lambda.$$

Each household's consumption of D imposes cost on the utility of N households, converted into dollars when divided by λ, the marginal utility of income. As will be confirmed shortly, this τ at the first-best optimum is the Pigovian tax rate.

In general, the government's second-best problem is to maximize utility by its selection of tax rates t_C, t_D, and t_L. At that second-best optimum, given the revenue requirement ($dG = 0$), there is no change that can raise utility. Totally differentiate the utility function (3), use $dV = -dL$, and set dU equal to zero:[3]

$$(6) \qquad dU = 0 = -\frac{\partial u}{\partial V} dL + \frac{\partial u}{\partial C} dC + \frac{\partial u}{\partial D} dD + \frac{\partial u}{\partial E} e' NdD.$$

Then use household first-order conditions,[4] the definition of τ in (5), and the production frontier (2) to get:

$$(7) \qquad 0 = ht_L dL + t_C dC + (t_D - \tau)dD.$$

Consider three special cases. First, suppose $t_L = t_C = 0$. Either government has some other lump-sum source of revenue, or, by happy coincidence, the Pigovian tax collects just

[3] I set $dU = 0$ to characterize the second-best optimum, whereas Bovenberg and de Mooij use dU to discuss the effect on utility of reducing t_D below the first-best Pigovian level. Both methods reveal whether t_D lies below τ, the marginal environmental damage, but the actual value of τ may depend on which point is evaluated. I am grateful to Gib Metcalf for pointing this out.

[4] First-order conditions imply $\partial u/\partial C = \lambda(1 + t_C)$, $\partial u/\partial D = \lambda(1 + t_D)$, and $\partial u/\partial V = \lambda h(1 - t_L)$.

enough revenue to finance G. Then, (7) implies $t_D = \tau$. This first-best outcome confirms that τ in equation (5) is indeed the first-best Pigovian tax.

Second, consider the case of Bovenberg and de Mooij, where $t_C = 0$ and the revenue requirement means $t_L > 0$. Then, (7) implies:

$$(8) \qquad t_D - \tau = -ht_L \frac{dL}{dD}.$$

Thus, the sign of dL/dD is crucial, and their paper devotes an entire section to it. In order to get definitive results for the change in L, they assume that a subutility function for consumption goods $Q(C, D)$ is homothetic and weakly separable from leisure.[5] They consider a small revenue-neutral change that would raise t_D and lower t_L. In brief, they note that any added tax on D is a partial consumption tax that raises the overall cost of consumption and reduces the real wage. It therefore affects the labor/leisure choice as well as the mix of C and D. The added t_D must exceed the fall in t_L, to collect the same revenue. Because it is more distorting, they argue, the increase in t_D affects actual labor supply more than the equal-revenue reduction in t_L. Thus, both D and L fall.

For present purposes, let us just accept the argument that dL/dD is positive. In this case (where $t_C = 0$), equation (8) means the second-best pollution tax lies below the marginal environmental damage ($t_D < \tau$).

Third, however, the same equation (7) can be employed to show the case where $t_L = 0$. In this case, t_C is used to raise the necessary revenue, and:

$$(9) \qquad t_D - \tau = -t_C \frac{dC}{dD}.$$

Assuming no perverse revenue effects, and $t_L = 0$, revenue neutrality requires that an increase in t_D be accompanied by a fall in t_C. Thus, dC/dD clearly is negative. As long as revenue needs mean that t_C is positive, then $t_D > \tau$, and the second-best pollution tax exceeds the marginal environmental damage. This result confirms the intuition that the dirt tax can help raise revenue.

More generally, equation (7) implies:

$$(10) \qquad t_D < \tau \quad \text{iff} \quad t_C < -ht_L \frac{dL}{dC}.$$

In the ongoing example, a revenue-neutral shift from labor tax toward dirt tax is likely to reduce D and increase C, but also reduce labor supply. Thus, dL/dC is negative, and the critical threshold for t_C is positive. Bovenberg and de Mooij choose a value ($t_C = 0$) that lies below this threshold, so their second-best pollution tax lies below the marginal environmental damage. But the result could have gone either way. If the preexisting t_C happens to equal $-ht_L dL/dC$, by coincidence, then the second-best pollution tax could exactly match τ.

II. Interpretations

The simple explanation for these results is that the labor tax is equivalent to a uniform tax t on both C and D. The budget constraint in (4) is the same whether labor income is multiplied by $(1 - t_L)$, or all expenditures are multiplied by $(1 + t)$, as long as $(1 + t) = 1/(1 - t_L)$. Government revenue also is unaffected by this switch. Start from the Bovenberg and de Mooij solution with $t_L > 0$, $t_C = 0$, and $t_D < \tau$. Then with no effect on any outcome whatsoever, any portion of the labor tax can be replaced by raising both t_C and t_D, until t_D matches or exceeds the marginal environmental damage.[6]

The alternative normalization can be used to help clarify Bovenberg and de Mooij. In equation (9), where $t_L = 0$, the result was $dC/dD < 0$ and, therefore, $(t_D - \tau) > 0$. Thus, under this normalization, the dirt tax is indeed used to raise revenue. Bovenberg and de Mooij show that labor supply falls, however, so the production frontier means dC/dD is smaller than one (in absolute value). Thus, from (9),

[5] In addition, to focus on the relevant externality and taxes, the framework assumes away any other distortions such as imperfect competition or government regulation.

[6] Ronnie Schöb (1997) makes a similar point.

the revenue-raising *component* of the dirt tax $(t_D - \tau)$ is less than t_C. The reason is that while both taxes distort the labor-leisure choice, the already-higher t_D also distorts the consumption mix.

In personal correspondence, Bovenberg says:

> To avoid confusion, we probably should have said that "optimal tax differentiation is less than the Pigovian rule would suggest." Our point is perhaps clearer in a model in which intermediate inputs pollute. In that case, the optimal pollution tax is always below the Pigovian tax, since the optimal tax on clean intermediate inputs is always zero. (Bovenberg and Goulder, 1996)

Another interpretation is provided by an equation in Agnar Sandmo (1975) that can be slightly rewritten to express the total tax on the dirty good as a weighted average of a revenue-raising Ramsey term (R) and the marginal environmental damage (τ):

$$t_D = \left(1 - \frac{1}{\eta}\right)R + \frac{1}{\eta}\tau, \tag{11}$$

where η is the marginal cost of public funds. With distorting taxes in the economy, a marginal dollar of revenue has a social cost that is more than a dollar ($\eta > 1$). Thus, the environmental component (τ/η) is less than the Pigovian rate (τ). Interestingly, an increase in the government revenue requirement means an increase in the distortionary effects of taxes, a higher η, more weight on the revenue-raising term, and less weight on the marginal environmental damage.[7]

Because Bovenberg and de Mooij set $t_C = 0$, they use the labor tax to acquire additional revenue. The revenue-raising term in (11) is zero, so $t_D = \tau/\eta < \tau$. With this normalization, if government needs more revenue, the labor tax would rise while the dirt tax actually would fall.

If, instead, the labor tax were zero, then R in (11) may be large and $t_D > \tau$. With this normalization, both t_C and t_D are raised to acquire more revenue. Thus, the intuition described in my introduction just uses a normalization different from that of Bovenberg and de Mooij.

What about the double-dividend hypothesis? Early writers used partial equilibrium models and often were not explicit about the experiment under consideration. In some cases, they had in mind a reform that would replace command and control regulation with a Pigovian tax. If this switch provides the same environmental protection, with the same effect on product prices, it would raise revenue that could be used to reduce distorting labor taxes. Bovenberg and de Mooij agree this reform would raise welfare.[8] In other cases, early writers may have had in mind an initial point that was suboptimal. If some taxes are more distorting than others, then a reform might well be able to increase a pollution tax, reduce a highly distorting tax, and raise welfare. Bovenberg and de Mooij also do not intend to refute this general proposition. Instead, their main point is that the early use of partial equilibrium models often did not recognize that additional environmental taxes can raise product prices in a way that exacerbates labor-supply distortions.

In this sense, early writers were correct to think that the tax on the dirty good could be increased in some circumstances, even perhaps above the marginal environmental damage, but wrong to think that it would necessarily be less distorting than other taxes.

[7] This interpretation, as suggested by a referee, appears in Bovenberg and van der Ploeg (1994). The higher marginal cost of public funds (η) means that all public goods are more expensive, including protection of the environment. Thus, the tax system is used less for the environment and more to try to raise revenue efficiently.

[8] In the terminology of Goulder (1995) and Parry (1995), this reform would have only the positive "revenue-recycling" effect of reducing other distorting taxes, without the negative "tax-interaction" effect of reducing the real net wage. This reform is equivalent to the "weak" version of the double-dividend hypothesis: if an uncorrected externality is subjected to initial taxation, then welfare is higher if the revenue is used to reduce other distorting taxes than if it is returned to consumers lump sum.

III. The Equivalence of Environmental Taxes and Subsidies

Finally, alternative normalizations are useful as a practical matter. Some countries may have large labor taxes (where the normalization of Bovenberg and de Mooij would be relevant), while others rely more on commodity taxes (where t_L is low and $t_D > \tau$). Also, in terms of reform, some instruments are easier to implement than others. Indeed, many tax-rate combinations can achieve the same second-best optimal quantities.

A. *No Need to Tax the Dirty Good*

In the first interpretation, as above, $Q(C, D)$ is a subutility function over two market goods. Suppose, however, that political constraints or administrative costs prevent the authorities from taxing the dirty good at all, so $t_D = 0$. No problem. By equation (7), just set:

$$t_C = \tau \frac{dD}{dC} - ht_L \frac{dL}{dC}. \tag{12}$$

To shift consumption away from D, this tax on C must be negative.[9] This solution works like an implicit deposit-refund system, or withholding tax. If the dirt tax is unenforceable (t_D must be zero), just raise the labor tax and give part of it back as a subsidy on clean consumption.[10]

This observation leads to one more refutation. One other version of the double-dividend hypothesis might claim that an environmental tax always leads to higher welfare than an environmental subsidy, because the revenue from a tax can be used to reduce other distorting taxes in the economy, while the environmental subsidy must be funded by *raising* other distorting taxes. Not so. This model shows that the two tax systems are equivalent. The tax on the dirty good raises its price, which reduces the real net wage and offsets the cut in the labor tax. Symmetrically, the subsidy to the clean good reduces its equilibrium price, which raises the real net wage and offsets the needed increase in the labor tax. Thus, the tax system with the subsidy to the clean good plus higher labor tax is equivalent in all respects to the tax system with the higher dirt tax and lower labor tax.

B. *No Need to Enforce Against Dumping*

In a second interpretation, $Q(C, D)$ represents the "technology" of household disposal. Then Q is a single consumption good, C represents the amount going into clean forms of disposal such as recycling or sanitary landfill, and D is the amount dumped illegally.[11] Instead of describing indifference curves between C and D, the $Q(C, D)$ function describes isoquants that show different combinations of clean disposal and dumping that are feasible and consistent with any given level of consumption Q; the rest of the model is unchanged. A difficult problem for policy makers (and for economists using enforcement models) is how to set the level of costly enforcement, the probability of detection, and the penalty for dumping (t_D). Results here suggest this problem can be entirely circumvented. An equivalent outcome can be achieved by adding a tax on all output Q (or equivalently, on labor) and a subsidy to proper disposal. This solution is an explicit, second-best deposit-refund system.

[9] To have the same effect on relative prices as the earlier tax on D, this solution must subsidize C. In the earlier case, denoted here by asterisks, the budget constraint was $hL(1 - t_L^*) = C + D(1 + t_D^*)$. Divide through by $(1 + t_D^*)$ and call the result $hL(1 - t_L) = C(1 + t_C) + D$. Then the new t_L must be $(t_L^* + t_D^*)/(1 + t_D^*)$, and $t_C = -t_D^*/(1 + t_D^*)$.

[10] Labor L can be taken to represent all resources that can be sold in the market or retained for use at home. Then t_L needs to tax all income to be a withholding tax on all spending.

[11] Fullerton and Thomas C. Kinnaman (1995) use such a function to solve for the optimal tax on output and subsidy to clean disposal (deposit-refund system) in a first-best model. Results here show equivalence in a second-best model. In this case, the units convention means that it costs a dollar to purchase *and dispose of* one unit in the form of C, or a dollar to purchase and dispose of one unit in the form of D. If clean disposal is more expensive, a dollar on C yields less consumption.

C. *No Need to Monitor Emissions*

In a third interpretation, $Q(C, D)$ is a constant returns-to-scale production function. Utility depends on consumption of Q, but the optimizations above simply substitute into that utility function the firm's production of Q, which uses a clean input C and emissions D. These emissions may be solid, liquid, or gaseous. The firm buys each unit of C on the market for a dollar (or $1 + t_C$, gross of tax). Each unit of emissions also entails some private cost for removal, transport, and disposal. By the units convention above, a unit of emissions is defined as the amount that costs a dollar (or $1 + t_D$, gross of tax). The utility function also could be amended to add other goods that are produced using only the clean input (labor).

Suppose the economy starts with a labor tax to raise revenue. The additional Pigovian tax would apply to emissions, and Bovenberg and de Mooij show that the second-best emissions tax t_D is less than marginal environmental damage τ. This emissions tax has an "output effect" that raises the cost of production, reducing demand for the good, and a "factor substitution effect" that induces the firm to cut emissions per-unit output. But emissions are not a purchased input with an invoice to help monitor and enforce the tax. An equivalent "two-part instrument" would provide a tax on output (to get the output effect) and a subsidy to clean inputs (to get the factor substitution effect). Both of these apply to market transactions, with invoices. Since labor is already subject to tax, however, this "subsidy" to the clean input really just means a lower tax here than in other nonpolluting industries. The combination (t_L, t_D) can be replaced by a system with a lower rate of tax on clean inputs used in Q, plus an excise tax on Q.

IV. Conclusion

Bovenberg and de Mooij obtain the correct analytical results with their normalization where the tax on the clean good is zero, but they leave the impression that the tax on the dirty good always lies below the Pigovian rate. Other normalizations have no effect on the equilibrium outcome, but they are very useful to help interpret these results. First, if the labor tax were zero, the total tax on the dirty good could exceed the Pigovian rate. It is the difference between the tax on the dirty good and the tax on the clean good that is less than the Pigovian rate. Second, even if the dirt tax were zero, the same second-best optimum can be achieved using a higher tax on labor and a subsidy to clean consumption. Finally, this last normalization is useful to show that a tax system with an environmental subsidy may be no different from one with an environmental tax—even in terms of revenue—since they can achieve the exact same equilibrium. A waste-end tax may be difficult to enforce, because of illegal dumping, and it raises product prices in a way that reduces the real net wage. A subsidy to proper disposal can achieve the same incentives, and it reduces product prices in a way that *offsets* the effect of the extra labor tax needed to pay for it.

REFERENCES

Bovenberg, A. Lans and de Mooij, Ruud A. "Environmental Levies and Distortionary Taxation." *American Economic Review*, September 1994, *84*(4), pp. 1085–89.

Bovenberg, A. Lans and Goulder, Lawrence H. "Optimal Environmental Taxation in the Presence of Other Taxes: General-Equilibrium Analyses." *American Economic Review*, September 1996, 86(4), pp. 985–1000.

Bovenberg, A. Lans and van der Ploeg, F. "Environmental Policy, Public Finance and the Labour Market in a Second-Best World." *Journal of Public Economics*, November 1994, *55*(3), pp. 349–90.

Fullerton, Don and Kinnaman, Thomas C. "Garbage, Recycling, and Illicit Burning or Dumping." *Journal of Environmental Economics and Management*, July 1995, *29*(1), pp. 78–91.

Goulder, Lawrence H. "Environmental Taxation and the Double Dividend: A Reader's Guide." *International Tax and Public Finance*, August 1995, *2*(2), pp. 157–83.

Lee, Dwight R. and Misiolek, Walter S. "Substituting Pollution Taxation for General Taxation: Some Implications for Efficiency in Pollution Taxation." *Journal of Environ-*

mental Economics and Management, December 1986, *13*(4), pp. 338–47.

Oates, Wallace E. "Pollution Charges as a Source of Public Revenues." Discussion Paper QE92-05, Resources for the Future, Washington DC, 1991.

______. "Green Taxes: Can We Protect the Environment and Improve the Tax System at the Same Time?" *Southern Economic Journal*, April 1995, *61*(4), pp. 915–22.

Parry, Ian W. H. "Pollution Taxes and Revenue Recycling." *Journal of Environmental Economics and Management*, November 1995, *29*(3), pp. S64–77.

Pigou, Arthur C. *A study in public finance*. London: Macmillan, 1947.

Sandmo, Agnar. "Optimal Taxation in the Presence of Externalities." *Swedish Journal of Economics*, March 1975, *77*(1), pp. 86–98.

Schöb, Ronnie. "Environmental Taxes and Preexisting Distortions: The Normalization Trap." *International Tax and Public Finance*, 1997 (forthcoming).

Terkla, David. "The Efficiency Value of Effluent Tax Revenues." *Journal of Environmental Economics and Management*, June 1984, *11*(2), pp. 107–23.

[10]

Environmental Levies and Distortionary Taxation: Reply

By A. LANS BOVENBERG AND RUUD A. DE MOOIJ *

In a clear and well-argued paper, Don Fullerton (1997) points out that the magnitude of the optimal pollution tax depends on the particular way the tax system is normalized. He shows that depending on the normalization—in particular the choice of the untaxed good—the optimal tax on pollution can lie either above or below the Pigovian tax. This suggests that one of the results we derived in Bovenberg and de Mooij (1994) is rather specific, namely that the optimal pollution tax typically lies below the Pigovian level if preexisting distortionary taxes are present. However, Fullerton confirms the main economic message of our paper: in the presence of distortionary taxes, environmental taxes tend to be more, rather than less, distortionary than other taxes. Indeed, environmental taxes typically exacerbate, rather than alleviate, preexisting tax distortions—even if revenues are employed to cut distortionary taxes.

In our previous note, we normalized the tax system by selecting the clean commodity as the untaxed good. Fullerton argues that other normalizations are equally valid and sometimes preferable. However, we believe—for two reasons—that for the purpose of our note, the normalization rule we adopted is the most appropriate. Most importantly, the normalization rule we adopted is the most appropriate one in the context of the double-dividend debate. Indeed, our normalization rule clearly isolates the focus of the double-dividend debate, i.e., tax differentiation between clean and dirty commodities. When one refers to pollution taxes in the context of the double-dividend debate, one has this tax differentiation in mind. To illustrate, a carbon tax is the additional tax on carbon compared to that on other commodities. When we talk about a carbon tax of $50 per ton, we do not include the labor tax that bears on carbon (and other commodities). In practice, if only for administrative reasons, consumption taxes are rather flat. Environmental taxes are the taxes that are imposed on top of these consumption (and labor) taxes.

The second reason we selected the clean commodity as the untaxed good is that it clearly reveals how the intuition of the double-dividend argument goes wrong. This latter argument implies that the government should resort more to environmental taxes if revenue needs increase. The intuition underlying this result is the one cited by Fullerton in the second paragraph of his contribution: if the government needs some more revenue, it should raise all taxes a little bit. Fullerton argues that nothing is wrong with this latter intuition. However, by selecting the clean good as the untaxed good, we show that something is indeed wrong with this intuition.

This can be illustrated with equation (11) in Fullerton's contribution. This equation writes the optimal pollution tax as a weighted average of a Ramsey term, R, and the Pigovian tax (the marginal environmental damage, τ), divided by the marginal cost of public funds, η. A more distortionary tax system, which implies a higher marginal cost of public funds, increases the weight of the Ramsey component, thereby raising the revenue-raising component. As regards the Ramsey component, Fullerton's intuition is correct: if the government needs more revenues, it should increase all taxes a bit.

Our normalization implies that the Ramsey component is zero.[1] We thus focus on the environmental component because it is here

* Bovenberg and de Mooij: CPB Netherlands Bureau for Economic Policy Analysis, Van Stolkweg 14 (2585 JR Den Haag), P.O. Box 80510, 2508 GM, The Hague, The Netherlands. The authors thank Gilbert van Hagen and Larry Goulder for helpful comments on an earlier draft.

[1] We assume homothetic utility with weakly separable leisure so that the Ramsey taxes on dirty and clean consumption are equal. Thus, the environmental component of the tax on dirty consumption corresponds to tax differentiation between dirty and clean consumption.

that the intuition of the double-dividend argument goes wrong. Whereas a higher marginal cost of public funds *increases* the weight of the Ramsey component, it *decreases* the weight of the Pigovian component. Indeed, with the marginal cost of public funds exceeding unity, the environmental component of the optimal tax lies below the Pigovian tax. Intuitively, scarcer public revenues as reflected in a higher marginal cost of public funds encourage the government to rely more on taxes that are efficient from a revenue-raising point of view, and to rely less on taxes aimed at environmental protection. Indeed, the higher marginal cost of public funds indicates that public goods, including the public good of the environment, become more expensive.

Our normalization thus shows that higher revenue needs should induce the government to *decrease*, rather than *increase*, the carbon tax (as commonly defined)—contrary to the intuition that the government should raise all taxes, including the carbon tax.

To conclude, Fullerton is correct in pointing out that the optimal pollution tax depends on the normalization rule adopted. However, the normalization rule determines also whether the government should raise all taxes if it needs more revenue. We believe that the particular normalization rule we adopted is most appropriate for showing why the double-dividend argument fails and why the government may want to reduce, rather than raise, environmental taxes (as conventionally defined) if revenues become scarcer.

REFERENCES

Bovenberg, A. Lans and de Mooij, Ruud A. ''Environmental Levies and Distortionary Taxation.'' *American Economic Review*, September 1994, *84*(4), pp. 1085–89.

Fullerton, Don. ''Environmental Levies and Distortionary Taxation: Comment.'' *American Economic Review*, March 1997, *87*(1), pp. 245–51.

[11]

International Tax and Public Finance, 4, 167–176 (1997)

Environmental Taxes and Pre-Existing Distortions: The Normalization Trap

RONNIE SCHÖB ronnie.schoeb@ces.vwl.uni-muenchen.de
Department of Economics, University of Munich, Schackstrasse 4, D-80539 Munich

Abstract

The double-dividend hypothesis claims that green taxes will both improve the environment and reduce the distortions of existing taxes. According to the earlier literature on the double dividend the tax rate for polluting goods should be higher than the Pigovian tax which fully internalizes the marginal social damage from pollution, in order to obtain a 'second dividend'. On the contrary, Bovenberg and de Mooij (1994) argue that environmental taxes typically exacerbate, rather than alleviate, pre-existing distortions. The optimal pollution tax should therefore lie below the Pigovian tax. This paper points out that there is no real contradiction between these apparently opposing policy recommendations. It will be shown that the difference in the results appears because, implicitly, different definitions of the second-best optimal pollution tax are chosen.

Keywords: Second-best Environmental Taxation, Distortionary Taxation, Double-dividend, Normalization

1. Introduction

In recent years, the prospect of a double dividend from green taxes has become very attractive. While it is taken for granted that green taxes improve the environment and hence yield a positive environmental dividend, there is an ongoing discussion about the existence of the 'second dividend' which relates to the effect of a green tax on the efficiency of the tax system.

According to Goulder (1995), we can distinguish a 'weak' form and a 'strong' form of the second dividend. The double-dividend hypothesis in its weak form claims that tax revenues from green taxes can be used to reduce *other distortionary taxes* like taxes on labour or capital income, and hence yield a second dividend. The idea of such an "excess benefit" originates with Tullock (1967), and was put forward by several papers in the mid-eighties (cf. Nichols 1984, Terkla 1984, and Lee and Misiolek 1986). The second dividend was considered originally to be a welcome side-effect of environmental tax policy only. A logical consequence of the existence of such a second dividend for policy recommendation is that the optimal pollution tax should be set higher than the Pigovian tax, which is equal to the marginal environmental damage of a polluting good. Going beyond the Pigovian tax further increases the environmental quality *and* raises additional public funds. These funds can be used to reduce the distortion from other taxes.[1]

The 'stronger' form of the second dividend concerns the effect of green taxes on the efficiency of the *whole tax system*. According to this definition, a positive second dividend exists if the excess burden of the tax system declines. Analysing the consequences of green taxes for the optimal tax structure, Bovenberg and de Mooij (1994) argue "that environmental taxes typically exacerbate, rather than alleviate, pre-existing distortions—even if revenues are employed to cut pre-existing distortionary taxes. [...] in the presence of existing distortionary taxes, the optimal pollution tax typically lies below the Pigovian tax ..." (Bovenberg and de Mooij 1994, p. 1085). Increasing a narrow-based green tax and reducing a broad-based tax like a tax on labour income will typically increase the overall distortion of the tax system. Hence, the second dividend is negative and the double-dividend hypothesis fails. Therefore they oppose the policy recommendation that going beyond the Pigovian tax increases welfare.[2]

As will be shown in this note, there is no real contradiction between these two apparently opposite conclusions, which have caused significant confusion in the debate on the double-dividend hypothesis. The difference in the results appears because, implicitly, different definitions of the pollution tax are chosen in evaluating second-best optimal environmental taxes. While the earlier contributions to the double-dividend debate focus on tax systems where only commodity taxes are present, the more recent contributions focus on tax systems where green taxes are introduced in addition to a labour tax. Consequently, the former approach includes a tax component which is raised for non-environmental reasons in its definition of the second-best optimal pollution tax while the latter defines the tax on a polluting good as the tax component which is imposed for environmental reasons only. The different definitions are due to different normalizations of the consumer price system chosen. Therefore, a comparison between the second-best optimal pollution tax and the first-best Pigovian tax turns out to be an inappropriate indicator for the existence of a second dividend.

Section 2 sets out an optimal taxation model similar to Sandmo (1975). In Section 3, this model will be used to analyse tax systems with different normalizations which may be characterized as a *labour tax system* and a *commodity tax system*, respectively. Section 4 then shows the differences and reconciles the two apparently opposing policy recommendations. Section 5 concludes.

2. The Model

Consider a closed economy with N households. Assume a linear technology to produce a private dirty good D, which consumption creates a negative externality, a private clean good C, which causes no externalities, and a public good G, with labour L being the only input into production. The notation is similar to Bovenberg and de Mooij (1994). Assuming perfect competition, we can normalize the wage rate to unity and choose units for all goods such that all producer prices are equal to one:

$$NL = NC + ND + G. \tag{1}$$

The preferences of a representative household depend on the consumption of the private commodities C and D, and on leisure V. Preferences also depend on the public good G

and on the environmental quality E. These preferences are described by a twice continuously differentiable, strictly quasi-concave utility function $u = (C, D, V, G, E)$. The time endowment is normalized to one, hence $V + L = 1$. The budget constraint of the representative household is given by

$$(1 + t_C)C + (1 + t_D)D = (1 - t_L)(1 - V), \quad (2)$$

where t_L denotes the tax rate on labour income while t_C and t_D denote the commodity taxes on the clean and the dirty good, respectively.

The consumption of D creates a negative externality on the environmental quality, which the household does not take into account when consuming the dirty good:

$$E = e(ND), \; de/d(ND) < 0. \quad (3)$$

The government maximizes welfare by maximizing the utility of a representative household. For convenience, we make use of the indirect utility function w which already takes into account the utility maximizing behaviour of the household. Hence, the government maximizes

$$W = w(t_C, t_D, t_L, G, E) \quad (4)$$

subject to the government budget constraint per capita, which is given by:

$$\frac{G}{N} = t_e C + t_D D + t_L L. \quad (5)$$

Without using a lump-sum tax, the government can only raise revenues by introducing taxes on the commodities C and D or by introducing a tax on labour.

3. The Optimal Tax Structure

To define the optimal tax structure, we can proceed in two alternative ways. As the demand functions are homogeneous of degree zero in consumer prices—we have no exogenously given income—we can normalize one consumer price at unity without loss of generality [cf. Dixit and Munk (1977) or Auerbach (1985)]. This is equivalent to normalize one tax rate to zero as we have already normalized all producer prices to unity. On the one hand, we can normalize the tax on the clean good to zero. In this case, we analyse a tax system with a labour tax and an additional tax on the dirty good. In what follows we refer to this as a labour tax system. On the other hand, we can normalize the labour tax to zero. In this case we analyse a commodity tax system.

3.1. A Labour Tax System

Maximizing (4) with respect to (5) for $t_C = 0$, using the Slutsky decompositions ($\partial I/\partial t_D = \partial I/\partial p_D = s_{ID} - D\partial I/\partial Y$ and $\partial I/\partial t_L = -\partial I/\partial p_L = -s_{IL} - L\partial I/\partial Y$) with $I = C, D,$

L, and s_{IJ}, $J = D, L$, denoting the Slutsky terms and using Cramer's rule we obtain the optimal tax structure in the presence of externalities:[3]

$$t_L = \frac{(1-\nu)(Ls_{DD} + Ds_{DL})}{s_{DD}s_{LL} - s_{DL}s_{LD}} \equiv t_L^R, \tag{6}$$

$$t_D = \frac{-(1-\nu)(Ds_{LL} + Ls_{LD})}{s_{DD}s_{LL} - s_{DL}s_{LD}} - \frac{\lambda}{\mu}N\frac{u_E}{\lambda}\frac{de}{d(ND)} \equiv t_D^R + \frac{\lambda}{\mu}t_P. \tag{7}$$

The shadow price λ denotes the *marginal utility of private income*. The shadow price μ denotes the *marginal utility of public expenditures*. The term ν,

$$\nu = \frac{\lambda}{\mu} + \sum_{I,i=L,D} t_i \frac{\partial I}{\partial Y} + \frac{\lambda}{\mu}N\frac{u_E}{\lambda}\frac{de}{d(ND)}\frac{\partial D}{\partial Y},$$

defines the *net social marginal utility of private income* Y of the representative household—measured in units of public expenditures. It can be attributed to Diamond [1975, see his eq. (6)]. However, the expression derived here also takes into account the impact of private income on the social evaluation of the externality. Note, that v is independent of the particular tax rate considered.

The optimal tax on labour consists of one term only, which relies on the efficiency of the tax system. The tax on the dirty good, however, consists of a term, which relies on the efficiency of the tax system and which we will call the Ramsey component, and an environmental component. The latter equals the marginal environmental damage weighted with the inverse of the marginal cost of public funds λ/μ. As the marginal environmental damage equals the (first-best) Pigovian tax, we will denote it by t_P.

With lump-sum taxes we obtain $\lambda = \mu$ and $\nu = 1$. There is no labour taxation and the optimal tax on the dirty good is equal to the marginal environmental damage. Only a Pigovian tax t_P is raised in addition to lump-sum taxes, which fully internalizes the external effect.[4]

Bovenberg and de Mooij (1994) assume that the utility function is separable between environmental quality, public good, leisure and consumption goods and homothetic in consumption goods. Under these rather restrictive assumptions, the Ramsey component of the dirty good becomes zero (see the appendix). If there is no lump-sum tax available, the inverse of the marginal cost of public funds is then given by:

$$\frac{\lambda}{\mu} = 1 + \frac{t_L}{L}\frac{\partial L}{\partial t_L}.^5 \tag{8}$$

If the labour supply curve is upward sloping, we have $\partial L/\partial t_L < 0$ and therefore for $t_L > 0$ we have $\lambda/\mu < 1$.[6] It turns out that the second-best optimal tax on the dirty good falls below the first-best Pigovian tax. Hence, it does not cover the total marginal environmental damage.

To see the intuition of this result, we have to analyse the consequences of a revenue-neutral shift from a broad-based labour tax to a narrow-based tax on the dirty good. Consider the whole consumption bundle and its consumption price index. It is obvious that a reduction in the labour tax and a revenue-neutral increase of t_D will not affect the real after-tax wage, if the household does not alter the composition of its consumption basket. However, if it substitutes the clean good for the dirty good, there will be a negative tax-base effect. Revenue-neutrality requires that the consumer price index will increase at a higher rate than the net wage. As a consequence the real after-tax wage actually falls. Labour supply falls and welfare decreases. Since the Pigovian tax completely internalizes the marginal environmental damage, the only effect of a marginal increase of the Pigovian tax is a higher marginal cost of public funds, i.e. a negative second dividend occurs.

3.2. *A Commodity Tax System*

Now we normalize the net wage rate to unity, i.e. $t_L = 0$. Maximizing (4) with respect to (5), the optimal tax structure in the presence of externalities is given by:

$$t_C = \frac{-(1-\hat{\nu})(Cs_{DD} - Ds_{DC})}{s_{DD}s_{CC} - s_{DC}s_{CD}} \equiv t_C^R, \tag{9}$$

$$t_D = t_D^R - \frac{\hat{\lambda}}{\mu} N \frac{u_E}{\lambda} \frac{de}{d(ND)} \equiv t_D^R + \frac{\hat{\lambda}}{\mu} t_P, \tag{10}$$

where t_i^R, $i = C, D$, denotes the Ramsey tax component, which relies on the efficiency of the tax system only. Note that although the real allocation is identical to the one described for a labour tax system, the marginal utility of income $\hat{\lambda}$ and hence $\hat{\nu}$ are different due to normalization. The marginal utility of public expenditures μ however is identical.

From eq. (10) it is no longer clear whether the tax on the dirty good lies above or below the Pigovian tax even if $\hat{\lambda}/\mu < 1$. According to this analysis, one could claim that going beyond the Pigovian tax is welfare improving. To see this, assume that the initial tax rate on the dirty good is equal to the Pigovian tax, $t_D = t_P$, and consider a marginal revenue-neutral tax reform which increases the tax on the dirty good. Total differentiation of eqs. (4) and (5) yields

$$\begin{aligned} d\tilde{W} &\equiv \frac{dW}{\hat{\lambda}} \\ &= N\left[-C + \frac{u_E}{\hat{\lambda}} \frac{de}{d(ND)} \frac{\partial D}{\partial t_C}\right] dt_C + N\left[-D + \frac{u_E}{\hat{\lambda}} \frac{de}{d(ND)} \frac{\partial D}{\partial t_D}\right] dt_D \end{aligned} \tag{11}$$

and

$$dG = N\left[C + t_C \frac{\partial C}{\partial t_C} + t_D \frac{\partial D}{\partial t_C}\right] dt_C + N\left[D + t_C \frac{\partial C}{\partial t_D} + t_D \frac{\partial D}{\partial t_D}\right] dt_D = 0. \tag{12}$$

Adding eq. (12) to eq. (11) and substituting in the definition for the Pigovian tax, we obtain:

$$d\tilde{W} = t_C \left[N \frac{\partial C}{\partial t_C} dt_C + N \frac{\partial C}{\partial t_D} dt_D\right]. \tag{13}$$

Assuming both goods to be Non-Giffen and the marginal tax revenues to be positive, the welfare change is positive if, due to the marginal revenue-neutral tax reform, the consumption of the clean good increases. The partial equilibrium models used by Nichols (1984) and Lee and Misiolek (1986) implicitly assume all cross price effects to be zero. In this case, the welfare change is guaranteed to be positive. Taxing the dirty good at the Pigovian tax, the reduced marginal environmental damage completely outweigh the partial loss in revenues due to reduced consumption of the dirty good $t_D \cdot \partial D/\partial t_D$. The additional public funds (assuming positive marginal revenues), however, can be used to reduce the distortion of taxing the clean good. This enhances the efficiency of the tax system and therefore welfare.

However, it need not be the case that the consumption of the clean good increases. In general, the welfare change is determined by the following condition:

$$\frac{d\tilde{W}}{dt_D}\begin{Bmatrix} < \\ = \\ > \end{Bmatrix} 0 \Leftrightarrow \frac{\dfrac{\partial C}{\partial t_D}}{\dfrac{\partial C}{\partial t_C}} \begin{Bmatrix} > \\ = \\ < \end{Bmatrix} \frac{\dfrac{\partial R}{\partial t_D}}{\dfrac{\partial R}{\partial t_C}}. \tag{14}$$

The welfare effect is positive if the clean good is an uncompensated substitute for the dirty good, i.e. $\partial C/\partial t_D > 0$. For C being an uncompensated complement to the dirty good, i.e. $\partial C/\partial t_D < 0$, the consumption of the clean good may actually decrease. To see this, assume that the government increases the tax on the dirty good by one unit. If the marginal revenue $\partial R/\partial t_D$ is very low, the additional funds the government raises are small. These have to be rebated by reducing the tax on the clean good, $dt_C < 0$. If the marginal revenue of the clean good $\partial R/\partial t_C$ is relatively high compared to $\partial R/\partial t_D$, the clean good will be reduced at a relatively small rate. The ratio of marginal tax revenues, $\partial R/\partial t_D/\partial R/\partial t_C$, is just the weight of the own-price effect $\partial C/\partial t_C$. If the weight is small, it might happen that, even in the case of a low cross price-effect, relative to the own-price effect, the increased consumption of the clean good resulting from a reduction in t_C is outweighed by the reduction in consumption resulting from an increase in t_D.

4. Reconciliation

Comparing eqs. (7) and (10) we find two different definitions of what the tax on the dirty good is even though we consider two identical tax systems which differ only with respect to normalization. The different definitions of the pollution tax are illustrated in Figure 1 for the case analysed by Bovenberg and de Mooij (1994). In a world without externalities the 45°-line OA indicates the optimal uniform commodity tax structure which is equivalent to pure labour taxation. The line O′A′ indicates the optimal commodity tax structure in the presence of externalities (whereby, for simplicity, the marginal environmental damage is kept constant). Moving up and to the right, the tax revenue increases ($R_2 > R_1$; $dR = 0$ indicates iso-revenue lines) and so does the marginal cost of public funds. The two lines converge [cf. eq. (7)]. B represents the summit of the utility hill which is represented by indifference contours. Moving up and to the right, private consumption decreases while public good provision increases first (on the Laffer-efficient side). This implies welfare

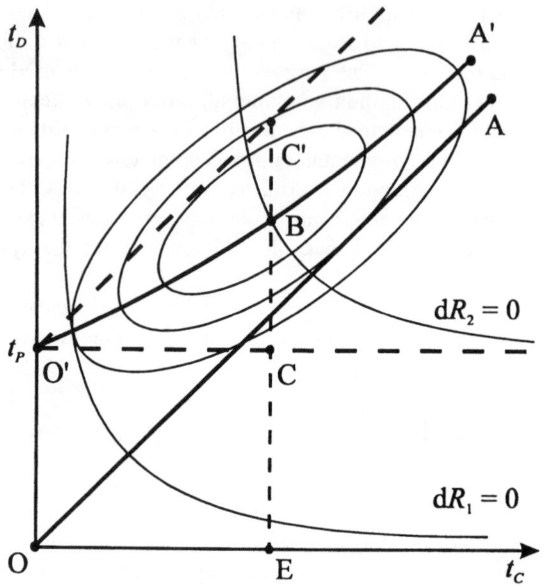

Figure 1. An optimal green tax system.

gains as long as the marginal rate of substitution between consumption and the public good is larger than the marginal cost of public good provision including the marginal excess burden (cf. Atkinson and Stern 1974). The summit B indicates the optimal tax structure which yields the revenues necessary for supplying the second-best optimal quantity of the public good.

Within an existing labour tax system, the tax rate t_D drives a wedge between the commodity prices of the clean and dirty good only. It does not cover the distortion the labour tax itself has already imposed on the price ratio of the dirty good and leisure. The tax rate t_D indicates only the *additional* wedge between the price of the dirty good and the price of leisure, which is given by the OA-line. In the optimum, the tax on the dirty good is therefore given by the vertical distance between the OA-line and the O′A′-line. Figure 1 shows that the optimal tax rate on the dirty good will decrease according to this definition as the marginal cost of public funds increases. A more cautious interpretation of the Bovenberg and de Mooij (1994) result is that adding a tax rate to the existing tax system OA, which is marginally smaller than the Pigovian tax t_P, is always better than adding the Pigovian tax (which would be indicated by a point on the line O′C′). Hence, the scope for environmental policy is smaller compared to the scope in a first-best world because, due to distortionary taxation, the environmental quality is already closer to the second-best optimum than the laissez-faire situation in a non-distorted economy.[7]

For the commodity tax system, however, the optimal tax rate t_D indicates the *total* wedge between the price of the dirty good and the price of leisure which is represented in Figure 1 as the difference between the O′A′-line and the abscissa, i.e. the distance BE. This tax rate explicitly covers the Ramsey component, i.e. the vertical distance between the OA-line and the abscissa. According to this definition, a tax rate which exceeds the Pigovian tax turns out to be optimal as long as the O′A′-line is upward sloping: The O′A′ line is strictly above the dotted horizontal line of the Pigovian tax (O′C). From this definition we learn that the total tax borne by the dirty good (in units of leisure) should be higher than the Pigovian tax.

5. Conclusions

We have chosen two different normalizations for the optimal tax structure in order to construct two reference tax systems, namely a tax system with labour taxes and a pure commodity tax system. It is seen that the difference of the first-best and second-best optimal tax on the polluting good depends on the normalization chosen. Therefore, we have to conclude that such a comparison provides an inappropriate indicator for the existence of a second dividend.[8] This becomes even clearer if we consider other possible normalizations. For example, we can normalize the sum of consumer prices to unity or even normalize the tax on the dirty good to zero.[9] In each case we get different looking answers on what should be the optimal tax on the polluting good.

Real tax systems consist of both income taxes and commodity taxes like value added taxes and excise taxes. In particular, goods with already high excise taxes as fuel are considered to be good candidates for imposing additional green taxes. Given that the tax system was optimized with respect to minimizing the excess burden of public revenues, we know from our analysis that additional green taxes should be lower than the marginal environmental damage. However, this should be not confused with comparing the nominal fuel tax with the marginal environmental damage which equals the first-best Pigovian tax.

Appendix

The separability and homogeneity assumptions made by Bovenberg and de Mooij (1994) imply that the Ramsey component has to be identically zero, i.e. $t_D^R = 0$ in eq. (7).

Proof: For the nominator of the Ramsey component we have $(Ds_{LL} + Ls_{LD}) = LD[(1 - t_L)s_{LL}/L - (1 - t_L)s_{DL}/D]/(1 - t_L) = LD(\varepsilon_{LL}^c - \varepsilon_{DL}^c)/(1 - t_L)$, whereby ε_{ij}^c denotes the compensated (cross-)price elasticities (note that $s_{LD} = -s_{DL}$). From the homogeneity condition we also know that $\varepsilon_{VV}^c + \varepsilon_{VC}^c + \varepsilon_{VD}^c = 0$ (cf. e.g. Deaton and Muellbauer 1980, p 62). Using the following condition for the compensated labour supply elasticity, $-(V/L)\varepsilon_{VV}^c = \varepsilon_{LL}^c$, and substituting into the former equation we have:

$$\begin{aligned}(Ds_{LL} + Ls_{LD}) &= -LD\left(\frac{V}{L}\varepsilon_{VV}^c + \varepsilon_{DL}^c\right)/(1 - t_L)\\ &= VD\left(\varepsilon_{VC}^c + \varepsilon_{VD}^c - \frac{L}{V}\varepsilon_{DL}^c\right)/(1 - t_L).\end{aligned}$$

Sandmo (1974, p. 705) shows that separability between leisure and consumption goods and homogeneity in consumption goods implies $\varepsilon^c_{DV} = \varepsilon^c_{DL} = \alpha V(1 - t_L)$, $\varepsilon^c_{VI} = \alpha I(1 + t_I)$ (whereby $\alpha = \beta / V$ in his notation). Substituting in yields

$$(Ds_{LL} + Ls_{LD}) = \frac{-VD}{(1 - t_L)}\alpha[(C(1 + t_C) + D(1 + t_D) - L(1 - t_L)]$$

Comparing the term in square brackets with eq. (1) shows that this term is identically zero. Hence, $t^R_D = 0$.

For a commodity tax system the separability and homogeneity assumptions guarantee uniform commodity taxes to be optimal in the absence of externalities [cf. Sandmo (1974)]. Ramsey components are thus equal if consumer prices are equal, as assumed here. ■

Acknowledgments

Comments by Michael Keen, Jack Mintz, Gerhard Orosel, Ray Rees and three anonymous referees are gratefully acknowledged. The usual disclaimer applies.

Notes

1. This view has recently been promoted by Pearce (1991) and Oates (1993).
2. In a previous version of this paper (Schöb 1994) I refer to the earlier contributions to the double-dividend literature as the environmental view and to the Bovenberg and de Mooij approach as the public finance view.
3. For a formal derivation of optimal tax rates, see e.g. Sandmo (1975). Note that $w_E = u_E$.
4. We assume throughout that the revenue requirement exceeds the tax revenues the government raises if it only imposes a Pigovian tax on the dirty good.
5. Eq. (8) can be derived by inserting $t_D = \lambda/\mu \cdot t_P$ [cf. eq. (7)] into the first-order condition for the labour tax.
6. The labour tax is positive if, for the compensated elasticities, we have: $\varepsilon_{LD} > \varepsilon_{DD}$.
7. As was pointed out by one referee, by interpreting the environment as a public good, this result restates the modified Samuelson rule (cf. Atkinson and Stern 1974). This rule shows that it is optimal to provide less of the public good than in a first-best world if the marginal cost of funds exceeds unity. Parry (1995) estimates the additional wedge to be between 63% and 78% of the marginal environmental damage.
8. A second dividend in the strong form can occur only if increasing the tax on the dirty good is welfare improving even if there are no externalities present. Hence, only a comparison of the actual tax rates—in the case of the dirty good: the actual tax rate minus the environmental component—with the second-best optimal Ramsey components may be used as an indicator for a positive second dividend.
9. Cf. Fullerton (1996), who independently derives very similar conclusions than those presented in this paper.

References

Auerbach, Alan J. (1985). "The Theory of Excess Burden and Optimal Taxation." In Alan J. Auerbach and Martin Feldstein, eds., *Handbook of Public Economics I*, pp. 61–127.

Atkinson, Anthony B. and Nicolas H. Stern. (1974). "Pigou, Taxation and Public Goods." *Review of Economic Studies* 41, 119–128.

Bovenberg, A. Lans and Ruud A. de Mooij. (1994). "Environmental Levies and Distortionary Taxation." *American Economic Review* 84, 1085–1089.

Deaton, Angus and John Muellbauer. (1980). *Economics of Consumer Behavior*. Cambridge: Cambridge University Press.

Diamond, Peter A. (1975). "A Many-Person Ramsey Tax Rule." *Journal of Public Economics* 4, 335–342.

Dixit, Avinash K. and Knud Jørgen Munk. (1977). "Welfare Effects of Tax and Price Changes: A Correction." *Journal of Public Economics* 8, 103–107.

Fullerton, Don. (1996). "Second Best Pollution Taxes." NBER Discussion Paper No. 5511, March, forthcoming in: *American Economic Review*.

Goulder, Lawrence H. (1995). "Environmental Taxation and the "Double Dividend:" A Reader's Guide." *International Tax and Public Finance* 2, 157–184.

Lee, Dwight R. and Walter S. Misiolek. (1986). "Substituting Pollution Taxation for General Taxation: Some Implications for Efficiency in Pollution Taxation." *Journal of Environmental Economics and Management* 13, 338–347.

Nichols, Albert L. (1984). *Targeting Economic Incentives for Environmental Protection*. Cambridge Mass. and London: MIT-Press.

Oates, Wallace E. (1993). "Polluting Charges as a Source of Public Revenues." In Herbert Giersch, eds., *Economic Progress and Environmental Concerns*. Berlin: Springer, pp. 135–152.

Parry, Ian W. H. (1995). "Pollution Taxes and Revenue Recycling." *Journal of Environmental Economics and Management* 29, S64–S77.

Pearce, David W. (1991). "The Role of Carbon Taxes in Adjusting to Global Warming." *Economic Journal* 101, 938–948.

Sandmo, Agnar. (1974). "A Note on the Structure of Optimal Taxation." *American Economic Review* 64, 701–706.

Sandmo, Agnar. (1975). "Optimal Taxation in the Presence of Externalities." *Swedish Journal of Economics* 77, 86–98.

Schöb, Ronnie. (1994). "Environmental Levies and Distortionary Taxation: Environmental View vs. Public Finance View." Department of Economics, University of Essex, Discussion Paper Series No. 436, November.

Terkla, David. (1984). "The Efficiency Value of Effluent Tax Revenues." *Journal of Environmental Economics and Management* 11, 107–123.

Tullock, Gordon. (1967). "Excess Benefit." *Water Resources Research* 3, 643–644.

[12]

ELSEVIER

Economics Letters 71 (2001) 137–142

economics letters

www.elsevier.com/locate/econbase

Tax normalizations, the marginal cost of funds, and optimal environmental taxes

Roberton C. Williams III*

Department of Economics, University of Texas, Austin, TX 78712, USA

Received 14 March 2000; accepted 20 September 2000

Abstract

Prior results on second-best optimal environmental taxes fail to hold under alternative tax normalizations, partly because the marginal cost of funds varies with the tax normalization. However, under any normalization, the optimal environmental tax typically lies below marginal damages. © 2001 Elsevier Science B.V. All rights reserved.

Keywords: Second-best environmental taxes; Marginal cost of funds; Tax normalizations

JEL classification: H21; H23

1. Introduction

The issue of how to set environmental taxes in an economy with pre-existing distortionary taxes has attracted a great deal of attention. The literature on this issue has demonstrated that in such a second-best setting, the optimal environmental tax will be lower than marginal environmental damages (the optimal level in a first-best setting), and that the degree to which it is lower depends on the size of the pre-existing distortions.[1]

However, much of this literature employs a normalization of the tax system in which clean (non-polluting) goods are untaxed, while labor income and dirty (polluting) goods are taxed. Jaeger (1999) shows that the optimal environmental tax differential (the difference in tax rates between dirty and clean goods) varies with the tax normalization. He concluded from this that the prior literature's result that this differential will be less than marginal environmental damages (MED) resulted from the tax normalization used. Given the importance of this question — this literature has had an

*Corresponding author. Tel.: +1-512-475-8522; fax: +1-512-471-3510.

E-mail address: rwilliam@eco.utexas.edu (R.C. Williams III).

[1]See, for example, Bovenberg and de Mooij (1994); Goulder (1995); Parry (1995).

0165-1765/01/$ – see front matter
PII: S0165-1765(00)00396-7

increasingly substantial influence on environmental policy — it would be troubling if the prior results were merely artifacts of the tax normalization.[2]

This paper investigates the normalization issue, employing an analytical general-equilibrium model that can consider an infinite range of possible tax normalizations. It confirms that the optimal environmental tax differential varies with the tax normalization. In addition, it shows that the prior literature's[3] result that the optimal tax differential equals MED divided by the marginal cost of public funds (MCPF) holds only under one possible tax normalization.

However, it also demonstrates that Jaeger's conclusion is incorrect. The ratio of the optimal tax differential to MED is constant across all possible tax normalizations, and will be less than one as long as there are pre-existing distortionary taxes and labor supply is not backward-bending.

In doing so, the paper shows that the MCPF varies with alternative tax normalizations. This last point has not been previously recognized by the literature on either the MCPF or second-best optimal environmental taxes, and is potentially important not just for environmental taxation, but for a broad range of other tax issues as well. It implies that researchers must be very careful not to use values for MCPF estimated under one tax normalization to reach conclusions about optimal taxation or public good supply in a context with a different tax normalization. It also indicates that comparisons of the MCPF between different tax systems (for example, comparing a consumption tax and an income tax) may prove to be highly misleading, due to the difference in normalization.

2. The model

A representative agent model is assumed, where households divide their time endowment (T) between leisure (l) and labor (L), which is used to produce a dirty consumption good (D), N clean goods ($C_1 \ldots C_N$), and a government-provided public good (G)[4]. The household utility function is

$$U(l, C, D, G) - \phi(D) \tag{1}$$

where U is continuous and quasi-concave. Each of the three goods is produced from labor under constant returns to scale, with units normalized such that one unit of labor can produce one unit of any of the goods.[5] Thus, production and the household time constraint are given by

$$T = l + L = l + \sum_i C_i + D + G \tag{2}$$

The government levies taxes on labor income (at the rate τ_L), consumption of the clean goods (at the rate τ_C), and consumption of the dirty good (at the rate τ_D). The unit normalization and assumption

[2] Fullerton (1997) and Schöb (1997) also considered the normalization issue, though with a different purpose than Jaeger (1999) or this paper; they demonstrated what was wrong with the conventional intuition that a higher government revenue requirement should imply heavier taxation of pollution. These two papers pointed out that under a normalization with no labor tax, the dirty-good tax rises with the government revenue requirement, but that this does not imply that the environmental tax differential rises, because the clean-good tax also rises.

[3] See, for example, Bovenberg and van der Ploeg (1994) or Parry (1995).

[4] This specification could also represent unproductive government spending (in which case).

[5] Note that this unit normalization is distinct from the tax normalization.

of competitive production implies that the pre-tax wage and pre-tax prices of the consumption goods will be equal, and we will normalize them to be 1. The consumer budget constraint is then

$$(1+\tau_C)\sum_i C_i + (1+\tau_D)D = (1-\tau_L)L \tag{3}$$

This system of taxes is redundant in the sense that there are an infinite number of combinations of rates for these three taxes that would yield an equivalent consumer budget constraint. Multiplying the consumer budget constraint by any non-zero constant α shows that the tax rates $(\tau_C', \tau_D', \tau_L')$ represent one such alternative normalization of the tax rates (τ_C, τ_D, τ_L) where

$$\tau_C' = \alpha(1+\tau_C) - 1, \quad \tau_D' = \alpha(1+\tau_D) - 1, \quad \tau_L' = 1 - \alpha(1-\tau_L) \tag{4}$$

This trivially shows that the optimal dirty-good tax varies with the tax normalization. In addition, it is straightforward to show that the optimal environmental tax differential $(\tau_D - \tau_C)$ also varies. If the tax rates (τ_C, τ_D, τ_L) are optimal, then under an alternative normalization (which will also be optimal), the environmental tax differential will follow.[6]

$$\tau_D' - \tau_C' = \alpha(\tau_D - \tau_C) \tag{5}$$

Tax revenue is used to finance a fixed level of the public good.[7] Thus, the government budget constraint is

$$\tau_C \sum_i C_i + \tau_D D + \tau_L L = G \tag{6}$$

The labor tax rate is assumed to vary to hold the level of G fixed for changes in the dirty-good tax. The result would be the same if the clean-good tax rate were varied instead.

Households maximize utility (1) subject to their time constraint (2) and budget constraint (3), taking prices, tax rates, the level of the public good, and the level of pollution as given. This yields the first-order conditions

$$U_C = (1+\tau_C)\lambda; \quad U_D = (1+\tau_D)\lambda; \quad U_l = (1-\tau_L)\lambda \tag{7}$$

where λ is the marginal utility of after-tax income. Together with the constraints given previously, these implicitly define the (uncompensated) demand functions

$$C_i(\tau_C, \tau_D, \tau_L); \quad D(\tau_C, \tau_D, \tau_L); \quad l(\tau_C, \tau_D, \tau_L) \tag{8}$$

Taking a total derivative of utility (1) with respect to τ_D, substituting in the first-order conditions (7), subtracting $(1+\tau_C)$ times the total derivative of the household time constraint (2) with respect to τ_D, and rearranging terms yield

[6] Jaeger's (1999) result that the optimal environmental tax differential varies with the tax normalization represents a special case of this result, as it considers only one possible renormalization.

[7] The model would yield the same result under the alternative assumption that government revenue is spent on a lump-sum transfer to households, as long as the purchasing power of that transfer is held constant.

$$\frac{1}{\lambda}\frac{dU}{d\tau_D}=\left(\tau_D-\tau_C-\frac{1}{\lambda}\frac{\partial\phi}{\partial D}\right)\frac{dD}{d\tau_D}-(\tau_L+\tau_C)\frac{dl}{d\tau_D} \tag{9}$$

As Parry (1995) showed, the cost of an environmental tax depends on the degree of complementarity between the polluting good and leisure. If the polluting good is a relative complement to leisure, then the cost of taxing it will be lower than if it is a relative substitute. However, if both consumption goods are equal net substitutes for leisure, then the second term can be shown to equal[8]

$$(\tau_L+\tau_C)\frac{dl}{d\tau_D}=\left(\frac{\eta}{1+\tau_C}-1\right)(\tau_D-\tau_C)\frac{dD}{d\tau_D} \tag{10}$$

where η is the marginal cost of public funds (MCPF), given by

$$\eta=\frac{(1-\tau_L)(1+\tau_C)}{1-\tau_L-(\tau_L+\tau_C)\varepsilon_L} \tag{11}$$

This is the marginal cost to households of raising government revenue through a change in the labor tax or clean-good tax; thus, it is the ratio of the loss to households from a marginal increase in either of these taxes to the marginal revenue raised.[9] ε_L is the (uncompensated) labor supply elasticity, given by

$$\varepsilon_L=\frac{\partial l}{\partial\tau_L}\frac{1-\tau_L}{L} \tag{12}$$

Substituting (10) into (9) and solving for the optimal environmental tax (tax differential between the clean good and the dirty good) yield

$$\tau_D-\tau_C=\frac{1+\tau_C}{\eta}\frac{1}{\lambda}\frac{\partial\phi}{\partial D} \tag{13}$$

Marginal environmental damages (MED) is the marginal loss of utility from a unit of pollution, in money units. Under the tax normalization $\tau_C=0$, expression (13) replicates the prior literature's finding that the optimal environmental tax is equal to MED divided by the MCPF. Under alternative tax normalizations, the prior literature's finding does not hold; in this general case, the ratio of the optimal environmental tax differential to MED is not $1/\eta$, but rather $1+\tau_C/\eta$.

One might interpret this result as suggesting that the ratio of the optimal environmental tax differential to MED will vary across alternative tax normalizations. In fact, this is not the case. Substituting in expression (4), rearranging, and canceling out α, one can show that under the alternative normalization $(\tau'_C, \tau'_D, \tau'_L)$ — which follows expression (4) — this ratio equals

[8] This derivation is contained in a separate mathematical appendix, available from the author.

[9] This is a 'non-environmental' definition of the MCPF; it omits the effects of both the environmental tax differential (calculating both the cost to households and the revenue change as if the dirty-good tax were equal to the clean-good tax) and any change in environmental quality.

$$\frac{1+\tau'_C}{\eta} = \frac{(1-\tau'_L) - (\tau'_L + \tau'_C)\varepsilon_L}{(1-\tau'_L)} = \frac{(1-\tau_L) - (\tau_L + \tau_C)\varepsilon_L}{(1-\tau_L)} \tag{14}$$

Thus, this ratio will remain constant across alternative tax normalizations. That is, η changes with τ_C such that the ratio $1 + \tau_C/\eta$ is constant. In addition, as long as the second term in the numerator is positive — which will be the case if labor supply is not backward-bending and the sum of the labor tax and clean good tax is positive — this ratio will be less than one. This indicates that the optimal tax differential will be less than MED, regardless of the tax normalization.

How is this result consistent with the result that the optimal tax differential varies with the tax normalization? The key insight is that changing the tax normalization will change the prices of the two consumer goods, and thus will change the marginal utility of income. As a result, MED — which is measured in money terms — will also change. Thus, the change in the optimal tax differential results not from a change in the ratio of that differential to MED — as Jaeger (1999) had concluded — but from a change in MED.

This result also might seem inconsistent with the earlier result from this paper that the ratio of the optimal tax differential to MED is not always equal to the MCPF. Again, there is no inconsistency; the MCPF varies under alternative tax normalizations. The reason for this is that the numerator of the MCPF — the marginal cost to households from increasing the tax rate — is implicitly measured relative to consumer prices, whereas the denominator — marginal tax revenue — is implicitly measured relative to producer prices. By changing the tax normalization, one alters the ratio of consumer to producer prices, and thus the MCPF changes as well. This result has not been noted previously in the literature either on the MCPF or on environmental taxation. It implies that researchers must be careful not to compare estimates of the MCPF taken from tax systems with different normalizations.

Thus, this paper has shown that while some of the prior results on optimal environmental taxes are sensitive to tax normalizations, the essential policy implication — that the optimal environmental tax differential will be lower in the presence of distortionary taxation — holds regardless of the normalization used.

Acknowledgements

The author would like to thank Larry Goulder and Don Fullerton for helpful comments on this paper.

References

Bovenberg, A.L., de Mooij, R., 1994. Environmental levies and distortionary taxation. American Economic Review 84, 1085–1089.

Bovenberg, A.L., van der Ploeg, F., 1994. Environmental policy, public finance and the labor market in a second-best world. Journal of Public Economics 55, 349–390.

Fullerton, D., 1997. Environmental levies and distortionary taxes: comment. American Economic Review 87, 245–251.

Goulder, L.H., 1995. Environmental taxation and the 'double dividend': A reader's guide. International Tax and Public Finance 2, 157–183.
Jaeger, W., 1999. Double Dividend Reconsidered. working paper, Williams College and University of Oregon
Parry, I., 1995. Pollution taxes and revenue recycling. Journal of Environmental Economics and Management 29, 64–77.
Schöb, R., 1997. Environmental taxes and pre-existing distortions: the normalization trap. International Tax and Public Finance 4, 167–176.

[13]

Environmental tax interactions when pollution affects health or productivity

Introduction

One of the most important tasks that economists face in environmental policymaking is the evaluation of the costs and benefits of existing and proposed regulations. For example, the EPA recently conducted extensive prospective and retrospective analyses of the costs of the Clean Air Act (Environmental Protection Agency, 1997, 1999). Those analyses, and others like them, will play an important role in determining future policies.

An extensive recent literature has called into question conventional analysis of the costs of environmental regulation. This literature has focused on two general-equilibrium effects that appear in an economy with pre-existing distortionary taxes.[1] The first, the *revenue-recycling effect*, appears when a pollution tax generates revenue for the government, permitting a reduction in distortionary taxes and thus an efficiency gain. This gain is offset by a loss from the *tax-interaction effect*, which arises because the pollution tax drives up the price of consumption goods, lowering the real wage and discouraging labor supply. This exacerbates the tax distortion in the labor market, creating an efficiency loss. As a result of these interactions, the economy-wide costs of regulation may differ substantially from the sum of firms' abatement costs.

As this paper will show, however, general-equilibrium interactions can have an equally large effect on the benefits of regulation. This effect has largely been ignored by the prior literature, which has implicitly assumed that improved environmental quality does not affect individuals' labor supply decisions, and therefore that the benefits of reduced pollution are unchanged from the first-best case. That assumption may be valid in certain cases, such as the protection of an endangered species with substantial existence value, which could be represented as a separable term in consumer utility. It is a much less reasonable assumption, however, for the wide range of cases in which pollution affects productivity or health.

Such cases are of substantial interest for environmental policy. For example, a significant proportion of the benefits of avoiding global warming appear in the form of avoided losses to agricultural productivity, while much of the damages from airborne pollutants such as sulfur dioxide and particulate emissions appear as damages to human health. In these cases, the benefits of pollution regulation also affect labor supply decisions, producing an additional tax-interaction effect[2] from the benefits of regulation. This *benefit-side tax-interaction effect* varies greatly depending on the effects of the pollutant in question, and can either magnify or diminish the benefits of pollution regulation.

This paper presents a model of environmental regulation that allows pollution to have a wide range of different effects, including not only direct effects on utility, but also productivity effects in different industries and a range of health effects.

It demonstrates that when reduced pollution leads to increased labor productivity, this encourages labor supply, and thus tax interactions will magnify the benefits of regulation. In contrast, if a cleaner environment boosts the productivity of a fixed factor, tax interactions reduce the benefit of regulation. When the benefits of reduced pollution appear in the form of reduced medical expenses, this creates an income effect that discourages labor supply, and thus tax interactions diminish the value of such benefits. If pollution increases time lost to illness (but does not affect medical expenses), the sign of the benefit-side tax-interaction effect is ambiguous, and depends on the labor tax rate and labor supply elasticities.

Though the model explicitly considers environmental regulation, its results and the concept of the benefit-side tax-interaction effect apply equally to other types of regulation affecting health or productivity.

The next section of the paper presents an analytically tractable general-equilibrium model that allows for a broad range of effects of pollution and derives an expression for the welfare effects of regulation. The following sections evaluate this expression for pollutants that affect only utility, pollutants that affect productivity, and pollutants that affect health. The final section discusses potential extensions to this model, suggests avenues for future work, and draws conclusions for policy decisions.

The model

This section presents a simple general-equilibrium model that incorporates a household labor–leisure decision along with a pollution externality. Thus, the model incorporates production of two goods, one of which has an associated pollution externality, and includes a government sector and distortionary income tax. The model uses a tax-reform approach; it examines the welfare effects of changes in the pollution tax while adjusting the labor tax rate to hold total tax revenue constant.

This model takes a similar approach to the analytical model used by Parry, Williams, and Goulder (1999) to examine the effects of carbon emissions regulation in a tax-distorted economy. This model is distinct, however, in that environmental quality appears not only as a separable term in the utility function, but also may affect production efficiency and the health of the representative agent. Furthermore, this model generalizes the production function, to allow for the possibility of profits in production.

Assumptions

A representative agent model is assumed, where households divide their time endowment (T) between leisure (l) and labor (L), which is used to produce the two consumption goods, X and Y. The household utility function is

$$U[V(l, X, Y), Q] \tag{1}$$

which is continuous and quasi-concave.[3] Q is environmental quality.

The consumption and/or production of good X causes a negative externality, while good Y causes no such externality. Environmental quality equals an exogenous baseline level minus emissions, with units normalized such that one unit of X creates one unit of emissions:

$$Q = \bar{Q} - X \tag{2}$$

Environmental quality can have several different effects. As noted above, it may directly affect utility. It may also affect production of one or both of the consumption goods. Thus, production of the two consumption goods will follow

$$X = F_X(L_X, Q) \tag{3}$$

and

$$Y = F_Y(L_Y, Q) \tag{4}$$

where L_X and L_Y are the labor used in production of goods X and Y, respectively.

Finally, the externality could affect the health of the population, either causing the representative agent to spend time sick (reducing the time available for labor or leisure) or by forcing expenditure on medical care (which is produced directly from labor, with one unit of labor producing one unit of medical care). This implies the household time constraint

$$T = L + l + S(Q) = L_X + L_Y + L_M + l + S(Q) \tag{5}$$

where $S(Q)$ represents time spent sick, which is decreasing in Q, and L_M is the labor used to produce medical care.

To control this externality, the government levies a corrective tax of τ_X per unit of the dirty good, X.[4] Both industries price output at marginal cost and pay labor its marginal product, and the gross wage is normalized to 1. The (tax-inclusive) price of good X is then

$$p_X = \frac{1}{\partial F_X / \partial L_X} + \tau_X \tag{6}$$

Since there is no tax on good Y, its price is given by

$$p_Y = \frac{1}{\partial F_Y / \partial L_Y} \tag{7}$$

If either production function is not homogenous of degree one in labor input, there will be profits in production of that good, which implicitly represent rents to a fixed factor in production. Total profits (π), which are assumed to accrue to households, follow

$$\pi = (p_X - \tau_X)X + p_Y Y - L_X - L_Y \tag{8}$$

Finally, the government levies a tax on all income at the rate τ_L in order to finance an exogenously fixed transfer to households (G). Thus, the household budget constraint is

$$(1 - \tau_L)(L + \pi + G) = p_x X + p_Y Y + M(Q) \tag{9}$$

where $M(Q)$ represents medical care required, which is decreasing in Q and is produced following $M = L_M$. The government's budget constraint is

$$G = \tau_L(L + \pi + G) + \tau_X X \tag{10}$$

Households maximize utility (1) subject to their time constraint (5) and budget constraint (9), taking government transfers, prices, the labor tax rate, and the environmental tax rate as given. This yields the first-order conditions

$$U_V V_X = p_X \lambda; \qquad U_V V_Y = p_Y \lambda; \qquad U_V V_l = (1 - \tau_L)\lambda \tag{11}$$

where the subscripts on U and V denote partial derivatives and λ is the marginal utility of income. These first-order conditions, together with the other equations given thus far, implicitly define the Marshallian demand functions

$$X(p_X, p_Y, \tau_L, \pi, Q); \qquad Y(p_X, p_Y, \tau_L, \pi, Q); \qquad l(p_X, p_Y, \tau_L, \pi, Q) \tag{12}$$

Note that because G is fixed, it has been omitted as an argument in these demand functions.

Effects of taxing the polluting good Taking a derivative of utility with respect to the corrective tax (τ_X) while allowing l, X, and Y to vary gives

$$\frac{dU}{d\tau_X} = U_V\left[V_X\frac{dX}{d\tau_X} + V_X\frac{dY}{d\tau_X} + V_l\frac{dl}{d\tau_X}\right] - U_Q\frac{dX}{d\tau_X} \tag{13}$$

Then substituting in the consumer first-order conditions (11) and dividing by λ yields

$$\frac{1}{\lambda}\frac{dU}{d\tau_X} = p_X\frac{dX}{d\tau_X} + p_Y\frac{dY}{d\tau_X} + (1 - \tau_L)\frac{dl}{d\tau_X} - \frac{1}{\lambda}U_Q\frac{dX}{d\tau_X} \tag{14}$$

Define

$$Z = \frac{\tau_L(\partial l/\partial\tau_L)}{(L + \pi + G) - \tau_L(\partial l/\partial\tau_L)} \tag{15}$$

This is the efficiency cost of raising an additional dollar of labor tax revenue, or the *marginal cost of public funds* (MCPF) minus one. The numerator is therefore the marginal deadweight loss in the labor market, while the denominator is the marginal revenue from a change in the tax rate.[5] Z applies in the case in which revenue is not returned to households, and is thus uncompensated. The corresponding term when the revenue is returned is the *marginal excess burden* (MEB) of the labor tax, which can be expressed as

$$Z' = \frac{\partial l^C/\partial\tau_L}{\partial l/\partial\tau_L} Z \tag{16}$$

where the superscript C denotes a compensated derivative.

The welfare effect of the tax on good X can now be expressed as[6]

$$\frac{1}{\lambda}\frac{dU}{d\tau_X} = \underbrace{(\tau_X - \tau_P)\frac{dX}{d\tau_X}}_{dW^P} + \underbrace{Z\left(X + \tau_X\frac{dX}{d\tau_X}\right)}_{dW^R} - \underbrace{(1+Z)\tau_L\frac{\partial l}{\partial p_X}}_{dW^I}$$

$$\underbrace{-(1+Z)\tau_L\left[\frac{\partial l}{\partial p_X}\left(\frac{dp_X}{d\tau_X} - 1\right) + \frac{\partial l}{\partial p_Y}\frac{dp_Y}{d\tau_X} + \frac{\partial l}{\partial \pi}\frac{d\pi}{d\tau_X} + \frac{\partial l}{\partial Q}\frac{dQ}{d\tau_X}\right] + Z\tau_L\left(\frac{d\pi}{d\tau_X} - \frac{\partial S}{\partial Q}\frac{dQ}{d\tau_X}\right)}_{dW^{IB}} \quad (17)$$

where τ_P is the Pigouvian tax level, equal to the marginal damage from emissions, including the effects on production, utility, and health, given by

$$\tau_P = \frac{\partial F_X}{\partial Q}(p_X - \tau_X) + \frac{\partial F_Y}{\partial Q}p_Y + \frac{1}{\lambda}\frac{\partial U}{\partial Q} - \frac{\partial M}{\partial Q} - \frac{\partial S}{\partial Q} \quad (18)$$

Expression (17) decomposes the welfare effect into three components that are well known from the prior literature: the *primary welfare effect* (dW^P), the *revenue-recycling effect* (dW^R), and the (*cost-side*) *tax-interaction effect* (dW^I), plus an additional term, the *benefit-side tax-interaction effect* (dW^{IB}). The primary welfare effect is the effect of the tax on the pollution externality. The revenue-recycling effect is the efficiency gain from using the pollution tax revenue to reduce the labor tax rate. Finally, the two tax-interaction effects result as changes in labor supply exacerbate or ameliorate the income tax distortion in the labor market. For the cost-side tax-interaction effect dW^I the pollution tax drives up the costs of producing consumer goods, lowering the real wage and discouraging labor supply.

The benefit-side tax-interaction effect dW^{IB} expresses the impact of changes in labor productivity or consumer health on labor supply decisions. This effect will vary substantially depending on what form the benefits of a better environment take. If Q enters only as a separable term in the utility function, as most prior work has assumed, it will not affect labor supply and thus this term will equal zero. But if environmental quality affects health or productivity, such changes will influence the labor supply decision and thus this effect will produce a welfare gain or loss.

Each of the two tax-interaction effects equals the distortionary wedge in the labor market (the labor tax) times the change in leisure resulting from the policy; the labor tax causes leisure to be underpriced, so an increase in leisure implies a welfare loss. Added to this is the value of any gain or loss in labor tax revenue, equal to the change in revenue times Z. Summing those elements for the effect of the pollution tax gives the third term in (17), and a similar sum for the effect of improved environmental quality gives the fourth term.

As the prior literature has shown (see, for example, Parry, 1995), the less substitutable the polluting good is for leisure, the lower the cost of environmental regulation. For simplicity, we consider the neutral assumption that goods X and Y are equal net substitutes for leisure.[7] This implies that the effect of a pollution tax can be expressed as

$$\frac{1}{\lambda}\frac{dU}{d\tau_X} = (1+Z)\tau_X\frac{dX}{d\tau_X} - \tau_P\frac{dX}{d\tau_X} - Z\left[(p_X - \tau_X)\frac{\partial F_X}{\partial Q} + p_Y\frac{\partial F_Y}{\partial Q}\right]\frac{dX}{d\tau_X} - Z'(1-\tau_L)\frac{d\pi}{d\tau_X}$$
$$-\left[(Z' - Z)\left(\frac{\partial S}{\partial Q} + \frac{\partial M}{\partial Q}\right) - Z'\tau_L\frac{\partial S}{\partial Q}\right]\frac{dX}{d\tau_X} \quad (19)$$

Thus, the cost of a pollution tax (the first term) is equal to 1 + Z times the primary cost of the policy, a familiar result from the prior literature. The total benefit of regulation is equal to the primary benefit (the second term) plus the benefit-side tax-interaction effects resulting from changes in labor productivity (the third term), fixed-factor rents (the fourth term), and individual health (the fifth term). Solving for the optimal pollution tax yields

$$\tau_X^* = \frac{\tau_P}{1+Z} + \frac{Z}{1+Z}\left[(p_X - \tau_X)\frac{\partial F_X}{\partial Q} + p_Y \frac{\partial F_Y}{\partial Q}\right] + \frac{Z'}{1+Z}(1-\tau_L)\frac{d\pi / d\tau_X}{dX / d\tau_X}$$
$$+ \frac{1}{1+Z}\left[(Z'-Z)\left(\frac{\partial S}{\partial Q} + \frac{\partial M}{\partial Q}\right) - Z'\tau_L \frac{\partial S}{\partial Q}\right] \qquad (20)$$

Here, the first term is the optimal tax in the absence of benefit-side tax interactions, while the next three terms represent the influence of benefit-side interactions from changes in labor productivity, fixed-factor rents, and individual health, respectively.

The following sections examine the implications of each of the different effects of environmental quality for the benefit-side tax-interaction effect, and therefore for the optimal pollution tax and the potential benefits of pollution regulation.

Labor supply–neutral externality

This section assumes that environmental quality appears as a separable term in the utility function, that it does not affect either health or production, and that production exhibits constant returns to scale. Thus, $\partial F_X / \partial Q$, $\partial F_Y / \partial Q$, $\partial S / \partial Q$, $\partial M / \partial Q$ and π all equal zero. The prior literature has assumed benefits of this form because in this case changes in environmental quality do not affect labor supply, and therefore there is no benefit-side tax-interaction effect. This can be seen by examining equation (19), where these assumptions imply that the terms representing the benefit-side interaction (all but the first two terms) equal zero. These assumptions also imply that all but the first term in equation (20) are equal to zero. Thus, in this case, the optimal pollution tax is equal to the Pigouvian tax divided by the MCPF.

As prior work (for example, Bovenberg and de Mooij, 1994) has noted, if environmental quality enters utility in a non-separable fashion, then this will affect the household labor-supply decision and thus change the optimal pollution tax. If environmental quality is a leisure complement (for example, if improved air quality makes outdoor leisure more attractive), then improved environmental quality will lead to a drop in labor supply, and thus the optimal pollution tax will be lower than if environmental quality is separable in utility. The opposite effect occurs if environmental quality is a complement to consumption (for example, if pollution reduces the utility derived from certain consumption goods).

Externality affecting production

This section assumes that environmental quality affects production of one or both consumption goods, but does not directly affect utility or health. Thus, $\partial U / \partial Q$, $\partial S / \partial Q$, and $\partial M / \partial Q$ all equal zero. Also assume for now that $d\pi / d\tau_X$ is equal to zero, an assumption that will be relaxed later in this section. In this case, improved environmental quality lowers the marginal production cost (and therefore the price) for one or both consumption goods, increasing the real wage and encouraging labor supply.

Under these assumptions, the last two terms in (19) equal zero, but the third term (the benefit-side tax-interaction effect) is equal to Z times the second term (the direct benefit from regulation). Thus, tax interactions produce a benefit-side gain, magnifying the benefits of the pollution tax to the same extent that the costs are magnified. In this case, both the cost-side and benefit-side interactions come from changes in the real wage; the cost-side effect arises because the tax-induced increase in the price of good X reduces the real wage, while the benefit-side effect arises because improved environmental quality raises labor productivity, boosting the real wage. Because both benefits and costs influence labor supply through the same channel—the real wage—they are both magnified to the same extent by tax interactions.

These assumptions also imply that the expression for the optimal tax (20) reduces to the Pigouvian tax. Because both the costs and benefits of the policy are magnified in the same proportion, the optimal pollution tax is the Pigouvian tax, just as in the first-best case.[8]

Bovenberg and van der Ploeg (1994) achieve a similar result through a somewhat different model. The results from this section generalize and extend their analysis in three respects.

First, their analysis assumed that environmental quality affects all industries equally. The model presented here demonstrates that the optimal pollution tax is the same as in the first-best case even if the effect of pollution differs across industries.

Second, this model calculates not only the optimal pollution tax, but also the welfare gain from implementing that tax, showing that in this case the optimal tax is the same as in the first-best case, but the potential gain from regulation is greater. Because both benefits and costs are equal to the MCPF times their first-best levels, the welfare gain from any given pollution tax—the benefits minus the costs—is also magnified, being equal to the MCPF times the gain in a first-best setting.

Third, this model allows for rents from production, and demonstrates that the optimal pollution tax is the same as in the first-best case only if changing the environmental tax leaves total producer rents unchanged. If total rents do change—for example, if improved environmental quality increases fixed-factor productivity—then the fourth term in (19) and the third term in (20) will no longer equal zero. Thus, as examination of expression (20) shows, if increased environmental quality increases rents, the optimal pollution tax will be lower than the Pigouvian level.[9] Unlike increased labor productivity, increased profits represent a benefit with no direct effect on labor supply, and will actually reduce labor supply due to the income effect. As a result, benefits in the form of increased profits are reduced by tax interactions. Since the costs are still magnified, if any benefits come in the form of increased rents, the optimal pollution tax will be less than the Pigouvian tax.[10] Global climate change may well have effects of this kind; to the extent that global warming decreases the productivity of farmland, preventing climate change will preserve landowners' rents.

Externality with health effects

This section considers the case where environmental quality affects health, but not productivity or utility. Thus, in this case, $\partial U/\partial Q$, $\partial F_X/\partial Q$, and $\partial F_Y/\partial Q$ equal zero. For simplicity, this section also assumes that production exhibits constant returns to scale, so $\pi = 0$. Under these assumptions, the third and fourth terms in expression (19) will equal zero, but the fifth term will not. The sign of this benefit-side interaction term will depend on the particular form of the health effect. If an improved environment lowers medical expenses, it will be negative, reducing the benefit of regulation, whereas if an improved environment reduces time lost to illness, then its sign will be ambiguous, depending on the tax rate and labor elasticities.

This result appears because both types of health damage cause an income effect. Reducing either medical expenses or time lost to illness makes households better off, causing increased consumption of leisure and exacerbating the labor market distortion. An offsetting effect occurs when an improved environment reduces time lost to illness because households have more time available for labor, thus generating a gain from additional labor tax revenues.

Under the assumptions in this section, the second and third terms in (20) will equal zero. The remaining expression will be less than the Pigouvian tax level. It may be more or less than the optimum tax in the case in which environmental quality has a separable effect on utility, depending on whether the last term in (20) is positive or negative. Assuming that the labor tax rate is 0.4, the MCPF is 1.11 (implying that $Z = 0.11$) and the MEB is 0.3,[11] suggests that this term will be negative, and thus that the optimal tax will be lower than it would be if environmental quality appeared only as a separable term in utility. Only if the MCPF is large relative to the MEB (if the uncompensated labor supply elasticity is large compared to the compensated elasticity), and if the fraction of benefits that appear as reduced medical costs are small relative to the gain from reduced time lost to sickness, will this last term be positive.

Conclusions

Prior research has shown that interactions with a tax-distorted labor market can significantly magnify the costs of pollution regulation, and the extent to which those costs are magnified will depend on the regulatory instrument used. This paper has shown that a similar principle holds on the benefit side. The benefit-side tax-interaction effect can magnify or diminish the benefits of reduced pollution, with the effect depending on just what form such benefits take. This effect is potentially very important; it can alter the benefits of environmental regulation to as great an extent as the second-best effects noted by the prior literature change the costs of regulation.

When reducing pollution boosts labor productivity, benefit-side interactions yield a welfare gain. When it boosts fixed-factor productivity or reduces medical expenses, these interactions yield a welfare loss. And when lowering pollution reduces time lost to illness, benefit-side interactions may yield either a welfare gain or loss, though typical parameter estimates suggest that it will be a loss.

Calculating the magnitude of these benefit-side tax interactions for the regulation of a particular pollutant should not be too difficult. The necessary parameter values—the proportion of damages coming from each of the several possible channels—are typically produced as intermediate steps in empirical studies that value pollution damages.[12]

Future studies should consider the benefit-side tax interactions as well as the cost-side tax interactions in estimating the optimal level of regulation and the potential gains from such regulation. Studies that fail to consider these second-best effects could prove to be substantially misleading.

While this model focuses only on environmental regulation, the insight it provides is more general. The benefit-side tax-interaction effect depends not on what is regulated, but on what form the benefits of regulation take. Thus, this effect will apply equally to a broad range of other policies that affect health or productivity, such as occupational health and safety rules or subsidies for research and development.

Notes

1. Among the many papers on this topic are Bovenberg and de Mooij (1994), Bovenberg and van der Ploeg (1994), Parry (1995), Goulder (1995), and Goulder, Parry, and Burtraw (1997).
2. The prior literature has referred to a single tax-interaction effect. This paper extends that concept to a general class of tax-interaction effects. These effects are general equilibrium welfare changes resulting from changes in the quantity demanded of a taxed good caused by forces outside the market for that good. The previously identified tax-interaction effect is a change in the demand for leisure caused when the cost of regulation drives up the price of consumer goods. The benefit-side tax-interaction effect introduced in this paper is a change in the demand for leisure resulting from improved environmental quality.
3. This model follows prior work by assuming that environmental quality is separable in utility from leisure and consumption. The implications of this assumption are discussed later.
4. Previous papers have shown that there is a substantial cost advantage to using an environmental tax in preference to a quota or system of grandfathered tradable permits, because of the efficiency gain from recycling the pollution tax revenues. See, for example, Goulder, Parry, and Burtraw (1997), Parry, Williams, and Goulder (1999), Goulder *et al.* (1999), and Fullerton and Metcalf (2001). Because this paper is not concerned with the distinction between taxes and quotas, it models only the use of a corrective tax.
5. This is a "non-environmental" definition of the MCPF; it omits the effects of changes in environmental quality and environmental tax revenue that would result from a change in the labor tax.
6. For full derivations of this and other expressions in this paper, see Williams (2000).
7. Other papers on this topic (e.g., Bovenberg and van der Ploeg, 1994 and Bovenberg and de Mooij, 1994) have assumed that utility is homothetic and that it is weakly separable between leisure and consumption. Together, those assumptions are sufficient to imply that all goods are equal net substitutes for leisure.
8. While the formula for the optimal pollution tax in this case is the same with or without distortionary taxation, equal to the marginal damage from pollution, the actual value for the optimal tax rate will generally differ, because introducing distortionary taxation may change the value of marginal damages.
9. This result is similar to that found by Williams (1999) in the context of optimal tariffs on international trade in a tax-distorted economy.
10. On the other hand, if improved environmental quality increases labor productivity but reduces rents (by reducing the productivity of a fixed factor such as land), the optimal second-best tax will exceed the Pigouvian tax. It is difficult to conceive of an example of such a case, however.
11. An uncompensated labor supply elasticity of 0.15 and an income elasticity of labor supply of –0.25, together with a labor tax rate of 0.4 imply these values for the MCPF and MEB. These elasticities are roughly consistent with those found by Fuchs, Krueger, and Poterba (1998) in a survey of labor economists. A labor tax rate of 0.4 is a standard assumption in the literature, as in Browning (1987).
12. The Environmental Protection Agency (1999), for example, provides estimates of the benefits of the Clean Air Act divided into numerous categories, including various effects on human health, effects on productivity (e.g., effects on timber growth), and direct effects on utility (e.g., changes in visibility).

References

Bovenberg, A. Lans and Ruud A. de Mooij, 1994. "Environmental Levies and Distortionary Taxation." *American Economic Review* 84(4):1085–9.

Bovenberg, A. Lans and Frederick van der Ploeg, 1994. "Green Policies and Public Finance in a Small Open Economy." *Scandinavian Journal of Economics* 96:343–63.

Browning, Edgar K., 1987. "On the Marginal Welfare Cost of Taxation." *American Economic Review* 77:11–23.

Environmental Protection Agency, 1997. "The Benefits and Costs of the Clean Air Act 1970 to 1990."

Environmental Protection Agency, 1999. "The Benefits and Costs of the Clean Air Act 1990 to 2010."

Fuchs, Victor R., Alan B. Krueger, and James M. Poterba, 1998. "Economists' Views about Parameters, Values and Policies: Survey Results in Labor and Public Economics." *Journal of Economic Literature* 36(3):1387–425.

Fullerton, Don and Gilbert Metcalf, 2001. "Environmental Controls, Scarcity Rents, and Pre-Existing Distortions." *Journal of Public Economics* 80:249–67.

Goulder, Lawrence H., 1995. "Environmental Taxation and the 'Double Dividend': A Reader's Guide." *International Tax and Public Finance* 2(2):157–83.

Goulder, Lawrence H., Ian W.H. Parry, and Dallas Burtraw, 1997. "Revenue-Raising vs. Other Approaches to Environmental Protection: The Critical Significance of Pre-Existing Tax Distortions." *Rand Journal of Economics* 28:708–31.

Goulder, Lawrence H., Ian W.H. Parry, Roberton C. Williams III, and Dallas Burtraw, 1999. "The Cost-Effectiveness of Alternative Instruments for Environmental Protection in a Second-Best Setting." *Journal of Public Economics* 72:329–60.

Parry, Ian W.H., 1995. "Pollution Taxes and Revenue Recycling." *Journal of Environmental Economics and Management* 29:S64–77.
Parry, Ian W.H., Roberton C. Williams III, and Lawrence H. Goulder, 1999. "When Can Carbon Abatement Policies Increase Welfare? The Fundamental Role of Distorted Factor Markets." *Journal of Environmental Economics and Management* 37:52–84.
Williams, Roberton C. III, 1999. "Revisiting the Cost of Protectionism: The Role of Tax Distortions in the Labor Market." *Journal of International Economics* 47:459–77.
Williams, Roberton C. III, 2000. "Environmental Tax Interactions When Pollution Affects Health or Productivity." NBER Working Paper No. 8049.

[14]

ELSEVIER

Journal of Public Economics 70 (1998) 343–364

JOURNAL OF PUBLIC ECONOMICS

Externalities and optimal taxation

Helmuth Cremer[a], Firouz Gahvari[b,*], Norbert Ladoux[a]

[a]IDEI and GREMAQ, University of Toulouse, Toulouse, France

[b]Department of Economics, University of Illinois at Urbana-Champaign, Champaign, IL 61820, USA

Received 30 April 1997; received in revised form 31 October 1997; accepted 20 March 1998

Abstract

This paper reexamines the optimal tax design problem (income and commodities) in the presence of externalities. The nature of the second–best, and the choice of the tax instruments, are motivated by the informational structure in the economy. The main results are: (i) environmental levies (linear or nonlinear) differ in formula from Pigouvian taxes by the expressions for the optimal tax on private goods; (ii) externalities do not affect commodity tax formulas (linear and nonlinear) for private goods; (iii) externalities do not affect the income tax structure if commodity taxes are nonlinear and affect it if commodity taxes are linear; and (iv) a general income tax plus strictly Pigouvian taxes are sufficient for efficient taxation *if* individuals of different types have identical marginal rates of substitution (at any given consumption bundle). © 1998 Elsevier Science S.A. All rights reserved.

Keywords: Optimal taxation; Externalities; Environmental levies; Second–best; Informational structure

JEL classification: H21; H23

1. Introduction

The role of public policy in combating environmental problems is a hotly debated issue among economists and noneconomists alike. The only consensus in

*Corresponding author. Tel.: +1-217-333-7651; Fax: +1-217-244-7368; E-mail: fgahvari@uiuc.edu

PII: S0047-2727(98)00039-5

academic circles is that *if* there is to be public intervention, it should be incentive-based rather than command and control. The most fully-developed incentive approach is the Pigouvian tax scheme. The idea is to levy a tax on an externality generating activity equal to its marginal social damage. This is a *first–best* remedy which, in the absence of other distortions in the economy (including distortionary taxes), moves the competitive equilibrium of the economy to its Pareto-efficient frontier. In a second–best environment, however, this prescription must be modified.

This problem was originally studied by Sandmo (1975), and more recently by Bovenberg and van der Ploeg (1994).[1] The main result that has emerged from this literature is what Sandmo dubbed the "additivity property" where the presence of externality only alters the tax formula for the externality generating good, leaving other tax formulas unaffected. Dixit (1985) has referred to Sandmo's result as an instance of the more general "principle of targeting". The idea is that one should best counter a distortion by thc tax instrument that acts on it directly. Bovenberg and van der Ploeg (1994) also emphasize this principle in their finding that, in addition to tax formulas for other goods, the formula for the labor income tax must also remain unaffected.

While this literature has been motivated by the recognition that second–best considerations may alter the characterization of optimal taxes, its treatment of the second–best has been quite arbitrary. In particular, it has assumed that the feasible tax instruments, including the income tax, are all linear. This is important. Atkinson and Stiglitz (1976) have taught us that the properties of optimal tax schemes depend crucially on the instruments allowed. The aim of the current paper is to reexamine the optimal tax problem in the presence of externalities while motivating the choice of the tax instruments by the informational structure in the economy.

We pose two basic questions. The first question concerns the nature of the optimal tax on an externality generating good when first–best taxes are not available. Under what circumstances does the tax differ from the Pigouvian tax and how? What factors determine the sign and the magnitude of this difference? The second question inquires into the properties of second–best taxes on "private" goods *and* on income in the presence of externalities. In particular, what are the interconnections between environmental levies and traditional tax instruments? The answers to these questions crucially depend on the delineation of the second–best itself; namely the extent and the nature of the constraints that prevent

[1] Bovenberg and van der Ploeg (1994) also examine the impact of externalities on the optimal level and composition of public spending. This latter issue is not the concern of the current paper. Nor are we concerned with the taxation of intermediate inputs as in Bovenberg and Goulder (1996). Bovenberg and de Mooij (1994) and Fullerton (1997) compare the *size* of a second–best tax relative to the "Pigouvian" tax. Their setup is also one of a "representative individual" facing linear taxes.

imposition of first–best taxes. We will consider two such specifications in this paper based on the informational constraints the government faces.

We model an economy with n private goods, labor supply and an externality generating good. The externality is created by the total consumption of the good in question. Many environmental problems are due to this type of externality; greenhouse effect is an example.[2] There are H types of persons in the economy who may *differ in two dimensions*: earning abilities and tastes. This is a generalization of Stiglitz's (Stiglitz, 1982, 1987) two-group optimal tax model where individuals differ only in earning abilities. In the tradition of the optimal tax literature, we assume that the types are not publicly observable. This makes first–best tax instruments unavailable. However, personal income levels are observable so that nonlinear income taxation is feasible.

In the first part of the paper (Section 3), we follow the implicit assumption of Stiglitz that personal consumption levels are publicly observable. This assumption allows commodity taxes to be levied in a nonlinear fashion. We then characterize the properties of second–best taxes in this environment. Answering our first question, we show that the tax on the externality generating good is *nonlinear* and differs in formula from the Pigouvian tax by the expression for the optimal tax on private goods. Recall that the first–best tax is linear with an *identical* rate for everybody; it is also strictly Pigouvian. Answering our second question, we show that the presence of the externality does not affect the formulas determining the optimal commodity taxes on private goods and income taxes. This finding is in agreement with Sandmo's additivity property.

We next extend Atkinson and Stiglitz's (Atkinson and Stiglitz, 1976) famous result [and Mirrlees's (Mirrlees, 1976) generalization of it] on the usefulness of commodity taxes in the presence of a general income tax, to a setting with externality. We prove that when individuals of different types have identical marginal rates of substitution (at any given consumption bundle), differential commodity taxation is not called for *and* the optimal tax on the externality generating good is strictly Pigouvian.

In the second part of the paper (Sections 4–6), we drop the assumption of public observability of personal consumption levels and examine the optimal tax problem anew. This is motivated by the nature of information typically available to tax administrations. While *total* purchases of a commodity are generally observed, individual consumption levels are often private information. As a rule, the tax administration does not know the identity of who buys how much of what good. Lack of public observability of personal purchases precludes the levying of nonlinear commodity taxes. The best that the government can do is to impose (possibly differential) linear commodity taxes.

Given this informational structure, we characterize Pareto-efficient allocations

[2]Meade (1952) has termed such externalities "atmosphere" externalities. For the issues pertaining to greenhouse effect and global warming, see Dornbusch and Poterba (1991).

that are constrained, in addition to resource balance and the standard self-selection constraints, by the linearity of commodity taxes. To do this, we derive an optimal revelation mechanism. For our purpose, a mechanism consists of a set of type-specific before-tax and after-tax incomes and a vector of commodity tax rates (same for everyone). This procedure determines the commodity tax rates right from the outset. A complete solution to the optimal tax problem per-se then requires only the design of an implementing income tax function.

We give a characterization for optimal commodity taxes and examine the properties of the marginal income tax rate. Answering our first question anew, we show that the optimal externality tax continues to differ in formula from the Pigouvian tax by the expression for the optimal tax on private goods. Regarding our second question, we show that while the tax formulas for private goods remain unaffected, the structure of income taxation changes. That is, the presence of externality has different implications for commodity and income taxation. This indicates that Sandmo's additivity property, and Dixit's Principle of targeting, is not a universal property. It depends on the nature of the tax instruments that are available (i.e. if linear or nonlinear) for direct as against indirect intervention.

Independently from the externality issue, the paper also makes a methodological contribution to the optimal tax literature. Building on Cremer et al. (1996), it studies Pareto-efficient tax structures in a model with H types of individuals and two unobservable characteristics. It derives general results on the properties of income and commodity taxes for two informational structures: public observability of consumption levels at (i) personal and (ii) aggregate levels.

2. The model

Consider an economy consisting of a continuum of individuals who can be grouped into H different and finite types. The types may differ in two characteristics: earning abilities and tastes. Each person, regardless of his type, is endowed with one unit of time. He has preferences over labor supply and $n+1$ consumer goods. All goods are produced by a linear technology subject to constant returns to scale. The $(n+1)$th good creates a negative consumption externality; the first n goods (labelled private goods) do not. The externality is created by the *total* consumption of y. This is the type Meade (1952) has termed "atmosphere" externalities. Normalize the population size at one and denote the proportion of persons of type j in the population by π^j. Further denote the vector of private goods by $\underline{x}=(x_1, x_2, \ldots, x_n)$, the externality generating good by y, the labor supply by L, and normalize producer prices of all consumer goods at one.

A person of type j has w^j as his wage and

$$\mho^j = U(\underline{x}, y, L, \theta^j) - \phi\left(\sum_{j=1}^{H} \pi^j y^j\right), \; j = 1, 2, \ldots, H, \tag{1}$$

as his utility function, where θ^j is a "taste" parameter. Note that while type j differs from type k ($k \neq j$), it is possible that $w^j = w^k$ or $\theta^j = \theta^k$. In words, we do not rule out the case where two types differ in one of the characteristics only. This is a very general specification assuming no particular correlation between the values of θ^j and w^j.[3]

We assume that U is strictly quasi-concave, twice continuously differentiable, strictly increasing in $\underline{x}$ and y, and strictly decreasing in L; while ϕ is convex and increasing. The following points must be noted regarding the specification of preferences in (1). First, for the purpose of exposition, we shall take the externality to be detrimental. Thus $\phi(\cdot)$ appears in (1) with a negative sign. Second, the seemingly equal weight assigned to $\phi(\cdot)$ is only in appearance; it imposes no restrictions. Since U depends on θ^j, this is a matter of normalization.[4] Third, allowing $\phi(\cdot)$ to also depend on θ^j will entail only a slight modification in the expressions derived below; it is of no consequence. Fourth, the main assumption is that of separability of preferences between consumption goods and the externality. This is adopted for ease of exposition and algebraic simplicity.[5]

In the tradition of the optimal income tax literature, we assume that an individual's type and labor input are not observable by the government. His before-tax income, $I = wL$, on the other hand, is. This rules out first-best taxation of types as a policy instrument while allowing nonlinear taxation of incomes. It is then convenient to introduce a type-specific utility function describing preferences over x_i's, y and I:

$$u^j(\underline{x}, y, I) \equiv U\left(\underline{x}, y, \frac{I}{w^j}, \theta^j\right), \tag{2}$$

where w^j is the wage of an individual of type j.

Given this framework, we set out to answer the two basic questions we posed in the Introduction. To do this, we specify two informational structures for the government; each delineating a different second-best environment.

3. Observable individual purchases

Suppose that in addition to before-tax incomes, I^j's, the government could also observe individual purchases, x_i^j's and y^j's, so that nonlinear commodity taxes are

[3] Specifically, if there are M "preferences types" and N "earning-ability types", there will be H ($\leq M \times N$) different individual types in the economy.

[4] For any nonunitary weight on $\phi(\cdot)$, one can divide U^j by that weight and return to (1).

[5] The assumption does not change the main conclusions of the paper. Without separability, the formulas that characterize the second-best tax on the externality generating good will include additional terms (reflecting the interaction between the externality and other goods). This matters only in places where the second-best tax is found to be strictly Pigouvian.

feasible. Tax structures will then be constrained by self-selection only.[6] We begin by considering the standard equivalent problem of the government first choosing optimal allocations subject to resource balance, self-selection and the relevant nonnegativity constraints. Having derived the optimal allocation, we then describe the tax structure that can implement it.

3.1. Pareto-efficient allocations

Let $\bar{R}$ denote the government's revenue requirement. Denote the utility level of a j-type individual by u^j when he chooses the allocation intended for him, and by u^{jk} when he chooses a k-type person's bundle. Thus denote

$$u^j = \boldsymbol{u}^j(\underline{x}^j, y^j, I^j), \tag{3a}$$

$$u^{jk} = \boldsymbol{u}^j(\underline{x}^k, y^k, I^k). \tag{3b}$$

One can then describe the set of Pareto-efficient allocations as follows. Maximize

$$\sum_{j=1}^{H} \gamma^j \mho^j, \tag{4}$$

with respect to $\underline{x}^j$, y^j and I^j; subject to the resource constraint

$$\sum_{j=1}^{H} \pi^j \Big(I^j - \sum_i x_i^j - y^j \Big) \geq \bar{R}, \tag{5}$$

and the self-selection constraints

$$u^j \geq u^{jk},\ j \neq k;\ j, k = 1, 2, \ldots, H, \tag{6}$$

where γ^j's are positive constants with the normalization $\Sigma_{j=1}^{H} \gamma^j = 1$.

Denote the Lagrangian expression by $\mathcal{L}$, and the (nonnegative) Lagrangian multipliers associated with the resource constraint (5) by μ, and with the self-selection constraints (6) by λ^{jk}. One can write[7]

$$\mathcal{L} = \sum_j \gamma^j \mho^j + \mu \Big[\sum_j \pi^j \Big(I^j - \sum_i x_i^j - y^j \Big) - \bar{R} \Big] + \sum_j \sum_{k \neq j} \lambda^{jk} (u^j - u^{jk}). \tag{7}$$

[6]This is the framework used by Stiglitz (1982), (1987) to discuss Pareto-efficient self-selection tax structures. Of course, in his setup, there is no externality. Moreover, he does not allow for taste differentiation and considers only two groups of persons who differ in earning abilities.

[7]To simplify notation, we use Σ_j for $\Sigma_{j=1}^{H}$ and $\Sigma_{k \neq j}$ for $\sum_{k=1, k \neq j}^{H}$ throughout the paper.

Substitute for U^j from (1) into (7), use $\sum_j \gamma^j = 1$ and rearrange the terms to rewrite the Lagrangian expression as

$$\mathscr{L} = \sum_j \Big(\gamma^j + \sum_{k \neq j} \lambda^{jk}\Big) u^j - \phi\Big(\sum_j \pi^j y^j\Big) + \mu\Big[\sum_j \pi^j \Big(l^j - \sum_i x_i^j - y^j\Big) - \bar{R}\Big] - \sum_j \sum_{k \neq j} \lambda^{jk} u^{jk}. \tag{8}$$

This yields the following first-order conditions for $j = 1, 2, \ldots, H$, and $i = 1, 2, \ldots, n$.

$$\frac{\partial \mathscr{L}}{\partial x_i^j} = \Big(\gamma^j + \sum_{k \neq j} \lambda^{jk}\Big) u_i^j - \mu\pi^j - \sum_{k \neq j} \lambda^{kj} u_i^{kj} = 0, \tag{9a}$$

$$\frac{\partial \mathscr{L}}{\partial y^j} = \Big(\gamma^j + \sum_{k \neq j} \lambda^{jk}\Big) u_y^j - \pi^j \phi' - \mu\pi^j - \sum_{k \neq j} \lambda^{kj} u_y^{kj} = 0, \tag{9b}$$

$$\frac{\partial \mathscr{L}}{\partial l^j} = \Big(\gamma^j + \sum_{k \neq j} \lambda^{jk}\Big) u_l^j + \mu\pi^j - \sum_{k \neq j} \lambda^{kj} u_l^{kj} = 0, \tag{9c}$$

where a subscript on u denotes a partial derivative. Note that the calculation of the derivatives of $\sum_j \sum_{k \neq j} \lambda^{jk} u^{jk}$ results in the transposition of their j and k indices. Manipulating first-order conditions (9a)–(9c), one can derive the following equations for $j = 1, 2, \ldots, H$, and $i, s = 1, 2, \ldots, n$.

$$\frac{u_y^j}{u_i^j} = \frac{1 + \phi'/\mu + \sum_{k \neq j} \lambda^{kj} u_y^{kj} / \mu\pi^j}{1 + \sum_{k \neq j} \lambda^{kj} u_i^{kj} / \mu\pi^j}, \tag{10a}$$

$$\frac{u_s^j}{u_i^j} = \frac{1 + \sum_{k \neq j} \lambda^{kj} u_s^{kj} / \mu\pi^j}{1 + \sum_{k \neq j} \lambda^{kj} u_i^{kj} / \mu\pi^j}, \tag{10b}$$

$$-\frac{u_l^j}{u_i^j} = \frac{1 - \sum_{k \neq j} \lambda^{kj} u_l^{kj} / \mu\pi^j}{1 + \sum_{k \neq j} \lambda^{kj} u_i^{kj} / \mu\pi^j}. \tag{10c}$$

The system of Eqs. (10a)–(10c) characterizes Pareto-efficient allocations constrained by self-selection. Note that these conditions, and our specification, are quite general. In particular, they are not based on the "single-crossing" property. The self-selection constraints associated with a j-type mimicking a k-type and a

k-type mimicking a j-type can simultaneously bind. It is also possible to have "bunching".

The left-hand sides of (10a)–(10c) are the familiar marginal rates of substitution between different goods. When individuals do their purchases in the market, they set these rates equal to the relative prices they face. This observation allows us to examine the properties of the tax functions which can implement these allocations.

3.2. First–best taxation

It will be instructive to start by examining the nature of first–best taxes. Our characterization of the second–best above allows us to do this most simply. At first–best allocations, self-selection is not a constraint on the government's problem. Thus set $\lambda^{kj}=0$ in Eqs. (10a)–(10c). This yields

$$\frac{u_y^j}{u_i^j} = 1 + \frac{\phi'}{\mu}; \frac{u_s^j}{u_i^j} = 1; -\frac{u_I^j}{u_i^j} = 1. \tag{11}$$

This tells us that the implementation of first–best outcome requires, as expected, no distortionary taxes on x_i^j's and I^j but a tax on y^j ($j=1, 2, \ldots ,H$) equal to ϕ'/μ. Note that the required tax rate on y is the same for everyone and equal to the marginal social damage associated with any person's purchase of a last unit of y. This is the case because the nature of the externality is such that only aggregate size of y matters.

In what follows, for concreteness, we shall follow the following terminology.

Definition 1. A tax is called Pigouvian if it is equal to ϕ'/μ (the marginal social damage of $\Sigma_j \pi^j y^j$).

3.3. Second–best taxation

When at least one of the self-selection constraints in (6) is binding, the optimal allocation is no longer first–best. The allocations to be implemented are thus characterized by (10a)–(10c) [rather than by (11)]. Consider (10a); the equation characterizing the second–best tax on y. It shows that any groups of persons, l, for whom $\lambda^{kl}\neq 0$, for some k, must pay a tax on y which will generally be different from ϕ'/μ. In a sense, this is to be expected. Our setting also requires that the tax treatment of private goods to depart from first–best (i.e. they should be taxed rather than go tax free). It is thus only logical that the same principle should hold for the tax treatment of nonprivate goods.

One can nevertheless make two important observations regarding the tax treatment of y. First, the formula characterizing the marginal tax on y differs from the Pigouvian tax by the expression for the optimal tax on private goods. Second, unless one places certain restrictions on preferences (see Section 3.3.1 below), different types of persons face different marginal tax rates on y depending on which self-selection constraints bind. Put another way, the optimal tax on y is nonlinear. Contrast these with first–best taxes where everyone, regardless of his type, faces a constant marginal tax rate equal to ϕ'/μ. While there may be some types of persons who would pay the Pigouvian tax here, this will not be the case for all types.[8]

Next, turn to (10b)–(10c), the equations characterizing optimal taxes on private goods and income. These equations do not contain any externality terms; they are identical to the equations governing optimal second–best taxes in the absence of the externality. In this sense, one may say that the presence of the externality does not change the structure of second–best taxes on private goods *and* income.[9]

This last result was originally derived by Sandmo (1975) in a setting with proportional income and commodity taxes. He dubbed it the "additivity property" whereby "the marginal social damage of commodity m enters the tax formula for that commodity additively, and does not enter the tax formulas for other commodities..." (p. 92). Later, Dixit (1985) referred to Sandmo's result as an instance of the more general "principle of targeting". As he put it, this principle states that "a distortion is best countered... by a tax instrument that acts directly on the relevant margin" (p. 314). Bovenberg and van der Ploeg (1994) emphasize this principle in their finding, again assuming linear taxes, that the formula for the labor income tax must also remain unaffected. While our result here is in accordance with this property, we will see in subsequent sections that this may not always be the case.[10]

3.3.1. Second–best Pigouvian taxes

An interesting case arises when individuals of different types have identical marginal rates of substitution between any given two consumer goods (at the same consumption bundle). That is, assume the following conditions hold everywhere.

$$\frac{u_y^{kj}}{u_i^{kj}} = \frac{u_y^j}{u_i^j},\ j = 1, 2, \ldots, H, \text{ and } i = 1, 2, \ldots, n, \tag{12a}$$

$$\frac{u_s^{kj}}{u_i^{kj}} = \frac{u_s^j}{u_i^j},\ i, s = 1, 2, \ldots, n. \tag{12b}$$

[8] The assumption that x_i^j's and y^j are publicly observable implies that the government will have no difficulty in levying nonlinear taxes.

[9] Of course, same formula does *not* mean same level.

[10] As a final observation for the general case, note that the famous "no distortion at the top" result of the optimal tax theory continues to hold here. If there exists a category of persons, h, whom nobody mimics at equilibrium, no incentive constraint will be binding towards it. Setting $\lambda^{kh}=0$ for all $k(\neq h)$ in (10a)–(10c) immediately implies that no distortionary taxes must be levied on these persons' income and consumption but that they should face a simple Pigouvian tax on their consumption of y. This is of course not surprising in view of the fact that *all* decision variables are individually observable here.

Conditions (12a)–(12b) are guaranteed when (i) preferences are separable between labor supply and other goods (as in Atkinson and Stiglitz) and (ii) tastes are homogeneous in the sense that the marginal rates of substitution of different persons (for nonleisure goods) are independent of the taste parameter θ^j.[11] Given (12a)–(12b), one can easily show that Eq. (10a) and Eq. (10b) will reduce to the corresponding ones in (11). This implies that the structure of *commodity taxes* that implement the second–best allocations characterized by (10a)–(10c) remains precisely the same as that in the first–best. That is, there should be no taxes on x_i^j's but that all types must face the same Pigouvian tax on y^j. [These preferences have no implications for the structure of income taxes].

This result is reminiscent of Atkinson and Stiglitz's (Atkinson and Stiglitz, 1976) seminal result, and its generalization by Mirrlees (1976), concerning the usefulness of commodity taxes in the presence of a general income tax. In the absence of externality, when conditions (12a)–(12b) hold, commodity taxes are not needed because they cannot be used as a basis for separation between individuals of different types. (See Stiglitz, 1982, 1987). That is, they cannot be used to relax otherwise binding self-selection constraints and effect a Pareto improvement. The same intuition applies to our setting when there is an externality present. Consumption of private goods must not be distorted, and the only adjustment needed for the externality generating good is the familiar Pigouvian one.[12]

[11]Preferences satisfying these properties are represented by

$$U(\underline{x}, y, L, \theta^j) = \Omega(\theta^j F(\underline{x}, y), L).$$

Atkinson and Stiglitz (1976) assume *identical* preferences at the outset. Mirrlees (1976) discusses taste differentiation.

[12]When conditions (12a)–(12b) do not hold, the characterization of the second–best tax on y becomes a complicated question. One can nevertheless shed some light on this issue by considering a two-group model with $w^h > w^l$. Assume preferences are given by

$$u^j(\underline{x}, y, I) = f(\underline{x}) + \theta^j h(y) - \varphi\left(\frac{I}{w^j}\right), \quad j = h, l,$$

and consider the case when redistribution is from the high- to low-ability persons. Setting $\lambda^{hl} > 0$ and $\lambda^{lh} = 0$ in (10a)–(10b), it immediately follows that

$$\frac{u_s^h}{u_h^h} = \frac{u_s^l}{u_i^l} = 1.$$

$$\frac{u_y^h}{u_l^h} = 1 + \frac{\phi'}{\mu}$$

$$\frac{u_y^l}{u_i^l} = 1 + \frac{\phi'}{\mu} + \frac{\lambda^{hl} h'(y^l)}{\mu \pi^l}(\theta^h - \theta^l).$$

These relationships tell us that (a) high-ability persons should face a Pigouvian tax on their consumption of y, while low-ability persons must face a tax greater (smaller) than Pigouvian if they, in comparison to h-types and for the same consumption bundle, have a lower (higher) marginal rate of substitution of y for x_i, and (b) private goods must go untaxed.

The following proposition summarizes the main results of this section.

Proposition 1. *Assume personal consumption levels are publicly observable. Then* (*i*) *if individuals of different types have identical marginal rates of substitution* (*at any given consumption bundle*), (*a*) *the optimal second–best tax on the externality good, y, is Pigouvian* (*same for everyone*), *and* (*b*) *private goods must not be taxed*;

(*ii*) *with nonidentical marginal rates of substitution, the optimal second–best tax on y is nonlinear with a formula that differs from the Pigouvian tax by the expression for the optimal tax on private goods;*

(*iii*) *the presence of the externality does not affect the formulas determining optimal commodity taxes on private goods and optimal income taxes.*

4. Observable aggregate purchases

The results of the previous section rests crucially on the assumption that personal consumption levels are publicly observable. This assumption allows the government to levy nonlinear commodity taxes. Moreover, as we saw in Section 3, such taxes are in fact necessary to implement Pareto-efficient allocations (constrained by self-selection). However, this assumption is rather hard to justify on informational grounds. It is more realistic to assume that the tax administration has information on anonymous transactions (i.e. aggregate sales of a commodity rather than who purchases how much). This is the standard assumption in the literature, so much so that it has been used as part of very definition of indirect taxes. (See, e.g., Atkinson and Stiglitz, 1980, p. 427). Under this circumstance, nonlinear commodity taxes are not feasible. If, for instance, the tax rate is linked to the quantity purchases, the buyer can avoid higher taxes by splitting the transactions. As a rule, only linear commodity taxes are available.[13]

Given this informational structure, one may proceed to characterize Pareto-efficient allocations that are constrained, in addition to resource balance, not only by the standard self-selection constraints but also by the linearity of commodity taxes. To do this, we derive an optimal revelation mechanism. For our purpose, a mechanism consists of a set of type-specific before-tax incomes, I^j's, aggregate expenditures on private goods, c^j's, and a vector of commodity tax rates (same for everyone). This procedure determines the commodity tax rates, $\underline{t}=(t_1, t_2, \ldots, t_n)$

[13]It should be pointed out that the informational requirement for nonlinear commodity taxation is much more stringent than for nonlinear income taxation. The latter type of taxes require information on each person's aggregate expenditure (or equivalently income) only. Nonlinear commodity taxes, on the other hand, require information on each person's expenditure on every single good. The linearity of commodity taxes is thus a direct implication of the informational structure typically available in the economy.

and t_y, right from the outset. A complete solution to the optimal tax problem per-se then requires only the design of a general income tax function. Note that instead of commodity taxes, the mechanism may equivalently specify the consumer prices of $\underline{x}$ and y, denoted by $\underline{p}=(p_1, p_2, \ldots, p_n)$ and q, where $p_i=1+t_i$ $(i=1, 2, \ldots, n)$ and $q=1+t_y$.[14]

To proceed further, it is necessary to consider the optimization problem of an individual for a *given* mechanism $(\underline{p}, q, c, I)$. This is necessitated by the fact that the mechanism determines personal consumption levels only indirectly, namely through prices. The mechanism assigns $(\underline{p}, q, c^j, I^j)$ to an individual who reports type j. The consumer then allocates c^j between the produced goods, $\underline{x}$ and y.

Formally, given any vector $(\underline{p}, q, c, I)$, an individual of type j solves

$$\max_{\underline{x}, y} \boldsymbol{u}^j(\underline{x}, y, I) \tag{13a}$$

$$\text{subject to} \sum_{i=1}^{n} p_i x_i + qy = c. \tag{13b}$$

The resulting demand functions are denoted by $\boldsymbol{x}_i^j(\underline{p}, q, c, I)$ and $\boldsymbol{y}^j(\underline{p}, q, c, I)$, and the indirect utility function by

$$\boldsymbol{v}^j(\underline{p}, q, c, I) \equiv \boldsymbol{u}^j(\underline{x}^j(\underline{p}, q, c, I), y^j(\underline{p}, q, c, I), I).$$

For ease of notation, we define

$$x_i^j = \boldsymbol{x}_i^j(\underline{p}, q, c^j, I^j), \tag{14a}$$

$$x_i^{jk} = \boldsymbol{x}_i^j(\underline{p}, q, c^k, I^k), \tag{14b}$$

with y^j, v^j, y^{jk} and v^{jk} defined similarly.

4.1. Pareto-efficient (constrained) allocations

Constrained Pareto-efficient "allocations" can be described as follows. Maximize

$$\sum_j \gamma^j \left[v^j - \phi\left(\sum_j \pi^j y^j \right) \right], \tag{15}$$

with respect to $p_2, p_3, \ldots, p_n$, q, c^j and I^j;[15] subject to the resource constraint

[14] Strictly speaking, this procedure does not characterize "allocations" as such; the optimization is over a mix of quantities *and* prices. However, given the commodity prices, utility maximizing individuals would choose the quantities themselves. We can thus think of the procedure as indirectly determining the final allocations.

[15] With one extra degree of freedom in setting commodity tax rates, t_1 is set equal to zero so that $p_1=1$.

$$\sum_j \pi^j\left[(I^j - c^j) + \sum_{s=2}^{n} (p_s - 1)x_s^j + (q-1)y^j\right] \geq \bar{R}, \tag{16}$$

and the self-selection constraints

$$v^j \geq v^{jk}, \quad j, k = 1, 2, \ldots, H. \tag{17}$$

As in Section 3, denote the Lagrangian expression by $\mathcal{L}$, and the Lagrangian multipliers associated with the resource constraint (16) by μ, and with the self-selection constraints (17) by λ^{jk}. We have

$$\begin{aligned}\mathcal{L} = &\sum_j \gamma^j\left[v^j - \phi\left(\sum_j \pi^j y^j\right)\right] \\ &+ \mu\left\{\sum_j \pi^j\left[(I^j - c^j) + \sum_{s=2}^{n}(p_s - 1)x_s^j + (q-1)y^j\right] - \bar{R}\right\} \\ &+ \sum_j \sum_{k \neq j} \lambda^{jk}(v^j - v^{jk}).\end{aligned} \tag{18}$$

Rearranging the terms, one may usefully rewrite the Lagrangian expression as

$$\begin{aligned}\mathcal{L} = &\sum_j \left(\gamma^j + \sum_{k \neq j} \lambda^{jk}\right)v^j - \phi\left(\sum_j \pi^j y^j\right) \\ &+ \mu\left\{\sum_j \pi^j\left[(I^j - c^j) + \sum_{s=2}^{n}(p_s - 1)x_s^j + (q-1)y^j\right] - \bar{R}\right\} \\ &- \sum_j \sum_{k \neq j} \lambda^{jk} v^{jk}.\end{aligned} \tag{19}$$

The first-order conditions are:

$$\begin{aligned}\frac{\partial \mathcal{L}}{\partial I^j} = &\left(\gamma^j + \sum_{k \neq j} \lambda^{jk}\right)v_I^j - \pi^j \frac{\partial y^j}{\partial I^j}\phi' \\ &+ \mu\pi^j\left[1 + \sum_{s=2}^{n}(p_s - 1)\frac{\partial x_s^j}{\partial I^j} + (q-1)\frac{\partial y^j}{\partial I^j}\right] - \sum_{k \neq j} \lambda^{kj} v_I^{kj} \\ = &\ 0, \quad j, k = 1, 2, \ldots, H,\end{aligned} \tag{20a}$$

$$\begin{aligned}\frac{\partial \mathcal{L}}{\partial c^j} = &\left(\gamma^j + \sum_{k \neq j} \lambda^{jk}\right)v_c^j - \pi^j \frac{\partial y^j}{\partial c^j}\phi' \\ &+ \mu\pi^j\left[-1 + \sum_{s=2}^{n}(p_s - 1)\frac{\partial x_s^j}{\partial c^j} + (q-1)\frac{\partial y^j}{\partial c^j}\right] - \sum_{k \neq j} \lambda^{kj} v_c^{kj} \\ = &\ 0,\end{aligned} \tag{20b}$$

$$\frac{\partial \mathcal{L}}{\partial p_i} = \sum_j \left(\gamma^j + \sum_{k \neq j} \lambda^{jk}\right) v_i^j - \left(\sum_j \pi^j \frac{\partial y^j}{\partial p_i}\right)\phi'$$

$$+ \mu \sum_j \pi^j \left[\sum_{s=2}^{n} (p_s - 1)\frac{\partial x_s^j}{\partial p_i} + x_i^j + (q-1)\frac{\partial y^j}{\partial p_i}\right] - \sum_j \sum_{k \neq j} \lambda^{jk} v_i^{jk}$$

$$= 0, \ i = 2, \ldots, n, \tag{20c}$$

$$\frac{\partial \mathcal{L}}{\partial q} = \sum_j \left(\gamma^j + \sum_{k \neq j} \lambda^{jk}\right) v_q^j - \left(\sum_j \pi^j \frac{\partial y^j}{\partial q}\right)\phi'$$

$$+ \mu \sum_j \pi^j \left[\sum_{s=2}^{n} (p_s - 1)\frac{\partial x_s^j}{\partial q} + y^j + (q-1)\frac{\partial y^j}{\partial q}\right] - \sum_j \sum_{k \neq j} \lambda^{jk} v_q^{jk}$$

$$= 0, \tag{20d}$$

where a subscript on v denotes a partial derivative. Eqs. (20a)–(20d) characterize the Pareto-efficient allocations constrained both by self-selection as well as the linearity of commodity tax rates. The next two sections discuss the properties of the commodity tax rates and the general income tax function that can implement these allocations.

5. Optimal commodity taxes

Denote the compensated demand for a good by a "tilde" over the corresponding variable. In Appendix A, we prove that an interior solution satisfies the following conditions.

$$\begin{pmatrix} t_y \\ t_2 \\ t_3 \\ \vdots \\ t_n \end{pmatrix} = A^{-1} \begin{pmatrix} -\sum_j \sum_{k \neq j} \lambda^{kj}(y^{kj} - y^j)\dfrac{v_c^{kj}}{\mu} \\ -\sum_j \sum_{k \neq j} \lambda^{kj}(x_2^{kj} - x_2^j)\dfrac{v_c^{kj}}{\mu} \\ -\sum_j \sum_{k \neq j} \lambda^{kj}(x_3^{kj} - x_3^j)\dfrac{v_c^{kj}}{\mu} \\ \vdots \\ -\sum_j \sum_{k \neq j} \lambda^{kj}(x_n^{kj} - x_n^j)\dfrac{v_c^{kj}}{\mu} \end{pmatrix} + \begin{pmatrix} 1 \\ 0 \\ 0 \\ \vdots \\ 0 \end{pmatrix} \frac{\phi'}{\mu}, \tag{21}$$

where

$$A = \begin{pmatrix} \sum_j \pi^j \frac{\partial \tilde{y}^j}{\partial q} & \sum_j \pi^j \frac{\partial \tilde{y}^j}{\partial p_2} & \sum_j \pi^j \frac{\partial \tilde{y}^j}{\partial p_3} & \cdots & \sum_j \pi^j \frac{\partial \tilde{y}^j}{\partial p_n} \\ \sum_j \pi^j \frac{\partial \tilde{x}_2^j}{\partial q} & \sum_j \pi^j \frac{\partial \tilde{x}_2^j}{\partial p_2} & \sum_j \pi^j \frac{\partial \tilde{x}_2^j}{\partial p_3} & \cdots & \sum_j \pi^j \frac{\partial \tilde{x}_2^j}{\partial p_n} \\ \vdots & \vdots & & \ddots & \vdots \\ \sum_j \pi^j \frac{\partial \tilde{x}_n^j}{\partial q} & \sum_j \pi^j \frac{\partial \tilde{x}_n^j}{\partial p_2} & \sum_j \pi^j \frac{\partial \tilde{x}_n^j}{\partial p_3} & \cdots & \sum_j \pi^j \frac{\partial \tilde{x}_n^j}{\partial p_n} \end{pmatrix}. \quad (22)$$

Note that the right-hand side of (21) also depends on the tax rates so that we only have an implicit "solution" here. Nevertheless (21) is illuminating in a number of ways. First, it shows that the optimal tax on y is not in general strictly Pigouvian. Again, given that the optimal tax rates on private goods are nonzero, this is to be expected. Second, the formula characterizing the tax on y contains both Pigouvian and non-Pigouvian elements. The non-Pigouvian part reflects the binding self-selection constraints. Similar expressions appear in the characterization of optimal tax rates on private goods. Third, the formulas for taxation of x_i^j's and y^j's differ only in that the latter entails a Pigouvian term. Thus Sandmo's (Sandmo, 1975) additivity property continues to hold in our setting for commodity taxes.[16]

5.1. Second–best Pigouvian taxes:

Section 3.3.1, and Proposition 1, establish that if preferences are such that individuals of different types have identical marginal rates of substitution between every two consumer goods, then private goods should not be taxed and the tax on the externality generating good must be Pigouvian. It is plain that the same result must hold here: If nonlinear commodity taxes are not useful, linear commodity taxes cannot be either.[17]

5.2. Independent demands

To gain further insights into the structure of optimal taxes we next concentrate on the special case where there are no cross-price and income effects. It is easy to see from (21) that one will now have

[16]The system of equations in (21) also yield first–best taxes. Setting $\lambda^{jk}=0$ in these equations immediately result in t_i's$=0$ and $t_y=\phi'/\mu$.

[17]Examination of (21) bears this out. Under this circumstance, from problem (13a)–(13b), $y^{kj}=y^j$ and $x_s^{kj}=x_s^j$ for all types k and j, and all goods s. One can easily see that, given these equalities, t_i's$=0$ and $t_y=\phi'/\mu$ will be a solution to (21).

$$t_y = \frac{\sum_j \sum_{k \neq j} \lambda^{kj}(y^{kj} - y^j)v_c^{kj}/\mu}{-\sum_j \pi^j \, \partial \tilde{y}^j/\partial q} + \frac{\phi'}{\mu}, \tag{23a}$$

$$t_i = \frac{\sum_j \sum_{k \neq j} \lambda^{kj}(x_i^{kj} - x_i^j)v_c^{kj}/\mu}{-\sum_j \pi^j \, \partial \tilde{x}_i^j/\partial p_i}, \quad i = 2, 3, \ldots, n. \tag{23b}$$

The formulas are strikingly simple, indicating a Pigouvian adjustment for t_y in comparison to t_i ($i=2, 3, \ldots, n$). One may thus loosely say, "everything else equal", t_y will exceed t_i by the Pigouvian element. Note also that the non-Pigouvian element of t_y and the tax on t_i are identical in form. The denominators in these expressions can be written in terms of elasticities. They will then yield a generalization of the famous "inverse elasticity" rule in a setting with heterogeneous tastes and in the presence of a general income tax. These considerations apply both to t_y and t_i.

It is also interesting to note that the non-Pigouvian element of t_y can take both positive as well as negative values so that t_y can be greater as well as smaller than the Pigouvian tax. To see this, note that from the properties of the Slutsky matrix, the denominator of the non-Pigouvian element is positive. It then follows that the optimal tax on y exceeds (is smaller than) the Pigouvian tax if $\Sigma_j \, \Sigma_{k \neq j} \, (y^{kj} - y^j)v_c^{kj}/\mu$ is positive (negative). A sufficient condition for this is that every mimicker, for whom the incentive compatibility constraint binds, would have a higher (lower) demand for y than the type whom he mimics. This makes quite a bit of sense, as the tax would then hurt a mimicker more (less) in comparison to the person he mimics. Of course, the cited condition is only sufficient. Less stringent conditions may also do.

5.3. Uniform tax rates:

If commodity taxes are restricted to be uniform (e.g., for political economy considerations), the optimal tax on y will continue to be given by Eq. (23a).[18] To see this, note that imposing $t_i=0$, ($i=1, 2, \ldots, n$) as an additional constraint on problem (15)–(17) does not change the structure of the remaining first-order conditions. The optimal tax on t_y will then be found by setting $t_i=0$ in (A11) in Appendix A. The resulting formula for the optimal tax rate will then be seen to be identical to the one given by Eq. (23a). Our discussion in Section 5.2 thus also applies here.The following proposition summarizes the main results of this section.

[18]Given the normalization rule that $t_1=0$, uniformity will also imply $t_i=0$, ($i=2, 3, \ldots, n$).

Proposition 2. *Assume aggregate (but not personal) consumption levels are publicly observable. Then*

(i) the optimal (linear) tax rate on y differs in formula from the Pigouvian tax by the expressions for the optimal tax on private goods, with the externality leaving the formulas for the optimal tax rates on private goods unaffected. The optimal tax rates are characterized by (21)–(22).

(ii) Assume individuals of different types have identical marginal rates of substitution (at the same consumption bundle). Then (a) the optimal second-best tax on y is Pigouvian, and (b) private goods must not be taxed.

(iii) Assume either income and cross-price effects are all zero, or that private goods must be taxed uniformly. Further assume that every mimicker, for whom the incentive compatibility constraint is binding, has a higher (lower) demand for y than the type whom he mimics. Then the optimal tax on y exceeds (is less than) the Pigouvian tax.

6. Income tax structure

The last question for us to examine is to determine if the presence of externality affects the structure of the optimal income tax schedule, and if yes, how. Denote the general income tax schedule facing a j-type person by $T(I^j)$ so that his net income is $c^j = I^j - T(I^j)$. The individual thus sets $-v_I^j/v_c^j = 1 - T'(I^j)$ where we have assumed the tax function is differentiable with T' denoting the marginal income tax rate.[19] Dividing Eq. (20a) by (20b), we can then immediately deduce that

$$1 - T'(I^j) = \frac{1 + \left[\sum_{i=2}^{n} \frac{\partial x_i^j}{\partial I^j} t_i + \frac{\partial y^j}{\partial I^j} t_y\right] - \frac{\phi'}{\mu}\frac{\partial y^j}{\partial I^j} - \frac{\sum_{k\neq j} \lambda^{kj} v_I^{kj}}{\mu \pi^j}}{1 - \left[\sum_{i=2}^{n} \frac{\partial x_i^j}{\partial c^j} t_i + \frac{\partial y^j}{\partial c^j} t_y\right] + \frac{\phi'}{\mu}\frac{\partial y^j}{\partial c^j} + \frac{\sum_{k\neq j} \lambda^{kj} v_c^{kj}}{\mu \pi^j}}, \tag{24}$$

Eq. (24) indicates that the marginal income tax rate is determined by three factors: incentive constraints, impacts of commodity taxes and the externality. The presence of the externality terms in (24) is quite telling. It shows that, with unobservable personal consumption levels, externality affects the shape of the income tax schedule. In particular, note that for the marginal income tax rate to be

[19] With a discrete distribution of types, the implementing tax function will generally be nondifferentiable at some points. There, we follow the standard terminology and continue to refer to $T'(I^j) \equiv 1 + v_I^j / v_c^j$ as the marginal income tax rate; see Stiglitz (1987).

independent of the externality, one must set $t_y = \phi'/\mu$. This, however, will be the case *if* conditions (12a)–(12b) hold.

This result is in sharp contrast to the corresponding result in Section 3 where, with observable consumption levels, we found that externality did not affect the expressions for the marginal income tax rate. The intuition is simple. If y^j's are publicly observable, one can "directly" set them at the desired level (using a nonlinear tax schedule to implement this level). The income tax instrument is not needed for this purpose. On the other hand, if y^j's are not publicly observable, they are "controlled" only indirectly. The income tax may then be used, in addition to the linear commodity tax on y, for this purpose. Specifically, the income tax affects y^j's and consequently this effect has to be taken into account in the design of the optimal income tax. (Any impact from income taxes on y^j's, when y^j's are observable, can be "neutralized" at no cost).

The foregoing result shows that Sandmo's additivity property, and Dixit's principle of targeting, does not hold in this setting. The reason for this is that the available direct instrument is more restrictive than the indirect instrument (a linear tax on the externality versus a nonlinear income tax). This is why in Section 3, where both instruments were nonlinear, the indirect instrument was not found useful. The same intuition applies to the findings of Sandmo (1975) and Bovenberg and van der Ploeg (1994) where all tax instruments (income as well as commodity) are linear and thus equally restrictive.

As a final observation on the shape of the optimal income tax schedule, assume that there exists a category of persons, *h*, whom nobody mimics at equilibrium.[20] This implies that no incentive constraint is binding towards this category, so that $\lambda^{kh} = 0$ for all $k(\neq h)$. It will then immediately follow from (24) that

$$1 - T'(I^h) = \frac{1 + \left[\sum_{i=2}^{n} \frac{\partial x_i^h}{\partial I^h} t_i + \frac{\partial y^h}{\partial I^h} t_y\right] - \frac{\phi'}{\mu}\frac{\partial y^h}{\partial I^h}}{1 - \left[\sum_{i=2}^{n} \frac{\partial x_i^h}{\partial c^h} t_i + \frac{\partial y^h}{\partial c^h} t_y\right] + \frac{\phi'}{\mu}\frac{\partial y^h}{\partial c^h}}. \tag{25}$$

Now, as was shown in Section 5, *if* preferences are separable and tastes are homogeneous, t_i's$=0$ and $t_y = \phi'/\mu$, so that $T'(I^h)=0$. However, in the absence of such restrictions on preferences, it is clear from (25) that in general

$$T'(I^h) \neq 0.$$

That is, the well-known "no distortion at the top" result no longer holds.[21] However, it must be emphasized that the distortion does not arise because of the

[20] When individuals differ in both earning abilities and tastes, this category may or may not exist.

[21] Recall that in Section 3, where all decision variables were individually observable, the result continued to hold. Under that informational structure, the first-best solution is available for the "top" person with no benefits from distorting his choice.

standard incentive constraints [Eqs. (17)]. Its source is the "incomplete control" of consumption levels through *linear* commodity taxes (which arises because individual consumption levels are not observable).The point is that changes in net and gross income (labor supply) affect consumption levels. In turn, these changes affect welfare through tax revenues generated from commodity taxes and through the externality.

The following proposition summarizes the main results of this section.

Proposition 3. *Assume aggregate* (*but not personal*) *consumption levels are publicly observable. Then*

(*i*) *in the absence of other restrictions, the externality affects the income tax structure;*

(*ii*) *the externality does not affect the income tax structure, if individuals of different types have identical marginal rates of substitution* (*at the same consumption bundle*);

(*iii*) *marginal income tax rate "at the top" will generally be nonzero; both positive and negative values are possible.*

7. Conclusion

This paper has reexamined the Pigouvian prescription for correcting externalities in a second–best environment. It has also examined the properties of optimal commodity and income taxes in the presence of externalities. It has shown that the answers to these questions depend crucially on the structure of information in the economy, via its determining the type of tax instruments that are available to the government.

Four main conclusions have emerged. First, environmental levies (linear or nonlinear) differ in formula from Pigouvian taxes by the expressions for the optimal tax on private goods. Second, externalities do not affect commodity tax formulas for private goods. This holds regardless of the public observability of individual consumption levels and thus applies to both linear and nonlinear commodity taxes. Third, externalities do not affect the income tax structure if commodity taxes are nonlinear and affect it if commodity taxes are linear. Fourth, a general income tax plus strictly Pigouvian taxes are sufficient for efficient taxation *if* individuals of different types have identical marginal rates of substitution (at any given consumption bundle).

An important implication of our second and third conclusions is that Sandmo's additivity property, and Dixit's Principle of targeting, breaks down when the tax instruments consist of linear commodity and nonlinear income taxes. In this case, while the tax formulas for private goods remain unaffected, income tax formulas change. The reason for this is that the available direct instrument is more restrictive than the (affected) indirect instrument (a linear tax on the externality versus a nonlinear income tax).

Acknowledgements

We thank two anonymous referees for helpful comments.

Appendix A

Derivation of (21): Multiply Eq. (20b) by y^j, sum over j and add the resulting equation to (20d). Then multiply (20b) by x_i^j, sum over j and add the resulting equation to (20c). Simplifying results in the following system of equations for $i=2, 3, \ldots, n$

$$\sum_j \left(\gamma^j + \sum_{k\neq j} \lambda^{jk}\right)(v_q^j + y^j v_c^j) - \phi' \sum_j \pi^j\left(y^j \frac{\partial y^j}{\partial c^j} + \frac{\partial y^j}{\partial q}\right)$$
$$+ \mu \sum_j \pi^j\left[\sum_{s=2}^n (p_s - 1)\left(y^j \frac{\partial x_s^j}{\partial c^j} + \frac{\partial x_s^j}{\partial q}\right) + (q-1)\left(y^j \frac{\partial y^j}{\partial c^j} + \frac{\partial y^j}{\partial q}\right)\right]$$
$$-\sum_j \sum_{k\neq j} \lambda^{kj}(v_q^{kj} + y^j v_c^{kj}) = 0, \tag{A1}$$

$$\sum_j \left(\gamma^j + \sum_{k\neq j} \lambda^{jk}\right)(v_i^j + x_i^j v_c^j) - \phi' \sum_j \pi^j\left(x_i^j \frac{\partial y^j}{\partial c^j} + \frac{\partial y^j}{\partial p_i}\right)$$
$$+ \mu \sum_j \pi^j\left[\sum_{s=2}^n (p_s - 1)\left(x_i^j \frac{\partial x_s^j}{\partial c^j} + \frac{\partial x_s^j}{\partial p_i}\right) + (q-1)\left(x_i^j \frac{\partial y^j}{\partial c^j} + \frac{\partial y^j}{\partial p_i}\right)\right]$$
$$-\sum_j \sum_{k\neq j} \lambda^{kj}(v_i^{kj} + x_i^j v_c^{kj}) = 0. \tag{A2}$$

Next make use of Roy's identity to set:

$$v_q^j + y^j v_c^j = 0, \tag{A3}$$

$$v_q^{kj} + y^{kj} v_c^{kj} = 0, \tag{A4}$$

$$v_i^j + x_i^j v_c^j = 0, \tag{A5}$$

$$v_i^{kj} + x_i^{kj} v_c^{kj} = 0, \tag{A6}$$

and the Slutsky equation to write:

$$\frac{\partial y^j}{\partial q} = \frac{\partial \tilde{y}^j}{\partial q} - y^j \frac{\partial y^j}{\partial c^j}, \tag{A7}$$

$$\frac{\partial x_s^j}{\partial q} = \frac{\partial \tilde{x}_s^j}{\partial q} - y^j \frac{\partial x_s^j}{\partial c^j}, \tag{A8}$$

$$\frac{\partial y^j}{\partial p_i} = \frac{\partial \tilde{y}^j}{\partial p_i} - x_i^j \frac{\partial y^j}{\partial c^j}, \tag{A9}$$

$$\frac{\partial x_s^j}{\partial p_i} = \frac{\partial \tilde{x}_s^j}{\partial p_i} - x_i^j \frac{\partial x_s^j}{\partial c^j}. \tag{A10}$$

Substituting from Eqs. (A3)–(A6) and (A7)–(A10) in (A1)–(A2), making use of the symmetry of the Slutsky matrix, setting $p_i - 1 = t_i$ and $q - 1 = t_y$, upon further simplification and rearrangement, one arrives at

$$\left(\sum_j \pi^j \frac{\partial \tilde{y}^j}{\partial q}\right) t_y + \sum_{i=2}^{n} \left(\sum_j \pi^j \frac{\partial \tilde{y}^j}{\partial p_i}\right) t_i = -\sum_j \sum_{k \neq j} \lambda^{kj} (y^{kj} - y^j) \frac{v_c^{kj}}{\mu} + \left(\sum_j \pi^j \frac{\partial \tilde{y}^j}{\partial q}\right) \frac{\phi'}{\mu}, \tag{A11}$$

$$\left(\sum_j \pi^j \frac{\partial \tilde{x}_s^j}{\partial q}\right) t_y + \sum_{i=2}^{n} \left(\sum_j \pi^j \frac{\partial \tilde{x}_s^j}{\partial p_i}\right) t_i = -\sum_j \sum_{k \neq j} \lambda^{kj} (x_s^{kj} - x_s^j) \frac{v_c^{kj}}{\mu} + \left(\sum_j \pi^j \frac{\partial \tilde{x}_s^j}{\partial q}\right) \frac{\phi'}{\mu}, \quad s = 2, \ldots, n. \tag{A12}$$

Eqs. (A11)–(A12) are one way of characterizing the optimal commodity tax rates: t_i's and t_y.

To arrive at (21), use the definition of **A** in (22) to write out Eqs. (A11)–(A12) in matrix notation:

$$\mathbf{A} \begin{pmatrix} t_y \\ t_2 \\ t_3 \\ \vdots \\ t_n \end{pmatrix} = \begin{pmatrix} -\sum_j \sum_{k \neq j} \lambda^{kj} (y^{kj} - y^j) \frac{v_c^{kj}}{\mu} + \left(\sum_j \pi^j \frac{\partial \tilde{y}^j}{\partial q}\right) \frac{\phi'}{\mu} \\ -\sum_j \sum_{k \neq j} \lambda^{kj} (x_2^{kj} - x_2^j) \frac{v_c^{kj}}{\mu} + \left(\sum_j \pi^j \frac{\partial \tilde{x}_2^j}{\partial q}\right) \frac{\phi'}{\mu} \\ -\sum_j \sum_{k \neq j} \lambda^{kj} (x_3^{kj} - x_3^j) \frac{v_c^{kj}}{\mu} + \left(\sum_j \pi^j \frac{\partial \tilde{x}_3^j}{\partial q}\right) \frac{\phi'}{\mu} \\ \vdots \\ -\sum_j \sum_{k \neq j} \lambda^{kj} (x_n^{kj} - x_n^j) \frac{v_c^{kj}}{\mu} + \left(\sum_j \pi^j \frac{\partial \tilde{x}_n^j}{\partial q}\right) \frac{\phi'}{\mu} \end{pmatrix}. \tag{A13}$$

Denote the first column vector of $\boldsymbol{A}$ by $\boldsymbol{a}_1$. Premultiplying (A13) by $\boldsymbol{A}^{-1}$ then yields

$$\begin{pmatrix} t_y \\ t_2 \\ t_3 \\ \vdots \\ t_n \end{pmatrix} = \boldsymbol{A}^{-1} \begin{pmatrix} -\sum_j \sum_{k \neq j} \lambda^{kj}(y^{kj} - y^j) \dfrac{v_c^{kj}}{\mu} \\ -\sum_j \sum_{k \neq j} \lambda^{kj}(x_2^{kj} - x_2^j) \dfrac{v_c^{kj}}{\mu} \\ -\sum_j \sum_{k \neq j} \lambda^{kj}(x_3^{kj} - x_3^j) \dfrac{v_c^{kj}}{\mu} \\ \vdots \\ -\sum_j \sum_{k \neq j} \lambda^{kj}(x_n^{kj} - xn^j) \dfrac{v_c^{kj}}{\mu} \end{pmatrix} + (\boldsymbol{A}^{-1}\boldsymbol{a}_1) \frac{\phi'}{\mu}, \qquad \text{(A14)}$$

which is readily seen to be the system of Eqs. (21) in the text.

References

Atkinson, A.B., Stiglitz, J.E., 1976. The design of tax structure: direct versus indirect taxation. Journal of Public Economics 6, 55–75.

Atkinson, A.B., Stiglitz, J.E., 1980. Lectures on Public Economics. McGraw-Hill, New-York.

Bovenberg, A.L., van der Ploeg, F., 1994. Environmental policy, public finance and the labor market in a second–best world. Journal of Public Economics 55, 349–390.

Bovenberg, A.L., de Mooij, R.A., 1994. Environmental levies and distortionary taxation. American Economic Review 84, 1085–1089.

Bovenberg, L., Goulder, L., 1996. Optimal environmental taxation in the presence of other taxes: general equilibrium analyses. American Economic Review 86, 985–1000.

Cremer, H., Pestieau, P., Rochet, J.C., 1996. Direct versus indirect taxation: The design of the tax structure revisited. Mimeo.

Dixit, A., 1985. Tax policy in open economies. In: Auerbach, A., Feldstein, M., (Ed.), Handbook of Public Economics. North-Holland, Amsterdam, pp. 313–374.

Dornbusch, R., Poterba, J.M., (Eds.), 1991. Global Warming: Economic Policy Responses. MIT Press, Cambridge, MA.

Fullerton, D., 1997. Environmental levies and distortionary taxation: Comment. American Economic Review 87, 245–251.

Meade, J.E., 1952. External economies and diseconomies in a competitive situation. Economic Journal 62, 54–67.

Mirrlees, J.A., 1976. Optimal tax theory: a synthesis. Journal of Public Economics 6, 327–358.

Sandmo, A., 1975. Optimal taxation in the presence of externalities. Swedish Journal of Economics 77, 86–98.

Stiglitz, J.E., 1982. Self-selection and Pareto efficient taxation. Journal of Public Economics 17, 213–240.

Stiglitz, J.E., 1987. Pareto efficient and optimal taxation and the new welfare economics. In: Auerbach, A., Feldstein, M., (Ed.), Handbook of Public Economics. North-Holland, Amsterdam, pp. 991–1042.

PART III

ENVIRONMENTAL TAX REFORMS AND THE ‘DOUBLE DIVIDEND’

[15]

JOURNAL OF ENVIRONMENTAL ECONOMICS AND MANAGEMENT **29**, S-64–S-77 (1995)

Pollution Taxes and Revenue Recycling*

IAN W. H. PARRY

Resources for the Future, 1616 P Street NW, Washington DC 20036

Received May 10, 1994; revised July 22, 1994

Discussions of environmental policy and the tax system have emphasized the value of pollution tax revenues, which can be used to reduce other tax distortions in the economy. However by raising private marginal production costs, environmental taxes also tend to reduce GDP and exacerbate the welfare costs of conventional taxes. For environmental taxes in consumption goods industries, the net welfare change from these two effects is negative unless this good is a relatively weak substitute for leisure. An estimate for the optimal pollution tax with full revenue recycling is 63 to 78% of marginal environmental damages.

1. INTRODUCTION

This paper examines two important policy questions raised by the interaction of environmental taxes with the rest of the tax system. First, is the welfare gain and hence the case for introducing an environmental tax, greater or less than that implied by a partial equilibrium analysis? Second, what is the optimal level of environmental taxation in second-best economies?

To address these questions two effects need to be considered, which will be called the "revenue effect" (RE) and the "interdependency effect (IE). The RE refers to the welfare gain from using environmental tax revenues to cut distortionary taxes, relative to the case where revenues are returned lump-sum (and have no efficiency consequences).[1] Thus it has been claimed that allowing for interactions with the tax system raises the welfare gain from environmental taxes, the so-called "double dividend hypothesis" (see Oates [15]. Repetto *et al.* [19], Pearce, [18], Terkla [22]).[2] One implication is that environmental taxes would still be worthwhile, even if the environmental benefits were very small.

Furthermore, Lee and Misiolek [12] incorporated the RE in the familiar partial equilibrium analysis of externalities, and showed that the optimal pollution tax is greater (less) than marginal environmental damages (MED) when the pollution tax Laffer curve is upward- (downward-) sloping. Thus Nordhaus [14] calculated that the optimal tax on carbon in response to the possibility of future global warming

* I am grateful to Karen Palmer and two anonymous referees for very helpful comments.

[1] The cases when pollution tax revenues are used to finance additional public spending, or reduced borrowing, are not considered here.

[2] Two other meanings have been attached to the double dividend hypothesis, one weaker, the other stronger, than above. The weak form just asserts that there is a benefit from using revenues to cut other distortionary taxes, relative to lump-sum replacement, which is always valid. The strong form asserts that not only is there a net gain from interactions with the tax system, but that this exceeds the cost of pollution abatement. For a good discussion of these issues see Goulder [9].

0095-0696/95 $12.00

would rise from a modest $5 per ton to $59 per ton, when the value of tax revenues is taken into account—more than a tenfold increase!

The crucial problem with all of this is that the IE is ignored. This refers to the likely exacerbation of preexisting tax distortions caused by the environmental tax. There are large tax wedges in the labor and capital markets, and the efficiency and revenue raised from these markets is reduced, to the extent that environmental taxes discourage employment and investment. Determining the net effect of the RE and IE in the aggregate and at the margin answers the two questions above. The focus here will be on (permanent) environmental taxes in consumption goods industries, and therefore interactions with the capital market are not relevant.

The next section examines environmental taxes on final goods. When pollution taxes substitute for labor tax revenues, and the polluting commodity is an average substitute for leisure, then the benefit from the RE is a fraction of the cost from the IE, where this fraction is the ratio of the post to pretax level of output. Indeed the RE could only outweigh the IE and the double dividend hypothesis could only be correct when the polluting commodity is a sufficiently weaker than average substitute for leisure. However, the pollution tax is still potentially welfare-improving, and the optimal level is on the order of 63% of MED.

Section 3 extends this analysis to allow for taxes on polluting inputs. To the extent that there is substitution in production, both the IE and RE are relatively weaker. However the double dividend hypothesis is still likely to fail. A best estimate for the optimal pollution tax in this case is 63 to 78% of MED.

These theoretical results are consistent with contribution in the optimal commodity tax literature. Bovenberg and de Mooij [2, 3] have recently shown that the existence of a labor tax reduces the welfare gain from a pollution tax (on both final and intermediate goods) and that the optimal pollution tax is less than MED, given an exogenous revenue requirement.[3] However, I feel that the diagrammatic approach used below, and the decomposition of the RE and IE, provides a more simple and intuitive treatment of the issues (rather than lumping the RE and IE together in one optimization model). Moreover, the analysis in Bovenberg and de Mooij [2, 3] is a little restrictive, because they assume that output from the polluting sector is an average substitute for leisure, which guarantees that the IE exceeds the RE in the aggregate and at the margin. The empirical results below are similar to those from the computable general equilibrium model used by Bovenberg and Goulder [4], which incorporates a detailed treatment of the U.S. tax system. They found that the optimal tax on carbon is 68% of MED (for an environmental damage of $25 per ton), when carbon tax revenues are used to cut the rate of personal income tax.[4]

Section 4 concludes.

2. ENVIRONMENTAL TAXES ON FINAL COMMODITIES

This section examines environmental taxes on final commodities, allowing for interactions with the labor market. The polluting industry is assumed to produce a consumption good, and therefore taxes on this good will have no spillover effects in

[3] See also Sandmo [20], Ng [13], and Bovenberg and van der Ploeg [5].

[4] In some further analysis, Goulder [10] found that the welfare gains from recycling revenues are well below the costs (gross of environmental benefits) of taxes on carbon, gasoline, and fuels.

the capital market (so long as they are permanent rather than transitory), hence capital can be excluded from the analysis. Also, any effect the tax may have on environmental R & D is ignored.[5] The economy is assumed to produce $X_1 \ldots X_K$ market commodities, where the production of X_j $(1 \leq j \leq K)$ involves the discharge of waste emissions which harm the environment, while all other commodities are environmentally clean.[6] For simplicity the environmental damage function is given by cX_j, where $c > 0$, although allowing for convex damages would be straightforward, and there is no internalization of environmental damages in the absence of policy intervention.[7] Each market is assumed to be competitive, which seems reasonable from Oates and Strassmann [16], who suggested that allowing for imperfect competition is unlikely to have much empirical effect on environmental policy analysis, because the markup over competitive prices in industries with monopoly power is typically small. Also, distortions caused by nonlabor taxes are ignored, since they are relatively much less important.[8] Finally, marginal costs are assumed to be constant in each market—a conventional assumption in optimal tax exercises, which is less restrictive than it may sound.[9]

Without loss of generality, the units of each commodity and labor can be defined such that their pretax prices are unity. If there is a proportional tax of m on labor income, then the aggregate household budget constraint can be written[10]

$$\sum_{i=1}^{K} X_i + (1 - m)N = (1 - m)T + G, \tag{1}$$

where N is leisure time, T is the household time endowment, or full income, and $T - N$ is labor supply. The labor tax is therefore equivalent to a tax on full income (which is not distortionary) plus a subsidy to leisure. G is an exogenous lump-sum transfer from the government, and for simplicity all revenues are assumed to be returned in such transfers, therefore $G = m(T - N)$.

The equilibrium in the only two distorted markets in the economy are shown in Fig. 1. In the upper panel, D_j and S_j are the demand and supply for X_j, and the initial output is X_j^0, where the demand and supply prices are equal. The marginal social cost curve is $S_j + c$. In the lower panel, D_N^0 and S_N are the demand and supply of leisure, which are, respectively, the mirror image of the supply of labor

[5] For a discussion of how pollution taxes might affect the incentive to invent cleaner technologies, see Parry [17].

[6] Obviously if there were important interactions between X_j and other polluting markets, these should be taken into account.

[7] This implies that (a) emitters do not bear any of the costs of their own pollution, (b) there is no scope for Coase-type [8] bargaining between polluters and victims, and (c) there is no altruism for the environment on behalf of consumers or producers. Alternatively, cX_j can be interpreted as that component of pollution damages which is not internalized by these factors.

[8] Revenues from excise taxes and customs duties are approximately 7% of Federal labor tax revenues (see "The Economic Report of the President" (1994)). State and local governments mainly rely on uniform sales taxes (which are approximately equivalent to labor taxes) and property taxes (which are a tax on capital).

[9] It would be straightforward to allow for upward-sloping marginal costs (see Harberger [11]). The Slutsky compensated price terms used below would be replaced by an analogous reduced-form coefficient, which shows how output in a particular market responds to changes in taxes, when there are potential interdependencies in the demand and supply for all goods.

[10] Allowing for nonproportional labor taxes would not affect the IE discussed below, or the amount of pollution tax revenues raised.

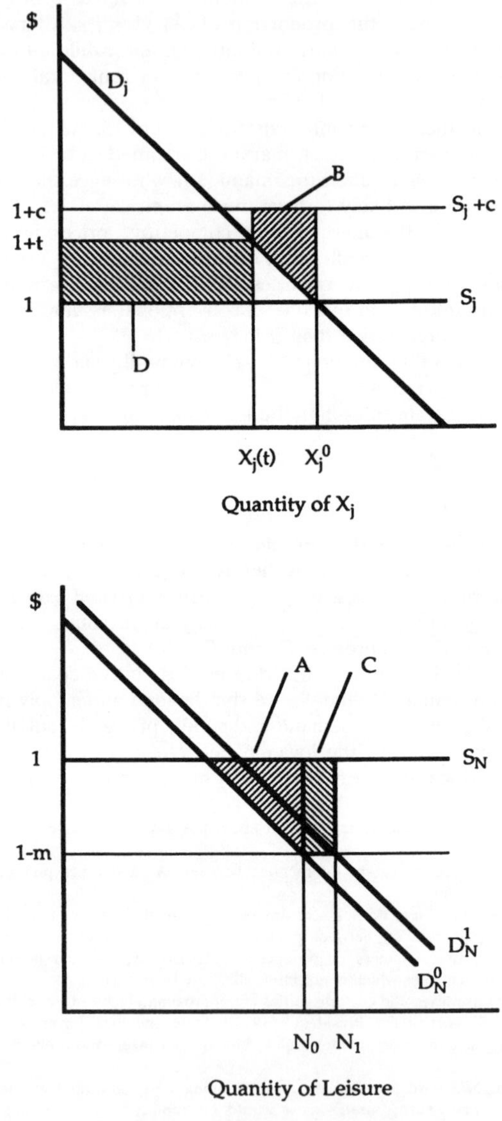

FIG. 1. The welfare effects of environmental taxes.

and the value marginal product of labor (ignore D_N^1 for the moment). The leisure subsidy drives a wedge of m between the supply and demand price of leisure, and the initial quantity of leisure is N_0. All the demand and supply curves in Fig. 1 are compensated, and the welfare cost of the leisure market distortion is therefore area A.

The Welfare Effects of Environmental Taxes

Suppose a specific tax of $t \leq c$ is now imposed on X_j, and the additional revenues are used to reduce the labor tax, therefore disposable income is constant. The resulting welfare change consists of the following three components:

(i) The gain from the reduction in output to $X_j(t)$, trapezoid B in Fig. 1. Assuming the demand curve is linear over the relevant range (which is a reasonable approximation at least for modest levels of taxation), this equals a rectangle with area $(c - t)(X_j^0 - X_j(t))$, plus a triangle with area $t(X_j^0 - X_j(t))/2$, where $X_j^0 - X_j(t) = -(dX_j/dp_j)t$ (p_j is the price of X_j). This gives

$$tX_j^0\eta_{jj}\left\{c - \frac{t}{2}\right\}, \tag{2}$$

where $\eta_{jj} = -(dX_j/dp_j)/X_j^0$ is the (magnitude of the) compensated own-price elasticity of demand for X_j evaluated at X_j^0. If $t = c$, the expression in (2) is just the well-known Harberger triangle. For later, it is helpful to note that $t\eta_{jj} = (X_j^0 - X_j(t))/X_j^0$ or

$$t\eta_{jj} = 1 - \frac{X_j(t)}{X_j^0}. \tag{3}$$

(ii) The welfare loss from the exacerbation of the leisure market distortion, when X_j and leisure are substitutes (the IE). Imposing the pollution tax shifts up the private marginal cost and hence the demand price for X_j, and in general this will shift out the demand for leisure.[11] Put another way, the labor supply curve shifts up, since the bundle of goods that a given nominal wage can purchase is smaller. In the lower panel in Fig. 1 the new leisure demand curve is shown as D_N^1, and leisure increases by $N_1 - N_0 = (dN/dp_j)t$ (assuming the cross-price term dN/dp_j is constant over the relevant range). Since the marginal social cost exceeds marginal benefit by m for each of these units, the welfare loss from the increase in leisure, rectangle C, is[12]

$$m\frac{dN}{dp_j}t. \tag{4}$$

The formulas in (2) and (4) are just a straightforward application of the more general formula for the welfare effect of a set of market distortions derived in Harberger [11].

[11] It is possible that X_j and leisure are complements and the demand for leisure will shift the other way. However this is only applicable to a narrow range of goods (such as skis and video cassette recorders) and will be ignored below.

[12] Figure 1 is not drawn to scale. The area of B and C will typically be very small relative to that of A.

Rectangle C is also the reduction in labor tax revenues indirectly caused by the environmental tax. The efficiency value per dollar of changes in aggregate tax revenues will be denoted by V (which is defined below). From the Slutsky symmetry property,

$$\frac{dN}{dp_j} = \frac{dX_j}{dw} \tag{5}$$

that is, the effect on leisure from a unit increase in the price of X_j equals the effect on X_j from a unit increase in the price of leisure (where $w = 1 - m$ is the price of leisure or net of tax wage). Therefore, using (4) and (5), and multiplying and dividing by $(1 - m)X_j^0$, the total welfare loss from the IE (rectangle C multiplied by $(1 + V)$) is

$$(1 + V)\frac{m}{1 - m}tX_j^0\eta_{jN}, \tag{6}$$

where $\eta_{jN} = (dX_j/dw)(1 - m)/X_j^0$ is the compensated elasticity of demand for X_j with respect to the price of leisure, evaluated at X_j^0.

(iii) The welfare gain from the pollution tax revenues raised (the RE). This is just the product of V and rectangle D in Fig. 1, which is

$$VtX_j(t). \tag{7}$$

Finally, when the price of leisure is increased, the demand for X_j will shift out. Since marginal social cost exceeds marginal benefit by $c - t$ in this market, this cause a welfare loss of

$$(c - t)\frac{dX_j}{dW}\Delta m, \tag{8}$$

where Δm is the reduction in labor tax. However, this feedback effect is relatively small so long as the proportionate reduction in labor tax is small (substituting (5) in (8) and comparing with (4)), and will be ignored in the analysis below.

When pollution tax revenues are used to reduce labor taxes, the appropriate formula for V is the "marginal welfare cost" of labor tax revenues. This is the addition to total welfare cost from a marginal increase in labor tax (or leisure subsidy), $-m(dN/dw)$, divided by the resulting increase in revenue, $(T - N) + m(dN/dw)$. Therefore

$$V = \frac{(m/1 - m)\epsilon}{1 - (m/1 - m)\epsilon}, \tag{9}$$

where $\epsilon = -(dN/dw)(1 - m)/(T - N)$ is the compensated labor supply elasticity, evaluated at the net of tax wage.[13] It is assumed that pollution tax revenues are small relative to aggregate labor tax revenues, hence the change in m and leisure are very small, and V can be taken as constant.

[13] This is essentially the same formula that was used by Browning [6] to estimate the marginal welfare cost of labor taxation. Browning [6] also suggests that allowing for a downward-sloping demand for labor (upward sloping supply of leisure) does not have much effect on estimates of V.

Rearranging (9) in terms of $m/(1-m)$ and substituting in (6), the cost of the IE can be expressed as

$$VtX_j^0 \frac{\eta_{jN}}{\epsilon}. \tag{10}$$

Unfortunately estimates of η_{jN} are not generally available for particular commodities, and therefore the IE cannot be calculated directly. However, a central estimate can be obtained when X_j is an average substitute for leisure at the pretax price. In this case

$$\eta_{jN} = \epsilon. \tag{11}$$

This follows because if labor supply increases by $\lambda\%$ in response to a compensated 1% increase in real wages, then aggregate consumption and hence average consumption must increase by $\lambda\%$.[15]

From (7) and (10), the benefit from the RE relative to the cost from the IE is simply

$$\frac{X_j(t)}{X_j^0} \frac{\epsilon}{\eta_{jN}}. \tag{12}$$

Therefore, when condition (11) holds, the benefit from the RE is a fraction of the cost of the IE, where this fraction is the ratio of the post- to pretax level of output. Only if X_j was a relatively weak substitute for leisure (that is, $\eta_{jN} < \epsilon(X_j(t)/X_j^0)$) could the RE exceed the IE and the double dividend hypothesis be correct.

The Optimal Environmental Tax

Differentiating (10) with respect to (the reduction in) X_j, the marginal cost from the IE is

$$MC_{\text{IE}} = \frac{V}{\eta_{jj}} \frac{\eta_{jN}}{\epsilon}, \tag{13}$$

[14] Deleted in proof.

[15] Differentiating the budget constraint in Eq. (1) with respect to the price of leisure, holding disposable income constant (which requires a compensation of N plus the recycling of extra tax revenues, $dG/dw = -m(dN/dw)$), gives

$$\sum_{i=1}^{K} \frac{dX_i}{dw} + \frac{dN}{dw} = 0.$$

Multiplying this equation by $(1-m)$ gives

$$\sum_{i=1}^{K} X_i \eta_{iN} = (T - N)\epsilon,$$

where $\eta_{iN} = (dX_i/dw)(1-m)/X_i$ is the compensated elasticity of demand for X_i with respect to the price of leisure. When all goods are equal substitutes for leisure, η_{iN} is constant across goods and equal to ϵ, since the aggregate value of consumption equals gross income.

(since $dX_j/dt = dX_j/dp_j$), which is a constant (all elasticities are defined at specific points). Differentiating (7) with respect to (the reduction in) X_j, the marginal benefit from the RE is

$$MB_{\mathrm{RE}} = V\left\{\frac{1}{\eta_{jj}}\frac{X_j(t)}{X_j^0} - t\right\}. \tag{14}$$

This is the product of V and the marginal pollution tax revenue, which is declining because the tax base ($X_j(t)$) shrinks with abatement, and the revenue loss (t) from marginal reductions in X_j is increasing.

The upper panel in Fig. 2 shows the MC_{IE} and MB_{RE} curves as a function of $X_j^0 - X_j(t)$, when condition (11) holds, where each has the same intercept (substituting $t = 0$ in Eq. (14)). If X_j was a relatively strong (weak) substitute for leisure, the MC_{IE} curve would be higher (lower) and, ignoring the externality, it would be optimal to subsidize (tax) X_j relative to other goods.[16] In the lower panel of Fig. 2, the $D_j - S_j$ curve is the marginal cost of reducing X_j, ignoring interactions with the tax system, which is just the gap between D_j and S_j in Fig. 1, or t. The Pigouvian tax would be $t' = c$, and the optimal level of abatement $X_j^0 - X_j(t')$. Adding on the net marginal cost from the IE and RE reduces the optimal level of abatement to $X_j^0 - X_j(t^*)$, and the optimal tax t^* is defined by

$$c = t^* + MC_{\mathrm{IE}} - MB_{\mathrm{RE}}. \tag{15}$$

Substituting (13) and (14) into (15) and using (3) gives

$$\bar{t}^* = \frac{1 + (V/c\eta_{jj})\{1 - (\eta_{jN}/\epsilon)\}}{1 + 2V}, \tag{16a}$$

where $\bar{t}^* = t^*/c$ denotes the optimal tax as a proportion of MED. When condition (11) holds, this simplifies to

$$\bar{t}^* = \frac{1}{1 + 2V} \tag{16b}$$

in which case the optimal tax is less than MED.[17] Estimates of the economy-wide compensated labor supply elasticity typically lie within a range of 0.2 to 0.4, while the (marginal) rate of tax on labor income, which depends on the rate of personal income tax, social security tax, and benefit withdrawal as income rises, is around 0.38 to 0.48 (see Browning [6]). From Eq. (9), this gives a median estimate for V ($\epsilon = 0.3$, $m = 0.43$) of 0.29, with lower and upper bounds of 0.14 and 0.59.[18]

[16] This is essentially the basic result from the optimal commodity tax literature (see, for example, Sandmo [21]).

[17] In Bovenberg and de Mooij [2, 3], environmental quality is treated as a public good which is separable from consumption and leisure in the utility function. The bottom line of this assumption is that a reduction in pollution leads to a negative income effect and a reduction in leisure, which dampens, though not overturns, their conclusion that the optimal environmental tax is less than MED. Whether it is appropriate to incorporate such income effects (usually they are excluded) is a difficult issue which has yet to be resolved.

[18] The above estimates are replicated from the second row in the lower half of Table 2 in Browning [6]. Results from computable general equilibrium models suggest that the marginal welfare cost of taxation lies between 10 and 60 cents per dollar (see for example Ballard *et al.* [1]).

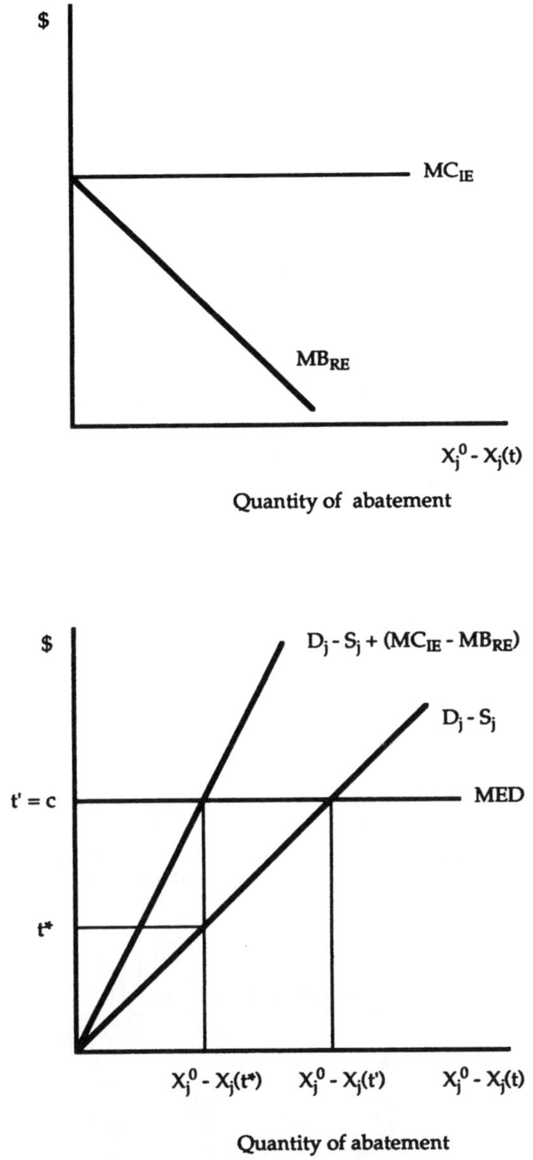

FIG. 2. The optimal environmental tax.

Table I shows simulations on the formulas in Eq. (16a) and (16b), under different assumptions about the degree of substitution with leisure, V, and $c\eta_{jj}$. This latter term is the proportionate reduction if X_j under a Pigouvian tax (substituting $t = c$ in Eq. (3)). The best estimate for the optimal pollution tax is 63% of MED, which is when X_j is an average substitute for leisure (condition (11) holds) and $V = 0.29$. This estimate is somewhat sensitive to V, and the lower and upper bounds are 46 and 78%, respectively (when (11) holds). The optimal tax is also sensitive to the degree of substitution with leisure and rises to 86–157% of MED if η_{jN} is 50% lower than average, and falls to 0–41% of MED when η_{jN} is 50% higher than average (assuming $V = 0.3$ and $c\eta_{jj}$ lies between 0.1 and 0.4).

3. ENVIRONMENTAL TAXES ON INTERMEDIATE GOODS

Sources of pollution are usually more directly related to inputs in the production process (such as chemicals and fuels) than final consumption goods. Therefore this section extends the previous analysis to allow for environmental taxes on an intermediate good. This good is denoted Z, is used in the production of X_j, and has a constant marginal production cost of unity. The environmental damage function is cZ. All other assumptions from the previous section are maintained, and there is no tax on X_j.

The Welfare Effects of Environmental Taxes on Intermediate Goods

The welfare change from imposing a specific tax of $u \leq c$ on Z consists of the following three components, which are analogous to those in (i) to (iii) above:

(i′) The trapezoid gain in the Z market, which has area

$$uZ_0\eta_{ZZ}\left\{c - \frac{u}{2}\right\}, \tag{2'}$$

where $\eta_{ZZ} = -(dZ/dp_Z)/Z_0$ is the (magnitude of the) unconditional own-price elasticity of demand for Z, evaluated at Z_0 (p_Z is the price of Z). This elasticity reflects the fall in demand for Z from both the reduction in X_j (the output effect) and the substitution of other factors for Z in production (the substitution effect).

TABLE I
The Optimal Pollution Tax (as a Proportion of MED)

		$\eta_j N/\epsilon$		
V	$c\eta_{jj}$	0.5	1	1.5
0.14	0.1	1.33	0.78	0.23
	0.4	0.92	0.78	0.64
0.29	0.1	1.57	0.63	0
	0.4	0.86	0.63	0.41
0.59	0.1	1.79	0.46	0
	0.4	0.79	0.46	0.13

As before

$$u\eta_{ZZ} = 1 - \frac{Z(u)}{Z_0}. \tag{3'}$$

(ii′) The welfare loss from the IE, when X_j and leisure are substitutes, which (including the value of reduced labor tax revenues) is given by

$$(1 + V)m\frac{\Delta N}{\Delta u}, \tag{17}$$

where $\Delta N/\Delta u$ is the increase in leisure induced by the tax. This can be broken down into

$$\frac{\Delta N}{\Delta u} = \frac{dN}{dp_j}\frac{\Delta p_j}{\Delta u} \tag{18}$$

where $\Delta p_j/\Delta u$ is the increase in price, or marginal cost, of X_j caused by the input tax. Substituting (5) and (18) into (17) and multiplying and dividing by $(1 - m)X_j^0$ gives

$$(1 + V)\frac{m}{1 - m}\frac{\Delta p_j}{\Delta u}X_j^0\eta_{jN}. \tag{6'}$$

(iii′) The welfare gain from the RE, which is

$$VuZ(u). \tag{7'}$$

Using a second-order Taylor series expansion, the increase in price of X_j is the product of u and the average of the pre- and posttax ratio of Z to X_j, that is,

$$\frac{\Delta p_j}{\Delta u} = \frac{u}{2}\{R_0 + R(u)\}, \tag{19}$$

where the input to output ratio $R(u)$ is

$$R(u) = \frac{Z_0 + u(dZ^c/dp_Z)}{x_j^0} \tag{20}$$

and dZ^c/dp_Z is the slope of the conditional (output constant) factor demand curve.[19] Therefore, to the extent there is substitution in production ($dZ^c/dp_Z < 0$), R declines with the imposition of the environmental tax.

[19] From a second-order Taylor series expansion, the increase in total cost (C) of producing X_j following an increase of u in the price of input Z is

$$u\frac{dC}{dp_Z} + \frac{u^2}{2}\frac{d^2C}{dp_Z^2}.$$

Using Shephard's lemma, $dC/dp_Z = Z_0$ and $d^2C/dp_Z^2 = dZ^c/dp_Z$ (see Varian [23], Chapter 3), dividing by X_j^0 to convert to per unit or marginal production costs, and substituting from (20) gives the expression in (19).

From (6′), (9), and (19), the welfare loss from the IE can be expressed as

$$VuZ_0\frac{\eta_{jN}}{\epsilon}\left\{1-\frac{u\eta_{ZZ}^c}{2}\right\}, \tag{10'}$$

where $\eta_{ZZ}^c = -(dZ^c/dp_Z)/Z_0$ is the (magnitude of the) conditional (or output constant) own-price elasticity of demand for Z, evaluated at Z_0. Hence $u\eta_{ZZ}^c$ is the proportionate reduction in Z due to the substitution effect only. Clearly

$$0 \le \frac{\eta_{ZZ}^c}{\eta_{ZZ}} \le 1, \tag{21}$$

that is, the elasticity of demand for Z when X_j is held fixed cannot exceed that when X_j is variable.

Dividing (7′) by (10′), the benefit from the RE relative to the cost of the IE is

$$\frac{Z(u)}{\{1-(u\eta_{ZZ}^c/2)\}Z_0}\frac{\epsilon}{\eta_{jN}}. \tag{12'}$$

Therefore, when there is no substitution in production ($\eta_{ZZ}^c = 0$) and condition (11) holds, the benefit from the RE equals the cost from the IE multiplied by the ratio of the post- to pretax levels of output of the polluting good, which is the same result as before. For a given reduction in Z, the RE is the same regardless of the strength of the substitution effect relative to the output effect. However, the greater the relative size of the substitution effect (the greater the η_{ZZ}^c/η_{ZZ}), the weaker is the IE, because the impact on the price of X_j, and hence the leisure market spillover, is smaller. Nevertheless, this makes little difference. Using (3′), (21), and (12′), the IE clearly exceeds the RE (when (11) holds).

The Optimal Environmental Tax on an Intermediate Good

Differentiating (10′) with respect to (the reduction in) Z gives

$$MC'_{\mathrm{IE}} = \frac{V}{\eta_{ZZ}}\frac{\eta_{jN}}{\epsilon}\{1-u\eta_{ZZ}^c\} \tag{13'}$$

(since $dZ/du = dZ/dp_Z$). Differentiating (8′) with respect to (the reduction in) Z gives

$$MB'_{\mathrm{RE}} = V\left\{\frac{1}{\eta_{ZZ}}\frac{Z(u)}{Z_0} - u\right\}. \tag{14'}$$

Again, when condition (11) holds, the marginal cost from the IE and the marginal benefit from the RE, as a function of the reduction in Z, have the same intercept. The MC'_{IE} curve is now downward sloping, because substitution in production reduces the impact of successive increases in tax on the price of X_j (that is, $R(u)$ is declining in Eq. (19)).[20]

[20] However, it still lies above the MB'_{RE} curve. This is because the latter is declining due to both the output effect and the substitution effect.

Substituting (13′) and (14′) into (15), and setting $u = t$, gives the following formula for the optimal pollution tax, when X_j is an average substitute for leisure,

$$\bar{u}^* = \left\{1 + V\left(2 - \frac{\eta_{ZZ}^c}{\eta_{ZZ}}\right)\right\}^{-1}, \tag{16b'}$$

where $\bar{u} = u/c$. Using (21), the optimal tax lies between 63 and 78% of MED, when $V = 0.29$. Therefore, to the extent there is substitution in production, the optimal tax is higher than in the previous case, although the difference is not very substantial. These results are highly consistent with Bovenberg and Goulder [4], who estimated that the optimal tax on carbon, with full revenue recycling, is 68% of MED.[21]

4. CONCLUSION

This paper has emphasized that the gains from using pollution tax revenues to substitute for labor tax revenues tends to be more than offset by the cost of exacerbating the preexisting distortion in the labor market. Of course the opposite conclusions apply for subsidies which result in increasing the demand for labor. That is, the interdependency effect will tend to work against the revenue effect, hence reducing the welfare cost of financing subsidies. Thus economists may have been overly pessimistic about the cost of subsidies for environmentally cleaner goods, such as public transportation.[22]

REFERENCES

1. C. L. Ballard, J. B. Shoven, and J. Whalley, General equilibrium computations of the marginal welfare costs of taxes in the United States, *Amer. Econom. Rev.* **75**, 128–138 (1985).
2. A. L. Bovenberg and R. A. de Mooij, Environmental levies and distortionary taxation, *Amer. Econom. Rev.* **84**, 1085–1089 (1994).
3. A. L. Bovenberg and R. A. de Mooij, "Environmental Policy in a Small Open Economy with Distortionary Taxes: A General Equilibrium Analysis," Research Center for Economic Policy, Erasmus University, Rotterdam (1993).
4. A. L. Bovenberg and L. H. Goulder, Integrating Environmental and Distortionary Taxes: General Equilibrium Analyses, working paper, Stanford University (1994).
5. A. L. Bovenberg and F. van der Ploeg, Environmental policy, public finance and the labor market in a second best world, *J. Public Econom.* **55**, 349–390 (1994).
6. E. K. Browning, On the marginal welfare cost of taxation, *Amer. Econom. Rev.* **77**, 11–23 (1987).
7. E. K. Browning, Subsidies financed with distorting taxes, *Nat. Tax J.* **45**, 121–134 (1992).
8. R. H. Coase, The problem of social cost, *J. Law Econom.* **3**, 1–44 (1960).
9. L. H. Goulder, Environmental Taxation and the "Double Dividend": A Reader's Guide, working paper, Stanford University (1994).
10. L. H. Goulder, Effects of Carbon Taxes in an Economy with Prior Tax Distortions: An Intertemporal General Equilibrium Analysis, *J. Environ. Econom. Management* **29**, 271–297 (1995).
11. A. C. Harberger, The measurement of waste, *Amer. Econom. Rev.* **54**, 58–76 (1964).

[21] This assumes MED is $25 per ton (see Table 6 in Bovenberg and Goulder [4], the "optimized benchmark" column). The optimal tax rises to 85% of MED when MED is $100 per ton. This is reflecting the significant reduction in m and hence ϵ, when a large amount of carbon tax revenues are recycled, which reduces V and hence $\bar{u}$ in Eq. (16b′).

[22] For example Browning [7] provides a thorough discussion of subsidies allowing for the revenue effect, but he ignored the interdependency effect.

12. D. R. Lee and W. S. Misiolek, Substituting pollution taxation for general taxation: Some implications for efficiency in pollution taxation, *J. Environ. Econom. Management* **13**, 338–347 (1986).
13. Y. K. Ng, Optimal corrective taxes or subsidies when revenue raising imposes an excess burden, *Amer. Econom. Rev.* **70**, 744–751 (1980).
14. W. D. Nordhaus, Optimal greenhouse-gas reductions and tax policy in the "DICE" model, *Amer. Econom. Rev.* **83**, 313–317 (1993).
15. W. E. Oates, Pollution charges as a source of public revenues, *in* "Economic Progress and Environmental Concerns" (H. Giersch, Ed.), Springer-Verlag, Berlin (1993).
16. W. E. Oates and D. L. Strassmann, Effluent fees and market structure, *J. Public Econom.* **24**, 29–46 (1984).
17. I. W. H. Parry, Pollution taxes and endogenous technological progress, *Resour. Energy Econom.* **17**, 69–85 (1995).
18. D. W. Pearce, The role of carbon taxes in adjusting to global warming, *Econom. J.* **101**, 938–948 (1991).
19. R. Repetto, R. C. Dower, R. Jenkins, and J. Geoghegan, "Green Fees: How a Tax Shift Can Work for the Environment and the Economy," World Resources Institute, Washington, DC (1992).
20. A. Sandmo, Optimal taxation in the presence of externalities, *Swedish J. Econom.* **77**, 86–98 (1975).
21. A. Sandmo, Optimal taxation—an introduction to the literature, *J. Public Econom.* **6**, 37–54 (1976).
22. D. Terkla, The efficiency value of effluent tax revenues, *J. Environ. Econom. Management* **11**, 107–123 (1984).
23. H. R. Varian, "Microeconomic Analysis," Norton, New York (1984).

[16]

JOURNAL OF ENVIRONMENTAL ECONOMICS AND MANAGEMENT **29**, 271–297 (1995)

Effects of Carbon Taxes in an Economy with Prior Tax Distortions: An Intertemporal General Equilibrium Analysis

LAWRENCE H. GOULDER*

Department of Economics, Stanford University, Stanford, California 94305-6072; Resources for the Future; and National Bureau of Economic Research, Cambridge, Massachusetts 02138

Received January 26, 1994; revised March 16, 1994

This paper analyzes the costs of carbon taxes in a model that recognizes interactions between this tax and pre-existing taxes. First we examine the extent to which costs of a U.S. carbon tax are reduced when its revenues finance cuts in income taxes. Such use of revenues significantly reduces, but does not eliminate, the overall policy costs. The positive overall costs reflect the carbon tax's focus on intermediate inputs and its relatively narrow base in comparison with income taxes. We also examine the sensitivity of the carbon tax's costs to the level of pre-existing taxes. For any given use of revenues, welfare costs rise significantly with pre-existing tax rates, indicating that models disregarding pre-existing taxes may substantially understate the costs of new environmental tax initiatives.

I. INTRODUCTION

A. *Overview*

In recent years policymakers and the general public have become increasingly concerned about the potential contributions of carbon dioxide (CO_2) emissions to the greenhouse effect and global climate change. These concerns have stimulated interest in a number of potential policy responses, including the introduction of a carbon tax, a tax on fossil fuels—oil, crude oil, and natural gas—in proportion to their carbon content.[1] The main rationale for a carbon tax is to internalize the externalities associated with fossil fuel combustion, yet the magnitudes of these externalities (and associated benefits from a carbon tax) are highly uncertain. At the same time that efforts are undertaken to reduce these uncertainties it is useful to assess the gross economic costs of the carbon tax—that is, the economic costs exclusive of the (highly uncertain) economic benefits associated with avoided environmental damages. These costs can be viewed as a lower bound on how large the environmental benefits would have to be to justify the carbon tax on efficiency grounds.

* I am grateful to Lans Bovenberg, Dale Jorgenson, Alan Manne, Paul Portney, Jim Poterba, Stephen Schneider, Larry Summers, Jim Sweeney, Peter Wilcoxen, three anonymous referees, and seminar participants at George Washington University, Harvard University, the NBER, Resources for the Future, the RAND Corporation, and Stanford University for helpful suggestions. I also thank Miguel Cruz, Jesse David, Alexander Dyck, and Steven Weinberg for excellent research assistance. Financial support from the National Science Foundation (Grant SBR-9310362), the IBM Corporation, and Resources for the Future is gratefully acknowledged.

[1] Since CO_2 emissions generally are proportional to the amount of carbon content, a tax based on carbon content is effectively a tax on CO_2 emissions. For a general discussion of the rationale for and potential effects of carbon taxes, see, for example, [23, 33, 42].

0095-0696/95 $12.00

Recent studies aiming to assess the gross costs of carbon taxes have generated many useful insights,[2] but they suffer an important limitation in disregarding interactions between carbon taxes and other, pre-existing taxes.[3] Two important interactions are generally overlooked. First, the studies tend to assume that the revenues earned from carbon taxes are returned in lump-sum fashion to the economy. In fact, revenues from carbon taxes could be used to finance reductions in other, distortionary taxes.[4] The reductions in other taxes yield offsetting efficiency gains by avoiding some of the distortions that the other taxes would otherwise generate. In this connection, work by Ballard *et al.* [1] and Jorgenson and Yun [22] indicates that, on average, the marginal efficiency costs of existing taxes is between 10 cents and 60 cents per dollar of revenue collected. This suggests that if environmental tax revenues were returned to the economy in a fairly *representative* way—by reducing typically distortionary taxes—there would be a significant efficiency benefit that offsets the "pure" efficiency cost of the carbon tax itself.[5] Recently, a number of authors—including Bovenberg and de Mooij [5, 6], Poterba [34], Weyant [46], Oates [29], and Pearce [32]—have emphasized the importance of accounting for these offsetting benefits in assessing the carbon tax.[6] Indeed, some studies have indicated that the gross cost of a revenue-neutral carbon tax policy possibly could be zero or even negative once the efficiency gains from carbon-tax-financed reductions in existing taxes are accounted for. Advocates of "green taxes" would certainly welcome such a result, since it would provide an efficiency rationale for a carbon tax even under the most conservative assumptions about its environmental benefits.

The second limitation from previous studies stems from implicit assumptions about pre-existing taxes. This drawback has a very different implication for the carbon tax's costs. Most simulation studies of these costs have assumed that the tax is imposed in an economy without pre-existing taxes.[7] This simplifying assumption

[2] For surveys of recent studies, see [13, 31, 46].

[3] The neglect of these interactions reflects a tradition in the field of public finance, where theoretical analysis of pollution taxes and other externalities issues has generally been kept separate from the analysis of ordinary distortionary taxes. An important exception to this tradition was provided by Sandmo [38], who considered optimal commodity taxation when an externality is associated with one of the commodities. More recent exceptions are offered by Oates [29] and Bovenberg and van der Ploeg [7].

[4] Of course, there are other options. The revenues could also be used to finance increases in Federal government spending or to reduce the Federal debt. The latter is equivalent to reducing future taxes, assuming that the government's debt cannot indefinitely grow faster than the interest rate (see, for example, [3]).

[5] We emphasize "representative" here because one can overstate the case for environmental taxes by linking such taxes to the reduction in a particularly burdensome pre-existing tax. If a particular existing tax generates especially large distortionary costs, then there is an independent efficiency rationale for reducing (or eliminating) this tax. The extraordinary costs of this tax are not a legitimate basis for endorsing a carbon tax. At the same time, we suggest that one would understate the case for a carbon tax if one required that the cost assessment be performed only in the case were revenues are returned in lump-sum fashion. This would bias upward the cost assessment, since it would neglect the fact that even "representative" replacement of the carbon tax revenues could generate significant cost offsets.

[6] Terkla [45], Lee and Misiolek [25], and Ballard and Medema [2] previously examined these issues in the context of other environmental taxes.

[7] There are exceptions, including the models of Shah and Larsen [40], Jorgenson and Wilcoxen [21], Whalley and Wigle [47], and Manne and Rutherford [27], and the OECD GREEN model [9]. Only the first two of these models have considered explicitly the significance of the form of revenue replacement or of pre-existing taxes. Subsection IB below discusses these two models.

may significantly bias the cost assessment. The distortionary costs of a tax on fossil fuels depend importantly on the level of prior taxes on (or subsidies to) these fuels. Basic partial equilibrium analysis suggests that the incremental gross efficiency cost of a given fuels tax is much higher when the tax is superimposed on high prior taxes on fuels than when it is imposed in a situation with no prior taxes.[8] Moreover, as discussed below, in a general equilibrium system prior taxes on *other* goods or factors are very important as well. Once one accounts for pre-existing taxes, the magnitude of the gross costs of a carbon tax are substantially higher than one would otherwise expect.

Thus, how carbon tax revenues are used and the nature of pre-existing taxes may importantly influence the costs of a carbon tax. In this paper we address these issues in evaluating the costs of carbon taxes, employing an intertemporal general equilibrium model of the U.S. economy. The general equilibrium framework is useful for addressing interactions among energy (fossil fuel) industries and between these industries and other sectors of the economy. The intertemporal focus permits attention to how the effects of taxes change over time as households and firms alter saving and investment decisions.

Three features of the model distinguish it from other economy-wide models applied to carbon taxes and are directly relevant to the problem at hand. First, the model contains a more detailed treatment of U.S. taxes than other economy-wide models applied to carbon taxes. Building on earlier tax modeling work,[9] it incorporates very specific tax instruments and addresses effects along a number of important dimensions, including firms' investment incentives, equity values, and profits,[10] and household consumption, saving, and labor supply decisions. This enables it to account for pre-existing tax distortions and to examine various options for using carbon tax revenues to finance reductions in distortionary taxes.

Second, the model incorporates nonrenewable resource supply dynamics and transitions from conventional to synthetic fuels within a disaggregated general equilibrium framework. Previously, such dynamics—including the depletion of oil and gas stocks, the associated increases in production costs, and the eventual replacement of conventional fuels by a "backstop" technology—have only been considered in optimization models, which involve highly aggregrated treatments of industries and final goods and which do not incorporate separate decision making by governments, firms, and households.[11] Recognizing the transition from conventional fossil fuels to synthetic fuels or backstop technologies is important for understanding the effects of a carbon tax, since there are significant differences in the carbon content of conventional fuels and synfuels.

[8] Similarly, if fuels face subsidies prior to the imposition of a carbon tax, this tax may reduce the gross distortions in fuels markets. Shah and Larsen [40] emphasize this point in considering the potential for carbon taxes in developing countries.

[9] See, for example, [17, 18].

[10] Here the model applies the asset price approach to investment developed by Summers [44].

[11] Although nearly all dynamic optimization models that consider exhaustibility are highly aggregated at the level of outputs, Manne and Rutherford [27] have managed to attain some disaggregation among products within a dynamic optimization framework. The OECD "GREEN" Model (see Burniaux *et al.*, [9]) is a disaggregated CGE (as opposed to optimization) model that considers resource exhaustibility. However, this model assumes static expectations and the resource extraction decisions are not based on intertemporal optimization.

Third, the model incorporates capital adjustment dynamics. In each industry, producers' investment decisions take account of the adjustment costs associated with the introduction of new capital. These costs render capital imperfectly mobile across industries and imply that firms will be less able to shift the burden of taxes to other sectors than would be the case under perfectly mobile capital. These dynamic considerations are important to understanding incidence and efficiency impacts.

The rest of this section indicates the relationship of this study to other empirical carbon tax studies that attend to tax interactions. Section II describes the model, while Section III discusses the data and parameters. In Section IV we present and interpret simulation experiments involving different carbon tax alternatives. The final section offers conclusions.

B. Relationship to Other Empirical Studies

Recently, a few authors have begun to consider the numerical significance of interactions between carbon taxes and existing distortionary taxes. Shah and Larsen [40] indicate that in many developing countries, prior subsidies to energy imply that introducing taxes on carbon will have small or even negative economic costs. Repetto *et al.* [37] examine several tax options and affirm that in many circumstances judicious revenue recycling can eliminate most or all of the GNP costs of green taxes. A limitation of these investigations is that they are partial equilibrium in nature, taking factor prices as given and disregarding interactions across product and factor markets. An attractive feature of the present investigation is its general equilibrium framework, which permits tax impacts to be evaluated in an integrated fashion.

Nordhaus [28] applies a highly aggregated global general equilibrium model to explore how the optimal value of a carbon tax might depend on the use of its revenues.[12] When revenues are devoted to reducing distortionary taxes, the optimal tax rate for the first decade rises to $59 per ton, as compared to about $5 per ton when revenues are returned in lump-sum fashion. That model calculates benefits from *reductions* in distortionary taxes based on an exogenous specification for avoided deadweight costs per dollar of revenue devoted to reductions in distortionary taxes. However, since the model does not actually contain distortionary taxes, it does not account for the costs associated with interactions between the carbon tax and *remaining* distortionary taxes in the system. As theoretical work and the numerical results from this paper should make clear, the remaining pre-existing distortionary taxes amplify the costs of carbon taxes—regardless of how the revenues from the carbon tax are returned to the economy. To assess the optimal carbon tax or the costs of various (suboptimal) carbon tax policies, it is thus essential to consider pre-existing taxes. Indeed, analytical work indicates that in a world with positive pre-existing taxes on labor and capital, the optimal carbon tax is lower than would be the case if there were no pre-existing factor taxes, contrary to the suggestion from the Nordhaus study.[13]

[12] Nordhaus has pioneered the integration of (environmental) benefits and (non-environmental) costs in applied simulation modeling of carbon taxes.

[13] See [7, 8]. In general, recycling the revenues through cuts in distortionary taxes mitigates this increase, but does not fully offset the effect.

Finally, Jorgenson and Wilcoxen [21] have used an intertemporal general equilibrium model of the United States to examine the costs of U.S. carbon taxes under alternative specifications for revenue recycling.[14] That model has a more solid econometric foundation than most other general equilibrium models, and it pays close attention to price-responsive technological change in different industries. The model applied in the present paper differs from the Jorgenson–Wilcoxen model in containing considerably more detail on U.S. taxes, in capturing the exhaustible nature of domestic fossil fuels and the transitions from exhaustible fuels to backstop technologies, and in recognizing the imperfect mobility of capital and associated capital adjustment dynamics.

Thus, the present model has unique features that make it especially well suited to analyzing the costs of carbon taxes in the presence of prior tax distortions. This study exploits these features, paying closer attention than previous studies to structural differences between carbon taxes and other taxes, and thereby providing a link with the theoretical tax literature. These structural elements underlie the differences between the gross costs of carbon and other taxes; equivalently, they explain the overall gross costs of revenue-neutral policies that combine a carbon tax with a reduction in another tax.

II. THE MODEL

A detailed appendix to this paper, available from the author upon request, documents the structure of the model and its solution method. This section briefly describes some important features.

The model generates an equilibrium path of prices and output for the U.S. economy. Equilibrium outcomes are calculated at yearly intervals, usually over the 80-year period beginning in 1990.

A. Industry and Consumer Good Disaggregation

The model distinguishes the 13 industries and 17 consumer goods shown in Table I. The energy industries consist of coal mining, oil and gas, petroleum refining, synthetic fuels, electric utilities, and gas utilities. The synthetic fuels industry is a "backstop" industry, at constant returns to scale, it produces shale oil, a perfect substitute for oil and gas.[15]

B. Producer Behavior

A nested production structure accounts for potential substitutions between different forms of energy as well as between energy and other inputs. Each industry produces a distinct output (X), which is a function of inputs of labor (L),

[14] See also [39], a study commissioned by the U.S. Environmental Protection Agency which considers the effects of carbon taxes under alternative methods for recycling the tax revenues. That study compared results from two econometric models (DRI and Project LINK), the model of Jorgenson and Wilcoxen [20], and this model.

TABLE I
Industry and Consumer Good Categories

	Industries
1.	Agriculture and noncoal mining
2.	Coal mining
3.	Crude petroleum and natural gas
4.	Synthetic fuels
5.	Petroleum refining
6.	Electric utilities
7.	Gas utilities
8.	Construction
9.	Metals and machinery
10.	Motor vehicles
11.	Miscellaneous manufacturing
12.	Services (except housing)
13.	Housing services
	Consumer Goods
1.	Food
2.	Alcohol
3.	Tobacco
4.	Utilities
5.	Housing services
6.	Furnishings
7.	Appliances
8.	Clothing and jewelry
9.	Transportation
10.	Motor vehicles
11.	Services (except financial)
12.	Financial services
13.	Recreation, reading, and misc.
14.	Nondurable, nonfood household expenditure
15.	Gasoline and other fuels
16.	Education
17.	Health

capital (K), an energy composite (E), and a materials composite (M), as well as the current level of investment (I):

$$X = f[g(L,K), h(E,M)] - \phi(I/K) \cdot I \tag{1}$$

The functions f, g, and h are CES in form. The energy composite is made up of the outputs of the energy industries, while the materials composite consists of the outputs of the other industries. Each of the individual inputs making up E and M is, in turn, a composite of a domestic and foreign good from the given industry. The aggregation functions for E and M and for their composite inputs are CES.

In Eq. (1), $\phi(I/K) \cdot I$ represents capital adjustment costs. The adjustment cost function, ϕ, is convex in I/K and has the form

$$\phi(I/K) = \begin{cases} \frac{1}{2} \cdot \beta \cdot (I/K - \delta)^2/(I/K), & I/K > \delta \\ 0, & I/K \leq \delta, \end{cases}$$

[15] The consumer goods are produced by combining the outputs of the 13 industries in given proportions. We obtain these proportions by aggregating the translation matrix provided in the May 1984 "Survey of Current Business."

where δ is the rate of economic depreciation. This function expresses the notion that installing new capital necessitates a loss of current output, as existing inputs (K, L, E, and M) that otherwise would be used to produce output are diverted to install the new capital. ϕ denotes a rate per unit of investment; total adjustment costs (loss of output) are $\phi \cdot I$.

Firms in each industry are price takers in the markets for inputs and outputs. Managers of firms are assumed to serve stockholders in aiming to maximize the value of the firm. The objective of firm-value maximization determines firms' choices of input quantities and investment levels in each period of time. The value of the firm can be expressed in terms of dividends and new share issues, which in turn depend on profits in each period. The firm's profits during a given period are given by

$$\pi = (1 - \tau_a)[pX - w(1 + \tau_L)L - \text{EMCOST} - i\text{DEBT} - \text{TPROP}] + \tau_a(\text{DEPL} + \text{DEPR}) \tag{2}$$

where τ_a is the tax rate on profits, p is the output price net of output taxes, w is the wage rate net of indirect labor taxes, τ_L is rate of the indirect tax on labor, EMCOST is the cost to the firm of energy and materials inputs, i is the gross-of-tax interest rate paid by the firm, DEBT is the firm's current debt, TPROP is property tax payments, DEPL is the current gross depletion allowance, and DEPR is the current gross depreciation allowance.

The following accounting or cash-flow identity links the firm's sources and uses of revenues:

$$\pi + \text{BN} + \text{VN} = \text{DIV} + \text{IEXP}. \tag{3}$$

The left-hand side is the firm's source of revenues, profits and new debt issue (BN), and new share issues (VN). The uses of revenues on the right-hand side are investment expenditure (IEXP) and dividend payments (DIV). Firms are assumed to pay dividends equal to a constant fraction, a, of profits net of economic depreciation, and to maintain debt equal to a constant fraction, b, of the value of the existing capital stock.[16] Thus

$$\text{DIV}_s = a[\pi_s + (p_{K,s} - p_{K,s-1})K_s - \delta p_{K,s}K_s] \tag{4}$$

$$\text{BN}_s \equiv \text{DEBT}_{s+1} - \text{DEBT}_s = b(p_{K,s}K_{s+1} - p_{K,s-1}K_s), \tag{5}$$

where p_K represents the purchase price of c units of capital. Investment expenditure is expressed by

$$\text{IEXP}_s = (1 - \tau_K)p_{K,s}I_s, \tag{6}$$

where τ_K is the investment tax credit rate (if any). In Eq. (3) new share issues, VN, are the residual, making up the difference between π + BN and DIV + IEXP. Arbitrage possibilities compel the firm to offer its stockholders a rate of return

[16] The best specification of firms' financial decisionmaking is a matter of some debate. For a survey and analysis of these issues, see [4, 35, 41].

comparable to the rate of interest on alternative assets:

$$(1 - \tau_s)\mathrm{DIV}_s + (1 - \tau_V)(V_{s+1} - V_s - \mathrm{VN}_s) = (1 - \tau_b)i_s V_s. \quad (7)$$

The parameters τ_e, τ_V, and τ_b are the personal tax rates on dividend income (equity), capital gains, and interest income (bonds), respectively. The return to stockholders consists of the current after-tax dividend plus the after-tax capital gain (accrued or realized) on the equity value (V) of the firm net of the value of new share issues. This return must be comparable to the after-tax return from an investment of the same value at the market rate of interest, i.

Define $r_s \equiv [(1 - \tau_b)/(1 - \tau_V)] \cdot i$, and define the discounting operator

$$d(t,s) \equiv \begin{bmatrix} 1, & s = t \\ \prod_{u=t+1}^{s} (1 + r_u)^{-1}, & s > t \end{bmatrix}$$

Recursive solution of the arbitrage condition (7) over a firm's infinite time horizon yields an expression for the firm's equity value as the discounted value of after-tax dividends less share issues[17]:

$$V_t = \sum_{s=t}^{\infty} \left[\left(\frac{1 - \tau_e}{1 - \tau_V} \right) \mathrm{DIV}_s - \mathrm{VN}_s \right] d(t,s). \quad (8)$$

Firms maximize V by choosing optimally in each period the levels of labor and intermediate inputs and the level of investment.[18]

C. Special Features of the Oil-Gas and Synfuels Industries

The production structure in the oil and gas industry is somewhat more complex than in other industries to account for the nonrenewable nature of oil and gas stocks. The production specification is

$$X = \gamma(Z) \cdot f[g(L,K), h(E,M)] - \phi(I/K) \cdot I, \quad (9)$$

where γ is a decreasing function of Z, the amount of cumulative extraction (or output) of oil and gas up to the beginning of the current period. Thus, the function $\gamma(Z)$ addresses *resource stock effects*, the fact that as Z rises (or, equivalently, as reserves are depleted), it becomes increasingly difficult to extract oil and gas resources, so that greater quantities of K, L, E, and M are required to achieve any given level of extraction (output). Increasing production costs ultimately induce oil and gas producers to remove their capital from this industry.[19]

[17] The derivation of this expression invokes the transversality condition, $\lim_{s \to \infty} V_s d(t,s) = 0$. This condition rules out eternal speculative bubbles by requiring that the value of the firm cannot indefinitely grow at a rate greater than the interest rate.

[18] Optimal investment involves balancing current costs of investment (both the acquisition costs of new capital and the adjustment costs) against the future benefits (the higher dividends made possible by a higher future capital stock).

[19] The attention to resource stock effects distinguishes this model from several other general equilibrium energy-environmental models. Many equilibrium models treat the domestic oil and gas industry as a constant-returns-to-scale production, disregarding resource stock effects or fixed factors. (See, for example, the model of Jorgenson and Wilcoxen [20, 21]). In their global energy-environment model, Manne and Richels [26] impose stock limits on resources such as oil and gas, but these limits have no effect on production costs prior to the point where the resource is exhausted.

The model incorporates a synthetic fuel—shale oil—as a backstop resource, a perfect substitute for oil and gas. As in other industries, in the synfuels industry producers choose input and investment levels to maximize the equity value of the firm. There is one difference, however; the technology for producing synthetic fuels on a commercial scale is assumed to become known only in the year 2010.

All domestic prices in the model are endogenous, except for the domestic price of oil and gas, which is given by the exogenous world price of oil gross of tariffs. Following the baseline assumptions of the Stanford Energy Modeling Forum [13], this world price is specified as $24 per barrel in 1990 and rising in real terms by $6.50 per decade. The supply of imported oil and gas is perfectly elastic at the given world price. As long as imports are the marginal source of supply to the domestic economy, domestic producers of oil and gas receive the world price (adjusted for tariffs or taxes) for their own output. However, rising oil and gas prices stimulate investment in synfuels. Eventually, synfuels production plus domestic oil and gas supply together satisfy all domestic demand, and the domestic oil and gas price is determined by the synfuels price (see subsection G below).

D. Household Behavior

Consumption, labor supply, and saving result from the decisions of an infinitely lived representative household maximizing its intertemporal utility with perfect foresight. In year t the household chooses a path of "full consumption" C to maximize

$$U_t = \sum_{s=t}^{\infty} (1+\omega)^{t-s} \frac{\sigma}{\sigma - 1} C_s^{\sigma - 1/\sigma}, \tag{10}$$

where ω is the subjective rate of time preference and σ is the intertemporal elasticity of substitution in full consumption. C is a CES composite of consumption of goods and services $\tilde{C}$ and leisure l:

$$C_s = \left[\tilde{C}_s^{(\nu-1)/\nu} + \alpha_C^{1/\nu} l_s^{(\nu-1)/\nu}\right]^{\nu/(\nu-1)}. \tag{11}$$

ν is the elasticity of substitution between goods and leisure; α_C is an intensity parameter for leisure. The household maximizes utility subject to the intertemporal budget constraint requiring that the present value of the consumption stream not exceed potential total wealth (current nonhuman wealth plus the present value of potential labor income and net transfers). In each period, overall consumption of goods and services $\tilde{C}$ is allocated across the 17 specific consumption categories of Table I according to fixed expenditure shares. Each of the 17 consumption goods is a composite of a domestically and foreign-produced consumption good of that type. Households substitute between domestic and foreign goods to minimize the cost of obtaining a given composite good.

The aggregate endowment of time is exogenous; it grows at a constant rate, g, which determines the long-run (steady-state) growth rate of the economy. This growth represents Harrod-neutral technical progress in producing labor or leisure services per unit of actual time.

E. The Government Sector

The government collects taxes, distributes transfers, and purchases goods and services (outputs of the 13 industries). Overall government expenditure is exogenous and increases at a constant rate, *g*, equal to the steady-state growth rate of the model. The model incorporates a wide array of tax instruments, including carbon taxes, output taxes, the corporate income tax, property taxes, sales taxes, and taxes on individual labor and capital income. In the benchmark year, 1990, the government deficit is approximately 2% of GNP. In the reference case (*status quo*) simulation, the deficit–GNP ratio is approximately constant.[20] In the policy experiments in this paper, we require that the real deficit and real government spending follow the same path as in the reference case. To meet its cash flow requirements, the government's real tax receipts under a policy change therefore must be the same as in the reference case. To meet this revenue neutrality requirement, we accompany the carbon tax with a reduction in another tax, either on a lump-sum basis or through reductions in marginal tax rates, as detailed in Section IV.

F. Foreign Trade

Except for oil and gas imports, which are perfect substitutes for domestically produced oil and gas, imported intermediate and consumer goods are imperfect substitutes for their domestic counterparts. Import prices are exogenous in foreign currency, but the domestic currency price changes with changes in the exchange rate. Export demands are modeled as functions of the foreign price of U.S. exports and the level of foreign income (in foreign currency). The foreign price is the price in U.S. dollars plus tariffs or subsidies, converted to foreign currency through the exchange rate. We impose the assumption of zero trade balance at each period of time. An exchange rate variable adjusts to reconcile the value of U.S. import demands with the value of foreign export demands.

G. Equilibrium

Equilibrium in each period satisfies four types of conditions:

(1) the aggregate demand for labor equals the aggregate supply;
(2) the demand for each industry output equals its supply;[21]
(3) the aggregate demand by firms for loanable funds equals the aggregate supply by households; and
(4) government tax revenues equal government spending less the government deficit.

[20] We assume that the real deficit grows at the steady-state growth rate, *g*. Along the baseline path and the economic path corresponding to policy changes, the growth rate of GNP generally differs from *g* in the short run but converges to *g* in the long run (steady state). Hence the deficit–GNP ratio is strictly constant only in the long run.

[21] Since oil and gas and synfuels are perfect substitutes, they generate a single supply–demand condition.

These conditions are met through adjustments in output prices, in the market interest rate, and in lump-sum taxes or tax rates.[22,23] The extended Newton–Raphson algorithm of Powell [36] is applied to attain equilibrium in each period. However, since agents are forward-looking, equilibrium in each period depends not only on current prices and taxes but on future magnitudes as well. We employ an iterative procedure similar to that employed by Fair and Taylor [12] to obtain perfect foresight expectations. The procedure is described in detail in [14].

III. DATA AND PARAMETERS

A. Data

Complete data documentation is contained in [10] and is available on request.[24] Industry input and output flows (used to establish production function share parameters) were obtained from 1986 input–output tables published in the February 1991 "Survey of Current Business." These tables were also the source for consumption, investment, government spending, import, and export values by industry. Data on industry capital stocks and employment levels were taken from tapes supplied by the Department of Commerce Bureau of Economic Analysis. Data on the carbon content of particular fossil fuels and synfuels were obtained from the 1989 Department of Energy "Annual Energy Outlook."

B. Parameters

Production function elasticities of substitution for the model were derived from estimates by Dale Jorgenson and Peter Wilcoxen. The Jorgenson–Wilcoxen esti-

[22] By Walras' Law, the required number of equilibrating variables is one less than the number of equilibrium conditions. The numeraire is the nominal wage.

[23] In general, output prices serve as equilibrating variables. However, in the market for "fuel resources" (oil/gas and synfuels), the equilibrating variable depends on the supply circumstances. Let p_R represent the fuel resource price—the price of oil/gas or of synfuels. Let p_W denote the (exogenous) price of imported oil/gas, and let p_S represent the synfuels price that would be necessary to generate a quantity of synfuels sufficient to satisfy the domestic demand for resources net of domestic oil and gas production. Thus, p_S is the price that would induce sufficient synfuels supply to drive oil and gas imports to zero. For the resources market, the following relationships hold:

$$p_R = p_W, \qquad p_S \geq p_W$$
$$p_R = p_S, \qquad p_S < p_W$$

When p_S exceeds p_W, domestic oil/gas production and synfuels are not sufficient to satisfy domestic resource demand. In this event, imports are the marginal source of supply, and the price received for a unit of resources is the exogenously specified world price, p_W (adjusted for tariffs). Under these conditions, the model employs the *quantity* of oil imports as the equilibrating variable that helps bring supplies and demands for resources into balance. In contrast, once synfuels production expands sufficiently to meet the entire domestic demand, oil/gas imports are zero and synfuels represent the marginal source of supply. Under these circumstances, the synfuels price p_S is the equilibrating variable for the resource market. This is the price that brings synfuels supply plus domestic oil and gas supply into balance with the total domestic demand.

[24] All data are available on request in machine-readable form.

mates of parameters for translog cost functions were transformed to elasticities of substitution more compatible with the CES form of our model.[25]

For the oil and gas industry, it is necessary to specify the function $\gamma(Z_t)$ which relates the costs of production to Z_t, the cumulative amount of extraction at time t. There is not sufficient information to estimate this function with precision; broad sensitivity analysis is critical here. For the central case specification, we specify the relationship.

$$\gamma(Z_t) = \gamma_0\left[1 - \left(Z_t/\bar{Z}\right)^{\varepsilon}\right], \tag{12}$$

with $\gamma_0 = 1.27$, $\varepsilon = 2$, and $\bar{Z} = 450$ billion barrels (about 100 times the 1990 production of oil and gas, where gas is measured in barrel-equivalents). The initial value for Z is 0.

Other important parameters apply to the household side of the model. The elasticity of substitution in consumption between goods and leisure, υ, is set to yield a compensated elasticity of labor supply of 0.5: $\upsilon = 0.69$. The intensity parameter α_C is set to generate a ratio of labor time to the total time endowment equal to .44.[26] The intertemporal elasticity of substitution, σ, equals .5.[27] Calibrating the model to 1990 flows leads to a value of 0.007 for time preference, ω. These parameters imply a value of 0.18 for the interest elasticity of savings between the current period and the next.

IV. SIMULATION RESULTS

A. Reference Case Simulation

To analyze the effects of carbon taxes, we first perform a reference case simulation. This simulation assumes *status quo* or business-as-usual conditions and forms a reference path for measuring effects of policy shocks. In the reference case, all tax rates and other policy variables are kept constant at their benchmark (1990) values. In the long run, the economy reaches a steady state: all quantities increase at a rate of 2% (governed by the growth rate of effective labor), and relative prices do not change. Two features of the model prevent steady-state or balanced growth in the short and medium run along the reference path. First, the depletion of oil and gas reserves implies rising unit costs of domestic oil and gas supply. In addition, the real prices of imported oil and gas are exogenously specified as increasing in real terms. These features lead to reductions, over time, in the share of oil and gas consumption relative to overall consumption. As indicated in Fig. 1, rising costs of domestic oil and gas production lead to

[25] Some differences between the specifications of the Jorgenson–Wilcoxen model and this model limit the reliability of the Jorgenson–Wilcoxen estimates in the present model. First, there are differences in industry classifications. In addition, the Jorgenson–Wilcoxen production specification assumes that capital is perfectly mobile in every period, whereas our production specification allows for short-run capital immobility. It would be preferable to employ parameters that are estimated under the same specification as that in the model. Such work is in progress.

[26] In calibrating the model, we assume the representative consumer works 1920 hours out of a potential 4638 waking hours each year.

[27] Econometric estimates of σ vary considerably; see, for example, [19, 24]. The value 0.5 falls between the lower estimates from time-series analyses and the higher ones from cross-sectional studies.

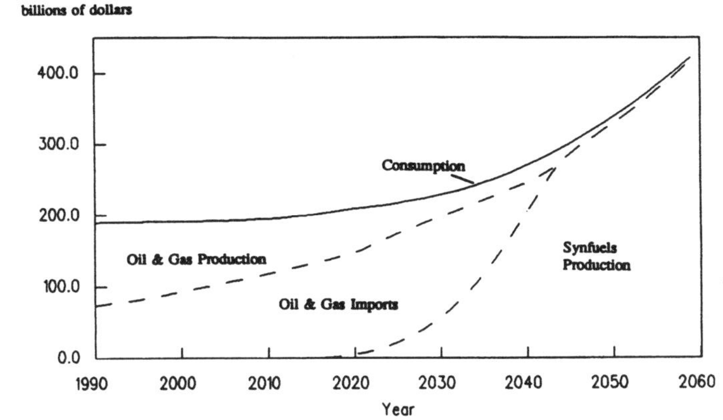

FIG. 1. Consumption of oil and gas and synthetic fuels (evaluated at 1990 prices).

diminishing output of domestic oil and gas, and rising import prices eventually cause synfuels to replace conventional fuels in the "resource" (oil/gas and its equivalent) market.

B. Effects of Carbon Taxes

Here we describe results from simulations to examine the two main issues in the paper: (1) the extent to which the gross costs of a carbon tax are reduced when revenues are returned through cuts in important distortionary taxes, and (2) the extent to which pre-existing taxes influence the gross costs of a carbon tax (for any given method of revenue replacement).

1. Implications of Alternative Revenue-Replacement Methods

We begin with the revenue-replacement (or "recycling") issue. To provide perspective, we present, in Fig. 2, the effects on emissions of unilateral U.S. carbon taxes of 25, 50, and 100 1990 dollars per ton of carbon, with the tax applying on a consumption basis in the sense that it applies to domestically produced and imported fossil fuels and exempts exported fuels.[28,29] In the simulations shown in the figure, revenue neutrality is assured through lump-sum tax reductions.[30] Marginal income tax rates are not changed. The solid line represents emissions

[28] For a discussion of alternative carbon tax designs and border adjustments, see [15].

[29] At 1990 prices, a $25/ton carbon tax amounts to $13.40 per short ton of coal, $2.93 per barrel of oil, and $0.35 per thousand cubic feet of natural gas. If there were no effect on pre-tax prices, a $25/ton tax would raise the prices of coal, oil, and natural gas by 72, 13, and 24 percent, respectively. The price increases reflect not only the direct impact of the tax but also an indirect effect associated with higher-priced fossil fuel inputs used in the production (extraction) of fossil fuels. See [15] for an analysis of these effects.

[30] The present value of the revenue yield (before lump-sum replacement) from the $25/ton, $50/ton, and $100/ton tax is $510 billion, $691 billion, and $766 billion, respectively.

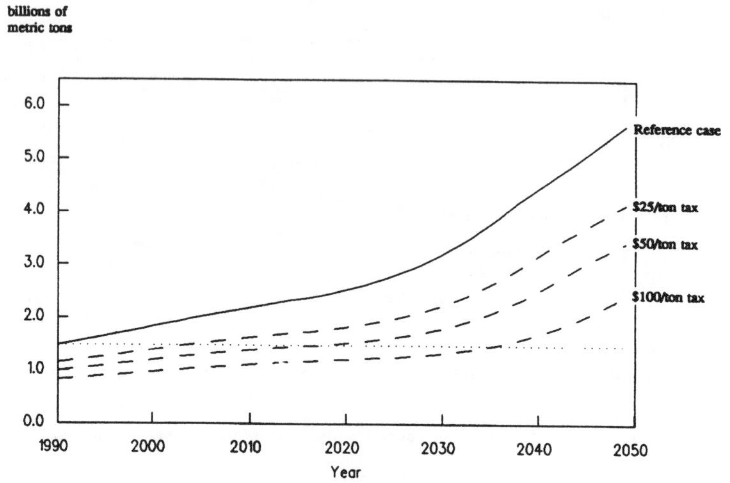

FIG. 2. Carbon emissions.

growth in the reference case. Emissions grow steadily over the 60-year interval displayed. Larger carbon taxes lead to more substantial emissions reductions. However, doubling the magnitude of the tax leads to less than a doubling of the emissions reduction. This reflects rising marginal costs to producers of reducing the use of fossil fuels and to consumers of substituting for fossil-fuel-intensive goods and services.

In Fig. 3, we compare the effects on GDP under alternative forms of replacement of the tax revenues. These simulations employ a carbon tax rate of $25 per ton. Three alternative revenue adjustments are considered. In the personal income tax adjustment simulation, the carbon tax revenues finance reductions in marginal tax rates on labor and capital (interest, dividend, and capital gains) income at the personal level. Marginal taxes on labor and on capital are reduced by 0.9%.[31] In the corporate tax replacement simulation, the corporate profits tax is reduced from .385 to .379. In the payroll tax replacement simulation, this tax is reduced by the same proportion (2.3%) in each industry.

This figure indicates that the GDP costs are reduced significantly when revenues are used to finance cuts in distortionary taxes. This is the case both in the short term, where the GDP losses are 25–40% smaller, and in the longer run, where they are 40–55% smaller. Over time, the cuts in distortionary taxes allow for improvements in intertemporal as well as in static (intersectoral) resource allocation. This helps explain why the gains relative to lump-sum tax replacement are proportionally larger in the long run than in the short run.

[31] The marginal tax on labor is reduced from .2302 to .2281, the marginal tax on dividend and interest income is reduced from .2289 to .2272, and the accrual-equivalent tax on capital gains is reduced from .0572 to .0568.

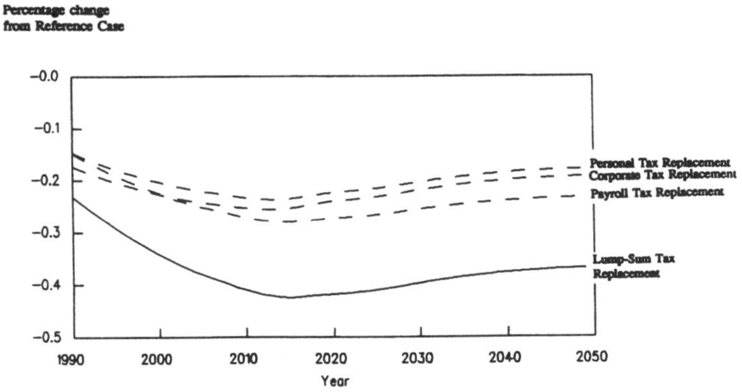

FIG. 3. Effects on GDP.

Table II shows effects on welfare. As with GDP effects, the welfare effects account only for the cost side of the ledger, disregarding the potential positive welfare impacts stemming from the avoided environmental damages associated with the carbon tax. The welfare measure is the equivalent variation per dollar of revenue earned by the carbon tax.[32] The first column of Table II displays the overall welfare effects of various revenue-neutral carbon tax policies. We include here results from an additional, "general" tax replacement simulation, in which *all* marginal taxes are reduced by a given proportion (0.362 percent).[33] This experiment gives a sense of how the distortionary cost of the carbon tax compares with the marginal distortionary cost of U.S. taxes in general. Compared with the case of lump-sum revenue replacement, the welfare loss is approximately 36% smaller when marginal taxes are reduced at the personal level, 37% smaller when the profits tax is reduced, 53% smaller when payroll taxes are reduced, and 42% smaller when all taxes are reduced.[34] Using the carbon revenues to finance cuts in distortionary taxes significantly reduces the overall economic losses. But it is important to note that the cuts in distortionary taxes do not entirely eliminate welfare costs of the revenue-neutral policy. This suggests that the gross distortion[35]

[32] The equivalent variation is the lump-sum payment which would enable the household to achieve the same level of intertemporal utility in the reference case (facing reference case prices and policy parameters) as under the policy change. Thus a positive equivalent variation implies that the policy change is welfare-improving. Thus, Table II indicates, for example, that in the case of a $25/ton carbon tax with lump-sum replacement, the welfare loss has a monetary equivalent of $0.516 per dollar of revenue earned by the tax.

[33] Performing this simulation is consistent with the notion, discussed in the introduction, that the costs of a carbon tax should be assessed by recycling the revenues through cuts in "representative" (as opposed to extraordinarily burdensome) taxes.

[34] The rankings for welfare costs differ somewhat from the GNP cost rankings. The policy of replacing revenues through payroll tax cuts ranks better in terms of welfare costs than in terms of GNP costs. Cutting payroll taxes leads to higher consumption of leisure than under lump-sum recycling. This favorable effect is accounted for in the welfare measure but not in the GNP measure.

[35] That is, the efficiency cost abstracting from environmental benefits.

TABLE II

Welfare Effects of $25 per Ton Carbon Tax under Alternative Methods for Revenue Replacement[a]

Type of revenue replacement	(1) Overall welfare change	(2) Welfare effect of carbon tax component	(3) Welfare effect of revenue-replacement component	(4) Sum of (2) and (3)
Lump-sum tax rebate	−0.516	−0.516	0.0	0.516
Personal income tax cut				
All marginal rates reduced	−0.332	−0.516	0.188	−0.328
Labor marginal rates reduced	−0.374	−0.516	0.144	−0.372
Capital marginal rates reduced	−0.279	−0.516	0.241	−0.275
Corporate income tax cut	−0.327	−0.516	0.194	−0.322
Payroll tax cut	−0.242	−0.516	0.275	−0.241
General tax cut	−0.299	−0.516	0.219	−0.297

[a] The welfare change is measured as the equivalent variation per dollar of gross revenue.

from the carbon tax tends to be greater than the avoided distortions associated with equal-revenue reductions in the personal income tax, corporate profits tax, or payroll tax.[36] Equivalently, it would appear that, at the margin, a carbon tax generates larger gross distortionary costs than are produced (at the margin) by the major types of income taxes it might partially replace. Hence the swap of a carbon tax for other taxes still entails a positive overall cost.

Columns 2 and 3 of Table II explore this issue further. These columns decompose the overall welfare effect of a revenue-neutral carbon tax policy. Here we separate the "pure" effect of the carbon tax from the "pure" effect of cutting existing taxes. The pure effect of the carbon tax, in column 2 of the table, is simply the welfare effect of the carbon tax under lump-sum revenue replacement. Similarly, the pure effect of the revenue-replacement component, in column 3 of the table, is the effect from the reduction of a given existing tax by the same magnitude as in column 1 but without the simultaneous imposition of a carbon tax; revenue losses here are made up with lump-sum tax increases. A comparison of the results in columns 2 and 3 shows that the welfare loss from the carbon tax itself (column 2) is significantly larger in absolute value than the welfare gain associated with the cut in existing taxes (column 3). Column 4 displays the sum of the effects in columns 2 and 3. If there were no interactions between the two components of the overall policy, the values in column 4 would be identical to the corresponding values in column 1. As the table indicates, the results in columns 1 and 4 are quite similar, implying that there is very little interaction between the carbon tax component and the tax cut component.

[36] A potential bias against carbon taxes in the model is its treatment of the world oil price as exogenous. If the model accounted for U.S. monopsony power, the costs would be offset to some degree through downward pressure exerted on the (net-of-tax) world oil price.

TABLE III
Sources of Excess Welfare Costs from the Carbon Tax

		(1) Welfare cost per dollar	(2) Excess cost per dollar	(3) Difference in excess cost	(4) Contribution
1.	Carbon tax	.516	.324		
				.028	8.6%
2.	Uniform gross output tax, fossil and synfuels industries	.488	.296		
				.186	57.4%
3.	Broad uniform gross output tax	.302	.110		
				.110	34.0%
4.	Personal income tax increase	.192	.0		

2. *Why Are the Gross Costs of a Carbon Tax Higher Than Those of "Traditional" Income Taxes?*

These results show the costs of a revenue-neutral carbon tax as remaining positive under a range of revenue-replacement (or recycling) options. Equivalently, the "pure" carbon tax has higher gross costs than the traditional income taxes it might replace. To what can this "excess cost" be attributed?

We examine this issue by performing further simulation experiments that isolate three structural features of a carbon tax that can contribute to its efficiency cost: (1) the *type* (or location) *of tax base* in comparison with the base of an income tax, (2) the *narrowness of the base* relative to a broader tax on outputs, and (3) the *lack of uniformity* of the tax rate per dollar of fuel.[37] Results from these experiments are summarized in Table III. All simulations in the table involve lump-sum revenue replacement. In addition to a \$25/ton carbon tax and personal income tax increase, this table considers a uniform gross output tax applicable to the fossil fuels and synfuels industries, and a broad uniform gross output tax applying (at a uniform rate) to all U.S. industries. As one moves from row 1 to row 4 of the table, the simulations remove in succession three structural differences between a carbon and income tax.

Column 1 of the table reports the welfare costs per dollar under each tax. The second column indicates the excess cost per dollar, that is, the difference between the welfare cost of the given tax and the welfare cost from an equal-revenue increase in the personal income tax. The third column shows the differences in excess costs across successive rows. Simulation 2 (the uniform tax on fossil and synfuels industries) differs from simulation 1 (the carbon tax) only in terms of the uniformity of the tax rate—the breadth and type of tax base are the same. Hence the difference in excess cost between rows 1 and 2 indicates the welfare effect associated with the *lack of uniformity* in the carbon tax rate (per dollar of output). Similarly, simulation 3 differs from simulation 2 only in terms of the breadth of the tax on gross output; hence the difference in excess cost between rows 2 and 3 indicates the welfare effect associated with the *narrowness of the base* relative to a

[37] The carbon tax is uniform per unit of carbon, but not per dollar of fuel, as indicated in Section III.

general gross output tax. Finally, the difference in excess cost between rows 3 and 4 isolates the significance of the *type of tax base* compared with an income tax. Specifically, it indicates the significance of taxing gross output (including intermediate inputs) as compared with net output under the income tax.

As can be seen from the table, more than half (about 57%) of the difference in cost can be related to the relative narrowness of the carbon tax base as compared to gross output tax that applies to all U.S. industries. At the same time, the application of the carbon tax to gross, rather than net, output accounts for about a third of its excess cost over the income tax. The lack of uniformity of the carbon tax rate explains a relatively small share of the excess cost.

These results reinforce the (often overlooked) insights from the theoretical tax literature. In particular, they remind us of the important contributions of Diamond and Mirrlees [11] and Stiglitz and Dasgupta [43], theoretical findings that taxes on intermediate inputs have larger welfare costs (apart from environmental benefits) than do equal-revenue taxes on primary factors or final goods.[38] The results also cohere with recent analytical results by Bovenberg and de Mooij [5, 6]; using a static model, these authors show analytically that an environmental tax on a particular commodity is generally more costly per dollar of revenue than a tax or labor income.[39]

It should be recognized that the theoretical results that support the present simulation outcomes stem from fairly simple models that may disregard important complicating factors. Neither Diamond and Mirrlees nor Bovenberg and de Mooij consider capital markets, in particular. Once capital markets are accounted for, it can no longer be established *a priori* whether a carbon tax or income tax (on labor and capital) is less costly per dollar of revenue.[40] Moreover, these theoretical findings assume constant-returns-to-scale production; it is possible that the results would differ under decreasing returns. The lack of complete generality from the theory gives further impetus for numerical simulation of the type performed here.

[38] The intuition for these results is that taxes on intermediate goods not only distort intermediate good choice but also compound factor market distortions. Labor market distortions are aggravated because intermediate good taxes cause commodity prices to rise and thereby reduce the real wage in terms of consumption. Capital market distortions are aggravated because intermediate good taxes raise the costs of producing capital goods and thereby reduce the real return to purchases of new capital.

[39] Intuition for the Bovenberg–de Mooij result is as follows. Consider a static model in which there is one labor market and one produced commodity. Suppose that initially there is a tax on labor but no commodity tax. Under these circumstances an infinitesimal commodity tax produces a non-infinitesimal excess burden. This is the case because, under the circumstances just described, the introduction of a commodity tax is formally identical to an increase in the labor tax. Now extend this example to allow for several commodities. Again suppose that initially there is a labor tax but no tax on any of the commodities. For simplicity, assume that elasticities of supply and demand are the same for all commodities. Now consider the effect of introducing (1) a uniform, but small tax on all commodities, or (2) introducing a small tax on just one of the commodities. Case 1 is formally quite similar to the case considered in the previous paragraph; it will generate non-infinitesimal excess burdens because this tax is equivalent to an increase in the wage tax. (This case would differ slightly from the previous case if elasticities of demand or supply differed across commodities.) Case 2 is relevant to the imposition of an environmental tax on one commodity. One of Bovenberg and de Mooij's insights is that, for a given revenue yield, the excess burden in Case 2 is non-infinitesimal and in fact is larger than in Case 1. The reason is that Case 2 generates both a labor market distortion and a distortion across commodities. These ideas are consistent with the results given above, where a carbon tax was shown to involve a larger gross welfare cost than a broader-based output tax with the same revenue yield.

[40] For a discussion of this issue, see [16].

It also signals the importance of sensitivity analysis; such analysis is performed in subsections 3 and 4 below.

It should also be noted that these simulation results do not rule out the possibility of finding some method of revenue recycling under which a revenue-neutral carbon tax policy will involve zero or negative welfare costs. It may be possible to locate an existing tax with an efficiency cost that is large enough that financing its reduction through a carbon tax is welfare-improving (even before considering environmental benefits). Indeed, simulations with the present model yield this result in certain cases.[41] The main results here pertain to revenue recycling through cuts in income taxes or in "representative" taxes.

The finding that revenue-neutral carbon taxes often give rise to positive gross welfare costs does not imply that these taxes are unwarranted. It does indicate, however, that under these forms of revenue replacement one cannot make the case for carbon taxes on efficiency grounds without invoking environmental benefits.

3. *The Significance of Pre-existing Distortions*

a. Findings. The second main issue examined in this paper is the potential importance of pre-existing taxes for regulating the costs of a carbon tax. We examine the significance of such taxes by performing simulations in which we specify alternative (and counterfactual) levels for pre-existing taxes. Results from these simulations are displayed in Figs. 4a and 4b, for carbon taxes of 1, 10, 25, and 50 dollars per ton. In each of these figures, we compare results under the actual benchmark data with results under counterfactual benchmarks in which all tax rates are either 50% lower or 50% higher than their actual values. Figure 4a shows effects under lump-sum replacement, while Fig. 4b shows effects when revenues are returned through reductions in the personal income tax.

Several important results emerge from Figs. 4a and 4b. First (as might be expected), the welfare costs under personal tax replacement (Fig. 4b) are always lower than under lump-sum replacement (Fig. 4a), for any given carbon tax rate or specification about the magnitude of pre-existing tax rates.

Second, the welfare cost of the carbon tax is directly related to the magnitude of pre-existing tax rates. The cost of the carbon tax is approximately 40% higher (35% lower) when pre-existing taxes are 50% higher (lower) than actual values.[42] This result may seem counterintuitive for the case of personal tax replacement (Fig. 4b); one might expect that higher pre-existing taxes should raise the payoff from recycling (that is, enlarge the compensating welfare benefit from returning the revenues through reductions in a pre-existing tax) and thus imply lower overall costs of the carbon tax. This is not the case, however, because higher pre-existing taxes also raise the pure cost of the carbon tax, as indicated by the results, in Fig. 4a, for lump-sum replacement.

[41] For example, under high elasticities of capital supply (a value above 1.5 for the household's intertemporal elasticity of substitution in consumption) the revenue-neutral combination of a carbon tax and reduction in capital income taxes yields a welfare gain.

[42] Shah and Larsen [40] obtain qualitatively similar results. In a partial equilibrium model with two goods (leisure and fuels), these authors derive analytical expressions for the welfare losses from carbon and other taxes. These expressions reveal the costs of a given carbon tax to be positively related to the magnitude of pre-existing income tax rates.

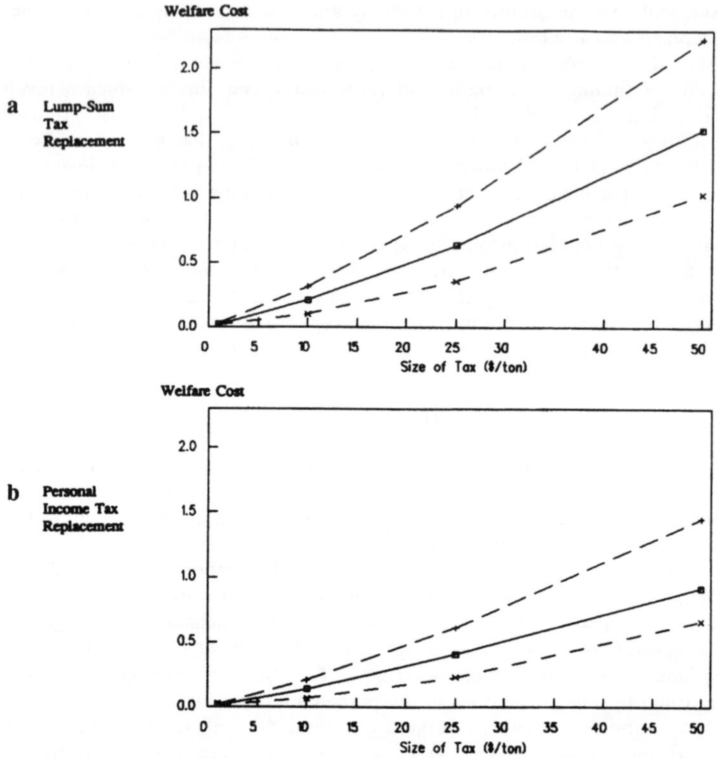

FIG. 4. Significance of pre-existing tax rates. (+) pre-existing tax rates, 1.5 × benchmark values; (□) pre-existing tax rates, benchmark values; (×) pre-existing tax rates, 0.5 × benchmark values. The welfare cost is the equivalent variation as a percentage of reference case human and nonhuman wealth.

Why do higher pre-existing tax rates raise the pure cost of the carbon tax? Bovenberg and de Mooij [5, 6] show analytically that a carbon tax (or other tax on a commodity linked to environmental damage) has important interactions with existing taxes because it is an implicit factor tax. In particular, a (new) carbon tax functions effectively as an increase in existing factor taxes. Thus it distorts not only the market for fossil fuels but also labor and capital markets. This implies that the higher the rates of pre-existing taxes on labor and capital, the greater the additional distortion introduced in these markets by introducing a carbon tax. In their model, Bovenberg and de Mooij indicate that higher pre-existing tax rates imply higher overall costs of a carbon tax, even when the revenues are rebated through reductions in pre-existing taxes. The relationships in Fig. 4 (which originally came as a surprise to the author) suggest that Bovenberg and de Mooij's result holds up in more realistic settings, since they emerge here from a complex, dynamic model that incorporates important details of an actual economy.[43]

b. Connections with optimal environmental taxes. The sensitivity to pre-existing taxes bears on the issue of the value of the optimal environmental tax. Lee and Misiolek [25] have pointed out that the optimal environmental tax must satisfy the requirement that the difference between marginal abatement costs and marginal environmental benefits per marginal dollar of revenues must equal the marginal excess burden of existing distortionary taxes. This can be written as

$$\frac{\partial C/\partial \tau_E}{\partial R/\partial \tau_E} - \frac{\partial B/\partial \tau_E}{\partial R/\partial \tau_E} = \lambda(\tau_D),$$

where $C(\tau_E, \tau_D)$ is total abatement cost, B is total environmental benefit, R is revenue, λ is the marginal excess burden of other taxes, and τ_E and τ_D are the rates of the environmental and existing distortionary tax. Note that C is a function of both τ_E and τ_D. If τ_D is zero, λ is zero and Eq. (13) reduces to

$$\partial C/\partial \tau_E = \partial B/\partial \tau_E, \tag{14}$$

which is the "Pigovian" rule for the optimal environmental tax; marginal abatement costs must equal marginal environmental damages. Let τ_E^* represent the tax rate that satisfies (14). Now consider the case where there are pre-existing taxes ($\tau_D > 0$). How does τ_E^{**}, the optimum when other taxes are present, differ from τ_E^*? Oates [29] points out that the tax elasticity at the Pigovian optimum is relevant here. If the derivative $\partial C/\partial \tau_E$ were independent of τ_D, one could determine from this elasticity whether τ_E^{**} is greater or less than τ_E^*. However, analytical results from Bovenberg and van der Ploeg [7] and the simulations results in Fig. 4 of this paper indicate that higher pre-existing taxes raise the value of $\partial C/\partial \tau_E$ evaluated at a given level of τ_E. This means that in the presence of other taxes, a lower value of τ_E may be required to satisfy (13).[44]

The results from Fig. 4 are relevant to recent work on optimal carbon taxes in particular. As mentioned in subsection IB, Nordhaus [28] finds that the optimal carbon tax profile is higher once one accounts for opportunities to recycle carbon tax revenues through cuts in distortionary taxes. Since the benchmark economy of the Nordhaus model does not contain distortionary taxes, the model cannot assess how pre-existing taxes raise the gross costs of a carbon tax (for any given recycling method). Hence, although the Nordhaus model calculates benefits associated with reductions in distortionary taxes (as part of revenue recycling), it disregards the

[43] These considerations also explain a key result from Fig. 4b—namely the fact that under recycling via personal tax cuts, the net welfare cost is positive even as the carbon tax rate approaches zero. If one were to ignore the connection between the carbon tax and other (e.g., factor) markets, one might suppose that a small carbon tax would have only negligible "pure" costs, while the return of its revenues in the form of reductions in pre-existing taxes would have non-negligible gains. By this reasoning, one would arrive at the incorrect conclusion that returning the revenues through cuts in pre-existing taxes would involve negative overall costs—provided the carbon tax rate is small enough.

[44] Thus, by influencing the marginal costs of environmental taxes, pre-existing taxes can imply that the optimal environmental tax rate is lower than the value prescribed by the Pigovian principle. This issue is explored analytically in detail by Bovenberg and van der Ploeg [7]. In their model τ_E^{**} is less than τ_E^* if and only if the marginal cost of public funds exceeds unity.

costs associated with remaining distortionary taxes in the economy. The simulation results from the present paper, as well as analytical results by Bovenberg and van der Ploeg [7], indicate that the latter cost is larger than the former benefit, implying that prior taxes lower, rather than raise, the value of the optimal carbon tax.[45]

4. *Further Sensitivity Analysis*

Our final simulations examine the sensitivity of results to important model parameters. Table IV displays the significance of these parameters for the effects of a \$25/ton carbon tax the revenues from which are returned either in lump-sum fashion or through reductions in marginal rates on personal income. To conserve space, we simply point out main results here; the reader may refer to the table for details.

A central result discussed previously is that returning carbon tax revenues through reductions in the personal income tax (or in any of several other important taxes) does not fully eliminate the cost of the revenue-neutral carbon tax package. This result is robust to all of the parameter specifications tried.

Welfare costs per dollar of revenue increase with the elasticity of energy demand, the elasticity of energy supply (as regulated by the stock effect),[46] and the energy intensity of production of capital. Higher energy sector elasticities broaden the scope for efficiency losses in energy sectors; hence the carbon tax entails higher costs. When revenues are recycled through personal tax cuts, welfare costs rise with higher labor supply elasticities (in keeping with predictions of simpler models). On the other hand, a higher intertemporal elasticity of substitution in consumption (which implies a larger interest elasticity of savings) is associated with lower welfare costs per dollar.[47]

While the costs of the carbon tax are significantly influenced by the values chosen for certain parameters, such costs generally are less sensitive to these parameters than to the assumption, discussed in the previous section, as to whether the economy contains any pre-existing taxes. These results suggest that modelers of the effects of carbon taxes, and of other energy taxes as well, need to pay as much attention to pre-existing distortions as to the specification of technological or preference parameters.

V. CONCLUSIONS

This paper has evaluated the costs of carbon taxes in a dynamic general equilibrium framework that recognizes tax interactions. The model used here differs from other numerical models that have investigated carbon taxes in that it

[45] In many cases policymakers do not confront the broad problem of optimizing the overall tax system, but instead concentrate on the more modest goal of making marginal improvements to suboptimal tax systems. Bovenberg and Goulder [8] find that in a realistic, "suboptimal" tax system, the optimal carbon tax is somewhat lower than that endorsed by the optimal tax formulae.

[46] The oil and gas industry is the only industry in which supply elasticities can be varied. The other industries involve constant returns to scale production (infinite supply elasticities).

[47] The more elastic the capital supply, the larger the offsetting benefits (avoided distortions) when revenues are returned through cuts in personal (including capital) taxes. On the other hand, lower capital adjustment costs are associated with higher welfare costs.

TABLE IV
Sensitivity Analysis

	Welfare cost per dollar of revenue	
	Lump-sum tax replacement	Personal income tax replacement
A. Central case	0.516	0.332
B. Energy sector parameters		
1. Long-run backstop cost		
a. \$40 per barrel-equivalent	0.551	0.347
b. \$70 per barrel-equivalent	0.436	0.291
2. Initial reserves of domestic oil & gas		
a. $\bar{Z} = 900$	0.557	0.368
b. $\bar{Z} = 225$	0.496	0.329
3. Carbon intensity of backstop		
a. 50% of reference value	0.475	0.299
b. Noncarbon backstop	0.346	0.198
4. Oil & gas stock effect		
a. $\varepsilon = 1.5$	0.507	0.328
b. $\varepsilon = 4.0$	0.536	0.343
5. Elasticities of energy demand		
a. Low (.5 × reference values)	0.360	0.177
b. High (1.5 × reference values)	0.633	0.435
6. Factor intensity of energy supply		
a. *K–L* Ratios Lowered 50%	0.483	0.297
b. *K–L* Ratios Raised 50%	0.592	0.406
C. General parameters		
1. Labor supply elasticities		
a. Low	0.444	0.296
b. High	0.558	0.360
2. Intertemporal substitution elasticity		
a. Low ($\omega = 0.3$)	0.499	0.336
b. High ($\omega = 1.0$)	0.531	0.188
3. Capital adjustment costs		
a. Low (zero)	0.569	0.366
b. High (2 × reference values)	0.477	0.309
4. Energy intensity of capital production		
a. Low (.5 × reference values)	0.504	0.317
b. High (2 × reference values)	0.532	0.338

Notes. (rows B1a and B1b) The long-run backstop cost is the long-run unit cost of backstop production when real input prices are at 1990 levels. In the central case, the long-run backstop cost is \$50 per barrel-equivalent. (rows B5a and B5b) In the low- (high-) elasticity simulation, the elasticity of substitution between composite energy ($\bar{E}$) and composite materials ($\bar{M}$) is lowered (raised) in all industries by 50%. (rows B6a and B6b) Capital–labor ratios are altered while maintaining the same total value added in each industry; increases (decreases) in capital are accompanied by decreases (increases) in labor. (rows C1a and C1b) In these simulations, the elasticity of substitution between leisure and consumption (ν) is changed. The compensated (uncompensated) elasticities of labor supply associated with the changes in this parameter are 0.25 (−0.14), 0.50 (0.03), and 0.80 (0.41) in the low-centrals and high-elasticity cases, respectively. (rows C3a and C3b) In the high adjustment cost scenario, we double the β parameter of the quadratic adjustment cost function (see Section II.B). In the low adjustment cost scenario, $\beta = 0$ for all industries except for synfuels. In the synfuels industry, β is halved. Zero adjustment costs for synfuels would imply implausibly rapid market penetration.

combines detailed attention to existing U.S. taxes with a close treatment of energy-sector dynamics, including exhaustibility and the conversion to synthetic fuels.

In recent years, proponents of environmental taxes have contemplated the possibility that the gross costs (i.e., the costs exclusive of environment benefits) of environmentally motivated taxes might shrink to zero or become negative once one accounts for the possibility of using the revenues from such taxes to reduce existing, distortionary taxes. If the avoided distortions from the reduction in existing taxes are larger than the (gross) distortions from the new environmental tax, then the overall gross costs of the policy package are negative and the environmental tax offers a "double dividend"—it not only (1) improves the environment but also (2) reduces the overall non-environmental costs of the tax system. This paper's results indicate that although judicious revenue recycling can significantly lower the costs of a carbon tax, the second dividend is not likely to obtain, at least for the major types of income taxes whose reductions might be financed from a carbon tax.[48] Under the revenue-replacement policies considered here, recycling the revenues does not bring the gross distortionary cost to zero. Simulations reveal that the carbon tax's application to intermediate goods (as compared with final goods under the income tax) and its relatively narrow tax base significantly contribute to the higher costs of a carbon tax relative to income taxes. These findings are consistent with theoretical results from the optimal tax literature. They also agree with numerical results from Shah and Larsen [40], but contrast with some of the empirical results from the Jorgenson–Wilcoxen model in [39].[49]

We also find that the welfare costs of carbon taxes are highly sensitive to initial conditions regarding the marginal rates on pre-existing taxes. For any given form of revenue-recycling, when carbon taxes are imposed in an economy with high existing marginal tax rates the welfare costs are significantly higher than when they are introduced in a world with low marginal rates. Thus, contrary to what some analysts have suggested, higher pre-existing tax rates weaken rather than strengthen the case for a carbon tax. This result conforms closely to recent results of Bovenberg and de Mooij [5, 6] in a simple analytical model. It reinforces the notion that a carbon tax functions as an implicit factor tax, so that higher rates for pre-existing taxes augment the potential of the carbon tax to exacerbate factor market distortions.

The finding of sensitivity to pre-existing taxes has at least four important implications. First, it indicates that even very small carbon taxes may generate significant gross costs; the supposition from partial equilibrium analysis that small

[48] As mentioned in Section IV, nothing in this analysis rules out the possibility that there exists some sufficiently burdensome prior tax that, if reduced via a carbon tax, could bring the overall gross costs of the carbon tax policy to zero. However, it should be kept in mind that if a given tax is unusually burdensome as assumed here, then one need not appeal to the carbon tax to justify its removal. Nor is its presence a reason to introduce a carbon tax.

[49] Shah and Larsen also find that the revenue-neutral combination of carbon tax and personal tax cut involves positive non-environmental costs overall [40, p. 17]. The Jorgenson–Wilcoxen model arrives at a welfare gain (negative cost) when carbon tax revenues are used to reduce personal income tax rates [39, p. 16]. It is difficult to pinpoint the source of this contrasting result since the paper does not include policy decompositions of the type in Table III, above, or analysis of how welfare results are influenced by changes in parameters.

taxes yield small welfare costs is wrong. Second, it indicates that previous analyses of carbon taxes which assume a first-best (no tax) starting point may substantially understate the costs of a carbon tax (and helps explain the observed differences between results of models with first-best and second-best initial conditions). Third, our results have implications for the analysis of other tax initiatives in second-best economies. Many of these findings apply directly to other environmentally motivated taxes such as BTU taxes. Fourth, the results suggest that the gross cost of carbon taxes may be larger in other economies with higher marginal rates for pre-existing taxes than those found in the U.S. Although these results indicate that carbon taxes may involve significant costs (even when revenues are recycled), they do not mean that such taxes lack justification on efficiency grounds. Rather, they imply that positive and possibly substantial environmental benefits must be invoked to justify the policy along the efficiency dimension.

These results should be kept in perspective. This study does not address distributional consequences—important considerations in deciding whether to introduce a carbon tax.[50] Nor does it assess the carbon tax's potential environmental benefits—the initial source of interest in this policy. Further research that reduces the uncertainties as to the magnitudes of these benefits will be extremely useful in the evaluation of the carbon tax option.

REFERENCES

1. C. Ballard, J. Shoven, and J. Whalley, General equilibrium computations of the marginal welfare costs of taxes in the U.S., *Amer. Econom. Rev.* **75**(1), 128–138 (1985).
2. C. Ballard and S. Medema, The marginal efficiency effects of taxes and subsidies in the presence of externalities: A computational general equilibrium approach, *J. Public Econom.* **52**, 199–216 (1993).
3. R. Barro, On the determination of the public debt. *J. Political Econom.* **87**, 940–971 (1979).
4. D. Bernheim and J. Shoven, Comparison of the cost of capital in the U.S. and Japan: The roles of risk and taxes, CEPR Discussion Paper 179, Stanford University (September 1989).
5. A. L. Bovenberg and R. de Mooij, Environmental taxation and labor market distortions, Working Paper, Ministry of Economic Affairs, The Hague (March 1992).
6. A. L. Bovenberg and R. de Mooij, Environmental levies and distortionary taxation, *Amer. Econom. Rev.* (1994).
7. A. L. Bovenberg and F. van der Ploeg, Environmental policy, public finance and the labour market in a second-best world, Working Paper, Tilburg University (October 1992).
8. A. L. Bovenberg and L. Goulder, Integrating environmental and distortionary taxes: General equilibrium analyses, Working Paper, Stanford University (March 1994).
9. J.-M. Burniaux, J. P. Martin, G. Nicoletti, and J. Oliveira-Martins, GREEN—A multi-region dynamic general equilibrium model for quantifying the costs of curbing CO_2 emissions: A technical manual, OECD Department of Economics and Statistics Working Paper 104, Paris (1991).
10. M. Cruz and L. Goulder, An intertemporal general equilibrium model for analyzing U.S. energy and environmental policies: Data documentation, unpublished manuscript, Stanford University (1992).
11. P. Diamond and J. Mirrlees, Optimal taxation and public production, I: Production efficiency, and II: Tax rules, *Amer. Econom. Rev.* **61** (1971).
12. R. Fair and J. Taylor, Solution and maximum likelihood estimation of dynamic nonlinear rational expectations models, *Econometrica* **51**(4), 1169–1185 (1983).

[50] Results by Poterba [33] and others indicate that a carbon tax (with lump-sum revenue replacement) is regressive. Revenue-recycling is relevant here. The regressive impact can be offset if carbon tax revenues are returned to the economy through income tax cuts targeted to lower income households or through cuts in regressive taxes such as payroll taxes.

13. D. Gaskins and J. Weyant, Eds., "The Costs of Controlling Greenhouse Gas Emissions," Stanford Univ. Press, Stanford, CA, (forthcoming).
14. L. Goulder, Second-best taxation and non-renewable resource supply: An integrative approach. Working Paper, Stanford University (March 1991).
15. L. Goulder, Carbon tax design and U.S. industry performance, *in* "Tax Policy and the Economy: 6" (James M. Poterba, Ed.), MIT Press, Cambridge, MA (1992).
16. L. Goulder, Energy taxes: Traditional efficiency effects and environmental implications, *in* "Tax Policy and the Economy: 8" (James M. Poterba, Ed.), MIT Press, Cambridge, MA (1994).
17. L. Goulder and L. Summers, Tax policy, asset prices, and growth: A general equilibrium analysis, *J. Public Econom.* **38**, 265–296 (1989).
18. L. Goulder and P. Thalmann, Approaches to efficient capital taxation: Leveling the playing field vs. living by the golden rule, *J. Public Econom.* **50**, 169–196 (1993).
19. R. Hall, Intertemporal substitution in consumption, *J. Political Econom.* **96**(2), 339–357 (1988).
20. D. Jorgenson and P. Wilcoxen, Environmental regulation and U.S. economic growth, *Rand J. Econom.* **21**(2), 314–340 (1990).
21. D. Jorgenson and P. Wilcoxen, Reducing U.S. carbon emissions: An econometric general equilibrium assessment, *in* "The Costs of Controlling Greenhouse Gas Emissions," (Darius Gaskins and John Weyant, Eds.), Stanford Univ. Press, Stanford, CA (forthcoming).
22. D. Jorgenson and K. Y. Yun, "Tax Policy and the Cost of Capital," Oxford Univ. Press, Oxford (1990).
23. L. Lave, Formulating greenhouse policies in a sea of uncertainty, *Energy J.* **12**(1), 9–21 (January 1991).
24. E. Lawrance, Poverty and the rate of time preference: Evidence from panel data, *J. Political Econom.* **99**(1), 54–77 (1991).
25. D. Lee and W. Misiolek, Substituting pollution taxation for general taxation: Some implications for efficiency in pollution taxation, *J. Environ. Econom. Management* **13**, 338–347 (1986).
26. A. Manne and R. Richels, "Buying Greenhouse Insurance: The Economic Costs of CO_2 Emissions Limits," MIT Press, Cambridge, MA (1992).
27. A. Manne, R. Richels, and T. Rutherford, International trade in oil, gas, and carbon emission rights: An intertemporal general equilibrium model, *Energy J.* **15**(1), 57–76 (1994).
28. W. Nordhaus, Optimal greenhouse-gas reductions and tax policy in the 'DICE' model, *Amer. Econom. Rev.* (Papers and Proceedings) **83**(2), 313–317 (1993).
29. W. Oates, Pollution charges as a source of public revenues, *Resources for the Future Discussion Paper* QE92-05, Resources for the Future, Washington, DC (November 1991).
30. OECD International Energy Agency, "Oil and Gas Information 1988–1990," Paris (1991).
31. OECD, The economic costs of reducing CO_2 emissions, *OECD Econom. Stud.* **19**, Paris (1992).
32. D. Pearce, The role of carbon taxes in adjusting to global warming, *Econom. J.* **101**, 938–948 (1991).
33. J. Poterba, Tax policy to combat warming: On designing a carbon tax, *in* "Global warming economic policy responses" (Rudiger Dornbusch and James M. Poterba, Eds.) MIT Press, Cambridge, MA (1991).
34. J. Poterba, Global warming: A public finance perspective, *J. Econ. Perspectives* **7**(4), 47–63 (1993).
35. J. Poterba and L. Summers, The economic effects of dividend taxation, *in* "Recent Advances in Corporate Finance" (Edward I. Altman and Marti G. Subramanyam, Eds.) Irwin, Homewood, IL (1985).
36. M. J. D. Powell, A hybrid method for nonlinear equations, *in* "Numerical Methods for Nonlinear Algebraic Equations" (P. Rabinowitz, Ed.) Ch. 6, Gordon and Breach, London (1970).
37. R. Repetto, R. Dower, R. Jenkins, and J. Geoghegan, Green fees: How a tax shift can work for the environment and the economy, World Resources Institute (November 1992).
38. A. Sandmo, Optimal taxation in the presence of externalities, *Swedish J. Econom.* **77** (1975).
39. R. Shackleton, M. Shelby, A. Cristofaro, R. Brinner, J. Yanchar, L. Goulder, D. Jorgenson, P. Wilcoxen, and P. Pauly, The efficiency value of carbon tax revenues, unpublished manuscript, U.S. Environmental Protection Agency (November 5, 1992).
40. A. Shah and B. Larsen, Carbon taxes, the greenhouse effect and developing countries, World Bank Policy Research Working Paper Series, 957, The World Bank, Washington, DC (1992).
41. H.-W. Sinn, Taxation and the cost of capital: The 'old' view, the 'new' view, and another view, *in* "Tax Policy and the Economy: 5" (David Bradford, Ed.) MIT Press, Cambridge, MA (1991).
42. R. Stavins, Project 88—Round II, Incentives for action: Designing market-based environmental strategies, public policy study sponsored by Senators Timothy Wirth and John Heinz, Washington, DC (May 1991).

43. J. Stiglitz and P. Dasgupta, Differential taxation, public goods, and economic efficiency, *Rev. Econom. Stud.* **38**(2) (April 1971).
44. L. Summers, Taxation and corporate investment: A q-theory approach, *Brookings Papers Econom. Activity*, 67–127 (January 1981).
45. D. Terkla, The efficiency value of effluent tax revenues, *J. Environ. Econom. Management* **11**, 107–23 (1984).
46. J. Weyant, Costs of reducing global carbon emissions, *J. Econom. Perspectives* **7**(4), 27–46 (1993).
47. J. Whalley and R. Wigle, The international incidence of carbon taxes, *in* "Global warming: economic policy responses" (Rudiger Dornbusch and James M. Poterba, Eds.) MIT Press, Cambridge, MA (1991).

[17]

Results from the Jorgenson–Wilcoxen model reducing US carbon emissions: An econometric general equilibrium assessment

Introduction

Our approach to EMF 12 differed in three important ways from the methodologies used by other participants. First, our results are based on a highly disaggregated intertemporal general equilibrium model of the United States. Using a disaggregated model allowed us to examine the effects of carbon taxes on narrow segments of the economy, such as particular industries or types of household. Second, all parameters in our model were obtained by econometric estimation using a data set spanning 39 years. Thus, the response of industries and consumers to changes in prices will be consistent with the historical record. Third, we model productivity growth at the industry level and allow it to be an endogenous function of relative prices. Allowing productivity growth to differ across industries permits the model to reflect a conspicuous feature of historical data. Together, these features allow us to shed light on several questions not addressed by most of the other participants. Some of our principle findings are as follows.

In the United States, the effects of a carbon tax will be very similar to the effects of a tax placed solely on coal. Of all fossil fuels, coal is the least expensive per unit of energy and produces the most carbon dioxide when burned. Thus, a tax levied on carbon emissions will raise the cost of coal-based energy far more in percentage terms than the price of energy derived from oil or natural gas. In response to this price change, the demand for coal will fall substantially. The demands for oil and natural gas will also decline, but by much smaller percentages.

Almost all coal consumed in the United States is used to generate electric power. As the price of coal rises, electric utilities will convert some generating capacity to other fuels. However, substitution possibilities are fairly limited, particularly in the short run, so the tax will raise the price of electricity significantly. Consumers and firms will substitute other inputs for electricity, leading to a fall in electricity demand.[1] Higher energy prices will lead to slower productivity growth, reduced capital formation, and a reallocation of labor to lower-wage industries, all of which will cause gross national product to be lower than it would have been in the absence of the tax.

The tax rate needed to achieve a fixed absolute emissions target, such as maintaining emissions at 1990 levels, will depend on how fast emissions grow in the absence of the tax. Baseline emissions growth, in turn, will depend on the rate of productivity growth, the rate of capital accumulation, the rate of growth of the labor force, any energy-saving biases in technical change, and the path of world oil prices. More rapid economic growth will generally lead to higher baseline emissions and will thus require higher tax rates if emissions are to be held at a fixed absolute level. Moreover, deeper absolute cuts in emissions will require sharply increasing tax rates.

A carbon tax large enough to have much effect on emissions will raise tens to hundreds of billions of dollars annually. How this revenue is used will affect the overall economic burden of the tax. By using the revenue to lower highly distortionary taxes elsewhere in the economy, the tax could actually increase output and economic welfare. In the remainder of this chapter we present an overview of our model and discuss each of these findings in detail.

An overview of the model

Our results are based on a set of simulations we conducted using a detailed model of the US economy designed specifically for examining the effects of energy and environmental policies. One feature of our approach which distinguishes it from many others is that we use a general equilibrium model. General equilibrium models are constructed by dividing the economy into a collection of interdependent sectors which interact through product and factor markets. The behavior of each sector is represented by an appropriate submodel. Prices and wages adjust until demands and supplies are equated in every market and the economy reaches equilibrium. Our model is composed of thirty-five producing sectors, a consumer sector, an investment sector, a government sector, and a foreign sector. In this section we present an overview of the model by describing the submodels used to represent each of these sectors. We also discuss our base case simulation.[2]

Production

Production is disaggregated into the thirty-five industrial sectors listed in Table 1. Most of these industries match two-digit sectors in the Standard Industrial Classification (SIC). Each industry produces a primary product and may produce one or more secondary products. This level of industrial detail makes it possible to measure the effect of changes in tax policy on relatively narrow segments of the economy. Since most anthropogenic carbon dioxide emissions are generated by fossil fuel combustion, a disaggregated model is essential for capturing differences in the response of each sector to a carbon dioxide control policy.

We derive the behavior of each of the industries from a hierarchical tier-structured transcendental logarithmic cost function. At the highest level, the cost of each industry's output is assumed to be a function of the prices of energy, materials, capital services, and labor. At the second level, we take the price of energy to be a function of prices of coal, crude petroleum, refined petroleum, electricity, and natural gas, and the price of materials to be a function of the prices of all other intermediate goods. Given this structure we derive factor demands for capital services, labor, and intermediate inputs from each of the thirty-five industries.

We estimated the parameters of each industry submodel econometrically, using a set of consistent inter-industry transactions tables constructed for the purpose. The tables describe the US economy for the period 1947 through 1985.[3] Estimating the production parameters over a long time series ensures that each industry's response to changes in prices is consistent with historical evidence.[4]

An unusual feature of our model is that productivity growth is determined endogenously.[5] Other models used to study global warming, for example, Manne and Richels (1992), take productivity growth to be exogenous. In our model the rate of productivity growth in each industry is determined endogenously as a function of input prices. In addition, each industry's productivity growth can be biased toward some inputs and away from others. Biased productivity

Table 1 Industry definitions

Number	Description
1	Agriculture, forestry, fisheries
2	Metal mining
3	Coal mining
4	Crude petroleum and natural gas extraction
5	Non-metallic mineral mining
6	Construction
7	Food and kindred products
8	Tobacco manufactures
9	Textile mill products
10	Apparel and other textile products
11	Lumber and wood products
12	Furniture and fixtures
13	Paper and allied products
14	Printing and publishing
15	Chemicals and allied products
16	Petroleum refining
17	Rubber and plastic products
18	Leather and leather products
19	Stone, clay, and glass products
20	Primary metals
21	Fabricated metal products
22	Machinery, except electrical
23	Electrical machinery
24	Motor vehicles
25	Other transportation equipment
26	Instruments
27	Miscellaneous manufacturing
28	Transportation and warehousing
29	Communication
30	Electric utilities
31	Gas utilities
32	Trade
33	Finance, insurance, and real estate
34	Other services
35	Government enterprises

growth is a common feature of historical data but is often ignored when modeling production. By allowing for biased productivity growth, our model is able to capture the evolution of industry input patterns much more accurately.

Although we allow for biased productivity growth, we do not impose that technical change be energy-saving in every industry. Most other participants in EMF 12 introduce energy-saving technical change through an exogenous parameter giving the rate of "Autonomous Energy Efficiency Improvements." The extent to which technical change is energy-saving is a source of considerable controversy. Manne and Richels (1992) suggest that engineering analysis shows technical change to be energy-saving, while Hogan and Jorgenson (1991) present econometric evidence that aggregate technical change may be slightly energy-using. However, these positions are not necessarily inconsistent. After the sharp increases in energy prices of the 1970s, the US economy became markedly less energy-intensive as producers and consumers substituted away from energy. To the engineers reported by Manne and Richels, this would have appeared as a shift toward energy-saving technology. Hogan and Jorgenson's study reports biases in technical change *after* accounting for movements induced by substitution. Our model is based on the same data set as Hogan and Jorgenson's work, and so has the technical change properties they describe.

In sum, the salient features of our model of producer behavior are as follows. First, production is disaggregated into thirty-five industries. Second, all parameters of the model are estimated econometrically from an extensive historical database developed specifically for this purpose. This allows the model to incorporate extensive historical evidence on the price responsiveness of input patterns, including changes in the mix of fossil fuels. Third, the model determines rates of productivity growth endogenously and allows for biased productivity change in each industry.

Consumption

We represent consumer behavior by assuming that households follow a three-stage optimization process. At the first stage, each household allocates full wealth (the sum of financial and human wealth, plus the imputed value of leisure time) across different periods.[6] We formalize this decision by introducing a representative agent who maximizes an additive intertemporal utility function subject to an intertemporal budget constraint. The portion of full wealth allocated to a particular period is called full consumption. At the second stage, households allocate full consumption to goods and leisure in order to maximize an indirect utility function. This allows us to derive demands for leisure and goods as functions of prices and full consumption. The demand for leisure implicitly determines labor supply, while the difference between current income and consumption of goods implicitly determines savings.

The third stage of the household optimization problem is the allocation of total expenditure among capital services, labor services, and the thirty-five commodities. At this stage, we relax the representative consumer assumption in favor of the approach of Jorgenson, Lau, and Stoker (1982) to derive separate systems of demand functions for households of different demographic characteristics. We distinguish among 1344 household types according to demographic characteristics such as the number of household members and the geographic region in which the household is located. The spending patterns of each household type are derived from a hierarchical tier-structured indirect utility function. This allows us to derive household demands for individual commodities.

As with production, the parameters of the behavioral equations for all three stages of our consumer model are estimated econometrically.[7] Our household model incorporates extensive time series data on the price responsiveness of demand patterns by consumers and also makes use of detailed cross-section data on the effects of demographic characteristics on consumer behavior. In addition, an important feature of our approach is that we do not impose that household demands be homothetic. As total expenditure increases, spending patterns may change even in the absence of price changes. This captures an important feature of cross-sectional expenditure data which is often ignored.

Investment and capital formation

We assume there is a single capital stock in the economy which is in fixed total supply in the short run. However, we also assume that capital is perfectly malleable and can be reallocated among industries and between industries and final demand categories at zero cost. Thus, the price of a unit of capital services will be equal in every industry and there will be a single economy-wide rate of return on capital.

In the long run the supply of capital is determined by investment. Our investment model is based on the assumption that investors have rational expectations and that arbitrage occurs until the present value of future capital services is equated to the purchase price of new investment goods. This equilibrium is achieved by adjustments in prices and the term structure of interest rates. New capital goods are produced from individual commodities according to a model identical to those for the industrial sectors, so the price of new capital will depend on commodity prices. We estimated the behavioral parameters for new capital goods production using final demand data for investment over the period 1947–1985. Thus, the model incorporates substitution among inputs in the composition of the capital.

Government and foreign trade

The two remaining parts of the model are the government and foreign sectors. To specify government behavior, we begin by computing total government spending on goods and services. We apply exogenous tax rates to taxable transactions in the economy and then add the capital income of government enterprises and non-tax receipts to obtain total government revenue.[8] Next we assume the government budget deficit can be specified exogenously and add the deficit to total revenue to obtain total government spending. To arrive at government purchases of goods and services, we subtract interest paid to holders of government bonds together with transfer payments to domestic and foreign recipients. We then allocate spending among commodity groups according to fixed shares constructed from historical data.

In the modeling of the foreign sector we begin by assuming that imports are imperfect substitutes for similar domestic commodities.[9] The mix of goods purchased by households and firms reflects substitution between domestic and imported products. We estimate the price responsiveness of this mixture econometrically from historical data. In effect, each commodity is assigned a separate elasticity of substitution between domestic and imported goods. Since the prices of imports are given exogenously, intermediate and final demands implicitly determine the quantity of imports of each commodity.

Exports are determined by a set of isoelastic export demand equations, one for each commodity, that depend on foreign income and the foreign prices of US exports.[10] Foreign prices are computed from domestic prices by adjusting for subsidies and the exchange rate. The demand elasticities in these equations are estimated from historical data. Without an elaborate model of international trade it is impossible to determine both the current account balance and the exchange rate endogenously, so we take the current account to be exogenous and the exchange rate to be endogenous.

Carbon dioxide emissions

For EMF 12, the most important remaining feature of the model is the way in which carbon dioxide emissions are calculated. We begin by assuming that carbon dioxide is produced in fixed proportion to fossil fuel use. For each fuel, Table 2 gives total domestic production, heat content per unit, and total heat produced.[11] Heat production is measured in quadrillion BTU.

Table 2 Domestic production and heat content of fossil fuels

Fuel	Unit	Domestic Production	MBTU per Unit	Total QBTU
Coal	ton	916.9×10^6	21.94	20.1
Oil	bbl	3033.2×10^6	5.80	17.6
Gas	kcf	17.8×10^9	1.03	16.8

We calculated the carbon content of each fuel by multiplying the numbers in Table 2 by figures from the Environmental Protection Agency on the amount of carbon emitted per million BTU produced from each fuel.[12] Total carbon emissions were then calculated using figures on total fuel production. Table 3 shows data for each fuel in 1987. For comparability with other studies, we measure CO_2 emissions in tons of contained carbon.[13]

Table 3 Carbon emissions data for 1987

Item	Unit of Measure	Fuel		
		Coal (ton)	Oil (bbl)	Gas (kcf)
Heat content	10^6 BTU/unit	21.94	5.80	1.03
Emissions rate	kg/10^6 BTU	26.9	21.4	14.5
	kg/unit	590.2	124.1	14.9
Domestic output	10^9 units	0.92	0.30	17.9
Carbon emissions	10^6	595.3	414.1	268.6

All prices in our model are normalized to unity in 1982, so quantities do not correspond directly to physical units. Moreover, the model has a single sector for oil and gas extraction. To convert the oil and gas data in Table 3 into a form appropriate for the model we added carbon production for crude petroleum and natural gas and divided by the industry's output for 1987 to obtain the industry's carbon coefficient. Similarly, the coefficient for coal was obtained by dividing total carbon production from coal by the model's 1987 value for coal mining output. These coefficients were used to estimate carbon emissions in each simulation.

The base case

To assess the effect of a carbon tax we must first determine the future path of the US economy in the absence of the tax. To construct such a scenario, which we will call a "base case", we adopted a set of default assumptions about the time path of each exogenous variable in the absence of changes in government policy. Since our model is based on agents with perfect foresight, values must be specified far into the future. Through 1990–2050, we forecast values of the exogenous variables on the basis of their behavior in the sample period. After 2050, we assume the variables remain constant at their 2050 values to allow the model to converge to a steady state by the year 2100.[14] Our projections for 1990–2050 were made as follows. First, all tax rates are set to their values in 1985, the last year in our sample period. Next, we assume that foreign prices of imports in foreign currency remain constant in real terms at 1985 levels. We then project a gradual decline in the government deficit through the year 2025, after which the nominal value of the government debt is maintained at a constant ratio to the value of the national product. Finally, we project the current account deficit by allowing it to fall gradually to zero by the year 2000. After that we project a current account surplus sufficient to produce a stock of net claims on foreigners by the year 2050 equal to the same proportion of national wealth as in 1982.

Some of the most important exogenous variables are those associated with growth of the US population and corresponding changes in the economy's time endowment. We project population by age, sex, and educational attainment through the year 2050, using demographic assumptions consistent with Social Security Administration projections.[15] After 2050 we hold population constant, which is roughly consistent with Social Security projections. In addition, we project the educational composition of the population by holding the level of educational attainment constant beginning with the cohort reaching age 35 in the year 1985. We transform our population projection into a projection of the time endowment by assuming that the pattern of relative wages across different types of labor remains as it was in 1985. Since capital formation is endogenous in our model, our projections of the time endowment effectively determine the size of the economy in the more distant future.

A summary of results

One policy often proposed for slowing global warming is to stabilize greenhouse gas emissions at 1990 levels. This corresponds to EMF 12 scenario 4, so we begin our discussion there. Subsequent sections will examine the effects of more stringent emissions targets, the consequences of using carbon tax revenue in different ways, and the sensitivity of results to assumptions embodied in the base case scenario.

Stabilizing emissions

To implement scenario 4 we introduced a tax on the carbon content of primary fossil fuels. The tax rate varied from year to year but was always chosen to be exactly enough to hold US carbon dioxide emissions at their 1990 value of 1576 million tons. We returned the revenue raised by the tax to households as a lump-sum rebate. The carbon tax we obtained is shown as a function of time in Figure 1. Base case emissions increase over time so the tax grows gradually over the next few decades. By 2020 our forecast of the US population crests and growth begins to slow, reducing the rate of carbon tax growth.[16] The tax produces significant reductions in carbon emissions, as shown in Figure 2. By 2020 emissions are 16% lower than they would have been without the tax. The tax also produces significant revenue: $31 billion annually by 2020.[17]

The direct effect of the tax is to increase purchasers' prices of coal and crude oil. By 2020, for example, the tax reaches $22.71 per ton of carbon. This amounts to a tax of $14.75 per ton of coal, $3.10 per barrel of oil, or $0.37 per thousand cubic feet of gas. Figure 3 shows the

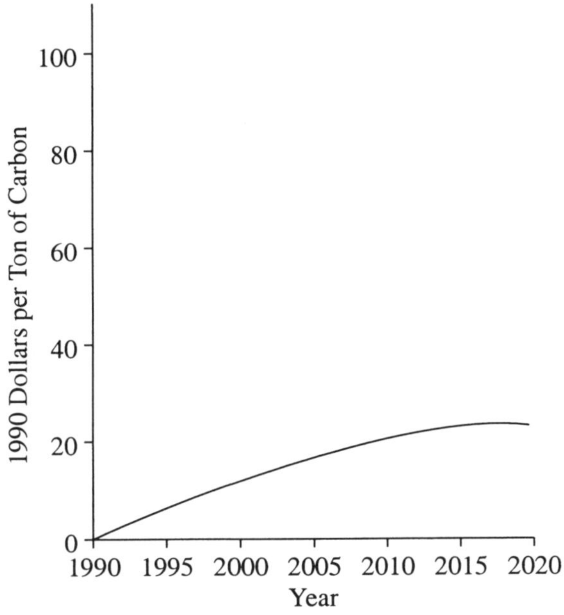

Figure 1 *Carbon tax under scenario 4*

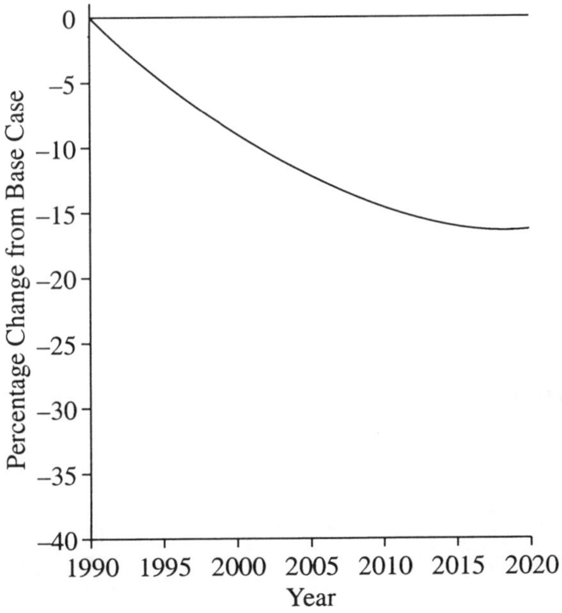

Figure 2 *Reduction in emissions under scenario 4*

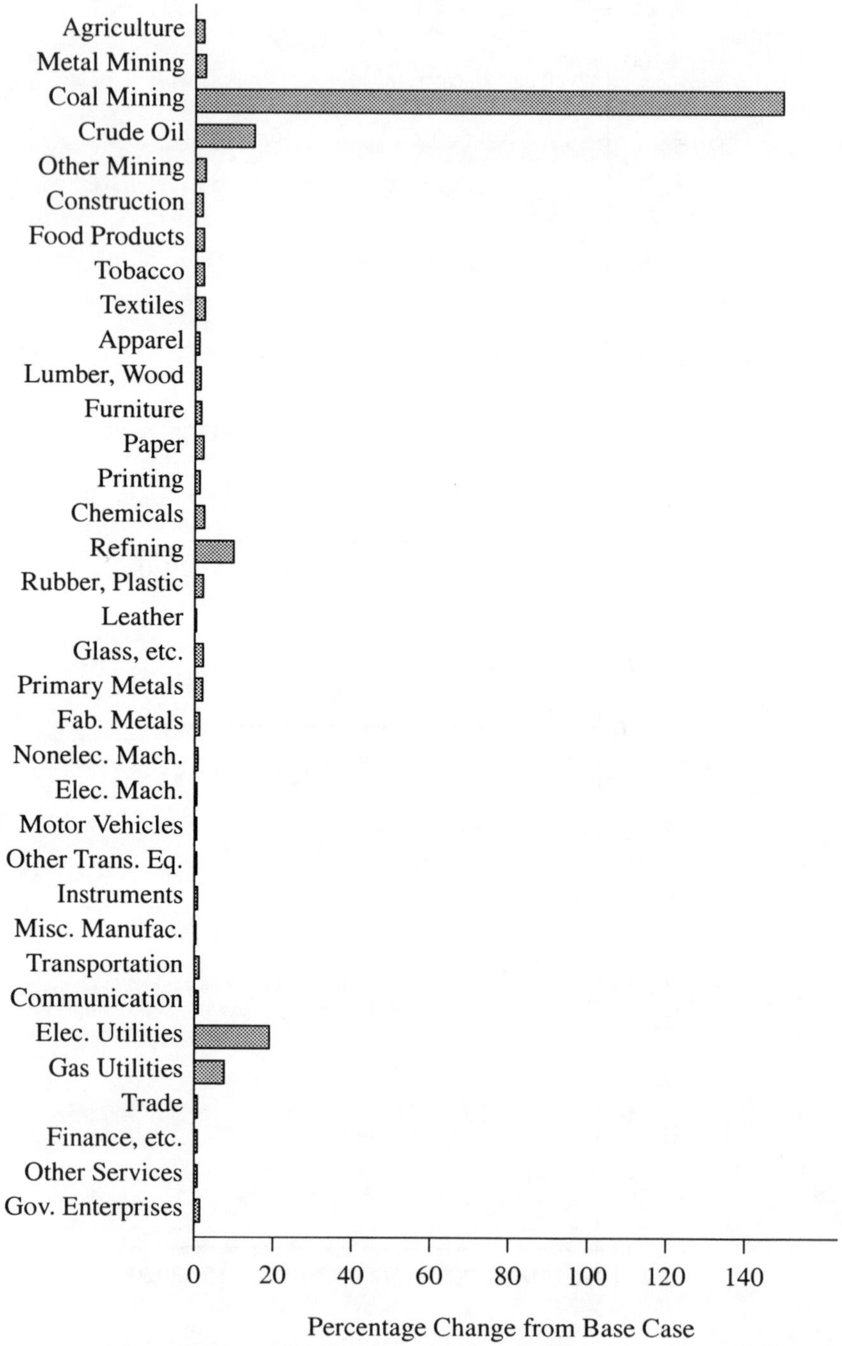

Figure 3 Change in prices at 2020 under scenario 4

effect of the tax on purchasers' prices of each industry's output in 2020. The price of coal rises by 47%, the price of electricity rises by almost 7% (coal accounts for about 13% of the cost of electricity), and the price of crude oil rises by around 4%. Other prices showing significant effects are those for refined petroleum and natural gas utilities. These rise, directly or indirectly, because of the tax on the carbon content of oil and natural gas.

Changes in relative prices affect demands for each good and lead to changes in industry outputs. Figure 4 presents percentage changes in industry outputs in 2020 relative to the base case. Most sectors show only small changes in output. Coal mining is an exception: its output falls by almost 30%. Coal is affected strongly for three reasons. First, coal emits more carbon dioxide than oil or natural gas per unit of energy produced. Thus, the absolute level of the tax per unit of energy content is higher on coal than other fuels. Second, the tax is very large relative to the base case price of coal: at the mine mouth the tax increases coal prices by around 50%. Oil is far more expensive per unit of energy, so in percentage terms its price is less affected by the tax. In fact, the price of crude oil rises only about 10%. Third, the demand for coal is relatively elastic. Most coal is purchased by electric utilities which can substitute other fuels for coal when the price rises. Moreover, the demand for electricity itself is relatively elastic so when the price of electricity rises, demand for electricity (and hence demand for coal) falls substantially.

For the rest of the economy, the main result of the tax is to increase the prices of electricity, refined petroleum, and natural gas, each by a few percent. This would have two effects. First, higher energy prices would mean that capital goods (which are produced using energy) would become more expensive. To the extent that domestic saving does not rise enough to compensate, higher prices for capital goods mean a slower rate of capital accumulation and lower GNP in the future. Second, higher energy prices discourage technical change in industries in which technical change is energy-using. Together, these two effects cause the capital stock to drop by 0.7% and GNP to fall by 0.5% (both relative to the base case) by 2020. Average annual GNP growth over the period 1990–2020 is 0.02 percentage points lower than in the base case. About half of this is due to slower productivity growth and half due to reduced capital formation.

Larger reductions

EMF 12 scenarios 2 and 3 specify more ambitious goals for carbon dioxide control. In scenario 2, emissions are required to decrease gradually until 2010, when they must be 20% below 1990 levels. In scenario 3, emissions must fall by 20% in 2010 and then by 50% by 2050. Figure 5 shows the paths of carbon taxes needed over time in scenarios 2, 3, and 4 while Figure 6 shows the paths of carbon emissions in each case. Table 4 compares key long-run results for these two simulations with results for scenario 4.

Comparing scenarios 2 and 3 with scenario 4 shows that increasing the stringency of the policy rapidly increases its cost. Moving from scenario 4 to scenario 2 doubles the effect of the policy: emissions fall by 32.90% instead of 16.12%. However, this comes at the cost of tripling the carbon tax and the loss of output. Moving from scenario 4 to scenario 3 raises costs even more sharply: the carbon tax and loss of GNP go up by more than a factor of 4 while the carbon reduction rises by only a factor of 2.4.

Comparing industry results across each of the scenarios shows that the more stringent policies have progressively larger effects on sectors other than coal mining. Doubling the emissions reduction by moving from scenario 4 to scenario 2 does not cause the reduction in coal output

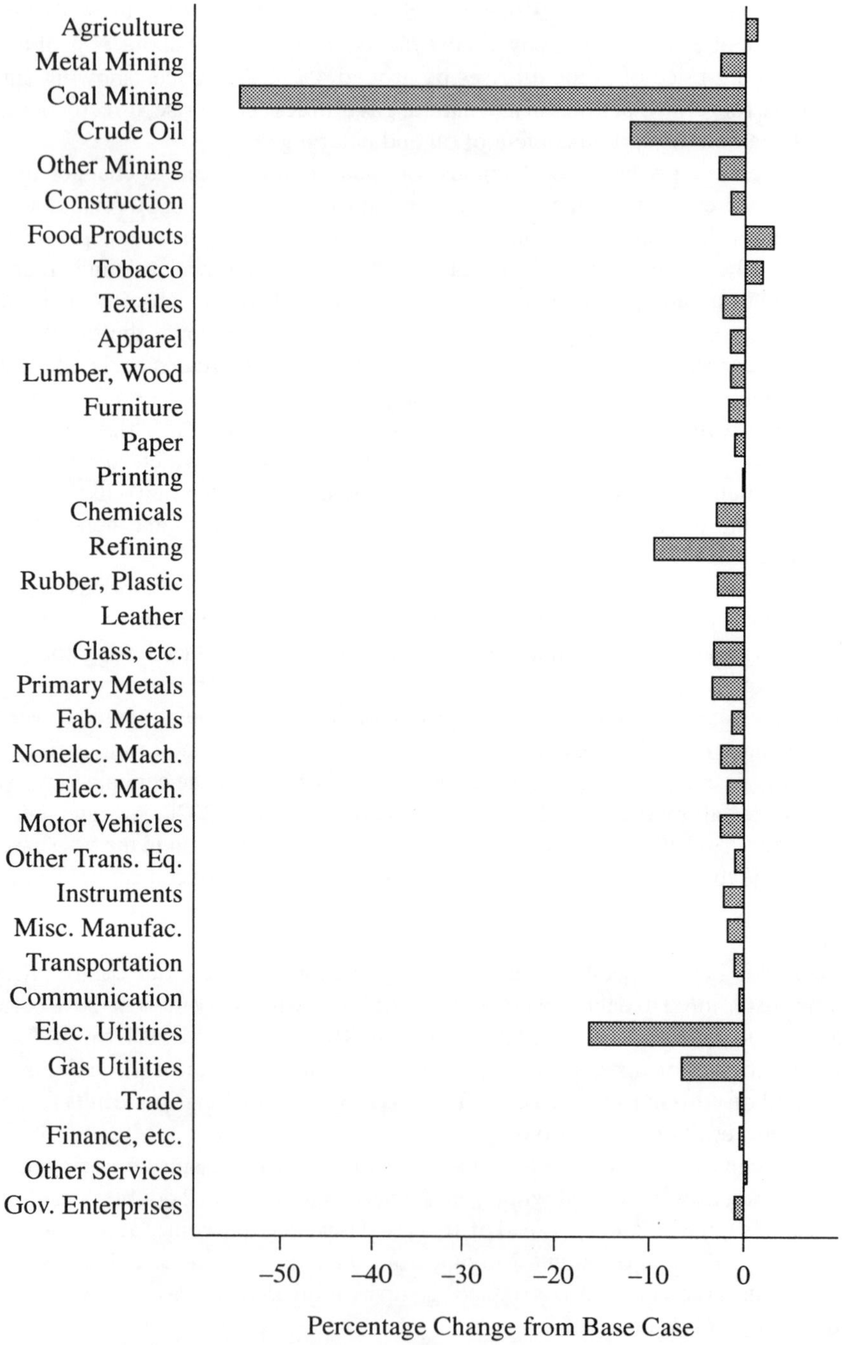

Figure 4 Change in output at 2020 under scenario 4

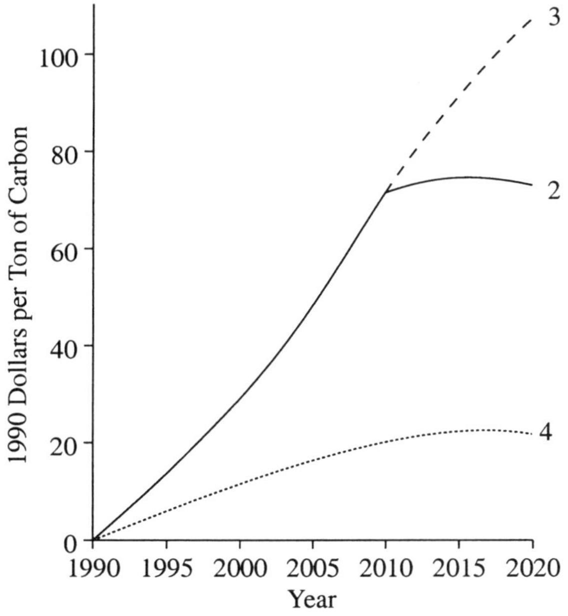

Figure 5 Carbon taxes under scenarios 2–4

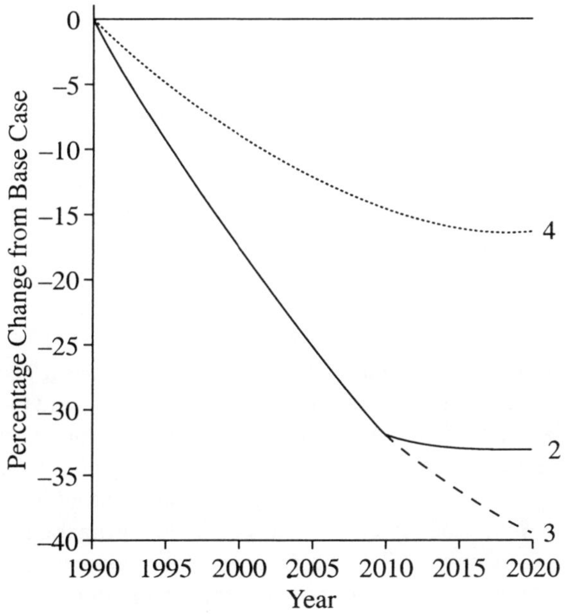

Figure 6 Reduction in emissions under scenario 4

Table 4 Selected results for scenarios 2–4 in 2020

Variable	Unit	Scenario		
		2	3	4
Carbon emissions	%Δ	–32.90	–39.19	–16.12
Carbon tax	$/t	74.49	108.78	22.71
Price of capital	%Δ	1.10	1.40	0.40
Capital stock	%Δ	–2.35	–2.95	–0.83
Tax revenue	$B	82.52	109.16	31.41
Real GNP	%Δ	–1.71	–2.36	–0.55
Coal price	%Δ	149.86	216.09	46.99
Coal output	%Δ	–55.03	–62.47	–29.28
Electricity price	%Δ	19.46	26.90	6.60
Electricity output	%Δ	–16.43	–21.74	–6.17
Oil price	%Δ	15.06	22.37	4.45
Oil output	%Δ	–12.35	–17.63	–3.90

to double. Coal users, particularly electric utilities, find it increasingly difficult to substitute away from coal. Thus, larger reductions in carbon emissions require progressively larger reductions in oil use. From scenario 4 to scenario 2, for example, the drop in oil use more than triples.

Use of carbon tax revenues

Even a modest carbon tax would raise substantial revenue. In the simulations above we assumed the proceeds were returned to households by a lump-sum rebate. This is probably not the most likely use of the revenue, nor is it likely to be the best use given that the federal budget deficit is large and that other government revenue is raised by distortionary taxes. Using the revenue to reduce a distortionary tax would lower the net cost of the carbon tax by removing inefficiency elsewhere in the economy.

To determine how large this efficiency improvement might be we constructed three simulations based on EMF 12 scenario 7. In each simulation we impose a carbon tax of $15 per ton in 1990 with the rate rising by 5% annually in subsequent years. The simulations differ in how the revenue was used. In the first simulation the revenue was returned to households by a lump-sum rebate; in the second it was used to lower taxes on labor; and in the third it was used to lower taxes on capital. Table 5 reports results from the three simulations.

The GNP results in Table 5 show that the disposition of revenue from a carbon tax has a very significant effect on its overall impact. In the lump-sum case, output in 2020 drops by 1.70% relative to the base case. When the revenue is returned by lowering the tax on labor the loss of GNP is less than half as much: only 0.69%. The improvement is due to an increase in employment brought about by the drop in the wedge between before- and after-tax wages. If the revenue were returned as a reduction in taxes on capital, GNP would actually increase above its base case level by 1.10%. In this case, the gain is due to accelerated capital formation generated by an increase in the after-tax rate of return on investment. These results suggest that a carbon tax would provide an opportunity for significant tax reform.

Table 5 Selected results of revenue experiments in 2020

Variable	Unit	Revenue Policy		
		Lump	Labor	Capital
Carbon emissions	%Δ	–32.24	–32.09	–31.65
Carbon tax	$/t	64.83	64.83	64.83
Price of capital	%Δ	0.97	–1.86	0.23
Capital stock	%Δ	–2.13	–1.36	1.89
Tax revenue	$B	79.65	79.82	80.35
Real GNP	%Δ	–1.70	–0.69	1.10
Coal price	%Δ	143.49	140.57	142.06
Coal output	%Δ	–54.14	–54.19	–53.45
Electricity price	%Δ	18.57	15.97	16.99
Electricity output	%Δ	–15.93	–15.37	–14.66
Oil price	%Δ	14.20	12.28	14.55
Oil output	%Δ	–11.92	–11.54	–11.39

Sensitivity to base case assumptions

Most EMF 12 scenarios required carbon dioxide emissions to be held indefinitely at a specified absolute level, such as that prevailing in 1990. In general, uncontrolled emissions will rise at the overall rate of economic growth less adjustments for increasing fossil fuel prices and energy-saving technical change. Achieving a fixed target in the face of continuously rising baseline emissions will require a growing carbon tax. At each point in time, the magnitude of the tax will depend on the size of the gap between uncontrolled emissions and the target. The more rapid the growth of uncontrolled emissions, the larger will be the gap and hence the larger will be the tax needed to keep emissions constant.

The growth of carbon emissions is determined by productivity growth, the rate of capital accumulation, the rate of labor supply growth, any energy-saving biases in technical change, and the path of world oil prices. For most models participating in EMF 12, many of these factors were exogenous. In fact, the EMF 12 study design includes a specified, exogenous GNP growth rate for each region. In our model, however, productivity growth, capital accumulation, and biases in the rate of technical change are all endogenous. Moreover, productivity growth and biased technical change occur at the level of individual industries rather than at the level of the economy as a whole. Thus, GNP growth is fundamentally endogenous in our model.

This difference in the treatment of growth makes direct comparisons of our results with those of the other EMF 12 participants difficult. Our base case estimate of US growth is substantially below the rate specified in the EMF 12 study design. As a result, our base case path of carbon emissions rises more slowly than it would if growth were faster. Thus, the carbon taxes needed to hold emissions at a fixed absolute level will tend to be lower in our model. To allow our results to be compared more easily with those of the other participants, and to explore the importance of GNP growth in general, EMF 12 scenario 12 was designed. Scenario 12 was identical to scenario 2 (a 20% reduction of emissions below 1990 levels), except that the growth rate of US GNP was set to the value predicted by our base case simulation. Thus, the results of other participants could be directly compared with ours.

The principle finding of scenario 12 was that the carbon taxes and GNP loss predicted by other participants dropped sharply. Comparing our results for scenario 2 to the scenario 12 results of others, our carbon tax moves from being particularly low to being near the middle of the group. Our prediction for loss of GNP due to the tax moves from the middle of the group to among the highest. This is precisely what might be expected given that our initial growth rate was relatively low. Our model incorporates stronger intertemporal links between current carbon taxes, capital accumulation, and productivity growth than most of the other models. Thus, our model should generate higher GNP losses than the others. Scenario 12 shows that after adjusting for base case emissions growth, this is in fact the case. More generally, scenario 12 emphasizes that overall economic growth will have a profound effect on the cost of controlling carbon dioxide emissions.

Conclusion

In summary, our approach to EMF 12 has three features that distinguish it from others: our model is disaggregated to the level of individual industries, our behavioral parameters are obtained by econometric estimation, and productivity growth and biased technical change are endogenous in our model. These features allow us to investigate several aspects of carbon taxes that other EMF 12 participants were unable to examine. In particular, we find that a carbon tax will have sharply differing effects in different industries. The tax will fall most heavily on coal mining, leading to a substantial drop in coal use by electric utilities and other industries. Outside the coal industry, the main effect of the tax will be to increase the price of electricity. This will reduce productivity growth and slow the rate of capital formation, leading to slower growth of US output.

The tax needed to attain any particular emissions target will depend heavily on how fast carbon dioxide emissions would have grown in the absence of the tax. Higher rates of GNP growth will lead to higher baseline emissions and will thus require higher carbon taxes. In addition, to achieve larger reductions in carbon emissions will require sharply increasing carbon taxes and will produce markedly higher losses of output.

Finally, a carbon tax large enough to have much effect on carbon emissions will raise considerable revenue. How this revenue is used will affect the overall economic burden of the tax. If the revenue were used to reduce distortionary taxes elsewhere in the economy, the impact of the tax on GNP would be reduced. In fact, it is possible that GNP would actually increase if the revenue were used to reduce taxes on capital.

Notes

1. In other words, consumers and firms will conserve energy as it becomes more expensive.
2. For more detail on the specification of the model or the base case simulation, see Jorgenson and Wilcoxen (1990b).
3. Data on inter-industry transactions are based on input–output tables for the US constructed by the Bureau of Economic Analysis (1984). Income data are from the US national income and product accounts, also developed by the Bureau of Economic Analysis (1986). The data on capital and labor services are described by Jorgenson (1990). Additional details are given by Wilcoxen (1988; Appendix C) and Ho (1989).
4. A detailed discussion of our econometric methodology is presented by Jorgenson (1984, 1986).
5. Our approach to endogenous productivity growth was originated by Jorgenson and Fraumeni (1981).
6. Full wealth is defined to be the sum of financial wealth, the present value of future labor earnings, and the imputed value of leisure time.
7. Details on the econometric methodology are given by Jorgenson (1984). Additional details are provided by Wilcoxen (1988) and Ho (1989).
8. The capital income of government enterprises is endogenous while non-tax receipts are exogenous.
9. This is the Armington (1969) approach. See Wilcoxen (1988) and Ho (1989) for further details on our implementation of this approach.
10. We take foreign income to be exogenous.
11. The data is taken from Energy Information Administration (1990).
12. Environmental Protection Agency (1990) internal memorandum.
13. To convert to tons of carbon dioxide, multiply by 3.67.
14. A more detailed discussion of the base case is given by Jorgenson and Wilcoxen (1992).
15. Our breakdown of the US population by age, sex, and educational attainment is based on the system of demographic accounts compiled by Jorgenson and Fraumeni (1989).
16. As noted above, our population projection is based on forecasts made by the Social Security Administration in which population growth approaches zero early in the twenty-first century.
17. All dollar amounts are in 1990 prices.

References

Armington, Paul S. (1969), "The Geographic Pattern of Trade and the Effects of Price Changes", *IMF Staff Papers*, 16: 176–99.

Bureau of Economic Analysis (1984), "The Input–Output Structure of the US Economy, 1977", *Survey of Current Business*, 64: 42–79.

Bureau of Economic Analysis (1986), *The Income and Product Accounts of the United States, 1929–1982: Statistical Tables*, Washington: US Department of Commerce.

Energy Information Administration (1990), *Annual Energy Review 1990*, Washington: US Department of Energy.

Environmental Protection Agency (1990), "Internal Memorandum on Carbon Emissions Coefficients."

Ho, Mun S. (1989), "The Effects of External Linkages on US Economic Growth: A Dynamic General Equilibrium Analysis", Ph.D. Dissertation, Harvard University.

Hogan, William W. and Dale W. Jorgenson (1991), "Productivity Trends and the Costs of Reducing Carbon Dioxide Emissions", *The Energy Journal*, 12: 67–85.

Jorgenson, Dale W. (1984), "Econometric Methods for Applied General Equilibrium Analysis", in Herbert E. Scarf and John B. Shoven, eds., *Applied General Equilibrium Analysis*, Cambridge: Cambridge University Press, 139–203.

Jorgenson, Dale W. (1986), "Econometric Methods for Modeling Producer Behavior", in Zvi Griliches and Michael D. Intriligator, eds., *Handbook of Econometrics*, Vol. 3, Amsterdam: North-Holland, 1841–915.

Jorgenson, Dale W. (1989), "Capital as a Factor of Production", in Dale W. Jorgenson and Ralph Landau, eds., *Technology and Capital Formation*, Cambridge: MIT Press, 1–35.

Jorgenson, Dale W. (1990), "Productivity and Economic Growth", in E.R. Berndt and J. Triplett, eds., *Fifty Years of Economic Measurement*, Chicago: University of Chicago Press, 19–118.

Jorgenson, Dale W. and Barbara M. Fraumeni (1981), "Relative Prices and Technical Change", in E.R. Berndt and B. Field, eds., *Modeling and Measuring Natural Resource Substitution*, Cambridge: MIT Press, 17–47.

Jorgenson, Dale W. and Barbara M. Fraumeni (1989), "The Accumulation of Human and Nonhuman Capital, 1948–1984", in R.E. Lipsey and H.S. Tice, eds., *The Measurement of Saving, Investment, and Wealth*, Chicago: University of Chicago Press, 227–82.

Jorgenson, Dale W. and Peter J. Wilcoxen (1990), "Intertemporal General Equilibrium Modeling of US Environmental Regulation", *Journal of Policy Modeling*, 12: 715–44.

Jorgenson, Dale W. and Peter J. Wilcoxen (1992), "Reducing US Carbon Dioxide Emissions: The Cost of Different Goals", in John R. Moroney, ed., *Advances in the Economics of Energy and Natural Resources*, Vol. 7, Greenwich: JAI Press, 125–58.

Jorgenson, Dale W., Laurence J. Lau, and Thomas M. Stoker (1982), "The Transcendental Logarithmic Model of Aggregate Consumer Behavior", in R.L. Basmann and G. Rhodes, eds., *Advances in Econometrics*, Vol. 1, Greenwich: JAI Press, 97–238.

Manne, Alan S. and Richard G. Richels (1992), *Buying Greenhouse Insurance: The Economic Costs of CO_2 Emissions Limits*, Cambridge: MIT Press.

Wilcoxen, Peter J. (1988), "The Effects of Environmental Regulation and Energy Prices on US Economic Performance", Ph.D. Dissertation, Harvard University.

[18]

COSTS OF ENVIRONMENTALLY MOTIVATED TAXES IN THE PRESENCE OF OTHER TAXES: GENERAL EQUILIBRIUM ANALYSES

A. LANS BOVENBERG* &
LAWRENCE H. GOULDER**

Abstract - *This paper employs analytical and numerical general equilibrium models to evaluate environmentally motivated tax policies, concentrating on whether the gross costs of these policies can be eliminated when revenues from the taxes are devoted to cuts in marginal income tax rates. Our analytical model shows that the prospects for a zero-or-negative-cost environmental tax reform depend on the magnitudes of prior inefficiencies in the relative taxation of labor and capital and on the extent to which reforms shift the tax burden from the more efficient (overtaxed) to the less efficient (undertaxed) factor. Numerical simulations indicate that the revenue-neutral substitution of BTU or gasoline taxes for typical income taxes usually entails positive gross costs to the economy. In the case of the gasoline tax, a significant tax-shifting effect lowers the policy's gross costs. This explains the lower costs of the gasoline tax compared with the BTU tax, despite its narrower base. Under neither policy is tax shifting substantial enough to eliminate the overall gross costs.*

INTRODUCTION

Interest in taxes as instruments of environmental protection has grown considerably in recent years. In many industrialized countries, environmentally motivated taxes either have been introduced recently or are being seriously contemplated. The actual and potential reforms include taxes on fossil fuels (such as carbon taxes and fossil-fuel-based BTU taxes) and taxes on gasoline.

The most important rationale for these taxes is their potential to provide environmental benefits by raising the prices of environmentally damaging activities and thereby reducing the levels of such activities. However, several analysts have pointed out recently that

*CPB Netherlands Bureau for Economic Analysis, 2508 GM Den Haag, The Netherlands.
**Department of Economics, Stanford University, Stanford, CA 94305.

these taxes might confer additional benefits, particularly if the environmental taxes are introduced in a revenue-neutral fashion. A number of authors, including Terkla (1984), Lee and Misiolek (1986), Pearce (1991), Oates (1993), Repetto *et al.* (1992), Ballard and Medema (1993), and Poterba (1993), have emphasized that the revenues from environmental taxes can be used to finance reductions in the marginal rates of other, distortionary taxes. In this way, an environmental tax reform could help reduce the distortionary costs associated with existing taxes. In this connection, Pearce indicated that environmental taxes might offer a "double dividend": not only might they improve the environment but they might also reduce certain costs of the overall tax system.

The second "dividend" has several possible interpretations. Some policy analysts have endorsed a strong notion, contending that the revenue-neutral swap of environmental taxes for ordinary income taxes involves negative gross costs.[1] This assertion is equivalent to the claim that whatever gross costs are directly associated with the introduction of an environmental tax are offset entirely by the cost savings stemming from the cuts in ordinary taxes, so that the gross cost of the revenue-neutral tax swap is actually negative. In a world where the magnitudes of the *benefits* from environmental taxes are highly uncertain, the idea that revenue-neutral environmental taxes involve negative costs is appealing; for if the costs are negative, one needs to establish only the *sign* (as opposed to magnitude) of the environmental benefits to be able to justify the tax swap on benefit-cost grounds. The reduction in information requirements is quite attractive, given the substantial uncertainties about magnitudes of environmental benefits.

This paper employs both analytical and numerical general equilibrium models to investigate the costs of revenue-neutral environmentally motivated tax reforms. We examine the extent to which the costs of environmental taxes are reduced when the revenues from these taxes are devoted to cuts in marginal income tax rates. Earlier analytical work[2] has tended to cast doubt on the possibility of the second dividend, emphasizing that environmental taxes are *implicit* taxes on labor and that, as a result, the revenue-neutral substitution of an environmental tax for a tax on labor usually does not reduce labor's tax burden.[3] Indeed, in these models, such a tax swap usually *increases* labor's tax burden because the environmental tax is less efficient in terms of raising revenue than an explicit labor tax. These considerations militate against the second dividend. However, these models usually consider only one primary productive factor (labor), and this restricts the scope for the second dividend. The first main contribution of this paper is to develop an analytical model that, in contrast with earlier models, allows for two primary factors of production—labor and capital. The generalization is important since it introduces a channel through which a revenue-neutral tax policy can shift the burden of taxes across the two factors. As shown later in this paper, tax shifting can enhance the prospects for the second dividend.

The second main contribution of this paper is to apply a numerical general equilibrium model to examine closely two environmentally motivated tax reforms, a BTU tax and a gasoline tax increase. The numerical model enables us to employ a realistic specification of taxes and to adopt a fairly detailed representation of production and demand. Outcomes from the numerical model are interpreted in light of the results from the analytical model. We find that the revenue-neutral substitution of a BTU or gasoline tax for typical income taxes usually entails positive gross costs. In the case of the gasoline tax increase, a significant tax-shifting effect serves to lower the policy's gross costs. This accounts for the lower gross cost of the gasoline tax compared with the BTU tax, despite the narrower base of the gasoline tax. At the same time, under a range of specifications for revenue-replacement methods, pre-existing tax rates, and parameter values, gross costs remain positive—the second dividend fails to materialize. Only under "unusual" combinations of parameter values and recycling methods is the tax-shifting effect strong enough to overcome the so-called tax burden effect, that is, the adverse cost impact associated with the relatively narrow bases of environmental taxes.

The rest of the paper is organized as follows. The next section presents the analytical model and its results. The third section describes the numerical model, while the fourth section presents its results. The final section offers conclusions.

COSTS OF REVENUE-NEUTRAL ENVIRONMENTAL TAX REFORMS: ANALYTICAL RESULTS

The Model

Here, we develop a simple model of an economy in which firms maximize profits under perfect competition. Production is described by a constant-elasticity-of-substitution (CES) production function $F(L,K,R)$ with the constant substitution elasticity σ. In contrast with earlier analytical models of the double-dividend issue (see Bovenberg and de Mooij, 1994), two (rather than one) primary nonpolluting production factors enter production: labor (L) and (clean) capital (K). The "polluting resource," R, harms environmental quality: $E = e(R)$, with $e_R < 0$, where the subscript denotes a partial derivative. R can be interpreted as the use of fossil fuels in production.[4]

The representative household maximizes utility $u[m(C,1-L),G,E]$.[5] The composite m of private consumption (C) and leisure $(1-L)$ is homothetic and weakly separable from public goods G and E, which denote public consumption and environmental quality. The household budget constraint is

1

$$C = wL + p_K\bar{K} + p_R\bar{R}$$

where $\bar{K}$ and $\bar{R}$ stand for the domestic endowments of (clean) capital and the polluting resource. We regard the economy as small and open. Whereas labor is immobile, capital and the polluting resource are mobile internationally. Hence, while the consumer wage, w, is endogenous, the required return on the world capital market p_K and the world market price of the polluting resource p_R are exogenous.[6]

The government budget constraint amounts to

2

$$G = t_K p_K K + t_R p_R R + t_L wL$$

where t_L, t_K, and t_R stand for the tax rates on labor, capital, and the polluting input, respectively. We assume (without loss of generality) that the consumption commodity is untaxed. Equilibrium on the balance of payments is given by

3

$$F(L,K,R) = G + p_K(K - \bar{K}) + p_R(R - \bar{R}) + C.$$

The welfare effects of a revenue-neutral change in the tax mix (i.e., a change in taxes such that $dG = 0$) are given by (see Appendix A)

4

$$\frac{du}{u_c} = -\frac{u_E}{u_c}[(-e_R)dR] + Ldw$$

where subscripts denote partial derivatives with respect to a particular variable. The first term at the right-hand side of equation 4 is the first (environmental) dividend, that is, the welfare effect of changes in environmental quality. The second term, which is the change in real (after-tax wage) income enjoyed by households, represents the second, nonenvironmental (or private), dividend. A positive second dividend implies that overall tax burden declines. Hence, the gross costs[7] of attaining higher environmental quality are negative.

We now analyze an environmental tax reform in which the government raises the tax on the polluting resource and uses the revenues to cut distortionary taxes on either labor or capital, while keeping government consumption fixed. In the case where the revenues from the environmental tax are employed to cut the tax on capital income, the solutions for private welfare (i.e., consumer wages), resource demand (which is inversely related to environmental quality), and capital demand are (see Appendix B)[8]

5

$$\tilde{w} = (\theta_K - \theta_R)\omega_R\frac{\sigma}{\Delta_K}\tilde{t}_R$$

6

$$\tilde{R} = \left[-1 + (\theta_K - \theta_R)\omega_R\frac{\eta_L + \sigma}{\Delta_K}\right]\sigma\tilde{t}_R$$

7

$$\tilde{K} = \left[1 + (\theta_K - \theta_R)\frac{\eta_L\omega_K + \sigma(l - \omega_R)}{\Delta_K}\right] \cdot \sigma\frac{\omega_R}{\omega_K}\tilde{t}_R$$

where $\Delta_K \equiv (1 - \theta_L)\omega_L - \eta_L(\theta_L\omega_L + \theta_R\omega_R + \theta_K\omega_K) - (\theta_R\omega_R + \theta_K(1 - \omega_R))\sigma > 0$, and $\tilde{t}_i = dt_i/(1 + t_i)$, $i = L,K,R$. For nontax variables, a tilde stands for a relative change. η_L represents the uncompensated wage elasticity of labor supply, while ω_i and θ_i, respectively, correspond to the production share of input i ($i = L, K, R$) and the tax rate as a percentage of the before-tax price (i.e., $\theta_i \equiv t_i/(1 + t_i)$).

The corresponding solutions for the case in which labor taxes, rather than capital taxes, are cut amount to (see Appendix B)

8

$$\tilde{w} = -[\theta_K\omega_K + \theta_R(1 - \omega_K)]\frac{\omega_R}{\omega_L}\tilde{t}_R$$

9

$$\tilde{R} = -\left[(1 - \omega_K) + (\theta_K\omega_K + \theta_R(1 - \omega_K))\frac{\omega_R\eta_L}{\Delta_L}\right] \cdot \frac{1}{\omega_L}\sigma\tilde{t}_R$$

10

$$\tilde{K} = -\left[1 + (\theta_K\omega_K + \theta_R(1 - \omega_K))\frac{\eta_L}{\Delta_L}\right] \cdot \frac{\omega_R}{\omega_L}\sigma\tilde{t}_R$$

where $\Delta_L \equiv (1 - \theta_L)\,\omega_L - \eta_L\,[\theta_L\omega_L + \theta_R\omega_R + \theta_K\omega_K] > 0$.

COSTS OF ENVIRONMENTALLY MOTIVATED TAXES

Environmental Taxation in an Optimal Tax System

First, we explore the impact of environmental taxes if the initial tax system is optimal from a nonenvironmental point of view. Such a tax system involves only labor taxes because pollution and capital taxes are "inefficient"[9] instruments for raising revenues. Intuitively, just like a labor tax, pollution and capital taxes are shifted to labor in the form of lower real wages, because the supplies of the polluting resource and capital to the economy are infinitely elastic. Hence, it is less costly to impose the labor tax, which distorts only the labor market, than the resource or capital tax, which distorts not only the labor market (to the same or greater degree) but also the resource and capital markets by changing the relative prices of the resource and capital.

Introducing a *small* pollution tax in this setting produces no first-order impacts on private welfare. To see this, note from expressions 5 and 8 that $\tilde{w}$ is zero when $\theta_K = \theta_R = 0$. This result follows also from the definition of the initial optimum. If the incremental revenue-neutral substitution of taxes altered nonenvironmental welfare, such welfare could be increased by changing the levels of taxes. This would contradict the notion that the initial situation was optimal from a nonenvironmental point of view.

To examine the welfare effects of *large* pollution levies, we turn to the case in which the environmental (resource) tax is positive in the initial equilibrium (but the tax on capital is still zero). With a positive initial pollution tax, the environmental dividend comes at the cost of a negative nonenvironmental (or second) dividend. This can be seen by substituting $\theta_K = 0$ and $\theta_R > 0$ into expressions 5 and 6 for a cut in capital taxes and into expressions 8 and 9 for a cut in labor taxes. The intuition behind the negative private dividend was suggested two paragraphs earlier: from a nonenvironmental point of view, pollution taxes are less "efficient" than explicit labor taxes. Pollution taxes thus raise the overall tax burden, as measured by the drop in private incomes. This is called the *tax burden* effect (see Bovenberg, 1995). Indeed, equations 5 and 8 indicate that the higher the initial levels of pollution taxes (that is, the higher is θ_R), the larger are the marginal costs of pollution taxes in terms of the burden on private incomes. Of course, higher pollution taxes also raise the supply of environmental quality, a public good, and the benefits from this public good may justify the higher tax burden. However, this does not deny the notion that an environmental tax reform imposes costs in terms of private incomes—which is the issue at the heart of the double-dividend debate.

Environmental Taxation in a Suboptimal Tax System

We now investigate the welfare effects in a setting where the initial tax system is *not* optimal from a nonenvironmental point of view. We will see that the suboptimality of the tax system yields another channel, through which environmental taxes influence private welfare, and introduces the possibility of a positive nonenvironmental dividend. In this new setting, capital (as well as labor) taxes are positive in the initial equilibrium. Thus, from an efficiency point of view (abstracting from the environmental dimension), capital taxes are too high.[10] With positive capital taxes and zero pollution taxes in the initial equilibrium, private welfare increases if and only if the demand for capital increases (substitute $\theta_R = 0$ and $\theta_K > 0$ into expressions 5 and 7 for a cut in capital taxes and expressions 8 and 10 for a cut in labor taxes). Intuitively, capital is "overtaxed" in the initial equilibrium and therefore yields a higher before-tax value marginal product per dollar than does labor. Hence, if a revenue-neutral environmental reform were to cause an increase in the supply of the more efficient factor, private welfare would rise. To determine whether this occurs, we must specify which taxes are reduced in exchange for the increase in the pollution tax.

Lowering Capital Taxes

If the pollution tax finances a cut in capital taxes, capital demand expands, which tends to raise private welfare (see expressions 5 and 7 with $\theta_R = 0$). Intuitively, the tax that is reduced directly stimulates capital demand, while the tax that is raised (i.e., the environmental tax) does not bear directly on capital but also affects labor demand. Thus, while the capital tax directly impacts the capital market, the burden of the environmental tax is spread over both the capital and labor markets. Hence, the revenue-neutral reform package shifts the burden away from the efficient factor (capital) to the inefficient factor (labor). This makes the tax system more efficient from a nonenvironmental point of view.

The reallocation of the tax burden between the efficient and the inefficient factors will be called the *tax shifting* effect. This effect is positive if it redistributes the burden of taxation away from the overtaxed to the undertaxed factor.[11] With zero initial pollution taxes, a positive tax shifting effect is a sufficient condition for a double dividend.

With positive resource taxes in the initial equilibrium, private welfare expands if and only if the tax shifting effect dominates the tax burden effect so that the efficiency gains associated with the shift in the tax burden away from the overtaxed factor are sufficiently large to offset other gross costs from the environmental tax. This means that the environmental tax reform yields a positive effect on private (nonenvironmental) welfare if and only if it moves the overall tax system closer to its nonenvironmental optimum.

Lowering Labor Taxes

If the government cuts the labor rather than the capital tax, the introduction of pollution taxes reduces private welfare (see expression 8 with $\theta_R = 0$). Here, both the tax shifting effect and the tax burden effect harm nonenvironmental welfare. In contrast with the case where capital taxes were lowered, in this case, the tax shifting effect reduces private welfare. This occurs because the tax burden is shifted the "wrong" way—from the inefficient factor (labor) to the efficient factor (capital). Whereas only the labor market is affected directly by the tax that is cut (i.e., the labor tax), the capital market bears part of the burden of the environmental tax. Hence, the overall effect of the revenue-neutral reform is to shift the burden from labor to capital.

Observations and Caveats

The analytical model presented shows that when the initial tax system is optimal from a nonenvironmental point of view, the second, nonenvironmental, dividend fails to materialize. This accords with results of simpler models (see Bovenberg and de Mooij, 1994). By introducing a second clean input in the present model, we have been able to consider an initial situation in which the relative taxation of clean factors (capital and labor) is not optimal. In such situations, a tax-shifting effect accompanies the tax burden effect. Tax shifting can either lower or raise the attractiveness of revenue-neutral environmental tax reforms: it can shift the burden toward already overtaxed factors and thereby exacerbate inefficiencies in the tax system, or it can shift the burden the other way and thereby help alleviate initial inefficiencies. In the latter case, the double dividend becomes a possibility. These theoretical results indicate that the presence or absence of the double dividend must be settled empirically, as it depends on initial conditions, the incidence of the pollution tax, and the way that environmental tax revenues are "recycled" to the economy.

To keep the analytical model tractable, we have imposed a number of simplifying assumptions, and some caveats are in order. First, we treated supplies of capital and the polluting resource as perfectly elastic, in keeping with the assumption of a small, open economy. The assumption that capital is perfectly elastically supplied underlies the idea that capital is initially overtaxed. If capital supply is less than perfectly elastic, labor can be the overtaxed factor initially, depending on elasticities of factor supply and demand and on the tax rates. If labor is initially overtaxed, the analytical results are reversed, although the economic logic remains the same. In this situation, the revenue-neutral substitution of an environmental tax for another tax produces a beneficial tax-shifting effect (and could generate a double dividend) to the extent that it helps shift the burden *away from* labor.

Bovenberg and van der Ploeg (1994) analyze this issue in a model in which capital is supplied perfectly *in*elastically. Their results complement those derived above in reinforcing the notion that the nature of the initial inefficiency (which factor is overtaxed) and the direction of tax shifting are key channels for assessing the double dividend.

The analytical model also abstracted from complications such as sectoral disaggregation, intermediate inputs, and dynamics. The numerical model incorporates these features. We find that the key features identified by the simpler analytical model—the tax shifting and tax burden effects—can largely explain the effects of revenue-neutral environmental tax reforms in the more complex numerical model.

BASIC FEATURES OF THE NUMERICAL MODEL

This section sketches out the main features of the numerical model. Some details on the model's structure and parameters are offered in Appendix C. A more complete description is contained in Goulder (1992). Cruz and Goulder (1992) provide data documentation.

The model is an intertemporal general equilibrium model of the U.S. economy with international trade. It generates paths of equilibrium prices, outputs, and incomes for the U.S. economy and the "rest of the world" under specified policy scenarios. All variables are calculated at yearly intervals beginning in the 1990 benchmark year and usually extending to the year 2070.

The model is unique in combining a fairly realistic treatment of the U.S. tax system and a detailed representation of energy production and demand. It incorporates quite specific tax instruments and addresses effects of taxation along a number of important dimensions; these include firms' investment incentives, equity values, and profits[12] and household consumption, saving, and labor supply decisions. The specification of energy supply incorporates the nonrenewable nature of crude petroleum and natural gas and the transitions from conventional to synthetic fuels.

Industry and Consumer Good Disaggregation

U.S. production divides into the 13 industries indicated in Table 1. The energy industries consist of coal mining, crude petroleum and natural gas extraction, petroleum refining, synthetic fuels, electric utilities, and gas utilities. The model distinguishes the 17 consumer goods listed in Table 1.

TABLE 1
INDUSTRY AND CONSUMER GOOD CATEGORIES

Industries:

1. Agriculture and Non-Coal Mining
2. Coal Mining
3. Crude Petroleum and Natural Gas
4. Synthetic Fuels
5. Petroleum Refining
6. Electric Utilities
7. Gas Utilities
8. Construction
9. Metals and Machinery
10. Motor Vehicles
11. Miscellaneous Manufacturing
12. Services (except housing)
13. Housing Services

Consumer Goods:

1. Food
2. Alcohol
3. Tobacco
4. Utilities
5. Housing Services
6. Furnishings
7. Appliances
8. Clothing and Jewelry
9. Transportation
10. Motor Vehicles
11. Services (except financial)
12. Financial Services
13. Recreation, Reading, and Miscellaneous
14. Nondurable, Non-Food Household Expenditure
15. Gasoline and Other Fuels
16. Education
17. Health

Producer Behavior

General Specifications

In each industry, a nested production structure accounts for substitution between different forms of energy as well as between energy and other inputs. Each industry produces a distinct output (X), which is a function of the inputs of labor (L), capital (K), an energy composite (E), and a materials composite (M), as well as the current level of investment (I):

11

$$X = f[g(L,K),h(E,M)] - \phi(I/K) \cdot I.$$

The energy composite is made up of the outputs of the six energy industries, while the materials composite consists of the outputs of the other industries:

12

$$E = E(\overline{x}_2,\overline{x}_3 + \overline{x}_4,\overline{x}_5,\overline{x}_6,\overline{x}_7)$$

13

$$M = M(\overline{x}_1,\overline{x}_8,\ldots,\overline{x}_{13})$$

where $\overline{x}_i$ is a composite of domestically produced and foreign made input i.[13] Industry indices correspond to those in Table 1.

Managers of firms choose input quantities and investment levels to maximize the values of their firms. The investment decision takes into account the adjustment (or installation) costs represented by $\phi(I/K) \cdot I$ in equation 11. ϕ is a convex function of the rate of investment, I/K.[14]

Special Features of the Oil and Gas and Synfuels Industries

The production structure in the oil and gas industry is somewhat more complex than in other industries to account for the nonrenewable nature of oil and gas stocks. The production specification is

14

$$X = \gamma(Z) \cdot f[g(L,K),h(E,M)] - \phi(I/K) \cdot I$$

where γ is a decreasing function of Z, the amount of cumulative extraction of oil and gas up to the beginning of the current period. This captures the idea that, as Z rises (or, equivalently, as reserves are depleted), it becomes increasingly difficult to extract oil and gas resources, so that greater quantities of K, L, E, and M are required to achieve any given level of extraction (output). Increasing production costs ultimately induce oil and gas producers to remove their capital from this industry.[15]

The model incorporates a synthetic fuel—shale oil—as a backstop resource, a perfect substitute for oil and gas. The technology for producing synthetic fuels on a commercial scale is assumed to become known in 2010. Thus, capital formation in the synfuels industry cannot begin until that year.

All domestic prices in the model are endogenous, except for the domestic price of oil and gas.[16] The path of oil and gas prices follows the assumptions of the Stanford Energy Modeling Forum.[17] The supply of imported oil and gas is taken to be perfectly elastic at the world price. As long as imports are the marginal source of supply to the domestic economy, domestic producers of oil and gas receive the world price (adjusted for tariffs or taxes) for their own output. However, rising oil and gas prices stimulate investment in synfuels. Eventually, synfuels production plus domestic oil and gas supply together satisfy all of the domestic demand. Synfuels then become the marginal source of supply, so that the cost of synfuels production, rather than the world oil price, dictates the domestic price of fuels.[18]

Household Behavior

Consumption, labor supply, and saving result from the decisions of a representative household maximizing its intertemporal utility, defined on leisure and overall consumption in each period. The utility function is homothetic and leisure and consumption are weakly separable (see Appendix C). The household faces an intertemporal budget constraint requiring that the present value of consumption not exceed potential total wealth (nonhuman wealth plus the present value of labor and transfer income). In each period, overall consumption of goods and services is allocated across the 17 specific categories of consumption goods or services shown in Table 1. Each of the 17 consumption goods or services is a composite of a domestically and foreign-produced consumption good (or service) of that type. Households substitute between domestic and foreign goods to minimize the cost of obtaining a given composite.

The Government Sector

The government collects taxes, distributes transfers, and purchases goods and services (outputs of the 13 industries). The tax instruments include energy taxes, output taxes, the corporate income tax, property taxes, sales taxes, and taxes on individual labor and capital income. In the benchmark year, 1990, the government deficit amounts to approximately two percent of gross domestic product. In the reference case (or status quo) simulation, the real deficit grows at the steady-state growth rate given by the growth of potential labor services. In the policy-change cases, we require that real government spending and the real deficit follow the same paths as those in the reference case. To make the policy changes revenue neutral, we accompany the tax rate increases that define the various policies with reductions in other net taxes, either on a lump-sum basis (increased exogenous transfers) or through reductions in marginal tax rates.

Foreign Trade

Except for oil and gas imports, imported intermediate and consumer goods are imperfect substitutes for their domestic counterparts.[19] Import prices are exogenous in foreign currency, but the domestic-currency price changes with variations in the exchange rate. Export demands are modeled as functions of the foreign price of U.S. exports and the level of foreign income (in foreign currency). The exchange rate adjusts to balance trade in every period.

Equilibrium and Growth

The solution of the model is a general equilibrium in which supplies and demands balance in all markets at each period of time. The requirements of the general equilibrium are that supply equal demand for labor inputs and for all produced goods,[20] that firms' demands for loanable funds match the aggregate supply by households, and that the government's tax revenues equal its spending less the current deficit. These conditions are met through adjustments in output prices, in the market interest rate, and in lump-sum taxes or marginal tax rates.[21]

Economic growth reflects the growth of capital stocks and of potential labor resources. The growth of capital stocks stems from endogenous saving and investment behavior. Potential labor resources are specified as increasing at an exogenous rate.

RESULTS FROM THE NUMERICAL MODEL

Here, we present the numerical model's assessment of the costs of environmentally motivated taxes in the presence of distortionary taxes. We concentrate on the gross efficiency costs of environmentally motivated taxes relative to "traditional" income taxes of equal revenue yield. This issue underlies the question of whether the revenue-neutral substitution of an environmental tax for an existing traditional tax implies gross costs overall.

Policies Considered

We examine the following four policies:

1. *A BTU tax*. This is a tax imposed on oil, natural gas, and coal in proportion to the BTU content of these fuels. The tax rate is 0.45 per million BTUs. The same tax rates apply to imported fuels as to their domestically produced counterparts. Exports of fuels are exempt from the tax.
2. *An increase in the gasoline tax (GAS)*. This is a specific, or per-unit, tax on the purchases of gasoline by consumers. "Gasoline and other fuels" is one of the 17 consumer goods distinguished in the model. The gasoline tax applies to household purchases of this good. This tax is increased to

0.692 per gallon from its original or benchmark value of 0.287 per gallon.

3. *An increase in marginal rates of the personal income tax* (PIT). The model includes marginal tax rates on individual wage income, dividend income, interest income, and capital gains income. These are the average marginal rates that apply in the benchmark year, 1994. The benchmark marginal rates on wage income, dividend income, interest income, and capital gains income are 0.230, 0.229, 0.229, and 0.057, respectively. Under this policy change, each of these rates is increased by 1.9 percent.
4. *An increase in the corporate income tax rate* (CIT). Here, the marginal rate on corporate profits is increased to 0.399 from its initial value of 0.385.

The first two policies fall in the category of environmentally motivated taxes. These are taxes on fuels rather than direct taxes on emissions. Other things equal, emissions taxes are preferable to fuel taxes as means of correcting externalities associated with emissions; in practice, however, monitoring and enforcement difficulties have tended to limit the use of emissions taxes.

To assess the effects of these taxes, we compare results under each simulated policy change with results from a baseline or reference case simulation (which assumes no change in tax policy). In the baseline simulation, all tax rates remain constant through time. All policies phase in the new tax rates over a three-year period, beginning in 1994.

Each policy is introduced in a revenue-neutral fashion: the path of tax revenues under each policy is made identical to the revenue path in the baseline. Revenue neutrality is achieved either through lump-sum reductions in personal income taxes or through reductions in the marginal tax rates on individual income.

For comparability, the tax changes under each policy are scaled to imply the same gross revenue impact—the same revenue yield, abstracting from the revenue-preserving reductions in other taxes. The gross revenue impact of these policies, over the infinite time horizon, is $1084 billion in present value. Over the first five years, these taxes yield gross revenues ranging from 55 to 69 billion 1990 dollars.

Simulation Results

Differences in Aggregate Economic Impacts

We begin by examining policies involving lump-sum replacement of revenues. Figures 1a–1c show the effects of the alternative policies on real gross national product (GNP), consumption, and investment. The figures indicate the percentage change in these variables relative to a reference case involving no policy change. The first year corresponds to 1995.

Figure 1a compares the GNP effects. Within the first nine years following implementation, the BTU and gasoline taxes imply larger reductions in GNP than the income tax alternatives. For example, in the year 2000 (five years after implementation), the BTU and gas taxes entail GNP reductions (relative to baseline) of about 0.21 and 0.18 percent, as compared with 0.15 and 0.08 percent under the personal and corporate tax increases. The GNP costs of the BTU tax remain larger than those

NATIONAL TAX JOURNAL VOL. L NO. 1

FIGURE 1. Aggregate Effects of Energy and Income Tax Policies; Revenue Replacement via Lump-Sum Tax Cuts (Percentage Changes from Reference Case)

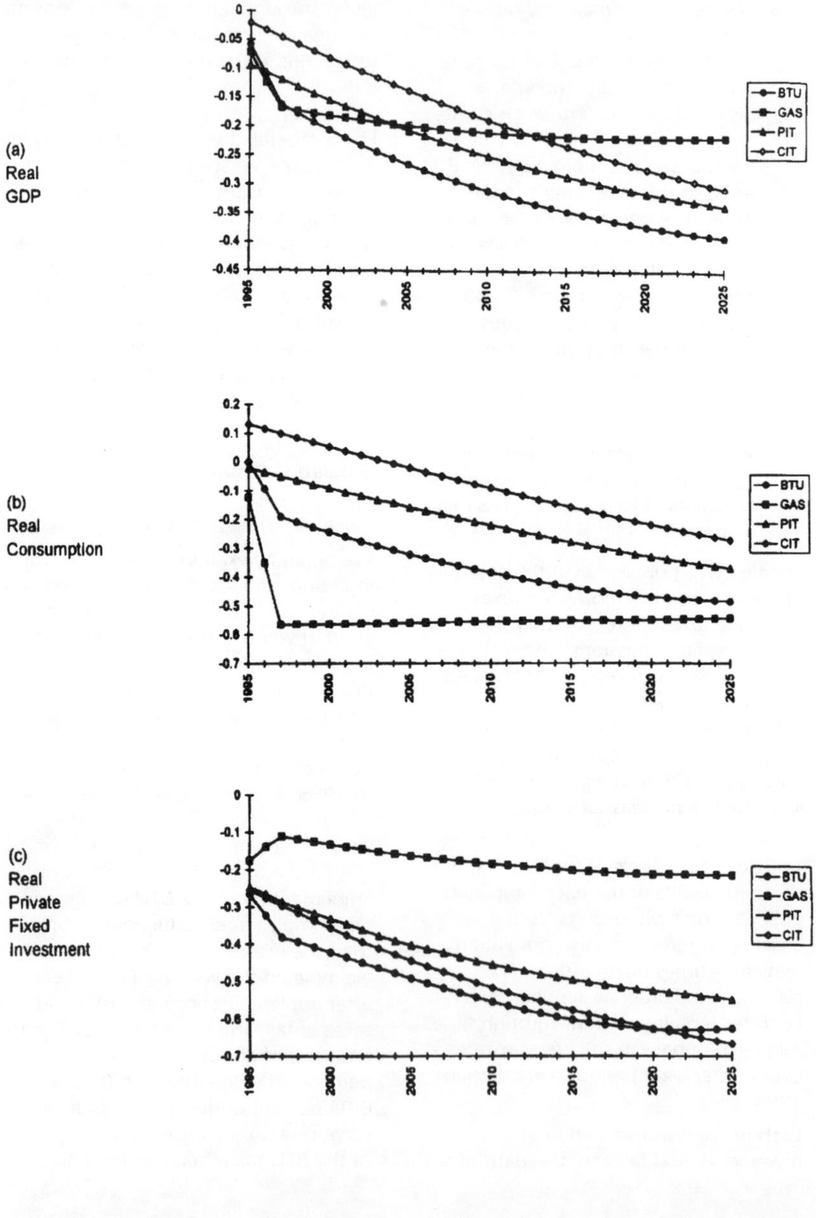

of the income tax alternatives. In contrast, the GNP costs of the gasoline tax eventually become smaller than those of the personal tax increase. The relatively benign long-term GNP impact of the gasoline tax reflects its more favorable impact on investment, as discussed below.

The impacts on consumption are compared in Figure 1b. As with the GNP losses, the losses in consumption are greatest for the energy tax policies. However, in contrast with the GNP results, the losses here are greater for the gasoline tax than the BTU tax. While the BTU tax raises the costs of production for intermediate, capital, and consumer goods, the gasoline tax targets only consumption. Thus, in comparison with the BTU tax, the gasoline tax yields GNP losses more in the form of reduced consumption than reduced investment.

Figure 1c contrasts the investment impacts. The investment losses of the gasoline tax are less severe than those of any of the other policies. Hence, the path of the capital stock is higher under the gasoline tax than under the other policies. This helps explain why, over time, the GNP path under the gasoline tax improves relative to the paths under the other policies.

Another way to examine the relative costs of the environmental and income taxes is to simulate policies in which an environmental tax replaces (at the margin) an income tax in a revenue-neutral fashion. Figures 2a–2c show results from such simulations. The simulations involve the same tax increases as above for the BTU, gasoline, and corporate taxes, but here the tax revenues are used to finance reductions in marginal rates of the personal income tax rather than lump-sum tax reductions. By comparing the results in figures 2a–2c with those of figures 1a–1c, one can observe that the effects from the new simulations involving personal income tax cuts are approximately the same as what would be obtained if one subtracted the effects of the personal income tax in Figures 1a–1c from the effects of the relevant other tax in those figures. The impacts of the component tax changes are close to additive.

We assess the aggregate (gross) welfare impact from these policies by employing the equivalent variation measure, which translates changes in utility from a given policy into a dollar equivalent.[22] Table 2 displays the welfare costs per dollar of revenue raised for each of the four policies.

The results in Table 2 for policies with lump-sum replacement indicate that the environmentally motivated taxes involve larger welfare costs than the income tax alternatives. Correspondingly, the results with replacement through personal income tax cuts indicate that a revenue-neutral swap of an environmental tax for a (marginal) reduction in the personal income tax involves costs overall: the environmental taxes fail to generate a second (double) dividend.

With lump-sum replacement, the cost of the personal income tax is about 57 percent of the cost of the BTU tax and 63 percent of the cost of the gasoline tax. Correspondingly, when the energy taxes are combined with revenue-preserving cuts in the income tax, welfare costs fall by about 40 percent relative to the case with lump-sum revenue replacement.[23] The BTU tax involves the highest welfare cost per dollar of revenue.

FIGURE 2. Aggregate Effects of Energy and Income Tax Policies; Revenue Replacement via Personal Income Tax Cuts (Percentage Changes from Reference Case)

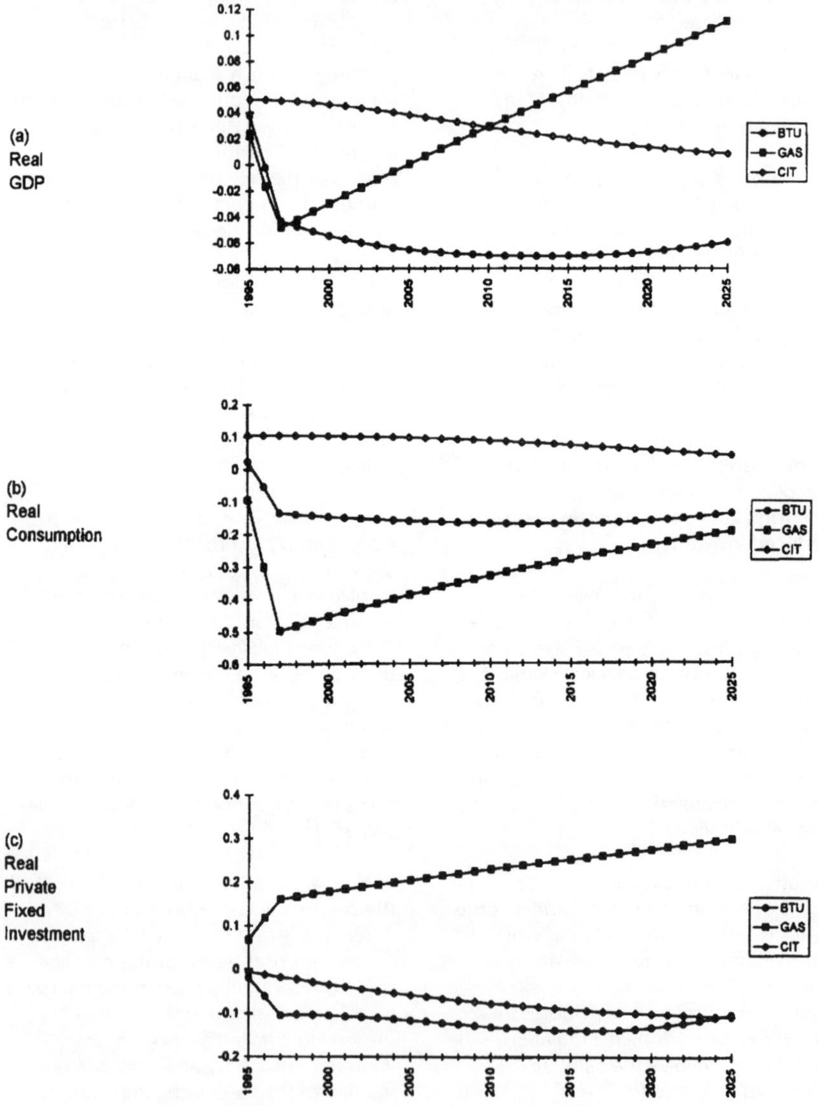

COSTS OF ENVIRONMENTALLY MOTIVATED TAXES

TABLE 2
WELFARE IMPACTS

	Welfare Cost per Dollar of Revenue	
	Lump-Sum Tax Replacement	Personal Income Tax Replacement
BTU tax	0.656	0.318
Consumer-level gasoline tax increase	0.594	0.253
Personal income tax increase	0.379	—
Corporate income tax increase	0.438	0.093

Explaining the "Excess Costs" of Environmental Taxes

A main result from these experiments is that the environmentally motivated taxes generate larger gross costs per dollar than income taxes. To what can these excess costs be attributed? The excess costs are consistent with analytical results by Bovenberg and de Mooij (1994) and Bovenberg and van der Ploeg (1994); these studies show that environmentally motivated taxes are implicit factor taxes that introduce comparable factor market distortions to those of income taxes, while introducing additional distortions into intermediate input choice (BTU tax) or consumer good choice (gasoline tax).[24]

The analytical model of the present paper introduced a further consideration, however: it showed that if initially the tax system is inefficient from a non-environmental point of view, the excess costs of an environmental tax may be reduced or even eliminated if the environmental tax poses a larger burden on the relatively inefficient (or relatively lightly taxed) factor than the tax it replaces. Equivalently, the costs of a revenue-neutral environmental tax reform are reduced to the extent that such substitution manages to shift the tax burden away from the highly taxed (efficient) factor. The costs of the revenue-neutral policy may even be negative: the double dividend is a possibility.

In the numerical model, labor is relatively lightly taxed in the sense that the marginal excess burden (MEB) per dollar of revenue raised is higher for the capital income tax than for the labor tax. In particular, under central case values for parameters, the MEB is \$0.43 for the capital income tax and \$0.31 for the labor income tax. Most numerical studies of the relative efficiency costs of labor and capital taxes in the U.S. economy obtain the same qualitative result.[25] This means that environmental taxes that fall heavily on labor (relative to the income tax) may have relatively low excess costs.

This information helps to explain the differences in the excess costs of the BTU and gasoline taxes. Table 3 shows the factor tax burden of the BTU, gasoline, and personal taxes, "alone" (that is, with lump-sum replacement of revenues) and in combination. The table also displays associated effects on equilibrium factor supplies. As indicated by effects on the returns to labor and capital, the burden of the gasoline tax falls primarily on labor,[26] while that of the BTU tax is shared more evenly by capital and labor. When the gasoline tax is used to finance reductions in the personal income tax, the real wage falls between 0.3 and 0.7 percent and the real return to capital increases from about 0.1 to 0.2 percent; in contrast, substituting the BTU tax for the income tax leads to less pronounced declines in the real wage and to reductions in the real return to capital. Thus, in an economy where labor is initially taxed relatively lightly, the gasoline tax reform leads to tax shifting that mitigates its

TABLE 3
IMPACTS OF TAXES ON FACTOR PRICES AND SUPPLIES
(PERCENTAGE CHANGES FROM BASELINE)

	Years after Policy Introduction			
	1	2	5	30
"Single-Tax" Policies:				
BTU tax, lump-sum replacement				
w	–0.250	–0.390	–0.446	–0.655
r	–0.083	–0.239	–0.179	–0.084
L	–0.124	–0.140	–0.121	–0.049
K	–0.017	–0.035	–0.092	–0.364
Gasoline tax increase, lump-sum replacement				
w	–0.722	–1.069	–1.058	–0.983
r	0.095	–0.007	–0.027	–0.005
L	–0.266	–0.335	–0.331	–0.298
K	–0.011	–0.019	–0.031	–0.069
Personal tax increase, lump-sum replacement				
w	–0.333	–0.347	–0.404	–0.655
r	–0.104	–0.108	–0.105	–0.053
L	–0.277	–0.274	–0.265	–0.212
K	–0.015	–0.030	–0.072	–0.313
Substitution of Environmental Tax for Personal Tax:				
BTU tax, personal tax replacement				
w	0.083	–0.042	–0.042	0.014
r	0.031	–0.125	–0.074	–0.053
L	0.157	0.139	0.149	0.163
K	–0.001	–0.005	–0.019	–0.037
Gasoline tax increase, personal tax replacement				
w	–0.375	–0.694	–0.571	–0.307
r	0.216	0.111	0.076	0.057
L	0.013	–0.057	–0.061	–0.084
K	0.004	0.012	0.041	0.252

Note: *w, r, L,* and *K,* respectively, refer to the after-tax real wage, after-tax real rate of return, aggregate real labor supply, and aggregate real capital stock.

excess costs. In contrast, the BTU tax reform yields relatively little tax shifting. This helps explain why the gasoline tax involves lower excess costs per dollar than the BTU tax. Our results are qualitatively similar to those obtained by Rotemberg and Woodford (1994) in a more aggregated model that addresses issues of imperfect competition. These authors find that the costs of energy taxes are considerably smaller when the taxes are imposed at the household level only (as with the gasoline tax here), as compared with the case where taxes are imposed on all energy (as with the BTU tax).

Theory also predicts that the excess costs of environmental taxes (i.e., the tax burden effect from the second section) are related to the breadth of the tax base. The broader the base of these taxes, the smaller are the distortions introduced in intermediate input choice or in consumer good choice and, thus, the lower the excess cost or tax burden effect. To test this prediction, we perform two additional simulations. First, we simulate a uniform, *broad-based* tax on intermediate inputs with the same gross revenue impact as the taxes already considered. Since the BTU tax is also a tax on intermediate inputs (of oil, natural gas, and coal), the main structural difference between the broad-based tax and the BTU tax is the breadth of base. Second, we simulate a uniform, broad-based consumption tax—applying to all consumer goods, not just consumer purchases of gasoline. This isolates the significance of the breadth of the tax base at the level of household consumption. Because these taxes are broad, they clearly would not be effective as instruments of environmental policy. We consider them now only to identify the significance of the breadth of the tax base.

Table 4 compares the excess costs of the narrow and broad taxes. The excess costs of the broad-based intermediate input tax are only a third as large as the excess costs of the BTU tax. Moreover, the excess costs of the broad-based consumption tax are *negative*: the consumption tax involves lower gross costs than the income tax. This is in keeping with the consumption tax's shifting of the tax burden onto (lightly taxed) labor. In contrast with the case of the gasoline tax, under the broad-based consumption tax policy, tax shifting does not have to offset the tax burden effect, that is, excess costs associated with distortions in consumer good choice. Hence, it yields negative excess costs.

Thus, the numerical results support the predictions from the analytical model. Both the BTU and gasoline tax produce excess costs relative to the income tax as a result of distortions in intermediate input choice (BTU tax) and consumer good choice (gasoline tax). In the case of the gasoline tax, tax shifting mitigates, but does not eliminate, the excess costs. Broader tax bases reduce the intermediate input or consumer good distortions and imply lower excess costs.

It is important to keep in mind that we abstract entirely from the (environmental) benefits from environmentally motivated taxes. The presence of excess costs (or, equivalently, the absence of the double dividend) does not eliminate the efficiency case for such taxes. But it does mean that environmental benefits must be invoked to make this case.

Sensitivity Analysis

Table 5 shows the sensitivity of results to key parameters. The first three columns show the welfare costs per dollar for the BTU, gasoline, and personal income taxes, when revenues are returned lump-sum. The last two columns contain the excess costs of the BTU or gasoline tax relative to the personal income tax.

TABLE 4
SIGNIFICANCE OF BREADTH OF TAX BASE

	Welfare Cost Per Dollar	Excess Cost Per Dollar
Taxes on Intermediate Inputs		
BTU tax	0.656	0.279
Broad intermediate input tax	0.474	0.097
Taxes on Consumption		
Gasoline tax increase	0.594	0.217
Broad consumption tax	0.211	–0.166
Tax on Income		
Personal income tax increase	0.377	—

TABLE 5
SENSITIVITY ANALYSIS

	Welfare Cost per Dollar of Revenue			Excess Cost per Dollar of Revenue	
	BTU Tax (1)	Gasoline Tax (2)	Personal Income Tax Increase (3)	BTU Tax (4)	Gasoline Tax (5)
1. Central Case	0.656	0.594	0.379	0.277	0.215
2. Labor-Leisure Substitution Elasticity (υ)					
a. low (υ = 0.50)	0.483	0.411	0.208	0.275	0.203
b. high (υ = 0.85)	0.705	0.647	0.426	0.279	0.221
3. Intertemporal Elasticity of Substitution in Consumption (σ_U)					
a. low (σ_U = 0.33)	0.427	0.388	0.165	0.262	0.223
b. high (σ_U = 0.66)	0.798	0.717	0.507	0.291	0.210
4. Energy Demand Elasticities					
a. low (–25%)	0.558	0.552	0.339	0.219	0.213
b. high (+25%)	0.802	0.776	0.491	0.311	0.285
5. Pre-Existing Tax Rates (τ_L, τ_K)					
a. low τ_L (–25%)	0.581	0.509	0.311	0.270	0.198
b. high τ_L (+25%)	0.729	0.668	0.444	0.285	0.224
c. low τ_K (–25%)	0.492	0.448	0.216	0.276	0.232
d. high τ_K (+25%)	0.833	0.758	0.548	0.285	0.210

Notes: Figures in columns 1–3 are the equivalent variation divided by the present value of gross tax revenues from the policy change. Figures in the last two columns are the difference in results for the energy tax in question (from column 1 or 2) and the personal income tax increase (column 3). Central case values for the labor-leisure substitution elasticity (υ) ana intertemporal elasticitity of substitution (σ_U) are 0.77 and 0.5, respectively. (See Appendix C for functional forms.) Values of 0.50, 0.77, and 0.85 imply uncompensated (compensated) wage elasticities of labor supply of –0.067 (0.588), 0.150 (0.936), and 0.214 (1.078), respectively, at benchmark prices. The variables τ_L and τ_K denote the marginal tax rates on individual labor and capital income; central case values are 0.23 and 0.229, respectively.

Higher values for labor-leisure substitution elasticity (υ) enlarge the potential for labor market distortions. The welfare costs per dollar of all three taxes rise with higher values for this elasticity. In addition, the excess costs per dollar increase with this elasticity, in keeping with the predictions of the theoretical model, although the effects on excess costs are fairly small.

The higher the value of the intertemporal elasticity of substitution in consumption (σ_U), the greater is the potential for efficiency or welfare losses under policies that distort the capital market, or intertemporal allocation of resources. For all three taxes considered, welfare costs rise with this elasticity. However, excess costs rise only for the BTU tax. The inverse relationship between σ_U and the gasoline tax's excess cost is consistent with the fact that the gasoline tax is effectively a narrow-based consumption tax whose burden falls primarily on labor. Relative to the personal income tax increase, it imposes a smaller additional tax burden on capital. Hence, the excess cost of the gasoline tax diminishes the larger the value of σ_U and the greater the potential for capital market distortions.

Higher energy demand elasticities raise welfare costs per dollar, with larger proportionate increases for the energy taxes. Hence, excess costs rise as well.

The effects of higher pre-existing labor and capital taxes are similar to those of higher labor and capital elasticities. Higher pre-existing labor taxes expand the potential for labor market distortions. Correspondingly, and in parallel with the effects of a higher labor-leisure substitution elasticity, welfare costs and excess costs rise with pre-existing tax rates. Higher pre-existing capital taxes expand the potential for capital market distortions. In parallel with the effects of higher values for σ, welfare costs rise, excess costs rise for the BTU tax, and excess costs fall for the gasoline tax.

Interestingly, although different parameter values can significantly affect the magnitudes of the excess costs of the energy taxes, excess costs are positive in all cases. Thus, for a fairly wide range of specifications for pre-existing taxes and parameter values, the double-dividend hypothesis fails. This does not mean that it is impossible to produce the double dividend with the numerical model. Indeed, the model does generate the double dividend under special parameter values and revenue-replacement methods. In particular, we can produce the double dividend under the gasoline tax increase if the intertemporal elasticity of substitution in consumption is 1.9 or higher and all revenues are returned in the form of reduced marginal tax rates on capital income. The high value for σ implies large gains to the extent that a revenue-neutral tax swap reduces the burden on capital. Combining the gasoline tax increase with a reduction in capital tax rates yields a significant reduction in capital tax burden. Although this demonstrates the possibility of a double dividend, we consider this circumstance relatively unusual, in terms of both assumed elasticities[27] and the recycling method.

Conclusions

This paper has employed analytical and numerical models to examine the costs of revenue-neutral environmental tax reforms. We find that the substitution of environmentally motivated taxes for traditional income taxes typically involves a (gross) cost: the double dividend does not materialize. This result runs contrary to what some analysts have suggested but is consistent with an emerging theoretical literature on the issue. Underlying this result is the fact that environmental taxes are implicit factor taxes that not only generate factor market distortions similar to those of income taxes, but also impose additional distortions of their own in other markets.

Earlier analytical work offered little scope for the double dividend, because it did not consider pre-existing inefficiencies in the tax treatment of labor and capital. In contrast with the earlier models, the analytical model in this paper is able to examine how the initial tax treatment of labor and capital affects the prospects for a double dividend. The model shows that, to the extent that a revenue-neutral tax reform shifts the burden of taxation to the less efficient (undertaxed) factor, the prospects for a double dividend are enhanced. The numerical model's simulations indicate that this tax shifting effect is pronounced in the case of a consumer gasoline tax but fairly small in the case of a BTU tax. In neither case, however, is the tax shifting effect strong enough to yield the double dividend. This result is robust to a range of assumptions about values for key parameters.

The absence of a double dividend does not vitiate the case for green taxes, but it does compel policy analysts to invoke environmental benefits to make the efficiency case for such taxes. Further research that helps reduce uncertainties as to the magnitudes of these benefits will be of considerable use to policymakers contemplating environmental tax reform.

Another fruitful area for research is the analysis of distributional effects. In this paper, we have concentrated on efficiency issues; by adopting a representative household framework, we have abstracted from distributional concerns. However, the pre-existing inefficiencies in the tax system that we analyze in this paper may originate because of concerns about distribution. A full understanding of prior inefficiencies seems to require attention to distribution. A complete evaluation of policy impacts requires such attention as well.[28]

In attending to distributional impacts, one should, in principle, account for the distribution of both costs and (environment-related) benefits. Such benefits can facilitate a political coalition supporting an efficiency-enhancing tax reform that involves shifting the tax burden from capital toward labor. An "ordinary" tax reform that finances cuts in capital taxes through higher labor taxes may not be feasible politically because it harms workers. However, an environmental tax reform with similar incidence effects might be supported by labor if workers value a cleaner environment. Thus, considerations of environmental benefits can relax distributional and political constraints for tax reform.

ENDNOTES

The authors are grateful to two anonymous referees for helpful comments, to Jesse David and Steven Weinberg for excellent research assistance, and to the National Science Foundation (Grant SBR-9310362), IBM Corporation, and Resources for the Future for financial support.

1 The modifier "gross" is employed to indicate that environmental benefits are not netted out. Clearly, environmental taxes generally yield both benefits (avoided environmental costs) and costs. This paper concentrates on the cost side of the ledger, in keeping with the focus of discussions of the double dividend.

2 See, for example, Bovenberg and de Mooij (1994), Bovenberg and van der Ploeg (1994), Parry (1995), Goulder (1995a), and Oates (1995).

3 The idea that intermediate taxes and commodity taxes are implicit factor taxes is not new. It is implicit, for example, in Diamond and Mirrlees (1971). However, this notion was often overlooked in initial discussions of the double dividend.

4 Alternatively, it can be regarded as manufactured capital that generates pollution when it is employed in production. Under either interpretation, production technologies are cleaner to the extent that they rely more on K and less on R.

5 The number of hours available for work has been normalized at unity.

6 The assumed exogeneity of p_K and p_R simplifies the analysis. However, as discussed in "Observations and Caveats" subsection below, the main channels exposed by this model also apply if supplies of K and R are less than infinite.

7 As mentioned in the Introduction, the modifier "gross" indicates that environmental benefits are not netted out.

8 The solutions are derived from a log-linearized model. Hence, they hold only for marginal changes in taxes.

9 We place the words inefficient and efficient in quotes to acknowledge the fact that we are abstracting from efficiency issues associated with environmental quality. A tax that is relatively inefficient when the environmental dimension is ignored may well be relatively efficient once the environmental dimension is considered.

10 There may be political economy (or distributional) reasons why the initial tax system is not optimal. The analysis in this section is closely related to the literature on tax reform, which explores the possibility of moving to a more efficient tax system starting from suboptimal systems.

11 In our analytical model, labor bears the ultimate burden of all taxes in terms of reduced real incomes because the supply of capital is infinitely elastic. Thus, the burden of taxation on the capital market is reflected only in a decline of the capital demand and not in a drop in the after-tax return on capital. The burden in terms of reduced incomes is shifted back onto labor. In a more general model, in which capital supply is less than infinitely elastic, the burden of taxation in the capital market would reduce not only capital demand but also the after-tax rate of return on capital. In this case, labor and capital would share the burden of taxation in terms of lower after-tax

incomes. See also "Observations and Caveats" subsection below.

[12] Here, the model applies the asset price approach to investment developed in Summers (1981).

[13] The functions *f*, *g*, and *h* and the aggregation functions for the composites *E*, *M*, and x_i are CES and exhibit constant returns to scale. Consumer goods are produced by combining outputs from the 13 industries in fixed proportions.

[14] ϕ represents adjustment costs per unit of investment. This function expresses the notion that installing new capital necessitates a loss of current output, as existing inputs (*K*, *L*, *E*, and *M*) are diverted to install new capital.

[15] The attention to resource stock effects distinguishes this model from other disaggregated general equilibrium energy environmental models. Many equilibrium models treat the domestic oil and gas industry as involving constant-returns-to-scale production, disregarding resource stock effects or fixed factors. In their global energy–environment model, Manne and Richels (1992) impose stock limits on resources such as oil and gas; however, these limits to do not affect production costs prior to the point where the resource is exhausted.

[16] Thus, inputs 3 (oil and gas) and 4 (synfuels) enter additively in the energy aggregation function shown in equation 12.

[17] The world price is $24 per barrel in 1990 and rises in real terms by $6.50 per decade. See Gaskins and Weyant (1996).

[18] For details, see Goulder (1994, 1995b).

[19] Thus, we adopt the assumption of Armington (1969).

[20] Since oil and gas synfuels are perfect substitutes, they generate a single supply-demand condition.

[21] Since agents are forward-looking, equilibrium in each period depends not only on current prices and taxes but on future magnitudes as well.

[22] Specifically, the equivalent variation is the increment to initial wealth, which, given the prices and policy environment of the reference case, would enable the household to enjoy the same level of utility as under the policy change. A positive equivalent variation thus implies that the policy change is welfare-improving. When referring to "welfare costs," we mean the negative of the equivalent variation.

[23] For example, in Table 2, the cost of the BTU tax falls from 0.656 per dollar under lump-sum replacement to 0.396 per dollar under personal tax replacement.

[24] These results are also very much in keeping with the results of Bovenberg and Goulder (1996) relating to *optimal* environmental taxes.

[25] See, for example, Ballard, Shoven, and Whalley (1985).

[26] The gasoline tax is effectively a narrow-based consumption tax. As such, its burden falls primarily on labor and existing (old) capital. For a discussion of the incidence of consumption taxes, see, for example, Auerbach and Kotlikoff (1987). Swapping the gasoline tax for existing income taxes reduces the tax burden on new investments (or new capital), as indicated by Table 3 and the investment paths in Figures 1 and 2.

[27] Estimated values for σ are typically below unity. Results from Hall (1988), for example, indicate that σ is below 0.2.

[28] See Kaplow (1996) for an analysis of these issues.

REFERENCES

Auerbach, Alan J., and Laurence J. Kotlikoff. *Dynamic Fiscal Policy*. Cambridge, MA: Cambridge University Press, 1987.

Armington, P. S. "A Theory of Demand for Products Distinguished by Place of Production." *International Monetary Fund Staff Papers*, 159–76. Washington, D.C.: IMF, 1969.

Ballard, Charles L., and Steven G. Medema. "The Marginal Efficiency Effects of Taxes and Subsidies in the Presence of Externalities: A Computational General Equilibrium Approach." *Journal of Public Economics* 52 No. 2 (September, 1993): 199–216.

Ballard, Charles L., John B. Shoven, and John Whalley. "General Equilibrium Computations of the Marginal Welfare Costs of Taxes in the United States." *American Economic Review* 75 No. 1 (March, 1985): 128–38.

Bovenberg, A. Lans. "Environmental Policy, Distortionary Taxation, and Employment: Pollution Taxes and the Double Dividend." In *Recent Advances in Environmental Economics*, edited by Carlo Carraro. Dordrecht: Kluwer, 1995.

Bovenberg, A. Lans, and Ruud A. de Mooij. "Environmental Levies and Distortionary Taxation." *American Economic Review* 84 No. 4 (September, 1994): 1085–9.

Bovenberg, A. Lans, and F. van der Ploeg. "Environmental Policy, Public Finance and the Labour Market in a Second-Best World." *Journal of Public Economics* 55 No. 3 (November, 1994): 49–70.

Bovenberg, A. Lans, and Lawrence H. Goulder. "Optimal Environmental Taxation in the Presence of Other Taxes: General Equilibrium Analyses." *American Economic Review 86 No. 4* (September, 1996): 985–1000.

Cruz, Miguel, and Lawrence H. Goulder. "An Intertemporal General Equilibrium Model for Analyzing U.S. Energy and Environmental Policies: Data Documentation." Stanford University. Unpublished manuscript, 1992.

Diamond, Peter, and James Mirrlees. "Optimal Taxation and Public Production I: Production Efficiency and II: Tax Rules." *American Economic Review* 61 No. 1 (March, 1971): 8–27 and No. 3 (June, 1971): 261–78.

Gaskins, Darius, and John Weyant. *Reducing Global Carbon Dioxide Emissions: Costs and Policy Options*. Stanford: Stanford University Press (forthcoming, 1996).

Goulder, Lawrence H. "An Intertemporal General Equilibrium Model for Analyzing U.S. Energy and Environmental Policies: Model Structure." Stanford University. Unpublished manuscript, 1992.

Goulder, Lawrence H. "Energy Taxes: Traditional Efficiency Effects and Environmental Implications." In *Tax Policy and the Economy* 8, edited by James Poterba. Cambridge, MA: MIT Press, 1994.

Goulder, Lawrence H. "Environmental Taxation and the 'Double Dividend:' A Reader's Guide." *International Tax and Public Finance* 2 No. 2 (August, 1995a): 157–83.

Goulder, Lawrence H. "Effects of Carbon Taxes in an Economy with Prior Tax Distortions: An Intertemporal General Equilibrium Analysis." *Journal of Environmental Economics and Management* 29 No. 3 Part 1 (November, 1995b): 271–97.

Hall, Robert. "Intertemporal Substitution in Consumption." *Journal of Political Economy* 96 No. 2 (April, 1988): 339–57.

Kaplow, Louis. "The Optimal Supply of Public Goods and the Distortionary Cost of Taxation." *National Tax Journal* 49 No. 4 (December, 1996): 513–33.

Lee, Dwight R., and Walter S. Misiolek. "Substituting Pollution Taxation for General Taxation: Some Implications for Efficiency in Pollution Taxation." *Journal of Environmental Economics and Management* 13 No. 4 (December, 1986): 338–47.

Manne, Alan S., and Richard G. Richels. *Buying Greenhouse Insurance: The Economic Costs of CO_2 Emissions Limits*. Cambridge, MA: MIT Press, 1992.

Oates, Wallace E. "Pollution Charges as a Source of Public Revenues." In *Economic Progress and Environmental Concerns*, edited by Herbert Giersch, 135–52. Berlin: Springer-Verlag, 1993.

Oates, Wallace E. "Green Taxes: Can We Protect the Environment and Improve the Tax System at the Same Time?" *Southern Economic Journal* 61 No. 4 (April , 1995): 915–22.

Parry, Ian W. H. "Pollution Taxes and Revenue Recycling." *Journal of Environmental Economics and Management* 29 No. 3 Part 2 (November, 1995): S64–77.

Pearce, David W. "The Role of Carbon Taxes in Adjusting to Global Warming." *Economic Journal* 101 No. 407 (July, 1991): 938–48.

Poterba, James M. "Global Warming: A Public Finance Perspective." *Journal of Economic Perspectives* 7 No. 4 (Fall, 1993): 47–63.

Poterba, James M., and Lawrence H. Summers. "The Economic Effects of Dividend Taxation." *In Recent Advances in Corporate Finance*, edited by Edward I. Altman and Marti G. Subramanyan. Homewood: Irwin, 1985.

Repetto, Robert, Roger C. Dower, Robin Jenkins, and Jacqueline Geoghegan. *Green Fees: How a Tax Shift Can Work for the Environment and the Economy*. Washington D.C.: World Resources Institute, 1992.

Rotemberg, Julio, and Michael Woodford. "Energy Taxes and Aggregate Economic Activity." In *Tax Policy and the Economy* 8, edited by James M. Poterba. Cambridge, MA: MIT Press, 1994.

Summers, Lawrence H. "Taxation and Corporate Investment: A q-Theory Approach." *Brookings Papers on Economic Activity* (January, 1981): 67–127.

Terkla, David. "The Efficiency Value of Effluent Tax Revenues." *Journal of Environmental Economics and Management* 11 No. 2 (June, 1984): 107–23.

APPENDIX A: WELFARE EFFECTS OF TAX REFORMS

Firms equalize the marginal product of each input to its user cost:

A1

$$F_L(1, K/L, R/L) = w(1 + t_L)$$

A2

$$F_K(1, K/L, R/L) = p_K(1 + t_K)$$

A3

$$F_R(1, K/L, R/L) = p_R(1 + t_R).$$

The last two first-order conditions yield the demands for K and R conditional on the level of employment:

COSTS OF ENVIRONMENTALLY MOTIVATED TAXES

A4

$$K = Lk[p_K(1 + t_K); p_R(1 + t_R)]R = Lr[p_K(1 + t_K); p_R(1 + t_R)].$$

Substituting equation A4 into A1, we find the producer wage in terms of the producer prices of capital and the polluting resource:

A5

$$w(1 + t_L) = \Omega(p_K(1 + t_K); p_R(1 + t_R))$$

where

A6

$$\frac{\partial\Omega}{\partial p_K(1 + t_K)} = -\frac{K}{L} \text{ and } \frac{\partial\Omega}{\partial p_R(1 + t_R)} = -\frac{R}{L}$$

The representative household maximizes utility $u[m(C, 1 - L), G, E]$ subject to the household budget constraint. This yields

A7

$$U_c = \lambda$$

A8

$$U_{1-L} = \lambda w$$

where λ represents the marginal utility of income.

The welfare effects of a revenue-neutral change in the tax mix (i.e., a change in taxes such that $dG = 0$) are derived by taking the total differential of utility:

A9

$$du = u_C dC - u_{1-L} dL + u_E e_R dR.$$

Substituting equations A7 and A8 into A9, we can write

A10

$$\frac{du}{u_C} = dC - wdL + \frac{u_E e_R dR}{u_C}.$$

Taking the total differential of balance of payments equilibrium (equation 3) and substituting equations A1, A2, and A3, we find

A11

$$w(1 + t_L)dL + p_K t_K dK + p_R t_R dR = dC.$$

Using equation A11 to eliminate dC from equation A10, we arrive at

A12

$$\frac{du}{u_C} = -\frac{u_E}{u_C}[(-e_R)dR] + [wt_L dL + p_R t_R dR + p_K t_K dK].$$

By taking the total differential of the government budget constraint (equation 2) (with $dG = 0$) and using equations A5 and A6, we find

A13

$$wt_L dL + p_R t_R dR + p_K t_K dK = L\, dw.$$

Substitution of equation A13 into A12 yields equation 4.

APPENDIX B: SOLUTION TO THE ANALYTICAL MODEL

Log-linearizing the production function and substituting the log-linearized version balance-of-payments equilibrium into A7 to eliminate output, we arrive at

B1

$$\omega_L \tilde{L} = \omega_C \tilde{C} - \omega_R \theta_R \tilde{R} - \omega_K \theta_K \tilde{K}$$

where ω_c decreases the share of consumption in output.

We want to express the endogenous variable at the right-hand side of equation B1 in terms of $\tilde{L}$ and $\tilde{w}$. To find the expressions for $\tilde{R}$ and $\tilde{K}$, we log-linearize A1, A2, and A3 to arrive at

B2

$$\tilde{R} = \tilde{L} + \sigma[(\tilde{w} + \tilde{t}_L) - \tilde{t}_R]$$

B3

$$\tilde{K} = \tilde{L} + \sigma[(\tilde{w} + \tilde{t}_L) - \tilde{t}_K].$$

Log-linearizing equation A5 and substituting A6, we find

B4

$$\omega_L(\tilde{w} + \tilde{t}_L) + \omega_R\tilde{t}_R + \omega_K\tilde{t}_K = 0.$$

Endogenous Capital Income Tax ($\tilde{t}_L = 0$)

Substitution of equation B4 into B3 to eliminate $\tilde{t}_K$ yields (with $\tilde{t}_L = 0$)

B5

$$\tilde{K} = \tilde{L} + \frac{\sigma}{\omega_K}[(1 - \omega_R)\tilde{w} + \omega_R\tilde{t}_R].$$

We now substitute equation B2 (with $\tilde{t}_L = 0$), B5 and the log-linearized household budget constraint,

B6

$$\omega_C\tilde{C} = \omega_L(1 - \theta_L)[\tilde{w} + \tilde{L}]$$

into B1 to eliminate, respectively, $\tilde{R}$, $\tilde{K}$, and $\tilde{C}$:

B7

$$[\theta_L\omega_L + \theta_R\omega_R + \theta_K\omega_K]\tilde{L} = [(1 - \theta_L)\omega_L - \sigma[\theta_R\omega_R + \theta_K(1 - \omega_R)]]\tilde{w} + (\theta_R - \theta_K)\omega_R\tilde{t}_R.$$

We can solve for $\tilde{L}$ and $\tilde{w}$ by using the labor supply function

B8

$$L = \eta_L\tilde{w}$$

This yields equation 5. Substituting equations 5 and B8 into B2 and B5, we find equations 6 and 7.

Endogenous Labor Income Tax ($\tilde{t}_K = 0$)

Substitution of equation B4 into B2 and B3 to eliminate $(\tilde{w} + \tilde{t}_L)$ yields (with $\tilde{t}_K = 0$)

B9

$$\tilde{R} = \tilde{L} - \frac{\sigma}{\omega_L}(1 - \omega_K)\tilde{t}_R$$

B10

$$\tilde{K} = \tilde{L} - \frac{\sigma}{\omega_L}\tilde{\omega}_R t_R.$$

Substituting equations B9, B10, and B6 into B1, we arrive at

B11

$$[\theta_L\omega_L + \theta_R\omega_R + \theta_K\omega_K]\tilde{L} = (1 - \theta_L)\omega_L\tilde{w} + [\theta_R(1 - \omega_K) + \theta_K\omega_K]\frac{\omega_R}{\omega_L}\sigma\tilde{t}_R$$

Using equation B8 to eliminate $\tilde{L}$ from B11, we find equation 8. Substitution of equation 8 into B8 and the result into B9 and B10 yields equations 9 and 10.

APPENDIX C: STRUCTURE AND PARAMETER VALUES OF THE NUMERICAL MODEL[1]

I. Structure
A. Production
1. Technology
a. General Features

Table C1 indicates the nested production structure. In each industry i, gross output X_i is produced using inputs of labor (L_i), capital (K_i), an energy composite $(\bar{E}_i)$ and a materials composite $(\bar{M}_i)$. The production function has the following form:

C1

$$X_i = f_i[g_{1i}(L_i, K_i), g_{2i}(\bar{E}_i, \bar{M}_i)] - \phi_i(I_i/K_i)I_i.$$

The functions f_i, g_{1i}, and g_{2i} are CES. Hence, the function f can be written as

TABLE C1
NESTED PRODUCTION STRUCTURE

X	=	$f(g_1, g_2) - \phi(I/K)I$	
g_1	=	$g_1(L, K)$	
g_2	=	$g_2(E, M)$	
E	=	$E(E_1, ..., E_5)$	
M	=	$M(M_1, ..., M_7)$	
E_i	=	$E_i(ED_i, EF_i)$	$i = 1,...,5$
M_i	=	$M_i(MD_i, MF_i)$	$i = 1,...,7$

Note: All functions are CES in form, except for $\phi(I/K)$, which is quadratic in I/K.

COSTS OF ENVIRONMENTALLY MOTIVATED TAXES

C2

$$f(g_1, g_2) = \gamma_f[\alpha_f g_1^{\rho_f} + (1 - \alpha_f)g_2^{\rho_f}]^{1/\rho_f}$$

where the industry subscript has been suppressed and where γ_f, α_f, and ρ_f are parameters. The parameter ρ is related to σ_f, the elasticity of substitution between g_1 and g_2: $\rho = (\sigma - 1)/\sigma$. Analogous expressions apply for the functions g_1 and g_2.

The second term in equation C1 represents the loss of output associated with installing new capital (or dismantling existing capital). Per-unit adjustment costs, ϕ, are given by

C3

$$\phi(I/K) = \frac{(\xi/2)(I/K - \delta)^2}{I/K}$$

where I represents gross investment (purchases of new capital goods) and ξ and δ are parameters. The parameter δ denotes the rate of economic depreciation of the capital stock.

The energy composite ($\bar{E}_i$) in equation 1 is a CES function of the specific energy products of the different energy industries:

C4a

$$\bar{E} = \bar{E}(E_1, E_2, \ldots, E_5)$$

C4b

$$= \gamma_{\bar{E}}\left[\sum_{j=1}^{5} \alpha_{\bar{E}j} E_j^{\rho_{\bar{E}}}\right]^{1/\rho_{\bar{E}}}$$

where $\sum_{j=1}^{5} \alpha_{\bar{E}j} = 1$. The subscripts to E in equations C4a and C4b correspond to energy industries as follows.

Subscript	*Energy Industry*
1	Coal Mining
2	Oil and Gas Extraction and Synthetic Fuels
3	Petroleum Refining
4	Electricity
5	Processed Natural Gas

Oil and gas and synthetic fuels combine as one input in the energy composite, reflecting the fact that these fuels are treated as perfect substitutes in production.[2]

Similarly, the materials composite ($\bar{M}_i$) in equation 1 is a CES function of the specific materials products of the seven nonenergy industries:

C5a

$$\bar{M} = \bar{M}(M_1, M_2, \ldots, M_7)$$

C5b

$$= \gamma_{\bar{M}}\left[\sum_{j=1}^{7} \alpha_{\bar{M}j} M_j^{\rho_{\bar{M}}}\right]^{1/\rho_{\bar{M}}}$$

where $\sum_{j=1}^{7} \alpha_{\bar{M}j} = 1$. The subscripts to M in equations C5a and C5b correspond to materials (nonenergy) industries as follows.

Subscript	*Materials Industry*
1	Agriculture and Mining (except coal mining)
2	Construction
3	Metals and Machinery
4	Motor Vehicles
5	Miscellaneous Manufacturing
6	Services (except housing)
7	Housing Services

The elements E_j ($j = 1,\ldots,5$) and M_j ($j = 1,\ldots,7$) in the E and M functions are themselves CES composites of domestically produced and foreign-made inputs:

C6

$$E_j = \gamma_{Ej}[\alpha_{Ej} ED_j^{\rho_{Ej}} + (1 - \alpha_{Ej}) EF_j^{\rho_{Ej}}]^{1/\rho_{Ej}}, \quad j = 1, \ldots, 5$$

C7

$$M_j = \gamma_{Mj}[\alpha_{Mj} MD_j^{\rho_{Mj}} + (1 - \alpha_{Mj}) MF_j^{\rho_{Mj}}]^{1/\rho_{Mj}}, \quad j = 1, \ldots, 7$$

where ED_j and EF_j denote domestic and foreign energy inputs of type j, and MD_j and MF_j denote domestic and foreign materials inputs of type j.

b. Endogeneity of γ in the Oil and Gas Production Function

In industries other than oil and gas, the element γ_f in the production function is parametric. In the oil and gas industry, γ_f is a decreasing function of cumulative oil and gas extraction:

C8

$$\gamma_{g,t} = \varepsilon_1[1 - (Z_t/\bar{Z})^{\varepsilon_2}]$$

where ε_1 and ε_2 are parameters, Z_t represents cumulative extraction as of the beginning of period t, and Z is the original estimated total stock of recoverable reserves of oil and gas (as estimated from the benchmark year). The following equation of motion specifies the evolution of Z_t:

C9

$$Z_{t+1} = Z_t + X_t.$$

Equation 8 implies that the production function for oil and gas shifts downward as cumulative oil and gas extraction increases. This addresses the fact that as reserves are depleted, remaining reserves become more difficult to extract and require more inputs per unit of extraction.

2. Behavior of Firms

In each industry, managers of firms are assumed to serve stockholders in aiming to maximize the value of the firm. The objective of firm-value maximization determines firms' choices of input quantities and investment levels in each period of time.

The value of the firm can be expressed in terms of dividends and new share issues, which in turn depend on profits in each period. The firm's profits during a given period are given by

C10

$$\pi = (1 - \tau_a)[pX - w(1 + \tau_L)L - EMCOST - iDEBT - TPROP]$$
$$+ \tau_a(DEPL + DEPR)$$

where τ_a is the tax rate on profits, p is the output price net of output taxes, w is the wage rate net of indirect labor taxes, τ_L is the rate of the indirect tax on labor, $EMCOST$ is the cost to the firm of energy and materials inputs, i is the gross-of-tax interest rate paid by the firm, $DEBT$ is the firm's current debt, $TPROP$ is the firm's property tax payments, $DEPL$ is the current gross depletion allowance, and $DEPR$ is the current gross depreciation allowance. $TPROP$ equals $\tau_p p_{K,s-1} K_s$, where τ_p is the property tax rate, p_K is the purchase price of a unit of new capital, and s is the time period. Current depletion allowances, $DEPL$, are a constant fraction β of the value of current extraction: $DEPL = \beta pX$. Current depreciation allowances, $DEPR$, can be expressed as $\delta^T K^T$, where K^T is the depreciable capital stock basis and δ^T is the depreciation rate applied for tax purposes.[3]

In equation C10, $EMCOST$ is given by

C11

$$EMCOST = \sum_{j=1}^{5}(1 + \tau_{Ej})(p_{ED,j}ED_j + p_{EF,j}EF_j)$$
$$+ \sum_{j=1}^{7}(1 + \tau_{mj})(p_{MD,j}MD_j + p_{MF,j}MF_j)$$

where the subscripts for energy and materials correspond to industries as indicated above; and where τ_E and τ_M denote the tax rates applying to the firm's use of intermediate inputs, and $p_{ED,j}$ and $p_{EF,j}$ ($p_{MD,j}$ and $p_{MF,j}$) are the pretax prices of domestic and foreign energy (materials) inputs of type j.[4]

The following accounting or cash-flow identity links the firm's sources and uses of revenues:

C12

$$\pi + BN + VN = DIV + IEXP.$$

The left-hand side is the firm's source of revenues: profits, new debt issue (BN), and new share issues (VN). The uses of revenues on the right-hand side are investment expenditure ($IEXP$) and dividend payments (DIV). Negative share issues are equivalent to share repurchases and represent a use rather than source of revenue.

Firms pay dividends equal to a constant fraction, a, of profits net of economic depreciation and maintain debt equal to a constant fraction, b, of the value of the existing capital stock. Thus,

C13

$$DIV_s = a[\pi_s + (p_{K,s} - p_{K,s-1})K_s - \delta p_{K,s}K_s]$$

C14

$$BN_s \equiv DEBT_{s+1} - DEBT_s = b(p_{K,s}K_{s+1} - p_{K,s-1}K_s).$$

Investment expenditure is expressed by

COSTS OF ENVIRONMENTALLY MOTIVATED TAXES

C15

$$IEXP_s = (1 - \tau_K)p_{K,s}I_s$$

where τ_K is the investment tax credit rate. Of the elements in equation C12, new share issues, VN, are the residual, making up the difference between $\pi + BN$ and $DIV + IEXP$.[5]

Arbitrage possibilities compel the firm to offer its stockholders a rate of return comparable to the rate of interest on alternative assets.

C16

$$(1 - \tau_e)DIV_s + (1 - \tau_v)(V_{s+1} - V_s - VN_s) = (1 - \tau_b)i_s V_s.$$

The parameters τ_e, τ_v, and τ_b are the personal tax rates on dividend income (equity), capital gains, and interest income (bonds), respectively. The return to stockholders consists of the current after-tax dividend plus the after-tax capital gain (accrued or realized) on the equity value (V) of the firm net of the value of new share issues. This return must be comparable to the after-tax return from an investment of the same value at the market rate of interest, i.

The firm's decision problem is completed by the equation of motion for the capital stock:

C17

$$K_{s+1} = (1 - \delta)K_s + I_s.$$

Capital is augmented by net investment. Cumulative extraction is augmented by the level of current output (or extraction). In the oil and gas industry, the equation of motion C9 also applies.

B. Household Behavior

Consumption, labor supply, and saving result from the decisions of an infinitely lived representative household maximizing its intertemporal utility with perfect foresight. The nested structure of the household's utility function is indicated in Table C2. In year t, the household chooses a path of "full consumption" C to maximize

C18

$$U_t = \sum_{s=t}^{\infty}(1 + \omega)^{t-s}\frac{\sigma_U}{\sigma_U - 1}C_s^{\frac{\sigma_U - 1}{\sigma_U}}$$

TABLE C2
NESTED UTILITY STRUCTURE

Function	Functional Form
$U_t(C_t, C_{t+1}, \ldots, C_s, \ldots)$	constant intertemporal elasticity of substitution
$C_s(\tilde{C}_s, l_s)$	CES
$\tilde{C}_s(\bar{C}_{1,s}, \ldots, \bar{C}_{i,s}, \ldots, \bar{C}_{17,s})$	Cobb–Douglas
$\bar{C}_{i,s}(CD_{i,s}, CF_{i,s})$	CES

Key:
U_t intertemporal utility evaluated from period t
C_s full consumption in period s
$\tilde{C}_s$ overall goods consumption in period s
l_s leisure in period s
$\bar{C}_{i,s}$ consumption of composite consumer good i in period s
$CD_{i,s}$ consumption of domestically produced consumer good i in period s
$CF_{i,s}$ consumption of foreign-produced consumer good i in period s

where ω is the subjective rate of time preference and σ_U is the intertemporal elasticity of substitution in full consumption. C is a CES composite of consumption of goods and services $\tilde{C}$ and leisure l:

C19

$$C_s = \left[\tilde{C}_s^{\frac{\nu-1}{\nu}} + \alpha_C^{\frac{1}{\nu}} l_s^{\frac{\nu-1}{\nu}}\right]^{\frac{\nu}{\nu-1}}$$

where υ is the elasticity of substitution between goods and leisure; α_C is an intensity parameter for leisure.

The variable $\tilde{C}$ in equation C19 is a Cobb–Douglas aggregate of 17 composite consumer goods:

C20

$$\tilde{C}_s = \prod_{i=1}^{17}\bar{C}_{i,s}^{\alpha_{\bar{C},i}}$$

where the $\alpha_{\bar{C},i}$ $(i = 1, \ldots, 17)$ are parameters. The 17 types of consumer goods identified in the model are shown in Table 2 of the main text.

Consumer goods are produced domestically and abroad. Each composite consumer good $\bar{C}_i$, $i = 1, \ldots, 17$, is a CES aggregate of a domestic and foreign consumer good of a given type:

C21

$$\tilde{C} = \gamma_{\tilde{c}}[\alpha_{\tilde{c}}CD^{\rho_{\tilde{c}}} + (1 - \alpha_{\tilde{c}})CF^{\rho_{\tilde{c}}}]^{1/\rho_{\tilde{c}}}.$$

In the above equation, *CD* and *CF* denote the household's consumption of domestically produced and foreign-made consumer goods of a given type at a given point in time. For simplicity, we have omitted subscripts designating the type of consumer good and the time period.

The household maximizes utility subject to the intertemporal budget constraint given by the following condition governing the change in financial wealth, *WK*:

C22

$$WK_{t+1} - WK_t = \bar{r}_t WK_t + YL_t + GT_t - \tilde{p}_t\tilde{C}_t$$

In the above equation, $\bar{r}$ is the average after-tax return on the household's portfolio of financial capital, *YL* is after-tax labor income, *GT* is transfer income, and $\tilde{p}$ is the price index representing the cost to the household of a unit of the consumption composite, $\tilde{C}$.

C. Government Behavior

A single government sector approximates government activities at all levels—federal, state, and local. The main activities of the government sector are purchasing goods and services (both nondurable and durable), transferring incomes, and raising revenue through taxes or bond issue.

1. Components of Government Expenditure

Government expenditure, *G*, divides into nominal purchases of nondurable goods and services (*GP*), nominal government investment (*GI*), and nominal transfers (*GT*):

C23

$$G_t = GP_t + GI_t + GT_t.$$

In the reference case, the paths of *real GP*, *GI*, and *GT* all are specified as growing at the steady-state real growth rate, *g*. In simulating policy changes, we fix the paths of *GP*, *GI*, and *GT* so that the paths of real government purchases, investment, and transfers are the same as in corresponding years of the reference case. Thus, the expenditure side of the government ledger is largely kept unchanged across simulations. This procedure is expressed by

C24a

$$GP^P_t / p^P_{GP,t} = GP^R_t / p^R_{GP,t}$$

C24b

$$GI^P_t / p^P_{GI,t} = GI^R_t / p^R_{GI,t}$$

C24c

$$GT^P_t / p^P_{GT,t} = GT^R_t / p^R_{GT,t}$$

The superscripts *P* and *R* denote policy change and reference case magnitudes, while p_{GP}, p_{GI}, and p_{GT} are price indices for *GP*, *GI*, and *GT*. The price index for government investment, p_{GI}, is the purchase price of the representative capital good. The price index for transfers, p_{GT}, is the consumer price index. The index for government purchases, p_{GP}, is defined below.

2. Allocation of Government Purchases

GP divides into purchases of particular outputs of the 13 domestic industries according to fixed expenditure shares:

C25

$$\alpha_{G,i}GP = GPX_i p_i \qquad i = 1,\ldots,13$$

where GPX_i and p_i are the quantity demanded and price of output from industry *i*, and $\alpha_{G,i}$ is the corresponding expenditure share. The ideal price index for government purchases, p_{GP}, is given by

C26

$$p_{GP} = \prod_{i=1}^{13} p_i^{\alpha_{G,i}}.$$

COSTS OF ENVIRONMENTALLY MOTIVATED TAXES

II. Parameter Values

A. Elasticities of Substitution in Production

Parameter:	σ_f	σ_{g1}	σ_{g2}	σ_E	σ_M	σ_x
Substitution margin:	g_1-g_2	L-K	E-M	E components	M components	domestic-foreign inputs
Producing Industry:						
1. Agriculture and Non-Coal Mining	0.7	0.68	0.7	1.45	0.6	2.31
2. Coal Mining	0.7	0.80	0.7	1.08	0.6	1.14
3. Oil and Gas Extraction	0.7	0.82	0.7	1.04	0.6	(infinite)
4. Synthetic Fuels	0.7	0.82	0.7	1.04	0.6	(not traded)
5. Petroleum Refining	0.7	0.74	0.7	1.04	0.6	2.21
6. Electric Utilities	0.7	0.81	0.7	0.97	0.6	1.0
7. Gas Utilities	0.7	0.96	0.7	1.04	0.6	1.0
8. Construction	0.7	0.95	0.7	1.04	0.6	1.0
9. Metals and Machinery	0.7	0.91	0.7	1.21	0.6	2.74
10. Motor Vehicles	0.7	0.80	0.7	1.04	0.6	1.14
11. Miscellaneous Manufacturing	0.7	0.94	0.7	1.08	0.6	2.74
12. Services (except housing)	0.7	0.98	0.7	1.07	0.6	1.0
13. Housing Services	0.7	0.80	0.7	1.81	0.6	(not traded)

B. Parameters of Stock Effect Function in Oil and Gas Industry

Parameter:	Z_0	$\bar{Z}$	ε_1	ε_2
Value:	0	450	1.27	2.0

Note: This function is parameterized so that γ_t approaches 0 as Z approaches $\bar{Z}$ (see equation C8). The value of $\bar{Z}$ is 450 billion barrels (about 100 times the 1990 production of oil and gas, where gas is measured in barrel-equivalents). $\bar{Z}$ is based on estimates from Masters *et al.* (1987). Investment in new oil and gas capital ceases to be profitable before reserves are depleted: the values of ε_1 and ε_2 imply that, in the baseline scenario, oil and gas investment becomes zero in the year 2031.

C. Utility Function Parameters

Parameter:	ω	σ_U	v	η
Value:	0.007	0.5	0.69	0.84

APPENDIX ENDNOTES

1 A more comprehensive description of the structure of the model is in Goulder (1992). Detailed documentation of the data and parameters for the model is provided in Cruz and Goulder (1992).

2 E_2 denotes the total quantity (in energy-equivalent units) of oil and gas plus synfuels:

$E_2 = E_{og} + E_{sf}$.

3 For convenience, we assume that the accelerated depreciation schedule can be approximated by a schedule involving constant exponential tax depreciation.

4 To simplify the exposition, we have not included in equations C10 and C11 subscripts identifying the given industry for which profits or input costs are calculated. It may be noted that the intermediate good taxes, τ_{Ej} and τ_{Mj}, may differ across industries using a particular good as well as across intermediate goods.

In equation C11, for $j = 2$, the expression $p_{Ej}(1 + \tau_{Ej}) E_j$ is shorthand for $p_{og}(1 + \tau_{og}) E_{og} + p_{sf}(1 + \tau_{sf}) E_{sf}$, where *og* refers to oil and gas and *sf* refers to synfuels. Since oil and gas and synfuels are perfect substitutes, it is always the case that gross-of-tax costs of these fuels to the firm are the same, that is, $p_{og}(1 + \tau_{og}) = p_{sf}(1 + \tau_{sf})$. However, when $\tau_{og} \neq \tau_{sf}$, the net-of-tax prices p_{og} and p_{sf} will differ.

5 For a discussion of alternative specifications, see Poterba and Summers (1985).

International Tax and Public Finance, 5, 7–39 (1998)

Environmental Taxes, International Capital Mobility and Inefficient Tax Systems: Tax Burden vs. Tax Shifting

RUUD A. DE MOOIJ radm@cpb.nl
OCFEB, Erasmus University Rotterdam; CPB Netherlands Bureau for Economic Policy Analysis

A. LANS BOVENBERG alb@cpb.nl
CPB Netherlands Bureau for Economic Policy Analysis, CentER, Tilburg University; OCFEB; CEPR

Abstract

This paper deals with the so-called 'double dividend' of an environmental tax reform. In a model with only labor and a polluting input as factors of production, we find that society faces a trade-off between internalizing environmental externalities and raising revenues in the least distortionary way. However, if capital enters the production structure, an ecological tax reform may render the tax structure more efficient from a non-environmental point of view, thereby raising not only environmental quality but also private incomes.

Keywords: Environmental tax reform; Double dividend; Tax burden; Tax shifting; Capital mobility

JEL codes: H22, Q28

1. Introduction

Recently, environmental tax reforms have received increasing attention. In particular, some economists have argued that substituting environmental taxes for pre-existing distortionary taxes on income may yield a 'double dividend', i.e. not only a cleaner environment but also a less distortionary way of revenue raising (see e.g. Pearce, 1991; Oates, 1991). Recent literature on the double dividend suggests, however, that environmental taxes typically exacerbate, rather than alleviate, pre-existing tax distortions (see Bovenberg and De Mooij, 1994ab; Bovenberg and Van der Ploeg, 1994ab; Goulder, 1995).

This paper extends these previous analyses by exploring how inefficiencies in the initial tax system affect the potential for a double dividend.[1] By modelling two non-polluting production factors (i.e. labor and capital), rather than just one, we are able to allow for an inefficient distribution of the tax burden over these two factors. Within such a setting, an environmental tax reform affects private welfare through two channels. First, it expands the supply of the public consumption good of the environment, thereby raising the overall tax burden. This *tax burden effect* is responsible for the failure of the double-dividend hypothesis in previous analyses that allowed for only one clean production factor (see Bovenberg and de Mooij, 1994a). With two clean production factors, however, an environmental tax reform affects private welfare through a second channel, namely the distribution of the tax burden over the two production factors. In particular, by redistributing the tax burden across the two factors, the reform affects the efficiency of the tax system as a revenue-raising device if the initial distribution of the tax burden is inefficient from a non-environmental point of view. This effect is called the *tax shifting effect*. If the reform shifts the tax burden from the overtaxed factor (i.e. the efficient factor) towards the undertaxed factor (i.e. the inefficient factor), the tax shifting effect alleviates initial inefficiencies in the tax system. However, it exacerbates these inefficiencies if the tax burden is moved on to the factor that is overtaxed already in the initial equilibrium. Hence, initial inefficiencies in the tax system provide both opportunities and dangers for environmental tax reforms. In particular, a double dividend is feasible if, by shifting the tax burden towards the undertaxed factor, the tax shifting effect makes the tax system more efficient from a non-environmental point of view and is large enough to offset the tax burden effect. In that case, the reduction in the excess burden associated with a more efficient revenue-raising system 'finances' the expansion of the supply of public consumption goods (due to a higher quality of the natural environment).

In illustrating these ideas, we allow for two extreme assumptions about the supply of capital. In the first model with two clean production factors, capital is perfectly mobile internationally. Hence, the capital supply is effectively infinitely elastic. In that case, the optimal source-based tax on capital is zero, while all distortionary taxes should be levied on labor. Accordingly, capital is overtaxed if the initial source-based tax on capital is positive. Since raising polluting taxes to cut initial taxes on capital tends to reduce the tax burden in the capital market, the tax shifting effect works in the right direction by improving the efficiency of the tax system as a revenue-raising device. Hence, a double dividend is obtained if the tax shifting effect dominates the tax burden effect. This is the case if two conditions are met. First, pre-existing capital taxes should be large compared to taxes on pollution. Second, compared to pollution, capital should be a poor substitute for labor. Recycling the revenues from the pollution tax through lower labor taxes, rather than capital taxes, does not yield a double dividend—as the tax shifting effect works in the wrong way. Thus, by redistributing the tax burden towards the capital market, an ecological tax reform exacerbates, rather than alleviates, the initial inefficiencies in the tax system.

In the second model capital is immobile internationally. Moreover, the supply of capital is completely inelastic so that the optimal tax on capital is 100%. Thus, capital is under- rather than overtaxed if the capital tax is below 100%. This production structure is similar to that of Bovenberg and Van der Ploeg (1994b), who also allow for a fixed factor in production. However, in contrast to Bovenberg and Van der Ploeg, who consider involuntary unemployment due to rigid consumer wages, we allow flexible wages to clear the labor market. Within this framework, we find that substituting environmental taxes for labor taxes may yield a double dividend. Intuitively, by shifting the tax burden from labor (the overtaxed factor) towards the fixed factor (the undertaxed factor), the government may improve the efficiency of the tax system as a revenue-raising device.

A numerical example illustrates our theoretical results. In particular, we calibrate the model for a typical European economy where we interpret the polluting input as energy used in production. Indeed, this seems to be the most natural interpretation of the polluting input. We find that energy taxes that raise after-tax energy prices for firms by 10%, from which the revenues are used to cut taxes on mobile capital, produce a double dividend: energy demand falls by 5.5%, while private incomes rise by 0.8% and employment rises by

0.16%. However, if labor taxes, rather than capital taxes, are reduced, private incomes fall by 0.4% while employment drops by almost 0.1%. Hence, the latter shift fails to produce a double dividend. A shift from labor taxes towards energy taxes, in contrast, may yield a double dividend in the presence of fixed capital (so that capital is immobile internationally). Indeed, we find that such a reform would reduce pollution by 7.8%, boost employment by 0.36% and raise private incomes by 0.05% if after-tax energy prices would be raised by 10%.

The rest of this paper is structured as follows. Section 2 discusses the model. Section 3 explores the effects of a shift in the tax mix away from labor towards pollution in a simple benchmark model which contains only labor as a clean production factor. Section 4 extends the benchmark model by incorporating internationally mobile capital. That section explores the consequences of substituting environmental taxes for taxes on either labor or capital. Section 5 discusses the model in which the supply of capital is fixed. Simulations are carried out in section 6 in order to illustrate our findings numerically. Finally, section 7 concludes.

2. The Model

2.1. Structure of the Model

This section discusses the model contained in Table 2.1. Notation is defined at the end of the table. The model describes a small open economy, which faces fixed world market prices for all commodities. Its static framework is used for an exercise in comparative statics. The model distinguishes three sectors, namely firms, households and the government. These sectors are discussed below.

Firms

Firm behavior is described by a representative firm that supplies a single commodity. The firm maximizes profits (I.1) subject to a neo-classical production function (I.2), which exhibits constant returns to scale with respect to its four inputs: labor (L), an input that causes pollution when used in production (the polluting input E), clean capital (K) and a fixed factor (H). The polluting input and clean capital are mobile internationally so that their market prices are fixed on world markets. We normalize units so that these prices are unity. Whereas clean capital and the polluting input are in effect supplied infinitely elastically, the supply of the fixed factor is completely inelastic. The fixed factor can be interpreted as land or immobile capital. Solving the firm's maximization problem, we find the implicit demand functions for labor (I.3), the polluting input (I.4) and clean capital (I.5).

Households

The representative household maximizes a homothetic utility function of the form (I.6) subject to its budget constraint (I.7). The household budget available for consumption

Table 2.1. The model.

Firms

Profits

$$\Pi = Y - (1 + T_L)WL - (1 + T_E)E - (1 + T_K)K \quad \text{(I.1)}$$

Production Function

$$Y = f[H, L, E, K] \quad \text{(I.2)}$$

First-Order Conditions

$$\frac{df}{dL} = (1 + T_L)W \quad \text{(I.3)}$$

$$\frac{df}{dE} = 1 + T_E \quad \text{(I.4)}$$

$$\frac{df}{dK} = 1 + T_K \quad \text{(I.5)}$$

Households

Utility Function

$$U = u[M, Q(V, C, G)] \quad \text{(I.6)}$$

Household Budget Constraint

$$WL_S + (1 - T_\Pi)\Pi + E^* + K^* = C \quad \text{(I.7)}$$

First-Order Conditions

$$\frac{\partial u}{\partial V} = \lambda W \quad \text{(I.8)}$$

$$\frac{\partial u}{\partial C} = \lambda \quad \text{(I.9)}$$

Labor Supply

$$L_S = 1 - V \quad \text{(I.10)}$$

Government

Government Budget Constraint

$$G = T_L WL + T_K K + T_E E + T_\Pi \Pi \quad \text{(I.11)}$$

Labor-Market Equilibrium

$$L = L_S \quad \text{(I.12)}$$

Environmental Quality

$$M = g(E) \quad \text{(I.13)}$$

Walras Law: Balance of Payments

$$Y = C + G + (E - E^*) + (K - K^*) \quad \text{(I.14)}$$

Endogenous: $Y, L, E, K, \Pi, V, C, L_S, W, M$, and T_L, T_K or T_Π
Exogenous: T_E, G, H, E^*, K^* and T_L, T_K or T_Π

Notation

Y = domestic output
H = fixed capital
E = polluting input demand
L = labor demand
K = demand for mobile capital
K^* = stock of domestically owned capital
E^* = domestic endowment of polluting inputs

T_L = ad-valorem tax on labor income
T_E = specific tax on pollution
T_K = ad-valorem tax on capital income
T_Π = tax on pure profits

W = market wage rate
V = leisure
M = environmental quality
G = public consumption

Π = pure profits (= return on the fixed factor)
L_S = labor supply
C = private consumption
λ = lagrange multiplier of the household budget constraint (= marginal utility of income)

consists of four components: after-tax labor income (WL_S), after-tax profits ($(1 - T_\Pi)\Pi$) and the after-tax returns on the domestic endowments of respectively, capital (K^*) and polluting inputs (E^*). All incomes from the fixed factor accrue to domestic households. Accordingly, international cross-ownership of rents is absent. Two public goods enter household utility, namely, public consumption (G) and environmental quality (M). The individual household takes the quantities of public goods as exogenously given. Hence, in optimizing utility, it adopts leisure (V) and consumption (C) as instruments. Environmental quality is weakly separable from private goods in utility. Changes in environmental quality thus do not affect private demand for consumption and leisure. Equations (I.8) and (I.9) represent the implicit expressions for labor supply and consumption demand, respectively. Here, λ denotes the marginal utility of private income. We normalize the time endowment to unity (see (I.10)).

Government

The government supplies public goods (G), which are financed by four taxes: a tax on labor income (T_L), a tax on capital (T_K), a tax on pure profits (T_Π), and a tax on the use of polluting inputs (T_E).[2] The tax rate on profits lies between zero and one. The government budget is assumed to be balanced (see (I.11)). In this paper, we examine the effects of a rise in the pollution tax under alternative options for recycling the revenues, namely, a reduction in the tax on labor income, a reduction in the tax on capital income and a reduction in the profit tax.

Labor-Market Equilibrium, the Environment and the Balance of Payments

Relation (I.12) represents the equilibrium condition on the labor market, while (I.13) formalizes the inverse relationship between the demand for polluting inputs and the quality of the environment. In line with the small-open-economy assumptions, possible spillovers of foreign pollution on the quality of the domestic environment are exogenously given. In accordance with the law of Walras, we find the equilibrium on the balance of payments (I.14) by combining the relations for output (I.1), profits (I.5), the household budget constraint (I.7), and the government budget constraint (I.11)

2.2. *Linearization*

To analyze the economic consequences of an environmental tax reform, we log-linearize the model around an initial equilibrium. Table 2.2 contains the log-linearized model. Notation is defined at the end of the table. A tilde ($\sim$) denotes a relative change, unless indicated otherwise. The supply of public goods (G) and the domestic endowments of capital and polluting inputs are fixed exogenously (i.e. $\tilde{G} = \tilde{K}^* = \tilde{E}^* = 0$).

Table 2.2. Linearized model.

Firms

Domestic Output

$$\tilde{Y} = w_H \tilde{H} + w_E \tilde{E} + w_L \tilde{L} + w_K \tilde{K} \qquad \text{(II.1)}$$

With mobile capital/no immobile capital

Polluting Input Demand

$$\tilde{E} = \tilde{L} - \epsilon^*_{EL}(\tilde{W} + \tilde{T}_L) - \epsilon^*_{EE}\tilde{T}_E - \epsilon^*_{EE}\tilde{T}_K \qquad \text{(II.2)}$$

Capital Demand

$$\tilde{K} = \tilde{L} - \epsilon^*_{KL}(\tilde{W} + \tilde{T}_L) - \epsilon^*_{KE}\tilde{T}_E - \epsilon^*_{KK}\tilde{T}_K \qquad \text{(II.3)}$$

Non-Profit condition

$$0 = w_L(\tilde{W} + \tilde{T}_L) + w_E \tilde{T}_E + w_K \tilde{T}_K \qquad \text{(II.4)}$$

With immobile capital/no mobile capital

Labor Demand

$$\tilde{L} = \tilde{H} - \epsilon_{LL}(\tilde{W} + \tilde{T}_L) - \epsilon_{LE}\tilde{T}_E \qquad \text{(II.2}'\text{)}$$

Polluting Input Demand

$$\tilde{E} = \tilde{H} - \epsilon_{EL}(\tilde{W} + \tilde{T}_L) - \epsilon_{EE}\tilde{T}_E \qquad \text{(II.3}'\text{)}$$

Profits

$$(1 + \theta_\Pi) w_\Pi \tilde{\Pi} = w_H \tilde{H} - w_L(\tilde{W} + \tilde{T}_L) - w_E \tilde{T}_E - w_K \tilde{T}_K \qquad \text{(II.4}'\text{)}$$

Households

Household Budget Constraint

$$w_L(1 - \theta_L)(\tilde{L} + \tilde{W}) + w_\Pi(\tilde{\Pi} - \tilde{T}_\Pi) = w_C \tilde{C} \qquad \text{(II.5)}$$

Labor Supply

$$\tilde{L}_S = \eta_{LL}\tilde{W} - \eta_L \frac{w_\Pi}{w_C}(\tilde{\Pi} - \tilde{T}_\Pi) \qquad \text{(II.6)}$$

Government

Government Budget Constraint

$$0 = w_L \tilde{T}_L + w_K \tilde{T}_K + w_E \tilde{T}_E + w_\Pi \tilde{T}_\Pi + \theta_\Pi w_\Pi \tilde{\Pi} + \theta_L w_L(\tilde{W} + \tilde{L}) + \theta_K w_K \tilde{K} + \theta_E w_E \tilde{E} \qquad \text{(II.7)}$$

Labor-Market Equilibrium

$$\tilde{L}_S = \tilde{L} \qquad \text{(II.8)}$$

Environmental Quality

$$\tilde{M} = -\gamma \tilde{E} \qquad \text{(II.9)}$$

Walras Law: Balance of Payments

$$\tilde{Y} = w_C \tilde{C} + w_G \tilde{G} + w_E(1 - \theta_E)\tilde{E} + w_K(1 - \theta_K)\tilde{K} \qquad \text{(II.10)}$$

Factor Demand Relations

This paper distinguishes between two versions of the model. First, we develop a model with mobile capital. Immobile capital does not enter this model. Relations (II.2) and (II.3) represent the factor demand equations for polluting inputs and capital. The elasticities, ε^*_{ij}, $(i, j = L, K, E)$ represent price elasticities of factor demand conditional on employment. Expression (II.4) represents the non-profit condition.

Second, we explore a model without mobile capital but in which immobile capital enters production. The alternative factor demand equations, represented by (II.2′) and (II.3′), express the demand for polluting inputs and capital conditional on this fixed factor. Expression (II.4′) represents the profit equation.

Table 2.2. Continued.

Endogenous:	$\tilde{Y}, \tilde{L}, \tilde{E}, \tilde{K}, \tilde{\Pi}, \tilde{L}_S, \tilde{C}, \tilde{W}, \tilde{M}$ *and* $\tilde{T}_L, \tilde{T}_K$ *or* $\tilde{T}_\Pi$
Exogenous:	$\tilde{H}, \tilde{T}_E$ *and* $\tilde{T}_L, \tilde{T}_K$ *or* $\tilde{T}_\Pi$ *and* $\tilde{K}^* = \tilde{E}^* = \tilde{G} = 0$

Parameters

ε_{ij} = uncompensated direct or indirect price elasticity of factor i with respect to the price j $(i, j = L, E, K)$ in the model with immobile capital

ε^*_{ij} = uncompensated direct or indirect price elasticity of factor i with respect to price j $(i, j = L, E, K)$ in the model with mobile capital

η_{LL} = uncompensated wage elasticity of labor supply

η_L = income elasticity of labor supply

$\eta^*_{LL} = \eta_{LL} + (1 - \theta_L)(w_L/w_C)\eta_L$ compensated labor supply elasticity

γ = elasticity that measures the effect of more polluting inputs on environmental quality

Taxes

$$\tilde{T}_E = \frac{dT_E}{1 + T_E}\ ;\ \tilde{T}_L = \frac{dT_L}{1 + T_L}\ ;\ \tilde{T}_K = \frac{dT_K}{1 + T_K}\ ;\ \tilde{T}_\Pi = \frac{dT_\Pi}{1 - T_\Pi}$$

$$\theta_L = \frac{T_L}{1 + T_L}\ ; \theta_E = \frac{T_E}{1 + T_E}\ ;\ \theta_K = \frac{T_K}{1 + T_K}\ ; \theta_\Pi = \frac{T_\Pi}{1 - T_\Pi}$$

Shares

$w_\Pi = (1 - T_\Pi)\Pi/Y$	$w_E = (1 + T_E)E/Y$	$w_C = C/Y$	$w_H = (1 + \theta_\Pi)w_\Pi$
$w_K = (1 + T_K)K/Y$	$w_L = (1 + T_L)WL/Y$	$w_G = G/Y$	$w^*_K = (1 + T_K)K^*/Y$
$w^*_E = (1 + T_E)E^*/Y$			

Relations between shares

$$w_H + w_E + w_L + w_K = 1 \quad \text{(S1)}$$

$$w_H = (1 + \theta_\Pi)w_\Pi = 1 - w_L - w_E - w_K \quad \text{(S2)}$$

$$(1 - \theta_L)w_L + w_\Pi + (1 - \theta_E)w^*_E + (1 - \theta_K)w^*_K = w_C \quad \text{(S3)}$$

$$w_G = \theta_L w_L + \theta_E w_E + \theta_K w_K + \theta_\Pi w_\Pi \quad \text{(S4)}$$

$$1 = w_c + w_G + (w_E - w^*_E)(1 - \theta_E) + (w_K - w^*_K)(1 - \theta_K) \quad \text{(S5)}$$

Labor Supply

Expression (II.6) reveals that a rise in the after-tax wage rate (W) boosts labor supply if the uncompensated wage elasticity (η_{LL}) is positive. Indeed, empirical evidence suggests that the value of the wage elasticity is positive, although rather small (Hausman, 1985). Hence, we will assume that this elasticity is positive. Depending on the income elasticity of labor supply (η_L), a rise in after-tax profits reduces labor supply because of a negative income effect. The quality of the environment does not directly affect private behavior because it is weakly separable from private goods in utility (see (I.6)).

2.3. Welfare

We measure the welfare effects of an environmental tax reform by the marginal excess burden, defined as the compensating variation divided by output. It corresponds to the additional transfer that must be provided to households to keep utility, after a policy shock, at its initial level (i.e. the level before the policy shock).[3] A positive excess burden thus implies a loss in welfare. The marginal excess burden, $\tilde{\beta}$, can be written as the sum of three market distortions (see appendix C):

$$\underset{\substack{\textit{labor-market}\\ \textit{distortion}}}{\tilde{\beta} = -\theta_L w_L \tilde{L}} \; - \underset{\substack{\textit{environmental}\\ \textit{distortion}}}{\left[\theta_E - \theta_E^P\right] w_E \tilde{E}} \; - \underset{\substack{\textit{capital-market}\\ \textit{distortion}}}{\theta_K w_K \tilde{K}} \tag{2.1}$$

where

$$\theta_E^P \equiv \frac{1}{1+T_E}\frac{U_M(-M_E)}{\lambda} \tag{2.2}$$

The first term on the right-hand side (RHS) of (2.1) involves the impact of the reform on the labor-market distortion. Employment yields a first-order welfare gain if the pre-existing labor income tax is positive. Intuitively, the labor tax drives a wedge between the marginal social benefits of employment in terms of additional production and the marginal social opportunity costs in terms of foregone leisure. Indeed, additional production due to more employment not only compensates workers for giving up their leisure, but also yields public revenues. The second term on the RHS of (2.1) denotes the environmental distortion, which is determined by the difference between two terms: On the one hand, a tax term representing the additional public revenues if polluting input demand increases and, on the other hand, a term representing the marginal social damage from pollution, defined in (2.2). If the first term exceeds the second term, a higher demand for the polluting input raises welfare—as the marginal social benefits exceed the marginal social costs. The tax rate that fully internalizes the environmental distortion is the Pigovian tax, i.e. $\theta_E = \theta_E^P$. At the Pigovian level, the loss in welfare on account of more pollution is exactly offset by the welfare gain on account of the broadening of the tax base. The third term on the RHS of (2.1) stands for the distortion in the capital market. In particular, the tax rate on capital drives a wedge between the marginal social benefits and costs of capital demand. Hence, an expansion of capital demand raises welfare.

Alternatively, the marginal excess burden can be written as (see appendix C):

$$\tilde{\beta} = \underset{\textit{blue}}{-[(1-\theta_L)w_L\tilde{W} + w_\Pi(\tilde{\Pi} - \tilde{T}_\Pi)]} + \underset{\textit{green}}{(\theta_E^P w_E \tilde{E})} \tag{2.3}$$

The term in square brackets on the RHS of (2.3) indicates that an increase in after-tax private incomes raises welfare. We call this the *blue* welfare component (private or non-environmental dividend). It is associated with the efficiency of the tax system as a revenue-raising device: a more efficient tax system reduces the overall tax burden on private agents and, therefore, boosts after-tax private incomes. Welfare may improve also on account of a *green* dividend, i.e. a better quality of the environment (see the last term on the RHS of (2.3)). If both the blue and the green dividend are positive, we speak about a *double dividend.*

3. Environmental Taxation in the Benchmark Model

This section analyses the consequences of an environmental tax reform in the benchmark model in which both the fixed factor, H, and mobile capital, K, are absent. Subsequently, we extend the benchmark model by incorporating mobile capital (section 4) or fixed capital (section 5), respectively. Hence, the benchmark model is a special case of the two extended models, which are solved in appendix A and appendix B, respectively.

In the benchmark model, the blue dividend is determined by the effect on wages only because profits are zero (see (2.3)). Moreover, in the absence of capital, the capital market distortion is zero (see (2.1)). We will discuss the effects of the ecological tax reform on blue and green welfare (see (2.3)) and on the labor-market and environmental distortions (see (2.1)).

The reduced-form equations for after-tax wages, employment, the demand for the polluting input and output are given in Table 3.1. The reduced-form coefficient in the third row of this table reveals that an environmental tax reform reduces the demand for the polluting input and thus yields a green dividend. If we start from an equilibrium without pollution taxes (i.e. $\theta_E = 0$), the introduction of a small tax leaves wages, and hence private welfare, unaffected (see the reduced-form coefficient in the first row of Table 3.1 with $\theta_E = 0$). The reason for constant wages is that the supply of the polluting input is effectively infinitely elastic because the market price of these inputs is fixed on the world market. Hence, the incidence of the pollution tax falls on the only immobile factor of production, labor, in the form of lower labor productivity. An environmental tax reform thus replaces an *explicit* by an *implicit* tax on labor, which leaves wages unchanged. Hence, the non-environmental costs and benefits coincide so that a small movement away from this equilibrium does not yield any first-order effects on blue welfare. On balance, starting from zero pollution taxes, an ecological tax reform improves overall welfare due to the single green dividend.

If the initial pollution tax is positive (i.e. $\theta_E > 0$), the wage rate declines so that the blue dividend is negative. Intuitively, the explicit labor tax is a more efficient instrument to raise public revenues than the implicit labor tax as the latter distorts not only the labor market but also reduces the demand for the polluting input, thereby (if $\theta_E > 0$) eroding the tax base. Indeed, the initial tax on pollution, θ_E, measures the gap between the social benefits and the non-environmental costs of pollution. Hence, the erosion of the tax base of the pollution tax measures the non-environmental (i.e. private) costs associated with a cleaner environment. We call the costs of a cleaner environment the *tax burden effect*: it reduces real wages and, given a positive uncompensated wage elasticity of labor supply, η_{LL}, employment drops. The environmental benefits, in contrast, leave labor supply unaffected: these benefits are public and thus independent of labor supply. Indeed, by improving the quality of the environment, pollution taxes expand the provision of public consumption goods. The overall burden of taxation is thus exacerbated.

Starting from positive pollution taxes, an environmental tax reform thus features a trade-off between a positive dividend (green welfare) and a negative dividend (blue welfare). Indeed, the reform improves overall welfare only if the value of the environmental improvement dominates the adverse effect on blue welfare due to the higher burden of taxation.

Table 3.1. Reduced-form coefficients for the pollution tax in the benchmark model.

	$\tilde{T}_E$
$\Delta\tilde{W}$	$-w_E\theta_E\dfrac{\sigma_L}{w_L}$
$\Delta\tilde{L}$	$-\theta_E w_E \eta_{LL}\dfrac{\sigma_L}{w_L}$
$\Delta\tilde{E}$	$-[\Delta + \theta_E w_E \eta_{LL}]\dfrac{\sigma_L}{w_L}$
$\Delta\tilde{Y}$	$-[\Delta + \theta_E \eta_{LL}]w_E\dfrac{\sigma_L}{w_L}$

where $\Delta \equiv (1-\theta_L)w_L - \eta_{LL}[\theta_L w_L + \theta_E w_E] > 0$

4. Environmental Taxation and Mobile Capital

This section extends the benchmark model by incorporating mobile capital (K) in the production function. The government can tax the associated capital income through a source-based capital income tax. In the absence of a fixed factor, the factor demand equations are expressed conditional on the level of employment (see (II.2) and (II.3)). To obtain a better understanding of what determines the own and cross price elasticities in these factor demand equations, Table 4.1 presents these elasticities for three separable production functions. It reveals that both a higher price of pollution (capital) and a lower price of labor reduce the pollution/labor ratio (capital/labor ratio) (i.e. ε^*_{EE} and $\varepsilon^*_{KK} > 0$; ε^*_{EL} and $\varepsilon^*_{KL} < 0$). The signs of the cross elasticities, ε^*_{KE} and ε^*_{EK} are ambiguous. In particular, a higher price of pollution boosts the demand for capital relative to that of labor if, compared to labor, capital is a better substitute for pollution. Likewise, the pollution/labor ratio expands on account of a higher price of capital if capital is a better substitute for pollution than it is for labor. If inputs are equally good substitutes for each other, the cross price elasticities are zero.

In the presence of capital, the welfare effects are determined not only by the labor-market and environmental distortions but also by the capital-market distortion (see (2.1)). Since profits are zero, blue welfare is determined by the effect on wages alone (see (2.3)). Alternatively, the private (blue) dividend can be decomposed in effects on the bases of pollution and capital taxes (see appendix C):

$$\tilde{\beta} = \underbrace{-\frac{1-\theta_L}{1-\theta_L-\theta_L\eta_{LL}}\left[\theta_E w_E\tilde{E} + \theta_K w_K\tilde{K}\right]}_{blue} + \underbrace{(\theta^P_E w_E\tilde{E})}_{green} \tag{4.1}$$

The rest of this section is organized as follows. Subsection 4.1 discusses the consequences

Table 4.1. Price elasticities of factor demands (conditional on employment) in the model with mobile capital.

	$Y = F[q(L, K), E]$	$Y = F[q(E, K), L]$	$Y = F[q(L, E), K]$
ϵ^*_{EL}	$-\dfrac{w_K\sigma_{LK} + w_L\sigma_E}{1 - w_E}$	$-\sigma_L$	$-\sigma_{EL}$
ϵ^*_{EE}	$(1 - w_E)\sigma_E$	$\dfrac{w_K\sigma_{EK} + w_E\sigma_L}{1 - w_L}$	σ_{EL}
ϵ^*_{EK}	$\dfrac{w_K(\sigma_{LK} - \sigma_E)}{1 - w_E}$	$\dfrac{w_K(\sigma_L - \sigma_{EK})}{1 - w_L}$	0
ϵ^*_{KL}	$-\sigma_{LK}$	$-\sigma_L$	$-\dfrac{w_E\sigma_{EL} + w_L\sigma_K}{1 - w_K}$
ϵ^*_{KE}	0	$\dfrac{w_E(\sigma_L - \sigma_{EK})}{1 - w_L}$	$\dfrac{w_E(\sigma_{EL} - \sigma_K)}{1 - w_K}$
ϵ^*_{KK}	σ_{LK}	$\dfrac{w_E\sigma_{EK} + w_K\sigma_L}{1 - w_L}$	σ_K

of pollution taxes if the revenues are used to cut labor taxes. Subsection 4.2 assumes that the capital tax is reduced.

4.1. Reducing Labor Taxes

Appendix A derives the solutions of a rise in pollution taxes, recycled through lower labor taxes. The reduced-form coefficients are presented in the first column of Table 4.2. We discuss the effects of environmental tax reforms starting from different initial equilibria.

Starting from Zero Non-labor Taxes

If the initial tax rates on the polluting input and capital are zero (i.e. $\theta_E = \theta_K = 0$), the reduced-form coefficient in the first row of Table 4.2 reveals that introducing a pollution tax leaves wages and thus blue welfare unaffected. Hence, zero taxes on the polluting input and capital are optimal from a non-environmental point of view and thus optimize blue welfare. Intuitively, both capital and the polluting input are perfectly mobile internationally and therefore supplied with infinite elasticity. Accordingly, the incidence of both the tax that is increased (i.e. the pollution tax) and the tax that is reduced (i.e. the labor tax) are borne by the only immobile factor of production, labor. If we start from zero non-labor taxes, all taxes are equally efficient instruments to raise revenues and a marginal change in the tax system does not yield any first-order effects on private welfare. Green welfare, however,

Table 4.2. Reduced-form coefficients for the pollution tax and the capital tax in the model with mobile capital.[a)]

	Reducing T_L	Reducing T_K
$\tilde{W}$	$-[\theta_E\Gamma_{EE}+\theta_K\Gamma_{EK}]\frac{w_E}{\Delta_L}$	$-[\theta_E(\Gamma_{EE}-\Gamma_{KE})-\theta_K(\Gamma_{KK}-\Gamma_{EK})]\frac{w_K}{\Delta_K}$
$\tilde{L}$	$-[\theta_E\Gamma_{EE}+\theta_K\Gamma_{EK}]\frac{w_E\eta_{LL}}{\Delta_L}$	$-[\theta_E(\Gamma_{EE}-\Gamma_{KE})-\theta_K(\Gamma_{KK}-\Gamma_{EK})]\frac{w_E\eta_{LL}}{\Delta_K}$
$\tilde{E}$	$-\left[\Gamma_{EE}+(\theta_E\Gamma_{EE}+\theta_K\Gamma_{EK})\frac{w_E\eta_{LL}}{\Delta_L}\right]$	$-(\Gamma_{EE}-\Gamma_{KE})$ $-[\theta_E(\Gamma_{EE}-\Gamma_{KE})-\theta_K(\Gamma_{KK}-\Gamma_{EK})]\frac{w_E\eta_{LL}}{\Delta_K}$
$\tilde{K}$	$-\left[\Gamma_{KE}+(\theta_E\Gamma_{EE}+\theta_K\Gamma_{EK})\frac{w_E\eta_{LL}}{\Delta_L}\right]$	$\frac{w_E}{w_K}(\Gamma_{KK}-\Gamma_{EK})$ $-[\theta_E(\Gamma_{EE}-\Gamma_{KE})-\theta_K(\Gamma_{KK}-\Gamma_{EK})]\frac{w_E\eta_{LL}}{\Delta_K}$
$\tilde{Y}$	$-\left[\left(1+\frac{\theta_E\eta_{LL}}{\Delta_L}\right)\Gamma_{EE}+\left(1+\frac{\theta_K\eta_{LL}}{\Delta_L}\right)\Gamma_{EK}\right]w_E$	$-\left(1+\frac{\theta_E\eta_{LL}}{\Delta_K}\right)(\Gamma_{EE}-\Gamma_{KE})w_E$ $+\left(1+\frac{\theta_K\eta_{LL}}{\Delta_K}\right)(\Gamma_{KK}-\Gamma_{EK})w_E$

where $\Delta_L \equiv (1-\theta_L)w_L - \eta_{LL}[\theta_L w_L + \theta_E w_E + \theta_K w_K] > 0$

$\Delta_K \equiv [(1-\theta_L)w_L - \theta_E w_L\Gamma_{KE} - \theta_K w_L \Gamma_{KK}] - \eta_{LL}[\theta_L w_L + \theta_E w_E + \theta_K w_K] > 0$

a) The elasticities Γ_{ij} for $i, j = E, K$, are defined in Table 4.3.

improves due to higher pollution taxes as pollution falls (see below). Hence, a single dividend emerges.

Starting from a Positive Pollution Tax: The Tax Burden Effect[4]

If we start from zero taxes on capital (i.e. $\theta_K = 0$) and a positive pollution tax (i.e. $\theta_E > 0$), further increases in the pollution tax amount to a shift in the tax mix away from the non-environmental optimum (in which $\theta_E = \theta_K = 0$). The resulting decline in non-environmental welfare implies a negative blue dividend (see the first column in Table 4.2). The reduced-form coefficient in the first row of Table 4.2 indeed reveals that wages (representing blue welfare) fall due to a green tax shift if the pollution tax is positive initially. The explanation is similar to that in section 3: at the margin, pollution taxes are less efficient instruments to raise public revenue than taxes on labor because they not only distort the labor market but also reduce the demand for the polluting input, thereby eroding the base of the pollution tax (i.e. the first term between square brackets on the RHS of (4.1)). This erosion of the tax base measures the tax burden effect. Overall welfare improves only if the magnitude of the tax burden effect is small compared to welfare improvement associated with the single green dividend. We thus again face a trade-off between a positive green dividend and a negative blue dividend.

The magnitude of the tax burden effect is determined by two elements: the initial tax rate on the polluting input and the fall in the demand for polluting inputs. The initial pollution tax measures the marginal costs of improving environmental quality. In particular, if pre-existing pollution taxes are large, a decline in the demand for the polluting input substantially reduces public revenues by eroding the tax base.

The second element determining the tax burden effect is the elasticity of polluting input demand, Γ_{EE}, defined below Table 4.3. This 'general equilibrium elasticity' measures the consequences for the pollution/labor ratio due to two price changes: first, a higher price of polluting inputs (measured by ε^*_{EE}) and, second, a lower price of labor induced by the rise in the price of polluting inputs along the factor-price frontier (measured by ε^*_{EL}).[5] A large elasticity, on the one hand, implies that the environment tax reform is successful in cutting pollution. On the other hand, in that case a high pollution tax imposes a heavy burden on the private sector as tax revenues fall substantially due to an eroding tax base. Hence, a trade-off exists between green and blue welfare: if an environmental tax reform is successful in enhancing environmental quality, it imposes a high burden on the private sector in terms of lower wages (see also the trade-off between the first and last terms on the RHS of (4.1)). To obtain a better understanding of the factors determining Γ_{EE}, Table 4.3 presents this elasticity in terms of Allen elasticities of substitution for three separable production functions. This table reveals that pollution unambiguously falls due to an environmental tax reform (i.e. $\Gamma_{EE} > 0$). In particular, both the higher price of pollution and the lower price of labor induce input substitution away from pollution towards labor. Furthermore, because an environmental tax reform shifts the tax burden from the immobile factor (which is rather inelastic in supply) to the mobile factor (which is infinitely elastic in supply), output unambiguously falls. This adverse production effect reinforces the fall in pollution on account of the substitution effect.

Starting from a Positive Capital Tax: The Tax Shifting Effect

If the initial equilibrium features a zero pollution tax (i.e. $\theta_E = 0$) and a positive tax rate on clean capital (i.e. $\theta_K > 0$), the tax system is sub-optimal, even from a non-environmental point of view. In that case, substituting pollution taxes for labor taxes may either exacerbate or alleviate preexisting tax distortions. In particular, an environmental tax reform reduces wages if capital demand falls (see the first row in Table 4.2 with $\theta_E = 0$). The effect on capital demand is determined by the cross price elasticity of capital demand, i.e. $\Gamma_{EK} = (w_K/w_E)\Gamma_{KE}$ (see the reduced-form for capital in the fourth row of Table 4.2 with $\theta_E = 0$). This elasticity measures the consequences for the capital/labor ratio due to a higher price of the polluting input and the associated lower price of labor. Table 4.3 presents expressions for this elasticity for three separable production functions. It reveals that capital demand typically falls. Intuitively, the tax that is cut involves the immobile factor (which is rather inelastic in supply), while the tax that is increased directly affects the mobile factor (which is infinitely elastic in supply). Consequently, output falls—especially if the more expensive mobile factor is a good substitute for the immobile factor. The adverse production effect typically reduces the demand for capital.[6]

The typical decline in capital demand hurts welfare by eroding the base of the tax on

Table 4.3. General equilibrium price elasticities of factor demands (conditinal on employment) of a higher price of the polluting input (or capital) and a lower price of labor.

	$Y = F[q(L, K), E]$	$Y = F[q(E, K), L]$	$Y = F[q(E, L), K]$
Γ_{EE}	$\frac{w_L\sigma_E + w_E w_K \sigma_{LK}}{w_L(1-w_E)}$	$\frac{w_E\sigma_L + w_L w_K \sigma_{EK}}{w_L(1-w_L)}$	$\frac{(1-w_K)\sigma_{EL}}{w_L}$
Γ_{KE}	$\frac{w_E}{w_L}\sigma_{LK}$	$\frac{w_E}{w_L}\frac{\sigma_L - w_L\sigma_{EK}}{1-w_L}$	$\frac{w_E}{w_L}\sigma_{EL}$
Γ_{EK}	$\frac{w_K}{w_L}\sigma_{LK}$	$\frac{w_K}{w_L}\frac{\sigma_L - w_L\sigma_{EK}}{1-w_L}$	$\frac{w_K}{w_L}\sigma_{EL}$
Γ_{KK}	$\frac{(1-w_E)\sigma_{LK}}{w_L}$	$\frac{w_K\sigma_L + w_L w_E \sigma_{EK}}{w_L(1-w_L)}$	$\frac{w_L\sigma_K + w_K w_E \sigma_{EL}}{w_L(1-w_K)}$
$\Gamma_{EE} - \Gamma_{KE}$	$\frac{\sigma_E - w_E\sigma_{LK}}{1-w_E}$	σ_{EK}	σ_{EL}
$\Gamma_{KK} - \Gamma_{EK}$	$\frac{w_E}{w_K}\sigma_{LK}$	$\frac{w_E}{w_K}\sigma_{EK}$	$\frac{w_E}{w_K}\frac{\sigma_K - w_K\sigma_{EL}}{1-w_K}$

where $\Gamma_{EE} \equiv \varepsilon^*_{EE} - \frac{w_E}{w_L}\varepsilon^*_{EL}$; $\Gamma_{KE} \equiv \varepsilon^*_{KE} - \frac{w_E}{w_L}\varepsilon^*_{KL}$

$\Gamma_{EK} \equiv \varepsilon^*_{EK} - \frac{w_K}{w_L}\varepsilon^*_{EL}$; $\Gamma_{KK} \equiv \varepsilon^*_{KK} - \frac{w_K}{w_L}\varepsilon^*_{KL}$

where $w_E\Gamma_{EK} = w_K\Gamma_{KE}$

capital. In this way, substituting pollution taxes for labor taxes exacerbates pre-existing distortions associated with capital taxation. We call this the *tax shifting effect* because the tax burden is shifted towards capital in terms of a lower capital demand. The tax shifting effect is measured by the second term between square brackets on the RHS of (4.1).

The magnitude of the tax shifting effect is determined by the initial tax rate on capital and the cross price elasticity of capital demand. High initial taxes on capital imply that the social costs associated with less capital demand are large. In particular, a fall in the demand for capital induces a large erosion of the tax base and, therefore, a substantial fall in private incomes. Second, the cross price elasticity of capital demand, Γ_{KE}, determines how large the fall in capital demand is.

Starting from an Arbitrary Equilibrium

We have now uncovered three channels through which a tax shift away from labor towards pollution affects welfare. First, substitution away from polluting inputs in combination with an adverse production effect contributes to green welfare (i.e. the final term on the RHS of (4.1)). Second, pre-existing taxes on the polluting input cause a tax burden effect. In particular, the fall in pollution raises the tax burden on private incomes, thereby adversely affecting blue welfare (see the first term in square brackets on the RHS of (4.1)). Third, if the capital income tax is initially positive, an environmental tax reform induces a tax shifting effect by affecting the base of the capital income tax. Through this channel, the tax distortion on the capital market is typically exacerbated so that blue welfare falls (see the second term between square brackets on the RHS of (4.1)). Overall, starting from an arbitrary equilibrium in which both capital and pollution taxes are positive, an environmental tax reform yields a green dividend. However, blue welfare typically falls so that there is no double dividend but rather a trade-off between two dividends. Accordingly, overall welfare improves only if the single green dividend dominates the adverse effects on blue welfare.

4.2. Reducing Capital Taxes

This subsection explores the consequences of shifting the tax burden away from capital taxes, rather than taxes on labor. The solutions are presented in the second column of Table 4.2 (see appendix A for a derivation).

Starting from Zero Non-labor Taxes

If taxes on polluting inputs and capital are zero (i.e. $\theta_E = \theta_K = 0$) a rise in pollution taxes leaves the wage rate unaffected (see the reduced-form in the first row of Table 4.2 with $\theta_E = \theta_K = 0$). Indeed, as we start from a tax system that is optimal from a non-environmental point of view (see subsection 4.1), a marginal change in the tax system away from this optimum does not yield any first-order effects on blue welfare.

Starting from a Positive Pollution Tax: The Tax Burden Effect

If the initial equilibrium features a positive pollution tax (i.e. $\theta_E > 0$) and zero taxes on capital (i.e. $\theta_K = 0$), further increases in the pollution tax typically shift the tax system further away from the non-environmental optimum, thereby harming blue welfare. Indeed, the reduced-form coefficient in the first row of Table 4.2 reveals that wages decline if the initial pollution tax is positive and the demand for polluting inputs falls. The effect on pollution is determined by the difference between two elasticities (see the third row in Table 4.2 with $\theta_E = \theta_K = 0$), which can be expressed as follows

$$\Gamma_{EE} - \Gamma_{KE} = \varepsilon^*_{EE} - \frac{w_E}{w_K}\varepsilon^*_{EK} \tag{4.2}$$

$\Gamma_{EE} - \Gamma_{KE}$ measures how the pollution-labor ratio changes due to a higher producer price of the polluting input (i.e. the first term on the RHS of (4.2)) and the associated lower producer price of capital (i.e. the second term on the RHS of (4.2)). Table 4.3 presents this general equilibrium elasticity for three separable production functions. It reveals that the shift from capital towards pollution taxes typically yields a green dividend by reducing pollution. If the term in (4.2) is indeed positive, we refer to this as the normal case. In the normal case, the reduction in pollution erodes the base of the environmental tax, thereby reducing the room to cut other, distortionary tax rates.

In the exceptional case that the term in (4.2) is negative, the introduction of a pollution tax, rather paradoxically, raises pollution. Intuitively, the revenues from the pollution tax are used to introduce a capital subsidy, which raises production and thereby pollution. In that case, compared to a pollution tax, a capital tax is a better instrument to cut pollution.[7] This exceptional case occurs if, compared to pollution, capital is a much better substitute for labor (see Table 4.3 if E is separable and σ_E is small compared to σ_{LK}). The tax reform then boosts production because the mobile factor that is elastic in demand (i.e. capital, which is a good substitute for labor) becomes cheaper while the mobile factor that is rather inelastic in demand (i.e. the polluting input which is a relatively poor substitute for labor) becomes more expensive. At the same time, the adverse substitution effect on the demand for the polluting input due to the higher cost of pollution is small because the polluting input is a poor substitute for the two other inputs (i.e. σ_E is relatively small). Accordingly, the positive output effect dominates the adverse substitution effect and pollution thus increases. In the exceptional case, the tax reform yields a positive blue dividend by expanding the base of the pollution tax but at the cost of a negative green dividend. Thus, the double dividend always fails if the initial equilibrium features a positive pollution tax and a zero capital tax: the blue and green dividends have opposite signs.

Starting from a Positive Capital Tax: The Tax Shifting Effect

Substituting pollution taxes for capital taxes is likely to produce a double dividend if such a reform starts from an initial equilibrium with a zero pollution tax (i.e. $\theta_E = 0$) and a positive tax on capital (i.e. $\theta_K > 0$). With this initial equilibrium, expression (4.1) reveals that the sign of the blue dividend depends on how the reform affects capital demand. This is determined by the difference between two elasticities (see the fourth row in Table 4.2 with $\theta_E = 0$), which can be written by using the definitions of the Γ's as

$$\Gamma_{KK} - \Gamma_{EK} = \varepsilon^*_{KK} - \frac{w_K}{w_E}\varepsilon^*_{KE} \tag{4.3}$$

The general equilibrium elasticity, $\Gamma_{KK} - \Gamma_{EK}$, measures how capital demand (scaled by the immobile input, labor) changes as a result of a higher price for the polluting input (measured by the second term on the RHS of (4.3)), and the lower price of capital (i.e. the first term on the RHS of (4.3)). Table 4.3 shows that (4.3) is typically positive so that the demand for capital expands. Intuitively, lower capital costs boost the demand for capital through positive substitution effects. In the normal case, this positive substitution effect dominates the arbitrary output effect. Hence, capital demand increases and private welfare rises.

The intuition behind the expansion of private welfare is that the environmental tax reform moves the tax system closer to a non-environmental optimum. In particular, in the initial equilibrium, one of the non-polluting factors, namely capital, is overtaxed compared to the other non-polluting factor, namely labor. Raising the pollution tax and reducing the capital tax typically reduces the tax burden on the overtaxed factor because, in contrast to the pollution tax, the capital tax directly impacts the capital market. The reallocation of the tax burden away from the overtaxed factor resulting in an expansion of capital demand is called the tax shifting effect.[8]

Only in the exceptional case that a negative output effect is strong enough to offset the positive substitution effect does the demand for capital decline so that private welfare falls. In this case, the tax shifting effect is negative since it works in the wrong way by further raising the burden of taxation on the capital market. This occurs if the polluting input is a much better substitute for labor than capital (see Table 4.3 if K is separable and σ_K is small compared to σ_{EL}). Intuitively, output contracts because the tax burden is shifted away from the input that is inelastic in demand (i.e. capital, which is a poor substitute for labor) towards the input that is in relatively elastic demand (i.e. the polluting input which is a relatively good substitute for labor). With only limited possibilities to substitute capital for other inputs, the adverse production effect dominates the substitution effect so that capital demand drops.

Starting from an Arbitrary Equilibrium

The welfare effects of an ecological tax reform starting from an arbitrary equilibrium can be decomposed into three parts. First, in the normal case, substitution effects produce a green dividend (see final term on the RHS of (4.1)). Second, with pre-existing taxes on the polluting input, the base of the environmental taxes erodes in the normal case, implying a positive tax burden effect. This reduces blue welfare (see first term between square brackets on the RHS of (4.1)). Third, with pre-existing taxes on capital income, a positive tax shifting effect creates the potential for an improvement in private welfare (see the second term between square brackets on the RHS of (4.1)).

In the normal case, substitution effects dominate output effects so that the demand for capital expands while the demand for the polluting input contracts. Consequently, both the tax shifting effect and the tax burden effect are positive. Blue welfare improves if the tax shifting effect is large compared to the tax burden effect so that the improvement in non-environmental efficiency of the tax system (i.e. the tax shifting effect)' finances' the costs of enhancing environmental quality (i.e. the tax burden effect). A double dividend requires that the initial capital tax is large compared to the initial pollution tax. Intuitively, large initial capital taxes indicate a substantial potential for non-environmental efficiency improvements, while small initial pollution taxes imply that environmental improvements are relatively cheap.

A double dividend is feasible only in the normal case, i.e. if substitution effects dominate output effects. In the exceptional case that large positive output effects cause pollution to rise, the green dividend is negative. In the other exceptional case, the blue dividend is negative as adverse production effects reduce capital demand.

Table 5.1. Price elasticities of factor demands in the model with fixed capital.

	$Y = F[q(L, H), E]$	$Y = F[q(E, H), L]$	$Y = F[q(L, E), H]$
ϵ_{LL}	$\frac{(1-w_E)\sigma_{LH}}{w_H}$	$\frac{w_H\sigma_L + w_L w_E \sigma_{EH}}{w_H(1-w_L)}$	$\frac{w_L\sigma_H + w_E w_H \sigma_{LE}}{w_H(1-w_H)}$
ϵ_{LE}	$\frac{w_E}{w_H}\sigma_{LH}$	$\frac{w_E}{w_H}\sigma_{EH}$	$\frac{w_E}{w_H}\frac{\sigma_H - w_H\sigma_{LE}}{1-w_H}$
ϵ_{EE}	$\frac{w_H\sigma_E + \sigma_{LH} w_L w_E}{w_H(1-w_E)}$	$\frac{(1-w_L)\sigma_{EH}}{w_H}$	$\frac{w_E\sigma_H + w_L w_H \sigma_{LE}}{w_H(1-w_H)}$
ϵ_{EL}	$\frac{w_L}{w_H}\sigma_{LH}$	$\frac{w_L}{w_H}\sigma_{EH}$	$\frac{w_L}{w_H}\frac{\sigma_H - w_H\sigma_{LE}}{1-w_H}$
$\epsilon_{LL} - \epsilon_{EL}$	σ_{LH}	$\frac{\sigma_L - w_L\sigma_{EH}}{1-w_L}$	σ_{LE}
$\epsilon_{EE} - \epsilon_{LE}$	$\frac{\sigma_E - w_E\sigma_{LH}}{1-w_E}$	σ_{EH}	σ_{LE}
ϵ_D	$\frac{\sigma_{LH}\sigma_E}{w_H}$	$\frac{\sigma_L\sigma_{EH}}{w_H}$	$\frac{\sigma_H\sigma_{LE}}{w_H}$

where $\epsilon_D \equiv \epsilon_{LL}\epsilon_{EE} - \epsilon_{LE}\epsilon_{EL} > 0$

5. Environmental Taxation and Fixed Capital

This section explores the model in which capital is immobile internationally. Hence, the model contains two factors of production that cannot cross international borders (i.e. labor and capital) and one input that is perfectly mobile across countries (i.e. the polluting input). Concerning capital, we take the extreme case in which it is fixed in supply—contrary to labor which is supplied with a finite wage elasticity.

The linearized factor demand equations for labor and polluting inputs (i.e. (II.2′) and (II.3′)) are expressed conditional on fixed capital, rather than on employment. To obtain more insight into the price elasticities in these factor demand equations, Table 5.1 presents them for three separable production functions. Comparing the elasticities in this table with the Γ's in Table 4.3, we find that they are equivalent except that the fixed factor in Table 5.1 plays the role of employment in Table 4.3. In view of this similarity, this section does not discuss the role of factor substitution in detail.

In the presence of a fixed factor, pure profits emerge. Profits can be interpreted as the return on fixed capital. Hence, blue welfare is no longer determined by wages alone. In particular, the marginal excess burden in (2.3) reveals that the effect on blue welfare depends on both after-tax wage income and after-tax profits.

Table 5.2. Reduced-form coefficients for the profit tax and the pollution tax in the model with a fixed factor.

	Reducing profit taxes	Reducing labor taxes
$\tilde{L}$	$-\left[\eta^*_{LL}\epsilon_{LE} - \frac{w_E}{w_C}\eta_L\theta_E\epsilon_D\right]/\Delta_H$	$\eta^*_{LL}(1-T_\Pi)(\epsilon_{LL}-\epsilon_{EL})w_E/\Delta_F$ $-\eta_{LL}\theta_E w_E\epsilon_D/\Delta_F$
$\tilde{E}$	$-\left[\eta^*_{LL}\epsilon_{EE} + \left(1-\frac{w_L}{w_C}\eta_L\theta_E\right)\epsilon_D\right]/\Delta_H$	$-\eta^*_{LL}(1-T_\Pi)(\epsilon_{EE}-\epsilon_{LE})w_L/\Delta_F$ $-[1-\theta_L-\eta_{LL}\theta_L]w_L\epsilon_D/\Delta_F$
$\tilde{W}$	$-\left[\epsilon_{LE} + \frac{w_E}{w_C}\eta_L(\theta_L\epsilon_{EL}+\theta_E\epsilon_{EE})\right]/\Delta_H$	$[(1-T_\Pi)(\epsilon_{LL}-\epsilon_{EL})-\theta_E\epsilon_D]w_E/\Delta_F$ $+(1-T_\Pi)\frac{w_L}{w_C}\eta_L Z w_E/\Delta_F$
$w_\Pi\tilde{\Pi}$	$-\frac{w_L}{w_C}\eta_L(1-T_\Pi)Z/\Delta_H$ $-w_E(1-T_\Pi)[\eta^*_{LL}+\epsilon_{LL}-\epsilon_{LE}]/\Delta_H$	$\eta_{LL}(1-T_\Pi)Zw_E w_L/\Delta_F$ $-(1-\theta_L)w_L(1-T_\Pi)(\epsilon_{LL}-\epsilon_{EL})w_E/\Delta_F$

where $Z \equiv \theta_L(\epsilon_{LL}-\epsilon_{EL}) - \theta_E(\epsilon_{EE}-\epsilon_{LE})$

$$\Delta_F \equiv \eta^*_{LL}(1-T_\Pi)w_L - \eta_{LL}w_L[\theta_L\epsilon_{LL}+\theta_E\epsilon_{LE}] + (1-\theta_L)w_L\epsilon_{LL} > 0$$

$$\Delta_H \equiv \eta^*_{LL} + \epsilon_{LL} + \frac{w_L}{w_c}\eta_L[\theta_L\epsilon_{LL}+\theta_E\epsilon_{LE}] > 0$$

5.1. *Reducing Profit Taxes*

The reduced-form coefficients in the first column of Table 5.2 present the consequences of higher pollution taxes, recycled through lower profit taxes (see appendix B for a derivation). The reduced-form coefficients in the third and fourth row reveal that such a shift reduces wages and profits, respectively. The reason is that, contrary to pollution taxes, profit taxes are non-distortionary. Shifting away from taxes on the return to fixed capital towards distortionary taxes on pollution thus harms private incomes.

5.2. *Reducing Labor Taxes*[9]

The consequences of higher taxes on the polluting input recycled through lower labor taxes are determined by the coefficients in the second column of Table 5.2. We discuss the reduced-form coefficients in this column by considering various initial equilibria.

Starting from a 100% Profit Tax and a Zero Pollution Tax

If the initial pollution tax is zero ($\theta_E = 0$) while profits are fully taxed away (i.e. $T_\Pi = 1$), the reduced forms in the third and fourth rows of Table 5.2 reveals that a shift from labor towards pollution taxes leaves private income unchanged. The reason is that the owners of the fixed factor receive zero profit income and thus cannot bear the burden of taxation. In fact, the government receives the return on fixed capital by imposing a 100% profit tax and, therefore, it bears the full burden of lower profits. As a result, labor is the only source of private income that can bear the burden of taxes. Just as in the benchmark model, therefore, the swap of pollution taxes for labor taxes boils down to substituting implicit for explicit taxes on labor income. In the absence of initial pollution taxes, employment and wages do not change due to such a shift and the blue dividend is zero (see also section 3). Because there is a single green dividend (see the second row of Table 5.2), an environmental tax reform thus amounts to a welfare improving exercise.

Starting from a Positive Pollution Tax: The Tax Burden Effect on Labor

If the initial pollution tax is positive ($\theta_E > 0$) but profits are fully taxed away (i.e. $T_\Pi = 1$), an environmental tax reform from labor towards pollution reduces wages and thus produces a negative blue dividend. Intuitively, by inducing substitution away from pollution, environmental taxes erode the pollution tax base thereby producing a tax burden effect. Accordingly, there exists a trade-off between a negative blue dividend (i.e. the private costs associated with the higher tax burden) and a positive green dividend. The magnitude of the tax burden effect depends on the initial pollution tax (θ_E) and on the substitution possibilities between pollution and the two other inputs, determined by ε_D.[10] As in the benchmark model, the tax burden effect is fully borne by wage incomes.

Starting from a Less Than 100% Profit Tax: The Tax Shifting Effect

If profits are not fully taxed away by the government (i.e. $T_\Pi < 1$), households receive not only labor income but also profit income. In that case, the ultimate burden of labor taxes and pollution taxes is not only borne by workers, but also by the owners of the fixed factor. Hence, labor and pollution taxes can be considered as implicit taxes on both labor and profit incomes. If we consider the role of these taxes as implicit taxes on profit income, compared to explicit profit taxes, they are less efficient as revenue-raising instruments. This is because, contrary to explicit profit taxes, implicit profit taxes distort the markets for polluting inputs and labor. Whether a reshuffling between labor and pollution taxes involves a more efficient way of taxing profit income thus depends on the marginal effects on these distortions.

To illustrate this, first consider the case that the initial pollution tax is zero (i.e. $\theta_E = 0$). The reduced-form equations for private incomes in Table 5.2 reveal that in that case blue welfare improves due to an environmental tax reform. The reason for this is as follows. If $\theta_E = 0$, the marginal improvement in environmental quality due to a lower demand for polluting inputs comes free. Hence, the tax burden effect is zero. In contrast, in the presence of positive labor taxes (i.e. $\theta_L > 0$), a marginal increase in employment alleviates distortions on the labor market. Indeed, the reduction in the labor tax lowers wage costs and, therefore, boosts labor demand if $\varepsilon_{LL} - \varepsilon_{EL} > 0$.[11] This rise in labor demand, however, is not a sufficient condition to induce an actual increase in employment. In particular, in order to stimulate labor supplys the market wage rate needs to rise, thereby ensuring a clearing labor market. This rise in wages involves a reduction in profits. Hence, an environmental tax reform changes the distribution of incomes in favor of workers and at the expense of capital owners (see the reduced-form coefficient for wages and profits in Table 5.2 with $\theta_E = 0$). Accordingly, we call this the tax shifting effect. The expansion of employment associated with the tax shifting effect broadens the base of the labor tax, thus increasing tax revenues endogenously if $\theta_L > 0$. Tax shifting from labor towards profits thus makes the tax system more efficient as a revenue-raising device and, therefore, yields a double dividend.[12]

Starting from an Arbitrary Equilibrium

If we start from an equilibrium in which $T_\Pi < 1$ and $\theta_E > 0$, an environmental tax reform exerts three different effects on blue welfare. First, there is a tax burden effect on labor. As illustrated above, as far as tax incidence bears on labor incomes it is more efficient from a non-environmental point of view to tax labor explicitly, rather than implicitly through pollution taxes if $\theta_E > 0$. Substituting pollution taxes for labor taxes thus reduces blue welfare on account of the tax burden effect on labor.

Second, in the presence of positive profit incomes, an environmental tax reform may shift the burden of taxation from labor towards the fixed factor. Due to this tax shifting effect, blue welfare may improve (see the first element in the term Z in the reduced form for blue welfare).

Finally, there is a third effect which is only present if both $T_\Pi < 1$ and $\theta_E > 0$. In particular, if households receive not only labor but also profit income, the tax burden associated with improvements in environmental quality may be distributed across these two sources of household income. Hence, the owners of the fixed factor share in the tax burden effect. Accordingly, we call the tax burden effect on profits and is represented by the second element in the term Z. The tax burden effect on profits determines the marginal distortionary effect of pollution taxes as an instrument to tax away profit income. Intuitively, higher pollution taxes reduce the demand for polluting inputs, thereby eroding the base of the pollution tax and reducing private incomes.[13]

An environmental tax reform from labor towards pollution yields a double dividend if the tax shifting effect is large compared to the sum of the total tax burden effect which is distributed across after-tax labor incomes and after-tax profits. The double dividend is feasible if four conditions are met. First, the fixed factor should be able to bear a large part of the tax burden. This requires a small profit tax and a large share of the fixed factor in production (implying that ε_D is small). Second, initial labor taxes should be large compared to pollution taxes. This implies that a rise in employment is valuable whereas a drop in pollution is cheap. Third, labor demand should be elastic relative to pollution demand. Finally, labor supply should be sufficiently elastic with respect to wages and profits.[14] These latter two conditions reveal that Ramsey principles are important for an environmental tax reform to improve non-environmental welfare.

6. Simulations

This section illustrates our findings by presenting some numerical simulations with the two different versions of the model. First, we consider the model in which all capital is perfectly mobile internationally. As the supply of capital is likely to be more elastic in the long run than in the short run, these simulations can, roughly speaking, be interpreted as the long-run consequences of environmental tax reforms (although other aspects may differ between the long run and the short run as well). In the second model, all capital is immobile and supplied inelastically. These outcomes could be interpreted as the short-term consequences of environmental tax reforms.

The calibration of the model requires empirical information about various shares, demand elasticities and other parameters. The shares in the model are based on a rough approximation of most Western European economies (see the first column in Table 6.1). Here, we take the polluting input to be energy. EU economies are characterized by a large share of labor income in GDP and large initial labor and capital taxes as compared to energy taxes. Indeed, T_L is set at 1, which implies a labor tax on the before-tax basis of 50%. The capital income tax on a before-tax basis is set at one third, which is also the tax rate on fixed capital. The factor demand elasticities are derived from a number of empirical studies (see e.g. Pindyk (1977), Berndt and Wood (1979), Griffin and Gregory (1981), Berndt and Hesse (1986), Hesse and Tarkka (1986), Ilmakunnas and Torma (1989)). In particular, the second column in Table 6.1 presents our parameterization for the demand elasticities based on this literature. These empirical estimates denote price elasticities conditional on the level of output. In order to find the elasticities used in our model, we need to transform these estimates into elasticities conditional on the fixed factor or labor, rather than on output. These transformed elasticities are presented in the third column of Table 6.1. All other calibrated parameters are given in the fourth column of Table 6.1

Given the uncertainty surrounding some price elasticities, we employ sensitivity analysis. In particular, the debate on the substitutability/complementarity between capital and energy calls for sensitivity analysis on the cross price elasticities of capital and energy demand. Furthermore, the sensitivity with respect to the cross price elasticity between labor and energy is employed. This also illustrates the importance of the empirical foundation of the production structure for the double-dividend debate.

The Model with Mobile Capital

The first two columns of Table 6.2 show the consequences of an increase in energy taxes that raise after-tax energy prices by 10% in the model with mobile capital.[15] The table reveals that energy demand falls by about 6%, which implies a positive green dividend. If the revenues from the energy tax are used to cut labor taxes, employment and wages fall by respectively 0.07% and 0.36%. Hence, there is no double dividend but rather a

Table 6.1. Calibration of the two models.

Shares	Basic parameters from empirical studies	Conditional on fixed capital (if $w_K = 0$)	Conditional on employment (if $w_H = 0$)	Other elasticities
$w_L = .7$	$e_{LL} = .25$	$\varepsilon_{LL} = 1.02$	$\varepsilon^*_{EL} = -.46$	$\eta_L = .3$
$w_E = .1$	$e_{LE} = -.03$	$\varepsilon_{LE} = .14$	$\varepsilon^*_{EE} = .58$	$\eta_{LL} = .2$
$w_H = .2$ if $w_K = 0$	$e_{LK} = -.06$	$\varepsilon_{EL} = .56$	$\varepsilon^*_{EK} = -.04$	$\eta^*_{LL} = .43$
$w_K = .2$ if $w_H = 0$	$e_{EL} = -.21$	$\varepsilon_{EE} = .72$	$\varepsilon^*_{KL} = -.67$	
$T_L = 1.0$	$e_{EE} = .55$		$\varepsilon^*_{KE} = -.02$	
$T_K = .5$	$e_{EK} = -.1$		$\varepsilon^*_{KK} = .71$	
$T_E = .1$	$e_{KL} = -.42$			
$T_\Pi = .33$	$e_{KE} = -.05$			
$w_C = .6$	$e_{KK} = .65$			
$w_G = .31$				

trade-off between a positive, green dividend and a negative, blue dividend. Compared to labor, energy is overtaxed from a non-environmental point of view in EU economies. This conclusion was also derived in the theoretical model of section 4 and denoted as the normal case.

If the revenues from the energy tax are used to cut capital taxes, rather than labor taxes, wages rise by 0.79%, whereas employment increases by 0.16%. These findings suggests that in the long run, compared to energy, capital is typically overtaxed in Western European countries. Hence, in using the terminology of section 4, we can say that the tax shifting effect dominates the tax burden effect.

If capital and energy are better substitutes for each other than in the base run simulation, substituting energy taxes for ordinary taxes on labor and capital becomes more favorable from a non-environmental point of view. This is illustrated by the third and fourth columns of Table 6.2. In particular, we find that a shift from labor towards energy taxes improves blue welfare in this case (wages rise by 0.14%). This is because, with easier substitution between capital and energy, such a shift in the tax system induces a large substitution effect towards capital. Accordingly, capital demand rises by 1.27%. The broadening of the base of the capital tax allows for further reductions in the endogenous labor tax and, therefore, higher after-tax wage incomes.[16]

If capital and energy would be poorer substitutes than in the base run simulation, substituting energy for labor taxes would be less favorable for blue welfare (see fifth and sixth columns of Table 6.2). However, the conclusion that capital is overtaxed compared to energy would still hold.

The Model with Fixed Capital

Table 6.3 presents the simulations of a rise in the energy tax that raises the after-tax energy price by 10% in the model with immobile capital that is fixed in supply. Again, we find that energy demand drops by around 6%. If the revenues would be used to reduce the

Table 6.2. Effects of a 10% increase in pollution taxes in the model with mobile capital, recycled through lower labor taxes or capital taxes.

	Base Run		K/E better substitutes $e_{KE} = -.25$ $e_{EK} = -.5$		K/E poorer substitutes $e_{KE} = .15$ $e_{EK} = .3$	
	Lower T_L	Lower T_K	Lower T_L	Lower T_K	Lower T_L	Lower T_K
wages (blue welfare)	−0.36	0.79	0.14	1.22	−0.85	0.37
employment	−0.07	0.16	0.03	0.16	−0.17	0.07
capital	−0.83	4.21	1.27	6.29	−2.93	2.12
pollution	−6.53	−5.54	−6.43	−7.46	−6.63	−3.63

Table 6.3. Effects of a 10% increase in pollution taxes in the model with fixed capital, recycled through lower labor taxes or capital taxes.

	Base Run		E/L better substitutes $e_{EL} = -.49, e_{LE} = -.07$		E/L poorer substitutes $e_{EL} = -.07, e_{LE} = -.01$	
	Lower T_L	Lower T_Π	Lower T_L	Lower T_Π	Lower T_L	Lower T_Π
wage rate	1.01	−1.0	3.38	0.24	0.47	−1.42
employment	0.36	−0.32	1.12	0.11	0.18	−0.50
pollution	−7.83	−4.59	−9.16	−2.55	−7.72	−5.59
gross profits	−2.29	−5.88	−6.59	−8.43	−1.33	−4.80
blue welfare	0.05	−1.06	0.30	−0.98	−0.01	−1.09

labor tax, wages and employment would rise by, respectively, 1.01% and 0.36%. Profits fall by 2.29%. The increase in wages dominates the drop in profits so that blue welfare rises by 0.05%. Hence, the tax shifting effect outweighs the tax burden effect. In the short run, EU economies thus slightly overtax labor compared to energy, even if environmental considerations are ignored. Recycling the revenues through lower profit taxes instead of labor taxes involves higher non-environmental costs in the short run, as shown in the second column of Table 6.3.

If labor and energy are much better substitutes than in the base run simulation, a shift from labor towards energy taxes is even more favorable for blue welfare (see third column of Table 6.3). Indeed, blue welfare rises by 0.3%. This is because employment rises more substantially (+1.12%) than in the base run simulation, as the substitution effect towards labor is larger. In addition, the fixed factor bears a larger part of the tax burden, resulting in a more substantial fall in profits of 6.59%. Consequently, the tax shifting effect from profit incomes towards wages is more substantial. The fourth column of Table 6.3 reveals that easier substitution between labor and energy also reduces the non-environmental costs associated with a shift from profit taxes towards energy taxes.

A number of empirical estimates suggest that, compared to capital, labor is a poorer substitute for energy. In particular, for nine European countries Hesse and Tarkka (1986) find a median substitution elasticity between energy and capital of 0.5, but a median elasticity of 0.2 between labor and energy. Hence, the results with easier substitution between E and

L as presented in the third and fourth columns of Table 6.3 may be unrealistic. The case with poorer substitution between energy and labor may be more relevant for most European countries. The fifth column in Table 6.3 reveals that this would be rather unfavorable for the double dividend in the short run. In particular, if labor and energy would be poorer substitutes than in the base run simulation, blue welfare may even fall (−0.01%) whereas the rise in wages and employment are mitigated (+0.47%) and +0.18%, respectively). Hence, with poor substitution between labor and energy, labor does not seem to be overtaxed.

7. Conclusions

Economists generally agree on the beneficial environmental effects of shifting the tax burden from labor towards polluting inputs. However, they often disagree on the consequences of such a reform for non-environmental welfare, i.e. private incomes. This paper focusses on this latter aspect. We find that, in a model for a small open economy with only labor and a polluting input as factors of production, non-environmental welfare declines. Hence, a trade-off seems to exist between environmental quality and private incomes: an increase in the supply of the public good of the environment is associated with a higher tax burden that reduces private incomes. However, other factors of production—such as capital—are important for the non-environmental consequences of environmental tax reforms as well. Indeed, this paper shows that incorporating capital creates the potential for a double dividend by inducing a so-called tax shifting effect: an environmental tax reform may move the tax system closer towards its non-environmental optimum if the tax system is sub-optimal initially.

The first tax shifting effect is illustrated in a model in which capital is perfectly mobile internationally. In that case, zero capital and pollution taxes are optimal from a non-environmental point of view so that the tax system is sub-optimal if capital is taxed initially. By expanding capital demand and reducing the demand for polluting inputs, a swap of pollution taxes for capital taxes boosts non-environmental welfare if the marginal welfare gain of additional capital dominates the tax burden effect, i.e. the marginal loss in non-environmental welfare due to a drop in polluting inputs. In that case, compared to polluting inputs, capital is overtaxed initially so that substituting pollution taxes for capital taxes shifts the tax system towards its non-environmental optimum. Our numerical simulations reveal that this is potentially important for EU economies.

The second tax shifting effect is illustrated in a model in which capital shares in bearing the burden of pollution taxes. In particular, the model includes immobile capital that is supplied inelastically. In that case, the initial distribution of taxes over labor and pollution may be inefficient from a non-environmental point of view as the incidence of taxes not only falls on labor but also on income from the fixed factor. Indeed, a swap of pollution taxes for labor taxes may shift the burden of taxation from labor towards the return on fixed capital, thereby improving non-environmental welfare. Accordingly, the incorporation of fixed capital increases the potential for a tax shifting effect and thus for a double dividend.

In reality, most capital is neither fixed nor perfectly elastic. Hence, the truth is somewhere between the two polar cases from this paper. Our cases show, however, that the potential for a double dividend from an environmental tax reform improves if capital is included in the analysis. Crucial elements in this respect are the degree of capital mobility, factor substitution and, most important, the initial inefficiencies. Equity considerations may be a reason for the presence of inefficient tax systems. Therefore, the distributional impacts of an ecological tax reform may be important when analyzing the feasibility of such a reform. This is an important issue for future research.

Appendix A: Solving the Model with Mobile Capital

This appendix solves the model from Table 2.2 if fixed capital is absent. To that end, we substitute equation (II.1) into (II.10) to eliminate $\tilde{Y}$:

$$w_L \tilde{L} = w_C \tilde{C} - w_E \theta_E \tilde{E} - w_K \theta_K \tilde{K} \tag{A1}$$

We will express the endogenous variables on the RHS of (A1) in terms of $\tilde{L}$ and $\tilde{W}$. To find $\tilde{C}$, we derive from (II.5) with $\tilde{T}_\Pi = \tilde{\Pi} = 0$:

$$w_C \tilde{C} = w_L (1 - \theta_L)(\tilde{W} + \tilde{L}) \tag{A2}$$

To find $\tilde{E}$ and $\tilde{K}$ in terms of $\tilde{L}$ and $\tilde{W}$, we use the factor demand relations for polluting inputs and capital from Table 2.2 in case the fixed factor is absent (i.e. (II.2) and (II.3), respectively). Two different versions of the model will be solved in this appendix. First, we derive the reduced forms for the case that the revenues from higher pollution taxes are used to reduce T_L endogenously. Subsequently, we do the same for the case that the revenues are used to cut T_K.

Endogenous Labor Tax

If the revenues from environmental taxes are used to cut the labor tax, we substitute (II.4) into (II.2) and (II.3) in order to eliminate the wage costs, $\tilde{W} + \tilde{T}_L$. This yields for polluting input demand and capital demand:

$$\tilde{E} = \tilde{L} - \Gamma_{EE} \tilde{T}_E - \Gamma_{EK} \tilde{T}_K \tag{A3}$$

$$\tilde{K} = \tilde{L} - \Gamma_{KE} \tilde{T}_E - \Gamma_{KK} \tilde{T}_K \tag{A4}$$

where

$$\Gamma_{EE} \equiv \varepsilon^*_{EE} - \frac{w_E}{w_L}\varepsilon^*_{EL} \ ; \ \Gamma_{EK} \equiv \varepsilon^*_{EK} - \frac{w_K}{w_L}\varepsilon^*_{EL}$$

$$\Gamma_{KE} \equiv \varepsilon^*_{KE} - \frac{w_E}{w_L}\varepsilon^*_{KL} \ ; \ \Gamma_{KK} \equiv \varepsilon^*_{KK} - \frac{w_K}{w_L}\varepsilon^*_{KL} \tag{A5}$$

Substituting (A2), (A3) and (A4) into (A1), we find a relation between $\tilde{L}$, $\tilde{W}$, and $\tilde{T}_E$ and $\tilde{T}_K$:

$$[\theta_L w_L + \theta_E w_E + \theta_K w_K]\tilde{L} - (1 - \theta_L) w_L \tilde{W}$$
$$= [\theta_E \Gamma_{EE} + \theta_K \Gamma_{EK}] w_E \tilde{T}_E + [\theta_E \Gamma_{KE} + \theta_K \Gamma_{KK}] w_K \tilde{T}_K \tag{A6}$$

where we used $w_K \Gamma_{KE} = w_E \Gamma_{EK}$. The relation for labor supply in (II.6) (with $\tilde{T}_\Pi = \tilde{\Pi} = 0$) and (A6) form a set of two equations and two endogenous variables $\tilde{L}$ and $\tilde{W}$. In matrix notation, we write them as:

$$\begin{pmatrix} \theta_L w_L + \theta_E w_E + \theta_K w_K & -(1-\theta_L) w_L \\ 1 & -\eta_{LL} \end{pmatrix} \begin{pmatrix} \tilde{L} \\ \tilde{W} \end{pmatrix} = \begin{pmatrix} (\theta_E \Gamma_{EE} + \theta_K \Gamma_{EK}) w_E & (\theta_E \Gamma_{KE} + \theta_K \Gamma_{KK}) w_K \\ 0 & 0 \end{pmatrix} \begin{pmatrix} \tilde{T}_E \\ \tilde{T}_K \end{pmatrix} \tag{A7}$$

By inverting the matrix on the LHS of (A7), we derive:

$$\Delta_L \begin{pmatrix} \tilde{L} \\ \tilde{W} \end{pmatrix} = \begin{pmatrix} -\eta_{LL} & (1-\theta_L) w_L \\ -1 & \theta_L w_L + \theta_E w_E + \theta_K w_K \end{pmatrix} \times \begin{pmatrix} (\theta_E \Gamma_{EE} + \theta_K \Gamma_{EK}) w_E & (\theta_E \Gamma_{KE} + \theta_K \Gamma_{KK}) w_K \\ 0 & 0 \end{pmatrix} \begin{pmatrix} \tilde{T}_E \\ \tilde{T}_K \end{pmatrix} \tag{A8}$$

where

$$\Delta_L \equiv (1-\theta_L) w_L - \eta_{LL} [\theta_L w_L + \theta_E w_E + \theta_K w_K] > 0 \tag{A8}$$

From (A8), we derive the reduced forms for employment and wages:

$$\Delta_L \tilde{L} = -\eta_{LL} [\theta_E \Gamma_{EE} + \theta_K \Gamma_{EK}] w_E \tilde{T}_E - \eta_{LL} [\theta_E \Gamma_{KE} + \theta_K \Gamma_{KK}] w_K \tilde{T}_K \tag{A10}$$

$$\Delta_L \tilde{W} = -[\theta_E \Gamma_{EE} + \theta_K \Gamma_{EK}] w_E \tilde{T}_E - [\theta_E \Gamma_{KE} + \theta_K \Gamma_{KK}] w_K \tilde{T}_K \tag{A11}$$

By substitution of (A10) into (A3) and (A4), we derive the reduced forms for polluting input demand and capital demand. The reduced form for output is found by substituting (A10) and the reduced forms for polluting inputs and capital into (II.1).

Endogenous Capital Income Tax

If the revenues from environmental taxes are used to cut the capital income tax, rather than the labor income tax, we substitute (II.4) into (II.2) and (II.3) to eliminate the capital income tax. Thus, we find for polluting input and capital demand

$$\tilde{E} = \tilde{L} - (\Gamma_{EE} - \Gamma_{KE}) \tilde{T}_E + \frac{w_L}{w_K} \Gamma_{EK} (\tilde{W} + \tilde{T}_L) \tag{A12}$$

$$\tilde{K} = \tilde{L} + \frac{w_E}{w_K} (\Gamma_{KK} - \Gamma_{EK}) \tilde{T}_E + \frac{w_L}{w_K} \Gamma_{KK} (\tilde{W} + \tilde{T}_L) \tag{A13}$$

Substituting (A12) and (A13) as well as (A2) into (A1), we find a relation between $\tilde{L}$, $\tilde{W}$, $\tilde{T}_E$ and $\tilde{T}_L$

$$\begin{aligned} &[\theta_L w_L + \theta_E w_E + \theta_K w_K] \tilde{L} - [(1-\theta_L) w_L - w_L (\theta_E \Gamma_{KE} + \theta_K \Gamma_{KK})] \tilde{W} \\ &\quad = [\theta_E (\Gamma_{EE} - \Gamma_{KE}) - \theta_K (\Gamma_{KK} - \Gamma_{EK})] w_E \tilde{T}_E \\ &\quad - [\theta_E \Gamma_{KE} + \theta_K \Gamma_{KK}] w_L \tilde{T}_L \end{aligned} \tag{A14}$$

Combining (A14) and (II.6) and applying the method of matrix inversion, we find the following reduced forms for employment and wages:

$$\begin{aligned}\Delta_K \tilde{L} &= -\eta_{LL}[\theta_E(\Gamma_{EE}-\Gamma_{KE})-\theta_K(\Gamma_{KK}-\Gamma_{EK})]w_E\tilde{T}_E \\ &\quad + \eta_{LL}[\theta_E\Gamma_{KE}+\theta_K\Gamma_{KK}]w_L\tilde{T}_L \qquad \text{(A15)}\end{aligned}$$

$$\begin{aligned}\Delta_K \tilde{W} &= -[\theta_E(\Gamma_{EE}-\Gamma_{KE})-\theta_K(\Gamma_{KK}-\Gamma_{EK})]w_E\tilde{T}_E \\ &\quad + [\theta_E\Gamma_{KE}+\theta_K\Gamma_{KK}]w_L\tilde{T}_L \qquad \text{(A16)}\end{aligned}$$

where

$$\begin{aligned}\Delta_K &\equiv (1-\theta_L)w_L-\theta_E w_L\Gamma_{KE}-\theta_K w_L\Gamma_{KK} \\ &\quad - \eta_{LL}[\theta_L w_L+\theta_E w_E+\theta_K w_K] \qquad \text{(A17)}\end{aligned}$$

By substituting (A15) into (A12) and (A13), we arrive at the reduced forms for polluting input demand and capital demand. The solution for output is found by substituting the reduced forms for employment, polluting inputs and capital into (II.1).

Appendix B: Solving the Model with Fixed Capital

This appendix solves the model from Table 2.2 if mobile capital is absent (i.e. $w_K = 0$). First, we solve the model if the labor tax is endogenously adjusted to balance the government budget. Second, we do the same if the profit tax is endogenous.

Endogenous Labor Tax

To solve the model, we derive three equations in terms of the three endogenous variables $\tilde{L}$, $\tilde{W}$ and $\tilde{T}_L$ and the exogenous taxes, $\tilde{T}_E$ and $\tilde{T}_\Pi$. First, we subtract (II.10) from (II.1) to eliminate $\tilde{Y}$

$$w_L\tilde{L} = w_C\tilde{C} - w_E\theta_E\tilde{E} \qquad \text{(B1)}$$

By substituting (II.3′) and (II.5) with $\tilde{H} = 0$ into (B1) to eliminate $\tilde{E}$ and $\tilde{C}$, respectively, we find:

$$\theta_L w_L\tilde{L} = w_L(1-\theta_L)\tilde{W} + w_\Pi(\tilde{\Pi}-\tilde{T}_\Pi) + w_E\theta_E[\epsilon_{EL}(\tilde{W}+\tilde{T}_L)+\epsilon_{EE}\tilde{T}_E] \qquad \text{(B2)}$$

Profits can be eliminated by substituting (II.4′) into (B2):

$$\begin{aligned}\theta_L w_L\tilde{L} &= w_L(1-\theta_L)\tilde{W} - w_\Pi\tilde{T}_\Pi - (1-T_\Pi)[w_L(\tilde{W}+\tilde{T}_L)+w_E\tilde{T}_E] \\ &\quad + w_E\theta_E[\epsilon_{EL}(\tilde{W}+\tilde{T}_L)+\epsilon_{EE}\tilde{T}_E] \qquad \text{(B3)}\end{aligned}$$

Second, by substituting (II.4′) into (II.6), we find for labor supply:

$$\tilde{L}_S = \eta_{LL}\tilde{W} + \frac{\eta_L}{w_C}(1-T_\Pi)[w_L(\tilde{W}+\tilde{T}_L)+w_E\tilde{T}_E+(1+\theta_\Pi)w_\Pi\tilde{T}_\Pi] \qquad \text{(B4)}$$

Relations (II.2′), (B3) and (B4) from three equations in terms of $\tilde{L}$, $\tilde{W}$, $\tilde{T}_L$, $\tilde{T}_E$ and $\tilde{T}_\Pi$. They can be written in matrix notation as:

$$\begin{pmatrix} 1 & \epsilon_{LL} & \epsilon_{LL} \\ 1 & -\left[\eta_{LL} + \eta_L(1-T_\Pi)\frac{w_L}{w_C}\right] & -\eta_L(1-T_\Pi)\frac{w_L}{w_C} \\ \theta_L w_L & -w_L[(1-\theta_L)-(1-T_\Pi)+\theta_E\epsilon_{LE}] & w_L[(1-T_\Pi)-\theta_E\epsilon_{LE}] \end{pmatrix} \begin{pmatrix} \tilde{L} \\ \tilde{W} \\ \tilde{T}_L \end{pmatrix}$$

$$= \begin{pmatrix} -\epsilon_{LE} & 0 \\ \eta_L(1-T_\Pi)\frac{w_E}{w_C} & \eta_L\frac{w_\Pi}{w_C} \\ -(1-T_\Pi)w_E + \theta_E w_E \epsilon_{EE} & -w_\Pi \end{pmatrix} \begin{pmatrix} \tilde{T}_E \\ \tilde{T}_\Pi \end{pmatrix} \tag{B5}$$

Applying Cramer's Rule to (B5), we find the following solutions for employment, the wage rate and the labor tax:

$$\Delta_F \tilde{L} = \eta^*_{LL}(1-T_\Pi)(\varepsilon_{LL}-\varepsilon_{EL})w_E\tilde{T}_E - \eta_{LL}\theta_E w_E \varepsilon_D \tilde{T}_E + w_\Pi \varepsilon_{LL}\eta^*_{LL}\tilde{T}_\Pi \tag{B6}$$

$$\begin{aligned} \Delta_F \tilde{W} = {} & [(1-T_\Pi)(\varepsilon_{LL}-\varepsilon_{EL}) - \theta_E\varepsilon_D]w_E\tilde{T}_E \\ & + (1-T_\Pi)\frac{w_L}{w_C}\eta_L[\theta_L(\varepsilon_{LL}-\varepsilon_{EL}) - \theta_E(\varepsilon_{EE}-\varepsilon_{LE})]w_E\tilde{T}_E \\ & + w_\Pi\varepsilon_{LL}\tilde{T}_\Pi + w_\Pi\frac{w_L}{w_C}\eta_L[\theta_L\varepsilon_{LL}+\theta_E\varepsilon_{LE}]\tilde{T}_\Pi \end{aligned} \tag{B7}$$

$$\begin{aligned} \Delta_F \tilde{T}_L = {} & -\eta_{LL}[(1-T_\Pi)w_E - \theta_L w_L \varepsilon_{LE} - \theta_E w_E \varepsilon_{EE}]\tilde{T}_E \\ & - [(1-T_\Pi)(\varepsilon_{LL}-\varepsilon_{EL}) - \theta_E\varepsilon_D]w_E\tilde{T}_E \\ & - (1-T_\Pi)\frac{w_L}{w_C}\eta_L w_E[\theta_L(\varepsilon_{LL}-\varepsilon_{EL}) - \theta_E(\varepsilon_{EE}-\varepsilon_{LE})]\tilde{T}_E \\ & - (1-\theta_L)w_L\left[\varepsilon_{LE} + (1-T_\Pi)\eta_L\frac{w_E}{w_C}\right]\tilde{T}_E \\ & - w_\Pi[\eta^*_{LL}+\varepsilon_{LL}]\tilde{T}_\Pi - w_\Pi\frac{w_L}{w_C}\eta_L[\theta_L\varepsilon_{LL}+\theta_E\varepsilon_{LE}]\tilde{T}_\Pi \end{aligned} \tag{B8}$$

where

$$\begin{aligned} \Delta_F \equiv {} & \eta_{LL}[(1-T_\Pi)w_L - \theta_L w_L \varepsilon_{LL} - \theta_E w_E \varepsilon_{EL}] \\ & + (1-\theta_L)w_L\left[\varepsilon_{LL} + (1-T_\Pi)\eta_L\frac{w_L}{w_C}\right] > 0 \end{aligned} \tag{B9}$$

$\epsilon_D \equiv \epsilon_{LL}\epsilon_{EE} - \epsilon_{LE}\epsilon_{EL}$ and $\eta^*_{LL} \equiv \eta_{LL} + \eta_L\frac{(1-\theta_L)w_L}{w_C}$ is the compensated elasticity of labor supply. The determinant in (B9) should be positive for the equilibrium to be stable. The reduced forms for pollution and profits are found by substituting (B7) and (B8) into (II.3′) and (II.4′), respectively.

Endogenous Profit Tax

If the profit tax would be endogenous while the labor tax is an exogenous policy variable, relations (II.2′), (B3) and (B4) form these equations in the three endogenous variables $\tilde{L}$, $\tilde{W}$ and $\tilde{T}_\Pi$. Hence, they can be written in matrix notation as:

$$\begin{pmatrix} 1 & \epsilon_{LL} & 0 \\ 1 & -\left[\eta_{LL} + \eta_L(1 - T_\Pi)\frac{w_L}{w_C}\right] & -\eta_L \frac{w_\Pi}{w_C} \\ \theta_L w_L & -w_L[(1-\theta_L) - (1 - T_\Pi) + \theta_E \epsilon_{LE}] & w_\Pi \end{pmatrix} \begin{pmatrix} \tilde{L} \\ \tilde{W} \\ \tilde{T}_\Pi \end{pmatrix}$$
$$= \begin{pmatrix} -\epsilon_{LE} & -\epsilon_{LL} \\ \eta_L(1 - T_\Pi)\frac{w_E}{w_C} & \eta_L(1 - T_\Pi)\frac{w_L}{w_C} \\ -(1 - T_\Pi)w_E + \theta_E w_E \epsilon_{EE} & -w_L[(1 - T_\Pi) - \theta_E \epsilon_{LE}] \end{pmatrix} \begin{pmatrix} \tilde{T}_E \\ \tilde{T}_L \end{pmatrix} \quad \text{(B10)}$$

Applying Cramer's Rule to (B10), we find the following solutions for employment, wages and the profit tax rate:

$$\Delta_H \tilde{L} = -\epsilon_{LL}\eta^*_{LL}\tilde{T}_L - \left[\eta^*_{LL}\epsilon_{LE} - \frac{w_E}{w_C}\eta_L\theta_E\epsilon_D\right]\tilde{T}_E \quad \text{(B11)}$$

$$\begin{aligned} \Delta_H \tilde{W} &= -\left[\epsilon_{LL} + \frac{w_L}{w_C}\eta_L(\theta_L\epsilon_{LL} + \theta_E\epsilon_{LE})\right]\tilde{T}_L \\ &\quad - \left[\epsilon_{LE} + \frac{w_E}{w_C}\eta_L(\theta_L\epsilon_{EL} + \theta_E\epsilon_{EE})\right]\tilde{T}_E \end{aligned} \quad \text{(B12)}$$

$$\begin{aligned} \Delta_H \tilde{T}_\Pi &= -\eta_{LL}[(1 - T_\Pi)w_E - \theta_L w_L \varepsilon_{LE} - \theta_E w_E \varepsilon_{EE}]\tilde{T}_E \\ &\quad - [(1 - T_\Pi)(\varepsilon_{LL} - \varepsilon_{EL}) - \theta_E\varepsilon_D]w_E\tilde{T}_E \\ &\quad - (1 - T_\Pi)\frac{w_L}{w_C}\eta_L w_E[\theta_L(\varepsilon_{LL} - \varepsilon_{EL}) - \theta_E(\varepsilon_{EE} - \varepsilon_{LE})]\tilde{T}_E \\ &\quad - (1 - \theta_L)w_L\left[\varepsilon_{LE} + (1 - T_\Pi)\eta_L\frac{w_E}{w_C}\right]\tilde{T}_E \\ &\quad - \eta_{LL}[(1 - T_\Pi)w_L - \theta_L w_L \varepsilon_{LL} - \theta_E w_E \varepsilon_{EL}]\tilde{T}_L \\ &\quad - (1 - \theta_L)w_L\left[\varepsilon_{LE} + (1 - T_\Pi)\frac{w_L}{w_C}\eta_L\right]\tilde{T}_L \end{aligned} \quad \text{(B13)}$$

where

$$\Delta_H = \eta^*_{LL} + \epsilon_{LL} + \frac{w_L}{w_C}\eta_L[\theta_L\epsilon_{LL} + \theta_E\epsilon_{LE}] > 0 \quad \text{(B14)}$$

The reduced forms for pollution and profits are found by substituting (B12) and (B13) into (II.3) and (II.4), respectively.

Appendix C: The Marginal Excess Burden

This appendix derives the marginal excess burden which is defined as the compensating variation ($d\beta$) relative to national income (Y). The compensating variation amounts to the transfer that needs to be provided to the household to keep its utility, after a policy shock, at its initial level:

$$0 = -\frac{\partial u}{\partial V}dL + \frac{\partial u}{\partial M}dM + \frac{\partial u}{\partial C}dC + \frac{\partial u}{\partial G}dG \tag{C1}$$

We assume that $dG = 0$. Substituting (I.8) and (I.9) into (C1) and adding the compensating variation, we arrive at:

$$0 = d\beta - WdL + (u_M/\lambda)dM + dC \tag{C2}$$

Dividing (C2) by Y and substituting the household budget constraint (II.5) to eliminate $\tilde{L}$ and $\tilde{C}$, we find:

$$\tilde{\beta} = -w_L(1-\theta_L)\tilde{W} - w_\Pi(\tilde{\Pi} - \tilde{T}_\Pi) + \theta_E^P w_E \tilde{E} \tag{C3}$$

where

$$\theta_E^P = \frac{1}{1+T_E}\frac{u_M(-M_E)}{\lambda} \tag{C4}$$

By subtracting (II.7) from (II.4′) we derive:

$$w_L(1-\theta_L)\tilde{W} + w_\Pi(\tilde{\Pi} - \tilde{T}_\Pi) = \theta_L w_L \tilde{L} + \theta_E w_E \tilde{E} + \theta_K w_K \tilde{K} \tag{C5}$$

Substituting (C5) into (C3), we arrive at the following alternative expression for the marginal excess burden:

$$\tilde{\beta} = -\theta_L w_L \tilde{L} - \theta_K w_K \tilde{K} - (\theta_E - \theta_E^P) w_E \tilde{E} \tag{C6}$$

To derive expression (4.1), we substitute labor supply (II.6) into (C5) to eliminate the wage rate and use the fact that profits are zero. This yields:

$$w_L(1-\theta_L)\tilde{L} = \eta_{LL}[\theta_L w_L \tilde{L} + \theta_E w_E \tilde{E} + \theta_K w_K \tilde{K}] \tag{C7}$$

Using (C7), we can eliminate employment from the marginal excess burden in (C6). Thus, we arrive at a third expression for the marginal excess burden

$$\tilde{\beta} = -\frac{1-\theta_L}{1-\theta_L-\theta_L\eta_{LL}}[\theta_K w_K \tilde{K} + \theta_E w_E \tilde{E}] + \theta_E^P w_E \tilde{E} \tag{C8}$$

Acknowledgments

We are grateful to Gilbert van Hagen, Sören B. Nielsen and two anonymous referees for helpful comments on an earlier draft.

Notes

1. Goulder (1995) suggests that an inefficient tax system may raise the scope for a double dividend, but does not model this formally.
2. Our paper ignores difficulties in the design of pollution taxes. In particular, we assume that the tax applies only to polluting inputs used by domestic firms. Foreign producers are not subject to the tax, i.e. the pollution tax is based on the origin principle. Pollution taxes based on the destination principle, which would involve import tariffs and export subsidies would feature bigger problems in tax design.
3. For infinitely small shocks, the compensating variation equals the equivalent variation (see e.g. Keller, 1980).
4. A similar case is explored by Bovenberg and Van der Ploeg (1994c) and Bovenberg and de Mooij (1994b). However, they do not analyze changes in the capital tax.
5. The production function exhibits constant returns to scale with respect to L, K and E. Hence, the factor-price frontier expresses producer wages in terms of the other input prices (see (II.4)).
6. Capital demand rises only if positive substitution effects, associated with the change in relative prices, dominate this adverse production effect. Substitution effects stimulate the demand for capital if, compared to the cheaper factor (i.e. labor), the more expensive factor (the polluting input) is a better substitute for capital. The adverse production effect is small if the mobile factor that is increased in price (the polluting input) is a poor substitute for the immobile factor and if the immobile factor accounts for a large production share compared to the more expensive mobile factor (i.e. $\sigma_L < w_L \sigma_{EK}$). In the rest of this subsection, we assume that this is not the case so that $\Gamma_{EK} > 0$.
7. Schöb (1994) finds a similar result for pollution taxes on consumption. In particular, he shows that a tax on a non-polluting consumption commodity that is complementary to the polluting consumption commodity may be a better instrument for environmental protection than a tax on the polluting commodity.
8. The ultimate burden of all taxes in terms of reduced real incomes is borne by labor because the supply of capital is infinitely elastic. Thus, the burden of taxation on the capital market is reflected only in a decline of capital demand and not a drop in the after-tax return on capital. The burden in terms of reduced incomes is shifted back unto labor. In a more general model in which capital supply would be less than infinitely elastic, the burden of taxation in the capital-market would reduce not only capital demand but also the after-tax return on capital. Hence, labor and capital would share the burden of taxation in terms of lower after-tax incomes (see also section 5).
9. A similar case is explored by Bovenberg and van der Ploeg (1994b). However, they assume that wages are fixed exogenously.
10. ε_D is large if the fixed factor is unimportant. In particular, if w_H approaches zero, ε_D goes to infinity (see Table 5.1).
11. Table 5.1 reveals that $\varepsilon_{LL} - \varepsilon_{EL}$ is always positive if pollution or the fixed factor are separable. However, this term may be negative if labor is separable. In particular, it is negative if producers find it much easier to substitute pollution than labor for the fixed factor. In this section, we rule out this possibility and assume that $\varepsilon_{LL} - \varepsilon_{EL} > 0$.
12. The compensated, rather than the uncompensated, elasticity of labor supply is relevant for the consequences for employment associated with the tax shifting effect (see the first element in the reduced-form for employment in Table 5.2). The reason is that the negative income effect on labor supply is offset by the fall in profits. Hence, only substitution effects matter. In case of the tax burden effect on labor, however, the uncompensated elasticity of labor supply is relevant for the employment effect. This is because the reduction in after-tax wages associated with the tax burden effect leaves profits unchanged (see the second element in the reduced-form for employment in Table 5.2).

13. The effect on pollution depends on $\varepsilon_{EE} - \varepsilon_{LE}$, which is typically positive thus indicating a fall in pollution (see Table 5.1). This term may be negative if polluting inputs are separable in production and, compared to labor, polluting inputs are a much better substitute for fixed capital. We, however, rule out this possibility and assume that own price effects dominate cross price effects.
14. Labor cannot bear the burden of taxation if it is supplied with infinite wage elasticity ($\eta_{LL} \rightarrow \infty$). Hence, in that case the effect on blue welfare is solely determined by the difference between the tax shifting effect and the tax burden effect on profits, both contained in the term Z. This term reveals that labor is overtaxed compared to pollution if $Z > 0$ (see also Bovenberg and Van der Ploeg (1994b)). In contrast, if labor is fixed in supply ($\eta_{LL} = \eta^*_{LL} = \eta_L = 0$), employment amounts to a fixed factor. In that case, the tax shifting effect is zero and a double dividend cannot be obtained.
15. Our linearized model is suitable only to explore the consequences of marginal policy changes. Although an increase of 10% is somewhat large, it should be stressed that our simulations are only illustrative.
16. This exceptional case corresponds to footnote 6 in the theoretical model of section 4.

References

Berndt, E. R., and D. O. Wood. (1979). "Engineering and Econometric Interpretations of Energy-Capital Complementarity." *American Economic Review* 69, 342–354.

Berndt, E. R., and D. M. Hesse. (1986). "Measuring and Assessing Capacity Utilization in the Manufacturing Sectors of Nine OECD Countries." *European Economic Review* 30, 961–989.

Bovenberg, A. L., and R. A. De Mooij. (1994a). "Environmental Levies and Distortionary Taxation." *American Economic Review* 84, 1085–1089.

Bovenberg, A. L., and R. A. De Mooij. (1994b). "Environmental Taxes and Labor-Market Distortions." *European Journal of Political Economy* 10, 655–683.

Bovenberg, A. L., and F. van der Ploeg. (1994a). "Environmental Policy, Public Finance and the Labour Market in a Second-Best World." *Journal of Public Economics* 55, 349–390.

Bovenberg, A. L., and F. van der Ploeg. (1994b). "Consequences of Environmental Reforms for Involuntary Unemployment and Welfare." *Environmental and Resource Economics* (forthcoming).

Bovenberg, A. L., and F. van der Ploeg. (1994c). "Green Policies in a Small Open Economy." *Scandinavian Journal of Economics* 96, 343–363.

Goulder, L. H. (1995). "Environmental Taxation and the "Double Dividend:" A Reader's Guide." *International Tax and Public Finance* 2, 155–182.

Griffin, J. M. (1981). "Engineering and Econometric Interpretations of Energy-Capital Complementarity: Comment." *American Economic Review* 71, 1100–1104.

Hausman, J. A. (1985). "Taxes and Labor Supply." In A. J. Auerbach and M. S. Feldstein (eds.), *Handbook of Public Economics 1*. Amsterdam: North Holland.

Hesse, D. M., and H. Tarkka. (1986). "The Demand for Capital, Labor and Energy in European Manufacturing Industry Before and After the Oil Price Shocks." *Scandinavian Journal of Economics* 88, 529–546.

Ilmakunnas, P., and H. Törmä. (1989). "Structural Change in Factor Substitution in Finnish Manufacturing." *Scandinavian Journal of Economics* 91, 705–721.

Keller, W. J. (1980). *Tax Incidence: A General Equilibrium Approach*. Amsterdam: North Holland.

Oates, W. E. (1991). Pollution Charges as a Source of Public Revenues, Resources for the Future Discussion paper no. QE92-05 (Washington, D.C., USA.

Parry, I. H. (1995). "Pollution Taxes and Revenue Recycling." *Journal of Environmental Economics and Management* 29, S64–S77.

Pearce, D. W. (1991). "The Role of Carbon Taxes in Adjusting to Global Warming." *Economic Journal* 101, 938–948.

Pindyck, R. S. (1979). "Interfuel Substitution and the Industrial Demand for Energy: An International Comparison." *The Review of Economic Studies* LXI.

Schöb, R. (1996). "Evaluating Tax Reforms in the Presence of Externalities." *Oxford Economic Papers* 48, 537–555.

[20]

ELSEVIER

European Economic Review 43 (1999) 1723–1746

EUROPEAN ECONOMIC REVIEW

www.elsevier.com/locate/econbase

Alleviating unemployment: The case for green tax reforms

Erkki Koskela[a], Ronnie Schöb[b,*]

[a] *Department of Economics, P.O. Box 54 (Unioninkatu 37), FIN-00014, University of Helsinki Finland*

[b] *Department of Economics, University of Munich, Schackstrasse 4, D-80539 Munich, Germany*

Received 1 May 1996; accepted 1 January 1998

Abstract

It has been argued recently that imposing taxes on pollution produces additional tax revenues which can be used to replace labour taxes and thus reap a double dividend in the form of improving environmental quality and alleviating unemployment. This paper analyses the employment effects of revenue-neutral green tax reforms by focusing on the revenue-recycling effect. Our model contains three features which are important when looking at the employment effects of green tax reforms. First, there is unemployment in equilibrium. Second, wages are determined endogenously. Third, various institutional arrangements for taxing unemployment benefits, for the price-indexation of unemployment benefits and the personal tax exemption are considered. It is shown that these institutional arrangements are crucial for the effectiveness of green tax reforms. A revenue-neutral green tax reform will boost employment if unemployment benefits are nominally fixed and taxed at a lower rate than labour income. Employment actually falls if unemployment benefits are price indexed and taxed at the same rate. A revenue-neutral green tax reform which increases the personal tax credit will never increase employment. © 1999 Elsevier Science B.V. All rights reserved.

JEL classification: H20; H30; J51

Keywords: Environmental tax reform; Tax shifting; Equilibrium unemployment; Trade union behaviour; Wage bargaining; Unemployment benefit taxation; Indexation

* Corresponding author. E-mail: ronnie.schoeb@ces.vwl.uni-muenchen.de.

PII: S0014-2921(98)00043-9

1. Introduction

Fighting unemployment has been at the top of the political agenda for the last decade. Europe suffers from persistently high levels of unemployment. At the end of 1997, the unemployment rates in the European Union were between 2.5% in Luxembourg and 20.0% in Spain, with an average unemployment rate for the EU member countries of 10.5%.[1] As well as other factors which are made responsible for the high unemployment, such as the mismatch of skills and the shortfall in demand, it is frequently claimed that the government's interventions in the labour market also significantly contribute to unemployment. High taxes on labour income combined with high levels of unemployment benefits distort labour supply and increase wage pressure in the wage negotiations between trade unions and employer organizations. Indeed, there is lot of empirical evidence showing that taxes have significant effects on unemployment. Surveying the empirical literature on this issue, a recent OECD (1995) study on taxation, employment ana unemployment concludes:

> 'Evidence that taxes on labour increase wage pressure and thereby increase unemployment (at least in the short-run) is, with some exceptions, reasonably convincing and in some countries, the increase in the tax wedge may have accounted for a significant proportion of the increase in unemployment.' (OECD, 1995, p. 68)

It is now widely accepted in political discussion that reducing the share of the tax burden borne by labour is a necessary policy measure for boosting employment. One possibility for lowering taxes is to reduce the size of the public sector. The other possibility is to shift the tax burden away from labour. One popular proposal for this is to increase consumption taxes as these taxes are also paid by other income groups. This will partly reduce the tax burden borne by labour while leaving the overall tax burden constant. Another possibility is to shift the tax burden to environmentally damaging behaviour. For the last two decades environmental problems have ranked high on the political agenda and the introduction of green taxes to fight pollution has become quite popular. It is therefore no surprise that it is politically very appealing to combine the two policy issues. Imposing taxes on pollution raises additional tax revenues which can be used to replace labour taxes and thus reap a double dividend in the form of improving the environmental quality and alleviating unemployment.

In the literature, however, we observe widespread pessimism as to whether there is a double dividend. Bovenberg and de Mooij (1994) and Bovenberg and

---

[1] These are standardized unemployment rates in the definition of the OECD, cf. Main Economic Indicators, June 1998, p. 40.

van der Ploeg (1994a) show that normally we can expect labour supply to fall as a result of a green tax reform. These authors develop their arguments using a model with market clearing in the labour market. With full-employment, however, the reduction of labour supply only indicates the willingness of society to produce fewer consumption goods in order to enjoy better environmental quality. The decrease in labour supply is always welfare improving.[2]

There are also some papers which find positive employment effects. In a model with production externalities, Bovenberg and van der Ploeg (1996) show that if green taxes are low initially, employment may increase if substitution between labour and resources within the production sector is easy. The shortcoming of their approach is, however, that the nominal net wage is exogenously fixed, so that both labour taxes and green taxes are assumed to be fully borne by the production sector.

Only recently have first attempts been made to consider green tax reforms within models which allow for unemployment in equilibrium and for endogenous wage setting. Schneider (1997) shows within an efficiency wage model that employment may increase due to an increase in green taxes. Nielsen et al. (1995) choose a monopoly union labour model where production externalities are present. In their model, however, marginal tax revenues of green taxes are always zero. Employment effects only result from changes in the provision of public goods and not because additional tax revenues are used to cut labour taxes. Carraro et al. (1996) use numerical simulations to study the effects of a carbon tax reform using a bargaining model for the labour market. They find some evidence in favour of a short-run employment dividend. Bovenberg and van der Ploeg (1995) look at the effects of revenue-neutral environmental tax reforms on wage formation, employment and environmental quality within a search theoretic framework where unemployment is caused by hiring costs. They show that, if an energy tax is levied on the polluting factor of production, a revenue-neutral cut in labour taxes may boost employment if the green tax reform succeeds in shifting the tax burden away from labour income to transfer income. Holmlund and Kolm (1997) examine the role of an environment tax reform for a small open economy with monopolistic competition. Assuming a Cobb–Douglas technology, they show for a two sector economy that a revenue-neutral tax reform on the production side, which increases the energy tax and reduces the labour tax, increases employment if tradable sector wages are higher than those in the non-traded sector. Koskela et al. (1998) allow for a CES production technology with production externalities and show that a green tax reform will boost employment if trade unions cannot increase or can only slightly increase the after-tax wage rate in wage negotiations.

[2] For surveys of the literature on the double dividend hypothesis, see e.g. Goulder (1995) and, with particular focus on the employment effects, Bovenberg (1995).

This paper considers the introduction of green taxes in a model where pollution is caused by the consumption of the dirty good and the nominal wage is endogenously determined in a bargaining process between a trade union and an employer organization. The main focus is on the impact the revenue-recycling effect has on the wage negotiations and employment. Wage negotiations are analysed using a 'right-to-manage' model. Trade unions and employer organisations bargain over wages and firms then choose the employment level that maximizes profits. Thereby, negotiations may take place on either an industrial or national level. This is an appropriate framework for analysing tax reforms in Europe, as in most European countries over three-quarters of the workforce earn wages that are covered by collective bargaining (cf. Layard et al., 1991).

The model contains three important features. First, there is involuntary unemployment in equilibrium. Second, wages are determined endogenously. Third, we explicitly distinguish between various institutional arrangements existing in the 15 EU member states, concerning the taxation of unemployment benefits, the type of tax exemption, and the price-indexation of unemployment benefits and tax exemptions. It will be shown that these institutional features, which have been largely neglected both in the literature on tax reforms and trade unions,[3] are crucial in terms of how green tax reforms actually work.

The paper is organized as follows. Section 2 gives a brief sketch of the institutional arrangements for unemployment benefit regulations and personal tax exemptions granted to workers in the EU member states. It also presents the basic model for the wage negotiations and provides comparative statics of the tax parameters for various institutional arrangements. Two different types of revenue-neutral green tax reforms are considered. In Section 3 the implications of a revenue-neutral green tax reform, which increases the tax rate on the dirty good and reduces the income tax accordingly, are analysed. Section 4 in turn develops the consequences of increasing the personal tax exemption. Finally, there is a brief conclusion.

2. The model

Consider a small open economy which consists of H households split into two groups. There are N workers and M shareholders. A worker's income consists of labour income if she is employed, and of unemployment benefits, paid by the government, if she is unemployed. Shareholder have internationally diversified portfolios, their total income consists of foreign profits π_f (which are kept

[3] For a rare exception see Bovenberg and van der Ploeg (1994b) and Pissarides (1998) who independently analyse the impact of different types of unemployment benefit indexations in models with alternative assumptions on the functioning of the labour market.

constant throughout the analysis) and domestic profits π. To finance the unemployment benefit payments and a fixed amount of some public goods G, the government imposes a tax t_L on income, and a so-called green tax t_D on the consumption of the dirty good D. Choosing the quantities of all commodities so that all producer prices are equal to unity, we can define a consumer price index P that only depends on the green tax. The partial derivative of the domestic consumer price level with respect to the tax on the dirty good is assumed to be positive, i.e.[4]

$$P_{t_D} > 0. \tag{1}$$

The environmental quality E depends negatively on the consumption of the dirty good D, i.e. $E(D)$, with $E' < 0$.

2.1. Firm behaviour

Firms produce output Q with labour as the only variable input, $Q = f(L)$. As they consider the wage rate and producer prices (normalized to unity) as given, they maximize profit with respect to labour input. The profit maximization of the firms,

$$\max_{L} \ \pi = Q(L) - wL \tag{2}$$

which, with a strictly concave production function, yields the labour demand function $L = L(w)$ with $L_w < 0$ and the output supply function $Q = Q(w)$ with $Q_w < 0$. The production process applies to the production of clean goods, the dirty good, and the (clean) public good G. In the following we assume that the wage elasticity of labour demand $\delta = -wL_w/L$ is constant.[5]

2.2. Trade union objective function

Trade unions act either on the industry level or on a national level. In the former case, Q represents the aggregate output of the industry; in the latter case, Q denotes the aggregate domestic output. The objective of the trade union is to maximize its members' real income. This consists of the *real after-tax wage*

---

[4] This assumption holds if the elasticity of substitution between the clean and the dirty goods is finite. If, e.g., preferences are given by a CES utility function, then

$$P_{t_D} = [1 + (1 + t_D)^{1-\sigma}]^{-\sigma/(1-\sigma)}(1 + t_D)^{-\sigma}$$

where σ is the elasticity of substitution between the clean good and the dirty good.

[5] This production function implicitly assumes that there is some fixed factor, e.g., capital, leading to decreasing marginal productivity of labour. Assuming a Cobb–Douglas production technology, e.g., guarantees a constant labour demand elasticity.

1728 E. Koskela, R. Schöb / European Economic Review 43 (1999) 1723–1746

income and the real after-tax unemployment benefits. Each worker inelastically supplies one unit of labour if employed, or zero labour if unemployed. In the former case the worker receives a wage income, in the latter case the unemployed member is entitled to unemployment benefits. As the actual form of the objective function depends on the various institutional arrangements, it is worthwhile discussing the variables which determine the trade union behaviour before modelling the labour market completely.

2.2.1. Labour income

The real after-tax wage depends on the nominal wage rate w, the income tax t_L, and the personal tax allowance a which is granted to each taxpayer. The personal tax allowance a may be either nominally fixed or price indexed.[6] If a is nominally fixed, the nominal after-tax wage is given by $w - t_L(w - a) = w(1 - t_L) + t_L a$. If the tax allowance is price indexed, it is given by $w(1 - t_L) + t_L aP$. Countries such as Portugal and Spain grant a tax credit instead of a personal tax allowance. The nominal after-tax wage is then given by $w(1 - t_L) + a$ and $w(1 - t_L) + aP$, respectively. To obtain the real after-tax wage $\tilde{w}$ the nominal after-tax wage has to be divided by the consumer price index P. Column 2 of Table 1 shows the type of tax exemptions granted in the 15 EU member states.

2.2.2. Unemployment benefits

In Europe, we can classify three types of unemployment benefits.[7] Most countries have introduced an unemployment insurance scheme where unemployment benefits are related to past contributions. Usually, unemployment insurance payments are limited to a certain maximum time period of unemployment. Either unemployment assistance or some type of guaranteed minimum income then replaces insurance payments.

In most countries, unemployment insurance is linked to previous gross earnings. An exception is Germany where unemployment benefits are linked to previous net earnings. Payments may be strictly proportional to earnings as e.g. in Belgium and Germany, or may increase linearly with previous earnings, starting from a minimum compensation, as e.g. in Austria and France. In most countries, unemployment benefits are subject to income taxation. In this case

---

[6] Price indexation may be institutionalized as e.g. in Belgium. It may also be the case that the government increases the personal tax allowance on a regular basis according to the preceding inflation rate as in the U.K.

[7] We focus here on unemployment benefits only. Depending on the availability and attractiveness of other social security contributions such as early retirement or disability benefits, these may be substitutes for unemployment benefits for individuals who become unemployed. In this case, the trade union has to take account of these substitutes and the frequency with which these alternative benefits are used by the unemployed or the government to hide unemployment in the unemployment statistics. For a survey, see Blöndal and Pearson (1995).

E. Koskela, R. Schöb / European Economic Review 43 (1999) 1723–1746 1729

the personal tax allowance (tax credit) is granted for the unemployed as well. In Austria, Germany and Portugal, unemployment benefits are exempted from taxation.

As we are interested in price changes and changes in the wage rate, we have to be careful about how price and wage changes interfere with the unemployment benefit payments. In the following we define unemployment benefits b as nominally fixed if they are determined by the wage rate and the income tax, which prevail before a tax reform takes place.[8] Unemployment benefits are determined by $b = \gamma w^0$ if they are proportional to previous gross earnings w^0, and by $b = \gamma w^0(1 - t_L^0)$ if they are proportional to previous net earnings $w^0(1 - t_L^0)$. Unemployment benefits in the U.K., as well as the unemployment assistance in many other countries, are fixed but are adjusted regularly according to the inflation rate. We refer to this as the case of price indexed unemployment benefits. Column 3 of Table 1 summarizes the institutional regulations with respect to the unemployment benefit payments.

Given the stylized facts as presented in Table 1, we distinguish four relevant cases for the 15 EU countries with respect to the nominal after-tax unemployment benefits.

1. *Cases A and A**: If unemployment benefits and the personal tax allowance are nominally fixed as e.g. in France or Germany, the nominal after-tax unemployment benefits are given by $b(1 - \alpha t_L) + \alpha t_L a$, where αt_L denotes the tax rate on unemployment benefits. The standard cases, here case A, always consider $\alpha < 1$, i.e. unemployment benefits are taxed at a lower rate than labour income. Cases with an asterisk here and in what follows consider the limiting case of $\alpha = 1$, where unemployment benefits are taxed at the same rate as labour income. Case A*, e.g., may be relevant for countries with a large income interval for the lowest tax bracket. If workers receive both labour income and unemployment benefits within a fiscal year, the marginal tax rate might be the same for both types of income.

2. *Cases B and B**: In some countries e.g., Belgium or Finland, unemployment benefits are nominally fixed, the personal tax allowance, however, is price indexed. In this case we have $b(1 - \alpha t_L) + \alpha t_L aP$ for the nominal after-tax unemployment benefits.

3. *Cases C and C**: If both unemployment benefits and the personal tax allowance are price indexed, as in the U.K., we have $bP(1 - \alpha t_L) + \alpha t_L aP$.

4. *Cases D and D**: In some countries such as Austria, Denmark, Italy, Portugal and Spain, a tax credit is granted instead of a tax allowance. If b is taxed sufficiently high, a tax credit implies that the same tax exemption applies to employed and unemployed workers. If both unemployment benefits and tax

---

[8] Bovenberg and van der Ploeg (1994b) refer to this case as nominal wage indexation.

Table 1
Tax exemption and unemployment benefit regulations in the EU

Country	Personal tax allowance, tax credit	Unemployment benefit rules	Case
Austria	Tax credit	(a) Linear indefinite; (b) non-taxable	D
Belgium	Tax allowance, Price indexed	(a) Proportional indefinite; (b) taxable	B
Denmark	Tax credit[1]	(a) Proportional 36/48 months; then fixed; (b) taxable	D
Finland	Tax allowance, Price indexed	(a) Linear 24 months; then fixed; (b) taxable	B
France	Tax allowance	(a) Linear 4–60 months; then fixed; (b) taxable, unemployment tax allowance	A/B
Germany	Tax allowance, Nominally fixed	(a) Proportional indefinite; (b) non-taxable[2]	A
Greece	Tax allowance	(a) Proportional 5–12 months; then fixed; (b) taxable	A/B
Ireland	Tax allowance	(a) Linear 15 months; then fixed; (b) taxable	A/B
Italy	Employment tax credit	(a) Proportional 6 months; (b) taxable, unemployment tax allowance	D
Luxembourg	Tax allowance	(a) Proportional 12–18 months; (b) taxable	A/B
Netherlands	Tax allowance	(a) Proportional 9–60 months; then fixed 24 months; (b) taxable	A/B
Portugal	Tax credit	(a) Proportional 10–30 months;[3] then fixed 5–15 months; (b) non-taxable	D
Spain	Tax credit	(a) Proportional 6–18 months; then fixed; (b) taxable	D
Sweden	Tax allowance	(a) Proportional 60 weeks; then fixed; (b) taxable	A/B
United Kingdom	Tax allowance fixed, but regularly adjusted	(a) Fixed, but regularly adjusted; (b) taxable	C

Sources: OECD (1991): Employment Outlook 1991, Tables 7.2 and 7.3; MISSOC (1996), Soziale Sicherheit in den Mitgliedstaaten der Europäischen Union, Chapters 4, 11 and 12; International Bureau of Fiscal Documentation (1995): European Tax Handbook 1995.

Legend: Unemployment benefits: (a) linear: Unemployment benefits increase linearly with gross earnings; proportional: Unemployment benefits increase proportionately with gross earnings; fixed: Unemployment benefits are fixed; (b) Unemployment benefits are subject to income taxation (taxable) or not (non-taxable); comments: (1) duration depending on age; (2) the tax value of the personal allowance is deducted from the amount of tax, i.e. in effect it is a tax credit; (3) benefits are paid proportional to earnings after tax and social security contributions, i.e. as taxes change so does the unemployment benefit.

credit are nominally fixed, we have therefore $b(1 - \alpha t_L) + a$.[9] If taxes paid on unemployment benefits are lower than the tax credit, the unemployed do not pay any taxes. This case can be represented by $\alpha = a = 0$.

Column 4 of Table 1 indicates which of the four cases each country belongs to. Dividing the nominal after-tax unemployment benefits by the consumer price index P yields the real net unemployment benefits $\tilde{b}$.

Having analysed the different real income components, we can specify the objective function of the trade union. Utilitarian trade unions are trying to maximize the real income of all N members. Each member is either employed and receives the real net wage $\tilde{w}$, or is unemployed and receives real net unemployment benefits $\tilde{b}$. The objective function of the trade union can be written as[10]

$$\tilde{V} = (\tilde{w} - \tilde{b})L + \tilde{b}N. \tag{3}$$

Within the bargaining process, the fall-back position of the trade union is given by

$$V^0 = \tilde{b}N, \tag{4}$$

i.e. all members remain at their reservation wage. In what follows we define $V \equiv \tilde{V} - V^0$ as part of the maximand under Nash bargaining representing the trade union's objective function. It should be noted, that one may also consider alternative fall-back positions of the trade union. As is shown in Binmore et al. (1986) within a dynamic context of strategic bargaining the fall-back position depends on the source of the incentive of the bargaining parties to reach an agreement. If the consequence of not reaching an immediate agreement is e.g., a delay of the outcome, the trade union's alternative wage includes income sources during the wage dispute. Some of the members may receive unemployment benefits and the rest strike support. For simplicity and in line with the literature we do not distinguish between strike support and unemployment benefits.[11]

2.3. Wage negotiations between trade unions and employer organizations

Usually, wages are determined in a bargaining process between trade unions and employer organizations. Then firms unilaterally determine employment. As

[9] In what follows, it does not matter whether the tax credit is nominally fixed or price indexed. Therefore, we focus on the former case only.

[10] The use of a linear objective function is for analytical convenience. It is often claimed that trade unions do not care about the level of employment if lay-offs follow an inverse seniority rule. In this case the objective function of the trade union would reduce to $\tilde{V} = \tilde{w}$ (cf. Oswald, 1993).

[11] Trade unions have strike funds which are accumulated by contributions from members in earlier periods. To analyse their determinations, however, would require a dynamic model which lies beyond the scope of the present paper.

we assume a small open economy the model allows us to analyse both wage negotiations which take place at the industry level as e.g., in the Benelux countries, and wage negotiations on a national level as e.g., in the Scandinavian countries.[12] In the following we use a 'right-to manage' model which represents the outcome of the bargaining by an asymmetric Nash bargaining with β representing the bargaining power of the trade union.[13] Assuming that the threat point of the employer organization is zero, the Nash bargaining maximand can be written as

$$\Omega = (\tilde{V} - V^0)^{\beta}\pi^{1-\beta}, \tag{5}$$

where the objective functions are defined by Eqs. (2)–(4).[14] Note that for $\beta = 1$ the model reduces to the case of a monopoly union.[15] Using $V \equiv \tilde{V} - V^0$, the first-order condition with respect to nominal wage is

$$\Omega_w = 0 \Leftrightarrow \beta\frac{V_w}{V} + (1-\beta)\frac{\pi_w}{\pi} = 0, \tag{6}$$

where variables with subscripts refer to partial derivatives (e.g., $V_w = \partial V/\partial w$). Provided that $\Omega_{ww} < 0$, Eq. (6) defines the negotiated nominal wage from Nash bargaining as a function of t_L, a, b, and t_D so that

$$w = w(t_L, a, b, t_D). \tag{7}$$

All these parameters affect Eq. (6) only via the first term of the right-hand side of Eq. (6) so that for parameter $\Psi = t_L, a, b, t_D$

$$\text{sign}\,(w_\Psi) = \text{sign}\,(\Omega_{w\Psi}) = \text{sign}\,(VV_{w\Psi} - V_wV_\Psi). \tag{8}$$

2.4. Comparative statics

In the following we will analyse how the negotiated nominal wage reacts to changes in taxes, the unemployment benefits, and the personal tax exemption. The trade union tries to maximize the rent, i.e. the surplus of real wages over real

[12] For a survey of the wage bargaining situation in the OECD countries, see Layard et al. (1991, p. 517ff).

[13] This approach can be justified either axiomatically (cf. Nash, 1950), or strategically (cf. Binmore et al., 1986).

[14] The following results are not affected if, alternatively, the managers of the firms maximize the real after-tax profit they pay to their share owners. Assuming that the foreign profits π_f the M share owners receive exceed the sum of personal tax allowances, from the viewpoint of a single firm or a centralized employer organization the relevant objective function to be considered in the Nash-bargaining maximand is real after-tax profit $\tilde{\pi} = (1 - t_L)\pi/P$. Of course, as was pointed out by one referee, this is only true for a small open economy as considered here. If wage negotiations affect the output price, the representation of the shareholder preferences becomes important.

[15] Cf. Oswald (1985) or Creedy and McDonald (1991). Note that in the monopoly union case, but not in the 'right-to-manage' model, labour demand elasticity has to exceed unity.

unemployment benefits. The calculations for the comparative statics results, presented in Table 2, are given in Appendix A.

If $\alpha < 1$, an increase in the income tax will lead to an increase in the nominal wage (cf. Eqs. (10-I) in Table 2). The wage surplus, lost by those dismissed, declines at a higher percentage than the benefits for those who remain in employment. It becomes profitable for the union to bargain for a higher nominal wage because the possible increase in labour income of those employed more than outweighs the income loss of those workers who are laid off.

This result holds only if unemployment benefits are taxed at a lower rate than labour income. If unemployment benefits are subject to the same tax rate, as in the limiting cases with $\alpha = 1$, the marginal net real wage income for the trade union and the net real unemployment benefits change by the same amount when the labour tax rate changes. This leaves the first-order condition of the bargaining solution unchanged. The labour tax rate has no effect on the optimal nominal wage.

Result 1. A rise in the labour income tax (i) will increase the nominal wage if the unemployment benefits are taxed at a lower rate than labour income, but (ii) will have no effect when unemployment benefits are taxed at the same rate as labour income.

An increase in the personal tax allowance a reduces the optimal nominal wage if $\alpha < 1$. Employed workers benefit more than unemployed workers as the differential $(1 - \alpha)t_L a$ can be interpreted as a subsidy on labour. This induces the trade union to accept a lower nominal wage as the marginal worker can now gain more from working than those already employed will lose from the necessary nominal wage reduction. If unemployment benefits are subject to the same tax rate, $\alpha = 1$, the personal tax allowance works like a lump-sum transfer to all members of the trade union. This leaves the arbitrage condition for the bargaining solution unchanged. Formally, both the objective function and the fall-back position of the trade union increase by the same amount.

Result 2. An increase in the personal tax allowance (i) will decrease the nominal wage if the unemployment benefits are taxed at a lower rate than labour income, but (ii) will have no effect when unemployment benefits are taxed at the same level as labour income.

If a represents a tax credit and if the tax payments of an unemployed exceeds the tax credit, a tax credit is also equivalent to a lump-sum transfer granted to all members of the trade union (case D).

Result 3. An increase in the personal tax credit will have no effect on the nominal wage, given that the taxes paid on unemployment benefits exceed the tax credit.

Table 2
Comparative statics of the nominal wage rate with Nash bargaining

	Cases A and A*	Cases B and B*	Cases C and C* $0 \leq \alpha < 1$	Cases D and D*
	Unemployment benefits and the personal tax allowance are nominally fixed	Unemployment benefits are nominally fixed, the personal tax allowance is price indexed	Unemployment benefits and personal tax allowances are price indexed	Unemployment benefits and the personal tax credit are nominally fixed
	$A: 0 \leq \alpha < 1$	$B: 0 \leq \alpha < 1$	$C: 0 \leq \alpha < 1$	$D: 0 \leq \alpha < 1$
	$A^*: \alpha = 1$	$B^*: \alpha = 1$	$C^*: \alpha = 1$	$D^*: \alpha = 1$
	France, Germany, Greece, Ireland, Luxembourg, Netherlands, Sweden	Belgium, Finland	United Kingdom	Austria, Denmark, Italy, Portugal, Spain
Objective function for the trade union V (9-I) [(3-I)–(4-I)]	$V = \frac{1}{P}[(1 - t_L)w + t_L a]L - \frac{1}{P}[b(1 - \alpha t_L P) + \alpha t_L a]L$	$V = \frac{1}{P}[(1 - t_L)w + t_L aP]L - \frac{1}{P}[b(1 - \alpha t_L) + \alpha t_L aP]L$	$V = \frac{1}{P}[(1 - t_L)w + t_L aP]L - \frac{1}{P}[bP(1 - \alpha t_L) + \alpha t_L aP]L$	$V = \frac{1}{P}[(1 - t_L)w]L - \frac{1}{P}[(1 - \alpha t_L)b]L$
(10-I)	$A: w_{t_L} > 0$ $A^*: w_{t_L} = 0$	$B: w_{t_L} > 0$ $B^*: w_{t_L} = 0$	$C: w_{t_L} > 0$ $C^*: w_{t_L} = 0$	$D: w_{t_L} > 0$ $D^*: w_{t_L} = 0$
(11-I)	$w_{t_D} = 0$	$B: w_{t_D} < 0$ $B^*: w_{t_D} = 0$	$w_{t_D} > 0$	$w_{t_D} = 0$
(12-I)	$A: w_a < 0$ $A^*: w_a = 0$	$B: w_a < 0$ $B^*: w_a = 0$	$C: w_a < 0$ $C^*: w_a = 0$	$w_a = 0$

Finally, consider a change in the tax on the dirty good. A higher tax increases the consumer price level – see Eq. (1) – and therefore influences real wages, real unemployment benefits and so on. If both unemployment benefits and the personal tax exemption are nominally fixed (cases A and D), all relevant variables are devalued by an increase in t_D. The arbitrage calculus of the bargaining solution remains unchanged. The same is true if $\alpha < 1$, as in this case the personal tax allowance does not enter the objective function. If unemployment benefits are nominally fixed but the personal tax allowance is price indexed (case B), the personal tax allowance remains constant in real terms while the wage rate devalues. The mechanism works in the same way as an increase in nominal personal tax allowances. If $\alpha < 1$, working becomes more attractive and the trade union will be willing to accept a lower nominal wage. As this is the only effect in case B, we have the paradoxical case that an increase in the consumer price level moderates wages.

If, however, unemployment benefits are also price indexed, there is a countervailing effect. As the latter effect dominates the former, the trade union will go for a higher nominal wage (case C).

Result 4. If the unemployment benefits are taxed at a lower rate than labour income, an increase in the tax on the dirty good will (i) increase the nominal wage if the unemployment benefits are price indexed, (ii) leave the nominal wage unchanged if unemployment benefits and personal tax allowances are nominally fixed, (iii) lower the nominal wage if the unemployment benefits are nominal fixed while the personal tax allowance is price indexed.

Note that the results hold even if the trade union is not interested in the level of employment, i.e. if its objective function is given by $\tilde{V} = \tilde{w}$ and hence $V = \tilde{w} - \tilde{b}$ (cf. Appendix B). As is shown in Oswald (1993), this may represent a trade union's objective function when lay-offs will be by inverse seniority within the firm.

Finally, note that an increase in the unemployment benefits, which increases the benefit-replacement ratio, makes the outside option for the trade union members more attractive. It becomes more profitable to bargain for a higher nominal wage. In all cases we have $w_b > 0$ (cf. Oswald, 1985).

In the next sections we will use the comparative static results to analyse revenue-neutral green tax reforms. Section 3 considers the case where additional revenues from increasing green taxes are recycled by reducing taxes on labour income. Section 4 will analyse the case where the additional tax revenues are used to increase the personal tax allowance or the personal tax credit, respectively.

1736 E. Koskela, R. Schöb / European Economic Review 43 (1999) 1723–1746

3. Revenue-neutral green tax reform I: Reducing the income tax

We can now analyse a revenue-neutral green tax reform which increases the tax on the dirty good and reduces the income tax correspondingly. The focus is on a comprehensive income tax t_L levied on both labour income and profit income. Revenue neutrality means that the government keeps the public good provision G constant. For case A, e.g., the government budget is given by

$$G = t_L(wL + \pi_f + \pi) + t_D D - (1 - \alpha t_L)b(N - L) - t_L a[M + L + \alpha(N - L)]. \tag{13A}$$

In general, a revenue-neutral green tax reform is described by

$$\mathrm{d}G = G_{t_L}\,\mathrm{d}t_L + G_{t_D}\,\mathrm{d}t_D + G_w\,\mathrm{d}w = 0, \tag{14}$$

where $\mathrm{d}w$ is determined by the reaction of the Nash bargaining solution to the tax rate changes. From the analysis of wage negotiation we know that the reaction of the nominal wage to a green tax reform is given by

$$\mathrm{d}w = w_{t_L}\,\mathrm{d}t_L + w_{t_D}\,\mathrm{d}t_D. \tag{15}$$

Substituting the RHS of Eq. (15) into Eq. (14) yields

$$\mathrm{d}G = G^*_{t_L}\,dt_L + G^*_{t_D}\,\mathrm{d}t_D = 0. \tag{16}$$

Here $G^*_{t_L}$ and $G^*_{t_D}$ denote the marginal tax revenues from the income tax and the tax on the dirty good, respectively, taking account of the impact tax rate changes have on the wage bargaining. Assuming that we are on the Laffer-efficient side of both tax revenue curves is equivalent to assuming that the marginal tax revenues of both taxes are positive, i.e.[16]

$$G^*_{t_L} > 0, \quad G^*_{t_D} > 0. \tag{17}$$

Using conditions (16) and (17), we have $\mathrm{sign}(\mathrm{d}t_L) = -\,\mathrm{sign}(\mathrm{d}t_D)$ for a revenue-neutral green tax reform. For the cases A, B, D, and in all limiting cases, the employment effects can easily be worked out from Eq. (15), see Table 3.

Proposition 1. A revenue-neutral green tax reform, which reduces the income tax rate, will increase employment if unemployment benefits are nominally fixed and taxed at a lower rate than labour income ($\alpha < 1$).

---

[16] While the first condition is quite reasonable as the income tax is imposed in order to raise tax revenues, we should point out that the second condition might not hold. If the environmental damage caused by the consumption of the dirty good is high, the government may be forced to levy such a high green tax that marginal tax revenues may actually become negative. Except for case B, a revenue-neutral green tax reform will never boost employment if the marginal tax revenue of a green tax is negative.

Table 3
Employment effects of a revenue-neutral green tax reform which reduces the income tax rate

Case	Changes in nominal wage	Employment effect
A, D	$dw = \underset{+}{w_{t_L}}\, \underset{-}{dt_L} < 0$	$dL > 0$
B	$dw = \underset{+}{w_{t_L}}\, \underset{-}{dt_L} + \underset{-}{w_{t_D}}\, \underset{+}{dt_D} < 0$	$dL > 0$
C	$dw = \underset{+}{w_{t_L}}\, \underset{-}{dt_L} + \underset{+}{w_{t_D}}\, \underset{+}{dt_D} \{\gtreqless\} 0$	?
A*, B*, D*	$dw = 0$	$dL = 0$
C*	$dw = \underset{+}{w_{t_D}}\, \underset{+}{dt_D} > 0$	$dL < 0$

Due to the reduction in the income tax, net wage income increases while net unemployment benefits remain constant. Hence it becomes profitable for the trade union to bargain for a lower nominal wage because the loss in wage income for all workers is more than outweighed by the gain from hiring more workers. As the nominal wage is not affected by changes in t_D, there is no countervailing effect in cases A and B.

In the limiting cases, where unemployment benefits are taxed at the same rate, the real after-tax wage for the trade union and the real after-tax unemployment benefits change proportionately, leaving the first-order conditions for the bargaining solution unchanged. Hence, an income tax cut has no effect on the optimal nominal wage or on employment and the results depend on the effect the green tax has on the wage negotiations only (for an interpretation see Section 2.4).

Proposition 2. If unemployment benefits are taxed at the same rate as labour income ($\alpha = 1$), *a revenue-neutral green tax reform, which reduces the income tax rate, will have no effect on employment if unemployment benefits are nominally fixed. It will reduce employment, if unemployment benefits are price indexed.*

The result for the case C is not that clear-cut. The reason for this ambiguity result lies in the fact that both the income tax and the green tax have a positive effect on nominal wages and thus a negative effect on employment. The revenue-neutral effects of a tax shift therefore depend upon their relative magnitudes. After some calculations, given in Appendix C, we obtain the following condition for case C:

$$\left.\frac{dL}{dt_D}\right|_{dG=0} \{\gtreqless\} 0 \Leftrightarrow \frac{\tau_{t_D}}{\tau_{t_L}} \{\gtreqless\} \frac{\varepsilon_{t_D}}{\varepsilon_{t_L}}, \tag{18}$$

where $\varepsilon_{t_L} = w_{t_L} t_L / w$ and $\varepsilon_{t_D} = w_{t_D} t_D / w$ denote the income tax elasticity and green tax elasticity of nominal wages, respectively; $\tau_{t_L} = (\partial G/\partial t_L) t_L / G$, and

$\tau_{t_D} = (\partial G/\partial t_D)t_D/G$ denote the income tax elasticity and green tax elasticity of tax revenues, respectively.

The ratio of the left-hand side indicates at what percentage the income tax has to decrease so that the public good provision G remains constant. The ratio of the right-hand side denotes the percentage the income tax has to decline to keep the nominal wage constant. If the revenue-neutrality requirement allows the government to cut the income tax at a higher (lower) rate than necessary to sustain the nominal wage, wage negotiations will lead to lower (higher) wages and will increase (decrease) employment accordingly.

Proposition 3. If unemployment benefits are price indexed, a revenue-neutral green tax reform, which reduces the income tax rate, will boost employment if the ratio of the tax revenue elasticities as given in Eq. (18), is larger than the ratio of the nominal wage elasticities.

Given the stylized facts presented in Table 1, Proposition 3 is relevant for the U.K. only. To some extent, however, it may also be relevant for other countries because the long-term unemployment benefits are often price indexed as they are determined by the minimum existence level to be sustained.

4. Revenue-neutral green tax reform II: Increasing the personal tax allowance or the personal tax credit

Instead of reducing the income tax, the government may also increase the tax exemption. Proceeding as in Section 3, we can derive the condition for the revenue-neutral green tax reform, where the personal tax allowance or the personal tax credit are increased:

$$dG = G_a^* da + G_{t_D}^* dt_D = 0. \tag{19}$$

G_a^* and $G_{t_D}^*$ now denote the marginal tax revenues from increasing the personal tax allowance and the tax on the dirty good, respectively. The assumption that we are on the Laffer-efficient side implies that the marginal tax revenue of an increase in the personal allowance is negative, while the marginal tax revenue of the tax on the dirty good is positive, i.e.

$$G_a^* < 0, \quad G_{t_D}^* > 0. \tag{20}$$

Using conditions (19) and (20) a revenue-neutral green tax reform has the property $\text{sign}(dt_D) = \text{sign}(da)$. Table 4 summarizes the employment effects for the various institutional arrangements.

As the comparison of Tables 3 and 4 shows, a revenue-neutral green tax reform which increases the personal tax allowance yields the same qualitative results as a reduction of the income tax (cases A, B, C) so that we can formulate

Table 4
Employment effects of a revenue-neutral green tax reform which increases the personal tax allowance or the personal tax credit

Case	Changes in nominal wage	Employment effect
A	$dw = \underset{-}{w_a}\ \underset{+}{da} < 0$	$dL > 0$
B	$dw = \underset{-}{w_{t_D}}\ \underset{+}{dt_D} + \underset{-}{w_a}\ \underset{+}{da} < 0$	$dL > 0$
C	$dw = \underset{+}{w_{t_D}}\ \underset{+}{dt_D} + \underset{-}{w_a}\ \underset{+}{da}\ \{\gtreqless\}0$	?
D	$dw = 0$	$dL = 0$
A*, B*, D*	$dw = 0$	$dL = 0$
C*	$dw = \underset{+}{w_{t_D}}\ \underset{+}{dt_D} > 0$	$dL < 0$

Proposition 4. A revenue-neutral green tax reform which increases the personal tax allowance will affect employment qualitatively in the same way as a revenue-neutral green tax reform which reduces the income tax rate.

Though the results are qualitatively the same as in the case of reducing the income tax, they differ quantitatively. To see this, we will split a green tax reform that increases the personal tax allowance into two succeeding tax reforms. First, we increase the green tax and reduce the income tax accordingly. Then, in a second step, we undo the reduction of the income tax and increase the personal tax allowance accordingly. This can be interpreted as an increase in the progressivity of the tax system. As Koskela and Vilmunen (1996) have shown, increasing progressivity in a revenue-neutral way will increase employment in popular models of trade union behaviour including the 'right-to manage' model (see also Holm and Koskela, 1997). An increase in progression moderates wages because it acts as a tax on wage increases. This result is not only a theoretical possibility but has also received an increasing amount of supporting empirical evidence.[17]

[17] This result cannot be seen directly from the calculations presented here. A revenue-neutral increase in progression will affect the nominal wage via the negative substitution effect so that the nominal wage falls and employment is boosted. For empirical evidence in Italy, see Malcomson and Sartor (1987); for the U.K., Lockwood and Manning (1993); for Sweden, Holmlund and Kolm (1995); and for Finland, Tyrväinen (1995).

Corollary 4. A revenue-neutral green tax reform will generally be more successful with respect to reducing unemployment if it rebates green tax revenues via increasing the personal tax allowance instead of reducing the income tax.

For countries where a personal tax credit is granted, Proposition 4 does not hold. As has been pointed out in Section 2, the nominal wage is not affected by a change in the tax credit as a tax credit is equivalent to a lump-sum transfer to all members of the trade union (given that $b\alpha t_L > a$). Hence, as unemployment benefits are nominally fixed in all countries that grant a tax credit instead of a tax allowance, employment remains constant as both the change in the tax credit and the change in the green tax do not affect wage negotiations.

Proposition 5. A revenue-neutral green tax reform which increases the personal tax credit will never have a positive effect on employment. It will be negative if unemployment benefits are price indexed.

Proposition 5 is important in showing that the question of how green tax revenues are rebated matters in countries such as Austria, Denmark, Italy, Portugal and Spain. If the decision is whether to rebate green tax revenues via a cut in the income tax or via an increase in the tax credit, only the former policy increases employment.

5. Concluding remarks

The paper analyses the employment effects of a green tax reform in a unionized labour market by focusing on the revenue-recycling effect. The model contains three important features which have not received enough attention in the literature. First, there is involuntary unemployment in equilibrium. Second, wages are endogenously determined in a bargain between trade unions and employers. Third, a distinction is made between various institutional arrangements concerning taxation of unemployment benefits, the type of tax exemption, price indexation of unemployment benefits and tax exemptions. Using the 'right-to-manage' model as the framework of analysis we have considered two different revenue-neutral green tax reforms: a rebate of green tax revenues via a reduction in labour taxes and a rebate via an increase in personal tax allowance or personal tax credit, respectively.

The main findings are as follows. First, the qualitative results are sensitive to institutional arrangements concerning taxation and indexation of unemployment benefits and the personal tax allowance. A revenue-neutral green tax reform will boost employment if unemployment benefits are nominally fixed and taxed at a lower rate than labour income. If unemployment benefits are price indexed, however, there is a negative effect on employment as a higher consumer price level increases nominal wages. Employment effects are indeterminate if unemployment benefits are price indexed and taxed at a lower rate than labour income. Employment actually falls if unemployment benefits are price indexed and taxed at the same rate as labour income.

Second, the employment effects of a revenue-neutral green tax reform are not sensitive to the question of whether green tax revenues are rebated via a cut in income taxes or an increase in the personal tax allowance – though the increase in personal tax allowances will increase employment more than the reduction in income taxes does. They are sensitive, however, in countries where tax credits are granted. In these countries, only a cut in the income tax lowers unemployment.

When employment is boosted, the tax burden is shifted away from labour income towards other income groups. In particular, if the indirect taxes increase, income from capital gains, savings or rents as well as income from social transfers bear a larger share of the tax burden.[18] More fundamentally, however, the change in the benefit–replacement ratio – the ratio between the after-tax real unemployment benefits and the after-tax real wage rate – rules the roost. It is the benefit–replacement ratio which decreases if the green tax reform succeeds in boosting employment.

Often it is stated that a green tax reform reaps a double dividend in the form of alleviating unemployment and improving environmental quality. Environmental quality, however, is affected by such a tax reform in two ways. First, an increase in the tax rate of the dirty good will affect the consumption of the dirty good negatively. Second, an increase in nominal income will lead to higher consumption, provided that the dirty good is a normal good. Intuitively, the environment improves if the substitution effect due to the change in relative consumer prices more than outweighs the positive income effect. The larger the employment effect is, however, the larger is the output change and the income effect, respectively. Thus these might be a trade-off between the environmental dividend and the employment dividend (cf. Schöb, 1996). This indicates that there is no free lunch, as obtaining a higher level of environmental quality goes along with a smaller employment effect.

[18] This effect is also pointed out in Bovenberg and van der Ploeg (1995). In their approach, however, the tax burden is shifted to transfer income only while in our model the burden of the green tax is also borne by profit income. The shift of the tax burden away from labour will become even stronger if the tax reduction is restricted to labour specific charges (e.g., unemployment insurance contributions) or labour specific tax allowances.

Concluding in terms of policy recommendations, our analysis suggests that there are good reasons for arguing that green tax reforms can alleviate unemployment by shifting the tax burden away from labour towards other income groups, or to put it in a more fundamental way, by decreasing the benefit-replacement ratio. However, as we have stressed, in order to be successful, green tax reforms require certain institutional arrangements concerning the taxation and price-indexation of unemployment benefits and the type of tax exemption granted.

Acknowledgements

The first author is indebted to the Research Unit on Economic Structures and Growth (RUESG) for financial support and to the CES in Munich for its great hospitality. An earlier version of this paper has been presented at seminars in Bergen, London, Munich, Prague, Tübingen, and Uppsala and at conferences in Copenhagen, Kassel, Lisbon and Tel Aviv. We would like to thank the participants of these seminars and conferences and, in particular, Louis Christofides, Clemens Fuest, Nils Gottfries, Bertil Holmlund, Andrew Oswald, Rüdiger Pethig, Agnar Sandmo, Dennis Snower, Marcel Thum and two anonymous referees as well as François Bourguignon, the editor of this journal, for many helplul comments. The usual disclaimer applies.

Appendix A. Some comparative statics of Nash bargaining

The following appendix shows some calculations which are necessary to understand the results of the comparative statics presented in Table 2. We proceed case by case.

*Cases A and A**: The partial derivative of the objective function (9-A), presented in Table 2, with respect to the nominal wage is given by

$$V_w = \frac{1}{P}\frac{L}{w}[(1-t_L)w(1-\delta) + [(1-\alpha t_L)b - (1-\alpha)t_L a)]\delta] \tag{A.1}$$

with δ being the wage elasticity of labour demand. Straightforward calculations utilizing Eq. (8) yield the partial derivatives as given in Table 2. In particular, we obtain

$$\operatorname{sign}(w_{t_L}) = \operatorname{sign}(VV_{wt_L} - V_w V_{t_L}) = \operatorname{sign}[(1-\alpha)(b-a)] \tag{A.2}$$

and

$$\operatorname{sign}(w_a) = \operatorname{sign}(VV_{wa} - V_w V_a) = -\operatorname{sign}[(1-t_L)t_L(1-\alpha)]. \tag{A.3}$$

*Cases B and B**: The partial derivative with respect to the nominal wage is given by

$$V_w = \frac{1}{P}\frac{L}{w}[(1-t_L)w(1-\delta) + (1-\alpha t_L)b\delta]. \tag{A.4}$$

Straightforward calculations, similar to case A, yield the results presented in Table 2.

*Cases C and C**: The partial derivative with respect to the nominal wage is given by

$$V_w = \frac{1}{P}\frac{L}{w}[(1-t_L)w(1-\delta) + [(1-\alpha t_L)bP - (1-\alpha)t_L aP)]\delta]. \tag{A.5}$$

Comparative statics is similar to the cases A and A* with the exception that

$$\begin{aligned}\operatorname{sign}(w_{t_D}) &= \operatorname{sign}(VV_{wt_D} - V_w V_{t_D}) \\ &= \operatorname{sign}[P_{t_D}[b(1-\alpha t_L) - (1-\alpha)t_L a]] > 0.\end{aligned} \tag{A.6}$$

*Cases D and D**: The partial derivative with respect to the nominal wage is given by

$$V_w = \frac{1}{P}\frac{L}{w}[(1-t_L)w(1-\delta) + (1-\alpha t_L)b\delta]. \tag{A.7}$$

Comparative statics are similar to the case A with the exception that

$$\operatorname{sign}(w_a) = \operatorname{sign}(VV_{wa} - V_w V_a) = 0 \quad \forall \alpha \in [0; 1]. \tag{A.8}$$

Appendix B. Comparative statics in a seniority model

If lay-offs follow some type of seniority rule, the trade union will act as though it were locally indifferent to the level of employment (cf. Oswald, 1993, p. 87). In our model the Nash maximand for case A then becomes

$$\Omega = \left[\frac{(1-t_L)w + (1-\alpha)t_L a - b(1-\alpha t_L)}{P}\right]^{\beta} \pi^{1-\beta}. \tag{B.1}$$

Using Eq. (8), straightforward calculations show that

$$VV_{wt_L} - V_w V_{t_L} = (1-\alpha)(b-a)/P^2 > 0 \Leftrightarrow w_{t_L} > 0, \tag{B.2}$$

$$VV_{wt_D} - V_w V_{t_D} = 0 \Leftrightarrow w_{t_D} = 0, \tag{B.3}$$

$$VV_{wa} - V_w V_a = (1-t_L)(1-\alpha)t_L/P^2 > 0 \Leftrightarrow w_a > 0. \tag{B.4}$$

The other cases can be proved analogously. A complete set of results is available from the authors upon request.

Appendix C. Derivation of the change in nominal wage for case C

Appendix C gives the calculations for deriving condition (18). Extending the revenue-neutrality condition (16) yields

$$\frac{\mathrm{d}G}{G} = \frac{G^*_{t_D} t_D}{G}\frac{\mathrm{d}t_D}{t_D} + \frac{G^*_{t_L} t_L}{G}\frac{\mathrm{d}t_L}{t_L} = 0 \tag{C.1}$$

and, by rearranging and using the definition given in Section 3, we obtain the following condition:

$$\frac{\mathrm{d}G/G}{\mathrm{d}t_D} = 0 \Leftrightarrow -\frac{\mathrm{d}t_L/t_L}{\mathrm{d}t_D/t_D} = \frac{\tau_{t_D}}{\tau_{t_L}}. \tag{C.2}$$

Condition (C.2) shows for a 1% increase in the green tax, at which percentage the income tax has to decrease to meet the revenue-neutrality requirement.

Analogously, we can derive the following condition for changes of the nominal wage [from Eq. (16)]:

$$\frac{\mathrm{d}w/w}{\mathrm{d}t_D}\{\gtreqless\}\,0 \Leftrightarrow \frac{\mathrm{d}t_L/t_L}{\mathrm{d}t_D/t_D}\{\gtreqless\} - \frac{\varepsilon_{t_D}}{\varepsilon_{t_L}}. \tag{C.3}$$

Substituting condition Eq. (C.2) in Eq. (C.3) and using $L_w < 0$ yields condition (18).

References

Binmore, K.G., Rubinstein, A., Wolinsky, A., 1986. The Nash bargaining solution in economic modelling. Rand Journal of Economics 17, 176–188.

Blöndal, S., Pearson, M., 1995. Unemployment and other non-employment benefits. Oxford Review of Economic Policy 11, 136–169.

Bovenberg, A.L., 1995. Environmental taxation and employment. De Economist 143, 111–140.
Bovenberg, A.L., de Mooij, R.A., 1994. Environmental levies and distortionary taxation. American Economic Review 84, 1085–1089.
Bovenberg, A.L., van der Ploeg, F., 1994a. Environmental policy, public finance and the labour market in a second-best world. Journal of Public Economics 55, 349–390.
Bovenberg, A.L., van der Ploeg, F., 1994b. Effects of the tax and benefit system on wage formation and unemployment. Mimeo., Tilburg University, April.
Bovenberg, A.L., van der Ploeg, F., 1995. Tax reform, structural unemployment and the environment. Fondazione Eni Enrico Mattei Discussion Paper No. 6/95.
Bovenberg, A.L., van der Ploeg, F., 1996. Optimal taxation, public goods and environmental policy with involuntary unemployment. Journal of Public Economics 62, 59–83.
Carraro, C., Galeotti, M., Gallo, M., 1996. Environmental taxation and unemployment: some evidence on the double dividend hypothesis in Europe. Journal of Public Economics 62, 141–181.
Creedy, J., McDonald, J., 1991. Models of trade union behaviour: A synthesis. Economic Record 67, 346–359.
Goulder, L.H., 1995. Environmental Taxation and the "double dividend": A reader's guide. International Tax and Public Finance 2, 157–184.
Holm, P., Koskela, E., 1997. Tax progression, structure of labour taxation and employment. Finanzarchiv 53, 28–46.
Holmlund, B., Kolm, A.-S., 1995. Progressive taxation, wage setting, and unemployment: Theory and Swedish evidence. Swedish Economic Policy Review 2, 423–460.
Holmlund, B., Kolm, A.-S., 1997. Environmental tax reform in a small open economy with structural unemployment. Working paper no. 1997/2. Department of Economics, Uppsala University, Uppsala.
International Bureau of Fiscal Documentation, 1995. European Tax Handbook 1995. Paris.
Koskela, E., Schöb, R., Sinn, H.-W., 1998. Polllution, factor taxation and unemployment. International Tax and Public Finance 5, 379–396.
Koskela, E., Vilmunen, J., 1996. Tax progression is good for employment in popular models of trade union behaviour. Labour Economics 3, 65–80.
Layard, R., Nickell, S., Jackman, R., 1991. Unemployment: Macroeconomic Performance and the Labour Market. Oxford University Press, Oxford.
Lockwood, B., Manning, A., 1993. Wage setting and the tax system – Theory and evidence for the United Kingdom. Journal of Public Economics 52, 1–29.
Malcomson, J.M., Sartor, N., 1987. Tax push inflation in a unionized labour market. European Economic Review 31, 1581–1596.
MISSOC, 1996. Soziale Sicherheit in den Mitgliedstaaten der Europäischen Union. Brussels, 1996.
Nash, J., 1950. The bargaining problem. Econometrica 18, 155–162.
Nielsen, S.B., Pedersen, L.H., Sørensen, P.B., 1995. Environmental policy, pollution, unemployment, and endogenous growth. International Tax and Public Finance 2, 185–205.
OECD, 1991. Employment Outlook 1991. Paris.
OECD, 1995. The OECD jobs study: Taxation, employment and unemployment. Paris.
Oswald, A.J., 1985. The economic theory of trade unions: An introductory survey. Scandinavian Journal of Economics 87, 160–193.
Oswald, A.J., 1993. Efficient contracts are on the labour demand curve. Labour Economics 1, 85–113.
Pissarides, C.A., 1998. The impact of employment tax cuts on unemployment and wages: The role of unemployment benefits and tax structure. European Economic Review 42, 115–183.

Schneider, K., 1997. Involuntary unemployment and environmental policy: The double dividend hypothesis. Scandinavian Journal of Economics 99, 45–59.
Schöb, R., 1996. Evaluating tax reforms in the presence of externalities. Oxford Economic Papers 48, 537–555.
Tyrväinen, T., 1995. Wage determination, taxes, and employment: Evidence from Finland. Bank of Finland Studies E3, Helsinki.

[21]

Scand. J. Economics 100(3), 593–610, 1998

Tax Reform, Structural Unemployment and the Environment*

A. Lans Bovenberg

Tilburg University, NL-5000 LE Tilburg, The Netherlands

Frederick van der Ploeg

University of Amsterdam, NL-1018 WB Amsterdam and Member of Parliament, The Hague, The Netherlands

Abstract

The effects of environmental tax reform, i.e., using the proceeds of a higher energy tax rate to lower the labour tax rate, on wage formation, employment and environmental quality are analysed in the context of a small open economy with structural unemployment caused by hiring costs. We find that such a reform may boost employment if it shifts the tax burden away from workers towards those without employment in the formal sector. Environmental tax reform succeeds in shifting the tax burden away from workers in the formal sector if higher energy taxes reduce earnings in the informal sector by reducing labour productivity.

I. Introdution

Many European economies suffer from high and persistent levels of unemployment. Commentators argue that high taxes on labour have contributed to unemployment. Environmental tax reform, i.e., raising taxes on pollution (and energy use, in particular) and using the proceeds to cut taxes on labour, is often seen as an attractive solution for cutting structural unemployment. Such a reform may yield a double dividend: not only an improvement in environmental quality but also a boost to employment.

Most work on environmental tax reform, e.g. Goulder (1995), including most of our own, e.g. Bovenberg and van der Ploeg (1994a,b), assumes market clearing. This is undoubtedly inappropriate for analysing the impact on structural unemployment. In Bovenberg and van der Ploeg (1994c, 1996) we explored how environmental tax reform affects involuntary unemployment, but did not model the underlying labour market imperfections that give rise to involuntary unemployment. Moreover, empirical studies suggest that the consumer wage is not exogenous but responds to, among other things, tax policy. Here we explicitly incorporate market imperfections which, together with the basic parameters character-

* We are grateful for the helpful comments of two anonymous referees.

ising preferences and technology, endogenously determine the wage level.

The scope for a double dividend depends mainly on how an environmental tax reform affects the threat point of employees in the bargaining process between employers and employees. This threat point, in turn, is determined by the income in unemployment. If income in unemployment is a fixed proportion of income in employment (implying a fixed replacement ratio), for example, taxes are borne completely by labour; see Layard and Nickell (1991). Hence, tax reform affects neither wage costs nor unemployment in equilibrium. The importance of the income regime applies to most models of structural unemployment, including union-firm bargaining, monopoly unions and efficiency wages.

We illustrate these insights and elaborate on these principles by formulating a search model of the labour market with individual worker-firm bargaining. In particular, we extend the matching model developed by Pissarides (1990) by including a polluting production factor. We also allow the unemployed to derive utility not only from unemployment benefits but also from leisure and from income from work in the informal sector.

Including other sources of utility than unemployment benefits is important. It implies that wage indexation of unemployment benefits does not necessarily mean that total unemployment income is fully indexed to wages. Hence, tax reform may affect structural unemployment, even if unemployment benefits are indexed to wages. Indeed, our analysis shows that the potential for a double dividend depends on the various elements that cause income in unemployment to be imperfectly linked to the wage level. In particular, the effects of environmental tax reform on income in employment (and hence the threat point of workers in the bargaining process) depends on three factors corresponding to the three sources of utility in unemployment: first, the manner in which unemployment benefits are indexed to wages and prices; second, the way utility of leisure changes with consumption of produced goods; and, third, how income that the unemployed earn from activities performed in the informal sector responds to changes in the formal economy.

Other papers that discuss the effects of environmental tax reform in the context of well-defined microeconomic models of structural unemployment include Nielsen *et al.* (1995), Koskela and Schöb (1996), and Holmlund and Kolm (1997).[1]

[1] Carraro *et al.* (1996) and Brunello (1996) employ computable general equilibrium models with wage bargaining to explore how environmental tax reforms impact employment. Carraro *et al.* (1996) find that employment, typically, declines in the long run but may rise in the short run. Brunello (1996) finds that a more competitive labour market enhances the positive employment effects of environmental tax reforms. However, if employment increases, pollution may rise. Hence, a double dividend fails to materialise.

Nielsen *et al.* (1995) adopt a monopoly union model with work sharing. In their model the marginal tax revenues from higher environmental taxes are zero, because pollution is rather elastic with respect to the price of pollution. Hence, environmental tax reform does not allow for a cut in the tax on labour income. In contrast, we allow the Laffer curve for green taxes to slope upwards.

Koskela and Schöb (1996) focus on pollution taxes on consumption. Using a model of wage bargaining between unions and employers, they show that the employment effects of environmental tax reform depend crucially on the taxation of unemployment benefits. In particular, such a tax reform boosts employment if unemployment benefits are not subject to the labour income tax and are not indexed to the consumer price index. In that case, the unemployed pay the higher pollution tax but do not get compensated by the lower tax on labour income. Hence, the environmental tax reform shifts the tax burden away from workers towards the unemployed. Also in our model, green tax reform increases employment if the tax burden is shifted to the unemployed. However, we study environmental taxes in production rather than consumption. Moreover, in contrast to Koskela and Schöb, we allow for untaxed income from the informal sector. Indeed, the channel through which green tax reform shifts the tax burden to the unemployed is quite different from that in Koskela and Schöb.

Holmlund and Kolm (1997) assume that income in unemployment is indexed to the consumer wage. Still, they show that environmental tax reform boosts employment if it relocates employment away from sectors where unions or firms exert relatively more market power.

International capital mobility enables capital to escape the burden of taxation by moving abroad. This reduces the scope for a double dividend, as environmental tax reform cannot shift the burden of taxation to capital. One of the purposes of this paper is to show that, even though capital is internationally mobile, a double dividend can be reaped.

In Section II we formulate a competitive model of a labour market with structural unemployment caused by hiring costs. Firms buy energy and capital on a competitive world market and are subject to both an energy and a labour tax. The unemployment benefit is indexed to the consumer wage. Earnings of the unemployed in the informal economy are related to the producer wage in the formal sector. The partial equilibrium effects of changes in the labour and energy tax rates on wage formation and the rate of unemployment are also analysed. Section III extends the analysis to allow for macroeconomic equilibrium in a small open economy. Section IV considers the consequences of environmental tax reform, i.e., using the revenue from a higher energy tax rate to reduce the labour tax rate without cutting the level of public consumption. The analysis is performed under various assumptions regarding the indexation of the unemployment benefit and income from the informal sector. Section V concludes with a summary of results.

II. Energy Use and Equilibrium Unemployment

We begin by considering the behaviour of individual people in a small open economy as they search for a job in a competitive labour market with frictions arising from hiring costs. We ignore on-the-job search and focus on trade between employers with vacant jobs and the unemployed seeking work. We extend the pioneering analysis of Pissarides (1990) by allowing for risk aversion, utility of leisure, various assumptions about indexation of unemployment benefits, and a polluting factor of production. In the remainder of the paper we refer to the polluting input as energy.

Matches in the Labour Market

The following constant-returns-to-scale matching function is at the heart of the analysis:

$$YN = \Xi(UN, VN) \tag{1}$$

where N, Y, U and V denote the exogenous labour force, the number of matches per unit of time, the unemployment rate, and the vacancy rate, respectively. Matching workers and jobs is a time-consuming and costly activity. The Poisson matching probability of a vacant job (Q) is given by:

$$Q(X) \equiv Y/V = \Xi(U/V, 1), \qquad \Xi_U > 0, \qquad Q' < 0 \tag{1'}$$

where $X \equiv V/U$ measures the tightness of the labour market. Steady-state equilibrium in the labour market requires that the flow into the pool of unemployed (i.e., $S(1-U)$, where S denotes the exogenous separation rate) equals the flow out of the pool of unemployed (i.e., XQU as XQ is the probability of an unemployed person finding a job). Hence, the equilibrium unemployment rate rises with the separation rate (S) and falls with the tightness of the labour market (X):

$$U = S/[S + XQ(X)] \tag{2}$$

where we assume that $0 < \xi \equiv -\mathrm{d}\log(Q)/\mathrm{d}\log(X) < 1$. In U–V space, equation (2) yields the familiar Beveridge curve. The bottom part of Figure 1 portrays (2) as a downward-sloping locus in U–X space, which shifts out if the separation rate rises or the matching technology worsens.

The production sector consists of many small firms, each of which has one job that is either vacant or occupied. If the job is occupied, the firm rents capital, K, at a rate R, imports a polluting factor of production (e.g.,

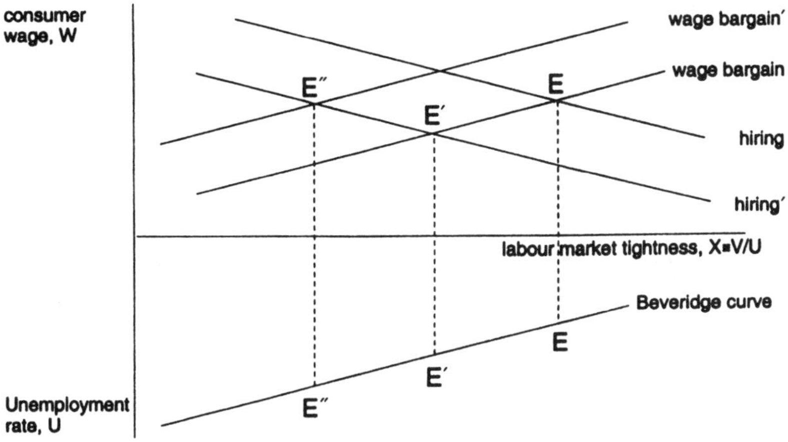

Fig. 1. Wage information and matches on the labour market

energy), E, at a price P, and employs one worker who is paid a wage W. Each operating firm thus employs one unit of labour and produces output $D = F(K,E)$, where $F_K, F_E > 0$, $F_{KK}, F_{EE} < 0$. Employment and the number of active firms thus equals L.[2] Firms set the marginal product of capital equal to the user cost of capital, which amounts to the sum of the interest rate on world capital markets, R, and the depreciation rate, δ ($F_K = R + \delta$). Firms also equate the marginal product of energy to the user cost of energy, which corresponds to the world energy price, P, plus an ad-valorem tax at the rate T_E ($F_E = P(1 + T_E)$). We assume that the interest rate (R) and the energy price (P) are exogenously determined on competitive world markets for capital and energy. Hence, the ad-valorem tax is equivalent to a specific tax on energy use. In the steady state, the present value of expected profits from an occupied job (J_O) equals the expected costs of filling a vacant job:

$$J_O = v(1 + T_L)W/Q(X) \tag{3}$$

where T_L denotes the payroll tax rate, W represents the consumer wage and Q^{-1} is the average duration of a vacancy. We assume that hiring costs are a fixed proportion, v, of the economy-wide producer wage. The alternative return on an occupied job must equal the instantaneous flow of profits from an occupied job plus the expected loss if a worker leaves:

[2]The aggregate production function amounts to $DL = F^*(KL, EL, L)$, where $F^*(\cdot)$ is concave and displays constant returns to scale. The firm-level production function $D = F(K, E) \equiv F^*(K, E, 1)$ is concave and shows decreasing returns to scale with respect to K and E. It thus follows that $K_{KK}F_{EE} - F_{KE}^2 > 0$.

$$R(J_O+K)=F(K,E)-\delta K-(1+T_L)W-(1+T_E)PE-SJ_O. \qquad (4)$$

where J_O+K amounts to the asset value of an occupied job. Combining (3) and (4) to eliminate J_O, we see that each firm sets the productivity of labour, A, equal to wage costs plus the expected capitalised value of its hiring costs:

$$A(R,P,T_E)\equiv F(K,E)-(R+\delta)K-P(1+T_E)E$$
$$=(1+T_L)W[1+(R+S)v/Q(X)]. \qquad (5)$$

Labour productivity declines if the world interest rate or the cost of energy rises ($\partial A/\partial R=-K<0$, $\partial A/\partial P=-(1+T_E)E<0$ and $\partial A/\partial T_E=-PE<0$). If we denote relative changes by lowercase letters (e.g., $x\equiv dX/X$), except $t_i\equiv dT_i/(1+T_i)$, $i=L,E$), and suppress changes in the world interest rate R and the world energy price P, we can write (5) in relative changes as:

$$x=-\varepsilon_{DL}[w+t_L-(\omega_E/\omega_L)t_E] \qquad (6)$$

where $\varepsilon_{DL}\equiv(\xi\psi)^{-1}>0$ declines with the share of hiring costs in total labour costs represented by $0<\psi\equiv(R+S)v[Q+(R+S)v]^{-1}<1$. The shares of labour and hiring costs and of energy costs in total production are given by $\omega_L\equiv A/F(K,E)$ and $\omega_E\equiv P(1+T_E)E/F(K,E)$, respectively.

The top part of Figure 1 shows the hiring schedule (6) as a downward-sloping locus. The inverse relationship between wage costs and labour market tightness can be explained as follows. An increase in wage costs reduces the expected benefits of an occupied job and, by increasing hiring costs, raises the costs of filling a vacant job. To re-establish arbitrage between the benefits and costs of hiring new workers, a less tight labour market must reduce hiring costs by reducing the expected duration of a vacancy. The smaller the share of hiring costs in total labour costs, ψ, and the smaller the effect of labour market tightness on the expected duration of vacancies (i.e., ξ is smaller) becomes, the less effective changes in labour market tightness are in bridging the gap between hiring costs and expected profits from an occupied job. Hence, larger movements in tightness are required to deal with changes in labour and/or energy costs.

Employment, L, rises and the unemployment rate, U, falls with labour market tightness:

$$l=U(1-\xi)x \quad \text{and} \quad u=-(L/N)(1-\xi)x. \qquad (2')$$

This relationship is portrayed as the Beveridge curve in the bottom part of Figure 1.

Wage Negotiations

J_U and J_E denote the present values of the expected incomes of unemployed workers (including the imputed income from non-market activities) and of employed workers, respectively. In equilibrium, the permanent income of an unemployed individual (i.e., the reservation wage, RJ_U) amounts to the instantaneous utility of an unemployed person (arising from utility of consumption and leisure) plus the gain in utility if a job is found:

$$RJ_U = V(B+Z)+\beta+XQ(X)(J_E-J_U) \tag{7}$$

where $V(\cdot)$ represents the instantaneous utility function of consumption, B the unemployment benefit, Z income from activities in the informal sector, β the utility of leisure, and XQ the probability of an unemployed individual finding a job. The permanent income of an employed worker corresponds to the instantaneous utility derived from wage income minus the loss in utility if the job is lost:

$$RJ_E = V(W)-S(J_E-J_U) \tag{8}$$

where S is the probability that an employed person loses a job. Subtracting (7) from (8), we find:

$$[R+S+XQ(X)]\,[J_E-J_U] = V(W)-V(B+Z)-\beta. \tag{9}$$

No individual will work unless it is worthwhile, i.e., $V(W)>V(B+Z)+\beta$. Hence, unemployment is more costly to those who currently experience it than to those who might expect to become unemployed in the future ($J_U<J_E$).

The rent of a realised job match corresponds to the sum of expected search costs for the firm and the worker (including foregone profit and wage incomes); if the match would split up, both firm and worker would have to engage in costly search activities before meeting another partner. The firm and worker share the rent that arises from frictions in the labour market by choosing the wage that minimises the Nash product of the net returns of the job $(J_E-J_U)^\rho J_O$, where $\rho\geq 0$ represents the bargaining power of the worker relative to that of the firm.[3] This yields the following first-order condition:[4]

$$\rho V'(W)J_O(1+T_L)^{-1} = J_E-J_U. \tag{10}$$

If the worker dominates the bargaining (i.e., $\rho\rightarrow\infty$), the productivity of labour equals the producer wage ($A = W(1+T_L)$). In that case, hiring costs play no role in the demand for labour. If the firm has all the bargaining power ($\rho=0$), in contrast, worker's utility ($V(W)$) is driven down to the

[3] The threat point corresponds to no match. This amounts to J_U for the worker and zero (i.e., the present value of expected profits from a vacant job in equilibrium) for the firm.

[4] Here, we have used $J_E-J_U=[V(W)-RJ_U]/(R+S)$ (from (8)) and $J_O=[A-W(1+T_L)]/(R+S)$ (from (4) and the definition of A in (5)), so that $\mathrm{d}(J_E-J_U)/\mathrm{d}W = V'(W)/(R+S)$ and $\mathrm{d}J_O/\mathrm{d}W = -(1+T_L)/(R+S)$.

reservation wage ($RJ_U = V(B+Z)+\beta$) since the permanent income of an employed worker is equal to that of an unemployed person ($J_E = J_U$). Using (3) and (9) to eliminate, respectively, J_O and ($J_E - J_U$) from (10), we find the following expression for the wage mark-up, M:

$$M \equiv [V(W)-V(B+Z)-\beta]/WV'(W) = \rho\nu[X+(R+S)/Q(X)]. \qquad (10'')$$

If hiring costs are zero ($\lambda = 0$), in equilibrium, workers are indifferent between being employed and unemployed ($V(W) = V(B+Z)+\beta$). Positive hiring costs drive a wedge between the utility of employment and that of unemployment. If the bargaining power of the worker (ρ) increases, the wage mark-up rises. A larger separation rate (S), a higher interest rate (R) or a tighter labour market (higher X) increase the expected capitalised value of the firm's hiring costs. This raises the rents from the job match and thus increases the wage mark-up. In addition, a tighter labour market improves the chances that an unemployed person finds a job. This raises the bargaining position of the worker, thereby raising the wage mark-up.

Assuming that utility is iso-elastic (i.e., $V(W) = W^{1-\sigma}/(1-\sigma)$),[5] we loglinearise equation (10'') for the wage mark-up:

$$w = \mu[\eta b+(1-\eta)z]+(\kappa/\lambda)x \qquad (11)$$

with $0<\kappa\equiv 1-(R+S)(XQ+R+S)^{-1}(1-\xi)<1$, $\lambda\equiv\sigma-1+M^{-1}>0$, $\mu\equiv V(B+Z)/[V(B+Z)+\beta] = [1+\beta(1-\sigma)(B+Z)^{\sigma-1}]^{-1}>0$,[6] and $\eta\equiv B/(B+Z)$. Bargaining yields a higher consumer wage if the reservation wage rises due to either a higher unemployment benefit or more pay in the informal sector. Hence, the wage schedule in the top part of Figure 1 shifts upwards if the unemployment benefit or pay in the informal economy rises. Also, a tighter labour market raises the wage, so that the wage curve slopes upwards.

Figure 1 shows how equilibrium is determined by the hiring locus (6), the wage schedule (11), and the Beveridge curve (2'). For example, a rise in the energy tax rate causes a decline in the productivity of labour ($a<0$) and shifts the hiring locus inwards. Hence, wages fall while the labour market becomes less tight and the unemployment rate rises (shift from E to E'). A higher interest rate or greater hiring costs affect both the hiring and the wage schedule. On the one hand, firms find it less attractive to hire and invest in a worker, and, on the other hand, the rent of a job match rises. Hence, the hiring locus shifts inwards and the wage schedule shifts upwards, so the labour market becomes less tight and unemployment rises (the equilibrium shifts from E to E'').

[5] The elasticity σ is inversely related to the substitution elasticity between leisure and consumption.

[6] This implies that $\lambda\mu = (B+Z)V'(B+Z)/[V(W)-V(B+Z)-\beta]$.

Unemployment Benefit and Pay in the Informal Economy

We assume that the unemployment benefit is indexed to market wages. In particular, a 1 percent increase in the market wage leads to a π_B percent rise in the unemployment benefit:

$$b = b^* + \pi_B w, \qquad \pi_B \geq 0 \tag{12}$$

where b^* stands for the autonomous relative change in the unemployment benefit and π_B denotes the indexation coefficient. If $\pi_B = 0$, the purchasing power of the unemployed is preserved by indexing the benefit to the price level. However, if $\pi_B = 1$, the benefit is fully indexed to the market wage so that the purchasing power of the unemployed moves in line with that of the employed.

Labour productivity, and thus pay, in the informal economy are positively related to labour productivity, that is labour costs inclusive of payroll taxes, in the formal economy:

$$z = z^* + \pi_Z (w + t_L), \qquad \pi_z \geq 0, \tag{12'}$$

where $z^* < 0$ corresponds to tightening the control on activities of the unemployed in the informal sector. This indexation rule makes sense if goods produced in the informal sector are perfect substitutes for goods supplied by the formal sector and workers dominate wage bargaining. Clearly, higher payroll taxes drive up labour costs in the formal sector and thus pay in the informal sector.

Comparative Statics

Using the hiring function (6), the wage schedule (11) and the indexation rules (12) and (12′) to solve for the relative changes in the wage and labour market tightness, we obtain:

$$\Delta w = \lambda\mu[\eta b^* + (1-\eta)z^*] - [\kappa\varepsilon_{DL} - \lambda\mu(1-\eta)\pi_Z]t_L - \kappa\varepsilon_{DL}(\omega_E/\omega_L)t_E \tag{13}$$

$$\begin{aligned}\Delta x = & -\lambda\mu\varepsilon_{DL}[\eta b^* + (1-\eta)z^*] - \lambda(1-\mu\eta\pi_B)\varepsilon_{DL}t_L \\ & -\lambda[1-\mu(\eta\pi_B + (1-\eta)\pi_Z]\varepsilon_{DL}(\omega_E/\omega_L)t_E\end{aligned} \tag{14}$$

where $\Delta \equiv \lambda\{1-\mu[\eta\pi_B + (1-\eta)\pi_Z]\} + \kappa\varepsilon_{DL} > 0$. Higher unemployment benefits or incomes in the informal sector make unemployment a less attractive option for workers. This strengthens their bargaining power, thereby pushing up wages and raising unemployment.

Both an energy tax and a labour tax raise unemployment if incomes during unemployment are not indexed to wages ($\pi_B = \pi_Z = 0$). Labour taxes raise wage costs directly while energy taxes increase wage costs per unit of output by reducing labour productivity. If unemployment incomes are not indexed to wages, the unemployed do not share in a decline in labour incomes. Hence, in the face of an unaffected outside option, workers resist cuts in after-tax wages. Consequently, a large share of the additional tax burden is shifted on to higher wage costs per unit of labour, thereby harming employment. In the extreme case where wage setting does not depend on the state of the labour market ($\kappa = 0$), workers escape the entire tax burden. Hence, after-tax incomes of employed and unemployed are protected at the expense of a higher rate of unemployment.

Workers absorb a larger share of the additional tax burden in terms of lower after-tax wages if income during unemployment is strongly indexed to wages. In fact, with full indexation of unemployment incomes ($\pi_B = \pi_Z = 1$) and zero utility of leisure ($\beta = 0$ and thus $\mu = 1$), workers bear the entire burden of the decline in labour productivity due to a higher tax rate on energy use. Accordingly, higher energy taxes do not affect wage costs per unit of output and thus leave unemployment unaffected. Intuitively, with full indexation of monetary incomes and no non-monetary income from leisure, incomes during unemployment decline proportionally with incomes in the formal economy. Hence, the threat point of workers worsens, inducing workers to accept lower after-tax wages.

With full indexation of unemployment incomes, not only a higher energy tax rate but also a higher labour tax rate does not raise unemployment if the unemployed do not participate in the informal economy ($\eta = 1$). However, if the unemployed benefit from untaxed income from the informal sector, they escape some of the additional tax burden on labour. This reduces the negative impact of the tax burden on the threat point, thereby preventing after-tax wages from fully absorbing the rise in the tax burden. Accordingly, wage costs rise, thereby reducing employment. Hence, if incomes from the informal sector are substantial and indexed to labour productivity in the formal economy, a higher labour tax rate reduces (formal) employment, whereas a higher energy tax rate leaves unemployment unaffected. Intuitively, in contrast to a labour tax, an energy tax hits the incomes of the unemployed who work in the informal sector by reducing labour productivity in the informal sector.[7]

---

[7] If we consider a consumer tax at a rate t_C, which hits consumption spending of both the employed and the unemployed, we find:

$$\Delta x = -\varepsilon_{DL}\lambda(1-\mu)t_C.$$

Hence, with full indexation of income during unemployment ($\pi_B = \pi_Z = 1$), a consumer tax and an energy tax exert similar effects on employment (even if there is a positive utility of leisure). The reason is that, in contrast to a labour tax and in analogy with an energy tax, a consumer tax hits incomes that are earned in both the informal sector and the formal economy.

With positive utility from leisure and easy substitution between leisure and consumption (i.e., $\beta > 0$ and $\sigma < 1$, so that $\mu < 1$), both taxes raise unemployment. The reason is that imputed income from leisure is untaxed and unrelated to labour productivity. Hence, the unemployed escape part of the tax burden. This strengthens the bargaining power of workers, so that workers bear less than 100 percent of the tax burden. However, if leisure is a poor substitute for consumption ($\sigma > 1$, so that $\mu > 1$) and incomes during unemployment are strongly indexed to wages (i.e., π_B and π_Z are close to unity), unemployment may decline as workers bear more than 100 per cent of the tax burden. Intuitively, by reducing consumption, a higher tax burden decreases the marginal utility of leisure compared to that of consumption. Hence, unemployment (i.e., leisure) becomes less attractive compared to work. Workers thus moderate wages in order to prevent unemployment. If the coefficient of relative risk aversion approaches unity ($\sigma = \mu = 1$) and incomes during unemployment are fully indexed, workers bear exactly 100 percent of the tax burden.

In the face of a gradual increase in labour productivity over the centuries, the structural rate of unemployment has not changed significantly. If we thus impose the restriction that labour productivity does not affect the unemployment rate, cf. King, Plosser and Rebelo (1988), we find that energy taxes also leave the unemployment rate unaffected. This restriction is met if utility from leisure is zero or the coefficient of relative risk aversion is unity ($\mu = 1$) and unemployment incomes are fully indexed. In this case, a higher labour tax rate raises unemployment as long as part of the income during unemployment is derived from activities in the informal sector ($1 - \eta > 0$).[8]

We can write expressions (13) and (14) in an alternative way in order to distinguish two distinct channels through which tax policy affects the labour market:

$$w = \delta b^{**} - \Omega t \qquad (13')$$

$$x = -\varepsilon_{DL}[(1 - \Omega)t + \delta b^{**}] \qquad (14')$$

where:

$$b^{**} = \eta b^* + (1 - \eta) z^* - (1 - \eta)\pi_Z(\omega_E/\omega_L)t_E \qquad (15)$$

$$t \equiv t_L + (\omega_E/\omega_L)t_E \qquad (16)$$

$\delta \equiv \lambda\mu/\Delta$ and $\Omega \equiv [\kappa\varepsilon_{DL} - \lambda\mu(1 - \eta)\pi_Z]/\Delta = 1 - \lambda(1 - \mu\eta\pi_B)/\Delta$. In particular, exogenous changes in fiscal policy affect after-tax wages through, first, the aggregate tax burden on labour, t, and, second, income in unemployment, b^{**}. To what extent workers bear the higher aggregate tax burden on

[8] In that case, the coefficient on t_L in (14) becomes $-\varepsilon_{DL}\lambda(1 - \eta)$.

labour in the form of lower after-tax wages depends on the tax-shifting coefficient Ω. If Ω is large, a higher tax burden is transmitted mainly to lower after-tax wages rather than higher wage costs. Hence, given the wage elasticity of labour demand, ε_{DL}, a large tax-shifting coefficient implies that a higher tax burden exerts only a relatively minor adverse impact on labour demand. Indeed, labour demand and therefore unemployment are not affected at all if the tax-shifting coefficient is unity. This is the case if the unemployed enjoy neither leisure nor income from the informal sector ($\eta = \mu = 1$) and unemployment benefits are indexed to after-tax wages ($\pi_B = 1$). In that case, the after-tax incomes of the unemployed develop parallel with those of the employed. Consequently, the unemployed fully share the higher tax burden with the employed.

Higher income during unemployment (b^{**}) boosts wages. This harms labour demand and raises unemployment. Three exogenous factors determine income during unemployment: the exogenous component of the unemployment benefit, b^*, the exogenous component of income from the informal sector, z^*, and the energy tax. The energy tax harms labour productivity in the formal sector. This reduces income during unemployment if the unemployed enjoy income from the informal sector ($\eta < 1$) and if this 'informal' income is positively related to labour productivity in the formal sector ($\pi_Z > 0$). Hence, if these conditions are met, a higher energy tax benefits employment by moderating wages, as the workers in the formal sector face a less attractive outside option.

Proposition 1. *A higher labour or energy tax rate boosts unemployment if incomes during unemployment are not indexed to wages. However, unemployment is unaffected if utility from leisure is absent and incomes during unemployment are fully indexed to wages. If informal incomes are present and indexed to labour productivity in the formal economy, a higher energy tax rate does not affect employment while a higher labour tax rate depresses employment. With positive utility of leisure, a higher labour or energy tax rate lowers (raises) unemployment if leisure and consumption are good (bad) substitutes in utility. If changes in productivity growth and the energy tax rate do not affect unemployment, a higher labour tax rate raises unemployment as long as the unemployed collect some income from the informal sector.*

III. Macroeconomic Equilibrium in a Small Open Economy

Government Budget and National Accounts

The government budget must be balanced, so that revenue from the energy tax and the labour (including cost of hiring) tax must be sufficient to cover government consumption, G, plus transfer payments to the unemployed:

$$T_E PEL + T_L W[1 + v(R+S)/Q(X)]L = G + (N-L)B. \tag{17}$$

Labour in the informal economy is, of course, untaxed. Considering relative changes in the government budget constraint (17), we obtain:

$$(1-\theta_L)(\omega_L t_L + \omega_E t_E) - \theta_E \omega_E \varepsilon_E t_E = \omega_G g + \omega_B (b^* + \pi_B w) - \alpha x \tag{18}$$

where $\omega_G \equiv G/LY$ denotes the national income share of public consumption, $\omega_B \equiv BUN/LY$ the national income share of unemployment benefits, $\theta_i \equiv T_i/(1+T_i)$, $i = L, E$, and $\alpha \equiv (1-\xi)[(L/N)\omega_B + U(\theta_L \omega_L + \theta_E \omega_E)] > 0$. The first term on the LHS of (18) represents the direct positive effects of a higher labour tax rate and a higher energy tax rate on public revenue, minus the adverse effect of a higher energy tax rate on labour productivity and thus on revenue from taxes on labour and hiring costs. The second term on the LHS of (18) captures the erosion in the energy tax base and the resulting fall in public revenue induced by a higher energy tax rate. The relative change in the demand for energy can be written as

$$e = -\varepsilon_E t_E. \tag{19}$$

so that the effect on the energy tax base is strong if the price elasticity of the demand for energy $\varepsilon_E \equiv -(1+T_E)PF_{KK}/(F_{KK}F_{EE} - F_{KE}^2) > 0$ is large.

The first two terms on the RHS of (18) stand for the rise in public expenditures arising from, respectively, a rise in public consumption and a higher level of the unemployment benefit. The last term on the RHS of (18) represents the beneficial effect of a high level of employment on public revenue. This effect operates through a broader base of the energy and labour taxes and a smaller volume of transfer payments. We assume that a higher energy tax rate boosts public revenue. This is the case if the initial labour tax rate and energy tax rate are not too large or the demand for energy is relatively inelastic (i.e., $\theta_L + \theta_E \varepsilon_E < 1$).

Aggregate private consumption, C, amounts to the consumption of the employed and consumption of the unemployed (i.e., $C = WL + (B+Z)(N-L)$). Walras' law then yields the following condition for equilibrium on the goods market:

$$[LD + Z(N-L) - \delta KL - vW(R+S)L/Q(X)] - C - G = PEL + RKL. \tag{20}$$

The LHS of (20) represents net exports of final goods, which corresponds to the excess of aggregate income in the formal economy (net of depreciation of capital and hiring costs) and the informal economy over the sum of aggregate private consumption and public consumption. External balance requires that net exports of final goods equal the value of capital and energy imports, represented by the RHS of (20).

Comparative Statics

The discussion of (13) and (14) assumes that increases in the labour or energy tax rate are accompanied by increases in government consumption. To discuss the implications of environmental tax reform, we substitute (13) and (14) into the government budget constraint (18) with $g = 0$ and solve for the relative change in the labour tax rate:

$$\Delta^* t_L = \Delta(\omega_G g + \omega_B b^*) + (\omega_B \pi_B + \alpha \varepsilon_{DL}) \lambda\mu[\eta b^* + (1-\eta) z^*]$$
$$- \{\Delta\omega_E(1-\theta_E \varepsilon_E - \theta_L) + \omega_B \pi_B \kappa (\omega_E/\omega_L) \varepsilon_{DL}$$
$$- \alpha\lambda[1-\mu(\eta\pi_B + (1-\eta)\pi_Z)](\omega_E/\omega_L) \varepsilon_{DL}\} t_E \qquad (21)$$

where $\Delta^* \equiv \Delta(1-\theta_L)\omega_L + \omega_B\pi_B[\kappa\varepsilon_{DL} - \lambda\mu(1-\eta)\pi_Z] - \alpha\varepsilon_{DL}\lambda(1-\mu\eta\pi_B)$. We assume that the Laffer curve for the labour tax rate is upward sloping ($\Delta^* > 0$). A reduction in public consumption thus permits a lower labour tax rate. In addition, a lower unemployment benefit allows for an even lower labour tax rate if the unemployment benefit is indexed to the consumer wage. The reason is that lower wages induce lower benefits and less unemployment which, in turn, leads to less transfer payments and an expansion of the labour tax base.

Substituting (21) into (13) and (14), we obtain the relative changes in the consumer wage and labour market tightness:

$$\Delta^{**} w = -\Omega t^* + \delta[1 - \varepsilon_{DL}\alpha(1-\theta_L)^{-1}\omega_L^{-1}] b^{**} \qquad (22)$$

$$\Delta^{**} x = -\varepsilon_{DL}\{(1-\Omega)t^* + \delta[1 + \omega_B\pi_B(1-\theta_L)^{-1}\omega_L^{-1}] b^{**}\} \qquad (23)$$

where:

$$t^* \equiv [\omega_G g + \omega_B b^* + \theta_E \omega_E \varepsilon_E t_E]/[(1-\theta_L)\omega_L] \qquad (24)$$

and $\Delta^{**} \equiv 1 + [\Omega\omega_B\pi_B - (1-\Omega)\alpha\varepsilon_{DL}](1-\theta_L)^{-1}\omega_L^{-1}$. These expressions indicate that the government can affect wages and employment through the aggregate tax burden t^*, and income in unemployment b^{**} (defined in (15)).

IV. Environmental Tax Reform

No Income from the Informal Sector and Zero Initial Energy Tax

If the initial tax rate on energy is zero, the environmental tax reform does not affect the aggregate tax burden, t^* (see (24)). Furthermore, if income from the informal sector is either absent ($\eta = 1$) or unrelated to labour productivity in the formal sector ($\pi_Z = 0$), the reform does not directly impact income during unemployment, b^* (see (15)). Hence, the environmental tax reform leaves the labour market unaffected. Intuitively, the energy tax amounts to an implicit labour tax because it reduces the productivity of labour. Accordingly, the environmental reform amounts to replacing an *explicit* labour tax by an *implicit* labour tax without affecting the overall tax burden on labour.

Income from the Informal Sector Related to Labour Productivity and Zero Initial Energy Tax

If income in the informal sector is positively related to labour productivity in the formal sector ($\pi_Z > 0$ with $\eta < 1$), the environmental tax reform boosts employment. In particular, the reform moderates wages by making the outside option for workers in the formal sector less desirable ($b^{**} < 0$, see (15)). The reason is that, compared to the labour tax, the energy tax imposes a heavier burden on the unemployed if the unemployed benefit from income from the informal sector ($\eta < 1$). In particular, the labour tax does not affect income from the informal sector (since this income escapes tax) and thus reduces incomes only in the formal sector. The energy tax, in contrast, decreases income in not only the formal but also the informal sector since informal incomes are linked to labour productivity. Consequently, an environmental reform implies a cut in income from unemployment. In other words, it amounts to replacing a labour tax by a tax which is in larger part borne by those outside the labour force. We call the shift in the tax burden away from the employed in the formal sector towards those who are not employed in the formal sector (i.e., the unemployed), the *tax-shifting* effect.[9] The tax-shifting effect makes a double dividend (i.e., not only a cleaner environment but also a higher level of employment) feasible.

In most cases, the double dividend comes at the expense of lower after-tax incomes in both employment and unemployment. However, if initial tax rates are high and the wage elasticity of labour demand is large (i.e., $\alpha\varepsilon_{DL} > (1-\theta_L)\alpha_L$), an environmental tax reform may produce a triple dividend, as incomes from employment and unemployment may rise in general equilibrium due to an expansion of the tax base; see Blanchard and Summers (1987). In this case, we have a Pareto-improving reform.

[9] One alternative interpretation of this result is that energy taxes are more difficult to evade than taxes on labour. Hence, replacing labour by energy taxes makes tax evasion in the informal sector less attractive, thereby expanding employment in the formal sector. Another interpretation is that income aspirations of workers are linked to labour productivity in the economy as a whole. If labour productivity increases, unions find it easier to organise workers for industrial actions, thereby raising the threat point of workers.

Positive Initial Energy Tax and No Income from the Informal Sector

If the initial tax on energy is positive, an environmental tax reform raises the aggregate tax burden, t^* (see (24)). Intuitively, a positive initial tax rate drives a wedge between the social benefits of energy use and the social costs of energy (abstracting from environmental benefits). Hence, a decline in energy demand due to higher energy taxes imposes costs so that a cleaner environment is no longer a free good. Indeed, these costs can be interpreted as an increase in the tax burden associated with a better quality of the public good of the environment. We call this increase in the overall tax burden the *tax-level* effect.

The magnitude of the tax increase depends on the elasticity of energy demand with respect to the price of energy, ε_E. Thus, the rise in the tax burden is substantial if a cleaner environment is expensive (i.e., the initial tax rate on energy and thus θ_E are large) and the improvement in environmental quality is substantial (i.e., the price elasticity of energy demand, ε_E, is large).

Without income from the informal sector, the energy and labour taxes imply the same relative tax burden on the employed versus the unemployed. Hence, the *tax-shifting* effect is absent so that the *tax-level* effect dominates. Intuitively, an environmental tax reform amounts to replacing an explicit labour tax by a higher implicit labour tax. An increase in the overall tax burden typically raises unemployment. Only if unemployment benefits are indexed to after-tax wages and the unemployed benefit from neither leisure nor income from the informal sector, does an increase in the overall tax burden leave unemployment unaffected. In that particular case, higher environmental quality does not raise unemployment because workers moderate wages sufficiently as the unemployed share in the costs of a cleaner environment. Hence, the costs of a cleaner environment amount to lower after-tax incomes rather than a lower level of employment.

Positive Initial Energy Tax and Income from the Informal Sector

In the general case, the employment effect depends on both the *tax-shifting* and the *tax-level* effects. Employment declines if the *tax-level* effect dominates. This is the case if incomes from the informal sector and the tax shift coefficient, Ω, are small. Moreover, both the initial energy tax and the price elasticity of energy demand should be large. In that case, the costs of a cleaner environment are high and are shifted on to those employed in the formal sector rather than the unemployed. This implies that workers in the formal sector do not sufficiently moderate wages so that the costs of a cleaner environment are shifted on to higher wage costs, thereby hurting employment. Only if the tax-shifting coefficient dominates are the costs of a cleaner environment borne by those out of employment, thereby inducing workers to moderate wages sufficiently.

Proposition 2. *Environmental tax reform boosts employment if the unemployed earn substantial incomes in the informal sector and the initial tax rate on energy is small. If these conditions are not met, employment declines.*

V. Concluding Remarks

A model of involuntary unemployment was developed to analyse the macroeconomic implications of environmental tax reform. We found that such reform boosts employment if it shifts the tax burden away from workers towards those without employment in the formal sector. Such a shift in the tax burden makes the outside option of workers in the formal sector less attractive, thereby moderating wages. Environmental tax reform succeeds in shifting the tax burden away from workers in the formal sector if higher energy taxes reduce earnings in the informal sector by reducing labour productivity.

Shifting the tax burden towards those outside formal employment is a necessary but not a sufficient condition for employment to expand. In particular, employment declines if initial pollution taxes are high and pollution is sensitive to higher green taxes. In that case, by increasing the supply of the public good of the environment, pollution taxes substantially raise the overall tax burden. In general, the overall employment impact depends on the balance between the tax-shifting and tax-burden effects. Employment expands if the increase in the overall tax burden associated with the costs of a cleaner environment can be shifted towards those outside employment in the formal sector.

References

Blanchard, O.J. and Summers, L.H.: Fiscal increasing returns, hysteresis, real wages, and unemployment. *European Economic Review 31*, 543–60, 1987.

Bovenberg, A.L. and van der Ploeg, F.: Environmental policy, public finance and the labour market in a second-best world. *Journal of Public Economics 55*, 349–90, 1994a.

Bovenberg, A.L. and van der Ploeg, F.: Green policies and public finance in a small open economy. *Scandinavian Journal of Economics 96*, 343–63, 1994b.

Bovenberg, A.L. and van der Ploeg, F.: Consequences of environmental tax reform for involuntary unemployment and welfare. 1994c; forthcoming in *Environmental and Resource Economics*.

Bovenberg, A.L. and van der Ploeg, F.: Optimal taxation, public goods and environmental policy with involuntary unemployment. *Journal of Public Economics 62*, 59–83, 1996.

Brunello, G.: Labour market institutions and the double dividend hypothesis. In C. Carraro and D. Siniscalco (eds.), *Environmental Fiscal Reform and Unemployment*, Kluwer Academic Publishers, Dordrecht, 1996.

Carraro, C., Galeotti, M. and Gallo, M.: Environmental taxation and unemployment: Some evidence on the double dividend' hypothesis in Europe. *Journal of Public Economics 62*, 141–81, 1996.

Goulder, L.: Environmental taxation and the double dividend: A reader's guide. *International Tax and Public Finance 2*, 157–83, 1995.

Holmlund, B. and Kolm, A.-S.: Environmental tax reform in a small open economy with structural unemployment. WP 5.97, Fondazione Eni Enrico Mattei, Milan, 1997.

King, R., Plosser, C. and Rebelo, S.: Production, growth and business cycles, I: The basic neoclassical model. *Journal of Monetary Economics 21*, 195–232, 1998.

Koskela E. and Schöb, R.: Alleviating unemployment: The case for green tax reforms. CES WP 106, University of Munich, Munich, 1996.

Layard, R., Nickell, S. and Jackman, R.: *Unemployment. Macroeconomic Performance and the Labour Market*. Oxford University Press, Oxford, 1991.

Nielsen, S.B., Pedersen, L.H. and Sørensen, P.B.: Environmental policy, pollution, unemployment and endogenous growth. *International Tax and Public Finance 2*, 185–205, 1995.

Pissarides, C.A.: *Equilibrium Unemployment Theory*. Basil Blackwell, Oxford, 1990.

First version submitted May 1996;
final version received July 1997.

[22]

Journal of Environmental Economics and Management **39,** 67–96 (2000)
doi:10.1006/jeem.1999.1093, available online at http://www.idealibrary.com on IDEAL®

Tax Deductions, Environmental Policy, and the "Double Dividend" Hypothesis

Ian W. H. Parry[1, 2]

Resources for the Future, Washington, DC

and

Antonio M. Bento[2]

University of Maryland, College Park, Maryland, and World Bank, Washington, DC

Received November 19, 1998; revised August 18, 1999

Recent studies find that environmental tax swaps typically exacerbate the costs of the tax system and therefore do not produce a "double dividend." We extend previous models by incorporating tax-favored consumption goods (e.g., housing, medical care). The efficiency gains from recycling environmental tax revenues are therefore larger because pre-existing income taxes distort both consumption decisions and factor markets. In this setting a revenue-neutral emissions tax (or auctioned permits) produces a double dividend. Moreover, the overall costs of environmental tax swaps are negative, for modest emissions reductions. The efficiency gains from emissions taxes over grandfathered permits are also much larger than previously recognized. © 2000 Academic Press

1. INTRODUCTION

In recent years there has been a good deal of debate among academics and policymakers about the interactions between environmental policies and the tax system. These debates arose in response to the so-called double dividend hypothesis, that is, the claim that environmental taxes could simultaneously improve the environment and reduce the economic costs of the tax system. The latter effect seemed plausible, if the revenues from taxes on carbon emissions, gasoline, traffic congestion, household garbage, fish catches, chemical fertilizers, and so on were used to reduce the rates of pre-existing taxes that distort labor and capital markets.

However, a number of recent analytical and numerical analyses have cast doubt on the validity of the double dividend hypothesis.[3] The basic point is that the

[1] Address correspondence to: Ian Parry, Resources for the Future, 1616 P Street, Washington, DC 20036. E-mail: parry@rff.org.

[2] We gratefully acknowledge the helpful comments and suggestions of Dallas Burtraw, Larry Goulder, Alan Krupnick, Gib Metcalf, Richard Newell, Wally Oates, Mike Toman, Rob Williams, and three referees.

[3] We do not go into the details of individual studies here since the rise and fall of the double dividend hypothesis has been discussed at length in other places. For recent surveys of the literature see Bovenberg and Goulder [5], Parry and Oates [30], Goulder [14, 16], and Oates [22]. Our discussion is concerned with models that assume a competitive labor market, which is probably a reasonable approximation for the U.S. economy. The general equilibrium welfare effects of environmental policies are more complex in countries where the labor market contains significant institutional distortions which make the real wage "sticky" (see, e.g., Bovenberg and van der Ploeg [3]).

0095-0696/00 $35.00

hypothesis ignores an important source of interaction between environmental taxes and pre-existing taxes. Since environmental taxes cause the costs and prices of products to rise they tend to discourage (slightly) labor supply and investment and thereby exacerbate the efficiency costs associated with tax distortions in labor and capital markets. In fact, aside from certain special cases, these studies find that the costs from this interaction effect dominate any efficiency benefits from recycling environmental tax revenues in other tax reductions. Thus, environmental tax swaps typically *increase* rather than *decrease* the efficiency costs of pre-existing tax distortions.

The models in the recent literature typically assume a uniform tax on labor (and possibly capital) income with no tax deductions. Thus, in these models the only source of price distortion created by the tax system is in factor markets. However, certain types of spending are (at least partially) deductible from labor taxes. This includes, among other things, spending on mortgage interest, employer-provided medical insurance, and other less tangible fringe benefits.[4] In practice, therefore, the tax system creates an additional source of price distortion: it effectively subsidizes tax-favored spending relative to all other, non-tax-favored spending. Indeed recent evidence points to the empirical significance of this second source of economic distortion. Feldstein [12] estimates that the efficiency costs of raising extra revenues through income taxes is much larger when the substitution between tax-favored consumption and ordinary (non-tax-favored) consumption is taken into account, besides the distortionary impact in the labor market.

This paper extends previous literature by exploring the implications of tax-favored consumption for the general equilibrium costs and overall welfare effects (benefits less costs) of environmental policies. We model a static economy where households allocate their time between leisure and labor supply. Labor, along with a clean input and a polluting input (e.g., energy or fossil fuels), are used to produce two consumption goods. Expenditure on one of the consumer goods is (partially) deductible from labor taxation. U.S. data on labor market and tax parameters are used to calibrate the model.

At first glance, one might think that if the distortionary costs of pre-existing taxes were greater than assumed in earlier studies, then the general equilibrium costs of new environmental policies would also be greater. However, we find the opposite result is typical for environmental taxes with revenues used to cut personal income taxes. That is, the presence of tax-favored consumption can substantially *reduce* the costs of environmental taxes (relative to their costs in the absence of tax deductions). In fact, results on the double dividend hypothesis established in the earlier literature can easily be overturned, even under conservative estimates for the costs of pre-existing taxes. In our benchmark simulations, ignoring any environmental benefits, the net impact of an environmental tax swap is to significantly reduce the overall economic costs of the tax system for pollution reductions of up to at least 50%. In other words the general equilibrium costs of the policy are less than the partial equilibrium costs, and by a potentially substantial amount. Indeed the overall costs of pollution taxes are negative for pollution reductions up to 19–33% in our benchmark simulations. A related point is that, in

[4] There are a variety of other major deductions from federal income taxes, such as those for pension and charitable contributions, accelerated depreciation, and so on. However, for reasons discussed below, we do not consider these other deductions to be relevant to our particular analysis.

contrast to typical results from earlier studies (e.g., Bovenberg and Goulder [4], Parry [25]), we find that the optimal environmental tax may easily exceed the Pigouvian tax.

These results arise because the welfare gain from using environmental tax revenues to reduce labor taxes is higher, and perhaps substantially so, when labor taxes distort the relative prices among consumption goods in addition to the price of labor. In contrast, roughly speaking, the interaction effect mentioned above does not change because environmental taxes have approximately the same impact on raising the price of consumption goods relative to leisure. Also, at least in the case when the pollution intensity is the same in the tax-favored and the non-tax-favored consumption sectors, the environmental tax does not alter the relative prices of the two consumption goods and hence does not exacerbate the costs of the subsidy to tax-favored consumption. Since the gains from recycling environmental tax revenues are larger, while the cost of the interaction effect is not, the costs of the environmental tax are lower—and possibly of opposite sign—than in earlier models.

We also explore the implications of tax-favored consumption for the costs of other policy instruments. We find that the costs of non-auctioned pollution emissions permits, or pollution taxes whose revenues are returned as a lump sum (rather than used to reduce distortionary taxes), could be significantly greater or significantly less than found in previous studies, depending on the relative pollution intensity of the tax-favored consumption sector. In addition, regardless of the relative pollution intensity, the welfare gain from using revenue-neutral emissions taxes (or auctioned emissions permits) instead of non-auctioned permits can be dramatically higher than suggested by earlier studies. This is due to the larger efficiency gain from using revenues from environmental policies to reduce labor taxes in the presence of tax-favored consumption. In many of our simulations there is much more at stake in whether environmental policies raise revenues, and how these revenues are recycled, than the (partial equilibrium) welfare gain from correcting the environmental externality.

Our results have important implications for policy. Clearly, if a side effect of an environmental tax is to produce significant efficiency gains by reducing the costs of the tax system, this can strengthen the case for implementing the environmental policy. To our knowledge, this is the first paper to demonstrate the possibility of such efficiency gains in a static general equilibrium model, without making some special assumptions (e.g., that the polluting good is a complement for leisure). Moreover, cost/benefit analyses of whether environmental policies are likely to enhance social welfare or not are often hampered by the difficulty of quantifying environmental benefits. If—due to the side benefit from reducing the costs of the tax system—the overall costs of an environmental tax would be small or negative, it may not be necessary to know the benefits from environmental improvement to justify a modest environmental tax on a cost/benefit criterion. *However*, as demonstrated in other studies (Parry [26], Parry et al. [29]), if revenues are *not* used to reduce distortionary taxes, the overall welfare effects of a Pigouvian tax can be negative, even when environmental benefits are significant.

As discussed below, our paper is simplified in a number of respects and is only meant to be a preliminary attempt at exploring the implications of tax deductions. Since our analysis is static it does not capture the impact of the tax system on distorting the consumption/saving decision or the choice among different investment goods. In this respect, our results may be conservative. Furthermore, the distortion between the marginal social benefit and marginal social cost in the market for tax-favored consumption is a good deal more complicated than assumed in our analysis. There are a number of externalities and other policy interventions that impinge on this market, although the empirical importance of these factors, and whether their net impact is to diminish or magnify the size of the subsidy distortion, is unclear. Another caveat is that the main effect of tax deductions in our analysis is to increase the efficiency gains from recycling environmental tax revenues over and above those in the labor market. For these deductions to make much difference, however, the tax expenditures involved must be significant relative to total labor tax revenues. This means that "small" tax expenditures, like those for employee parking, only trivially affect our results. However, as we discuss, these types of deductions become more significant if they apply directly to the market that is being regulated.

The rest of the paper is organized as follows. Section 2 discusses the welfare effects of alternative environmental policies in the presence of tax-favored consumption. Section 3 describes our numerical model, and Section 4 provides the simulation results. Section 5 discusses possible generalizations to the analysis, and Section 6 offers conclusions.

2. CONCEPTUAL FRAMEWORK

In this section we explain the different components of the welfare effects of alternative environmental policies in the presence of (partially deductible) labor taxation, with the aid of diagrams and certain key formulas. This provides a conceptual framework for interpreting the subsequent numerical results. We provide a more rigorous mathematical model, and the derivation of the formulas, in Appendices A and B.[5] At the end of this section we relate our results to those in earlier studies.

Assumptions

Consider a static economy where two final goods X and Y are produced using labor and intermediate goods. X denotes "tax-favored" consumption and represents an aggregate of consumption goods that are (at least partially) deductible from labor taxes. As discussed in Section 3, these "goods" include (mortgage interest paid on) owner-occupied housing and non-wage compensation such as employer-provided medical insurance. Y denotes an aggregate of consumption goods that do not receive preferential tax treatment.

There is a polluting intermediate good Z (e.g., coal) and a clean intermediate good C, both of which are produced using labor. Household utility is adversely

[5] The mathematical derivations of the welfare effects (see Appendix A) are similar to those in several recent models of environmental policies in the presence of labor taxes (e.g., Goulder et al. [17], Parry et al. [29]). In particular, the analytical model of Parry et al. would be almost equivalent to that in the current paper, following the introduction of a subsidy for one of the two consumption goods in their household and government budget constraints. Thus, we think there is more value added from using a diagrammatic approach in this section, in which the intuition is more transparent, and we relegate the (partially repetitive) mathematical proofs to the Appendix.

affected by pollution. For now, assume that pollution damages per unit of Z are a constant ϕ (this assumption is relaxed later). In addition we assume that production is competitive and characterized by constant returns to scale, therefore supply curves are perfectly elastic.[6]

We represent the tax system by assuming the government levies two taxes on gross labor earnings: a "comprehensive" labor tax t_C and a "non-comprehensive" tax t_N. Expenditure on X is deductible from the non-comprehensive tax but not expenditure on Y. Neither good is deductible from the comprehensive tax.[7] The government returns all revenues in a lump-sum transfer (G) to the household sector.

The (aggregate) household budget constraint amounts to

$$(1 - t_N)p_X X + p_Y Y = (1 - t_N - t_C)L + G, \tag{2.1}$$

where p_X and p_Y are the producer prices of X and Y, which we normalize to unity in the initial equilibrium, and L is labor supply. Note that the tax system effectively taxes labor income and subsidizes the consumption of X.

Figure 1 depicts the equilibrium in each of the three distorted markets in the economy. These are the polluting input market (upper panel), the market for tax-favored consumption (middle panel), and the labor market (bottom panel). Demand and supply curves are denoted by D and S and initial quantities by subscript 0. MSC^Z denotes the marginal social cost of the polluting input, which equals the supply price plus environmental damages per unit. In the labor market the demand curve is perfectly elastic, while the supply curve is upward sloping, reflecting the increasing marginal social cost of labor time.[8]

The Welfare Effects of Environmental Policies

Suppose a tax of $\tau = \phi$ is imposed on the polluting input and, for the moment, that the revenue consequences of this policy are neutralized by changing the lump-sum transfer. The general equilibrium welfare change from this policy consists of three components (see Appendix A for a proof):

(i) *Pigouvian welfare gain.* Imposing a tax of $\tau = \phi$ on the polluting input reduces the quantity to Z_1 in Figure 1a. This reduces environmental damages by rectangle *abcd*.[9] It also produces economic costs of triangle *acd*, which we call the

[6] These are standard assumptions. The distortions created by non-competitive market structures are typically not large enough to greatly influence the overall welfare impacts of environmental policies (Oates and Strassmann [23]). In addition, the assumption of perfectly elastic supply curves seems reasonable for most industries in the long run.

[7] In practice some components of X, such as non-wage compensation, are deductible from all labor taxation, that is both personal income and payroll taxes. Other components of X, such as mortgage interest, are deductible from income taxes but not payroll taxes. This issue is discussed further in Section 3.

[8] Our assumption of constant returns to scale and that labor is the only primary input imply a flat labor demand curve. On the supply curve, a worker well to the left of L_0 has a relatively low opportunity cost to being in the labor force, and someone well to the right of L_0 would have a relatively high cost to being in the labor force. The latter may represent, for example, the partner of a working spouse who enjoys looking after the house and children.

[9] The change in Z is general equilibrium, that is, after the environmental tax revenues have been returned in extra transfers.

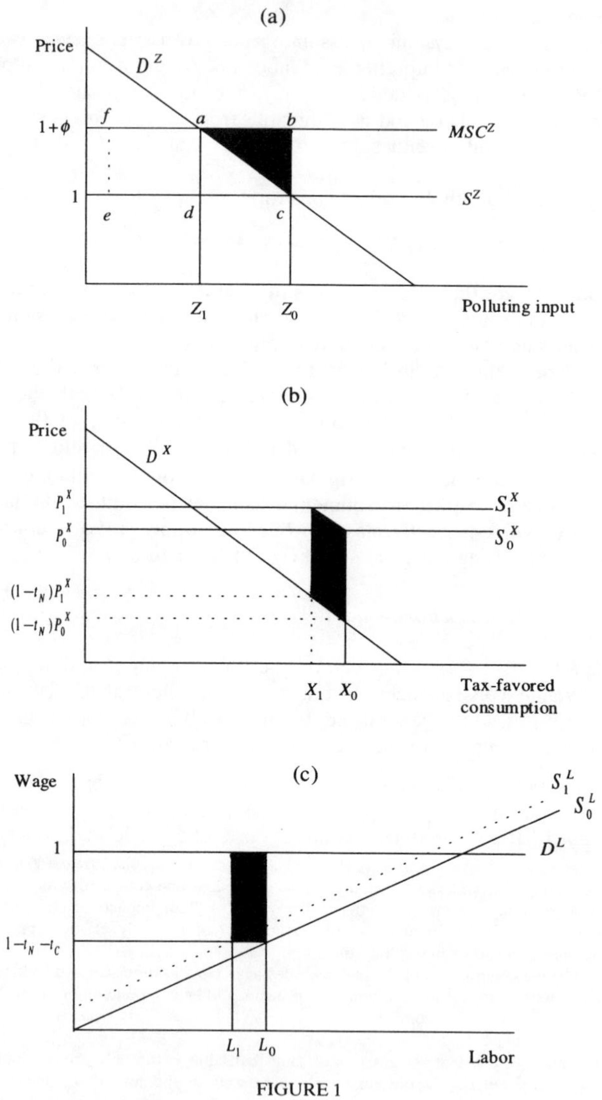
(a)
Price
D^Z
$1+\phi$
f
a
b
MSC^Z
1
e
d
c
S^Z
Z_1
Z_0
Polluting input
(b)
Price
D^X
P_1^X
P_0^X
S_1^X
S_0^X
$(1-t_N)P_1^X$
$(1-t_N)P_0^X$
X_1
X_0
Tax-favored consumption
Wage
(c)
S_1^L
S_0^L
1
D^L
$1-t_N-t_C$
L_1
L_0
Labor

FIGURE 1

primary cost of the policy. This equals the reduction in consumer surplus (trapezoid acZ_0Z_1), less the reduction in production costs (rectangle dcZ_0Z_1). Environmental benefits less the primary cost leaves the *Pigouvian welfare gain*, equal to the shaded triangle.

(ii) *Subsidy-interaction effect.* In the market for tax-favored consumption there is a wedge of $t_N p^X$ between the supply price (equal to the marginal social cost of X) and the demand price (equal to the marginal social benefit). The environmental tax raises the private costs of producing X, and this shifts the supply curve from S_0^X to S_1^X. The demand price increases from $(1 - t_N)p_0^X$ to $(1 - t_N)p_1^X$, and output falls to X_1. This produces a welfare gain equal to the shaded parallelogram. That is, for each unit reduction in X the reduction in social costs exceeds the reduction in consumer benefits by the wedge between the supply and demand price, $t_N p^X$.[10] We refer to this welfare effect as the *subsidy-interaction effect*. As explained below, the subsidy-interaction effect is relatively small when the prices of X and Y increase in the same proportion. But it becomes empirically important when the relative pollution intensity differs markedly across the X and Y industries.

(iii) *Tax-interaction effect.* The position of the labor supply curve in Figure 1c depends on the prices of consumption goods. In particular, the increase in price of X and Y caused by the environmental tax reduces the amount of consumption that can be purchased from a given nominal (net-of-tax) wage. That is, the environmental tax indirectly reduces the return to work effort relative to leisure, and this typically causes the labor supply curve to shift upward (slightly) to S_1^L. Labor supply falls from L_0 to L_1, and this produces a welfare loss equal to the shaded rectangle, which has been termed the *tax-interaction effect* (Goulder [14]). This rectangle equals the wedge between the gross wage, unity (or value marginal product of labor) and the net wage, $1 - t_N - t_C$ (or cost of a unit of foregone leisure) multiplied by the reduction in labor supply.

For the environmental tax with lump-sum replacement these three components constitute the general equilibrium welfare effect of the policy (Appendix A). If instead one of the two labor taxes adjusts to maintain budget balance, an additional welfare effect comes into play.

(iv) *Revenue-recycling effects.* Suppose the net revenue raised by the environmental tax is rectangle *fade* in Figure 1a.[11] If this revenue is used to reduce the non-comprehensive tax instead of increasing the lump-sum transfer, this produces two sources of welfare gain. First, this raises (slightly) the net-of-tax wage, leading to an increase in labor supply. Second, it also reduces (slightly) the relative subsidy for X and therefore induces a substitution out of tax-favored consumption and into

[10] This is a simple application of the familiar formulas for the general equilibrium welfare effect of a new tax in the presence of pre-existing price distortions (see, e.g., Harberger [19, Chaps. 2 and 3] and Appendix A below). Note that a new tax causes a second-order welfare effect (i.e., triangle) in the market where it is imposed (in this case the polluting input market). It causes a first-order effect (a rectangle or parallelogram) in any other market of the economy where quantities change and there is a pre-existing distortion.

[11] This is somewhat less than the revenue raised in the polluting input market, ϕZ_1, due to the loss of labor tax revenues in Figure 1c. The direct revenues from the environmental tax are likely to easily dominate the loss of labor tax revenues, except when environmental taxes approach prohibitive levels (Parry [25]).

non-tax-favored consumption.[12] The combined welfare gain from these two effects, per dollar of revenue recycled, is denoted MEB^N. This is equivalent to the marginal excess burden (MEB) of non-comprehensive labor taxation, that is, the welfare cost from raising an extra dollar of revenue from the non-comprehensive tax (to finance transfer spending). The total welfare gain from using the pollution tax revenues to cut the non-comprehensive labor tax is therefore MEB^N times rectangle *fade*, and we refer to this as the *strong revenue-recycling effect*.

Suppose instead that net revenues are used to reduce the comprehensive labor tax. In this case there is a similar welfare gain in the labor market, but no gain from reducing the subsidy wedge in the market for tax-favored consumption. Therefore (for the same amount of revenues raised) there is a welfare gain of MEB^C times rectangle *fade*, where MEB^C is the MEB for the comprehensive labor tax and $MEB^C < MEB^N$. For this case we say there is a *normal revenue-recycling effect*.[13]

Emissions Permits

Now suppose the quantity of the polluting input is reduced to Z_1 in Figure 1a by issuing the appropriate quantity of pollution permits. This policy induces the same Pigouvian welfare gain as the environmental tax. It also induces an analogous subsidy-interaction effect and tax-interaction effect because it raises the price of the polluting input to the same level $(1 + \phi)$. The permit policy creates rents of rectangle ϕZ_1. If the permits were auctioned the rents would accrue to the government and the welfare effect of the policy would be identical to that of the environmental tax in our model.

Instead, in keeping with practice so far in U.S. pollution control programs, we assume the permits are given out for free to existing firms. Still, the government does (indirectly) receive a minor fraction of the rents because rents are reflected in firm profits (which are subject to corporate income tax) and ultimately non-labor household income (which is subject to personal income tax). Typically this revenue gain is (slightly) less than the reduction in labor tax revenues in our simulation results, so there is no net revenue-recycling effect.

Relation to Previous Studies

In previous studies (e.g., Goulder et al. [17], Bovenberg and de Mooij [2], Parry [25]) there is no allowance for tax-favored spending and hence no distortion in the X market in Figure 1b.[14] The general equilibrium cost of a revenue-neutral

[12] The welfare gain in the labor market is (approximately) equal to the increase in labor supply multiplied by the wedge between the gross and net wage. The welfare gain in the X market equals (approximately) the reduction in X multiplied by the rate of non-comprehensive tax.

[13] The tax-interaction effect and normal revenue-recycling effect are familiar from earlier studies. For ease of exposition, we use a slightly different definition here. Other studies (e.g., Parry [25], Goulder et al. [17]) add on the welfare loss from the reduction in labor tax revenues to the cost of the tax-interaction effect, rather than subtracting it from the revenue-recycling effect, as we have above.

[14] Lawrence Goulder has used a sophisticated dynamic numerical model of the U.S. economy to conduct a number of exercises that examine the effects of environmental taxes (see, e.g., Goulder [15]). Although it treats the tax system in some detail, it is not disaggregated enough to incorporate tax deductions for medical insurance and mortgage interest.

pollution tax in these models therefore consists of the primary costs, the tax-interaction effect, and the normal revenue-recycling effect. These studies typically find that the tax-interaction effect dominates the (normal) revenue-recycling effect; that is, the net impact of environmental tax swaps is to reduce the labor supply and increase the costs of pre-existing taxes. These studies therefore cast doubt on the "double dividend" hypothesis, that is, the claim that an environmental tax could both improve the environment and reduce the costs of the tax system at the same time.[15]

Our numerical results below differ from those in these earlier studies to the extent that the strong and normal revenue-recycling effects differ and, to a lesser extent, because of the subsidy-interaction effect. The ratio of the strong to the normal revenue-recycling effect equals $MEB^{\mathrm{N}}/MEB^{\mathrm{C}}$. In Appendix B we derive the following formula for MEB^{N} (when $\tau = 0$ and we ignore feedback effects on the environment):

$$MEB^{\mathrm{N}} = \frac{(t/(1-t))\varepsilon_{\mathrm{L}}^{\mathrm{H}} + (t_{\mathrm{N}}/(1-t_{\mathrm{N}}))s_X\eta_X^{\mathrm{H}}}{1-(t/(1-t))\varepsilon_{\mathrm{L}}^{\mathrm{M}} - s_X\{1+(t_{\mathrm{N}}/(1-t_{\mathrm{N}}))\eta_X^{\mathrm{M}}\}} \qquad (2.2)$$

where $\varepsilon_{\mathrm{L}}^{\mathrm{M}}$ and $\varepsilon_{\mathrm{L}}^{\mathrm{H}}$ are the uncompensated (Marshallian) and compensated (Hicksian) labor supply elasticities, η_X^{M} and η_X^{H} are the uncompensated and compensated own price elasticity of demand for tax-favored consumption (expressed as positive numbers), s_X is the share of tax-favored consumption in total consumption, and $t = t_{\mathrm{C}} + t_{\mathrm{N}}$ is the total labor tax wedge. Setting $t_{\mathrm{N}} = 0$ gives

$$MEB^{\mathrm{C}} \cong \frac{(t/(1-t))\varepsilon_{\mathrm{L}}^{\mathrm{H}}}{1-(t/(1-t))\varepsilon_{\mathrm{L}}^{\mathrm{M}}} \qquad (2.3)$$

The formula in (2.3) has been discussed at length in other studies (see, e.g., Browning [7] and Snow and Warren [35]), and we do not go into details here.[16] For our purposes the key point here is that (comparing (2.2) and (2.3)) the increase in the MEB because of tax-favored consumption depends on three key parameters, which we discuss below: the relative size of the tax-favored sector, the (compensated and uncompensated) demand elasticity for tax-favored consumption, and the subsidy wedge.

[15] This hypothesis stems from earlier analyses that essentially "tack on" the revenue-recycling effect to a partial equilibrium analysis of environmental taxes. Since they are not general equilibrium, these analyses fail to capture the crucial tax-interaction effect.

[16] These formulas are for an increase in labor taxation to finance an extra dollar of the lump-sum transfer. If the extra revenue were not returned to households (for example, it went out of the economy in foreign aid), all the elasticities would be uncompensated, while if the extra public spending was sufficient to keep household utility constant, all the elasticities would be compensated. In our case the formulas depend on both uncompensated and compensated elasticities because the extra revenue to be recycled from an incremental increase in labor tax ($L + t\,dL/dt$ in the case of (2.3)) does not fully compensate households for the loss in surplus from the tax increase (L). The formula in (2.3) is exact when $t_{\mathrm{N}} = 0$, as in previous studies. The MEB for the comprehensive tax in our model is a little more complicated because of a cross-price effect in the X market; however, in quantitative terms the difference is very small.

3. NUMERICALLY SOLVED MODEL

We now develop a numerical model to compare, quantitatively, the welfare impacts of alternative environmental policies. Subsections A and B describe the assumed functional forms and model calibration. We consider "low," "medium," and "high" scenarios for the costs of pre-existing taxes.

Functional Forms

The household has the following constant elasticity of substitution (CES) form for utility:

$$U = \left\{\alpha_U C^{(\sigma_U - 1)/\sigma_U} + (1 - \alpha_U)(\bar{L} - L)^{(\sigma_U - 1)/\sigma_U}\right\}^{\sigma_U/(\sigma_U - 1)} - \phi(Z) \quad (3.1)$$

$$C = \left\{\alpha_C X^{(\sigma_C - 1)/\sigma_C} + (1 - \alpha_C) Y^{(\sigma_C - 1)/\sigma_C}\right\}^{\sigma_C/(\sigma_C - 1)}, \quad (3.2)$$

where C denotes composite consumption or sub-utility from the consumption of goods and the σ's and α's are parameters. σ_U and σ_C denote the elasticities of substitution between composite consumption and leisure, and between individual consumption goods, respectively. The α's are share parameters. $\phi(\cdot)$ is disutility from the pollution caused by the dirty input Z, where $\phi' > 0$, $\phi'' \geq 0$.

There are three notable restrictions embedded in this utility function—Section 5 discusses when it might be appropriate to relax these assumptions and how this would affect the results. First, the separability assumption in (3.1) simplifies our analysis by ruling out possible feedback effects of changes in environmental quality on the labor/leisure decision and the choice among consumption goods. Second, the weak separability between leisure and consumption goods and the homothetic property of the function in (3.2) together imply that X and Y are equal substitutes for leisure (Deaton [10]). This seems a reasonable benchmark assumption, given that we know of no evidence to suggest that the degree of substitution between tax-deductible consumption and leisure is significantly stronger or weaker than the degree of substitution between all other consumption goods and leisure. Third, we do not further disaggregate consumption goods into those that are produced by relatively clean and relatively dirty industries.[17]

X and Y are produced using the polluting intermediate good (Z), a clean intermediate good (H), and labor, according to the following CES production functions:

$$X = X\left\{\alpha_D^X Z_X^{(\sigma_X - 1)/\sigma_X} + \alpha_C^X C_X^{(\sigma_X - 1)/\sigma_X} + \alpha_L^X L_X^{(\sigma_X - 1)/\sigma_X}\right\}^{\sigma_X/(\sigma_X - 1)}$$

$$Y = Y\left\{\alpha_D^Y Z_Y^{(\sigma_Y - 1)/\sigma_Y} + \alpha_C^Y C_Y^{(\sigma_Y - 1)/\sigma_Y} + \alpha_L^Y L_Y^{(\sigma_Y - 1)/\sigma_Y}\right\}^{\sigma_Y/(\sigma_Y - 1)}, \quad (3.3)$$

[17] Of course, it may be appropriate to revise these central case assumptions somewhat in light of future econometric investigations. At any rate, we have to make some assumptions to estimate the costs of environmental policies, and we believe our benchmark assumptions provide the most logical starting point.

where σ_X and σ_Y are the elasticities of substitution between inputs in the two industries, the α's are input share parameters, and

$$Z = Z^X + Z^Y; \qquad H = H^X + H^Y. \tag{3.4}$$

Pollution is proportional to Z, but we relax this assumption later.

Labor is the only input used to produce Z and H, and the marginal product of labor in each of these intermediate goods industries is taken to be constant and normalized to unity. Thus

$$Z = L^Z; \qquad H = L^H. \tag{3.5}$$

Labor market equilibrium requires

$$L^X + L^Y + L^Z + L^H = L. \tag{3.6}$$

That is, labor demanded by final and intermediate good industries equals labor supplied by households.

As discussed above, the government provides a lump-sum transfer (G), levies a comprehensive tax (t_C) and non-comprehensive tax (t_N) on labor income, and reduces Z by either a pollution tax (τ) or pollution permits. We assume the government budget must balance. In the case of the pollution tax this constraint is

$$G = (t_C + t_N)L - t_N p_X X + \tau Z. \tag{3.7}$$

That is, government spending equals labor tax revenues less deductions plus pollution tax revenue.

Households choose X, Y, and L to maximize utility subject to the budget constraint given by (2.1). This generates the demand functions for goods and the labor supply function. Firms choose inputs to minimize production costs, and this determines costs per unit of output, or producer prices. In equilibrium demand and supply are equated in the final goods, intermediate goods, and labor markets, and the household and government budget constraints are satisfied.[18]

Model Calibration

The consumption/leisure substitution elasticity (σ_U) is calibrated to be consistent with estimates of labor supply elasticities. The econometric evidence on labor supply elasticities has been reviewed many times and we do not go into the details here (see, e.g., Killingsworth [20]). For our purposes there are several important points. First, for our highly aggregated model the labor supply response to changes in net wages represents the impact on average hours worked per employee and the impact on the participation rate, averaged across all members (male and female) of the labor force. Second, there is still a fair amount of uncertainty over the economy-wide labor supply elasticity, and therefore it is prudent to consider a range of values. Third, our model should be consistent with estimates for both the compensated and uncompensated labor supply elasticity. In our medium scenario for the MEB of pre-existing taxes, we choose the consumption/leisure elasticity and the initial ratio of labor supply to the time endowment to imply an uncompen-

[18] We used GAMS with MPSGE to solve the model.

TABLE I
Estimated Losses in Personal Income Tax Revenues by Function (1995)

	In $billion	% of labor income
Included categories		
Health	64.4	5.7
Employer provided medical insurance	60.7	
Medical expenses	3.7	
Housing	57.9	5.1
Mortgage interest on owner-occupied houses	51.3	
Exemption from passive loss rules for $25,000 of rental loss	4.3	
Credit for low income housing investments	2.3	
Miscellaneous[a]	17.7	1.6
Total	140.0	12.4
Excluded categories (greater than $10 billion)		
Pension contributions (employer and employee)	55.5	
Set-up basis of capital gains at death	28.3	
Deductions for state and local income tax	27.3	
Accelerated depreciation of machinery and equipment	19.4	
Charitable contributions	18.9	
Deferral of capital gains on home sales	17.1	
OASI benefits for retired workers	16.9	
Property tax on owner occupied homes	14.8	
Interest deduction for state and local debt	12.4	
Interest on life insurance savings	10.4	
Total	221.0	19.6

Source: "Statistical Abstract of the United States," 1994, Table 523. Gross labor income in 1995 is calculated by adding wages and salaries ($3442 billion), other labor income ($402 billion), employer contributions for social insurance ($365 billion), and sales and excise tax revenues ($298 billion). This gives $4507 billion. These figures are from Table B-28 of the "Economic Report of the President" (1999) and Table 478 of the "Statistical Abstract of the United States." We divide the above revenue losses by 0.25 and express the result relative to gross labor income, to obtain the shares reported on the last column.

[a] Includes group life insurance (2.9), childcare (2.9), employee parking (1.9), workman's compensation benefits (4.5), disability insurance benefits (1.9), and benefits for dependents and survivors (3.6).

sated and a compensated labor supply elasticity of 0.15 and 0.4, respectively. These are typical values used in previous studies of environmental policies (e.g., Goulder et al. [17]). In our low and high MEB scenarios we use values of 0.1 and 0.2 for the uncompensated and 0.3 and 0.5 for the compensated elasticity, respectively.[19] Following other studies (Lucas [21], Goulder et al. [17]), we assume a marginal tax wedge in the labor market of 40% which reflects the combined effects of personal, payroll, and sales taxes.

Table I shows estimates of federal revenue losses (or tax expenditures) for various categories due to deductions and exemptions built into the income tax system for 1995. The two largest components of tax-favored spending are employer-provided medical insurance and homeowner mortgage interest. Spending on

[19] These values are roughly consistent with a recent survey of opinion among labor economists by Fuchs et al. [13], assuming a weight of 0.6 and 0.4 for the male and female elasticities reported in their Table 2.

these goods amounted to about 6% and 5%, respectively, of gross labor income in 1995.[20] There are a variety of other quantifiable items (e.g., deductions for childcare and employee parking) that add about another 1.6%. In addition, there are other categories that are difficult to measure, such as business lunches and trips, employer-provided health clubs, debt-financed spending secured by real estate, and so on. In short, it is tricky to pin down really accurately the relative size of the tax-favored consumption sector. We assume $s_X = 0.11, 0.13$, and 0.15 in our low, medium, and high MEB scenarios, respectively.[21]

We exclude from our analysis a variety of other tax expenditures, shown in the lower half of Table I. These include deductions for savings and investment—pension contributions, interest on state and local bonds, capital gains at death, corporate income tax deductions, and interest on life insurance savings. Incorporation of these deductions would require a dynamic model with investment in different types of assets that are taxed or subsidized at different rates and is beyond the scope of this paper. Deductions for state and local income taxes affect the overall level of labor taxation—and this is implicitly taken into account in our estimates of labor tax rates—but do not distort the allocation of consumption expenditures. We also exclude charitable contributions, implicitly assuming that there are external benefits that just offset the tax subsidy at the margin. Finally, property taxes and (to some extent) capital gains taxes on home sales can be deducted from income taxes. These provisions affect the size of the price distortion in the housing sector but not the share of housing services in labor income.

If all tax-favored consumption were fully deductible from labor taxes, the subsidy wedge in the market for tax-favored consumption would be 40% in our model. This is not quite the case, however, and we assume a subsidy of 30%.[22] As discussed in Section 5, we abstract from a number of other complications that affect the overall size of the subsidy wedge.

The overall demand elasticities for tax-favored consumption depend on the elasticity of substitution between tax-deductible consumption and other consump-

[20] Direct estimates of these items overstate tax-favored spending; for example, mortgage payments include repayment of principal, which is not tax-deductible. They also reflect payments of all taxpayers, including those that do not itemize deductions and therefore do not receive the tax subsidy. Total health care expenditures include those for seniors who are not in the labor force.

[21] At first glance it might seem that tax-favored consumption should also include black market activities where cash transactions are not reported as taxable income (possible examples include the hiring of nannies and gardeners). However, since these activities are not observed they are implicitly counted as leisure activities and hence are captured in studies that estimate how taxes affect the substitution from observed labor supply into leisure.

[22] In particular mortgage interest is only deductible from the personal income tax and not the payroll tax. It is subsidized at the marginal rate of income tax (averaged across individuals), which is around 25 percent. Our assumptions about tax rates and s_X imply government revenue is 34–37% of total spending in our benchmark, which is approximately consistent with the ratio of total tax receipts to net national product. Note that our strong revenue-recycling effect implicitly assumes that environmental tax revenues are used to cut the rate of personal income tax. The revenue-recycling effect would be somewhat smaller if revenues were used to cut the payroll tax, since this tax has fewer deductions.

Certain sector-specific tax provisions further complicate the wedge between the demand and supply price in the housing market. In particular, property taxes are levied on the value of the housing stock. However, differences in average property tax rates between jurisdictions are reflected in differences in the value of local services. To this extent, property taxes act like a user fee and are not distortionary. Moreover, a quarter of the property tax liability is essentially nullified by the deductibility from income taxes.

TABLE II
Alternative Scenarios for Key Parameters

Parameter	Low MEB	Medium MEB	High MEB
s_X	0.11	0.13	0.15
η_X^M	1.00	1.20	1.40
η_X^H	0.89	1.12	1.35
ε_L^M	0.10	0.15	0.20
ε_L^H	0.30	0.40	0.50
MEB^N	0.31	0.46	0.56
MEB^C	0.21	0.30	0.38

Note. See Section 2 for notational definitions.

tion goods, and s_X, as follows: $\eta_X^M = (1 - s_X)\sigma_C + s_X$ and $\eta_X^H = (1 - s_X)\sigma_C$.[23] Various studies have estimated demand elasticities for individual components of X. For example, in a careful study Rosen [33] estimated the (uncompensated) demand elasticity for home mortgages to be unity. A recent estimate of the demand elasticity for health insurance is 1.8 (Gruber and Poterba [18]).[24] We choose σ_C to imply values of 1, 1.2, and 1.4 for the uncompensated demand elasticity for X in our low, medium, and high MEB scenarios.

Table II summarizes our key parameter values. They imply an MEB from the non-comprehensive tax equal to 0.31, 0.46, and 0.56 in the low, medium, and high scenarios. In earlier studies that neglect tax-favored consumption (e.g., Goulder et al. [17]) the MEB is around 0.3, which equals our MEB for the comprehensive tax in the medium scenario. At first glance it may seem surprising that the presence of tax-favored consumption increases the MEB so much, when tax-favored consumption is only around 13% of the size of the labor market. However, this is counteracted to some extent because tax-favored consumption is much more sensitive to changes in tax rates than to labor supply.[25]

Our estimates of the MEB with tax deductions are approximately consistent with those recently obtained by Parry [27] in a more detailed study, and we refer the reader to this paper for more discussion about underlying parameter values. However, they are well below estimates of the MEB in Feldstein's [12] seminal article, which were typically above unity. To calculate the MEB, Feldstein used estimates of the elasticity of people's taxable income with respect to changes in income tax rates. This elasticity reflects substitution effects into all of the tax deductions listed in Table I. As discussed above, for our analysis it is appropriate to exclude many of these categories—in fact over 60% of them—although the deductions for investment and savings would be relevant for a dynamic analysis.[26]

[23] These formulas can be obtained after differentiating the expenditure and indirect utility functions for CES utility functions (see Varian [36, p. 130]) and some manipulation.

[24] Earlier studies typically find significantly lower estimates; however, Gruber and Poterba suggest that these studies contain a number of methodological problems.

[25] In terms of our MEB formulas, the extra terms in (2.2) compared with (2.3) are still significant because, even though s_X is small, the η's are much larger than the ε's.

[26] Moreover, the most recent estimates of the taxable income elasticity are significantly lower than those used in Feldstein's original analysis (see Carroll [9]).

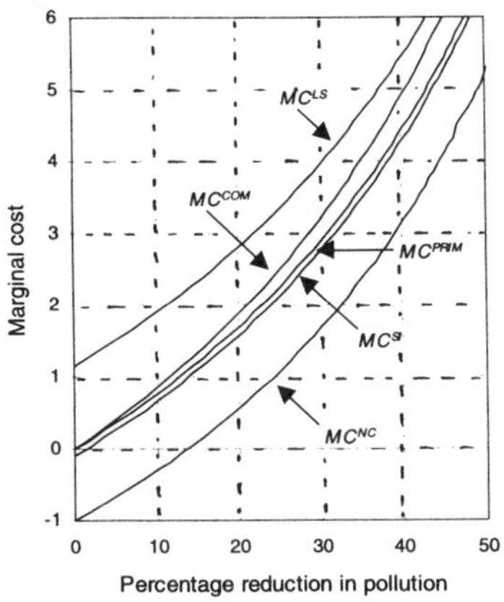

FIG. 2. Marginal costs.

We take the elasticities of substitution in the X and Y industries (σ_X and σ_Y) to be unity. This is a standard assumption, and, as discussed below, our results are not sensitive to other values. In our initial simulations the factor input ratios are the same in both consumption goods industries, but this is relaxed later on. Finally, we assume the initial value of output in each intermediate good industry amounts to 10% of the value of total final output. The relative costs of environmental policies are not especially sensitive to alternative assumptions about the size of the polluting intermediate good (e.g., energy) relative to GDP.[27]

4. RESULTS

This section presents our simulation results illustrating how the tax system affects the costs, overall welfare impacts, and optimal levels of environmental policies.

Marginal Costs

In Figure 2 we compare the marginal cost of reducing pollution under alternative policy instruments up to 50% below pre-regulation levels. Marginal costs are expressed as a percentage of the initial value product of the polluting input. For this figure we mainly focus on qualitative results, and since these are essentially the same under all three MEB scenarios, we illustrate just the medium MEB case.

MC^{PRIM} indicates marginal costs in a first-best case when we set pre-existing taxes and the subsidy to zero. This curve reflects primary costs only and is the same

[27] That is, primary costs and the tax-interaction and revenue-recycling effects increase in roughly the same proportion as we increase or decrease the breadth of the polluting intermediate good, leaving relative costs unaffected (Goulder et al. [17]).

under both the pollution tax and pollution permits.[28] MC^{PRIM} has a zero intercept and is upward sloping, reflecting the increasing marginal cost of substituting other inputs for the polluting input in production and the increasing marginal cost of reducing the amount of consumption.

MC^{SI} shows marginal costs when we allow for the 30% subsidy for X, but still set labor taxes at zero.[29] The difference between this curve and MC^{PRIM} reflects the (marginal) subsidy-interaction effect. This effect is a welfare gain (the parallelogram in Figure 1b) because the pollution tax reduces the output of X, thus offsetting to some extent the distortionary effect of the subsidy. However, in practical terms the subsidy-interaction effect is negligible. This is because the prices of X and Y increase in the same proportion, and hence the reduction in X reflects substitution into leisure only and not into other consumption. Subsequent simulations show, however, that the subsidy-interaction effect can be important when the relative pollution intensity differs significantly between the tax-favored and non-tax-favored production sectors.

MC^{LS} indicates marginal cost under the pollution tax with both labor taxes but with no revenue-recycling effect; that is, environmental tax revenues are neutralized by adjusting the lump-sum transfer. The difference between this curve and MC^{SI} reflects the (marginal) tax-interaction effect. This effect causes a substantial upward shift of the marginal cost curve (see Goulder et al. [17] and Parry [26] for more discussion).

MC^{COM} shows marginal costs under the pollution tax with revenues used to reduce the comprehensive tax (holding government transfers constant in real terms). It equals MC^{LS} less the (marginal) benefit from the normal revenue-recycling effect. Comparing MC^{COM} with MC^{SI}, we can infer that the tax-interaction effect dominates the normal revenue-recycling effect at the margin (except at zero pollution reduction). Again, this result is familiar from other studies (Goulder et al. [17], Parry [25]). The gap between MC^{LS} and MC^{COM} decreases with the amount of pollution reduction, since the erosion of the pollution tax base reduces the marginal revenue-recycling effect. Indeed the marginal revenue-recycling effect eventually becomes negative if pollution is reduced by more than a certain amount. Beyond this point the pollution tax Laffer curve is downward sloping and MC^{COM} rises above MC^{LS}.

Finally, MC^{NC} is the marginal cost curve for the pollution tax with revenues used to reduce the non-comprehensive labor tax.[30] This curve equals MC^{LS} less the (marginal) benefit from the strong revenue-recycling effect. It has a negative intercept and marginal costs are negative up to a pollution reduction of 13% in our medium cost scenario. Thus, even if there were no environmental benefits it would still be optimal to reduce pollution by 13% in this case. Up to a point, therefore, the environmental tax swap reduces the overall costs of the tax system, not counting environmental benefits. The environmental tax essentially allows the

[28] To calculate the primary costs we recalibrate the distribution parameters such that the initial quantities of goods and leisure are the same as in the model with non-zero taxes. However, the substitution elasticity parameters, which crucially determine the relative costs of policies, are the same across the models with and without the labor taxes. Pollution tax revenues are returned as a lump sum.

[29] For this case the pre-existing subsidy is financed by a lump-sum tax.

[30] To avoid cluttering Figure 2, we omit marginal costs for emissions permits in the presence of pre-existing taxes. The effects of this policy are explained below.

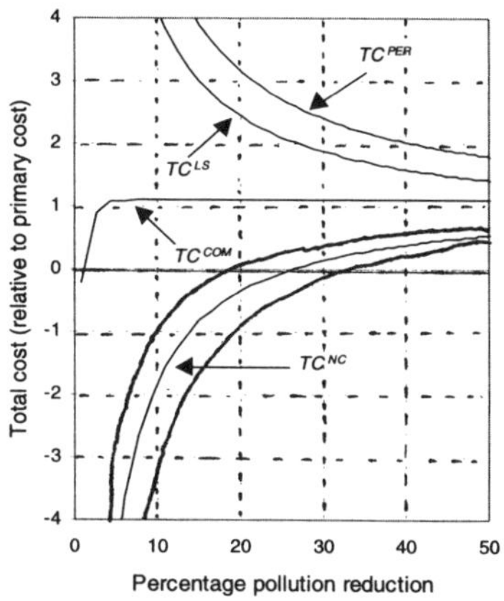

FIG. 3. Total costs.

burden of the tax system to be spread more evenly across the two consumption sectors, because tax-favored consumption is produced with the polluting input.

Total Costs

Figure 3 shows the total (as opposed to marginal) costs of reducing pollution under various policies, expressed relative to the total primary costs. When a cost curve lies above (below) unity, the net impact of the tax system is to raise (lower) the overall cost of a policy above (below) its primary costs.

The most novel feature of Figure 3 is the total cost curves for the pollution tax with revenues used to reduce the non-comprehensive labor tax. The thicker curve, denoted TC^{NC}, indicates the medium MEB scenario, and the upper and lower dotted curves correspond to the low and high MEB scenarios (or low and high substitution elasticities in the utility function), respectively. These curves lie below the horizontal axis for pollution reductions up to 19–33%. When total costs are negative the welfare gain from reducing the costs of the tax system more than offsets the primary cost of the policy. Goulder [14] refers to this as a "strong" double dividend from environmental taxes. When total costs are positive but less than unity, there is still a net welfare gain from interactions with the tax system. For example, in the medium MEB scenario, if the reduction in pollution is below 50%, interactions with the tax system reduce the overall costs of the pollution tax by over 50%.[31]

[31] Thus, for more modest levels of pollution taxation there is potential for a sizable double dividend, but this declines at higher levels of pollution taxation. The reason for this is clear from Figure 1. At modest levels of pollution taxation, the net revenues raised, and hence the (strong) revenue-recycling effect, are large relative to the primary cost triangle *acd*. But at high levels of pollution taxation the base of the tax is much smaller, and this reduces the size of the strong revenue-recycling effect relative to primary costs. At 100% pollution reduction there are no revenues raised under any policies, and the total costs of all the policy instruments we consider become equal and exceed primary costs.

In contrast, if revenues are instead used to reduce the comprehensive labor tax, total costs are indicated by TC^{COM} in the medium-cost scenario. In this case there is no potential for a double dividend; the general equilibrium costs of this policy exceed the primary costs by around 11%.[32] Figure 3 clearly shows that, by neglecting the welfare gain from the reduced subsidy for tax-favored consumption, previous studies may dramatically overstate not only the magnitude of costs from environmental tax swaps, but also the sign of the welfare change. For example, for a pollution reduction of 20% in the medium-MEB scenario, previous studies would estimate costs equal to 111% of primary costs; in contrast, our analysis predicts a welfare *gain* equal to 40% of primary costs.

When the revenue effects of environmental taxes are neutralized by lump-sum transfers, total costs are given by TC^{LS} in the medium MEB case. The overall costs of this policy are infinitely larger than the primary costs for an incremental amount of pollution reduction. This reflects the positive intercept of the marginal cost curve for this policy in Figure 2. As the extent of pollution reduction increases, total costs fall relative to the primary cost. This is because the primary cost triangle *acd* in Figure 1a increases relative to the cost of the tax-interaction effect, the shaded rectangle (for more discussion see Goulder et al. [17]). Finally, TC^{PER} is the (general equilibrium) total cost of reducing pollution by emissions permits, relative to the primary cost, when government budget balance is maintained by adjusting the comprehensive labor tax. Although we assume that 40% of permit rents accrue to the government in tax revenue, this is not quite enough to compensate for the reduction in labor tax revenues; hence tax rates must be increased slightly to maintain government budget balance, and TC^{PER} lies above TC^{LS}.[33]

Previous studies have emphasized the potentially strong efficiency case for using (revenue-neutral) pollution taxes—or equivalently in our analysis, auctioned emissions permits—over non-auctioned emissions permits (see, e.g., Parry [26], Goulder et al. [17], Parry et al. [29]). This case is based on a comparison of total cost curves that (roughly speaking) correspond to TC^{COM} and TC^{PER} in Figure 3. However, when recycling the revenues from the pollution tax or permit sales produces a welfare gain in the market for tax-favored consumption, in addition to the welfare gain in the labor market, the appropriate comparison is between the TC^{NC} curves and (approximately) TC^{PER} in Figure 3. In this case, the efficiency cost savings from using the pollution tax or auctioned permits over free pollution permits is potentially much more dramatic. For example, if pollution is reduced by 20%, the cost of emissions permits is more than 300% of primary costs; in contrast, the pollution tax or auctioned permits produces an economic gain equal to about 40%

[32] Previous studies (Goulder et al. [17], Parry [26]) find somewhat higher cost ratios for this policy. This is because they use slightly different definitions to compare welfare differences between first best and second best outcomes. The difference between the TC^{NC} and TC^{COM} curves in Figure 3 is a little larger than can be explained by the difference between the strong and normal revenue recycling effects alone. The reason is a little technical. When the recycling of pollution tax revenues reduces the subsidy distortion for tax-favored consumption, this raises the relative attractiveness of work effort to leisure at the margin. As a result the overall reduction in labor supply is slightly smaller when there is a strong rather than a normal revenue-recycling effect (in fact the overall change in labor supply is slightly positive for modest pollution reductions).

[33] If the non-comprehensive tax is adjusted to maintain budget balance, total costs are slightly higher than indicated by TC^{PER}.

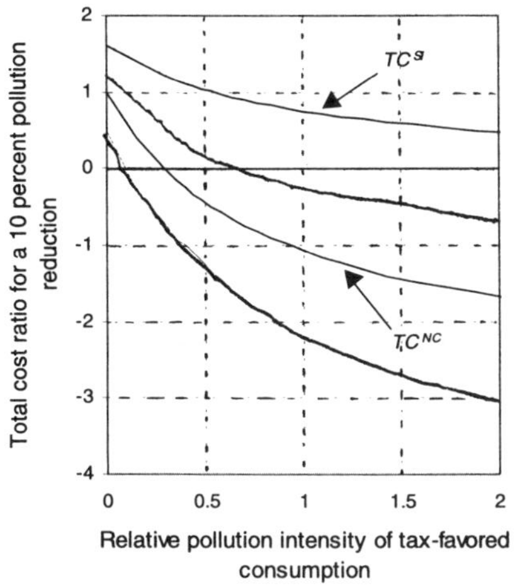

FIG. 4. Varying the pollution intensity of tax-favored consumption.

of primary costs in the medium-MEB scenario. Consistent with earlier studies, however, the cost saving from using the pollution tax over emissions permits is relatively less dramatic at higher levels of pollution reduction.

Relative Pollution Intensities

We now relax the assumption of equal pollution intensities in the tax-favored and non-tax-favored production sectors. This affects the costs of policies by changing the relative size of the subsidy-interaction effect. Along the horizontal axis in Figure 4 we vary the (initial) ratio of the polluting input to the clean input in the tax-favored sector, relative to the same ratio in the non-tax-favored sector (keeping the total amount of pollution the same). This ratio is less (greater) than unity when tax-favored consumption is cleaner (more polluting) than non-tax-favored consumption.

The TC^{SI} curve shows the total costs of reducing pollution by 10% in the medium-MEB case, expressed relative to the primary costs, when there is a 30% subsidy for X but labor taxes are zero. The gap between this curve and unity isolates the subsidy-interaction effect. As the relative pollution intensity in the tax-favored sector falls (moving left along the horizontal axis), the welfare gain from the subsidy interaction effect declines and becomes negative (this occurs when the TC^{SI} curve rises above unity and the pollution intensity ratio is less than 0.57). This is because the pollution tax drives up the price of non-tax-favored consumption by a proportionally greater amount, hence reducing and eventually reversing the direction of the change in tax-favored consumption.

The TC^{NC} curve shows the total costs of the pollution tax with the strong revenue-recycling effect relative to primary costs, for a 10% pollution reduction (again the upper and lower dotted curves correspond to the low- and high-MEB scenarios, respectively). As the relative pollution intensity of tax-favored consumption falls, the costs of this policy increase as the subsidy-interaction effect declines and becomes negative. In fact, when the intensity ratio falls below 0.60, 0.35, or 0.10 in the low-, medium-, and high-MEB scenarios, total costs are positive; hence the strong double dividend disappears.

Thus our results are sensitive to the relative pollution intensity of the tax-favored sector. In the limiting case when polluting inputs are used exclusively in the non-tax-favored sector, the environmental tax shift no longer reduces the costs of pre-existing taxes. Moreover, if non-auctioned emissions permits were used to reduce these pollutants, the general equilibrium costs (relative to primary costs) would be substantially higher than implied by Figure 3, since these policies serve to exacerbate the distortion in prices between the tax-favored and non-tax-favored sectors. Having said this, even if the tax-favored sector is relatively less polluting, it is still possible to generate a significant double dividend for modest levels of pollution taxes. For example, when the pollution intensity in the tax-favored sector is only 50% of that for the rest of the economy, a revenue-neutral tax that reduces pollution by 10% produces a net economic gain equal to 40% of primary costs in our medium-MEB scenario.

Some pollutants—e.g., chemical pesticides and fertilizers used in agricultural production—are used exclusively in the non-tax-favored sector, and environmental taxes on these pollutants would not yield the double dividend in our analysis. However, pollutants associated with energy production may, if anything, be used more intensively in the tax-favored sector. This is because the housing sector is responsible for a disproportionate amount of energy consumption. At any rate, estimating the relative intensity of use for different pollutants in the tax-favored sectors would be a useful topic for future research.[34]

Welfare under the Pigouvian Rule

In Figure 5 we compare the overall welfare impacts of the different environmental policies (i.e., environmental benefits minus economic costs), sticking, for simplicity, with the medium-MEB scenario and equal pollution intensities across sectors. We postulate different values for the marginal environmental benefit from reducing pollution, and the corresponding Pigouvian pollution reduction is shown along the horizontal axis.[35] The vertical axis shows the ratio of the general equilibrium welfare gains from this pollution reduction to the Pigouvian welfare gain (i.e., the shaded triangle in Figure 1a).

Again, the novel feature from this figure is the curve for the pollution tax with the strong revenue-recycling effect, W^{NC}. This curve lies above unity, while the curves for all the other policies lie below unity. That is, the general equilibrium

[34] Such estimation can become quite involved and is really beyond the scope of this paper. For example, measuring the relative energy intensity of tax-favored consumption would require estimating energy costs as a fraction of the value of health and housing output, taking account of energy used in the upstream production of all intermediate inputs used by these industries. It would also require estimating the extent to which extra spending on housing translates into more energy demand for space heating and cooling, lighting, and so on.

[35] That is, the pollution reduction from imposing a tax equal to marginal environmental benefits. Marginal benefits are taken as constant, which seems a reasonable approximation for some pollutants, such as sulfur and carbon (see Burtraw et al. [8] and Pizer [32]).

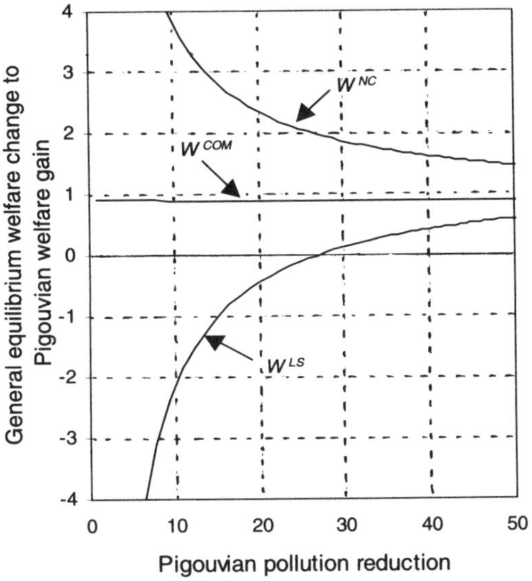

FIG. 5. Welfare under the Pigouvian rule.

welfare gain is higher than the Pigouvian welfare gain for this policy and less for all other policies. Previous studies find that even with the (normal) revenue-recycling effect, the welfare gain from Pigouvian pollution policies is typically less than the Pigouvian welfare gain. In contrast, the welfare gain from the pollution tax with strong revenue recycling is more than double the Pigouvian welfare gain for pollution reductions below 25%. Finally, we note again the potentially striking difference between policies that do and do not produce the (strong) revenue-recycling effect. For pollution reductions below 25% a pollution tax with lump-sum replacement *reduces* welfare, despite environmental benefits.

Optimal Policies

Our final diagram, Figure 6, shows the second-best optimal pollution reduction under alternative policies, expressed relative to the optimal Pigouvian pollution reduction (for the medium-MEB scenario and alternative assumptions about marginal environmental benefits). When these curves lie above (below) unity the optimal (second-best) pollution reduction is greater (less) than would be implied by a partial equilibrium analysis. As consistent with our earlier results, the optimal levels of policies differ substantially when (marginal) environmental benefits are more modest relative to (marginal) primary costs. For example, when environmental benefits imply the optimal Pigouvian (or partial equilibrium) pollution reduction is 15%, in a general equilibrium analysis this would be zero under the tax with lump-sum replacement, 13.5% under the tax with normal revenue recycling, and 22.5% under the tax with strong revenue recycling.

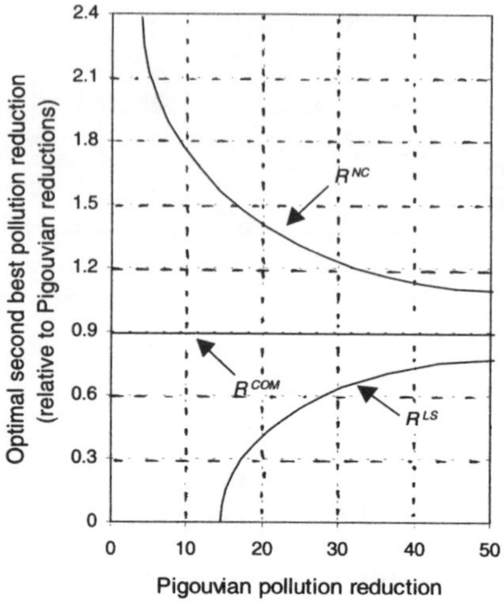

FIG. 6. Optimal policies.

Further Sensitivity Analysis

Previous studies (e.g., Goulder et al. [17], Parry [26]) have found that—*for a given reduction in pollution*—the size of the tax-interaction and revenue-recycling effects relative to the partial equilibrium costs of environmental policies are not really affected by changing the degree of substitution between pollution and other inputs. In other words these three effects are all changed in roughly the same proportion, leaving the relative total cost curves in Figure 3 unaffected.[36] We find the same result in our analysis. Similarly, increasing the possibilities for substitution by allowing for end-of-pipe treatment does not have much effect on relative costs.[37]

5. FURTHER DISCUSSION

In this section we comment on how the results would be affected by various extensions to the analysis (for more discussion of some of these issues see, e.g., Bovenberg and Goulder [5], Goulder [16], Parry [28]).

[36] We can see this from Figure 1. Suppose that we pivot the D^Z curve about point c such that it now intersects the vertical line at Z_1 halfway between points a and d. This halves the primary cost of reducing pollution from Z_0 to Z_1. But it will also halve the tax required to reduce the polluting input to Z_1 and hence halve the revenue-recycling effect. Similarly, this will roughly halve the effect of the tax on product prices and hence the tax-interaction effect.

[37] We expanded our model to allow firms to reduce emissions per unit of the dirty good by employing labor, such that the primary costs of reducing pollution by 10% were halved. The ratio of the general equilibrium costs to primary costs under the emissions tax with the strong revenue-recycling effect fell from -1.90 to -1.85.

Non-Separable Environmental Effects

Our assumption that environmental quality is separable in the utility function implies that changes in environmental quality do not have feedback effects on current labor supply decisions or the choice among consumption goods. This seems plausible for some cases, for example, when the environmental impacts of current emissions do not occur for several decades (climate change, nuclear waste), or when pollution affects ecological rather than economic variables.

But there are some notable counter-examples. Reducing work-related traffic congestion may produce a positive feedback effect on labor supply, by reducing the time costs of commuting. Cleaner air improves human health and this may have feedback effects on the demand for health care and labor supply.[38] On the other hand, a more pleasant environment (beaches, national parks, etc.) may increase the value of leisure pursuits relative to work time. A fruitful area for future research would be to explore empirically the extent to which these sorts of feedback effects could dampen or magnify the tax interactions discussed above.

Substitution between Polluting Goods and Leisure

We have assumed that goods produced by relatively clean and relatively polluting industries have the same degree of substitution with leisure. If pollution is concentrated in industries that are relatively weak (strong) leisure substitutes, the tax-interaction effect is smaller (larger) (see, e.g., Bovenberg and Goulder [5], Parry [25]). Yet many pollutants are associated with energy production, and to our knowledge there is not clear evidence that energy-intensive goods as a group are significantly weaker or significantly stronger leisure substitutes than consumption goods as a whole. However, there are some special cases where incorporating relatively weak leisure substitutes would be important. These include externalities associated with necessity goods, such as smoke from cigarettes, and pollutants associated with agricultural production.

Parry [25] shows that the tax-interaction effect[39] is (approximately) proportional to the price elasticity of the polluting good with respect to leisure divided by the price elasticity for aggregate consumption with respect to leisure. Thus, if the cross-price elasticity for cigarettes was, say, 40% of that for consumption goods as a whole, the tax-interaction effect for cigarettes would be 40% of that in our benchmark simulations.[40]

Substitution between Tax-Favored Goods and Leisure

The preference structure in (3.1) and (3.2) implies that tax-favored goods and non-tax-favored goods exhibit the same degree of substitution with leisure (Deaton

[38] The direction of the health feedback effects is unclear, however. For example, if older people live longer because of better health, medical expenditures over their lifetime could still increase. Similarly, Williams [37] finds that the labor supply effects of improved health are ambiguous.

[39] In his terminology this is the "interdependency effect."

[40] A value for the ratio of cross-price elasticities might be obtained without doing a detailed econometric study. If we maintain the assumption of weak separability between consumption and leisure (which is reasonable in some cases), but allow for non-homothetic preferences, then from Deaton [10] we know that this elasticity ratio is simply equal to the expenditure elasticity of demand for the polluting good.

[10]). Suppose we relax the assumption of unitary expenditure elasticities implied by the homothetic functional form in (3.2). This alters the strong revenue-recycling effect, but only very slightly—if we keep the model consistent with evidence on the uncompensated price elasticity.[41] However, suppose that we relax the assumption of weak separability between consumption goods and leisure in (3.1). If people obtain better housing at the expense of other consumption goods, if anything this is likely to increase rather than decrease the value of leisure time relative to labor time. Thus, since the environmental tax with the strong revenue-recycling effect reduces the relative consumption of tax-favored consumption, this could produce an additional efficiency gain through a positive feedback effect on labor supply. In this respect, our results on the welfare effects of this policy may be conservative.

Capital

In principle, another useful extension would be to introduce capital as a second factor input. This would require a considerably more complex dynamic analysis in which the taxation of capital distorts the choice between current and future consumption, in addition to the choice between tax-favored assets and other capital assets.[42] In this setting the welfare gain from revenue-neutral environmental taxes may be significantly larger than in our static analysis, though this will depend on the relative pollution intensity of tax-favored capital goods.

Non-Tax Distortions in the Housing and Health Markets

The size of the subsidy wedge for tax-favored consumption (the height of the parallelogram in Figure 1b) is much more complicated in practice than we have assumed. There may be efficiency gains from this subsidy; for example, it may offset market failures due to asymmetric information in health insurance, and positive externalities to neighbors if houses are better maintained when owned rather than rented. In addition, there are a variety of regulations that raise the price of tax-favored consumption goods. These include building codes, rent controls, and zoning restrictions in the housing market, and occupational licensing and drug regulations in the health market. All of these effects reduce the overall wedge between the marginal social cost and marginal social benefit from tax-favored consumption. However, what matters is the impact on the price of tax-favored goods relative to non-tax-favored goods—the price effect will tend to be offset to the extent that other regulations raise the relative price of non-tax-favored goods.

Unfortunately, the quantitative importance of these factors is often difficult to pin down (see, e.g., Rosen [33], Pauly [31]). Moreover, there are other factors that operate in the opposing direction. For example, housing receives additional subsidies because imputed income is not subject to tax, low-income households receive public assistance, and complementary services such as roads and schools are

[41] If we keep the same value for the uncompensated own price elasticity of demand for tax-favored consumption, then through the Slutsky equation, changing the income elasticity implies different values for the compensated price elasticity η_X^H in (2.2). If the income elasticity is between 0 and 2 (and evidence suggests it is closer to unity than either of these values), then η_X^H varies between 0.94 and 1.2 in our medium-MEB scenario. This implies values for MEB^N of between 0.45 and 0.47.

[42] Note, however, that at least in terms of size the labor market is easily the more important market. It accounts for about 70% of total factor income in the United States.

usually subsidized. Government programs subsidize health care for the poor and elderly. Also, these goods may confer some negative externalities, such as habitat destruction and congestion caused by housing development, and the crowding out of lower income workers from the health insurance market as prices rise in response to demand for higher quality from the better off. In short it is difficult to assess whether on balance these additional factors would increase or reduce the overall subsidy wedge for tax-favored consumption, let alone by how much.

Other Tax Deductions

A key theme of this paper is that the presence of tax expenditures, when significant relative to total labor tax revenues, can substantially raise the efficiency gains from recycling environmental tax revenues in income tax reductions. However, there are a variety of other tax expenditures that—although small in size—could still significantly affect the welfare impact of environmental policies, if they apply directly to the market that is being regulated. Some examples might include favorable depletion allowances for petroleum and other minerals, favorable capital gains treatment for farm income, exclusion of interest on state and local bonds for pollution control and waste disposal facilities, and reimbursed employee parking expenses.[43] To the extent that the tax system effectively subsidizes activities with negative externalities, the prospects for a double dividend from imposing revenue-neutral taxes on these activities is enhanced.

6. CONCLUSIONS

This paper uses a simple numerical model to demonstrate the potential importance of tax-favored consumption for the general equilibrium welfare effects of environmental policies. When part of consumer spending is deductible from labor taxes, the tax system distorts the allocation of consumption in addition to the labor market. In this setting the welfare gain from using environmental tax revenues to reduce labor taxes can be significantly higher than implied by earlier models that do not allow for tax-favored consumption. As a result, the cost savings from using revenue-neutral environmental taxes or auctioned pollution permits over non-auctioned pollution permits can be dramatically higher than suggested by previous studies. In fact, under certain conditions, the overall costs of an environmental tax swap can be negative. These conditions include the requirement that at least some of the polluting input is used in the production of tax-favored goods and a level of pollution taxes that is not too high. Our results suggest that taxes on carbon, for example, might be worthwhile to implement—if set at modest levels—even in the absence of clear evidence of the benefits of limiting atmospheric accumulations of carbon dioxide.[44]

[43] For more detail on these types of tax expenditures see Office of Management and Budget [24].

[44] Of course, this crucially assumes that all new sources of revenues will be used to cut distortionary taxes. Some recent public choice analyses suggest that at least part of new revenues sources are likely to be used for public spending (Becker and Mulligan [1], Brett and Keen [6]). In this case the prospects for a double dividend are likely to be smaller, unless the additional spending generates social benefits well in excess of dollar outlays. On the other hand, a number of environmental taxes in Holland have been implemented in a revenue-neutral fashion. In Germany the new Social Democratic/Green Party coalition government is proposing similar environmental tax swaps.

In some sense our results are paradoxical. The presence of tax-favored consumption raises the costs of the tax system, and normally one would expect this to imply a smaller optimal size of government (Feldstein [11]). In contrast we find that the welfare gains from environmental protection through revenue-neutral taxes (or auctioned pollution permits) can be significantly *greater* in the presence of tax-favored consumption. However, it is important to emphasize that this result depends entirely on a pre-existing inefficiency of the tax system on "non-environmental" grounds that the environmental tax swap improves. A first best response to this inefficiency would be to implement direct tax reforms, such as cutting back the deductions for employer-provided health insurance and mortgage interest. Yet, probably because of opposition from adversely affected interest groups, these types of direct reforms have proved difficult to implement, at least in the United States.

We emphasize again the preliminary nature of our findings. There is uncertainty about key parameters underlying the market for tax-favored consumption, including the demand elasticity, the relative pollution intensity, and the influence of non-tax factors on the overall level of distortion in the market. In addition our analysis is simplified in a number of respects. For example, we ignore the possibility of feedback effects on labor supply from environmental improvement, and we do not model the impact of the tax system on distorting the consumption/investment margin and the choice among alternative investment assets. Nonetheless our analysis clearly illustrates that the presence of tax deductions can substantially affect the overall welfare impacts of environmental policies, under a wide range of assumptions about parameter values. In short, tax deductions are important to incorporate into any comprehensive efficiency analysis of environmental policies.

Finally, we note that the results may have less relevance for countries other than the United States. For example, in Britain mortgage interest tax relief has now been phased out, and most people rely on the National Health Service rather than (subsidized) private health insurance.

APPENDIX A: FORMAL DERIVATION OF WELFARE EFFECTS

Here we provide a formal derivation of the welfare effects discussed in Section 2 for the pollution tax with lump-sum replacement and with the strong revenue-recycling effect. For simplicity we focus on incremental policy changes (rather than the non-marginal changes shown in Figure 1). All variables are as defined in the text.

Suppose household utility is

$$U(X, Y, \bar{L} - L) - \phi(Z), \tag{A1}$$

and the household faces the budget constraint

$$(1 - t_N)p_X(\tau)X + p_Y(\tau)Y = (1 - t_N - t_C)L + G, \tag{A2}$$

where the prices of goods depend on the pollution tax τ.[45] Households choose X, Y, and L to maximize (A1) subject to (A2), taking Z as given. The solution to this

[45] Since firms are competitive and supply curves are perfectly elastic we do not need to explicitly model firm behavior. The tax on the polluting input is fully passed on to consumers in the form of higher product prices.

problem is the (uncompensated) demand and labor supply functions. These functions can be expressed as

$$X(\tau, t_N, t_C, G), \qquad Y(\tau, t_N, t_C, G), \qquad L(\tau, t_N, t_C, G). \tag{A3}$$

The derived demand for the polluting good can also be expressed as a function of the exogenous variables:

$$Z(\tau, t_N, t_C, G). \tag{A4}$$

Substituting (A3) and (A4) into (A1) gives

$$V(\tau, t_N, t_C, G) - \phi(Z(\tau, t_N, t_C, G)), \tag{A5}$$

where V is indirect utility from non-environmental goods. From Roy's identity,

$$\frac{\partial V}{\partial \tau} = -\lambda Z \qquad \frac{\partial V}{\partial t_N} = -\lambda(L - X) \qquad \frac{\partial V}{\partial t_C} = -\lambda L \qquad \frac{\partial V}{\partial G} = \lambda, \tag{A6}$$

where λ is the marginal utility of income and we have normalized p_X to unity.

(i) *Pollution Tax with Lump-Sum Replacement*

Differentiating (A5) with respect to τ and holding t_N and t_C constant, and using (A6) gives

$$\frac{1}{\lambda}\frac{dV}{d\tau} = -Z + \frac{dG}{d\tau} - \frac{\phi'}{\lambda}\frac{dZ}{d\tau}, \tag{A7}$$

where

$$\frac{dZ}{d\tau} = \frac{\partial Z}{\partial \tau} + \frac{\partial Z}{\partial G}\frac{dG}{d\tau}. \tag{A8}$$

The government budget constraint is

$$G = (t_N + t_C)L - t_N X + \tau Z. \tag{A9}$$

Totally differentiating (A9) and holding t_N and t_C constant, we can obtain

$$\frac{dG}{d\tau} = (t_C + t_N)\frac{dL}{d\tau} - t_N\frac{dX}{d\tau} + Z + \tau\frac{dZ}{d\tau}, \tag{A10}$$

where the first two price coefficients on the right-hand side are analogous to (A8). From (A7) and (A10),

$$\frac{1}{\lambda}\frac{dV}{d\tau} = \left(\frac{\phi'}{\lambda} - \tau\right)\left(-\frac{dZ}{d\tau}\right) - t_N\frac{dX}{d\tau} + (t_C + t_N)\frac{dL}{d\tau}. \tag{A11}$$

The left-hand side of this expression is the general equilibrium (marginal) welfare effect (in dollars), and the terms in the right hand-side correspond to the Pigouvian welfare gain, the subsidy-interaction effect, and the tax-interaction effect discussed in Section 2.

(ii) *Pollution Tax with Strong Revenue-Recycling Effect*

The difference between this policy and the previous one is that the extra revenue, $dG/d\tau$, is used to reduce t_N rather than to increase the lump-sum transfer. Thus, the welfare effect is equal to that in (A11) plus

$$\frac{1}{\lambda}\left\{-\frac{\partial V}{\partial G}+\frac{\partial V}{\partial t_N}\left(-\frac{dt_N}{dG}\right)\right\}\frac{dG}{d\tau}; \tag{A12}$$

that is, we subtract off the gain in utility from increasing G and add on the gain in utility from reducing t_N. Totally differentiating (A9) with respect to t_N and G, we can obtain (setting $\tau = 0$)

$$\frac{dt_N}{dG} = \left\{L + t\frac{dL}{dt_N} - t_N\frac{dX}{dt_N} - X\right\}^{-1}, \tag{A13}$$

where $t = t_C + t_N$,

$$\frac{dL}{dt_N} = \frac{\partial L}{\partial t_N} + \frac{\partial L}{\partial G}\frac{dG}{dt_N}, \tag{A14}$$

and similarly for dX/dt_N. Substituting (A13) and (A6) in (A12) gives

$$MEB^N\frac{dG}{d\tau}, \tag{A15}$$

where

$$MEB^N = \frac{-t(dL/dt_N) + t_N(dX/dt_N)}{L - X + t(dL/dt_N) - t_N(dX/dt_N)}. \tag{A16}$$

MEB^N is the MEB of the non-comprehensive tax, that is, the welfare loss from raising an extra dollar of revenue from increasing t_N. The numerator in (A16) is the welfare loss in the labor market from an incremental increase in t_N (i.e., the wedge between the gross and net wage multiplied by the reduction in labor supply) plus the welfare loss from the increase in tax-favored consumption (i.e., the subsidy wedge between the supply and demand price for X times the increase in X). The denominator is the additional revenue from an incremental increase in t_N (from differentiating $(t_C + t_N)L - t_N X$).

Differentiating (A9) with respect to τ and G and substituting in (A15) gives

$$MEB^N\left\{Z + t\frac{dL}{d\tau} - t_N\frac{dX}{d\tau}\right\} \tag{A17}$$

when $\tau = 0$. This is the (marginal) strong revenue-recycling effect. It equals the MEB times the revenue raised by increasing the pollution tax, net of the reduction in labor tax revenue and the implicit change in subsidy payments for X.

APPENDIX B: DERIVING A FORMULA FOR THE MEB

From the Slutsky equations,

$$\frac{\partial L}{\partial t_{\mathrm{N}}} = \frac{\partial L^{\mathrm{H}}}{\partial t_{\mathrm{N}}} - \frac{\partial L}{\partial G}(L - X); \qquad \frac{\partial X}{\partial t_{\mathrm{N}}} = \frac{\partial X^{\mathrm{H}}}{\partial t_{\mathrm{N}}} - \frac{\partial X}{\partial G}(L - X), \qquad \text{(B1)}$$

where H denotes a Hicksian (compensated) price effect. From (B1), (A14), the analogous expression for dX/dt_{N}, and (A16),[46]

$$MEB^{\mathrm{N}} = \frac{(t/L)\,\partial L^{\mathrm{H}}/\partial(1-t) - s_X(t_{\mathrm{N}}/X)\,\partial X^{\mathrm{H}}/\partial(1-t_{\mathrm{N}})}{1 - (t/L)\,\partial L/\partial(1-t) - s_X\{1 - (t_{\mathrm{N}}/X)\,\partial X/\partial(1-t_{\mathrm{N}})\}}, \qquad \text{(B2)}$$

where $s_X = X/L$. Finally, we can obtain Eq. (2.2) by substituting the following formulas for the Marshallian and Hicksian labor supply elasticities ($\varepsilon_{\mathrm{L}}^{\mathrm{M}}$ and $\varepsilon_{\mathrm{L}}^{\mathrm{H}}$), and the Marshallian and Hicksian own price elasticities of demand for X (η_X^{M} and η_X^{H}), expressed as positive numbers:

$$\varepsilon_{\mathrm{L}}^{\mathrm{M}} = \frac{\partial L}{\partial(1-t)}\frac{1-t}{L}; \qquad \varepsilon_{\mathrm{L}}^{\mathrm{H}} = \frac{\partial L^{\mathrm{H}}}{\partial(1-t)}\frac{1-t}{L};$$
$$\eta_X^{\mathrm{M}} = -\frac{\partial X}{\partial(1-t_{\mathrm{N}})}\frac{1-t_{\mathrm{N}}}{X}; \qquad \eta_X^{\mathrm{H}} = -\frac{\partial X}{\partial(1-t_{\mathrm{N}})}\frac{1-t_{\mathrm{N}}}{X}. \qquad \text{(B3)}$$

REFERENCES

1. G. S. Becker and C. B. Mulligan, "Efficient Taxes, Efficient Spending and Big Government," Discussion Paper, University of Chicago, Chicago, IL (1997).
2. A. L. Bovenberg and R. A. de Mooij, Environmental levies and distortionary taxation, *Amer. Econom. Rev.* **84** 1085–1089 (1994).
3. A. L. Bovenberg and F. van der Ploeg, Consequences of environmental tax reform for unemployment and welfare, *Environ. Res. Econom.* **12**, 137–150 (1994).
4. A. L. Bovenberg and L. H. Goulder, Optimal environmental taxation in the presence of other taxes: General equilibrium analyses, *Amer. Econom. Rev.* **86**, 985–1000 (1996).
5. A. L. Bovenberg and L. H. Goulder, Environmental taxation, *in* "Handbook of Public Economics" (A. Auerbach and M. Feldstein, Eds.), 2nd ed., New York, North Holland (1998).
6. C. Brett and M. Keen, "Political Uncertainty and the Earmarking of Environmental Taxes," Discussion paper, University of Essex, Colchester, UK (1998).
7. E. K. Browning, On the marginal welfare cost of taxation, *Amer. Econom. Rev.* **77**, 11–23 (1987).
8. D. Burtraw, A. J. Krupnick, E. Mansur, D. Austin, and D. Farrell, "The Costs and Benefits of Reducing Acid Rain," Discussion Paper No. 97-31, Resources for the Future, Washington, DC (1997).
9. R. Carroll, "Tax Rates, Taxpayer Behavior, and the 1993 Tax Act," paper presented at the National Tax Association Meetings, Austin, TX (1998).
10. A. Deaton, Optimal taxes and the structure of preferences, *Econometrica* **49**, 1245–1259 (1981).
11. M. Feldstein, How big should government be? *Nat. Tax J.* **50**, 197–214 (1997).
12. M. Feldstein, Tax avoidance and the deadweight loss of the income tax, *Rev. Econom. Statist.*, to appear.
13. V. R. Fuchs, A. B. Krueger, and J. M. Poterba, Economists' views about parameters, values and policies: Survey results in labor and public economics, *J. Econom. Lit.* **36**, 1387–1425 (1998).

[46] Note that $\partial L/\partial t_{\mathrm{N}} = -\partial L/\partial(1-t)$, $\partial X/\partial t_{\mathrm{N}} = -\partial X/\partial(1-t_{\mathrm{N}})$, and the same applies for the Hicksian price effects.

14. L. H. Goulder, Environmental taxation and the "double dividend": A reader's guide, *Internat. Tax Pub. Finance* **2**, 157–183 (1995).
15. L. H. Goulder, Effects of carbon taxes in an economy with prior tax distortions: An intertemporal general equilibrium analysis, *J. Environ. Econom. Management* **29**, 271–297 (1995).
16. L. H. Goulder, "Environmental Policy Making in a Second-Best Setting," Discussion Paper, Stanford University, CA (1999).
17. L. H. Goulder, I. W. H. Parry, and D. Burtraw, Revenue-raising vs. other approaches to environmental protection: The critical significance of pre-existing tax distortions, *RAND J. Econom.* **28**, 708–731 (1997).
18. J. Gruber and J. M. Poterba, Tax incentives and the decision to purchase health insurance, *Quart. J. Econom.* **CIX**, 701–734 (1994).
19. A. C. Harberger, "Taxation and Welfare," University of Chicago Press, Chicago, IL (1974).
20. M. R. Killingsworth, "Labor Supply," Cambridge Univ. Press, Cambridge, UK (1983).
21. R. E. Lucas, Supply-side economics: An analytical review, *Oxford Econom. Papers* **42**, 293–316 (1990).
22. W. E. Oates, Green taxes: Can we protect the environment and improve the tax system at the same time? *Southern Econom. J.* **61**, 914–922 (1995).
23. W. E. Oates and D. L. Strassmann, Effluent fees and market structure, *J. Public Econom.* **24**, 29–46 (1984).
24. Office of Management and Budget, "Fiscal Year 1996 Federal Budget," OMB, Washington, DC (1999).
25. I. W. H. Parry, Pollution taxes and revenue recycling, *J. Environ. Econom. Management* **29**, S64–S77 (1995).
26. I. W. H. Parry, Environmental taxes and quotas in the presence of distorting taxes in factor markets, *Res. Energy Econom.* **19**, 203–220 (1997).
27. I. W. H. Parry, "Tax, Deductions, Consumption Distortions, and the Marginal Excess Burden of Taxation," Discussion Paper, Resources for the Future, Washington, DC (1999).
28. I. W. H. Parry, The double dividend: When you get it and when you don't, *Nat. Tax Association Proc.*, to appear.
29. I. W. H. Parry, R. C. Williams, and L. H. Goulder, When can carbon abatement policies increase welfare? The fundamental role of distorted factor markets, *J. Environ. Econom. Management* **37**, 52–84 (1999).
30. I. W. H. Parry and W. E. Oates, Policy analysis in the presence of distorting taxes, *J. Policy Anal. Management*, to appear.
31. M. V. Pauly, Taxation, health insurance, and market failure in the medical economy, *J. Econom. Lit.* **24**, 629–675 (1986).
32. W. A. Pizer, "Prices vs. Quantities Revisited: The Case of Climate Change," Discussion Paper 98-02, Resources for the Future, Washington, DC (1997).
33. H. S. Rosen, Housing decisions and the U.S. income tax: An econometric analysis, *J. Public Economy* **11**, 1–23 (1979).
34. H. S. Rosen, Housing subsidies: Effects on housing decisions, efficiency, and equity, *in* "Handbook of Public Economics" (Alan J. Auerbach and Martin Feldstein, Eds.), Vol. 1, North Holland, New York (1985).
35. A. Snow and R. S. Warren, The marginal welfare cost of public funds: Theory and estimates, *J. Public Econom.* **61**, 289–305 (1996).
36. H. R. Varian, "Microeconomic Analysis," 2nd Ed., Norton, New York (1984).
37. R. C. Williams, "The Effect of Pre-Existing Taxes on the Benefits of Regulations Affecting Health or Productivity," Working Paper, Stanford University (1998).

PART IV

ENVIRONMENTAL INSTRUMENT CHOICE IN A SECOND-BEST SETTING

[23]

ELSEVIER

Resource and Energy Economics 19 (1997) 203–220

RESOURCE and ENERGY ECONOMICS

Environmental taxes and quotas in the presence of distorting taxes in factor markets

Ian W.H. Parry *

Resources for the Future, 1616 P Street NW, Washington, DC 20036, USA

Accepted 6 June 1996

Abstract

Environmental quotas tend to compound the welfare cost of pre-existing tax distortions in the labor market. Under plausible parameters, this source of welfare loss can easily be large enough to outweigh the entire partial equilibrium welfare gain from the quota. Environmental taxes induce the same interaction effect, however they also raise government revenues. If the revenues are used to reduce distortionary taxes, then most of this interaction effect can be offset. Therefore, revenue-raising can be a necessary condition for environmental policies to increase welfare. © 1997 Elsevier Science B.V.

JEL classification: Q28; H21; H23

Keywords: Environmental tax; Environmental quota; Pre-existing labor tax; General equilibrium welfare effect

1. Introduction

An understanding of how environmental policies affect economic efficiency is crucial, both for choosing amongst alternative types of policy instruments, and for judging the appropriate level of policy intervention. Up till very recently, environmental policies have usually been evaluated in partial equilibrium models, or at least in models which do not pay attention to the complications posed by distortions in other markets of the economy. Yet public finance economists have

* Phone: (202)328-5151; e-mail: parry@rff.org.

0928-7655/97/$17.00
PII S0928-7655(96)00012-7

long emphasized the importance of evaluating regulatory policies in general equilibrium models, which do capture the secondary efficiency effects in other distorted markets (Lipsey and Lancaster, 1956–57; Harberger, 1974a,b). The most important source of 'other distortions' are those caused by the tax system, particularly in the labor and capital markets. Indeed a number of recent contributions have shown that the overall welfare effects and optimal level of environmental taxes in the presence of distorting taxes in factor markets, can differ significantly from those implied by partial equilibrium models.

Analytical work by Bovenberg and de Mooij (1994), Bovenberg and van der Ploeg (1994) and Parry (1995a), has shown that the potential welfare gain from a revenue-neutral pollution tax in the presence of a pre-existing tax on labor income is generally less than the partial equilibrium effect. [1] The overall effect of the tax can be decomposed into two effects – the *revenue-recycling* and *tax-interaction* effects – in addition to the partial equilibrium (or Pigouvian) effect, described in first-best, textbook analyses. [2] The revenue-recycling effect is the welfare gain from using the pollution tax revenues to reduce the pre-existing distortionary tax (relative to when the revenues are returned as lump sum transfers). However, introducing the tax drives up the relative price of (polluting) consumption goods and induces some substitution out of employment and into leisure. This causes a welfare loss (the tax-interaction effect), since the labor tax creates a wedge between the marginal social benefit and marginal social cost of labor. In general the tax-interaction effect dominates the revenue-recycling effect, and only if the polluting good is a sufficiently weaker than average substitute for leisure could the net effect from interactions with the tax system be positive. The optimal environmental tax in these models is typically around 70% of the Pigouvian tax (or marginal environmental damages). [3]

Goulder (1995b), and Bovenberg and Goulder (1996a,b,c) have examined the welfare effects of revenue-neutral environmental taxes in a dynamic general equilibrium model, which incorporates a detailed treatment of the tax system and energy sector. The revenue-recycling and tax-interaction effects are more complex in this type of model. Nevertheless the same conclusion – that the potential welfare gains from environmental taxes are lower when full allowance is made for interactions with the tax system – is generally robust.

These analytical and empirical contributions have revealed the fundamental flaw in the widely held view that there was a 'double dividend' from environmental taxes. This hypothesis asserted that environmental taxes could simultaneously correct market failures and reduce the welfare costs of the tax system, when the

[1] This result is implicit in earlier contributions by Sandmo (1975) and Ng (1980).

[2] See Parry (1995a) (who used a slightly different terminology), Goulder (1995a) and Oates (1995).

[3] Subsidies for goods with positive externalities have symmetrical effects (Sandmo, 1975; Ng, 1980; Parry, 1995b) that is the optimal subsidy is somewhat below marginal environmental benefits.

revenues are used to cut other taxes. The crucial problem with this argument is that it ignores the efficiency loss from the tax-interaction effect. This effect is generally large enough so that, despite revenue-recycling, the overall impact of environmental taxes is to compound the welfare costs of the tax system. [4]

This paper expands on this literature by comparing the welfare effects of environmental taxes with non-auctioned environmental quotas in the presence of a tax on labor income. For a given amount of environmental improvement, the quota causes the same partial equilibrium and tax-interaction effect as the environmental tax, but no revenue-recycling effect. This is a potentially crucial asymmetry, because we show that the revenue-recycling and tax-interaction effects can easily be large relative to the partial equilibrium effect. Therefore, under plausible parameters, the tax-interaction effect can more than offset the entire Pigouvian gain from the quota, and only the environmental tax is potentially welfare-improving.

Thus the analysis suggests that the complications posed by pre-existing tax distortions can be a key consideration in instrument choice. This has important implications for the potential choice between a carbon tax versus a system of (freely allocated) carbon permits as a policy to address the possibility of future global warming. It also suggests that the costs of the existing permit program to abate sulfur dioxide emissions could be greatly reduced if the permits were auctioned rather than grandfathered. The results are also relevant to the choice of instrument to regulate fisheries; traffic congestion; the destruction of natural habitat; and so on. More generally, they suggest that the welfare costs of almost *any* (non-revenue-raising) government regulation may be substantially greater, when allowance is made for the effect on compounding pre-existing tax distortions. Indeed a parallel result has recently emerged in the context of monopoly pricing. Browning (1995) estimated that the welfare costs from monopoly pricing in the U.S. are several orders of magnitude greater, in a model which incorporates pre-existing taxes in the labor market.

The next two sections examine the efficiency effects of an environmental tax and quota on a final consumption good, in the presence of a tax on labor income. Section 4 extends the analysis to incorporate the regulation of a (polluting) intermediate good. Section 5 cautions that the general equilibrium welfare effects of environmental policies are considerably more complex than suggested by the simple analytical model used below. Three ways in which the analysis might be usefully extended are discussed. However the basic point – that, despite environmental benefits, revenue-raising can be a necessary condition for environmental policy to be welfare-improving – is likely to be robust. Section 6 summarizes.

[4] The rise and fall of the double dividend hypothesis is discussed in detail by Oates (1995) and Goulder (1995a).

2. The regulation of consumption goods

2.1. The model [5]

A one-period model is assumed in which $X_1, \ldots, X_k$ consumption goods are produced in the economy, using labor and possibly intermediate goods. One of these goods, X_1, causes damage to the environment of c per unit which is not internalized by the private sector, while all other goods are environmentally clean. As usual, we assume that (private) marginal production costs are constant (for given producer prices). [6] Also, besides the environmental externality, the only other source of distortion in the economy is assumed to be a (proportional) tax of m on labor income. Therefore, there are no imperfections due to monopoly pricing, regulations, other taxes, etc. The government has an exogenous spending requirement of G, which is just returned to households as a lump sum transfer. [7]

Choosing units such that the marginal rate of transformation between all consumption goods and leisure is unity, the aggregate household budget constraint can be expressed as

$$\sum_{i=1}^{k} X_i + (1-m)N = (1-m)T + G \tag{1}$$

where N is leisure and T is the household time endowment ($T-N$ is labor supply). Thus the labor tax is equivalent to a tax on T (which is not distortionary) plus a subsidy for leisure.

We assume that the government budget must balance, and therefore any changes in revenues directly or indirectly caused by the environmental policy are offset by adjusting the rate of the pre-existing tax. This is the conventional approach in the optimal tax literature. An alternative is to assume that revenue changes are just neutralized by lump sum transfers, and therefore have no efficiency consequences. However this approach is problematic because it implies there would be no welfare cost to financing regulatory subsidies, and a whole

[5] The model used here is the same as in Parry (1995a), which first decomposed the revenue-recycling and tax-interaction effects. However that paper only looked at environmental taxes, and did not examine the size of these effects relative to the partial equilibrium effect.

[6] The above type of model readily generalizes to incorporate upward sloping supply curves (Harberger, 1974b; Stern, 1987). In this case the Slutsky demand coefficients used below would be replaced by an analogous reduced form coefficient, which shows how output in a particular market responds to tax changes, when allowance is made for interdependencies in demand and supply across all commodities.

[7] The analysis would be the same if G were a public good, so long as the quantity of government spending is held constant.

range of commodity subsidies which are inefficient in a partial equilibrium sense might then be justified (Parry, 1995b). [8]

Environmental regulation causes no first-order effect on disposable household income since aggregate tax revenues are constant, and therefore all the demand coefficients and elasticities below are (Slutsky) compensated. We also ignore any efficiency effects from changes in the distribution of income. [9] Finally, to facilitate empirical estimation the demand for X_1 and N are taken to be linear over the relevant range, and therefore the welfare change formulas below are second-order approximations. [10]

2.2. Pollution taxes

Suppose a tax of $t < c$ is now introduced on X_1. The resulting welfare effect consists of three components: [11]

(i) *The Pigouvian effect.* This is illustrated in Fig. 1 where D_1, S_1 and $S_1 + c$ are the demand, supply and marginal social cost curves respectively, and X_1^0, $X_1(t)$ and X_1^* are the free market, regulated and Pigouvian levels of output respectively. The tax produces a welfare gain equal to the shaded trapezoid – since it reduces the output of a commodity for which marginal social cost exceeds marginal social benefit – which has area [12]

$$W^{\mathrm{P}} = \left(c - \frac{t}{2}\right)\left(X_1^0 - X_1(t)\right) \tag{2}$$

(ii) *The revenue-recycling effect.* This is the welfare gain from using the pollution tax revenues to reduce the labor tax, relative to when they are returned lump sum and have no efficiency consequences. Let the efficiency cost of raising an additional dollar of (labor) tax revenue be denoted V (this is defined below). The revenue-recycling effect is the product of V and pollution tax revenue, or

$$W^{\mathrm{R}} = VtX_1(t) \tag{3}$$

which is the shaded rectangle in Fig. 1.

[8] This is because these subsidies reduce the price of consumption relative to leisure, and the tax-interaction effect – which is now a welfare gain – can dominate the partial equilibrium loss.

[9] These can occur when households differ in their propensity to consume goods and leisure out of additional income. However, in general these effects are thought to be small, and are usually ignored in empirical analysis.

[10] The purpose here is just to indicate broad orders of magnitude for interactions with the tax system. In general, more precise estimation requires specification of the household utility function and solving the model by numerical simulation.

[11] As in Parry (1995a), a graphical analysis is used below to clarify the intuition on this topic, which has been so poorly understood (Oates, 1995). The formulas used below are a simple application of the 'triangles and rectangles' approach developed by Harberger (1974a,b) and others. A more rigorous derivation from utility and production functions is available from the author on request.

[12] The formula in Eq. (2) also applies when $t > c$.

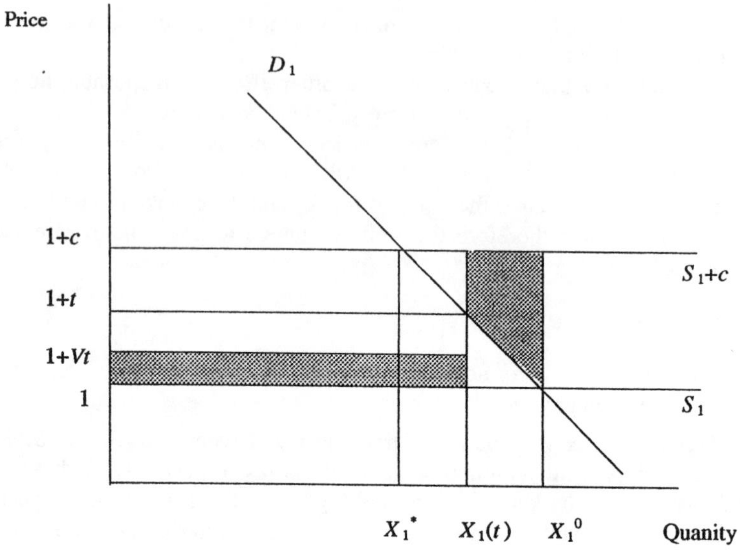

Fig. 1.

(iii) *The tax-interaction effect.* This is illustrated in Fig. 2, where D_N^0, S_N and N^0 are the initial demand, supply and quantity of leisure respectively.[13] D_N^0 is downward sloping because of declining marginal utility from leisure, and S_N is perfectly elastic given our assumption of constant marginal production costs. The leisure subsidy drives a wedge of m between the supply and demand price of leisure, which produces a welfare cost of area *abc*.

Typically goods and leisure are substitutes, in which case the demand for leisure will shift out (slightly) when the price of X_1 is driven up by the environmental tax.[14] In Fig. 2 the post-regulation demand and quantity are D_N^1 and N^1 respectively. Since there is a wedge of m between the marginal social cost and marginal social benefit of leisure, the increase in leisure leads to a welfare loss of rectangle *bedc*. This rectangle is also the reduction in labor tax revenue indirectly caused by the environmental tax, since $N^1 - N^0$ units are no longer

[13] The demand and supply of leisure are just the mirror image of the supply of and demand for labor respectively.

[14] From Eq. (1) leisure and aggregate consumption, and hence the average consumption good, must be substitutes. Complementarity with leisure is possible for narrowly-defined (polluting) goods such as a lawn mower, but these cases are not considered here. Another interpretation is that the increase in price of X_1 reduces the real wage and therefore reduces labor supply (Bovenberg and de Mooij, 1994).

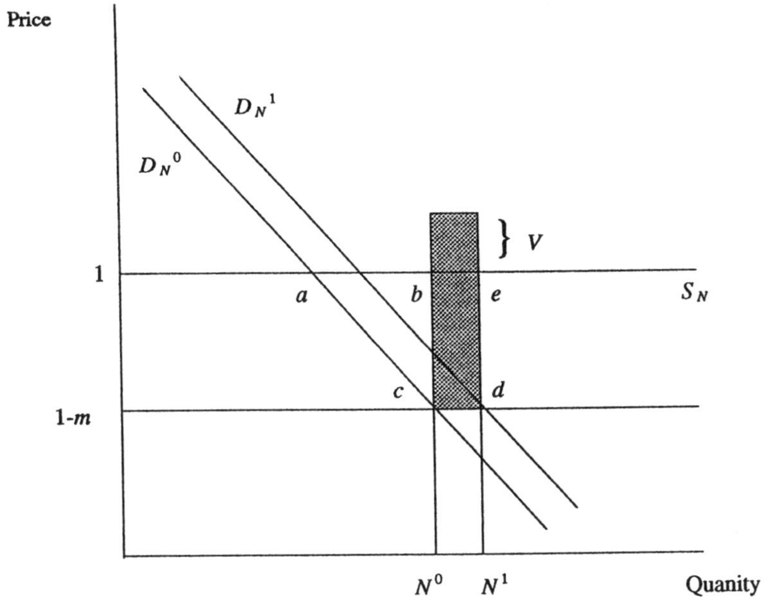

Fig. 2.

paying the tax of m. Therefore the total welfare loss from the tax-interaction effect is *bedc* multiplied by $1 + V$, which is the shaded rectangle. This has area [15]

$$W^1 = (1 + V) m (N^1 - N^0) \tag{4}$$

Labor tax revenue is initially $m(T - N^0)$, and therefore marginal tax revenue is $T - N^0 - m(\mathrm{d}N/\mathrm{d}m)$. Also, the welfare loss from the increase in leisure induced by an incremental increase in m is $m(\mathrm{d}N/\mathrm{d}m)$. Therefore, the efficiency cost of raising an extra dollar of labor tax revenue, or marginal welfare cost of taxation, is[16]

$$V = \frac{m(\mathrm{d}N/\mathrm{d}m)}{T - N^0 - m(\mathrm{d}N/\mathrm{d}m)}. \tag{5}$$

Using the Slutsky symmetry property, the increase in leisure is

$$N^1 - N^0 = \frac{\mathrm{d}X_1}{\mathrm{d}(1 - m)} t \tag{6}$$

[15] Fig. 2 is not drawn to scale: the shaded rectangle is typically very small relative to triangle *abc*. However, what matters is its size relative to the trapezoid in Fig. 1.

[16] For a comprehensive discussion of the marginal welfare cost of taxation see Browning (1987). V is taken as constant in the current analysis, which is a reasonable approximation when environmental tax revenues are small relative to labor tax revenues (Parry, 1995a).

where $1-m$ is the demand price of leisure. Using Eqs. (4)–(6) the tax-interaction effect can be expressed, after some manipulation [17]

$$W^{I} = \phi V t X_1^0; \quad \phi = \frac{\eta_{1N}^0}{\epsilon^0} \tag{7}$$

where

$$\eta_{1N}^0 = \frac{\mathrm{d}X_1}{\mathrm{d}(1-m)} \frac{1-m}{X_1^0}$$

is the elasticity of demand for X_1 with respect to the price of leisure (evaluated at X_1^0) and

$$\epsilon^0 = \frac{\mathrm{d}(T-N^0)}{\mathrm{d}(1-m)} \frac{1-m}{T-N^0}$$

is the labor supply elasticity (evaluated at $T-N^0$).

$T-N^0$ equals aggregate consumption, [18] therefore ϵ^0 can also be interpreted as the elasticity of demand for aggregate, and hence average, consumption with respect to the price of leisure. If X_1 were an average substitute for leisure, then $\phi = 1$ and comparing (7) with (3) the tax-interaction effect exceeds the revenue-recycling effect because $X_1^0 > X_1(t)$. Only if X_1 were a relatively weak substitute for leisure ($\phi < 1$) could the revenue-recycling effect dominate, and the overall welfare effect of the tax exceed the Pigouvian effect.

2.3. Environmental quotas

Suppose, instead of the tax, that a non-auctioned quota is used to restrict output to $X_1(t)$ in Fig. 1. The Pigouvian welfare gain is the same trapezoid, given by Eq. (2). Also, since the price of X_1 relative to leisure increases by the same amount, the tax-interaction effect is again the shaded rectangle in Fig. 2, or Eq. (7). [19] However – despite the taxation of quota rents – there is no revenue-recycling effect. The rents created by the quota are $cX_1(t)$ in Fig. 1. These are ultimately received as profits by households, but only at the expense of real labor earnings. That is for a given labor supply, aggregate real output and hence real gross income paid to households is the same in the tax and quota case. Therefore, so long as all

[17] Note that $1+V = V(T-N^0)/m(\mathrm{d}N/\mathrm{d}m)$ from (5) and that $\mathrm{d}N/\mathrm{d}m = \mathrm{d}(T-N)/\mathrm{d}(1-m)$.

[18] This follows from Eq. (1), and because the initial government budget constraint is $G = m(T-N^0)$.

[19] We abstract from transactions costs which may hinder the trading of quotas amongst firms. These would reduce the Pigouvian gain from the quota, but would not affect the increase in price of X_1 (which is determined by $X_1(t)$), and hence the tax-interaction effect.

income is taxed at the same rate, income tax revenues are the same, regardless of the respective shares of rent and labor earnings in total income. [20]

3. Empirical analysis

3.1. Welfare under the Pigouvian rule

First of all, suppose that X_1 is an average substitute for leisure ($\phi = 1$) and that the Pigouvian rule is adopted, therefore $t = c$ and output is X_1^* in Fig. 1. The Pigouvian welfare gain is now a triangle with area

$$W^{\mathrm{P}} = \frac{c}{2}\left(X_1^0 - X_1^*\right) \tag{2a}$$

Using Eqs. (2a), (3) and (7), the size of the tax-interaction effect, and tax-interaction effect net of the revenue-recycling effect, expressed relative to the Pigouvian effect, are

$$\frac{W^{\mathrm{I}}}{W^{\mathrm{P}}} = \frac{2V}{x_1^*} \tag{8}$$

and

$$\frac{W^{\mathrm{I}} - W^{\mathrm{R}}}{W^{\mathrm{P}}} = 2V \tag{9}$$

respectively, where $x_1^* = (X_1^0 - X_1^*)/X_1^0$ is the proportionate reduction in X_1.

To estimate V, Eq. (5) is easily manipulated to give

$$V = \frac{(m/(1-m))\epsilon^0}{1 - (m/(1-m))\epsilon^0} \tag{5a}$$

which is (essentially) the formula used by Browning (1987). Based on the existing empirical literature, he concluded that the most likely ranges for the (marginal) rate of labor tax and compensated labor supply elasticity are 0.38–0.48 and 0.2–0.4 respectively. From (5a) this gives a range of (approximately) 0.15–0.6 for the marginal welfare cost of taxation, with a central estimate of 0.3.

Table 1 compares the welfare loss from interactions with the tax system under

[20] In the U.S. non-labor income is taxed at a slightly lower rate than labor income. (Both are subject to income taxes, but the effects of corporate taxation on the former are outweighed by the effects of social security taxation on the latter.) Thus for a given level of real income, a quota which increases the share of non-labor income at the expense of labor income would reduce overall tax revenues and lead to a negative revenue-recycling effect. By ignoring this, the above analysis (slightly) understates the asymmetry between pollution taxes and quotas.

Table 1
Welfare loss from interactions with the tax system under the Pigouvian rule (relative to the Pigouvian effect)

Policy	x_1 *	V		
		0.15	0.3	0.6
Quota	0.05	6	12	24
	0.2	1.5	3	6
	0.6	0.5	1	2
Tax		0.3	0.6	1.2

quota and tax, expressed relative to the Pigouvian triangle, using Eqs. (8) and (9). The startling result is that the welfare loss from the tax-interaction effect can easily exceed the entire Pigouvian welfare gain from an environmental quota (this occurs when the cell entry exceeds unity). For example when $V=0.3$, the tax-interaction effect is 12 times, 3 times and the same size as the Pigouvian effect, when the proportionate reduction in output is 5%, 20% and 60% respectively. Even under a very low estimate for the marginal welfare cost of taxation ($V=0.15$), the tax-interaction effect is still crucial to determining at least the magnitude, if not the sign, of the general equilibrium effect from the quota. In the case of the Pigouvian tax, the net loss from interactions with the tax system is much smaller, but can still offset a large amount of the Pigouvian gain. For example, when $V=0.3$ the tax-interaction effect net of the revenue-recycling effect is 60% of the Pigouvian triangle.

The intuition behind the quota result is straightforward. Most of the substitution away from X_1 will lead to higher demand for other consumption goods rather than leisure – that is, the base of the shaded rectangle in Fig. 2 is small relative to the base of the Pigouvian triangle. However, the welfare cost per additional unit of leisure is large because taxes effectively drive a substantial wedge between the marginal social cost and marginal social benefit of leisure (around 40%) – that is, the height of the rectangle can be large relative to the height of the triangle. [21]

3.2. *Welfare under the optimal environmental tax*

The above results may be unduly pessimistic because they calculate welfare effects at the Pigouvian level of regulation, rather than the second-best optimal

[21] As mentioned above, the results are consistent with Browning (1995), who found that the welfare loss in the labor market caused by monopoly pricing is much larger than the Harberger triangles in the product markets. Previous empirical studies in environmental economics emphasized the relative importance of the revenue-recycling effect, but did not take into account the – even more important – tax-interaction effect. For example, Nordhaus (1993) estimated that revenue-recycling increased the optimal tax on carbon from $5 per ton to $59 per ton.

level. Therefore this subsection compares taxes and quotas when regulation is equivalent to that of the optimal environmental tax, maintaining the assumption that $\phi = 1$.

Adding Eqs. (2) and (3), subtracting Eq. (7), and differentiating with respect to the reduction in $X_1(t)$, gives the following formula for marginal welfare under the environmental tax:

$$c - \frac{t}{2} - Vt + \left(\frac{1}{2} + V\right)\left(X_1^0 - X_1(t)\right)\frac{\mathrm{d}t}{\mathrm{d}X_1(t)}.$$

Equating this with 0, and noting that

$$X_1^0 - X_1(t) = -\frac{\mathrm{d}X_1}{\mathrm{d}t}t = \frac{t}{c}x_1^* X_1^0 \tag{10}$$

gives the following formula for the optimal environmental tax (Parry, 1995a):

$$\frac{t}{c} = \frac{1}{1+2V}. \tag{11}$$

This lies between 45% and 77% of the Pigouvian tax, given our range for V. Under this level of regulation, the welfare loss from interactions with the tax system under the environmental quota and tax, relative to the Pigouvian effect, are (from Eqs. (2), (3), (7), (10) and (11))

$$\frac{W^{\mathrm{I}}}{W^{\mathrm{P}}} = \frac{2V(1+2V)}{(1+4V)x_1^*} \tag{8b}$$

and

$$\frac{W^{\mathrm{I}} - W^{\mathrm{R}}}{W^{\mathrm{P}}} = \frac{2V}{1+4V} \tag{9b}$$

respectively.

Table 2 shows calculations of Eqs. (8b) and (9b). The welfare loss from interactions with the tax system is now much smaller for the pollution tax,

Table 2
Welfare loss from interactions with the tax system under the second-best optimal tax (relative to the Pigouvian effect)

Policy	x_1^*	V		
		0.15	0.3	0.6
Quota	0.05	4.88	8.73	15.53
	0.2	1.22	2.18	3.88
	0.6	0.41	0.73	1.29
Tax		0.19	0.27	0.35

Table 3
Sensitivity with respect to ϕ

Policy	x_1^*	ϕ 0.5	ϕ 1.5
Quota	0.05	6.0	18.0
	0.2	1.5	4.5
	0.6	0.5	1.5
Tax	0.05	−5.4	6.6
	0.2	−0.9	2.1
	0.6	0.1	1.1

between 19% and 35% of the Pigouvian gain. However, the tax-interaction effect is still crucial for the magnitude, and possibly the sign, of the general equilibrium welfare effect from the quota (again a cell entry greater than unity indicates that the overall welfare impact of the policy is negative).

3.3. Degree of substitution with leisure

The above calculations assume that the regulated commodity is an average substitute for leisure. In general this may be the best assumption we can make, since it is usually very difficult to estimate the degree of substitution between particular goods and leisure.[22] However, it is useful to examine how sensitive the results are to relaxing this assumption.

Returning to the case when the Pigouvian rule $t=c$ is adopted, the relative effect from interactions with the tax system under the environmental quota and tax are (using Eqs. (2a), (3), (7) and (10) when $\phi \neq 1$)

$$\frac{W^{\mathrm{I}}}{W^{\mathrm{P}}} = \frac{2\phi V}{x_1^*} \tag{8c}$$

and

$$\frac{W^{\mathrm{I}} - W^{\mathrm{R}}}{W^{\mathrm{P}}} = \frac{2V(\phi - 1 + x_1^*)}{x_1^*} \tag{9c}$$

respectively.

Table 3 calculates these formulas when the elasticity of demand for X_1 with respect to the price of leisure is 50% below and 50% above that for the average good, and assuming the central estimate of 0.3 for V. Clearly the results are sensitive to ϕ, for example under the Pigouvian tax when $x_1^* = 0.2$, there is a net

[22] See for example Deaton and Muellbauer (1980, Ch. 3). The numerical models discussed in the introduction restrict utility – by assuming leisure is weakly separable and preferences are homothetic over consumption goods – such that all goods are equal substitutes for leisure.

loss from interactions with the tax system equal to 210% of the Pigouvian effect if $\phi = 1.5$, and a gain of 90% if $\phi = 0.5$. However, even in the scenario when X_1 is a relatively weak substitute for leisure, the tax-interaction effect exceeds the Pigouvian effect from an environmental quota when $x_1^* = 0.05$ and 0.2, and offsets 50% of it when $x_1^* = 0.6$.

4. The regulation of intermediate goods

This section extends the previous analysis to examine the welfare effect of environmental regulations imposed on an intermediate good (gasoline, coal, pesticides, etc.). We assume this good, denoted Z, is produced competitively with constant marginal cost (normalized to unity), is used in the production of X_1, and causes an environmental damage of c per unit. All other assumptions from before are maintained, and there is no regulation of X_1.

4.1. Environmental taxes and quotas

Suppose the Pigouvian tax of $t = c$ is imposed on Z, and the revenues are used to reduce the labor tax. Analogous to before, the general equilibrium welfare effect consists of:

(i) The Pigouvian welfare gain triangle, given by

$$W^P = \frac{c}{2}(Z^0 - Z^*) \tag{2'}$$

where Z^* is the Pigouvian level of output. The reduction in Z consists of the familiar substitution effect (the replacement of Z for other inputs in production) plus the output effect (the fall in demand for Z from the reduction in X_1).

(ii) The welfare gain from the revenue-recycling effect, which is

$$W^R = VcZ^*. \tag{3'}$$

(iii) The welfare loss from the tax-interaction effect. This occurs because the increase in cost of Z drives up the price of X_1, thereby inducing some substitution into leisure. [23] Denoting the price increase by Δp_1, then analogous to (7), the tax-interaction effect can be expressed

$$W^I = \phi V X_1^0 \Delta p_1. \tag{7'}$$

To a second-order approximation, the price of X_1 increases by the product of c and the average of the ex ante and ex post ratio of Z to X_1 (see Appendix A).

[23] Despite possible substitution of labor for Z in the production of X_1, the tax-interaction effect is positive, assuming X_1 and leisure are substitutes. This is because the aggregate quantity of leisure is determined by the price of leisure relative to consumption, and must increase when the price of X_1 increases.

This ratio falls by $\mu(Z^0 - Z^*)/X_1^0$, where μ is the fraction of the total reduction in Z due to the substitution effect. Therefore

$$\Delta p_1 = \frac{c}{X_0}\left(Z^0 - \frac{\mu}{2}(Z^0 - Z^*)\right). \tag{12}$$

From Eqs. (12) and (7′), the tax-interaction effect is

$$W^{\mathrm{I}} = \phi V c Z^0\left\{1 - \frac{\mu z^*}{2}\right\} \tag{7″}$$

where $z^* = (Z^0 - Z^*)/Z^0$ is the proportionate reduction in Z. Comparing Eq. (7″) with Eq. (3′), we have essentially the same result as before. That is, the tax-interaction effect exceeds the revenue-recycling effect, except possibly in the case when final output from the polluting sector is a relatively weak substitute for leisure ($\phi < 1$). [24]

Again, a non-auctioned environmental quota which has the equivalent Pigouvian welfare effect in Eq. (2′), causes the same tax-interaction effect (Eq. (7″)), but no revenue-recycling effect.

4.2. Empirical comparison

Using Eqs. (2′), (3′) and (7″), the welfare loss from interactions with the tax system (relative to the Pigouvian effect) under the environmental quota and tax are

$$\frac{W^{\mathrm{I}}}{W^{\mathrm{P}}} = \frac{2\phi V\{1 - \mu z^*/2\}}{z^*} \tag{8′}$$

and

$$\frac{W^{\mathrm{I}} - W^{\mathrm{I}}}{W^{\mathrm{P}}} = \frac{2V\{\phi(1 - \mu z^*/2) - (1 - z^*)\}}{z^*}. \tag{9′}$$

Table 4 shows simulations on Eqs. (8′) and (9′), assuming X_1 is an average substitute for leisure and $V = 0.3$. If Z is used in fixed proportions to output, then all of the reduction in Z is due to the output effect and $\mu = 0$ (third column). In this case, the relative welfare loss from interactions with the tax system is the same as in Table 1. [25] The other extreme is when all the reduction in Z is due to the substitution effect, that is $\mu = 1$ (fourth column). This has some impact on reducing the tax-interaction effect, for example the relative welfare cost of

[24] Again, it has long been recognized in optimal tax models (which do not decompose the revenue-recycling and tax-interaction effects) that in general the welfare effect from interactions with the tax system is negative for taxes on intermediate goods (Diamond and Mirrlees, 1971).

[25] For a given reduction in final output, regulating a factor input is equivalent to regulating final output, when the factor is used in fixed proportions (Wisecarver, 1974).

Table 4
Intermediate goods

Policy	z^*	μ	
		0	1
Quota	0.05	12	11.7
	0.2	3	2.7
	0.6	1	0.7
Tax	0.05	0.6	0.3
	0.2	0.6	0.3
	0.6	0.6	0.3

interactions with the tax system are reduced from 60% to 30% under the Pigouvian tax. However, for the quota it makes little empirical difference to the previous conclusion that the tax-interaction effect can easily dominate the Pigouvian welfare gain. For example, the tax-interaction effect is still 11.7 and 2.7 times as large as the Pigouvian triangle when the proportionate reduction in Z is 5% and 20% respectively.

5. Generalizing the analysis

In practice the general equilibrium welfare effects of environmental policies are considerably more complex than suggested by the simple analytical model used above. This section briefly discusses three ways in which the analysis might be extended. However, the basic result – that revenue-raising can be a necessary condition for environmental policy to increase welfare – is likely to be robust in more general models.

5.1. Interactions with the capital market

The other market in the economy which is substantially distorted by taxes is the capital market. To the extent that an environmental policy reduces investment rather than consumption, it will compound the welfare cost of taxes on capital rather than labor (Bovenberg and Goulder, 1996b). Therefore, assuming the marginal welfare cost of taxation is greater for capital than for labor, [26] incorporating capital into the above analysis is likely, if anything, to increase the welfare loss from the tax-interaction effect. On the other hand, if environmental tax revenues are used to reduce taxes on capital, the revenue-recycling effect, and hence the asymmetry between taxes and quotas, will be larger.

[26] See for example Lucas (1990).

5.2. Non-tax distortions

Market imperfections due to non-tax factors such as monopoly pricing, government regulations, imperfect information and externalities, are quite pervasive in the economy. Therefore, a specific environmental regulation could potentially cause efficiency effects in a variety of other markets in addition to the labor and capital markets. However, taken individually these other efficiency effects are likely to be empirically unimportant, unless the market is severely distorted *and* closely related to that being regulated. In this connection, Oates and Strassmann (1984) suggest that pre-existing distortions in product markets due to monopoly pricing do not substantially affect the overall welfare effect of environmental policies. This is mainly because the price wedges caused by imperfect competition are much smaller than those caused by the tax system. Nevertheless, a recent paper by Browning (1994) suggests that the aggregate impact of non-tax distortions could be significant. He estimated that non-tax distortions effectively increase the overall distortion in the labor market from 43% to around 55%. Therefore, by ignoring these non-tax factors, the above analysis may significantly *understate* the revenue-recycling and tax-interaction effects.

5.3. Command and control regulations

Command and control regulations are much more prevalent in practice than the pure taxes and quotas analyzed above. Like quotas, they do not raise revenues. They also increase marginal production costs, and hence increase the relative price of consumption goods, and induce a tax-interaction effect similar to that discussed above. However by constraining the method of abatement, they typically lead to production inefficiency and higher (partial equilibrium) abatement costs than the equivalent quota. A useful extension to the analysis would be to consider the contribution of the tax-interaction effect, relative to that from production inefficiency, in the overall abatement costs from command and control regulations.

6. Summary

By increasing the relative price of consumption goods, environmental policies typically induce some substitution into leisure, which compounds the welfare cost of tax distortions in the labor market. Under plausible parameters, this effect can dominate the partial equilibrium effect of the policy. Therefore, despite environmental benefits, the overall welfare impact from imposing the Pigouvian quota could be negative. However, an environmental tax raises revenues and if these are used to reduce the labor tax, most of this interaction effect can be offset. Thus in some cases only revenue-raising environmental policies can potentially increase welfare.

Acknowledgements

This paper is a revised version of an earlier draft, 'Environmental Policy in a Second Best World'. I am grateful to Larry Goulder, Mark Harrison, Larry Sjaastad, David Starrett, and seminar participants at Chicago, Maryland, NBER and Resources for the Future for very helpful comments.

Appendix A. Deriving Eq. (12)

From a second-order Taylor series expansion, the change in total cost (ω) of producing X_1, following a change of c in the price of input Z is

$$c\frac{\mathrm{d}\omega}{\mathrm{d}p_Z}+\frac{c^2}{2}\frac{\mathrm{d}^2\omega}{\mathrm{d}p_Z^2}$$

where p_Z is the price of Z. Dividing by X_1^0 to convert to marginal production costs and substituting $\mathrm{d}\omega/\mathrm{d}p_Z = Z^0$ (from Shephard's lemma) and $c(\mathrm{d}^2\omega/\mathrm{d}p_Z^2) = \mu(Z^* - Z^0)$, gives Eq. (12).

References

Bovenberg, A.L. and R.A. de Mooij, 1994, Environmental levies and distortionary taxation, American Economic Review 84, 1085–1089.

Bovenberg, A.L. and L.H. Goulder, 1996a, Optimal environmental taxation in the presence of other taxes: An applied general equilibrium analysis, American Economic Review, forthcoming.

Bovenberg, A.L. and L.H. Goulder, 1996b, Costs of environmentally motivated taxes in the presence of other taxes: General equilibrium analyses (Stanford University, Stanford, CA).

Bovenberg, A.L. and L.H. Goulder, 1996c, Integrating environmental and distortionary taxes: General equilibrium analysis (Stanford University, Stanford, CA).

Bovenberg, A.L. and F. van der Ploeg, 1994, Environmental policy, public finance and the labor market in a second best world, Journal of Public Economics 55, 349–390.

Browning, E.K., 1995, The welfare cost of monopoly and other output distortions (Department of Economics, Texas A&M University, College Station, TX).

Browning, E.K., 1994, The non-tax wedge, Journal of Public Economics 53, 419–433.

Browning, E.K., 1987, On the marginal welfare cost of taxation, American Economic Review 77, 28–38.

Deaton, A. and J. Muellbauer, 1980, Economics and consumer behavior (Cambridge University Press, New York).

Diamond, P. and J. Mirrlees, 1971, Optimal taxation and public production II: Tax rules, American Economic Review 61, 261–278.

Goulder, L.H., 1995a, Environmental taxation and the 'double dividend': A reader's guide, International Tax and Public Finance 2, 157–184.

Goulder, L.H., 1995b, Effects of carbon taxes in an economy with prior tax distortions: An intertemporal general equilibrium analysis, Journal of Environmental Economics and Management 29, 271–297.

Harberger, A.C., 1974a, Taxation, resource allocation and welfare, In: Taxation and welfare (University of Chicago Press, Chicago, IL).

Harberger, A.C., 1974b, The measurement of waste, In: Taxation and welfare (University of Chicago Press, Chicago, IL).

Lipsey, R.G. and K. Lancaster, 1956–57, The general theory of the second best, Review of Economic Studies 24, 11–32.

Lucas, R.E., 1990, Supply-side economics: An analytical review, Oxford Economic Papers 42, 293–316.

Ng, Y.K., 1980, Optimal corrective taxes or subsidies when revenue-raising imposes an excess burden, American Economic Review 70, 744–751.

Nordhaus, W.D., 1993, Optimal greenhouse gas reductions and tax policy in the 'DICE' model, American Economic Review 83, 313–317.

Oates, W.E., 1995, Green taxes: Can we protect the environment and improve the tax system at the same time? (Presidential Address), Southern Economics Journal 915–922.

Oates, W.E. and D.L. Strassmann, 1984, Effluent fees and market structure, Journal of Public Economics 24, 29–46.

Parry, I.W., 1995a, Pollution taxes and revenue recycling, Journal of Environmental Economics and Management 29, S64–S77.

Parry, I.W., 1995b, The effects of environmental subsidies in the presence of distorting taxes (Resources for the Future, Washington, DC).

Sandmo, A., 1975, Optimal taxation in the prescence of externalites, Swedish Journal of Economics, 77, 86–98.

Stern, N.H., 1987, Aspects of the theory of tax reform, In: D. Newberry and N.H. Stern, eds., The theory of taxation for developing countries (Oxford University Press, New York).

Wisecarver, D., 1974, The social costs of input market distortions, American Economic Review 64, 359–372.

[24]

RAND Journal of Economics
Vol. 28, No. 4, Winter 1997
pp. 708–731

Revenue-raising versus other approaches to environmental protection: The critical significance of preexisting tax distortions

Lawrence H. Goulder*

Ian W.H. Parry**

and

Dallas Burtraw***

Using analytical and numerical general equilibrium models, we show that preexisting factor taxes produce a "tax-interaction effect" that substantially increases the costs of pollution taxes and quotas. Under policies that raise revenue and recycle it through cuts in marginal factor tax rates, this effect is partially offset by a "revenue-recycling effect." Grandfathered pollution quotas, such as those used under the 1990 Clean Air Act Amendments to regulate electric utilities' SO_2 emissions, do not benefit from this offset. The cost differential between policies that do or do not exploit the revenue-recycling effect depends crucially on the extent of emissions reduction. We examine these theoretical findings empirically in the context of U.S. policies to reduce SO_2 emissions.

1. Introduction

■ Regulators often must choose between taxes and quotas as instruments of environmental protection. A number of considerations are relevant to this choice, but in the last decade researchers have devoted considerable attention to the differing implications of these two types of instruments for the generation and disposition of revenue.[1]

* Stanford University, Resources for the Future, and NBER; goulder@leland.stanford.edu.

** Resources for the Future; parry@rff.org.

*** Resources for the Future; burtraw@rff.org.

The authors gratefully acknowledge the helpful comments and suggestions of Don Fullerton, Roger Gordon, Alan Krupnick, Gib Metcalf, Robert Porter, Sjak Smulders, David Starrett, George Tolley, two anonymous referees, and seminar participants at Harvard University, Resources for the Future, the University of Chicago, the University of California–Berkeley and the University of California–Santa Barbara. We also thank Koshy Mathai, Akila Weerapana, and Roberton Williams for outstanding research assistance, and the National Science Foundation (grant nos. SBR-9310362 and SBR-9613458), Environmental Protection Agency (grant no. R825313-01), and IBM Corporation for financial support.

[1] Other considerations relevant to this choice include administrative ease, monitoring and enforcement costs, the probability distribution of policy errors in the face of uncertainty, effects on the distribution of rents and other income, and political feasibility. An extensive literature examines how these other considerations might influence instrument choice. See, for example, Hahn (1986), Nichols (1984), Stavins (1991), and Weitzman (1974).

Oates and Schwab (1988), Poterba (1993), Repetto et al. (1992), and others have emphasized that emissions taxes generate revenues that in principle can be used to finance cuts in existing, distortionary taxes, which in turn avoids some of the deadweight cost associated with distortionary taxation. They point out that, in contrast, emissions quotas or emissions permits that are given out free (or grandfathered) do not bring in revenues and thus cannot finance cuts in distortionary taxes. Numerical investigations by Terkla (1984) and Ballard and Medema (1993), along with those reported in Repetto et al. (1992) and Shackleton et al. (1996), indicate that such "revenue recycling" can substantially lower the aggregate social cost of environmental regulation relative to the case where no revenues are raised or, equivalently, where revenues are returned lump sum rather than used to cut marginal tax rates. The efficiency benefit from using revenues to finance cuts in the marginal rates of existing taxes has been termed the *revenue-recycling effect* (Goulder, 1995).

Recent explorations in second-best environmental taxation suggest that the presence or absence of the revenue-recycling effect may be more important to the choice of environmental policy instruments than previously thought. Beyond indicating that policies that fail to enjoy this effect will be at an efficiency disadvantage, this work calls in question the potential of such policies to generate improvements in overall efficiency (aggregate social benefits from environmental improvement net of social costs of pollution abatement). Analytical work by Bovenberg and de Mooij (1994), Bovenberg and van der Ploeg (1994), and Parry (1995) has shown that environmental taxes, by driving up the price of (polluting) goods relative to leisure, tend to compound the distortions caused by taxes in labor markets, thereby producing a negative welfare impact termed the *tax-interaction effect*.[2] The presence of the tax-interaction effect makes the revenue-recycling effect (along with the environmental benefits) more crucial to overall efficiency gains. This analytical work indicates that environmental taxes that fail to exploit the revenue-recycling effect—as in the case where revenues are returned to the economy through lump-sum tax cuts rather than through cuts in marginal tax rates—may be unable to generate an efficiency improvement no matter what level of pollution reduction is attempted! Reinforcing these analytical insights are numerical results from Bovenberg and Goulder (1996) indicating that a carbon tax whose revenues are returned lump sum cannot improve economic efficiency (regardless of the size of the carbon tax) if the marginal environmental benefits from carbon abatement are less than \$50 per ton.

Like environmental tax policies in which revenues are returned lump sum, regulation through emissions quotas or grandfathered emissions permits also fails to exploit the revenue-recycling effect. Yet, as discussed below, such regulation still produces a (costly) tax-interaction effect similar to that of environmental taxes. This suggests that in a second-best setting, the serious limitations to efficiency that apply to environmental tax policies in which revenues are returned lump sum may apply equally to emissions quotas or grandfathered emissions permits. These considerations suggest the usefulness of grouping policies according to whether they take advantage of the revenue-recycling effect. We apply the label "RR policies" to policies that exploit this effect, and the label "NRR policies" to those that do not. The former include policies involving

[2] In general, the negative welfare impact of the tax-interaction effect dominates the positive influence of the revenue-recycling effect and implies that, overall, environmental regulations are more costly in a second-best setting with preexisting distortionary taxes than in a first-best situation where no other taxes are present. This implies that the optimal second-best pollution tax is usually lower than the "Pigouvian" tax rate or marginal environmental damage. Bovenberg and Goulder (1996) and Parry (1995) find the optimal tax to be about 30% below the Pigouvian rate under plausible parameters and preexisting tax rates. These results are consistent with earlier theoretical contributions in the optimal tax literature. See, for example, Sandmo (1975), Ng (1980), and Auerbach (1985).

emissions taxes or auctioned emissions permits—policies that generate revenues and devote the revenues to financing cuts in existing distortionary taxes. The latter include emissions quotas or grandfathered emissions permits, as well as emissions tax policies with revenues returned to the economy in lump sum fashion. It will be convenient at times to refer to the former as revenue-raising policies and the latter as non-revenue-raising policies, but it should be kept in mind that the distinguishing criterion is whether the revenue-recycling effect is exploited, not simply whether revenues are raised.[3]

This article examines the choice between RR policies (emissions taxes or auctioned emissions quotas) and NRR policies (emissions quotas or grandfathered emissions permits) in a second-best setting where distortionary taxes are present. We demonstrate how the efficiency impacts of these policies are governed by the tax-interaction and revenue-recycling effects. Our analysis shows that preexisting taxes significantly raise the gross (exclusive of environment-related benefits) costs of both types of policies relative to what these costs would be in a first-best setting. In addition, the analysis reveals that preexisting taxes substantially alter both the relative and absolute overall efficiency impacts of these two types of policies. For NRR policies, preexisting taxes significantly influence the prospects for overall efficiency gains. We begin with a simple model that yields analytical results and then extend it gradually to gain greater realism. As we extend the original model, we give up the opportunity to obtain analytical solutions and must solve through numerical simulation. For concreteness we gauge model parameters and industry definitions to approximate circumstances faced by U.S. policy makers in the drafting of provisions of the 1990 Clean Air Act Amendments applying to sulfur dioxide emissions from coal-fired electric power plants. But the insights apply to other settings, including the abatement of carbon emissions on the national or international level through taxes or tradeable permits.

The article is organized as follows. Section 2 lays out the central theoretical issues and obtains initial results using an analytical model. This model has a similar focus to the graphical analysis in Parry (1997)—the only previous article we know of on this topic—but differs from it in providing an explicit utility-maximizing basis for the welfare results. Section 3 extends the original model, where the extensions include attention to intermediate inputs and a broader set of options for pollution abatement. The extended model is applied numerically in Section 4. This section explores further how tax interactions affect the net welfare gains from pollution-abatement policies, and it examines when these interactions can offset the entire "Pigouvian" welfare gain from pollution abatement. Section 5 analyzes further the sensitivity of the results to parameters and model specifications. Section 6 offers conclusions.

2. Analytical foundations and results

■ **The basic model.** A representative agent model is assumed in which household utility is

$$U(X, Y, H) + V(Q), \tag{1}$$

where $U(\cdot)$ is quasi-concave, $V(\cdot)$ is concave, and both functions are continuous. X and Y are market goods, H is hours of leisure or nonmarket time, and Q is the quality of the environment. Separability between environmental and nonenvironmental goods implies that the demand functions for X, Y, and H are independent of Q. This assumption is discussed in Section 5.

[3] For a related discussion, see Fullerton and Metcalf (1996).

X and Y are produced by competitive firms using labor as the only input. The marginal product of labor in both industries is constant and unaffected by environmental quality. Normalizing units to imply transformation rates of unity, we can write the economy's resource constraint as

$$T = X + Y + H, \tag{2}$$

where T is the household time endowment ($T - H$ is labor supply).

The production of X causes waste emissions that harm the environment; that is,

$$Q = Q(X), \tag{3}$$

where $Q_X < 0$. The numerical model discussed below relaxes the assumption that waste emissions are proportional to final output. From (1) and (3), we can define marginal environmental damages from production of X in terms of dollars by

$$D(X) = \frac{1}{\lambda}V'Q_X, \tag{4}$$

where λ is the marginal utility of income. We make the usual assumption that $D'(X) \geq 0$. In the absence of policy intervention, there is assumed to be no internalization of environmental damages by firms or households.

Finally, the government has an exogenous total revenue requirement TR, levies a proportional tax of τ_L on labor income, and regulates X. For our purposes it does not matter what TR is used for; we assume it is returned to households as a lump-sum transfer.

□ **RR policy: pollution tax with revenues used to cut marginal tax rates.** Suppose a tax of τ_L per unit is imposed on X. Normalizing the gross wage to unity, we can express the household budget constraint as

$$(1 + \tau_X)X + Y = (1 - \tau_L)(T - H) + TR. \tag{5}$$

Households are assumed to maximize utility (1) subject to their budget constraint (5), taking environmental quality as given. This yields the first-order conditions

$$U_X = (1 + \tau_X)\lambda; \qquad U_Y = \lambda; \qquad U_H = (1 - \tau_L)\lambda. \tag{6}$$

From (5) and (6) we can implicitly derive the (uncompensated) demand functions

$$X(\tau_X, \tau_L); \qquad Y(\tau_X, \tau_L); \qquad H(\tau_X, \tau_L). \tag{7}$$

Government revenues are the sum of labor and pollution tax revenues. Therefore, government budget balance requires

$$TR = \tau_L(T - H) + \tau_X X. \tag{8}$$

We now consider a policy involving an incremental increase in τ_X, where τ_L adjusts to maintain government budget balance. Totally differentiating the resource constraint (2) yields the following condition for the aggregate quantity effects of the policy change:

$$\frac{dH}{d\tau_X} + \frac{dX}{d\tau_X} + \frac{dY}{d\tau_X} = 0, \tag{9}$$

where

$$\frac{dH}{d\tau_X} = \frac{\partial H}{\partial \tau_X} + \frac{\partial H}{\partial \tau_L}\frac{d\tau_L}{d\tau_X} \tag{10}$$

and where analogous expressions apply for $dX/d\tau_X$ and $dY/d\tau_X$.

Differentiating (1) and using (3) and (7), we obtain the following expression for the welfare effect of the policy change:

$$\frac{dU}{d\tau_X} = \{U_X + V'Q_X\}\frac{dX}{d\tau_X} + U_Y\frac{dY}{d\tau_X} + U_H\frac{dH}{d\tau_X}.$$

Substituting the expressions for marginal environmental damage (4), marginal utility from consumption (6), and the aggregation property (9) gives

$$\frac{1}{\lambda}\frac{dU}{d\tau_X} = -(D - \tau_X)\frac{dX}{d\tau_X} - \tau_L\frac{dH}{d\tau_X}. \tag{11}$$

We now decompose the second term on the right-hand side of (11). Totally differentiating the government budget constraint (8), using (7) and (10), we can obtain

$$\frac{d\tau_L}{d\tau_X} = -\frac{X + \tau_X\dfrac{dX}{d\tau_X} - \tau_L\dfrac{\partial H}{\partial \tau_X}}{T - H - \tau_L\dfrac{\partial H}{\partial \tau_L}}. \tag{12}$$

This expression is the reduction in labor tax that can be financed by a marginal increase in the environmental tax, while maintaining budget balance. Substituting (10) and (12) in (11) gives

$$\frac{1}{\lambda}\frac{dU}{d\tau_X} = \underbrace{(D - \tau_X)\left(-\frac{dX}{d\tau_X}\right)}_{dW^P} + \underbrace{M\left\{X + \tau_X\frac{dX}{d\tau_X}\right\}}_{\partial W^R} - \underbrace{(1 + M)\tau_L\frac{\partial H}{\partial \tau_X}}_{\partial W^I}, \tag{13}$$

where

$$M = \frac{\tau_L\dfrac{\partial H}{\partial \tau_L}}{T - H - \tau_L\dfrac{\partial H}{\partial \tau_L}}. \tag{14}$$

The numerator in (14) is the partial equilibrium welfare loss from a marginal increase in the labor tax. This is the increase in leisure multiplied by τ_L, the wedge between the gross and net wage. The denominator is the partial equilibrium increase in government revenues from a marginal increase in the labor tax (from differentiating $\tau_L(T - H)$

with respect to τ_L). Therefore, M is the (partial equilibrium) efficiency cost of raising an additional dollar of revenue by increasing the labor tax, or marginal excess burden of labor taxation.[4]

Equation (13) decomposes the welfare impact of the policy change into three components. The first is the *Pigouvian effect, dW^P*. This is the general equilibrium reduction in X from a marginal increase in the environmental tax, multiplied by the wedge between marginal social cost and the demand price, or marginal social benefit. The second is the gain from the (marginal) revenue-recycling effect, ∂W^R. This is the product of the efficiency value per dollar of tax revenue (the marginal excess burden of taxation) and the incremental pollution tax revenue. The third is the (marginal) tax-interaction effect, ∂W^I. When X and leisure are substitutes, an increase in the demand price of X increases leisure, which exacerbates the welfare cost of the labor tax by $\tau_L(\partial H/\partial \tau_X)$.[5] This also reduces labor tax revenues by $\tau_L(\partial H/\partial \tau_X)$. The tax-interaction effect is the welfare loss from these two impacts.

We now compare the revenue-recycling and tax-interaction effects. ∂W^I can be manipulated to give the following approximation (see Appendix A):

$$\partial W^I = \phi_X M X; \qquad \phi_X = \frac{\eta^c_{XH} + \eta_U}{\dfrac{X}{X+U}\eta^c_{XL} + \dfrac{Y}{X+Y}\eta^c_{YH} + \eta_U}, \tag{15}$$

where η^c_{XH} and η^c_{YH} are the compensated elasticities of demand for X and Y with respect to the price of leisure, and η_U is the income elasticity of labor supply. ϕ_X is a measure of the degree of substitution between X and leisure relative to that between aggregate consumption and leisure. ϕ_X equals unity when X and Y are equal substitutes for leisure (η^c_{XH} equals η^c_{YH}) and is greater (less) than unity when X is a relatively strong (weak) substitute for leisure (that is, η^c_{XH} is greater (less) than η^c_{YH}). Comparing (15) with ∂W^R in (13), we see that the (marginal) revenue-recycling effect equals the tax-interaction effect when $\tau_X = 0$, but dominates it for $\tau_X > 0$, if X and Y are equal substitutes for leisure. Therefore, the net effect from interactions with the tax system is generally negative, unless X is a sufficiently weak substitute for leisure (ϕ_X is sufficiently below unity).[6]

□ **NRR policy: grandfathered pollution quotas.** Now consider, in contrast with the pollution tax case, the situation where a binding, nonauctioned quota is imposed. We define this quota by a virtual tax τ_X; that is, by the tax that would induce the equivalent reduction in X as the quota. This quota produces rents of $\pi = \tau_X X$, which are retained by households (who own firms). The numerical model incorporates the taxation of these rents, but for the moment we simplify by ignoring this possibility. Therefore π appears as an exogenous lump-sum component of income in the household budget constraint. The household demand functions can now be summarized by

$$X(\tau_X, \tau_L, \pi); \qquad Y(\tau_X, \tau_L, \pi); \qquad H(\tau_X, \tau_L, \pi). \tag{7a}$$

---

[4] One plus the marginal excess burden of taxation would equal the marginal cost of public funds.

[5] From the resource constraint (2), leisure and aggregate consumption ($X + Y$) are substitutes. Hence, on average, consumption goods and leisure are substitutes.

[6] The predominance of the tax-interaction effect has recently been discussed by Parry (1995). The result has long been implicit in optimal tax models (for example, Sandmo, 1975), which do not decompose the revenue-recycling and tax-interaction effects. In the special case when X and leisure are complements, $\phi_x < 0$ and the tax-interaction effect is an efficiency gain.

The key difference compared with the previous case is that the quota policy generates no revenue. Therefore the government budget constraint is

$$TR = \tau_L(T - H). \tag{8a}$$

Again we consider a revenue-neutral incremental increase in τ_X. We can obtain the analogous aggregation property (9), and welfare change expression (11), except that

$$\frac{dH}{d\tau_X} = \frac{\partial H^I}{\partial \tau_X} + \frac{\partial H}{\partial \tau_L}\frac{d\tau_L}{d\tau_X}, \tag{10a}$$

where

$$\frac{\partial H^I}{\partial \tau_X} = \frac{\partial H}{\partial \tau_X} + \frac{\partial H}{\partial \pi}\frac{d\pi}{d\pi_X}$$

and so on. I denotes a coefficient that takes into account the income effect from the increase in household rents.[7] Differentiating the government budget constraint (8a), using (7a) and (10a), yields

$$\frac{d\tau}{d\tau_X} = \frac{\tau_L \dfrac{\partial H^I}{\partial \tau_x}}{T - H - \tau_L \dfrac{\partial H}{\partial \tau_L}}. \tag{12a}$$

Since $\partial H^I/\partial \tau_X$ is positive (in general), the revenue-neutral quota induces an overall increase, rather than a decrease, in the labor tax.

Following a procedure analogous to the above gives the following expression for the general equilibrium welfare change from the policy:

$$\frac{1}{\lambda}\frac{dU}{d\tau_X} = \underbrace{(D - \tau_X)\left(-\frac{dX}{d\tau_X}\right)}_{dW^P} - \underbrace{(1 + M)\tau_L\frac{\partial H}{\partial \tau_X}}_{\partial W^I}. \tag{13a}$$

The quota policy leads to a Pigouvian welfare effect and a tax-interaction effect. However, the key difference between (13a) and (13) is that the quota does not generate a revenue-recycling effect to counteract the tax-interaction effect.[8,9]

---

[7] In the pollution tax case, this income effect is gained when the revenues are returned in labor tax reductions.

[8] $\partial H^I/\partial \tau_x$ is (slightly) less than the compensated cross-price effect on leisure. Households suffer an overall income loss because the additional quota rents ($X + \tau_x(dX/d\tau_x)$) do not fully offset the income effect from an uncompensated increase in the price of X (when $\tau_x > 0$). This net income loss reduces the overall substitution into leisure, since leisure is a normal good.

[9] The model could be extended to include capital as well as labor. In an extended model the tax-interaction effect stems from the environmental regulation's compounding of preexisting distortions in both capital and labor markets. For RR policies this is partly offset by the revenue-recycling effect, with the extent of offset depending on the scope of preexisting distortions in factor markets and the way the revenues are recycled. On this see Bovenberg and Goulder (1997).

□ **Welfare implications of instrument choice.** The traditional Pigouvian analysis implies that environmental regulation can increase welfare so long as marginal environmental damages are positive. This is true for the pollution tax in the above model, when X and Y are equal substitutes for leisure ($\phi_X = 1$). In the pollution quota case, however, where there is no revenue-recycling effect, the incremental welfare change from regulation is positive at $\tau_X = 0$ when $dW^P > dW^I$. When X and Y are equal substitutes for leisure, this condition is expressed by (see Appendix A):

$$D' \geq \left\{ \frac{\dfrac{\tau_L}{1-\tau_L}\epsilon^c}{1 - \dfrac{\tau_L}{1-\tau_L}\epsilon^u} \right\} \frac{1}{\eta}, \tag{16}$$

where ϵ^c and ϵ^u are respectively the compensated and uncompensated labor supply elasticity, η is the (magnitude of the) own price elasticity of demand for X, and D' is marginal environmental damage expressed relative to the price or marginal private cost of X.

Some quick calculations show that this can be crucial to welfare impacts. In the numerical model of sulfur dioxide regulation discussed below, the benchmark parameter values are $\tau_L = .4$, $\epsilon^c = .4$, and $\epsilon^u = .15$. Substituting these values in (16), if the elasticity of demand for the polluting good is .5, 1, or 2, then marginal environmental damages must exceed 60, 30, or 15% respectively of marginal production costs, or else any level of quota necessarily reduces welfare (when X and Y are equal substitutes for leisure).

Hence this simple analytical model indicates that the magnitude and even the sign of the welfare effects can hinge critically on whether a revenue-raising or non-revenue-raising instrument is used. Below, we examine these issues further using a numerical model that enables us to avoid some of the simplifying assumptions of the present model.

3. A numerical model

■ The analytical results indicate that the NRR policies face a significant disadvantage relative to the RR policies, especially when marginal environmental benefits of pollution reduction are "low" relative to production cost. To explore this issue further, we now extend the model to incorporate intermediate inputs (in addition to consumer goods) and to recognize firms' abilities to reduce emissions through abatement expenditure (which reduces the intensity of emissions per unit of output). The extended model does not afford analytical results; hence we obtain solutions numerically. However, the model enables us to consider impacts of large (as opposed to incremental) policy changes, and it facilitates sensitivity analysis. In special cases the numerical model's structure reduces to that of the analytical model; this makes it possible to identify (in Section 5) the significance of the new features in the numerical model.

The extended model has the following elements. The production sector involves competitive producers. There are two intermediate goods, electricity (E) and a "general intermediate good" (G). In addition, there are two consumer goods: an electricity-intensive good (C_I) and a non-electricity-intensive good (C_N). The intermediate goods and consumer goods are produced using inputs of labor, electricity, and the general intermediate good. Electricity production entails emissions of sulfur dioxide (SO_2). Firms can reduce such emissions either by reducing levels of electricity output or by purchasing abatement services or equipment, which reduces emissions per unit of output. A representative household allocates its time between labor and leisure. The government imposes taxes on labor income and, in policy simulations, regulates SO_2 emissions, either through emissions taxes or emissions quotas. Government revenues finance fixed transfers to households.

The full set of equations of the model is provided in Appendix B. Here we present the behavioral specifications governing producer and household behavior, along with the equilibrium conditions.

□ **Production technologies.** We assume competitive, price-taking firms and a constant-elasticity-of-substitution (CES) production technology in all industries. Production follows

$$X_i = (\alpha_{Li}x_{Li}^{\rho_i} + \alpha_{Ei}x_{Ei}^{\rho_i} + \alpha_{Gi}x_{Gi}^{\rho_i})^{1/\rho_i}, \qquad i = G, E, C_I, C_N, \tag{17}$$

where X_i is output from industry i, x_{ji} is the use of good j by industry i, and ρ_i and the α_{ji}'s are parameters. ρ is related to σ, the elasticity of substitution: $\rho = (\sigma - 1)/\sigma$.

Producers make input decisions in accordance with profit maximization. This assumption is becoming increasingly appropriate for the electricity industry in light of the substantial moves in recent years to deregulate the industry and foster competition. For producers in industries other than electricity, profit is the value of output minus expenditure on labor, energy, and materials (see Appendix B). In the electricity industry, the expression for profit is slightly more complex to account for pollution charges and abatement expenditure. In this industry profit (π) is given by

$$\pi_E = p_E X_E - p_L x_{LE} - p_E x_{EE} - p_G x_{GE} - p_Z Z - \tau_S S, \tag{18}$$

where p_L, p_E, and p_G represent the prices of inputs of labor, electricity, and the general intermediate input, respectively. Z and S represent abatement services and SO_2 emissions, respectively; p_Z is the unit price of abatement services (assumed to be equal to the price of labor), and τ_S is the tax rate applied to SO_2 emissions.

We abstract from the heterogeneity among firms in given industries and, in particular, the considerable heterogeneity among electric power producers. Considerations of heterogeneity can importantly influence the choice among policy instruments. For example, heterogeneity gives an efficiency advantage to tradeable permits relative to fixed emissions quotas, since trades can bring about equality of marginal abatement costs. (On this see, for example, Tietenberg (1985) and Blinder (1987).) Our focus is on the presence or absence of the revenue-recycling effect, which adds a further efficiency consideration that is largely independent of the extent of heterogeneity across firms.[10]

The relationship between electricity output, pollution emissions, and abatement services is

$$S/X_E = \alpha_S - \alpha_Z (Z/X_E)^{\beta}, \tag{19}$$

where α_S, α_Z, and β are parameters. This formulation asserts that in the absence of expenditure on abatement services or equipment (that is, when Z is zero), the ratio of

[10] Thus, for example, the efficiency consequences of a system of auctioned tradeable permits (which raises revenue) relative to a system of grandfathered permits (which does not raise revenue) are largely independent of the extent of heterogeneity in firms' abatement costs.

SO_2 emissions to electricity output is α_S.[11] To the extent that the firm devotes resources to abatement, this ratio falls. Our data on abatement costs for U.S. electricity producers (see below) indicate that β is less than unity: there are increasing marginal costs to SO_2 reduction.

We consider two types of pollution regulation: a tax τ_S on SO_2 emissions (RR policy) and a fixed quota on such emissions (NRR policy). In the tax case, firms choose the level of abatement such that, at the margin, the costs of abatement are equal to the avoided charges on pollution (see Appendix B). In the quota case, each firm j maximizes profits subject to the constraint that $S_j = \bar{S}_j$.[12] As shown in Appendix B, in this case the firm's behavior—and in particular the quantity of abatement equipment purchased (Z)—is identical to what the firm would choose if pollution level S had been enforced through a pollution tax. As indicated earlier, this means we can model the pollution quota case as a tax on emissions, with the "revenues" (quota rents) returned in lump-sum fashion to owners of electricity firms (households). The crucial difference between the case of an actual emissions tax and that of an emissions quota (or virtual emission tax) is that significant government revenues are earned only in the former case; thus the revenue-recycling effect is enjoyed only in that case.[13]

□ **Household behavior.** In its treatment of household behavior, the extended model differs from the earlier model in distinguishing the goods that directly confer utility (the consumption goods) from other (intermediate) goods. The electricity-intensive consumption good corresponds to direct household use of electricity, with the other consumption good representing all other goods-and-services consumption. As before, household behavior reflects utility-maximizing decisions of a representative household that allocates overall time between work and leisure and allocates income between consumption of the two consumer goods. Income is net-of-tax wage income plus—in the case of an emissions quota policy—net-of-tax rents. The utility function is

$$\begin{aligned} U &= U(H, C_I, C_N, S) \\ &= (\alpha_H H^{\rho_u} + \alpha_{\bar{C}} \bar{C}^{\rho_u})^{1/\rho_u} + V(S), \end{aligned} \tag{20}$$

where

$$\bar{C} = (\alpha_{CI} C_I^{\rho_{\bar{C}}} + \alpha_{CN} C_N^{\rho_{\bar{C}}})^{1/\rho_{\bar{C}}}. \tag{21}$$

The parameter ρ_U is related to σ_U, the elasticity of substitution between leisure and overall consumption, $\bar{C}$: $\rho_U = (\sigma_U - 1)/\sigma_U$. $\bar{C}$ is a CES composite of the two consumption goods, with the substitution between them controlled by $\rho_{\bar{C}}$. Utility depends on SO_2 emissions (S) as well as ordinary goods and leisure. The household regards S as exogenous. The impact of S on utility is represented by the function V, which is treated as separable from the effects of goods and leisure (as in the analytical model).

□ **The government's budget constraint.** As in the analytical model, all policies we consider are revenue neutral: the government must obtain enough revenue to maintain fixed transfers to households. To the extent that any policy change (e.g., the introduction

[11] With greater industry disaggregation, one could link emissions to the use of specific fuels by the electricity industry. In Section 5 we apply an extended model that distinguishes coal and other fuel inputs to electricity and connects SO_2 emissions to the use of the coal input.

[12] In keeping with the assumption of homogeneous producers, we assume that the aggregate emissions reduction is achieved by equal reductions by all producers.

[13] In fact the quota policy has a slight revenue impact, as discussed in Section 4.

of a tax on SO_2 emissions) would cause revenues to depart from this required revenue level, such revenue impacts are offset through adjustments to the marginal tax rate on labor income. The government's budget constraint is

$$TR = \tau_L(T - H) + \tau_R RENT + \tau_S S. \tag{22}$$

RENT denotes the total rents generated by government policy; these are positive in the case of the emissions quota or NRR policy. For the sake of realism, we assume here that these rents are taxed, and for simplicity we assume that τ_R, the tax rate on rents, has the same value as τ_L, the tax rate applying to labor income. (A pure NRR policy would not collect taxes on the rents; we consider the pure case in Section 5.) In the case of the emissions quota, τ_S is zero. This policy affects the government's budget only indirectly: by producing taxable quota rents and by affecting the real wage and labor supply (which alters labor tax revenues).

□ **Equilibrium conditions.** The production and household specifications above give rise to a set of supply and demand functions of producers and the household (see Appendix B). Exploiting the constant-returns-to-scale nature of production, we reduce the number of equilibrium conditions to (1) aggregate labor demand equals aggregate supply, (2) government revenue equals transfers to households, and (3) aggregate emissions equals $\bar{S}$. Solving the model involves finding the vector of "primary" prices satisfying these conditions. These prices uniquely determine all other prices and thus determine all demands and supplies. The primary prices are p_L, τ_S, and $\Delta\tau_L$ (the adjustment to the labor tax rate necessary to match revenues with the required level of household transfers).

□ **Data.** The benchmark dataset for the model is intended to represent roughly the situation in the United States in the year 2000. We develop this dataset by scaling observed 1990 data on input uses, output levels, and consumption patterns to the year 2000, assuming a real growth rate of 2.6% for all flows.[14] Elasticities of substitution in the production functions and utility function are taken from the disaggregated general equilibrium dataset developed by Cruz and Goulder (1992). The remaining parameters of the model—the α distribution parameters—are calibrated by using the identifying restriction that under benchmark policy conditions, the model must replicate the projected benchmark data. (For a discussion of calibration methods for general equilibrium models, see Shoven and Whalley (1992).) Table 1 displays benchmark data flows, data sources, and parameter values.

The baseline situation against which policy outcomes are compared assumes no abatement of SO_2; in other words, there is no (explicit or virtual) tax on SO_2 emissions in the baseline. This obviously differs from actual circumstances, but using this baseline permits the clearest assessments of impacts of alternative regulations. Developing baseline values of SO_2 emissions is a bit tricky because regulatory constraints on such emissions were introduced under the 1990 Clean Air Act Amendments and in fact have been in place for some "new sources" of electric power since 1971. Following NAPAP (1991), we assume that aggregate SO_2 emissions in the year 2000 would be 20 million tons in the absence of the 1990 Clean Air Act Amendments; that is, in the baseline scenario. In actuality, the amendments will limit average annual emissions to 10 million tons in the year 2000 and after.

[14] This is the average real growth for the United States over the period 1985–1994, as reported in Table 699 of the 1985 *Statistical Abstract of the United States*.

TABLE 1 Benchmark Data and Parameters for the Numerical Model

	E	G	C_I	C_N	Leisure Time[a]	Total Input Value
Input-output flows (S in millions of tons per year; all other flows in millions of 1990 dollars per year)						
E	42.6	90,943.3	49,437.6	46.2	0	140,469.8
G	64,088.6	4,877,379.6	154,662.3	3,142,264.4	0	8,238,395.0
L	74,838.1	3,270,072.0	0	0	4,568,288.0	7,913,198.1
Total expenditure	138,969.4	8,238,395.0	204,099.8	3,142,310.6		
Rents	1,500.3	0	0	0		
Total output value	140,469.7	8,238,395.0	204,099.8	3,142,310.6		
S (tons × 10^6)	20.4	0	0	0		
Parameter values						
$\sigma_E = \sigma_G = .8$						
$\sigma_{CI} = \sigma_{CN} = .9$						
$\sigma_{\bar{c}} = .85$; $\sigma_U = .79$[b]						

Sources: Input-output flows are from U.S. Department of Commerce, Bureau of Economic Analysis, *Survey of Current Business,* "Use of Commodities by Industries," April 1994. Flows related to electric utilities were split into coal-fired and non-coal-fired utilities based on data from Table 7.1 of the Department of Energy, Energy Information Administration, *Monthly Energy Review,* September 1990. The input composition of the two consumer goods C_I and C_N is based on Table B of the May 1984 *Survey of Current Business.* Sulfur emissions data derive from Table 369 of the 1993 *Statistical Abstract of the United States.*

[a] Benchmark leisure time in 1990 is assumed to be 1.4 times observed work time.

[b] σ_U is calibrated to generate an uncompensated wage elasticity of labor supply of .15.

We consider a range of values for the abatement cost parameter, α_Z. For a central value, we calibrate this parameter so that electricity producers' (private) marginal costs of abatement of SO_2 are $300 per ton in 1990 dollars when aggregate abatement is 10 million tons (from an unconstrained level of emissions of 20 million tons).[15]

An important parameter is σ_U, the elasticity of substitution between leisure and composite consumption in the utility function. Different values of this parameter imply different values for the elasticity of labor supply, the marginal excess burden of taxation, and hence the size of the tax-interaction effect (see Section 2). We employ several values for σ_U. We use .96 as the central value because it implies what seem to be the most reasonable values (.15 and .40, respectively) for the uncompensated and compensated elasticities of labor supply in the baseline or status quo ante situation.[16] The marginal excess burden from taxation associated with this value of σ_U is .30.[17]

[15] This is within the range of estimates from various studies. RDI (1995), USEPA (1995a), and EPRI (1995) respectively estimate marginal abatement costs to be $195, $462, and $339–493 (1990 dollars) by the year 2010, when the full, 10-million-ton abatement requirement is in force. Emissions allowance prices today are lower than these values, in part because these future costs are discounted to the present.

[16] The labor supply elasticities represent changes in the economywide effective labor supply induced by changes in the net of tax rate. The effective labor supply incorporates changes in the labor participation rate, average hours per worker, and effort on the job. Our preferred values are based on a recent survey of estimates by Russek (1996). We prefer a slightly higher value for the compensated elasticity than Russek's central value (.3), since the studies he discusses do not account for induced changes in effort.

[17] This is consistent with results from other studies (see, for example, Browning (1987) and Ballard, Shoven, and Whalley (1985)).

4. Results from the numerical model: RR versus NRR policies

■ **Relative costs of RR and NRR policies: crucial determinants.** This section contrasts the costs and net efficiency gains from an RR policy (emissions tax) and a comparable NRR policy (emissions quota). We compare costs in the two panels of Figure 1. Each panel shows the marginal social cost[18] of SO_2 emissions abatement under four different assumed values—0, .2, .4 (our preferred estimate),[19] and .6—for the preexisting marginal tax rate, τ_L.

Several key findings emerge from the figures. First, as predicted by the analytical model, for both policies the social costs are increasing and nonlinear functions of τ_{L0}, the initial labor tax rate. The larger the preexisting tax rate, the larger the marginal tax-interaction effect for any given amount of abatement. The *total* social cost of emissions abatement (the area under the marginal cost curve from zero to the level of abatement) is highly sensitive to the preexisting tax rate. For example, compared with the first-best case ($\tau_{L0} = 0$), under the RR policy the cost of a five-million-ton reduction is 1.1, 1.3, and 2.8 times higher than the cost in the first-best case when τ_{L0} is .2, .4, and .6. Achieving given emissions targets is more costly under NRR policies because these policies do not enjoy the revenue-recycling effect.

Second, the marginal social cost curve for the NRR policy has a positive intercept (except when the preexisting tax rate is zero), while the curve for the RR policy has a zero intercept. Under the RR policy, for an initial increment of abatement, the tax-interaction effect is exactly offset by the revenue-recycling effect; hence the zero intercept.[20] The NRR policy has a positive intercept because there is no offsetting revenue-recyling effect.[21]

The positive intercept has significant policy implications. The intercept of the marginal social cost curve represents a threshold value for the marginal environmental *benefits* (assuming such marginal benefits are constant or decreasing with the amount of SO_2 abatement). If marginal environmental benefits are below this critical value, then no amount of emissions abatement through the NRR policy can be efficiency improving! For example, according to panel (b) of Figure 1, if the preexisting labor tax is .4, the marginal benefits from SO_2 abatement must be at least \$104 per ton for any quota policy to yield an overall welfare gain.

□ **Relative costs over the entire possible range of pollution abatement.** In Figure 2 we superimpose the marginal social cost curves for the RR and NRR policies, displaying these costs over the range from 0 to 100% abatement (20 million tons) of SO_2 emissions. Panel (a) shows that marginal social costs rise faster for the RR policies. For substantial levels of abatement, marginal costs under RR policies exceed those of NRR policies. This occurs because marginal tax revenue declines with abatement under the RR policy. This reflects the reduction in the emissions tax base as the emissions

[18] In the second-best setting we examine, marginal social cost includes firms' private marginal costs of abatement plus costs stemming from the tax-interaction and revenue-recycling effects. We calculate the marginal social cost using the equivalent variation measure. For details, see our earlier working paper, Goulder, Parry, and Burtraw (1996).

[19] Taxes on labor include federal and state income taxes and social security (payroll) taxes. Browning (1987, 1994) uses a value of .43.

[20] The numerical model's nested utility function implicitly assumes that the consumption goods are equal substitutes for leisure. If this were not the case, the tax-interaction and revenue-recycling effects would not necessarily be equal at the initial incremental amount of abatement, and thus the intercept under the RR policy could be nonzero. These considerations do not affect the relative impacts of RR and NRR policies.

[21] In fact the quota policy has a slightly negative revenue-recycling effect. The policy leads to an erosion of the labor tax base, which loses revenue. This loss is offset almost entirely by the revenues earned on policy-generated (taxable) quota rents. The net effect is quite small.

FIGURE 1

MARGINAL ABATEMENT COSTS AND THE PREEXISTING TAX RATE

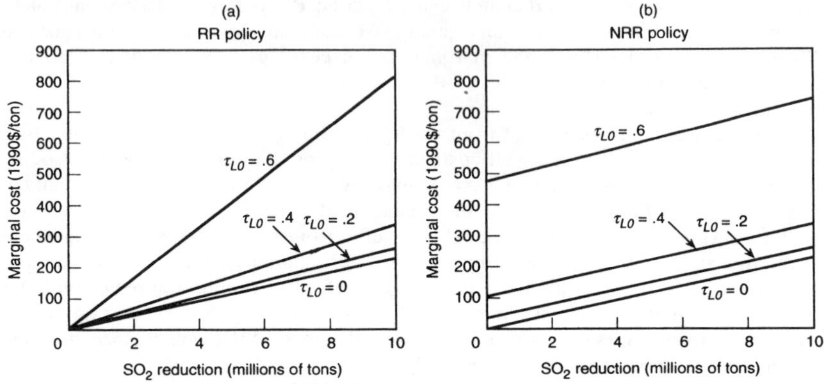

tax and the extent of abatement rise. Eventually marginal tax revenue becomes zero, and at this point (the peak of the emissions tax Laffer curve) the RR and NRR curves cross. To the right of this point, marginal tax revenue from the emissions tax is negative, and the revenue-recycling effect has a negative welfare impact at the margin. Indeed, if one pursues emissions reductions to the point of 100% abatement, the total costs of the two types of policies are identical. At this point neither policy earns any revenue, and there is no difference between them.

These results demonstrate that the relative cost advantage of the RR policies diminishes with the extent of abatement. These ideas are borne out by panel (b) of Figure 2, which indicates the implications of second-best considerations for both the absolute and relative costs of RR and NRR policies. The two solid lines in the figure are the ratios of total costs in a second-best setting (with $\tau_{LO} = .4$) to total costs in a first-best setting (with $\tau_{LO} = 0$), for the NRR and RR policies. For the RR policies, second-best considerations imply approximately 30% higher costs regardless of the extent of emissions abatement, so this ratio is constant. For the NRR policies, the ratio begins at infinity, in keeping with the fact that the intercept of the *marginal* cost function is positive for the NRR policy in a second-best world, but zero in a first-best world (see Figure 1 for $\tau_{LO} = .4$ and $\tau_{LO} = 0$). As the level of abatement approaches 100%, the ratio of total costs approaches the ratio for the RR policy.

In this connection it is noteworthy that the 1990 Clean Air Act Amendments call for a 10-million-ton (approximately 50%) reduction in SO_2 emissions. These regulations fall in the NRR category, since emissions allowances are given out free (grandfathered) rather than auctioned. Significant distributional or political objectives may be served by grandfathering but, as indicated by panel (b) of Figure 2, they come at a high efficiency cost. At 10 million tons of abatement, annual total costs under the NRR approach are 71% (or $907 million) higher than they would be in a first-best world. As indicated in this figure, over half of this extra cost ($533 million) could be avoided by adopting the RR policy instead of the NRR policy.[22]

Although this article points out the efficiency drawbacks of the NRR element of SO_2 emissions regulation under the 1990 Clean Air Act Amendments, it is not intended

[22] The costs of a 10-million-ton reduction are $2.182 and $1.649 billion under the grandfathering (NRR) and auctioning (RR) of emissions allowances, respectively.

FIGURE 2

COSTS OVER THE ENTIRE RANGE OF POSSIBLE EMISSIONS REDUCTIONS

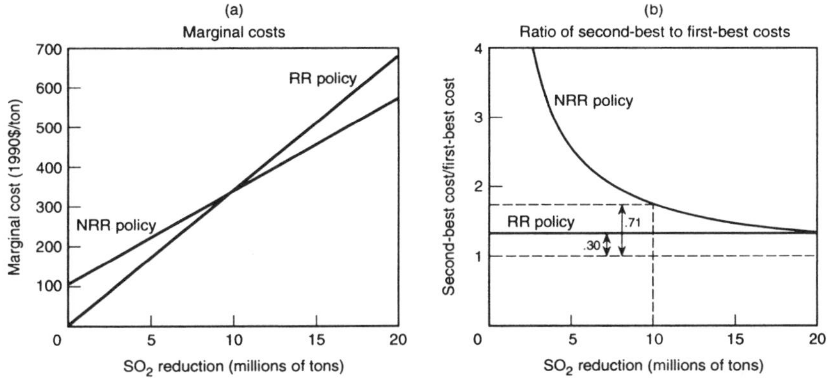

to be a wholesale critique of this legislation. The 1990 legislation achieved major reforms in environmental regulation by introducing emissions-allowance trading, a flexible, incentive-based approach to regulation. This approach has several theoretical advantages over the traditional, less-flexible methods (see, for example, Tietenberg (1985)), and empirical studies already indicate that it will generate dramatic reductions in overall compliance costs, compared to conventional approaches (see, for example, Burtraw (1996) and Ellcrman and Montero (1996)).

□ **Net benefits from RR and NRR policies.** We now consider environmental benefits in addition to the costs of regulation, to illustrate differences in the *net* benefits of the RR and NRR policies. We consider a wide range of values for the marginal environmental benefits from emissions reductions: \$100, \$250, and \$1000 per ton. These values are consistent with the range of estimates reported in recent years.[23]

Table 2 indicates the net benefits. The first panel shows, for the RR policy, the optimal level of abatement corresponding to each marginal benefit assumption, along with the corresponding total abatement cost and net welfare gain (total environmental benefit minus total abatement cost). The second panel provides this same information for the NRR policy. Except when 100% abatement is justified, welfare gains are smaller under the NRR policy. For the low (\$100 per ton) value of marginal benefits, the net benefit or welfare gain under the NRR policy is zero, since optimal abatement is zero (marginal benefits are below the minimal marginal abatement cost of \$104 per ton). With the intermediate benefit value, the optimal level of abatement under the NRR policy is again below that under the RR policy (since marginal abatement costs are higher under the NRR policy), and net benefits under the NRR policy are only about half of those under the RR policy. If marginal benefits are high (\$1,000 per ton), under both policies 100% abatement is optimal and total abatement costs are the same.

An important issue is the extent to which optimal abatement in a second-best setting differs from the first-best level. To examine this issue, we consider the level of

[23] The range is approximately that implied in the survey by Portney (1990). Some recent estimates exceed \$1,000 per ton, due to greater predicted health benefits and an improved characterization of visibility benefits. See USEPA (1995b) and Chestnut, Dennis, and Latimer (1994). However, Crandall, Reuter, and Steger (1996) argue that these recent estimates are biased upward.

TABLE 2 **Welfare Effects Under Alternative Policies**

	Marginal Environmental Benefit		
	$100/ton	$250/ton	$1,000/ton
RR policy			
Optimal abatement	3.0	7.5	20.0
Total abatement cost	146.3	922.9	6,708.3
Net welfare (efficiency) gain	153.7	952.1	13,291.7
NRR policy			
Optimal abatement	0	6.3	20.0
Total abatement cost	0	1,104.5	6,708.3
Net welfare (efficiency) gain	0	470.5	13,291.7
% of RR net welfare gain	0	49.4	100.0
RR policy and "Pigouvian" level of abatement			
Abatement	3.9	9.7	20.0
Assumed total abatement cost	191.9	1,199.5	5,180.0
Actual total abatement cost	247.7	1,550.5	6,708.3
Net welfare (efficiency) gain	142.3	874.5	13,291.7
% of RR net welfare gain	92.6	91.8	100.0
NRR policy and "Pigouvian" level of abatement			
Abatement	3.9	9.7	20.0
Assumed total abatement cost	191.8	1,199.2	5,179.9
Actual total abatement cost	576.1	2,082.5	6,708.3
Net welfare (efficiency) gain	−186.1	342.5	13,291.7
% of RR net welfare gain	−121.1	36.0	100.0

Note: Abatement figures are in millions of tons of SO_2. Costs and welfare changes are in millions of 1990 dollars.

abatement that would take place if, in determining the optimal level of abatement, regulators ignored tax interactions and incorrectly identified firms' private marginal abatement costs with the marginal social costs of abatement. The third and fourth panels consider the "Pigouvian level of abatement," the level at which *private* marginal abatement costs are equal to the marginal benefits from abatement. When marginal environmental benefits are low or moderate, choosing the Pigouvian level of abatement can *reduce* welfare relative to the no-regulation status quo! The fourth panel of the table indicates, for example, that when (gross) marginal benefits of abatement are $100 per ton, introducing an emissions quota at the Pigouvian level generates a net welfare loss of $186.1 billion. When marginal benefits are $185 or below, excessive abatement under the Pigouvian approach leads to net welfare losses under the quota policy. These results illustrate the importance of accounting for tax interactions in choosing the level of pollution abatement.

5. Further sensitivity analysis

■ We have considered how preexisting tax rates and the magnitude of marginal environmental benefits affect the relative costs and overall efficiency impacts of NRR and RR policies. Table 3 reports results from an expanded sensitivity analysis that

TABLE 3 **Marginal Abatement Costs Under Alternative Parameter Values (1990$/ton)**

	RR Policy			NRR Policy		
SO_2 Reduction (millions of tons)	0	5	10	0	5	10
1. Central case	1.6	165.8	334.8	104.3	219.1	335.8
2. Utility parameters						
a. $\sigma_u = 1.68$ (implying $\epsilon_u = .45$, $\epsilon_c = .7$)	2.1	212.9	430.1	232.5	333.0	433.0
b. $\sigma_u = .24$ (implying $\epsilon_u = -.15$, $\epsilon_c = .1$)	1.3	135.8	274.1	22.4	146.7	274.3
c. $\sigma_u = .80$, $T = 10.189 \times 10^{12}$ (implying $\epsilon_u = .15$, $\epsilon_c = .6$)	1.6	165.8	334.8	155.5	245.8	336.3
d. $\sigma_u = 2.38$, $T = 4.669 \times 10^{12}$ (implying $\epsilon_u = .15$, $\epsilon_c = .2$)	1.6	165.8	334.7	53.0	192.5	335.3
e. σ_c doubled	1.6	165.0	333.6	103.9	218.4	334.9
f. σ_c halved	1.6	166.2	335.3	104.5	219.4	336.2
3. Production elasticities						
a. Elasticities doubled	1.5	157.5	322.0	99.5	211.0	326.3
b. Elasticities halved	1.7	170.1	341.2	106.9	223.2	340.5
4. Abatement function parameters						
a. α_z doubled	.4	42.6	85.1	27.2	56.1	85.1
b. α_z halved	5.6	596.7	1,252.4	359.6	800.6	1,272.6
5. Size of regulated industry (E)						
a. Size quadrupled	1.7	173.3	345.7	108.8	226.2	343.8
b. Size halved	1.5	156.0	319.9	98.6	209.6	324.7
6. Quota rents not taxed	n/a	n/a	n/a	172.7	254.9	336.6
7. Alternative model structures						
a. Numerical model collapsed to match analytical model	1.2	142.2	335.4	133.2	232.9	371.4
b. Numerical model expanded to consider coal and other fuels explicitly	.9	97.0	213.6	26.2	114.5	219.8

considers how other preference and production parameters, model specifications, or policy assumptions might affect the relative costs of these two policies.

Rows 2a–2f of the table show the implications of changes in household utility parameters. In the experiments in rows 2a and 2b, we raise and lower σ_u to yield the indicated higher and lower values of the uncompensated and compensated labor supply elasticities, ϵ_u and ϵ_c. Larger values for σ_u imply easier substitutability between consumption and leisure (reflected in higher labor supply elasticities), and this implies larger tax-interaction and revenue-recycling effects. Thus, higher values for σ_u raise marginal social costs by a greater amount under the NRR policy than under the RR policy. In rows 2c and 2d, we alter both σ_u and the household's time endowment T in order to change the compensated labor supply elasticity ϵ_c while holding the uncompensated elasticity ϵ_u constant. Thus, we isolate the significance of changes in ϵ_c. When ϵ_u is held constant, changes in ϵ_c have no impact on results under RR policies: for these policies no lump-sum transfer or provision of untaxed rents is involved, and the efficiency cost depends entirely on the uncompensated elasticity (see Bovenberg and de Mooij, 1994). Rows 2e and 2f show the impacts of changes in σ_C, the elasticity of substitution between the electricity-intensive and non-electricity-intensive consumer goods. A higher value for this elasticity also implies a lower private cost of avoiding electricity use. Hence the social cost of avoiding SO_2 emissions is lower as well.

Higher elasticities of substitution in production (row 3a) mean that electricity (and associated SO_2 emissions) can more easily be substituted for other intermediate inputs. Hence, marginal social costs of abatement fall with higher values for these parameters.

Rows 4a and 4b examine impacts of alternative values for the parameter α_z in the SO_2 abatement function. A lower value for α_z means that a given amount of abatement equipment has a smaller effect on the emissions-output ratio, implying higher private marginal costs of abatement. Smaller values of α_z thus enlarge the tax-interaction effect and widen the differences in costs between RR and NRR policies, especially at lower levels of abatement.

Results in row 5 show that the relative cost disadvantage of the NRR policy is not sensitive to different assumptions about the size of the polluting industry in the overall economy.[24] This disadvantage depends on the relative magnitudes of the tax-interaction and revenue-recycling effects, not on their absolute magnitudes.[25] Each of these effects increases roughly in proportion to the size of the polluting sector.

The simulations reported thus far assumed that quota-induced rents are taxed at the same rate as labor. The taxation of rents partly offsets the adverse revenue impact associated with the quota's negative impact on the labor tax base. Row 6 presents results from simulations where quota rents are not taxed. In this circumstance the government cannot reduce costs by recycling revenues from taxes on quota rents, and thus the economy's marginal costs are higher at each level of abatement.

Rows 7a and 7b consider alternative model specifications. Results in row 7a are from a "collapsed" version of the numerical model that matches the analytical model. This version has no intermediate inputs and no separate abatement function.[26] The marginal costs from this collapsed version correspond to the marginal costs predicted by equation (13a) of the analytical model.[27] By comparing results in rows 7a with those in row 1 for the RR policy and row 6 for the NRR policy,[28] we can observe the importance of intermediate inputs and a separate abatement function. For both types of policies, marginal social costs (and the tax-interaction effect) are lower in the original model than in the scaled-down model. Intermediate inputs and a separate abatement function expand the opportunities for emissions abatement and lower the costs of achieving given emissions reductions.

Row 7b presents results from a more disaggregated version of the numerical model that contains coal and "other fuels" as intermediate inputs, in addition to G and E. In

---

[24] For details on these simulations, see our earlier working paper, Goulder, Parry, and Burtraw (1996).

[25] This result may depend on the specification of demand and supply elasticities. In our model, these elasticities are constant over a wide range. This contributes to fairly constant relative magnitudes of the tax-interaction and revenue-recycling effects.

[26] In this version of the numerical model, we treat E and G as consumer goods that are produced with the same production parameters as those for C_I and C_N in the original numerical model. Baseline SO_2 emissions and consumption of E and G are the same as the original model's baseline levels for SO_2, C_I, and C_N, respectively. We calibrate the utility function parameter σ_C so that private marginal costs of abatement at 10 million tons of abatement are $300 per ton, as in the original model.

[27] For the NRR policy, we compare the results in Table 3 with the marginal costs predicted by a modified version of equation (13a). For details, see Goulder, Parry, and Burtraw (1996). The predicted marginal costs are $131.6, $231.8, and $369.9 million, at 0, 5, and 10 million tons of abatement, respectively. These are within 1.2% of Table 3's marginal costs, which were obtained directly from the equivalent variation measure of the changes in household utility associated with incremental changes in abatement.

[28] Row 6 applies for the quota policy since the analytical model's formulas assume no taxes on quota rents.

the original numerical model the abatement function linked SO_2 emissions with electricity output (and abatement expenditure); the expanded model's greater disaggregation enables us to use a more realistic abatement function relating emissions to the level of coal input in the electricity industry.[29] This model specification leads to somewhat lower marginal costs than in the original specification, in keeping with the widened opportunities for input substitution.

A further potential area for sensitivity analysis deserves mention. We have assumed that emissions (or environmental quality) are separable from consumption or leisure in utility. Relaxing this assumption would affect the results. If environmental quality and leisure are gross complements, then regulations improving the environment will generate a larger tax-interaction effect, other things equal, because policies' adverse impacts on labor supply will be magnified. The reverse is true if leisure and environmental quality are gross substitutes. The case of gross complements seems more likely, since a cleaner environment can make leisure or recreational activities more attractive. Further empirical work that helps identify these relationships would be of considerable value to policy makers.

6. Conclusions

■ Using analytical and numerical general equilibrium models, this article indicates that the tax-interaction effect—the factor market impact of environmental regulations imposed in markets for produced goods—may critically influence the efficiency consequences of environmental regulations. In a world with prior taxes on factors, the tax-interaction effect implies significantly higher costs of regulation relative to what would apply in a first-best world with no preexisting taxes. The revenue-raising (RR) policies defined here enjoy a revenue-recycling effect that offsets much of the tax-interaction effect. The non-revenue-raising (NRR) policies defined here, in contrast, enjoy no such offset. As a result, the gross costs of achieving given reductions in pollution are higher under NRR policies than under RR policies.

The implications of tax interactions for the absolute and relative costs of these policies are not trivial. U.S. environmental regulations enforce annual reductions of about 10 million tons of SO_2 emissions from coal-fired electric power plants. Our calculations indicate that preexisting taxes make the costs of these regulations approximately 71% (or \$907 million) higher than they would in a first-best setting. More than half of this additional cost (or \$533 million) could be avoided if emissions allowances were auctioned rather than grandfathered.

In fact, the sign of the welfare impact of environmental regulations can depend on whether policies enjoy the revenue-recycling effect. If marginal environmental benefits fail to exceed a critical threshold value, any pollution abatement through one of the NRR policies is efficiency reducing. In the context of SO_2 regulation in the United States, we find that the use of an NRR policy (grandfathered emissions allowances) implies that efficiency gains disappear entirely if marginal environmental benefits are below \$104 per ton. In addition, we show that adopting a Pigouvian or first-best approach to environmental regulation can lead to welfare-reducing policies, even when environmental benefits are as high as \$185 per ton. The disadvantage of the NRR policies relative to the RR policies shrinks the larger the marginal environmental benefits and the larger the optimal amount of abatement. In the limiting case where environmental benefits justify 100% abatement, there is no difference in welfare impacts

[29] In the expanded version, X_E (electricity output) in the abatement cost function is replaced by $x_{coal,E}$, the use of coal by the electricity industry. We calibrate α_S to yield the same baseline emissions as in the original model and calibrate α_Z to yield marginal abatement costs of \$300 per ton at 10 million tons of SO_2 emissions.

of the NRR and RR policies. All of these results are largely independent of the size of the polluting or regulated sector relative to the overall economy.

Of course, NRR policies may have attractions along other dimensions. For example, grandfathered tradeable-permits programs may have important political advantages: grandfathering may be crucial to winning the consent of existing polluters and gaining necessary support for a regulatory program. Our results do not deny these attractions but simply indicate that they may come at a higher efficiency cost than previously had been recognized.

These insights on the importance of preexisting tax distortions have very general applicability.[30] They suggest that almost any government regulation that lowers real factor returns (by raising the price of consumer goods) might have considerably higher aggregate cost than would be implied by a first-best or partial equilibrium analysis. Existing studies in industrial organization, agricultural economics, labor economics, and international trade could be highly misleading to the extent that they evaluate regulatory policies using models that disregard preexisting tax distortions.

Appendix A

■ The derivations of equations (15) and (16) follow.

□ **Equation (15).** Using (13) and (14), $\partial W^I = M(T - H)(\partial H/\partial\tau_x)/(\partial H/\partial\tau_L)$. Substituting the Slutsky equations, and making use of the Slutsky symmetry property, we can obtain

$$\partial W^I = \frac{-M(T-H)\left\{\dfrac{\partial X^c}{\partial\tau_L} + \dfrac{\partial H}{\partial I}X\right\}}{\dfrac{\partial H^c}{\partial\tau_L} - \dfrac{\partial H}{\partial I}(T-H)}, \qquad \text{(A1)}$$

where c denotes a compensated coefficient and I is disposable household income. Differentiating (2) yields

$$\frac{\partial H^c}{\partial\tau_L} = -\left\{\frac{\partial X^c}{\partial\tau_L} + \frac{\partial Y^c}{\partial\tau_L}\right\}. \qquad \text{(A2)}$$

Substituting (A2) in (A1), and using (2), we obtain (15), where

$$\eta^c_{XH} = -\frac{\partial X^c}{\partial\tau_L}\frac{1-\tau_L}{X}; \qquad \eta^c_{YH} = \frac{\partial Y^c}{\partial\tau_L}\frac{1-\tau_L}{Y}; \qquad \eta_{LI} = -\frac{\partial H}{\partial I}\frac{(1-\tau_L)(T-H)}{T-H}. \qquad \text{(A3)}$$

□ **Equation (16).** From (13a) and (14), $dW^P > dW^I$ when

$$D' > \left\{\frac{\tau_L\dfrac{\partial H^c}{\partial\tau_L}}{T - H - \tau_L\dfrac{\partial H}{\partial\tau_L}}\right\}\left\{\frac{\dfrac{\partial H^I}{\partial\tau_X}}{\left(\dfrac{X}{(T-H)}\right)\dfrac{\partial H^c}{\partial\tau_L}}\right\}\left\{\frac{-1}{\dfrac{p_X}{X}\dfrac{dX}{d\tau_X}}\right\}, \qquad \text{(A4)}$$

where p_x is the price of X and $D' = D/p_x$. The first bracket component of (A4) is easily manipulated to match the bracketed term in (16), where

$$\epsilon^c = -\frac{\partial(T-H)^c}{\partial\tau_L}\frac{1-\tau_L}{T-H}; \qquad \epsilon^u = -\frac{\partial(T-H)}{\partial\tau_L}\frac{1-\tau_L}{T-H}.$$

When $\tau_x = 0$, $\partial H^I/\partial\tau_x = \partial H^c/\partial\tau_x$ (see footnote 7). Using this, (A2), (2), and the Slutsky symmetry property, we can express the second bracketed term in (A4) as

[30] They apply, for example, to issues of monopoly pricing: Browning (1995) estimates that the welfare loss from monopoly pricing in the U.S. economy is substantially larger once allowance is made for the effect of compounding tax distortions in the labor market. See also Oates (1995) for other potential applications.

$$\frac{\left(\frac{\partial X^c}{\partial \tau_L}\frac{1-\tau_L}{X}\right)}{\left(\frac{X}{X+Y}\right)\left(\frac{\partial X^c}{\partial \tau_L}\frac{1-\tau_L}{X}\right)+\left(\frac{Y}{X+Y}\right)\left(\frac{\partial Y^c}{\partial \tau_L}\frac{1-\tau_L}{Y}\right)}. \tag{A5}$$

From (A3), this term is equal to unity when $\eta^c_{XH} = \eta^c_{YH}$. Hence we obtain (16), where $\eta = -(dX/d\tau_x)(p_x/X)$.

Appendix B

■ The numerical model follows.

□ **Production functions and optimal input intensities.** In the G, C_I, and C_N industries, profit is given by $p_iX_i - p_Lx_{Li} - p_Ex_{Ei} - p_Gx_{Gi}$. Differentiating profit with respect to the variable inputs x_{mi} ($m = L, E, G$) yields the marginal productivity condition, $p_i\ (\partial X_i/\partial x_{mi} = p_m)$. Evaluating this condition with the functional form in (17) yields the optimal input intensities

$$a_{mi} \equiv \frac{x_{mi}}{X_i} = \alpha_{mi}^{1/1-\rho_i}\left(\frac{p_m}{p_i}\right)^{-1/1-\rho_i} \tag{B1}$$

for $m = L, E, G$.

For the electricity (E) industry, we first indicate optimal input and abatement choices where the firm faces a pollution tax. Electricity producers maximize profits (equation (18)) subject to the emissions-output relationship (equation (19)). Substituting (19) and the production function (17) into the profit equation and differentiating by the choice variables x_{LE}, x_{GE}, x_{EE}, and Z yield the first-order conditions

$$\begin{aligned}
a_{LE} &\equiv x_{LE}/X_E = \left[\alpha_{LE} + \alpha_{EE}\left(\frac{p_E\alpha_{LE}}{p_L\alpha_{EE}}\right)^{\rho_E/(\rho_E-1)} + \alpha_{GE}\left(\frac{p_G\alpha_{LE}}{p_L\alpha_{GE}}\right)^{\rho_E/(\rho_E-1)}\right]^{-1/\rho_E}\\
a_{GE} &\equiv x_{GE}/X_E = a_{LE}\left(\frac{p_G\alpha_{LE}}{p_L\alpha_{GE}}\right)^{1/\rho_E-1}\\
a_{EE} &\equiv x_{EE}/X_E = a_{LE}\left(\frac{p_E\alpha_{LE}}{p_L\alpha_{EE}}\right)^{1/\rho_E-1}.
\end{aligned} \tag{B2}$$

We model the pollution quota as a virtual pollution tax whose revenues are retained as rents by the firm.[31] The equivalence to firm behavior between the virtual tax and the quota can be seen as follows. Under the pollution quota, the firm's profit function is

$$\pi_E = p_EX_E - p_Lx_{LE} - p_Gx_{GE} - p_Ex_{EE} - p_ZZ. \tag{B3}$$

Firms maximize (B3) subject to the constraint imposed by the emissions quota $\bar{S}$:

$$X_E[\alpha_s - \alpha_Z\ (Z/X_E)^\beta] = S. \tag{B4}$$

The Lagrangian expression corresponding to this maximization problem is

$$\mathcal{L} = p_EX_E - p_Lx_{LE} - p_Gx_{GE} - p_Ex_{EE} - p_zZ - \lambda\{X_E[\alpha_s - \alpha_z(Z/X_E)^\beta] - \bar{S}\}. \tag{B5}$$

Let the (virtual) pollution tax be set equal to λ, the shadow price on the emissions constraint. In this case, the Lagrangian expression is identical to the maximization problem under the pollution tax case, except for the constant $\tau_s\bar{S}$. Thus the first-order conditions from this maximization problem are the same as those under the pollution tax, implying that firms' behavior under the pollution quota can be modelled through a virtual pollution tax. Under the virtual tax, the firm regards and responds to the tax as if it is a cost, but in fact the tax "revenues" are rebated as rents to the firm.

□ **Household utility function, labor supply, and consumer good demands.** The representative household maximizes utility (20) subject to the budget constraint:

[31] Pollution quotas are implemented by the government's giving a fixed number of pollution permits to existing firms. Since rents are enjoyed only by firms with permits and the number of permits is fixed, the existence of rents does not trigger further entry.

$$P_{CI}C_I + P_{CN}C_N = P_L(1 - \tau_L)(T - H) + (1 - \tau_R)RENT + TR. \tag{B6}$$

Equations (B7)–(B12) express the solution to the household's maximization problem:

$$a_{I\dot{C}} = \left[\alpha_{CI} + \alpha_{CN}\left(\frac{\alpha_{CI}p_{CN}}{\alpha_{CN}p_{CI}}\right)^{\rho_{\dot{C}}/\rho_{\dot{C}}-1}\right]^{1/\rho_{\dot{C}}} \tag{B7}$$

$$a_{N\dot{C}} = \left[\alpha_{CN} + \alpha_{CI}\left(\frac{\alpha_{CN}p_{CI}}{\alpha_{CI}p_{CN}}\right)^{\rho_{\dot{C}}/\rho_{\dot{C}}-1}\right]^{1/\rho_{\dot{C}}} \tag{B8}$$

$$p_{\dot{C}} = p_{CI}a_{I\dot{C}} + p_{CN}a_{N\dot{C}} \tag{B9}$$

$$H = \frac{p_L(1 - \tau_L)T + TR + (1 - \tau_R)RENT}{p_L(1 - \tau_L) + \left[\dfrac{\alpha_\ell p_{\dot{C}}}{\alpha_{\dot{C}}p_L(1 - \tau_L)}\right]^{1/\rho_u - 1} p_{\dot{C}}} \tag{B10}$$

$$L = T - H \tag{B11}$$

$$\bar{C} = (p_{\dot{C}})^{-1}[p_L(1 - \tau_L)L + (1 - \tau_R)RENT + TR]. \tag{B12}$$

Combining (B12) with (B7) or (B8) yields the optimal levels of C_I and C_N.

□ **The government sector.** Government revenues finance a fixed level of real government transfers, *TR*. Revenues (*REV*) depend on whether the policy is an actual emissions tax (τ_S^a) or an emissions quota (virtual tax, τ_S^v). Under the pollution tax policy, revenues are

$$REV = \tau_L L + \tau_S^a S. \tag{B13}$$

Under the emissions quota policy, revenues are

$$REV = \tau_L L + \tau_R RENT, \tag{B14}$$

where *RENT* equals $\tau_S^v S$. Under all policies, the tax on labor is equal to the initial tax rate plus $\Delta\tau_L$, the rate change necessary to yield total revenues equal to the given level of spending (fixed real transfers):

$$\tau_L = \tau_{LO} + \Delta\tau_L. \tag{B15}$$

□ **Prices.**

$$p_{CI} = a_{LCI}p_L + a_{ECI}p_E + a_{GCI}p_G \tag{B16}$$

$$p_{CN} = a_{LCN}p_L + a_{ECN}p_E + a_{GCN}p_G \tag{B17}$$

$$p_G = a_{LG}p_L + a_{EG}p_E + a_{GG}p_G \tag{B18}$$

$$p_E = a_{LE}p_L + a_{EE}p_E + a_{GE}p_G + p_Z(Z/X_E) + \tau_S(S/X_E). \tag{B19}$$

The electricity price p_E equals unit input cost (first three terms) plus unit abatement expenditure (fourth term) plus whatever tax costs or rents may apply. The last term in (B19) represents the unit tax cost in the pollution tax case and the unit rent in the quotas case.

□ **Aggregate supplies and demands.** Since production of the intermediate inputs *E* and *G* follows constant returns to scale, the supplies of these goods are demand determined. Thus $X_G = G\_AD$ and $X_E = E\_AD$, where *G_AD* and *E_AD* denote the aggregate demands. The aggregate demands *G_AD* and *E_AD* are given by

$$G\_AD = a_{GG}X_G + a_{GE}X_E + a_{GI}C_I + a_{GN}C_N \tag{B20}$$

$$E\_AD = a_{EG}X_G + a_{EE}X_E + a_{EI}C_I + a_{EN}C_N. \tag{B21}$$

Equations (B20) and (B21) are solved simultaneously to obtain *G_AD* and *E_AD*.

L_AD, the aggregate demand for labor, is given by

$$L\_AD = a_{LG}G\_AD + a_{LE}E\_AD + Z + a_{LI}C_I + a_{LN}C_N. \tag{B22}$$

□ **Equilibrium conditions.** The equilibrium conditions are

$$L\_AD = L$$
$$S = \bar{S} \qquad \text{(B23)}$$
$$REV = TR.$$

Solving the model involves finding the vector of primary "prices" satisfying the equilibrium conditions. These prices uniquely determine all quantities and other prices of the system. The primary prices are p_L τ_S and $\Delta\tau_L$. We use p_L as the numeraire and solve explicitly for only the latter two primary prices. By Walras's Law, one of the equilibrium conditions is redundant: we need only apply the latter two equilibrium conditions to determine τ_s and $\Delta\tau_L$.

References

AUERBACH, A.J. "The Theory of Excess Burden and Optimal Taxation." In A.J. Auerbach and M.S. Feldstein, eds., *Handbook of Public Economics,* Vol. 1. Amsterdam: North-Holland, 1985.

BALLARD, C., SHOVEN, J.B., AND WHALLEY, J. "General Equilibrium Computations of the Marginal Welfare Costs of Taxes in the U.S." *American Economic Review,* Vol. 75 (1985), pp. 128–138.

———, AND MEDEMA, S.G. "The Marginal Efficiency Effects of Taxes and Subsidies in the Presence of Externalities: A Computational General Equilibrium Effect." *Journal of Public Economics,* Vol. 52 (1993), pp. 199–216.

BLINDER, A.S. *Hard Heads, Soft Hearts: Tough-Minded Economics for a Just Society.* Reading, Mass.: Addison-Wesley, 1987.

BOVENBERG, A.L. AND DE MOOIJ, R.A. "Environmental Levies and Distortionary Taxation." *American Economic Review,* Vol. 84 (1994), pp. 1085–1089.

——— AND GOULDER, L.H. "Optimal Environmental Taxation in the Presence of Other Taxes: General Equilibrium Analyses." *American Economic Review,* Vol. 86 (1996), pp. 985–1000.

——— AND ———. "Costs of Environmentally Motivated Taxes in the Presence of Other Taxes: General Equilibrium Analyses." *National Tax Journal,* Vol. 50 (1997), pp. 59–87.

——— AND VAN DER PLOEG, F. "Environmental Policy, Public Finance and the Labour Market in a Second-Best World." *Journal of Public Economics,* Vol. 55 (1994), pp. 349–390.

BROWNING, E.K. "On the Marginal Welfare Cost of Taxation." *American Economic Review,* Vol. 77 (1987), pp. 11–23.

———. "The Non-Tax Wedge." *Journal of Public Economics,* Vol. 53 (1994), pp. 419–433.

———. "The Welfare Cost of Monopoly and Other Output Distortions." Working Paper, Department of Economics, Texas A&M University, 1995 (forthcoming, *Journal of Public Economics*).

BURTRAW, D. "The SO_2 Emissions Trading Program: Cost Savings Without Allowance Trades." *Contemporary Economic Policy,* Vol. 14 (1996), pp. 79–94.

CHESTNUT, L.G. DENNIS, R.L., AND LATIMER, D.A. "Economic Benefits of Improvements in Visibility: Acid Rain Provisions of the 1990 Clean Air Act Amendments." Proceedings of the International Specialty Conference, *Aerosols and Atmospheric Optics, Volume A.* Air & Waste Management Association, 1994.

CRANDALL, R.W., REUTER, F.H., AND STEGER, W.A. "Clearing the Air: EPA's Self-Assessment of Clean-Air Policy." *Regulation,* Vol. 4 (1996), pp. 35–46.

CRUZ, M. AND GOULDER, L.H. "An Intertemporal General Equilibrium Model for Analyzing U.S. Energy and Environmental Policies: Data Documentation." Unpublished manuscript, Stanford University, 1992.

ELECTRIC POWER RESEARCH INSTITUTE (EPRI). *The Emission Allowance Market and Electric Utility SO_2 Compliance in a Competitive and Uncertain Future.* EPRI TR-105490, prepared by K. White, Energy Ventures Analysis, Inc., and Van Horn Consulting, Palo Alto, Calif., 1995.

ELLERMAN, A.D. AND MONTERO, J.P. "Why Are Allowance Prices So Low? An Analysis of the SO_2 Emissions Trading Program." CEEPR 96-001, Massachusetts Institute of Technology, 1996.

FULLERTON, D. AND METCALF, G. "Environmental Controls, Scarcity Rents, and Pre-Existing Distortions." Working paper, University of Texas at Austin, 1996.

GOULDER, L.H. "Environmental Taxation and the 'Double Dividend': A Reader's Guide." *International Tax and Public Finance,* Vol. 2 (1995), pp. 157–183.

———, PARRY, I.W.H., AND BURTRAW, D. "Revenue-Raising vs. Other Approaches to Environmental Protection: The Critical Significance of Pre-Existing Tax Distortions." NBER Working Paper no. 5641, 1996.

HAHN, R.W. "Trade-offs in Designing Markets with Multiple Objectives." *Journal of Environmental Economics and Management,* Vol. 13 (1986), pp. 1–12.

NG, Y.K. "Optimal Corrective Taxes or Subsidies When Revenue-Raising Imposes an Excess Burden." *American Economic Review,* Vol. 70 (1980) pp. 744–751.

NICHOLS, A.L. *Targeting Economic Incentives for Environmental Protection.* Cambridge, Mass.: MIT Press, 1984.

OATES, W.E. "Green Taxes: Can We Protect the Environment and Improve the Tax System at the Same Time?" *Southern Economic Journal,* Vol. 61 (1995), pp. 914–922.

——— AND SCHWAB, R.M. "Economic Competition Among Jurisdictions: Efficiency Enhancing or Distortion Inducing?" *Journal of Public Economics,* Vol. 35 (1988), pp. 333–354.

PARRY, W.H. "Pollution Taxes and Revenue Recycling." *Journal of Environmental Economics and Management,* Vol. 29 (1995), pp. S64–S77.

———. "Environmental Taxes and Quotas in the Presence of Distorting Taxes in Factor Markets." *Resource and Energy Economics,* Vol. 19 (1997), pp. 203–220.

PORTNEY, P.R. "Economics and the Clean Air Act." *Journal of Economic Perspectives,* Vol. 4 (1990), pp. 173–181.

POTERBA, J.M. "Global Warming Policy: A Public Finance Perspective." *Journal of Economic Perspectives,* Vol. 7 (1993), pp. 47–63.

REPETTO, R., DOWER, R.C., JENKINS, R., AND GEOGHEGAN, J. *Green Fees: How a Tax Shift Can Work for the Environment and the Economy.* Washington, D.C.: World Resources Institute, 1992.

RESOURCE DATA INTERNATIONAL, INC. (RDI). *RDI's Phase I 1995 Databook Performance Under the Clean Air Act Amendments of 1990.* Boulder, Colo., 1995.

RUSSEK, F.S. "Labor Supply and Taxes." Staff Memorandum, Congressional Budget Office, Washington, D.C., 1996.

SANDMO, A. "Optimal Taxation in the Presence of Externalities." *Swedish Journal of Economics,* Vol. 77 (1975), pp. 86–98.

SHACKLETON, R., SHELBY, M., CRISTOFARO, A., BRINNER, R., YANCHAR, J., GOULDER, L., JORGENSON, D., WILCOXEN, P., AND PAULY, P. "The Efficiency Value of Carbon Tax Revenues." In D. Gaskins and J. Weyant, eds., *Reducing Global Carbon Dioxide Emissions: Costs and Policy Options.* Stanford: Stanford University Energy Modeling Forum, 1996.

SHOVEN, J.B. AND WHALLEY, J. *Applying General Equilibrium.* New York: Cambridge University Press, 1992.

STAVINS, R., ED., *Project 88—Round II. Incentives for Action: Designing Market-Based Environmental Strategies.* Public policy study sponsored by Senators Timothy Wirth and John Heinz, Washington, D.C., 1991.

TERKLA, D. "The Efficiency Value of Effluent Tax Revenues." *Journal of Environmental Economics and Management,* Vol. 11 (1984), pp. 107–123.

TIETENBERG, T.H. *Emissions Trading: An Exercise in Reforming Pollution Policy.* Washington, D.C.: Resources for the Future, 1985.

U.S. ENVIRONMENTAL PROTECTION AGENCY (USEPA). *Economic Analysis of the Title IV Requirements of the 1990 Clean Air Act Amendments.* Prepared by ICF Resources Incorporated, Washington, D.C., 1995a.

———. *Human Health Benefits from Sulfate Reductions Under Title IV of the 1990 Clean Air Act Amendments.* Prepared by L.G. Chestnut (Contract no. 68-D3-0005) for the U.S. Environmental Protection Agency, 1995b.

U.S. NATIONAL ACID PRECIPITATION ASSESSMENT PROGRAM (NAPAP). *1990 Integrated Assessment Report.* Washington, D.C.: Council on Environmental Quality, 1991.

WEITZMAN, M.L. "Prices vs. Quantities." *Review of Economic Studies,* Vol. 41 (1974), pp. 477–491.

[25]

Journal of Environmental Economics and Management **37**, 52–84 (1999)
Article ID jeem.1998.1058, available online at http://www.idealibrary.com on IDEAL®

When Can Carbon Abatement Policies Increase Welfare? The Fundamental Role of Distorted Factor Markets

Ian W. H. Parry[1]

Resources for the Future, Washington, DC 20036

Roberton C. Williams, III

Stanford University

and

Lawrence H. Goulder

Stanford University, Resources for the Future, and NBER

Received September 23, 1997; revised September 1998

This paper employs analytical and numerical models to assess the welfare effects of a revenue-neutral carbon tax and (nonauctioned) carbon emissions permits, taking into account preexisting tax distortions in factor markets. The presence of preexisting taxes significantly raises the general equilibrium costs of both policies. This cost increase is much greater under emissions permits, since this policy does not generate revenues to reduce distortionary taxes. Under our central estimates emissions permits cannot increase welfare unless environmental damages exceed about $18 per ton of carbon. In contrast, an appropriately scaled carbon tax is welfare-improving so long as environmental damages are positive. © 1999 Academic Press

1. INTRODUCTION

The prospect of global climate change from the continued atmospheric accumulation of carbon dioxide (CO_2) and other greenhouse gases has prompted analysts to consider a number of policy options for mitigating emissions of CO_2. The issue has attained heightened importance since the signing of the Kyoto Protocol in December 1997, when 160 nations resolved to reduce emissions of CO_2 and other greenhouse gases. This paper focuses on alternative ways that the United States might achieve significant reductions in CO_2 emissions.

The crucial point of departure from previous studies of CO_2 abatement policies[2] is the present paper's focus on connections between the efficiency impacts of CO_2 abatement policies and preexisting tax distortions. The motivation for this focus

[1]Address correspondence to: Dr. Ian Parry, Resources for the Future, 1616 P Street NW, Washington, DC 20036. Phone: (202)328-5151. Fax: (202)939-3460; E-mail address: parry@rff.org. The authors gratefully acknowledge the helpful comments and suggestions of Gary Becker, Dallas Burtraw, Jenny Ligthart, two referees and an associate editor. We also thank the National Science Foundation (grant number SBR-9613458) for financial support.

[2]See, for example, Nordhaus [27] and Manne and Richels [21].

0095-0696/99 $30.00

stems from recent studies of environmental regulation in a second-best setting. These papers have shown that the efficiency costs of environmental regulations are higher in a world with preexisting factor market distortions than they would be in the absence of such distortions.[3] The higher costs reflect two effects. First, by raising the costs of production in the affected industry, environmental regulations give rise to higher prices of output in that industry and thus a higher price of consumption goods in general. This implies a lower real wage and a reduction in labor supply. If there are preexisting taxes on labor, the reduction in labor supply has a first-order—that is, nonincremental—efficiency cost, which has been termed the *tax-interaction effect*.

The second welfare effect arises under environmental policies that raise revenues and use the revenues to finance cuts in the marginal rates of preexisting distortionary taxes. When marginal rates of prior taxes are lowered, some of the distortionary costs of these taxes are avoided. The efficiency benefit produced by this "recycling" of revenues has been termed the *revenue-recycling effect*. This effect partly offsets the tax-interaction effect.

These considerations are highly relevant to the choice among alternative instruments for reducing emissions of CO_2. The most frequently cited instruments for dealing with CO_2 emissions are carbon taxes, carbon quotas (or "carbon caps"), and marketable carbon emissions permits.[4] All of these policies generate a (costly) tax-interaction effect, but only some of them can exploit the offsetting revenue-recycling effect. Carbon taxes, as well as carbon quotas or tradeable permits that are auctioned by the government, enjoy the revenue-recycling effect as long as the revenues obtained are used to finance cuts in marginal tax rates of distortionary taxes such as the income tax. In contrast, grandfathered (nonauctioned) carbon quotas and permits fail to raise revenues and thus cannot exploit the revenue-recycling effect. Carbon taxes whose revenues are returned through lump-sum transfers to households also fail to enjoy this effect. This paper shows that the inability to make use of the revenue-recycling effect can put the latter policies at a substantial efficiency disadvantage relative to the former policies.[5] Indeed, the absence of the revenue-recycling effect may make it impossible for the latter policies to generate overall welfare (i.e., efficiency) gains, despite the benefits from avoided future

[3]See, for example, Bovenberg and de Mooij [3], Bovenberg and van der Ploeg [4], Goulder [15], Goulder *et al.* [16], Parry [31, 32], and (in a somewhat different context) Browning [9]. Earlier papers by Terkla [40], Lee and Misiolek [19], and Ballard and Medema [1] examine policies in which revenues from environmental taxes finance reductions in distortionary taxes, although these papers do not explicitly address the ways that preexisting distortionary taxes raise the costs of new environmental taxes.

[4]See, for example, Tietenberg [41], Poterba [35], Hoel [18], and Oates and Portney [29].

[5]Some earlier analyses of carbon taxes have recognized the potential importance of the revenue-recycling effect. Repetto *et al.* [36] and Nordhaus [25] indicate that the costs of a carbon tax are much lower when revenues are returned through cuts in marginal tax rates than when revenues are returned as a lump sum. These studies make a valid point about the relative costs of policies that do or do not exploit the revenue-recycling effect. However, the absolute costs of carbon tax policies are not fully captured in these studies because they do not integrate preexisting taxes in the analysis, and thus they cannot account for the tax-interaction effect. The presence or absence of the revenue-recycling effect can be linked to whether policy-generated rents are captured by the government and returned to taxpayers (as in the case of a pollution tax) or instead left in producers' hands (as in the case of pollution quotas or freely offered pollution permits). On this see Fullerton and Metcalf [14].

climate change![6] These results bear directly on current CO_2 abatement policy discussions in the United States and Europe, where grandfathered tradeable carbon permits are gaining serious consideration.

In this paper we use analytical and numerically solved general equilibrium models to contrast the effects of two sorts of policies, where the crucial difference between the two policies is the presence or absence of the revenue-recycling effect. These policies are a carbon tax with revenues devoted to cuts in marginal tax rates and a nonauctioned carbon emissions quota (or, equivalently, a free emissions permit program). To our knowledge, this is the first study to compare these carbon abatement policies in the presence of preexisting distortionary taxes. As mentioned, the first policy exploits the revenue-recycling effect, while the second does not. For simplicity, we apply the labels "carbon tax" and "carbon quota" to these policies, since it is cumbersome to refer repeatedly to the presence or absence of the revenue-recycling effect. It should be kept in mind that, as indicated above, some policies involving quotas or tradeable permits would share efficiency properties of our former category, while some policies involving taxes or tradeable permits would share efficiency properties of our latter category.

We begin by deriving analytical formulas indicating that the efficiency costs associated with the tax-interaction effect can be quite large relative to the direct costs of carbon abatement considered in typical policy models. We then perform numerical simulations that show that the absence of the revenue-recycling effect makes the carbon quota policy significantly more costly than the carbon tax. Under central values for parameters, the marginal costs of emissions abatement begin at approximately \$18 per ton under the quota, as compared with \$0 per ton under the revenue-neutral carbon tax.[7] The quota's minimal marginal cost of \$18 per ton has some powerful implications for policy. Estimated marginal benefits from carbon abatement are typically below \$18 per ton (see, in particular, Nordhaus [23, 27]). If marginal benefits are indeed below this value, then only the carbon tax can produce an overall welfare improvement in our model; a carbon quota (or set of grandfathered tradeable permits) necessarily reduces welfare, and potentially by a large amount. Clearly, there is enormous uncertainty as to the potential gains from reducing carbon emissions; as discussed below, under more extreme scenarios for climate change, benefit estimates can easily exceed \$18 per ton. Yet even when marginal damages are quite large, there is still a very strong efficiency argument for preferring a carbon tax over a (nonauctioned) quota. When marginal damages are \$75 per ton, for example, the maximum welfare gain under the quota is only half of that under the tax.

We would emphasize that the absolute costs of the carbon quota, and its cost relative to that of the carbon tax, are sensitive to different assumptions about labor supply elasticities, which are difficult to pin down accurately. Nonetheless, even

[6] The impossibility of efficiency gains was demonstrated through numerical simulations performed by Bovenberg and Goulder [5]. They found that any carbon abatement through a carbon tax policy that recycles the revenues in lump-sum fashion (and thus does not exploit the revenue-recycling effect) will be efficiency reducing, if the marginal environmental benefits from carbon abatement do not exceed a strictly positive threshold value. This restriction on environmental benefits does not apply to carbon tax policies involving recycling through cuts in marginal rates. The present study differs from the Bovenberg–Goulder study in decomposing the tax-interaction and revenue-recycling effects and in examining quota policies (and the treatment of quota rents) in some detail.

[7] This study measures emissions in terms of carbon rather than CO_2.

under extremely conservative values for labor supply elasticities, the marginal cost of the quota at zero abatement still significantly exceeds the central estimate of $5 per ton for marginal environmental benefits in Nordhaus [27]. Our analysis also abstracts from a number of potentially significant considerations, such as capital accumulation, technological innovation, and preexisting sources of distortion in the economy due to nontax factors. However, as we discuss at the end of the paper, generalizing the analysis may well strengthen rather than weaken our empirical results.

Our results are consistent with—but in some ways more striking than—the results obtained by Goulder *et. al* [16] in a study of the sulfur dioxide (SO_2) permit program under the 1990 Clean Air Act Amendments. Goulder *et al.* found that, under central estimates for marginal environmental benefits from SO_2 reductions, a system of grandfathered (freely allocated) SO_2 permits allows for an improvement in welfare relative to the unregulated status quo. The present study indicates that the prospects for welfare gains through quotas or nonauctioned permits are much dimmer in the CO_2 context. Quotas or nonauctioned permits have a greater chance at yielding welfare gains in the SO_2 case because the central estimates for marginal environmental benefits are relatively high (compared with marginal abatement costs) in this case. In contrast, central estimates for marginal environmental benefits from CO_2 reductions are fairly low relative to marginal abatement cost.[8]

The rest of the paper is organized as follows. Section 2 develops and applies our analytical model. This model is fairly simple, containing two final goods, a clean and dirty intermediate input, and one primary factor, labor. In Section 3, we describe an extended version of the original model that distinguishes different fossil fuels and identifies different nonfuel intermediate goods. Section 4 applies the extended model, which is solved numerically. The numerical solution method enables us to consider large (nonincremental) policy changes, and this turns out to be relevant to the relative costs of the different policies. Section 5 discusses the sensitivity of the results to alternative values for important parameters. Section 6 concludes and discusses some limitations of the analysis.

2. THE ANALYTICAL MODEL

Here we present an analytically tractable model that reveals the welfare impacts of carbon taxes and nonauctioned carbon quotas in a second-best setting. This model shares some features of analytical models developed by Parry [31, 32] and Goulder *et al.* [16]. However, the present model is distinct from Parry's in deriving results explicitly from utility maximization. In addition, it differs from the model of Goulder *et al.* in incorporating a more flexible relationship between the levels of pollution emissions and the level of output produced by the regulated industry.

[8]Another option for reducing carbon emissions is to mandate certain technologies that require less fossil fuel input and thus entail lower emissions. Fullerton and Metcalf [14] analyze the efficiency impacts of a particular technology restriction, along with emissions taxes and quotas, in a second-best setting. The paper shows that incremental abatement through a technology restriction need not be any more costly than incremental abatement under a pollution tax. Our analysis differs from that in Fullerton and Metcalf by concentrating specifically on CO_2 emissions reductions and in examining not only incremental emissions abatement but also large amounts of abatement. As emphasized below, the relative costs of quotas and taxes depend importantly on the extent of emissions abatement.

2.1. *Model Assumptions*

A representative household allocates its time endowment $(\bar{L})$ between labor supply (L) and leisure or nonmarket time $(l = \bar{L} - L)$. It also purchases two consumption goods, C_F and C_N. C_F represents an aggregate of final output from industries that use fossil fuels (F) intensively, and C_N is an aggregate of all other consumption goods. We ignore capital accumulation in the economy, which means that we just focus on behavior in one period, rather than solving a dynamic problem (see Section 4). The household utility function is given by

$$u(C_F, C_N, l) - \phi(F), \tag{2.1}$$

where $u(\cdot)$, utility from nonenvironmental goods, is continuous and quasi-concave. ϕ is disutility from current, anthropogenically caused additions to the stock of CO_2 in the atmosphere, caused by combustion of fossil fuels. These damages represent the present discounted value of the expected utility losses due to induced changes in future global climate.[9] The separability in (2.1) implies that future climatic change does not affect the relative attractiveness of leisure and the two types of consumption.[10]

C_F and C_N are produced under constant returns to scale. The production functions are given by

$$C_F = C_F(L_F, F_F, N_F); \quad C_N = C_N(L_N, F_N, N_N); \tag{2.2}$$

where N is a "clean" (nonpolluting) intermediate good. Labor is the only input used to produce the intermediate goods F and N, and the marginal product of labor in each of these two industries is taken to be constant. We assume that production in all four industries is competitive. The use of fossil fuels in the C_F and C_N industries leads to a proportional amount of carbon emissions. This is a standard assumption in energy models: unlike the case of SO_2, there are no economically viable scrubber technologies to reduce CO_2 emissions per unit of fuel input. Aggregate fossil fuel use is

$$F = F_F + F_N. \tag{2.3}$$

We choose units to imply one ton of carbon per unit of F.

We do not consider heterogeneity in the costs of emissions abatement among producers within a given industry. If regulators have imperfect information about these costs, in general they will be unable to achieve production efficiency in the allocation of quotas: marginal costs of abatement are likely to differ across producers. Under these circumstances a carbon tax or a system of tradeable carbon

[9]Although we focus on the costs to the United States of carbon abatement policies, we use environmental damage estimates for the world economy. This seems appropriate, since we are dealing with a globally dispersed pollutant.

[10]If pollution were to alter the tradeoff (marginal rate of substitution) between consumption and leisure (as would be the case if pollution affects consumer health or labor productivity), then the benefits of reduced pollution could be magnified or diminished by tax interactions. For more details on this point see Bovenberg and van der Ploeg [4] and Williams [43].

permits would have an efficiency advantage over fixed carbon quotas, apart from the advantages associated with revenue-recycling emphasized here.[11]

Finally, we assume that the government spends G as lump-sum transfers to households. G represents nominal transfers, but in policy experiments we assume that the government adjusts G to hold real transfers constant. The government also levies a proportional tax of t_L on labor income and regulates carbon emissions by using either a tax or a nonauctioned quota. The government budget is assumed to balance, and therefore any revenue consequences from regulation are neutralized by adjusting the rate of t_L.

Denoting the demand prices of C_F and C_N by p_F and p_N, and normalizing the gross wage to unity, we can write the household budget constraint as

$$p_F C_F + p_N C_N = (1 - t_L)L + G. \tag{2.4}$$

Households choose C_F, C_N, and L to maximize utility (2.1) subject to (2.4) and the time endowment. From the resulting first-order conditions and the household budget constraint, we obtain the (implicit) uncompensated demand and labor supply functions

$$C_F(p_F, p_N, t_L); \quad C_N(p_F, p_N, t_L); \quad L(p_F, p_N, t_L). \tag{2.5}$$

Substituting (2.5) into (2.1) gives the indirect utility function:

$$V = v(p_F, p_N, t_L) - \phi(F). \tag{2.6}$$

From Roy's Identity:

$$\frac{\partial v}{\partial p_F} = -\lambda C_F; \quad \frac{\partial v}{\partial p_N} = -\lambda C_N; \quad \frac{\partial v}{\partial t_L} = -\lambda L \tag{2.7}$$

where the Lagrange multiplier λ is the marginal utility of (nonlabor) income.

Consider a policy—either a carbon tax or a quota—that creates a wedge of τ_F per unit between the demand and supply price of fossil fuels. Under constant returns to scale and competition, the general equilibrium increase in final product prices[12] that results from an incremental increase in τ_F is (see Appendix A)

$$\frac{dp_F}{d\tau_F} = \frac{F_F}{C_F}, \quad \frac{dp_N}{d\tau_F} = \frac{F_N}{C_N}, \tag{2.8}$$

that is, the ratio of fossil fuel input to final output. Finally, the equilibrium quantity of fossil fuels can be expressed as a function of the policy variables (see Appendix A):

$$F(\tau_F, t_L) = F_F(\tau_F, t_L) + F_N(\tau_F, t_L), \tag{2.9}$$

where $dF/d\tau_F < 0$. These functions summarize the effect of changes in τ_F on fossil fuel use through (a) the input-substitution effect, that is, the replacement of

[11] Policy analysts have paid considerable attention to this heterogeneity issue and the associated potential gains from trades. Perhaps as a result, tradeable carbon permits seem to enjoy more political support than nontradeable quotas.

[12] That is, the increase that applies when all prices and quantities are treated as variable.

labor and N for fossil fuels in production of C_F and C_N; (b) the output-substitution effect, that is, the change in derived demand for fossil fuels from changes in the quantities of C_F and C_N caused by the effect of τ_F on final product prices. Changes in t_L affect fossil fuels through their effect on the quantity of final consumption goods, in response to a change in the relative price of leisure.

2.2. *Carbon Tax*

Suppose τ_F^t represents a tax per unit paid by firms purchasing fossil fuels. Given the fixed proportions between fuel use and emissions, this is equivalent to a tax of τ_F^t per ton on carbon emissions. In this case, the government budget constraint is

$$\tau_F^t F + t_L L = G \tag{2.10}$$

that is, the sum of carbon tax revenues and labor tax revenues equals government spending. Consider a policy change involving an incremental change in τ_F^t and t_L. The change in the labor tax necessary to hold government spending fixed in real terms can be expressed as (see Appendix A for derivation)

$$\frac{dt_L}{d\tau_F^t} = -\frac{(1 - s_G)F + \tau_F^t \, dF/d\tau_F^t + t_L \, \partial L/\partial \tau_F^t}{L + t_L \, \partial L/\partial t_L}, \tag{2.11}$$

where s_G is the share of government transfers in household income, given by

$$s_G = \frac{G}{G + (1 - t_L)L}.$$

We now define two concepts that describe the burden of the labor tax. These will be useful in expressing the tax-interaction effect. First we define

$$Z = \frac{-t_L \, \partial L/\partial t_L}{L + t_L \, \partial L/\partial t_L}. \tag{2.12}$$

Z is the partial equilibrium efficiency cost of raising an additional dollar of labor tax revenue when this additional revenue is devoted to an increase in government consumptive expenditure. $Z + 1$ is usually referred to as the *marginal cost of public funds* (MCPF).[13] The numerator of (2.12) is the welfare loss from an incremental increase in t_L; it is the wedge between the gross wage (equal to the value marginal product of labor) and net wage (equal to the marginal social cost of labor in terms of foregone leisure), multiplied by the reduction in labor supply. The denominator is marginal labor tax revenue (from differentiating $t_L L$).

[13] The MCPF includes both the "direct" cost (equal to unity) of removing revenue from the private sector, plus the additional deadweight loss (Z) created by the distortionary tax. For a discussion of the MCPF concept and its relationship with the MEB concept presented below, see Hakonsen [17].

If instead the revenue from the labor tax is used to provide (lump-sum) transfers to households, the partial equilibrium efficiency cost is

$$Z'' = \frac{-t_L\,\partial L^c/\partial t_L}{L + t_L\,\partial L/\partial t_L} = \frac{(t_L/(1-t_L))\varepsilon^c}{1-(t_L/(1-t_L))\varepsilon^u};$$
$$\varepsilon^c = \frac{\partial L^c}{\partial(1-t_L)}\frac{1-t_L}{L} \quad \text{and} \quad \varepsilon^u = \frac{\partial L}{\partial(1-t_L)}\frac{1-t_L}{L}, \qquad (2.12'')$$

where superscript c denotes a compensated price effect and ε^c and ε^u are the compensated and uncompensated labor supply elasticities, respectively. Z'' is usually defined as the *marginal excess burden* (MEB) of the labor tax (see Hakonsen [17]). Z'' depends on both the compensated and uncompensated elasticities because the recycling of the tax revenue through lump-sum transfers partly compensates for the lost income associated with the higher labor tax rate.

The welfare effect of the policy change is obtained by differentiating the utility function (2.6) with respect to τ_F^t, allowing t_L to vary. This gives

$$\frac{dV}{dt_F^t} = \frac{\partial v}{\partial p_F}\frac{dp_F}{d\tau_F^t} + \frac{\partial v}{\partial p_N}\frac{dp_N}{d\tau_F^t} + \frac{\partial v}{\partial t_L}\frac{dt_L}{\partial\tau_F^t} - \phi'(F)\frac{dF}{d\tau_F^t}.$$

Substituting (2.3), (2.7), (2.8), (2.11), and (2.12) gives

$$\frac{1}{\lambda}\frac{dV}{d\tau_F^t} = \underbrace{\left(\frac{\phi'}{\lambda} - \tau_F^t\right)\left(-\frac{dF}{d\tau_F^t}\right)}_{dW^P} + \underbrace{Z\left\{F + \tau_F^t\frac{dF}{d\tau_F^t}\right\}}_{\partial W^R}$$
$$\underbrace{-(1+Z)t_L\left(-\frac{\partial L}{\partial\tau_F^t}\right) - Z''Fs_G}_{\partial W^I}. \qquad (2.13)$$

Thus, the welfare effect (in dollars) can be separated into three terms. The first, dW^P, is the *primary welfare gain*, representing the effect within the fossil fuel market. This is the environmental benefit from reduced fuel combustion net of the reduction in consumer surplus to users of fossil fuels. More specifically, this gain is the incremental reduction in fossil fuel multiplied by the gap between the marginal social cost ($q_F + \phi'/\lambda$) and marginal social benefit or demand price ($q_F + \tau_F^t$) of fossil fuels (where q_F is the supply price of F). The second, ∂W^R, is the (marginal) *revenue-recycling effect*, or efficiency gain from using additional carbon tax revenues to reduce the labor tax. This equals marginal carbon tax revenue multiplied by the marginal cost of public funds minus one. The third, ∂W^I, is the (marginal) *tax-interaction effect*. This effect has three components. $t_L(-\partial L/\partial\tau_F^t)$ is the efficiency loss from the reduction in labor supply stemming from the reduced real wage (which, in turn, results from the higher final goods prices caused by τ_F^t). This reduction in labor supply reduces revenue from the labor tax. The cost of replacing this revenue is $Zt_L(-\partial L/\partial\tau_F^t)$, the second component of ∂W^I. Finally, because τ_F^t raises the price of consumption, nominal government spending must rise to hold real spending constant. The third component, $Z''Fs_G$, is the efficiency loss from raising this additional revenue.[14]

The tax-interaction effect can be expressed as (see Appendix A)

$$\partial W^I = ZF + Z''F(1 - s_G)(\mu - 1); \qquad \mu = \frac{h_F \eta_{Fl}^c + h_n \eta_{Nl}^c}{s_F \eta_{Fl}^c + s_N \eta_{Nl}^c} \tag{2.14}$$

where η_{Fl}^c and η_{Nl}^c are the compensated elasticities of demand for C_F and C_N with respect to the price of leisure; h_F and h_N are the shares of fossil fuels in the C_F and C_N sectors ($h_F + h_N = 1$); and s_F and s_N are the shares of C_F and C_N in the value of total output ($s_F + s_N = 1$). μ is a measure of the degree of substitution between fossil-fuel-intensive consumption and leisure, relative to that between aggregate consumption and leisure. In general, both η_{Fl}^c and η_{Nl}^c are positive, because from the household budget constraint (2.4), aggregate consumption and leisure are inversely related. If C_F and C_N are equal substitutes for leisure (that is, $\eta_{Fl}^c = \eta_{Nl}^c$), then $\mu = 1$ and the second term in (2.14) goes to zero. In this case (comparing ∂W^I—that is, μZF—with ∂W^R), the tax-interaction effect equals the revenue-recycling effect when $\tau_F^t = 0$, but exceeds it when $\tau_F^t > 0$ (since $dF/d\tau_F^t < 0$). Therefore, taking into account the preexisting labor tax raises the slope but does not affect the intercept (equal to zero) of the marginal cost of carbon emissions reduction.[15] Since C_F is carbon-intensive, the share of fossil fuels used in the C_F sector exceeds the share of C_F in total production ($h_F > s_F$). Therefore, if C_F were a stronger (weaker) substitute for leisure than Y (that is, η_{Fl}^c is greater (less) than η_{Nl}^c), then μ would be greater (less) than 1, and the marginal cost of emissions reduction would have a positive (negative) intercept.[16]

2.3. *Carbon Quota*

Suppose instead that carbon emissions are reduced by a quota (or nonauctioned permits). We define this quota by τ_F^q, the wedge it creates between the demand and supply price of fossil fuels. (τ_F^q can also be regarded as a "virtual tax".) Since price exceeds marginal private cost by τ_F^q for each unit of F, τ_F^q produces quota rents of $\pi = \tau_F^q F$. These rents accrue to households, who own firms. We will generally assume that this rent income is taxed at the same rate as labor income. (In the sensitivity analysis of Section 5, we will consider the case in which quota rents are

[14] The last term of the tax-interaction effect in (2.13) differs from that in Parry [32] and Goulder *et al.* [16]. In these earlier papers, the analytical model assumed that government spending was constant in nominal terms. In contrast, the present paper holds government spending constant in real terms.

[15] This is the same qualitative result as that for a revenue-neutral pollution tax on a final good (Goulder *et al.* [16]). Note that, despite substitution of labor for fossil fuels in production of final goods, the aggregate effect on labor supply is still negative. This occurs because, given our assumptions of constant returns to scale and labor as the only primary factor input, the aggregate demand for labor is perfectly elastic, and changes in the quantity of labor are determined purely by changes in the real household wage (the nonsubstitution theorem is satisfied; Varian [42, p. 354]). Any policy that causes final goods prices to increase, and hence the real wage to fall, will therefore reduce the labor supply.

[16] For more discussion about how the costs of emissions taxes depend on the relative degree of substitution between output from the polluting sector and leisure, see Bovenberg and van der Ploeg [4] and Parry [31].

not taxed.) Under these conditions the government budget constraint is

$$t_L(\pi + L) = G. \tag{2.10}$$

If instead, rent income were taxed at 100%, or the quotas were sold by the government at a price of τ_F^q, then the carbon quota would be equivalent to the carbon tax in this model.

Following a procedure analogous to before the one already described, we can express the welfare change from a marginal tightening of the quota (that is, an increase in τ_F^q) as (see Appendix A)

$$\frac{1}{\lambda}\frac{dV}{d\tau_F^q} = \underbrace{\left(\frac{\phi'}{\lambda} - \tau_F^q\right)\left(-\frac{dF}{d\tau_F^q}\right)}_{dW^P} + \underbrace{t_L Z'\left\{F + \tau_F^q \frac{dF}{d\tau_F^q}\right\}}_{\partial W^R}$$
$$\underbrace{- (1 + Z')t_L\left(-\frac{\partial L}{\partial \tau_F^q}\right) - Z'' F s_G}_{\partial W^I}, \tag{2.13'}$$

where

$$Z' = \frac{-t_L\, \partial L/\partial t_L}{L + t_L\, \partial L/\partial t_L + \pi}. \tag{2.12'}$$

Comparing (2.13′) with (2.13), one will observe that the quota yields the same primary welfare effect as the tax. It also induces the analogous tax-interaction effect, since it increases the price of consumption goods in the same way as the carbon tax. The key difference is that it generates a revenue-recycling effect only indirectly—through the taxation of quota rents. Under the quota, the revenue-recycling effect is equal to the fraction t_L of the revenue-recycling effect under the carbon tax. Therefore when C_F and C_N are equal substitutes for leisure, the revenue-recycling effect will only partially offset the tax-interaction effect for the first unit reduction in carbon; hence the marginal cost of emissions reduction will now have a positive intercept. If the environmental benefits from carbon abatement are below this intercept, then a carbon quota cannot increase welfare.[17]

When C_F and C_N are equal substitutes for leisure, this threshold benefit level ($\bar{B}$) can be expressed as (see the Appendix A)

$$\bar{B} = Z''(1 - t_L)\frac{d\tau_F^q}{dF}F^0. \tag{2.15}$$

In the numerical model below, the benchmark parameter values we use for t_L, ε^c, and ε^u are 0.4, 0.3, and 0.15, implying $Z'' = 0.22$. In addition, $d\tau_F^q/dF = \$0.085$ per million tons, and initial emissions are 1423 million tons. Substituting these

[17] t_L in the expression for ∂W^R in (2.13′) represents the fraction of quota rents that the government obtains through income taxation and uses to cut other taxes. In the case of a revenue-neutral auctioned quota, t_L would be unity in this expression (as in Eq. (2.13)). Alternatively, in the case of carbon tax, where the revenues are returned as lump sum transfers rather than used to cut distortionary taxes, $t_L = 0$. The marginal cost of public funds in (2.12′) is slightly different from that in (2.12), because increasing t_L now affects tax revenues from rent income as well as labor income.

values in (2.12″), the analytical model predicts that the quota cannot increase welfare unless environmental benefits exceed \$16 per ton.

3. THE NUMERICAL MODEL

The simplicity of the model in Section 2 contributes to the transparency of the results, but it also limits the model's ability to gauge the empirical importance of the second-best issues of interest. In this section we introduce some extensions to the original analysis to gain a better sense of the significance of these issues. We extend the analysis in two main ways. First, we consider the effects of "large" policy changes, that is, policy changes that produce greater than incremental reductions in emissions. As will be shown below, the relative (as well as absolute) costs of carbon taxes and quotas depend importantly on the extent of carbon abatement achieved through these policies. To consider large changes, we must specify functional forms for the utility and production functions and solve the model numerically. The second extension is to disaggregate further the intermediate goods in production. We disaggregate fossil fuels into oil, coal, and natural gas to allow for emissions reductions not only through substitution of nonfuel inputs for fossil fuels (collectively), but also through substitution of low-carbon fuels (such as natural gas) for high-carbon fuels (such as coal). We also distinguish between energy-intensive and non-energy-intensive nonfuel inputs. This disaggregation allows us to perform a rich sensitivity analysis, which is not possible in the analytical model.

Subsection A describes the behavioral assumptions for households, firms, and the government, and the equilibrium conditions of the extended model. The complete set of equations for the model is presented in Appendix B. Section 3.2 describes the calibration of the model.

3.1. *Model Structure*

There are six intermediate goods. Fossil fuels are divided into coal (F_C), petroleum (F_P), and natural gas (F_N). Coal is the most carbon-intensive fuel per unit of energy and natural gas the least. The remaining intermediate goods are electricity (E), an aggregate of other energy-intensive intermediate goods (I), and an aggregate of non-energy-intensive intermediate goods (N).[18] As in the analytical model, there are two consumption goods: C_N represents final output from industries that use N intensively, and C_I represents final output from industries that use the other five intermediate goods (notably energy) intensively. Labor time is the sole primary factor of production and equals the household time endowment net of leisure. All of the intermediate goods and labor are used as inputs in the production of intermediate goods. Final goods are produced using only intermediate goods as inputs.

[18] Energy-intensive intermediate goods are those for which a relatively large proportion of energy goods (fossil fuels and electricity) are used as inputs, such as metals processing and transportation. Non-energy-intensive intermediate goods are those with a relatively low proportion of energy inputs, such as services and agriculture.

As before, labor is taxed at a proportional rate of t_L. The tax revenue is used to provide a fixed level of lump-sum transfers to households. Carbon emissions are proportional to the use of each of the three fossil fuels, with a different carbon content for each. Again, we consider two instruments: a tax and a quota on carbon emissions.

i. *Firm Behavior*

We assume competitive producers that take input and output prices as given. Production functions in all industries have the following nested constant elasticity of substitution (CES) form:

$$X_j = \left[\left(\sum_{i \in m} \alpha_{i,j} X_{i,j}^{\rho_{jm}} \right)^{\rho_j/\rho_{jm}} + \left(\sum_{i \in g} \alpha_{i,j} X_{i,j}^{\rho_{jg}} \right)^{\rho_j/\rho_{jg}} + \alpha_{L,j} X_{L,j}^{\rho_j} \right]^{1/\rho_j} . \quad (3.1)$$

$m = \{I, N\}$, $g = \{F_N, F_C, F_P, E\}$, $j = \{F_N, F_C, F_P, E, I, N, C_I, C_N\}$, where the ρ's and the α_j's are parameters; $\rho = (\sigma - 1)/\sigma$, and σ is the elasticity of substitution between factors in production. This function divides inputs into three groups: energy (fossil fuels and electricity), materials (the two remaining intermediate goods), and labor, with different elasticities of substitution between inputs in different groups. Because this production function possesses constant returns to scale, supply curves in all industries are perfectly elastic for given input prices.

Producers choose input quantities to maximize profits. In the case of the carbon quota, this is subject to the constraint on emissions. Profits equal the value of output minus expenditures on labor and intermediate goods used in production, less any charges per unit of carbon emissions (τ_c).[19] Thus, profit for industry j (π_j) is given by

$$\pi_j = (p_j - \beta_j \tau_C) X_j - \sum_I p_i X_{i,j}, \quad (3.2)$$

where p_i and p_j are the prices of inputs and outputs, respectively, and β_j represents the carbon emissions per unit of good j. β_j is zero for all goods except F_N, F_C, and F_P. Note that because this production function exhibits constant returns to scale, profits will equal zero under the carbon tax, but will equal the quota rents under the emissions quota. Total carbon emissions are

$$e = \beta_{FN} X_{FN} + \beta_{FC} X_{FC} + \beta_{FP} X_{FP}. \quad (3.3)$$

ii. *Household Behavior*

We assume the following nested CES utility function:

$$U = U(l, C_I, C_N, e) = (\alpha_l l^{\rho_u} + \alpha_F C^{\rho_u})^{1/\rho_u} + \phi(e), \quad (3.4)$$

where

$$C = (\alpha_{C_I} C_I^{\rho_C} + \alpha_{C_N} C_N^{\rho_C})^{1/\rho_C}. \quad (3.5)$$

[19] We assume here that carbon taxes are levied on the producers of fossil fuels imposed at source, in keeping with most carbon tax proposals.

l is leisure time and the α's and ρ's are parameters. ρ_U and ρ_C are related to the elasticities of substitution between aggregate consumption and leisure and between the two consumption goods, respectively, in the same manner as in the production function. e denotes carbon emissions.[20]

The household maximizes utility subject to the budget constraint

$$p_{C_I} C_I + p_{C_N} C_N = p_L L(1 - t_L) + \pi(1 - t_R) + G, \tag{3.6}$$

where t_L is the tax rate on labor income, t_R is the tax rate on rent income, $L = \bar{L} - l$ is labor supply, π is the total rent generated by a quota policy, G is government transfers to households (fixed in real terms), and p_C is the composite price of consumption. This constraint requires that expenditure on consumption equal after-tax income in the form of wages, rents, and government transfers. Except in the sensitivity analysis in Section 5, we assume that the tax rates on labor income and rent income are the same: $t_R = t_L$.[21]

iii. *Government Policy*

The numerical model considers the same two types of emissions regulation considered in the analytical model: a tax of τ_t on carbon emissions, and an emissions quota yielding a virtual tax of τ_q. As shown in Appendix B and in the analytical model, firms behave identically under the carbon tax and under the quota for a given level of abatement. The crucial difference between the two policies is that the tax directly raises revenue for the government and uses those revenues to finance reductions in preexisting tax rates.

The government's budget constraint is given by

$$G = t_L L + t_R \pi + \tau_t e. \tag{3.7}$$

Under a carbon tax, π is equal to zero, while under a carbon quota, τ_t equals zero. As before, any revenue consequences of carbon regulation are neutralized by adjusting the tax rates t_L and (if applicable) t_R so as to maintain a fixed level of real transfers.

iv. *Equilibrium Conditions*

The requirements of general equilibrium are that the demand for labor and for each good equal supply, that the government's revenue requirement be satisfied, and that carbon emissions equal a specified target (if applicable). We can reduce the set of equilibrium conditions to three equations: aggregate labor demand equals aggregate supply, government revenue equals expenditures, and carbon

[20] As in the analytical model, the damages from climate change are assumed to be separable in utility from goods and leisure. Weak separability between goods and leisure and homothetic preferences over consumption goods together imply that C_I and C_N are equal substitutes for leisure (see Deaton [11]). Since there is no obvious reason or empirical evidence to suggest that energy-intensive goods are relatively strong or relatively weak substitutes for leisure, we regard this as a reasonable simplification.

[21] The effective taxes on labor earnings (primarily personal income and payroll taxes) and nonlabor earnings (personal and corporate income taxes) are roughly the same. For example, Lucas [20] estimates them to be 40% and 36%, respectively.

emissions equal the target level.[22] The model is solved by adjusting the primary prices: the pretax wage (p_L); the tax rate on labor income (t_L); and the tax rate on carbon emissions (τ_t), or virtual tax rate (τ_q), such that these three conditions hold.

3.2. *Calibration of the Model*

The benchmark data set, summarized in Table I, approximates the U.S. economy in the year 1995, the most recent year for which the relevant energy data were available. We developed this data set by aggregating 1987 data from the *Survey of Current Business* on input uses, output levels, and consumption patterns into the six intermediate and two final goods industries in the model. We then scaled the data up to the year 1995, using data from the *Survey of Current Business* on growth rates in the different industries modeled and information on 1995 electricity and fossil fuel use from the 1997 *Annual Energy Update*.[23]

In the model, the sensitivity of labor supply to the after-tax wage is controlled by the parameter σ_U. Based on the existing literature, we set $\sigma_U = 1.20$, which implies an uncompensated and compensated labor supply elasticity of 0.15 and 0.3, respectively.[24] The baseline labor tax rate is taken to be 40%, which is meant to account for taxes at both the Federal and state levels.[25]

The elasticities of substitution in production of intermediate and final goods are aggregated from those estimated by McKibbin and Wilcoxen [22]. We adjusted the outer-nest elasticities (elasticity of substitution between labor, materials, and energy) so as to produce, in the absence of preexisting labor taxes, a schedule of marginal costs of carbon emissions abatement that closely matches the curve derived by Nordhaus [24] from a survey of existing studies. The resulting elasticities are given in Table IB.

[22] Our assumptions of competition and constant returns to scale imply product prices equal marginal cost and perfectly elastic supply curves. The computational algorithm used to solve the model only uses the government budget and carbon emissions conditions. By Walras's law, if these two conditions are satisfied, then the aggregate excess demand for labor must also equal zero. As a check on the computation, we verify that the third equilibrium condition holds, and that the result is consistent with the appropriate homogeneity conditions in prices and quantities.

[23] We scaled up non-energy-industry data to 1993, using industry-specific growth rates, and then scaled the data up to 1995 levels, using the rate of GDP growth from 1993–95, thus implicitly assuming that both nonenergy industries grew at the same rate from 1993–95. Energy industry data were scaled up based on 1995 use of each fuel and of electricity. We used Kuroda's method to ensure that the resulting data set met the necessary adding-up conditions. As shown in Section 5, our results are largely insensitive to the relative sizes of different industries.

[24] These elasticities also reflect the assumption that, in the initial data set, nonsleep leisure time equals 0.3 times hours worked. The labor supply elasticities are median estimates from the econometric literature (see the survey in Russek [37]). They represent the effects of changes in net wages on the participation rate and average hours per worker. We regard these values as conservative, since they do not capture the effect of changes in net wages on effort per hour. Other tax simulation models often assume somewhat higher values. For example, Bhattarai and Whalley [2] assume an uncompensated elasticity of 0.25.

[25] Other studies use comparable values. See, for example, Lucas [20] and Browning [7]. The sum of Federal income, state income, payroll, and consumption taxes amounts to around 36% of net national product. This average rate is relevant for the participation decision. The marginal tax rate, which affects effort level and hours worked per employee, is higher because of various tax deductions. Our values for tax rates and labor supply elasticities imply a marginal excess burden of labor taxation equal to 0.22 (when additional spending is returned as a lump-sum transfer).

TABLE I

Benchmark Data for the Numerical Model

A. Input-output flows (in millions of 1995 dollars, except for carbon emissions in millions of tons)

	F_C	F_P	F_N	E	I	N	C_I	C_N	l	Total input value
F_C	2874.4	33.1	0.5	7,729.2	3,267.6	1,453.4	490.8	9.7		15858.7
F_P	414.8	107,334.5	22,258.5	9,823.6	26,620.8	26,553.9	10,092.9	5,538.3		208637.2
F_N	10.5	21,371.3	36,113.9	8,987.5	11,196.6	12,315.4	2,761.8	202.8		92959.9
E	653.7	3,710.2	814.9	48.3	25,181.9	41,148.8	34,003.6	44.5		105605.9
I	1,569.9	22,155.8	1,512.5	10,879.4	338,137.4	469,948.4	116,320.4	8,778.8		969302.5
N	4892.5	33,651.2	16,157.5	38,359.5	233,261.9	3,326,713.5	291,455.2	2,699,669.1		6644160.3
L	5,442.9	20,381.1	16,102.1	29,778.5	331,636.4	2,766,027.0			932,167.0	4101534.9
Total output value	15,858.7	208,637.2	92,959.9	105,605.9	969,302.5	6,644,160.3	455,124.7	2,714,243.2		
e	507.3	598.7	317.6							1423.6

B. Parameter values

	Elasticity of substitution among energy, labor, and materials	σ_E elasticity of substitution in energy (fuels and electricity) nest	σ_M elasticity of substitution in materials nest
F_C	0.25	0.16	0.53
F_P	0.19	0.20	0.20
F_N	0.21	0.89	0.20
E	0.18	0.20	0.95
I	0.17	0.82	0.27
N	0.18	0.53	1.51
C_I	0.19	0.59	0.26
C_N	0.22	0.97	0.76

$\sigma_C = 0.5$, $\sigma_U = 1.2$ (elasticities of substitution between final goods and between consumption and leisure, respectively).

The carbon content for each of the three fossil fuel intermediate goods (β) is calculated by dividing the 1995 emissions of carbon from the burning of each fuel, as reported in the 1997 *Annual Energy Outlook*, by the quantity of each fuel burned. The α distribution parameters were calibrated based on the assumed elasticities of substitution and the identifying restriction that each industry utilized the cost-minimizing mix of inputs, or, equivalently, the restriction that in the absence of an emissions-control policy, the model will replicate the benchmark data.[26]

3.3. *Policy Proposals and Carbon Damage Scenarios*

The Kyoto Protocol calls for industrialized nations (the so-called Annex I countries) to achieve significant reductions in a basket of greenhouse gases (including CO_2) by 2008–2012. The United States, in particular, must achieve a level of emissions about 7% below 1990 levels. Under business-as-usual conditions, emissions are projected to grow significantly from the present time until 2008–2012; hence meeting the Kyoto targets would compel the United States to reduce its emissions by considerably more than 7%. In our numerical simulations, we consider emissions reductions ranging from 0% to 25%, a range that seems relevant to the reductions required by the Kyoto Protocol.

We consider a range of estimates for benefits from carbon abatement. Central estimates in the literature are typically below $20 per ton (for example, $5 per ton in Nordhaus [27]).[27] The "low" values for the central estimates reflect the notion that continued accumulation of greenhouse gases will not produce extreme changes in climate over the next century, and the idea that most economic activities are not exceptionally sensitive to modest climate change. In addition, discounting over long periods of time substantially reduces the benefit estimates, which are present values. However, under extreme values for climate change, sensitivity of the economy to such change, or discount rates, much higher benefit estimates arise. Under an extreme scenario, Nordhaus [23], for example, estimates benefits to be $66 per ton.[28] The simulations below aim to span a wide range of benefit scenarios, considering a range from $0 to $100 per ton. In all cases, we assume that marginal benefits are constant over the range of emissions reductions.[29]

4. NUMERICAL RESULTS

4.1. *Marginal Costs of Emissions Reduction*

Figure 1 shows how the preexisting labor tax affects the marginal cost of reductions in carbon emissions. The bottom curve is the marginal cost when there is no distortionary labor tax. This curve is roughly the same in real terms as that in

[26] For a discussion of calibration methods for general equilibrium models, see Shoven and Whalley [39].

[27] The first benefit estimate was $7 per ton, by Nordhaus [23]. Other estimates include $12 (Peck and Teisberg [33]) and $20 (Fankhauser [12]).

[28] The estimates have also been criticized for neglecting some ecosystem impacts, potentially adverse effects on the distribution of world income, and the possibility of nonlinearities within the climate system. Nordhaus [26] provides insightful commentary on these issues.

[29] This seems a reasonable approximation (see Pizer [34]).

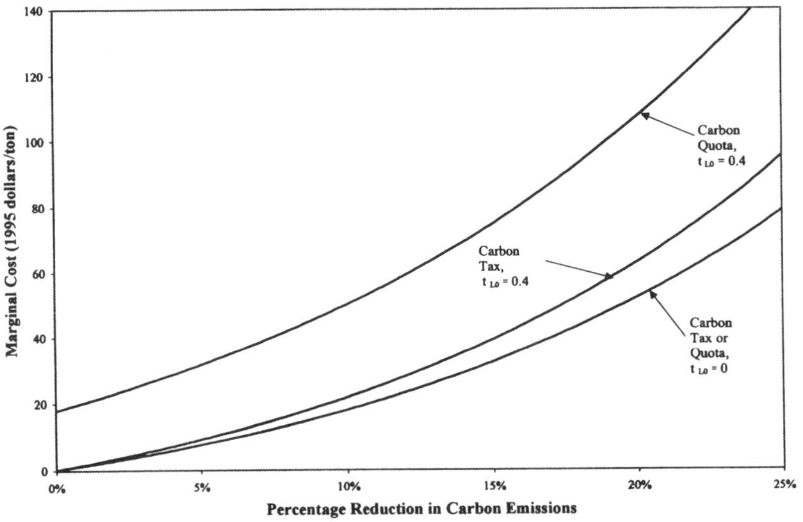

FIG. 1. Marginal cost of emissions reduction.

Nordhaus [24]. The curve is upward sloping, reflecting the increasing difficulty of substituting fossil fuels for other inputs in production. In a first-best world, the same curve applies whether the reduction is achieved by a tax or by a quota. In a second-best world, in contrast, the marginal cost curves differ significantly. In our central-case scenario, which assumes a preexisting labor tax (t_{L0}) of 40%, the quota policy shifts up the marginal cost curve, giving it a positive intercept. This upward shift reflects the tax-interaction effect. Under the carbon tax, the marginal cost curve pivots upward but retains the zero intercept that applies in the first-best case. The middle curve in Fig. 1 represents marginal costs under the carbon tax. The zero intercept reflects the fact that the revenue-recycling effect exactly offsets the tax-interaction effect at the first increment of abatement. The zero intercept implies that the carbon tax can increase welfare as long as marginal benefits from emissions reduction are positive. In contrast, under the quota, marginal benefits must exceed a strictly positive value ($17.8 per ton under central-case values for parameters) to increase welfare. These qualitative results were anticipated by the analytical model. The value of the intercept of the marginal cost under the quota is almost identical in both analytical and numerical models.[30]

[30]The intercept of the quota curve is somewhat lower than that implicit in the numerical model of Bovenberg and Goulder [5], which incorporates a much more detailed treatment of the tax system. In their model, a carbon tax with revenues recycled through lump-sum transfers is welfare-reducing unless marginal benefits from emissions reduction exceed $55 per ton. This policy would be equivalent to the above quota policy if there were no taxation of quota rents. When we assume no taxes on quota rents in the present model, the intercept of the marginal cost curve rises to $29.4 per ton (see Section 5). The bulk of the difference is due to our assumption of a lower (compensated) labor supply elasticity than in their model (we assume 0.3 for this elasticity, while Bovenberg and Goulder assume 0.6). In addition, Bovenberg and Goulder [5] incorporate preexisting taxes on gasoline, which increases marginal abatement costs.

4.2. *Average Costs of Emissions Reduction*

Here we examine the significance of preexisting distortionary taxes for the costs per ton of emissions reductions. Figure 2 displays these average costs under the tax and quota, expressed relative to the average cost of the same emissions reduction in a first-best setting with no preexisting labor tax.[31] For both policies, preexisting taxes imply higher costs at all levels of abatement than would occur if the labor tax were zero. At all levels of abatement, the cost of the carbon tax is about 22% higher when the preexisting labor tax is 0.4 than when there is no preexisting labor tax.[32] Under the quota policy, preexisting taxes have a much greater impact. The

[31] We compare average costs, rather than total costs, because baseline (unregulated) emissions are higher in the absence of a labor tax—eliminating the labor tax encourages labor supply.

[32] The ratio of average costs between the first- and second-best settings is constant with respect to the amount of emissions reduction, in the carbon tax case. This is because the marginal net loss from the tax-interaction and revenue-recycling effects changes in proportion to the slope of the primary marginal cost of emissions reduction.

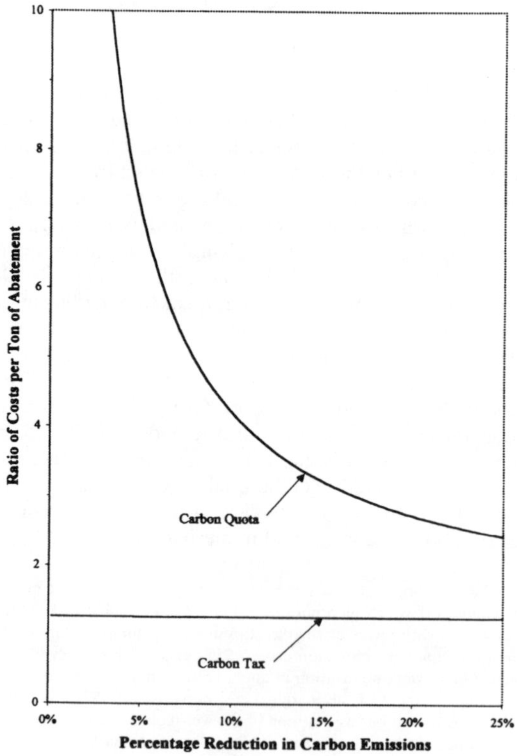

FIG. 2. Ratio of second-best to first-best costs.

average cost of a 5% emissions reduction, for example, is six times as high with preexisting taxes than without; the average cost of a 15% emissions reduction is 2.6 times as high. The very high ratios reflect the fact that the marginal costs of abatement begin at a strictly positive level in a second-best setting, whereas they start at zero in the absence of prior taxes, as shown in Fig. 1.

Figure 2 shows that, on efficiency grounds, preexisting taxes put the quota policy at a considerable disadvantage relative to the tax policy. For all levels of emissions reduction up to 25%, the cost of the quota is more than double that of the tax. Whatever the benefits of reducing carbon emissions, there is a strong efficiency case for preferring the carbon tax to the carbon quota. Note that the relative discrepancy between the tax and quota declines with the level of abatement. The marginal tax-interaction effect is approximately constant, but marginal tax revenue and hence the marginal revenue-recycling effect are declining. This occurs because the carbon tax base (F in (2.13)) declines with abatement. Eventually, marginal tax revenue would become negative (when the downward sloping part of the Laffer curve is reached). In the limit, at 100% emissions reduction, the total costs of the tax and quota are identical. At this point, no revenues are raised under the tax, and hence there is no revenue-recycling effect and no difference between the tax and quota policies.[33]

Our results indicate that in a second-best setting, under a carbon quota (or grandfathered tradeable permits), even "small" amounts of abatement involve large costs. Thus, for example, the total cost of using a quota to reduce emissions by 5% is (a substantial) $1.75 billion per annum. These costs reflect the presence of a significant tax-interaction effect (that is not offset by a revenue-recycling effect).[34]

4.3. *Welfare Impacts under Second-Best Optimal Emissions Reduction*

The second-best optimal emissions reduction is easily inferred from Fig. 1: it is where a given (constant) marginal benefits curve intersects the applicable marginal cost curve. The second-best optimal emissions reduction under the tax is slightly less than 90% of the optimal reduction when there is no preexisting labor tax. Under the carbon quota, the optimal emissions reduction is zero if damages are below $17.8 per ton. If damages are "high," say $60 per ton, the optimal emissions reduction is 12.3% and 19.5% respectively, under the quota and tax, and 21.7% if there were no labor tax.

Figure 3 shows the maximum welfare gain—that is, the welfare gain from the second-best optimal emissions reduction—under each policy as a function of environmental damages per ton of emissions. For any level of damages, the maximum welfare gain under the carbon tax is around 75% of the maximum gain when there is no labor tax. However, for the carbon quota, the maximized welfare gain is much less; even if damages are $70 per ton, the maximum welfare gain is only $6 billion, or 36% of the maximum gain in a first-best setting.

[33] For more discussion of this see Goulder *et al.* [16].

[34] Results similar to those in Figs. 1 and 2 were obtained by Goulder *et al.* [16], in their study of the SO_2 permit program. They estimated that the threshold benefit level below which an SO_2 quota cannot increase welfare is $103 per ton. In their equivalent of Fig. 2, the cost of the 50% emissions reduction mandated by the program is 70% higher because of preexisting taxes.

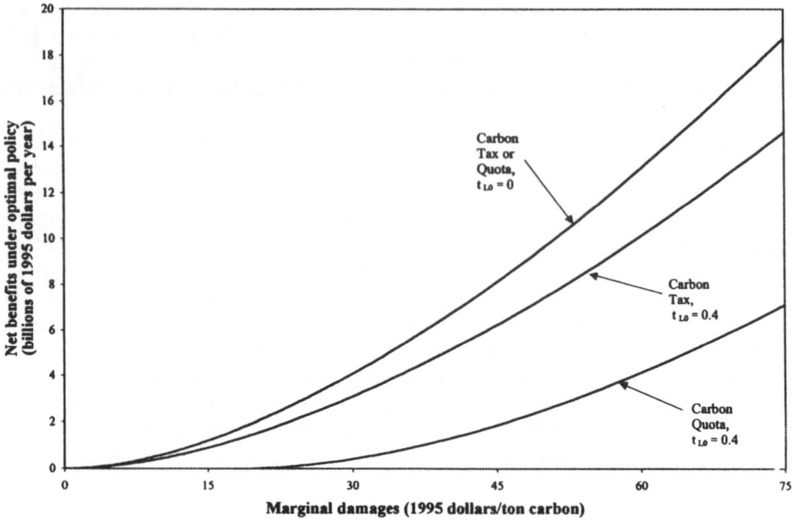

FIG. 3. Net welfare gain from the optimal level of regulation.

4.4. *Welfare Impacts under the Pigouvian Rule*

Figure 4 shows the welfare impact under the carbon tax and quota, if the Pigouvian or first-best rule is followed: that is, if the regulation reduces carbon emissions by the same fraction as the optimal policy in a world without labor taxes. Under the carbon tax, the welfare change is always positive, and around 75% of that when there is no preexisting labor tax, for any level of damages. However, imposing the carbon quota at the Pigouvian level *reduces* welfare, unless damages exceed $55 per ton. This welfare loss can be substantial; for example, it is $2.1 billion, if damages per ton are $20. Even if damages are $100 per ton, the welfare gain from the quota is only $8.9 billion, or 30% of the gain when there is no preexisting labor tax. Thus, following the optimal policy rule implied by a first-best analysis can lead to perverse welfare impacts.

5. SENSITIVITY ANALYSIS

Table II summarizes the sensitivity of marginal abatement costs to a range of values for important parameters. We vary the elasticity of substitution among the intermediate inputs in production, the labor supply elasticity, the preexisting labor tax rate, and the share of fossil fuels in the economy. In addition, we consider the implications of allowing quota rents to remain untaxed.

The elasticity of substitution among intermediate inputs in the outer nest of the production function drives the primary marginal cost of abatement. The larger the value of this parameter, the easier it is to substitute other intermediate goods for

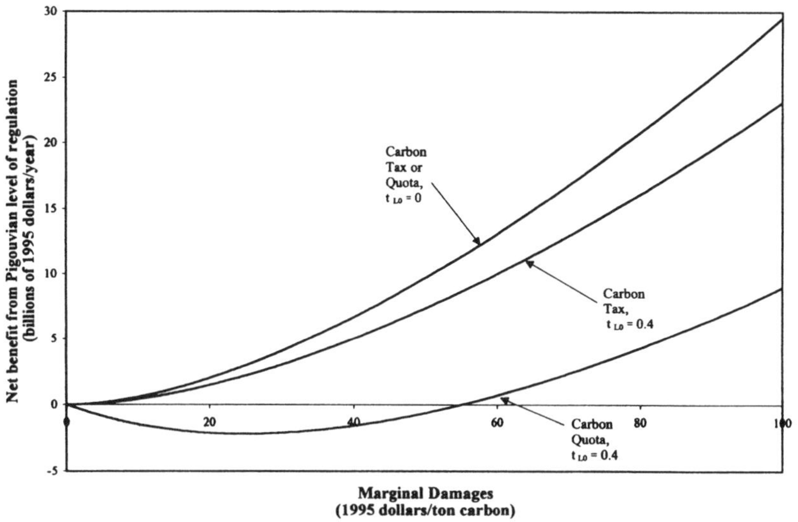

FIG. 4. Net welfare gain under the Pigouvian rule.

fossil fuels, and the lower the (marginal) cost of emissions reduction. The overall marginal cost equals the primary marginal cost plus the marginal net loss from the tax-interaction and revenue-recycling effects. As shown in rows 1a and b, this curve is somewhat sensitive to the production elasticity. However, even when this elasticity is increased by 50%, the marginal cost under the quota still has a substantial intercept of \$14.8 per ton.

The second row displays results when we vary the consumption/leisure substitution parameter σ_U. We alter this parameter so as to yield uncompensated labor supply elasticities ranging from 0 to 0.3, and associated compensated labor supply elasticities of 0.15–0.45. (These values roughly span the range of existing economy-wide econometric estimates.) This substantially affects costs under the quota. The intercept of the marginal cost function, in particular, varies between \$8.3 and \$29.8 per ton. This variation reflects the fact that the tax-interaction effect is directly related to the consumption/leisure elasticity. However, a larger consumption-leisure elasticity also implies a larger revenue-recycling effect, and hence the overall costs of the carbon tax are less sensitive to this change than those of the quota.

In the experiments reported in rows 3 and 4, we vary σ_U and the labor time endowment so as to alter either the uncompensated labor supply elasticity alone (row 3) or the compensated elasticity alone (row 4). These simulations indicate that the costs of the carbon quota are somewhat more sensitive to the compensated than to the uncompensated labor supply elasticity. This is because the recycling of quota rents offsets most of the income effect associated with higher consumption goods prices. The cost under the emissions tax is only sensitive to the uncompen-

TABLE II

Marginal Abatement Costs under Alternate Parameter Values and Model Specifications

	Carbon emission quota			Carbon tax		
	0%	10%	20%	0%	10%	20%
Central Case	17.8	50.0	107.1	0.1	21.7	63.0
1. Outer-nest production elasticities						
a. Elasticities 3/2 of base elasticity	14.8	37.2	73.1	0.1	16.7	44.6
b. Elasticities 2/3 of base elasticity	21.0	66.5	157.1	0.3	28.0	89.4
2. Both labor-supply elasticities						
a. $\varepsilon^u = 0.00$, $\varepsilon^c = 0.15$	8.3	32.9	78.2	0.1	19.8	57.6
b. $\varepsilon^u = 0.30$, $\varepsilon^c = 0.45$	29.8	71.5	143.6	0.3	24.6	70.7
3. Compensated labor supply elasticity						
a. $\varepsilon^u = 0.15$, $\varepsilon^c = 0.20$	12.2	41.3	94.6	0.2	21.9	63.4
b. $\varepsilon^u = 0.15$, $\varepsilon^c = 0.45$	26.6	63.8	128.3	0.2	21.9	63.5
4. Uncompensated labor supply elasticity						
a. $\varepsilon^u = 0.00$, $\varepsilon^c = 0.30$	16.2	45.6	98.1	0.1	19.8	57.7
b. $\varepsilon^u = 0.25$, $\varepsilon^c = 0.3$	19.4	55.1	119.7	0.2	23.6	68.1
5. Baseline tax rate						
a. $t_L = 0.5$	32.5	77.3	155.1	0.3	25.9	74.5
b. $t_L = 0.3$	10.5	36.5	83.4	0.1	20.1	58.1
c. $t_L = 0.0$	0.1	18.1	51.9	0.1	18.1	51.9
6. Share of fossil fuels in GDP						
a. share doubled	17.7	49.0	101.0	0.1	21.7	61.5
b. share halved	20.4	64.9	156.2	0.6	26.6	86.0
7. Quota rents not taxed	29.4	69.4	140.0	n/a	n/a	n/a

sated elasticity, since the increase in goods prices and reduction in labor tax rate are both uncompensated changes.

Thus, the absolute costs of the carbon quota and its cost relative to that of the carbon tax can be sensitive to different assumptions about labor supply elasticities. Nonetheless, even under extremely conservative values for labor supply elasticities, the marginal cost of the quota at zero abatement is still significantly above the central estimate of $5 per ton for marginal environmental benefits in Nordhaus [27] (see row 2a).

For a higher initial tax rate (row 5), the distortion between marginal social benefit and marginal social cost in the labor market is greater. Hence the revenue-recycling and tax-interaction effects are larger. Thus, increasing the tax rate leads to a more-than-proportionate increase in marginal costs.[35]

Row 6 illustrates that marginal costs from proportionate emissions reductions are not sensitive to changing the share of the fossil fuel sector in gross domestic product. While this change increases the sensitivity of consumption goods prices to fossil fuel prices, it also means that a ton of emissions reduction can be achieved with a smaller change in fossil fuel prices. Hence the cost of emissions reduction remains roughly the same.

[35]This is because the (marginal) tax-interaction and revenue-recycling effects are proportional to the marginal welfare cost of taxation, and this increases more than in proportion to the tax rate.

Our previous experiments assumed that the rents generated by an emissions quota are taxed at the same rate as labor income. Thus, even the quota policy generates government revenue and enjoys a small revenue-recycling effect.[36] Row 7 indicates that if quota rents are not taxed, the marginal cost of emissions reduction is greater, and the intercept is higher. Thus, the efficiency disadvantage of the quota is reduced to the extent that taxes are imposed on quota rents. However, as shown in Section 2.2, these rents would have to be taxed 100% for the quota to suffer no efficiency disadvantage relative to the carbon tax.

6. CONCLUSIONS AND CAVEATS

In this paper we have used analytical and numerical general equilibrium models to examine the efficiency impacts of revenue-neutral carbon taxes and quotas (or grandfathered carbon permits) in a second-best setting with preexisting labor taxes. For each of these policies, the efficiency costs are considerably higher than would be the case in the absence of prior taxes. These higher costs reflect the tax-interaction effect: the efficiency cost stemming from the regulation's impact on labor supply as a result of higher output prices and a reduction in the real wage.

Preexisting taxes imply especially high costs in the case of carbon quotas or grandfathered carbon permits. While emissions taxes and auctioned permits enjoy a revenue-recycling effect that offsets much of the tax-interaction effect, quotas and grandfathered permits policies do not exploit the revenue-recycling effect. The associated efficiency disadvantage can be very large: our central estimate is that, in the presence of prior labor taxes, achieving a 5% reduction in carbon emissions is almost 6 times as costly under a carbon quota as under a carbon tax; a 15% reduction is 2.6 times as costly.

Indeed, carbon quotas or grandfathered carbon permits may be unable to generate positive overall welfare gains. Our central estimate is that the marginal social cost of emissions reductions begins at $17.8 per ton for these policies. By comparison, typical estimates of marginal social benefits from carbon emissions reductions are below this level. This suggests that policies like carbon quotas and grandfathered carbon permits may be welfare-reducing, regardless of the level of carbon abatement. In contrast, carbon tax policies can be welfare-improving (provided that the level of abatement is not too great) because the marginal social costs of emissions reduction start at zero. In general, our results indicate that ignoring preexisting tax distortions can give rise to highly misleading conclusions about the sign as well as the magnitude of the welfare impacts from carbon abatement policies.

Some limitations to our analysis deserve mention. The analytical and numerical models are static, ignoring in particular the dynamics of capital accumulation. Considering capital as well as labor would introduce another relevant consideration in assessing the overall efficiency impacts: now these impacts would also depend on (1) preexisting inefficiencies in relative taxation of labor and capital, and (2) the extent to which carbon abatement policies might reduce these inefficiencies by

[36] For example, at a 10% emissions reduction, it generates rent tax revenues of $9.7 billion. However, the quota reduces the labor tax base, causing a loss of labor tax revenues that more than offsets the rent tax revenue, so the overall revenue change is −$1.6 billion. In contrast, a carbon tax with the same effect on emissions produces a net revenue gain of $13 billion.

shifting the tax burden from one factor to another. Bovenberg and Goulder [6] indicate that for the U.S. economy, capital appears to be overtaxed relative to labor; that is, the marginal excess burden of capital taxes appears to be higher than that of labor taxes. In this setting, carbon abatement policies that ultimately shift the tax burden toward labor will induce a beneficial tax-shifting effect that mitigates the efficiency costs. The reverse is true if abatement policies shift more of the tax toward capital. Empirical analysis by Bovenberg and Goulder suggests that abatement policies tend to shift the burden toward capital, since the energy sector is relatively capital intensive. Thus our exclusive focus on labor may have biased downward our assessment of efficiency costs.

Another limitation of our analysis is that it ignores preexisting distortions attributable to nontax factors such as noncompetitive market structures. Browning [8] suggests that nontax distortions add another 30% to the distortion in the labor market created by taxes. If so, incorporating nontax distortions into our analysis would significantly increase the importance of second-best interactions and reduce the efficiency gains from carbon abatement policies.[37]

In other respects, however, our analysis may understate the welfare gains from carbon abatement policies. First, by employing static models we disregard dynamic issues associated with the benefits from carbon abatement. Marginal damages from carbon emissions (or benefits from emissions abatement) could increase with CO_2 concentrations (for example, the concentration-damage relationship could exhibit significant threshold effects). If this is the case, and if CO_2 concentrations continue to rise, then marginal damages from CO_2 emissions (marginal benefits from abatement) will increase over time. Under such circumstances, a carbon quota might be able to yield welfare gains at some future date, when marginal damages are significantly higher. (However, in efficiency terms, it will always be better to adopt the carbon tax.) Second, carbon abatement policies—particularly carbon taxes—can produce dynamic efficiency gains by stimulating the invention and diffusion of less-carbon-intensive production technologies. This is especially important, to the extent that there are failures in the research market that have not been fully corrected by other government policies.[38] Third, the prospects for welfare gains also improve if one considers ancillary benefits from carbon abatement policies, such as benefits from the reduction in other fossil-fuel-related pollutants (e.g., sulfur oxides, nitrogen oxides, and particulates).

Finally, our analysis ignores distributional considerations. The decision whether to introduce a carbon tax or carbon quota fundamentally affects the distribution of wealth between taxpayers, on the one hand, and owners and employees of fossil-fuel-producing firms, on the other. Quota policies leave rents in producers' hands, while carbon taxes effectively tax these rents away. Some analysts might invoke these distributional impacts to favor the quota over the tax. The second-best issues examined in this paper do not diminish the importance of these distributional considerations, but at the same time they indicate that forgoing the redistribution toward taxpayers has efficiency costs that are much greater than would be suggested by a first best analysis.

[37] On the significance of monopoly price distortions, in particular, see also Oates and Strassmann [30].
[38] For further discussion of this issue, see, for example, Fischer *et al.* [13].

APPENDIX A: ANALYTICAL DERIVATIONS

Deriving Equation (2.8)

Given constant returns to scale, payments to inputs in the C_F industry exhaust value product (from Euler's theorem), that is,

$$p_F C_F = (\tau_F + q_F) F_F = q_N N_F + L_F, \qquad \text{(A1)}$$

where q_F and q_N are the supply prices of the intermediate goods F and N, and the purchase price of fossil fuels includes the carbon tax. Totally differentiating (A1) gives

$$dp_F C_F + p_F dC_F = d\tau_F F_F + (\tau_F + q_F) dF_F + q_N dN_F + dL_F, \qquad \text{(A2)}$$

because q_F and q_N are determined by marginal product of labor in the F and N industries, and the gross wage, which are all constant. From differentiating the production function (2.2), we obtain

$$dC_F = \frac{\partial C_F}{\partial L_F} dL_F + \frac{\partial C_F}{\partial F_F} dF_F + \frac{\partial C_F}{\partial N_F} dN_F. \qquad \text{(A3)}$$

Also, from the first-order conditions for profit maximization, the marginal products equal the input price divided by the product price, or

$$\frac{\partial C_F}{\partial L_F} = \frac{1}{p_F}; \quad \frac{\partial C_F}{\partial F_F} = \frac{\tau + q_F}{p_F}; \quad \frac{\partial C_F}{\partial N_F} = \frac{q_N}{p_F}. \qquad \text{(A4)}$$

Substituting (A4) in (A3), multiplying through by p_F, and subtracting from (A2) gives the expression for $dp_F/d\tau_F$ in (2.8). The same procedure gives the analogous expression for $dp_N/d\tau_F$.

Deriving Equation (2.9)

From the cost minimization problem for firms in the C_F and C_N industries, we can derive the demands for inputs, conditional on the level of output, and input prices. Input prices can be summarized by τ_F, since q_F, q_N and the gross wage are all fixed. Therefore, the conditional demands for fossil fuel are

$$F_F(\tau_F, C_F); \quad F_N(\tau_F, C_N). \qquad \text{(A5)}$$

In equilibrium, the final output produced by firms equals that demanded by households. Therefore, substituting the expressions for C_F and C_N from (2.5) into (A5), and noting from (2.8) that changes in product prices are determined by changes in τ_F, the equilibrium quantity of fossil fuels is summarized by (2.9).

Deriving Equation (2.11)

Fixing government spending in real terms implies that

$$dG = \frac{G}{p_C} dp_C, \qquad \text{(A6)}$$

where p_C is the composite price of consumption, which is arbitrarily normalized so that

$$p_C = p_F s_F + p_N s_N. \tag{A7}$$

s_F and s_N are the expenditure shares for the two consumption goods, given by $s_F = p_F C_F / I$, $s_N = p_N C_N / I$, where I denotes household income which is given by $I = G + (1 - t_L)L$.

Taking a total derivative of (A7) for a change in τ_F^t, substituting in (2.8) and (2.9), rearranging, and substituting into (A6) give

$$\frac{dG}{d\tau_F^t} = s_G F. \tag{A8}$$

Totally differentiating (2.10) and substituting in (A8) and $dF/d\tau_F^t = \partial F/\partial \tau_F^t + (\partial F/\partial t_L)(dt_L/d\tau_F^t)$ give (2.11).

Deriving Equation (2.14)

Using (2.5), (2.12), and (2.13), the tax-interaction effect can be expressed as

$$\begin{aligned} \partial W^I &= -\frac{L}{L + t_L(\partial L/\partial t_L)} \left(\frac{\partial L/\partial t_L}{\partial L/\partial t_L} \right) t_L \frac{\partial L}{\partial \tau_F^t} + ZFs_G \\ &= \frac{ZL}{\partial L/\partial t_L} \left\{ \frac{\partial L}{\partial p_F} \frac{dp_F}{d\tau_F^t} + \frac{\partial L}{\partial p_N} \frac{dp_N}{d\tau_F^t} \right\} + Z'' F s_G. \end{aligned}$$

Substituting the Slutsky equations, (2.8) and (2.9) give

$$\partial W^I = ZL \left\{ \frac{(\partial L^c/\partial p_F)(F_F/C_F) + (\partial L^c/\partial p_N)(F_N/C_N) - (\partial L/\partial I)F}{(\partial L^c/\partial t_L) - (\partial L/\partial I)L} \right\} + Z'' F s_G, \tag{A9}$$

where c denotes a compensated coefficient. From the Slutsky symmetry property:

$$\frac{\partial L^c}{\partial p_F} = \frac{\partial C_F^c}{\partial (1 - t_L)}; \quad \frac{\partial L^c}{\partial p_N} = \frac{\partial C_N^c}{\partial (1 - t_L)}. \tag{A10}$$

Taking a total derivative of household utility (2.1) while holding the level of utility constant gives

$$\frac{\partial L^c}{\partial t_L} = -\frac{\partial L^c}{\partial (1 - t_L)} = -\left\{ \frac{p_F}{1 - t_L} \frac{\partial C_F^c}{\partial (1 - t_L)} + \frac{p_N}{1 - t_L} \frac{\partial C_N^c}{\partial (1 - t_L)} \right\}. \tag{A11}$$

Making these substitutions in (A9) and rearranging, we obtain (2.14), where

$$\eta_{FI}^c = \frac{\partial C_F^c}{\partial (1 - t_L)} \frac{1 - t_L}{C_F}; \quad \eta_{NI}^c = \frac{\partial C_N^c}{\partial (1 - t_L)} \frac{1 - t_L}{C_N};$$

$$h_F = \frac{F_F}{F}; \quad h_N = \frac{F_N}{F}.$$

Deriving Equation (2.13′)

Following an approach similar to that as used to derive (2.11) in the case of the quota yields

$$\frac{dt_L}{d\tau_F^q} = -\frac{t_L\{F + \tau_F^q\, dF/d\tau_F^q + \partial L/\partial\tau_F^q\} - Fs_G}{L + \pi + t_L\, \partial L/\partial t_L}. \qquad (2.11')$$

The indirect utility function now includes net income from quota rents, $(1 - t_L)\pi$. Equations (2.7) and (2I.8) are the same as before, except that $\partial Lv/\partial t_L = -\lambda(L + \pi)$. Differentiating the indirect utility function with respect to τ_F^q, making substitutions analogous to those already mentioned, and using

$$\frac{\partial v}{\partial[(1 - t_L)\pi]}\frac{d[(1 - t_L)\pi]}{d\tau_F^q} = \lambda\left\{(1 - t_L)\left[F + \tau_F^q\frac{dF}{d\tau_F^q}\right] - \pi\frac{dt_L}{d\tau_F^q}\right\}$$

give, after some manipulation, (2.13′).

Deriving Equation (2.15)

Using (2.12′) and (2.13′), when $\tau_F^q = \pi = 0$, gives

$$\partial W^I - \partial W^R = t_L\frac{L(-\partial L/\partial\tau_F^q) + t_L F\,\partial L/\partial t_L}{L + t_L\,\partial L/\partial t_L}. \qquad (A12)$$

Changes in τ_F^q affect rents, therefore

$$\frac{\partial L}{\partial\tau_F^q} = \frac{\partial L^u}{\partial\tau_F^q} + \frac{\partial L}{\partial I}\frac{\partial[(1 - t_L)\pi]}{\partial\tau_F^q} = \frac{\partial L^u}{\partial\tau_F^q} + \frac{\partial L}{\partial I}(1 - t_L)F^0, \qquad (A13)$$

where "u" denotes uncompensated. Substituting (A13) and the Slutsky equations for $\partial L^u/\partial\tau_F^q$ and $\partial L/\partial t_L$ in (A12), and multiplying and dividing by $t_L\,\partial L^c/\partial t_L$ give

$$\partial W^I - \partial W^R = F^0\left\{\frac{(\partial L^c/\partial\tau_F^q)L}{(\partial L^c/\partial t_L)F^0} - t_L\right\}\frac{t_L(-\partial L^c/\partial t_L)}{L + t_L\partial L/\partial t_L}. \qquad (A14)$$

Substituting

$$\frac{\partial L^c}{\partial\tau_F^q} = \frac{\partial L^c}{\partial p_F}\frac{dp_F}{d\tau_F^q} + \frac{\partial L^c}{\partial p_N}\frac{dp_N}{d\tau_F^q},$$

(2.8), (A10), (A11), and the definitions of η_{FI}^c and η_{NI}^c, when these elasticities are equal, in (A14) gives (2.15), where

$$\varepsilon^u = \frac{\partial L}{\partial(1 - t_L)}\frac{1 - t_L}{L}; \quad \varepsilon^c = \frac{\partial L^c}{\partial(1 - t_L)}\frac{1 - t_L}{L}.$$

APPENDIX B: THE NUMERICAL MODEL

Except where otherwise noted, i ranges over L, F_N, F_C, F_P, E, I, and N, which represent inputs in production. Similarly, j ranges over F_N, F_C, F_P, E, I, G, C_P, and C_N, which represent goods produced.

I. *Parameters*

Firm Behavior Parameters

a_{ij}	distribution parameter for input i in production of good j
ρ_j, ρ_{jm}, ρ_{jg}	substitution parameters for production of good j, in outer nest, materials nest, and energy nest, respectively (note: $\rho = (\sigma - 1)/\sigma$ where σ is the elasticity of substitution)

Household Behavior Parameters

$\bar{L}$	total labor endowment
α_l, α_{CF}, α_{C_N}, α_{C_I}	distribution parameters for utility function
r_C, r_U	substitution parameters for utility function

Government Policy Parameters

$\bar{e}$	carbon emissions target
$\bar{e}_j$	carbon quota for industry j
G	government spending (transfers to households, in real terms)

Emissions Parameters

b_j	emissions of carbon per unit of good j used (note: b_j is nonzero only for j ranging over F_N, F_C, and F_P)

II. *Endogenous Variables*

a_{ij}	use of input i per unit of output of good j
C_I and C_N	aggregate demands for energy-intensive and nonintensive final goods
C	aggregate demand for composite consumption good
AD_i	aggregate demand for good i
X_j	aggregate supply of good j
L	aggregate labor supply
l	leisure or nonmarket time
p_C	price of composite final good
p_j	price of good j
π	total carbon quota rents
REV	government revenue
e_i	carbon emitted from use of good i (note: here i ranges only over F_N, F_C, and F_P)

e_i	total carbon emissions
U	total consumer utility
ϕ	utility associated with carbon emissions
X_{ij}	use of good i in production of good j

III. *Equations*

Production Functions and Optimal Input Intensities

In all industries, output is produced according to

$$X_J = \left[\left(\sum_{i\in m} \alpha_{i,j} X_{i,j}^{\rho_{jm}}\right)^{\rho_j/\rho_{jm}} + \left(\sum_{i\in g} \alpha_{i,j} X_{i,j}^{\rho_{jg}}\right)^{\rho_j/\rho_{jg}} + \alpha_{L,j} X_{L,j}^{\rho_j}\right]^{1/\rho_j} \tag{B1}$$

$$m = \{I, N\}, \quad g = \{F_N, F_C, F_P, E\}, \quad j = \{F_N, F_C, F_P, E, I, N, C_I, C_N\}.$$

Profit for industry j is given by

$$\pi_j = (p_j - \beta_j \tau_t) X_j - \sum_I p_i X_{i,j}. \tag{B2}$$

Differentiating profit with respect to the inputs X_{ij} yields the first order conditions for the optimal input mix:

$$a_{ij} \equiv \frac{X_{ij}}{X_j} = \left(\frac{p_j - \beta_j \tau_t}{p_{ij}}\right)^{1/(i-\rho_j)}$$

$$i = \{g, m, L\} \text{ (note: } \beta_j = 0 \text{ for } j = E, I, N, C_I, C_N), \tag{B3}$$

where X_m and X_g are the composite material and energy inputs, and p_m and p_g are the prices of these composite inputs. The makeup of the composites is given by

$$a_{ijm} \equiv \frac{X_{ij}}{X_{mj}} = \alpha_{ij}^{1/(1-\rho_{jm})}\left(\frac{p_{mj}}{p_i}\right)^{1/(1-\rho_{jm})} \quad i = \{I, N\};$$

$$a_{ijg} \equiv \frac{X_{ij}}{X_{gj}} = \alpha_{ij}^{1/(1-\rho_{jg})}\left(\frac{p_{gj}}{p_i}\right)^{1/(1-\rho_{jg})} \quad g = \{F_N, F_C, F_P, E\} \tag{B4}$$

Equations (B2)–(B4) assume that carbon regulation is accomplished through a carbon tax. Firm behavior will be identical under a carbon quota. In this case, profit for industry j is

$$\pi_j = p_j X_j - \sum_I p_i X_{i,j}, \tag{B5}$$

with the constraint that industry emissions equal the industry emissions quota $\bar{e}_j$:

$$\beta_j X_j = \bar{e}_j. \tag{B6}$$

Maximizing profit under this constraint yields the Lagrangian function

$$p_j X_j - \sum_I p_i X_{i,j} - \lambda_j(\beta_j X_j - \bar{e}_j). \tag{B7}$$

If the carbon quota is set such that the shadow price of carbon emissions λ_j equals τ_t the Lagrangian function in Eq. (B7) is equal to the profit function in Eq. (B2) with an additional constant term $\tau_t \bar{e}_j$, which represents quota rents.[39] Therefore, the first-order conditions resulting from this maximization will be the same as from maximizing Eq. (B2), implying that the carbon quota can be modeled as a virtual carbon tax in determining firm behavior.

Finally, substituting Eqs. (B1), (B3), and (B4) into Eq. (B2) and differentiating with respect to the quantity produced, X_j yields an equation for the output price:

$$p_j = \sum_i p_i a_{ij} + \tau \beta_j, \tag{B8}$$

where τ is either the carbon tax or the virtual carbon tax, depending on whether the pollution-control policy is a tax or a quota. Solving this equation simultaneously for all intermediate goods yields the price vector for the intermediate goods.

Household Utility Function: Labor Supply and Final Good Demands

The representative household's utility function is

$$U = U(l, C_I, C_N, e) = \left(\alpha_l l^{\rho_u} + \alpha_C C^{\rho_u}\right)^{1/\rho_u} + \phi(e), \tag{B9}$$

where C represents composite consumption:

$$C = \left(\alpha_{C_I} C_I^{\rho_C} + \alpha_{C_N} C_N^{\rho_C}\right)^{1/\rho_C}. \tag{B10}$$

The household maximizes utility subject to the budget constraint

$$p_{C_I} C_I + p_{C_N} C_N = p_L(1 - t_L)L + (1 - t_R)\pi + G \tag{B11}$$

and the time endowment $l + L = \overline{L}$. This maximization yields the following equations, which express the household's behavior:

$$a_{C_I} \equiv \frac{C_I}{C} = \left[\alpha_{C_I} + \alpha_{C_N}\left(\frac{\alpha_{C_I} p_{C_N}}{\alpha_{C_N} p_{C_I}}\right)^{\rho_C/(\rho_C - 1)}\right]^{1/\rho_C} \tag{B12}$$

$$a_{C_N} \equiv \frac{C_N}{C} = \left[\alpha_{C_N} + \alpha_{C_I}\left(\frac{\alpha_{C_N} p_{C_I}}{\alpha_{C_I} p_{C_N}}\right)^{\rho_C/(\rho_C - 1)}\right]^{1/\rho_C} \tag{B13}$$

$$p_C = p_{C_I} a_{C_I} + p_{C_N} a_{C_N} \tag{B14}$$

[39] This assumes that the shadow price of carbon emissions will be the same across all polluting industries, as would be the case under a tradeable quota, but would not necessarily be the case under a nontradeable quota. If the shadow price differed across industries, firm behavior could still be modeled with a virtual tax, but the virtual tax would also vary across industries. In the rest of this analysis, we assume that the virtual tax is constant across industries.

$$l = \frac{p_L(1 - t_L)\bar{L} + p_C G + (1 - t_R)\pi}{p_L(1 - t_L) + p_C[\alpha_l p_C/\alpha_C p_L(1 - t_L)]^{1/(\rho_U - 1)}} \tag{B15}$$

$$L = \bar{L} - l \tag{B16}$$

$$C = p_C^{-1}[p_L(1 - t_L)L + p_C G + (1 - t_R)\pi]. \tag{B17}$$

Combining (B17) with (B11) or (B12) yields the optimal levels of C_I and C_N.

Government

Government revenues finance government transfers to households G, which are fixed in real terms. Revenues (REV) are determined by

$$REV = t_L L + \tau_t e + t_R \pi, \tag{B18}$$

where $\pi = \tau_q \bar{e}$, τ_q is the virtual carbon tax in the emissions quota case, and τ_t is the actual carbon tax. Under a carbon tax, the reverse is true.

Throughout most of this analysis, we assume that the tax on rents is the same as the tax on labor income; thus

$$t_R = t_L. \tag{B19}$$

Aggregate Demand and Supply

Aggregate demand for the two final goods is determined by the household, through Eq. (B17) and Eq. (B11) or (B12). Aggregate demand for labor and for the six intermediate goods is determined from the use of each good in production, yielding

$$AD_i = \sum_j X_{ij}. \tag{B20}$$

Since production of all goods follows constant returns to scale, supplies of both final goods and the six intermediate goods are determined by demand. Thus

$$X_{C_I} = C_I \tag{B21}$$

$$X_{C_N} = C_N \tag{B22}$$

$$X_i = AD_i \quad \text{for } i \text{ ranging over } F_N, F_C, F_P, E, I, \text{ and } N. \tag{B23}$$

Solving this last equation simultaneously for all values of i yields aggregate supplies and demands for the intermediate goods.

IV. *Equilibrium Conditions*

The equilibrium conditions are

$$L = AD_L \tag{B24}$$

$$e = \bar{e} \tag{B25}$$

$$REV = G. \tag{B26}$$

To solve the model, we compute the values of τ and t_L that satisfy (B25) and (B26), using p_L as the numeraire. By Walras's Law, if two of the three equilibrium conditions hold, the third will also hold, so the vector of primary prices that satisfies (B25) and (B26) also satisfies (B24).

REFERENCES

1. C. L. Ballard and S. G. Medema, The marginal efficiency effects of taxes and subsidies in the presence of externalities: A computational general equilibrium approach, *J. Public Econom.* **52**, 199–216 (1993).
2. K. Bhattarai and J. Whalley, "Discreteness and the Welfare Cost of Labor Supply Tax Distortions," NBER working paper no. 6280, Cambridge, MA (1997).
3. A. L. Bovenberg and R. A. de Mooij, Environmental levies and distortionary taxation, *Amer. Econom. Rev.* **84**, 1085–1089 (1994).
4. A. L. Bovenberg and F. van der Ploeg, Environmental policy, public finance and the labor market in a second-best world, *J. Public Econom.* **55**, 349–390 (1994).
5. A. L. Bovenberg and L. H. Goulder, Optimal environmental taxation in the presence of other taxes: general equilibrium analyses, *Amer. Econom. Rev.* **86**, 985–1000 (1996).
6. A. L. Bovenberg and L. H. Goulder, Costs of environmentally-motivated taxes in the presence of other taxes: General equilibrium analyses, *Nat. Tax J.* **50**, 59–88 (1997).
7. E. K. Browning, On the marginal welfare cost of taxation, *Amer. Econom. Rev.* **77**, 11–23 (1987).
8. E. K. Browning, The non-tax wedge, *J. Public Econom.* **53**, 419–433 (1994).
9. E. K. Browning, The welfare cost of monopoly and other output distortions, *J. Public Econom.* **66**, 127–144 (1997).
10. M. Cruz and L. H. Goulder, An intertemporal general equilibrium model for analyzing U.S. energy and environmental policies: data documentation, unpublished manuscript, Stanford University (1992).
11. A. Deaton, Optimal taxes and the structure of preferences, *Econometrica*, **49**, 1245–1259 (1981).
12. S. Fankhauser, The social costs of greenhouse gas emissions: An expected value approach, *Energy J.* **15**, 157–184 (1994).
13. C. Fischer, I. W. H. Parry, and W. A. Pizer, "Instrument Choice for Environmental Protection When Technological Innovation is Endogenous," discussion paper, Resources for the Future, Washington, DC (1998).
14. D. Fullerton and G. Metcalf, "Environmental Controls, Scarcity Rents, and Pre-existing Distortions," NBER working paper no. 6091, Cambridge, MA (1997).
15. L. H. Goulder, Effects of carbon taxes in an economy with prior tax distortions: An intertemporal general equilibrium analysis, *J. Environ. Econom. Management* **29**, 271–297 (1995).
16. L. H. Goulder, I. W. H. Parry and D. Burtraw, Revenue-raising vs. other approaches to environmental protection: The critical significance of pre-existing tax distortions, *RAND J. Econom.* **28**, 708–731 (1997).
17. L. Hakonsen, An investigation into alternative representations of the marginal cost of public funds, *International Tax and Public Finance* **5**, 329–343 (1998).
18. M. Hoel, Efficient international agreements for reducing emissions of CO_2, *Energy J.* **12**, 93–107 (1991).
19. D. R. Lee and W. S. Misiolek, Substituting pollution taxation for general taxation: Some implications for efficiency in pollution taxation, *J. Environ. Econom. Management* **13**, 338–347 (1996).
20. R. E. Lucas, Supply-side economics: An analytical review, *Oxford Econom. Papers* **42**, 293–316 (1990).
21. A. S. Manne, and R. Richels, "Buying Greenhouse Insurance," MIT Press, Cambridge, MA (1992).
22. W. McKibbin and P. Wilcoxen, The theoretical and empirical structure of G-cubed, unpublished manuscript, Brookings Institution, Washington, DC (1992).
23. W. D. Nordhaus, To slow or not to slow: The economics of the greenhouse effect, *Econom. J.* **101**, 920–937 (1991).
24. W. D. Nordhaus, The cost of slowing climate change: A survey, *Energy J.* **12**, 37–65 (1991).
25. W. D. Nordhaus, Optimal greenhouse gas reductions and tax policy in the "DICE" Model, *Amer. Econom. Rev.* **83**, 313–317 (1993).

26. W. D. Nordhaus, Reflections on the economics of climate change, *J. Econom. Perspectives* **7**, 11–26 (1993).
27. W. D. Nordhaus, Managing the global commons: The economics of climate change, MIT Press, Cambridge, MA (1994).
28. W. E. Oates, Green taxes: Can we protect the environment and improve the tax system at the same time? *Southern Econom. J.* **61**, 914–922 (1995).
29. W. E. Oates and P. R. Portney, Economic incentives and the containment of global warming, *Eastern Econom. J.* **18**, 85–98 (1992).
30. W. E. Oates and D. L. Strassmann, Effluent fees and market structure, *J. Public Econom.* **24**, 29–46 (1984).
31. I. W. H. Parry, Pollution taxes and revenue recycling, *J. Environ. Econom. Management* **29**, S64–S77 (1995).
32. I. W. H. Parry, Environmental taxes and quotas in the presence of distorting taxes in factor markets, *Res. Energy Econom.* **19**, 203–220 (1997).
33. S. C. Peck and T. J. Teisberg, Global warming uncertainties and the value of information: An analysis using CETA, *Res. Energy Econom.* **15**, 71–98 (1993).
34. W. A. Pizer, "Prices vs. Quantities Revisited: The Case of Climate Change," discussion paper no. 98-02, Resources for the Future, Washington, DC (1997).
35. J. M. Poterba, Global warming: A public finance perspective, *J. Econom. Perspectives* **7**, 47–63 (1993).
36. R. Repetto, R. C. Dower, R. Jenkins and J. Geoghegan, "Green Fees: How a Tax Shift Can Work for the Environment and the Economy," World Resources Institute, Washington, DC (1992).
37. F. Russek, "Taxes and Labor Supply," working paper, Congressional Budget Office, Washington, DC (1996).
38. A. Sandmo, Optimal taxation in the presence of externalities, *Swedish J. Econom.* **77**, 86–98 (1975).
39. J. B. Shoven and J. Whalley, "Applying General Equilibrium," Cambridge Univ. Press, Cambridge, England (1992).
40. D. Terkla, The efficiency value of effluent tax revenues, *J. Environ. Econom. Management* **11**, 107–123 (1984).
41. T. H. Tietenberg, Economic instruments for environmental regulation, *in* "Economic Policy Towards the Environment" (Dieter Holm, Ed.), Blackwell, Cambridge, MA (1991).
42. H. R. Varian, "Microeconomic Analysis," Norton, New York (1992).
43. R. C. Williams, "The Impact of Pre-existing Taxes on the Benefits of Regulations Affecting Health or Productivity," working paper, Stanford University, Stanford, CA (1997).

[26]

ELSEVIER

Journal of Public Economics 80 (2001) 249–267

JOURNAL OF PUBLIC ECONOMICS

www.elsevier.nl/locate/econbase

Environmental controls, scarcity rents, and pre-existing distortions

Don Fullerton[a], Gilbert E. Metcalf[b,*]

[a]*Department of Economics, University of Texas at Austin, and NBER, Austin, TX, USA*
[b]*Department of Economics, Tufts University, and NBER, Medford, MA 02155, USA*

Received 31 March 1999; received in revised form 31 December 1999; accepted 31 January 2000

Abstract

One might suppose that an emissions tax has an advantage over command and control (CAC) regulations since it raises revenue that can be used to cut other distorting taxes. In this paper, we show that the focus on revenue raising is misplaced. In a simple analytical general equilibrium model, we show that the same welfare effects of environmental protection can be achieved, by taxes that raise revenue, certain command and control regulations that raise no revenue, and even subsidies that cost revenue. Instead, the pre-existing labor tax distortion is exacerbated by policies that generate privately-retained scarcity rents.

Keywords: Emissions tax; Scarcity rents; Command and control regulations

JEL classification: H2; Q2

1. Introduction

A large literature considers the choice among environmental policy instruments such as emission taxes, abatement subsidies, tradeable permits, or command and control (CAC) regulations. For a given amount of environmental protection, one might naturally suppose that the emissions tax has the important advantage that the revenues can be used to reduce other distorting taxes on labor or capital incomes.

*Corresponding author. Tel.: +1-617-627-3685; fax: +1-617-627-3917.
E-mail address: gmetcalf@tufts.edu (G.E. Metcalf).

0047-2727/01/$ – see front matter
PII: S0047-2727(00)00087-6

In contrast, CAC regulations raise no revenue at all. Using this logic, an environmental subsidy would rank lowest on efficiency grounds, since the government must cover the cost of the subsidy by *raising* other distorting taxes.[1]

A related literature on the 'double-dividend hypothesis' does not compare instruments for a given amount of environmental protection, but instead considers whether a pollution tax can *increase* environmental protection and also raise revenue that can be used to reduce other distorting taxes. Again, note the role of revenues in this early statement of the hypothesis (Pearce, 1991, p. 940):

> Governments may then adopt a fiscally neutral stance on the carbon tax, using revenues to finance reductions in incentive-distorting taxes such as income tax, or corporation tax. This 'double-dividend' feature of a pollution tax is of critical importance in the political debate about the means of securing a 'carbon convention'.

As shown in Bovenberg and de Mooij (1994) and Parry (1995), the pollution tax itself raises product prices, which reduces the real net wage and further distorts labor supply. Thus the double dividend is in doubt, but raising revenue is still considered important for cutting labor tax rates and offsetting that effect.[2]

In this paper, we offer a different perspective on the role of revenue. Using an analytical general equilibrium model similar to those in a number of papers listed above, we compare different policy instruments and show an important sense in which the revenue from an environmental tax is *irrelevant*. Specifically, earlier studies typically show that the incremental environmental policies that are least costly are those that raise revenue. Although these studies show that raising revenue is not a sufficient condition for zero marginal costs of abatement at the origin (see, for example, cases of emissions taxes with lump-sum recycling of the revenue), they can leave the impression that raising revenue is necessary. This paper demonstrates that raising revenue is neither necessary nor sufficient.[3]

---

[1]Tullock (1967) first suggested that emission taxes have no excess burden but instead have 'excess benefit', and that the revenue may be 'free' (p. 643). Terkla (1984) also considers the 'efficiency value of effluent tax revenues'. The idea that subsidies are inferior on the basis of the lost revenue appears in, for example, Ballard and Medema (1993, p. 215) and Rosen (1995, p. 102).

[2]Other papers that discuss the revenue value of pollution taxes include Lee and Misiolek (1986), Repetto et al. (1992), Bovenberg and Goulder (1996), Parry (1997), and Goulder et al. (1997). The 'double dividend' is reviewed in Goulder (1995) and Oates (1995).

[3]We thank Larry Goulder for helping us clarify the differences among papers in this literature. Those earlier papers compare only two kinds of policies. They find that the 'revenue-raising' (RR) policy results in substantially higher welfare than the 'non-revenue-raising' (NRR) policy. Goulder et al. (1997) are careful to distinguish between revenue-recycling effects and revenue raising. Revenue-recycling refers to the use of environmental tax revenues to cut other distorting taxes as opposed to returning the monies in a lump sum fashion. However, the use of 'revenue raising' and 'non-revenue raising' can lead the casual reader to obscure the difference between revenue raising and revenue-recycling.

We use our model to provide comparable analyses of at least five kinds of environmental policies including: a tax, a subsidy, tradeable permits, a CAC policy that restricts emissions, and a different CAC policy that restricts technology. In this way, we are able to show that *some* non-revenue-raising policies perform just as well as revenue-raising policies. In particular, the same welfare-raising effects of environmental protection can be achieved, without exacerbating pre-existing labor tax distortions, by a tax that raises revenue, the CAC technology restriction that raises no revenue, and even a subsidy that costs revenue. Thus, raising revenue is *not* necessary for raising welfare. Instead, the exacerbation of the pre-existing tax distortion is associated with policies that generate privately-retained scarcity rents. Such policies include both the quantity-restricting CAC regulation and the marketable permit policy in which the permits are given to existing polluters. The problem with such policies is that the output price must rise by more than necessary to cover the cost of abatement technologies; below we show that price must rise by an additional amount equal to scarcity rents that arise as a result of the emissions restrictions. The higher output price reduces the real net wage and exacerbates the labor tax distortion. That higher price is not such a problem if government captures the rents by using a pollution tax or by selling the permits, because then the labor tax can be reduced.[4]

Thus the NRR policy in those earlier papers performs poorly because it generates rents and fails to capture them. Public revenues from an environmental policy help indicate where the scarcity rents accrue, and so revenues are positively related to the welfare performance of alternative policies (Schöb, 1996). Revenue is not the key determinant, however, because other NRR policies can avoid the creation of those rents and provide the same welfare gain as RR policies.

Many other papers with heterogeneous abatement costs have shown that imperfect CAC regulations can be many times more expensive than the minimum total abatement cost made possible by incentive-based policies like taxes or permits.[5] Thus, when we show that a perfectly-designed CAC regulation can avoid the creation of scarcity rents and perform just as well as an environmental tax, we certainly do not mean to endorse CAC regulations. Instead, the point is just that the difference is not due to revenue. Moreover, if policymakers are to limit themselves to imperfect CAC regulations, they could avoid ones that unnecessarily hand out profits. Those profits are not just a transfer, because they raise product prices and exacerbate labor distortions.

[4]The rents interpretation is also consistent with the revenue-recycling interpretation described above. It does, however, have three useful features. Firstly, it avoids any confusion about the necessity of revenue raising for welfare improvements. Secondly, it provides a useful link to the political economy literature on instrument choice in papers such as Buchanan and Tullock (1975) and Maloney and McCormick (1982). Thirdly, it provides a conceptual link to other literature on import quotas and tariffs that have high excess burden by creating scarcity rents (e.g. Bizer and Stuart, 1987).

[5]See Atkinson and Lewis (1974), Seskin et al. (1983), and other studies surveyed in Cropper and Oates (1992, p. 686).

2. The model

Our goal is to analyze and compare the impacts of five different kinds of policies such as tradeable pollution permits, a command and control (CAC) limit on emissions, a tax on emissions, a subsidy to clean production, or a CAC restriction on technology. In particular, we wish to compare all such policies within a single model. For this purpose, we develop a simple static model with N identical individuals who own a single resource and sell it in the market to earn income that can be used to buy two different goods.[6] We assume perfect certainty, no transactions costs, and constant returns to scale production.[7]

For simplicity we refer to the resource as time available for labor supply, but under some conditions it can be interpreted more generally as a fixed total amount of labor, capital, land, and any other resource that can be sold in the market (in amount L) or used at home (in amount L_H). Distinction among these inputs is not necessary for any of the points we make below. The resource kept at home could be interpreted either as leisure or as a resource used in home production.

Each individual receives utility from per-capita amounts of a nonpolluting good (X), a polluting good (Y), and leisure (L_H), and from the total amounts of a government-provided nonrival public good (G), and another nonrival public good called environmental quality (E). The per-capita amount X is produced using just labor L_X, while Y is produced using labor L_Y and emissions Z. One might write a production function for the dirty good where both the output and the waste by-product are produced using inputs like labor, capital, and other resources. Using a device common in environmental economics, however, we simply move the waste emissions to the other side of the equation. In other words, we view emissions as an input to production, with its own downward sloping marginal product curve (since successive units of emissions are less crucial to production). Total emissions (NZ) negatively affect the environment through:

$$E = e(NZ), \quad \text{where } e' < 0. \tag{1}$$

The other goods are produced according to:

$$X = L_X \tag{2a}$$

$$Y = F(L_Y, Z) \tag{2b}$$

[6] If government cannot observe individual differences, then it cannot use individual-specific lump sum taxes. We abstract from heterogeneity, but still assume that the government cannot use lump sum taxes. For an interpretation that incorporates heterogeneity, see Kaplow (1996).

[7] These considerations might also affect the choice among policy instruments. Other models have analyzed uncertainty (Weitzman, 1974), monitoring and enforcement costs (Russell, 1990), and transactions costs (Stavins, 1995). The large literature on the choice among policy instruments is reviewed in Bohm and Russell (1985).

$$G = NL_G. \tag{2c}$$

We define a unit of X as the amount that can be produced using one unit of labor. The numeraire good is L, or equivalently X. Then Y is produced in a constant returns to scale function (F), using clean labor (L_Y) and emissions (Z). The elasticity of substitution between these two inputs will help determine pollution abatement possibilities. Emissions may include gaseous, liquid, or solid wastes that require some private costs for removal and disposal. These private costs must come in the form of resources, so we define one unit of emissions as the amount that requires one unit of private resources ($Z = L_Z$).[8] Thus, the private cost of Z is always 1. We define a unit of Y such that its initial competitive equilibrium price is $p_Y = 1$. Finally, labor (L_G) is also used to produce the public good. The combination of these production relationships provides the overall resource constraint:

$$NL = NX + N(L_Y + L_Z) + G. \tag{3}$$

Individuals maximize:

$$\mathscr{L} = U(X, Y, L_H, G, E) + \lambda[(1 - t_L)L + M - X - p_Y Y] \tag{4}$$

by their choice of X, Y, and L_H, where t_L is the tax rate on resource (labor) supply, and M is nonlabor income (discussed below). Taxable labor supply is $L = L_X + L_Y + L_Z + L_G$. A subscript on U indicates a partial derivative (marginal utility), and U_H is the partial of U with respect to L_H, so these individuals set $U_X = U_Y / p_Y = U_H/(1 - t_L) = \lambda$, the marginal utility of income.

Our approach is to start at an initial competitive equilibrium with an existing tax on labor, but without any policy correction for the external effect of Z on E, and then to analyze small changes. As shown in Appendix A, the general equilibrium impact of changes on utility following a restriction on emissions is given by:

$$\frac{dU}{\lambda L} = t_L \hat{L} - \mu\left(\frac{Z}{L}\right)\hat{Z} \tag{5}$$

where a hat over a variable indicates a proportional change (e.g. $\hat{L} = dL/L$), and where μ is defined as $-NU_E e'/\lambda$. This term μ is the dollar value of lost utility to all individuals from a marginal increase in emissions, that is, 'marginal environmental damage'.

This equation is a variation on Eq. (5) in Bovenberg and de Mooij (1994). The left-hand side is the dollar value of the change in utility (dU/λ), divided by total

[8]Note that emissions are positively related to the use of these resources: L_Z is not to clean up or reduce emissions, but just to cart it away. Abatement is undertaken by substituting away from Z and into L_Y. This overall production function is still constant returns to scale, since Z is a linear function of L_Z. The private cost for emissions helps justify our assumption of an internal solution with a finite choice for Z, even without corrective government policy.

income (L). On the right-hand side are two terms. The policy under consideration is a mandated reduction in emissions, or some incentive that reduces emissions, so $\hat{Z}<0$. Thus the second term on the right-hand side of (5) is an unambiguous increase in utility from abating pollution. The impact will depend on the importance of the externality (size of μ), the reduction in Z, and the initial size of Z relative to the size of the economy. In the first term, however, utility is also affected by a pre-existing labor tax ($t_L>0$). If the policy reduces labor supply, utility will fall by the exacerbation of a pre-existing labor distortion. The overall effect on welfare depends on the change in labor and on the relative size of these two terms.

In order to derive an expression for the change in labor supply, $\hat{L}$, we need to trace the effect of the policy on the price of emissions, the price of output, and thus on the real net wage. We also need to trace the effect of the policy on income flows that might also affect labor supply. These income effects include the possibility that the policy generates private profits.

Any policy to reduce Z will raise the marginal product of Z above its private cost. If the government imposes a tax on emissions, or sells a limited number of emission permits, then the firm faces an effective 'price' p_Z that equals the private resource cost plus the tax or the price of the permit. The price p_Z is simply the marginal product of emissions in equilibrium. For these two policies, the scarcity rent goes to the government.

If the limited number of permits are handed out for free, however, then the scarcity rent goes to the permit recipient. These permits can be used by the recipients, to yield a marginal product of emissions greater than the private cost of emissions, or they can be sold. Either way, the policy has generated a private profit (i.e. producer surplus). We define these profits as:

$$\Pi=(p_Z-1)Z. \tag{6}$$

The rules for the initial allocation of these permits do not matter in our model, because our N identical agents must own whatever firm or other entity is given the permits. These profits become part of nonlabor income, M, in Eq. (4).

These profits may arise for some kinds of command-and-control (CAC) policies as well. One example is a 'new source performance standard' that requires an expensive technology for new firms only, raising the marginal cost of production (and thus the equilibrium price of output) without affecting the cost of production for old firms. The result is an entry barrier that provides profits to old firms.[9] Our model does not distinguish new firms from old firms, but profits can arise in other ways. For the simplest example, consider the special case where production of Y

[9]See Buchanan and Tullock (1975) or Maloney and McCormick (1982). Nielsen et al. (1995) investigate a tax reform in which regulation with grandfathering is replaced by environmental taxes. They also stress the role of rents.

uses fixed combinations of L_Y and Z. Then a restriction on Z is equivalent to a restriction on Y. What happens if all firms are required to produce at 90% of last year's level? The result is a government-mandated cartel that allows all firms to charge a price greater than marginal cost.[10]

We start at a competitive equilibrium with no environmental policy and zero profits, and we introduce a new policy such as $\hat{Z} < 0$. Any generated profits might affect consumer behavior and government revenue. Thus, prior to any policy, $p_Z = 1$ and Π in Eq. (6) is zero. The change in profits ($d\Pi$) equals ($Zdp_Z + p_ZdZ - dZ$), which equals Zdp_Z (since the initial p_Z is 1).

The government budget constraint is:

$$G = Nt_L L + Nt_\Pi \Pi \quad (7)$$

where t_Π is a tax on profits. We can then set this tax rate (exogenously) to 1.0 for any case where government receives the scarcity rent, such as for an emissions tax or sale of permits, and we set it to zero for the other extreme where private parties keep the rents. This specification also allows us to consider the case where a pre-existing corporate profits tax rate would take part of the firm's private profits. We do not adjust this tax rate endogenously to help maintain the necessary revenue to pay for G, but its existence greatly affects the amount by which the labor tax might have to be adjusted. Suppose, for example, that a permit or CAC policy generates profits but also reduces labor supply and thus labor tax revenue. If the tax rate on profits is zero, then the government will have to raise the labor tax rate and exacerbate labor supply distortions. If t_Π equals 1, then the government may be able to reduce the labor tax rate.

Differentiate the government budget (Eq. (7)), set $dG = 0$, and use $d\Pi = Zdp_Z$ to get:

$$\hat{t}_L = -\left(\frac{t_L}{1-t_L}\right)\hat{L} - t_\Pi\left(\varphi\frac{Z}{Y}\right)\hat{p}_Z \quad (8)$$

where $\hat{t}_L = dt_L/(1-t_L)$ and $\varphi = p_Y Y/(X + p_Y Y) = p_Y Y/(1-t_L)L$ is the share of consumer expenditures on the dirty good. Eq. (8) indicates the rate at which government has to change the labor tax. To evaluate this expression, we need to solve for $\hat{L}$ and $\hat{p}_Z$.

To determine specific effects on labor supply, we follow Bovenberg and de Mooij (1994) by assuming that G and E are separable in utility from leisure and

[10] These profits still arise with substitution between L_Y and Z. In our model, with perfect competition and constant returns to scale, identical firms would have no reason to buy or sell permits from each other anyway, so the tradeable permit equilibrium (with scarcity rents) must be functionally equivalent to the CAC equilibrium (with each firm's emissions limited to 90% of last year's level). The point is that the firm does not have to sell the permit to receive a profit: a mandated restriction still raises the marginal product of Z above its cost.

consumption, and that the combination of consumption goods is homothetic and separable from leisure:

$$U = U(V[Q(X, Y), L_H], G, E) \tag{9}$$

where Q is a homothetic function of X and Y.[11] The household budget is given by:

$$X + p_Y Y = (1 - t_L)L + (1 - t_\Pi)\Pi. \tag{10}$$

Define w as the real net wage, so $w = (1 - t_L)/p_Q$ where p_Q is a price index on $Q(X, Y)$. This index assigns the weight φ to p_Y, so $\hat{p}_Q = \varphi \hat{p}_Y$. Totally differentiate w to get:

$$\hat{w} = -\hat{t}_L - \varphi \hat{p}_Y. \tag{11}$$

This equation says that the real net wage falls if either the tax on labor were to rise, or if the price of consumption goods were to rise. In Appendix B, we show how the change in the price of emissions affects the price of Y, the real net wage, and labor supply. In addition, we show how labor supply ultimately depends on the policy shock (emission restriction):

$$\begin{aligned} \hat{L} &= (1 - t_\Pi)\left\{\frac{(1 - t_L)\varphi(\eta - \varepsilon)}{(1 - t_\Pi)\varphi(\eta - \varepsilon) - [\sigma_Q(1 - \varphi) + \sigma_Y(L_Y/Z)](1 - t_L - \varepsilon t_L)}\right\}\hat{Z} \\ &\equiv (1 - t_\Pi)\Omega\hat{Z} \end{aligned} \tag{12}$$

where σ_Q is the elasticity of substitution between X and Y in consumption, σ_Y is the elasticity of substitution between L_Y and Z in production of Y, ε is the uncompensated labor supply wage elasticity, and η is the labor supply income elasticity.[12] The term in curled brackets (Ω) must be positive if we assume that leisure is a normal good ($\eta < 0$), labor supply is not backward bending ($\varepsilon \geq 0$), and t_L is on the normal side of the Laffer Curve $[(1 - t_L - \varepsilon t_L) > 0]$.[13]

The point of this equation is that environmental policy raises the cost of emissions, and thus the cost of output, in a way that reduces w and affects

[11] These assumptions imply that both goods are equal substitutes for leisure. Thus, when starting from a zero pollution tax, we show below that the introduction of a small pollution tax raises the price of Y and affects the real net wage and labor supply in a way that exactly offsets the reduction in the labor tax rate. This special case allows for a simple analytical solution to our model, but it is a central special case. If Y were a relative complement (or substitute) to leisure, then the pollution tax would reduce labor supply by less (or more) than exactly enough to offset the reduction in the labor tax rate. Also, even with equal substitutes, an increase in a pre-existing pollution tax would reduce labor by more than enough to offset the reduction in the labor tax rate.

[12] This equation could also be expressed in terms of the compensated elasticity $\varepsilon^C = \varepsilon - \eta$. Fullerton and Metcalf (1997) use $\varepsilon = 0.1$ and $\eta = -0.2$, for example, so their compensated elasticity is 0.3.

[13] This last term will be positive if the initial point is on the normal side of the Laffer curve. Define revenue as $R = Lt_L$, totally differentiate, and rearrange to get $\hat{R}/\hat{t}_L = (1 - t_L)/t_L - \varepsilon$.

equilibrium labor supply. With Ω positive and $\hat{Z}$ negative, the equation says that equilibrium labor supply must fall. Notice that the tax on profits t_Π is very important for damping the impact of a price change on labor supply. In the limit when all profits are taxed away, labor supply is not affected at all.

3. Interpretation of results

We now use the welfare effect in Eq. (5) to compare several policies. Firstly, consider a CAC restriction on emissions with no capture of rents ($t_\Pi = 0$). This policy is equivalent, in our model, to handing out a limited number of tradeable pollution permits. Since $\hat{Z}$ is negative in Eq. (5), the second term in brackets $[-\mu(Z/L)\hat{Z}]$ is the unambiguous gain from correcting the externality. The first term is $t_L\hat{L}$, the loss from the labor distortion. For reasonable parameter values, Fullerton and Metcalf (1997) show that the first term loss can exceed the second term gain. In this case, the very first step toward correcting the pollution externality has a net *negative* effect on welfare.[14] Regardless of whether the negative labor supply effect is large enough to offset the positive environmental effect, however, the point is that the negative labor supply effect arises from creating scarcity rents ($d\Pi > 0$) and leaving them in private hands ($t_\Pi = 0$).

Further intuition is provided by Neary and Roberts' (1980) result that a regulation can be interpreted as a 'virtual' tax. This virtual tax is either recycled lump sum, by grandfathered permits, or it can be captured by government and used to reduce labor taxes. What is crucial is the way the tax is recycled, not whether the revenue appears explicitly in the government budget.

Secondly, suppose the government sells some of the permits or otherwise captures part of the rents ($0 < t_\Pi < 1$). Then (12) shows that labor supply still falls. The negative labor supply effect is smaller, but it can still offset part or all of the positive environmental effect. With t_Π strictly positive, this policy is a 'revenue-raising' policy, but it can provide a net welfare loss (Fullerton and Metcalf, 1997). Thus revenue raising is not sufficient for positive welfare effects (Goulder et al., 1997).

Thirdly, suppose that government captures *all* of the rents ($t_\Pi = 1$) by using an emissions tax, selling all of the permits, or imposing a 100% profits tax. Then (12) shows that $\hat{L}$ is zero. The first term in (5) disappears, leaving only the positive welfare effect of improving the environment.

---

[14]Similar numerical results were obtained by Parry (1997) and Goulder et al. (1997), where a pollution quota has a 'tax-interaction effect' (raising output prices that reduce the real net wage) and no 'revenue-recycling effect' (lowering the labor tax rate to raise the real net wage). The net effect on welfare also can be negative even *with* $t_\Pi = 1$, if revenues are used for lump-sum rebates or for reduction of a tax on a fixed factor (Bovenberg and Goulder, 1996).

Fourthly, consider a subsidy per unit of abatement from a baseline level. Schöb (1996) shows that this policy is equivalent to the combination of a *tax* per unit of emissions (the subsidy foregone) plus a lump-sum transfer to firms (the subsidy rate times baseline emissions). The higher opportunity cost of emissions still raises the equilibrium output price and therefore lowers the real net wage, but this negative effect on labor supply is exacerbated by the transfer (since leisure is a normal good). This policy performs quite poorly in simulations of Ballard and Medema (1993) or Parry (1998).

Some might attribute this last result to the fact that the subsidy loses revenue instead of raising revenue, but we attribute it to the creation and handout of rents. To demonstrate this point, we now show that a revenue *losing* subsidy can be just as effective as a revenue *raising* policy.

Fifthly, therefore, consider a different kind of subsidy. To simplify, we revert temporarily to a model with no abatement in production ($Y = Z$). We then consider a subsidy (s) to consumption of the clean good (X), so the household budget constraint becomes $X(1 - s) + p_Y Y = (1 - t_L)L$. This policy tilts consumers toward purchase of X, and therefore away from Y. It reduces the overall price index, which would raise the real net wage, but the necessary increase in the labor tax offsets that effect. Since the added tax on labor is equivalent to a tax on *both* goods, the tax on labor plus subsidy to the clean good is just a renormalization (Fullerton, 1997; Schöb, 1997). It is identical to the tax on pollution with complete capture of rents. This policy has no effect on the real net wage and no effect on the pre-existing labor distortion. It has only the positive effect of improving the environment.

Sixthly, return to the model of emissions in production, and consider a similar renormalization: a subsidy to the clean input (L_Y).[15] Instead of raising the cost of production, like the subsidy per unit of abatement, this subsidy reduces the cost of production. If it is financed by a tax on output of Y, this 'two-part instrument' is equivalent to the tax on emissions (Fullerton and Wolverton, 1999). This subsidy does not create scarcity rents, so it does not exacerbate labor distortions.

A final type of policy is a technology restriction, considered in the next section.

4. A technology restriction

Do all command and control policies raise production costs and exacerbate the labor supply distortion? If environmental authorities hand out a limited number of permits, or otherwise restrict the quantity of emissions, they create a scarce resource. Whoever owns the 'rights' to those limited emissions earns a scarcity rent. Similarly, a 'new source performance standard' erects a barrier to entry by

[15] An example is a subsidy for the use of low-sulfur coal, but note that our simple model has only two inputs. With more inputs, the subsidy would have to apply to all inputs other than emissions.

raising costs for new firms only. Suppose instead, however, that the authorities were to impose a technological requirement on the production process for *all* firms. For example, suppose every firm must have a scrubber on every smokestack. This rule might raise costs, but it does not restrict entry, and it does not provide an advantage to existing firms. We show below that this type of requirement reduces equilibrium emissions, even though it does not legally restrict emissions. It cannot generate profits in our model, because other firms have access to the exact same constant-returns-to-scale technology and would enter to share those profits.

This technological restriction can be analyzed in our model as a forced change in emissions (Z) per unit of output (Y), or equivalently, a forced change in the ratio of inputs (L_Y/Z). In other words, instead of the policy $\hat{Z}<0$, we analyze the policy $(\hat{L}_Y-\hat{Z})>0$. Firms have a number of ways to comply with this restriction. They can cut emissions, or they can just use more of the clean input. They could even increase emissions, so long as they increase clean inputs more. In order to look at the firm's problem in terms of levels, rather than changes, suppose the initial equilibrium quantities are $Y^0=F(L_Y^0, Z^0)$. Then the new policy restricts the choice of L_Y and Z such that

$$\left(\frac{L_Y}{Z}-\frac{L_Y^0}{Z^0}\right)\geq r>0. \tag{13}$$

The initial ratio (L_Y^0/Z^0) is taken as given by policy makers, existing firms, and even entrants.[16] Policy makers specify the required increase in that ratio (r). Any existing firm or entrant takes those two parameters (L_Y^0/Z^0 and r) as given.

The initial equilibrium has no restriction ($r=0$), and we find a new equilibrium with a small increase in r. Perhaps surprisingly, we find that a small increase in r has no effect on production costs and therefore no effect on the price of Y. It thus has no effect on the real net wage or the pre-existing labor supply distortion. In general, the firm chooses L_Y and Z to minimize:

$$\mathscr{L}=p_L L_Y+p_Z Z+\xi_1[Y-F(L_Y,Z)]+\xi_2\left(r-\left(\frac{L_Y}{Z}-\frac{L_Y^0}{Z^0}\right)\right). \tag{14}$$

Define C^* as the optimized cost function. By the envelope theorem, ξ_1 is the marginal cost of production ($\partial C^*/\partial Y$) while ξ_2 is the shadow price of the regulatory constraint ($\partial C^*/\partial r$). We want to know how the policy (r) affects the marginal cost of production (ξ_1), that is, the magnitude of $\partial\xi_1/\partial r$. Second partials are invariant to the order of differentiation, so:

$$\frac{\partial^2 C^*}{\partial Y\partial r}=\frac{\partial\xi_1}{\partial r}=\frac{\partial\xi_2}{\partial Y}. \tag{15}$$

[16] Because of constant returns to scale, in this model, the same ratio of inputs would be used by all firms. The ratio matters, but not the initial level of each input.

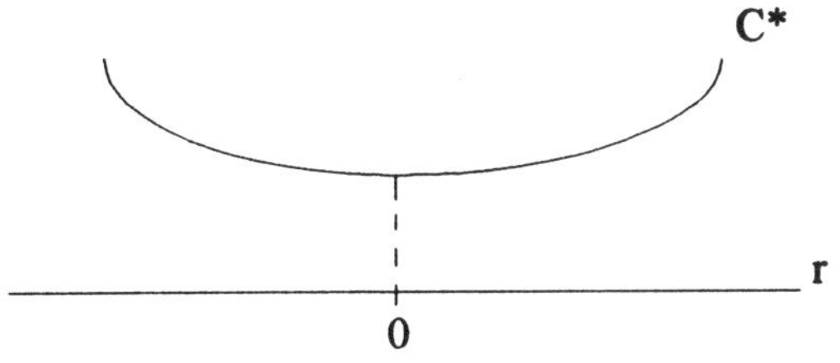

Fig. 1. Marginal cost and regulation.

Thus, to see how marginal cost changes with r, we need only consider how the shadow price on the regulatory constraint changes with Y. At the initial point where $r = 0$, and therefore the initial $\xi_2 = 0$, constant returns to scale in $F(L_Y, Z)$ implies that output Y can vary with *no change* in the factor ratio (given factor prices). In other words, changes in Y have no impact on ξ_2. Since $\partial\xi_2/\partial Y = 0$ at that point, Eq. (15) implies that $\partial\xi_1/\partial r = 0$. And with competition among firms, no change in marginal cost means no change in output price. Thus the policy does not affect the real net wage.

In the absence of profits, labor supply is $\hat{L} = \varepsilon\hat{w} = 0$. Also, since the price of Y is unchanged, the demand for Y must be unchanged. Essentially, firms switch from $Z = L_Z$ into L_Y with no change in total use of resources L, and no change in output. But since Z falls, welfare unambiguously increases.

How can an environmental restriction leave the marginal cost of production unchanged? To provide some intuition, Fig. 1 shows how the optimized cost function C^* is related to the regulatory parameter r. Because of constant returns to scale, this total cost can be taken for one unit of output and interpreted as marginal cost. This cost is minimized by the firm's unrestricted choices at the initial point where $r = 0$, so it must be higher at any $r \neq 0$. Thus costs *are* higher with $r \neq 0$, as one would expect. But, evaluated at $r = 0$, the curve is flat. From the initial starting point, a small change in r has no perceptible effect on cost. As the policy becomes restrictive, however, it would begin to raise the cost of production. Since the marginal cost of environmental protection is the increment to production cost, we have just shown that the marginal cost curve for this type of environmental protection starts at the origin.[17] A small but finite restriction has only second-order

[17] This 'origin property' is shared by the emissions tax (when revenues are used to cut the labor tax). While both the emissions tax and the technology restriction reduce pollution per unit output, only the emissions tax can also reduce output optimally. Thus, as shown by Goulder et al. (1999), a *large* policy of technology restriction can become more expensive per marginal unit of abatement than the emission tax and can even become more expensive than the quota (CAC quantity restriction or handout of permits). This distinction between large and small policies is important, but it is not the same as the distinction between starting at the origin and starting away from the origin.

effect on cost, but it has first-order effect on environmental benefits (since μ is strictly positive). We do not find the optimal degree of protection, that is, where the rising marginal cost curve intersects the falling marginal benefit curve. We only show that, for positive initial marginal benefits of protection, the first small restriction unambiguously raises welfare.[18]

The technology restriction $(\hat{L}_Y - \hat{Z}) > 0$ generates a cross-subsidy within the firm. Emissions may be reduced, such that the marginal product F_Z rises above private cost ($p_Z = 1$), but, to produce the same output, labor is increased such that its marginal product F_L falls *below* private cost ($p_L = 1$). Implicitly, profits on emissions are offset by losses on use of labor, as necessary to satisfy the restriction, with no net profits.

Thus the technology restriction is equivalent to the revenue-neutral combination of a small 'virtual' tax on Z and subsidy to L_Y (using Neary and Roberts (1980)).[19] In one case the government collects the 'profits' on Z to cover 'losses' on L_Y, and in the other case the government forces the firm to use profits on Z to cover its own losses on L_Y. The two outcomes are equivalent. Again, this result clarifies that the important distinction is not whether the policy raises revenue, but whether it generates privately-retained rents.

5. Conclusion

We have considered a number of environmental policies in a simple general equilibrium model to assess how these policies interact with pre-existing distortions. Whether we analyze tradeable pollution permits, direct controls on emissions, subsidies for non-polluting activities, or mandated technology adoptions, we find a common theme in our results. The magnitude of the welfare gain (or possibly the loss) due to new environmental policies in the face of pre-existing distortions depends critically on (1) whether the policy generates scarcity rents and (2) whether those rents are captured by the government and used to lower other distorting taxes. Environmental policies enhance welfare by reducing pollution but

[18]The pollution tax has both a substitution effect (by raising the cost of Z relative to L_Y) and an output effect (by raising the price of Y and discouraging purchases). In contrast, this technological restriction reduces pollution only through the mix of inputs. Walls and Palmer (1997) show that full equivalence to the pollution tax can be restored by placing a tax on output. Also, our model does not capture differences among firms' abatement costs. If these costs differ, then to remain efficient, a technology-based CAC policy would have to specify which firms must change which technologies. Information problems may become prohibitive. Finally, note that the pollution tax might provide more dynamic efficiency through incentives to invent new technologies.

[19]de Mooij and Bovenberg (1998) show that a shift from a capital tax to a pollution tax can induce inflow of mobile capital, increase output, and ultimately increase pollution. In our closed economy model, the cross-subsidy has no effect on production cost, so it cannot change output price or output. With $\hat{Y}=0$, and $(\hat{L}_Y - \hat{Z}) > 0$, we must have L_Y rise and pollution fall.

can reduce welfare by discouraging labor supply. The net welfare change depends on the relative size of these two factors. The key to understanding the impact on labor supply is to focus on the real net wage. When a policy generates scarcity rents, it leads to an increase in the price level that reduces the real net wage and hence labor supply. The only way to avoid this adverse effect on efficiency is for government to capture the rents (through a 100% tax on profits, or the sale of all tradeable permits), or to avoid generating the rents (through mandated technologies for all existing firms and entrants). Thus, much of the focus in our paper is on the sources and disposition of these scarcity rents.

Recognizing the importance of scarcity rents clarifies a source of possible confusion in the 'instrument choice' and 'double dividend' literature. Much of the emphasis in this literature has been the role that the revenue from the Pigouvian tax plays in allowing a reduction in other tax rates. Our analysis of different policies shows that this emphasis is misplaced. Following the assumption in that literature that the budget is balanced by adjusting the labor tax rate, we demonstrate equivalent welfare results whether government were to (1) raise revenue by taxing pollution or selling tradeable permits, (2) lose revenue by subsidizing the clean alternative to the polluting good or input, or (3) collect no revenue by using a technology mandate. Small changes in any of these three directions have no effect on the real net wage or on the labor market distortion.

Acknowledgements

The authors gratefully acknowledge the comments of Richard Arnott, Lans Bovenberg, Larry Goulder, Dan Hamermesh, Michael Hanemann, Ian Parry, Jon Skinner, Kerry Smith, Pete Wilcoxen, and three anonymous referees. This research was partially supported by grants to the first author from the Environmental Protection Agency (EPA R824740-01-0) and to the second author from the National Science Foundation (NSF SBR-9514989). This paper is part of NBER's research program in Public Economics. Any opinions expressed are those of the authors and not those of the EPA, the NSF, or the National Bureau of Economic Research.

Appendix A. Impact of the emissions restriction on utility (Eq. (5))

First totally differentiate utility (holding G fixed):[20]

$$dU = U_X dX + U_Y dY - U_H dL + U_E e'N dZ. \tag{A.1}$$

[20]This G is required in the model to justify the collection of taxes (see Eq. (7)).

To balance the government's budget, a policy that reduces labor must also specify how the lost labor tax revenue will be recovered. Substituting the consumer's first order conditions into (A.1) yields:

$$dU = \lambda dX + \lambda p_Y dY - \lambda(1 - t_L)dL + U_E e' N dZ. \tag{A.2}$$

Totally differentiate the resource constraint (3), with $dG = 0$, to get $dX = dL - dL_Y - dL_Z$, and substitute into (A.2):

$$dU/\lambda = t_L dL - \mu dZ + (p_Y dY - dL_Y - dL_Z) \tag{A.3}$$

where $dL_Z = dZ$, and where μ is defined as $-NU_E e'/\lambda$. Next, totally differentiate the production function for Y:

$$dY = F_L dL_Y + F_Z dZ \tag{A.4}$$

where F_L and F_Z are the marginal products of L_Y and Z. Assuming profit maximization (and a zero initial tax on emissions), these marginal products are equal to factor prices divided by output price: $F_L = F_Z = 1/p_Y = 1$. Thus, from (A.4), the expression in parentheses in (A.3) is zero. We divide (A.3) by L (and use $\hat{L} \equiv dL/L$) to get (5) in the text.

Appendix B. Impact of the emissions restriction on labor supply (Eq. (12))

First we show how p_Y is related to the cost of Z by using the zero-profits condition to show that $\hat{p}_Y = (Z/Y)\hat{p}_Z$.[21] Then, using (8) in (11), we have:

$$\hat{w} = \left(\frac{t_L}{1 - t_L}\right)\hat{L} - (1 - t_\Pi)\varphi\left(\frac{Z}{Y}\right)\hat{p}_Z. \tag{B.1}$$

Labor is chosen by maximizing the sub-utility function $V(Q, L_H)$ subject to:

$$Q = wL + (1 - t_\Pi)\Pi/p_Q. \tag{B.2}$$

We can write the labor supply function resulting from this maximization problem as $L = L(w, (1 - t_\Pi)\Pi/p_Q)$. That is, labor supply depends on uncompensated effects of the real net wage, and it depends on additional income effects of real net profits. Totally differentiating this function yields:

$$\hat{L} = \varepsilon\hat{w} + (1 - t_\Pi)\eta\varphi\left(\frac{Z}{Y}\right)\hat{p}_Z \tag{B.3}$$

where ε is the uncompensated labor supply elasticity, and η is the income

---

[21] Profits are created by $p_Z > 1$, but the firm breaks even on output given that higher cost of Z. The zero-profits condition is $p_Y Y = L_Y + p_Z Z$. Totally differentiate, and use the fact shown above (at Eq. (A.4)) that $dY = dL_Y + dZ$, to get $dp_Y Y = dp_Z Z$. Initial prices are one, so $\hat{p}_Y = (Z/Y)\hat{p}_Z$.

elasticity of labor supply. Substituting Eq. (B.1) into (B.3) gives the labor supply response as a function of $\hat{p}_Z$:

$$\hat{L} = \frac{(1 - t_\Pi)(1 - t_L)(\eta - \varepsilon)\varphi}{1 - t_L - \varepsilon t_L} \left(\frac{Z}{Y}\right) \hat{p}_Z. \tag{B.4}$$

Next, we need to relate $\hat{p}_Z$ to the emissions restriction. In general, this relationship depends on the demand for emissions, which depends on the demand for the output. The demand for Y is based on the consumer's maximization of $Q(X, Y)$, where we define σ_Q as the elasticity of substitution between X and Y in consumption. Given this definition, and given that the price of X always equals 1, we have the basic behavioral relationship:

$$\hat{Y} = \hat{X} - \sigma_Q \hat{p}_Y. \tag{B.5}$$

We need to eliminate $\hat{X}$ from this expression. Totally differentiate the household budget constraint (10), without holding any variables constant, and rearrange to solve for $\hat{X}$. Substitute that expression into (B.5), and rearrange to get:

$$\hat{Y} = \hat{L} + \hat{w} + \varphi(1 - t_\Pi)\hat{p}_Y - \sigma_Q(1 - \varphi)\hat{p}_Y. \tag{B.6}$$

The first two terms give the income effect on Y from the change in labor income, which implicitly incorporates the government's adjustment of t_L. The third term represents the income effect of profits on the demand for Y. The last term is the substitution effect.

Next, substitute Eqs. (B.1) and (B.4) into (B.6) to obtain $\hat{Y}$ as a function of $\hat{p}_Y$:

$$\hat{Y} = \left\{ \frac{(1 - t_\Pi)\varphi(\eta - \varepsilon) - \sigma_Q(1 - \varphi)(1 - t_L - \varepsilon t_L)}{1 - t_L - \varepsilon t_L} \right\} \hat{p}_Y \equiv \gamma_Y \hat{p}_Y. \tag{B.7}$$

The expression γ_Y represents the full general equilibrium response of Y to a change in its price, incorporating household behavior as well as the government budget constraint. We combine Eqs. (B.4) and (B.7) to obtain:

$$\begin{aligned} \hat{L} &= (1 - t_\Pi) \left\{ \frac{(1 - t_L)\varphi(\eta - \varepsilon)}{(1 - t_\Pi)\varphi(\eta - \varepsilon) - \sigma_Q(1 - \varphi)(1 - t_L - \varepsilon t_L)} \right\} \hat{Y} \\ &\equiv (1 - t_\Pi)\Delta \hat{Y}. \end{aligned} \tag{B.8}$$

Next we relate changes in output to changes in emissions. Let σ_Y represent the elasticity of substitution in production of Y between the two inputs (L_Y and Z). Then, by definition:

$$\hat{L}_Y - \hat{Z} = \sigma_Y(\hat{p}_Z - \hat{p}_L). \tag{B.9}$$

The price of labor is fixed, however, so Eq. (B.9) can be written as:

$$\hat{L}_Y = \hat{Z} + \sigma_Y \hat{p}_Z. \tag{B.10}$$

We showed above that $dY = dL_Y + dZ$ (Eq. (A.4)), so the percentage change in output of Y can be expressed as a weighted average of the percentage changes in the two inputs:

$$\hat{Y} = \left(\frac{L_Y}{Y}\right)\hat{L}_Y + \left(\frac{Z}{Y}\right)\hat{Z}. \tag{B.11}$$

Recall that the firm makes zero profits on output, given the raised price of emissions necessary to cover the scarcity rents, so:

$$p_Y Y = p_L L_Y + p_Z Z. \tag{B.12}$$

Evaluated at initial prices of one (prior to the regulation), we have $Y = L_Y + Z$. Substitute Eq. (B.10) into (B.11) and use the relationship $Y = L_Y + Z$ to obtain:

$$\hat{Y} = \hat{Z} + \sigma_Y\left(\frac{L_Y}{Y}\right)\hat{p}_Z. \tag{B.13}$$

Now recall that the full equilibrium effect on Y, in Eq. (B.7), is $\hat{Y} = \gamma_Y \hat{p}_Y$ and that $\hat{p}_Y = (Z/Y)\hat{p}_Z$. Together, these two relationships imply:

$$\hat{p}_Z = \left(\frac{Y}{Z\gamma_Y}\right)\hat{Y}. \tag{B.14}$$

Substituting (B.14) into (B.13) provides the equilibrium relationship between Y and Z:

$$\hat{Y} = \left(\frac{\gamma_Y}{\gamma_Y - \left(\frac{L_Y}{Z}\right)\sigma_Y}\right)\hat{Z}. \tag{B.15}$$

Finally, we substitute Eq. (B.15) into (B.8) and use the expression for γ_Y to get (12) in the text.

References

Atkinson, S.E., Lewis, D.H., 1974. A cost-effectiveness analysis of alternative air quality control strategies. Journal of Environmental Economics and Management 1 (3), 237–250.

Ballard, C.L., Medema, S.G., 1993. The marginal efficiency effects of taxes and subsidies in the presence of externalities: a computational general equilibrium approach. Journal of Public Economics 52 (2), 199–216.

Bizer, D.S., Stuart, C., 1987. The public finance of a protective tariff: the case of an oil import fee. American Economic Review 77 (5), 1019–1022.

Bohm, P., Russell, C.F., 1985. Comparative analysis of alternative policy instruments. In: Kneese, A.V., Sweeney, J.L. (Eds.). Handbook of Natural Resource and Energy Economics, Vol. 1. Elsevier, New York, pp. 395–460.

Bovenberg, A.L., Goulder, L.H., 1996. Optimal environmental taxation in the presence of other taxes: general equilibrium analyses. American Economic Review 86 (4), 985–1000.

Bovenberg, A.L., de Mooij, R.A., 1994. Environmental levies and distortionary taxation. American Economic Review 84 (4), 1085–1089.

Buchanan, J.M., Tullock, G., 1975. Polluters' profits and political response: direct controls versus taxes. American Economic Review 65 (1), 139–147.

Cropper, M.L., Oates, W.E., 1992. Environmental economics: a survey. Journal of Economic Literature 30 (2), 675–740.

Fullerton, D., 1997. Environmental levies and distortionary taxation: comment. American Economic Review 87 (1), 245–251.

Fullerton, D., Metcalf, G.E., 1997. Environmental Controls, Scarcity Rents, and Pre-Existing Distortions. NBER, Working paper no. 6091.

Fullerton, D., Wolverton, A., 1999. The Case for a Two-Part Instrument: Presumptive Tax and Environmental Subsidy. In: Panagariya, A., Portney, P.R., Schwab, R.M. (Eds.), Environmental and Public Economics: Essays in Honor of Wallace E. Oates. Edward Elgar Publishing, Cheltenham, UK, pp. 32–57.

Goulder, L.H., 1995. Environmental taxation and the 'double dividend': a reader's guide. International Tax and Public Finance 2 (2), 157–183.

Goulder, L.H., Parry, I.W.H., Burtraw, D., 1997. Revenue-raising versus other approaches to environmental protection: the critical significance of preexisting tax distortions. RAND Journal of Economics 28 (4), 708–731.

Goulder, L.H., Parry, I.W.H., Williams, R.C., Burtraw, D., 1999. The cost-effectiveness of alternative instruments for environmental protection in a second-best setting. Journal of Public Economics 72 (3), 329–360.

Kaplow, L., 1996. The optimal supply of public goods and the distortionary cost of taxation. National Tax Journal 49 (4), 513–533.

Lee, D.R., Misiolek, W.S., 1986. Substituting pollution taxation for general taxation: some implications for efficiency in pollution taxation. Journal of Environmental Economics and Management 13 (4), 338–347.

Maloney, M.T., McCormick, R.E., 1982. A positive theory of environmental quality regulation. Journal of Law and Economics 25 (1), 99–123.

de Mooij, R., Bovenberg, A.L., 1998. Environmental taxes, international capital mobility, and inefficient tax systems: tax burden versus tax shifting. International Tax and Public Finance 5 (1), 7–39.

Neary, J.P., Roberts, K.W.S., 1980. The theory of household behaviour under rationing. European Economic Review 13 (1), 25–42.

Nielsen, S.B., Pedersen, L.H., Sørensen, P.B., 1995. Environmental policy, pollution, unemployment, and endogenous growth. International Tax and Public Finance 2 (2), 185–205.

Oates, W.E., 1995. Green taxes: can we protect the environment and improve the tax system at the same time? Southern Economic Journal 61 (4), 914–922.

Parry, I.W.H., 1995. Pollution taxes and revenue recycling. Journal of Environmental Economics and Management 29 (3), S64–S77.

Parry, I.W.H., 1997. Environmental taxes and quotas in the presence of distorting taxes in factor markets. Resource and Energy Economics 19 (3), 203–220.

Parry, I.W.H., 1998. A second-best analysis of environmental subsidies. International Tax and Public Finance 5 (2), 153–170.

Pearce, D., 1991. The role of carbon taxes in adjusting to global warming. The Economic Journal 101 (407), 938–948.

Repetto, R., Dower, R.C., Jenkins, R., Geoghegan, J., 1992. Green Fees: How a Tax Shift Can Work for the Environment and the Economy. World Resources Institute, Washington, DC.

Rosen, H., 1995. In: 4th Edition. Public Finance. Richard Irwin, Chicago.

Russell, C., 1990. Monitoring and enforcement. In: Portney, P.R. (Ed.), Public Policies for Environmental Protection. Resources for the Future. Johns Hopkins University Press, Baltimore, pp. 243–274.

Schöb, R., 1996. Choosing the right instrument. Environmental and Resource Economics 8 (4), 399–416.
Schöb, R., 1997. Environmental taxes and pre-existing distortions: the normalization trap. International Tax and Public Finance 4 (2), 167–176.
Seskin, E.P., Anderson, R.J., Reid, R.O., 1983. An empirical analysis of economic strategies for controlling air pollution. Journal of Environmental Economics and Management 10 (2), 112–124.
Stavins, R.N., 1995. Transaction costs and tradeable permits. Journal of Environmental Economics and Management 29 (2), 133–148.
Terkla, D., 1984. The efficiency value of effluent tax revenues. Journal of Environmental Economics and Management 11 (2), 107–123.
Tullock, G., 1967. Excess benefit. Water Resources Research 3, 643–644.
Walls, M., Palmer, K., 1997. Upstream Pollution, Downstream Waste Disposal, and the Design of Comprehensive Environmental Policies. Resources for the Future, Discussion paper 97-51.
Weitzman, M.L., 1974. Prices vs. quantities. Review of Economic Studies 41 (4), 477–491.

ELSEVIER Journal of Public Economics 72 (1999) 329–360

JOURNAL OF PUBLIC ECONOMICS

The cost-effectiveness of alternative instruments for environmental protection in a second-best setting

Lawrence H. Goulder[a,b,c,*], Ian W.H. Parry[b], Roberton C. Williams III[a], Dallas Burtraw[b]

[a]Stanford University, Stanford, CA, USA
[b]Resources for the Future, 1616 P Street NW, Washington, DC 20036, USA
[c]NBER, Cambridge, MA, USA

Received 31 January 1998; received in revised form 30 August 1998; accepted 30 September 1998

Abstract

This paper employs analytical and numerical general equilibrium models to examine the significance of pre-existing factor taxes for the costs of pollution reduction under a wide range of environmental policy instruments. Pre-existing taxes imply significantly higher abatement costs for every instrument considered, but the cost-impact of such taxes differs sharply across instruments. Prior taxes can eliminate the cost-advantage of market-based instruments (emissions taxes and permits) over technology mandates or performance standards, particularly if the former policies fail to generate revenues and use the revenues to finance cuts in the prior distortionary taxes. The cost differences between instruments are highly sensitive to the extent of pollution abatement: for most policies, abatement costs converge to the same value as pollution abatement approaches 100 percent.

Keywords: Environmental instrument choice; General equilibrium efficiency analysis; Second-best regulation

JEL classification: D58; H21; L51

*Corresponding author. Tel.: +1-650-723-3706.
E-mail address: goulder@Leland.Stanford.edu (L.H. Goulder)

PII: S0047-2727(98)00109-1

1. Introduction

Environmental policy makers often must choose among alternative instruments for reducing emissions of pollution. A number of considerations affect this choice, including administrative ease, the costs of monitoring and enforcement, the probability distribution of policy errors in the face of uncertainty, effects on the distribution of income, and political feasibility.[1]

In recent years another important consideration has emerged: namely, the implications of pre-existing distortionary taxes (such as income, payroll, and sales taxes) for the costs of pollution abatement under various instruments. The potential significance of pre-existing taxes to environmental policy has been suggested by recent analyses of environmentally motivated taxes in a second-best setting. This work has shown that pre-existing factor (income) taxes tend to raise the costs of environmental tax initiatives, even when the revenues from environmental taxes are used to finance cuts in factor taxes.[2] Two welfare effects underlie these results. By driving up the price of (polluting) goods relative to leisure, environmental taxes tend to compound the factor-market distortions created by pre-existing taxes, thereby producing a negative welfare impact termed the *tax-interaction effect*. At the same time, environmental taxes whose revenues are recycled through cuts in marginal tax rates reduce the distortions caused by the pre-existing taxes, which contributes to a positive welfare impact. Typically this *revenue-recycling effect* only partly offsets the tax-interaction effect, implying that the overall impact of pre-existing taxes is to raise costs.[3]

These welfare impacts are also relevant to the choice between environmental taxes and other environmental policy instruments, and a few recent studies have taken some first steps in analyzing instrument choice in this second-best context. Parry (1997) employed an analytical model to investigate the choice between emissions taxes and emissions permits (or quotas), while Goulder et al. (1997) and Parry et al. (1998) used analytical and numerical general equilibrium models to examine this choice in the context of sulfur dioxide and carbon dioxide abatement,

[1]An extensive literature examines how these considerations might influence instrument choice. See, for example, Hahn (1986), Nichols (1984), Stavins (1991), and Weitzman (1974).

[2]See, for example, Bovenberg and de Mooij (1994), Parry (1995), Oates (1995), and Goulder (1995a), (1995b). A related insight is that the optimal environmental tax rate in a second-best setting with distortionary taxes is typically lower than in a first-best world. See, for example, Bovenberg and van der Ploeg (1994), Parry (1995), and Bovenberg and Goulder (1996).

[3]Of course, the new revenues could be devoted to purposes other than reducing marginal rates of existing taxes. They could be used, for example, to increase government spending, to finance lump-sum tax cuts, or to reduce the deficit. These different methods of recycling the revenues can have very different efficiency consequences. In the case where emissions tax revenues are returned as lump-sum tax cuts, the revenue-recycling effect does not materialize and there is no offset to the tax-interaction effect.

respectively.[4] These studies show that while both taxes and non-auctioned emissions permits (or quotas) produce the costly tax-interaction effect, only taxes can generate the offsetting revenue-recycling effect. As a result, pre-existing taxes disproportionately raise the costs of non-auctioned permits. These studies show that the cost disadvantage of non-auctioned permits can be very important to overall efficiency. Indeed, Parry et al. (1998) estimate that reducing carbon emissions through carbon permits will be efficiency-*reducing* unless the marginal benefits from carbon abatement exceed US$18 per ton. These papers demonstrate the significance of second-best considerations in connection with the control of two important pollutants – sulfur dioxide and carbon dioxide. However, the studies examine only two policy instruments.

A recent paper by Fullerton and Metcalf (1997) expands the domain of instrument choice to include a 'technology restriction' policy (specifically, a constraint on the ratio of emissions to labor input).[5] They use an analytical model to show that initial, incremental abatement involves zero cost under the technology restriction policy, but involves strictly positive costs under the pollution-permit policy. Their model is limited, however, in that it cannot examine the costs of non-incremental abatement.

The present paper investigates how the costs and overall efficiency impacts of different environmental policy instruments are affected by pre-existing taxes and the extent of pollution abatement. Using analytical and numerical general equilibrium models, we examine the cost-effectiveness of emissions taxes, emissions permits (or quotas), fuels taxes, performance standards, and mandated technologies.

Our paper extends the prior literature on instrument choice in several ways. First, it extends prior first-best cost-effectiveness analyses (that is, analyses ignoring prior distortionary taxes[6]) by deriving both analytical and numerical results in a unified, general equilibrium framework, and by considering both

[4]Previously, Ballard and Medema (1993) examined instrument choice in a second-best setting, employing a numerical general equilibrium model to evaluate the efficiency impacts of pollution taxes and subsidies to pollution abatement. They demonstrated that pollution taxes are generally more efficient than abatement subsidies. The difference is due in part to the pollution tax's ability to raise revenue that can be used to reduce marginal rates of existing taxes. This fiscal issue is reflected in the *revenue-recycling effect* discussed below.

[5]They also consider a policy that subsidizes all goods in the economy other than a polluting good. In their model this is formally equivalent to a tax on the polluting good.

[6]Throughout this paper, the term 'first-best' refers to a setting with no prior distortionary taxes. Strictly speaking, the absence of distortionary taxes does not guarantee a first-best situation: environmental resources, in particular, may not be efficiently priced or regulated. However, we find it useful to apply this label to provide a contrast with the second-best setting involving prior distortionary taxes.

incremental and 'large' pollution reductions.[7] The attention to both small and large changes is important: we show that the relative costs of different instruments depend importantly on the extent of abatement. Indeed, while relative costs differ significantly at low levels of abatement, for all instruments except for the fuel tax, the costs per unit of abatement converge to the same value as the extent of abatement approaches 100 percent.

Second, the paper extends the emerging literature on instrument choice in a second-best setting. In contrast with the studies by Parry, by Goulder et al., and by Parry et al., we consider not only emissions taxes and permits but also technology mandates, performance standards, and fuel (input) taxes. And in contrast with Fullerton and Metcalf (1997), we consider abatement beyond the initial increment (as well as some additional instruments). We find that pre-existing taxes raise the costs of abatement under each of the instruments considered, relative to its costs in a 'first-best' (no-prior-tax) world. This extra cost is an increasing function of the magnitude of pre-existing tax rates, and for plausible tax rates and parameter values the cost increase is substantial (27 percent or more). Importantly, pre-existing taxes do not raise the costs of all instruments by the same proportion, and thus prior taxes influence the relative attractiveness of different instruments. The cost-impact of pre-existing taxes is particularly large for (non-auctioned) emissions permits; here the cost increase can be several hundred percent. This result has important policy implications. Economists have long argued that tradable emissions permits and emissions taxes are more cost-effective than performance standards, technology mandates, and other traditional forms of regulation (see, for example, Cropper and Oates, 1992). Our results suggest that tradable emissions permits will yield substantial cost savings over performance standards or technology mandates only if the permits are auctioned, with revenues used to cut other taxes.

Finally, the paper applies the numerical model to analyze nitrogen oxide (NO_x) emissions regulation under the 1990 Clean Air Act Amendments. These regulations have relied primarily on performance standards and are expected to yield emission reductions of approximately 20 percent in 2005 relative to the forecasted baseline emissions. Our results suggest that pre-existing taxes raise the cost of this reduction by about US$1.3 billion (1990 dollars) in the year 2005. At the same time, our results cast doubt on the possibility of achieving the same emissions reductions at lower cost under a policy of tradable emissions permits. In addition to investigating policy costs in the context of NO_x regulation, we consider alternative scenarios in order to bring out general principles applicable to other pollutants.

[7]The most extensive prior analysis of a broad range of instruments appears to be Spulber (1985). That study involves only analytical methods and (accordingly) considers only small changes. Tietenberg (1985) and Lester et al. (1997) (chapt. 7) also consider a large set of instruments, but these studies do not offer a unified general-equilibrium analysis.

A caveat is in order. Our analysis abstracts from heterogeneity in firms' abatement cost schedules and associated information problems faced by regulators. These issues can be very important to the choice of policy instruments and should be considered along with the second-best issues investigated here.

The paper is organized as follows. Section 2 presents an analytical model that reveals the different efficiency impacts of the policy instruments. This model is extended in later sections to introduce more realism and gauge the empirical importance of these differences in efficiency. Section 3 presents the extended model, which is solved numerically. Section 4 provides results from simulations with the extended model. The final section offers conclusions.

2. The analytical model

This section uses an analytical model to compare the costs of environmental policy instruments in the presence of distortionary taxes. Detailed derivations for all of the results below are provided in a separate mathematical appendix available from the authors on request.

2.1. Model assumptions

We develop a static model in which a representative household enjoys utility from a polluting consumption good (X), a non-polluting consumption good (Y), and leisure, with leisure equal to the household time endowment ($\bar{L}$) less labor supply (L). Emissions (E) from producing X cause environmental damages that reduce consumer utility. The household utility function is given by:

$$U = u(X,Y,\bar{L} - L) - \phi(E), \tag{2.1}$$

where $u(.)$ is utility from non-environmental goods and is quasi-concave, and $\phi(.)$ is disutility from waste emissions and is weakly convex. The separability assumption in (2.1) implies that the demands for X and Y and the supply of labor do not vary with changes in E.[8] X and Y are produced by competitive firms using

[8]Relaxing this assumption would complicate the tax-interaction effect discussed below. If, compared with consumption, leisure is a relatively strong (weak) substitute for environmental quality, then this effect is weakened (strengthened). There is little empirical evidence on the relative ease of substitution between leisure, overall consumption, and environmental quality. Under these circumstances it seems reasonable to assume separability, which implies that changes in environmental quality do not affect the relative attractiveness of consumption and leisure. For a discussion of the significance of the separability assumption, see Espinosa and Smith (1995).

labor, which is the only factor of production.[9] We assume that the marginal product of labor is constant in each industry and normalize output to imply marginal products (and a wage rate) of unity. This normalization implies that the unit cost of producing X or Y is unity.

Firms can reduce waste emissions per unit of output through 'end-of-pipe' treatment, which requires the purchase of abatement equipment or services. We assume that such equipment or services are produced directly from labor. Emissions per unit of X are $e_0 - a$, where e_0 is baseline emissions per unit (that is, emissions per unit in the absence of regulation) and a is the reduction in per-unit emissions from utilizing abatement equipment or services. Economy-wide emissions, E, are therefore equal to $(e_0 - a)X$. Thus, total emissions fall as a result of reduced production of X (the *output-substitution effect*) and increased abatement activity (the *abatement effect*).

The total cost (C) of abatement activity to the firm is given by:

$$C = c(a)X, \tag{2.2}$$

where $c(a)$ is a convex function representing the per-unit cost of abatement activity.

The government levies a proportional tax of t_L on labor earnings, regulates emissions, and provides a lump-sum transfer G to households. G denotes the nominal transfer; we assume that the government adjusts G so that real transfers are held constant for all policy changes. We also assume government budget balance; any revenue consequences of environmental policies are offset by adjusting t_L.

The household budget constraint is:

$$p_X X + Y = (1 - t_L)L + G, \tag{2.3}$$

where p_X is the demand price of X (equal to unity in the absence of regulation). Households choose X, Y and L to maximize utility (2.1) subject to the budget constraint (2.3), taking environmental damages as given. From the resulting first-order conditions and (2.3) we obtain the uncompensated demand and labor supply functions:

$$X(p_X, 1 - t_L, G), \quad Y(p_X, 1 - t_L, G), \quad L(p_X, 1 - t_L, G). \tag{2.4}$$

Substituting these equations into (2.1) gives the indirect utility function:

$$V = \mathrm{v}(p_X, 1 - t_L, G) - \phi(E). \tag{2.5}$$

[9] In an extended model that considered other primary factors (such as capital), our quantitative results would vary to the extent that pre-existing taxes on these factors differed and the environmental policy imposed a different burden on these factors. This issue is examined in detail in Bovenberg and Goulder (1997).

Throughout this paper the term 'costs' refers to the gross efficiency costs of environmental policies, that is, the costs before netting out environment-related benefits from changes in $\phi(.)$.

We now define two concepts relating to the burden of the labor tax. These will be useful in expressing the tax-interaction effect. First, define:

$$M \equiv \frac{-t_L(\partial L/\partial t_L)}{L + t_L(\partial L/\partial t_L)}. \tag{2.6}$$

This is the (partial equilibrium) efficiency cost from raising an additional dollar of labor tax revenue in order to finance government consumption expenditure. It equals the *marginal cost of public funds* minus one.[10] The numerator of (2.6) is the efficiency loss from an incremental increase in t_L. This equals the wedge between the gross wage (the value marginal product of labor) and the net wage (the marginal social cost of labor in terms of foregone leisure), multiplied by the reduction in labor supply. The denominator is marginal labor tax revenue (from differentiating $t_L L$).

The corresponding expression when revenue is returned to households as lump-sum transfers is the partial equilibrium *marginal excess burden* of the labor tax, given by:

$$M' \equiv \frac{-t_L(\partial L^C/\partial t_L)}{L + t_L(\partial L/\partial t_L)} = \frac{\varepsilon^C t_L/(1-t_L)}{1-\varepsilon^U t_L/(1-t_L)}, \quad \varepsilon^C \equiv \frac{\partial L^C}{\partial(1-t_L)}\frac{1-t_L}{L},$$

$$\varepsilon^U \equiv \frac{\partial L}{\partial(1-t_L)}\frac{1-t_L}{L}, \tag{2.6'}$$

where the superscript C denotes a compensated derivative and ε^C and ε^U denote the compensated and uncompensated labor supply elasticities.[11] Below we provide and interpret key equations that decompose the efficiency cost of the various policies.

2.2. Emissions tax (with revenues returned through cuts in distortionary tax rates)

Consider a revenue-neutral tax of t_E imposed on emissions, with revenues from

[10]It is a partial equilibrium concept because it does not take into account the indirect effect of the labor tax on emissions and emissions tax revenue. We assume that M is positive, in keeping with evidence that the uncompensated labor supply for the whole economy is positive (see below).

[11]In this case, there is an income effect from the increased government transfers to households, and thus expression (2.6′) depends on both the compensated and uncompensated derivatives of labor supply, whereas (2.6) depends only on the uncompensated derivative. Browning (1987) provides a comprehensive discussion of the formula in (2.6′). For a discussion of the relationship between the marginal excess burden and marginal cost of public funds, see Hakonsen (1998).

this tax used to finance cuts in the distortionary tax, t_L. The government budget constraint is:

$$t_E E + t_L L = G, \tag{2.7}$$

that is, revenues from the emissions tax and (reduced) labor tax exactly finance the given level of government spending. The profit per unit of X is:

$$p_X - \{1 + c(a) + t_E(e_0 - a)\}, \tag{2.8}$$

and in equilibrium profits are zero. The emissions tax raises the marginal cost (and thus the price) of X because it induces firms to incur abatement costs $c(a)$ and because it exacts a tax payment of $t_E(e_0 - a)$. Firms choose a, the emissions abatement per unit of X, to maximize profits. This gives the first-order condition:

$$t_E = c'(a). \tag{2.9}$$

Eq. (2.9) states that abatement activity occurs until the marginal abatement cost per unit of X equals the emissions tax rate. Eqs. (2.4) and (2.9) imply $E = E(t_E, t_L)$.

We now consider an incremental, revenue-neutral increase in t_E. The efficiency cost of this policy can be expressed as:

$$-\frac{1}{\lambda}\frac{dv}{dt_E} = \underbrace{c'(a)\left(\frac{da}{dt_E}\right)X}_{dW^A} + \underbrace{\left(-\frac{dX}{dt_E}\right)t_E(e_0 - a)}_{dW^O} - \underbrace{M\left\{E + t_E\frac{dE}{dt_E}\right\}}_{\partial w^R}$$
$$+ \underbrace{\left[(1+M)t_L\left(-\frac{\partial L}{\partial p_X}\right) + M'Xs_G\right]\frac{dp_X}{dt_E}}_{\partial W^I}, \tag{2.10}$$

where λ is the marginal utility of income and s_G is the share of government transfers in household income, given by $s_G = G/[G + (L - t_L)L]$. The first two terms on the right-hand side comprise the *primary cost* of this policy. The term labeled dW^A represents the cost from the *abatement effect.* This is the efficiency cost associated with firms' expenditure on end-of-pipe abatement activities. The term labeled dW^O represents the cost from the *output-substitution effect.* This is the efficiency cost associated with households substituting away from (the now higher-priced) X to other goods and leisure. This effect equals the reduction in consumption of X multiplied by the increase in marginal production cost of X caused by the emissions tax. (In the expanded model of Section 3, which includes intermediate inputs, a third channel for emissions reduction – the *input-substitution effect* – also applies.)

Table 1 summarizes the extent that these effects are utilized under the emissions tax and other policies. The emissions tax exploits all of these effects 'fully' in that it induces the most cost-effective level of adjustment along each of these dimensions. As discussed below, under the other policies some of the

Table 1
Determinants of primary costs by policy

Instrument	Abatement effect	Input-substitution effect	Output-substitution effect
Emissions tax	Full	Full	Full
Emissions permits	Full	Full	Full
Performance standard	Full	Full	Partial
Technology mandate	Full	Partial	Partial
Fuels tax	None	Full	Full

dimensions are exploited either partially or not at all, which implies higher primary costs to achieve given emissions abatement targets.

In a first-best (no-prior-tax) setting, the relative cost-effectiveness of different policies can be explained fully in terms of the differences in primary costs. But in a second-best setting (with pre-existing distortionary taxes), two additional cost terms come into play. These are represented by ∂W^{R} and ∂W^{I} in (2.10). ∂W^{R} is the efficiency gain from using the additional emissions tax revenue to finance cuts in the distortionary labor tax. This is the (marginal) *revenue-recycling effect.* It equals the product of the marginal cost of public funds minus one and the marginal revenue from the emissions tax. ∂W^{I} is the efficiency loss from the *tax-interaction effect.* The emissions tax increases the price of X, implying an increase in the price of consumption and thus a reduction in the real wage. This reduces labor supply and produces a marginal efficiency loss of $t_{L}(-\partial L/\partial p_{X})(\mathrm{d}p_{X}/\mathrm{d}t_{E})$, which is the tax wedge between the gross and net wage multiplied by the reduction in labor supply. The reduction in labor supply also reduces tax revenues. The efficiency cost of replacing the lost revenue is M times the lost tax revenues. Finally, as the price of consumption rises, nominal government spending must increase in order to hold real spending constant. The cost of raising this extra revenue is M' times the change in nominal government spending, Xs_{G}. The combined efficiency loss from these three sources is the tax-interaction effect. As discussed below, the tax-interaction effect usually dominates the revenue-recycling effect: pre-existing distortionary taxes raise the costs of a given emissions tax, even when revenues are recycled through cuts in these prior taxes.

2.3. Emission permits

Now consider the impact of a set of (non-auctioned) tradable emission permits. In this model, with homogeneous producers, this policy is equivalent to one where the government chooses an overall acceptable level of emissions and allocates emissions permits so that each firm is entitled to a level of emissions proportional to its baseline emissions. The key difference between this policy and the emissions tax is that it does not raise revenues for the government, and that, consequently, the policy does not allow for a reduction in the distortionary tax, t_{L}. If emissions permits were auctioned by the regulator, their effects would be identical in this model to those of an emissions tax.

Under the non-auctioned permit policy, the government budget constraint is:

$$t_L L = G. \tag{2.7a}$$

The permit policy can be represented as a virtual tax on emissions, where the 'revenues' from this tax are rebated to firms in lump-sum fashion. Such revenues correspond to the rents generated by the permit policy.[12] We use t_E^v to denote the virtual tax. The cost of an incremental increase in the virtual tax can be decomposed as follows:

$$-\frac{1}{\lambda}\frac{dv}{dt_E} = \underbrace{c'(a)\left(\frac{da}{dt_E^v}\right)X}_{dW^A} + \underbrace{\left(-\frac{dX}{dt_E^v}\right)t_E^v(e_0 - a)}_{dW^O} + \underbrace{\left[(1+M)t_L\left(-\frac{\partial L}{\partial p_X}\right) + M'Xs_G\right]\frac{dp_X}{dt_E^v}}_{\partial W^I}. \tag{2.10a}$$

A comparison of (2.10a) with (2.10) reveals that the permit involves a primary cost (dW^A plus dW^O) analogous to that under the emissions tax. In a first-best setting, where only the primary costs matter, the tax and permit policies have equivalent efficiency impacts (Table 1).

The permit policy also induces a similar tax-interaction effect (∂W^I) because, like an emissions tax, it drives up the price of consumption goods and reduces the real wage. The key difference from the emissions tax is the absence of the revenue-recycling effect, which implies that a given emissions reduction is more costly under the non-auctioned permit policy than under the emissions tax.[13]

2.4. Fuel tax

Next, consider a revenue-neutral tax of t_X per unit on the production of X. We refer to this as a fuel tax, implicitly regarding the pollution-related good X as a fuel. The general equilibrium cost of an incremental increase in the fuel tax is:

[12] The limited supply of emissions permits implies reduced output, which gives rise to economic rents.

[13] Parry (1997) and Goulder et al. (1997) examine in detail the significance of the revenue-recycling effect to the relative costs of permits and taxes.

$$-\frac{1}{\lambda}\frac{\mathrm{d}v}{\mathrm{d}t_X} = \underbrace{t_X\left(-\frac{\mathrm{d}X}{\mathrm{d}p_X}\right)}_{\mathrm{d}W^{\mathrm{O}}} - \underbrace{M\left(X + t_X\frac{\mathrm{d}X}{\mathrm{d}t_X}\right)}_{\partial W^{\mathrm{R}}} + \underbrace{(1+M)t_{\mathrm{L}}\left(-\frac{\partial L}{\partial p_X}\right) + M' s_{\mathrm{G}} X}_{\partial W^{\mathrm{I}}}. \tag{2.10b}$$

This expression differs from (2.10), which applies to the emissions tax, in that the abatement effect is missing. Under this policy, profits per unit of X are:

$$p_X - \{1 + t_X + c(a)\}. \tag{2.8a}$$

The first-order conditions for profit maximization imply $a = 0$. Because this policy does not raise the price of emissions, it gives firms no incentive to engage in end-of-pipe abatement expenditure and the policy generates only the output-substitution effect. For this reason the fuel tax fails to generate the efficient emissions-output ratio. As demonstrated in the numerical simulations below, the primary cost of the fuel tax exceeds that of the emissions tax and permit, for a given level of emissions reduction. This reflects the fuel tax's inability to exploit the abatement effect. The fuel tax also generates the tax-interaction and revenue-recycling effects because it increases the price of good X and raises revenue. Whether the fuel tax is more or less costly than the emissions permit depends on whether the fuel tax's failure to exploit the abatement effect is as important as the permit's failure to exploit the revenue-recycling effect. The numerical results of Section 4 will show that these relative costs depend importantly on the level of abatement.

2.5. Command-and-control policies

The literature on environmental regulation distinguishes two main types of command-and-control (CAC) policies: technology mandates and performance standards. Technology mandates require firms to adopt a specific pollution abatement technology, such as a catalytic converter on new cars or desulfurization equipment on new coal-fired power plants. Performance standards require firms to achieve a ratio of emissions to a measure of input or output that does not exceed a given maximum; examples here are the standards for NO_x emissions from power plants, which limit the ratio of such emissions to energy input. In the present analytical model, spending on abatement is the only way to reduce emissions per unit of output. Thus, technology mandates and performance standards are equivalent here. For now we refer to these policies as the technology mandate, but it should be kept in mind that the results here hold for the performance standard as well. The extended model incorporates intermediate inputs and thus allows input substitution, permitting us to distinguish the two types of policies.

If the policy mandated by the government is the most cost-effective among the available technology alternatives, we will refer to the policy as the least-cost mandated technology. If instead the regulators compel firms to adopt a technology that is not the most cost-effective, we will label the policy as a higher-cost mandated technology. We employ the parameter θ to represent the proportion by which the cost of the higher-cost technology mandate exceeds that of the least-cost mandate. Specifically, we represent the cost of the abatement effect under technology mandate by $\theta c(a)$, where $\theta = 1$ under the least-cost policy and $\theta > 1$ under the higher-cost policy.[14]

The general equilibrium cost of the technology mandate is:

$$-\frac{1}{\lambda}\frac{\mathrm{d}v}{\mathrm{d}a} = \underbrace{\theta c'(a)X}_{\mathrm{d}W^{\mathrm{A}}} + \underbrace{\left[(1+M)t_{\mathrm{L}}\left(-\frac{\partial L}{\partial p_X}\right) + M' s_{\mathrm{G}} X\right]\frac{\mathrm{d}p_X}{\mathrm{d}a}}_{\partial W^{\mathrm{I}}}. \qquad (2.10\mathrm{c})$$

The cost is higher than under the emissions tax for two main reasons. First, this policy involves a higher primary cost because it does not fully utilize the output-substitution effect, $\mathrm{d}W^{\mathrm{O}}$.[15] Under the technology mandate, the regulator specifies both the type of technology, indexed by θ, and the required level of end-of-pipe abatement per unit of output, indicated by a. Profits per unit of X are:

$$p_X - \{1 + \theta c(a)\}. \qquad (2.8\mathrm{b})$$

Unlike the emissions tax, the technology mandate does not charge firms for their 'residual emissions' – the per-unit emissions that the firm continues to generate after the policy is introduced. In contrast, under the emissions tax, if a firm produces another unit of output, it incurs not only the cost of the additional inputs and additional abatement expense but also the tax on residual emissions. Thus, when $\theta = 1$ the price of output will be lower under the technology mandate than under the emissions tax, as is evident from comparing the unit cost of good X under the technology mandate and under the emissions tax (the bracketed terms in (2.8) and (2.8b)). Because the price of output is too low under the technology

[14] This is an ad hoc assumption because θ is imposed exogenously rather than determined by the model. We include the higher-cost policy as a reminder that the compliance costs of command-and-control policies are likely to be significantly higher in a more general model that captures heterogeneity in the costs of emissions reduction among firms and imperfect information among regulators about firms' costs of abatement.

[15] As indicated by (2.10c), the output-substitution effect is absent for incremental changes in a. However, this effect is non-zero for larger changes.

mandate, it does not fully exploit the output-substitution effect, and this contributes to higher primary costs.

In addition, the technology mandate involves higher second-best costs than those under the emissions tax. For a small or moderate θ, the output price is lower under the technology mandate than under the emissions tax, so the tax-interaction effect is smaller. However, since the revenue-recycling effect is absent, the overall second-best costs are higher. Although both primary costs and second-best costs are higher, the ratio of these costs is the same as the corresponding ratio under the emissions tax, as discussed below. Thus, the higher costs of the technology mandate reflect both higher primary costs and higher second-best costs.

2.6. The cost impact of pre-existing taxes

We now explore how pre-existing taxes affect the overall costs of emissions reductions under each policy. Here we compare overall efficiency costs (including second-best effects) to the primary costs alone. While previous subsections observed only incremental changes, here we consider large changes. We assume demand, supply and marginal cost curves are linear in order to obtain second-order cost approximations. These restrictions are avoided in the numerical simulations presented in Section 4.

2.6.1. Emissions tax

The ratio of the general equilibrium cost of the emissions tax relative to the primary cost is:

$$\frac{\Delta W^{A} + \Delta W^{O} - \Delta W^{R} + \Delta W^{I}}{\Delta W^{A} + \Delta W^{O}} = 1 + M. \tag{2.11}$$

Since $M > 0$, this term will be greater than 1, indicating that the costs associated with the tax-interaction effect are only partly offset by the revenue-recycling effect. Thus, despite the fact that the revenues from the emissions tax are devoted to cuts in distortionary taxes, pre-existing taxes raise the policy's costs. This is the case because the policy raises revenues from a narrow-based (emissions) tax at the expense of revenues from a broad-based (labor) tax, and narrow-based taxes involve higher costs.[16]

Under this policy, the net efficiency impact from the combination of the

[16] This is now a familiar result. Thus, given the initial conditions specified here, such reforms yield an environmental 'dividend' but not a double (i.e., second) dividend in the form of a reduction in the overall efficiency cost of the tax system. For more discussion, see the surveys by Oates (1995), Goulder (1995b), and Bovenberg and Goulder (1997) and the references therein. Formula (2.11) assumes that X and Y are equal substitutes for leisure. If X were instead a relatively weak substitute for leisure, the revenue-recycling effect could exceed the tax-interaction effect (Parry, 1995).

tax-interaction and revenue-recycling effects is proportional to primary cost. The magnitude of the tax-interaction effect depends on the change in output price, which in turn is determined by the primary cost and the charge on residual emissions. The size of the revenue-recycling effect depends on the charge on residual emissions. When the revenue-recycling effect is subtracted from the tax-interaction effect, the contributions from the charge on residual emissions cancel, and thus the net efficiency impact is proportional to primary cost.

Table 2 offers an intuitive summary of the contribution of the second-best effects to the overall costs of the emissions tax and other policies. Because the emissions tax applies to residual emissions, it leads to a 'large' impact on output prices, and the tax-interaction effect is large. The revenue-recycling effect is large as well. The overall second-best contribution is described as moderate, because the revenue-recycling effect offsets much of the tax-interaction effect.

2.6.2. Emissions permits

The general equilibrium cost of the permit policy expressed relative to the primary cost is:

$$\frac{\Delta W^{A} + \Delta W^{O} + \Delta W^{I}}{\Delta W^{A} + \Delta W^{O}} = 1 + M + \frac{2M'[1 - (\Delta E/E_0)]}{\Delta E/E_0}. \tag{2.11a}$$

This expression exceeds $1+M$ in (2.11) so long as the proportionate emissions reduction, $\Delta E/E_0$, is less than unity. Thus, interactions with the tax system raise the cost of the permit proportionately more than they raise the costs of the emissions tax because non-auctioned permits do not generate the efficiency benefit from the revenue-recycling effect. In fact, using our benchmark assumptions of $t_L = 0.4$, $\varepsilon^C = 0.4$ and $\varepsilon^U = 0.15$ (see below), Eq. (2.11a) implies that when the proportionate reduction in emissions is 10 percent, the general equilibrium costs of emissions permits are 6.5 times the primary costs! Thus, as indicated in Table 2,

Table 2
Second-best contributions to overall costs

Instrument	Impact on output price	Tax-interaction effect[a]	Revenue-recycling effect[a]	Proportional net second-best contribution[a]
Emissions tax[b]	Large	Large	Large	Moderate
(Non-auctioned) emissions permits	Large	Large	0	Potentially huge
Performance standard	Moderate	Moderate	0	Moderate
Technology mandate	Moderate	Moderate	0	Moderate
Fuels tax[b]	Large	Large	Large	Moderate

[a]Relative to primary cost.
[b]It is assumed that revenues from the tax are used to finance cuts in rates of pre-existing taxes. See text for discussion.

the contribution of prior taxes to the costs of emissions permits is potentially huge. However, in the limit as the proportionate emissions reduction approaches unity, the cost discrepancy between the emissions permit and emissions tax declines to zero. This happens because at 100 percent emissions reduction the emissions tax generates no revenue and hence no revenue-recycling effect.

2.6.3. Fuel tax

The ratio of general equilibrium costs to primary costs under the fuel tax is again $1 + M$. Just as under the emissions tax, there is a large tax-interaction effect and a large and partly offsetting revenue-recycling effect. Thus, the proportional net impact of the tax-interaction and revenue-recycling effects is the same as under the emissions tax, as summarized in Table 2. However, since primary costs are higher under the fuel tax (as discussed in Section 2.4 above), the overall costs (including second-best costs) are higher.

2.6.4. Technology mandate

The general equilibrium cost of the technology mandate expressed relative to the primary cost is:

$$\frac{\Delta W^{A} + \Delta W^{I}}{\Delta W^{A}} = 1 + M. \tag{2.11b}$$

The proportional increase in cost under this policy is the same as that under the emissions tax, which is lower than that under the emissions permit. Like the emissions permit, the technology mandate does not generate the revenue-recycling effect. However, this is compensated for by the fact that the tax-interaction effect is relatively weaker than under the emissions tax and permit. Thus the overall second-best impact under this policy is moderate (Table 2). Note that θ does not enter (2.11b): although θ directly affects the primary costs of a CAC policy, it has no effect on the ratio of overall costs to primary costs.

2.6.5. Summary

This analysis has decomposed the overall efficiency costs of different instruments into primary costs (reflecting the abatement and output-substitution effects) and the second-best tax-interaction and revenue-recycling effects. In a first-best setting, the emissions tax and permit policies have identical primary costs. The fuel tax and technology mandate have higher primary costs because they do not fully exploit the potential channels for emissions reduction.

In a second-best setting, the cost-rankings change significantly. Second-best interactions substantially raise the cost of the permit policy relative to other policies because the permit policy does not generate the revenue-recycling effect to counteract the tax-interaction effect. The technology mandate does not produce the revenue-recycling effect either, but this is compensated for by the fact that it produces a relatively weak tax-interaction effect. At 'low' levels of emissions abatement, the marginal revenue-recycling effect is very large and becomes an especially important determinant of relative policy costs.

3. The numerical model

We now extend the previous model by incorporating intermediate inputs in production. This yields a new channel for emissions reduction: now emissions can be reduced not only through output-substitution and abatement effects but also by way of the *input-substitution effect* – altering the mix of intermediate inputs. Incorporating intermediate goods provides greater realism and allows the performance standard and technology mandate to have different economic impacts.

The numerical model distinguishes two intermediate goods: a polluting intermediate good (D) and a 'clean' intermediate good (N). As before, there are two final consumption goods: C_N represents final output from industries that use N relatively more intensively, and C_D is final output from industries that use D relatively more intensively. The extended model is solved numerically to obtain 'exact' welfare assessments, in contrast with the second-order approximations obtained above. This is potentially important for 'large' reductions in emissions. (A full model description is in our earlier working paper (Goulder et al., 1998) and in an appendix available from the authors on request.)

3.1. Model structure

3.1.1. Household behavior

As in the previous model, a representative household derives utility from consumption (of C_N and C_D) and from leisure, according to the constant-elasticity-of-substitution (CES) utility function:

$$U = U(l, C_D, C_N, E) = \left(\alpha_l l^{(\sigma_U - 1)/\sigma_U} + \alpha_F C^{(\sigma_U - 1)/\sigma_U}\right)^{\sigma_U/(\sigma_U - 1)} - \phi(E), \qquad (3.1)$$

where C is composite consumption, defined by

$$C = \left(\alpha_{C_D} C_D^{(\sigma_C - 1)/\sigma_C} + \alpha_{C_N} C_N^{(\sigma_C - 1)/\sigma_C}\right)^{\sigma_C/(\sigma_C - 1)}, \qquad (3.2)$$

and where $l \equiv \bar{L} - L$ represents leisure time, E is aggregate emissions, and the α's are parameters.[17] σ_U and σ_C are the elasticities of substitution between goods and

[17]Homothetic preferences over consumption goods, together with separability between consumption goods and leisure, imply that consumption goods are equal substitutes for leisure (Deaton, 1981).

leisure and between the two consumption goods, respectively. The household maximizes utility subject to the budget constraint:

$$p_{C_D}C_D + p_{C_N}C_N = p_L L(1 - t_L) + \pi(1 - t_R) + p_C G, \tag{3.3}$$

where t_L is the tax rate on labor income, t_R is the tax rate on rent income, L is labor time, π is policy-generated rent (applicable under the permit policy), G is (constant) real government spending in the form of transfers to households, and p_C is the composite price of consumption. Except in the sensitivity analysis in Section 5, the tax rates t_L and t_R are assumed to be the same. Taxes finance a fixed real level of government transfers to households.

3.1.2. *Firm behavior*

We use a CES form for production functions in all industries:

$$X_j = \left(\sum_i \alpha_{i,j} X_{i,j}^{(\sigma_j - 1)/\sigma_j}\right)^{\sigma_j/(\sigma_j - 1)}, \quad i = \{D,N,L\},\ j = \{D,N,C_D,C_N\}, \tag{3.4}$$

where X is output, the $\alpha_{i,j}$'s are share parameters, and the σ_j's are the elasticities of substitution between factors in production. Pollution emissions from industry j, E_j, follow

$$E_j = \beta_D X_{D,j}\left[1 - \alpha_E\left(\frac{A_j}{\beta_D X_{D,j}}\right)\right]^{\gamma}, \tag{3.5}$$

where A_j is real expenditure (in the form of additional labor input) by industry j on emissions abatement, α_E and γ are parameters describing the emissions abatement technology, and β_D represents emissions per unit of the polluting intermediate good. This emissions function is homogenous of degree one in abatement spending and in the amount of the polluting intermediate good used, which is consistent with the assumption of constant returns in production. The parameter γ determines the curvature of the abatement cost function. This function is assumed to be convex: $\gamma < 1$. Our central case value for γ is 0.5, implying that marginal abatement costs are linear.

Producers choose the profit-maximizing input quantities and abatement subject to any constraints imposed by pollution regulation, taking input and output prices as given. Profits equal the value of output minus expenditures on labor, intermediate inputs and abatement, less any tax charged per unit of residual emissions (τ_e) or per unit of output (τ_j). Thus, profit for industry j (π_j) is:

$$\pi_j = (p_j - \tau_j)X_j - \sum_i p_i X_{i,j} - \tau_e E_j - A_j, \tag{3.6}$$

where p_i and p_j are the prices of inputs and outputs, respectively. Note that because the production function and abatement function both exhibit constant returns to scale, profits will equal zero under all policies except the permit policy, under which profits equal permit rents.

3.1.3. Government policy

With this extended model we examine five policies: an emissions tax, a set of emissions permits, a fuel tax, a performance standard, and a technology mandate. These correspond to the policies examined earlier, except that by including intermediate inputs we now can distinguish the performance standard and technology mandate. As before we distinguish between a least-cost and higher-cost technology mandate.[18] The fuel tax is now levied on a (polluting) intermediate input rather than on a final good.

We assume that each policy is implemented in a way that avoids introducing additional efficiency losses attributable to the uneven treatment of industries. Therefore, in all cases policies are introduced so as to ensure that the private marginal cost of emissions reduction is equated across industries. Hence the emissions tax policy applies the same tax rate to all industries, the emissions permit is set such that the shadow price of the permit is constant across industries, and so forth.

The government's budget constraint is:

$$p_C G = t_L(T - l) + t_R \pi + \tau_e \sum_j E_j + \sum_j \tau_j X_j. \tag{3.7}$$

The tax rates t_L and t_R on labor and rent income are adjusted to hold government revenue constant.

3.1.4. Equilibrium conditions

In general equilibrium, supply must equal demand for all produced goods, government revenue must equal government transfer payments, and pollution emissions must equal a specified target. Because production and abatement functions are linearly homogeneous, the supply of each good is perfectly elastic at given factor prices and tax rates. Under these conditions the set of equilibrium conditions reduce to three equations: aggregate labor demand equals aggregate supply, government revenue equals expenditures, and aggregate pollution emissions equal the target level.[19]

3.2. Data and parameters

Table 3 summarizes our benchmark data set, which depicts the United States economy in 1990. Production data were obtained from the Commerce Department

[18] In the presence of heterogeneity a similar distinction could be made for the performance standard.
[19] More details on the solution of the numerical model are provided in Goulder et al. (1998).

Table 3
Benchmark data for the numerical model. Input–output flows (in millions of 1990 dollars per year except as otherwise noted)

	D	N	C_D	C_N	Leisure time	Total output value
D	91,441.0	111,842.7	156,881.1	6264.3		366,429.1
N	88,073.5	4,741,097.5	464,159.9	2,670,485.6		7,963,816.5
L	186,914.7	3,110,876.3			1,832,106.1	5,129,897.1
Total output value	366,429.1	7,963,816.5	621,041.0	2,676,750.0		
Emissions (millions of tons)	23.0					

$\sigma_D = \sigma_N = 0.8$ (elasticities of substitution in intermediate goods production).
$\sigma_{C_D} = \sigma_{C_N} = 0.9$ (elasticities of substitution in final goods production).
$\sigma_C = 0.85$, $\sigma_U = 0.96$ (elasticities of substitution between final goods and between consumption and leisure, respectively).
$\alpha_E = 1.55 \times 10^{-4}$ (effectiveness of technological abatement).
$\gamma = 0.5$ (curvature of abatement cost function – implies linear marginal abatement costs).

Bureau of Economic Analysis. The pollution-related intermediate good comprises fossil fuels (oil, coal, and natural gas), while the clean intermediate good includes all other intermediates. The consumer good C_D is a composite of the consumer goods whose production involves intensive use of fossil fuels (utilities, motor vehicles, and gasoline), while the good C_N embraces all other final goods.

Elasticities of substitution in the production functions and the inner nest of the consumer utility function are taken from the disaggregated general equilibrium data set developed by Cruz and Goulder (1992). The α distribution parameters for production functions were calibrated based on assumed elasticities of substitution and the identifying restriction that firms adopt cost-minimizing mixes of inputs.

An important preference parameter is σ_U, the consumption-leisure substitution elasticity. We choose the value for this parameter, along with the labor time endowment, to imply uncompensated and compensated labor supply elasticities of 0.15 and 0.4, respectively. These are typical estimates from the literature and are meant to represent the effects of changes in the real wage on average hours worked and the labor force participation rate.[20] We assume a pre-existing tax rate on labor and rent income of 40 percent.[21] These parameters imply a marginal

[20]These values are roughly consistent with a recent survey of opinion among labor economists by Fuchs et al. (1998), assuming a weight of 0.6 and 0.4 for the male and female elasticities reported in Table 2 of that survey.

[21]The effective tax rates on labor and profit income are roughly the same: labor is subject to personal income and payroll tax, while capital is subject to personal and corporate income tax. Total revenues from income taxes amount to about 36 percent of net national product. The marginal tax rate is higher because of various deductions. Other studies assume factor income rates of around 40 percent (Browning, 1987; Lucas, 1990).

excess burden of labor taxation in our model equal to 0.3, which is consistent with other studies (see, e.g., Browning, 1987).

Our central case values for pollution-related parameters are based on characteristics of NO_x emissions. The pollution content for the polluting intermediate good (the β_D parameter) is derived by dividing the actual 1990 emissions of NO_x, as given by Pechan et al. (1996), by the quantity of the polluting good. The parameter α_E, which expresses the effectiveness of abatement, was calibrated so that 2.2 million tons of emissions abatement (relative to initial emissions of 23.0 million tons) could be achieved at a marginal cost of US$500 per ton, a figure extrapolated from Pechan et al. (1996). Although our model is benchmarked based on characteristics of NO_x emissions, in Section 4.4 below we adopt different data assumptions to examine how alternative characteristics of pollution generation or abatement might affect policy costs.

4. Numerical results

To facilitate comparisons among policies we use the emissions tax costs as a reference point, comparing the costs of other policies to these costs. We emphasize the rankings of policy costs, as opposed to absolute costs, and examine how the rankings depend on parameters of the abatement-cost, production, and utility (consumer demand) functions. These parameters affect cost by determining the relative contributions of the abatement, and input-substitution, and output-substitution effects. We abstract from heterogeneity in firms' production technologies (and thus in abatement costs). Such heterogeneity can affect – perhaps dramatically – the relative costs of command-and-control policies by imposing additional informational burdens or by affecting the extent to which regulations equate marginal abatement costs across firms or industries.

4.1. First-best costs

We first examine costs in a first-best setting ($t_L = 0$), where only the primary costs apply. Fig. 1a shows costs under the different policy instruments, expressed as the ratio of the total costs of the policy in question to the total costs under the emissions tax.[22] The curve for the permit policy is constant at unity; that is, the costs of the emissions tax and permit policy are identical at all levels of emissions reduction. In the absence of distortionary taxes, the tax-interaction and revenue-recycling effects do not apply, and thus the source of differences in cost impacts – the revenue-recycling effect – is absent.

The first-best cost of the performance standard exceeds that of the emissions tax.

[22]These are calculated by setting the labor tax in the numerical model equal to zero and returning any government revenues from the policies as lump sum transfers to households.

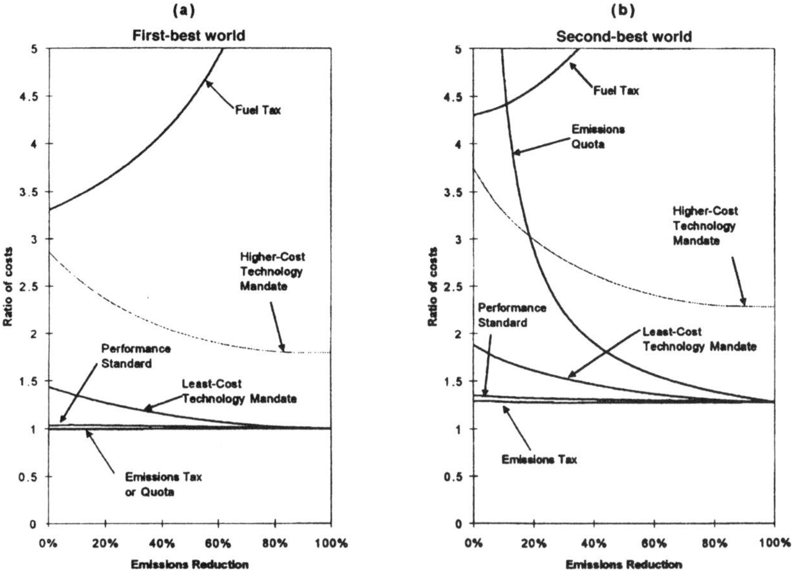

Fig. 1. Ratio of cost under policy alternative to cost under first-best emissions tax.

This is the case because the performance standard does not charge firms for residual emissions; hence the output-substitution effect is inefficiently weak. However, the cost discrepancy between the two instruments is very small because the output-substitution effect plays a relatively small role in reducing NO_x emissions.[23]

The cost of the least-cost technology mandate is higher than that of the performance standard. The technology mandate is the more restrictive of the two policies because firms have no incentive to reduce emissions by input-substitution. We assume that the abatement costs under the higher-cost technology mandate are twice those under the least cost mandate (i.e., $\theta = 2$). Under this assumption, the general equilibrium total costs of the higher-cost mandate in the first-best setting turn out to be roughly twice those of the least-cost mandate at all levels of emissions reduction.

Finally, the first-best cost of the fuel tax exceeds that of the emissions tax. Under the fuel tax, the abatement effect is absent. The bulk of NO_x emissions reductions under the emissions tax come from the abatement effect, and thus the fuel tax is much more costly than the emissions tax.

[23]In the central case, a 50 percent reduction in emissions under an emissions tax achieves 79.0 percent of that reduction through the abatement effect, 18.5 percent through the input-substitution effect, and only 2.5 percent through the output-substitution effect.

Importantly – and perhaps surprisingly – the costs of the least-cost technology mandate and performance standard converge to those of the emissions tax and permit policy at 100 percent emissions reduction. This finding is robust to different parameter assumptions, as confirmed in the sensitivity analysis below.[24] In contrast with the emissions tax case, under the performance standard firms are not charged for their residual emissions, and thus the output-substitution effect is not fully utilized. This difference declines in importance at higher levels of emissions reduction. At 100 percent emissions reduction, there are no residual emissions, and both policies have the same effect on the price of the polluting good and the same output-substitution effect. Thus, their costs converge to the same value.[25] Like the performance standard, the technology mandate fails to fully utilize the output-substitution effect. Furthermore, the technology mandate fails to exploit the input-substitution effect, and thus has higher costs. However, the importance of this effect converges to zero as emissions reductions approach 100 percent. Thus the technology mandate's costs also converge to those of the other policies.

4.2. The significance of pre-existing taxes

Fig. 1b shows the general equilibrium costs of the policy instruments in a second-best setting with $t_L = 0.4$ initially. These costs are expressed relative to those of the emissions tax in a first-best world. By comparing results of Fig. 1b with those in Fig. 1a, one observes the impact of pre-existing taxes.

For the emissions tax, second-best costs exceed first-best costs by a constant factor of 1.27 – the tax-interaction and revenue-recycling effects contribute to a 27 percent increase in the costs of the emissions tax.[26] The second-best costs of the performance standard, technology mandate and fuel tax exceed those of the emissions tax by the same proportions as in Fig. 1a; pre-existing taxes raise the costs of all these policies by about 27 percent. The net impact of the tax-

[24]The form of our abatement cost function (Eq. (3.2)) implies that firms can entirely eliminate emissions at finite cost. For many pollutants, for example lead and chlorofluorocarbons, this is a realistic assumption, since there are substitute inputs or alternative processes that yield the same economic services and involve nearly zero costs. But the assumption is not always apt. Williams (1998b) examines the scenario where marginal abatement costs approach infinity as emissions approach zero and finds that the convergence result still holds in some cases.

[25] Fig. 1a also shows that the relative inefficiency of the fuel tax is larger, the greater the extent of emissions reduction. This is not necessarily a general result, but arises because of our assumed functional forms. For details, see Goulder et al. (1998).

[26]The 27 percent increase is not entirely attributable to the net impact of the tax-interaction and revenue-recycling effects. We find that when one moves from a first-best to a second-best setting, primary costs rise. In our numerical simulations about half of the 27 percent increase reflects the increase in primary costs.

interaction and revenue-recycling effects is proportional to primary cost.[27]

The results of Fig. 1b for the impact of prior taxes are particularly striking in the case of the permit policy. Here, interactions with the tax system raise the overall costs by a larger amount, reflecting the fact that permits do not generate a revenue-recycling effect to counteract the tax-interaction effect. The differences in costs are especially great at modest levels of abatement. For emissions reductions below 24 percent, the cost of the permit policy is more than double that of the tax. However, under the emissions tax the marginal revenue-recycling effect declines with the level of emissions reductions as the tax base is eroded. At 100 percent abatement, no emissions tax revenues are raised and there is no revenue-recycling effect; thus the total costs of the emissions tax and permit are equal.[28]

Four points deserve emphasis. First, only the permit policy has positive marginal costs at initial, incremental abatement. An incremental amount of abatement increases the effective tax on labor through the tax-interaction effect. In a world with prior labor taxes, an incremental increase in the effective labor tax yields a first-order welfare cost – marginal costs are not incremental. In contrast, under the emissions tax marginal costs are zero at initial abatement, so the ratio of total costs of the permit and emissions-tax policies is infinite. For all the other instruments, at initial abatement the tax-interaction and revenue-recycling effects either are zero or they exactly offset each other, so that marginal costs are zero.[29]

[27]For the two tax instruments, this proportionality occurs because the revenue-recycling effect exactly offsets the portion of the tax-interaction effect resulting from the charge on residual emissions, leaving a net second-best effect that is proportional to the first-best cost of the tax, as discussed in Section 2. The technology mandate and performance standard do not charge firms for residual emissions; hence under these policies the increase in price of final output only depends on the costs of abatement and input substitution – the first-best costs. Thus, in these cases, the tax-interaction effect itself is proportional to the first-best cost of the policy. Since these policies do not involve a revenue-recycling effect, the overall second-best effect is proportional as well.

[28]Note that the numerical model incorporates an indirect revenue-recycling effect from the taxation of permit rents. This equals 40 percent of the revenue-recycling effect under the emissions tax. Thus, the difference between the tax and permit is smaller than predicted by the analytical model, which ignores the taxation of permit rents.

[29]In the case of the performance standard and technology mandate, the tax-interaction and revenue-recycling effects are both zero at initial abatement. Thus the marginal cost curves emerge from the origin. A similar result was obtained by Fullerton and Metcalf (1997) under their technology-restriction policy, which resembles the performance standard considered here. The permit policy's marginal cost curve does not emerge from the origin because it has an efficiency loss from the tax-interaction effect and no offsetting revenue-recycling effect. There are other cases under which the net impact of the tax-interaction and revenue-recycling effects is strictly positive at incremental abatement. These include the case where the government introduces an emissions tax and returns the revenues in lump-sum fashion, and the case where the government policy increases the returns to a perfectly inelastic factor of production (Williams, 1998c, and, in the context of trade policy, Williams, 1998a). What is common to all these cases is that the government policy has effectuated a lump-sum transfer to the private sector, either by generating untaxed scarcity rents (the case emphasized by Fullerton and Metcalf), by providing explicit lump-sum transfers, or by generating additional rents to fixed factors. In a world with distortionary taxes, lump-sum transfers from the government to the private sector are costly in efficiency terms because the government ultimately must finance such transfers through distortionary taxes.

Thus, for these other policies, the ratio of total costs is finite at initial, incremental abatement.

Second, the efficiency consequences of the permit policy depend importantly on the fact that permits are not auctioned, which means that the revenue-recycling effect is not exploited. If permits were auctioned and the revenues used to finance cuts in the marginal rates of pre-existing taxes, the efficiency impacts would be the same as that of the emissions tax.

Third, these results bear importantly on the evaluation of tradable permits systems. A key attraction of such systems is that they help achieve a more efficient allocation of abatement effort by promoting an equilibrium in which producers' marginal costs of abatement are equal. Typical estimates indicate that allowing for trades can reduce costs of compliance by 30 percent or more relative to the costs of a system with fixed emissions permits (that is, with no trades).[30] The results of Fig. 1b indicate that second-best considerations can have an equal or larger impact on costs. *The decision whether to grandfather or auction the permits can be as important to policy costs as the decision about whether to allow trades.*

Finally, the presence or absence of the revenue-recycling effect is also very important to the costs of emissions taxes. If revenues from an emissions tax were returned as lump-sum payments rather than used to reduce pre-existing tax rates, the revenue-recycling effect would not materialize and the costs of the emissions tax in our model would be the same as those of the (non-auctioned) emissions permit. Thus, Fig. 1b indicates that the cost of achieving a given abatement target can depend as much on how revenues are recycled as on the choice of whether to introduce an emissions tax or a fuels tax, particularly when modest levels of abatement are involved.

Regulations promulgated under the 1990 Clean Air Act Amendments are expected to yield about a 20 percent economy-wide reduction in NO_x emissions (relative to the projected baseline) in 2005.[31] These regulations rely mainly on performance standards. Our modeling suggests that pre-existing taxes raise the cost of these regulations in 2005 by about US$1.3 billion (1990 dollars). Fig. 1b suggests that achieving this overall reduction would be considerably more costly under (non-auctioned) tradable permits than under performance standards, unless the performance standards were imposed in an extremely inefficient way.[32]

[30]Tietenberg (1985) surveyed 11 studies, with costs under command and control estimated to be over six times larger on average as costs under the ideal least-cost approach. Numerous other studies have found significant cost savings from tradable pollution permit programs, although costs under these programs typically exceed the theoretical minimum by a substantial amount, in part because of flaws in program design (Hahn, 1989).

[31]This estimate is extrapolated from Pechan et al. (1996).

[32]Here we compare costs of achieving reductions in NO_x emissions by performance standards alone and by permits alone. There have been several recent proposals to superimpose regional permit-trading programs on existing regulations (which mainly involve performance standards). Calculating the costs of this mix of regulations requires attention to regional issues as well as considerably more industry disaggregation than that of the present model. In future work we hope to perform such cost calculations.

4.3. Alternative scenarios

We now examine the impacts of alternative parameterizations that change the relative importance of the output-substitution, input-substitution and abatement effects. The first alternative reduces α_E in (3.2) in order to quadruple the marginal abatement cost relative to the central case at given levels of abatement.[33] Fig. 2a shows the implications of this change for the second-best cost of each policy relative to the first-best emissions tax. Changing this parameter has virtually no effect on the curves for the emissions permit or performance standard, relative to the corresponding curves in Fig. 1b.[34] However, this change significantly raises the relative cost of the technology mandates, since technology mandates achieve a much greater proportion of emissions reduction through spending on abatement than does the emissions tax. In contrast, the absolute cost of the fuel tax remains unchanged in this scenario, since it does not utilize the abatement effect. Hence this policy's relative cost is now lower.

In Fig. 2b we quadruple the value of the substitution elasticity between consumer goods to increase the relative importance of the output-substitution effect. This has very little impact on the position of the curves relative to those in Fig. 1b because it is still the case that only a small fraction of the emissions

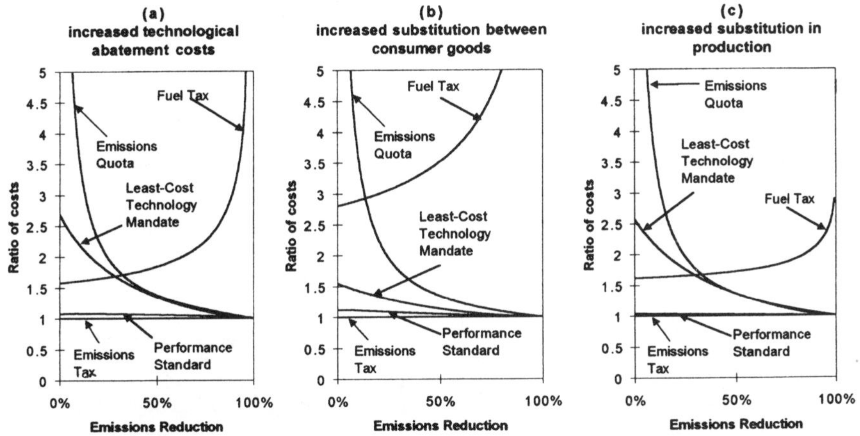

Fig. 2. Cost ratios under alternative parameter assumptions.

[33]This variable differs widely among pollutants. For instance, the abatement effect is relatively less important in the context of reducing SO_2 emissions than for NO_x emissions. Some of the reduction in SO_2 emissions following the 1990 Clean Air Act Amendments has come from installing abatement technologies (scrubbers) but a more substantial part has come from substituting in favor of cleaner inputs (lower sulfur coal). In the case of CO_2, there are no commercially available abatement technologies.

[34]That is, the *ratio* of the cost under each policy to the cost under the emissions tax does not change. The *absolute* costs are of course greater in this alternative scenario.

reduction is due to the output substitution effect. Indeed, for all major pollutants, the bulk of emission reduction comes from reducing the emissions-output ratio, rather than by substituting away from pollution-related goods in consumption.

In Fig. 2c we quadruple the elasticity of substitution in production, which increases the importance of the input-substitution effect. This has virtually no impact on the relative cost of the emissions permit or performance standard. The technology mandate, however, derives relatively little of its emissions reductions from the input-substitution effect, so its cost relative to the emissions tax rises, even though its absolute cost falls slightly. In contrast, the relative cost of the fuel tax falls because it relies on the input substitution effect much more than the emissions tax does.

4.4. *Efficiency impacts*

We now consider the net efficiency impacts – environmental benefits less economic costs – of the different policies (under central values for parameters). Here we posit a range of values for the (constant) marginal benefits from reductions in NO_x emissions (or marginal damages from such emissions), and calculate the optimal level of abatement and net efficiency gain associated with each posited value.

Fig. 3a displays, in a first-best world, the ratio of the maximum efficiency gain

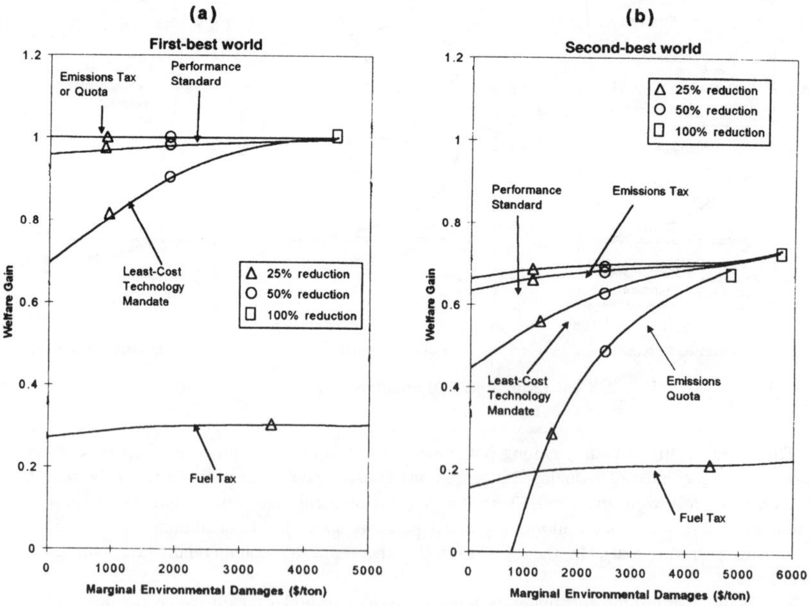

Fig. 3. Ratio of maximum welfare gain under given instrument to maximum gain under first-best tax.

under each policy to the efficiency gain under the optimal emissions tax. Fig. 3b offers complementary information: the ratio of the maximum gain under each policy in a second-best world to the maximum gain from an emissions tax in a first-best world. Thus, the differences in the ratios for Fig. 3a,b reveal the significance of pre-existing taxes. On each graph, the horizontal axis depicts the posited value for marginal pollution damages, while the triangles, circles, and rectangles respectively show, for each policy, the level of marginal damages that implies optimal emissions reductions of 25, 50, and 100 percent.

In the first-best case, the initial marginal cost for each policy is zero; hence there is scope for an efficiency gain so long as marginal pollution damages (marginal benefits from abatement) are positive. The potential efficiency gains are largest under the emissions tax and permit, as expected, since these policies have the lowest primary costs. Policies with higher primary costs produce lower potential efficiency gains.

The level of marginal damages necessary to justify a given level of emissions reduction also varies among the different policies. Marginal costs of emissions reductions are lowest for the emissions tax and permit; hence a given level of emissions reduction is justified at a lower level of marginal benefits. The other policies have higher marginal costs and thus require higher levels of marginal damages to justify a given level of emissions reduction. When marginal damages justify a 100 percent emissions reduction under the other policies, the efficient level of emissions reduction under the fuel tax is less than 50 percent.

In the second-best case shown in Fig. 3b, the same principles apply, but since the costs of all policies are higher, the potential overall efficiency gains are substantially lower. Under emissions permits, second-best elements have the most profound impact on marginal costs and, consequently, on potential efficiency gains. In fact, tradable permits cannot produce an efficiency gain unless marginal damages exceed a certain threshold value. This stems from the fact that, in the second-best case, the initial marginal cost of a permit policy is strictly positive, in contrast with the other policy instruments examined here.

As in the first-best situation, in a second-best world the efficient level of emissions reduction associated with a given value for marginal damages varies across policies. The sharpest differences are between the fuel tax and other policies. At values for marginal damages that justify nearly 100 percent emissions reduction for the other policies, the optimal emissions reduction under the fuel tax is only about 25 percent. This reflects the fact that marginal abatement costs rise most sharply under the fuel tax.

4.5. Further sensitivity analysis

Table 4 summarizes the sensitivity of the numerical results to a range of values for other important parameters. We vary the compensated and uncompensated labor supply elasticities, the initial labor tax rate, and the curvature parameter for

Table 4
Sensitivity analysis. Ratio of total costs under each policy to total costs under the emissions tax

	Emissions quota	Performance standard	Least-cost technology mandate	Fuel tax
1. Central case				
25% reduction	1.992	1.035	1.238	3.677
50% reduction	1.345	1.025	1.112	4.348
75% reduction	1.123	1.014	1.036	5.804
2a. Uncompensated labor supply elasticity=0.0 ($\sigma_U = 0.6$)				
25% reduction	1.983	1.035	1.236	3.700
50% reduction	1.346	1.025	1.112	4.410
75% reduction	1.123	1.013	1.036	6.022
2b. Uncompensated labor supply elasticity=0.3 ($\sigma_U = 2.4$)				
25% reduction	1.997	1.035	1.237	3.656
50% reduction	1.350	1.025	1.112	4.294
75% reduction	1.126	1.014	1.036	5.705
3a. Compensated labor supply elasticity=0.2 ($\sigma_U = 2.4$, $T=3.587\times10^{12}$)				
25% reduction	1.499	1.035	1.237	3.672
50% reduction	1.174	1.025	1.111	4.315
75% reduction	1.062	1.014	1.036	5.645
3b. Compensated labor supply elasticity=0.6 ($\sigma_U = 0.8$, $T=7.795\times10^{12}$)				
25% reduction	2.490	1.035	1.238	3.683
50% reduction	1.522	1.025	1.112	4.388
75% reduction	1.187	1.014	1.036	6.010
4a. Initial labor tax rate=0.2				
25% reduction	1.369	1.035	1.236	3.692
50% reduction	1.130	1.025	1.112	4.363
75% reduction	1.046	1.013	1.035	5.803
4b. Initial labor tax rate=0.6				
25% reduction	3.240	1.033	1.234	3.652
50% reduction	1.845	1.024	1.114	4.682
75% reduction	1.332	1.013	1.039	[a]
5a. Abatement cost curvature parameter $\gamma=0.6667$				
25% reduction	1.776	1.022	1.122	3.876
50% reduction	1.256	1.011	1.041	6.457
75% reduction	1.087	1.005	1.012	10.832
5b. Abatement cost curvature parameter $\gamma=0.3333$				
25% reduction	2.268	1.057	1.559	3.641
50% reduction	1.475	1.063	1.430	2.710
75% reduction	1.202	1.054	1.199	2.496

[a] In this case, for emissions reductions over 60% government revenues are insufficient to cover expenditures for any value of the labor tax rate, and thus no equilibrium exists.

the abatement cost function. The table displays the ratio of the total cost under each policy to the total cost under the emissions tax in a second-best setting, under a range of parameter values. These cost ratios are shown for emissions reductions of 25, 50, and 75 percent.

In the second and third rows we vary labor supply elasticities and pre-existing tax rates. Higher elasticities imply a greater degree of substitution between consumption and leisure, and this strengthens the tax-interaction and revenue-recycling effects. The costs of emissions permits are more sensitive to these elasticities than the costs of the emissions tax and fuel tax, since emissions permits do not generate the (offsetting) revenue-recycling effect. The costs of the performance standard and technology mandate are also less sensitive to these elasticities than emissions permits, since the tax-interaction effect is less important for these policies. For similar reasons, the relative costs of emissions permits are more sensitive to higher rates of pre-existing taxes, which strengthen the tax-interaction and revenue-recycling effects.

The final set of rows considers cases where firms' marginal cost curves are concave (row 5a) or convex (row 5b) in abatement expenditure, as opposed to linear (see (3.2)).[35] When these curves become concave (convex), the importance of the abatement effect is increased (decreased). Consequently, the relative costs of the performance standard and technology mandate increase (decrease) while the relative costs of the fuel tax are reduced (increased). This occurs because the performance standard and technology mandate rely relatively heavily on the abatement effect, while the fuel tax does not utilize this effect.

5. Conclusions

This paper has employed analytical and numerical general equilibrium models to compare, in first- and second-best settings, the cost-effectiveness of a range of environmental policy instruments. We find that, in both first- and second-best settings, the relative costs of the different instruments depend crucially on the level of emissions reduction. Indeed, for all of the instruments except the fuel tax, the costs of abatement converge as the level of abatement approaches 100 percent.

Pre-existing taxes significantly raise the costs of all environmental policies relative to their costs in a first-best world. The cost increase is proportionally larger for (non-auctioned) emissions permits than for the other policy instruments. Earlier work on instrument choice has emphasized the superiority of tradable emissions permits relative to command-and-control policies like performance standards and mandated technologies. Our results indicate that pre-existing taxes can undo the cost advantage of tradable permits over these other instruments.

[35]For more details on this simulation, see Goulder et al. (1998).

Indeed, numerical results suggest that achieving the NO_x emissions reductions required under the 1990 Clean Air Act Amendments would be more costly under tradable permits than under performance standards unless the permits were auctioned.

Some limitations in the present study deserve attention. First, our analysis does not incorporate heterogeneity among polluting firms within a given industry. The significance of heterogeneity extends beyond the issue, discussed above, of the attractiveness of allowing trades in emissions rights. Heterogeneity augments the information burdens faced by regulators and consequently implies that mandated technologies will tend to be less efficient than suggested here, because regulators will have a difficult time discerning what technology is most appropriate. In addition, heterogeneity implies that many forms of regulation will involve serious costs of standard-setting, monitoring, and enforcement. To the extent that it is easier, for example, to monitor fuels or the use of mandated equipment than it is to monitor emissions, the fuel tax and mandated technology would enjoy an advantage over other policies. Thus, heterogeneous production and the associated information problems produce additional cost considerations that could importantly affect the relative attractiveness of the policies we have considered.[36]

Second, our analysis is static. Clearly the various policy instruments will differ in terms of their impacts for investments in research and development and the associated potential to reduce future costs of abatement. These dynamic effects may have significant welfare consequences that are not captured by our analysis.[37]

Finally, this study concentrates solely on efficiency issues. A comprehensive evaluation of alternative policy instruments must also take account of distributional impacts. Indeed, some would maintain that political feasibility is influenced far more by distributional concerns than by efficiency calculations. Future work that integrates efficiency and distributional issues in a second-best context may provide additional useful and highly practical policy insights.

Acknowledgements

The authors gratefully acknowledge helpful comments from Jesse David, Carolyn Fischer, Don Fullerton, Koshy Mathai, Robert Stavins, and Michael Toman. We also thank the National Science Foundation (grants SBR-9310362 and SBR-9613458) and Environmental Protection Agency (grant R825313-01) for financial support.

[36] See, for example, Tietenberg (1985).

[37] For a theoretical investigation of the dynamic implications of instrument choice, see Milliman and Prince (1989) and Fischer et al. (1998). For a recent empirical examination, see Newell et al. (1998).

References

Ballard, C.L., Medema, S.G., 1993. The marginal efficiency effects of taxes and subsidies in the presence of externalities: a computational general equilibrium approach. Journal of Public Economics 52, 199–216.

Bovenberg, A.L., de Mooij, R.A., 1994. Environmental levies and distortionary taxation. American Economic Review 84, 1085–1089.

Bovenberg, A.L., van der Ploeg, F., 1994. Environmental policy, public finance and the labor market in a second-best world. Journal of Public Economics 55, 349–390.

Bovenberg, A.L., Goulder, L.H., 1996. Optimal environmental taxation in the presence of other taxes: general equilibrium analyses. American Economic Review 86, 985–1000.

Bovenberg, A.L., Goulder, L.H., 1997. Environmental taxation. In: Auerbach, A., Feldstein, M. (Eds.), Handbook of Public Economics, 2nd ed. North-Holland, New York (forthcoming).

Browning, E.K., 1987. On the marginal welfare cost of taxation. American Economic Review 77, 11–23.

Cropper, M., Oates, W., 1992. Environmental economics: a survey. Journal of Economic Literature 30, 675–740.

Cruz, M., Goulder, L.H., 1992. An intertemporal general equilibrium model for analyzing U.S. energy and environmental policies: data documentation. Unpublished manuscript, Stanford University.

Deaton, A., 1981. Optimal taxes and the structure of preferences. Econometrica 49, 1245–1259.

Espinosa, J.A., Smith, V.K., 1995. Measuring the environmental consequences of trade policy: a nonmarket CGE analysis. American Journal of Agricultural Economics 77 (3), 772–777.

Fischer, C., Parry, I.W.H., Pizer, W.A., 1998. Instrument choice for environmental protection when technological innovation is endogenous: discussion paper No. 99-04, Resources for the Future, Washington, DC.

Fuchs, V.R., Krueger, A.B., Poterba, J.M., 1998. Economists' views about parameters, values and policies: survey results in labor and public economics. Journal of Economic Literature 36 (3), 1387–1425.

Fullerton, D., Metcalf, G., 1997. Environmental controls, scarcity rents, and pre-existing distortions. NBER Working Paper 6091, Cambridge, MA, July.

Goulder, L.H., 1995. Effects of carbon taxes in an economy with prior tax distortions: an intertemporal general equilibrium analysis. Journal of Environmental Economics and Management 29, 271–297.

Goulder, L.H., 1995. Environmental taxation and the 'double dividend': a reader's guide. International Tax and Public Finance 2, 157–183.

Goulder, L.H., Parry, I.W.H., Burtraw, D., 1997. Revenue-raising vs. other approaches to environmental protection: the critical significance of pre-existing tax distortions. RAND Journal of Economics 28 (4), 708–731.

Goulder, L.H., Parry, I.W.H., Williams III R.C., Burtraw, D., 1998. The cost-effectiveness of alternative instruments for environmental protection in a second-best setting. National Bureau of Economic Research Working Paper 6464 (March).

Hahn, R.W., 1986. Trade-offs in designing markets with multiple objectives. Journal of Environmental Economics and Management 13, 1–12.

Hahn, R.W., 1989. Economic prescriptions for environmental problems: how the patient followed the doctor's orders. Journal of Economic Perspectives 3 (2), 95–114.

Hakonsen, L., 1998. An investigation into alternative representations of the marginal cost of public funds. International Tax and Public Finance 5, 329–343.

Lester, J.A., Dodds, D.E., Zerbe, R.O. Jr., 1997. Environmental Economics and Policy. Addison-Wesley, New York.

Lucas, R.E., 1990. Supply-side economics: an analytical review. Oxford Economic Papers 42, 293–316.

Milliman, S.R., Prince, R., 1989. Firm incentives to promote technological change in pollution control. Journal of Environmental Economics and Management 17, 247–265.

Newell, R.G., Jaffe, A.B., Stavins, R.N., 1998. The induced innovation hypothesis and energy-saving technological change. Quarterly Journal of Economics, forthcoming.

Nichols, A.L., 1984. Targeting Economic Incentives for Environmental Protection. MIT Press, Cambridge, MA.

Oates, W.E., 1995. Green taxes: can we protect the environment and improve the tax system at the same time?. Southern Economic Journal 61, 914–922.

Parry, I.W.H., 1995. Pollution taxes and revenue recycling. Journal of Environmental Economics and Management 29, S64–S77.

Parry, I.W.H., 1997. Environmental taxes and quotas in the presence of distorting taxes in factor markets. Resource and Energy Economics 19, 203–220.

Parry, I.W.H., Williams, R.C., Goulder, L.H., 1998. When can carbon abatement policies increase welfare? The fundamental role of distorted factor markets. Journal of Environmental Economics and Management (forthcoming).

Pechan, E.H. et al., 1996. Emission reduction and cost analysis model for NO_x (ERCAM-NOX) (Report No. 96.09.002/1763), September.

Spulber, D.F., 1985. Effluent regulation and long-run optimality. Journal of Environmental Economics and Management 12, 103–116.

Stavins, R. (Ed.), 1991. Project 88 – Round II, incentives for action: designing market-based environmental strategies. Public policy study sponsored by Senators Timothy Wirth and John Heinz, Washington, DC, May.

Tietenberg, T.H., 1985. Emissions Trading: An Exercise in Reforming Pollution Policy. Resources for the Future, Washington, DC.

Weitzman, M.L., 1974. Prices vs. quantities. Review of Economic Studies 41, 477–491.

Williams, R.C., 1998a. Revisiting the cost of protectionism: the role of tax distortions in the labor market. Journal of International Economics (forthcoming).

Williams, R.C., 1998b. Costs of emissions reduction under different instruments as emissions approach zero. Stanford University, unpublished.

Williams, R.C., 1998c. The effect of pre-existing taxes on the benefits of regulations affecting health or productivity. Working paper, Stanford University.

[28]

International Tax and Public Finance, 5, 153–170 (1998)

A Second-Best Analysis of Environmental Subsidies

IAN W. H. PARRY* parry@rff.org
Resources for the Future, 1616 P Street NW, Washington, DC 20036

Abstract

This paper examines the complications posed by pre-existing tax distortions in the economy, for the evaluation of a variety of subsidy policies that affect the environment. These complications include not only the efficiency cost of financing the subsidy by distortionary taxation, but also the interaction effects between the subsidized market and markets with pre-existing taxes. Studies that ignore both of these effects, or only incorporate the first type of effect, can be highly misleading.

JEL codes: Q28, H21, H23

Keywords: externalities, subsidies, pre-existing taxes, welfare impacts

I. Introduction

Most environmental problems, from air and water pollution to the depletion of fish stocks and traffic congestion, are caused by the harmful external effects of production and consumption activities. The most direct way to reduce such environmental damage is by regulating the source of the externality using taxes or some form of quantity control. Thus, most of the environmental policy literature is concerned with these types of policy instruments, and little attention has been paid to the effects of environmental subsidies.

Nevertheless, there are a variety of actual or proposed subsidy policies which (intentionally or otherwise) affect the environment, and it is important to understand their consequences. In particular we distinguish the following four types of subsidies:

(i) *Pigouvian subsidies*, that directly increase efficiency by encouraging activities with positive (rather than negative) externalities. Examples of such activities include afforestation, which can reduce soil erosion, flooding and atmospheric concentrations of greenhouse gases; and the renovation of waterfronts and historical buildings, which can increase the utility of passers by.[1]

(ii) *Indirect subsidies*, which improve the environment by encouraging the production of (relatively) clean goods, that are close substitutes for goods with harmful externalities. Although not the most efficient policy, such subsidies may be appealing in the presence of political or administrative obstacles to direct regulation. This may explain mass transit subsidies, which reduce the pollution and congestion costs of cars; the favorable tax treatment of cleaner fuels such as ethanol, methanol and natural gas; and subsidies for solar power plants and wind farms.

(iii) *Production-reducing subsidies*, which directly discourage productive activities with harmful externalities. For example under the Conservation Reserve Program and Wetland

* I am grateful to Michael Keen and three anonymous referees for very helpful comments and suggestions. I also thank Brian Kropp for excellent research assistance.

Reserve Program in the U.S., farmers are paid not to produce on land in environmentally sensitive areas, such as habitat for endangered species.

(iv) *Environmentally unfriendly subsidies* that, unlike the above subsidies, compound rather than alleviate environmental problems. For political or other reasons, these subsidies are quite pervasive.[2] For example fossil fuel combustion, the major cause of air pollution, is typically encouraged in developing countries by direct energy subsidies and underpricing of electricity.[3] Agricultural subsidies in the OECD countries can increase land clearance and lead to loss of wildlife, forests and public amenities. They also increase the derived demand for chemical fertilizers and pesticides. Throughout the world farmers are charged well below the marginal social cost of irrigation supply, thereby exacerbating problems of salinization and waterlogging (Repetto, 1986). Subsidies for mining and timber harvesting on public lands are also common, especially in developing countries.

In general it is straightforward to extend the Pigouvian (or partial equilibrium) analysis of externalities to incorporate these types of policies.[4] However, a number of very recent papers have shown that the effects of environmental taxes and quotas can be significantly affected by pre-existing tax distortions, particularly in the labor market.[5] This paper expands this growing literature, to incorporate the above types of environmental policies. In particular, we examine: (a) the welfare effects, and optimal level of these subsidies, in the presence of a pre-existing tax on labor income; (b) why, and to what extent, existing studies which do not fully account for interactions with the tax system, may be misleading.

In the presence of a pre-existing labor tax, the welfare effect of a revenue-neutral Pigouvian subsidy can be decomposed into a *revenue-financing* and *tax-interaction* effect, in addition to the welfare effect within the subsidized market, which we call the *primary* welfare effect.[6] The revenue-financing effect is the welfare cost of financing the subsidy by increasing the distortionary labor tax (relative to increasing a lump sum tax). The tax-interaction effect is the welfare gain from the increase in labor supply, induced by the increase in the real household wage when the price of the subsidized consumption good falls. In general the revenue-financing effect exceeds the tax-interaction effect, and the optimal level of subsidy is still positive, but somewhat below that implied by a first-best analysis.[7] Numerous papers *have* emphasized the drawback of financing subsidies through distortionary taxation, but *have not* recognized the advantage from the tax-interaction effect.[8] However, under plausible parameters the revenue-financing and tax-interaction effects can be larger than the primary welfare gain. Therefore these studies can be misleading not only about the overall welfare effect of such subsidies, but also about the sign of the welfare effect. This is a very general point, and for example applies to the evaluation of subsidies for health care, agricultural commodities and low-income housing.[9]

Production-reducing subsidies are effectively a tax on production combined with a lump sum transfer. That is, they raise the relative price of consumption goods, and therefore the tax-interaction effect re-inforces rather than offsets the revenue-financing effect. For these subsidies, marginal environmental benefits have to be above a threshold amount before *any* level of subsidy is welfare-improving.[10] As regards environmentally unfriendly subsidies, many studies claim that they lead to a double cost, because they exacerbate environmental externality problems, and increase the revenue requirement from distortionary taxes.[11]

However these studies overstate the overall costs, because the subsidy produces an efficiency gain through the tax-interaction effect, which can offset much of the latter cost.

The next section develops a general equilibrium model with pre-existing tax distortions in the labor market, and illustrates the marginal welfare impacts of the above types of subsidy. Section III uses a linearized version of the model to illustrate that the costs of (non-marginal) subsidies (gross of environmental effects) can differ substantially from those implied by an analysis which ignores pre-existing tax distortions, or that incorporates the revenue-financing but not the tax-interaction effect. Approximate calculations of the second-best optimal level of subsidy are presented. Section IV summarizes the main points of the paper.

II. Analytical Model

A. *Model Assumptions*[12]

A single period, closed economy, representative household model is assumed. Households allocate their time endowment (T) between labor supply (L) and leisure or non-market time ($T - L$), and purchase two consumption goods (X and Y). The utility function is given by:

$$U = u(X, Y, T - L) + \phi(Z) \tag{1}$$

where $u(.)$, utility from non-environmental goods, is continuous and strictly quasi-concave. $\phi(.)$ is utility from environmental quality (Z), and this function is continuous. The only restriction on household utility is that environmental and non-environmental goods are separable, which implies that the demand functions for X and Y, and the supply of labor, are independent of Z.[13]

X and Y are produced by competitive firms using labor supplied by households. Labor is chosen to be the numeraire, and the gross wage is normalized to unity. We assume that the marginal product of labor in each industry is constant, and therefore (private) marginal production costs are constant (since the gross wage is fixed). The units of X and Y are defined such that marginal costs, or producer prices, are also unity. In equilibrium firm profits are zero. The production of X and Y may affect the environment, and the environmental quality function is given by:

$$Z = Z(X, Y) \tag{2}$$

with partial derivatives Z_X and Z_Y respectively (this function is restricted below). As usual, we assume that neither households nor firms consider the environmental consequences of their decisions.

The government is assumed to have an exogenous spending requirement of G per household (which is fixed relative to producer prices). In addition the government taxes labor income at rate t and imposes some type of subsidy in the X market.[14] For the moment, we assume this is a production (or equivalently consumption) subsidy of s per unit. G is assumed to be a lump sum transfer to households.[15] We assume the government budget must balance, and therefore any changes in revenues directly or indirectly caused by the subsidy policy are offset by adjusting the rate of labor tax. The government budget constraint is therefore:

$$G + sX = tL \tag{3}$$

The (per capita) household budget constraint amounts to

$$(l - s)X + Y = (1 - t)L + G \tag{4}$$

As usual, households are assumed to maximize utility (1), subject to the budget constraint (4), taking government parameters and environmental quality as given. From the resulting first order conditions and household budget constraint, we obtain the uncompensated household demand and labor supply functions:

$$X(s, t, G); \qquad Y(s, t, G); \qquad L(s, t, G) \tag{5}$$

and from (2) and (5)

$$Z = Z(X(s, t, G),\ Y(s, t, G)) \tag{6}$$

Substituting (5) and (6) into (1) gives the indirect household utility function:

$$V = v(s, t, G) + \phi(Z(X(s, t, G), Y(s, t, G))) \tag{7}$$

From Roy's Identity

$$\frac{\partial v}{\partial s} = \lambda X; \qquad \frac{\partial v}{\partial t} = -\lambda L \tag{8}$$

where the Lagrange multiplier λ is the marginal utility of income ($\lambda = \partial V/\partial G$). Finally, using (5) and (6) we can define the following total derivatives (when G is constant):

$$\frac{dX}{ds} = \frac{\partial X}{\partial s} + \frac{\partial X}{\partial t}\frac{dt}{ds}; \quad \frac{dY}{ds} = \frac{\partial Y}{\partial s} + \frac{\partial Y}{\partial t}\frac{dt}{ds}; \quad \frac{dZ}{ds} = Z_X\frac{dX}{ds} + Z_Y\frac{dY}{ds} \tag{9}$$

B. The Revenue-Financing and Tax-Interaction Effects

Consider a revenue-neutral policy change consisting of an incremental increase in s and t. Differentiating (3) with respect to s and t, and using (5) and (9), we can obtain:

$$\frac{dt}{ds} = \frac{X + s\frac{dX}{ds} - t\frac{\partial L}{\partial s}}{L + t\frac{\partial L}{\partial t}} \tag{10}$$

Equation (10) is an expression for the increase in labor tax required to maintain budget balance, following an incremental increase in the subsidy. dX/ds is the total effect on X from the policy change, while the effects on labor supply from a change in s and t are kept separate.

We define:

$$M = \frac{-t\frac{\partial L}{\partial t}}{L + t\frac{\partial L}{\partial t}} \tag{11}$$

This is the partial equilibrium efficiency cost of raising an additional dollar of revenue from labor taxation, or marginal welfare cost of taxation.[16] The numerator is the reduction in labor supply following an incremental increase in t, multiplied by the wedge between the gross and net wage, or between the value marginal product of labor and the marginal cost of labor in terms of foregone leisure. The denominator is marginal tax revenue (from differentiating tL).[17]

The welfare effect of the policy change is obtained by differentiating the utility function (7) with respect to s, allowing t to vary to maintain budget balance (G is constant). This gives

$$\frac{dV}{ds} = \frac{\partial v}{\partial s} + \frac{\partial v}{\partial t}\frac{dt}{ds} + \phi'(Z)\frac{dZ}{ds}$$

Substituting from (8), (10) and an expression for $1 + M$ from (11), gives the following decomposition for the general equilibrium welfare change from a revenue-neutral increase in the subsidy:

$$\frac{1}{\lambda}\frac{dV}{ds} = \underbrace{\frac{\phi'(Z)}{\lambda}\frac{dZ}{ds}}_{dW^E} - \underbrace{s\frac{dX}{ds}}_{dW^P} - \underbrace{M\left[X + s\frac{dX}{ds}\right]}_{\partial W^R} + \underbrace{(1+M)t\frac{\partial L}{\partial s}}_{\partial W^I} \tag{12}$$

dW^E is the welfare effect (in dollars) from the overall incremental change in environmental quality (see below). dW^P is the efficiency loss in the X market (gross of environmental effects), or *primary cost*; that is the overall increase in X multiplied by the wedge between the supply and demand price, or between marginal production cost and marginal benefit to consumers. We call $dW^E - dW^P$ the *primary welfare* effect. The next two terms separate out the overall effect in the labor market into two components. ∂W^R is the welfare loss from the (marginal) *revenue-financing* effect. This is the product of the marginal welfare cost of taxation and the incremental increase in the subsidy payment. Finally, ∂W^I is the (marginal) *tax-interaction* effect. Since the subsidy reduces the price of good X, it increases the real household wage. In general, this increases labor supply (see below), producing a welfare gain of $t(\partial L/\partial s)$. In addition, labor tax revenues increase leading to a efficiency gain of $Mt(\partial L/\partial s)$. The combined effect is ∂W^I.[18]

We now compare the revenue-financing and tax-interaction effects. The formula for ∂W^I can be manipulated to give (see Appendix A)

$$\partial W^I = \beta M X, \qquad \text{where } \beta = \frac{\eta^c_{XL} + \eta_{LI}}{f_X\eta^c_{XL} + f_Y\eta^c_{YL} + \eta_{LI}}; \tag{13}$$

η^c_{XL} and η^c_{YL} are respectively the (compensated) elasticity of demand for X and Y with respect to the price of leisure; η_{LI} is the income elasticity of labor supply; f_X and f_Y are the share of spending on X and Y in total spending respectively, and $f_X + f_Y = 1$. β is a measure of the degree of substitution between X and leisure relative to that between aggregate consumption and leisure. From (13), $\beta = 1$ when X and Y are equal substitutes for leisure ($\eta^c_{XL} = \eta^c_{YL}$), and is greater (less) than unity when X is a relatively strong (weak) substitute for leisure (η^c_{XL} is greater (less) than η^c_{YL}). Comparing (12) and (13), when $s = 0$, $\partial W^I = \partial W^R$ if $\beta = 1$. Therefore for small levels of subsidy, the cost of financing the subsidy by distortionary taxation is approximately offset by the tax-interaction effect, when the subsidized good is an average substitute for leisure. That is, the net effect on labor supply is zero. At positive levels of subsidy ∂W^R exceeds ∂W^I, because $s(dX/ds)$, the subsidy paid to incremental increases in X, is positive. Thus for a non-marginal increase in the subsidy, the net effect from interactions with the tax system is typically negative (labor supply falls), unless X is a sufficiently stronger than average substitute for leisure (β is sufficiently above unity).[19]

C. *Applications to Subsidy Policies*

1. *Pigouvian Subsidies*

Suppose X has a positive externality and Y is environmentally neutral, that is $Z_X > 0$ and $Z_Y = 0$. From (9) and (12):

$$dW^E - dW^P = \left\{\frac{\phi'}{\lambda}Z_X - s\right\}\frac{dX}{ds} \tag{14a}$$

where $(\phi'/\lambda)Z_X$ is the marginal environmental benefit (in dollars) from a unit increase in X. If X is an average substitute for leisure, then at $s = 0$, ∂W^R and ∂W^I cancel out, and the subsidy is potentially welfare improving so long as marginal environmental benefits are positive. For $s > 0$, in general $\partial W^R > \partial W^I$, therefore the (marginal) welfare effect, and optimal level of subsidy is less than would be implied by an analysis which ignored pre-existing taxes. Studies which incorporate the revenue-financing effect—but neglect the tax-interaction effect—are overly pessimistic about these type of subsides: they misleadingly imply that marginal environmental benefits must exceed the marginal revenue-financing effect at s = 0, for a subsidy to be potentially welfare-improving.

2. *Indirect Subsidies*

Now suppose X is environmentally-neutral but the production of Y adversely affects the environment, that is $Z_X = 0$ and $Z_Y < 0$. From (9) and (12):

$$dW^E - dW^P = \frac{\phi'}{\lambda}Z_Y\frac{dY}{ds} - s\frac{dX}{ds} \tag{14b}$$

that is, the subsidy distorts the X market, but improves the environment by reducing the production of Y ($dY/ds < 0$ when X and Y are substitutes). The revenue-financing and tax-interaction effects are the same as in the previous case. In this two good model, a revenue-neutral subsidy for the clean good is actually equivalent to a revenue-neutral tax on the environmentally harmful good. This is because they have identical effects on the relative price of goods and the net wage, for a given amount of government revenue (see Appendix A). Therefore, even though the subsidy only improves the environment indirectly, it is no less efficient than a direct environmental tax.[20] However in a more general setting with three or more goods, the subsidy is less efficient than direct taxation of the harmful externality, unless it is levied on all goods in the economy without the externality.

3. Production-Reducing Subsidies

To examine this type of subsidy, suppose that $Z_X < 0$, $Z_Y = 0$ and the pre-subsidy level of output is X_0. A subsidy of s per unit reduction in output of X is equivalent to a lump sum payment of sX_0 to producers of X, plus a tax of s per unit of production, since this is the subsidy payment forgone by producing an extra unit. Obviously, the resulting profits may create incentives for the entry of new firms into the industry, and this is the traditional argument against these types of subsidies.[21] However in the case of the Conservation Reserve Program and the Wetland Reserve Program in the U.S., subsidies for reducing production in environmentally sensitive areas are limited to existing farmers (moreover, the presence of a factor in inelastic supply—land—would restrict entry).[22] The analysis below ignores the possibility of new entry.

Under a production-reducing subsidy, the equilibrium price of X is the marginal production cost plus s, since this is now opportunity cost to firms of producing an additional unit. Therefore the household budget constraint is

$$(l + s)X + Y = (l - t)L + \pi + G \tag{4'}$$

where $\pi = s(X_0 - X)$ is profits created by the subsidy in the X industry, which are ultimately distributed to households (π is taken as given by the individual household). The government budget constraint is[23]

$$G + s(X_0 - X) = tL \tag{3'}$$

Repeating the derivation of equation (12), gives the following decomposition of the marginal welfare effect from increasing s:[24]

$$\frac{1}{\lambda}\frac{dV}{ds} = \underbrace{\left\{\frac{\phi'}{\lambda}Z_X + s\right\}\frac{dX}{ds}}_{dW^E - dW^P} - \underbrace{M\left\{X_0 - X - s\frac{dX}{ds}\right\}}_{\partial W^R} + \underbrace{(1 + M)t\frac{\partial L}{\partial s}}_{\partial W^I} \tag{12'}$$

Increasing the subsidy now reduces $X(dX/ds < 0)$. The primary welfare effect consists of the gain from decreased environmental damage, less the primary cost from reducing X (there is now a wedge of s between the marginal benefit and marginal production cost of X). The (marginal) revenue-financing effect is initially zero, since $X = X_0$ when $s = 0$. However it is increasing with s, both because the base of the subsidy, and the payment for incremental reductions in X, are increasing. The most important point from equation (12′) is that the tax-interaction effect is now a welfare loss rather than a gain. This is because the subsidy raises the price of X, thereby reducing the real wage and labor supply ($dL/ds < 0$). Therefore the tax-interaction effect now reinforces rather than offsets the revenue-financing effect, and marginal environmental benefits must be above a certain threshold level before the subsidy can be welfare-improving.

4. *Environmentally Unfriendly Subsidies*

Now suppose $Z_X < 0$ and $Z_Y = 0$. The primary welfare effect is analogous to equation (14a), except that the environmental effect is now negative. That is, the subsidy compounds environmental damage, causes excessive production of X, and adds to the revenue requirement from distortionary labor taxes. However, this third source of loss is—at least in part—neutralized by the gain from the tax-interaction effect. Thus the "double dividend" from removing these types of subsidies is less than implied by an analysis that neglects the tax-interaction effect.

III. The Empirical Significance of Pre-Existing Taxes

This section illustrates the potential empirical significance of the revenue-financing and tax-interaction effects, for the overall cost, and optimal level of environmental subsidies. To do this, we use a linearized approximation of the previous model; that is, demand curves are taken to be linear over the relevant range.[25] In addition, we make the common empirical assumption that all goods are equal substitutes for leisure, prior to the introduction of the environmental policy.[26] The empirical results from the model are discussed below; all derivations and formulas used are in Appendix B.

For the graphs presented, the only parameters needed for calibration are the labor tax rate t, and the compensated and uncompensated labor supply elasticities. We use data for the U.S. Following Browning (1987) we assume the labor tax $t = 0.43$, which is approximately the value used in other studies. This reflects the combined effects of federal and state income taxes, social security taxes, and consumption taxes. The appropriate labor supply elasticities capture the effects of higher net wages on hours worked and the participation decision. Based on surveys of the existing literature we assume an uncompensated and compensated labor supply elasticity of 0.15 and 0.35 respectively (see for example CBO (1996)). These three parameters generate a marginal welfare cost of labor taxation of 0.3 for spending on the lump sum transfer (see Appendix), which is broadly consistent with other studies (for example Browning (1987), Ballard et al. (1985)).

A. *Gross Costs*

In Figure 1(a), the horizontal axis is the proportionate increase in output induced by a revenue-neutral production subsidy for good X. TC_1 is the total cost of a Pigouvian,

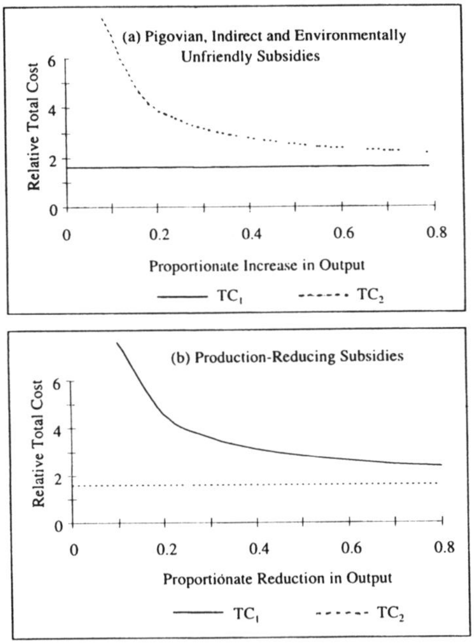

Figure 1. Gross cost of subsidies (expressed relative to the primary cost).

indirect or environmentally unfriendly subsidy, gross of environmental benefits (that is, the primary cost plus the revenue-financing effect less the tax-interaction effect), and expressed relative to the primary cost. This line is constant at 1.6; that is, the net loss from the revenue-financing and tax-interaction effects raises the gross cost of the subsidy by 60%. Therefore, these results suggest that an analysis which does not take into account pre-existing tax distortions, will significantly understate the general equilibrium gross cost of these types of subsidies.

TC_2 is the estimated gross cost of the subsidy if the tax-interaction effect is ignored, relative to the primary gross cost. This curve always lies above TC_1, and is more than twice as high as TC_1 when the proportionate increase in output is less than 37.5%. Therefore studies which incorporate the revenue-financing effect but neglect the tax-interaction effect, can substantially overstate the overall gross costs of these subsidies. Moreover, ignoring the tax-interaction effect would imply the subsidy is welfare-reducing when it actually increases welfare, if total environmental benefits (relative to the primary cost) lie between TC_1 and TC_2.

The intuition behind these results is straightforward. From (12), the size of the (marginal) revenue-financing effect relative to the (marginal) primary cost is:

$$\frac{\partial W^R}{dW^P} = \frac{MX + Ms(dX/ds)}{s(dX/ds)}$$

This ratio is arbitrarily large for sufficiently small s (since $MX > 0$).[27] The tax-interaction effect can also be relatively important because, even though the effect on aggregate labor supply from the fall in price of consumption is small, the welfare loss per unit of labor is relatively large because of the large tax wedge between the gross and net wage.

Figure 1 (b) shows the overall cost of a production-reducing subsidy relative to the primary cost, as a function of the proportionate reduction in output. TC_1 is the "correct" curve, which incorporates the welfare loss from both the revenue-financing and the tax-interaction effect. The height of this curve is well above 1.6, implying that the pre-existing tax raises the gross cost of production-reducing subsidies by substantially more than for the other three types of subsidy. This is because the tax-interaction effect re-inforces rather than counteracts the revenue-financing effect. TC_2 is the relative cost if the tax-interaction effect is ignored. In this case, this curve understates the overall cost of the subsidy, since the tax-interaction effect is a loss rather than a gain.[28]

B. Second-Best Optimal Subsidy

This subsection discusses to what extent the second-best optimal subsidy differs from the first-best optimal subsidy (when there is no pre-existing tax). We simplify by assuming that marginal environmental benefits are constant. Environmentally unfriendly subsidies are ignored, since the first-best and second-best optimal level of such subsidies is always zero in the model.

1. Pigouvian Subsidy

The second-best optimal Pigouvian subsidy in the linearized model is equal to marginal environmental benefits divided by one plus twice the marginal welfare cost of taxation (see the derivation of equation (A11) in Appendix B). Given the value of labor market parameters this is equal to 62.5% of the first-best subsidy, equal to marginal environmental benefits.[29] At the margin there is a net loss from interactions with the tax system, because the marginal revenue-financing effect is increasing[30] while the marginal tax interaction effect is constant.

2. Indirect Subsidies

In this case marginal environmental benefits from increasing X are $-(Z_Y\phi'/\lambda)(dY/dX)$; that is, the (monetary) reduction in environmental damages caused by the effect of a unit increase in X on decreasing Y. Again, the optimal subsidy on X is equal to this expression for marginal benefits divided by one plus twice the marginal welfare cost of taxation.[31]

3. Production-Reducing Subsidy

The second-best optimal production-reducing subsidy is a non-linear function of marginal environmental damages. It is easier to express the optimal subsidy implicitly, by comparing

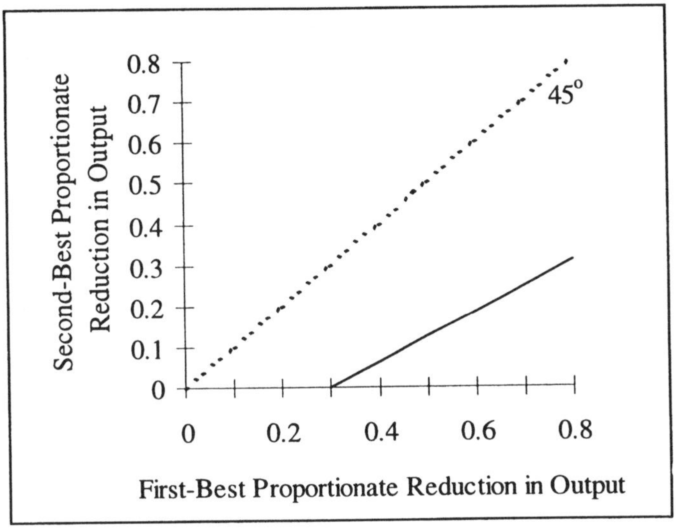

Figure 2. Optimal output reduction under production-reducing subsidy.

the first-best and second-best optimal proportionate reduction in output, for a given marginal environmental benefit. This is done in Figure 2. The solid curve is the second-best reduction in output, which is well below the first-best reduction, indicated by the 45° line. Indeed if marginal benefits are not large enough to imply a first-best output reduction in excess of 30%, then a production-reducing subsidy cannot increase welfare. This is because the marginal tax-interaction effect re-inforces rather than counteracts the marginal revenue-financing effect, implying the overall marginal cost curve from reducing production has a positive intercept.

IV. Conclusion

Subsidy policies that affect the environment, either positively or adversely, are quite pervasive. This paper has emphasized that the efficiency effects of such policies depend crucially on the existence of tax distortions in the labor market. Subsidies that reduce the relative price of consumption goods increase the real household wage, and produce an efficiency gain by encouraging labor supply. This tax-interaction effect generally offsets most, but not all of the efficiency cost of paying for the subsidy by distortionary taxation (the revenue-financing effect). The optimal level of such subsidies is positive, but somewhat below the first-best level. Subsidies for reducing environmentally harmful production produce a negative tax-interaction effect, which compounds the revenue-financing effect. Marginal environmental benefits must exceed a threshold level before such subsidies can be welfare-improving. Studies of environmental subsidies that ignore the implications of pre-existing tax distortions, or which incorporate the revenue-financing effect but not the tax-interaction effect, can be very misleading about general equilibrium welfare impacts.

Appendix A: Derivations in the General Model

Deriving Equation (13)

Using (11) and (12), we can obtain:

$$\partial W^I = -ML\frac{\partial L/\partial s}{\partial L/\partial t}$$

Substituting the Slutsky equations for the uncompensated price coefficients gives

$$\partial W^I = ML\frac{(-\partial L^c/ds) - (\partial L/\partial I)X}{(\partial L^c/\partial t) - L(\partial L/\partial I)} \tag{A1}$$

where "c" denotes a compensated coefficient and I is disposable household income. From the Slutsky symmetry property $-\partial L^c/\partial s = \partial X^c/\partial(1-t)$, and from differentiating the household budget constraint (4) for a compensated price change:[32]

$$\frac{\partial L^c}{\partial t} = -\frac{\partial L^c}{\partial(1-t)} = -\left\{\frac{\partial X}{\partial(1-t)} + \frac{\partial Y}{\partial(1-t)}\right\}$$

Making these substitutions in (A1), and multiplying by $1-t$, we obtain (13), where

$$\eta^c_{XL} = \frac{\partial X^c}{\partial(1-t)}\frac{1-t}{X};\ \eta^c_{YL} = \frac{\partial Y^c}{\partial(1-t)}\frac{1-t}{Y};\ \eta_{LI} = \frac{\partial L}{\partial I}\frac{(1-t)L}{L};$$

$$f_X = \frac{X}{L};\ f_Y\frac{Y}{L}$$

Note that $L = X + Y$ is total spending.

Equivalence between Tax on X and Subsidy for Y

Suppose a tax of τ is introduced on Y instead of a subsidy of s on X. Analogous to (4), the household budget constraint is

$$X + (1+\tau)Y = (1-t')L + G \tag{A2}$$

where t' denotes the new rate of labor tax. Government budget balance requires that:

$$\tau Y + t'L = G$$

Equating this with (3) gives

$$t' = t - \frac{\tau Y + sX}{L} \tag{A3}$$

where $t' - t$ is the difference in the labor tax because the government gains rather than loses revenue from the environmental policy. Substituting (A3) in (A2) gives (4); that is, exactly the same household budget constraint, for a given level of G, t and s.

Appendix B: The Linearized Model

For the empirical exercises below, it is helpful to use a slightly different decomposition to that in (12). Multiplying out (10) and adding $t(\partial L/\partial G)dG$ to both sides gives

$$\left\{L + t\frac{dL}{dt}\right\} dt = \left\{X + s\frac{dX}{ds} - t\frac{dL}{ds}\right\} ds$$

where

$$\frac{dL}{dt} = \frac{\partial L}{\partial t} + \frac{\partial L}{\partial G}\frac{dG}{dt}; \qquad \frac{dL}{ds} = \frac{\partial L}{\partial s} - \frac{\partial L}{\partial G}\frac{dG}{ds} \tag{A4}$$

These coefficients define the effect on labor supply of changes in s and t when the revenue consequences are neutralized by adjusting the lump sum transfer. Repeating the derivation of equation (12) gives the same decomposition, except that $\partial L/\partial t$ and $\partial L/\partial s$ are replaced by the coefficients in (A4). That is, the marginal welfare cost of taxation and the marginal tax-interaction effect are given by:

$$M' = \frac{-t(dL/dt)}{L + t(dL/dt)}; \qquad \partial W^I = (1 + M')t\frac{dL}{ds} \tag{A5}$$

From differentiating the government budget constraint, $dG/dt = L + t(dL/dt)$, and substituting into (A4) gives

$$\frac{dL}{dt} = \frac{(\partial L/\partial t) + (\partial L/\partial G)L}{1 - t(\partial L/\partial G)}$$

Substituting this into (A5) gives

$$M' = \frac{-t(\partial L^c/\partial t)}{1 + t(\partial L/\partial t)}$$

where $\partial L^c/\partial t = \partial L/\partial t + (\partial L/\partial G)L$ is the compensated price coefficient, from the Slutsky equation. This formula is easily manipulated to give

$$M' = \frac{(t/1 - t)\varepsilon^c}{1 - (t/1 - t)\varepsilon^u} \tag{A6}$$

where $\varepsilon^c = [\partial L^c/\partial(1-t)](1-t)/L$ and $\varepsilon^u = [\partial L/\partial(1-t)](1-t)/L$ are the compensated and uncompensated labor supply elasticities respectively. (A6) defines the efficiency cost of raising an additional dollar of revenue and returning it to households as a lump sum transfer.[33] Given $t = 0.43$, $\varepsilon^c = 0.35$ and $\varepsilon^u = 0.15$, then $M' = 0.3$.

Total Costs of Subsidies (Gross of Environmental Benefits)

We assume that M' is constant, which is reasonable when the proportionate change in labor tax is small.

Proof. Taking logs of (A5) and differentiating with respect to M' and t gives

$$\frac{dM'}{M'} = \frac{dt}{t} - \frac{2(dL/dt)dt}{L + t(dL/dt)}$$

since dL/dt is constant. Substituting (A5) gives

$$\frac{dM'}{M'} = \frac{dt}{t}(1 + 2M')$$

The term in brackets is 1.6 when $M' = 0.3$. Therefore, so long as the proportionate change in t is small, the proportionate change in M' is small.

Linearity implies that

$$X - X_0 = \Delta X = s\frac{dX}{ds} \tag{A7}$$

and we define the proportionate increase in output of X by $\Delta x = \Delta X / X_0$. Also, using (A5):

$$\partial W^I = -M\frac{dL/ds}{dL/dt}L$$

where $\frac{dL/ds}{dL/dt}L$ is taken to be constant because of linearity and the proportionate change in t and hence labor supply is small. Equating this with (13) when X is initially an average substitute for leisure, that is $\beta = 1$ and $X = X_0$, gives

$$\partial W^I = MX_0 \tag{A8}$$

Integrating dW^P, ∂W^R and ∂W^I between 0 and s, using (12), (A7) and (A8) gives:

$$\Delta W^P = s\Delta X/2; \qquad \Delta W^R = MsX; \qquad \Delta W^I = MsX_0 \tag{A9}$$

From (A9), the gross cost of the subsidy relative to the primary cost in Figure 1(a) is given by:

$$\frac{\Delta W^P + \Delta W^R - \Delta W^I}{\Delta W^P} = 1 + 2M' = TC_1$$

and if the tax-interaction effect is ignored

$$\frac{\Delta W^P + \Delta W^R}{\Delta W^P} = 1 + \frac{2M'(1 - \Delta x)}{\Delta x} = TC_2$$

Following the same integration procedure for the production-reducing subsidy using (12′) instead of (12), gives $\Delta W^P = s\Delta X/2$, $\Delta W^R = Ms\Delta X$, and $\Delta W^I = MsX_0$; and therefore in Figure 1(b)

$$\frac{\Delta W^P + \Delta W^R - \Delta W^I}{\Delta W^P} = 1 + 2M'\{1 + (1/\Delta x)\} = TC_1$$

$$\frac{\Delta W^P + \Delta W^R}{\Delta W^P} = 1 + 2M' = TC_2$$

Note that TC_2 for the production-reducing subsidy is the same expression for TC_1 for the other subsidies.

Optimal Pigouvian Subsidy

Let marginal environmental benefits $Z_X\phi'/\lambda$ in (14a) be a constant b. Differentiating $\Delta W^P + \Delta W^R - \Delta W^I$ from (A9) with respect to s gives:

$$\frac{\Delta X}{2} + \frac{s}{2}\frac{dX}{ds} + M'(X - X_0) + M's\frac{dX}{ds} \tag{A10}$$

Equating with $b(dX/ds)$ (environmental benefits from a marginal increase in s) and substituting from (A7) gives:

$$s = \frac{b}{1 + 2M} \tag{A11}$$

the optimal Pigouvian subsidy.

Optimal Production-Reducing Subsidy

Following the same procedure for the production-reducing subsidy, except differentiating with respect to s instead of X gives

$$-b\frac{dX}{ds} = \frac{\Delta X}{2} - \frac{s}{2}\frac{dX}{ds} + M\Delta X - Ms\frac{dX}{ds} + MX_0$$

where b denotes marginal environmental damages. Substituting $-s(dX/ds) = \Delta X$ and manipulating gives

$$\Delta x = \frac{\Delta x^P - M}{1 + 2M} \tag{A12}$$

where $\Delta x^P = -(dX/ds)b/X_0$ is the proportionate reduction in output under the first-best subsidy equal to b. Equation (A12) is plotted in Figure 2.

Optimal Indirect Subsidy

This can be derived by repeating the derivation of (A10), except using $b\Delta Y$ for environmental benefits, where $b = -Z_Y\phi'/\lambda$. This gives:

$$s = \frac{d(dY/dX)}{1 + 2M'}$$

where $dY/dX = (dY/ds)/(dX/ds)$.

Notes

1. There are a number of other activities which, although they do not affect the environment, may still have positive externalities. For example, the consumption of certain "basic needs" goods by the poor may raise the utility of wealthier, paternalistic citizens (see for example Harberger (1984)); new products and production processes invented by one firm may provide spillover benefits to other firms that can copy or imitate them; and artistic activities may provide external cultural benefits.

2. See Gupta et al. (1995), and the references therein.
3. Larsen and Shah (1992) estimate that total world energy subsidies are around \$230 billion, and removing these subsidies would reduce global carbon dioxide emissions by the same amount as imposing a carbon tax of \$50–90 per ton in OECD countries.
4. See for example the discussion in Piacentino and Smith (1994) and Gupta et al. (1995).
5. See Bovenberg and de Mooij (1994), Bovenberg and van der Ploeg (1994), Bovenberg and Goulder (1996, 1997), Goulder (1995), Goulder et al. (1997), Fullerton (1996), Fullerton and Metcalf (1996), Schöb (1996), and Parry (1996, 1997). These studies build on earlier contributions by Sandmo (1975) and Ng (1980).
6. An analogous decomposition for environmental taxes is presented in Goulder et al. (1996) and Parry (1995).
7. This result is implicit in other papers (Sandmo, 1975; Ng, 1980). However these models do not decompose the revenue-financing and tax-interaction effects, and therefore do not make transparent the flaw in other papers which ignore the tax-interaction effect.
8. See for example Repetto (1986, 1988), Piacentino and Smith (1994), Ballard and Medema (1983), Browning (1992).
9. We do not analyze spending on public goods to improve the environment, such as litter collection, national parks, and the clean up of rivers. Since public goods do not affect the relative price of consumption, they do not induce a tax-interaction effect (although they affect the supply of labor indirectly if they are complements or substitutes for leisure). For a public good which is separable in utility, the optimal quantity of spending is where the social benefits per dollar equals one plus the marginal welfare cost of taxation (Atkinson and Stern, 1974; Wildasin, 1984; Ballard and Fullerton, 1990). Due to the tax-interaction effect, the same rule is *not* applicable to the subsidy policies analyzed here.
10. We do not analyze subsidies for the adoption of pollution-reducing technologies. However, to the extent that the technology increased (reduced) marginal production costs and hence the final product price, there would be a welfare-reducing (-increasing) tax-interaction effect.
11. See for example, Gupta et al. (1995), Repetto et al. (1986, 1988).
12. The model below has a similar structure to that in Section II of Goulder et al. (1996), in their analysis of emissions taxes and permits.
13. This is a standard simplifying assumption. If instead environmental quality and leisure were complements (substitutes) the net effect on leisure, and hence the net welfare loss from interactions with the tax system, of a subsidy which improved environmental quality would be greater (less).
14. Alternatively the government could raise revenue from consumption taxes, with a lower rate applied to X than Y. This tax system is equivalent to a labor tax plus a subsidy for X, in the absence of non-labor income.
15. If G were market distorting, the analysis below would need to consider the spillover effect of the subsidy in this market in addition to that in the labor market.
16. Some authors refer to this as the marginal excess burden of taxation, and others use the marginal cost of public funds, which is equivalent to $1 + M$.
17. Marginal tax revenue is assumed to be positive, that is the labor tax Laffer curve is upward sloping. This condition is easily satisfied for the labor market parameters from the U.S. assumed in Section III.
18. When the labor tax is increased, this will cause a feedback effect in the X market. However, the efficiency consequences of this, and the change in subsidy payment, are captured in the total derivative terms dZ/ds and dX/ds in dW^P and ∂W^R. Since the change in labor supply is decomposed into two terms, these, and the corresponding welfare effects, are labeled with a "∂" rather than a "d".
19. Symmetrical results hold for an environmental tax (Bovenberg and de Mooij, 1994; Goulder et al., 1997). In this case, the welfare gain from using environmental tax revenues to reduce the labor tax is generally outweighed by the loss from the tax-interaction effect (that is, the reduction in labor supply induced by the fall in the real wage when the price of (polluting) goods is increased).
20. This point has been made previously by Fullerton (1996).
21. See for example Baumol and Oates (1988), Ch. 14.
22. The other drawback to production-reducing subsidies is that the environmental improvement from the reduced production can be difficult to measure (Baumol and Oates, 1988). However this is not the case with agricultural land set-asides, which are relatively easy to monitor with aerial photography.
23. We assume no taxation of profits, since the agricultural sector is not subject to corporate taxation.

24. That is, using (3′) and (4′) instead of (3) and (4). The derivatives with respect to s in (12′) incorporate the income effect from the increase in π.
25. The objective is to indicate broad orders of magnitude, in a transparent manner. More precise estimates could be obtained by specifying a utility function and solving the model by numerical simulation.
26. See for example Bovenberg and Goulder (1996, 1997) and Goulder et al. (1997). This is implied by their assumptions that utility is weakly separable in goods and leisure, and the sub-utility function for goods is homothetic.
27. The relative importance of the revenue-financing effect was recognized in earlier studies, for example Browning (1992), Alston and Hurd (1990).
28. TC_2 in Figure 1(b) is the same as TC_1 in Figure 1(a) (see Appendix B), that is, the sum of the revenue-financing and tax-interaction effects for the production-reducing subsidy equals the revenue-financing effect for the other types of subsidy, when expressed relative to the primary cost. The revenue-financing effect is smaller in the former case because the base of the subsidy is only the reduction in output, compared with the whole (and increasing) level of output in the latter case.
29. Parry (1995) derived the symmetrical formula for the optimal environmental tax. He discusses the sensitivity of the optimal tax to alternative assumptions about the marginal welfare cost of taxation, and the degree of substitution with leisure. In Bovenberg and Goulder (1996), the optimal tax is a little closer to the first-best optimal tax. This difference is because they assumed a constant elasticity of substitution utility function, implying demand curves are non-linear, in contrast to the above assumption.
30. This is because the base of the subsidy is increasing, and the subsidy payment for incremental increases in output is increasing.
31. For more discussion of the optimal subsidy on clean goods that are substitutes for dirty goods see Fullerton (1996).
32. Note that the change in revenues following the increase in gross wage, $t[\partial L/\partial(1-t)] - s\partial X/\partial(1-t)$, are returned to households.
33. Again, this is ignoring feedback effects in the X market. For a comprehensive discussion of this formula see Browning (1987). His formula is slightly different as he allows for non-proportional tax increases and, instead of a lump sum transfer, he assumes the additional spending is sufficient to keep household utility at the same level of utility.

References

Alston, J. M., and B. H. Hurd. (1990). "Some Neglected Social Costs of Government Spending in Farm Programs." *American Journal of Agricultural Economics* 72, 149–156.

Atkinson, A. B., and N. H. Stern. (1974). "Pigou, Taxation and Public Goods." *Review of Economic Studies* 41, 119–128.

Ballard, C. L., and D. Fullerton. (1992). "Distortionary Taxes and the Provision of Public Goods." *Journal of Economic Perspectives* 6, 117–131.

Ballard, C. L., and S. G. Medema. (1993). "The Marginal Efficiency Effects of Taxes and Subsidies in the Presence of Externalities." *Journal of Public Economics* 52, 199–216.

Ballard, C. L., J. B. Shoven and J. Whalley. (1985). "General Equilibrium Computations of the Marginal Welfare Costs of Taxes in the United States." *American Economic Review* 75, 128–138.

Baumol, W. J., and W. E. Oates. (1988). *The Theory of Environmental Policy* (Second edition). Cambridge, UK: Cambridge University Press.

Bovenberg, A. L., and R. A. de Mooij. (1994). "Environmental Levies and Distortionary Taxation." *American Economic Review* 84, 1085–1089.

Bovenberg, A. L., and F. van der Ploeg. (1994). "Environmental Policy, Public Finance and the Labor Market in a Second Best World." *Journal of Public Economics* 55, 349–390.

Bovenberg, A. L., and L. H. Goulder. (1996). "Optimal Environmental Taxation in the Presence of other Taxes: An Applied General Equilibrium Analysis." *American Economic Review* 86, 985–1000.

Bovenberg, A. L., and L. H. Goulder. (1997). "Costs of Environmentally Motivated Taxes in the Presence of other Taxes: General Equilibrium Analysis." *National Tax Journal* 50, 59–88.

Browning, E. K. (1987). "On the Marginal Welfare Cost of Taxation." *American Economic Review* 77, 11–23.

Browning, E. K. (1992). "Subsidies Financed with Distorting Taxes." *National Tax Journal* 45, 121–134.

CBO. (1996). "Labor Supply and Taxes." Congressional Budget Office Memorandum, Washington, DC.

Fullerton, D. (1996). "Environmental Levies and Distortionary Taxation: Comment." *American Economic Review* 87, 245–251.

Fullerton, D., and G. Metcalf (1996). "Environmental Controls, Scarcity Rents and Pre-Existing Distortions." University of Texas, Austin, TX.

Goulder, L. H. (1995). "Effects of Carbon Taxes in an Economy with prior Tax Distortions: An Intertemporal General Equilibrium Analysis." *Journal of Environmental Economics and Management* 29, 271–297.

Goulder, L. H., I. W. H. Parry and D. Burtraw. (1997). "Revenue-Raising vs. Other Approaches to Environmental Protection: The Critical Significance of Pre-Existing Tax Distortions." *RAND Journal of Economics* 28, 708–731.

Gupta, S., K. Miranda and I. W. H. Parry. (1995). "Public Expenditure Policy and the Environment: A Review and Synthesis." *World Development* 23, 515–528.

Harberger, A. C. (1984). "Basic Needs versus Distributional Weights in Social Cost-Benefit Analysis." *Economic Development and Cultural Change* 32, 455–474.

Larsen, B. J., and A. Shah. (1992). "World Fossil Fuel Subsidies and Global Carbon Emissions." World Bank, Washington, DC.

Ng, Y. K. (1980). "Optimal Corrective Taxes or Subsidies when Revenue-Raising Imposes an Excess Burden." *American Economic Review* 70, 744–751.

Parry, I. W. H. (1995). "Pollution Taxes and Revenue Recycling." *Journal of Environmental Economics & Management* 29, S64–S77.

Parry, I. W. H. (1997). "Environmental Taxes and Quotas in the Presence of Distortionary Taxes in Factor Markets." *Resource and Energy Economics* 19, 203–220.

Piacentino, D., and S. Smith. (1994). "Taxes and Subsidies in Environmental Fiscal Reform." Institute for Fiscal Studies, London, U.K.

Repetto, R., (1986). *Skimming the Water: Rent-Seeking and the Performance of Public Irrigation Systems*. World Resources Institute, Washington, D.C.

Repetto, R. (1988). *The Forest for the Trees? Government Policy and the Misuse of Forest Resources*. World Resources Institute, Washington, D.C.

Sandmo, A. (1975). "Optimal Taxation in the Presence of Externalities." *Swedish Journal of Economics* 77, 86–98.

Schöb, R. (1996). "Environmental Levies and Distortionary Taxation: The Normalization Trap." University of Munich, Munich, Germany.

Wildasin, D. E. (1984). "On Public Good Provision with Distortionary Taxation." *Economic Inquiry* 22, 557–543.

PART V

EFFICIENCY–DISTRIBUTION TRADE-OFFS IN ENVIRONMENTAL POLICY

[29]

THE OPTIMAL SUPPLY OF PUBLIC GOODS AND THE DISTORTIONARY COST OF TAXATION

LOUIS KAPLOW*

Abstract *- The conventional view of economists is that the optimal supply of public goods must directly take into account the cost of financing them with distortionary taxes, notably, the income tax. However, this article demonstrates, under standard simplifying assumptions, that it is possible to finance a public good in a manner that results in no additional distortion, by using an adjustment to the income tax that offsets the benefits of the public good. In this case, it is optimal to supply the public good whenever the simple cost-benefit test is satisfied. The article also shows that if a different tax adjustment is made, the difference in outcome will be purely redistributive; thus, any change in distortionary costs will be accompanied by an opposing change in redistributive benefits. In this case, the cost-benefit test should be modified to reflect both of these changes. Finally, it is explained that the present analysis is fully applicable to determining the optimal level of environmental taxes.*

*Harvard Law School and the National Bureau of Economic Research, Cambridge, MA 02138.

INTRODUCTION

The conventional view of economists is that the optimal supply of public goods is not determined by the simple cost-benefit test—which asks whether the sum of individuals' benefits exceeds a project's direct cost—because financing public goods involves the use of distortionary taxes, notably, the income tax. This view dates from Pigou (1947), who stated that the benefits of public goods must exceed their direct costs by an amount sufficient to outweigh the distortionary cost of taxation. Pigou's argument has been formalized and refined in subsequent work, beginning with important contributions by Atkinson and Stern (1974), Diamond and Mirrlees (1971), and Stiglitz and Dasgupta (1971) and continuing more recently with, for example, Ballard and Fullerton (1992), Fullerton (1991), and Mayshar (1990). In particular, this literature emphasizes the income effect of taxation: because taxation reduces individuals' incomes, it may induce more work effort, which increases the revenue produced by preexisting taxes.[1] Accordingly, the literature uses estimates of the elasticity of labor supply to compute an appropriate "marginal cost of funds" for purposes of adjusting the simple cost-benefit formula.

This article reexamines the relationship between the optimal supply of public goods and the distortionary cost of income taxation. The article first demonstrates that, under standard simplifying assumptions (including the separability of leisure), there exists a way to modify the income tax to finance a public good such that there is no additional distortion. Suppose that the preexisting income tax schedule is adjusted so that, at each income level, the tax change just offsets the benefits from the public good. By construction, an individual's *net* reward from any level of work effort will be unaltered: any reduction in disposable income due to the tax adjustment is balanced by the benefit from the public good. Because an individual's after-tax utility as a function of his work effort will thus be unchanged, his choice of work effort—and utility level—will also be unaffected.

To complete the argument, observe that the increase in tax revenue due to this adjustment in the tax schedule will equal the sum of individuals' benefits from the public good. Hence, if the sum of benefits from the public good exceeds its direct cost, the government will have surplus revenue, which can be rebated in a manner that makes everyone better off. In this case, therefore, the simple cost-benefit formula indicates whether the public good should be supplied. There should be no adjustment to account for the distortionary cost of labor income taxation because labor supply does not change. Although this argument will be qualified, it will be explained that the necessary adjustments have little to do with the usual view concerning the distortionary cost of raising funds.

The second part of the analysis addresses the situation in which a public good is not financed by the foregoing tax adjustment that offsets the benefits from the public good. When a different tax adjustment is made to finance the public good, there generally will be a change in distortionary costs. But in such cases there also will be an opposing change in redistributive benefits. (For example, the literature sometimes stipulates that higher marginal income tax rates will finance a public good that produces a uniform monetary benefit; this combination does increase distortionary costs but it also creates redistributive benefits because the poor gain at the expense of the rich.)

In general, it will be explained that the act of supplying of a public good financed with a non-offsetting tax adjustment can be decomposed into (1) financing the public good with a tax adjustment that does offset the benefits of the public good (as described above) and (2) a further, *purely redistributive* adjustment to the tax system. How one should modify the cost-benefit test to account for this second component will depend upon whether increasing the degree of redistribution raises social welfare, which is determined by the policymaker's distributive preferences and the preexisting level of redistribution (and not by the marginal cost of funds).

The next two sections of this article will focus on the point that there is no change in labor supply when the tax adjustment offsets the benefits of the public good. Illustrations will be followed by a more general analysis, accompanied by a discussion of qualifications. After this, the point about the need to examine redistribution in the case of more general methods of finance will be presented. (It will be observed, however, that the offsetting-benefit case may, at least roughly, be descriptively accurate and thus be more relevant for policy analysis.) After developing these ideas, the argument will be related to the existing literature on the subject as well as to prior literatures on a number of closely related topics: Musgrave's (1959) proposed separation of the allocation and distribution functions of government, the Kaldor–Hicks compensation test, benefits taxation, the use of distributive weights in cost-benefit analysis, and optimal income taxation.

Finally, it will be explained that the present analysis of distortionary costs is fully applicable to another important problem: the assessment of environmental taxes. For example, if one were to implement a Pigouvian tax at the first-best level and achieve budget balance with a distribution-neutral adjustment to the income tax, there would be a Pareto improvement in the basic case. And, as above, the difference in outcome that would arise from using some other income tax adjustment would be purely redistributive. This result is contrary to the suggestion of a growing literature which, like that on public goods, typically examines some stipulated income tax adjustment that entails redistribution and documents the efficiency cost from the resulting distortion while not considering the distributive benefit.

ILLUSTRATIONS

Proportional Case

Suppose initially that there is in place a proportional income tax under which individuals pay taxes equal to 30 percent of their earnings. Now consider supplying a public good that produces benefits that increase with income; specifically, assume that the benefits equal one percent of income. (Individuals with more income might use the good more or place a greater value on its use; for example, police protection of private property may be more valuable to higher-income individuals who have more property to protect.[2]) Next, we can construct a tax adjustment that offsets the benefits of the public good. Because these benefits equal one percent of income, the tax adjustment that offsets these benefits consists of requiring that an additional one percent of income be paid in tax—that is, raising the income tax rate from 30 to 31 percent.[3]

Consider now the effect of adjusting the income tax in this manner combined with the effect of providing the public good. For each additional dollar an individual might earn, he will have one cent less than otherwise available for private consumption, 69 cents instead of 70 cents. However, the individual will benefit in an amount worth one additional cent due to the availability of the public good, raising his aggregate marginal benefit from earning a dollar back to 70 cents.[4] *That is, his net utility benefit from earning an additional dollar will be precisely what it was before—without the public good and the tax adjustment.* Because each individual's net benefit from any level of labor effort is thus unchanged, labor supply will be unaffected, and each individual's utility will be the same as it was before.

Finally, consider the government's budget. Because labor supply is unchanged, the tax adjustment, which absorbs each individual's benefits from the public good, will increase government revenue by the sum of individuals' benefits. If this sum exceeds the direct cost of supplying the good—which is to say, if the simple cost-benefit test is passed—there will be a government surplus. Then, the surplus can be rebated *pro rata* to achieve budget balance in a manner that makes all individuals better off.[5]

Uniform Case

Suppose that the public good provides a uniform monetary benefit to individuals, say, a park producing a per capita benefit of $100.[6] Here, the tax adjustment that offsets (absorbs) the benefits from the public good consists of adding $100 to the tax each individual owes (rather than increasing the marginal tax rate, as in the previous example).[7] It is obvious that this tax adjustment would involve no distortion.[8] Thus, as long as the park costs less than $100 per capita—again, if the simple cost-benefit test is passed—there will be a government surplus that can be rebated in a manner that makes everyone better off. (Although uniform tax changes of the sort considered here, akin to uniform lump-sum taxes, are often ruled out because they are deemed to be objectionable on distributive grounds, when the uniform tax change finances a public good that produces uniform benefits, such an objection is inapposite; after all, a Pareto improvement results.[9])

Discussion

How can one explain the difference between the result in these examples and that in the recent literature on public goods? Essentially, the present examples involve *matching the distributive incidence of the method of finance to the incidence of the public good.* When the public good is worth more to high-income individuals, the offsetting (benefit-absorbing) tax adjustment requires that they pay more; when the benefit is uniform, so is the tax. The literature, by contrast, typically stipulates a public good (usually without exploring its distributive incidence) and stipulates one or more tax mechanisms.[10] It so happens that the combinations that are usually selected often result in greater distortion.[11]

For instance, one can obtain the standard distortionary result by combining a tax adjustment that increases marginal income tax rates with a public good that produces uniform monetary benefits.[12] This combination involves a tax adjustment that does not offset the benefit of the public good; instead, the rich pay an amount in excess of their benefits, so they are worse off, and the poor pay less than they benefit, so they are better off. In other words, this assumed combination involves more distortion because it involves greater redistribution. But if redistribution is greater, the resulting beneficial effect on social welfare must be considered along with the distortionary cost of the tax adjustment, as will be emphasized below. Nevertheless, the literature, often implicitly and sometimes explicitly, ignores redistributive benefits.[13] (In many models appearing in the literature, there would not be a redistributive benefit because individuals are assumed to be identical, but one must keep in mind that this assumption is merely for analytical simplicity.[14])

ANALYSIS

Generalizing the Argument

This section will explain when and why the use of a tax adjustment that offsets the benefits of a public good will involve no distortion. A more formal presentation and a worked-out example of the proportional case appear in the Appendix.

OPTIMAL SUPPLY OF PUBLIC GOODS

It is useful to begin by defining more precisely the offsetting adjustment to the labor income tax (taken here to refer to the combination of the tax itself and government transfer programs). Essentially, the offsetting adjustment is a benefits tax, which is set equal to the monetary value of the benefit of the public good to individuals at each income level.[15] In more technical terms, the tax adjustment equals individuals' marginal rate of substitution.

When a public good is financed using an offsetting adjustment to the income tax scheme, each individual's monetary benefit from the public good just equals the additional tax he pays. If individuals who earn $20,000 have a benefit worth $126, they will be paying an additional $126 in taxes; if those earning $21,000 enjoy a benefit of $135, their additional tax will be $135. Thus, the direct effect of the public good combined with such a tax is to leave everyone as well off as before, as long as each individual chooses to earn the same level of income.

Next, consider whether there can be any distortion or other revenue effect due to a change in labor supply, the focus of the recent literature on public goods provision. It can readily be demonstrated that there will in fact be no effect on behavior when the tax adjustment is offsetting, if one assumes that individuals' utility functions are weakly separable in the disutility of labor. (This assumption is stated precisely in the Appendix and is relaxed in the discussion below.) Labor effort does not change because, for any level of before-tax income one might earn, the offsetting tax adjustment leaves individuals with the same utility from the combination of private and public goods as they had in the absence of the public goods and the offsetting tax adjustment. In particular, there is now more utility from public goods and less from private goods. The offsetting tax adjustment is constructed so that the reduction in expenditures on private goods for a given level of before-tax income produces a reduction in utility just equal to the increase in utility from the public goods. *Thus, any chosen level of labor effort will produce precisely the same utility with public goods and the offsetting tax adjustment as it produced without them.* Because individuals' utility-opportunity sets are unaffected, their choice of labor remains the same. (In the preceding example, an individual who must decide between earning $20,000 and $21,000 will receive the same utility from each choice after the reform as he did before the reform; thus, whichever level of labor supply was chosen before will be selected afterward.)

This logic should be familiar from the illustrations offered previously. In the first, the monetary benefit from the public good and the supplemental tax both increased at a rate equal to one percent of income. In the second, both the monetary benefit from public good and the offsetting tax increase were uniform—independent of income. The present, more general case simply allows for any relationship between the monetary benefit from the public good and income.

Up to this point, it has been shown that, if one provides a public good and imposes a tax that soaks up each individual's benefits from the public good, individuals' utility levels and behavior will remain the same. Now, one can ask whether this method of finance produces a budget surplus or deficit. If the simple cost-benefit test is satisfied, there will be a surplus, for the revenue yielded by the tax adjustment precisely equals the sum of individuals' monetary benefits from the public good and the only new expenditure is the direct cost of supplying the public good. One can rebate this surplus uniformly to produce a Pareto improvement.[16]

Qualifications

The qualifications that follow will be familiar to some readers from the optimal income taxation literature. It should be emphasized at the outset that these qualifications concern only how the simple cost-benefit test should be adjusted in light of certain complications; they do not affect the validity of the central argument in this article. In particular, neither the direction nor the magnitude of the appropriate adjustments to the cost-benefit test is indicated by a general measure of the mar-ginal cost of funds, which, in turn, would depend on the uncompensated elasticity of labor supply. Moreover, the qualifications do not affect the argument elabor-ated upon below that, when taxes are not offsetting, there is a general tendency for distortionary and distributive effects to run in opposing directions, requiring that both effects be considered.

Relative complementarity of private and public goods with leisure. The simple cost-benefit rule should be adjusted when private and public goods do not have the same degree of complementarity with leisure.[17] This possibility is absent in the preceding analysis because the utility function is assumed to be weakly separable in leisure.[18] This caveat is analogous to Atkinson and Stiglitz's (1976) result that optimal commodity taxes are zero in the presence of an optimal nonlinear income tax except to the extent that commodities are substitutes for or complements with leisure. To pursue the analogy, interpret private goods as one set of commodities and public goods as another; applying a higher (lower) relative tax on public goods would correspond to reducing (increasing) their supply relative to that indicated by the simple cost-benefit test.

To illustrate the phenomenon, it might be argued that there should be smaller public libraries than otherwise would be efficient, because libraries make leisure more attractive, reinforcing the adverse incentive effect of the income tax. Conversely, there perhaps should be greater police protection of private property than otherwise would be efficient, because this increases the value of goods that are purchased from the fruits of labor. The relevant point for present purposes is that this qualification, however important it may be in some instances, does not justify the type of adjustment to cost-benefit analysis proposed in the literature. The marginal-cost-of-funds adjustment depends most directly upon the income and substitution effects of taxation on labor effort; it is not suggested that the validity and direction of any adjustment depend upon whether public goods are leisure substitutes or complements.

Heterogeneity of preferences. The analysis may also need qualification when the benefits of public goods vary *within* income classes due to differences in tastes or opportunities.[19] Then, individuals having the same income but different preferences would need to pay different offsetting taxes in order to make feasible a Pareto improvement whenever the simple cost-benefit test was satisfied. If differences in benefits are observable, offsetting taxes can take the differences into account. For example, if a project will benefit a particular region, the corresponding adjustment to the tax system would apply solely to that region. (Financing local public goods with local taxes tends to accomplish this result.)

But often, differences in preferences are neither directly observable nor readily elicited; indeed, a substantial literature is addressed to this problem.[20] Moreover, even if detailed information were available, perfectly offsetting taxes may be administratively impractical. To this extent, compensation is inevitably imperfect, so there will be "redistribution." But this redistribution is not of a conventional sort—such as results from changing the progressivity of the overall tax/expenditure system. If it were, it could be offset by adjusting the income tax schedule. Rather, any unavoidable redistribution is *within* income groups, so-called horizontal inequity.[21] For example, physically weak individuals might benefit more from police protection than physically stronger ones (holding income constant). In this instance, the public good may be equality enhancing in a relevant sense, and thus more should be provided than otherwise. In other instances, a public good may create disparities in "effective" income between individuals with equal nominal income, in which case public goods provision may be less desirable than otherwise. Note, however, that the appropriate adjustment to the simple cost-benefit test is unrelated to the conventional view in the literature, for the adjustment is not based on the distortionary cost of taxation.[22]

APPLICATION TO POLICY

In order to explore further the policy relevance of the foregoing analysis, which assumes that public goods will be financed by tax adjustments that offset the benefits from the public goods, this section considers how analysis should proceed when such adjustments are not used and then examines whether it is plausible that such offsetting tax adjustments will if fact be used.

Policy Analysis When Tax Adjustments Do Not Offset Benefits from Public Goods

Initially, observe that, when a tax adjustment does offset the benefits from a public good, the net result is *distribution-neutral*: because individuals at each income level pay additional taxes in an amount that equals their benefits from the public good, it follows that the combination of the public good and the tax adjustment involves no redistribution. If some other finance mechanism is used, however, the distribution will change.

To elaborate, consider the prospect of supplying a public good that is to be financed by some method T (where T refers to the adjustment to the income tax and transfer payment system that provides the revenue for the project). Decompose this reform into two components:

(1) Finance the public good by an offsetting tax adjustment, T_0.
(2) Reform the tax system, changing the tax scheme from T_0 to T.

The first component consists of the hypothetical reform already considered. It involves no additional distortion of labor effort and no redistribution; in the basic case, it is properly evaluated using the simple cost-benefit test. One would now supplement this evaluation by considering the second component, which consists of a *purely redistributive* (revenue-neutral) reform of the tax/transfer system. Thus, in the example of the park that produces uniform monetary benefits of $100 and is presumed to be financed by raising the marginal income tax rate, one would now evaluate the greater redistribution that results from raising the marginal income tax rate instead of raising taxes by a uniform dollar amount. In this regard, there is a familiar trade-off: increased redistribution entails more distortion. If, according to the policymaker's social welfare function, the preexisting regime provided too little redistribution, an increase in redistribution would count as a supplemental net benefit despite the increase in distortionary cost. If, instead, there previously was too much redistribution, the prospect of additional redistribution and the accompanying distortion would constitute a net cost.

Knowledge that the aggregate reform —the public good and the tax adjustment, taken together—causes distortion thus provides little guidance, because the existence of distortion is associated with greater redistribution. Whether the net effect is good or bad depends upon the extent of preexisting redistribution and the policymaker's judgment about the optimal extent of redistribution. Analogously, reforms that reduce distortion are not per se desirable on this account, because such reforms entail correspondingly less redistribution. Therefore, when the tax adjustment does not offset the benefits of the public good, there can be no presumption that the appropriate "adjustment" to the cost-benefit test is even in the *direction* indicated by conventional analysis.[23]

To summarize, the proposed two-part decomposition is analytically useful for the general case in which a public good may not be financed by a tax adjustment that offsets the benefits from the public good. The first step of the analysis involves assessing the merits of the public good, and the second step involves determining whether any change in the extent of redistribution is desirable. To a significant extent, these conceptually distinct questions are also separable in practice because either component can be implemented independently: the public good could be financed with an offsetting tax adjustment T_0 instead of with T, and the extent of redistribution could be increased or reduced without regard to whether the public good is provided.

The Likelihood That Actual Tax Adjustments Will Offset Benefits from Public Goods

It seems plausible that the preexisting tax/transfer regime will reflect some equilibrium of political forces that, among other things, entails a level of redistribution. In this case, one's best guess might be that projects will be financed in a manner that is, on net, distribution-neutral. And, as just explained, distribution-neutral finance consists precisely of using a tax adjustment that offsets the benefits from the public good.[24] Moreover, when the extent of redistribution does change, one would expect the change to result from a realignment of political forces. Furthermore, one would expect such a realignment to produce a change in redistribution even if no new project were to be implemented.

The increasing use of distribution tables in assessing government policy and in packaging proposals suggests that politicians do keep an eye on distribution. The 1986 tax reform was explicitly formulated to be distribution-neutral (changes unfavorable to the rich were consciously balanced by targeted tax rate reductions), and the 1993 tax reform, enacted shortly after a change in the ruling political party, was designed to increase redistribution (although it contained what was believed to be a regressive gasoline tax increase, which was offset by progressive income tax adjustments).

It remains true that the legislature is not in the business of fine-tuning the tax system each time a program is enacted or repealed. But the distortions examined in the existing literature arise only after the tax system is adjusted (which, lately, happens quite often). When such adjustments are made, the legislature can (and, given the preceding observations, likely would) take into account any significant changes in the distribution of income. To be sure, one would not expect tax adjustments to offset the benefits of new public projects completely and precisely. Nevertheless, if one had to guess, it seems plausible that roughly, on average, and over time, changes in the level of public goods will tend to be accompanied by tax adjustments that offset changes in the distributive incidence of the benefits produced by those goods.[25]

RELATIONSHIP TO PRIOR LITERATURE

The present argument is related to—and draws upon the insights of—a range of prior literature. Most familiar to many readers will be Musgrave's (1959) proposed separation of the allocation and distribution functions of government. This view, in turn, is related to the Kaldor–Hicks hypothetical compensation test, under which a project is deemed to be desirable if it constitutes a potential Pareto improvement—that is, if the winners could compensate the losers. Although still seen as helpful, these ideas are not generally accepted as valid in a second-best world: public goods are financed by distortionary taxation, and losers are not directly compensated by winners. Thus, the modern literature on public goods provision emphasizes the need to account for tax distortions, and other writing on cost-benefit analysis advocates the use of distributive weights to account for the redistributive effects of public projects.[26]

The offsetting tax construct suggested here is a scheme of benefits taxation (often referred to as Lindahl pricing). If such taxation is used, compensation is not merely hypothetical. Thus, in the analytical section, it was shown under standard simplifying assumptions that financing public goods with an offsetting tax adjustment results in an actual Pareto improvement whenever the Samuelson (1954) cost-benefit test is met.

Benefits taxation has received relatively little attention for two reasons: it is difficult to implement because each individual's benefits cannot readily be measured, and the actual tax system seems to be (and should be) redistributive rather than grounded in a benefits principle. The present article offers a different perspective on each of these points. The infeasibility of pure benefits taxation was admitted in the discussion of heterogeneous preferences, but it was emphasized that the only necessary differences between taxes paid and benefits received consist of differences *within* income groups. As a result, there need not arise the distortion associated with the labor income tax, which arises from redistribution among individuals at *different* income levels.

The suggestion that the actual tax system involves redistribution, not pure benefits taxation, also does not disrupt the present argument. The relevant question is not the redistributive character of the entire tax system but of the marginal decision to finance more of a public good. As noted previously, this decision might be distribution-neutral even when the preexisting regime is redistributive. More importantly, when finance is not distribution-neutral, it does not follow that the cost-benefit test should be modified in the manner suggested in the recent literature to account for the distortionary cost of taxation. There generally is a redistributive effect directly opposed to the distortionary effect. Thus, if the simple cost-benefit test requires modification, one cannot ascertain even the direction of the adjustment without assessing both of these effects and determining whether the status quo involves too little or too much redistribution.

Less familiar branches of prior literature are also directly relevant to the present inquiry. In particular, the construct of offsetting taxes is used in Hylland and Zeckhauser's (1979) important (but surprisingly overlooked) article arguing that distributive objectives should not affect program choice in cost-benefit analysis.[27] Whereas Hylland and Zeckhauser emphasize that distributive effects are not inherent, the present article emphasizes that distortion is not inherent and underscores the point that distortionary effects tend to be accompanied by offsetting distributive effects.[28] Hylland and Zeckhauser's analysis has been extended in Christiansen (1981) and Boadway and Keen (1993), who investigate public goods provision in the presence of optimal nonlinear income taxes.[29] Unfortunately, insights from these prior investigations do not appear in the extensive literature on public goods provision. The present article attempts an integration. It differs from the optimal tax literature in two respects. First, using an argument like the original one of Hylland and Zeckhauser, this article emphasizes a result that holds without regard to whether the initial income tax is optimal.[30] Second, the current investigation addresses how one should analyze the public goods problem when neither assumption—the presence of an optimized income tax or the use of an offsetting tax adjustment—holds; in particular, it highlights the existence of generally opposing influences on social welfare, one from distortionary effects and the other from distributive effects.

The dominant literature in the past few decades, which is referred to throughout this article, is concerned with determining an appropriate adjustment to the simple cost-benefit test to account for the distortionary cost of taxation. This literature generally makes little reference to the others discussed in this section. In particular, the conventional approach focuses on distortion, ignoring the fact that distributive concerns are the primary motivation for using distortionary income taxation. As a result, the literature presents measures—often embodied in a marginal cost of funds—that provide an incomplete and misleading basis for policy.

To further illustrate the problem, consider the case in which public goods substitute for private consumption.[31] The literature suggests that such an assumption would produce the Pigouvian result that public goods provision is distortionary, requiring benefits to exceed costs by at least the distortionary cost of taxation. For example, Ballard and Fullerton (1992) explain that, in such a case, the income effect of the tax (which raises labor supply and thus produces a positive revenue effect) would be fully offset by the opposing income effect of the public good, leaving only the substitution effect of the tax, which entails distortion. But if an offsetting tax is used to finance the public good, whenever there is a substitution effect due to the tax, it will be precisely offset by that due to the public good, so there would be no labor supply effect. The standard distortionary effect identified in the literature, therefore, arises because it is implicitly assumed that the finance mechanism (say, a proportional income tax) will have a more progressive incidence than the benefits of the public good (taken to be uniform).[32] But if this assumption is to be made, the distributive benefit of the more progressive tax/ expenditure system should be included in the final account. When that is done, the marginal cost of funds is not the appropriate adjustment to the simple cost-benefit test.

ENVIRONMENTAL TAXES

Analogous to the past decades of literature on public goods provision that emphasizes distortionary costs of taxation is a rapidly growing literature that examines the effects of environmental taxes, taking into account how any revenue raised will allow the government to reduce the level of other, distortionary taxes.[33] The framework of the present article can be applied directly to this context. After all, correcting externalities may be viewed as a public good. That the revenue produced by a corrective tax is positive rather than negative, as when financing a tangible public project, does not affect the analysis in any fundamental way. (It implies that the offsetting tax adjustment to the income tax will offset both the benefits from correcting the externality and the incidence of the environmental tax.)

In particular, one can decompose any corrective tax scheme—consisting of a corrective tax and an income tax adjustment T' that achieves budget balance—into two components:

(1) Impose the corrective tax and make an offsetting (distribution-neutral) tax adjustment, T_0'.
(2) Reform the income tax system, changing the scheme from T_0' to T'.

As before, the first component, which is both distribution- and revenue-neutral, involves no change in distortion (aside from influencing the level of the externality). Under the standard simplifying assumptions, familiar, first-best reasoning would be valid. This suggests (contrary to the environmental tax literature) that the optimal Pigouvian tax will tend to be that which fully internalizes the externality.[34] The second component, as before, is a purely redistributive tax change, and it can be evaluated as such. If the actual tax adjustment is not offsetting, it follows (as in the public goods case) that one cannot ascertain even the direction of any adjustment to the first-best Pigouvian tax without first determining whether the existing extent of redistribution is too little or too much.

To illustrate the argument, consider a gasoline tax and suppose that the demand for gasoline is proportional to income. This gasoline tax, in addition to reducing gasoline use, would have an effect on labor supply similar to that of a proportional income tax. The reason is that, because gasoline demand rises proportionately with income, the gasoline taxes one must pay also rise proportionately with income. The gasoline tax, therefore, would not succeed in raising revenue without distorting the labor-leisure choice. Moreover, if one restored the prior budget balance (or degree of imbalance) with an offsetting tax adjustment, this would entail an equal-proportionate reduction in the income tax. This offsetting adjustment would, in turn, have an effect on labor supply precisely opposite to that of the gasoline tax.

In addition, the income tax adjustment would need to offset the benefits from controlling the externality, just as the tax adjustment in the case of public goods absorbed the benefits from the public goods. Therefore, the combined income tax adjustment will eliminate any effects on labor supply from both the environmental tax itself and from the effects of that tax on environmental benefits. Thus, as with public goods, finance by an offsetting tax adjustment eliminates distortionary (and distributive) effects. Finally, if the gasoline tax indeed corrects an externality, precisely the concern in the traditional analysis of Pigouvian taxes, the government will have a surplus after the tax adjustment because the positive net benefits will be in the government's coffers due to the income tax adjustment that absorbs all the benefits.

Now, suppose that the gasoline tax is regressive. Finance by an offsetting tax would involve adjusting the income tax schedule to raise less revenue but in a somewhat more progressive manner. The net effect of the regressive gasoline tax and the progressive adjustment to the income tax would be to raise the same revenue with the same distributive effect and the same labor-leisure distortion as that which existed previously. On the other hand, if the income tax were reduced in a proportional rather than an offsetting manner, there would be less distortion through use of the regressive gasoline tax, but there also would be less redistribution. This illustrates the more general and by now familiar point that, when there is change in the distortionary cost of taxation, there also will be a countervailing change in the extent of redistribution. The existence of a change in distortionary costs depends on the assumption that the tax adjustment will not be offsetting, and, when this is the case, a proper policy evaluation must consider both the distortionary and distributive effects.

The perspective on Pigouvian taxes offered here is related to the argument of Atkinson and Stiglitz (1976) that it is not optimal to employ differential commodity taxes in the presence of an optimal nonlinear income tax (subject to the previously noted qualifications). Taxing a commodity more heavily will distort the labor-leisure choice because bundles of goods will be made more expensive; by adjusting the nonlinear income tax instead, the same revenue can be raised, with the same distributive incidence and effect on labor supply, but without distorting individuals' choices among goods. Consumer choices are optimal when price ratios reflect full social costs—producers' costs plus any external costs—and nothing else.

Conclusion

A substantial literature is concerned with determining how to modify the simple cost-benefit test for public goods provision to account for the distortionary cost of taxation. The present article argues, however, that the proposed adjustment, based upon the marginal cost of funds, is inappropriate.

The correct analysis of public goods supply follows from two findings. First, under standard simplifying assumptions, there exists a way to modify the income tax to finance a public good such that there is no additional distortion. The method of finance involves adjusting the income tax so that, at each income level, tax increases just offset the benefits from the public good; the net effect is distribution-neutral. It is also suggested that, roughly speaking, public goods might plausibly be financed in this manner. If this is the case, no adjustment to the simple cost-benefit test should be made. (Qualifications to this conclusion are noted, but they entail subtle adjustments that are unrelated to the conventional view of the distortionary cost of taxation.)

Second, when public goods are not financed in the manner just described, it is explained that the distortionary cost identified in the literature will arise, but it will be accompanied by a countervailing change in redistributive benefits that has been ignored. In this case, policy analysis should have two components: assessing the merits of the public good according to cost-benefit analysis and determining whether the change in redistribution is desirable. This latter step does not involve an adjustment for the marginal cost of funds because distortion is only half of the story. Instead, distortionary costs must be balanced against redistributive benefits. Greater redistribution will, on net, be desirable when the policymaker believes that there is too little redistribution to begin with (and, conversely, when initially there is too much). *Ceteris paribus,* knowledge that the distortion associated with a particular method of finance is positive indicates that redistribution is greater, but this does not answer the question of whether the result is beneficial.

Regardless of the actual method of finance (the actual method often is unknown to the analyst), the assumption that public goods will be financed by income tax adjustments that offset the benefits from the public goods provides a useful way of conceptualizing the problem of public goods supply. The approach reveals that neither distortionary nor redistributive effects are inherent when changing the level of public goods, and it makes clear how analysis should proceed when distortion and redistribution are involved.

The present analysis also casts the recent literature on environmental taxes in a different light. When the income tax adjustment used to balance the budgetary impact of Pigouvian taxes is designed to offset the distributive effects of the latter, conventional first-best analysis is correct (under standard, simplifying assumptions). And, when the income tax adjustment is different, for any change in the net distortion of labor supply, there will be opposing redistributive effects that must be considered.

ENDNOTES

I am grateful for comments from Alan Auerbach, Lucian Bebchuk, David Bradford, Peter Diamond, Don Fullerton, Larry Goulder, Carl Shapiro, Steven Shavell, Jonathan Skinner, Jeff Strnad, workshop participants, and referees, and for support from the John M. Olin Center for Law, Economics, and Business at Harvard Law School.

1 The literature also indicates that the supply of public goods may itself affect revenue because of the interaction between public goods and the demand for private goods, a factor that has received comparatively little attention. In particular, much analysis of distortionary taxation assumes that public goods enter utility in an additively separable manner, in which case this interaction does not arise. See, e.g., Ballard, Shoven, and Whalley (1985) and Stuart (1984). (The interaction also does not arise in models that simply omit public goods from individuals' utility functions.) Browning (1987) and Wildasin (1984) emphasize the revenue effect of public goods. Some of the limitations imposed by assuming separability are analyzed in Ahmed and Croushore (1994).

2 Benefits could be proportional to income either because those with more income get more direct benefit from the public good, as explained in the text, or due to an income effect (i.e., the same good is worth more, measured in dollars, to those with higher income due to the declining marginal utility of income). The latter case would be

applicable if benefits were additively separable, as commonly assumed in the literature. See note 1. Both cases are illustrated in the Appendix.

3 More realistically, one might suppose that the benefits are a function of disposable (after-tax) income. In that case, benefits equal to one percent of disposable income would be offset by a tax increase of 0.7 percent on before-tax income (because, prior to the adjustment, after-tax income was only 70 percent of before-tax income). The offsetting tax adjustment would be complicated further if the preexisting tax was not linear (with a zero intercept). The simplifications in the example are for expositional clarity; the general argument to follow shows that they are inessential.

4 As already stated in note 2, the individual might directly benefit from the public good (those with more income to consume may make more use of the public good or gain more from its presence) or it may be that his marginal utility of private consumption is higher on account of the tax adjustment. As will become clear in the more general analysis, what matters is that an individual's *utility* benefit from earning an additional dollar is the same with the public good and tax adjustment as it was in the absence of the them. (Both cases are illustrated in the Appendix.)

5 For an account of the income effect of providing this rebate, see note 16.

6 A uniform *utility* benefit—as implied by the common additively separable specification—does not imply a uniform *monetary* benefit. Indeed, when the utility from consumption is logarithmic, there is a proportional benefit, as previously considered. See note 37.

7 This can be accomplished by adjusting the level of exemptions and tax brackets; for poor persons who pay no tax, welfare payments could be cut by $100.

8 There would be an income effect due to the tax increase, which would tend to increase labor supply, but there is an offsetting income effect from the public good.

9 See note 14. As a further example of contemporary interest, suppose that the government decided to provide free basic health care at a level most individuals would purchase in any event, financed by a uniform increase in the tax schedule. This would be equivalent to a requirement of compulsory purchase from the government. Even if the government revenue requirement grew by hundreds of billions of dollars, there need not be any distortion involved in financing the reform. See Summers (1989).

10 It might be supposed that the common assumption that the public good enters utility in an additively separable manner (see note 1) indicates that there is a neutral distributive incidence, which thus may be ignored. If this were true, however, it would be natural to consider a uniform (in dollar amount) tax increase rather than an increase in the tax rate. In any event, it is not the case that an additively separable public good produces a uniform benefit when measured in dollars (which is relevant for present purposes). This case is discussed further in the Appendix.

11 Of course, this is not necessarily the case, as the recent literature has emphasized. See, e.g., Ballard and Fullerton (1992) and Fullerton (1991).

12 For the average individual, there would be an offsetting income effect from the public good—the tax reduces income whereas the public good increases effective income by $100—but no offsetting substitution effect.

13 For examples of the latter, see, e.g., Auerbach (1985) and Ballard and Fullerton (1992).

14 The representative individual approach appears, for example, in Atkinson and Stern (1974) and Stiglitz and Dasgupta (1971). If all individuals really were identical, then the optimal tax scheme would be a uniform tax, and there would be no distortionary cost. However, a uniform tax is ruled out, and instead it is assumed that an income tax must be used; this approach is motivated by our understanding that individuals are not in fact identical and, as a result, the income tax is distributively superior. (See Drèze and Stern's (1987) and Oakland's (1987) surveys of the theories of cost-benefit analysis and public goods.) Under this rationale, however, distributive benefits should not be ignored.

There is sometimes confusion about lump-sum taxation: the lump-sum taxes familiar from the second theorem of welfare economics are individualized, and it is generally agreed that these are infeasible, or at least subject to error, because differences in individuals' ability are not observable. It is not the case, however, that *uniform* lump-sum taxes raise serious problems of feasibility, particularly with regard to financing a modest change in the level of public goods. The present tax/transfer system already has a uniform component because the intercept of the tax/transfer schedule is not zero: the tax system has exemptions and the welfare system provides positive transfers. See, e.g., Mirrlees (1994). Both can be raised or reduced (and adjustments are in fact made with some regularity). As a result, *if* a public good did produce uniform monetary benefits, it is plausible to imagine financing it by a uniform tax adjustment of the sort discussed in the text.

15 Here, as in other work on the subject, individuals are assumed to differ only in their ability, and preferences are taken to be independent of ability. The case of heterogeneous preferences is addressed in the text below, and the possibility that preferences depend on ability is considered in note 17.

OPTIMAL SUPPLY OF PUBLIC GOODS

16 More precisely, one can uniformly decrease the tax schedule slightly until one reaches the point at which the budget balances. As one rebates the surplus, there will be effects on behavior (an income effect). But as long as changes in labor effort are continuous (except perhaps for a set of individuals having measure zero), there will exist a modification that involves a positive rebate to everyone while balancing the budget.

17 Another qualification arises when individuals' tastes vary in a manner related to their unobservable ability. In that instance, public goods preferred more by the less (more) able would be more (less) desirable than otherwise (Mirrlees, 1976). For example, if higher ability increases appreciation for sophisticated art, the optimal subsidy for lowbrow art would exceed that for highbrow art.

18 More formally, the assumption implies, in the model in the Appendix, that $\partial U/\partial l$ is unaffected when the offsetting tax keeps $v(c,g)$ constant. But if c and g can interact differently with l, rather than through the common subutility function $v(c,g)$, the combination of a higher g and lower c could affect the marginal disutility of effort; the direction of the effect depends on the relative complementarity of c and g to l. See Boadway and Keen (1993) and Christiansen (1981). (Although their analyses assume that optimal nonlinear income taxation is employed, this limitation is immaterial for present purposes, as will be discussed below.)

19 See Boadway and Keen (1993) and Hylland and Zeckhauser (1979). If public goods produce separable benefits, as many studies assume, heterogeneity would not affect social welfare in a utilitarian framework. (Heterogeneity would affect the distribution of welfare, but not individuals' marginal utilities of income or labor effort.)

20 The most important source of unobservable differences probably is variation in preferences rather than in opportunities. While a strict utilitarian would wish to account for this, others may argue that such heterogeneity should be ignored in setting government policy.

21 Such redistribution can be understood as presenting a more refined problem of vertical equity or, equivalently, from an *ex ante* perspective, one involving the imposition of risk. See Kaplow (1989). The vertical equity comparison is also suggested in Atkinson's (1980) discussion of how measuring the inequality resulting from a reform can be misleading if one examines the postreform averages for groups of prereform equals who are not treated equally by the reform.

22 Also, the adjustment does not entail a simple weighting of costs and benefits to reflect the income levels of winners and losers because the winners and losers are, by assumption, *within* income groups.

23 Similarly, knowing that the chosen tax adjustment involves, say, a particularly high level of distortion is, by itself, a misleading basis for policy because, *ceteris paribus,* tax adjustments cause greater distortion when they produce more redistribution.

24 If the preexisting regime were thought to reflect a desire to implement the optimal distributive scheme, the assumption that offsetting taxes would be used is also a plausible approximation. (Moreover, when the preexisting regime is optimal, distortionary and distributive effects will have an offsetting influence on social welfare in any event, as discussed in note 30 with reference to the prior optimal nonlinear income taxation literature.)

25 The competing assumption most common in the current literature—that finance will involve a proportional income tax or a uniform increase in the rates of all taxes without regard to the distributive incidence of the benefits of the goods being financed—has not, to my knowledge, been defended as descriptively accurate, and recent tax reforms in the United States do not suggest that this is the case.

26 On the latter, see Weisbrod (1968) and Drèze and Stern (1987).

27 The idea is also used by Shavell (1981) to show that distributive objectives should not affect the choice of legal rules regulating activity that produces externalities.

28 Put another way, some literature on cost-benefit analysis advocates the use of distributive weights, implicitly assuming that the finance mechanism is nonredistributive; other literature on cost-benefit analysis advocates an adjustment for the distortionary cost of taxation, implicitly assuming redistributive finance. The present effort can be seen as integrating both aspects of the problem.

29 Mirrlees (1976, 1994) and Tuomala (1990) briefly analyze public goods provision with optimal nonlinear income taxation. There also has been work restricting attention to linear taxation. See, e.g., King (1986) and Wilson (1991).

30 The argument in the optimal tax literature follows automatically from the fact that deviations from the social optimum involve no first-order welfare loss. That is, *any* marginal change in the tax schedule will produce distortionary and distributive effects on social welfare that precisely offset.

31 Formally, this case assumes that the utility, v, of private consumption (c) and public goods (g) can be expressed as $v(c,g) = v(c + b(g))$, where $b(g)$ is the consumption value of public goods. The other special case emphasized in the literature, involving public goods that produce additively separable benefits, is discussed in the Appendix. Many public goods do not produce additively separable benefits but rather substitute for consumption to some extent. For example, road repair reduces costs of automobile repair; greater police protection reduces spending on private security measures;

more and better parks reduce expenditures on private yards. See Ahmed and Croushore (1994), Aschauer (1985), and Browning (1987).

32 Ballard's (1991) survey identifies consensus on the view that, if a project is a close substitute for cash, the marginal cost of funds for labor taxes or lump-sum taxes will be higher than for a project producing separable benefits. He further suggests that an evaluator needs to know the marginal cost of funds and the (nontax) costs and benefits of the project. The marginal cost of funds is understood to be independent of the particular project, implying that there is some given tax source (such as a proportional increase in all taxes).

33 On the revenue benefits from Pigouvian taxes, see, e.g., Ballard and Medema (1993) and Cordes, Nicholson, and Sammartino (1990). For more elaborate analyses that account for general equilibrium effects and the effect of environmental taxes on labor supply, thereby reaching different conclusions, see, e.g., Bovenberg and de Mooij (1994), Bovenberg and van der Ploeg (1994), Bovenberg and Goulder (1996), and Goulder (1995). There is an analogous literature that considers the optimal level of Pigouvian subsidies. See, e.g., Browning (1993) and Ng (1980). And there is a literature that assesses the distributive consequences of environmental taxes, motivated by the general concern that such consequences provide an independent ground for evaluation. See, e.g., Casler and Rafiqui (1993).

The argument in the text also implies that distributive effects should not play a role in assessing the desirability of legal rules that regulate harm-causing behavior. See Shavell (1981). (Legal rules enforced by private suits are like Pigouvian taxes, where the victim receives the proceeds, whereas rules that stipulate fines owed to a public authority are tantamount to the tax enforcement mechanism for a Pigouvian tax.)

34 For a formal statement of the problem analyzed in this section, see note 35. Because the analysis is essentially the same, the qualifications raised in the context of public goods are equally applicable here.

The "conventional" view in this literature has gone through two stages. Earlier writing emphasized the possibility of an environmental "double dividend"—a corrective tax both internalizes an externality and allows reduced reliance on preexisting distortionary taxes. More recent work, emphasizing how environmental taxes themselves affect labor supply, suggests a more complicated story in which there typically is no double dividend. For a discussion of the literature, see, e.g., Goulder (1995).

REFERENCES

Ahmed, Shaghil, and Dean Croushore. "The Marginal Cost of Funds with Nonseparable Public Spending." *Public Finance Quarterly* 24 No. 2 (April, 1996): 216–36.

Aschauer, David A. "Fiscal Policy and Aggregate Demand." *American Economic Review* 75 No. 1 (March, 1985): 117–27.

Atkinson, Anthony B. "Horizontal Equity and the Distribution of the Tax Burden." In *The Economics of Taxation*, edited by Henry Aaron and Michael J. Boskin, 3–18. Washington, D.C.: The Brookings Institution, 1980.

Atkinson, Anthony B., and Nicholas H. Stern. "Pigou, Taxation, and Public Goods." *Review of Economic Studies* 41 No. 1 (January, 1974): 119–28.

Atkinson, Anthony B., and Joseph E. Stiglitz. "The Design of Tax Structure: Direct Versus Indirect Taxation." *Journal of Public Economics* 6 Nos. 1-2 (July–August, 1976): 55–75.

Auerbach, Alan J. "The Theory of Excess Burden and Optimal Taxation." In *Handbook of Public Economics,* vol. 1, edited by Alan J. Auerbach and Martin Feldstein, 61–127. Amsterdam: North-Holland, 1985.

Ballard, Charles L. "Marginal Efficiency Cost Calculations for Different Types of Government Expenditure: A Review." The University of Melbourne General Paper No. G-96. Parkville, Victoria, Australia: Impact Research Centre, 1991.

Ballard, Charles L., and Don Fullerton. "Distortionary Taxes and the Provision of Public Goods." *Journal of Economic Perspectives* 6 No. 3 (Summer, 1992): 117–31.

Ballard, Charles L., and Steven G. Medema. "The Marginal Efficiency Effects of Taxes and Subsidies in the Presence of Externalities: A Computational General Equilibrium Approach." *Journal of Public Economics* 52 No. 2 (September, 1993): 199–216.

Ballard, Charles L., John B. Shoven, and John Whalley. "General Equilibrium Computations of the Marginal Welfare Costs of Taxes in the United States." *American Economic Review* 75 No. 1 (March, 1985): 128–38.

Boadway, Robin, and Michael Keen. "Public Goods, Self-Selection and Optimal Income Taxation." *International Economic Review* 34 No. 3 (August, 1993): 463–78.

Bovenberg, A. Lans, and Ruud A. de Mooij. "Environmental Levies and Distortionary

Taxation." *American Economic Review* 84 No. 4 (September, 1994): 1085–9.

Bovenberg, A. Lans, and Lawrence H. Goulder. "Optimal Environmental Taxation in the Presence of Other Taxes: General Equilibrium Analysis." *American Economic Review* 86 No. 4 (September, 1996): 985–1000.

Bovenberg, A. Lans, and Frederick van der Ploeg. "Environmental Policy, Public Finance, and the Labour Market in a Second-Best World." *Journal of Public Economics* 55 No. 3 (November, 1994): 349–90.

Browning, Edgar K. "On the Marginal Welfare Cost of Taxation." *American Economic Review* 77 No. 1 (March, 1987): 11–23.

Browning, Edgar K. "Subsidies Financed with Distorting Taxes." *National Tax Journal* 46 No. 2 (June, 1993): 122–34.

Casler, Stephen D., and Aisha Rafiqui. "Evaluating Fuel Tax Equity: Direct and Indirect Distributional Effects." *National Tax Journal* 46 No. 2 (June, 1993): 197–205.

Christiansen, Vidar. "Evaluation of Public Projects Under Optimal Taxation." *Review of Economic Studies* 48 No. 3 (July, 1981): 447–57.

Cordes, Joseph J., Eric M. Nicholson, and Frank J. Sammartino. "Raising Revenue by Taxing Activities with Social Costs." *National Tax Journal* 43 No. 3 (September, 1990): 343–56.

Diamond, Peter A., and James A. Mirrlees. "Optimal Taxation and Public Production II: Tax Rules." *American Economic Review* 61 No. 3 (June, 1971): 261–78.

Drèze, Jean, and Nicholas Stern. "The Theory of Cost-Benefit Analysis." In *Handbook of Public Economics,* vol. 2, edited by Alan J. Auerbach and Martin Feldstein, 909–89. Amsterdam: North-Holland, 1987.

Fullerton, Don. "Reconciling Recent Estimates of the Marginal Welfare Cost of Taxation." *American Economic Review* 81 No. 1 (March, 1991): 302–8.

Goulder, Lawrence H. "Environmental Taxation and the 'Double Dividend:' A Reader's Guide." *International Tax and Public Finance* 2 No. 2 (August, 1995): 157–83.

Hylland, Aanund, and Richard Zeckhauser. "Distributional Objectives Should Affect Taxes but Not Program Choice or Design." *Scandinavian Journal of Economics* 81 No. 2 (1979): 264–84.

Kaplow, Louis. "Horizontal Equity: Measures in Search of a Principle." *National Tax Journal* 42 No. 2 (June, 1989): 139–54.

Kaplow, Louis. "Should the Government's Allocation Branch Be Concerned About the Distortionary Cost of Taxation and Distributive Effects?" NBER Working Article No. 4566. Cambridge, MA: National Bureau of Economic Research, 1993.

King, Mervyn A. "A Pigouvian Rule for the Optimum Provision of Public Goods." *Journal of Public Economics* 30 No. 3 (August, 1986): 273–91.

Mayshar, Joram. "On Measures of Excess Burden and Their Application." *Journal of Public Economics* 43 No. 3 (December, 1990): 263–89.

Mirrlees, James A. "Optimal Tax Theory: A Synthesis." *Journal of Public Economics* 6 No. 4 (November, 1976): 327–58.

Mirrlees, James A. "Optimal Taxation and Government Finance." In *Modern Public Finance*, edited by John M. Quigley and Eugene Smolensky, 213–31. Cambridge, MA: Harvard University Press, 1994.

Musgrave, Richard A. *The Theory of Public Finance*. New York: McGraw-Hill, 1959.

Ng, Yew-Kwang. "Optimal Corrective Taxes or Subsidies when Revenue Raising Imposes an Excess Burden." *American Economic Review* 70 No. 4 (September, 1980): 744–51.

Oakland, William H. "Theory of Public Goods." In *Handbook of Public Economics,* vol. 2, edited by Alan J. Auerbach and Martin Feldstein, 485–535. Amsterdam: North-Holland, 1987.

Pigou, Arthur C. *A Study in Public Finance*. London: Macmillan, 1947.

Samuelson, Paul A. "A Pure Theory of Public Expenditure." *Review of Economics and Statistics* 36 (November, 1954): 387–9.

Shavell, Steven. "A Note on Efficiency vs. Distributional Equity in Legal Rulemaking: Should Distributional Equity Matter Given Optimal Income Taxation?" *American Economic Review* 71 No. 2 (May, 1981): 414–8.

Stiglitz, Joseph E., and Partha Dasgupta. "Differential Taxation, Public Goods, and Economic Efficiency." *Review of Economic Studies* 38 No. 114 (April, 1971): 151–74.

Stuart, Charles. "Welfare Costs per Dollar of Additional Tax Revenue in the United States." *American Economic Review* 74 No. 3 (June, 1984): 352–62.

Summers, Lawrence H. "What Can Economics Contribute to Social Policy? Some Simple Economics of Mandated Benefits." *American Economic Review, Papers and Proceedings* 79 No. 2 (1989): 177–83.

Tuomala, Matti. *Optimal Income Tax and Redistribution*. Oxford: Clarendon Press, 1990.

Weisbrod, Burton A. "Income Redistribution Effects and Cost-Benefit Analysis." In *Problems in Public Expenditure Analysis*, edited by Samuel B. Chase, 177–209. Washington, D.C.: The Brookings Institution, 1968.

Wildasin, David E. "On Public Good Provision with Distortionary Taxation." *Economic Inquiry* 22 No. 2 (April, 1984): 227–43.

Wilson, John Douglas. "Optimal Public Good Provision with Limited Lump-Sum Taxation." *American Economic Review* 81 No. 1 (March, 1991): 153–66.

APPENDIX

Individuals have utility functions $U(v(c,g),\ell)$, where c is consumption, g the level of expenditures on the public good, and ℓ labor effort. Individuals' wages (ability) w have density $f(w)$. Each individual chooses ℓ to maximize $U(v(c,g),\ell)$ subject to the budget constraint

1

$$c = w\ell - T(w\ell,g)$$

where $T(w\ell,g)$ is the tax (which may be negative) that an individual pays as a function of the income, $w\ell$, he earns, which is all that the government observes.[1] The term T is also a function of g to denote that, when the government changes the level of the public good, it also must change the tax schedule. (It is assumed that initially the budget balances, and it is required that, after all adjustments, the budget must again be in balance.)

Examples

Before proceeding with the general case, some illustrations will be useful. Consider first the special case in which

2

$$U = v(c(1 + g)) - z(\ell).$$

Assume that there is initially a proportional income tax at rate t_0, the revenue from which finances the public good at the level g_0. Substituting from the budget constraint (equation 1), the initial level of utility can be expressed as

3

$$U = v(w\ell(1 - t_0)(1 + g_0)) - z(\ell).$$

(Observe that, in this case, as in the illustration in the body of the article, the value of the public good is proportional to income.)

Suppose that we increase the level of the public good by Δg. At income $w\ell$, this will raise the value of individuals' "effective income" by $w\ell(1 - t_0)\Delta g$. Now consider an increase in the tax rate (which, as in the illustration in the body of the article, is a proportional one) given by

4

$$\Delta t = \frac{(1 - t_0)\Delta g}{1 + g_0 + \Delta g}.$$

It is straightforward to show that this tax rate adjustment reduces individuals' effective income and thus their utility to the prior level, for any given amount of earned income, $w\ell$: that is, $w\ell(1 - t_0)(1 + g_0) = w\ell(1 - t_0 - \Delta t)(1 + g_0 + \Delta g)$.[2] Therefore, every individual's utility function after the reform precisely equals his utility function (expression 3) before the reform for every ℓ. Thus, each individual, in choosing a level of labor supply, ℓ, is maximizing the same function before and after, so labor supply will be unaffected.

Finally, observe that total tax revenue will, by construction of the offsetting tax Δt, just equal the sum of individuals' benefits (measured in dollars) from the change in the

OPTIMAL SUPPLY OF PUBLIC GOODS

level of the public good, Δg. Hence, if the Samuelson (1954) cost-benefit test is met, there will be a surplus, which can be rebated in a manner that makes all individuals better off.

Another special case is where utility is additively separable in private consumption (c), public goods (g), and labor (ℓ). More formally, $U(c,g,\ell) = v_1(c) + v_2(g) - z(\ell)$. Here, the level of the public good will not affect labor supply. Nonetheless, the offsetting tax, which absorbs the benefits from the public good, will keep labor supply constant. To see this, note that one can keep labor supply constant by using a tax adjustment that produces offsetting income and substitution effects for all levels of income. It turns out that the offsetting (benefit-absorbing) tax in this case has just this feature. As an example (which is worked out in note 3), suppose that the utility from consumption is given by the natural logarithm of consumption. Then the benefits from the public good, which are constant when measured in *utility*, will rise proportionately with income when measured in *dollars*. Thus, a proportional tax rate adjustment will be offsetting in the manner described.[3] (This again parallels the illustration in the body of the article.)

General Case

If utility is weakly separable in labor (leisure), as specified above and discussed in the text, then *any marginal change in g that produces positive unweighted net benefits—i.e., for which the integral ("sum") of individuals' marginal rates of substitution (v_g/v_c) exceeds the cost—will result in a Pareto improvement when financed through an appropriate change in the tax schedule T.*

Holding ℓ fixed, examine how utility changes with a marginal change in g.

5

$$\frac{\partial U}{\partial g} = \frac{\partial U}{\partial v}(v_c c_g + v_g).$$

From the budget constraint (equation 1),

6

$$c_g = \frac{dT(w\ell,g)}{dg}.$$

Now, set the tax adjustment as follows (which, as discussed below, equals the marginal rate of substitution):

7

$$\frac{dT(w\ell,g)}{dg} = \frac{v_g}{v_c}$$

Using equations 6 and 7 to substitute into 5, it follows that $\partial U/\partial g = 0$ for any given w and ℓ. Thus, for any ability level (w), each choice of ℓ produces the same utility when g is raised and T is adjusted in an offsetting manner as it does when g is not raised. Because individuals' opportunity sets are thus unaffected, they will choose the same ℓ.[4]

It remains to determine whether a balanced budget results. Revenue is given by

8

$$R = \int T(w\ell(w),g)f(w)dw$$

where $\ell(w)$ denotes the amount of labor effort chosen by individuals of ability w. Because ℓ is unaffected by g when taxes are adjusted in the assumed manner,

9

$$\frac{dR}{dg} = \int \frac{dT(w\ell(w),g)}{dg} f(w)dw = \int \frac{v_g}{v_c} f(w)dw.$$

The right side is the integral of individuals' marginal rates of substitution. If this total exceeds one (the cost of the public good, expressed as a one unit increase in g), there is a budget surplus. To complete the argument, the adjusted tax schedule can be uniformly decreased until the point at which the budget balances.[5] Then, a marginal increase in g financed by this modified tax schedule will increase the utility of all individuals.[6]

Comments

The offsetting tax adjustment for any wl was stipulated in expression 7 to equal individuals' marginal rate of substitution, v_g/v_c. Observe that, for any level of g, $v(\cdot,\cdot)$ is a function of (only) wl, just as is the tax schedule. In particular, v does *not* depend on l or w independently (this relates to the assumed separability of the utility function). This implies that the marginal rate of substitution and thus the tax adjustment that absorbs benefits from the public good at each level of income are the same for all individuals. Those with different wages, w, will in general earn different levels of income, but each type of individual faces the same tax *schedule*, as a function of income, and the same subutility (v) *schedule*, both initially and as the level of the public good is adjusted.

To reinforce the intuition that labor supply is unaffected, it is helpful to think about the $v(wl,g)$ schedule changing in stages. Each individual begins with the same v schedule. If one were to increase g without adjusting the tax schedule, this common v schedule would shift up in some manner (depending upon the incidence of the public good). Next, the offsetting tax adjustment, $dT(wl,g)/dg$, is designed such that, at every level of income, wl, the common v schedule is shifted down to exactly where it was initially. (That is, at each level of wl, one asks how much income one would have to take from individuals so that their subutility, v, falls by just the amount it rose due to the increase in the public good, g.[7] By definition, this amount is given by the marginal rate of substitution.) Because the v schedule ends up being the same as it was before the changes, every individual, when choosing l, is maximizing the same function after the reform as he was initially.

APPENDIX ENDNOTES

[1] This formulation can readily be restated for the case of externalities and environmental taxes. The utility function would then be $U(v(c,g,e),l)$, where c is now interpreted as a vector of consumption goods and e is a vector of externalities. (Each element of e is simply the total consumption of the corresponding element of c; only some of the elements of e need affect utility.) The budget constraint becomes

$$\rho c = wl - T(wl,g,\rho)$$

where ρ is a price vector that includes Pigouvian taxes and subsidies. Now, as one adjusts a commodity tax toward the level of the first-best Pigouvian tax, one adjusts the tax schedule in a manner analogous to that described below, so that, for each level of income, wl, individuals' subutility functions, v, have the same value as before the adjustment. Such an adjustment will ensure that labor effort and utility are unchanged. The net revenue from the adjustment will be the sum of individuals' compensating variations, which will be positive (producing a surplus) if one moves to the first-best Pigouvian tax vector. For further discussion, see Kaplow (1993).

[2] Starting with the right side and substituting for Δt using expression 4, we have

$$wl\left(1 - t_0 - \frac{(1-t_0)\Delta g}{1 + g_0 + \Delta g}\right)(1 + g_0 + \Delta g) = wl\Big((1-t_0)(1+g_0+\Delta g) - (1-t_0)\Delta g\Big) = wl\,(1-t_0)(1+g_0).$$

[3] Let $v_1(c) = \ln(c)$, which implies that the marginal utility of consumption is inversely proportional to consumption. Then, if all individuals receive the same utility benefit from the public good, the *monetary* benefit of the good will be strictly proportional to disposable income. Now, if one raises the level of the public good by Δg, there will be a constant utility benefit, say, β, for all individuals. (i.e., $\beta = v_2(g_0 + \Delta g) - v_2(g_0)$) Simply set the tax adjustment $\Delta t = (1-t_0)(1-e^{-\beta})$. Then, the fall in utility from the tax adjustment equals $\ln\{wl(1-t_0)\} - \ln\{wl(1-t_0-(1-t_0)(1-e^{-\beta}))\}$; the

OPTIMAL SUPPLY OF PUBLIC GOODS

latter term is just ln $\{wl\,(1-t_0)e^{-\beta}\}$, so the difference is $-\ln\{e^{-\beta}\}$ or just β. That is, the fall in utility from the tax adjustment will just equal the increase in utility from the public good, and this will be true at every income level. Thus, each individual's utility as a function of labor, l, is the same both before and after the public good and tax adjustment are introduced; hence, behavior is unchanged. Here, by contrast to the previous case, the public good itself has no effect on labor supply, so it is necessary that the tax adjustment itself have no effect on labor supply.

4 Equivalently, one can show that the derivative of individuals' first-order condition for the choice of l with respect to g, after using expression 7 to substitute for the tax change, equals zero. (The only qualification is that some individuals may have multiple optima. Assuming that they make the same choice independent of the regime or that such individuals comprise a set of measure zero, the conclusion is unaffected.)

5 As the surplus is rebated, there will be effects on behavior (an income effect). But as long as changes in labor effort are continuous (except perhaps for a set of individuals having measure zero—see note 38), there will exist a modification that involves a positive rebate to everyone while balancing the budget.

6 Similarly, if benefits are less than costs, welfare can be improved by reducing public goods and reducing taxes in an offsetting manner. When the sum of individuals' marginal rates of substitution is less than one, there might exist some method of financing the public good (other than an offsetting tax) that would increase welfare. The work of Christiansen (1981) and Boadway and Keen (1993) shows that this is not the case in the presence of an optimal nonlinear income tax. (The intuition is that, in such an instance, any small adjustment to the tax system—including an offsetting tax—to raise or rebate a given amount of revenue will have the same effect on welfare.) But if the prevailing tax regime were not optimal, it would be possible to increase the level of public goods and improve welfare even when the project was otherwise undesirable if the adjustment to the tax system moved it sufficiently closer to the optimal system. But any such benefit is more naturally attributed to the tax reform itself rather than to providing more of the public good.

7 As explained in the preceding paragraph, because labor enters U in a weakly separable manner, this amount of income is the same for all types, even though different types would have different levels of l at a given level of income.

[30]

International Tax and Public Finance, 2: 207–219 (1995)

The Double Dividend and the Role of Inequality Aversion and Macroeconomic Regimes

S. PROOST
Center for Economic Studies, Catholic University of Leuven, Naamsestraat 69, 3000 Leuven Belgium
D. VAN REGEMORTER
Center for Economic Studies, Catholic University of Leuven, Naamsestraat 69, 3000 Leuven Belgium

Abstract

The introduction of the European Community's carbon-energy tax in a small open economy is analyzed by comparing two kinds of revenue recycling. We use a dynamic general-equilibrium model with different regimes for the labor market, several income groups, and a crude valuation of environmental benefits. This allows for a more comprehensive empirical test of the double-dividend hypothesis, including equity aspects. It is shown that the weak double-dividend hypothesis can fail when equity aspects are taken into account.

Key words: tax reform, general equilibrium, environment, double dividend, climate change

1. Introduction

This paper analyzes the introduction of the proposed European Community (EC) carbon-energy tax in the tax and transfer system of a small open economy like Belgium. The European energy-carbon tax can be considered to be an international agreement of the minimum national tax type.[1] In order to reach the stabilization of emissions promised by the EC in Rio de Janeiro, all EC-member states have agreed to introduce a national carbon tax of a given magnitude in their tax system but may decide themselves on how they will use the extra tax proceeds.

The way the countries use these tax proceeds is important and remains at the heart of what has become known as the double-dividend debate (Goulder, 1994). The double-dividend hypothesis states that the introduction of an environmental tax entails gross costs (abatement expenditures and price distortions between energy sources) that can be compensated by two types of dividends. The first dividend is the environmental benefit. The second benefit is the efficiency gain that can be made by using the tax revenue to substitute existing distortionary taxes. The strong double-dividend hypothesis claims that this second dividend is even larger than the gross costs—so that the precise knowledge of the environmental benefits is unnecessary in order to justify the environmental tax. Bovenberg (1994) surveys the different theoretical models that can be used to discuss the double-dividend hypothesis and shows that the strong double-dividend hypothesis can occur only under strict and rather unlikely assumptions about the functioning of the economy. This certainly holds for a small open economy.

This paper contributes to the literature in two ways. On the conceptual level, it argues that the double-dividend discussion should include the equity dimension in discussing costs and benefits of alternative recycling options. It is argued that even the generally accepted weak double-dividend proposition (replacing a lump-sum subsidy by a decrease in distortionary taxes) can fail due to equity effects. The paper adds to the empirical literature by explicitly including environmental benefits and equity concerns in the welfare function. Furthermore it tests for the importance of the macroeconomic regime.

We study this question using a dynamic (two-period) applied general-equilibrium (AGE) model. Proost and Van Regemorter (1992b) analyzed a related question with a representative consumer AGE-model for Belgium. They used this model to study the effects of a unilateral Belgian carbon tax. This exercise yielded insights on the sectoral impacts of a carbon tax. In an economy with only one type of individual there can be no conflict of interests in the revenue recycling decision: all efficiency gains accrue to all consumers. In reality we observe that the equity aspects will very often dominate the tax-reform discussions. This can be explained by the order of magnitude of the efficiency gains of a tax reform. This efficiency gain will be only a small fraction of the total environmental tax revenue collected (Proost and Van Regemorter, 1992a). For each social group there is more at stake in the income distribution aspects of the tax-recycling decision than in the total efficiency effects of the different recycling options. We have therefore extended the model to several income groups. It is a dynamic, multisectoral model that allows us to study fixed-price regimes for the labor market. In this case study, labor supply is fixed.

Section 1 of this paper surveys the different elements that enter our tax-reform discussion. Section 2 briefly presents the model structure. Section 3 provides results, and Section 4 concludes.

2. Insights into optimal directions of tax reform

We first consider the existing tax system to which the EC energy-carbon tax is added. The existing tax system is the result of a series of historical compromises and is probably suboptimal. Even if it were optimal, the introduction of an additional tax might require a reoptimization of the whole system in order to arrive at some bliss point designated by optimal tax theory. We limit our amibitions to comapring only two alternative tax recycling strategies that all include the same energy-carbon tax.

The two tax-reform strategies are indexed LT and SS and differ in their uses of the net tax revenue of the same EC energy-carbon tax ($10 per equivalent barrel of oil):

- LT = the revenue is used to increase the welfare payments (this is a lump-sum type of tax reform that benefits more the poor—5.5 percent in the flexible-wage case);
- SS = the revenue is used to finance a reduction of the social security contributions of the employers by approximately five percentage points (from 29 percent to 24 percent in the flexible-wage case).

In all simulations the payment of unemployment benefits gets absolute priority over the possibilities to increase the other welfare payments or over the possibility to reduce the social security contributions. This way of closing the government budget is important because the payment of unemployment benefits can give rise to vicious effects on the labor market.

More refined tax-reform strategies could also be elaborated. The two we selected are more or less archetypes used in the policy discussions. A strategy of indirect tax reform is missing because the EC framework prohibits large unilateral VAT or excise changes. Of course, we could also discuss the appropriate rate of the carbon tax itself. Here the tax rate is taken as given and it is assumed that other European countries also implement the carbon-energy tax.

We will compare two tax-reform strategies by using a welfare function incorporating three effects: environmental benefits, effects on the total value of private goods (here defined as efficiency effects), and equity effects. We test the sensitivity of the welfare ranking to the degree of income inequality aversion and to the macroeconomic regime of the economy.

First we discuss the overall specification of the welfare function, and then we analyze in more detail the importance of three factors that have been somewhat neglected in the carbon-tax recycling discussion: the valuation of the environmental benefits, the importance of the macroeconomic regime, and the income-distribution dimension.

Throughout this paper, we use the following notations for the welfare function of the policymaker (here expressed for the reference state 0):

$$W(0/s, \epsilon) = WP(0/s, \epsilon) + WE(0/s, \epsilon) \qquad (1)$$

The function consists of two parts: the welfare in relation to the quantity and distribution of private goods (private welfare) and the welfare level in relation to the quality and distribution in valuations[2] of environmental goods (environmental welfare). The quality of the environment enters the welfare function in an additive way; there is thus no feedback from the quality of the environment to the allocation or private goods.[3]

We examine the welfare effect of two exogenous parameters. First is the macroeconomic regime of the economy s—s = flexible (FL) or fixed (FI) wages. The second parameter is the degree of inequality aversion ϵ. Two values will be used for ϵ.[4] When only efficiency is used as a criterion, $\epsilon = 0$: the marginal utility of income is equal. If $\epsilon = 1$, however, utility of income is measured on a logarithmic scale (marginal utility of income equals the inverse of real income). We assume that both terms of the welfare function are normalized by the marginal utility of income so that for small welfare changes, the normalized changes in welfare represent equivalent income changes.

The reference state will be compared to new equilibria (index 1 instead of 0) obtained with the EC-energy carbon tax of $10 per barrel of oil and a recycling strategy (LT or SS). The difference in welfare with the reference state can be written as the sum of four effects:

$$\begin{aligned} W(1, r = SS/s, \epsilon) - W(0/s, \epsilon) = {} & \\ & + WP(1, r = LT/s, \epsilon) - WP(0/s, \epsilon) \\ & + WE(1, r = LT/s, \epsilon) - WE(0/s, \epsilon) \\ & + WP(1, r = SS/s, \epsilon) - WP(1, r = LT/s, \epsilon) \\ & + WE(1, r = SS/s, \epsilon) - WE(1, r = LT/s, \epsilon) \end{aligned} \qquad (2)$$

We generalize here some concepts introduced by Goulder (1994) for the case without equity concerns ($\epsilon = 0$):

- The first effect represents the gross costs of the carbon tax: what is the loss in private welfare when an environmental tax is used and all revenue is recycled via lump-sum transfers. In our terminology the magnitude of this effect also depends on the income inequality aversion ϵ.
- The second effect is the first dividend of the carbon tax: the improvement in the environmental welfare given that the tax is recycled in a lump-sum way.
- The third effect represents the second dividend of the carbon tax: the improvement in private welfare when we replace the revenue recycling via transfers by a reduction of distortionary taxes.
- The fourth effect is the change in environmental welfare that can accompany a change in recycling strategy.

The *strong form of the double-dividend hypothesis* states that the sum of the gross costs plus the third effect is positive. Recycle the environmental tax revenue by reducing existing distortionary taxes and a welfare gain will result that makes it unnecessary to know the environmental benefits. This hypothesis is now rejected by most theoretical models (Bovenberg and Van Der Ploeg, 1994a). The *weak form of the double-dividend* is in general accepted: reducing a lump-sum subsidy in order to decrease distortionary taxes always generates a positive efficiency effect (Goulder, 1994). Efficiency is here defined as the total value of private goods available: the third effect in (2) would be positive for $\epsilon = 0$.

We discuss now the impact of three important factors on the double-dividend hypothesis: the valuation of environmental benefits, the macroeconomic regime, and the degree of income inequality aversion.

2.1. The shift to greener preferences or the importance of the first benefit

The main reason that the EC proposed an energy-carbon tax is the concern for global warming. The society has become more aware of this environmental problem only recently. We introduce environmental-benefit considerations in our selection of alternative tax-reform strategies because, even for a fixed energy-carbon tax rate, the recycling strategy can strongly influence the total emission of pollutants (see the fourth effect in equation (2)). We distinguish not only the direct CO_2-related efffects but also the side effects on other pollutants. We assume that the CO_2 emission variations can be values at the EC energy-carbon tax rate. Variations in the emission of other pollutants are valued by the avoided cost of other emission reduction.[5]

2.2. The importance of the macroregime of the economy for the second dividend

Dreze (1985) has shown that the tax-reform policy has, in principle, to take into account the macroeconomic regime of the economy: do price adjustments clear all markets? We will concentrate on classical unemployment, in which the real wage is fixed at too high a level. In the European context and certainly in the Belgian context, wages (including the social security contributions of the workers) are indexed to the consumer price index. Hence, real-wage cuts may be hard to achieve. We discuss environmental tax reform for two regimes of the economy: flexible wages and fixed real wages.

In the case of *full flexibility of the labor market*, Bovenberg and De Mooij (1994) and Bovenberg and Van Der Ploeg (1994a) have shown that, in a small open economy, there is no strong second dividend. The intuition is that labor is the only production factor that is not mobile and thus bears in the end always the additional pollution abatement costs of the production sector. The additional costs are reflected in a lower net wage, which harms the supply of labor.

There are two ways out to increase labor supply and employment: either levying high environmental taxes on nonactive population groups (living on transfers) or to decrease other public expenditures and use the additional public revenue to decrease taxes on labor supply. Both strategies involve a cost as either the income distribution or the supply of public goods is harmed. Another way out is to introduce a fixed production factor to which the tax can be shifted.

In the case of *fixed real wages*,[6] there is a larger initial distortion on the labor market so that there is a larger potential for efficiency gains. Bovenberg and Van Der Ploeg (1994b) use a model for a small open economy with a fixed factor, an imported polluting input and a fixed real wage. They show that a beneficial welfare effect can be obtained only under strict conditions of which the possibiliity of tax shifting to the immobile factor is an important one. Another important element is the inefficiency of the initial tax system. As in the case of flexible wages, an environmental tax imposed on industry lowers total productivity, and this implies a downward shift of the demand curve for labor if there is no other production factor paying for this.

In our case study labor supply is fixed, and we compare tax-reform strategies across flexible and fixed wages. Fixed labor supply combined with flexible wages implies that efficiency gains associated with a reduction of the labor taxes are absent. Hence other elements dominate the choice between tax recycling strategies. In the case of fixed real wages, in contrast, lowering taxes on the use of labor may yield important efficiency gains.

2.3. *The income-distribution dimension*

Any tax reform will also be primarily concerned with the effects on the distribution of income.[7] A reform will be accepted only if the benefits and costs are to some extent distributed in an equitable way. The concern for income distribution is also at the heart of the existing tax system: in the absence of income-distribution concerns, the optimal tax system would be limited to a combination of a head tax and corrective taxes for externalities, without distorting taxes, second-dividend concerns about the reduction of distortionary taxes would be irrelevant.

Coming back to the double-dividend terminology of Goulder (1994), introducing income distribution concerns requires that the gross costs, the environmental benefit, and the recycling benefit are all weighed by the welfare weights of the different economic agents affected.

Now even the weak form of the double-dividend proposition no longer necessarily holds. If lump-sum subsidies accrue relatively more to the poor, the associated equity benefit could compensate the efficiency losses of a higher distortionary tax and invalidate the weak double-dividend propostion.

3. The model used

For this study we extended the model developed by Dewatripont, Erlich, Ginsburgh, and Van Regemorter (1991) to include several income groups, a more elaborate description of the tax and transfer system, a distinction between energy forms, and the emissions of different air pollutants. A model description with only one type of consumer can be found in Proost and Van Regemorter (1992b). We develop a dynamic perfect-foresight AGE model for an open economy that covers two periods. The first period represents the medium-run adaptations (say, five to seven years) and the second period captures the full adjustment taking place in the long run (say, another seven years). The institutional framework is perfect competition with the possibility, however, of labor-market disequilibrium in the medium run.

There are two types of goods: tradables and nontradables. All commodities are in principle considered as tradable. All factors of production (labor and production capacities) are nontradable. The model is solved as a Negishi welfare optimum.

The model contains four types of agents: households, firms, the government, and the rest of the world. Four homogeneous groups of consumers are modeled. These groups have the same utility functions but differ in labor productivity, in the probability of becoming unemployed and in their shares of the initial capital stock and welfare payments (see Table 1). A more detailed description of the model can be obtained from the authors.

4. Results

4.1. Scenario description

The EC energy-carbon tax takes the form of an increase in excises on all energy products consumed. It is an excise and is applied to all sectors and all households. The excise equals $10 per barrel of oil equivalent. Half of the excise of proportional to the carbon content of the fuel; the other half is proportional to the energy content. This excise is kept constant in real terms and is added to the energy prices of a given reference scenario. This implies an average increase for industrial energy prices of 50 percent and of 20 percent for the energy prices of private consumers.

In all the scenarios we consider, it is assumed that an identical energy-carbon tax of $10 per barrel is imposed on the trade partners, which feature flexible wages and recycle revenues by increasing welfare payments. Because we deal only with an AGE model for Belgium, we had to use an artefact to mimic the behavior of the foreign economies. The actions of the trade partners affect Belgium only via the demand functions for Belgian exports and via the supply functions of imports to Belgium. We assume that the import and export behavior of our trade partners reacts in the same way to tax reform strategies as the Belgian economy would do.

Table 1. Data by income class (in percent).

	Class 1	Class 2	Class 3	Class 4
Distribution of consumers:				
Consumers	11.2%	25.8%	35.7%	27.3%
Active population	5.0	23.3	42.6	29.1
Unemployed	14.6	33.1	41.6	10.7
Distribution of income:				
Relative labor efficiency	0.49	0.77	0.91	1.33
Share in capital income	3.1	18.2	16.1	62.6
Share in transfer income	18.7	26.3	29.5	25.5
Average taxation rates:				
Labor income	0	6.4	22.6	34.8
Capital income	24.1	24.1	24.1	24.1

This procedure is more justified when the major trade partners have a similar type of economy as the home country, when partners adopt similar tax-reform policies, and when the economy is very open. This is indeed the case for Belgium: 80 percent of its total export and import (except energy products imported at a fixed price) is with EC member countries and its exports and imports amount each to some 80 percent of its GDP.

4.2. *Results*

In Table 2 alternative domestic tax reform policies are compared for two macroeconomic regimes: flexible wages and fixed wages at home.

4.2.1. The case of flexible wages and no income-inequality aversion. We first concentrate in some more detail on the first column of Table 2 that reports results for the lump-sum transfer scenario in which all variations in net public revenue are handed back by a proportional variation of the welfare-transfer payments (exclusive of unemployment benefits). Only for the first recycling policy do we report results for the two period (the first two columns). In the other columns results concern the first period. Welfare computations are, however, always reported for both periods jointly.

The results shown in the left half of Table 2 (first column) are in line with the results of the literature: low aggregate economic effects and a restructuring to less energy-intensive industries. This restructuring requires extra investment in the first period (+2.4 percent). The extra investment efforts are only moderate because the energy-intensive sectors are the most capital-intensive sectors.

Regarding the welfare effects, a clear efficiency loss occurs if environmental benefits are ignored (line private welfare $\epsilon = 0$ shows -2.95 percent loss). This is expected because an additional tax on an imported input (energy) is a new distortion (see Dixit, 1985, and Diamond and Mirrlees, 1971). With a fixed import price of energy, there is also no role for a disguised import tax. The same holds true for the tax on private energy use: this is an extra distortion that, together with the carbon tax on industry, is used to increase a lump-sum transfer.

Table 2. The choice of tax reform strategy as a function of the macroeconomic regime.

Difference in % Reference Scenario for Period 1	Flexible Wages at Home: Transfers (LT) 1 per	Flexible Wages at Home: Transfers (LT) 2 per	Flexible Wages at Home: Social Security (SS)	Fixed Wages at Home: Transfers (LT)	Fixed Wages at Home: Social Security (SS)
GDP	+0.2	−0.6	+0.2	−7.0	−5.1
Consumption	−0.9	−1.0	−0.9	−4.7	−3.7
Investment	2.37	−5.2	2.3	−20.6	+14.2
Energy-intensive sectors	−2.5	−1.7	−2.5	+11.9	−8.8
Real wage cost	−5.2	−6.2	−4.5	−0.2	−3.3
Unemployment (1,000)	0	0	0	238	176
CO_2 emissions	−12.2	−10.7	−13.3	−18.5	−17.0
Private welfare ($\epsilon = 0$)	−2.95		−3.12	−15.7	−12.4
Private welfare ($\epsilon = 1$)	−0.6		−1.35	−8.6	−7.1
Private welfare + environmental welfare ($\epsilon = 1$)	0.31		−0.53	−7.8	−6.2
Private consumers Class 1	2.3	2.3	−0.5	−6.4	−6.8
Private consumers Class 2	−0.9	−0.9	−1.1	−6.2	−5.2
Private consumers Class 3	−1.8	−1.8	−1.2	−5.5	−4.3
Private consumers Class 4	−1.8	−1.9	−1.4	−6.4	−4.5
Employer SS contribution (changes in share in GDP)	−0.48	−0.43	−2.08	+0.07	−1.96
Direct tax (changes in share in GDP)	−0.67	−0.69	−0.13	−0.41	+0.04
Indirect tax (changes in share in GDP)	+2.68	+2.49	+2.63	+2.80	+2.72

Due to the assumption of fixed-labor supply and flexible wages, reducing the social security payments (the third column in Table 2) does not lead to a reduction in distortions. Therefore most economic effects are more or less comparable to the transfer scenario. The loss in private welfare is even somewhat higher: this is a second-order effect due to distortions present in other markets than the labor market. Finally, we would like to point to the important decrease in the real-wage cost of the firms that would be necessary in the first period to restore equilibrium in the labor market.

It is useful to restate the results in terms of the *double-dividend discussion* in the upper left side of Table 3. This table has been constructed by using the type of welfare evaluations reported in Table 2. As defined by equation (2), the total welfare effect of a tax reform can be decomposed into three effects: gross costs, a first benefit, and a second benefit (representing the sum of the effects on private and on enviroinmental welfare). The sum of the gross costs and the first benefit gives the total welfare effect of the lump-sum transfers recycling scenario. Adding the second benefit gives you the total welfare effect when environmental tax revenues are recycled by reducing social security contributions. The gross costs, that only take into account private welfare, are negative as they correspond to the

Table 3. Carbon taxes and the double-dividend hypothesis.

Differences in Welfare (Income Equivalents) (% Difference with Reference Scenario)		Flexible Wages at Home: No Inequality Aversion ($\epsilon = 0$)	Flexible Wages at Home: Inequality Aversion ($\epsilon = 1$)
1	Gross costs (including recycling via lump-sum transfers and without environmental benefits)	−3.26	−0.61
2	First dividend (increase in environmental benefits)	+1.35	+0.92
1+2	Total (via increase of lump-sum transfers)	−1.91	+0.31
3	Second dividend[a] (via reduction of social security contributions employers)	−0.19	−0.84
1+2+3	Total (via reduction of social security contributions)	−2.1	−0.53
		Fixed Wages at Home (Flexible Wages Abroad and Transfers as Recycling Strategy Abroad)	
		No Inequality Aversion ($\epsilon = 0$)	Inequality Aversion ($\epsilon = 1$)
1	Gross costs (including recycling via lump-sum transfers and without environmental benefits)	−17.3	−9.3
2	First dividend (increase in environmental benefits, high assumption)	+2.0	+1.4
1+2	Total (via increase of lump-sum transfers)	−15.3	−7.9
3	Second dividend (via reduction of social security contributions employers)	+3.6	+1.7
1+2+3	Total (via reduction of social security)	−11.7	−6.2

[a]The second dividend contains here the sum of the changes in private welfare and in environmental welfare that are due to the change in recycling.

already mentioned loss in overall productivity. They are partially compensated by the first benefit that corresponds to the valuation of decreased emissions. These emissions are valued at a rate somewhat higher than the environmental tax that is introduced. The fact that despite this high valuation, the sum of gross costs and the first dividend is still negative corresponds to the idea that the optimal environmental tax is likely to be smaller than the sum of marginal damages. This confirms results demonstrated theoretically and empirically by Bovenberg and Goulder (1994) for a carbon tax in the United States. The second benefit is here slightly negative as this corresponds to the second-order effects on distorted markets. That the weak double-dividend assumption does not hold here has mainly to do with the absence of distortions on the labor market so that reducing social security contributions cannot bring any efficiency gain.

4.2.2. The case of flexible wages and income-inequality aversion. When the government is interested not only in total equivalent income variations but attaches a higher weight to poor households ($\epsilon = 1$), the welfare results improve. The reason is that higher energy taxes are paid more or less porportionally to income, but the welfare payments are more concentrated in the lowest income group (see Table 1). The welfare ranking can be improved further by taking into account the environmental benefits (the line private welfare + environmental welfare) in Table 2. There is an overall welfare gain when income distribution effects and environmental benefits are taken into account. Of course, these results depend strongly on the valuation of environmental benefits and on the degree of inequality aversion.

The major difference between the two tax-reform scenarios lies in the income distribution effects: reducing social security contributions benefits much more the rich. In terms of the *double-dividend discussion* (see upper right side of Table 3), the gross costs are now much smaller, and the lump-sum transfer recycling scenario generates a small positive total welfare effect. The second dividend is now strongly negative as recycling through lowered social security contributions has no efficiency gains but has adverse equity effects. The weak double-dividend hypothesis fails here for equity reasons.

4.2.3. The case of fixed wages and no income-inequality aversion. The right side of Table 2 compares tax-reform strategies under the assumption of fixed real wages in the first period. The tax-reform strategy matters much more for efficiency reasons because there is an important initial distortion on the labor market, which has an excess supply. The strategy of recycling via increased transfer payments produces catastrophic economic results: the strategy reduces GDP by 7 percent and creates greater unemployment. That this happens is not a surprise: the increased energy tax on households is shifted to the firms via the constant real-consumption wage. The higher real-wage cost (via the increased energy taxes on households) and the higher energy costs of the firms work together to ensure that production becomes insufficiently profitable. Thus, investments decline, the production capacity adapts insufficiently, and unemployment surges.

The decrease in activity is particularly important in the energy-intensive sectors because they have the highest cost handicap compared to the rest of the world. It is assumed that the rest of the world has flexible wages and uses a transfer scenario—thus, the cost handicap could be important.

The negative welfare results are somewhat mitigated by the better environmental performance: carbon emissions drop by 50 percent more in the fixed-real-wage scenario than they do in the case with flexible wages. Part of this effect has to do with a higher carbon leakage, for which no correction was applied. Also of interest is that the net gain in public revenue (+2.4 percent of GDP) seems to have been absorbed completely by the increase in unemployment benefits so that ultimately, due to the tax-base effects, the lump-sum transfer payments decrease rather than increase!

Reducing the social security contributions for employers appears at first to be a win-win solution. It is a better tax-reform strategy than the other, but overall welfare still decreases rather than increases. The reduction in social security rates is, however, insufficient to obtain the drop in the employer's labor cost that is needed to improve employment (real wage cost decreases by 3.3 percent instead of the necessary 4.5 to 5 percent). The possibilities of reducing the wage cost are limited because the energy carbon-tax base is eroded (by some 18 percent rather than 10 to 12 percent in the flexible-wages case) and the increased unemployment benefits have to be financed. If we had protected welfare payments in real terms, results would have been even worse, as there would have been no room for a reduction of the social security contributions of employers.

This confirms the theoretical results of Bovenberg and Van Der Ploeg (1993b), who state that a necessary condition to have a positive employment effect is that pollution taxes are borne by the fixed factor when the real wage is protected. In our model there is no fixed factor as virtually all sectors need at least replacement investments already within the first period. These replacement investments will not be financed as long as no sufficient return is offered.

We can reframe these results in terms of the *double-dividend discussion* in the lower left side of Table 3. The gross costs now dominate all other effects as the carbon tax aggravates an existing distortion. The demand for labor curve is shifted leftward so that the unemployment gap increases rather than decreases. The first benefit is larger as there is a stronger decrease in emissions due to the decline (in fact partly migration) in energy-intensive industries. The second benefit is positive as reducing the social security benefits has an important positive efficiency effect when there is an excess supply on the labor market.

4.2.4. The case of fixed wages and income-inequality aversion. In the case of fixed wages the efficiency losses dominate the equity considerations. Recycling the revenues via reduced social security considerations produces such important efficiency gains that this scenario is preferred to the increased welfare scenario. In fact as we have seen above, actual lump-sum transfers decrease rather than increase in the lump-sum-transfer recycling scenario.

5. Conclusions

This paper has analyzed alternative ways to use the revenue (tax-reform strategies) of an EC energy-carbon tax for a small open economy. This is a test of the double-dividend hypothesis. It is shown that in order to test the double-dividend hypothesis in a welfare-theoretic framework, researchers must broaden concepts, to include the income-distribution dimension. Once this is done, efficiency effects of recycling can be dominated by equity effects, and the weak double-dividend proposition does not necessarily hold: increasing lump-sum welfare payments can be more appropriate than reducing distortionary taxes mainly borne by the rich—even if the latter strategy entails clear efficiency gains.

The double-dividend hypothesis is tested with the help of a dynamic, multisectoral AGE that can simulate two macroeconomic regimes (flexible wages and fixed real wages) and contains several income groups but a fixed labor supply. To this model were added estimates of environmental benefits for the major air pollutants.

As long as no price rigidities distort the labor market, the choice of a tax-reform strategy is not important for the aggregate economic results. The choice of strategy matters mainly for income distribution: net tax proceeds can be used to increase welfare payments or to decrease direct tax rates.

When real wages are fixed, the gross costs of an energy carbon tax are high. Reducing the social security taxes on employers is a better strategy than to increase welfare payments. The main problem is the real wage cost, which cannot be decreased sufficiently.

In conclusion, the regime of the labor market, together with the aversion to income inequality should be the main determinants affecting the choice of a tax-reform strategy. The strong version of the double-dividend assumption was rejected everywhere. The weak version of the double-dividend was verified only in those cases where efficiency gains dominate distribution effects.

Acknowledgments

This work has been supported by the Belgian Ministry of Economic Affairs, Energy Program, under contract 91-05. S. Proost has been supported by the National Fund for Scientific Research. The views defended here are the authors' own and are not necessarily those of the Ministry. We thank L. Bui and R. McDougall (our discussants at the IIPF meeting in Harvard, August 1994), L. Bovenberg, I. Mayeres, E. Schokkaert, and T. Rutherford as well as three anonymous referees for their comments on a previous version.

Notes

1. Alternative types of international agreements are studied in Hoel (1992) and empirically in Eyckmans, Proost, and Schokkaert (1994).
2. The environmental quality is assumed identical for all income groups, but their valuation can be different. Equity concerns come in here as the policy maker can attach a different weight to the valuations of the different income groups. In the empirical model, however, we assume identical valuations for environmental quality among income groups.
3. This assumption can be easily generalized but makes the exposition of double-dividend notions more complex (see Mayeres and Proost, 1994).
4. The private goods welfare function is of the utilitarian type. The degree of inequality aversion is introduced by choosing a particular cardinalization of the utility function by analogy to the isoelastic utility function used by Atkinson (1970).
5. The methodological problems are discussed in more detail in Proost and Van Regemorter (1994). The marginal damage estimates of pollutants used (expressed in ECU 1988 per ton) are: 18 for CO_2, 2,225 for NO_x and 325 for SO_2.
6. Assuming fixed real wages is a simplistic explanation of unemployment. Rigid real wages have to be explained by the functioning of the labor market, and this richer structure should be included in the model as in Bovenberg and Van Der Ploeg (1994c).
7. Optimal marginal tax reform as a function of the degree of inequality aversion and the macroeconomic regime has been studied by Van De Gaer, Schokkaert, and De Bruyne (1992).

References

Atkinson, A.B. (1970). "On the Measurement of Inequality." *Journal of Economic Theory* 2, 244–263.

Bovenberg, A.L. (1994). "Environmental Policy, Distortionary Labor Taxation, and Employment: Pollution Taxes and the Double Dividend." Paper presented at the International Workshop on Environmental Taxation, Revenue Recycling and Unemployment, December, Milan.

Bovenberg, A.L., and R.A. de Mooij. (1994). "Environmental Levies and Labour-Market Distortions." *American Economic Review* 94(4).

Bovenberg, A.L., and L. Goulder. (1994). "Costs of Environmentally Motivated Taxes in the Presence of Other Taxes: An Applied General Equilibrium Analysis." Working Paper, Stanford University, May.

Bovenberg, A.L., and R. Van Der Ploeg. (1994a). "Green Policies and Public Finance in a Small Open Economy." *Scandinavian Journal of Economics* 96(3), 343-363.

Bovenberg, A.L., and R. Van Der Ploeg. (1994b). "Consequences of Environmental Tax Reform for Involuntary Unemployment and Welfare." CentER, D.P. No. 9408, Tilburg University, The Netherlands.

Bovenberg, A.L., and R. Van Det Ploeg. (1994c). "Tax Reform, Structural Unemployment, and the Environment." Mimeo, CentER, Tilburg University, The Netherlands.

Dewatripont, C., Z. Erlich, V. Ginsburgh, and D. Van Regemorter. (1991). "The Effects of Unemployment of Reducing Social Security Contributions: A General Equilibrium Analysis for Belgium." In H. Don, T. Van De Klundert, J. Van Sinderen (eds.), *Applied General Equilibrium Modelling* (pp. 135-153). Dordrecht: Kluwer.

Diamond, P.A., and J.A. Mirrlees. (1971). "Optimal Taxation and Public Production I: Production Efficiency, and II: Tax Rules." *American Economic Review* 61, 8-27, 261-278.

Dixit, A. (1985). "Tax Policy in Open Economies." Ini A.J. Auerbach and M. Feldstein (eds.), *Handbook of Public Economics* (pp. 313-374). Amsterdam: Elsevier.

Dreze, J.H. (1985). "Second-Best Analysis with Markets in Disequilibrium." *European Economic Review* 29, 263-301.

Eyckmans, J., S. Proost, and E. Schokkaert. (1994). "A Comparison of Three International Agreements on Carbon Emission Abatement." In E. Van Ierland (ed.), *International Environmental Economics* (Vol. 4). Amsterdam: Elsevier.

Goulder, L. (1994). "Environmental Taxation and the Double-Dividend." Paper presented at the Fiftieth Congress of the IIPF, Harvard University.

Hoel, M. (1992). "Carbon Taxes: An International Tax or Harmonised Taxes." *European Economic Review* 36, 400-406.

Mayeres, I., and S. Proost. (1994). "Optimal Tax Rules for Congestion Type of Externalities." D.P., CES, KULeuven, Belgium.

McDougall, R., and G.A. Meagher. (1994). "Distributional Effects of a Carbon Tax in Australia." Paper presented at the Fiftieth Congress of the IIPF, Harvard University.

Proost, S., and D. Van Regemorter. (1992a). "CO_2 Emissions and Taxation: Macroeconomic, Public Finance and Welfare Impacts in the EC." *European Economy*, special issue 1, 91-124.

Proost, S., and D. Van Regemorter. (1992b). "Economic Effects of a Carbon Tax, with a General Equilibrium Illustration for Belgium." *Energy Economics*, April.

Proost, S., and D. Van Regemorter. (1994). "Testing the Double Dividend Hypothesis for a Carbon Tax in a Small Open Economy." Paper presented at the 50th Congress of the IIPF, August 1994, Cambridge, MA.

Van De Gaer D., E. Schokkaert, and G. De Bruyne. (1992). "Marginal Tax Reform in Different Macroeconomic Regimes." *Public Finance* 47 (Supplement), 256-270.

[31]

Neutralizing the Adverse Industry Impacts of CO_2 Abatement Policies
What Does It Cost?

A. Lans Bovenberg and Lawrence H. Goulder

2.1 Introduction

Most studies of U.S. CO_2 abatement policies have focused on the aggregate costs and benefits of these initiatives. Yet the desirability and political feasibility of these policies tend to hinge critically on their distributional impacts. A full assessment of CO_2 abatement options therefore requires attention to distributional impacts.

Some studies—including Poterba (1991), Bull, Hassett, and Metcalf (1994), Schillo et al. (1996), and Metcalf (1998)—have focused on the distribution of impacts of CO_2 abatement policies across household income groups. In these papers, the instrument for CO_2 abatement is usually a carbon tax. This tax is generally found to produce a regressive impact, although this impact is fairly small, especially when one ranks households by measures of lifetime income (such as expenditure) rather than by annual income (which includes transitory shocks and lifetime variations that make annual income a bad indicator of permanent income). Moreover, as indicated by Schillo et al. (1996) and Metcalf (1998), the government can reduce the regressive effect by lowering personal income tax rates at the bottom end of the income scale and by raising public transfers.

A second important distributional dimension is the variation in impacts

A. Lans Bovenberg is professor of economics at the CentER for Economic Research, Tilburg University, and a research fellow of the Centre for Economic Policy Research, London. Lawrence H. Goulder is associate professor of economics at Stanford University, a research associate of the National Bureau of Economic Research, and a university fellow of Resources for the Future.

The authors are grateful to Gilbert Metcalf, Ruud de Mooij, Peter Orszag, Ian Parry, Jack Pezzey, Robert Stavins, Roberton Williams III, and conference participants for helpful comments, and to Derek Gurney and Rudolf Schusteritsch for excellent research assistance.

across industries. CO_2 abatement policies such as carbon taxes or carbon quotas can reduce net output prices in the fossil fuel (carbon supplying) industries and raise costs in industries that intensively employ fossil fuels as inputs. These price and cost impacts have the potential to seriously harm profits, employment, and equity values. The distribution of impacts along these dimensions crucially influences political feasibility, since representatives of fossil fuel producers carry significant weight in the political process.[1] CO_2 abatement policies that pose serious burdens on these industries may stand little chance of political survival.[2]

This paper explores the distributional impacts of various U.S. CO_2 abatement policies in terms of their impacts on profits and equity values for the industries supplying fossil fuels (the coal industry and crude petroleum and natural gas industry) and the industries that rely heavily on fossil fuels as intermediate inputs (e.g., petroleum refining and electric utilities). We examine a range of abatement policies, including policies designed to avoid adverse consequences for the regulated industries. As discussed later, some of the adverse consequences can be avoided through industry-specific corporate tax cuts, direct transfers, and the government's free provision (or "grandfathering")[3] of emissions permits to firms. A main purpose of our paper is to assess the efficiency cost of avoiding adverse impacts through such policies.

To perform this investigation we employ an intertemporal general equilibrium model of the United States.[4] The general equilibrium framework

1. Indeed, the industry-distribution impacts may be more important politically than the household-distribution impacts, since the stakes for each firm from these policies are high, while the impacts of abatement policies on households, although important in the aggregate, are fairly small for each individual household. Under these circumstances, affected firms may be more willing to incur the costs of political mobilization than affected households are. This discussion invokes the notion of political mobilization bias, an idea originated by Olson (1965). For a discussion of this bias and other political transactions cost issues, see Williamson (1996). For an analysis of the implications of political mobilization bias for legislators' choice of environmental policy instruments, see Keohane, Revesz, and Stavins (1998). For a general discussion of political resistance to market-based environmental policy instruments, see Pezzey (1988).

2. This will be the case irrespective of the efficiency properties of abatement policies. In the real world, winners often cannot compensate losers through costless, lump-sum transfers. Hence the most efficient policies—those with the largest net benefits in the aggregate—may not yield actual Pareto improvements: They may only be potentially Pareto-improving. In such a world, political feasibility may require designing policies that avoid serious negative impacts on key stakeholders. This may involve a sacrifice of some of the efficiency gains from the most efficient policy.

3. Grandfathering is a special case of free provision. It is a legal rule whereby "old" entities (e.g., firms subject to previous environmental rules) are exempt from new regulatory requirements and remain bound only to the earlier (and perhaps more lax) regulatory provisions. Under grandfathering, the free provision of permits is linked to current production factors. Newly entering firms are not eligible for a free provision, and investments in new capital are not rewarded.

4. This is the same model as that in Goulder (1995a) and Bovenberg and Goulder (1996, 1997), with some extensions to allow for attention to the industry-specific revenue-recycling and tradable-permits provisions described below.

is especially useful for assessing the incidence of carbon policies. Nearly all of the studies of distributional impacts of carbon policies have employed a partial equilibrium framework that ignores behavioral responses to environmental taxes.[5] These studies impose exogenous incidence assumptions and cannot analyze how behavioral responses affect pollution, efficiency, and distribution. An applied general equilibrium analysis, in contrast, derives tax incidence endogenously from the model-generated behavioral responses. An important distributional consideration is the impact of CO_2 abatement policies on returns to labor and capital. A general equilibrium framework is appropriate for this purpose, since it captures important links between energy markets and factor markets. The model used here is especially useful in this regard because it incorporates forward-looking investment behavior and the adjustment costs associated with the installation or removal of physical capital. These features enable us to consider the capitalization effects of unanticipated policies.[6] Most other general equilibrium models treat capital as perfectly mobile, and thus they cannot successfully examine impacts on profits or equity values. In such models, the impacts on industries are measured largely in terms of the effects on outputs. The results from this paper show that output effects are unreliable indicators of distributional effects.

Earlier analyses of CO_2 abatement policies reveal a tension between promoting economic efficiency, on the one hand, and avoiding serious adverse distributional consequences to key industries, on the other. Goulder, Parry, and Burtraw (1997), Farrow (1999), Fullerton and Metcalf (1998), and Parry, Williams, and Goulder (1999) show that policies that raise revenues and use these revenues to finance cuts in preexisting distortionary taxes have lower costs than policies that do not generate and recycle revenues in this way. The differences in the costs of the two types of policies can be large enough to determine whether the overall efficiency impact—environment-related benefits minus economy-wide costs of abatement—is positive or negative.[7] Yet the latter, less efficient policies impose a smaller financial burden on the regulated industries because they do not charge firms for every unit of their pollution.[8] These considerations suggest a conflict be-

5. An exception is Jorgenson, Slesnick, and Wilcoxen (1992).

6. Our model does not incorporate adjustment costs for industry-specific labor; indeed, labor is perfectly mobile across industries. To the extent that labor faces adjustment costs, one should explore capitalization effects on labor along lines similar to this paper's exploration of such effects on capital.

7. Parry, Williams, and Goulder (1999) show that while a carbon tax with revenues recycled through cuts in marginal income tax rates produces efficiency gains, reducing CO_2 emissions through a system of freely provided (grandfathered) CO_2 permits may be an efficiency-reducing proposition: For any level of emissions reduction, the environmental benefits will fall short of society's costs of abatement!

8. Two revenue-raising policies are an emissions tax and a system of auctioned emissions permits, where the permits are initially auctioned. Under these policies, firms endure costs of emissions abatement and, for whatever emissions they continue to produce, must either pay a tax or purchase permits. In contrast, under a system of freely provided emissions

tween efficiency and political feasibility: The efficient policy—the carbon tax—appears less politically acceptable because it puts too much of a burden on politically mobilized, fossil fuel industries, while the politically more acceptable policy of grandfathered carbon (or CO_2) permits involves serious inefficiencies.

The present study finds that the choice between efficiency and insulating profits of key industrial stakeholders (to enhance political feasibility) may be less problematic than previously thought. We find that desirable distributional outcomes at the industry level can be achieved at relatively low cost in terms of efficiency; without substantial added cost to the overall economy, the government can implement carbon abatement policies that protect profits and equity values in fossil fuel industries. The key to this conclusion is that CO_2 abatement policies have the potential to generate rents that are very large in relation to the potential loss of profit. Under a standard carbon tax policy, these potential rents do not materialize; instead they become revenues collected by the government. In contrast, under a policy involving freely allocated emissions permits, or a policy in which some (inframarginal) emissions are exempted from a carbon tax, firms realize some of the potential rents.[9] Because the potential rents are very large in relation to potential lost profit, the government can protect firms' profits and equity values in fossil fuel industries by enabling firms to retain only a very small fraction of the potential rents. Thus, the government needs to freely allocate (as opposed to auction) only a small percentage of CO_2 emissions permits or, similarly, must exempt only a small fraction of emissions from the base of a carbon tax.[10] Each of these gov-

permits requiring equivalent emissions reductions, firms endure the same costs of abatement but do not pay for remaining emissions. Hence, the burden on polluting firms is smaller.

9. Buchanan and Tullock (1975) pointed out that environmental policies can generate significant rents to firms to the extent that such policies cause output to be restricted. They showed that because of such rents, regulated firms can experience higher profits than in the absence of regulation. Our findings in this paper are consistent with Buchanan and Tullock's analysis. Fullerton and Metcalf (1998) emphasize the importance of rents to the overall efficiency costs of policies to reduce pollution. They indicate that efficiency costs are substantially higher under policies producing rents that are not taxed away, in comparison with policies that do not produce rents that are left in private hands. A parallel line of investigation was conducted by Goulder, Parry, and Burtraw (1997), who show that policies that fail to tax away rents are at a disadvantage in terms of efficiency because they fail to generate revenues that can be used to reduce preexisting distortionary taxes. Such policies thus fail to exploit an efficiency-enhancing revenue-recycling effect. In the present study, we examine the extent to which policy-generated rents affect the impacts of CO_2 abatement policies on the profitability and equity values of regulated firms.

10. Correspondingly, if the government were to freely allocate 100 percent of the emissions permits, or exempt 100 percent of inframarginal emissions from the base of a carbon tax, it wouid generate substantial windfalls to firms: The rents produced and enjoyed by producers would be many times larger than the income losses otherwise attributable to the policy. The government does not need to be nearly this generous in order to safeguard firms' profits and equity values. Our focus on the use of inframarginal exemptions to accomplish distributional objectives is in the spirit of Farrow (1999), who employs a model along the lines of Bovenberg

ernment policies involves only a small sacrifice of potential government revenue. Such revenue has an efficiency value because it can be used to finance cuts in preexisting distortionary taxes. Since these policies give up little of this potential revenue, they involve only a small sacrifice in terms of efficiency. In suggesting that the revenue sacrifice is small relative to potential revenues, our findings complement those obtained in a paper by Vollebergh, de Vries, and Koutstaal (1997), who employ a partial equilibrium model to compare the potential tax revenues and abatement costs that could stem from a carbon tax in the European Union.[11]

Because the potential rents are quite large, it is also possible to devise policies that, with relatively little loss of efficiency, protect not only the fossil fuel industries, but also certain industries (such as petroleum refining and electric utilities) that intensively use fossil energy. These industries would suffer significant profit losses under a standard carbon tax.

We also find that there is a very large difference between preserving firms' profits and preserving their tax payments. Allowing firms to enjoy a dollar-for-dollar offset to their payments of carbon taxes (e.g., through industry-specific cuts in corporate tax rates) substantially overcompensates firms, raising profits and equity values significantly relative to the unregulated situation. This reflects the fact that producers can shift onto consumers most of the burden from a carbon tax. The efficiency costs of such policies are far greater than the costs of policies that do not overcompensate firms. To maintain firms' profits, the government needs to offer tax relief representing only a small fraction of carbon tax payments.[12]

The remainder of the paper is organized as follows. Section 2.2 provides a brief description of the numerical general equilibrium model employed to evaluate the various policy alternatives. Section 2.3 then indicates the links in the model between the various policy alternatives and firms' profits and equity values. Section 2.4 briefly describes the model's data and parameters. Section 2.5 indicates the policies under consideration, and section 2.6 conveys and discusses the results from numerical simulations. The final section offers conclusions.

---

and de Mooij (1994) with one factor of production (labor). Our analysis differs from Farrow's in its consideration of imperfectly mobile capital and its attention to the implications of pollution-abatement policies for firms' profits and equity values.

11. Vollebergh, de Vries, and Koutstaal (1997) calculate the tax revenues and abatement costs that would stem from a carbon tax sufficient to reduce CO_2 emissions by 13 percent in the countries of the European Union. Their results indicate that the revenues from this tax would be many times the policy-generated abatement costs. This suggests that exempting a small share of inframarginal emissions from the carbon tax (or grandfathering a small share of the permits under a permits policy) would be sufficient to compensate the fossil fuel suppliers involved.

12. Felder and Schleiniger (1999) consider the efficiency costs of meeting the constraint that there be no "monetary transfers" (i.e., no change in overall tax payments) as a result of a carbon tax policy. Using a numerical general equilibrium model of Switzerland, they meet this constraint through industry-specific output subsidies or labor subsidies.

2.2 The Model

This section outlines the structure of the intertemporal general equilibrium model employed in this study. The model is an intertemporal general equilibrium model of the U.S. economy with international trade. It generates paths of equilibrium prices, outputs, and incomes for the U.S. economy and the rest of the world under specified policy scenarios. All variables are calculated at yearly intervals beginning in the benchmark year 2000 and usually extending to the year 2075.

The model combines a fairly realistic treatment of the U.S. tax system and a detailed representation of energy production and demand. It incorporates specific tax instruments and addresses effects of taxation along a number of important dimensions. These include firms' investment incentives, equity values, and profits;[13] and household consumption, saving, and labor-supply decisions. The specification of energy supply incorporates the nonrenewable nature of crude petroleum and natural gas and the transitions from conventional to synthetic fuels.

U.S. production divides into the 13 industries indicated in table 2.1. The energy industries consist of (1) coal mining, (2) crude petroleum and natural gas extraction, (3) petroleum refining, (4) synthetic fuels, (5) electric utilities, and (6) gas utilities. The model also distinguishes the 17 consumer goods shown in the table.

2.2.1 Producer Behavior

General Specifications

In each industry, a nested production structure accounts for substitution between different forms of energy as well as between energy and other inputs. Each industry produces a distinct output (X), which is a function of the inputs of labor (L), capital (K), an energy composite (E), a materials composite (M), and the current level of investment (I):

(1) $$X = f[g(L,K),h(E,M)] - \phi(I/K)\cdot I.$$

The energy composite is made up of the outputs of the six energy industries, while the materials composite consists of the outputs of the other industries:

(2) $$E = E(\bar{x}_2,\bar{x}_3 + \bar{x}_4,\bar{x}_5,\bar{x}_6,\bar{x}_7),$$

(3) $$M = M(\bar{x}_1,\bar{x}_8,\dots,\bar{x}_{13}),$$

13. Here the model applies the asset-price approach to investment developed in Summers (1981).

Table 2.1 Industry and Consumer Goods

	Gross Output, Year 2000[a]	
	Level	Percent of Total
Industries		
1. Agriculture and noncoal mining	993.6	6.2
2. Coal mining	50.5	0.3
3. Crude petroleum and natural gas	193.7	1.2
4. Synthetic fuels	0.0	0.0
5. Petroleum refining	324.6	2.0
6. Electric utilities	234.6	1.5
7. Gas utilities	211.5	1.3
8. Construction	1508.8	9.5
9. Metals and machinery	799.1	5.0
10. Motor vehicles	541.2	3.4
11. Miscellaneous manufacturing	3365.2	21.3
12. Services (except housing)	5183.6	32.8
13. Housing services	2420.8	15.3
Consumer goods		
1. Food		
2. Alcohol		
3. Tobacco		
4. Utilities		
5. Housing services		
6. Furnishings		
7. Appliances		
8. Clothing and jewelry		
9. Transportation		
10. Motor vehicles		
11. Services (except financial)		
12. Financial services		
13. Recreation, reading, and miscellaneous		
14. Nondurable, nonfood household expenditure		
15. Gasoline and other fuels		
16. Education		
17. Health		

[a] Billions of year 2000 dollars.

where $\overline{x}_i$ is a composite of domestically produced and foreign made input i.[14] Industry indices correspond to those in table 2.1.

Managers of firms choose input quantities and investment levels to max-

14. The functions f, g, and h, and the aggregation functions for the composites E, M, and $\overline{x}_i$, feature a constant elasticity of substitution (CES) and exhibit constant returns to scale. Consumer goods are produced by combining outputs from the 13 industries in fixed proportions.

imize the value of the firm. The investment decision takes account of the adjustment (or installation) costs represented by $\phi(I/K) \cdot I$ in equation (1), where ϕ is a convex function of the rate of investment I/K.[15]

Special Features of the Oil and Gas and Synthetic Fuels Industries

The production structure in the oil and gas industry is somewhat more complex than in other industries to account for the nonrenewable nature of oil and gas stocks. The production specification is

$$X = \gamma(Z) \cdot f[g(L,K),h(E,M)] - \phi(I/K) \cdot I, \tag{4}$$

where γ is a decreasing function of Z, the cumulative extraction of oil and gas up to the beginning of the current period. This captures the idea that as Z rises (or, equivalently, as reserves are depleted), it becomes increasingly difficult to extract oil and gas resources, so that greater quantities of K, L, E, and M are required to achieve any given level of extraction (output). Each oil and gas producer perfectly recognizes the impact of its current production decisions on future extraction costs.[16] Increasing production costs ultimately induce oil and gas producers to remove their capital from this industry.

The model incorporates a synthetic fuel—shale oil—as a backstop resource, a perfect substitute for oil and gas.[17] The technology for producing synthetic fuels on a commercial scale is assumed to become known in 2020. Thus, capital formation in the synthetic fuels industry cannot begin until that year.

All domestic prices in the model are endogenous, except for the domestic price of oil and gas. The path of oil and gas prices follows the assumptions of the Stanford University Energy Modeling Forum.[18] The supply of imported oil and gas is taken to be perfectly elastic at the world price. So long as imports are the marginal source of supply to the domestic economy, domestic producers of oil and gas receive the world price (adjusted for tariffs or taxes) for their own output. However, rising oil and gas prices stimulate investment in synthetic fuels. Eventually, synthetic fuel production plus domestic oil and gas supply together satisfy all of the domestic demand. Synthetic fuels then become the marginal source of supply, so that the cost of synthetic fuel production rather than the world oil price dictates the domestic price of fuels.[19]

15. The function ϕ represents adjustment costs per unit of investment. This function expresses the notion that installing new capital necessitates a loss of current output because existing inputs (K, L, E, and M) are diverted to install new capital.

16. We assume representative oil and gas firms: initial resource stocks, profit-maximizing extraction levels, and resource-stock effects are identical across producers.

17. Thus, inputs 3 (oil and gas) and 4 (synthetic fuels) enter additively in the energy aggregation function shown in equation (2).

18. The world price is $19 per barrel in 2000 and rises in real terms by $5.00 per decade. See Gaskins and Weyant (1996).

19. For details, see Goulder (1994, 1995a).

2.2.2 Household Behavior

Consumption, labor supply, and saving result from the decisions of a representative household maximizing its intertemporal utility, defined on leisure and overall consumption in each period. The utility function is homothetic, and leisure and consumption are weakly separable (see the appendixes). The household faces an intertemporal budget constraint requiring that the present value of consumption not exceed potential total wealth (nonhuman wealth plus the present value of labor and transfer income). In each period, overall consumption of goods and services is allocated across the 17 specific categories of consumption goods or services shown in table 2.1. Each of the 17 consumption goods or services is a composite of a domestically and foreign-produced consumption good (or service) of that type. Households substitute between domestic and foreign goods to minimize the cost of obtaining a given composite.

2.2.3 The Government Sector

The government collects taxes, distributes transfers, and purchases goods and services (outputs of the 13 industries). The tax instruments include energy taxes, output taxes, the corporate income tax, property taxes, sales taxes, and taxes on individual labor and capital income. In the benchmark year, 2000, the government deficit amounts to approximately 2 percent of GDP. In the reference case (or status quo) simulation, the real deficit grows at the steady-state growth rate given by the growth of potential labor services. In the policy-change cases, we require that real government spending and the real deficit follow the same paths as in the reference case. To make the policy changes revenue-neutral, we accompany the tax-rate increases that define the various policies with reductions in other taxes, either on a lump-sum basis (increased exogenous transfers) or through reductions in marginal tax rates.

2.2.4 Foreign Trade

Except for oil and gas imports, imported intermediate and consumer goods are imperfect substitutes for their domestic counterparts.[20] Import prices are exogenous in foreign currency, but the domestic-currency price changes with variations in the exchange rate. Export demands are modeled as functions of the foreign price of U.S. exports and the level of foreign income (in foreign currency). The exchange rate adjusts to balance trade in every period.

2.2.5 Equilibrium and Growth

The solution of the model is a general equilibrium in which supplies and demands balance in all markets at each period of time. The requirements

20. Thus, we adopt the assumption of Armington (1969).

of the general equilibrium are that supply equal demand for labor inputs and for all produced goods, that firms' demands for loanable funds match the aggregate supply by households, and that the government's tax revenues equal its spending less the current deficit. These conditions are met through adjustments in output prices, in the market interest rate, and in lump-sum taxes or marginal tax rates.[21]

Economic growth reflects the growth of capital stocks and of potential labor resources. The growth of capital stocks stems from endogenous saving and investment behavior. Potential labor resources are specified as increasing at an exogenous rate.

2.3 Relationships between Carbon Abatement Policies, Profits, and Equity Values

An important component of this study is the impact of CO_2 abatement policies on the profitability of firms that supply fossil fuels. The first part of this section describes in fairly general terms the model's treatment of firms' profits and equity values, while the second part focuses on how abatement policies affect these elements. In all of this section, we concentrate on the fossil fuel industries: coal, and oil and gas.

2.3.1 Profits, Dividends, and Equity Values

Let α denote the (fixed) ratio of carbon emissions to units of fuel (output) in the industry in question, and let τ_c denote the carbon tax rate per unit of emissions. Then the carbon tax τ_c requires a payment of $\tau_c\alpha$ per unit of output X. The equity value of the firm can be expressed in terms of dividends and new share issues, which in turn depend on profits in each period. The firm's profits during a given period are given by

$$(5) \qquad \pi = (1 - \tau_a)[(p - \tau_c\alpha)X - w(1 + \tau_L)L - EMCOST - iDEBT - TPROP + LS] + \tau_a(DEPL + DEPR),$$

where τ_a is the corporate tax rate (or tax rate on profits), p is the output price, w is the wage rate net of indirect labor taxes, τ_L is rate of the indirect tax on labor, $EMCOST$ is the cost to the firm of energy and materials inputs, i is the gross-of-tax interest rate paid by the firm, $DEBT$ is the firm's current debt, $TPROP$ is property tax payments, LS is a lump-sum receipt (if applicable) by the firm, $DEPL$ is the current gross depletion allowance, and $DEPR$ is the current gross depreciation allowance. $TPROP$ equals $\tau_p p_{K,s-1} K_s$, where τ_p is the property tax rate, p_K is the purchase price of a unit of new capital, and s is the time period. Current depletion allow-

21. Since agents are forward-looking, equilibrium in each period depends not only on current prices and taxes but on future magnitudes as well.

ances, *DEPL*, are a constant fraction β of the value of current extraction: $DEPL = \beta pX$. Current depreciation allowances, *DEPR*, can be expressed as $\delta^T K^T$, where K^T is the depreciable capital stock basis and δ^T is the depreciation rate applied for tax purposes.[22]

The firm's sources and uses of revenues are linked through the cash-flow identity

$$\pi + BN + VN = DIV + IEXP. \tag{6}$$

The left-hand side represents the firm's sources of revenues: profits, new debt issue (*BN*), and new share issues (*VN*). The uses of revenues on the right-hand side are investment expenditure (*IEXP*) and dividend payments (*DIV*). Negative share issues are equivalent to share repurchases and represent a use rather than a source of revenue.

Firms pay dividends equal to a constant fraction, *a*, of profits gross of capital gains on the existing capital stock and net of economic depreciation. They also maintain debt equal to a constant fraction, *b*, of the value of the existing capital stock. Thus,

$$DIV_s = a[\pi_s + (p_{K,s} - p_{k,s-1})K_s - \delta p_{K,s} K_s], \tag{7}$$

$$BN_s \equiv DEBT_{s+1} - DEBT_s = b(p_{K,s} K_{s+1} - p_{K,s-1} K_s). \tag{8}$$

Investment expenditure is expressed by

$$IEXP_s = (1 - \tau_K) p_{K,s} I_s, \tag{9}$$

where τ_K is the investment tax credit rate. Of the elements in equation (6), new share issues, *VN*, are the residual, making up the difference between $\pi + BN$ and $DIV + IEXP$.[23]

Arbitrage possibilities compel the firm to offer its stockholders a rate of return comparable to the rate of interest on alternative assets:

$$(1 - \tau_e) DIV_s + (1 - \tau_v)(V_{s+1} - V_s - VN_s) = (1 - \tau_b) i_s V_s. \tag{10}$$

The parameters τ_e, τ_v, and τ_b are the personal tax rates on dividend income (equity), capital gains, and interest income (bonds), respectively. The return to stockholders consists of the current after-tax dividend plus the after-tax capital gain (accrued or realized) on the equity value (*V*) of the firm net of the value of new share issues. This return must be comparable to the after-tax return from an investment of the same value at the market rate of interest, *i*.

Recursively applying equation (10) subject to the usual transversality

22. For convenience, we assume that the accelerated depreciation schedule can be approximated by a schedule involving a constant rate of exponential tax depreciation.

23. This treatment is consistent with the "old view" of dividend behavior. For an examination of this and alternative specifications, see Poterba and Summers (1985).

condition ruling out eternal speculative bubbles yields the following expression for the equity value of the firm:

$$V_t = \sum_{s=t}^{\infty}\left[\frac{1-\tau_e}{1-\tau_v}DIV_s - VN_s\right]\mu_t(s), \tag{11}$$

where

$$\mu_t(s) \equiv \prod_{u=t}^{s}\left[1 + \frac{r_u}{1-\tau_v}\right]^{-1}.$$

Equation (11) indicates that the equity value of the firm is the discounted sum of after-tax dividends net of new share issues.

2.3.2 Abatement Policies and Equity Values

A Standard Carbon Tax

Abatement policies affect equity values by altering firms' profits and the stream of dividends paid by firms. A carbon tax, in particular, will tend to lower the profits of firms in the industries on which the tax is imposed. Figure 2.1 heuristically indicates the carbon tax's implications for the coal industry.[24]

The line labeled S_0 in the figure is the supply curve for coal in the absence of a tax. This diagram accounts for the quasi-fixed nature of capital resulting from capital-adjustment costs. The supply curve S_0 should be regarded as an average of an infinite number of supply curves, beginning with the curve depicting the marginal cost of changes in supply in the first instant and culminating with the marginal cost of changing supply over the very long term, when all factors are mobile. This curve therefore indicates the average of the discounted marginal costs of expanding production, given the size of the initial capital stock. We draw the supply curve as upward sloping, in keeping with the fact that in all time frames except the very long run capital is not fully mobile and production exhibits decreasing returns in the variable factors—labor and intermediate inputs.[25]

The supply curve represents the marginal costs associated with increments in the use of variable factors to increase supply. Capital is the fixed factor underlying the upward-sloping supply curve. The return to this factor is the producer surplus in the diagram. With an upward-sloping supply curve, this producer surplus is positive. The existence of producer surplus does not necessarily imply supernormal profits. Indeed, in an initial long-

24. Pezzey and Park (1998, fig. 1) offer a somewhat similar analysis for policies involving tradable emissions permits.

25. In the long run, in contrast, capital is fully mobile, production exhibits constant returns to scale, and the supply curve is infinitely elastic.

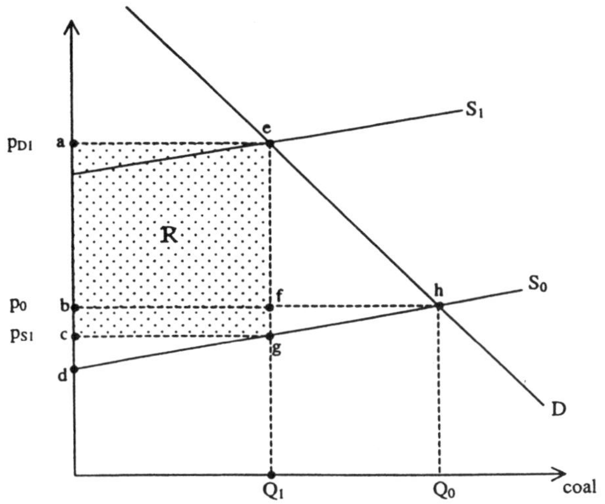

Fig. 2.1 CO_2 abatement and profits

run equilibrium, the producer surplus is just large enough to yield a normal return on the capital stock. To illustrate, at the initial equilibrium with a market price p_0 and aggregate quantity supplied Q_0, the producer surplus amounts to the triangular area *bhd.* On a balanced-growth path, this producer surplus yields a normal (market) return on the initial capital stock so that the value of the initial capital stock equals the price of investment (and thus Tobin's q is unity).

Now consider the impact of an unanticipated carbon (coal) tax. The introduction of this tax shifts the supply curve upward to S_1. As a direct consequence, the output price paid by coal consumers increases from p_0 to p_{D1}. However, since supply is not infinitely elastic, the suppliers of coal are not able to shift the entire burden of the tax onto demanders. Indeed, the producer price of coal declines to p_{S1}. This causes producer surplus to shrink to the area *cgd.* Since this triangle is smaller than the initial producer surplus, the return on the initial capital stock (valued at the price of investment goods) falls short of the market rate of return. Hence, to satisfy the arbitrage condition, Tobin's q falls below unity and the owners of the capital stock suffer a capital loss.

This analysis is complicated by the fact that the carbon tax can finance reductions in other taxes, which may imply reductions in costs to firms. This will tend to offset the carbon-tax-induced losses in profits and the associated reductions in equity values. To the extent that the carbon tax revenues finance general (economy-wide) reductions in personal or corporate income taxes, the reductions in tax rates will be small and thus will exert only a small impact on costs to the fossil fuel industries. If the revenues are recycled through tax cuts targeted for the fossil fuel industries, however, the changes in marginal rates can be significant and the beneficial offsetting impact on profits and equity values may be more pronounced.

Effects of Rent-Generating Policies

In figure 2.1, the shaded rectangle *R* (with area *aegc*) represents the firms' payments of the carbon tax. If the government forgoes some of the carbon tax revenue, and allows producers to retain this potential revenue as a rent, the impact on profits, dividends, and equity values can be fundamentally different. Consider, for example, the case in which the government restricts CO_2 emissions through a system of carbon permits. Since such emissions are proportional to coal combustion, the government can accomplish a given percentage reduction in emissions from coal by restricting coal output by that same percentage through the sale of a limited number of coal-supply permits. For comparability, suppose that the number of permits restricts supply to the level Q_1 in the figure. If the permits are auctioned competitively, then the government (ideally) collects the revenue *R* from sale of the permits and the effects on firms are the same as under the carbon tax. In contrast, if the permits are given out free (or grandfathered), then the area *R* represents a rent to firms. The government-mandated restriction in output causes prices to rise, but there is no increase in costs of production (indeed, marginal production costs are lower).

As suggested by figure 2.1, this rent can be quite large and, indeed, can imply substantial increases in profits and equity values to the regulated industries. In the figure, the postregulation profits enjoyed by the firm are given by the sum of areas *R* and *cgd.* Here postregulation profits are many times higher than the profit prior to regulation (*bhd*). Owners of industry-specific capital enjoy a capital gain as Tobin's *q* jumps above unity. Intuitively, by restricting output, government policy allows producers as a group to exploit their market power and reap part of the original consumer surplus.

Using comparable diagrams, it is straightforward to verify that the magnitude of the profit increase under a system of grandfathered emissions permits depends on

1. The extent of abatement (or number of permits issued relative to "business-as-usual" emissions). The regulation-induced increase in profit is represented by the difference between the areas of the rectangle *aefb* and the triangle *fhg.* For incremental restrictions in supply, the former will be larger than the latter (if demand is less than infinitely elastic). Thus, producers must gain. However, this is not necessarily the case as the magnitude of the required reduction in supply gets larger. If the demand curve has a "choke price" (a price above which demand is strictly 0), then the potential rent will shrink to 0 as the extent of abatement approaches 100 percent.

2. The elasticity of supply. The potential to enjoy significant additional profits from restrictions on output is larger, the higher the elasticity of supply. In this case, most of the burden associated with reductions in output is borne by consumers, and a large share of the rents rectangle R represents an increase in producer surplus—that is, most of R will lie above p_0. In contrast, if supply is inelastic (as in the case where adjustment costs are substantial), very little of the rents rectangle R represents an increase in producer surplus because much of it extends below the initial output price p_0. In this case, restrictions in output do not enable producers to expropriate much of the consumer surplus. Thus, the rectangle *aefb* will be smaller than the triangle *fhg*, and profits will fall.

A small income share of the fixed factor (i.e., capital in our model) contributes to a large supply elasticity. A large supply elasticity (or flat supply curve) implies that the producer surplus *bhd* (i.e., the income to the fixed factor) is small while most of the area R will lie above p_0. Hence the additional profits will be large compared to the initial producer surplus.

3. The elasticity of demand. If demand is highly elastic, the policy-induced reduction in output gives firms relatively little market power—only a small part of R will lie above p_0. In contrast, if demand is inelastic, the abatement policy enables firms to exercise substantial market power. In this case, much of R will lie above p_0, and firms will be able to expropriate a considerable amount of the consumer surplus. The aggregate elasticity of demand for a given fossil fuel will reflect the elasticities of substitution inherent in the production functions of domestic users of coal. In addition, the response of demand will reflect the extent to which the government insulates domestic fossil fuel producers from foreign competition. In particular, the elasticity of demand will be smaller, and the potential to enjoy large rents larger, to the extent that the government accompanies taxes on domestic production with levies on imports on fossil fuels and subsidies to exports of such fuels. Carbon taxes or auctioned emissions permits applicable to imported fuels cause the imported fuel prices to rise in tandem with the prices of domestic fuels, thus preventing domestic consumers from shifting demand to imported fuels. Export subsidies ensure that the prices of exported fuels do not rise relative to foreign fuel prices, and thus they help to sustain foreign demand for domestically produced fuels.

Under rent-generating policies, the rectangle R corresponds, in a dynamic context, to

$$\sum_{s=t}^{\infty}(1 - \nu)(1 - \tau_a)(p_{D1,t} - p_{S1,t})Q_{1,t}\mu_t(s), \tag{12}$$

where the factors $1 - \nu$ and $1 - \tau_a$ address the fact that the rents are subject to the personal and corporate income taxes, respectively. Here $Q_{1,t}$ represents gross output (under the policy change) at time t.

A system of grandfathered permits is not the only form of regulation that would enable firms to capture much of *R*. Firms could capture some of *R* under a carbon tax policy in which inframarginal emissions (emissions below some trigger level) are exempt from the tax, while all emissions beyond that level face the tax.[26]

In sum, the impact on firms' profits and equity values can be fundamentally different, depending on how much of the area *R* is retained by firms rather than collected by the government. It also depends on how much of the area *R* lies above the initial equilibrium price. This, in turn, will depend on the extent of abatement and on elasticities of supply and demand. We return to these issues in the discussion of policy results in section 2.6.

2.4 Data and Parameters

Data documentation is in Cruz and Goulder (1992), which is available on request. Industry input and output flows (used to establish share parameters for production functions) were obtained from the 1988 input-output table from the Bureau of Economic Analysis of the U.S. Department of Commerce. This table is also the source for consumption, investment, government spending, import, and export values by industry. Data on industry capital stocks derive from Bureau of Economic Analysis (1994). Employment by industry was obtained from the October 1990 Survey of Current Business. To form the benchmark data set, these data are projected to the year 2000, based on the average growth of real GDP from the relevant historical period to 1998. Data on the carbon content of fossil fuels were obtained from the 1998 U.S. Department of Energy *Annual Energy Outlook.*

Elasticities of substitution determine the industry and household price elasticities of demand. We derive the production function elasticities by transforming parameters of translog production functions estimated by Dale Jorgenson and Peter Wilcoxen (personal communication). The capital-adjustment cost parameters are based on Summers (1981).

Other important parameters apply to the household side of the model. The elasticity of substitution in consumption between goods and leisure, ν, is set to yield a compensated elasticity of labor supply of 0.4.[27] The intertemporal elasticity of substitution in consumption, σ, equals 0.5.[28] The intensity parameter α_c is set to generate a ratio of labor time to the total time endowment equal to 0.44. These parameters imply a value of 0.19 for the interest elasticity of savings between the current period and the next.

26. Farrow (1999) describes and evaluates a policy of this sort. See also Pezzey (1992).

27. This lies midway in the range of estimates displayed in the recent survey by Russek (1996).

28. This value falls between the lower estimates from time-series analyses (e.g., Hall 1988) and the higher ones from cross-sectional studies (e.g., Lawrance 1991).

2.5 Abatement Policies Investigated

In nearly all simulations, the tool for abatement is the carbon tax (although we also consider CO_2 quotas or tradable permits, as discussed later). All policies are unanticipated and phased in smoothly (with equal increments to the carbon tax) over a 3-year period beginning in the base year, 2000. The carbon tax is levied "upstream"; that is, the tax is imposed on suppliers of fossil fuels (producers of coal and of oil and gas). To prevent an adverse impact on the international competitive position of fossil-fuel-producing industries, exports of fossil fuels are exempt from the carbon tax, while imports of these fuels are subject to the carbon tax. Nearly all proposals for a U.S. carbon tax include export and import elements of this type.

The policies differ in two main ways: (1) the way the gross revenues from the carbon tax are recycled to the private sector, and (2) the extent to which the policies create and leave rents for the regulated firms. We normalize the carbon tax so that discounted carbon emissions are the same across the policies.[29] We do not allow for public debt policy. Hence, all gross revenues from the carbon tax are immediately returned to the private sector.

2.5.1 Starting Point: Policies without Distributional Adjustments

The first set of policies involves broad-based revenue recycling and thus does not attend to distributional concerns. These policies involve three alternative ways to recycle the revenues: higher lump-sum transfers to households, lower personal income tax rates, and lower corporate income tax rates. We implement these recycling options by using the recycling instrument to endogenously balance the government budget.

The other policies involve additional elements to address important distributional considerations. Thus these policies involve not only environmental neutrality (the reductions in emissions are normalized across policies) and revenue neutrality (all gross revenues are recycled), but also some form of distributional neutrality. The attention to distributional neutrality is motivated by concerns about equity and political feasibility.

2.5.2 Imposing the Requirement of Equity-Value Neutrality

The first group of policies to attend to distributional neutrality adds the constraint that the real[30] value of equity of the principally affected industries must not be changed (i.e., reduced) at the time the abatement policy

29. In the simulations, we have approximated environmental neutrality by scaling the results of a uniform carbon tax of $25 per ton carbon by discounted emissions reductions. We find that efficiency outcomes from the model are close to linear within the small range of variation in emissions reductions, so that this type of scaling does not significantly affect the interpretation of results.

30. To express the equity values in real terms, we adopt the ideal price index that is associated with the utility function of the representative household.

is announced and implemented. We call this the requirement of *equity-value neutrality.* The most vulnerable industries are fossil-fuel-supplying industries (coal, and oil and gas), the petroleum refining industry, and the electric utilities industry.[31] The constraint on the value of equity can be interpreted as the requirement that industry-specific production factors not be hurt by the carbon tax. In the model, labor is perfectly mobile across industries, while capital is subject to adjustment costs. Since capital is the only the industry-specific production factor, the effect on the value of capital represents the impact of the carbon tax on industry-specific production factors. Unanticipated policies yield instantaneous changes in the value of industry-specific wealth, as measured by changes in the equity values of various industries.

We consider three mechanisms for achieving equity-value neutrality: (1) industry-specific cuts in corporate tax rates, (2) lump-sum transfers to capital employed in particular industries, and (3) inframarginal exemptions to the carbon tax. Our model abstracts from uncertainty and from heterogeneity across firms in a given industry. In such a model, a policy involving emissions permits, in which a certain fraction of the permits is given out free (rather than auctioned), is equivalent to a carbon tax policy in which the same fraction of (inframarginal) emissions is exempt from the carbon tax.[32] Thus, the third policy can be interpreted as one in which the government controls emissions through emissions permits and freely allocates, or grandfathers, some of these permits. We simulate this policy by imposing a $25 per ton carbon tax and rebating to the firm a share of its tax payment, with the share corresponding to the percentage of emissions that are exempt from the tax. The rebate is lump-sum from the firm's point of view. Under this simulation, output and emissions from the coal and the oil and gas industries rise through time. Hence, this corresponds to an emissions permit policy in which the number of permits in circulation increases through time.

In our simulations, the policies with inframarginal exemptions have the potential to produce dramatic impacts on profits and equity values. For this reason, we perform additional policy experiments involving inframarginal exemptions of various magnitudes. In these experiments, we do not aim to achieve equity-value neutrality, but instead focus on how profits, equity values, and other important variables are affected by the magnitude of the exemptions. The policies introduced under this heading are an emissions permit system in which 100 percent of the permits are grandfathered,

31. Thus we focus on four of the six energy industries identified in the model. We give less attention to the natural gas-delivery industry, which experiences considerably smaller impacts from the abatement policies, and the synthetic fuels industry, which does not emerge significantly until 2025.

32. They are equivalent under appropriate scaling of the two policies: The limit on emissions under the permits program must be the same as the level of emissions that occurs under the carbon tax.

and a carbon tax with inframarginal exemptions equal to 50 or 90 percent of first-period emissions under the unregulated status quo. The rents generated by each of these policies face the same taxes as other producer income and thus are subject to the corporate income tax.

These policies involve three instruments to achieve three targets. The carbon tax rate assures environmental neutrality (the same emissions reductions), the adjustment to the personal income tax rate yields revenue neutrality (all additional revenues from the carbon tax must be recycled), and the industry-specific corporate income tax cuts, lump-sum payments, or inframarginal exemptions bring about equity-value neutrality.

2.5.3 Imposing the Requirement of Tax-Payment Neutrality

In the political arena, a popular indicator of distributional neutrality is the tax payment of a particular industry.[33] According to this alternative notion of distributional neutrality, a given industry's overall tax payments from carbon taxes, corporate taxes, property taxes, and indirect labor taxes should remain constant. We term this *tax-payment neutrality.* As instruments for this type of neutrality we consider industry-specific corporate tax cuts and explicit lump-sum transfers to sector-specific capital. As with the simulations involving equity-value neutrality, the tax-payment neutrality simulations involve policy packages in which three instruments achieve three targets.

2.6 Simulation Results

2.6.1 Policies without Distributional Adjustments

Policy 1: Lump-Sum Recycling

We begin by examining the effects of the $25 per ton carbon tax with lump-sum recycling. Results are displayed in column (1) of table 2.2. The table shows the impacts on prices, output, and after-tax profits for years 2002 (2 years after implementation) and 2025.

The coal industry experiences the largest impact on prices and output. In this industry, prices rise by approximately 54 percent by the time the policy is fully implemented (year 2002) and the price increase is sustained at slightly above that level. The price increase implies a reduction in output of about 24 percent in the long run. The other major impacts on prices and output are in the oil and gas, petroleum refining, and electric utilities industries. Although the carbon tax is imposed on the oil and gas industry, the price increase is considerably smaller than in the coal industry, reflecting the lower carbon content (per dollar of fuel) of oil and gas as

33. Indeed, in several countries, such as Denmark and the Netherlands, additional environmental taxes raised from energy-intensive industries are earmarked for technology subsidies to this sector.

Table 2.2 **Industry Impacts of CO_2 Abatement Policies (percentage changes from reference case)**

	No Distributional Adjustments Revenue-Recycling via			Equity-Value Neutrality Imposed via		
	Lump-Sum Transfer (1)	PIT Rate Reduction (2)	CIT Rate Reduction (3)	Industry-Specific CIT Rate Cut (4)	Industry-Specific Lump-Sum Payment (5)	Partial Grandfathering of Emissions Permits (6)
Gross of tax output price (2002, 2025)						
Coal mining	54.5, 57.0	54.5, 57.0	54.5, 57.1	54.3, 55.9	54.5, 57.0	54.5, 57.0
Oil and gas	13.2, 8.3	13.2, 8.3	13.2, 8.3	13.2, 8.3	13.2, 8.3	13.2, 8.3
Petroleum refining	6.4, 5.1	6.4, 5.1	6.4, 5.1	6.3, 4.7	6.4, 5.1	6.4, 5.1
Electric utilities	2.5, 5.6	2.5, 5.5	2.5, 5.7	2.5, 5.1	2.5, 5.5	2.5, 5.5
Average for other industries	−0.6, −0.6	−0.6, −0.7	−0.6, −0.7	−0.6, −0.6	−0.6, −0.7	−0.6, −0.7
Output (2002, 2025)						
Coal mining	−19.2, −23.6	−19.1, −23.3	−19.2, −23.5	−18.9, −21.9	−19.1, −23.3	−19.1, −23.3
Oil and gas	−2.0, −3.9	−2.1, −4.4	−1.3, −2.5	1.5, −0.4	−2.1, −4.4	−2.1, −4.3
Petroleum refining	−7.9, −5.6	−7.8, −5.3	−7.9, −5.3	−7.8, −5.0	−7.8, −5.3	−7.8, −5.3
Electric utilities	−3.0, −5.7	−3.0, −5.4	−3.0, −5.5	−2.9, −5.0	−3.0, −5.4	−3.0, −5.4
Average for other industries	−0.2, −0.3	−0.1, 0.1	−0.1, 0.1	−0.1, 0.1	−0.1, 0.1	−0.1, 0.1
After-tax profits (2002, 2025)						
Coal mining	−32.5, −25.8	−32.3, −25.5	−32.0, −25.1	−19.9, −12.0	−32.3, −25.5	−16.6, −10.4
Oil and gas	−2.3, −3.5	−2.3, −3.9	−0.3, −0.4	−6.6, −9.1	−2.3, −3.8	1.3, −1.8
Petroleum refining	−9.2, −3.9	−9.1, −3.6	−8.1, −2.7	−5.5, −0.9	−9.1, −3.6	−9.1, −3.6
Electric utilities	−7.7, −5.2	−7.4, −4.8	−7.1, −4.2	−5.2, −2.7	−7.4, −4.8	−7.4, −4.8
Average for other industries	−0.9, −1.1	−0.7, −0.7	0.2, 0.2	−0.7, −0.7	−0.7, −0.7	−0.7, −0.8

	Inframarginal Exemptions			Tax Payment Neutrality Imposed via	
	Exempt 100% of Actual Emissions (100% Grandfathering of Emissions Permits) (7)	Exempt 50% of BAU Emissions (8)	Exempt 90% of BAU Emissions (9)	Industry-Specific CIT Rate Cut (10)	Industry-Specific Lump-Sum Payment (11)
Gross of tax output price (2002, 2025)					
Coal mining	54.5, 57.0	54.5, 57.0	54.5, 57.0	54.3, 56.0	54.5, 57.0
Oil and gas	13.2, 8.3	13.2, 8.3	13.2, 8.3	13.2, 3.0	13.2, 8.3
Petroleum refining	6.4, 5.1	6.4, 5.1	6.4, 5.1	6.4, 2.0	6.4, 5.1
Electric utilities	2.4, 5.5	2.5, 5.5	2.5, 5.6	2.5, 5.6	2.5, 5.6
Average for other industries	−0.6, −0.6	−0.6, −0.7	−0.6, −0.6	−0.6, −0.4	−0.6, −0.6
Output (2002, 2025)					
Coal mining	−19.0, −23.3	−19.1, −23.4	−19.1, −23.4	−19.4, −23.3	−19.1, −23.5
Oil and gas	−2.0, −4.2	−2.1, −4.3	−2.1, −3.5	7.5, 23.9	−2.0, −4.1
Petroleum refining	−7.8, −5.4	−7.8, −5.4	−7.8, −5.4	−8.0, −2.8	−7.9, −5.5
Electric utilities	−3.0, −5.5	−3.0, −5.4	−3.0, −5.5	−3.0, −5.0	−3.0, −5.6
Average for other industries	−0.1, −0.1	−0.1, 0.0	−0.1, −0.1	−0.2, −0.2	−0.2, −0.2
After-tax profits (2002, 2025)					
Coal mining	542.7, 526.9	555.9, 351.5	957.2, 653.0	−19.9, −12.8	−32.4, −25.7
Oil and gas	21.4, 9.4	18.0, 5.5	34.3, 13.7	25.7, 45.7	−2.3, −3.6
Petroleum refining	−9.1, −3.8	−9.1, −3.7	−9.2, −3.8	−10.5, −2.6	−9.2, −3.8
Electric utilities	−7.5, −5.0	−7.4, −4.9	−7.5, −5.0	−8.6, −4.7	−7.6, −5.1
Average for other industries	−0.7, −0.9	−0.7, −0.8	−0.8, −0.9	−1.0, −1.0	−0.9, −1.0

Table 2.3 **Equity-Value and Efficiency Impacts**

	No Distributional Adjustments Revenue-Recycling via			Equity-Value Neutrality Imposed via		
	Lump-Sum Transfer (1)	PIT Rate Reduction (2)	CIT Rate Reduction (3)	Industry-Specific CIT Rate Cut (4)	Industry-Specific Lump-Sum Payment (5)	Partial Grandfathering of Emissions Permits[a] (6)
Equity values of firms (year 2000) (percentage changes from reference case)						
Agriculture and noncoal mining	−0.7	0.2	1.4	0.1	0.1	0.1
Coal mining	−28.4	−27.8	−27.2	0.0	0.0	0.0 (0.043)
Oil and gas	−4.8	−5.0	−0.7	0.0	0.0	0.0 (0.150)
Petroleum refining	−5.2	−4.5	−3.3	0.0	0.0	−4.5
Electric utilities	−6.3	−5.4	−4.4	0.0	0.0	−5.4
Natural gas utilities	−1.4	−0.4	0.6	−0.3	−0.4	−0.4
Construction	−0.3	1.5	2.1	1.8	1.5	1.5
Metals and machinery	−1.2	−0.4	1.0	−0.6	−0.4	−0.4
Motor vehicles	−0.6	0.2	1.6	0.2	0.2	0.2
Miscellaneous manufacturing	−0.8	−0.1	1.4	−0.2	−0.1	−0.1
Services (except housing)	−0.8	0.2	1.2	0.2	0.1	0.1
Housing services	0.0	0.4	0.1	0.4	0.4	0.4
Total	−0.8	−0.1	0.9	0.1	0.1	0.0
Efficiency cost						
Absolute (billions of year 2000 dollars)	−817	−471	−374	−345	−482	−506
Per ton of CO_2 reduction	102.6	60.0	47.7	46.9	61.4	64.4
Per dollar of carbon tax revenue	.73	.42	.34	.30	.43	.50

compared with coal. There are significant increases in prices and reductions in output in the petroleum refining and electric utilities industries as well, in keeping with the significant use of fossil fuels in these industries. The reductions in output are accompanied by reductions in annual after-tax profits. Associated with these output reductions is a reduction in CO_2 emissions of approximately 18 percent.[34]

34. This is the reduction in emissions associated with domestic consumption of fossil fuels. It accounts for the carbon content of imported fossil fuels, and excludes the carbon content of exported fossil fuels. These figures do not adjust for changes in the carbon content of imported or exported refined products. The percentage change in emissions is the percentage change between the reference case and policy-change case in the present value of emissions,

Table 2.3 (continued)

	Inframarginal Exemptions			Tax-Payment Neutrality Imposed via	
	Exempt 100% of Actual Emissions (100% Grandfathering of Emissions Permits) (7)	Exempt 50% of BAU Emissions (8)	Exempt 90% of BAU Emissions (9)	Industry-Specific CIT Rate Cut (10)	Industry-Specific Lump-Sum Payment (11)
Equity values of firms (year 2000) (percentage changes from reference case)					
Agriculture and noncoal mining	0.0	0.0	−0.1	−0.2	−0.4
Coal mining	1,005.4	709.1	1,284.0	1,283.3	4,283.7
Oil and gas	29.2	22.3	43.1	43.2	117.2
Petroleum refining	−4.7	−4.7	−4.8	−4.8	−12.1
Electric utilities	−5.7	−5.6	−5.7	−5.8	−12.9
Natural gas utilities	−0.8	−0.6	−0.8	−0.9	−1.1
Construction	1.0	1.1	0.8	0.7	0.2
Metals and machinery	−0.5	−0.6	−0.7	−0.7	−0.9
Motor vehicles	0.1	0.0	−0.1	−0.2	−0.4
Miscellaneous manufacturing	−0.2	−0.3	−0.4	−0.4	−0.6
Services (except housing)	−0.1	−0.1	−0.2	−0.3	−0.5
Housing services	0.1	0.3	0.3	0.2	0.1
Total	1.1	0.7	1.3	1.2	4.5
Efficiency cost					
Absolute (billions of year 2000 dollars)	−751	−549	−611	−355	−713
Per ton of CO_2 reduction	95.1	69.7	77.4	61.1	89.9
Per dollar of carbon tax revenue	—	.79	1.64	.32	.64

[a]Numbers in parentheses are proportion of emssions permits required to achieve equity-value neutrality.

The reductions in after-tax profits are associated with reductions in equity values. As shown in table 2.3, the largest equity-value impacts are in the coal industry, where such values fall by approximately 28 percent. The reductions in equity values in the oil and gas, petroleum refining, and electric utilities industries are also substantial, in the range of 4.8 to 6.3 percent. As indicated in the table, the impacts on equity values of other industries are relatively small.

---

where the emissions stream is discounted using the after-tax interest rate. If marginal environmental damages from emissions are constant, the percentage changes in discounted emissions will be equivalent to percentage changes in damages.

Table 2.3 also indicates efficiency impacts. We employ the equivalent variation to measure these impacts. This is a gross measure because our model does not account for the benefits associated with the environmental improvement from reduced emissions. As indicated in the table, the policy implies a gross efficiency loss of approximately $103 per ton of emissions reduced, or $0.73 per dollar of discounted gross revenue from the carbon tax.

Policy 2: Personal Income Tax Recycling

Policy 2 recycles the revenues through personal income tax (PIT) cuts rather than via lump-sum payments. As shown in column (2) of table 2.2, such recycling does not alter the impacts of the carbon tax on prices and output very much. Furthermore, such recycling only slightly attenuates the impacts on profits and equity values in the most affected industries. However, as indicated in table 2.3, this form of recycling reduces the economy-wide efficiency costs by over 40 percent. The equivalent variation is approximately $60 per ton of emissions reduced, and $0.42 per dollar of discounted carbon tax revenues. The reason for the smaller efficiency losses with PIT recycling is that, by lowering the marginal rates of the PIT, this recycling helps lower the distortionary costs of the PIT. This efficiency consequence has been termed the *revenue-recycling effect.* Despite the lower distortionary taxes, the carbon tax package still imposes gross efficiency costs because it tends to raise output prices and thereby reduce real returns to labor and capital. This *tax-interaction effect* tends to dominate the revenue-recycling effect. Hence the carbon tax still involves an overall economic cost (abstracting from the environmental benefits), even when the revenues are devoted to cuts in the PIT.[35]

Policy 3: Corporate Income Tax Recycling

The carbon tax revenue can be used instead to reduce the corporate income tax (CIT). This type of recycling further reduces the gross efficiency costs of emission reductions to 34 percent of discounted carbon tax revenues. Thus, CIT recycling appears to be more efficient than PIT recycling. This indicates that in the model the CIT is more distortionary than the PIT in the initial equilibrium. Although there is considerable disagreement as to the distortionary impacts of the CIT, these results are consistent with the prevailing results from other applied general equilibrium analyses.[36] In

35. This exemplifies the now-familiar result that, abstracting from the value of the environmental improvement they generate, green taxes tend to be more costly than the ordinary taxes they replace. Although this is the central result, the opposite outcome can arise when the preexisting tax system is suboptimal along nonenvironmental dimensions (e.g., involves overtaxation of capital relative to labor) and the introduction of the environmental reform helps alleviate the nonenvironmental inefficiency. For analysis and discussion of this issue see Bovenberg and de Mooij (1994), Parry (1995), Goulder (1995b), Bovenberg and Goulder (1997, 2000), and Parry and Bento (2000).

36. See, for example, Jorgenson and Yun (1991), and Goulder and Thalmann (1993).

the U.S. economy, taxes on capital investment such as the CIT appear to be more distortionary than labor income taxes or the PIT (a tax on both capital and labor income).

A cut in the CIT rate benefits the owners of capital because it reduces the tax burden on earnings from the installed capital stock. As a result, compared to the cases with lump-sum recycling or PIT recycling, in the most affected industries (coal, oil and gas, petroleum refining, and electric utilities), firms' equity values fall less. Indeed, the value of equity in the oil and gas sector is almost unaffected by this policy package. While CIT recycling significantly changes the impact on equity values, it makes relatively little difference to output patterns. This indicates that changes in industry output are an unreliable measure of the impact of environmental policy on the real earnings of industry-specific production factors.

2.6.2 Policies Achieving Equity-Value Neutrality

We now consider policies that introduce an additional instrument to alter the distributional impacts. We start with results from policies that impose the requirement of equity-value neutrality.

Policy 4: Industry-Specific Cuts in the Corporate Income Tax

Policy 4 achieves equity-value neutrality through industry-specific adjustments to CIT rates (with the remainder of the revenues recycled via cuts in the PIT). This appears to be an efficient way to attain such neutrality. In fact, as indicated in table 2.3, the gross efficiency losses are smaller than in the case where this constraint is not imposed (policy 2), suggesting that there is no trade-off between efficiency and distributional neutrality in this case. Two factors help explain this result. First, in our model the CIT is more distortionary than the PIT, as indicated by the difference in efficiency costs of policies 2 and 3. Under policy 4, the efficiency benefit from cutting the CIT rate is offset by the need to finance these cuts through the PIT—that is, the PIT cannot be lowered as much under this policy as under policy 2, which involves no CIT cuts. Since the CIT is more distortionary than the PIT, there is an overall efficiency benefit from this tax swap.

A second reason for the relatively low efficiency cost relates to tax distortions in the fossil fuel industries. The carbon tax significantly raises the overall taxation of energy industries relative to other industries. On nonenvironmental grounds, these industries are overtaxed relative to other industries. Targeted CIT cuts undo some of the nonenvironmental distortions attributable to the carbon tax. We have verified this effect by performing an additional simulation experiment that (like policy 3) recycles some carbon tax revenues through reductions in the overall CIT rate, but also (like policy 4) recycles sufficient revenues in the form of additional CIT cuts for the energy industries to preserve equity values in those industries. This policy involves an efficiency cost of $40.9 per ton, significantly lower than the efficiency cost per ton under policy 3. The difference between this policy and policy 3 is that this policy includes the additional targeted CIT cuts. Thus there is a (gross) efficiency benefit from reducing the "excess" taxation of energy industries under the carbon tax.[37] This is a second reason why policy 4's efficiency cost is lower than that of policy 2.

Policy 5: Industry-Specific Lump-Sum Transfers

Policy 5 produces equity-value neutrality through industry-specific lump-sum transfers. This appears to be an inexpensive way to ensure distributional neutrality: Relatively small lump-sum transfers ensure that the real value of equity is not affected by the carbon tax. These small transfers absorb relatively little revenue, allowing PIT rates to be cut almost as much as under policy 2. The cost of emissions abatement (relative to policy 2) is raised by only a small amount, from \$60.0 to \$61.4 per ton.

Policy 6: Grandfathered Emissions Permits

As discussed in section 2.2, emissions quotas or permits, by forcing firms to restrict output, can create rents for the regulated industries. At the same time, there are costs to these industries connected with the reduction in output and the associated need to remove capital or retire capital prematurely.[38] The question arises whether the policy-induced rents might be sufficient to compensate firms for the other costs associated with abatement.[39]

We consider this issue with policy 6. Here we introduce a carbon tax, but grant firms exemptions to this tax for a certain percentage of their actual emissions. It deserves emphasis that the value of the exemption, although tied to actual emissions in the industry (in the aggregate), is exogenous from the firm's point of view. As discussed in section 2.5, this experiment can also be interpreted as a policy in which the government introduces a tradable permits program, but grandfathers a percentage of the permits. The special case (considered later) in which the firm enjoys a 100 percent (inframarginal) exemption from the carbon tax corresponds to the case of fully grandfathered emissions permits.[40]

37. We are grateful to Ruud de Mooij for suggesting this diagnostic experiment.

38. There are other transition costs, such as the unemployment costs that may result from reduced output. These are not captured in our analysis.

39. This policy imposes equity-value neutrality only for the coal and oil and gas industries, since the carbon tax (and its exemptions) or emissions permits apply only to these industries. The government would need to invoke additional instruments to achieve equity-value neutrality in other industries.

40. Three modeling assumptions underlying this correspondence should be noted. First, the equivalence between a carbon tax policy and a carbon emissions-permits policy would not hold in a more general model in which regulators faced uncertainty. In the presence of uncertainty, taxes and permits policies intended to lead to a given level of emissions will generally yield different aggregate emissions ex post. Second, we assume that a cost-effective allocation of emissions responsibilities is achieved under the permits policy. This implicitly assumes that any differences in abatement costs (associated with heterogeneity in firms' pro-

Perhaps surprisingly, only a very small percentage of emissions permits need to be grandfathered in order to achieve equity-value neutrality. Only 15 percent need to be grandfathered in the oil and gas industry, and an even smaller percentage—4.3 percent—must be grandfathered in the coal industry! As a result, the goal of distributional neutrality can be achieved at a small cost in terms of efficiency. Earlier research has made clear that there is a trade-off between efficiency and political feasibility associated with the implementation of an emissions permit program: Efficiency requires the auctioning of permits (no grandfathering), whereas political feasibility calls for grandfathering. These results indicate that the trade-off may be relatively benign; it only takes a small amount of grandfathering, and a small sacrifice in efficiency, to preserve equity values in the industries that otherwise would suffer most from CO_2 abatement regulations.[41]

Why does a small amount of grandfathering go a long way? As suggested by the discussion in section 2.3, the gain offered to regulated firms by exemptions to a carbon tax or by the free allocation of emissions permits is enhanced to the extent that elasticities of supply are high and elasticities of demand are low. In this model, the elasticity of supply is determined by the share of cash flow (payments to owners of the quasi-fixed factor, capital) in overall production cost, along with the specification of adjustment costs. We find that for the coal and oil and gas industries, cash flow in the unregulated situation is quite small relative to production cost, which contributes to a higher supply elasticity. In addition, although adjustment costs restrict the supply elasticity in the short run, under our central values for parameters the average elasticity (taking into account the medium and long runs) is fairly high. Indeed, the long-run elasticity in the coal industry is infinite because of the assumption of constant returns to scale.[42] These conditions imply that most of the cost from abatement policies is shifted onto demand.

duction methods) are ironed out through trades of permits. Third, our model does not distinguish between new and old firms (although it does distinguish between installed and newly acquired capital). The model's treatment of grandfathering is most consistent with a situation in which only established firms enjoy the freely offered emissions permits, where these permits are linked to the (exogenous) initial (or old) capital stock.

41. Table 2.3 reveals that it is more costly to achieve equity-value neutrality through partial grandfathering of emissions permits (policy 6) than through lump-sum payments to firms (policy 5). The difference can be attributed to differences in the treatment of importers of fossil fuels under the two policies. Both policies can be interpreted as a carbon tax plus an inframarginal lump-sum rebate. Under policy 5, the rebate or lump-sum payment is offered only to domestic fossil fuel producers. In contrast, under policy 6, the rebate (via grandfathering) is offered both to domestic fossil fuel producers and to importers of fossil fuels. Under policy 6, the government is somewhat more generous and forgoes more tax revenue; hence the added efficiency cost. Another difference between the policies is that the petroleum refining and electric utilities industries receive direct compensation under policy 5, but enjoy no protection under policy 6. This would tend to raise the costs of policy 5 relative to policy 6. However, this cost impact is more than offset by the differences just described in the treatment of importers.

42. In the oil and gas industry, the presence of a fixed factor implies decreasing returns even in the long run.

Table 2.4 **Price Responses under Carbon Tax**

	2000	2001	2002	2004	2010	2025	2050
Coal industry							
Gross of carbon tax output price	1.1769	1.360	1.546	1.551	1.560	1.570	1.570
Net of carbon tax output price	0.986	0.978	0.973	0.978	0.995	0.995	0.998
Crude petroleum and natural gas industry							
Gross of carbon tax output price	1.046	1.090	1.132	1.125	1.109	1.083	1.059
Net of carbon tax output price	1.000	1.000	1.000	1.000	1.000	1.000	1.000

Note: Table shows ratio of price under policy change to reference-case price. Results are for policy 2, a $25 per ton carbon tax with revenues recycled through reductions in personal income tax rates. Coal and oil and gas price responses are very similar under the other carbon tax policies.

Table 2.4 bears this out. It displays the impact of a revenue-neutral carbon tax policy (policy 2) on gross and net output prices in different years. In the coal industry, the net-of-tax coal price falls a bit (relative to the reference-case price) in the short run, but the carbon tax is fully shifted in the long run. Even in the short run, over 90 percent of the tax is shifted onto consumers of coal. In the oil and gas industry, the tax is entirely forward-shifted in all years, reflecting the fact that the United States is regarded as a price-taker with respect to oil and gas.[43]

In terms of the analysis of section 2.3, the ability to shift forward the costs of regulation means that most of the *R* rectangle lies above the initial price. When the initial producer surplus or cash flow is small in relation to production cost, owners of the quasi-fixed factor (capital) can be fully compensated for the costs of regulation if they are given just a small piece of the *R* rectangle through grandfathering.

This is confirmed in table 2.5. The table shows the dynamic equivalent of the *R* rectangle under policy 2 (carbon tax with recycling through personal income tax cuts) and policy 6. To enhance comparisons between policies 2 and 6, we will interpret each policy as involving emissions permits; policy 2 is the case of emissions permits with no grandfathering, while policy 6 involves partial grandfathering to yield equity-value neutrality. (As mentioned, one could also interpret these as carbon tax policies, where policy 2 includes no inframarginal exemption and policy 6 involves sufficient exemptions to preserve equity-value neutrality.) Column (2) of table 2.5 shows that policy 2 causes equity values to fall by $4.9 billion in the coal industry. This policy requires the firm to purchase $119 billion of

43. The real net-of-tax price of oil and gas is the only exogenous price in the model. This price is assumed to increase at a rate of 2.7 percent per year (in keeping with baseline assumptions employed by the Energy Modeling Forum at Stanford University). Hence, the ratio of the (constant) real carbon tax rate to the (rising) net-of-tax price declines through time. This explains why, in table 2.4, the percentage increase in the gross-of-tax price of oil and gas declines after 2004.

Table 2.5 **Carbon Payments and Equity Values**

	Industry Equity Value		Present Value of Potential Carbon Payments	α – (Fraction of Tax Payments Exempted or Permits Grandfathered)	Present Value of Actual Carbon Payments [(1 – α) (3)]	Present Value of Inframarginal Exemption or Grandfathered Permits [α (3)]
	Level	Difference from Reference Case				
	(1)	(2)	(3)	(4)	(5)	(6)
Coal industry						
Reference case	17.6	—	—	—	—	—
Standard carbon tax (policy 2)	12.7	−4.9	119.5	—	119.5	—
Carbon tax with inframarginal exemption, carbon permits with partial grandfathering (policy 6)	17.6	—	119.6	0.043	114.5	5.1
Oil and gas industry						
Reference case	187.5	—	—	—	—	—
Standard carbon tax (policy 2)	178.0	−9.5	65.8	—	65.8	—
Carbon tax with inframarginal exemption, carbon permits with partial grandfathering (policy 6)	187.5	—	66.0	0.150	56.1	9.9

Note: Values in billions of year 2000 dollars. Values columns (4)–(6) are net of deductions to corporate and personal income taxes, as indicated in equation (12).

carbon emissions permits. "Potential carbon payments" (col. [3]) is the analog to the *R* rectangle: It is the permit price times the number of permits employed in the coal industry. For the coal industry, this value is $119 billion. Under policy 2, all of the permits are in fact auctioned, and thus the actual carbon payments are the same as the potential payments. Note that this number is very large in relation to the reduction in equity values—$4.9 billion—suffered by the industry. If only a small fraction of the $119 billion could be retained by firms, they would be compensated for the $4.9 billion loss. Under policy 6, firms can in fact retain a fraction of *R*. Enabling firms to retain just 4.3 percent of the potential carbon payments is worth an amount comparable to the $4.9 billion and prevents any reduction in equity values.

Thus, in the coal industry, a very small amount of grandfathering preserves equity values. This reflects the fact that the potential tax payment (the *R* rectangle) is large relative to the loss in equity value in the absence of grandfathering. This, in turn, reflects the small share of cash flow in production cost and the large elasticity of supply, as discussed previously. The result is similar in the oil and gas industry. However, in this industry the potential carbon payments are not as large in relation to the loss of equity value. Hence, the firm must be relieved of a somewhat larger fraction (15 percent) of these payments to suffer no loss of equity value.

While policy 6 preserves profits in the fossil fuel industries, it does not insulate all industries from negative impacts on profits. The petroleum refining and electric utilities industries—which use fossil fuels (carbon) most intensively—also endure noticeable losses of profit and equity values, as indicated by table 2.3. Protecting these industries would require expanded policies involving additional instruments.[44]

Policies 7–9: Other Policies Involving Inframarginal Exemptions

The emissions permits policy just analyzed is one of many potential policies that offer inframarginal exemptions to the regulated firms. Before investigating policies imposing tax-payment neutrality, it seems worthwhile to examine some related policies that grant inframarginal exemptions from carbon taxation. Under policy 7 we consider the limiting case where 100 percent of actual emissions are (inframarginally) exempt from the carbon tax or, equivalently, where all emissions permits are grandfathered. The results are shown in tables 2.2 and 2.3. Full grandfathering leads to very large increases in equity values in the regulated industries—especially the coal industry. These large increases are consistent with the predicted magnitudes of the rents these policies generate and the associated increases in the discounted value of after-tax cash flow.

We also consider some policies that offer exemptions based on business-as-usual (BAU) emissions. In particular, we examine the case where firms receive exemptions from emissions corresponding to 50 or 90 percent of their first-period emissions in the unregulated situation. These simulations differ in two ways from the earlier experiments involving exemptions. First, the exemptions are tied to BAU emissions rather than to the actual emissions occurring under the new policy. Second, the exemptions are constant through time. (In the earlier experiments, actual emissions tend to grow with time, which means that the number of permits in circulation grows as well.) Since we model a growing economy in which outputs of all industries tend to increase through time (even under a carbon tax), the exemption represents a diminishing percentage of actual output.

These policies (8 and 9) are less generous to firms than the policy involving 100 percent grandfathering, but more generous than policy 6, which grandfathered just enough permits to assure equity-value neutrality. As shown in table 2.3, offering a permanent exemption equal to 50 percent of

44. One possible extension is to employ input subsidies for selected downstream industries. Such a subsidy could insulate downstream users from higher fuel prices. We are grateful to Ruud de Mooij for suggesting this option to us. Another possibility would be to give downstream users some of the carbon (fossil fuel) permits. This effectively is a lump-sum transfer to downstream users; such users could sell the permits to fossil fuel suppliers and earn revenues that compensate them for the higher costs of fossil fuels.

first-year BAU emissions is enough to increase equity values of firms relative to the unregulated situation: Equity values rise by a factor of 7 in the coal industry and by approximately 22 percent in the oil and gas industry. A permanent exemption equal to 90 percent of first-year BAU emissions raises equity values by more than a factor of 12 in the coal industry and by approximately 43 percent in the oil and gas industry. The government forgoes more revenues under these policies than under policy 6; accordingly, the efficiency costs of these policies are somewhat higher than under policy 6.

2.6.3 Policies Achieving Tax-Payment Neutrality

Policy 10: Industry-Specific Cuts in the Corporate Income Tax

Policy experiments 10 and 11 invoke additional instruments (relative to policy 2) to yield tax-payment neutrality for the coal, oil and gas, petroleum refining, and electric utilities industries. In experiment 10, we introduce industry-specific CIT cuts to achieve such neutrality, with a constraint that the CIT cuts cannot bring the industry's tax rate below 0. It turns out that this constraint is binding for the coal industry; under this policy, the CIT rate for this industry reaches 0 before tax-payment neutrality is achieved. This reflects the fact that this industry's carbon tax payments are very large relative to CIT payments under the status quo. In the oil and gas industry, tax-payment neutrality is achieved when the CIT rate is lowered to 0.17 from its initial value of 0.42.

The CIT reductions that move toward tax-payment neutrality (in the coal industry) or achieve such neutrality (in the oil and gas industry) are much larger than the reduction necessary to achieve equity-value neutrality (policy 4), and they imply extremely large increases in equity values relative to the unregulated situation. The reason is as follows. As mentioned earlier, the "average" of short-, medium-, and long-run elasticities of supply in the model is fairly high. Thus, overall, firms are able to shift onto demanders a large fraction of the carbon tax. Because producers bear only a small share of the tax burden, only a small CIT cut is needed to undo the potential impact of a carbon tax on profits and equity values. In contrast, a CIT cut that achieves tax-payment neutrality vastly overcompensates firms in terms of the real burden of the carbon tax to producers—most of the tax is shifted onto consumers.

Policy 11: Industry-Specific Lump-Sum Transfers

When we maintain tax-payment neutrality through lump-sum recycling, the efficiency costs are fairly high. As in the case with industry-specific CIT cuts, lump-sum recycling substantially overcompensates firms in terms of profits and equity values. Again the reason is that most of the carbon tax's burden falls on demanders rather than suppliers. But the case

Table 2.6 Sensitivity Analysis

	Policy 1: Carbon Tax with Recycling via Lump-Sum Transfer			Policy 2: Carbon Tax with Recycling via PIT Rate Reduction			Policy 6: Carbon Tax with Partial Grandfathering of Emissions Permits for Equity-Value Neutrality[a]			Policy 7: Carbon Tax with 100% Inframarginal Exemption (Emissions Permits with 100% Grandfathering)		
A. Carbon Tax Rate ($)	12.50	25.00	50.00	12.50	25.00	50.00	12.50	25.00	50.00	12.50	25.00	50.00
Change in equity value of firms, year 2000 (%)												
Coal mining	−17.0	−28.4	−42.8	−16.6	−27.8	−41.9	0.0 (0.037)	0.0 (0.043)	0.0 (0.053)	554.9	1,005.4	1,749.6
Oil and gas	−2.6	−4.8	−9.3	−2.8	−5.0	−9.4	0.0 (0.151)	0.0 (0.150)	0.0 (0.141)	14.7	29.2	56.7
Petroleum refining	−2.7	−5.2	−9.6	−2.3	−4.5	−8.4	−2.4	−4.5	−8.4	−2.5	−4.7	−8.9
Electric utilities	−3.4	−6.3	−11.2	−2.8	−5.4	−9.5	−2.9	−5.4	−9.6	−3.1	−5.7	−10.3
Efficiency cost per ton of CO_2 reduction	93.1	102.6	126.0	51.7	60.0	77.9	60.2	64.4	83.0	82.5	95.1	109.4
B. Elasticity of Demand	Low	Medium	High	Low	Medium	High	Low	Medium	High	Low	Medium	High
Change in equity value of firms, year 2000 (%)												
Coal mining	−19.0	−28.4	−43.2	−18.2	−27.8	−42.9	0.0 (0.032)	0.0 (0.043)	0.0 (0.058)	1,104.9	1,005.4	840.5
Oil and gas	−5.1	−4.8	−4.5	−5.3	−5.0	−4.5	0.0 (0.151)	0.0 (0.150)	0.0 (0.154)	28.7	29.2	28.9
Petroleum refining	−4.6	−5.2	−5.8	−3.8	−4.5	−5.3	−3.8	−4.5	−5.3	−4.2	−4.7	−5.5
Electric utilities	−4.4	−6.3	−8.3	−3.3	−5.4	−7.6	−3.3	−5.4	−7.6	−3.7	−5.7	−7.9
Efficiency cost per ton of CO_2 reduction	151.9	102.6	60.7	86.6	60.0	38.3	94.5	64.4	38.8	140.0	95.1	48.8
C. Adjustment Costs	Low	Medium	High	Low	Medium	High	Low	Medium	High	Low	Medium	High
Change in equity value of firms, year 2000 (%)												
Coal mining	−26.2	−28.4	−31.1	−25.5	−27.8	−30.5	0.0 (0.040)	0.0 (0.043)	0.0 (0.067)	1,065.4	1,005.4	901.3
Oil and gas	−4.8	−4.8	−5.7	−5.0	−5.0	−5.9	0.0 (0.136)	0.0 (0.150)	0.0 (0.158)	30.3	29.2	26.2
Petroleum refining	−5.0	−5.2	−5.4	−4.3	−4.5	−4.7	−4.3	−4.5	−4.7	−4.6	−4.7	−5.0
Electric utilities	−6.1	−6.3	−6.5	−5.2	−5.4	−5.4	−5.2	−5.4	−5.5	−5.6	−5.7	−5.9
Efficiency cost per ton of CO_2 reduction	101.6	102.6	102.1	57.9	60.0	59.8	62.0	64.4	65.5	90.2	95.1	89.5

[a]Numbers in parentheses are proportion of emissions permits required to achieve equity-value neutrality.

with lump-sum recycling is considerably more costly than the previous case because it lacks the beneficial influence on efficiency associated with the cut in marginal CIT rates.

The efficiency costs, however, do not become as large as with full lump-sum recycling to households (policy 1). The reason is that part of the lump-sum transfers to firms are taxed away by the PIT on dividend income when firms pay out these lump-sum transfers as dividends. Since the PIT rate endogenously balances the government budget, the additional tax revenue associated with the higher dividend income is returned to households in the form of a lower PIT rate. In contrast, under full lump-sum recycling to households (policy 1), the PIT rate stays constant.

It may be noted that ensuring tax neutrality through lump-sum transfers does not have much consequence for industry-specific output, employment, and investment. Lump-sum transfers decouple interindustry allocation from interindustry distribution.

These experiments indicate that imposing tax-payment neutrality substantially overcompensates firms. While equity concerns might justify compensating firms for lost profits or equity values, they seem to offer little justification for tax-payment neutrality. The real-world backing for tax-payment neutrality may stem from the misperception that leaving firms' tax revenues unchanged is necessary to neutralize the real burden from regulation.

2.6.4 Sensitivity Analysis

Table 2.6 indicates how key parameters affect results under policies 1, 2, 6, and 7. Panel A of the table illustrates the implications of the size of the carbon tax (or extent of abatement). Here we consider carbon tax rates of $12.50 and $50.00, as well as the previously considered central-case value of $25.00. Impacts on equity values increase with the size of the carbon tax, but somewhat less than linearly. The results for the 100 percent-exemption case indicate that considerable rents are generated even when the carbon tax is $12.50—in this situation, equity values in the coal mining industry rise by almost a factor of six. Under all three policies, efficiency costs per ton (or average abatement costs) increase as the carbon tax rises from $12.50 to $50.00, attesting to rising marginal costs of abatement. The efficiency rankings of the three policies do not change as the carbon tax rate changes.

Panel B reveals the significance of alternative values for elasticity of demand for energy. The high-elasticity case involves a doubling in each industry of the elasticities of substitution between the energy composite E and the materials composite M, as well as the elasticity of substitution among the specific forms of energy. The low-elasticity case halves each of these elasticities in each industry. For the coal industry, the high-, central-, and low-elasticity of substitution cases yield general equilibrium elasticities of demand of 0.26, 0.41, and 0.64, respectively, under policy 2. Under every policy, the efficiency costs per ton of abatement are lower, the larger the elasticity of demand. The efficiency rankings of policies remain invariant across the various demand-elasticity scenarios. The numbers in parentheses in the columns associated with policy 6 are the proportion of emissions permits required to achieve equity-value neutrality. In keeping with the analysis of section 2.2, this proportion tends to rise with the elasticity of demand.

Panel C examines the implications of alternative assumptions for the elasticity of supply. We regulate this elasticity by altering the parameter ξ in the adjustment cost function for each industry; see equation (A2) in appendix A. This parameter determines the marginal adjustment cost, which is inversely related to the elasticity of supply. The low-adjustment-cost (high-elasticity-of-supply) case reduces this parameter by 25 percent in all industries; the high-adjustment-cost (low-elasticity-of-supply) case doubles it everywhere.[45] Efficiency costs per ton do not vary substantially with this parameter. As predicted by the analysis in section 2.2, the proportion of emissions permits required to achieve equity-value neutrality rises with adjustment costs (or falls with the elasticity of supply).

2.7 Conclusion

This paper indicates that the government can implement carbon abatement policies and at the same time protect profits in key industries without substantial costs to the budget and thus to economy-wide efficiency. In particular, the government has to grandfather only a small fraction of tradable pollution permits or exempt a small fraction of inframarginal emissions from a carbon tax to protect the value of capital in industries that are especially vulnerable to impacts from carbon taxes.

In the coal and oil and gas industries, initial cash flow is fairly small in relation to total cost. This small cost share contributes to a high supply elasticity and the ability to shift a large share of the tax burden onto demand. The ability to shift a significant portion of the tax burden implies that only a very small fraction of the potential rents associated with CO_2 policies needs to be earmarked for the fossil fuel industries in order to preserve profits and equity values. These equity values can be safeguarded through policies that depart only slightly from the most efficient carbon tax (or auctioned carbon permits) policies. The efficiency sacrifice is small.

The simplest programs involving freely allocated emissions permits or inframarginal exemptions to the carbon tax protect only the fossil-fuel-supplying industries; downstream industries are not protected. In our model, the downstream industries that suffer the largest proportionate re-

45. We were unable to obtain a solution for the model when adjustment cost parameters were reduced by more than 25 percent.

ductions in equity values are the electric utilities and petroleum refining industries. To protect these industries, other policy instruments would need to be invoked. We find that the potential carbon revenues are very large in relation to the revenue that would be required to protect profits in the fossil fuel industries and the electric utilities and petroleum refining industries. As a result, in our simulations the profits of this broader group of energy industries can be protected at relatively small efficiency cost.

Some caveats are in order. First, our model's aggregation may mask significant losses in some industries (such as aluminum manufacturing) that are not explicitly identified. To protect these industries, additional compensation methods would be required.

Second, our model assumes pure competition. If, in contrast, industries producing fossil fuels already exercise considerable market power before the carbon tax is introduced, they may have already enjoyed much or all of the potential rents. In this case, CO_2 abatement policies may be unable to generate significant additional rents, and thus the opportunities for achieving equity-value neutrality at low cost may be considerably more limited.

Third, in our model capital is the only factor that is not perfectly mobile. To the extent that labor also is imperfectly mobile, there can be serious transition losses from policy changes, and such losses may have significant political consequences. Overcoming barriers to political feasibility requires attention to these losses.

Finally, it is worth emphasizing that the forces underlying the political feasibility of CO_2 abatement policies are complex. Protecting the profits of key energy industries may not be sufficient to bring about political feasibility.

Notwithstanding these qualifications, the present analysis offers significant hope that some major distributional concerns related to CO_2 abatement policies can be eliminated at low cost. Hence the price tag on removing key political obstacles to domestic CO_2 abatement policies may be lower than previously thought.

Appendix A
Structure of the Numerical Model

Production

Technology: General Features

Equations (1)–(3) of the text indicate the nested production structure. The second term in equation (1) represents the loss of output associated with installing new capital (or dismantling existing capital). Per-unit adjustment costs, ϕ, are given by

(A1) $$\phi(I/K) = \frac{(\xi/2)(I/K - \delta)^2}{I/K},$$

where I represents gross investment (purchases of new capital goods) and ξ and δ are parameters. The parameter δ denotes the rate of economic depreciation of the capital stock. The production function for the oil and gas industry, equation (4), contains the additional element γ_f, which is a decreasing function of cumulative oil and gas extraction:

(A2) $$\gamma_{g,t} = \varepsilon_1[1 - (Z_t/\overline{Z})^{\varepsilon_2}],$$

where ε_1 and ε_2 are parameters, Z_t represents cumulative extraction as of the beginning of period t, and $\overline{Z}$ is the original estimated total stock of recoverable reserves of oil and gas (as estimated from the benchmark year).

The following equation of motion specifies the evolution of Z_t:

(A3) $$Z_{t+1} = Z_t + X_t.$$

Equation (A2) implies that the production function for oil and gas shifts downward as cumulative oil and gas extraction increases. This addresses the fact that as reserves are depleted, remaining reserves become more difficult to extract and require more inputs per unit of extraction.

Behavior of Firms

In each industry, managers of firms are assumed to serve stockholders in aiming to maximize the value of the firm. The objective of firm-value maximization determines firms' choices of input quantities and investment levels in each period of time.

The equation of motion for the firm's capital stock is

(A4) $$K_{s+1} = (1 - \delta)K_s + I_s.$$

Household Behavior

Consumption, labor supply, and saving result from the decisions of an infinitely lived representative household maximizing its intertemporal utility with perfect foresight. The model employs a nested utility function. In year t the household chooses a path of full consumption C to maximize

(A5) $$U_t = \sum_{s=t}^{\infty}(1 + \omega)^{t-s}\frac{\sigma_U}{\sigma_U - 1}C_s^{(\sigma_U-1)/\sigma_U},$$

where ω is the subjective rate of time preference and σ_U is the intertemporal elasticity of substitution in full consumption. C is a CES composite of consumption of goods and services $\tilde{C}$ and leisure ℓ:

(A6) $$C_s = [\tilde{C}_s^{(\nu-1)/\nu} + \alpha_C^{1/\nu}\ell_s^{(\nu-1)/\nu}]^{\nu/(\nu-1)},$$

where ν is the elasticity of substitution between goods and leisure; and α_C is an intensity parameter for leisure.

The variable $\tilde{C}$ in equation (A6) is a Cobb-Douglas aggregate of 17 composite consumer goods:

(A7) $$\tilde{C}_s = \prod_{i=1}^{17} \overline{C}_{i,s}^{\alpha_{\overline{C}i}},$$

where the $\alpha_{\overline{C},i}(i = 1, \ldots, 17)$ are parameters. The 17 types of consumer goods are shown in table 2.1.

Consumer goods are produced domestically and abroad. Each composite consumer good $\overline{C}_i$, $i = 1, \ldots, 17$, is a CES aggregate of a domestic and foreign consumer good of a given type:

(A8) $$\overline{C} = \gamma_{\overline{C}}[\alpha_{\overline{C}}CD^{\rho_{\overline{C}}} + (1 - \alpha_{\overline{C}})CF^{\rho_{\overline{C}}}]^{1/\rho_{\overline{C}}}.$$

In this equation, *CD* and *CF* denote the household's consumption of domestically produced and foreign-made consumer good of a given type at a given point in time. The parameter $\rho_{\overline{C}}$ is related to $\sigma_{\overline{C}}$, the elasticity of substitution between *CD* and *CF*, $\rho_{\overline{C}} = (\sigma_{\overline{C}} - 1)/\sigma_{\overline{C}}$. For simplicity, we have omitted subscripts designating the type of consumer good and the time period.

The household maximizes utility subject to the intertemporal budget constraint given by the following condition governing the change in financial wealth, *WK*:

(A9) $$WK_{t+1} - WK_t = \bar{r}_t WK_t + YL_t + GT_t - \tilde{p}_t\tilde{C}_t,$$

where $\bar{r}$ is the average after-tax return on the household's portfolio of financial capital, *YL* is after-tax labor income, *GT* is transfer income, and $\tilde{p}$ is the price index representing the cost to the household of a unit of the consumption composite, $\tilde{C}$.

Government Behavior

A single government sector approximates government activities at all levels—federal, state, and local. The main activities of the government sector are purchasing goods and services (both nondurable and durable), transferring incomes, and raising revenue through taxes or bond issues.

Components of Government Expenditure

Government expenditure, *G*, divides into nominal purchases of nondurable goods and services (*GP*), nominal government investment (*GI*), and nominal transfers (*GT*):

(A10) $$G_t = GP_t + GI_t + GT_t.$$

In the reference case, the paths of real *GP*, *GI*, and *GT* all are specified as growing at the steady-state real growth rate, *g*. In simulating policy changes, we fix the paths of *GP*, *GI*, and *GT* so that the paths of real government purchases, investment, and transfers are the same as in corresponding years of the reference case. Thus, the expenditure side of the government ledger is largely kept unchanged across simulations. This procedure is expressed by

(A11a) $$GP_t^P / p_{GP,t}^P = GP_t^R / p_{GP,t}^R,$$

(A11b) $$GI_t^P / p_{GI,t}^P = GI_t^R / p_{GI,t}^R,$$

(A11c) $$GT_t^P / p_{GT,t}^P = GT_t^R / p_{GT,t}^R,$$

where the superscripts *P* and *R* denote policy change and reference case magnitudes, while p_{GP}, p_{GI}, and p_{GT} are price indexes for *GP*, *GI*, and *GT*. The price index for government investment, p_{GI}, is the purchase price of the representative capital good. The price index for transfers, p_{GT}, is the consumer price index. The index for government purchases, p_{GP}, is defined in the next section.

Allocation of Government Purchases

GP divides into purchases of particular outputs of the 13 domestic industries according to fixed expenditure shares:

(A12) $$\alpha_{G,i} GP = GPX_i p_i \quad i = 1,\ldots,13,$$

where GPX_i and p_i are the quantity demanded and price of output from industry *i*, and $\alpha_{G,i}$ is the corresponding expenditure share. The ideal price index for government purchases, p_{GP}, is given by

(A13) $$p_{GP} = \prod_{i=1}^{13} p_i^{\alpha_{G,i}}.$$

Appendix B

Parameter Values of the Numerical Model

Table 2B.1 Elasticities of Substitution in Production

	Parameter					
	σ_f	σ_{g1}	σ_{g2}	σ_E	σ_M	σ_x
Substitution margin	g_1-g_2	$L-K$	$E-M$	E components	M components	Domestic-foreign inputs
Producing industry						
1. Agricultural and noncoal mining	0.7	0.68	0.7	1.45	0.6	2.31
2. Coal mining	0.7	0.80	0.7	1.08	0.6	1.14
3. Oil and gas extraction	0.7	0.82	0.7	1.04	0.6	(Infinite)
4. Synthetic fuels	0.7	0.82	0.7	1.04	0.6	(Not traded)
5. Petroleum refining	0.7	0.74	0.7	1.04	0.6	2.21
6. Electric utilities	0.7	0.81	0.7	0.97	0.6	1.0
7. Gas utilities	0.7	0.96	0.7	1.04	0.6	1.0
8. Construction	0.7	0.95	0.7	1.04	0.6	1.0
9. Metals and machinery	0.7	0.91	0.7	1.21	0.6	2.74
10. Motor vehicles	0.7	0.80	0.7	1.04	0.6	1.14
11. Miscellaneous manufacturing	0.7	0.94	0.7	1.08	0.6	2.74
12. Services (except housing)	0.7	0.98	0.7	1.07	0.6	1.0
13. Housing services	0.7	0.80	0.7	1.81	0.6	(Not traded)

Table 2B.2 Parameters of Stock Effect Function in Oil and Gas Industry

	Parameter			
	Z_0	$\bar{Z}$	ε_1	ε_2
Value	0	450	1.27	2.0

Note: This function is parameterized so that γ_f approaches 0 as Z approaches $\bar{Z}$; see equation 8. The value of $\bar{Z}$ is 450 billion barrels (about 100 times the 1990 production of oil and gas, where gas is measured in barrel-equivalents). $\bar{Z}$ is based on estimates from Masters et al. (1988). Investment in new oil and gas capital ceases to be profitable before reserves are depleted. The values of ε_1 and ε_2 imply that, in the baseline scenario, oil and gas investment becomes 0 in the year 2050.

Table 2B.3 Utility Function Parameters

	Parameter			
	ω	σ_u	ν	η
Value	0.007	0.5	0.69	0.84

References

Armington, P. S. 1969. A theory of demand for products distinguished by place of production. *IMF Staff Papers,* 159–76.

Bovenberg, A. Lans, and Ruud A. de Mooij. 1994. Environmental levies and distortionary taxation. *American Economic Review* 84 (4): 1085–89.

Bovenberg, A. Lans, and Lawrence H. Goulder. 1996. Optimal environmental taxation in the presence of other taxes: General equilibrium analyses. *American Economic Review* 86 (4): 985–1000.

———. 1997. Costs of environmentally motivated taxes in the presence of other taxes: General equilibrium analyses. *National Tax Journal* 50 (1): 59–87.

———. 2000. Environmental taxation and regulation in a second-best setting. In *Handbook of public economics,* ed. A. Auerbach and M. Feldstein, 2nd ed. Amsterdam: North-Holland, forthcoming.

Buchanan, James M., and Gordon Tullock. 1975. Polluters, profits and political response: Direct controls versus taxes. *American Economic Review* 65: 139–47.

Bull, N., K. Hassett, and G. Metcalf. 1994. Who pays broad-based energy taxes? Computing lifetime and regional incidence. *Energy Journal* 15:145–64.

Bureau of Economic Analysis. U.S. Department of Commerce. 1994. *Survey of Current Business,* August.

Cruz, Miguel, and Lawrence H. Goulder. 1992. An intertemporal general equilibrium model for analyzing U.S. energy and environmental policies: Data documentation. Stanford University. Unpublished manuscript.

Farrow, Scott. 1999. The duality of taxes and tradeable permits: A survey with applications in central and eastern Europe. *Environmental and Development Economics* 4:519–35.

Felder, Stefan, and Reto Schleiniger. 1999. Environmental tax reform: Efficiency and political feasibility. Faculty of Economics, Institute for Social Medicine, Otto-Von-Guericke-Universität Magdeburg. Working paper. January.

Fullerton, Don, and Gilbert Metcalf. 1998. Environmental controls, scarcity rents, and pre-existing distortions. University of Texas at Austin. Working paper.

Gaskins, Darius, and John Weyant, eds. 1996. *Reducing global carbon dioxide emissions: Costs and policy options.* Stanford, Calif.: Energy Modeling Forum, Stanford University.

Goulder, Lawrence H. 1994. Energy taxes: Traditional efficiency effects and environmental implications. In *Tax policy and the economy,* vol. 8, ed. James M. Poterba. Cambridge, Mass.: MIT Press.

———. 1995a. Effects of carbon taxes in an economy with prior tax distortions: An intertemporal general equilibrium analysis. *Journal of Environmental Economics and Management* 29:271–97.

———. 1995b. Environmental taxation and the "Double Dividend": A reader's guide. *International Tax and Public Finance* 2 (2): 157–83.

Goulder, Lawrence H., Ian W. H. Parry, and Dallas Burtraw. 1997. Revenue-raising vs. other approaches to environmental protection: The critical significance of pre-existing tax distortions. *RAND Journal of Economics* 28:708–31.

Goulder, Lawrence H., and Phillipe Thalmann. 1993. Approaches to efficient capital taxation: Leveling the playing field vs. living by the golden rule. *Journal of Public Economics* 50:169–86.

Hall, Robert. 1988. Intertemporal substitution in consumption. *Journal of Political Economy* 96 (2): 339–57.

Jorgenson, Dale W., Daniel T. Slesnick, and Peter J. Wilcoxen. 1992. Carbon taxes and economic welfare. *Brookings Papers on Economic Activity, Microeconomics,* 393–431.

Jorgenson, Dale W., and K. Y. Yun. 1991. *Tax reform and the cost of capital.* Oxford: Oxford University Press.

Keohane, Nathaniel, Richard Revesz, and Robert Stavins. 1998. The choice of regulatory instruments in environmental policy. *Harvard Environmental Law Review* 22 (2): 313–67.

Lawrance, Emily. 1991. Poverty and the rate of time preference: Evidence from panel data. *Journal of Political Economy* 99 (1): 54–77.

Masters, Charles, Emil Attanasi, William Dietzman, Richard Meyer, Robert Mitchell, and David Root. 1988. World resources of crude oil, natural gas, natural bitumen, and shale oil. In *Proceedings of the twelfth World Petroleum Congress,* vol. 5, 3–27. New York: Wiley.

Metcalf, Gilbert E. 1998. A distributional analysis of an environmental tax shift. NBER Working Paper no. 6546. Cambridge, Mass.: National Bureau of Economic Research.

Olson, Mancur. 1965. *The logic of collective action.* Cambridge, Mass.: Harvard University Press.

Parry, Ian W. H. 1995. Pollution taxes and revenue recycling. *Journal of Environmental Economics and Management* 29:S64–S77.

Parry, Ian W. H., and A. Bento. 2000. Tax deductions, environmental policy, and the "double dividend" hypothesis. *Journal of Environmental Economics and Management* 39 (1): 67–96.

Parry, Ian W. H., Roberton C. Williams III, and Lawrence H. Goulder. 1999. When can CO_2 abatement policies increase welfare? The fundamental role of pre-existing factor market distortions. *Journal of Environmental Economics and Management* 37:52–84.

Pezzey, John. 1988. Market mechanisms of pollution control: "Polluter pays," economic and practical aspects. In *Sustainable environmental management: Principles and practice,* ed. R. K. Turner. London: Belhaven Press.

———. 1992. The symmetry between controlling pollution by price and controlling it by quantity. *Canadian Journal of Economics* 25 (4): 983–91.

Pezzey, John C. V., and Andrew Park. 1998. Reflections on the double dividend debate: The importance of interest groups and information costs. *Environmental and Resource Economics* 11 (3/4): 539–55.

Poterba, James M. 1991. Tax policy toward global warming: On designing a carbon tax. In *Economic policy responses to global warming,* ed. R. Dornbusch and J. Poterba. Cambridge, Mass.: MIT Press.

Poterba, James M., and Lawrence H. Summers. 1985. The economic effects of dividend taxation. In *Recent advances in corporate finance,* ed. E. Altman and M. Subramanyam. Homewood, Ill.: Irwin.

Russek, Frank S. 1996. Labor supply and taxes. Macroeconomic Analysis Division, Washington, D.C. Congressional Budget Office. Working paper.

Schillo, Bruce, Linda Giannarelli, David Kelly, Steve Swanson, and Peter Wilcoxen. 1996. The distributional impacts of a carbon tax. In *Reducing global carbon dioxide emissions: Costs and policy options,* ed. D. Gaskins and J. Weyant. Stanford, Calif.: Energy Modeling Forum, Stanford University.

Summers, Lawrence H. 1981. Taxation and corporate investment: A *q*-theory approach. *Brookings Papers on Economic Activity,* no. 1, 67–127.

Vollebergh, Herman R. J., Jan L. de Vries, and Paul R. Koutstaal. 1997. Hybrid carbon incentive mechanisms and political acceptability. *Environmental and Resource Economics* 9:43–63.

Williamson, Oliver E. 1996. The politics and economics of redistribution and efficiency. In *The mechanisms of governance.* Oxford: Oxford University Press.

Name index